DICTIONARY OF
AMERICAN BIOGRAPHY

American Council of Learned Societies

American Philosophical Society, Philadelphia, Pennsylvania
American Academy of Arts and Sciences, Cambridge, Massachusetts
American Antiquarian Society, Worcester, Massachusetts
American Oriental Society, New Haven, Connecticut
American Numismatic Society, New York, New York
American Philological Association, Swarthmore, Pennsylvania
Archeological Institute of America, New York, New York
Society of Biblical Literature and Exegesis, Haverford, Pennsylvania
Modern Language Association of America, New York, New York
American Historical Association, Washington, District of Columbia
American Economic Association, Evanston, Illinois
American Philosophical Association, Middletown, Connecticut
American Anthropological Association, Chicago, Illinois
American Political Science Association, Evanston, Illinois
Bibliographical Society of America, Albany, New York
Association of American Geographers, Minneapolis, Minnesota
American Sociological Society, Washington, District of Columbia
American Society of International Law, Washington, District of Columbia
College Art Association of America, New York, New York
History of Science, South Hadley, Massachusetts
Linguistic Society of America, Washington, District of Columbia
Mediaeval Academy of America, Cambridge, Massachusetts
Population Association of America, Washington, District of Columbia

Dictionary of

American Biography

PUBLISHED UNDER THE AUSPICES OF

American Council of Learned Societies

EDITED BY

Dumas Malone

Jasper—Larkin

VOLUME X

NEW YORK

Charles Scribner's Sons

MCMXLIII

Prompted solely by a desire for public service the New York Times Company and its President, Mr. Adolph S. Ochs, have made possible the preparation of the manuscript of the Dictionary of American Biography through a subvention of more than $500,000 and with the understanding that the entire responsibility for the contents of the volumes rests with the American Council of Learned Societies.

Printed in the United States of America

CONTRIBUTORS TO VOLUME X

Charles G. Abbot	C. G. A.
Lawrence F. Abbott	L. F. A.
Thomas P. Abernethy	T. P. A.
Adeline Adams	A. A.
James Truslow Adams	J. T. A.
Robert Greenhalgh Albion	R. G. A.
Carroll S. Alden	C. S. A.
William H. Allison	W. H. A.
Frank Maloy Anderson	F. M. A.
J. Douglas Anderson	J. D. A.
John Clark Archer	J. C. A—h—r.
Percy M. Ashburn	P. M. A.
Joseph Cullen Ayer	J. C. Ay—r.
Joy Julian Bailey	J. J. B.
Frank Collins Baker	F. C. B—r.
Newton D. Baker	N. D. B.
Hayes Baker-Crothers	H. B-C.
Thomas S. Barclay	T. S. B.
Claribel R. Barnett	C. R. B.
Harold K. Barrows	H. K. B—s.
George A. Barton	G. A. B—n.
Ernest Sutherland Bates	E. S. B.
Howard K. Beale	H. K. B—e.
Samuel Flagg Bemis	S. F. B.
C. C. Benson	C. C. B.
Elbert J. Benton	E. J. B.
Percy W. Bidwell	P. W. B.
F. C. Billard	F. C. B—d.
Edith R. Blanchard	E. R. B.
G. Alder Blumer	G. A. B—r.
Ernest Ludlow Bogart	E. L. B.
Charles K. Bolton	C. K. B.
Herbert E. Bolton	H. E. B.
Robert W. Bolwell	R. W. B.
Earl D. Bond	E. D. B.
Archibald L. Bouton	A. L. B.
Sarah G. Bowerman	S. G. B.
Jeffrey R. Brackett	J. R. B.
Herman Branderis	H. B.
Agnes B. Brett	A. B. B.
William Bridgwater	W. B.
W. E. Britton	W. E. B.
Elsie M. S. Bronson	E. M. S. B.
J. Thompson Brown	J. T. B.
L. Parmly Brown	L. P. B.
Oswald E. Brown	O. E. B.
C. A. Browne	C. A. B.
Solon J. Buck	S. J. B.
F. Lauriston Bullard	F. L. B.
Edmund C. Burnett	E. C. B.
Isabel M. Calder	I. M. C.
Robert G. Caldwell	R. G. C.
Arthur E. Case	A. E. C.
Charles W. Chadwick	C. W. C.
Charles Lyon Chandler	C. L. C.
Dora Mae Clark	D. M. C.
R. C. Clark	R. C. C—k.
Walter G. Clippinger	W. G. C.
Frederick W. Coburn	F. W. C.
Fannie L. Gwinner Cole	F. L. G. C.
John R. Commons	J. R. C.
Royal Cortissoz	R. C.
Robert C. Cotton	R. C. C—n.
E. Merton Coulter	E. M. C.
Jesse H. Coursault	J. H. C.
Isaac J. Cox	I. J. C.
Katharine Elizabeth Crane	K. E. C.
Merle E. Curti	M. E. C.
Robert E. Cushman	R. E. C.
Stuart Daggett	S. D.
George Dahl	G. D.
Elmer Davis	E. D.
Ned H. Dearborn	N. H. D.
Edward S. Delaplaine	E. S. D.
Herman J. Deutsch	H. J. D.
Irving Dilliard	I. D.
Eleanor Robinette Dobson	E. R. D.
Dorothy Anne Dondore	D. A. D.
Margaret Elder Dow	M. E. D.
William Howe Downes	W. H. D.
Stella M. Drumm	S. M. D.
W. E. Burghardt Du Bois	W. E. B. D.
Raymond S. Dugan	R. S. D.
Andrew G. Du Mez	A. G. D-M.
Walter Prichard Eaton	W. P. E.
Edwin Francis Edgett	E. F. E.
Joseph D. Eggleston	J. D. E.
L. Ethan Ellis	L. E. E.
Charles R. Erdman, Jr.	C. R. E., Jr.
Barton Warren Evermann	B. W. E.
John O. Evjen	J. O. E.
Charles Fairman	C. F.
Hallie Farmer	H. F.
George Haws Feltus	G. H. F.
Vergilius Ferm	V. F.
James Fisher	J. F.
Edward A. Fitzpatrick	E. A. F.
Percy Scott Flippin	P. S. F.

Contributors to Volume X

Blanton Fortson	B. F.	Rufus M. Jones	R. M. J.
Louis H. Fox	L. H. F.	James R. Joy	J. R. J.
John H. Frederick	J. H. F.	Paul Kaufman	P. K.
John C. French	J. C. F.	Louise Phelps Kellogg	L. P. K.
Robert D. French	R. D. F.	R. W. Kelsey	R. W. K.
J. Nelson Frierson	J. N. F.	W. W. Kemp	W. W. K.
William L. Frierson	W. L. F.	William J. Kerby	W. J. K.
Claude M. Fuess	C. M. F.	John Kieran	J. K.
John F. Fulton	J. F. F.	Richard R. Kirk	R. R. K.
Elmer H. Funk	E. H. F.	Edward Chase Kirkland	E. C. K.
Philip J. Furlong	P. J. F.	Harry Lyman Koopman	H. L. K.
Katharine Jeanne Gallagher	K. J. G.	R. S. Kuykendall	R. S. K.
Paul N. Garber	P. N. G.	William Coolidge Lane	W. C. L.
Curtis W. Garrison	C. W. G.	Conrad H. Lanza	C. H. L—a.
George Harvey Genzmer	G. H. G.	Kenneth S. Latourette	K. S. L.
W. J. Ghent	W. J. G.	Hugh T. Lefler	H. T. L.
Julius Goebel	J. G.	Ernest E. Leisy	E. E. L.
Armistead Churchill Gordon, Jr.	A. C. G., Jr.	William R. Leonard	W. R. L.
Harris P. Gould	H. P. G.	Charles Lee Lewis	C. L. L.
Dorothy Grafly	D. G.	Arnold J. Lien	A. J. L.
Gladys Graham	G. G.	Harlow Lindley	H. L.
Evarts B. Greene	E. B. G.	Anna Lane Lingelbach	A. L. L.
Anne King Gregorie	A. K. G.	George W. Littlehales	G. W. L.
Sidney Gunn	S. G.	Charles Sumner Lobingier	C. S. L.
J. Sam Guy	J. S. G.	Francis Taylor Long	F. T. L.
J. G. deR. Hamilton	J. G. deR. H.	Ella Lonn	E. L.
William A. Hammond	W. A. H.	Charles H. Lyttle	C. H. L—e.
Elizabeth Deering Hanscom	E. D. H.	Alexander McAdie	A. M.
Alvin F. Harlow	A. F. H.	Henry N. MacCracken	H. N. M.
Rebecca S. Harris	R. S. H.	Arthur S. McDaniel	A. S. M.
Freeman H. Hart	F. H. H.	Philip B. McDonald	P. B. M.
Mary Bronson Hartt	M. B. H.	Walter M. McFarland	W. M. M.
Paul L. Haworth	P. L. H.	W. J. McGlothlin	W. J. M.
Earl L. W. Heck	E. L. W. H.	Reginald C. McGrane	R. C. M.
Atcheson L. Hench	A. L. H.	Oliver McKee, Jr.	O. M., Jr.
Stephen J. Herben	S. J. H.	Andrew C. McLaughlin	A. C. McL.
Frederick C. Hicks	F. C. H.	Harley Farnsworth MacNair	H. F. M.
Granville Hicks	G. H.	W. E. McPheeters	W. E. M.
Norman E. Himes	N. E. H.	Warren B. Mack	W. B. M—k.
Oliver W. Holmes	O. W. H.	James D. Magee	J. D. M.
Lucius H. Holt	L. H. H.	W. C. Mallalieu	W. C. M.
Frank E. Horack	F. E. H—k.	Dumas Malone	D. M.
Orren C. Hormell	O. C. H.	Frederick H. Martens	F. H. M.
Walter Hough	W. H.	Albert P. Mathews	A. P. M.
Leland Ossian Howard	L. O. H.	David M. Matteson	D. M. M.
F. W. Howay	F. W. H.	Francis O. Matthiessen	F. O. M.
Harry M. Hubbell	H. M. H.	Bernard Mayo	B. M.
Albert Hyma	A. H.	Lawrence S. Mayo	L. S. M.
Joseph D. Ibbotson	J. D. I.	Robert Douthat Meade	R. D. M.
Asher Isaacs	A. I.	Robert L. Meriwether	R. L. M—r.
Olive M. Jack	O. M. J.	George P. Merrill	G. P. M.
Theodore H. Jack	T. H. J.	Frank J. Metcalf	F. J. M.
Joseph Jackson	J. J.	Herman H. B. Meyer	H. H. B. M.
Arthur C. Jacobson	A. C. J.	William Snow Miller	W. S. M.
J. Franklin Jameson	J. F. J.	Edwin Mims	E. M.
Walter Louis Jennings	W. L. J—s.	Catherine Palmer Mitchell	C. P. M.
Willis L. Jepson	W. L. J—n.	Wilmot B. Mitchell	W. B. M—l.
		Carl W. Mitman	C. W. M.

Contributors to Volume X

Frank Monaghan	F. M—n.	A. M. Sakolski	A. M. S.
Fulmer Mood	F. M—d.	Verne Lockwood Samson	V. L. S.
Robert E. Moody	R. E. M.	Durward V. Sandifer	D. V. S.
Albert B. Moore	A. B. M.	Wallace S. Sayre	W. S. S.
Hugh A. Moran	H. A. M.	Joseph Schafer	J. S—r.
Samuel Eliot Morison	S. E. M.	Lawrence H. Schmehl	L. H. S.
Richard L. Morton	R. L. M—n.	H. W. Schoenberger	H. W. S—r.
William B. Munro	W. B. M—o.	Eldor Paul Schulze	E. P. S.
H. Edward Nettles	H. E. N.	Thorsten Sellin	T. S.
Allan Nevins	A. N.	Joseph Seronde	J. S—e.
A. R. Newsome	A. R. N.	Harry Shaw, Jr.	H. S., Jr.
Robert Hastings Nichols	R. H. N.	William Bristol Shaw	W. B. S.
Roy F. Nichols	R. F. N.	Augustus H. Shearer	A. H. S.
Harold J. Noble	H. J. N.	Guy Emery Shipler	G. E. S.
Walter B. Norris	W. B. N.	Fred W. Shipman	F. W. S.
Frank M. O'Brien	F. M. O.	George N. Shuster	G. N. S.
John Rathbone Oliver	J. R. O.	Kenneth C. M. Sills	K. C. M. S.
Francis R. Packard	F. R. P.	St. George L. Sioussat	St. G. L. S.
Mildred B. Palmer	M. B. P.	Albert William Smith	A. W. S.
Edward L. Parsons	E. L. P—s.	David Eugene Smith	D. E. S.
James W. Patton	J. W. P—n.	W. E. Smith	W. E. S—h.
Charles O. Paullin	C. O. P.	Herbert Weir Smyth	H. W. S—h.
Frederic Logan Paxson	F. L. P.	Albert Sonnichsen	A. S.
Cecilia H. Payne	C. H. P.	J. Duncan Spaeth	J. D. S.
Charles E. Payne	C. E. P.	Charles Worthen Spencer	C. W. S.
Haywood J. Pearce, Jr.	H. J. P., Jr.	LaVerne Ward Spring	LaV. W. S.
C. C. Pearson	C. C. P.	Harris Elwood Starr	H. E. S.
Edmund L. Pearson	E. L. P—n.	Wendell H. Stephenson	W. H. S.
James H. Peeling	J. H. P.	Wayne E. Stevens	W. E. S—s.
Dexter Perkins	D. P.	John A. Stevenson	J. A. S.
Frederick T. Persons	F. T. P.	Randall Stewart	R. S.
A. Everett Peterson	A. E. P.	Lionel Summers	L. S.
James M. Phalen	J. M. P—n.	William A. Sumner	W. A. S.
George Morris Piersol	G. M. P.	Frank A. Taylor	F. A. T.
David deSola Pool	D. deS. P.	A. Grace Teeter	A. G. T.
Julius W. Pratt	J. W. P—t.	David Y. Thomas	D. Y. T.
Edward Preble	E. P.	Milton Halsey Thomas	M. H. T.
Leon C. Prince	L. C. P.	Herbert Thoms	H. T.
J. M. Purcell	J. M. P—l.	Irving L. Thomson	I. L. T.
Richard J. Purcell	R. J. P.	Charles J. Turck	C. J. T.
Albert J. Ramaker	A. J. R.	Alonzo H. Tuttle	A. H. T.
James G. Randall	J. G. R.	John G. Van Deusen	J. G. V-D.
P. O. Ray	P. O. R.	Harold L. Van Doren	H. L. V-D.
Charles Dudley Rhodes	C. D. R.	Irene Van Fossen	I. V-F.
Leon J. Richardson	L. J. R.	Arnold J. F. van Laer	A. J. F. v-L.
Irving B. Richman	I. B. R.	Henry R. Viets	H. R. V.
Robert E. Riegel	R. E. R.	Harold G. Villard	H. G. V.
Clarence W. Rife	C. W. R.	Michael Z. Vinokouroff	M. Z. V.
Doane Robinson	D. R.	John D. Wade	J. D. W.
William A. Robinson	W. A. R.	Frederick C. Waite	F. C. W.
William M. Robinson, Jr.	W. M. R., Jr.	J. Herbert Waite	J. H. W.
J. Magnus Rohne	J. M. R.	Frank K. Walter	F. K. W.
Ernest Rob Root	E. R. R.	Estelle Frances Ward	E. F. W.
Winfred Trexler Root	W. T. R.	W. P. Webb	W. P. W.
Marvin B. Rosenberry	M. B. R.	F. Estelle Wells	F. E. W.
Frank Edward Ross	F. E. R.	Allan Westcott	A. W.
John E. Rothensteiner	J. E. R.	Edward M. Weyer	E. M. W.
Constance Rourke	C. R.	Melvin J. White	M. J. W.

Contributors to Volume X

Jeanne Elizabeth Wier	J. E. W.	James A. Woodburn	J. A. W.
Harry Emerson Wildes	H. E. W.	Helen Sumner Woodbury	H. S. W.
Mary Wilhelmine Williams	M. W. W.	Robert S. Woodworth	R. S. W.
Samuel C. Williams	S. C. W.	Thomas Woody	T. W.
Walter Williams	W. W.	William H. Worrell	W. H. W.
Mildred E. Williamson	M. E. W.	Helen Wright	H. W.
Samuel Williston	S. W.	Herbert F. Wright	H. F. W.

DICTIONARY OF

AMERICAN BIOGRAPHY

Jasper — Larkin

JASPER, WILLIAM (*c.* 1750–Oct. 9, 1779), Revolutionary soldier, was born of humble and obscure parents. The place of his birth is presumed to have been in the vicinity of Georgetown, S. C., as he was living there on July 7, 1775, when he enlisted in a company that was being recruited by Francis Marion for service in the 2nd South Carolina Infantry commanded by William Moultrie. His character and ability seem to have impressed his superior officers, for immediately upon his enlistment he was advanced to the grade of sergeant. In September 1775 he was assigned to duty with his company at Fort Johnson, where he remained, with the exception of a brief interval at Dorchester, S. C., until the spring of 1776. At the latter date he was transferred to Fort Sullivan (now Fort Moultrie), where he assisted in reinforcing and rebuilding the fortifications. During the bombardment by the British fleet under Sir Peter Parker, on June 28, 1776, he distinguished himself by recovering the flag after it had been shot from its staff and, in the face of a deadly fire, attaching it to a sponge-staff and remounting it upon the walls of the fort. For this act of rare bravery he was presented with a sword by Governor Rutledge and offered a commission which he declined on the ground that his lack of education would be an embarrassment to him as an officer. Moultrie then gave him a roving commission as a scout, a service for which his restless and adventurous character eminently fitted him. Holding this commission successively under Moultrie, Marion, and Lincoln, he made three trips into the British lines in Georgia, bringing back important information each time, and after the capture of Savannah by the British rendered valuable services as a scout in the Black Swamp and the morasses of the Coosawhatchie and the Tulifinnee. He accompanied D'Estaing and Lincoln in the assault upon Savannah in 1779 and was killed, on Oct. 9, while planting the colors of the 2nd South Carolina Infantry upon the Spring Hill redoubt.

Jasper's career has been made the subject of so much laudatory and fantastic writing that it is difficult to arrive at an accurate estimation of his character. Moultrie's appraisal of him as "a brave, active, stout, strong, enterprising man, and a very great partizan" (Moultrie, *post,* II, 24) would seem to be a just one. As a scout he was adventurous, trustworthy, and loyal, and "a perfect Proteus in ability to alter his appearance"; he could wear all disguises with admirable ease and dexterity; and he was equally as remarkable for his cunning as for his bravery (Garden, *post,* p. 91). It is said that he could neither read nor write, but the gist of a letter of his, "ill-written and worse spelt," is reproduced in Francis Bowen's "Life of Benjamin Lincoln" (p. 316). An impressive monument has been erected to his memory in Savannah, and one of the redoubts at Fort Moultrie, supposedly on the site of his valiant act in rescuing the flag, is called "Jasper Battery" in his honor.

[Chas. C. Jones, *Sergeant William Jasper. An Address delivered before the Ga. Hist. Soc.* (1876); Wm. Moultrie, *Memoirs of the Am. Revolution, so far as it related to the States of North and South-Carolina, and Georgia* (2 vols., 1802); John Drayton, *Memoirs of the Am. Revolution* (2 vols., 1821); Alexander Garden, *Anecdotes of the Revolutionary War in Am.* (1822); Wm. Gilmore Simms, *The Life of Francis Marion* (1844); Francis Bowen, "Life of Benj. Lincoln" in *Lib. of Am. Biography,* ed. by Jared Sparks (1847); *S. C. Hist. and Geneal. Mag.,* Oct. 1909, p. 229.] J. W. P—n.

JASTROW, MARCUS (June 5, 1829–Oct. 13, 1903), rabbi and lexicographer, born in Rogasen, Posen, was the fifth of the seven children of

Abraham and Yetta (Rolle) Jastrow. His elementary and secondary education, gained in his native town and the city of Posen, led on to the Universities of Berlin and Halle; from the latter he received the degree of Ph.D. in 1855. Two years later he was awarded his rabbinical diploma, and in 1858, on May 16, he married Bertha Wolfsohn. His first position was that of teacher in a Jewish religious school at Berlin. In 1858, on the recommendation of the historian Graetz he became rabbi of the German synagogue in Warsaw, where he devoted himself to uniting the Polish and the German Jewish elements. When, in the Russian repression of the peaceful movement for a measure of Polish home rule, five civilians fell victims to the troops on Feb. 27, 1861, Jastrow joined in the great patriotic demonstration made at their funeral, even though it was on the Sabbath, and 10,000 copies of the rousing Polish sermon he preached at the memorial service were secretly distributed among the Polish patriots. On Nov. 10 of that year, on the factitious charge of participating in the funeral procession of the Catholic archbishop, he was arrested as a patriot leader and held prisoner in the citadel of Warsaw for over three months, twenty-three days of which he spent in solitary confinement. He was released on Feb. 12, 1862, to be banished as a foreigner. Returning to Germany to regain his shattered health, he became rabbi at Mannheim. In November, his order of banishment was revoked, and his Warsaw congregation enthusiastically called him back. Two months later, active revolution broke out in Poland and the position of Jastrow, ardent devotee of Polish patriotism, became untenable. His passport was taken from him, and he was compelled to return to Germany. In the rabbinate in the dull little town of Worms (1864–66), in the Germany of Bismarck, his political independence made his position uncomfortable, and he was glad to respond to a call of the Rodeph Shalom congregation in Philadelphia.

There his scholarly, conservative Jewish attitude, which had been strongly influenced by Rabbi Michael Sachs in Berlin, impelled him to constant and vigorous controversy with that American reform Judaism which, in emphasizing the modernizing and occidentalizing of Judaism, was destroying its distinctive historic individuality. Against this he marshaled the battery of his learning, powerful personality, and vibrant emotional and intellectual Jewish convictions. To the end of preserving Judaism by creating an informed Jewish will to survive, he taught religious philosophy, Jewish history, and Biblical exegesis in the Maimonides College, which he helped organize in 1867, promoted the formation of the Young Men's Hebrew Association (1875), contributed innumerable educational articles to the Jewish press, made his synagogue a powerful center of conservative Judaism, and took an active part in all Jewish community activities.

From 1876, his health being severely impaired, he limited his activity to his ministry, and the painstaking preparation of his monumental *Dictionary of the Targumim, the Talmud Babli and Yerushalmi and the Midrashic Literature,* originally issued in parts (1886–1903), and reprinted in 1926. This great work of 1736 crowded double-columned pages is a concise and lucid dictionary, with references, of a millennium of Hebrew and Jewish Aramaic literature. To compile it, Jastrow was often obliged to establish the correct reading of his texts. Though he used the earlier work of Jacob Levy, his dictionary is highly original, especially in its philology, for he tried to show the possibility of Semitic derivations for many words which were usually explained as borrowed from Persian, Greek, or other sources. In 1892, his health being broken, he was made rabbi emeritus of his congregation and devoted himself altogether to scholarly work. When, however, at the end of the century, modern Herzlian Zionism was born, his patriotic passion, his championship of the cause of the oppressed, his fearless devotion to what he conceived to be the truth, his strong Jewish historic consciousness and belief in his people and their religion, led Jastrow, old and physically broken as he was, fervently to espouse what was then an unpopular cause. From 1892 to his death he also did devoted work for the Jewish Publication Society as chairman of its committee on a new English translation of the Hebrew Bible, and edited the department of Talmud for the *Jewish Encyclopedia.* His other literary labors, which have been altogether overshadowed by his *Dictionary,* included some political works in German on Polish conditions; *Kazania Polskie* (1863), a volume of Polish sermons; *Vier Jahrhunderte aus der Geschichte der Juden* (Heidelberg, 1865), a revision (with H. Hochheimer) of Benjamin Szold's prayer book, *Abodat Yisrael* (1871); and a translation of Szold's *Songs, Prayers and Meditations for Divine Services* (1885). He had seven children, one of whom was Morris Jastrow [*q.v.*]. Characteristic of his Jewish traditionalism was his last request to be robed in a plain white shroud, and buried in an unornamented, wooden coffin, with no words of eulogy spoken over him.

[*Hebrew Leader* (N. Y.), Apr. 1–July 1, 1870; *Jewish Exponent* (Phila.), Oct. 16, 1903; Henrietta Szold, in *Jewish Encyc.*, vol. VII (1904); and in *Pubs. Am. Jewish Hist. Soc.*, vol. XII (1904); H. S. Morais, *The Jews of Phila.* (1894); *Who's Who in America*, 1903–05; *Public Ledger* and *Phila. Press*, Oct. 14, 1903.]

D. deS. P.

JASTROW, MORRIS (Aug. 13, 1861–June 22, 1921), Semitic scholar, son of Marcus Jastrow [*q.v.*] and Bertha Wolfsohn, was born at Warsaw, Poland. His father, a distinguished Rabbi and Talmudic scholar, removed to Philadelphia, Pa., in 1866, where he became Rabbi of the Synagogue Rodeph Shalom. Morris grew up in Philadelphia and was graduated at the University of Pennsylvania in 1881. After three years of study in France and Germany he received the degree of Ph.D. at the University of Leipzig in 1884. After his return to America he occupied the post of lecturer to his father's congregation for a year and then determined to withdraw from the ministry. In 1892 he was elected professor of Semitic languages in the University of Pennsylvania and in 1898, librarian of the University. Both of these positions he held until his death. In 1893 he married Helen Bachman of Philadelphia, a woman of literary tastes, whose enthusiasm stimulated his scholarly work.

Jastrow was one of the most active and influential of the Orientalists of his time. His first publication was in the field of Arabic philology, being the interpretation of two grammatical writings of Abu Zakarijja, but Assyriology and religion had for him a far greater fascination than other fields of Semitic research and he soon began to publish interpretations of cuneiform inscriptions. This type of research he continued through his life, publishing his results sometimes in book form (as, for example, in his *Babylonian-Assyrian Birth-Omens*, Geissen, 1914), but oftener as articles in one of the journals devoted to Oriental research. His last work of this kind was an article translating and annotating the then recently discovered Assyrian laws, which appeared in the *Journal of the American Oriental Society* in February 1921, four months before his death. His interest in religion was as great as his interest in philology and he soon projected a series of handbooks on different religions. To this series he himself contributed a volume, *The Religion of Babylonia and Assyria* (1898), which at once took its place as the only authoritative work on the subject. A German edition was soon called for, and in making this, he incorporated the large mass of ever-increasing new material. In the researches incident to this work, he was led to endeavor to understand the texts which treated of liver-divination by reading them with a sheep's liver before him. As a result his work on the origin and development of liver-divination was epoch-making. The first volume of his *Religion Babyloniens und Assyriens* appeared in 1905, the second in 1912. The work contains altogether nearly 1800 pages. It was his *magnum opus* and has so far been the best book on the subject. Many of the more important conclusions in this work were put into a more popular form for English readers in a volume entitled *Aspects of Religious Belief and Practice in Babylonia and Assyria* (1911). His interest in Assyriology naturally led him to consider the influence of Babylonian and Assyrian culture upon Israel. For years many articles from his pen testified to this interest and in 1914 a volume entitled *Hebrew and Babylonian Traditions*, the Haskell Lectures of the previous year, was published, followed later by *A Gentle Cynic, being the Book of Ecclesiastes* (1919); *The Book of Job* (1920); and *The Song of Songs, Love Lyrics of Ancient Palestine* (1921, posthumously published). These books reveal a rare combination of skill in linguistics, in textual and higher criticism, and in fine literary insight.

As secretary of the American Committee on the History of Religions, Jastrow organized courses of lectures by eminent scholars, each of whom produced a monograph on one of the great religions. He was thus instrumental in calling into existence an important series of books on different religions in addition to the series, already mentioned, of which he was editor. His interest in the study of religion in the widest sense had been manifested as early as 1901, when he contributed to the Contemporary Science Series, published in London, a volume entitled *The Study of Religion* (1901). Few American scholars have done as much as he to promote interest in the study of the history of religion. The range and volume of his literary activity, however, is indicated by his bibliography, which contains more than two hundred titles and includes *The War and the Bagdad Railway* (1917), and *The War and the Coming Peace* (1918), and *Zionism and the Future of Palestine* (1919).

[The following articles, published in the *Jour. Am. Oriental Soc.*, Dec. 1921, were reprinted separately in a volume entitled *In Memoriam, Morris Jastrow, Jr.* (1921); Julian Morgenstern, "Morris Jastrow, Jr., as a Biblical Critic"; G. A. Barton, "The Contributions of Morris Jastrow, Jr., to the History of Religion"; A. T. Clay, "Prof. Jastrow as an Assyriologist"; and A. T. Clay and J. A. Montgomery, "Bibliography of Morris Jastrow, Jr." See also *Jewish Encyc.* (1925), vol. VII; *Public Ledger* (Phila.), June 23, 1921; *N. Y. Times*, June 23, 1921.]

G. A. B—n.

JAY, ALLEN (Oct. 11, 1831–May 8, 1910), Quaker preacher, educational leader, was born in Mill Creek, near the southern line of Miami County, Ohio, the son of Isaac and Rhoda (Cooper) Jay. He came of a long and distinguished line of colonial Quaker ancestors from Nantucket, North and South Carolina, and Pennsylvania. He was born before his great-great-grandfather, Paul Macy, died, so that their two lives spanned the years from 1740 to 1910. His education began in a log schoolhouse in Western Ohio, and was continued by the training and discipline of a pioneer Quaker school. To this was added a short period in an Ohio academy, one year in Friends Boarding School, Richmond, Ind., and three months in Antioch College. He possessed an alert and virile mind, which continued to develop and to accumulate knowledge for the whole period of his life. In 1850 he settled in Marion, Ind., and on Sept. 20, 1854, he married Martha Sleeper. They both taught in pioneer schools in Indiana. Jay was recorded a minister of the Society of Friends in Greenfield Meeting, Indiana, in 1864. From that time until his death he was one of the most widely known and best loved of all Quaker ministers in America. He traveled extensively on preaching tours, visiting more than once all sections of the Society of Friends in America and in Europe.

In 1868 he was made superintendent of the Baltimore Association, an organization formed after the Civil War, under the leadership of Francis T. King of Baltimore, for the educational and spiritual reconstruction of the Quaker sections in North Carolina. The Association expended over $138,000 and did a notable work, especially along educational lines, for which Jay showed peculiar gifts. During these years in North Carolina, from 1868 to 1874, he discovered his two chief interests, educational leadership and public ministry. After spending more than a year on an important preaching tour in England, Ireland, Scotland, and on the Continent of Europe, he became in 1877 treasurer of what is now Moses Brown School, Providence, R. I., and the organizer and director of its religious life. In 1881 he was called to similar work in Earlham College, Richmond, Ind. He developed unusual gifts for soliciting educational funds and endowments and was responsible not only for large additions to the financial assets of Earlham College, but as well to those of most of the Quaker colleges of the Western states and of Guilford College in North Carolina. He also brought inspiration and creative leadership to Quaker education throughout America, and had an important part in the reawakening of Quakerism in America in the seventies and eighties of the nineteenth century. He was an important influence in the extension of Bible schools and foreign-mission work and was one of the founders of the American Friends Peace Association and of the Five Years Meeting. His first wife died Apr. 27, 1899, and on Nov. 25, 1900, he married Naomi W. Harrison. His life came to an end at Richmond, Ind.

[*Autobiog. of Allen Jay* (1908); *Friends Review, American Friend*, and *The Friend* (London), for the years 1864 to 1910; *Minutes of the Baltimore Association*, 1868–74; *Minutes of Quinquennial Conferences*, 1887 and 1893; *Minutes of Five Years Meeting*, 1887 to 1912; *Quaker Biogs.*, n.d., vol. III; *Indianapolis News*, May 9, 1910.] R. M. J.

JAY, Sir JAMES (Oct. 27, 1732–Oct. 12 or 20, 1815), physician, was born in New York City, the third son of Peter and Mary (Van Cortlandt) Jay. Chief Justice John Jay [*q.v.*] was a younger brother. James received the degree of M.D. at the University of Edinburgh in 1753, publishing a dissertation, *De Fluore Albo* (1753), which shows greater familiarity with former writers on the subject than with first-hand information. Upon his return to New York, he set up practice as a physician, but his career there was not happy (Jones, *post*, II, 223), and he decided to go to England, consenting (1762) to make a collection there for the benefit of King's College. Upon his arrival, he met Rev. William Smith [*q.v.*], there on a similar errand for the College of Philadelphia; thenceforth they worked jointly, agreeing to divide the contributions at the end. Aided by the King, they raised some £10,000 for each of the colleges (*Ibid.*, II, 224, 475–80). On Mar. 25, 1763, upon his presentation of an address from the Governors of King's College, Jay was knighted by George III (W. A. Shaw, *The Knights of England*, 1905, II, 292). A premature attempt of the Governors to secure the funds Jay had collected, instigated by a jealous London agent, resulted in a law-suit (subsequently dropped by the college), a breach between Jay and the Governors, and the failure of the college to acknowledge him as a benefactor. Jay's explanation was set forth in two *Letters* (published in 1771 and 1774, *post*).

During the first years of the Revolution, Jay's sympathies were apparently with the American cause. He invented an ink for secret correspondence, which he used in communicating military information obtained in England. In July 1778, upon his return to America, he lent the clothier-general in Boston $20,000 in Continental currency (*Clinton Papers, post*, VI, 497–500; VII, 543–47, 562–63). Owing to depreciation, only a small part of his actual loan was repaid, and in 1813 he addressed to Congress a petition for reimbursement, a pamphlet of sixteen pages reciting his services to the government, upon which a settlement was made to him (*American State Papers, Claims,* 1834, p. 421). He was a member of the New York Senate from October 1778 to April 1782, and he joined with John Morin Scott [*q.v.*] in securing the passage of the Act of Attainder of Oct. 22, 1779, confiscating the property of the leading New York Loyalists (Jones, II, 524–40). In April 1782 by prearrangement he was captured in New Jersey and brought into the King's lines, where he conversed with Governor Robertson and William Smith [*q.v.*], the historian, regarding his dread of the French and his project for reuniting the colonies with Great Britain. Nothing came of his plans, for he was suspected as a spy, but he was released by Sir Guy Carleton and allowed to go to England (Diary of William Smith, MS., at New York Public Library, March–May 1782; *Royal Gazette,* New York, Apr. 17, 1782). This episode led to a somewhat general distrust of his patriotism—his brother John Jay wrote of him, in September 1782: "If after making so much bustle in and for America, he has, as it is surmised, improperly made his peace with Britain, I shall endeavour to forget that my father has such a son" (Jones, II, 540). The brothers had little communication with each other after the Revolution. For some time Sir James continued to practise in England and on the Continent, but he spent the last years of his life at Springfield, N. J. In 1791 his name appeared in the charter of the College of Physicians and Surgeons, and from 1807 to 1811 he was a trustee. He died at Springfield (on Oct. 12, 1815, according to the New York *Evening Post* of Nov. 2, 1815; his gravestone says Oct. 20). The materials available lead to the judgment that Sir James was a man of talent, ability, and sincerity, but proud, vain, at times overbearing, and because of infelicities of personality, undeservedly disliked and misunderstood.

His publications include: *An Humble Representation . . . in Behalf of the Lately Erected Colleges of New York and Philadelphia* (1762), with the Rev. William Smith; *A Letter to the Governors of the College of New York* (1771); *Reflections and Observations on the Gout* (1772); *A Letter to the Universities of Oxford and Cambridge, &c.* (1774); and his petition, *To the Honorable the Senate and House of Representatives in Congress Assembled* (1813).

[Thomas Jones, *Hist. of N. Y. during the Rev. War* (2 vols., 1879), ed. by E. F. De Lancey; *Public Papers of George Clinton,* vols. VI, VII, VIII (1902–04); Robert Bolton, *Hist. of the County of Westchester* (2 vols., 1848); *A Hist. of Columbia Univ.* (1904); Herbert and Carol Schneider, *Samuel Johnson, President of King's College* (4 vols., 1929); manuscript minutes of the Governors of King's College.] M. H. T.

JAY, JOHN (Dec. 12, 1745–May 17, 1829), statesman, diplomatist, was the sixth son, in a family of eight children, of Peter and Mary (Van Cortlandt) Jay, and was born in New York City. He was the younger brother of James Jay [*q.v.*]. The families of both his father and mother were among the most influential in the colony. His paternal grandfather, Augustus Jay, was a French Huguenot exile who settled in New York about 1686. His father, Peter Jay, was a rich and reputable colonial merchant. John Jay, never of a democratic nature or persuasion, grew up under the most careful family protection. His education went on, with private tutors, under the watchful guidance of his father. Bookish and pious in temperament, the boy is described in contemporary family letters as "serious," "grave," "sedate." Self-confidence and self-satisfaction, rather than ambition, were characteristic of his career. In after life he never once solicited an appointment to public service—except for a successful application for a commission in the New York militia—though he attained, aside from the presidency of the United States, the most important offices which his country could bestow. After graduating from King's College in 1764 he prepared for the bar in the office of Benjamin Kissam of New York. Lindley Murray, a fellow student in the same office, wrote, in his autobiography, of Jay: "He was remarkable for strong reasoning powers, comprehensive views, indefatigable application, and uncommon firmness of mind" (Pellew, *post,* pp. 15–16). These qualities, with a certain lucidity of literary expression —the styles of Jay and Hamilton were similar —marked him from the beginning as a man of unusual intellectual power. His fellow citizens early sought out his service. As years went on Jay's self-confidence begat a not disagreeable vanity, and literary facility sometimes gave way to pretentious oracular utterance.

Following his admission to the bar in 1768, Jay lived the pleasant life of a serious, well-established and well-liked lawyer (he was associated for a time with Robert R. Livingston), prosperously busy, surrounded by friends and clubmates. His was a town-man's life. It drew its principal interest from proper social contacts. There is no indication that he had a liking for sports or strenuous physical exercise, though he was fond of animals, and, of necessity, a horseback rider. Possessed of a fairly wiry and robust constitution, he was nevertheless frequently ailing in health throughout his long life. As a young man he was tall, slender, and graceful, with highly arched eyebrows, a prominent Gallic nose, a pleasing mouth, and a long chin; he had an honest and a refined face, neither grave nor light, with a certain spiritual beauty. He married, on Apr. 28, 1774, Sarah Van Brugh Livingston, the youngest daughter of William Livingston [*q.v.*], later the revolutionary governor of New Jersey.

Jay's first public employment was as secretary, in 1773, of a royal commission for settling the boundary between New Jersey and New York. The dispute was eventually settled by means of a mixed arbitration, a device which must have appealed to Jay's philosophic disposition; it may have been the example for the mixed commissions which were later such prominent features of Jay's Treaty of 1794 with Great Britain, and were repeated in principle in other American treaties thereafter. The advent of the American Revolution put an end forever to Jay's law practice and started his career of public life. He became a conservative member of the New York committee (of fifty-one) of correspondence and soon was sent as a delegate of his colony to the first, and later to the second, Continental Congress. As an indefatigable worker in the Congress he reflected the interests of the conservative colonial merchants who were opposed to independence because they feared it might be followed by an upheaval of mob rule and democracy. But once the Declaration was adopted, in Jay's absence attending the New York provincial congress, he threw his life and fortune unreservedly into the scales, and no man became more jealous against any imputation of the permanency or completeness of American independence. Jay's part in the peace negotiations of 1782 testified abundantly to his conviction. In the spring of 1776 his energies were absorbed in affairs of the new state of New York rather than in the second Continental Congress. As a member of the provincial congress, he not only helped to ratify the Declaration of Independence, but also provided the guiding hand which drafted the constitution of the state. He served until 1779 as chief justice of New York, interpreting the constitution which he had drafted. He was also a colonel in the state militia, but never saw active service.

Jay resumed his seat in the Continental Congress in December 1778, and on the tenth of that month was elected president of the Congress, a position which he continued to hold until elected minister plenipotentiary to Spain, Sept. 27, 1779. Jay's career as a diplomatist begins—if we omit his experience as a member of the secret committee of the Second Continental Congress, for corresponding with foreign powers—with his departure for Spain. He was the most able and distinguished man whom the Congress could spare for this important mission to plead for recognition and assistance at the Court of Madrid, taking with him, as he did, the prestige of "the first office on the continent." After a perilous voyage by way of the West Indies, Jay reached Cadiz, with his wife, on Jan. 22, 1780. From the beginning the mission was a hopeless one. Spain had no intention of recognizing the independence of the United States, much less of making an alliance with the insurrectionists, or even of joining with her ally, France, in a Franco-American combination. Floridablanca had tied Vergennes to a secret treaty, by the terms of which France had agreed not to make a peace with Great Britain except jointly with Spain, and with Gibraltar secured for Spain. On the other hand, France had agreed with the United States not to make peace with Great Britain except jointly with the United States and on the basis of the absolute and unlimited independence of that republic. Thus was the cause of American independence chained to the European rock of Gibraltar. With Jay the Spanish ministry would go no farther than to continue its policy of secret assistance in munitions and money in order to keep the American insurrection going; and Floridablanca made a "loan" (without taking titles for payment) of approximately $170,000. This relieved Jay of the cruel embarrassment caused by the writing of drafts on him by Congress under the unwarranted expectation that he would have meanwhile gotten some money out of Spain. "His two chief points," Floridablanca wrote, concerning Jay, to the Spanish ambassador at Paris, "were: Spain, recognize our independence; Spain, give us more money" (Bemis, *Pinckney's Treaty,* p. 38).

In the spring of 1782 Jay was summoned to Paris by Franklin to assume his post as joint commissioner for negotiating a peace with Great Britain. Despite "bad roads, fleas, and bugs" he reached the city, after a pleasant journey overland, on June 23. The most controversial question in the study of Jay's diplomatic career is whether he upset the American diplomatic apple-cart which had been so cleverly trundled along by Franklin in his preliminary conversations with the British peace representatives, before the arrival of Jay. The latter insisted that the British representative, Richard Oswald, be expressly empowered to treat with representatives of the United States of America, not of the "Colonies," which designation had at first seemed sufficient to Franklin, and to Vergennes, whose good faith Jay suspected. Jay privately communicated to Shelburne, the British prime minister, advice to close quickly with the Americans, recognizing them as plenipotentiaries of the United States. His insistence won out in the end, but delayed the negotiations—in the early course of which Franklin had craftily been proposing the cession of Canada, without provoking active opposition—until after the relief of Gibraltar had greatly strengthened the British negotiating position.

It is not possible to say that Lord Shelburne would have agreed to Franklin's ideas as to the desirability of ceding Canada, and Shelburne's instructions make it certain that if articles of independence should not have been agreed to, the situation was to remain the same as if the negotiation had never been opened, namely one of warfare against a rebellion of colonies. Whether in that instance the world would have construed unsuccessful negotiations with plenipotentiaries of the United States, as a definitive recognition of American independence is extremely doubtful.

Jay and Adams convinced Franklin that they should sign the preliminary articles of peace, as agreed on with Great Britain, without the privity of the French Minister. In this they certainly violated their own instructions to negotiate only with the full confidence of the French ministry. They did not violate the Franco-American treaty of alliance, for the peace was not to go into effect until preliminaries of peace should also have been ratified between Great Britain and France. France could not make peace till Spain was ready. Undoubtedly the American preliminaries, together with the relief of Gibraltar, opened the way for Vergennes to bring Spain into line. Articles between Spain and Great Britain, and between France and Great Britain, were signed on Jan. 20, 1783, without the cession of Gibraltar. The preliminaries of peace thus became complete. Hostilities ceased. Jay further had participated in the peace negotiations by suggesting to the British the reconquest of West Florida before the armistice; and a secret article was inserted in the preliminaries providing that, in case of such reconquest, the southern boundary of the United States should commence at the latitude of the Yazoo River, instead of thirty-one degrees north latitude. Jay's object in making this suggestion was to keep Spain away from the east bank of the Mississippi by keeping Great Britain in West Florida. In the definitive peace treaty of 1783 this was not included, as Florida had been yielded to Great Britain by Spain.

Jay declined the post of minister to Great Britain after the war, as well as that to France, in order to return home and resume his law practice and the delights of private life. When he arrived in New York, July 24, 1784, he found that Congress had already drafted him into service as secretary of foreign affairs. For the position, which amounted to that of minister of foreign affairs of the United States, Jay was the best qualified man available. He put aside personal desires and accepted the unremunerative responsibility which had been thrust upon him. Jay remained in this office until after the adoption of the Constitution and the organization of the new government. In fact, as secretary *ad interim* he administered the business of the new Department of State until Mar. 22, 1790, pending the arrival of Thomas Jefferson to be sworn in as secretary. In addition to the negotiation of treaties of commerce with Prussia and Morocco, and discussions of the same with Austria, Denmark, Portugal, and Tuscany, the handling of the hopeless Barbary corsairs question, and negotiation of a consular convention with France, Jay's principal diplomatic problems as secretary of foreign affairs were connected with Great Britain and with Spain. The dispute with the former involved the retention of the Northwest Posts, in which British garrisons had remained in defiance of the terms of the treaty of peace. The British justified their position on the ground that Congress had not complied with its own treaty obligations in respect to facilitating the payment of pre-war debts to English creditors, and to the proper protection of the Loyalists. We know now that, on the day before the proclamation of the treaty of peace by George III, secret orders were sent out from Whitehall not to evacuate the posts. Without going into the controversy which arose, or the mutual recriminations, during a time that Great Britain refused to send a diplomatic representative to the United States, it may be said that Jay—who naturally remained ignorant of secret orders which have only recently been disclosed—was so impressed by the laxity of Congress in enforcing its own obligations that he could not make progress with Great Britain on this issue; it continued into the national period and was not actually settled until Jay's Treaty of 1794.

With Spain the controversy was somewhat similar. Spanish garrisons continued to occupy alleged American soil up to the latitude of the mouth of the Yazoo River, although the boundary of the United States as laid down by the Anglo-American treaty of peace stipulated the line of thirty-one degrees between the Mississippi and the Apalachicola. Spain also closed the navigation of the Mississippi where it flowed between exclusively Spanish banks. In justice to the Spanish contention it should be recognized that Spain's title to the lower east bank of the Mississippi was at least as good as that of the United States, and that her right to close the navigation of the river was not and could not be estopped by anything in the treaty of peace between the United States and Great Britain. A protracted negotiation between Gardoqui, first Spanish diplomatic representative accredited to the United States, and Jay, between 1784 and 1789, reached no settlement of the question. When in Spain, Jay had not believed in acknowledging exclusive Spanish navigation of the Mississippi, even though, upon instructions received from Congress, he had made such an offer as a condition of Spanish recognition of American independence and the making of a treaty. But during the period of the Confederation Jay became convinced, as did Washington, that the only way to come to terms with Spain was to forbear to use the navigation of the river for a period of twenty-five years or so, while the West could fill up with a population of fighting men. He reached an agreement in principle with Gardoqui on that basis, coupled with some articles of alliance by which each guaranteed the territory of the other power. Congress refused to ratify the Mississippi articles, and Jay never revealed the mutual guaranty clauses to Congress once he saw that the main Mississippi article would not succeed.

Jay's position as secretary of foreign affairs was weakened in power and effect by the impotence of the Union under the Articles of Confederation. He became one of the strongest advocates of a new government under a stronger constitution. After the adoption of the Constitution of 1787 he joined with Hamilton and Madison in the writing of the "Federalist" papers. Illness prevented him from contributing more than five essays—on the Constitution and foreign affairs. When Jefferson arrived to take the post of secretary of state, Jay had already been nominated chief justice of the United States.

The first five years were the formative period of the Supreme Court so far as procedure was concerned. The most important case decided by Jay was *Chisholm* vs. *Georgia,* which involved the suability of a state by a citizen of another state. Jay in his decision pointed out that the Constitution specifically gave a citizen of one state the right to sue another state, and that suability and state sovereignty were incompatible. It was a vigorous exposition of nationalism, too vigorous for the day. Georgia lost the case by default, but before any judgment could be executed, her sister states, alarmed, quickly passed the Eleventh Amendment to the Constitution. While chief justice, Jay was frequently consulted by the President on state decisions, and it was he who wrote (albeit subject to Hamilton's suggestions) a first draft of the famous neutrality proclamation of 1793. After the proclamation, actually indited by Edmund Randolph [*q.v.*], and before the appropriate legislation by Congress for the enforcement of neutrality, Jay, in making a charge to the grand jury at Richmond, May 22, 1793, laid down the principle that the proclamation of the President must implicitly be held declaratory of existing law, that is, of the law of nations (Johnston, *post,* III, 478).

It was while still holding the office of chief justice that Jay was sent on the celebrated diplomatic mission to arrange a peaceful settlement of existing controversies with Great Britain. The war crisis, which arose in the spring of 1794, was caused principally by the British occupation of the Northwest Posts, and the still pending question of private debts to British creditors, together with the spoliations made by British cruisers on American neutral shipping during the Anglo-French war. By this time Alexander Hamilton [*q.v.*] had come to be the principal influence in Washington's administration. Hamilton's new credit system depended on tariff revenues, and nine-tenths of these came from imposts on imported British goods. War with Great Britain, or even suspension of commercial intercourse for any extended period, such as the Republicans advocated, would have meant, in Hamilton's words, cutting up credit by the roots; the collapse of credit would have brought the downfall of the new government, and with it the possible end of American nationality. Jay spent the summer of 1794 in England coming to an arrangement with Lord Grenville on terms mainly suggested by Hamilton. The resulting treaty might more appropriately have gone down in history as Hamilton's than as Jay's Treaty. Without securing any acknowledgment of the illegality of British maritime procedure under which the spoliations had been made, the United States agreed that all spoliation claims which should not receive ultimate justice after running the gamut of British courts of law, should go to a mixed claims commission for settlement; similarly all British claims for the collection of private debts should go to a mixed commission, and the United States should be answerable for payment of the awards in sterling money; British troops were to evacuate the Northwest Territory; commissions were to settle boundary controversies on the northeast and the northwest frontier; and the free navigation of the Mississippi, with particular trade privileges for British ships, was guaranteed the citizens and subjects of each nation. By refusing to enforce in the face of Great Britain the rules of international law accepted in the Franco-American treaty of 1778, the United States gave great umbrage to France; this led to a serious but not vital controversy with that country, in which there is something to be said for the French point of view. Jay's Treaty was the price paid by the Federalists for the maintenance of peace and financial stability at a time when both were vitally necessary for the establishment of American nationality under the new Constitution. He was vilified for his part in the negotiation and Hamilton was stoned while speaking in defense of the treaty; but the Senate ratified it, Washington proclaimed it, and history has justified it as a sort of necessary evil.

While chief justice, Jay had already been a candidate of the Federalist party against George Clinton [*q.v.*] for the governorship of New York, in 1792, and had been defeated by the action of a partisan board of electoral canvassers which threw out many Federalist ballots on technicalities. When he returned home from England in 1795 he found himself already nominated and elected governor. There was little choice but to accept. Jay's two terms, of six years altogether, furnished the state with an upright and conservative administration. Despite the ordinary petty political disputes in which Jay, as a Federalist governor, must needs have his share, no overwhelming political issue arose. In 1800 the victory of the Republicans in the next gubernatorial election was imminent, and Jay had decided to retire from public life. He declined to become a candidate for reëlection, and refused to be considered for renomination as chief justice of the United States. In view of John Marshall's subsequent career in that office, Jay's reasons for declining it are interesting if not amusing: he felt that the Supreme Court lacked "the energy, weight, and dignity which are essential to its affording due support to the national Government" (Johnston, IV, 285).

The presidential election of 1800 afforded an opportunity to test the purity of Jay's political virtue. Believing that the presidency depended on the vote of New York, where the newly elected Republican legislature would be sure to choose Jeffersonian electors, Alexander Hamilton urged Governor Jay to call a special session of the expiring (Federalist) legislature that would choose Federalist electors. Jay refused to countenance this trickery. On Hamilton's letter proposing the plan, he wrote the indorsement: "Proposing a measure for party purposes which I think it would not become me to adopt." The remaining twenty-eight years of Jay's life were spent in complete retirement, saddened by the early death of his wife. He settled down at his 800-acre farm at Bedford, Westchester County, N. Y. Here he died May 17, 1829. He had two sons, Peter Augustus Jay and William Jay [*qq.v.*]. Only one of his five daughters married and she had no children that survived.

Jay was a very able man but not a genius. His principal and invaluable contribution to American public life flowed from his character as he steadfastly performed the day's work. He brought consistent intellectual vigor and moral tone into every office which he held. He belonged to a school of rigid self-disciplinarians and high-minded men who invested the foundations of American nationality with a peculiar mantle of righteousness and dignity. He was second to none of the "Fathers" in the fineness of his principles, uncompromising moral rectitude, uprightness of private life, and firmness, even fervor, of religious conviction. A communicant of the Episcopal Church, he did not scruple to unite with his fellow Christians of other denominations. He owned slaves, to emancipate them; and as governor of New York he signed the act for the abolition of slavery in that state. In retirement Jay took an active interest in church affairs; he became president in 1818 of the Westchester Bible Society, and, in 1821, of the American Bible Society. As a political sage in retirement at Bedford he left these lines: "The post, once a week, brings me our newspapers, which furnish a history of the times. By this history, as well as by that of former times, we are taught the vanity of expecting, that from the perfectability of human nature and the lights of philosophy the multitude will become virtuous or wise, or their demagogues candid and honest" (William Jay, *post*, I, 431).

[The best biography is by a descendant, George Pellew, *John Jay* (1890), and is based on the Jay family papers which in their entirety have not been exploited by any non-family writer. A selected part of these was published by H. P. Johnston, *Correspondence and Public Papers of John Jay* (4 vols., 1890–93). There is a group of Jay papers relating to the Treaty of 1794, in the N. Y. Hist. Soc. The son, William Jay, wrote a filial biography, *The Life of John Jay* (2 vols., 1833), which published for the first time the papers more fully printed by Johnston. Wm. Whitelock, *The Life and Times of John Jay* (1887) is not adequate. Jay as chief justice is portrayed in Henry Flanders, *The Lives and Times of the Chief Justices of the Supreme Court of the U. S.*, vol. I (1855). There are two interesting short sketches: W. W. Spooner, *Historic Families of America* (1907); and Elbert Hubbard, *Little Journeys to the Homes of Famous People* (1922). S. F. Bemis has dealt with Jay's diplomacy in *The Am. Secretaries of State and their Diplomacy,* vol. I (1927), in *Jay's Treaty; a Study in Commerce and Diplomacy* (1923), and *Pinckney's Treaty; a Study of America's Advantage from Europe's Distress* (1926). An account of Jay's participation in the peace negotiations of 1782, written by a descendant, John Jay, is in Justin Winsor, *Narrative and Critical Hist. of America,* vol. VII (1888). For the Supreme Court in Jay's time see Charles Warren, *The Supreme Court in U. S. History,* I (1922). See also *Memorials of Peter A. Jay, Compiled for his Descendants by his Great-grandson, John Jay* (1905, reprinted 1929).] S. F. B.

JAY, JOHN (June 23, 1817–May 5, 1894), lawyer, author, diplomat, grandson of Chief Justice John Jay [*q.v.*], and the only son who grew to maturity of Judge William Jay [*q.v.*] and Hannah Augusta (McVickar) Jay, was born in New York City. His early years were spent happily in his grandfather's home at Bedford. Prepared for college at Dr. Muhlenberg's Institute, Flushing, L. I., he was graduated from Columbia in 1836, studied law, was admitted to the bar in 1839, and practised in New York City for about twenty years. On the death of his father in 1858 he retired from practice to give the rest of his life to the care of the ancestral estate and to public service.

Oppressed or suffering humanity everywhere had his sympathy. While still a student in Columbia College he was manager of the New York Young Men's Anti-Slavery Society. As a young lawyer he was particularly prominent in the seven-years struggle (1846–53) to procure the admission of St. Philip's Church (negro) to the Protestant Episcopal Convention. He served as secretary of the Irish Relief Committee during the potato famine in 1847. After the enactment in 1850 of the Fugitive-Slave Law he acted as counsel for many black fugitives. At a mass meeting in the Broadway Tabernacle, Jan. 30, 1854, he framed the resolutions that were adopted opposing the repeal of the Missouri Compromise. In the following year he was an enthusiastic leader in the organization of the new Republican party in New York State. Though he was an exponent of peace like his father, nevertheless when the Civil War became a reality, he declared, in an address to his Mount Kisco neighbors, July 4, 1861, that "a whipped hound should be the emblem of the Northern man who whimpers for a peace that can only be gained by dishonour" (*The Great Conspiracy,* 1861, p. 48). He favored enlistment of the blacks in the Union army, the proclamation of emancipation, the organization of the Freedmen's Bureau, and the adoption of the Thirteenth Amendment. On the other hand, he showed a liberal attitude toward the defeated South in favoring an allotment in the National Cemetery at Antietam for fallen Confederate soldiers (*Documents of the Senate of the State of New York,* 1868, no. 82). As minister to Austria, 1869–74, he had the difficult task of bringing order out of a calumniating chaos in connection with the United States Commission to the International Exhibition held in Vienna in 1873 (see his article, "The American Foreign Service," *International Review,* May–June 1877). After his return he was appointed chairman of a commission to investigate the New York Custom House for the Treasury Department, he was vice-president of the Civil Service Reform Association of the State of New York, a member, 1884–87, of the state Civil Service Commission, and one of the framers of the state's first civil-service law. A stout defender of the public schools, he assailed the Roman Catholic Church for its attempts "to overthrow our common school system, to tax the people for Romish schools where children will be bent like the twig, moulded in the confessional, educated as subjects of the Pope, owing to him their chief allegiance" (*Rome, the Bible and the Republic,* 1879, p. 13). In his presidential address before the American Historical Association (1890), he maintained that the only sure guarantee of America's continued greatness was that every teacher in the common schools should be well grounded in American history. That Jay was well grounded himself is evidenced in all of his writings, especially in an excellent piece of historical research, *The Peace Negotiations of 1782 and 1783,* published by the New York Historical Society in 1884, and under slightly different titles as a chapter in Volume VII of Justin Winsor's *Narrative and Critical History of America* (1888) and in *Papers of the American Historical Association,* vol. III (1888). In November 1877 he contributed "Motley's Appeal to History" to the *International Review,* an article which precipitated a controversy by its criticism of Grant's administration.

Jay was one of the founders of the Union League Club and its president in 1866 and 1877; he was the first president (1883-94) of the Huguenot Society of America, one of the founders (1852) of the American Geographical and Statistical Society, an active member of the New York Historical Society, the Metropolitan Museum of Art, and the National Academy of Design. He married, June 23, 1837, Eleanor Kingsland Field, of New York City.

[*N. Y. Tribune, N. Y. Times,* May 6, and (N. Y.) *Evening Post,* May 7, 1894; J. T. Scharf, *Hist. of Westchester County* (1886), vol. I; W. W. Spooner, *Hist. Families of America* (1907); "Slavery and the War," a collection of twenty-one pamphlets by Jay presented by him to various libraries including the Lib. of Cong.; *Ann. Report Am. Hist. Asso., 1894* (1895); *Proc. Huguenot Soc. of America*, vol. III, pt. I (1896); *The Union League Club Dinner Given to Hon. John Jay . . . on . . . His Seventieth Birthday* (1887).]

A. E. P.

JAY, PETER AUGUSTUS (Jan. 24, 1776–Feb. 20, 1843), lawyer, was the eldest child of John Jay and the brother of William Jay [*qq.v.*]. His mother was Sarah Van Brugh Livingston, daughter of William Livingston [*q.v.*], later governor of New Jersey, at whose residence, "Liberty Hall," Elizabeth Town, Peter was born and with whom he lived during his childhood years. He attended school in his native town and also at Poughkeepsie, N. Y., and in 1790 entered Columbia College, where his father had preceded him, graduating in 1794. The appointment, in the year of his graduation, of his father as special envoy to Great Britain, gave the son an opportunity to visit that country as the envoy's secretary, to meet such celebrities as Pitt, Fox, Lord Grenville, and Lord Mansfield, to watch Erskine in a trial at Old Bailey, and to see Kemble and Mrs. Siddons at Drury Lane in *The Merchant of Venice*. Returning to New York after his father's negotiation of the treaty, he studied law with his cousin, Peter Jay Munro, with whom, upon his admission to the bar in 1797, he formed a partnership, and he ultimately built up a large and lucrative practice. In the autumn of 1802, on account of pulmonary trouble, he again went abroad, this time to southern Europe. Happening to be in Paris when the Louisiana Purchase Treaty was signed, he was entrusted with the transmission not only of that document but of Napoleon's order to evacuate the territory. On his way back he visited La Rochelle, the home of his Huguenot ancestors, who, he found, were remembered, and in his diary he deplores the decline of that once prosperous port. On the voyage across the Atlantic his ship was stopped several times by British frigates, but finally, after nearly forty days, he arrived in New York with the precious documents. The following winter he visited Bermuda and on July 29, 1807, he was married to Mary Rutherfurd Clarkson, daughter of Gen. Matthew Clarkson [*q.v.*] of New York City, and they had eight children. He was a prominent member of the Episcopal Church and served it in various capacities. He defended, unsuccessfully, those charged with causing a riot during the Columbia College Commencement exercises at Trinity Church in 1811. From 1812 to 1817 and again in 1823 he was a trustee of the college. He was a Federalist in his early years and always remained one at heart; in New York politics he was anti-Clintonian. He was nominated for Congress in 1812 by the "Peace and Commerce" party, but his election was declared void and another contest the following year resulted in his defeat by a narrow margin. He was nevertheless elected to the state Assembly in 1816 as a Federal Republican and supported legislation for the Erie Canal and the abolition of slavery in New York. In 1820 he was appointed by Governor Clinton, though a political opponent, recorder (criminal court judge) of New York City, holding the office for a year only, but receiving a testimonial from the bar. In 1821 he was a member of the convention which framed New York's revolutionary constitution. He voted against the final draft, naming as its chief defects "making the right of suffrage universal, rendering the Judges of the Supreme Court dependent, and vesting the power of appointment, in almost all instances, in the Legislature" (*Memorials, post,* p. 150). He was president of the New York Hospital from 1827 to 1833 and in the latter year served as one of the commissioners who fixed the boundary between New York and New Jersey. In 1840 he became president of the New York State Historical Society and was instrumental in establishing it in a permanent home. Philip Hone described him as "always wise, always honest, but sometimes a little prejudiced" (*Diary, post,* I, 55).

[*Memorials of Peter A. Jay Compiled for His Descendants by His Great-grandson John Jay* (1905); *The Diary of Philip Hone* (2 vols., 1889), ed. by Bayard Tuckerman; *Proc. N. Y. Hist. Soc. for the Year 1843* (1844); W. W. Spooner, *Historic Families of America* (n.d.); *N. Y. Tribune,* Feb. 22, 23, 1843.]

C. S. L.

JAY, WILLIAM (June 16, 1789–Oct. 14, 1858), judge, author, moral reformer, was born in New York City, the son of John Jay [*q.v.*] and Sarah Van Brugh Livingston, and a brother of Peter Augustus Jay [*q.v.*]. Following a thorough classical training under Thomas Ellison, rector of St. Peter's Church in Albany, and preparation for college from Henry Davis, afterwards president of Hamilton College, he entered Yale in 1804. After his graduation (1807) he undertook the study of law in the office of John B. Henry, Albany, but impaired eyesight prevented active practice and he turned to agricultural pursuits on his father's 800 acres at Bedford.

In 1818 he was appointed judge of the court of Westchester County, and with one short interruption held that office until 1843, when he was removed through the influence of pro-slavery Democrats. His charges to the jury always commanded attention because of his "full exposition of the law, without the slightest concession to the popular current of the day" (New York *Evening Post,* Oct. 15, 1858). Active with tongue and pen in championing the cause of emancipation, he was agitating for the abolition of the slave trade in the District of Columbia twenty-two years before congressional action brought it about. The first number of the *Emancipator,* May 1, 1833, had a contribution from Judge Jay. The same year the New York City Anti-Slavery Society was established with his support, and largely through his persuasive arguments a National Anti-Slavery Convention in Philadelphia inaugurated a country-wide campaign that was based on strictly constitutional grounds. Like Wilberforce he opposed the plan to colonize the former slaves in Africa, declaring that those who favored that plan were not moved by "the precepts of the Gospel" but by "prejudice against an unhappy portion of the human family" (*An Inquiry into the Character and Tendency of the American Colonization, and American Anti-Slavery Societies,* two editions, 1835). To the advocates of gradual emancipation he revealed its dangers, arguing that it must be either "immediate emancipation or continued slavery" (*Ibid.*). In other pamphlets he reproved certain bishops of the Protestant Episcopal Church, of which he himself was a communicant, for their use of the Bible to prop up slavery; and he vigorously assailed the American Tract Society, of which he was a life director, for its attempt to sidestep the slavery issue in the interest of harmony. A collection of his arguments, *Miscellaneous Writings on Slavery,* was published in 1853. He was far in advance of his age in the advocacy of arbitration to settle international disputes. His pamphlet of 1842, *War and Peace: the Evils of the First and a Plan for Preserving the Last,* was reprinted as a timely contribution during the World War peace discussion of 1919. The American Peace Society continued him as its president for a decade.

Amid his various humanitarian activities, he took time to write *The Life of John Jay: with Selections from his Correspondence and Miscellaneous Papers* (2 vols., 1833) and in 1850 published *Reply to Remarks of Rev. Moses Stuart . . . on Hon. John Jay, and an Examination of his Scriptural Exegesis, Contained in his Recent Pamphlet Entitled "Conscience and the Constitution"* (1850). Other writings are essays on the Sabbath as a civil and divine institution, duelling, temperance, Sunday schools and their development, and a commentary (unpublished) on the Old and New Testaments. His pamphlets in support of Bible Societies (he was one of the founders of the American Bible Society in 1816) brought him into acrimonious controversy with Bishop J. H. Hobart [*q.v.*]. Jay was also a devoted agrarian with an enthusiasm for experiments in tillage, drainage, horticulture, and stock-raising on the Bedford estate. He married, Sept. 4, 1812, Hannah Augusta McVickar, daughter of a New York merchant. John Jay, 1817–1894 [*q.v.*], was their only surviving son.

[Bayard Tuckerman, *William Jay and the Constitutional Movement for the Abolition of Slavery* (1893), containing a list of Jay's writings as an appendix; F. B. Dexter, *Biog. Sketches Grads. Yale Coll.,* vol. VI (1912), also with a list of writings; G. B. Cheever, *The True Christian Patriot* (1860); Frederick Douglass, *Eulogy of the Late Hon. William Jay* (1859); A. H. Partridge, *"The Memory of the Just": A Memorial of the Hon. Wm. Jay* (1860); newspaper obituaries, particularly those in (N. Y.) *Eve. Post,* Oct. 15, and *N. Y. Tribune,* Oct. 16, 1858.]
A. E. P.

JAYNE, HORACE FORT (Mar. 17, 1859–July 8, 1913), biologist, was born in Philadelphia, the son of David and Hannah (Fort) Jayne. His father, son of a Baptist minister, was brought up in Monroe County, Pa., at a time when educational facilities there were decidedly limited. It is indicative of his ability that he prepared himself to enter the University of Pennsylvania and completed the medical course there about 1825. For some years he practised medicine in New Jersey. In 1831 he introduced the first of the proprietary remedies which bear his name and which made his fortune. Returning to Philadelphia, he established a wholesale drug company for the manufacture and sale of his family medicines and became one of the richest men in that city.

Horace, the younger of his two sons, shared many of his father's capabilities. He was a brilliant and enthusiastic student and at the age of twenty received the degree of bachelor of arts from the University of Pennsylvania. In 1882 he was graduated with highest honors from the medical school of that institution, receiving the Henry C. Lea prize for the best thesis ("The Variations in the Arteries of the Arm") and the Anomaly Prize. For the next two years he studied at Leipzig and at Jena where his association with Dr. Ernst Haeckel stimulated his interest in the study of biology. Returning to the United States, he studied for one year (1883–84) at Johns Hopkins University and was at the same time an instructor in biology at the University of Pennsylvania. In 1884 he became professor of vertebrate morphology there. In addition to his teaching he served as dean of the college faculty (1889–94), dean of the faculty of philosophy (1890–94), and as secretary of the faculty of the school of biology (1884–89). During all the years of his connection with the university he gave liberally of his time and personal means toward furthering its interests. All the money he received in payment for his services he immediately returned. He took an active part in the founding of the biology school and gave $50,000 for a building to house it.

In 1894 he became director of The Wistar Institute of Anatomy and Biology, Philadelphia, a research institution organized by the university and Gen. Isaac J. Wistar. He remained there for more than ten years, continuing his investigations in comparative mammalian morphology, and serving as professor of zoölogy, 1896–1904. Although well grounded in all branches of biology, his main interest lay in comparative anatomy. His best-known book is *Mammalian Anatomy—A Preparation for Human and Comparative Anatomy* (1898). Other publications are "Descriptions of Some Monstrosities Observed in North American Coleoptera" in *Transactions of the American Entomological Society* (vol. VIII, 1880), and "Revision of the Dermestidae of the United States" in *Proceedings of the American Philosophical Society* (vol. XX, 1883). In these two papers the author's name appears as Horace F. Jayne, but he dropped the "F" in later years.

His private life was unusually happy. He was married on Oct. 10, 1894, to Caroline Augusta Furness, a talented daughter of Henry Howard Furness [*q.v.*], the Shakesperian scholar. Their home, "Lindenshade," at Wallingford, near Philadelphia, and their theatrical studio, "The Green Room," in Philadelphia, were the scenes of many original social events to which invitations were eagerly sought. His wife's death in 1909 was a shock from which he never recovered. He could not regain either his health or his enthusiasm for life, and he died suddenly from heart failure in his fifty-fifth year.

[*Autobiog. of Isaac Jones Wistar* (1914), vol. II; *Entomological News,* Oct. 1913; *Makers of Philadelphia* (1894), ed. by Charles Morris; *Who's Who in America,* 1912–13; *Evening Bulletin* (Phila.), Jan. 22, 1907, July 9, 1913.]
F. E. W.

JEANES, ANNA T. (Apr. 7, 1822–Sept. 24, 1907), philanthropist, the youngest of the ten children of Isaac Jeanes, a Philadelphia merchant, and his wife, Anna, was born in the family homestead, "Fox Chase," then one of the suburbs of Philadelphia. Her mother died when Anna was four, and she was brought up by an older sister. Outwardly her life was uneventful. For nearly fifty years she lived in the house where she was born. She then moved to 1023 Arch Street, which was her residence until about two years before her death, when she went to spend her last days in the Friends' Boarding Home, Germantown, which she herself had established. She was a little, energetic woman, with a keen sense of humor and a musical laugh, of retiring disposition, strong-willed, a devoted member of the liberal branch of the Society of Friends. She was interested in art, and painted a little; was a great reader, especially in Oriental literature; and was a member of the Philadelphia Academy of Natural Sciences, the Philadelphia Zoological Society, and the Philadelphia Academy of Fine Arts. She published anonymously a collection of poems, *Fancy's Flight,* which circulated chiefly among her friends, but discloses deep religious feeling, and some gift for poetic expression. She also published *The Sacrificer and the Non-Sacrificer* (1886). In it she tries to show that the Eastern religions, including the Hebrew, contain two opposing points of view; that of the "Sacrificer," which beholds Deity as actuated by human passions, a Being to be appeased by sacrifice; and that of the "Non-Sacrificer," which conceives of God as the personification of love, a Being to be communed with and trusted. Although the founder of the Christian religion was a prophet of the non-sacrificing point of view, the other view entered into Christianity through the doctrine of the atonement. Her conclusion is that "Faith in the Goodness of God, and obedience to His law in the heart, is the natural religion of the soul."

Her independence, resoluteness, and determination to have her own way at any cost, often made her seem eccentric. Disturbed by the people in the adjoining house, she bought it, and let it lie idle. The family homestead she permitted to remain vacant for years, because she could not bear the thought of strangers in the place endeared to her by memories of her parents. When she built the Friends' Boarding Home, she spurned the suggestion that she employ an architect, and planned it herself. Electricity and magnetism were the hobbies of her old age, and she spent much time in making experiments.

Three of her brothers were prosperous merchants. She outlived them, and all the accumulated family wealth came to her. Her disposition of it brought her into nation-wide notice. Long deeply interested in the colored race, just before her death she gave $1,000,000 to establish the Negro Rural School Fund, Anna T. Jeanes Foundation. Her will disposed of property estimated to be worth $5,000,000, the most of which went to some thirty charitable institutions or enterprises. A bequest to Swarthmore College on condition that the institution abandon participation in intercollegiate athletic contests, created much discussion all over the country, and was not accepted. She left $20,000 to the trustees of the Fair Hill Burying Ground "to encourage the practice of cremation," and directed that her own body be cremated.

[J. H. Dillard, "Fourteen Years of the Jeanes Fund," *South Atlantic Quart.*, July 1923; *Friends' Intelligencer,* Eleventh Mo., 9, 1907; *Philadelphia Record,* Sept. 25, 1907, and other Philadelphia papers for Sept. 26, 28, and Oct. 1, 1907.] H. E. S.

JEFFERS, WILLIAM NICHOLSON (Oct. 16, 1824–July 23, 1883), naval officer, was born at Swedesboro, N. J., son of John Ellis Jeffers, a lawyer of Massachusetts birth, and Ruth, daughter of Amos Westcott of New Jersey. His eagerness for sea service was quickened by his maternal uncles, who were naval officers, and he secured a midshipman's appointment, Sept. 25, 1840, and until 1845 served in the *United States* and *Congress* on the Pacific and Brazil stations. He studied at the Naval Academy from Oct. 10, 1845, to July 11, 1846, graduating fourth in a class of forty-seven. At this time he published a book, *The Armament of our Ships of War.* In the steamer *Vixen,* during the Mexican War, he took part in all the important operations against shore defenses. Again at the Naval Academy as instructor, 1848–49, he published two textbooks, *Nautical Routine and Stowage; with Short Rules in Navigation* (1849), in collaboration with J. M. Murphy, and *A Concise Treatise on the Theory and Practice of Naval Gunnery* (1850). In 1852–53 and again in 1857 he was engaged in survey work in Honduras for a proposed "interoceanic railway," and later, 1859–60, as hydrographer in surveys for a canal route across the Chiriqui Isthmus. Meantime he was in the Brazil Squadron, 1853–56, commanding the *Water Witch* in a survey expedition up the Parana and La Plata Rivers. The firing on this vessel by a Paraguayan battery led to the naval punitive expedition of 1857. On Jan. 30, 1855, he had been made lieutenant. In the Civil War he commanded the steamer *Philadelphia,* April to May 1861, in the Potomac; then served in the *Roanoke* on the Atlantic blockade; and, commanding the gunboat *Underwriter,* took an active part in operations, January to February 1862, in the North Carolina sounds, receiving commendation for "zeal and intelligence" (*Official Records, post,* 1 ser. VI, 638). His special studies in ordnance were doubtless partly responsible for his transfer to the command of the *Monitor,* Mar. 13, 1862, just after her engagement with the *Merrimac.* In this vessel he participated in the bombardment of Drury's Bluff, May 15, and in other operations on the James River. His report on the *Monitor* (*Official Records,* 1 ser. VII, 410–13), gave a detailed and highly valuable study of the defects of her type and the remedies. Made lieutenant commander July 16, 1862, he was engaged in ordnance duty during the remainder of the war, first at Philadelphia, and after September 1863, as inspector and in charge of experiments at the Ordnance Yard, Washington. Among other activities he assisted in preparing the powder-ship *Louisiana* for explosion, Dec. 24, 1864, off Fort Fisher. After eight years of routine duties, chiefly in sea command, he was chief of the bureau of ordnance, 1873–81. Though criticized for caution and willingness to await results of foreign experiments, he took at this time a leading part in the modernization of naval ordnance, altering 11-inch Dahlgren smooth-bores to 8-inch rifles and 100-lb. Parrot guns to breech-loaders, and working out details of breech-loading systems for all calibers to 12-inch. In addition to books already mentioned, he edited *Inspection and Proof of Cannon* (1864), and *Ordnance Instructions for the United States Navy* (4th ed., 1866, 5th ed., 1880), and wrote *Nautical Surveying* (1871), and *Care and Preservation of Ammunition* (1874). Popular and uniformly courteous, he had a firm spirit, illustrated by his refusal to admit the suffering of his last illness. He was married, Sept. 17, 1850, to Lucie LeGrand Smith, daughter of Surgeon S. B. Smith of the United States Army, by whom he had a son who died at seven, and a daughter. His death occurred in Washington, and he was buried in the Naval Cemetery, Annapolis, Md.

[Family sources and a biog. sketch (MS.), by Prof. Marshall Oliver, U. S. N.; *War of the Rebellion: Official Records (Navy)*; L. R. Hamersly, *The Records of Living Officers of the U. S. Navy and Marine Corps* (3rd ed., 1878); *Naval Encyc.* (1881); *Army and Navy Jour.*, July 28, 1883; *Washington Post,* July 24, 1883]. A. W.

JEFFERSON, JOSEPH (1774–Aug. 4, 1832), actor, was born in Plymouth, England. His father, Thomas Jefferson, whom Garrick is reputed to have placed on the stage, was manager of the Plymouth Theatre. His mother was a Miss May, a woman of great beauty and charm, who died when he was an infant. Joseph was well trained as a player in his father's company, but disliking his stepmother and being republican in sympathy, he came to America in 1795, engaged by Charles Stuart Powell, manager of the new Federal Street Theatre in Boston, at seventeen dollars a week. This engagement failing (the theatre had not prospered), he joined the company of the John Street Theatre in New York, appearing there first on Feb. 10, 1796, as Squire Richard in *The Provoked Husband.* In New York he lodged at the house of a Mrs. Fortune, a Scotch woman, on John Street, and speedily married her daughter, Euphemia. Another daughter, Esther, later married William Warren, thus allying the two actor families. Jefferson remained at the John Street, and then the Park Theatre, till 1803, playing comedy rôles, especially old men, and being greatly esteemed by his fellow players and the public. In 1803 he was offered the place of comedian in the company of the Chestnut Street Theatre, Philadelphia, and accepted, perhaps because in New York he was overshadowed by John Hodgkinson. For the next twenty-five years, familiarly known as "Old Jefferson" because of his skill in playing elderly parts, he was a pillar in the fine company at the Chestnut Street and a beloved citizen of the town. In Philadelphia he reared his family of eight children (a ninth died in infancy). Seven of these children went on the stage. He brought to the theatre the best traditions and to private life dignity and kindliness and virtue, so that his influence was doubly strong in establishing the playhouse in America. In 1830, after Warren had left the Chestnut Street management and the theatre had fallen on hard days, Jefferson was stung by the failure of a younger public to support his benefit, and left both theatre and the city. For two years he wandered to other towns and suffered in quick succession the loss of two daughters and his son John, who was acting with him. Then his wife died. Broken by gout, bereavement, and grief at his fallen fortunes, Jefferson himself died in Harrisburg, Pa., in the summer of 1832. He was said physically to resemble President Jefferson, and the two men had met and attempted to discover a common ancestry. His acting style was evidently easy, natural, and free from excesses, and gained its comic force from the delicacy of his inflections and byplay, and the charm and rich playful humor of his personality.

[Wm. Winter, *Life and Art of Jos. Jefferson* (1894); *The Autobiog. of Jos. Jefferson* (1890); Wm. B. Wood, *Personal Recollections of the Stage* (1855); Jos. Cowell, *Thirty Years Passed Among the Players in England and America* (1844); *Poulson's Am. Daily Advertiser,* Aug. 8, 1832.] W. P. E.

JEFFERSON, JOSEPH (Feb. 20, 1829–Apr. 23, 1905), actor, grandson of Joseph Jefferson [*q.v.*], was born in Philadelphia, Pa., the son of Joseph Jefferson and Cornelia Frances Thomás, a French exile from Santo Domingo who had married an actor, Thomas Burke, and was a widow with one son when Jefferson married her in 1826. Joseph Jefferson, III, therefore had English, Scotch, and French blood. His father, though an actor, was more interested in painting. From Joseph I he inherited a sunny, optimistic nature, sense of humor, and personal integrity, but no acting genius. To his son he passed on the kindly, humorous, happy disposition, the personal integrity, a love of art, and the acting genius which he had missed. During young Joe's early years, the father was acting and scene-painting in New York and the East, and the boy made his début at the age of four in Washington. "Jim Crow" Rice, a famous early interpreter of negro songs and dances, brought little Joe on in a bag, dumped him out on the stage blacked and dressed exactly like himself, and the child gave an imitation of his song and dance. In 1837 the father moved west with his wife, two children, and his stepson, Charles Burke. They went first to Chicago, then a mere village, and later down the middle border. The family acted in barns, halls, log houses even, and lived the hard life of frontier players. This life was the only schooling young Jefferson ever had. His father died suddenly, of yellow fever, in Mobile, Nov. 24, 1842, at the age of thirty-eight. The family were without funds, and young Joe, at the age of thirteen, was the man of the family, barnstorming the primitive South in rôles beyond his years, and even following the American army into Mexico. He did not get back to New York till September 1849, when, a seasoned trouper of twenty, he came forward at Chanfrau's Theatre as Hans in *Somebody Else.* His half brother, Charles Burke, was also in the company. Some success in New York inspired him to organize a company and take a tour through the South. Later he played in Philadelphia and Baltimore, and by 1856 he had saved enough money for a trip to Europe, to study the theatre there. In November 1856 he became a member of Laura Keene's company in New York and his hard apprenticeship was over. In this skilled company he made a hit as Dr. Pangloss in *The Heir at Law* and in October 1858 appeared as Asa Trenchard in *Our American Cousin,* in which E. A. Sothern appeared as Lord Dundreary. Both men became famous as a result of this play. In September 1859 he joined Dion Boucicault at the Winter Garden, where he first appeared as Caleb Plummer in Boucicault's version of *The Cricket on the Hearth,* and then as Salem Scudder in *The Octoroon.*

In February 1861 his wife died, and Jefferson was much broken in health. He accordingly set out for Australia, where he remained four years, acting his successful rôles and recovering his health. In 1865 he went to London and there carried out a long-cherished dream—to secure a new version of *Rip Van Winkle* in which he could play. There had been several stage versions of the story acted in America, the best by James Henry Hackett and Jefferson's half-brother, Charles Burke. Jefferson induced Boucicault to make a new version, based on Burke's, he himself suggesting the famous scene with the ghosts, in which only Rip speaks. The new play was acted on Sept. 4, 1865, at the Adelphi Theatre, London, and Jefferson's performance was immediately recognized as one of those rare and precious things which come only once in a generation. He first acted the rôle in America at the Olympic, New York, Sept. 3, 1866, and with the same effect. From that time on, Jefferson gradually shelved all his other rôles with the exception of Caleb Plummer, Dr. Pangloss, and one or two more, until 1880, when he made a new acting version of *The Rivals* in which he elevated Bob Acres from a rustic boob to a quaint and whimsical eccentric. Thereafter he chiefly alternated Rip and Bob as his repertoire. This revival of *The Rivals* was made in Philadelphia at the Arch Street Theatre, with Mrs. Drew as Mrs. Malaprop. From 1866 on, too, his annual tours of the country became triumphs; every child in America was taken to see *Rip* as a part of its education; Jefferson's fame and his fortune grew, and because of his whimsical, kindly, honest, and sparkling personality as well as his art, he became one of the best-loved figures in American life. From 1875 to 1877 he reappeared with great success in London. In later years his tours were confined to the autumn and spring. In summer, after 1889, he lived at "Crow's Nest" near Grover Cleveland, his friend, on Buzzards Bay, Mass., and in winter on his plantation in Louisiana or at his home in Palm Beach, Fla. He inherited his father's love for painting, and also for fishing, and spent much of his leisure indulging these hobbies. In 1893 he succeeded Edwin Booth as president of the Players' Club, and hence as acknowledged head of the actors of America. In these later years, too, he was in much demand as a lecturer, for in spite of his complete lack of a formal education he had formulated the laws of his art and could express them with apt phrase and illustration better, perhaps, than almost any other player since Talma, as may be seen by consulting his fascinating *Autobiography,* published serially in the *Century Magazine* from November 1889 to October 1890, and in 1890 reprinted in book form.

Jefferson

Jefferson's last appearance on the stage was in Paterson, N. J., May 7, 1904, as Caleb Plummer and Mr. Golightly in *Lend Me Five Shillings.* He had been on the stage for seventy-one years! He became ill the following winter, at his residence at Palm Beach, and died on Shakespeare's birthday, in 1905. His grave is near his Cape Cod home. He was twice married: first to Margaret Clements Lockyer, in 1850, who died in 1861, and second, in 1867, to Sarah Isabel Warren, a distant cousin. She died in 1894. His first son, Charles Burke Jefferson, was for many years his manager. His fifth child, Thomas, became an actor, and two sons by his second marriage went on the stage, thus making five generations of the Jefferson family in the theatre.

Jefferson had proved himself a skilled actor in over a hundred rôles before he became identified with *Rip Van Winkle.* He was one of the leading contributors, through the medium of comedy, to a more naturalistic art, getting constantly away from hard-and-fast classifications and presenting rounded, individual characters, in whom laughter and tears could mingle. Far more than the tragedians, such as Forrest and Booth, he was constantly assuming rôles drawn from contemporary life, or rôles with local flavor, and his share was large in preparing the ground for the modern theatre. As for his Rip, all who saw it, and then saw the attempts of others, even of his own son Thomas, to play the part after his death, can testify to the enormous contribution his personality made to that play, personality rendered effective by the perfection of his art. You, like the Dutch children and the dogs, couldn't help loving this whimsical vagabond. There was something of the woods and waterfalls about him. There was an eerie poetry in his scene with the ghosts (a scene technically suggesting Eugene O'Neill's *Emperor Jones*). And in his return, an old man, struggling for recognition, there was heartbreaking pathos which slipped with consummate mastery into a final vagabond mirth again. Jefferson's Rip was the perfect union of an actor's own personality with an appealing character—and like all perfect things there was heartache in it. In later years, perhaps the nearest approach to such a union on our stage, imparting an analogous warmth of tender emotion, humor, and elfin poetry, was Maude Adams' Peter Pan. But, of course, Jefferson's Rip touched deeper stops. The play itself has not stood the test of time; it seemed old-fashioned even before Jefferson's death. It will have to be drastically rewritten before another actor can hope with any success to restore it to our American repertoire, where in some form or other it occupied a place from 1828 to 1904. But during those years, and especially from 1866 on, as played by Joe Jefferson (the American public characteristically expressed their affection by refusing ever to call him Joseph), *Rip Van Winkle* held before us a practical ideal of dramatic entertainment drawn from native sources, and humor, pathos, even poetry, extracted from the common lot. More than can be reckoned, perhaps, Jefferson's embodiment of this rôle was a milestone in the development of our modern theatre. Both as man and artist, he richly deserved the honor and the love America gave him.

[*The Autobiog. of Jos. Jefferson* (1890); Wm. Winter, *Life and Art of Jos. Jefferson* (1894), the authoritative source book for the history of the Jefferson family of actors; Francis Wilson, *Jos. Jefferson* (1906); Eugénie Paul Jefferson, *Intimate Recollections of Jos. Jefferson* (1909); G. C. D. Odell, *Annals of the N. Y. Stage*, vols. II–VII (1927–31); *N. Y. Times*, Apr. 24, 1905.]

W. P. E.

JEFFERSON, THOMAS (Apr. 2/13, 1743–July 4, 1826), statesman, diplomat, author, scientist, architect, apostle of freedom and enlightenment, was born at "Shadwell" in Goochland (now Albemarle) County, Va., then on the fringe of western settlement. Whether or not the first Jefferson in the colony came from Wales, as the family tradition held, a Thomas Jefferson was living in Henrico County in 1677 and married Mary Branch. Their son Thomas, who married Mary Field, lived at "Osbornes" in what is now Chesterfield County, where on Feb. 29, 1707/08 Peter Jefferson was born. The family was not aristocratic or wealthy and Peter had largely to shift for himself. Becoming a surveyor, he removed to Goochland County, where by 1731 he was a magistrate. Four years later he patented 1000 acres on the south side of the Rivanna River and shortly thereafter purchased from William Randolph of "Tuckahoe," for a bowl of punch, 400 acres more, containing the site north of the river upon which he erected a plain frame house. Thither in 1739 he brought his wife and there Thomas, his third child, was born.

Jane Randolph, who became Peter Jefferson's wife at nineteen, first-cousin of William of "Tuckahoe" and the eldest surviving child of Isham Randolph of "Dungeness" and his wife, Jane Rogers, connected her husband with perhaps the most distinguished family in the province and assured the social standing of his children. Peter Jefferson's career closely followed that of Joshua Fry [*q.v.*], under whom he served as deputy surveyor in Albemarle, with whom he continued the boundary line between Virginia and North Carolina and made the first accurate map of Virginia, and whom he succeeded as burgess and county lieutenant (Harrison, *post*). Thomas Jefferson had great respect for his father's map and from him doubtless acquired much of his zest for exploring and drawing and his liking for untrodden paths. From him he inherited a vigorous, if less powerful, body, and perhaps his fondness for mathematical subjects. Of the ten children of Peter Jefferson, eight survived his death, Aug. 17, 1757. He left Thomas, the elder of his two sons, 2750 acres of land and an established position in the community.

Seven of the first nine years of Jefferson's life were spent at "Tuckahoe," on the James a few miles above the present Richmond, whither his father removed in pursuance of a promise to William Randolph to act as guardian of the latter's son. Here he began his education at the "English school." The red hills of Albemarle became his permanent home, however, at the age of nine and held ever thereafter an unrivaled place in his affections. At this time he began the study of Latin and Greek under the Rev. William Douglas, who also introduced him to French. Of Douglas' abilities Jefferson later expressed a low opinion. After the death of his father, he studied with the Rev. James Maury, whom he later described as "a correct classical scholar." Whoever may deserve the credit for it, Jefferson gained an early mastery of the classical tongues and ever found the literature of Greece and Rome a "rich source of delight." In March 1760 he entered the College of William and Mary, from which he was graduated two years later. Here, at the seat of the provincial government, he was enabled to view history in the making and politics in practice (H. B. Adams, *The College of William and Mary*, 1887). His chief intellectual stimulus while a student came from his association with Dr. William Small, who held first the chair of mathematics and then *ad interim* that of philosophy. Small aroused in him the interest in scientific questions which was destined to remain active all his life, and introduced him to the "familiar table" of Gov. Francis Fauquier and to George Wythe [*q.v.*], most noted teacher of law of his generation in Virginia, under whose guidance Jefferson prepared himself for practice.

During these years he appears to have been a recognized member of the close-knit social group that the children of the great families of Virginia constituted. He visited homes, made wagers with girls, gossiped about love affairs, served at weddings. Tall, loose-jointed, sandy-haired, and freckled, he was not prepossessing in appearance, but he was a skilled horseman, played on the violin, and seems to have been a gay companion. The strain of seriousness in his nature, however, was soon apparent; it may have been accentuated by the unhappy outcome of his love affair with Rebecca Burwell (Chinard, *Thomas Jefferson,* pp. 17–18). Before he became a prominent actor on the stage of public life, he had formulated for himself a stern code of personal conduct and had disciplined himself to habits of study as few of his contemporaries ever found strength to do (Chinard, *Literary Bible,* p. 12). Some time after 1764, perhaps, he began to apply historical tests to the Bible, lost faith in conventional religion, though without questioning conventional morality, and for inspiration turned to the great classical writers (*Ibid.,* pp. 34–35). That he prepared himself with unusual care for his profession, by the study of legal history as well as of procedure, is apparent from the notebook in which he abridged his legal reading (Chinard, *The Commonplace Book of Thomas Jefferson,* 1927). He was admitted to the bar in 1767, and, despite his dislike of court practice, was quite successful in the law until on the eve of the Revolution he abandoned it as a profession. His legal training, however, left a permanent impress upon him. In his most famous state papers he is the advocate pleading a cause and buttressing it with precedents.

On Jan. 1, 1772, Jefferson was married to Martha (Wayles) Skelton, then in her twenty-fourth year, the daughter of John Wayles of Charles City County and his wife, Martha Eppes. She was the widow of Bathurst Skelton and had borne him a son, who died in infancy. In the ten years of their married life she bore Jefferson six children, only three of whom survived her and only two of whom, Martha and Mary (or Maria), attained maturity. She is reputed to have been beautiful, and certainly her second husband lavished upon her notable devotion. The young couple began their married life in the only part of "Monticello" then finished, the southeastern "pavilion." Jefferson had moved to his adored mountain-top after the nearby house at "Shadwell" burned, together with his cherished library, in 1770, and had begun the building operations which were to extend over a generation. The 2750 acres in Albemarle left him by his father were doubled by 1794 and probably much earlier. From the estate of his father-in-law he acquired in behalf of his wife, soon after his marriage, holdings practically equivalent to his own. With them, however, went a huge debt from the effects of which he never entirely escaped. Throughout most of his mature life he was the owner of approximately ten thousand acres of land and from one to two hundred slaves. Nothing if not methodical, he made periodical records of everything connected with his plantations—his slaves, his horses and cattle, the trees planted, the temperature at "Monticello," the dates at which birds and flowers first appeared.

In 1770 Jefferson was appointed county lieutenant of Albemarle, and in 1773, by the College of William and Mary, surveyor of the county. In May 1769 he was elected a member of the House of Burgesses, as he continued to be until the House ceased to function in 1775, though he did not attend in 1772. He says he had been intimate for almost a decade with Patrick Henry, and appears to have been sympathetic with the orator as the representative of the upper counties against the aristocracy. Never an effective public speaker, Jefferson did greatest service in legislative bodies on committees, where his marked talents as a literary draftsman were employed. Identified from the outset with the aggressive anti-British group, he was one of those who drew up the resolves creating the Virginia Committee of Correspondence and was appointed a member of the committee of eleven, though not of the select committee of three. In 1774 he was one of the champions of the resolution for a fast day, on the day the Boston Port Act was to go into effect, which resolution led to the dissolution of the House. In 1775 he was on the committee appointed to draw up an address to Dunmore rejecting Lord North's conciliatory offer, and says that he drafted the address adopted (Ford, *post,* I, 455–59). Prevented by illness from attending the Virginia convention of 1774, after he had drawn up the resolutions of his county and been appointed a delegate, he sent a paper, later published as *A Summary View of the Rights of British America* (Ford, I, 421–47), which proved to be his greatest literary contribution to the American Revolution next to the Declaration of Independence and which reveals, as perhaps no other document does, his point of view in that struggle. Though approved by many, it was not adopted because regarded as too advanced. Emphasizing the "natural" right of emigration and the right of conquest, exercised by the first English settlers in America as by the Saxons in England, he denied all parliamentary authority over the colonies and claimed that the only political tie with Great Britain was supplied by the King, to whom the colonists had voluntarily submitted. The aids rendered by the mother country, he felt, had been solely for commercial benefit and were repayable only in trade privileges. He advocated, not separation, but freedom of trade in articles that the British could not use, and the relinquishment of all British claims in regard to taxation. This powerful pamphlet, distinctly legalistic in tone, reveals no adequate conception of the value of early English protection or of the contemporary British imperial problem. Throughout his career as a Revolutionary patriot he emphasized "rights as derived from the laws of nature," not a king; and here, as elsewhere, he strove for the "revindication of Saxon liberties" (Chinard, *Commonplace Book,* p. 57).

Elected by the Virginia convention to serve in Congress in case Peyton Randolph was required at home, Jefferson sat in that body during the summer and autumn of 1775. Though he drew drafts of several papers, these were too strongly anti-British in tone to be acceptable while there was hope of conciliation. He was not present in Congress from Dec. 28, 1775, to May 14, 1776. Probably called home by the illness of his mother, who died Mar. 31, and by the needs of his family, he also had duties to perform as county lieutenant and commander of the militia of Albemarle, to which office he had been appointed by the Virginia Committee of Safety on Sept. 26 (Chinard, *Thomas Jefferson,* p. 66; Randall, *post,* I, 140–41). Following the famous resolutions introduced into Congress on June 7 by Richard Henry Lee, Jefferson was elected four days later, with John Adams, Franklin, Roger Sherman, and Robert R. Livingston, to draw up a declaration of independence. The reasons for the prominence in this connection of one so young as Jefferson, and especially for his selection over Lee, have been much disputed (Randall, I, 144–59). Now only thirty-three years old, he had been a "silent member" on the floor of Congress, though outspoken and decisive in committees. The "reputation of a masterly pen," however, stood him in good stead and opened the door of dangerous but glorious opportunity.

More changes in his draft of the Declaration were made at the instance of Adams, and particularly of Franklin, than he later remembered, and some were made by Congress itself, but this most famous American political document as a composition belongs indisputably to Jefferson (Fitzpatrick, *post;* Becker, *post*). The philosophical portion strikingly resembles the first three sections of George Mason's Declaration of Rights, itself a notable summary of current revolutionary philosophy. Jefferson probably availed himself of this, but he improved upon it. The doctrines are essentially those of John Locke, in which the more radical of the patriots were steeped. Jefferson himself did not believe in absolute human equality, and, though he had no fears of revolution, he preferred that the "social compact" be renewed by periodical, peaceful revisions. That government should be based on popular consent and secure the "inalienable" rights of man, among which he included the pursuit of happiness rather than property, that it should be a means to human well-being and not an end in itself, he steadfastly believed. He gave here a matchless expression of his faith. The charges against the King, who is singled out because all claims of parliamentary authority are implicitly denied, are in general an improved version of those that had already been drawn up by Jefferson and adopted as the preamble of the Virginia constitution of 1776. Relentless in their reiteration, they constitute a statement of the specific grievances of the revolting party, powerfully and persuasively presented at the bar of public opinion. The Declaration is notable for both its clarity and subtlety of expression, and it abounds in the felicities that are characteristic of Jefferson's unlabored prose (Becker, *post,* ch. V). More nearly impassioned than any other of his important writings, it is eloquent in its sustained elevation of style and remains his noblest literary monument.

Desiring to be nearer his family and feeling that he could be more useful in furthering the "reformation" of Virginia than in Congress, Jefferson left the latter body in September 1776, and, entering the House of Delegates on Oct. 7, served there until his election to the governorship in June 1779. While a member of Congress, he had submitted to the Virginia convention of 1776 a constitution and preamble, only the latter of which was adopted. His proposed constitution was in some respects, especially in its failure to provide for popular participation in the election of senators, less democratic than the one adopted (W. C. Ford, in the *Nation,* Aug. 7, 1890, pp. 107–09). With the new constitution and government, which were marked by little change in law and social organization, he was, however, profoundly dissatisfied. To him the Revolution meant more than a redress of grievances. Against the continuance of an established church, divorced from England, which the conservatives favored, he desired the entire separation of church and state. He was determined to rid his "country," as he long called Virginia, of the artificial aristocracy of wealth and birth, and to facilitate through education the development of a natural aristocracy of talent and virtue and an enlightened electorate. He felt that the legal code should be adapted to republican government "with a single eye to reason, & the good of those for whose government it was formed." Because of his skill as a legislator, the definiteness of his carefully formulated program, and the almost religious zeal with which he pressed it, he immediately assumed the leadership of the progressive group which Patrick Henry had relinquished when he became governor and which George Mason willingly conceded to a more aggressive man. He deserves the chief credit not only for an unparalleled program but also for legislative achievements that have rarely been equaled in American history.

He struck the first blow at the aristocratic system by procuring the abolition of land-holding in fee-tail. On Oct. 12, 1776, he moved the revision of the laws. Elected to the board of revisors with four others, of whom only Wythe and Edmund Pendleton served to the end, he labored two years with scholarly thoroughness on his share of the revision, including the law of descent and the criminal law. The report of the board (June 18, 1778), comprised 126 bills, the substance of at least 100 of which was ultimately enacted (Lingley, *post,* p. 188 note; Ford, II, 199–239; Hening, XII). Primogeniture was abolished in 1785. His bill for Establishing Religious Freedom (Ford, II, 237–39), presented in 1779 by John Harvie of Albemarle and passed, with slight modifications in the preamble (Hening, XII, 84–86), in 1786 when Jefferson was in France, was regarded by him as one of his greatest contributions to humanity. In its assertion that the mind is not subject to coercion, that civil rights have no dependence on religious opinions, and that the opinions of men are not the concern of civil government, it is indeed one of the great American charters of freedom.

Jefferson's educational bills, which represented the constructive part of his program, were unsuccessful. Of his extraordinary Bill for the More General Diffusion of Knowledge (Ford, II, 220–29), which summarizes his educational philosophy, only the part dealing with elementary schools was acted on, in 1796, and a provision was inserted that in effect defeated its purpose. His attempts to amend the constitution of his old college and to establish a public library (*Ibid.,* II, 229–37) entirely failed. During his governorship, however, as a visitor of William and Mary, he effected the abolishment of the professorships of Hebrew, theology, and ancient languages and the establishment of professorships of anatomy and medicine, law, and modern languages, the two latter being the first of their kind in America (C. J. Heatwole, *A History of Education in Virginia,* 1916, pp. 90–91). Though he did not originate the idea of removing the capital to Richmond, he framed a bill for that purpose and the measure which was passed in 1779 (Hening, X, 85) included his preamble and provisions for handsome public buildings such as he had favored. His plans for his state were never fully carried out, but he may properly be termed the architect of Virginia government.

His election to the governorship (June 1, 1779) in succession to Patrick Henry was the natural consequence of his preëminence as a legislator and his unchallenged leadership of the progressive group. The philosophical qualities that made him so conspicuous as a planner and prophet were of little avail to him, however, as an executive. Resourceful in counsel, he was ever hesitant and reluctant in the exercise of authority, the very necessity of which he deplored. His position as a war-governor was rendered the more difficult by the constitutional limitations upon his authority and the diminution of the state's resources. In handling the countless details of his office he was extraordinarily industrious and conscientious (H. R. McIlwaine, *Official Letters of the Governors of the State of Virginia,* II, 1928). His chief weaknesses were his unwillingness, even in time of acute crisis, to use means of doubtful legality and his characteristic reliance upon the militia (Eckenrode, *post,* ch. VIII). He managed sufficiently well during the first year of his governorship and was duly reëlected, but in the spring of 1781, when the British seriously invaded Virginia, the state was at their mercy. Richmond being in British hands, the legislature was called to meet at Charlottesville May 24. Jefferson proceeded to "Monticello" and last exercised the functions of his office June 3, interpreting his term to continue only one year and not until his successor qualified. As he put it, he "resigned" the governorship, recommending that the military and civil agencies be combined by the election of Gen. Thomas Nelson, but his act was a virtual abdication. On June 4, Tarleton made a raid on "Monticello." The supposed governor and the legislators who were his guests all escaped, Jefferson the last among them. He returned the next day, but soon removed his family to "Poplar Forest," where late in June he was thrown from his horse and disabled. Thus did his administration come to an unheroic end.

What was left of the Assembly, meeting beyond the mountains at Staunton, elected Nelson and ordered (June 12, 1781) that an investigation of Jefferson's conduct as governor be made at the next session. Judging from the heads of charges proposed by his neighbor and subsequent supporter, George Nicholas (Randall, I, 354–55; Jefferson Papers, Library of Congress), there was no allegation of personal cowardice, such as was made later by political enemies. The conduct of the assemblymen, indeed, had been marked by even greater prudence. All the charges had to do with the lack of military precaution and expedition. After the crisis actually arose, Jefferson seems to have done everything possible and with as great speed as could have been expected. Whether or not he had made such previous preparation for an impending crisis as he might have is questionable. By autumn, however, the storm had stilled. On Dec. 12 a committee appointed by the House of Delegates to inquire into his conduct as governor reported that no information had been offered them except rumors, which they regarded as groundless, and on Dec. 19 resolutions of thanks were finally adopted. Though formally vindicated, Jefferson did not for years recover his prestige in Virginia. For a time the state government passed into conservative hands, but during his long absence in France (1784–89) the progressives, under the able leadership of Madison, again gained ascendancy, and Jefferson came to be regarded as the prophet of the new order, as indeed he was.

Persuaded that public service and private misery were inseparable, Jefferson retired to his neglected farms, his cherished books, and his beloved family, convinced that nothing could again separate him from them. He took advantage of the leisure forced upon him by his fall from his horse to organize the careful memoranda about Virginia which he had made over a long period of years. Arranging these in the order of the queries submitted in 1781 by Barbé de Marbois, secretary of the French legation, he somewhat corrected and enlarged them during the winter of 1782–83, and at length had them printed in France in 1784–85. The *Notes on the State of Virginia* (Ford, III, 68–295) went through many editions and laid the foundations of Jefferson's high contemporary reputation as a universal scholar and of his present fame as a pioneer American scientist. Unpretentious in form and statistical in character, this extraordinarily informing and generally interesting book may still be consulted with profit about the geography and productions, the social and political life, of eighteenth-century Virginia. With ardent patriotism as well as zeal for truth Jefferson combatted the theories of Buffon and Raynal in regard to the degeneracy of animal and intellectual life in America, and he manifested great optimism in regard to the future of the country, but he included "strictures" on slavery and the government of Virginia. In 1783 he drafted another proposed constitution for his state (Ford, III, 320–33), which was published in 1786 and ultimately bound with the *Notes* as an appendix.

But for the death of his wife, Sept. 6, 1782, he might have remained in philosophic retirement. He lavished upon his motherless daughters extraordinary tenderness and solicitude, but he was now glad to abandon "Monticello" and seek relief from personal woe in public activity. Appointed peace commissioner to Europe, Nov. 12, 1782, he was prepared to sail when, his mission having become unnecessary, his appointment was withdrawn. In June 1783 he was elected a delegate to Congress and during six months' service in that body the following winter he was a member of almost every important committee and drafted no fewer than thirty-one state papers (Ford, I, xxviii–xxx). Some of these were of the first importance, especially his Notes on the Establishment of a Money Unit (*Ibid.*, III, 446–57), in which he advocated the adoption of the dollar, to be divided into tenths and hundredths, and his successive reports on the government of the western territory (*Ibid.*, III, 407–10, 429–32). The report of Mar. 22, 1784, which has been ranked second in importance only to the Declaration of Independence among Jefferson's state papers (*Ibid.*, III, 430, note), contained practically all the features of the epoch-making Ordinance of 1787. If it had been adopted as Jefferson presented it, slavery would have been forbidden in all the western territory after 1800, and the secession of any part of that region would have been rendered indisputably illegal. Jefferson had earlier drafted a deed of cession of the northwestern territory claimed by Virginia, and he drew up a land ordinance which failed of adoption. Certainly he was a major architect of American expansion.

As a member of Congress he drafted a report on the definitive treaty of peace which was eventually adopted (Ford, III, 349–50). He drew up, on Dec. 20, 1783, a report which was agreed to as the basis of procedure in the negotiation of treaties of commerce, and was himself appointed, May 7, 1784, to assist Franklin and Adams in this work. Arriving in Paris on Aug. 6 with his daughter Martha, he was appointed in 1785 Franklin's successor as minister to France and remained in that country until October 1789. Rightly regarded in France as a savant, he carried on the tradition of Franklin, but until the end of his own stay he was overshadowed by Franklin's immense reputation. Jefferson's attitude toward his predecessor, whom he regarded as the greatest American, was one of becoming modesty without a tinge of jealousy. During his ministry he was likewise overshadowed by Lafayette, who was regarded as the French symbol of American ideas and ideals and the protector of American interests. Jefferson took full advantage of Lafayette's invaluable cooperation and associated with him on terms of intimacy and affection, content to be relatively inconspicuous if he might be useful.

Though he later characterized his official activities in France as unimportant, Jefferson proved a diligent and skilful diplomat. He and his colleagues succeeded in negotiating, in 1785, a treaty of commerce with Prussia. Early in 1786 he joined Adams in London, but their efforts to negotiate a treaty were futile. He made careful note of English domestic gardening and mechanical appliances, but of their architecture and manners had no kind word to say. He supported Thomas Barclay in the negotiation of a treaty with Morocco in 1787, but was convinced that the Barbary pirates could be restrained only by force and worked out a scheme for concerted action on the part of a league of nations. This was accepted by Congress, but aroused no enthusiasm in Europe. He negotiated with France a consular convention, signed Nov. 14, 1788, which was the first of the sort agreed to by the United States (Woolery, *post,* ch. IV). Though he could not hope to make much of a breach in the wall of commercial exclusiveness, he gained some relaxation of French duties on American products, and by his arguments against the tobacco monopoly of the Farmers General, which he attacked as a system, made a definite impression on Vergennes and his successor, Montmorin (F. L. Nusbaum, in *Political Science Quarterly,* December 1925, pp. 497–516). Jefferson left Europe with the feeling that the French had granted all the commercial concessions possible, that they had few interests in America, and that they had great sentimental attachment to the young Republic. He was convinced that the United States should be friendly to France, both because of gratitude and because of her value as a counterpoise against the British, whom he regarded as hostile in sentiment and entirely selfish in policy. He gained the impression, however, that Great Britain and Spain would pay much for American neutrality if they should become involved in European controversy. The hope that the United States would ultimately gain great advantages from the troubles of Europe profoundly affected his subsequent foreign policy, predisposing him to ways of peace (Bemis, *American Secretaries of State,* II, 9–13).

At a time when there was a flood of sentimental French writings about America, Jefferson endeavored to present the American cause adequately and accurately. These motives in part caused him to distribute his own *Notes on the State of Virginia,* and the Virginia statute of religious freedom. Appealed to for information by many writers, he furnished extensive materials in particular to his former neighbor, Philip Mazzei [*q.v.*], whose *Recherches Historiques et Politiques sur les États-Unis* (4 vols., 1788) was the most accurate work of the period on America, and to Démeunier, whose article, "États-Unis," in the *Encyclopédie Methodique: Économie Politique et Diplomatique* (1786), greatly embarrassed the American minister by its inaccuracies and its fulsome praise of him. To interested friends at home, he wrote about inventions in dozens of letters; and for the younger Madison, Monroe, and others he continually purchased books. In 1787 he went into northern Italy to see the machines used there for cleaning rice, smuggled out samples of rice seed to South Carolina and Georgia, forwarded information about the olive tree, and at Nîmes gazed for hours at the Maison Carrée, "like a lover at his mistress." To his native Virginia he sent a plan for the new state capitol, modeled on this temple, and thus served to initiate the classical revival in American architecture. On another tour in 1788, he made numerous observations in Germany (H. A. Washington, *post,* IX, 373). This keen-eyed, serious-minded, reflective traveler purposed that his mission should prove educative to his fellow citizens as well as himself and never lost sight of his obligation to be useful.

Though greatly impressed with French manners, he was strongly opposed to any aping of them by Americans. He was attracted by the cuisine and wines and found the French a temperate people, but thought their life lacking in domestic happiness and on the whole rather futile. Life for him was empty when not purposeful. He thought little of French science, but was enthusiastic about their arts—architecture, painting, and, most of all, music, which he valued the more perhaps because a fractured wrist had ended his days as a violinist. It is doubtful whether he ever mastered French as a spoken language, but he read it well enough. Distressed by the inequality of conditions, he came to think less than ever of royalty, nobility, and priests. His experiences and observations did not give him a new philosophy, for, like the French reformers, he had already drunk at the fountain of liberal English political thought. Many of the writings of Condorcet (see especially A. O'Connor, *Oeuvres de Condorcet,* 1847, VIII, 1–13), might have come from Jefferson's own pen; he shared with Du Pont de Nemours the passionate desire to remove economic and intellectual barriers; like the early revolutionists, he had profound faith in the indefinite perfectibility of mankind and made a veritable religion of enlightenment. From his stay in France he gained, not new doctrines, but an emotional stimulus, returning to America strengthened in his civic faith.

The course of the Revolution until his departure Jefferson followed closely and reported in detail. Though he strove to maintain strict official neutrality, this skilled political architect suggested to Lafayette's aunt, Mme. de Tessé, a desirable course of procedure for the Assembly of Notables (H. A. Washington, II, 133–34), and to Lafayette himself he submitted a proposed charter for France (June 3, 1789, Ford, V, 199–202). A meeting of the leaders of the Patriot party, arranged by Lafayette, met at Jefferson's house in the effort to arrive at a compromise on the questions of the royal veto and the constitution of the Assembly (H. A. Washington, III, 116–17; Ford, I, 143). Intimate and sympathetic with the moderate reformers, he deplored the violence of later days but retained the conviction that the Revolution had done far more good than ill; and, in his ripe old age, he declared that every traveled man would prefer France as a place of residence to any country but his own.

Having been granted a leave of absence to settle his private affairs and to take home his two daughters, the younger of whom, Mary, had joined him in Paris in 1787, Jefferson sailed in October 1789 and arrived at "Monticello" two days before Christmas, to be welcomed tumultuously by his rejoicing slaves. Soon after he landed, he received from Washington the offer of the appointment to the Department of State, then being temporarily administered by John Jay [*q.v.*]. Jefferson's dislike for publicity and shrinking from censure made him reluctant to enter the storm of politics, from which in France he had been relatively aloof, but on patriotic grounds he at length accepted the eminently appropriate appointment. After giving his daughter Martha in marriage to her cousin, Thomas Mann Randolph [*q.v.*], he proceeded to New York, where, on Mar. 22, 1790, he became the first secretary of state under the Constitution.

Though he had kept in close touch with American developments through extensive correspondence, Jefferson was not fully aware of the conservative reaction which had taken place in his own country while he was in the midst of political ferment in France. He had seen nothing threatening in the commotions that had marked the last years of the Confederation, but thought dangerous liberty distinctly preferable to quiet slavery and had regarded the government, despite its imperfections, as "without comparison the best existing or that ever did exist" (Ford, IV, 423–25). None the less, he had viewed with distinct favor the movement for strengthening the federal government and had given the new Constitution his general approval, objecting chiefly to the absence of a bill of rights, which was later supplied, and the perpetual re-eligibility of the president. He had denied that he was of the party of federalists, but had stated that he was much farther from the anti-federalists (Ford, V, 75–78). He cannot be justly charged with factiousness because he came to be regarded, before his retirement from office, as the leader of the group opposed to the policies of Alexander Hamilton [*q.v.*]. To distinguish themselves from their opponents, whom they termed monarchists, Jefferson and his sympathizers soon called themselves Republicans. They may have subsequently exaggerated their charges for political effect, but he believed until the end of his life that his early fears of an American monarchy were warranted and it would seem that they were at the time not unnatural and not without foundation (Ford, I, 156–57; Dunbar, *post*). Undoubtedly he was distressed by the social atmosphere in which he found himself. He had enjoyed a considerable social experience in monarchical France, where theoretical democracy and even republicanism were fashionable, but in the aristocratic Federalist court, at first in New York and soon in Philadelphia, he was ever ill at ease.

With Hamilton, nearly fourteen years his junior, who had already assumed the first place in the counsels of the government, he strove at the outset to cooperate. His subsequent statement that he was duped by his colleague in connection with the Assumption Bill is unconvincing as well as uncomplimentary to his own intelligence. His contemporary letters show clearly that he was at the time convinced that some compromise was essential for peace and the preservation of the Union. When at length better provision for Virginia was made in the bill, and the location of the Federal City on the banks of the Potomac was agreed to, he gave his approval to the measure. He did not yet fully perceive that Hamilton's whole financial policy was least advantageous to the agrarian groups in which—for broad social rather than narrow economic reasons—he himself was most interested.

The first serious difference of opinion between the two men was over a question of foreign policy. Fully convinced that the British would not yield the Northwest posts or grant commercial privileges unless forced to do so, Jefferson favored the employment of commercial discrimination as a weapon against them. This policy, advocated in Congress by Madison, was opposed by Hamilton, who feared the loss of revenue from British imports. The movement in Congress for discrimination was strengthened by successive able reports of Jefferson on matters of commercial policy, but thanks to Hamilton it was blocked in February 1791 and ultimately abandoned (Bemis, *Jay's Treaty,* chs. I–IV). Meanwhile, the Secretary of the Treasury had maintained a surprising intimacy with George Beckwith, the unofficial British representative (1789–91), with whom the Secretary of State properly refused to have anything to do.

In February 1791, at the request of his chief, Jefferson drew up an opinion on the constitutionality of the Bank of the United States (Ford, V, 284–89) to which Hamilton replied, though neither paper was published until long afterward. Jefferson, who opposed monopolistic tendencies anyway, argued that the powers assumed by Hamilton's bill were not among those enumerated in the Constitution as belonging to the federal government, nor within either of its general phrases, which he interpreted narrowly and literally. He subsequently declared that he did not view constitutions with "sanctimonious reverence," and he favored their periodical revision, but this critic of the Scriptures here set up the Constitution as a sort of sacred law. His fears that liberal construction might result in the unbridled power of the federal government were undoubtedly heightened by his growing distrust of Hamilton, and this perhaps led him to go to extremes in the statement of his own theoretical position. Strict construction had its uses as a check on the tyranny of the national majority, but thoroughgoing application of Jefferson's arguments would have rendered the federal government feeble and inflexible, as he himself in practice later found. None the less, he had suffered a second defeat at the hands of Hamilton.

In the spring of 1791 Thomas Paine's *Rights of Man* appeared in America, with an extract from a private note of the Secretary of State as a preface. Jefferson's statement that he was glad that something was to be said publicly against "the political heresies" that had sprung up was interpreted both as an approval of Paine, who was anathema to the Anglomen in America, and as a reflection upon John Adams [*q.v.*], whose expatiations on the faults of democratic systems, indeed, Jefferson had definitely in mind. His statement of regret (Ford, V, 353–55) that he and his old friend had been "thrown on the public stage as public antagonists," may be accepted as sincere by others, as it was by Adams. The incident, however, identified Jefferson with criticism of the aristocratic tendencies of the government and in the end was politically advantageous to him. Fortuitous circumstances thus served to make a popular figure of one who abhorred controversy, who preferred to work behind the scenes, and who lacked the personal aggressiveness commonly associated with political leadership.

In May–June 1791 he and Madison made a trip to New England, during which they doubtless gave thought to politics; and, on Oct. 31, Philip Freneau [*q.v.*] published in Philadelphia the first number of the *National Gazette,* in opposition to the *Gazette of the United States,* published by John Fenno [*q.v.*]. Jefferson, knowing Freneau to be an ardent democrat, had given him the small post of translator in the Department of State, as Hamilton had already given Fenno the more lucrative printing at his disposal and was later to give him personal financial assistance. With the increasingly bitter criticism of Hamilton in Congress during the winter of 1791–92 Jefferson afterward claimed that he had nothing to do, except that he expressed hostility in conversation with and letters to his friends. His leadership even at this time was probably less active than has been commonly supposed, but he had undoubtedly become the symbol of anti-Hamiltonianism, and, though more scrupulous of proprieties than his colleague, served to inspire forces which he did not now or ever essay to command.

Hamilton had established with George Hammond, who presented in November 1791 his credentials as British minister, an intimacy similar to that which Beckwith had enjoyed. Hammond, forced by Jefferson to admit that he had no power to negotiate a new treaty, unwisely undertook to debate with the American Secretary the infractions of the treaty of peace. Jefferson's magnificent reply of May 29, 1792 (*American State Papers, Foreign Relations,* I, 1832, pp. 201–37), which completely demolished the mediocre case of the Britisher, was submitted in draft to Hamilton in advance, and, with the latter's relatively minor criticisms, to Washington, who heartily approved it. To Hammond, however, the Secretary of the Treasury lamented the "intemperate violence" of Jefferson, and stated that the reply had not been read by Washington and did not represent the position of the government. Thus fortified by assurances which nullified Jefferson's arguments, the British minister submitted the matter to his superiors at home, who felt safe in ignoring it (Bemis, *Jay's Treaty,* ch. V). The full extent of Hamilton's intrigue has only recently been disclosed, but Jefferson was undoubtedly aware that he owed his undeserved defeat to his colleague.

By the summer of 1792 the hostility of the two men had become implacable. In the spring Jefferson had expressed in no uncertain terms to Washington his opinion that the causes of public discontent lay in Hamilton's policy, particularly in the "corruption" that had accompanied the financial measures of the latter and that had extended to the legislature itself (Ford, I, 176–78). A formal list of the objections Jefferson had cited was submitted by the President to Hamilton on July 29 and was replied to by the latter three weeks later. In the meantime, Hamilton, smarting under the barbs of Freneau, had made an anonymous attack on the democratic editor and through him upon Jefferson. Washington's letters to his two secretaries, deploring the dissensions within the government, elicited lengthy replies in which each man presented his case, not only to his chief but also to posterity (see J. Sparks, *The Writings of George Washington,* X, 1836, pp. 249–55, 515–26; *The Works of Alexander Hamilton,* 1904, II, 426–72, VII, 303–06; Ford, *Writings of Thomas Jefferson,* VI, 101–09, 123–24). Washington did not succeed in stilling the troubled waters. Hamilton, indeed, during the autumn of 1792 published in the *Gazette of the United States* a series of ferocious anonymous attacks on his colleague, with the definite object of driving him from office. Jefferson, with greater dignity or greater discretion, refrained from newspaper controversy, leaving his defense to his friends. He played a direct part, however, in drafting the resolutions of William Branch Giles [*q.v.*], presented early in 1793, which were severely critical of Hamilton's conduct of the Treasury (P. L. Ford, in the *Nation,* Sept. 5, 1895; *Writings of Jefferson,* VI, 168–71).

His hostility to Hamilton, apart from his justifiable resentment at the interference of the latter in the conduct of his department, was like that of a religious devotee to an enemy of his faith. He was convinced that Hamilton's system "flowed from principles adverse to liberty, and was calculated to undermine and demolish the republic, by creating an influence of his department over the members of the legislature." Hamilton's hostility to Jefferson, apart from resentment that his power had been challenged, was like that of a practical man of affairs who found specific projects impeded by one whom he regarded as a quibbling theorist. Washington, reluctant to admit the existence of parties, valued both men and wanted both to remain in office, utilized both, and followed the policies of neither exclusively. The invaluable service rendered by each in his own field of activity vindicates the judgment of the patient President.

Yielding to the request of his Chief, Jefferson remained in office until the last day of 1793, during a critical period of foreign affairs. Though the course of the Revolution in France had been followed with growing concern by the conservative groups in America, popular opinion was still rather favorable to the French when war broke out in Europe (Feb. 1, 1793) and a new minister, Edmond Charles Genet [*q.v.*], came to the United States. Jefferson was determined that his country should take no action that would imply opposition to the principles of the French Revolution, but he fully shared the feeling of Washington and Hamilton that American neutrality was imperative. He successfully urged the avoidance of the word "neutrality" in Washington's proclamation, however, in order to offend the French as little as possible and in the hope of gaining from the British some concessions in the definition of contraband. He also prevailed upon Washington to receive Genet without qualification and to postpone consideration of the treaty until the French should demand execution of the guarantee, which he thought they would not do. He finally yielded to the opinion of Hamilton that payments on the debt to France should not be anticipated, but urged a softening of the refusal. Though he received Genet kindly, rejoiced in the popular enthusiasm for democracy that the fiery emissary kindled, and, through letters of introduction, came dangerously near conniving with the Frenchman in his projected expeditions against

Canada and Louisiana, he strove with diligence to maintain neutrality and bore with patience the immense labors that the American position imposed upon him. When Genet persisted in intolerable practices and criticisms Jefferson lost patience with him and joined his colleagues in asking his recall.

Though he protested vigorously against British infringements of American neutral rights during the war, Jefferson was unable as secretary of state to solve the problem of British relations, and he regarded Jay's Treaty, which was later negotiated under the influence of Hamilton, as an ignominious surrender of American claims. The negotiations instituted by him with Spain were equally unsuccessful during his term of office, though the American objectives which he had formulated were attained in the treaty of 1795. His tangible achievements as secretary of state were not commensurate with his devoted labors, but he had fully justified Washington's confidence in him. If in the heat of the controversy with Hamilton he was at times guilty of extravagant assertion, he performed an inestimable service to the Republic by calling attention to the dangers of his colleague's policy, by formulating the chief grounds of opposition to it, and by inspiring the forces that were to effect its modification after it had achieved its most significant results.

Now in his fifty-first year, Jefferson felt that his second retirement from public life was final. Soon he gathered all the members of his immediate family under the paternal roof, and he at length resumed building operations at "Monticello," following revised plans that had grown out of his architectural observations abroad. By a system of crop rotation he tried to restore his lands, he experimented with mechanical devices, built a grist-mill, set up a nail-factory, and directed his large but relatively unprofitable establishment with characteristic diligence and attention to minute details. His renewed and increased enthusiasm for agriculture quite got the better of his love of study. At no other period of his mature life did he read so little and write so rarely. His days on horseback soon restored his health to the vigor that he feared it had permanently lost, and he brought some order into his tangled finances. During his years as an office-holder he had largely lived upon his small salary, yet the profits from his plantations and even sales of slaves and lands had been insufficient to rid him of the old Wayles debt, which in 1795 was increased by a judgment against the executors as security for the late Richard Randolph. Like so many of his fellow Virginians, Jefferson was unable to realize upon his assets and was eaten up by interest to British creditors. His personal generosity, however, which had been manifested in Philadelphia by loans to friends more distressed than he, continued unabated.

To Madison, whom he regarded as the logical Republican candidate for the presidency, he wrote, Apr. 27, 1795, that the "little spice of ambition" he had had in his younger days had long since evaporated and that the question of his own candidacy was forever closed (Ford, VII, 10). He remained, however, the symbol and the prophet of a political faith and when the leaders of his party determined to support him in 1796 did not gainsay them. He would have been willing to go into the presidency for a while, he said, in order "to put our vessel on her republican tack before she should be thrown too much to leeward of her true principles" (Jan. 1, 1797, Ford, VII, 98), but he was surprisingly content to run second to Adams, who was his senior and whom he perhaps regarded as the only barrier against Hamilton. After it appeared that Adams had won, and that he was second by three votes, he even suggested that some understanding in regard to future elections be reached with the President-Elect (Randall, II, 320–28). He proved himself a more realistic observer and a better political strategist, however, when he wrote Madison: "Let us cultivate Pennsylvania & we need not fear the universe" (Ford, VII, 109).

The vice-presidency provided a salary which Jefferson undoubtedly needed, enabled him to spend much time at "Monticello," and afforded him relative leisure. The chief significance of his service as presiding officer of the Senate lies in the fact that out of it emerged his *Manual of Parliamentary Practice* (1801), subsequently published in many editions and translated into several languages, and even now the basis of parliamentary usage in the Senate. Despite the conciliatory spirit that marked his early relations with Adams, Jefferson played no part in the conduct of the administration, in which the hand of Hamilton was soon apparent. Since the Vice-President belonged to the opposing group, his complete abstention from politics was not to be expected. He was characteristically discreet in public utterance, but his general attitude toward the questions of the day was undoubtedly well known; and he was inevitably the target of the Federalist press, which continued to regard him as the personification of his party. The publication in the United States in May 1797 of a private letter of his to Philip Mazzei (Apr. 24, 1796, Ford, VII, 72–78), which originally appeared in a Florentine paper and was somewhat altered in form by successive translations, gave wide currency to his earlier criticisms of the Federalists. Certain vehement phrases were interpreted as reflecting upon Washington and served to alienate the latter from his former secretary. Jefferson made no effort to disavow a letter which was in substance his (Ford, VII, 165), and suffered in silence while the Federalist press termed him "libeler," "liar," and "assassin" (Bowers, p. 352), and he was practically ostracized by polite society.

He had approved of Monroe's conduct in France, which aroused so much hostile Federalist comment, and felt that the bellicose spirit which swept the country after the publication of the "X. Y. Z. despatches" was aggravated by the Hamiltonians, with a view to advancing their own interests and embroiling the United States on the side of the British. He himself was sympathetic with Elbridge Gerry [*q.v.*], the Republican commissioner who proved more amenable than his colleagues to French influence, and suggested that Gerry publish an account of his experiences. At all times, however, Jefferson was a patriotic American, and he had now no enthusiasm for the existing order in France. He was glad to drop the disastrous French issue when, at the height of the war fever, the Federalists provided a better one by passing the Alien and Sedition Acts. Jefferson rightly regarded hysterical hostility to aliens, such as his friends Volney and Joseph Priestley, and attacks upon freedom of speech as a menace to the ideals he most cherished. Since the Sedition Law was applied chiefly to Republican editors, partisan as well as philosophical motives were conjoined in his opposition.

His most notable contribution to the campaign of discussion consisted of the Kentucky Resolutions of 1798, which, it appeared years later, he drafted. The Virginia Resolutions, drawn by Madison, were similar in tenor. The constitutional doctrines advanced in these famous documents—that the government of the United States originated in a compact, that acts of the federal government unauthorized by the delegated powers are void, and that a state has the right to judge of infractions of its powers and to determine the mode of redress—were in later years emphasized as their most important feature. The dominant purpose of the framers, however, was to attack the offensive laws as an unconstitutional and unwarranted infringement upon individual freedom, a denial of rights that could not be alienated. The language of what was in effect a party platform was in the nature of the case extravagant, but Jefferson and Madison had no intention of carrying matters to extremes, and such indorsement as their party ultimately received was of their protest, not of their method (F. M. Anderson, in *American Historical Review,* October 1899, pp. 45–63, January 1900, pp. 225–52). More important from the practical point of view than any promulgation of constitutional theory was the immense stimulus given by Jefferson and the other Republican leaders to the establishment of newspapers such as their opponents had attacked.

Nominated by a congressional caucus for the presidency and by no means indifferent to the outcome as he had been four years earlier, Jefferson owed his success in the election of 1800 as much to Federalist dissensions as to any formal issues that had been raised. To the Republican victory, his running mate, Aaron Burr [*q.v.*], also made no small contribution. By fault of the electoral machinery, soon to be remedied, the two Republicans received an identical vote and the choice of a president was left to the Federalist House of Representatives. Despite the personal hostility of many of the Federalists to Jefferson, the feeling, to which Hamilton greatly contributed, that he was the safer man of the two, and a tacit understanding that he would not revolutionize the government, caused Congress ultimately to yield to the undoubted desire of the Republicans and to elect him (Beard, *Economic Origins of Jeffersonian Democracy,* pp. 402–14). His own reference to the "revolution" of 1800 was one of his political exaggerations, but the elevation to the highest executive office of one who, almost twenty years before, had unheroically relinquished the reins of gubernatorial power undoubtedly marked a revolution in his own political fortunes. The popular success of Jefferson, whose diffidence and lack of spectacular qualities would have constituted in a later day an insuperable handicap, and whose relative freedom from personal ambition makes it impossible to characterize him as a demagogue, was due in considerable part to his identification of himself with causes for which time was fighting, and to his remarkable sensitiveness to fluctuations in public opinion, combined with an ability to utilize and to develop agencies of popular appeal. As a practical politician he worked through other men, whom he energized and who gave him to an extraordinary degree their devoted cooperation. His unchallenged leadership was due, not to self-assertiveness and imperiousness of will, but to the fact that circumstances had made him a symbolic figure, and that to an acute intelligence and unceasing industry he joined a dauntless and contagious faith. The long struggle between his partisans and the Federalists has been variously interpreted as one between democracy and aristocracy, state rights and centralization, agrarianism and capitalism. His election, however, had more immediate significance in marking the vindication of political opposition, the repudiation of a reactionary régime, and the accession of more representative leaders to power.

Jefferson, the first president inaugurated in Washington, had himself drawn a plan for the city, part of which survives in the Mall. As secretary of state, to whom the commissioners of the District were responsible, he had suggested the competition for the new federal buildings and he was considerably responsible for the selection of classical designs. As president he created for Benjamin H. Latrobe [*q.v.*] the office of surveyor of public buildings and fully cooperated in planning for the future development of a monumental city. In his day, pomp and ceremony, to which on principle and for political reasons he was opposed, would have been preposterous in the wilderness village. Remaining until the last at Conrad's boarding-house, where his democratic simplicity was almost ostentatious, he walked to the nearby Senate chamber of the incompleted capitol, to receive the oath of office from his cousin and inveterate political foe, Chief Justice John Marshall. Though aware of the last efforts of the Federalists to renew the Sedition Act and entrench themselves in the judiciary, he felt that after the long "contest of opinion" the danger of monarchy was now removed, and in his benevolent inaugural (Ford, VII, 1–6) he sought to woo the more moderate of his opponents by making acquiescence in the will of the majority as easy as possible. Though he challenged the assertion that a republican government could not be strong, he defined its functions as essentially negative. It should restrain men from injuring one another, he said, but otherwise leave them to regulate their own concerns. He declared against special privileges and urged encouragement, not of industry, but of agriculture and of commerce "as its handmaid." He reiterated his conviction that the federal government should chiefly concern itself with foreign affairs, leaving to the states the administration of local matters. War, he felt, could be avoided by peaceable coercion through the weapon of commerce.

Inaugurated in his fifty-eighth year, he made his official residence in the boxlike and incompletely plastered Executive Mansion, though he continued to spend as much time as possible at "Monticello," where he was still directing building operations. His beautiful second daughter, now the wife of her cousin John Wayles Eppes [*q.v.*], though far less prolific than her sister, had also by this time made him a grandfather. She was to sadden her father's life by her untimely death in 1804. Generally deprived of adequate feminine supervision while in Washington, Jefferson lived there in sartorial indifference and dispensed generous but informal hospitality, as he was accustomed to do at home, to the consternation of diplomats jealous of precedence (Ford, VIII, 276–77; Henry Adams, *post,* II, ch. XVI; *American Historical Review,* July 1928, pp. 832–35). His manners, after he had overcome his constitutional diffidence, were easy though not polished. To hostile observers his democratic simplicity was a pose, to his friends the naturalness of one who had achieved and thought enough to dare to be himself. His loose gait and habit of lounging, together with his discursive though highly informing conversation, doubtless contributed to the common but erroneous impression among his foes that this most scholarly of politicians was a careless thinker. "His external appearance," according to an admirer, "had no pretensions to elegance, but it was neither coarse nor awkward, and it must be owned that his greatest personal attraction was a countenance beaming with benevolence and intelligence" (Margaret Bayard Smith, *First Forty Years of Washington Society,* 1906, pp. 385–86).

Chief in his harmonious official family were Madison, the secretary of state, and Gallatin, who as secretary of the treasury was to carry out with considerable success his program of economy. Jefferson found nearly all the minor offices filled by Federalists and, though anxious to conciliate his former foes, sympathized with his own followers in their insistence that the balance be restored. This could only be done by removals, for, as he said, vacancies "by death are few; by resignation none." He proceeded to treat as null and void Federalist appointments which seemed to him of questionable legality, such as those of the "midnight judges" and others made by Adams after the latter's defeat was apparent. Finding his policy a political success, he extended it, until by the summer of 1803 the balance was restored and removals ceased. No non-partisan standard was adopted, however, and the Republicans came to dominate the civil service as the Federalists had done. Since

Jefferson's appointments involved some recognition of party service, they constituted a technical introduction of the spoils system. The standards of the federal service, however, were not perceptibly lowered, and, except in New England, the people were generally satisfied (Fish, *post,* ch. II).

Though Jefferson, whose voice could hardly be heard upon a public occasion anyway, abandoned the custom of delivering messages in person, he maintained over Congress indirect and tactful but efficacious control. The repeal of the Federalist Judiciary Act of 1801 was distinctly a measure of the administration. The severe rebuke administered to him and Madison by Marshall in *Marbury* vs. *Madison* (1803) did not predispose him to concede the right of the Supreme Court to invalidate an act of Congress. Indeed, in pardoning victims of the Sedition Law, he himself pronounced that statute unconstitutional, as he felt he was called upon to do (Beveridge, *Life of John Marshall,* III, 605–06). He throughly approved of the use of the weapon of impeachment against offensively partisan judges and deeply regretted its practical failure, notably in the case of Justice Samuel Chase [*q.v.*]. Though the federal judges learned better to observe the proprieties, Jefferson never receded from his position that the Federalists, from the battery of the judiciary, were endeavoring to beat down the works of Republicanism and defeat the will of the people, as in a sense they were.

Rumors of the retrocession of Louisiana by Spain to France led Jefferson to write the American minister to France, Robert R. Livingston [*q.v.*], on Apr. 18, 1802, that the possessor of New Orleans was the natural enemy of the United States and that by placing herself there France assumed an attitude of defiance (Ford, VIII, 143–47). Following the independent announcement by the Spanish intendant, Oct. 16, 1802, of the closure of the Mississippi and Federalist talk in Congress of warlike measures, he despatched Monroe to France as special minister. The purchase which Livingston and Monroe made, and for which Jefferson gave them full credit, was a diplomatic triumph of the first magnitude but it required him to disregard many scruples and to compromise cherished constitutional principles. In his proper anxiety to preserve the freedom of navigation of the Mississippi, he felt compelled at one time to consider a rapprochement with Great Britain, his traditional foe, and ultimately to increase the debt which he was striving so hard to reduce. He was confident that the Constitution did not empower the federal government to acquire or incorporate territory, and that broad construction would make blank paper of that supreme safeguard against tyranny. After the treaty was negotiated he favored the submission of a constitutional amendment, but yielded to the insistence of his political friends that no amendment was necessary and that delay was perilous, doubtless consoling himself with the thought that in Republican hands the Constitution was safe. The ratification of the treaty, effected in response to overwhelming public opinion, has been interpreted as a death-blow to strict construction (H. Adams, *post,* II, 90–91). The Louisiana Purchase marked the lowest, or highest, point of Jefferson's pragmatic statesmanship. He had assured the physical greatness of his country and the future success of his party, which was symbolized by his own triumphant reëlection. Western discontent was stilled and the Federalists were reduced to sectional impotence. For all of this his momentary theoretical inconsistency seemed to his partisans a small price to pay, but his subsequent silence about the greatest constructive accomplishment of his presidency implies that he viewed it with little pride. The purchase served, however, to facilitate the expedition for which he had already commissioned Meriwether Lewis [*q.v.*] and prepared elaborate instructions (Ford, VIII, 192–202). He himself wrote for the *History of the Expedition under the Command of Captains Lewis and Clark* (1814), the best biography of his former secretary, and no one more than he rejoiced in the discoveries the explorers made.

Livingston and Monroe had bought a vaguely defined region which they soon persuaded themselves included West Florida as well as Louisiana. Jefferson subsequently embodied similar views in a pamphlet which determined the attitude of the administration and its supporters (in *Documents Relating to the Purchase & Exploration of Louisiana,* 1904; Cox, *post,* pp. 80–87). The Mobile Act of Feb. 24, 1804, assumed the acquisition of West Florida, but Jefferson, finding that the Spanish were not acquiescent as he had expected, practically annulled its offensive features by proclamation and soon afterward sent Monroe on what proved to be a futile mission to Spain. In his public message to Congress, on Dec. 4, 1805 (Ford, VIII, 384–96), he adopted an uncharacteristic tone of belligerency, apparently with the idea of frightening the Spanish, then, by revealing to Congress his purpose to acquire Florida by what John Randolph of Roanoke [*q.v.*] regarded as a bribe to France, confounded his supporters and alienated that vitriolic leader, already incensed by the settlement of the Yazoo claims. A proposal went to Napoleon too late to be of any use and the perplexing question of Florida remained unsettled during Jefferson's administration. His tortuous and uncandid policy had served only to diminish his influence in Congress and weaken his hand against the British (Cox, pp. 660–68).

His policy of peaceable negotiation did not extend to the Barbary pirates, to whom he applied more force than had any previous American president. Following the repudiation of his treaty by the Bey of Tripoli in 1801, Jefferson dispatched against him a naval force which blockaded his ports. Subsequently Jefferson also employed naval force against the Sultan of Morocco. The treaty at length negotiated with Tripoli, though it included provisions for the ransom of American prisoners, granted the United States the most favorable terms yet given any nation by that piratical power (Woolery, *post,* ch. II).

Long before the trial of Aaron Burr [*q.v.*] in 1807 on charges of treason, Jefferson had lost faith in his former associate, but he gave little heed to the mystifying western expedition of the adventurer until it was well on its way. On Nov. 27, 1806, Jefferson issued a proclamation of warning against an illegal expedition against Spain, and, after Burr's arrest, publicly expressing himself as convinced of the latter's guilt, exerted powerful influence to bring about his conviction. Burr's trial in Richmond before John Marshall [*q.v.*] developed into a political duel between the Chief Justice and the President. Burr's counsel, including Luther Martin [*q.v.*], raised against Jefferson a cry of persecution which echoed through the land, and, attacking the credibility of the chief witness for the prosecution, the vulnerable James Wilkinson [*q.v.*], through him assailed the man who had appointed him to command the army and had sent him to protect Louisiana against the Spanish. Marshall was distinctly hostile to Jefferson throughout the proceedings and, by his definition of treason, made the conviction of Burr impossible. Jefferson wished to press the charge of misdemeanor, in order to find grounds for the impeachment of the Chief Justice, but had to abandon his plans because the whole case rested on Wilkinson. Though Marshall's conduct was by no means unexceptionable, this famous trial proved more discomforting to Jefferson than to the Chief Justice and strengthened the hands of his political enemies, who not improperly charged him with an original indifference which gave way to credulity, and with a measure of vindictiveness wholly inconsistent with his expressed convictions in regard to the sacred rights of the individual.

The difficulties which Jefferson faced during his second administration as the head of a neutral nation in a time of ruthless general European war, were unescapable and could probably have been successfully met by no American statesman. During his first term, though he had done little to prepare for a possible conflict of arms, he had managed sufficiently well by employing ordinary diplomatic methods. Until 1805 the British had in practice granted sufficient concessions to permit large prosperity to the American carrying trade, and in effect they later modified the Rule of 1756 (1805). The impressment of seamen, however, remained a grievance, which the British would do nothing to remove. Then, in the battle of Orders in Council and Napoleonic decrees, the neutral American Republic, unable to meet both sets of requirements and threatened with the confiscation of commercial vessels in case either were violated, was placed in an intolerable position.

Of the possible courses of action open to him, war never commended itself to Jefferson, who did not want to take sides with either of the European rivals, though, after the *Leopard* fired on the *Chesapeake* in June 1807, a declaration against the British might have been supported by the American people. In this instance, Jefferson's belligerency vented itself in a proclamation, regarded by his foes as pusillanimous, denying to British armed vessels the hospitality of American waters (Ford, IX, 89–99). He had previously sent William Pinkney [*q.v.*] to London to serve with Monroe on a mission extraordinary, and had tried to strengthen the hands of the negotiators by the Non-Importation Act of 1806, which was to become effective some months later. His reliance was on diplomacy, supplemented by the threat of economic pressure, and when diplomacy failed he fell back on economic pressure. The only other apparent alternatives were intolerable submission or some sort of cooperation with the British against Napoleon. The Embargo constituted perhaps Jefferson's most original and daring measure of statesmanship; it proved to be his greatest practical failure (Sears, *post*). Adopted in December 1807, after an inadequate debate and by an overwhelming vote because of his political dominance and still enormous popularity, the measure, which Jefferson is thought to have drawn, combined with the Non-Intercourse Act to bring about a theoretical suspension of foreign commerce for an indefinite period.

The attempts to enforce the Embargo involved an exercise of arbitrary power by the federal government and an inevitable and increasing infringement on individual rights which were contrary to Jefferson's most cherished ideals. He opposed war in large part because of the corruption and repression which were its accompaniments, little realizing that his peaceful substitute would be attended with the same evils and that negative heroism would in the end prove galling. He counted too heavily on British liberal opinion, which had opposed the Orders in Council as affecting the United States, and he did not anticipate the developments in Spain and the Spanish colonies which did so much to relieve the pressure on Great Britain. He claimed, with considerable justification, that the Embargo was not in effect long enough to attain its objective, and it may well be that under other circumstances some measure of the sort might prove an efficacious weapon. But in 1808–09, employed by a weak power, it served chiefly to impoverish the sections that supported Jefferson most loyally, to give a new lease on life to partisan opposition in New England, and to bring his second executive venture to an inglorious consummation. Forced to yield to a rebellious Congress, on Mar. 1, 1809, he signed the Non-Intercourse Act, which partially raised the Embargo, and shortly afterward retired to Albemarle, discredited and disillusioned, though unconvinced that he had erred in policy. He correctly described himself as a wave-worn mariner approaching the shore, as a prisoner emerging from the shackles, and declared that Nature had intended him for the tranquil pursuits of science, in which he found infinite delight (Memorial Edition, XII, 258–60).

During the past eight years this earnest advocate of the freedom of the press had been subjected to a flood of personal calumny. Long regarded in ecclesiastical circles, especially in New England, as the embodiment of foreign infidelity, he not unnaturally aroused a storm of indignation, soon after his first inauguration, by offering to Thomas Paine [*q.v.*] passage to America on a sloop-of-war and by expressing the hope that his "useful labours" would be continued (Ford, VIII, 18–19). The following year an indefensible assault was launched by a disgruntled pamphleteer, whose pen Jefferson himself had previously subsidized. To the charges of cowardice, dishonesty, and personal immorality made in 1802 by James Thomson Callender [*q.v.*] in the Richmond *Recorder* almost every subsequent story reflecting on Jefferson's private life can ultimately be traced. Given nationwide currency by the Federalist press, these were discussed in 1805 in the House of Representatives of Massachusetts, where a motion to dismiss the printers of the House for publishing in the *New-England Palladium* (Jan. 18, 1805) libels on the President failed of adoption. One only of these charges was admitted by Jefferson (W. C. Ford, *Thomas Jefferson Correspondence,* 1916, p. 115). This referred to an instance of highly improper conduct on his part, while yet a young man and single, for which he made restitution. Of the other allegations of immorality, it is quite sufficient to say that Jefferson, a model husband and father, was "more refined than many women in the delicacy of his private relations" (Henry Adams, I, 324).

For the wide acceptance, by persons of the better sort, of the extravagant charges of an unscrupulous drunkard, the sensitive President was disposed to blame his old theological foes, especially in New England. There his followers were assaulting the ancient alliance between church and state, for the final overthrow of which they deserve considerable credit. It may well be, as Henry Adams says (*History,* I, 310), that Jefferson did not understand the New Englanders, but it is certain that they did not understand him. Though sanguine in temperament, he was as serious-minded and almost as devoid of humor as any Puritan; and had he lived a generation later he would have been more at home in liberal religious circles in New England than anywhere else in America. He loathed Calvinism, but he objected to Unitarianism only because it also was another sect. At many times he paid grateful tribute to Epicurus and Epictetus, but as early as 1803 he began to select from the Gospels the passages which he believed came from Jesus. Toward the end of his life this amateur higher critic placed parallel texts, in four languages, in a "wee-little book," which he entitled the "Morals of Jesus" (published in 1904 as *House Doc. No. 755,* 58 Cong., 2 Sess.). This proved, he felt, that he was "a *real Christian,* that is to say a disciple of the doctrines of Jesus" (Ford, X, 5–6).

During the remaining seventeen years of his life, Jefferson ventured only a few miles from his haven at "Monticello." The Embargo and its aftermath were ruinous to him, as to so many Virginia planters, and because of the demands of incessant hospitality he could not live as simply as he desired. After the War of 1812, however, the sale of his library of some 10,000 volumes to the government, for the Library of Congress, served for several years to relieve his financial burdens; and his grandson, Thomas

Jefferson Randolph [*q.v.*], took over the management of his lands. Laborious correspondence occupied a disproportionate amount of his time, but he enjoyed exchanging ideas with John Adams (with whom his old friendship was beautifully restored), his friends in France, Thomas Cooper, and others, and has left in the letters of these years a mine of treasure. He gave his counsel to his disciples Madison and Monroe, when they asked it; and some of his expressions on public policy, as, for example, on the Missouri Compromise (to John Holmes, Ford, X, 157), and on the attitude of the United States toward Europe and the Latin-American republics (Oct. 24, 1823, Ford, X, 277–79) are notable.

The chief public problem to which he addressed himself, however, was that of education in Virginia, which he again called his "country." He never ceased to advocate a comprehensive state-wide plan of education, such as he had proposed in 1779. "Enlighten the people generally," he wrote Du Pont de Nemours in 1816, "and tyranny and oppressions of both mind and body will vanish like evil spirits at the dawn of day" (Memorial Edition, XIV, 491). Popular education, however, he regarded as more than a defensive weapon and a guarantor of freedom. His proposals of 1779 had been marked by a unique provision whereby youths of great promise were to be advanced from one grade of instruction to another without cost, and he hoped that these "geniuses . . . raked from the rubbish" would serve the state as governors or enlarge the domains of human knowledge. He formulated, as perhaps no other American of his generation, an educational philosophy for a democratic state; and in his last years he declared himself in favor of a literacy test for citizenship (Washington Edition, VI, 343; Memorial Edition, XIV, 491–92).

Having failed in his earlier efforts to transform the College of William and Mary, by 1800 at least Jefferson had hopes of establishing in the more salubrious upper country a university on a broad, liberal, and modern plan. Whatever interest he may have had, during his presidency, in the creation of a national university contingent upon the amendment of the Constitution (Honeywell, *post,* p. 63), after 1809 Virginia was central in all his thoughts. Indeed, his regret that so many of his "countrymen" went to be educated among "foreigners" (as at Princeton) or were taught at home by "beggars" (Northern tutors) was partly due to the fear that their political principles were being contaminated. His representations may have stimulated Gov. John Tyler to send to the Assembly in 1809 his strong message on education (Bruce, *post,* I, 85) which resulted in the establishment, the following year, of the Literary Fund. Jefferson regarded this as an inadequate provision for general education but it later made possible the creation of an institution of higher learning.

By happy chance, Jefferson in 1814 became associated as a trustee with the unorganized Albemarle Academy. Transformed into Central College, this became the germ from which the University of Virginia developed, under his adroit management at every stage. His letter of Sept. 7, 1814, to Peter Carr (Cabell, *post,* pp. 348 ff.), outlining in masterly fashion his views of a state system, probably inspired the resolution, adopted by the General Assembly on Feb. 24, 1816, which required a report on a scheme of public instruction. Shortly thereafter, Jefferson himself drafted a bill (Honeywell, appendix H), which contained most of the features of his more famous proposal of 1779 and included a provision for a university. This was rejected and for a time it appeared that, after an appropriation for elementary schools (which Jefferson always felt should be supported locally), no funds would be available for a higher institution. At length, in 1818, by a compromise, appropriations were authorized for elementary, but not for intermediate, schools and for a university.

Jefferson was appointed a member, and became chairman, of the Rockfish Gap Commission, empowered to recommend a site. By skilful use of geographical arguments, he gained the victory for Central College in August 1818. The report, which he had drafted beforehand, incorporated his ideas of what a university should be and remains one of his greatest educational papers (Cabell, pp. 432 ff.). After a legislative battle in which he acted only behind the scenes, the report was adopted, and in 1819 the University of Virginia was chartered. Though the services of Joseph C. Cabell and John H. Cocke [*qq.v.*] in launching the institution were invaluable, Jefferson, who was inevitably appointed a member of the first board of visitors and elected rector, remained until his death the dominant factor in its affairs. He received architectural suggestions from Benjamin H. Latrobe and to a lesser extent from William Thornton [*qq.v.*], but the plan of an academical village was his own. Many of the specifications were drawn up by him and the "pavilions," "hotels," dormitories, colonnades, and arcades were constructed under his immediate supervision. At his death, only the Rotunda, modeled by him on the Pantheon at Rome, was incomplete.

The courses of study followed closely those of

Jefferson's suggestions that seemed immediately practicable and at no later time went far beyond his anticipations. Upon the organization of the institution, he left his most characteristic impress perhaps in the establishment of independent, diploma-conferring "schools," capable of indefinite expansion, in the provision for entire freedom in the election of courses, in the complete disregard of the conventional grouping of students into classes, in the arrangement for a rotating chairmanship of the faculty, without a president, and in the prohibition of honorary degrees (Bruce, I, 321–34). Despite his insistence that Republican, rather than Federalist, principles be taught in the school of law, to a remarkable extent he freed the institution from hampering restrictions and made it in spirit a university. He can hardly be blamed that it subsequently suffered because of the lack of contributing colleges, the need of which he clearly envisaged, and that circumstances combined to make it a more aristocratic institution than he had anticipated or desired. Though he was disappointed in his full hopes of drawing from Europe to the faculty "the first characters in science," the mission of Francis Walker Gilmer [*q.v.*] was measurably successful, the new institution had from the outset a flavor of cosmopolitanism, and several of the first professors achieved distinction. The "Old Sachem" lived to see the university opened and for more than a year in operation.

During his own lifetime, Jefferson received not only American but also international recognition as a man, and as a patron, of learning. Elected president of the American Philosophical Society on Jan. 6, 1797 (*Transactions of the American Philosophical Society,* IV, 1799, pp. xi–xiii), he remained the head of this notable organization until 1815 and actively cooperated with it in the advancement and dissemination of knowledge. By introducing to his colleagues, on Mar. 10, 1797, his megalonyx he fired the "signal gun of American paleontology" (*Ibid.*, IV, no. XXX; *Science,* Apr. 19, 1929, p. 411). To them he read on May 4, 1798, a description of a mouldboard of least resistance for a plow (*Ibid.*, IV, no. XXXVII), for which invention he received in 1805 a gold medal from a French society (*Mémoires de la Société d'Agriculture du Département de Seine et Oise,* VII, xlix–lviii). In due course he became associated with an extraordinary number of important societies in various countries of Europe, as he had long been with the chief learned, and almost all the agricultural, societies of America. Much but by no means all of his recognition was due to his political prominence. His election, Dec. 26, 1801, as *associé étranger* of the Institute of France, if due to his position at all, was due to his presidency of the American Philosophical Society. This signal honor, which during his lifetime was shared by no other man of American birth and residence, may best be attributed to his reputation in France as the most conspicuous American intellectual. He himself interpreted it as "an evidence of the brotherly spirit of Science, which unites into one family all its votaries of whatever grade, and however widely dispersed throughout the different quarters of the globe" (Chinard, *Jefferson et les Idéologues,* p. 21). He corresponded throughout his life with an extraordinary number of scientists and philosophers in other lands, as well as in America, and sought to make available in his own country the best of foreign thought and discovery.

Modern scholars have recognized Jefferson as an American pioneer in numerous branches of science, notably paleontology, ethnology, geography, and botany. Living before the age of specialization, he was for his day a careful investigator, no more credulous than his learned contemporaries, and notable among them for his effort in all fields to attain scientific exactitude. In state papers he is commonly the lawyer, pleading a cause; in the heat of political controversy he doubtless compromised his intellectual ideals and certainly indulged in exaggeration; but his procedure in arriving at his fundamental opinions, the habits of his life, and his temperament were essentially those of a scholar. As secretary of state, he was in effect the first commissioner of patents and the first patent examiner (Wyman, *post*). He himself invented or adapted to personal uses numerous ingenious devices, the best known of which is his polygraph.

At home in French, Italian, and Spanish, as well as Greek and Latin, he wrote *An Essay towards Facilitating Instruction in the Anglo-Saxon and Modern Dialects of the English Language* (1851), and during a generation he amassed an extraordinary collection of Indian vocabularies, only to have them cast upon the waters by thieves in 1809. He owned one of the best private collections of paintings and statuary in the country, and has been termed "the first American connoisseur and patron of the arts" (Kimball, *Thomas Jefferson, Architect,* p. 86). Besides the Virginia state capitol, "Monticello," and the original buildings of the University of Virginia, he designed wholly or in part numerous Virginia houses, among them his own "Poplar Forest," "Farmington," "Bremo," "Barboursville," and probably the middle section of

"Brandon." Before the advent of professional architects in America, he began to collect books on architecture and discovered Palladio, from whom his careful and extensive observations abroad never weaned him. Always himself a Romanist, he did more than any other man to stimulate the classical revival in America. His own work, while always ingenious, is academic, precise, and orderly, but, because of the fortunate necessity of using brick and wood, the new creation was a blend, with a pleasing domesticity (*Ibid.*, pp. 82–83). He created a definite school of builders in Virginia, sought to establish formal instruction in architecture, stimulated and encouraged, among others, Bulfinch and Thornton, and, except for the fact that he accepted no pay for his services, was as truly a professional as they. It is probably no exaggeration to say that he was "the father of our national architecture" (*Ibid.*, p. 89).

Few other American statesmen have been such careful and unremitting students of political thought and history as was Jefferson, or have been more concerned with ultimate ends. Yet he has left no treatise on political philosophy, and all general statements about his theoretical position are subject to qualification. It is impossible to grant eternal validity to the "principles" adduced by him to support his position in particular circumstances; he was always more interested in applications than in speculation, and he was forced to modify his own philosophy in practice. But, despite unquestionable inconsistencies, the general trend of his policies and his major aims are unmistakable. A homely aristocrat in manner of life and personal tastes, he distrusted all rulers and feared the rise of an industrial proletariat, but, more than any of his eminent contemporaries, he trusted the common man, if measurably enlightened and kept in rural virtue; though pained and angered when the free press made him the victim of its license, he was a passionate advocate of human liberty and laid supreme stress on the individual; though he clearly realized the value of union, he emphasized the importance of the states and of local agencies of government; an intellectual internationalist, he gave whole-hearted support to the policy of political isolation, and anticipated the development on the North American continent of a dominant nation, unique in civilization. He is notable, not for his harmony with the life of his age, but rather for his being a step or several steps ahead of it; no other American more deserves to be termed a major prophet, a supreme pioneer. A philosophical statesman rather than a political philosopher, he contributed to democracy and liberalism a faith rather than a body of doctrine. By his works alone he must be adjudged one of the greatest of all Americans, while the influence of his energizing faith cannot be measured.

Regarded by Hamilton as ambitious and temporizing, by Marshall as untrustworthy, loved by John Adams despite rivalry and misunderstanding, honored as a kindly master by a group of disciples the like of which has assembled around no other American statesman, Jefferson, by the very contradictions of his subtle and complex personality, of his bold mind and highly sensitive nature, has both vexed and fascinated all that have attempted to interpret him. As Henry Adams said: "Almost every other American statesman might be described in a parenthesis. A few broad strokes of the brush would paint the portraits of all the early Presidents with this exception, . . . but Jefferson could be painted only touch by touch, with a fine pencil, and the perfection of the likeness depended upon the shifting and uncertain flicker of its semi-transparent shadows" (*History,* I, 277).

The last years of this most enigmatical and probably the most versatile of great Americans were marked by philosophical serenity in the face of impending financial disaster. Ruined by the failure in 1819 of his friend Wilson Cary Nicholas [*q.v.*], whose note for $20,000 he had indorsed, he tried vainly to find a purchaser for his lands, and secured legislative permission, in the last year of his life, to dispose of most of them by the common method of a lottery. The public strongly protested against this indignity to him and some voluntary contributions were made, so the project was abandoned. Jefferson died believing that his debts would be paid, fortunately not realizing that "Monticello" was soon to pass from the hands of his heirs forever. A beloved and revered patriarch in the extensive family circle, he retained extraordinary intellectual vigor and rode his horse daily until almost the end of his ordered and temperate life. His death occurred, with dramatic appropriateness, on the fiftieth anniversary of the Declaration of Independence, shortly after noon and a few hours before that of John Adams. His daughter, Martha Randolph, with ten of her children and their progeny, and his grandson, Francis Eppes, survived him. On the simple stone over his grave in the family burying-ground at "Monticello" he is described as he wished to be remembered, not as the holder of great offices, but as the author of the Declaration of Independence and the Virginia statute for religious freedom, and the father of the University of Virginia.

[The Jefferson manuscripts in the Lib. of Cong. comprise, in addition to other important items, 236 vols. of correspondence (*c.* 40,000 pieces), partially calendared in the *Calendar of the Correspondence of Thos. Jefferson* (Parts I–III, 1894–1903). The collection in the Mass. Hist. Soc. consists of 67 vols. (*c.* 10,000 pieces), and some of his most interesting personal records, including account books, his Garden Book, his Farm Book, and the catalogue of his library. Other papers are in the Mo. Hist. Soc., St. Louis, the library of the Univ. of Va., and various other depositories, and some are still in private hands.

P. L. Ford, *The Writings of Thos. Jefferson* (10 vols., 1892–99) is the most useful edition, but this should be supplemented by the more extensive Memorial Ed. (20 vols., 1903–04), and by the edition of H. A. Washington (9 vols., 1853–54). Both the "Autobiography" and the preface to "The Anas" were written in old age and carry less authority than contemporary documents. The following are valuable sources: "The Jefferson Papers," *Collections of the Mass. Hist. Soc.* 7 ser., vol. I (1900); *Thos. Jefferson Correspondence, Printed from Originals in the Collections of Wm. K. Bixby*, with notes by W. C. Ford (1916); G. Chinard, *The Commonplace Book of Thos. Jefferson* (1927), *The Literary Bible of Thos. Jefferson* (1928), *The Letters of Lafayette and Jefferson* (1929), the *Correspondence of Jefferson and Du Pont de Nemours with an Introduction on Jefferson and the Physiocrats* (1931); D. Malone, *Correspondence between Thos. Jefferson and P. S. du Pont de Nemours, 1798–1817* (1930); P. Wilstach, *Correspondence between John Adams and Thos. Jefferson* (1925). Numerous letters to and from Jefferson are contained in G. Chinard, *Volney et L'Amérique* (1923), *Jefferson et Les Idéologues* (1925), and *Trois Amitiés Françaises de Jefferson* (1927). John P. Foley, *The Jefferson Cyclopedia* (1900) is a useful compilation.

Of the older biographies, H. S. Randall, *The Life of Thos. Jefferson* (3 vols., 1858), though eulogistic, is still extremely valuable, as is S. N. Randolph, *The Domestic Life of Thos. Jefferson* (1871), which contains many family letters. The most important of the recent biographies are G. Chinard, *Thos. Jefferson: The Apostle of Americanism* (1929) and A. J. Nock, *Jefferson* (1926), both of which emphasize the intellectual aspect of his career. More general treatments are P. L. Ford, *Thos. Jefferson* (1904); D. S. Muzzey, *Thos. Jefferson* (1918). A hostile Federalist work is Theo. Dwight, *The Character of Thos. Jefferson, as Exhibited in His Own Writings* (1839). C. G. Bowers, *Jefferson and Hamilton* (1925), is dramatic and favorable; F. W. Hirst, *Life and Letters of Thos. Jefferson* (1926), is eulogistic.

For genealogical materials, the family background, and his early life, see *Tyler's Quart. Hist. and Genealog. Mag.*, Jan., Apr., July, Oct. 1925; Jan., July 1926; Wm. C. Bruce, *John Randolph of Roanoke* (1922), I, 9 ff.; E. Woods, *Albemarle County in Va.* (1901); *Wm. and Mary Quart. Hist. Mag.*, Jan. 1921, p. 34, and F. Harrison, *Ibid.*, Jan. 1924, p. 15. For his public career and political position, see *Jour. of the House of Burgesses of Va., 1766–76* (3 vols., 1905–06); W. W. Hening, *The Statutes at Large . . . of Va.* (13 vols., 1809–23); Carl Becker, *The Declaration of Independence* (1922); J. C. Fitzpatrick, *The Spirit of the Revolution* (1924), chs. I, II; H. J. Eckenrode, *The Revolution in Va.* (1916); C. R. Lingley, "The Transition in Va. from Colony to Commonwealth," *Columbia Univ. Studies in Hist., Economics and Pub. Law*, vol. XXXVI, no. 2 (1910); B. Faÿ, *L'Esprit Révolutionnaire en France et aux États-Unis à la Fin du XVIIIe Siècle* (1925); L. B. Dunbar, *A Study of "Monarchical" Tendencies in the U. S.* (1922); S. F. Bemis, *Jay's Treaty* (1923), *Pinckney's Treaty* (1926), *The Am. Secretaries of State and Their Diplomacy*, II (1927), 3–93; W. K. Woolery, "The Relation of Thos. Jefferson to Am. Foreign Policy, 1783–1793," *Johns Hopkins Univ. Studies in Hist. and Pol. Science*, vol. XLV, no. 2 (1927); Chas. A. Beard, *Economic Origins of Jeffersonian Democracy* (1915); C. R. Fish, *The Civil Service and the Patronage* (1905); A. J. Beveridge, *The Life of John Marshall* (4 vols., 1916); I. J. Cox, *The W. Fla. Controversy, 1798–1813* (1918); L. M. Sears, *Jefferson and the Embargo* (1927); Henry Adams, *Hist. of the U. S. of Am.*, vols. I–IV (1889–90); C. E. Merriam, *A Hist. of Am. Pol. Theories* (1910), ch. IV; V. L. Parrington, *Main Currents in Am. Thought*, I (1927), 342–56; E. S. Brown, *Wm. Plumer's Memorandum of Procs. in the U. S. Senate* (1923); *The Defense of Young and Mims, Printers to the State . . .* (Boston, 1805).

For the Univ. of Va., see N. F. Cabell, *Early Hist. of the Univ. of Va. as Contained in the Letters of Thos. Jefferson and Jos. C. Cabell* (1856); P. A. Bruce, *Hist. of the Univ. of Va.*, vols., I, II (1922); R. J. Honeywell, *The Educational Work of Thos. Jefferson* (1931). For architecture, see Fiske Kimball, "Thos. Jefferson as Architect: Monticello and Shadwell," *Architectural Quart. of Harvard Univ.*, June 1914, *Thos. Jefferson and the First Monument of the Classical Revival in Am.* (1915), *Thos. Jefferson, Architect* (1916); W. B. Bryan, *A Hist. of the Nat. Capital*, vol. I (1914). For his scientific work, see Wm. E. Curtis, *The True Thos. Jefferson* (1901), ch. XII; Alex. F. Chamberlain, "Thos. Jefferson's Ethnological Opinions and Activities," *Am. Anthropologist*, July–Sept. 1907; Geo. T. Surface, "Thos. Jefferson: a Pioneer Student of Am. Geography," *Bulletin of the Am. Geog. Soc.*, Dec. 1909; F. A. Lucas, "Thos. Jefferson—Paleontologist," *Nat. Hist.*, May–June, 1926; H. F. Osborn, "Thos. Jefferson, The Pioneer of Am. Paleontology," *Science*, Apr. 19, 1929; Wm. I. Wyman, "Thos. Jefferson and the Patent System," *Jour. of the Patent Office Soc.*, Sept. 1918. For a personal picture, see D. Malone, "Polly Jefferson and Her Father," *Va. Quart. Rev.*, Jan. 1931. Probably better than any portrait is the life mask of Jefferson, reproduced in C. H. Hart, *Browere's Life Masks of Great Americans* (1899).] D. M.

JEFFERY, EDWARD TURNER (Apr. 6, 1843–Sept. 24, 1927), railroad executive, was born at Liverpool, England, the son of William S. and Jane (McMillan) Jeffery. With his parents he emigrated to the United States in 1850 and after a brief period of schooling began to work for the Illinois Central Railroad in 1856. The next twenty years he spent in the Chicago shops, where he rose to the rank of assistant superintendent of machinery. In 1877 he reached his first important position, that of general superintendent and chief engineer, and in the same year he married Virginia Osborne Clarke. He was made general manager of the company in 1885, and although his work was generally recognized as excellent, he resigned in 1889, probably as a result of a conflict with Harriman over certain proposed changes in rates (*Railroad Gazette*, Sept. 6, 1889). Having no alternate position available upon his resignation from the Illinois Central, Jeffery threw himself into work for the proposed world's fair at Chicago and made a trip to Europe to view the Paris exposition of 1889 in order that he might describe it for the benefit of the people interested in a similar fair at Chicago. The formal account of his trip appeared in his pamphlet: *Paris Universal Exposition, 1889* (n.d.). After his return to the United States he was one of the most active supporters of the Chicago plans. With DeW. C. Cregier and T. B. Bryan he appeared before Congress to ask recognition and support for Chicago as the site of the exposition (see *Arguments Before a Special Committee of the United States Senate . . . for the Location . . . of the World's Exposition of 1892* (1890), and in 1891 he was appointed chairman of the committee on buildings and grounds.

Jeffery severed his connection with the Chicago exposition in 1891 to become president and general manager of the Denver & Rio Grande Railroad. He managed the road so well that it was able to weather the financial difficulties of the panic of 1893. He made the most significant decision of his life in the winter of 1900–01, when George Jay Gould bought control of the Denver & Rio Grande. Would he accept the orders of the dictatorial Gould or would he insist upon his own idea of sound railroading? His decision to support Gould can undoubtedly be traced to his experiences on the Illinois Central. With Gould in control, a new road, the Western Pacific Railway, was chartered to connect Ogden, the western terminus of the Denver & Rio Grande, with San Francisco. Jeffery became president of the Western Pacific in 1905 and carried it to completion in 1911. The new line was well built but unprofitable. The failure of the road to pay dividends reacted adversely on the Denver & Rio Grande, which had advanced much of the cost of construction and had guaranteed certain of the Western Pacific bonds. Both roads were foreclosed and sold in 1915, and the succeeding years found the Denver & Rio Grande in continual financial difficulties. Meantime Jeffery had resigned the presidency of the latter in 1912 to become chairman of the board of directors, and had taken similar action in respect to the Western Pacific in 1913. In 1917 he retired from all active railroad management. Obviously the Denver & Rio Grande had been wrecked. An investigation by the Interstate Commerce Commission (113 *Interstate Commerce Reports,* 75–160) baldly denounced the officers of the roads but absolved them from the charge of acting for the benefit of themselves or of the bankers. The minority stockholders of the Denver & Rio Grande instituted court proceedings to gain damages from Gould, Jeffery, and others (*Rogers et al.* vs. *Gould et al.*, 206 *A.D.*, N. Y., 433, and 210 *A.D.*, 15), but received an adverse decision of the court in 1926. Jeffery died the following year in New York City.

[The main events of Jeffery's career appear in *Who's Who in America,* 1926–27; the *Railway Age Gazette,* Jan. 12, 1917, the *Railway Age,* Oct. 1, 1927; and the *N. Y. Times,* Sept. 25, 1927. See also: *Report of the President to the Board of Directors of the World's Columbian Exposition* (1898); Ernest Howard, *Wall Street Fifty Years after Erie* (1923), written by a minority stockholder of the Denver & Rio Grande; B. J. Hendrick, "The Passing of a Great Railroad Dynasty," the best of the magazine articles on the Gould fiasco, in *McClure's Mag.,* Mar. 1912.]

R. E. R.

JEFFREY, JOSEPH ANDREW (Jan. 17, 1836–Aug. 27, 1928), banker, manufacturer, was born in Clarksville, Clinton County, Ohio. His father, James Jeffrey, of New England ancestry, was a native of Monmouth County, N. J., and as a young man had gone to the Ohio country, where he established a farm and married Angeline Robinson, whose father was one of the first settlers of Warren County. Until he was seventeen years old Jeffrey remained with his parents, moving with them to Auglaize County, Ohio, where, in St. Mary's, he completed his high-school education. Business seems to have had a strong attraction for him, and after leaving school he entered a country store near his home and served as a clerk for four years. Then followed a year of several business experiences which carried him eventually, in 1858, to Columbus, Ohio. Here he entered the office of Rickly & Brother, private bankers, and for eight years served as bookkeeper, teller, and cashier, respectively. He forsook these banking activities, however, in 1866, to become manager of the firm of Rickly, Howell & Company, wholesale and retail carpet and furniture dealers of Cincinnati. Three years later he returned to Columbus and with F. C. Sessions reëntered the banking business, founding what is now known as the Commercial National Bank. About 1877, while walking along one of the business streets of Columbus, he chanced to notice displayed in an empty store window a crude model of a machine invented by Francis M. Lechner, to be used in coal mines. It was called a cutter bar and was designed to undercut coal seams. Seeing great possibilities in the device, Jeffrey proceeded to organize the Lechner Mining Machine Company for the purpose of manufacturing the machine. In 1883 he sold his banking interest, and acquired the controlling interest in the Lechner Company. From that time on it enjoyed a healthy and rapid growth. Gradually the plant was extended and new mining machinery and mechanical handling equipment were added to its output, so that at Jeffrey's death it was the world's largest manufactory of coal-mining machinery, the plant covering thirty-five acres of ground. During this period, too, the company name was changed to the Jeffrey Manufacturing Company. In 1900 Jeffrey retired as president but he served as chairman of the board of directors for the remainder of his life. In addition to his interest in the Jeffrey Company, he owned the Ohio Malleable Iron Company of Columbus, was a director in a number of Columbus banks, and took an active interest in the city's charitable institutions. On Oct. 2, 1866, he married Celia C. Harris of Columbus, and at the time of his death was survived by three sons and two daughters.

[*Jeffrey Service*, Sept., Oct. 1928; W. A. Taylor, *Centennial Hist. of Columbus and Franklin County* (1909), vol. II; *Franklin County at the Beginning of the Twentieth Century* (1901); *A Centennial Biog. Hist. of the City of Columbus and Franklin County, Ohio* (1901); *Columbus Evening Dispatch*, Aug, 27, 1928; *Ohio State Jour.*, Aug. 28, 1898.] C. W. M.

JEFFREY, ROSA GRIFFITH VERTNER JOHNSON (1828–Oct. 6, 1894), poet, novelist, was the daughter of John Y. Griffith, himself a writer of both prose and verse, and well known for his Indian stories, which received the distinction of being widely copied in English journals of his day. She was born in Natchez, Miss. Her mother, daughter of the Rev. James Abercrombie, a Philadelphia clergyman of note, died when the baby was only nine months old. The child was immediately adopted by a maternal aunt, Rosa Vertner, and spent an unusually happy girlhood, near Port Gibson, Miss., on her aunt's beautiful country estate "Burlington," which she affectionately described later in her poem "My Childhood's Home." By the time she was ten years old she had shown such talent—"she prattled in rhyme long before she could write" (Julia Deane Freeman, *Women of the South Distinguished in Literature*, 1861, p. 245)—that the Vertners decided to move to Kentucky for her better education. She entered the Episcopal Seminary of Bishop Smith at Lexington, which enjoyed a considerable reputation in the South, and was commended as "a polished scholar and intelligent student of history and literature." At the age of fifteen she wrote "The Legend of the Opal" (published in *Poems*, 1857), and at seventeen she was married to Claude M. Johnson of Louisiana, a man of wealth, position, and broad cultural interests, by whom she had six children. During her married life she was known as a social leader in Southern cities, including Washington, D. C. In 1850 she became a contributor to the *Louisville Journal* under the pen name of "Rosa," and here were first printed many of the poems that were to make her "the first Southern woman whose literary work attracted attention throughout the United States" (Frances E. Willard and Mary E. Livermore, *Portraits and Biographies of Prominent American Women*, 1901, I, 418). *Poems* appeared in 1857, and its success called for a second edition the next year. After the death of her husband in 1861, Mrs. Johnson moved with her children to Rochester, N. Y., where she met and married (1863) Alexander Jeffrey of Edinburgh, Scotland. She remained in Rochester during the period of the Civil War, afterwards returning to the Vertner home in Lexington, Ky. Her first novel, *Woodburn*, appeared in 1864, and from then until 1884, when her last work, *Marah*, was published, she produced both poetry—*Daisy Dare and Baby Power* (1871), *The Crimson Hand* (1881)—and fiction, and, although they were never published, several dramas. She died in Lexington at the age of sixty-six.

While the poems of "Rosa" are far too expansive, sentimental, and florid for the taste of a later day than her own, they have an authentic spontaneity and exuberance which mark her as a natural poet. Her inspiration was so apparently exhaustless, and so slightly restrained by the simple metres which she always used, that such poems as "Hasheesh Visions" and "Daisy Dare" ran into an astounding number of stanzas. Her poetry seems the undisciplined flowering of an extremely happy and responsive nature. Beauty, wealth, and charm held at bay the rigors of life which might have deepened a fine talent into something much more.

[J. W. Davidson, *The Living Writers of the South* (1869); M. T. Tardy, *Southland Writers* (1870), vol. I; *The South in the Building of the Nation* (1909), vol. XI; *Reg. of the Ky. State Hist. Soc.*, Jan. 1911; J. W. Townsend, *Ky. in Am. Letters 1784–1912* (1913), vol. I.] G. G.

JEFFRIES, BENJAMIN JOY (Mar. 26, 1833–Nov. 21, 1915), ophthalmic surgeon, was the son of Dr. John and Anne Geyer (Amory) Jeffries, and a descendant of David Jeffries who came to Boston from England in 1677. Benjamin was the last of five generations of Jeffries who lived in Boston, attended Harvard College, and attained prominence in the history of New England. The second of the line, David Jeffries, was a stanch patriot, a deacon in the Old South Church, and treasurer of the town of Boston, but his son John [*q.v.*], at the time of the American Revolution, espoused the cause of England, made his house the rendezvous of British officers, and served as surgeon with the British forces in America. After the war, while living in London as a refuge for a period, this same John Jeffries, in 1785, in company with a Frenchman, Jean Pierre Blanchard, made the first balloon crossing of the English channel. The fourth of the line, Benjamin's father, was an eminent physician of his day. Together with Dr. Edward Reynolds, in 1824, he founded the

Massachusetts Eye and Ear Infirmary, the third oldest institution of its kind in North America.

While Benjamin had a cumulative family reputation to sustain, there is no doubt that he succeeded in impressing his personality upon his times. Graduating from Harvard College in 1854, and from Harvard Medical School in 1857, he went to Vienna to study ophthalmology under Arlt and Jaeger, and dermatology under Hebra. In 1859, he returned to Boston to practise these specialties, and in course of time he limited his efforts to ophthalmology, in which he acquired a large practice. For thirty-six years he served as ophthalmic surgeon at the Eye and Ear Infirmary, where he justly earned the reputation of being one of the skilful surgeons of his day. He was one of the original members of the American Ophthalmological Society, and he gave much time and energy to keeping the usefulness of this society at a high level. In 1872, he married Marian Shimmin of Boston, by whom he had two children, a son, who died during his freshman year at college, and a daughter.

Among his earlier published writings were: *Diseases of the Skin: The Recent Advances in Their Pathology and Treatment* (1871), Boylston Prize Essay; *The Eye in Health and Disease* (1871); *Animal and Vegetable Parasites of the Human Skin and Hair* (1872). After 1878, he devoted himself to the subject of color vision, and about half of his thirty-four scientific papers dealt with this topic. His treatise, *Color Blindness, Its Dangers and Its Detection* (1879, revised edition 1883), was long the standard authority on this subject, and it led to many important public measures safeguarding travel by land and by sea. Jeffries was noted for the honest and conscientious service that he gave to each of his patients. While critical of things he felt to be wrong, yet his fairness won him popularity among the laity and respect from his colleagues. Until the last few years of his life, he continued to see his patients in the same house where his father lived and practised before him, a house filled with most interesting collections from colonial days.

[J. T. L. Jeffries, *Jeffries of Mass., 1658–1914* (n.d.); *Mag. of Am. Hist.*, Jan. 1885; *Proc. Bunker Hill Monument Asso., 1906* (1906); *Boston Medic. and Surgic. Jour.*, Dec. 9, 1915; *Trans. Am. Ophthalmological Soc.*, vol. XIV, pt. 2 (1916); *Who's Who in America*, 1914–15; *Harvard Coll., Report of the Class of 1854* (1894); *Harvard Grad. Mag.*, Mar. 1916; *Boston Transcript*, Nov. 22, 1915; *N. Y. Times*, Nov. 24, 1915.] J. H. W.

JEFFRIES, JOHN (Feb. 5, 1744/45–Sept. 16, 1819), physician, scientist, was born in Boston, Mass., the son of David and Sarah (Jaffrey) Jeffries and the great-grandson of an earlier David Jeffries who emigrated from England to Boston in 1677. John graduated from Harvard in 1763, studied medicine under home practitioners and in England and Scotland, and received the degree of M.D. from Marischal College, Aberdeen, at the age of twenty-five. Returning to Boston, he practised there until 1771, when he became assistant surgeon on a British naval vessel, serving in that capacity until 1774. When Boston was evacuated he withdrew to Halifax in company with many Loyalists. From 1775 to 1779 he was a surgeon in British military hospitals; he then went to England and was appointed surgeon-major and as such served with British troops in the campaign around Savannah and Charleston. Returning to England he practised successfully and also became interested in levitation, as it was then called, or aerostation. He seems to have been the first to attempt to gather scientific data of the free air. His observations were made with care and, since he had sufficient means, he was able to secure instruments of high grade. His flights were made with the French aeronaut Blanchard, who received distinguished honors, but it was Jeffries who paid all the bills, accepted the responsibility, and made the observations. Two ascents, the one over London, Tuesday, Nov. 30, 1784, and the other across the English Channel, were made for scientific purposes. The first took place in the presence of the Prince of Wales, the Duchess of Devonshire, and other notables. Jeffries and Blanchard stepped into the car of the balloon, rose a few yards, then, descending, affixed oars with which it was hoped to steer the balloon. Rising, they bumped against the top of a chimney, knocking off the funnels, but ultimately cleared all obstacles and in a few moments were above the city streets crowded with people. Jeffries had provided himself with thermometer, barometer, electrometer, hygrometer, timepiece, mariner's compass, telescope, several yards of thin ribbon, a sharp knife, scissors, a small phial two thirds full of common water, and six four-ounce bottles filled with distilled water, with glass stoppers and numbered, so that they could be emptied and afterwards corked at different elevations. This was done at the suggestion of Cavendish, who subsequently made a chemical analysis of the air. Twelve observations of temperature, pressure, and humidity were made. These constitute the first scientific data for free air, to a height of 9,309 feet. The values agree closely with modern determinations.

The second voyage is the one commonly associated with Jeffries. From Dec. 17, 1784, until Jan. 6, 1785, stormy weather held the aviators at Dover; but on Jan. 7, a clear, fine morning with frost and light NNW wind, the balloon was filled and at 1 P. M. the ascent was begun. In fifteen minutes the balloon had risen about half a mile and it was necessary to untwist the tubes to prevent undue expansion of the balloon. At 1:50 the tubes were again twisted, the aviators being one third of the way over and the balloon falling. Casting out the sand ballast, they rose again and at 2 o'clock were nearly half way across. At 2:15 the balloon started to fall, and it was necessary to cast away the wings, the ornaments of the car, and all the apparatus but the barometer. At 2:30 the balloon was only about three-fourths distended and was falling. Biscuits, apples, oars, and finally the moulinet were thrown out, then the anchors and cords; then outer clothes of the occupants. They were now beneath the plane of the French cliffs, about five miles from shore, approaching it rapidly. Suddenly they were carried upward to a greater height than previously experienced and at 3 o'clock passed over the high ground between Cape Blanc Nez and Calais. At a little before 4 o'clock, after some interference with tree tops, the adventurers landed in the forest of Guines, not far from Ardres. They were received with much enthusiasm and were conveyed to Calais, where they were later entertained by the mayor and other dignitaries. Blanchard was given the freedom of the city, and apologies were made to Jeffries because similar honors could not be paid to him without leave from the Court. On Jan. 11, 1785, they reached Paris, and two days afterwards Jeffries was complimented by the King, and on Jan. 15 he dined with Franklin at Passy. The days in Paris were a continuous round of receptions, dinners, and theatre parties. He met Commander John Paul Jones at Franklin's dinner table and each complimented the other for bravery. Returning to Dover, he was given the freedom of the city and made a Baron of the Cinque Ports, and on Mar. 5, was back in London.

Returning to Boston about 1790, Jeffries established a large and profitable practice. He was married, first, about 1770, to Sarah Rhoads, by whom he had three children, and, second, Sept. 8, 1787, at London, to Hannah Hunt, by whom he had eleven children. Benjamin Joy Jeffries [*q.v.*] was a grandson.

[B. J. Jeffries, in *Mag. of Am. Hist.*, Jan. 1885; *New-Eng. Jour. of Medicine and Surgery*, Jan. 1820, pp. 63–72; *Medic. Dissertations . . . of the Mass. Medic. Soc.*, III (1822), 415–17; "Brief Memoirs and Notices of Prince's Subscribers," *New-Eng. Hist. and Geneal. Reg.*, Jan. 1861; C. H. Turnor, *Astra Castra: Experiments and Adventures in the Atmosphere* (London, 1865); John Jeffries, *A Narrative of the Two Aerial Voyages of Dr. Jeffries with Mons. Blanchard; with Meteorological Observations and Remarks* (London, 1786); *A Report of the Record Commissioners of the City of Boston containing Boston Births from A. D. 1700 to A. D. 1800* (1894), p. 253; *The Writings of Benj. Franklin* (1905–07), ed. by A. H. Smyth, see index in vol. X; T. F. Harrington, *The Harvard Medic. School* (1905), I, 41–44; J. T. L. Jeffries, *Jeffries of Mass. 1658–1914* (n.d.); E. A. Jones, *The Loyalists of Mass.* (1930); *Columbian Centinel* (Boston), Sept. 22, 1819; information from family records.] A. M.

JEMISON, MARY (1743–Sept. 19, 1833), "the White Woman of the Genesee," captured and adopted in girlhood by Indians, with whom she thereafter lived, was born at sea while her parents, Thomas and Jane (Erwin) Jemison, were on their way from Belfast to Philadelphia. On Apr. 5, 1758, at their farm near the junction of Sharps Run and Conewago Creek, Pennsylvania, Mary, her parents, three of the other children, and some neighbors were captured by a party of Shawnee Indians and French soldiers. Most of the captives were killed, but Mary's life was spared. She was taken to Fort Duquesne, and given to two Seneca women who adopted her as a sister in the place of a brother killed in battle, naming her *Dehgewanus*. For five years she lived in the Ohio country, and in the third year of her captivity was married to a Delaware warrior named Sheninjee, by whom she had two children. Late in 1762 she accompanied three Indian brothers to the tribal home at Little Beard's town on the Genesee River near the present Geneseo, N. Y. When at the close of the French and Indian War a bounty was offered for the return of prisoners, a chief of the tribe wished to take Mary to the English at Fort Niagara, but her Indian family refused to give her up, and she, having developed a deep affection for them, was not unwilling to stay. Some four years later, Sheninjee having died, she became the wife of an old chief, Hiokatoo, by whom she had six children. During the Revolution her home was frequently the stopping place of Walter Butler and Joseph Brant [*qq.v.*]. At its close she was offered her freedom by her Indian brother, but preferred to remain with the tribe. In 1797 she was granted a tract of her own choice on the Gardeau Flats along the Genesee, near Castile, N. Y., where she had lived since the destruction of Little Beard's town by Sullivan's army in 1779. Her husband, Hiokatoo, died in 1811, at the age of 103; in that year and the year following two of her sons were killed in a drunken rage by the third, who was himself similarly killed a few years later.

In 1817 she was naturalized and her land-title confirmed by act of the New York legislature. At this time she was leasing the greater part of her land to white settlers and living with a married daughter, though continuing to plant, hoe, and harvest her own corn. One of the most extensive landholders in her section of the state, noted for her kindness and generosity, she was a figure of great interest to the settlers. In 1823, James Everett Seaver, M.D., was commissioned at the instance of a group of citizens, to interview her and write the story of her life. The resulting book, *A Narrative of the Life of Mrs. Mary Jemison* (Canandaigua, N. Y., 1824), went through twenty-two editions in the next hundred years, and her story became a tradition in Western New York. In 1831, the Senecas having sold their Genesee lands, she moved to the Buffalo Creek Reservation. In the last months of her life she professed the Christian religion, and she was buried near the Seneca Mission Church. Her remains were moved in 1874 to the estate of William Pryor Letchworth, now Letchworth Park, near her old home on the Genesee. There, in 1910, a bronze statue by H. K. Bush-Brown was erected to her memory.

According to her biographer, she spoke English distinctly, "with a little of the Irish emphasis," though she had completely lost the art of reading. "Spirits and tobacco I have never used," she said to Dr. Seaver, "and I have never attended an Indian frolic." For her husband, Hiokatoo, she had such veneration that she would not speak of his notoriously cruel exploits, but sent Dr. Seaver to her cousin, George Jemison, for an account of his career. She adhered to the Indian customs and manner of dress until her death.

[J. E. Seaver, *A Narrative of the Life of Mary Jemison* (22nd ed., revised by C. D. Vail, 1925), with notes correcting errors in earlier editions; E. W. Vanderhoof, *Hist. Sketches of Western N. Y.* (1907); *Red Man* (Carlisle, Pa.), Sept. 1913; *Twelfth Ann. Report, Am. Scenic and Hist. Preservation Soc.* (1907) and *Sixteenth* . . . (1911); *Rochester Hist. Soc. Pub. Fund Ser.*, vol. III (1924).] E. R. D.

JENCKES, JOSEPH [See JENKS, JOSEPH, 1602–1683].

JENCKES, JOSEPH (1632–Jan. 4, 1717), founder of Pawtucket, pioneer iron manufacturer of Rhode Island, was born in England, probably in the neighborhood of Hammersmith where his father, Joseph Jenks [*q.v.*], was a skilled ironworker. The elder Jenks was induced to emigrate to America to undertake the development of the iron ore which had been discovered near Lynn, Mass., and a few years later, probably about 1650, his son followed and was associated with his father in the iron works there. He met and married Esther, the daughter of William Ballard, a none too Puritanical lady, evidently, as it is recorded that in 1652 she was brought before the Quarterly Court "for wearing silver lace." Another paragraph in the old records reveals something of Joseph's democratic temper. He was brought before the Court in 1660 for treasonable utterances. King Charles II had just come to the throne and Jenckes was heard to declare with heat that "if he hade the King heir, he wold cutte of his head and make a football of it."

The date of Joseph Jenckes's move to Rhode Island may not be stated with certainty. Bog iron had been discovered in the colony and this probably led him to move to the new locality. It is known that he purchased land on the Pawtuxet River in 1669 "for the employ of his saw-mill." Two years later, in 1671, he bought sixty acres near Pawtucket Falls. Here he set up a sawmill and a forge. He was prosperous in his work and others came to settle in the district, thus developing the community known as Pawtucket. In 1675, when King Philip and his Indians opened warfare on the colonists, the settlement at Pawtucket was at once in danger, and most of the inhabitants sought refuge in the larger and better protected town of Providence. Joseph Jenckes's home and forge were in the path of destruction and were burned in 1676. When Philip's efforts to dislodge the English from his lands failed, Jenckes and other colonists returned to rebuild their ruined homes. Jenckes took active part in the affairs of the colony. In 1679 he was a deputy to the General Assembly, and with the exception of a few years he was Assistant from 1680 to 1698. He was the father of six daughters and four sons. All of the latter were men who held places of respect and distinction in Rhode Island, his namesake, Joseph [*q.v.*], serving as governor for five years. Both Jenckes and his wife died in 1717.

[See Alonzo Lewis, *The Hist. of Lynn* (1829); Massena Goodrich, *Hist. Sketch of the Town of Pawtucket* (1876); J. O. Austin, *The Geneal. Dict. of R. I.* (1887); and the *New-Eng. Hist. and Geneal. Reg.*, July 1855. Joseph Jenckes is known to have spelled his name as it is given here.] E. R. B.

JENCKES, JOSEPH (1656–June 15, 1740), governor of Rhode Island, was the son of Joseph Jenckes (1632–1717) and the grandson of Joseph Jenks [*qq.v.*]. His father, founder of what is now the city of Pawtucket in Rhode Island, married Esther, the daughter of William Ballard of Lynn, Mass. Joseph, the eldest of their ten children, was born and grew to manhood in Pawtucket. He adopted the profession of land-surveying, his ability soon making him a distinguished man in the colony. For several years (1691, 1698, 1700–08) he was a deputy to the General Assembly, acting for two years of that time as speaker (1698–99, 1707–08). Later (1708–12), he held the more responsible post of assistant. In 1715 he was elected deputy governor and continued as such for twelve years. His competence as a surveyor proved of great value to his fellow colonists. In 1710 he was empowered to treat with Colonel Dudley on the matter of the Massachusetts boundaries, and on the strength of his success in this affair, he was in 1720 appointed to act, together with the colony's agent in England, to settle the much more difficult question of the Connecticut boundaries. His efforts in London were entirely satisfactory to his constituents, but the boundary disagreement dragged on for years.

On the death of Governor Cranston, who had held office for thirty successive terms, Joseph Jenckes was chosen in 1727 to succeed him. He continued as governor for five years, announcing in 1731 that he would refuse reëlection. He would scarcely have obtained it in any case. The finances of Rhode Island had become involved by the introduction of paper money, and when a bill to emit sixty thousand pounds additional currency was passed by the General Assembly, the Governor noted his dissent on the document. This veto was declared ineffectual by the paper-money party which overruled his action. After hot dispute both the Governor and the General Assembly appealed to the home government. The latter's reply, which found that within limits neither the governor nor the Crown could change such an act of the Assembly, confirmed Jenckes's opponents and ended his political career. During his life Jenckes had given much attention to military as well as political affairs and progressed through the various ranks from lieutenant to colonel. From 1707 to 1711 he acted as Major of the Main Land. He was twice married. His first wife was Martha Brown, a grand-daughter of Chad Brown, the associate of Roger Williams. She died leaving nine children. In 1727 he married a widow, Alice (Smith) Dexter, who died childless in 1736. Jenckes was a man of extraordinary size and strength. Seven feet two inches tall and splendidly proportioned, he was an imposing figure in any gathering.

[S. G. Arnold, *Hist. of the State of R. I.*, vol. II (1860); J. O. Austin, *Geneal. Dict. of R. I.* (1887); E. R. Potter and S. S. Rider, *Some Account of the Bills of Credit . . . of R. I.* (1880); *Records of the Colony of R. I.*, vols. III and IV (1858–59).] E. R. B.

JENCKES, THOMAS ALLEN (Nov. 2, 1818–Nov. 4, 1875), jurist and legislator, born in Cumberland, R. I., was the son of Thomas B. and Abigail W. (Allen) Jenckes, and a descendant of Joseph Jenks [*q.v.*]. He was educated at Brown University, from which institution he graduated with distinction at the age of twenty. For one year thereafter he served as a tutor at Brown, meanwhile pursuing the study of law. He was admitted to practice in 1840, and having formed a partnership with Edward H. Hazard of Providence, he rose rapidly in his profession. In due course he gave special attention to patent law, a field in which he proved to be peculiarly qualified by his mechanical aptitudes, and was retained as counsel in much of the important patent litigation of his time, including the suits which arose out of the Sickles and Corliss patents relating to the steam-engine and the more famous Day and Goodyear rubber controversies. At an early age he disclosed a *flair* for politics; he served as one of the secretaries in the "Landholders Convention" of 1841 and in the Rhode Island constitutional convention of 1842. In the same year, 1842, he was appointed secretary of the governor's council and subsequently did service in both houses of the state legislature. This service led to his election as a member of the national House of Representatives in 1862, and he took his seat at the opening of the Thirty-eighth Congress. He was three times reëlected to represent the first Rhode Island congressional district.

During his four terms Jenckes served on two important committees—patents and judiciary. His services in connection with the revision and improvement of the laws relating to patents and copyrights were of great and enduring value. He was actively associated with civil-service reform in its earliest stages and indeed he has a fair claim to be ranked as the first American legislator to grasp the significance of this reform. In 1865 he introduced a bill for the selection of public employees by competitive examinations, a measure which he had framed after a study of the English practice and after an elaborate correspondence with Sir Charles Trevelyan and Sir Stafford Northcote, both of whom had played an important part in the English movement for civil-service reform. This bill was defeated, but Jenckes persisted and in 1866 obtained the appointment of a joint committee to study the subject of retrenchment in governmental expenditures. This committee appointed a sub-committee on civil service, with Jenckes at its head, and a bill based on its recommendations was presented to the House in 1868; but this too was defeated, although by a narrow margin.

Meanwhile, however, President Grant had been persuaded to take an interest in the movement. In his second annual message the President expressed himself in favor of a law which would govern "the manner of making all appointments." This executive approval led Congress in 1871 to attach a rider to the appropriation bill giving the president authority "to prescribe such rules and regulations for the admission of persons into the civil service of the United States as will best promote the efficiency thereof" (*The Statutes at Large,* XVI, 1871, 514). This rider also authorized the appointment of a civil-service commission and made an appropriation therefor. But the victory for civil-service reform was not yet won, for Congress presently declined to continue the appropriation for the commission's work.

Jenckes was also closely identified with the movement for a national bankruptcy law and was successful in securing the enactment of such a measure after several years of effort. He initiated competitive examinations for admission to West Point. When the impeachment of President Andrew Johnson was voted by the House, his name was proposed as one of the managers to prosecute the impeachment proceedings before the Senate, and he came within a few votes of being chosen. By reason of his independence, integrity, and sound judgment, he became one of the outstanding members of the Fortieth and Forty-first congresses, becoming widely recognized as one of the best lawyers in the House. Consequently, when it was decided to undertake an investigation of the Crédit Mobilier charges against various members of Congress, Jenckes, who was now no longer a member of the House, was selected as one of the counsel to assist in the prosecution of the inquiry. Much was expected of him in this capacity, by reason of his legal talents and high reputation; but ill health prevented him from assuming a leading part in the proceedings. He died on Nov. 4, 1875. To his contemporaries he was a somewhat austere figure, aloof and objective, but with intellectual power and legal acumen that commanded the highest respect everywhere. He was always in earnest and rarely lost his temper or self-control. In spite of a large law practice which made heavy demands upon his time he gave much of his energy to the public service for more than thirty years and by his great capacity for work was able to make his mark in both fields. He married in 1842 Mary J. Fuller of Attleboro, Mass. They had seven children.

[For biographical information see *In Memoriam: Thos. Allen Jenckes, Born Nov. 2, 1818—Died Nov. 4, 1875* (n.d.); G. E. Jenks, *Geneal. of the Jenks Family of Newport, N. H.* (n.d.); *Biog. Dir. Am. Cong.* (1928); the *Providence Jour.,* Nov. 5, Dec. 13, 1875, Jan. 5, June 21, 1876. References to his work in the cause of civil-service reform may be found in C. R. Fish, *The Civil Service and the Patronage* (1905) and in the various biographies of the period.]

W. B. M—o.

JENIFER, DANIEL OF ST. THOMAS (1723–Nov. 16, 1790), pre-Revolutionary leader and statesman of the early national period, was born in Charles County, Md. His father, Dr. Daniel Jenifer, was of English ancestry, and his mother, the daughter of Samuel and Elizabeth Hanson and the sister of John Hanson [*q.v.*], was a direct descendant of a Swedish Colonel Hanson who died with Gustavus Adolphus on the battlefield of Lützen. John, the son of Colonel Hanson, emigrated from Sweden to America in 1642. His great-grandson, Daniel of St. Thomas Jenifer, the origin of whose distinctive name is unknown, was possessed of unusual wealth for the time and made his home on his large estate, known as "Stepney," in Charles County. Besides serving as agent and receiver-general for the last two lord proprietors of Maryland, he held many offices of public trust. In his young manhood he was justice of the peace of his home county, and, later, of the western circuit of the province. In 1760 he was placed upon the commission for the settlement of the boundary dispute with Pennsylvania and Delaware. In 1766 he was made a member of the provincial court, and from 1773 until the opening of the Revolution he sat upon the governor's council. Though at first inclined to be conciliatory and desirous of peace with England, he at length took a stand for independence and in 1775 was chosen president of the Maryland Council of Safety and showed great activity in securing aid for the Revolutionary cause. When the state government was set up in 1777 he was made president of the Senate. The following year he was elected to the Continental Congress, of which he was a member until 1782, serving on various committees, including the admiralty board and the committee to consider the cession of western lands. Nationalistic in bent, he favored a permanent union of the states, opposed the emission of paper money, and desired that Congress be given the power to tax. Beginning in 1782 he was for some years intendant of the Maryland revenues and financial agent of the state. He was likewise one of the commissioners from Maryland who, in 1785, met, first at Alexandria and then at Mount Vernon, to settle with Virginia the question of navigation of the parts of Chesapeake Bay and the Potomac shared by the two states. Two years later he was sent as a delegate from Maryland to the Federal convention in Philadelphia, but he played only a very minor part in framing the new constitution. The most important stand he took was for a three years' term for members of the House of Representatives, for he felt that too frequent elections would cause popular indifference to civic duties and would make men of prominence unwilling to assume office. He favored the completed constitution and signed it, and when Luther Martin declared that he would be hanged if the people of Maryland would approve the document, Jenifer humorously advised him to remain in Philadelphia lest he hang in his home state. Jenifer never married but lived in jolly bachelorhood at "Stepney," for many years exchanging visits with George Washington, who appears to have been rather attached to him. Indeed, he was a general favorite, for, according to a contemporary, he was always in a good humor and never failed to be pleasing company. His death took place at Annapolis. Daniel of St. Thomas Jenifer had a brother Daniel. The latter had two sons, Daniel of St. Thomas and Daniel.

[Sources include: J. T. Scharf, *Hist. of Md.* (1879); G. A. Hanson, *Old Kent* (1876); E. S. Delaplaine, *The Life of Thos. Johnson* (1927); *The Records of the Federal Convention of 1787* (3 vols., 1911), ed. by Max Farrand; *Archives of Md.*, especially vol. III (1895); *The Diaries of Geo. Washington* (1925), ed. by J. C. Fitzpatrick; *Maryland Gazette* (Annapolis), Nov. 18, 1790; Calvert papers in the lib. of the Md. Hist. Soc.; Jenifer papers, "Letter Book of the Intendant of Revenue for Md.," and papers of the Continental Congress in the Manuscripts' Div., Lib. of Cong.] M. W. W.

JENKINS, ALBERT GALLATIN (Nov. 10, 1830–May 21, 1864), congressman and Confederate soldier, was probably of the same ancient Welsh family as Micah Jenkins [*q.v.*]. His father, Capt. William Jenkins, operated a line of sailing vessels from the James River to South America; his mother, Janetta McNutt, was of Highland Scotch extraction. In 1825 Captain Jenkins moved to Cabell County, Va. (now W. Va.), where he acquired an estate of 4,441 acres, extending "seven miles along the river front and as far back into the hills as they would pay taxes" (Huntington *Herald-Advertizer, post*). On this property, in 1830, was born his second son, Albert Gallatin. Here near the Ohio, Captain Jenkins built in 1835 his stately mansion, "Green Bottom," whence Albert Gallatin Jenkins, "Congressman and country gentleman," went forth to battle, "never to return—alive, except for one brief furlough" (Huntington *Herald-Advertizer, post*). The old home, much damaged through the vicissitudes of time, still stands as "Cabell County's one great monument" to the ante-bellum days. Jenkins was graduated from Jefferson College, Canonsburg, Pa., in 1848, and from Harvard Law School in 1850. After practising law at Charleston, Va., and farming, he was chosen a delegate to the National Democratic Convention at Cincinnati, 1856, and served in the Thirty-fifth and Thirty-sixth congresses, 1857–61. In 1858 he was married to Virginia, daughter of J. B. Bowlin of St. Louis, Mo.

Though Jenkins was a slaveholder and Southern Democrat, he had a bitter mental struggle before he decided to bear arms against the Union. Resigning his seat in Congress in April 1861, he went to western Virginia and was elected captain of a cavalry company. Like many of the new officers, he had received no military training; so he proceeded to master "Hardee's" military manual. In June Jenkins attracted notice by raiding Point Pleasant, Va., and capturing some prominent Unionists. But in August, "apparently incautiously advancing into an ambush" (Lee to H. A. Wise, *Official Records, post,* 1 ser., vol. V, p. 824), his men were badly routed, despite his brave effort to rally them. This defeat, however, was probably due as much to the incompetence of his commander, Floyd, as to Jenkins' inexperience, and seems to have little affected his reputation. As lieutenant-colonel and, later, colonel of the 8th Virginia, he continued his demoralizing raids through the mountain counties, winning enduring fame as a leader of independent cavalry.

Early in 1862 he was elected a representative to the first Confederate Congress but was soon sent back to western Virginia with a brigadier-general's commission. In late August and September he led his brigade on his most famous raid, a daring five-hundred-mile ride through western Virginia and into Ohio, where he was the only Confederate general, except Morgan, to unfurl the Stars and Bars. He captured 300 prisoners, destroyed the official records in many counties, 5,000 stand of arms, and many stores, yet all the while pursued "a policy of such clemency as won us many friends" (Loring's official report, *Official Records,* 1 ser., vol. XII, pt. II, p. 756). In 1863 his brigade was chosen to lead the advance guard into Pennsylvania. They captured Chambersburg and reconnoitered to Harrisburg before being ordered to Gettysburg. At Gettysburg Jenkins was severely wounded. Returning to his mountain command in the fall of 1863, on May 9, 1864, he was opposed to Crook's superior force at Cloyd's Mountain, Va. While he, with drawn sword, was trying to prevent the retreat of a Virginia regiment, they fled. Left behind, he was wounded and captured. A Federal surgeon amputated his arm at the shoulder, but he was unable to withstand the shock and died on May 21.

[See extensive papers and memoranda in possession of Roy Bird Cook, Charleston, W. Va.; *Confed. Mil. Hist.* (1899), vol. II; *Herald-Advertizer* (Huntington, W. Va.), Aug. 25, 1929; *Huntington Herald*, June 22, 1900; *War of the Rebellion, Official Records* (*Army*).]
R. D. M.

JENKINS, CHARLES JONES (Jan. 6, 1805–June 14, 1883), jurist, governor of Georgia, was born in the Beaufort district, S. C., the only child of Charles Jones Jenkins, who was the ordinary of Beaufort district and had previously served as clerk of the court of common pleas. About 1816 the family moved to Jefferson County, Ga. Young Jenkins was an earnest student and received the best educational advantages. He attended the famous school of Moses Waddell, whom he followed to Athens, Ga., when Waddell became president of Franklin College, completed his preparation there, and entered Franklin College. In February 1822 he took his dismissal in order to enter Union College at Schenectady, N. Y., where he graduated in 1824. He read law with J. MacPherson Berrien [*q.v.*] and was admitted to the bar in April 1826. Beginning practice in Sandersville he was immediately successful. In 1829 he moved to Augusta, where, in 1832, he joined the prosperous firm of Augustus B. Longstreet [*q.v.*] and William M. Mann. In 1830 he went to the lower house of the legislature from Richmond County and in 1831 was elected attorney general of the state. This office he soon resigned to seek reëlection to the legislature, but was twice defeated before his successful candidacy of 1836. With the exception of the term of 1842, he served continuously in the house from 1836 until his resignation in 1850, and during this time was speaker of the house for four terms. He was an ardent Union Whig and, in the state constitutional convention of 1850, wrote and championed the resolutions endorsing the compromise measures of 1850, commonly known as the "Georgia platform." The historian Fielder, a contemporary, called him the "Madison" of this convention (Fielder, *post*, p. 72). In September 1850 Fillmore offered him a position in the cabinet, but he declined. (Toombs to Fillmore, in Phillips, *post*, p. 212). In 1852 the Georgia Whigs bolted the Scott presidential ticket and voted for Webster, who had died in October, and Jenkins (Avery, *post*, p. 25). A few days after the election Jenkins pronounced to the Whigs of Augusta a *Eulogy on the Life and Services of Henry Clay* (1853). In 1853 he was the candidate of the Whig or "Union" party for governor but was defeated. Although he deprecated the drift toward secession he was removed from active politics by his appointment to the Georgia supreme court, on which he served during the entire war.

He declined the presidency of the constitutional convention of 1865, charged with restoring Georgia to the Union, but, as chairman of the committee on business, he directed the difficult work of readjustment. In November 1865 he was accorded the unique honor of a unanimous election as governor. In his inaugural address he declared entire acceptance of the results of the war and pleaded for reconciliation. Within two years he virtually restored the credit of the state. He opposed ratification of the Fourteenth Amendment. When the reconstruction acts of 1867 were passed he sought an injunction in the Supreme Court restraining Secretary Stanton from executing them, but the court declined to interfere. Because he refused to sign a warrant on the state treasury for the payment of the expenses of the reconstruction convention, he was removed by General Meade on Jan. 13, 1868. Jenkins, on leaving the state, sequestered the executive documents, state moneys, and the executive seal, which were not restored until the Democratic governor James M. Smith took office in 1872. In appreciation the state legislature presented Jenkins with a gold facsimile of the executive seal inscribed, "In Arduis Fidelis." After some months in Canada and eighteen months' residence abroad, he had returned to Georgia late in 1870. He retired to his home at Summerville, near Augusta, and only returned to public life for brief service as president of the constitutional convention of 1877. Avery, the Georgia historian, writing in 1881, said that "no man in the state has enjoyed a larger measure of respect than Mr. Jenkins." (Avery, *post*, p. 20.)

He was married twice: first, to a sister of Seaborn Jones of Burke County, Ga., and, after she died, to a daughter of Judge Barnes of Philadelphia.

[C. C. Jones, *The Life and Services of Ex-Gov. C. J. Jenkins* (1884); W. J. Northen, *Men of Mark in Ga.*, vol. III (1910); I. W. Avery, *The Hist. of the State of Ga.* (copr. 1881); Herbert Fielder, *A Sketch of the Life and Times and Speeches of Joseph E. Brown* (1883); "The Correspondence of Robert Toombs, Alexander H. Stephens and Howell Cobb" edited by U. B. Phillips in *Ann. Rept. of the Am. Hist. Asso. for the year 1911*, vol. II (1913); *Atlanta Constitution*, June 16, 1883.]
H. J. P., Jr.

JENKINS, EDWARD HOPKINS (May 31, 1850–Nov. 6, 1931), agricultural chemist, was born in Falmouth, Mass., the son of John and Chloe (Thompson) Jenkins. He studied at Phillips Academy, Andover, and entered Yale University, from which he received the degree of A.B. in 1872. After carrying on graduate work there until 1875 he went to Germany, where he studied at the University of Leipzig (1875–76), and later at the Forest School, Tharandt, Saxony. Returning to Yale, he received from that institution in 1879 the degree of Ph.D.

In the meantime, 1877, he became chemist of the Connecticut Agricultural Experiment Station at New Haven, with which he remained connected throughout his long career. In 1884 he was made vice-director, in 1900, director, and in 1923 director emeritus. During his administration there were established departments of entomology, forestry, and genetics, and the tobacco substation at Windsor. In addition to his other duties, he served as director of the Storrs Agricultural Experiment Station from 1912 until his retirement from active service in 1923. He was chairman of the state sewage commission, 1897–1903, president of the Association of Agricultural Colleges and Experimental Stations in 1913, and was chiefly responsible for the organization of the Association of Official Seed Analysts, of which he was the first president. He was also a charter member of the Association of Official Agricultural Chemists, one of its early presidents, and a member of its first committee on food standards, appointed in 1897. He was president of the Connecticut Forestry Association, and was connected with many local, state, and national organizations. Of the reports of the state sewage commission he was editor, or joint editor. As director of the Experiment Station he planned and conducted studies which added materially to knowledge on various subjects, and he was author, or co-author, of numerous papers, many of them published in the reports of the Connecticut Agricultural Experiment Station. They deal particularly with the chemical composition of fertilizers, feeding stuffs, foods and drugs, plant nutrition, and the cultivation of tobacco. In this last-named industry he was especially interested, and results of experiments in growing and curing tobacco were published by him in Station reports from 1893 to 1904. He was the first to introduce into the Northern states the practice of growing tobacco under cloth for cigar wrapper purposes. A member of the board of editors of the first edition of the *Century Dictionary,* he prepared the definitions of chemical terms; he was the author of the section on agriculture in N. G. Osborn's *History of Connecticut in Monographic Form* (1925); and was a contributor to the *Dictionary of American Biography.*

His scrupulous integrity made him economical and circumspect in the use of public funds; he was sympathetic and helpful in his relation to his colleagues, but never impinged upon their freedom; his modesty, kindliness, invariable good humor, and fine feeling made him a delightful companion. His tastes were inclusive and his gifts varied; he contributed sketches anonymously to periodicals, and wrote verses and humorous skits, which were known only to his friends. On June 18, 1885, he was married to Elizabeth Elliot Foote of Guilford, Conn. He died suddenly at his home in New Haven.

[*Am. Men. of Sci.* (4th ed., 1927); *Rus* (4th ed., 1930); *Yale Alumni Weekly,* Nov. 13, 20, 1931; *Science,* Nov. 27, 1931; *Forty-Ninth Report of the Conn. Agric. Experiment Station . . . for the Year 1925*; records of Class of 1872, Yale; *Cat. of the Officers and Grads. of Yale Univ., 1701–1924*; *Who's Who in America,* 1930–31.]

W. E. B.

JENKINS, HOWARD MALCOLM (Mar. 30, 1842–Oct. 11, 1902), editor, historical writer, son of Algernon Sydney and Anna Maria (Thomas) Jenkins, was born at Gwynedd, Montgomery County, Pa., where the first American ancestor of his father's family had been among the early Welsh settlers. His father served as a justice of the peace for nearly forty years. He was educated at the Friends' School of Gwynedd and at the Gwynedd Boarding School. For one winter after leaving the latter he taught school, but his interest in public affairs, together with marked literary ability, drew him toward journalism as a profession. With Wilmer Atkinson [*q.v.*], whose sister Mary Anna he married three years later, he bought the Norristown *Republican* in 1862, which was soon merged with the *Herald and Free Press.* Jenkins served as editor until 1866. Meanwhile he entered the emergency service of the Pennsylvania militia, called out in 1862 and 1863 when Lee invaded Pennsylvania. In 1866 he moved to Wilmington and founded with Atkinson the first daily paper in Delaware, the *Wilmington Daily Commercial.* It was during this period that he enjoyed the friendship of Bayard Taylor. After the sale of the *Daily Commercial* in 1877 he became an editorial contributor to the West Chester *Village Record,* the Philadelphia *Times,* and other newspapers, and for nearly ten years was editor of the Philadelphia *American.* His work during this period shows wide knowledge of state and national politics as well as of foreign affairs, discriminating appreciation of cultural movements, and humane interest in social betterment. For five years (1891–96) he was associated with Charles Heber Clark in the management of the *Manufacturer.* Meanwhile he had become interested in the possibilities of a publication that might be influential in unifying and directing the efforts of the Society of Friends. Accordingly he purchased the *Friends' Journal* in 1884, which the following year was merged with an older paper, the *Friends' Intelligencer*. He served as editor-in-chief until his death in 1902 and in this capacity became a distinguished and much-loved leader of the Society of Friends.

His work in the field of Pennsylvania local history was extensive. In addition to writing numerous pamphlets and magazine articles, he edited *Historical Collections Relating to Gwynedd* (1884), a useful collection of source material, and had nearly completed the editing of the three-volume history, *Pennsylvania: Colonial and Federal* (posthumously published, 1903) at the time of his death. He also compiled *The Family of William Penn* (1899) and *Genealogical Sketch of the Descendants of Samuel Spencer of Pennsylvania* (completed by A. H. Jenkins and posthumously published, 1904), and contributed Volume I to J. R. Young's *Memorial History of the City of Philadelphia* (1895), though his name does not appear on the title-page. He also had many interests in educational and philanthropic fields and especially enjoyed his service on the board of managers of Swarthmore College, from which institution four of his children graduated. Insisting upon the need of special training he said, "Each of us, if we are to earn our own way, must bring to market something of real service to society." He contributed to his generation a leadership in the movements to secure justice for the negro, the Indian, and the prisoner; to bring about lasting peace; and to promote constructive plans for the betterment of mankind.

[Memoirs of Jenkins by two of his sons, T. A. Jenkins and A. H. Jenkins, were published respectively in the *Friends' Intelligencer*, Dec. 27, 1902, and in the *Geneal. Sketch of Samuel Spencer of Pa.* (1904), previously mentioned. See also: *Who's Who in America*, 1901–02; and the *Public Ledger* (Phila.), Oct. 12, 13, 1902.] A. L. L.

JENKINS, JAMES GRAHAM (July 18, 1834–Aug. 6, 1921), lawyer, judge, was born at Saratoga Springs, N. Y., the son of Edgar Jenkins, a merchant, and Mary Elizabeth (Walworth) Jenkins. His mother's father was Reuben Hyde Walworth [*q.v.*], a justice of the supreme court of New York and a distinguished chancellor of that state. James was educated in the private schools of his native city and commenced the study of law in the offices of Ellis, Burrill & Davison, New York City. Upon his admission to the bar he immediately commenced the practice of his profession and two years later (1857) removed to Milwaukee. He was married in 1870 to Alice Mary Miller, daughter of Andrew Gilbraith Miller, then United States district judge for the eastern district of Wisconsin. During the time Jenkins was engaged in practice he was successively the law partner of Jason Downer, later a justice of the Supreme Court, Edward G. Ryan, later chief justice of the supreme court of Wisconsin, Senator Matthew Hale Carpenter, Theodore B. Elliott, and Gen. Frederick C. Winkler. It would be difficult to select from the roll of Wisconsin lawyers a more distinguished group. At the time of his appointment to be United States district judge for the eastern district of Wisconsin (July 2, 1888), he was generally recognized as the leader of the bar. When Walter Q. Gresham resigned the office of United States circuit judge for the seventh judicial circuit to become a member of President Cleveland's cabinet (March 1893) Jenkins was appointed to succeed him and continued to serve in that capacity until his retirement to private life in 1905.

Jenkins' name is associated with two important cases: *Pillsbury* vs. *Pillsbury Washburn Company, Ltd.* (24 *U. S. Appeal Reports*), and *Farmers Loan & Trust Company* vs. *Northern Pacific Railway Company* (60 *Fed.*, 803). The first case, which involved matters generally classified under unfair competition or unfair trade, remains a landmark in the history of American jurisprudence. The principles there laid down, amplified and extended, have so far governed the law of that subject. The second case, generally known as the Northern Pacific receivership, involved Jenkins in a controversy with Congress. John C. Spooner, counsel for the receiver, filed a petition in the court over which Jenkins presided. Upon the petition the court issued the famous injunctional or strike order which enjoined the employees then in the service of the receiver from combining and conspiring to quit the services of the receiver with the object and intent of crippling the property in their custody. This order became the subject of investigation by a subcommittee of the House of Representatives. The committee attempted to summon Jenkins before it. He declined to comply on the ground that the committee was not authorized to inquire into any matters affecting his personal or official integrity. The case was later appealed to the Supreme Court of the United States and there, with very slight modification, the decree was affirmed.

After his retirement from the bench, Jenkins was for seven years (1908–15) dean of the law school of Marquette University, Milwaukee. Throughout his life he was an influential leader of the Democratic party and was its candidate for governor in 1879. In 1881 he received the vote of his party in the legislature of Wisconsin for United States senator. While his party in the state was in a hopeless minority, his interest in it never waned. He was active in its councils and gave much of his time and energy to its support upon the stump. He was of medium height, commanding presence, and distinguished bearing, and he enjoyed to an unusual degree a deserved popularity with the people of his state. He died in Milwaukee, Wis.

["In Memoriam, Jas. Graham Jenkins," 175 *Wis. Reports,* lii; *A Memorial of Jas. Graham Jenkins Prepared on Behalf of Alice Mary Jenkins* (1922); P. M. Reed, *Bench and Bar of Wis.* (1882); John R. Berryman, *Hist. of the Bench and Bar of Wis.* (1898), vol. II; the *Milwaukee Jour.*, Aug. 7, 1921.] M. B. R.

JENKINS, JOHN (Feb. 15, 1728–November 1785), pioneer, surveyor, the son of John and Lydia (Allen) Jenkins, was probably born in East Greenwich, Conn. He was married, in February 1751, to Lydia Gardner of New London. In 1753 the Susquehanna Company of Connecticut was formed to settle the territory in Pennsylvania claimed by the colony of Connecticut by the grant in its original charter, but disputed by the proprietaries of Pennsylvania. Jenkins, who had explored the Wyoming Valley that year, was its leading spirit and chief commissioner. He went to Albany, N. Y., during the congress of the colonies in 1754 and with his fellow commissioners obtained from the chiefs of the Six Nations a deed to the disputed lands on the Susquehanna River including Wyoming and the country westward to the Alleghanies. For this they paid the chieftains £2,000. The following year Jenkins was sent to survey the Wyoming Valley but found the savages engaged in strife with the settlers. The settlement of the country by the Susquehanna Company was accordingly postponed.

In 1762, believing the time propitious for the colonization of Wyoming, Jenkins headed a band of settlers who were purchasers from the Susquehanna Company. They arrived in the summer of that year, but on Oct. 15, 1763, were driven out by the Indians who massacred some of the party. In 1768 a meeting of the company was held at Hartford, Conn., with Jenkins presiding, which resolved that the forty proprietors of the five proposed townships should proceed to Wyoming and commence the settlement, and that 200 more should follow in the next spring. The plan was carried out in January 1769, when Jenkins, accompanied by his son John [*q.v.*], started for the Susquehanna and began the settlement of the town of Kingston. He held all the lands from the township line to Kingston and Exeter, at the head of the Wyoming Valley. At Pittson Ferry Bridge, he and others constructed the stronghold, known as Jenkins' Fort. He was a member of the Connecticut Assembly from Westmoreland County in 1774, 1775, and 1777. On July 1, 1778, the day before the Wyoming "massacre," he was driven out of his land and fled to Orange County, N. Y., where he died. After his retirement from Wyoming Valley, his son took his place as leader of the Connecticut settlers.

[See Isaac A. Chapman, *A Sketch of the Hist. of Wyoming* (1830); Chas. Miner, *Hist. of Wyoming, in a Series of Letters from Chas. Miner, to his Son Wm. Penn Miner, Esq.* (1845); Geo. Peck, *Wyoming: Its Hist., Stirring Incidents, and Romantic Adventures* (1858); *Hist. of Luzerne, Lackawanna, and Wyoming Counties, Pa.* (1880); H. C. Bradsby, *Hist. of Luzerne County, Pa.* (1893); *Geneal. and Family Hist. of the Wyoming and Lackawanna Valleys, Pa.* (1906), ed. by H. E. Hayden, Alfred Hand, and J. W. Jordan; and *Pa. Archives,* 2 ser., vol. XVIII (1893). According to Peck, *ante,* Jenkins was born in Wales and came to America about 1735.] J. J.

JENKINS, JOHN (Nov. 27, 1751 o.s.–Mar. 19, 1827), soldier, pioneer, surveyor, the eldest son of John Jenkins [*q.v.*] and Lydia Gardner, was born at Gardner's Lake, in New London, Conn. As a youth he accompanied his father to the Wyoming Valley, Pa., with the band of settlers who, by attempting to establish the claims of Connecticut to that region, kept alive the strife which has been called the Pennamite War. He was, in turn, farmer, surveyor, conveyancer, school teacher, merchant, and ironmonger. For many years he was the agent of the Susquehanna Company of Connecticut, which his father had been instrumental in forming, and also commanded the Forty Fort, the stronghold of the settlers. He took an active interest in the Revolution from the beginning. In 1777 he was taken prisoner by Indians and Tories and was carried first to Niagara, subsequently to Montreal, and finally to Albany. While his captors were planning to hold a Grand Council to decide what disposition to make of him, he escaped and after great suffering and fatigue, reached his home in Wyoming in June 1778. Almost immediately after his return he joined Captain Spalding's company as lieutenant and was with Colonel Hartley at Tioga Point in September 1778, participating in the battle of Indian Hill, near Wyalusing. He is said to have been called into conference with Washington, and to have assisted him in planning General Sullivan's punitive expedition against the Indians who committed the massacre at Wyoming (1778). He served with Sullivan throughout the campaign, receiving the formal thanks of that commander for his services as guide and for his gallant conduct in the battle of Newtown, Aug. 29, 1779. With his company he joined Washington's army on the Hudson in the spring of 1781 and was in the battle of King's Bridge, July 3, 1781. He accompanied the army to Yorktown, being present at the surrender of Cornwallis. Shortly afterward he resigned his command and returned to his home, where as the leader of the Connecticut settlers he actively defended his family and friends against the Indians and the "Pennamites."

In 1783 Jenkins appeared before the Supreme Executive Council of Pennsylvania to press the claims of the Susquehanna Company of Connecticut. Three years later he defended himself before the same body against charges of Pennsylvania settlers in the Wyoming Valley that he had acted tyrannically and had threatened bodily harm to those who opposed him. In the same year, 1786, he laid out the towns of Athens and Tioga Point, in Bradford County, and in 1787, having established himself in Exeter, he was elected sheriff of Luzerne County after it had been organized. He owned a plot of land six miles square in the disputed territory, within the townships of Blakely, Carbondale, and Greenfield, but refused it under Pennsylvania title and consequently suffered great loss. He continued his fight against the state, even going to Congress, but finally he concluded to relinquish his claims. Jenkins married Bethiah Harris, of Colchester, Conn., June 23, 1778. Such was his popularity in his community that although he was a Democrat, and the county generally was Federalist, he was several times elected to public office. He died at his home in Exeter.

[H. C. Bradsby, *Hist. of Bradford County, Pa.* (1891), and *Hist. of Luzerne County, Pa.* (1893); *Hist. of Luzerne, Lackawanna, and Wyoming Counties, Pa.* (1880); George Peck, *Wyoming: Its Hist., Stirring Incidents and Romantic Adventures* (1858); *Geneal. and Family Hist. of the Wyoming and Lackawanna Valleys, Pa.* (1906), ed. by H. E. Hayden, Alfred Hand, and J. W. Jordan; *Pa. Archives*, 2 ser., vol. XVIII (1893); Isaac A. Chapman, *A Sketch of the Hist. of Wyoming* (1830); Chas. Miner, *Hist. of Wyoming, in a Series of Letters from Chas. Miner to his Son Wm. Penn Miner, Esq.* (1845).] J. J.

JENKINS, JOHN STILWELL (Feb. 15, 1818–Sept. 20, 1852), lawyer, newspaper editor, author, was probably the son of Ira Jenkins, an Albany merchant and banker, who about 1830 removed to central New York and in 1836 was elected second president of the village of Clyde in Wayne County, and Rebecca (Van Heusen) Jenkins. John Stilwell Jenkins was born in Albany. He entered Hamilton College at Clinton, N. Y., as a member of the sophomore class in 1835 but left college at the end of the year to take up the study of law. He was admitted to the bar and seems to have begun to practice at Jordan in Onondaga County but soon removed to Weedsport and subsequently to Auburn and Sennett in Cayuga County. He married the grand-daughter of Gen. John Fellows of the Revolutionary army in 1843. Becoming interested in newspaper work, he established and edited the *Cayuga Tocsin*, a Democratic newspaper which opposed the further extension of slavery. In 1847 the paper was merged with the *Cayuga Patriot* under the name of the *Cayuga New Era*, to the editorial pages of which Jenkins also contributed. His novelette, "Alice Howard," appeared in a Philadelphia periodical in 1846. He was a prolific writer or rather compiler of books, doubtless stimulated by the appearance of several publishing houses in Auburn in the decade of the forties. *The New Clerk's Assistant* (1846), a volume of practical legal forms, passed through many editions and sold to the number of 30,000 copies. His *History of Political Parties in the State of New York* (1846) is an abridgment and popularization of the two-volume work on the same subject published four years before by Jabez D. Hammond, to whom he dedicated the volume. *Lives of the Governors of the State of New York* (1851) is a similar work on the history and politics of the empire state. *The History of the War between the United States and Mexico, from the Commencement of Hostilities to the Ratification of the Treaty of Peace* (1848), purporting to be the first account of the struggle between the two republics, was based upon the official reports of the officers of the army and sold to the number of 35,000 copies. *United States Exploring Expedition* (1851), intended to be the first of a series of works on exploration, is a condensation of Charles Wilkes's *Narrative of the United States Exploring Expedition, 1838–42* (5 vols., 1845), and William Francis Lynch's *Narrative of the United States' Expedition to the River Jordan and the Dead Sea* (1849). *The Life of Silas Wright, Late Governor of the State of New York* (1847), *The Life of General Andrew Jackson* (1847), *James Knox Polk, and a History of His Administration* (1850), and *The Life of John Caldwell Calhoun* (1850), are eulogistic accounts of the leaders of the Democratic party of his day, written too soon after the decease of the subjects to have permanent value. *The Lives of Patriots and Heroes Distinguished in the Battles for American Freedom* (1847), *The Generals of the Last War with Great Britain* (1849), and *The Heroines of History* (1851), are biographical works so general in character as to be without value. At the time of his death, Jenkins was engaged upon a "Pictorial History of New York," and a work on "The Practice in Justices' Courts," neither of which was completed. He died at the home of his father in Syracuse after a surgical operation at the age of thirty-four. He was survived by his wife and four children.

[*Cat. of the Corporation, Officers, and Students, of Hamilton Coll., Clinton,* 1835–36; C. E. Fitch, ed., *Encyc. of Biog. of N. Y.*, vol. II (1916); Elliot G. Storke, *Hist. of Cayuga County, N. Y.* (1879), and "Hist. of the Press of Cayuga County, from 1798 to 1877," in *Cayuga County* (N. Y.) *Hist. Soc. Colls.*, vol. VII (1889); *Syracuse Standard*, Sept. 22, 1852; *Syracuse Jour.*, Sept. 23, 1852.] I. M. C.

JENKINS, MICAH (Dec. 1, 1835–May 6, 1864), Confederate soldier, was born on Edisto Island, S. C. The Jenkinses belonged to an ancient Welsh family, claiming descent from the last Prince Llewellyn. Joseph Jenkins, the first of Micah's South Carolina ancestors, landed about 1670; in 1791 one of his descendants bought "Brick House" Plantation of Edisto Island, which is still in possession of the family. Micah was the third son of Capt. John Jenkins, Edisto "planter and baron," and Elizabeth Clark. He entered the South Carolina Military Academy in 1851, and was graduated, when nineteen, at the head of his class. The next year, 1855, he helped to establish the King's Mountain Military School, at Yorkville, S. C., which continued in successful operation until the outbreak of the Civil War. To the cause of secession Jenkins gave himself with intense enthusiasm. He assisted in organizing and was elected colonel of the 5th South Carolina Regiment, which was among the first regiments to enter the Confederate service, and at Manassas was posted on the right and fought conspicuously. The next year "Jenkins' Palmetto Sharpshooters," a new regiment of picked men which he had organized, quickly attracted notice in the battles around Richmond. At Seven Pines, Jenkins acted as commander of a brigade, including the "Sharpshooters." Gen. D. H. Hill, in giving an account of the operations, reported that Jenkins' brigade, because of the latter's skilful handling of it, "rendered more service than any two engaged" (Thomas, *post*, p. 26). After Frayser's Farm, in which the "Sharpshooters" lost all but 125 men, he was promoted brigadier-general, July 22, 1862; and after Second Manassas, where Jenkins was severely wounded, General Lee, riding up to him, said, "I hope yet to see you one of my lieutenant-generals" (Thomas, *post*, p. 26).

In 1864 Jenkins, being ordered to East Tennessee, commanded Hood's division at Chickamauga. From Chattanooga he accompanied Longstreet in his campaign against Knoxville. Returning to Virginia, he was in time to command his old brigade in the second day of the Wilderness. As he rode into battle by the side of Longstreet, he exclaimed, "I am happy; I have felt despair of the cause for some months, but am relieved, and feel assured that we will put the enemy back across the Rapidan before night" (Longstreet, *post*, p. 563). Before he had finished speaking he was mortally wounded by mistaken fire of the Confederates, being shot near the same spot and in the same way as was Stonewall Jackson. Wade Hampton described Jenkins as the "finest soldier I ever saw" (Thomas, *post*, p. 26). A surviving war-time portrait shows him with dark moustache and eyes, and handsome, resolute face. Married in 1856 to Caroline, daughter of Gen. D. F. Jamison, later president of the South Carolina secession convention, he was survived by four sons, including Maj. Micah Jenkins, cited for bravery at San Juan Hill, and Major-Gen. John M. Jenkins, U. S. A.

[J. P. Thomas, *Career and Character of Gen. Micah Jenkins, C. S. A.* (1903), and *The Hist. of the S. C. Mil. Acad.* (1893); *War of the Rebellion, Official Records* (*Army*); *Confed. Mil. Hist.* (1899), V, 404–06; Jas. Longstreet, *From Manassas to Appomattox* (1896); *S. C. Hist. and Geneal. Mag.*, Oct. 1919; *Charleston Mercury*, May 9, 12, 1864; information as to certain facts from Jenkins' son, Gen. John M. Jenkins, Washington, D. C.] R. D. M.

JENKINS, NATHANIEL (June 7, 1812–May 20, 1872), inventor, manufacturer, was born in Boston, Mass., the son of Nathaniel and Mary (Wheeler) Jenkins. He was educated in the city public schools and then became a coppersmith's apprentice. After completing his full term and working for several years for different masters, he organized in 1837 his own coppersmith's business in Boston under the firm name of Rice, Jenkins & Company. For the succeeding seventeen years he carried on this business acquiring a large control in 1853 and changing the firm name to Jenkins & Company. The following year, however, he disposed of his interest in this company and established himself in Boston as a silversmith and clock-maker and carried on the business successfully for ten years. In the meantime, around 1860, he undertook some experimental work in an attempt to find a suitable packing material which would withstand the destructive effect of hot water and steam in faucets and valves. After a very complete and thorough search extending over four years he eliminated all materials except rubber compounds, and in 1864 he gave up silversmithing and opened a place of business at 52 Sudbury Street, Boston, to engage in the invention and production of water faucets fitted with renewable packings of rubber. For two years he labored diligently and was then rewarded on May 8, 1866, with a United States patent, No. 54,554, for a rubber compound packing which would stand hot water and steam as well (*House Executive Document 109,* 39 Cong., 2 Sess., II, 708). At about the same time he invented a steam valve and as this seemed to possess greater possibilities, he concentrated his efforts on the production of this device and the packing compound for steam and hot-water joints. He also continued with his inventive work and obtained several additional patents for improvements on these products in 1866 and 1867. Finally on Oct. 6, 1868, he was granted patent No. 82,844 (*House Executive Document 52,* 40 Cong., 3 Sess., II, 506) for the type of steam globe valve now known throughout the world as the Jenkins valve. As Jenkins designed it, an India-rubber compounded packing was employed for sealing the joint of the valve. The valve parts were arranged in such a way that should the packing weaken or be destroyed, the metallic portions of the joint would come into contact and effect a tight union. Jenkins took his son Charles into partnership with him in 1868. Four years later he died, and immediately thereafter, to continue the business, his two sons Charles and Alfred B. Jenkins formed a partnership under the firm name of Jenkins Brothers. About forty years later the business of Jenkins Brothers was incorporated under the laws of the state of New Jersey, Alfred B. Jenkins serving as president until his death. Nathaniel Jenkins married Mary W. Tucker of Roxbury, Mass., on Oct. 4, 1835, and at the time of his death was survived by three sons and a daughter.

[*Boston Daily Jour.,* May 20, 1872; *Boston Daily Advertiser,* May 21, 1872; Patent Office records; correspondence with the firm of Jenkins Brothers.]

C. W. M

JENKINS, THORNTON ALEXANDER (Dec. 11, 1811–Aug. 9, 1893), naval officer, was born in Orange County, Va. There he prepared for college but was forced to work as a merchant clerk for two or three years until, upon warm testimonials from friends, including Mrs. Dolly Madison, he was appointed midshipman, Nov. 1, 1828. After service in the West Indies against pirates, 1828–33, he took his examination for lieutenant, 1834, standing first among eighty-two candidates, though he was not promoted until 1839. He was on coast survey duty, 1834–42; in the Brazil and Mediterranean squadrons, 1842–45; and in 1845–46 went abroad with another officer to study European lighthouse systems, the results of which were published in a comprehensive report (1846). Later he was secretary of the first temporary lighthouse board, 1850–52, framed the law of 1852 for the administration of the lighthouse service, and was secretary of the permanent board, 1852–58, 1861–62. Meanwhile he had served during the Mexican War as executive in the *Germantown,* heading her landing parties at Tuxpan and Tabasco, and in command of the hospital ship *Relief* and the supply station at Salmadena Island. He had charge of Gulf Stream observations for the Coast Survey, 1848–52, and commanded the *Preble* in the Paraguayan Expedition, 1858–59, and later in the West Indies, where in 1861 he assisted in saving for the Union the forts at Key West and the Dry Tortugas. In the Civil War he commanded the *Wachusett* in the James River, June–September, 1862, taking part in the actions at Coggin's Point and City Point. He was promoted captain in July, and in November, commanding the *Oneida,* joined the blockade below Mobile, where he was senior officer, Nov. 12–Dec. 28. In February 1863, he became Farragut's flag captain on the Mississippi, commanding the *Hartford* at the passing of Port Hudson and Grand Gulf, Mar. 14–19. Subsequently, transferred to the *Richmond,* he commanded the forces below Port Hudson, and was senior naval officer at its surrender, July 8. The day before, on board the *Monongahela,* he received a slight wound in the hip while passing the batteries at College Point. After taking the *Richmond* to New York for refitting, he was again on the Mobile blockade, December 1863–February 1865, acting during the greater part of this period as senior officer, and in the *Richmond* commanding the 2nd division at the battle of Mobile Bay. Farragut in his report (August 12) of the battle speaks in warmest terms of Jenkins' "ability and most untiring zeal," while one of his subordinates in this campaign, Lieutenant Perkins (C. S. Alden, *George Hamilton Perkins, U. S. N.; His Life and Letters,* 1914, p. 202), describes him as "one of the kindest and best of men." After duty on the James River until the close of the war, he was chief of the Bureau of Navigation, August 1865–April 1869. Secretary Welles remarked upon his appointment that he was "one of the most faithful, industrious, laborious, and best informed officers in the service" (*Diary of Gideon Welles,* 1911, III, 569). He was made rear admiral on July 13, 1870, and commanded the Asiatic Squadron from May 1872, until his retirement, Dec. 11, 1873. Before and during his service as bureau chief he was author of a number of government publications in his special field of navigation, notably a *Code of Flotilla and Boat Squadron Signals for the United States Navy* (1861); *Instructions for Hydrographic Surveyors* (1868); *The Rule of the Road at Sea and in Inland Waters* (1869); *The Barometer, Thermometer, Hygrometer, and Atmospheric Appearances at Sea and on Land as Aids in Foretelling Weather* (1869); and *Ships' Compasses* (1869). After his retirement he made his home in Washington. He was married first to a Miss Powers, and second to a daughter of Paymaster Thornton of the navy. By his second marriage he had three daughters and two sons.

[*War of the Rebellion: Official Records (Navy)*; L. R. Hamersly, *The Records of Living Officers of the U. S. Navy and Marine Corps* (4th ed., 1890); L. G. Tyler, *Encyc. of Va. Biog.* (1915), vol. III; *Army and Navy Jour.*, Aug. 12, 1893; *Washington Post*, Aug. 10, 1893.]
A. W.

JENKS, GEORGE CHARLES (Apr. 13, 1850–Sept. 12, 1929), writer of dime novels, journalist, was born in London, England, son of George Stilwell and Eliza (Miller) Jenks. After serving an apprenticeship with a London printer, he came to America in 1872 and worked at printing for ten years. He was a writer on the *Pittsburgh Press* for six years; then moved to New York in 1895, where he became correspondent of the *Pittsburgh Dispatch* and *Gazette-Times*, and an author of fiction and motion pictures. He wrote dramatic criticism, engaged in private theatricals, and in the occasional directorship of small theatres. Books signed with his own name include an *Official History of the Johnstown Flood* (1889) with Frank Connelly, and a few novels in conventional form: *The Climax* (1909), from the play by Edward Locke; *The Deserters* (1911), with Anna A. Chapin; and *Stop Thief!* (1913), with Carlyle Moore. He also gave lectures on the work of the writers of fiction. Paradoxically, he owes his fame to work done under pseudonyms. His career as a writer of dime novels and "nickel weeklies" began as early as 1886, when he was writing, under his own name, for the pioneer firm in this branch of fiction: Beadle & Adams. Years later, in an article, "Dime Novel Makers" (*Bookman*, New York, October 1904), he gave a good-humored description of his fellow dime-novelists of the early period, not, however, admitting his own share in this work.

Writing for the firm of Street & Smith, Jenks was one of the group of authors who related the preposterous but highly popular adventures of *Nick Carter*. This detective was the creation of John Russell Coryell, Frederic V. R. Dey, Eugene T. Sawyer, Jenks, and others. From October 1896 to June 1911 Jenks (with others) wrote a weekly novelette about a character called *Diamond Dick*. Priority is always doubtful in these stories, but Samuel S. Hall had used this name as early as 1882. Despite the similarity in name to E. L. Wheeler's *Deadwood Dick*, the new tales were successful. Years after the dime novels had vanished, the names of only five or six out of their thousands of characters remained in the minds of readers, and Jenks's youthful hero was one of the survivors. *Diamond Dick, Jr., The Boys' Best Weekly*, sold at five cents a copy, with a colored picture showing Dick befriending the innocent or baffling the wicked. He had a broad-brimmed hat; long, golden curls; fancy jacket; broad sash; white breeches and high, black boots—a costume never worn by anybody outside a Wild West show. There was a Western flavor in his adventures, indicated by the titles: *Diamond Dick's Sack of Sand; or, Turning the Tables on the Mining Wolves*, and *The Shade of Diamond Dick; or, The Ghost of the Mine*. The stories were signed W. B. Lawson, a pseudonym also attached to many of the Jesse James stories.

Jenks was married thrice: in 1878 to Sarah Jane Lambert, who died in 1895; in 1897 to Elizabeth J. Aylward, who died in 1897; and in 1899 to Katharine Baird, who survived him. He had a cheerful, kindly temperament which not only made him well liked by his associates, but enabled him to keep his poise in the midst of literary over-production. His physical strength—he grew to be very large—was such that, at a moment's notice, he could attack his type-writer with a tremendous vigor, and finish a fifteen-thousand-word story in two sittings. He saw the amusing side of the manufacture of five-cent thrillers, but had the necessary ability to take his own work seriously. He found genuine excitement in the exploits of his hero. While he might get only one hundred dollars for a novel of 80,000 words, his industry helped him achieve what seemed to him, as contrasted with his boyhood, a great success; frequently to visit Europe with his family; and finally to retire to a country home at Owasco, N. Y. Nevertheless, his facility in writing led to a deterioration, even from the standards of the dime novel.

[*Who's Who in America*, 1928–29; *N. Y. Times*, Sept. 14, 1929; information as to certain facts from surviving members of his family, and from his publisher.]
E. L. P—n.

JENKS, JEREMIAH WHIPPLE (Sept. 2, 1856–Aug. 24, 1929), economist, teacher, was the son of Benjamin Lane and Amanda (Messer) Jenks and was descended on his father's side from Joseph Jenks [*q.v.*]. After attending the public schools of St. Clair, Mich., his birthplace, he entered the University of Michigan, graduating in 1878. He chose a legal career and while teaching Greek, Latin, and German at Mount Morris College, Mount Morris, Ill., he carried on studies which resulted in his being admitted to the Michigan bar in 1881. But then the new field of political economy attracted him so strongly that in 1883 he gave up his professorship and went to Germany for graduate work. He received the degree of Ph.D. at Halle in 1885, publishing in the same year his thesis, *Henry C. Carey als Nationalökonom.* Upon his return to the United States he taught political science and English literature (1886–89) at Knox College and for two years was professor of economics and social science at Indiana University (1889–91). The appointment as professor of political economy at Cornell which he received in 1891, at the age of thirty-five, gave him wider scope and it soon became evident that the practical application of economic theories to the solution of current political problems absorbed more of his interest than did research in pure theory. It was not until 1899, however, that he got his first opportunity to make a first-hand study of an economic question. The "trust problem" was then under wide consideration. When the United States Industrial Commission was established, Jenks was chosen as its adviser on industrial combinations. He prepared a study, *Industrial Combinations and Prices* (vol. I of the commission's reports), and also a volume on *Industrial Combinations in Europe* (vol. XVIII). *The Trust Problem* (1900) was based largely on data brought out in the course of the commission's work.

This was the beginning of Jenks's excursions into the field of practical economics. He was the first American economist of academic training and connections to devote a large part of his life to service on government boards and commissions. After the Spanish-American War, the War Department, having on its hands the administration of the Philippine Islands, sent Jenks to the Orient to study currencies, taxation, and police systems. His observations were published in *Certain Economic Questions in the English and Dutch Colonies in the Orient* (Washington, 1902). In 1903 he served the Mexican government as an expert on currency reform, and in 1904 he made his second trip to the Orient as the representative of the Commission on International Exchange which had been created at the request of the Chinese and Mexican governments. In the latter position he won the friendship of many prominent Chinese and acquired a permanent interest in Oriental affairs. Later he became a member of the American Asiatic Association and of the China Society of America.

In 1907 Congress by the establishment of the Immigration Commission provided for an extensive economic and social survey and Jenks was one of the three members of the commission selected by President Roosevelt to cooperate with six members of Congress. He plunged into his new task with characteristic energy and thoroughness. It was owing largely to his experience and advice that the commission rejected hearings as a method of collecting evidence and relied instead upon field studies by its own experts. Jenks was particularly interested in the white slave trade and the facts which his investigations revealed were used as a basis for federal legislation. He was able to shape to a considerable extent the commission's general recommendations. Later in collaboration with W. Jett Lauck he published a useful college textbook, *The Immigration Problem* (1911), based on the voluminous reports of the commission.

After a service of over twenty years at Cornell University, Jenks resigned in 1912 to accept an appointment as professor of government at New York University. A second series of foreign missions began in 1918. The year previous he had been named as one of the three members of the High Commission for Nicaragua, to act as its umpire. In this capacity he made a number of visits to Nicaragua and in 1925 assisted in the revision of its banking laws. Meanwhile the new German Republic had availed itself of his services as one of a group of experts in a survey of economic conditions preliminary to plans for currency stabilization. His activity as a traveler and investigator continued until the end of his life; in 1928 at the age of seventy-two he revisited China to familiarize himself at first hand with the progress made under the nationalist régime. He was a voluminous writer. Besides the works on trusts and on immigration and the official reports cited above, he was the author of *Principles of Politics* (1909), a series of lectures delivered at Columbia University, and of numerous books dealing with educational, religious, and business subjects. His writings on economic questions show that he was chiefly interested in the collation of significant facts and their exposition rather than with the formulation of principles or with the criticism of existing economic theories. In his discussion of economic problems he took a conservative attitude. Averse to partisanship, he often softened the force of his conclusions by qualifying phrases. He was gifted with a charming personality, was sincerely interested in people, and had many loyal friends, particularly among the young men with whom he came into contact in his university work. He was married, on Aug. 28, 1884, to Georgia Bixler of Bedford Springs, Pa. He died in New York City.

[*Who's Who in America,* 1928–29; *Am. Econ. Rev.,* Dec. 1929; *Univ. of Mich. Cat. of Grads. . . . 1837–1921* (1923); the *Mich. Alumnus,* Oct. 5, 1929; G. E. Jenks, *Geneal. of the Jenks Family of Newport, N. H.* (1888); *Cornell Alumni News,* June 19, 1912; *N. Y. Times,* Aug. 25, 1929.] P. W. B.

JENKS, JOSEPH (1602–March 1683 N.S.), inventor, the descendant of an old Welsh family, was probably born in Colnbrook, England, though accounts vary in regard to the place of his birth. He was by trade an iron-worker and was employed at Hammersmith when, in 1642, Robert Bridges of Lynn, Mass., succeeded in forming a company in England to finance the first iron works to be established in America. Bog iron had been found in considerable quantities at Saugus, near Lynn, and the colonists were eager to make use of it. As a skilled worker Jenks was induced to come to America to assist in the development of the new enterprise. He was a man of unusual inventive ability, and not content with casting the much-needed utensils and tools required by the settlers, he was soon occupied with new and original projects. In 1646 he petitioned the Court "for liberty to make experience of his abillityes and Inventions for the making of engines for mills, to goe with water . . . and mills for the making of sithes . . . with a new Invented Sawemill" (Lewis, *post,* p. 92). His reputation as a metal worker spread in the colony, and when, in 1652, a mint was set up in Boston, he was chosen to cut the dies for the first coins. His daughter-in-law is said to have provided the design of a pine tree which gave to the new piece of money its popular name. In 1654 the Boston selectmen arranged to have Jenks make "an Ingine to carry water in case of fire" (*Ibid.,* p. 100), said to be the first fire-engine in America. Meanwhile the iron works sold to Jenks the right to build a forge of his own for the manufacture of scythes. It was here in 1655 that he produced a scythe of a distinctly new type, "for the more speedy cutting of grasse." This was an improvement on the old English model, and its adequacy is suggested by the fact that there has been little change in the shape or size of scythes since that time.

In 1667 Jenks was petitioning for aid "to commence a wire factory." He was not successful in obtaining financial support in this venture, however, The iron works had not proved in the long run a remunerative project. There were plenty of people who needed its wares, but few with ready money to pay for them. Litigation caused by the flooding of adjoining property arose, and there is a tradition that the settlers became apprehensive lest a scarcity of wood might result from the amount of charcoal consumed. In any case, the works, after continuing with some difficulty, suspended operations about 1688. Jenks was a widower when he came to America. He had left in England a son [see Jenckes, Joseph, 1632–1717] who later joined his father, learned the parental trade, and established himself in Rhode Island where he became the founder of the city of Pawtucket. After coming to Lynn the elder Jenks married a certain Elizabeth, whose family name is unknown. They had four children, two sons and two daughters. He died at Saugus at the age of eighty-one.

[See Alonzo Lewis, *The Hist. of Lynn* (1829); Robt. Grieve, *An Illustrated Hist. of Pawtucket, Central Falls, and Vicinity* (1897); Massena Goodrich, *Hist. Sketch of the Town of Pawtucket* (1876); G. E. Jenks, *Geneal. of the Jenks Family of Newport, N. H.* (1888); *New-Eng. Hist. and Geneal. Reg.,* July 1855. Although the family name is variously spelled, it seems likely that the most authentic spellings for Joseph Jenks and his descendants are those given here.] E. R. B.

JENKS, TUDOR STORRS (May 7, 1857–Feb. 11, 1922), author, was born in Brooklyn, N. Y., the son of Grenville Tudor and Persis Sophia (Smith) Jenks, and a direct descendant of Joseph Jenks [*q.v.*]. He was graduated from the Polytechnic Institute, Brooklyn (1874), from Yale (1878), and received the degree of LL.B. from Columbia (1880). He then studied art for a year in Paris but returned to New York to practise law, 1881–87. He married, Oct. 5, 1882, Mary Donnison Ford of Brooklyn. Being interested in literature as well as in law he began the writing of juvenile books, of which he produced a large number: *The Century World's Fair Book for Boys and Girls* (1893); *Captain John Smith* (1904); *In the Days of Chaucer* (1904); *The Book of Famous Sieges* (1909); *Chemistry for Young People* (1909).

With all his versatility in subject matter, Tudor Jenks rarely wrote a dull book. His facts are generally accurate and he had a happy method of presenting them to young people. His aim was to teach history, literature, and popular science, and with them patriotism. In 1887 Jenks became associate editor of the *St. Nicholas* and remained on its staff until 1902, when he resumed the practice of law. At the time of his death he was a member of the firm of Jenks & Rogers. He was a witty conversationalist and had a mind full of odd bits of knowledge. In Bronxville, N. Y., where he lived after 1897, his neighbors had the habit of calling him on the telephone for information and advice. His chief recreation was drawing and painting—the walls of his home were decorated with his landscapes —and he left many scrapbooks of sketches. He had pronounced educational theories. He sent none of his three daughters to school, educating them privately, although he believed in college for boys. One who knew him well says of his appearance that he had "a look of great serenity and kindliness, as though he looked at life squarely without sentimentality and found it good."

[*Who's Who in America,* 1921–22; *Quarter-Centenary Record of the Class of 1878, Yale Univ.* (1905); obituary in the *N. Y. Evening Post,* Feb. 13, 1922; information as to certain facts from Jenks's daughter, Mrs. Edgerton Hazard, N. Y. City.] S. G. B.

JENKS, WILLIAM (Nov. 25, 1778–Nov. 13, 1866), Congregational clergyman, was a son of Capt. Samuel and Mary (Haynes) Jenks and a direct descendant of Joseph Jenks [*q.v.*], a machinist who came from Hammersmith, England, about 1643. William was born in Newton, Mass., but after the death of his mother when he was four years old, the family moved to Boston, where he grew up. He was educated at Dr. Samuel Cheney's school, the Boston Latin School, and Harvard College where he graduated in 1797. As private tutor and teacher in various schools he fitted twenty-five boys for Harvard, studied theology, and officiated for eight years as reader in Christ Church, Cambridge (1797–1805). On Dec. 26, 1805, he was ordained at the First Church, Bath, Me., where he remained as pastor for about thirteen years. During this period he was also an army chaplain in the War of 1812 and secretary of the board of trustees and later professor of Oriental languages and English literature in Bowdoin College (1812–16). In 1818 he returned to Boston, opened a private school, and became a pioneer in religious work among seamen. His chapel on Central Wharf was the progenitor of several other institutions for sailors and out of another founded by him at the West End, grew the City Missionary Society and the Shawmut Church. He was also instrumental in founding the Salem Street and Green Street churches and was pastor of the latter from 1826 to 1845.

During his Green Street pastorate Jenks issued his *Comprehensive Commentary on the Holy Bible* (6 vols., 1835–38), a work of great importance in its day. It had an immediate sale of 20,000 copies and passed through several editions. He was one of the earliest members of the American Antiquarian Society, of which he was a corresponding secretary from 1812 to 1816, a member of the council for eleven years, of the committee on publication for fourteen years, and senior vice-president for the last thirteen years of his life. In 1813 he read before the society the first address to be printed, and on its fiftieth anniversary he delivered another entitled "American Archæology." He was elected to the Massachusetts Historical Society, Aug. 27, 1821, was its librarian from 1823 to 1832, and a member of its publication committee in 1825 and in 1852. The idea of the American Oriental Society originated with him (*Proceedings of the American Oriental Society, post,* p. xiv), and he was one of its vice-presidents from its inception in 1842. He was a member of the New-England Historic Genealogical Society and from 1853 to 1858 was chairman of its publishing committee. To the publications of all of these societies he was a prolific contributor. In addition he was the author of many historical and literary articles and pamphlets among which was his pseudonymous *Memoir of the Northern Kingdom* (1808), an anti-Jeffersonian tract of considerable felicity. His knowledge was extensive and varied, but his biblical and oriental scholarship was outstanding. His private library was considered one of the best in New England.

He was a champion of popular education and a friend of the Indian and the negro. A stanch adherent of the New England theology and in his views of church government a strong Congregationalist, yet he was tolerant toward other faiths and an upholder of the right of private judgment. Oil portraits of Jenks may be seen in the rooms of the New-England Historic Genealogical Society and the Congregational Library of Boston. He was diminutive in stature, but courtly and dignified in bearing, with a certain slight formality which was softened by his constant kindliness of spirit. For many years he went about armed with a huge ear trumpet, the badge of his only infirmity. On Oct. 22, 1797, he married Betsey, daughter of Ezekiel and Sarah (Wood) Russell, who died Sept. 14, 1850. Of their sixteen children, seven sons and six daughters survived them.

[*New-Eng. Hist. and Geneal. Reg.,* July 1874; *Memorial Biogs. of the New-Eng. Hist. Geneal. Soc.,* vol.

VI (1905); *Proc. Mass. Hist. Soc.*, 1866–67, 1867–69; *Proc. Am. Antiquarian Soc.*, Nov. 15, 1866; *Proc. Am. Oriental Soc.*, May 22, 1867; *Boston Transcript*, Nov. 16, 1866.]
F. T. P.

JENNEY, WILLIAM LE BARON (Sept. 25, 1832–June 15, 1907), architect, inventor, was born at Fairhaven, Mass., the son of William P. and Elizabeth Le Baron (Gibbs) Jenney. He was educated at Phillips Academy, Andover, Mass., the Lawrence Scientific School, and the École Centrale des Arts et Manufactures in Paris, where he studied art and architecture and graduated with high honors in 1856. Returning to the United States, he became an engineer for the Tehuantepec Railroad Company of New Orleans on the Isthmus of Tehuantepec, but after a year went again to France and spent eighteen months in additional study in architecture. At the outbreak of the Civil War he returned to the United States and enlisted in the Federal army. Shortly after his enlistment, on Aug. 19, 1861, he was appointed captain additional aide de camp and assigned to engineering duty on the staff of General Grant. He served with Grant from Cairo to Corinth and then, at General Sherman's request, was transferred to his command and put in charge of the engineering work at Memphis, Tenn. Subsequently he became chief engineer of the XV Army Corps and continued to serve on the staff of General Sherman until he resigned on May 19, 1866, with the rank of major. After doing some miscellaneous engineering work in western Pennsylvania, he went to Chicago in 1868 and established himself as an engineer and architect. Among his first architectural works were a large church and several large office buildings. In the latter he introduced a change over existing designs in that he provided for attractive entrances, light and commodious hallways, and no dark office rooms. About 1883 he was appointed architect for the Home Insurance Company of New York to design an office building, to be built in Chicago, which was to be fire-resistant and to have the maximum number of well-lighted small offices. For this building (erected 1884) he devised a skeleton construction in which each story —walls, partition and floors—was carried independently on columns. This proved to be "the first high building to utilize as the *basic* principle of its design the method known as skeleton construction," and as such was "the true father of the skyscraper" (*The Octagon,* January 1932, p. 20). The columns for the building were of cast-iron and in it were used for the first time a few Bessemer steel beams. In appreciation of the service he had rendered the industry in this pioneer application of structural steel, the Bessemer Steamship Company of New York later named one of its vessels for him (*Brickbuilder,* February 1897). Jenney also devised many of the appointments that are now common to good office buildings, such as tile office vaults, rapid metal elevators, and a system of plumbing of a most approved type. In 1891 he took William B. Mundie into partnership. Following the completion of the Home Insurance Building, his services were in constant demand. He designed and built in Chicago the Siegel Cooper & Company department store, the Y. M. C. A. Building, the Chicago National Bank Building, the Horticulture Building at the World's Columbian Exposition, and the New York Life Building. The last work in which he was actively interested was the erection of the Illinois memorial on the battlefield of Vicksburg. His poor health prevented his completing this undertaking however, and he retired in 1905 to Los Angeles, Cal., where he died. Shortly before his retirement the firm had become Jenney, Mundie & Jensen. He was the author of numerous magazine articles, and in 1869 published *Principles and Practice of Architecture.* On May 8, 1867, he married Elizabeth H. Cobb of Cleveland, Ohio, who with two sons survived him.

[*Am. Architect and Building News,* July 6, 1907; *Arch. Record,* Aug. 1907; *Who's Who in America,* 1906–07; T. E. Tallmadge, *The Story of Architecture in America* (1927); *Inter Ocean* (Chicago), June 16, 1907; *War of the Rebellion: Official Records (Army)*; *Memorials of Deceased Companions of the Commandery of the State of Ill., Mil. Order of the Loyal Legion of the U. S.,* vol. II (1912); obituary in *Brickbuilder,* June 1907, repr. in *Am. Inst. Arch. Quart. Bull.,* July 1907; reports of two committees of architects appointed to investigate the construction of the Home Insurance Bldg., summarized in *The Octagon,* Jan. 1932.]
C. W. M.

JENNINGS, HENNEN [See JENNINGS, JAMES HENNEN, 1854–1920].

JENNINGS, JAMES HENNEN (May 6, 1854–Mar. 5, 1920), mining engineer, son of James Rody and Katharine Sharpe (Hennen) Jennings, was born in Hawesville, Ky., whither his father had come from New Orleans to develop the coal resources. Although christened James Hennen, he dropped the former name early in life. Across the Ohio River in Indiana lived another coal-mining family of which Hamilton Smith [*q.v.*] was a member, and he inspired Jennings to become an engineer. After several years at school in England, Jennings entered Harvard and was graduated in 1877 from the Lawrence Scientific School. His first position was at the North Bloomfield hydraulic gold mine in California, where Smith was consulting engineer and H. C. Perkins was manager. Next, Jennings was assistant to Ross E. Browne, surveyor at the New Almaden quicksilver mines. For a time "the blue-eyed Kentucky giant" was again with Perkins and then, with the backing of Perkins and Smith, he developed a small gravel-gold mine in Sierra County, gaining a substantial profit. He then became superintendent of the New Almaden, and having met Mary Lucretia Coleman, daughter of one of the owners of the Idaho mine at Grass Valley, married her on Oct. 7, 1886. In the next year, on the recommendation of Smith, he was made manager of the El Callao gold mine in Venezuela, succeeding Perkins there, and after two years he was appointed, again on the recommendation of Smith, to be consulting engineer to H. Eckstein & Company at Johannesburg, South Africa. Perkins joined him three years later as manager of the Rand Mines, an affiliated group. The famous Rand gold district was then in its early development, and American engineers accustomed to large-scale production on a systematic basis were brought in, despite the jealousy of British engineers. Recognizing the necessity of increasing the extraction from the low-grade ores, Jennings summoned Charles Butters from California to design and operate a chlorination plant at the Robinson mine. He soon perceived that this process would not solve the problem, however, and recognizing the importance of the work of MacArthur, Forrest, and Alfred James in developing the cyanide process for recovering gold, he entered into an agreement with them to erect a plant, which treated the tailings of the Robinson mine. It was the general adoption of this process that made the Rand a profitable gold-producing district. Jennings had the faculty of gathering about him able assistants and with their aid contributed materially to enlarged operations at depth, to hand-picking of the ore, and to the introduction of electrical appliances. Having an analytical mind, he took broad views of problems, attaining his ends more by tact and quiet moderation than by brilliance. Economical consolidations of the operating companies were effected, and in 1898 Jennings went to the London office of Wernher, Beit & Company as consulting engineer.

After the Boer War, he returned to Africa in 1902, for a year, to assist in the work of reorganization, with which his younger brother, Sidney, was also associated in an engineering capacity. As chairman of a committee of fifteen, he reported to Joseph Chamberlain on the condition and future of the mines; he also assisted prominently in the establishment of the South Africa School of Mines and of the South Africa Association of Engineers. Upon his return to England he was chosen president of the Institution of Mining and Metallurgy, and was awarded the gold medal of the Institution, unusual honors for an American. In London he served on a committee for the reorganization of the Royal College of Science. Leaving Wernher, Beit & Company in 1905, he returned to the United States and established a home in Washington. In association with Professor Nathaniel S. Shaler [*q.v.*] he contributed to the development of the Conrey Placer Mining Company, which was one of the assets of the Gordon McKay bequest to the scientific departments of Harvard University. His valued cooperation was given generously to government departments and public service, especially to the United States Bureau of Mines during the war. His contributions to scientific literature were chiefly concerned with gold—the methods of mining it and its power as a balance wheel in regulating prices. Among them were "The History and Development of Gold Dredging in Montana" (*Bulletin 121, Department of the Interior, Bureau of Mines,* 1916, and *The Gold Industry and Gold Standard* (1918). In 1918 he was chairman of a committee appointed by the Secretary of the Interior to study the gold situation; its report was published as *Bulletin 144, Department of the Interior, Bureau of Mines* (1919). Besides his wife, a son and a daughter survived him.

[T. A. Rickard, *Interviews with Mining Engineers* (1922); W. R. Ingalls in *Mining and Metallurgy* (N. Y.), May 1920; *Trans. Am. Inst. Mining and Metallurgical Engineers,* vol. LXVI (1922); *Engineering and Mining Jour.,* Mar. 13, 27, May 1, 1920; *Mining Congress Jour.* (Washington, D. C.), Apr. 1920; *Who's Who in America,* 1920–21; *Evening Star* (Washington, D. C.), Mar. 6, 1920.]

P. B. M.

JENNINGS, JOHN (*c.* 1738–Jan. 14, 1802), public official, Revolutionary soldier, and a prominent figure in the Pennamite War in Pennsylvania, is believed to have been a native of Philadelphia and to have been the son of Solomon Jennings. In 1761 he was elected sheriff of Northampton County (*Pennsylvania Archives,* 2 ser. IX, 1896, pp. 318–19) and was several times returned to the office, the last time in 1778. In 1766, with Captain Long and Major Smallman he journeyed from Fort Pitt to Fort Chartres, in the Illinois country, thence down the Mississippi River to New Orleans. As sheriff of Northampton County Jennings was called upon to eject the Connecticut settlers from the lands in the Wyoming Valley which they had purchased from the Susquehanna Company of Connecticut and thus he became prominent in the Pennamite War. After the few Connecticut settlers fled from the territory in 1763, owing to the Indian attacks, two proprietary manors were laid out at Wyoming, and these, in 1768, were leased for seven years to three principal settlers—Charles Stewart, Amos Ogden, and John Jennings, In the following January, forty members of the Connecticut company started for the disputed territory. Both contestants erected forts, and Jennings, with only a posse, was expected to turn out the intruders, so he resorted to stratagem. Inviting three leaders of the Yankee party into his block house for a conference, he arrested them, having previously sent to the capital for processes in blank. The captured leaders were taken to Easton and for a time the civil power had triumphed. Subsequently, however, two of the Yankee leaders reëntered the settlement and began to burn the houses and to carry away goods and cattle. Once more Jennings dispersed the intruders.

On Jan. 1, 1783, Jennings was listed as a private in the 3rd Regiment of the Continental Line, and in the following February he was elected quartermaster of the 1st Company, 2nd Battalion, of the Northampton County militia. Shortly after this he settled in Philadelphia, where he became secretary (or clerk) of the Mutual Assurance Company, one of the early fire insurance companies in America. In 1791 he was clerk to the commissioners of bankrupts and "register of sweeps" in Philadelphia and in 1794 he was made deputy United States marshal for the district of Pennsylvania. In 1796 he was elected an alderman in Philadelphia and in the same year he was appointed associate justice of the mayor's court. The latter office he held until his death in 1802.

[J. T. Scharf and Thompson Westcott, *Hist. of Phila.* (1884), III, 2115; T. F. Gordon, *The Hist. of Pa.* (1829); F. Ellis, *Hist. of Northampton County, Pa.* (1877); Chas. Miner, *Hist. of Wyoming* (1845), pp. 106–15; *Pa. Archives,* 1 ser., vol. IV (1853), 5 ser., vol. VIII (1906), 6 ser., vol. XI (1907); *Minutes of the Provincial Council of Pa.,* vol. IX (1852); *Phila. Gazette and Daily Advertiser,* Jan. 16, 1802; manuscript journal of John Jennings in the library of the Hist. Soc. of Pa.]

J. J.

JENNINGS, JONATHAN (1784–July 26, 1834), first governor of Indiana, the son of Jacob Jennings and Mary (Kennedy) Jennings, was born either in Hunterdon County, N. J., or in Rockbridge County, Va. His father had served as a surgeon in the Revolution and continued to practise medicine after he became an itinerant Presbyterian minister. While Jonathan was a small boy the family moved to Fayette County, Pa., where he received his elementary schooling. Later he attended a grammar school at Canonsburg, Washington County, Pa. In 1806 he decided to migrate to the Northwest Territory. Embarking at Pittsburgh he went down the Ohio to Jeffersonville. Shortly after his arrival he was admitted to the bar and began practising law. Dissatisfied with this location, a year later, he proceeded to Vincennes, where he found employment as clerk in the territorial land office under Nathaniel Ewing. In 1809 he left Knox County to take up his residence in Clark County. In that year he became a candidate for territorial representative to Congress on the platform of "no slavery in Indiana" and won the close election held on May 22. In 1811 he married Ann Gilmore Hay, the daughter of John Hay of Clark County, who accompanied her husband on horseback through fifteen hundred miles of wilderness to Washington. In 1811 and again in 1813 he was reëlected territorial delegate. After the passage of the enabling act on Apr. 19, 1816, a constitutional convention met at Corydon, elected him as president, and drafted Indiana's first constitution within the short time of nineteen days. On Aug. 5 he was elected governor against Thomas Posey. In 1818, along with Lewis Cass and Benjamin Parke, he negotiated the St. Marys treaties of cession with the Potawatomi, the Wea, the Miami, and the Delaware. His enemies contended that the Governor had vacated his office as chief executive of the state when he served as commissioner for those treaties, but the state legislature refused to institute impeachment proceedings against him. In 1819 he was reëlected but, in 1822, resigned in order to run for representative to Congress from the second congressional district. He was successful and continued to hold the same office until 1830, when he was defeated. Having lost his first wife in March 1826 he had married, on Oct. 19, 1827, Clarissa Barbee of Paducah, Ky., with whom he retired to his farm near Charlestown after 1830. In 1832, he again served as commissioner, with Marks Crume and John W. Davis, to conclude land cessions from several bands of the Potawatomi. In his last years he became involved in financial difficulties and was only saved from actual want by the generosity of loyal friends. He died on his farm and was buried in a country cemetery in Charlestown, Ind.

["Governors Messages and Letters. Messages and Papers of Jonathan Jennings, Ratliff Boon, Wm. Hendricks," edited by Logan Esarey (1924), *Ind. Hist. Colls.*; John Tipton Letters in the Indiana State Library at Indianapolis; Letters of Jonathan Jennings in the W. H. English Coll. of The Lib. of the Univ. of

Chicago; L. V. Rule, *Forerunners of Lincoln* (1927); J. H. B. Nowland, *Sketches of Prominent Citizens* (1877); W. W. Woollen, *Biog. and Hist. Sketches of Early Ind.* (1883); J. H. Jennings, *A Geneal. Hist. of the Jennings Families in England and America,* vol. II (1899); M. C. Morrison, *Ann Gilmore Hay* (1925); Logan Esarey, *A Hist. of Ind.,* 2nd ed., vol. I (1918); J. P. Dunn, *Indiana; a Redemption from Slavery* (1888); J. B. Dillon, *A Hist. of Ind.* (1859); W. M. Cockrum, *Pioneer Hist. of Ind.* (1907); Charles Kettleborough, "Constitution Making in Ind.," vol. I (1916), *Ind. Hist. Colls.*]
J. J. B.

JEROME, CHAUNCEY (June 10, 1793–Apr. 20, 1868), clock-maker, inventor, was born in Canaan, Litchfield County, Conn., the son of Lyman and Sallie (Noble) Jerome. His father was a blacksmith and wrought-iron maker, in very poor circumstances, and Jerome's early life was an extremely hard one. After obtaining some education in the district school during three winters, at the age of nine he was taken into his father's shop and taught to make nails. When he was eleven years old his father died, and because his mother was unable to support him he was compelled to leave home and work for the neighboring farmers. After four years of such employment he went to live with a house carpenter in Plymouth, Conn., to learn that trade, and while so engaged he obtained permission to work for himself during the dull winter months, making dials for grandfather clocks. He soon became skilled in this work but his progress was interrupted by the War of 1812, in which he served with a company of Plymouth militiamen on guard duty at New London and New Haven. Shortly after peace was declared he married, in February 1815, Salome Smith, daughter of Capt. Theophilus Smith of Plymouth, and with his bride moved to Farmington, Conn., where for about a year and a half he engaged in his trade of carpentry.

In the winter of 1816 he obtained employment with Eli Terry, who was making his patent shelf clocks in his factory at Plymouth, and the following spring he bought some clock parts, mahogany, and veneers, and in a small shop started a clock-making business of his own. For five years he led a rather hand-to-mouth existence, peddling his clocks from farmhouse to farmhouse, and in 1822 he moved to Bristol, Conn., where he built a small shop for making clock cases only. He had considerable difficulty disposing of these and was without the necessary means to purchase movements to place in them, but in the fall of 1824 he succeeded in forming a clock company with his brother Noble, and Elijah Darrow. About six months later he devised the so-called "bronze looking-glass clock," which became extremely popular and resulted in starting him on the road to financial success. Business increased rapidly from 1827 to 1837, during which time more clocks were made by Jerome's company than by any of its competitors. Because of the opposition of the South to Yankee clocks, he started a clock assembling plant in Richmond, Va., in 1835, to which he shipped cases and clock movements made at his factory in Bristol. In 1836 he established a similar plant in Hamburg, S. C. The breakdown of all business in the great panic of 1837 materially affected his business, but this shrinkage was somewhat offset by his timely invention of a one-day brass clock movement, which could be made and sold more cheaply than the one-day wood clock. He began its manufacture in 1838 and by 1841 the company had made clear profits of $35,000. In 1842 he purchased a defunct carriage factory in New Haven, Conn., and fitted it up for making clock cases, retaining at Bristol his plant for the manufacture of movements. Three years later, however, after a fire had partially destroyed his Bristol factory, he carried on the entire business in New Haven. During the succeeding five years it grew to large proportions. The clocks were so good and so much in demand that many small manufacturers used Jerome's clock labels for their own poor clocks, and to protect himself he was drawn into a number of lawsuits. In 1850 he was induced to form a joint stock company with the Benedict & Burnham Company of Waterbury, and the new firm was called the Jerome Manufacturing Company. This change proved to be the beginning of Jerome's downfall. The business was very profitable for a year or two but misplaced confidences brought about the complete failure of the company in 1855 and left Jerome a veritable pauper. To the entrance of P. T. Barnum [*q.v.*] into the concern Jerome attributed this disaster (see Jerome's *History, post,* pp. 106–16). At the age of sixty-two he was compelled to start all over again at the bench. He moved to Waterbury and worked one year for the Benedict & Burnham Company. He was then induced by an unscrupulous individual to take up clock making in another Connecticut town, but two years later he returned to New Haven and spent the remaining ten years of his life in obscurity, dying in very straitened circumstances. In 1860 he published a *History of the American Clock Business for the Past Sixty Years and a Life of Chauncey Jerome Written by Himself*. He was survived by three children.

[In addition to the book mentioned above see W. I. Milham, *Time & Timekeepers* (1923); E. E. Atwater, *Hist. of the City of New Haven* (1887), p. 577; G. H.

Baillie, *Watchmakers and Clockmakers of the World* (London, 1929); U. S. Nat. Museum records.]

C. W. M.

JERVIS, JOHN BLOOMFIELD (Dec. 14, 1795–Jan. 12, 1885), engineer, was born at Huntington, N. Y., the son of Phoebe Bloomfield and Timothy Jervis (or Jarvis). When John was three the family removed to Rome, N. Y., where he grew up, attending the common school and working with the timber crews of his father's lumbering business. He served as an expert axeman on the survey for the Erie Canal, of which Benjamin Wright was chief engineer, and then as rodman. His promotion was rapid. In 1819 he was made a resident engineer in charge of construction of seventeen miles of the middle section of the canal. In 1823 he was made superintendent of fifty miles of completed canal with the responsibility of maintaining the flow of traffic in this section. In 1825 he became principal assistant on the projected Delaware & Hudson canal and railway system of which Wright was now the first chief engineer. Jervis with John B. Mills made an examination of the surveyed route and recommended the construction that was finally adopted for the canal. The system was built to convey anthracite coal from the Lackawaxen Valley in Pennsylvania to the Hudson River for cheap transport to the New York market and as constructed consisted of a canal from Rondout on the Hudson to Honesdale, Pa. (108 miles), and a railway from Honesdale to the mines at Carbondale, Pa. (16 miles).

On the resignation of Wright in 1827, Jervis became chief engineer at a salary of $4,000 a year. Since the engineering of the canal was then practically completed, he was directed to devote his attention to the location and planning of the railway. At this time there was no railway worthy of the name in America and practically nothing was known of the primitive developments in England. Jervis' report is most interesting in that the total absence of precedent forced him to present a complete argument for and against every method that he proposed to employ. He compared the efficiency of single- and double-rail tracks, discussed the relative costs of locomotive and horse power, compared stationary engines with locomotives, and recommended the use of inclined planes and stationary engines for the steep ascents, and locomotive engines on the level middle section of the route. Very few essential details escaped his consideration, and to govern the speed of cars descending the planes he invented a successful contrivance of rotating sails that he geared to the cable sheaves to slow them down. In addition to building the road he trained the operating personnel (which included Horatio Allen) and drew up the specifications for all equipment including the "Stourbridge Lion," the first locomotive to run in America.

Jervis left the Delaware & Hudson Company in May 1830 to become chief engineer of the Mohawk & Hudson Railway. He located a line for this company that permitted the use of locomotives over the whole route and dispensed with the inclined planes. His observation of the severe action of the heavy four-wheel locomotive "John Bull" led him to devise a better method of suspension of locomotive weight. In 1832 the West Point Foundry Company built the "Experiment" according to Jervis' plans, employing his most important invention, the swiveling, four wheel, "bogie" truck to support the forward end of the locomotive. J. Snowden Bell, railroad historian, in his foreword to the *Development of the Locomotive* (1925) describes the swivel truck which Jervis used on the "Experiment" as the first and the most radical and universally approved advance in locomotive design. The "Experiment" was also one of the first locomotives to have six wheels and was in its day the fastest locomotive in the world, capable of speeds of sixty and eighty miles an hour. Upon the completion of the Mohawk & Hudson Railway and of the Schenectady & Saratoga (of which he was also chief engineer), Jervis became chief engineer of the Chenango (New York) Canal, April 1833. This was the first canal in the country to employ artificial reservoirs to supply water to the upper levels, and in this connection Jervis did considerable original work to determine the percentage of total rainfall that could be depended upon to replenish this supply of water. His determination of forty per cent. of the total was higher than the constant used for similar works in Europe and was used successfully in the design of this canal. Some of Jervis' constants for the computation of rainfall and run-off were given in standard engineering handbooks as late as 1900.

While he was with the Chenango Canal, Jervis was consulted regarding the enlargement of the Erie Canal and in 1836 he became the chief engineer of the eastern division of the Erie Canal enlargement. The canal board increased the width of the locks to eighteen feet over Jervis' objection and in September 1836 he resigned to accept the position of chief engineer on the Croton (N. Y.) Aqueduct. In this position he directed the completion of the dam, the Ossining Bridge, the Harlem River Bridge, and the distributing reservoir. In 1846 he was employed by the city of Boston, Mass., to investigate (with Walter Johnson of Philadelphia) the possible sources of a water supply for the city. The Cochituate River was recommended and work on this project was begun in 1846 with Jervis as consulting engineer. He held this position until the completion of the work in 1848. Meanwhile, in 1847, he became chief engineer for the proposed Hudson River Railroad and directed its construction to Poughkeepsie. He remained with the company until 1850 when he spent four months in Europe. He was next engaged on the construction of the Michigan Southern & Northern Indiana Railroad of which he was chief engineer until 1858. During this time he also built the Chicago & Rock Island Railway. In 1861 he became general superintendent of the Pittsburgh, Fort Wayne & Chicago Railway, then in the hands of trustees for the bondholders. He resigned in 1864 but remained with the company as consulting engineer until 1866 when he retired to his home at Rome, N. Y., where he lived until his death. Jervis was married, in 1834, to Cynthia Brayton of Western, N. Y. She died in 1839 and he was later married to Elizabeth R. Coates. His home and personal library at Rome became the Jervis Library by his bequest. Port Jervis, N. Y., is named for him and in 1927 the Delaware & Hudson named their finest locomotive (No. 1401) the "John B. Jervis" in his honor. Jervis was the author of *Description of the Croton Aqueduct* (1842); *Report on the Hudson River Railroad* (1846); *Letters Addressed to the Friends of Freedom and the Union* (1856); *Railway Property: A Treatise on the Construction and Management of Railways* (1861); and *The Question of Labour and Capital* (1877).

[*Proc. Am. Soc. of Civil Engineers,* vol. XI (1885); *A Century of Progress: Hist. of the Delaware and Hudson Company, 1823–1923* (1925); G. A. Jarvis and others, *The Jarvis Family* (1879); *Science,* Mar. 27, 1885; *Railroad Gazette,* Jan. 23, 1885; *Van Nostrand's Engineering Mag.,* Feb. 1885; *Engineering News,* Jan. 17, Nov. 28, 1885; *N. Y. Tribune,* Jan. 14, 1885.] F. A. T.

JESSE, RICHARD HENRY (Mar. 1, 1853–Jan. 22, 1921), educator, was born on the Ball Farm, the birthplace of Washington's mother, in Lancaster County, Va. His parents, William T. and Mary (Claybrook) Jesse, were descendants of early Virginia families. After preparatory study in an academy founded by his father in Lancaster County, and also in Hanover Academy, he entered the University of Virginia, completing his work in this institution in 1875. The next year he taught French and mathematics in Hanover Academy, and from 1876 to 1878 he served as principal of an endowed high school, Washington Academy, at Princess Anne, Md. He then accepted the deanship of the academic department of the University of Louisiana, gave up his intention of studying law, and began a notable educational career. Largely as a result of his foresight and energy, the property given by Paul Tulane to promote higher education in New Orleans was used in 1884 to further a university for the state, the University of Louisiana becoming the Tulane University of Louisiana. He served as professor of Latin here from 1884 to 1891, when he became president of the University of Missouri.

During the seventeen years of his presidency, he labored with courageous singleness of purpose to make the institution serve the practical needs of the state. He stood firmly against the interference of partisan politics and sectarian religion in university affairs. Faculty members were chosen with a view only to their worth in teaching and research. The college (now school) of education, established in his administration, was a pioneer in its field, and the school of journalism, advocated by President Jesse and established shortly after his administration, was the first in America. His interests extended to the secondary schools. Evidence of his influence is found in his successful efforts to abolish the university preparatory school and to foster accredited secondary schools, and in his membership on the well-known Committee of Ten of the National Education Association, which made a large contribution to secondary school curricula. Various positions of honor and influence held by him were: chairmanship of the Section for Higher Education of the National Education Association (1898); presidency of the Missouri State Teachers Association (1899); presidency of the Southern Association of Colleges and Secondary Schools (1903, 1905); and presidency of the National Association of State Universities (1905–06).

Strenuous work broke down his health. In accordance with the advice of his physicians, he resigned as president in December 1907, at the age of fifty-four, and retired from his administrative duties six months later. He lived the remainder of his days close to the campus, occasionally contributed articles to periodicals, and was a source of inspiration to his associates. On July 13, 1882, he married Addie Henry Polk of Princess Anne, Md.; they were parents of three sons and three daughters. An open-communion Baptist, he was deeply religious and a firm believer in Providence. In political belief, he was a Jeffersonian democrat. A key to his success may be found in his own words: "When the cause is thoroughly good, and commends itself to my sober judgment, I do not know how to give up, and no man ought to learn how."

[*Official Retirement of President Richard Henry Jesse* (1908), containing an account of the growth of the University of Missouri during his administration; H. L. Conard, *Encyc. of the Hist. of Mo.*, vol. III (1901); W. F. Switzler, Hist. of the Univ. of Mo. (MS.), in archives of the university; *Who's Who in America,* 1920–21; *Am. Law Rev.*, May, June 1911; *Mo. Alumnus,* Dec. 1913, Apr. 1914; *Educ. Rev.*, June 1911; *Univ. of Mo. Exercises at the Inauguration of Albert Ross Hill, LL.D.* (1909); *N. Y. Times,* Jan. 24, 1921.] J. H. C.

JESSUP, HENRY HARRIS (Apr. 19, 1832–Apr. 28, 1910), missionary, the son of Hon. William and Amanda (Harris) Jessup, was born at Montrose, Pa. He was a descendant of John Jessup who emigrated from England and was living in Hartford, Conn., as early as February 1637. Later he was one of the original settlers of Southampton, L. I. William Jessup was a prominent lawyer, an apostle of temperance, and an active member of the Presbyterian Church. Henry's early education was obtained in the local schools. At the age of fourteen he enrolled in Cortland Academy, Homer, N. Y., and after one year there he entered Yale College. He received the degree of B.A. in 1851 and spent the following year as a teacher in Montrose. Entering Union Theological Seminary, New York, he graduated in 1855. While in college his attention had been directed to foreign missions, especially through the visit of Rev. David T. Stoddard [*q.v.*], of Persia, and in the summer of 1852 he decided to become a missionary. In March 1853, he formally volunteered for this service, and on Nov. 1, 1855, he was ordained at Montrose to the ministry of the Presbyterian Church, his father making an address on the occasion. The next month he sailed from Boston for Syria, under appointment of the American Board. He arrived in Beirut Feb. 7, 1856, by way of Smyrna, and proceeded shortly thereafter to the city of Tripoli to begin active service. He remained there until 1860, devoting himself particularly to the acquisition and use of the Arabic language, in which he became remarkably expert. In 1857–58 he made a visit to America where he married, Oct. 7, 1857, Caroline, daughter of Dr. Wynans Bush of Branchport, N. Y. He arrived again in Tripoli, with his wife, on Apr. 27, 1858.

In 1860, during the Druse wars, the Jessups removed to Beirut. Mrs. Jessup was taken ill in 1864, and a sea voyage was prescribed for her. Accordingly, he set sail on June 30, with her and two of their three small children. She failed rapidly, however, and died at Alexandria, Egypt, where she was buried. Mr. Jessup went on with the two children to America and returned to Beirut in January of the next year. On Oct. 1, 1868, he was married at Hartford, Conn., to Harriet Elizabeth, daughter of the Rev. David Stuart Dodge. Five children were born of this marriage. The second Mrs. Jessup died in April 1882. In 1870 the Syrian mission work was transferred by the American Board to the Presbyterian Board, and Jessup served the latter thereafter. He was for thirty years acting pastor of the Syrian Church of Beirut and superintendent of its school; secretary of the Asfuriyeh Hospital for the Insane from its foundation; was for some time missionary editor of the Arabic journal *El-Neshrah;* and was one of the founders, in 1866, of the Syrian Protestant College (now the American University of Beirut). Save for seven visits to America, four of which were regular furloughs, he gave himself wholly to his life-work in Syria. He declined in 1857 a professorship in Union Seminary; in 1870, a secretaryship of the Presbyterian Board; and in 1883, the post of United States minister to Persia. During his furlough in 1879 he served as moderator of the Presbyterian Assembly at Saratoga, N. Y. On July 23, 1884, he married Theodosia Davenport Lockwood, daughter of the Rev. Peter Lockwood of Binghamton, N. Y.

Jessup was the author of *The Women of the Arabs* (copr. 1873), *Syrian Home Life* (1874), *The Mohammedan Missionary Problem* (1879), *The Greek Church and Protestant Missions* (1891), *The Setting of the Crescent and the Rising of the Cross* (1898), and *Fifty-three Years in Syria* (2 vols., 1910). He died and was buried in Beirut.

[Biog. material in Jessup's *Fifty-three Years in Syria*; H. G. Jesup, *Edward Jessup of West Farms, Westchester County, N. Y., and His Descendants* (1887); "Obit. Record of Yale Grads.," *Bull. of Yale Univ.*, July 1910; alumni records of Yale Univ.; *Missionary Rev. of the World,* July, Aug. 1910; *Assembly Herald,* June 1910; *A Memorial of Theodosia Davenport Jessup* (Am. Mission Press, Beirut, Syria, 1908); records of the Board of Foreign Missions of the Presbyt. Ch.] J. C. A—h—r.

JESUP, MORRIS KETCHUM (June 21, 1830–Jan. 22, 1908), capitalist, philanthropist, was born at Westport, Conn., the fourth son of Charles and Abigail (Sherwood) Jesup, and a descendant of Edward Jessup who emigrated from England and settled in Stamford, Conn., some time before 1649. Charles Jesup was a graduate of Yale (1814), a merchant of New York and Westport, and was much interested in Sunday schools and the work of the American

Tract Society. The conventional nineteenth-century Connecticut pattern of Morris's boyhood was interrupted by the financial panic of 1837, almost coincident with his father's early death, and by his mother's brave efforts, with slender resources, to hold the family together until the children could become self-supporting. Removal to New York City was the first step in the family's new program, and for the boy Morris this was a most important change. He attended several private schools in the city, but at the age of twelve he entered the office of the Rogers Locomotive Works. Here he gained experience that was helpful when in 1854, with a partner, he started a small business handling railroad supplies on commission, under the firm name of Clark & Jesup. This developed into the house of M. K. Jesup, with which for ten years John Stewart Kennedy [*q.v.*] was associated. Among the railroads with which Jesup had business relations at this period (1857–67) were the Chicago & Alton, the Southern, and the Atlantic Coast Line. The next twenty years of his active business career were devoted to banking and in that calling his fortune was made. For eight years, 1899–1907, he was president of the Chamber of Commerce of the State of New York.

For the general public, the significant part of Jesup's life opened in 1884 with his retirement from business. At that time he began to develop interests, and to formulate plans for their promotion, in which many groups were to share. His abilities were now wholly at the service of the community, although he held no public office. The American Museum of Natural History (to which he gave $1,000,000 in his lifetime and an equal sum by his will) seems to have been continually in his thoughts. He was one of the incorporators in 1868, became a trustee the following year, and president in 1881. His great desire was to make the Museum an instrument of popular education and a center of research. At first, because of his Puritan up-bringing, an advocate of Sunday closing, he came to see the wrong involved in excluding any part of the public from the museum's privileges on any day of the week and when the doors were thrown open on Sunday no one rejoiced more than he in the museum's enhanced usefulness. He supported the Carl Lumholtz expedition, 1890–97, to study the Indians of Northern Mexico, and the Jesup North Pacific Expedition, beginning in 1897, to study migrations between Asia and North America. As president of the Peary Arctic Club he did much to make the discovery of the North Pole possible, although he died before Peary had achieved his quest. He early came to the aid of the forest preservation movement in New York State which resulted in the Adirondack Preserve. He was also an enthusiastic supporter of the Audubon Society, of which he was president from 1897 to 1908.

Among educational institutions which he aided, he was identified especially with the Syrian Protestant College at Beirut and with Union Theological Seminary in New York. To the former he gave the Maria De Witt Jesup Hospital Foundation. He stoutly upheld the Seminary in the controversies with the Presbyterian Church over the Briggs and McGiffert heresy cases. He made large contributions also to Hampton and Tuskegee, as well as to Yale, Harvard, Williams, and Princeton. He was treasurer of the John F. Slater Fund for the Education of Freedmen (1883–1908), and was a member of the General Education Board. He was early interested in the Five Points House of Industry and in the railroad work of the Young Men's Christian Association. His support was given to Anthony Comstock in his fight against indecent publications and he stanchly defended that crusader when other friends had apparently deserted the cause. In all religious efforts in New York for many years he was counted a leader. On Apr. 26, 1854, he married Maria Van Antwerp De Witt, daughter of the Rev. Thomas De Witt.

[H. G. Jesup, *Edward Jessup of West Farms, Westchester County, N. Y. and His Descendants* (1887); E. C. Birge, *Westport, Conn.* (1926), pp. 8–12; Wm. A. Brown, *Morris Ketchum Jesup, a Character Sketch* (1910); *Tribute of the Chamber of Commerce of the State of N. Y. to the Memory of Morris K. Jesup* (1908); *Resolutions in Appreciation of Morris Ketchum Jesup by the Trustees of the Am. Museum of Nat. Hist.* . . . (1908); H. F. Osborn, *The Am. Museum of Natural Hist.: Its Origin, Its Hist.* (1911), pp. 27–35; *N. Y. Times* and *Sun* (N. Y.), Jan. 23, 1908; *Nation*, Jan. 23, 1908; *Outlook*, Feb. 1, 1908; *Science*, Feb. 7, 1908.]

W. B. S.

JESUP, THOMAS SIDNEY (Dec. 16, 1788–June 10, 1860), soldier, was born in Berkeley County, Va. (now W. Va.), the son of James Edward and Ann (O'Neill) Jesup, and a descendant of Edward Jessup who emigrated from England and was in Stamford, Conn., as early as 1649. Thomas was commissioned from Ohio as a second lieutenant in the 7th Infantry on May 3, 1808, and as a first lieutenant, Dec. 1, 1809. During the War of 1812 he served as brigade-major and adjutant-general on the staff of Gen. William Hull [*q.v.*]. He was promoted captain, Jan. 20, 1813, and major, 19th Infantry, on Apr. 6, 1813. For distinguished and meritorious service in the battle of Chippewa, he was brevetted lieutenant-colonel on July 5, 1814, and for gallant conduct and distinguished skill in the battle of Niagara (Lundy's Lane), where he was severely wounded, he was brevetted colonel on July 25, 1814. In December of that year he was sent to Connecticut, ostensibly to recruit, but really to watch the Hartford Convention. Convinced that a resolution to secede could not be passed, he was able to dispel President Madison's fears (Jesup, *post,* p. 152). He was promoted lieutenant-colonel on Apr. 30, 1817, and served as such until Mar. 27, of the following year, when he was appointed adjutant-general of the army with the rank of colonel. On May 8, 1818, while serving at Brownsville, Tex., he was appointed quartermaster-general with the rank of brigadier-general by President Monroe. Soon after taking office, on July 17, 1818, he defined the principal objects of the quartermaster's department to be: "to insure an ample and efficient system of supply, to give the utmost facility and effect to the movements and operations of the Army, and to enforce a strict accountability on the part of all officers and agents charged with monies and supplies" (Rodenbough, *post,* p. 51). A better conception of the duties of the department has never been put into so few words. On May 8, 1828, he was commissioned major-general. He acted as a second to Henry Clay in the latter's bloodless duel with John Randolph of Roanoke on Apr. 8, 1826.

On May 19, 1836, by direction of President Jackson, he was assigned to the command of the United States troops and the troops of Georgia and Alabama then operating against the Indians in the Creek country, and on Dec. 8, 1836, he succeeded Brigadier-General Richard Keith Call in command of the army in Florida. He was wounded in the face during a fight with the Seminole Indians at Jupiter Inlet on Jan. 24, 1838. Relieved by Gen. Zachary Taylor in May 1838, he resumed his duties as quartermaster-general at Washington. Soon after his return, some senators questioned his conduct of the Seminole War with a view to provoking an inquiry. Senator Thomas H. Benton of Missouri, then chairman of the Senate committee on military affairs, ably championed Jesup and showed what he had accomplished in the face of great obstacles, to the satisfaction of the Senate and the country. Under the able direction of Jesup, the quartermaster department was organized upon a sound military and business basis. He put into effect practical directions, regulations, and blank forms for all the varied operations of his department. These were embodied in the elaborate edition of the *Army Regulations* issued in 1821, and many have not been changed in their essential characteristics since that time. During the Mexican War, he displayed characteristic qualities. He purchased and provided ships, boats, wagons, and animals in large numbers for the forces in the field, and went to the theatre of operations himself to renovate the supply system. When no funds were available for the purchase of tents and he could not wait for duck, he supplied ordinary muslin for what little shelter it might afford the expeditionary forces in Mexico. Officers of the quartermaster's department have always venerated him. His long service, forty-two years, as quartermaster-general has never been equaled by the head of any other department or corps in the army. Fort Jesup, La., established in 1822 and abandoned in 1846, and Camp Jesup, near Atlanta, Ga., an inactive quartermaster depot, were named in his honor. A lake in Orange County, Fla., also bears his name. He married Ann Heron Croghan of Louisville, Ky., daughter of Major William and Lucy (Clark) Croghan, the latter a sister of George Rogers Clark and William Clark [*qq.v.*]. He died in Washington, D.C. and was succeeded as quartermaster-general by Lieutenant-Colonel Joseph E. Johnston [*q.v.*]. On Dec. 26, 1912, his remains were placed in the Arlington National Cemetery.

[J. F. Rodenbough, *The Army of the U. S.* (1896); T. H. Benton, *Thirty Years' View* (2 vols., 1854–56); F. B. Heitman, *Hist. Reg. and Dict. of the U. S. Army* (1903); J. H. Smith, *The War with Mexico* (2 vols., 1919); L. D. Ingersoll, *Hist. of the War Dept. of the U. S.* (1879); H. G. Jesup, *Edward Jessup . . . and His Descendants* (1887); records and documents in library of the Quartermaster-General's Office, Washington; *Evening Star* (Washington), June 11, 1860.]

R. C. C—n.

JETER, JEREMIAH BELL (July 18, 1802–Feb. 18, 1880), Baptist clergyman, editor, was born in Bedford County, Va., the son of Pleasant and Jane Eke (Hatcher) Jeter. The father, of Huguenot ancestry, was a rolling stone and thriftless dreamer, and the mother, a daughter of Rev. Jeremiah Hatcher, was forced to bear the brunt of the hardships of a growing family, which came to number three sons, Jeremiah being the oldest, and four daughters. His schooling was limited to rural or small village schools; his *Recollections* give interesting revelations of his youthful crudity and naïveté. Beginning to preach at nineteen, he was ordained in May 1824 and spent some time in evangelistic preaching. His first long settlement was with the Morattico Church, Lancaster County, Va. Early in this pastorate he lost his first wife, Margaret P. Waddy, whom he had married on Oct. 5, 1826. In December 1828, he married Sarah Ann Gaskins, who lived until Oct. 29, 1847.

Jeter's reputation as minister and preacher

was made and maintained through two long pastorates in Richmond, Va., separated by a short service (1849–52) at the Second Baptist Church, St. Louis. His first Richmond pastorate, at the First Baptist Church (1836–49), was one of marked influence. Probably its most significant accomplishment was the separation of its fourteen hundred negro members and their organization into the First African Church. There was strong opposition to the project and legal difficulties arose, but Jeter carried it through with such good judgment that the moral victory of his success strengthened his position as a leader in church and community. In 1844, he attended the Baptist Triennial Convention at Philadelphia. He was a leader in the separation of the Southern element and in the organization, May 1845, of the Southern Baptist Convention. During his pastorate at Grace Street, Richmond (1852–70), he immediately regained his earlier influence in that city. In the troublous years of the Civil War, he was devoted to the Confederate cause. He became chief proprietor and editor of the *Religious Herald* in 1865, and for the last decade of his life devoted himself primarily to his editorial task. Although dogmatic in his opinions, he lifted many of the Southern Baptists out of provincialism to a vision of the broader interests of the Christian religion. No paper was more prophetic of the religious South as it was actually to develop during the quarter century following Jeter's own lifetime. He wrote several memoirs and a few rather mediocre theological works; but his *Campbellism Examined* (1855) is an interpretation always to be taken into account for any adequate understanding of the relations between the Baptists and the Campbellite movement.

He was married a third time, June 1849, to Charlotte E. Wharton, who was his wife during the St. Louis and the first half of the Grace Street pastorates. She died on Aug. 19, 1861, and on May 5, 1863, he married Mrs. Mary C. Dabbs, who survived him. With her, in 1872–73, he spent some time traveling in Europe, his specific object being to investigate, for the Foreign Mission Board of the Southern Baptist Convention, conditions in the Baptist mission at Rome.

[Wm. E. Hatcher, *The Life of J. B. Jeter* (1887), embodies many excerpts from Jeter's own *Recollections of a Long Life* (1891), which was first published in the *Religious Herald*; see also G. B. Taylor, *Va. Bapt. Ministers,* 3 ser. (1912); *The State* (Richmond), Feb. 18, 1880.]

W. H. A.

JEWELL, HARVEY (May 26, 1820–Dec. 8, 1881), lawyer, was born in Winchester, N. H., the eldest of the ten children of Pliny and Emily (Alexander) Jewell, and a descendant of Thomas Jewell of England who was given a grant of land near Quincy, Mass., in 1639. His father, grandfather, and great-grandfather were all tanners, and he and three brothers were associated with their father in this trade. His father and mother, in addition to rearing and educating a large family, were prominent in all useful activities of their locality, his father being one of the leading men of Winchester, town moderator, and Whig member of the state legislature. He was also interested in genealogy and compiled *The Jewell Register, Containing a List of the Descendants of Thomas Jewell* (1860). Marshall Jewell [*q.v.*], Harvey's brother, became governor of Connecticut, United States minister to Russia, and postmaster-general under President Grant.

Harvey Jewell attended school at Keene Academy, N. H., graduated from Dartmouth in 1844, was then appointed usher in the Mayhew School in Boston, and while there studied law with Lyman Mason. He was admitted to the bar of Suffolk County in 1847 and became a partner of David A. Simmons, in Boston. After the death of Simmons in 1863, he was associated with Walbridge A. Field until the latter was made chief justice of the Massachusetts supreme court; with William Gaston until he became governor of Massachusetts; and with E. O. Shepard for the remainder of his life. He was influential in the Whig and Republican parties in Massachusetts, justice of the peace in Boston for many years after 1850, a member of the Boston Municipal Council in 1851 and 1852, and representative in the Massachusetts legislature, 1861–62, 1866–71, being a member of many important House committees, especially the judiciary, of which he was chairman. He was also speaker of the House from 1868 to 1871, which position he filled with marked ability.

In the state Republican convention of 1871, Jewell was a candidate for governor, the other candidates being William B. Washburn and Gen. Benjamin F. Butler. In order to defeat Butler he withdrew from the candidacy and threw his support to Washburn. His association legally, for almost thirty years, with commercial affairs in Boston, had given him practical knowledge of maritime law, and this experience, together with good judgment and attractive and dignified personality, made his appointment by President Grant to the Court of Commissioners of Alabama Claims eminently fitting. His service with the court extended from Feb. 26, 1875, until Dec. 29, 1876, when the court was adjourned, and during this time he lived in Washington, D. C. His opinions delivered for the court are characterized by concise simplicity and exceptional clearness of thought. After the adjournment of the court, he returned to Boston and resumed the practice of law, remaining actively connected with many positions of trust until his death. On Dec. 26, 1849, he married Susan Bradley, of Concord, N. H., and they had three daughters.

[*Mass. Reg.*, 1850–69; *Mass. Manual for the Gen. Court*, 1861–71; *Biog. Encyc. of Mass. of the Nineteenth Century*, vol. II (1883); W. T. Davis, *Bench and Bar of the Commonwealth of Mass.* (1895), vol. I; G. T. Chapman, *Sketches of the Alumni of Dartmouth Coll.* (1867); *Report of the Secretary of State, with Accompanying Papers, Relating to the Court of Commissioners of Alabama Claims* (1877); J. B. Moore, *Hist. and Digest of the Internat. Arbitrations to Which the U. S. has been a Party* (1898), vol. V; the *Granite Monthly*, Jan. 1883; *Boston Transcript*, Dec. 8, 9, 1881.] O. M. J.

JEWELL, MARSHALL (Oct. 20, 1825–Feb. 10, 1883), manufacturer, governor of Connecticut, postmaster-general, son of Pliny and Emily (Alexander) Jewell, was born in Winchester, N. H. Harvey Jewell [*q.v.*] was his elder brother. Brought up in his father's tanyard, obtaining a limited education at the town's common schools, Marshall worked as a day-laborer until at the age of eighteen he went to Woburn, Mass., to learn the currier's trade. In 1847, the tanning business being dull, he learned telegraphy and worked at it in Boston, Rochester, N. Y., and Akron, Ohio, showing such ability that he was placed in charge of the construction of the Louisville and New Orleans telegraph line. Here he formed the political opinions that drew him into the ranks of the Republican party on its organization. Returning north in 1849 he was for a time superintendent of the telegraph line between Boston and New York. His father's leather-belting business, established in Hartford, Conn., in 1845, had grown so rapidly that on Jan. 1, 1850, he became a partner. The business soon became one of the foremost in the state with a trade extending through the United States and Europe. In its interest he traveled widely in the United States from 1852 to 1857, and in Europe in 1859, 1860, 1865, 1866, and 1867. His purchases of leather on the eve of the Civil War placed the firm in a commanding position. While always active in his father's firm, he was interested in other enterprises such as the Phoenix Fire Insurance Company, the Traveler's Insurance Company, the Hartford Bank, the New York and New England Railroad, the Weed Sewing Machine Company, and Landers, Frary & Clark. He was part owner of the Hartford *Evening Post*, president of the Jewell Pin Company, and president of the Southern New England Telephone Company. In addition he owned large tanneries in the West, and after 1860 was a special partner in the dry-goods firm of Charles Root & Company of Detroit.

Jewell first entered politics in 1867 when as a candidate for the Connecticut state Senate he was defeated. After a vigorous campaign in 1868 he was defeated for the governorship by James E. English [*q.v.*]. Elected in 1869, 1871, and 1872, he was a straightforward and businesslike governor, winning many friends by his shrewdness and unfailing good-humor. On his retirement from state office, President Grant appointed him minister to St. Petersburg in December 1873. While in Russia he investigated the process of producing Russia leather, learning methods which proved of value to the American leather industry. A trade-mark convention which he negotiated helped to make American inventions more secure against fraudulent practices in Russia. Appointed postmaster-general in December 1874, he investigated the European postal systems before entering upon his duties. During his administration of the office he initiated the fast mail service between New York and Chicago (*Harper's Weekly*, Oct. 9, 1875). His good business sense led him to attack the system of fraudulent contracts and straw bids, and to distribute offices in the interests of efficiency. A disgusted place-broker remarked profanely, "Why, . . . he ran the post-office as though it was a factory" (*Nation*, New York, July 20, 1876). During the prosecution of the Whiskey Ring cases he stood squarely by Secretary Benjamin H. Bristow. Partisan politicians, fearful for the results of the approaching election, influenced Grant to request his resignation in July 1876. As chairman of the Republican National Committee, an office which he held at the time of his death, he was an effective supporter of Garfield in the campaign of 1880 (T. C. Smith, *The Life and Letters of James Abram Garfield*, 1925, II, ch. 26). Jewell was married, Oct. 6, 1852, to Esther E. Dickinson of Newburgh, N. Y., who with two daughters survived him.

[*Biog. Encyc. of Conn. and R. I. of the Nineteenth Cent.* (1881); F. C. Norton, *The Govs. of Conn.* (1905); J. H. Trumbull, *The Memorial Hist. of Hartford County, Conn., 1633–1884* (1886), vol. I; *Proc. in Joint Convention of the Court of Common Council . . . of Hartford on the Death of the Hon. Marshall Jewell, Feb. 12, 1883* (n.d.); Pliny Jewell and Joel Jewell, *The Jewell Reg.* (1860); W. R. Cutter, *Geneal. and Family Hist. of the State of Conn.* (1911), vol. I; *Harper's Weekly*, Apr. 4, 1868; *Hartford Daily Courant*, Feb. 12, 1883.] R. E. M.

JEWETT, CHARLES COFFIN (Aug. 12, 1816–Jan. 9, 1868), bibliographer and librarian, brother of John Punchard Jewett [*q.v.*], was born in Lebanon, Me., where his father, the Rev. Paul Jewett, was settled as a Congregational minister. His mother was Eleanor Masury Punchard of Salem. Prepared for college in Salem, he enrolled first at Dartmouth but transferred to Brown University, where he graduated in 1835. After two years of teaching he entered Andover Theological Seminary and graduated in 1840, with the intention of becoming a missionary. After another year of teaching, however, he was appointed librarian at Brown, and subsequently elected professor of modern languages and literature. In 1843–45 he visited Europe, studying, inspecting libraries, and purchasing books for the University Library at John Carter Brown's expense. On his return he devoted himself to teaching until March 1848, when he resigned to become assistant secretary and librarian under Joseph Henry [*q.v.*] in the recently founded Smithsonian Institution. His *Notices of Public Libraries in the United States of America,* published by the Institution in 1851, was the first extended collection of facts and statistics on American libraries.

His plans for building up at the Institution a comprehensive bibliographical collection included the compilation of a union catalogue of American libraries by clipping and mounting titles from printed catalogues, and the development of an original method of preparing stereotype plates of individual book titles which by successive new combinations might be used for printing catalogues of various different libraries, joint catalogues of two or more libraries, and even a union catalogue of all the libraries in the country (*Proceedings of the American Association for the Advancement of Science,* vol. IV, 1851; Smithsonian Report for 1850, pp. 32–41 and 80–83, separately printed as *A Plan for Stereotyping Catalogues by Separate Titles,* 1851; Jewett's fuller paper, *On the Construction of Catalogues of Libraries . . . with Rules and Examples,* 1852, 2nd ed., 1853). In 1853 the New York Conference of Librarians, over which he presided, discussed the new plan with enthusiasm and recommended that the Smithsonian Institution publish at stated intervals joint catalogues of all libraries that would cooperate (*Norton's Literary and Educational Register,* 1854, pp. 49–94; S. S. Green, *The Public Library Movement in the United States,* 1913, pp. 1–10), but the time was not yet ripe, and mechanical invention was not yet sufficiently advanced, for such an undertaking.

Jewett's original bibliographical projects had been warmly approved by Henry, but when he insisted that the Smithsonian should become primarily a great reference library instead of an instrument of scientific investigation, he came into sharp conflict with the Secretary and the Regents, and Henry at length summarily removed him, July 10, 1854 (Smithsonian Report for 1854, p. 21). Leaving Washington, he was soon occupied in the congenial task of selecting and purchasing books for the newly established Public Library at Boston. He was appointed superintendent in 1858 and thenceforward to the end of his life directed the policy and further growth of the library. He inaugurated the practice, then unusual, of permitting easy access to the books with the fewest possible restrictions and introduced many new and simplified methods, such as the use of separate slips instead of a bound volume for recording loans. The catalogues prepared under his direction marked a distinct advance in library practice and met with praise from experts both at home and abroad (W. W. Greenough in *Sixteenth Annual Report* of the Boston Public Library, 1868, pp. 77–80). His publications, in addition to those already mentioned, include: *Close of the Late Rebellion in Rhode Island* (1842), an account of personal experiences in the Dorr War, published anonymously; *Catalogue of the Library of Brown University* (1843); and *Facts and Considerations Relative to Duties on Books* (1846). His *Plan for Stereotyping Catalogues* was translated into Italian and printed in Florence in 1888. Jewett was married, Apr. 5, 1848, to Rebecca Green Haskins. He died from apoplexy at his home in Braintree.

[Jewett's annual reports, 1847–53, in the *Ann. Report* of the Smithsonian Inst., and his annual reports as librarian of the Boston Pub. Lib.; R. A. Guild, in *Ann. Report of the Board of Regents of the Smithsonian Inst., 1867* (1868), pp. 128–30, *In Memoriam: Charles Coffin Jewett* (1868), repr. from *Providence Evening Press,* Jan. 10, 1868, memorial sketch in *Library Journal,* Nov. 1887, and *Hist. Sketch of the Library of Brown Univ.* (1861); H. G. Wadlin, *The Public Library of Boston; a History* (1911); C. A. Cutter, in *Pub. Libraries in the U. S. A.* (U. S. Bur. of Educ., 1876), pt. 1, p. 538; F. C. Jewett, *Hist. and Geneal. of the Jewetts of America* (1908), vol. I; *Boston Transcript,* Jan. 9, 1868; *Boston Morning Journal,* Jan. 10, 1868.]

W. C. L.

JEWETT, CLARENCE FREDERICK (Sept. 1, 1852–May 3, 1909), projector of historical works, was born at Claremont, N. H., the son of Frederick and Josephine (Forehand) Jewett. He went to school with George H. and Oscar Walker and later sold their atlases in Boston. In time he associated himself with Henry W. Burgett under the firm name of C. F. Jewett & Company. Both men were visionaries who could, it was said, sell anything "not too light to go by mail or too heavy to go by freight." Their first venture was the *Standard History of Essex County, Mass.* (1878), edited by Dr. Henry Wheatland. This was followed by *The History of Worcester County, Mass.* (2 vols., 1879). Their next work (much improved in appearance) was *The Memorial History of Boston,* four quarto volumes, edited by Justin Winsor, and issued in 1880–81. Jewett, claiming that the idea came from him and not from his firm, sold his rights to James R. Osgood & Company, and his action was sustained by the court. The *Memorial History* eventually went to Ticknor & Company and later to Frederick E. Belcher. A handsome two-volume work, *The History of the American Episcopal Church, 1587–1883,* by Bishop W. S. Perry, followed in 1885. All these productions bore Jewett's name as publisher or "projector" upon the title-page. Jewett then fostered the *Narrative and Critical History of America,* a monumental work of the best scholarship, in eight volumes (1886–89). He obtained letters of commendation from all but one of the justices of the Supreme Court in Washington, considered at the time a great feat of enterprise. At the same period he started *The Memorial History of Hartford County, Conn.* (2 vols., 1886).

These were high pressure years; the books which he planned were well written and profusely illustrated. His associates, the Osgoods, were allied with a firm engaged in making plates for book illustrations. This accounts for the many pictures in all of Jewett's works, but to him is due credit for the historical value of the pictures selected for reproduction.

Meanwhile Jewett had married Mary Robinson, an intelligent and versatile woman, and they settled in Brookline, a suburb of Boston. He next undertook an autobiography of Benjamin F. Butler, whose sensational administration of New Orleans during the Civil War, and whose career as a politician, made the publishing venture attractive. The contract, signed Sept. 15, 1889, called for two printed pages of matter daily. Butler sent in sixty-three pages and soon asked for their return for revision. He then finished the book, broke his contract with Jewett, and sold the manuscript known as *Butler's Book* to another firm. Jewett applied to the court to have the publication stopped. There were eminent lawyers on both sides. The case was dismissed without prejudice Oct. 11, 1892, Judge Holmes stating that in his opinion the breach of contract had been proved, but that certain rights of the defendants deserved consideration.

Jewett, at the end of his resources, left for South America. On the voyage he became the hero of a shipwreck, but, having booked his passage under the name of "Mr. Cabot of Boston," he could not accept public recognition. Upon his return to the United States, he went into land development schemes in Oregon (1895) but was soon in difficulties and disappeared for a time from public view. He settled in New York City about 1899 and became treasurer of the Cherry Hill Gold Mining Company. He died at his home in New York on May 3, 1909. His portrait represents an abnormally sensitive, refined man, with a highly developed brain. His eyes suggest fanatical zeal, but evidence of a strong character is lacking.

[No printed record of Jewett's career has been found. For *Butler's Book* see Equity and Probate Records of Suffolk County, Mass., Case No. 3,592 (Equity); for Oregon lands see "Clippings and Cases" in Identification Dept., Boston Police Headquarters; for Cherry Hill Gold Mining Company, see *N. Y. Tribune,* Jan. 17, 1902, p. 6, col. 1; for publishing companies see Osgood-Ticknor papers in the Boston Athenæum. A photograph of Jewett is in the Greenough Collection at the Athenæum.] C. K. B.

JEWETT, DAVID (June 17, 1772–July 26, 1842), commander in the Brazilian navy, was born in the north parish of New London, Conn., the son of Patience Bulkley and David Hibbard Jewett, who served as a surgeon for the American army in the Revolution. He was the descendant of Joseph Jewett who emigrated from Yorkshire, England, in 1638 and settled in Rowley, Mass. During a voyage to Spain, on which he accompanied a relative, young David acquired the inclination for a sea-faring life that never left him. He returned home to study navigation and to serve his country in its early struggles. In the naval war against France, with his twenty-four gun command, the *Trumbull,* he captured and sent home a number of prizes. He served as commander in the United States navy from Apr. 6, 1799, to June 3, 1801, when he was discharged under the peace establishment act. In June 1815 he entered the service of the United Provinces of the Rio de la Plata (now the Argentine Republic) in command of the four-hundred-ton bark, *Invencible,* with which he captured several Spanish vessels. After returning to Buenos Aires from his successful cruise in the *Invencible,* he sailed for Port Soledad in the Falkland Islands (then called the Isles Malouines) in command of the *Heroína,* an armed vessel belonging to the United Provinces. Barely escaping shipwreck he landed there in October 1820, took possession of the islands in the name of the United Provinces, and set up the claim for legal title that was used in the later international disputes over ownership. He spent some months on the islands and returned to Buenos Aires in 1821. In the following year he left the employ of the United Provinces with the thanks of the government for his services. In 1822 he became a captain in the navy of Brazil, which had been declared an independent empire a month before. After a turn of duty before Montevideo he took a prominent and active part under Lord Cochrane in driving the Portuguese fleet out of Bahia, Brazil. He was promoted to be chief of division in the Brazilian navy on Oct. 12, 1823, and succeeded the English admiral, John Taylor, who had served in the Brazilian navy for some time, in command of the naval forces that crushed, at Pernambuco, the organization called the Confederation of the Equator. Unlike his Connecticut countryman, Charles W. Wooster, who was then serving in the Chilean navy, Jewett seems always to have been on friendly terms with Lord Cochrane. He continued the rest of his life in the Brazilian naval service and made numerous prolonged visits to the United States in behalf of the Brazilian government. In 1827, on one of these trips, he married Mrs. Eliza McTiers, the daughter of Augustine H. Lawrence, an alderman of New York City. He contracted for and superintended the building of certain ships of war, and contributed a large share to the upbuilding of the strength and tradition of the Brazilian navy.

[Archives of the Brazilian Ministry of Marine; A. J. Carranza, *Campañas Navales de la República Argentina,* vol. III (1916), pp. 169–85; T. M. da Silva, *Apontamentos para a Historia da Marinha de Guerra Brazileira,* vol. II (1882), pp. 78, 220, 334–57, 398; C. L. Chandler, *Inter-American Acquaintances* (1915); F. C. Jewett, *Hist. and Geneal. of the Jewetts of America* (1908), vol. I.] C. L. C.

JEWETT, HUGH JUDGE (July 1, 1817–Mar. 6, 1898), railroad president, was born at "Lansdowne," Harford County, Md., where he received his early education. He was the son of John and Susannah (Judge) Jewett and was descended from Joseph Jewett who emigrated to America in 1638 and settled in Rowley, Mass. He studied at Hopewell Academy, Chester County, Pa., and was admitted to the bar at Elkton, Md., in 1838. Later he removed to Ohio where he practised law in St. Clairsville for several years. In 1848 he moved to Zanesville, where he soon achieved a reputation for ability to handle cases involving financial questions. He was elected president of the Muskingum County branch of the state bank in 1852 and later became identified with other banking interests in Zanesville. An earnest Democrat, he began to take part in politics. In 1853 he was elected to the Ohio state Senate, but he resigned in 1855 to accept an appointment as United States district attorney for the southern district of Ohio. The following year he was a delegate to the National Democratic Convention. After several unsuccessful candidacies for public office he served one term in the state House of Representatives, 1868–69, and briefly, 1873–74, as representative to Congress. He was mentioned as a possible presidential candidate of the Democratic party in 1880.

Meanwhile he was developing a special knowledge of railroad affairs. In 1855 he was elected a director of the Central Ohio Railroad Company, becoming vice-president and general manager in 1856 and president in 1857. The panic of the year 1857 struck the railroad and Jewett was appointed receiver. In 1869 he was elected to the presidency of the Little Miami and Columbus & Xenia Railroads. The following year he was made vice-president of the Pittsburgh, Cincinnati & St. Louis Railway, later leased by the Pennsylvania Railroad, and shortly afterward he became president of the Cincinnati & Muskingum Valley Railroad. In 1874 he was elected president of the Erie Railway Company at $40,000 a year, the largest salary paid to a railroad president up to that time. In return he agreed to devote his whole time to the road for a period of ten years. The Erie was then in a thoroughly discredited and embarrassed financial position. It was owned almost entirely by English investors but was managed by an American board which distributed as dividends money which should have gone into improvements. The panic of 1873 and the rate war of 1874 forced the road into bankruptcy and Jewett was made receiver. In 1878 it was sold under foreclosure for $6,000,000 to a reconstruction company and was reorganized as the New York, Lake Erie & Western Railroad Company. Jewett was made president of the new board and succeeded in extricating the corporation from the worst of its embarrassments and obtained its release from the jurisdiction of the courts. The road had been crippled, however, by the serious railroad strike of 1877 and by rate wars, so that it was not possible to make it profitable. Jewett moreover followed the policy of putting the earnings back into the property rather than distributing them as dividends. During the ten years of his presidency he replaced the iron with steel rails, changed the gauge from six feet to standard, completed the double track from New York to Buffalo, improved the terminals, and extended the system in order to effect needed connections with the West. This policy did not please the stockholders and in 1884, upon the expiration of his ten-years' contract, he was succeeded by John King. He then retired to his family homestead in Maryland, where he lived for the rest of his life, though he usually spent the winters in New York City. He died Mar. 6, 1898, at Augusta, Ga., and was survived by his wife and six children. He married twice, his first wife being Sarah Jane Ellis, by whom he had four children, and his second wife, Mrs. Sarah Elizabeth Kelly (née Guthrie) by whom he had three children.

[E. H. Mott, *Between the Ocean and the Lakes: The Story of Erie* (1899); *Mag. of Western Hist.*, Nov. 1888; H. V. Poor, *Manual of the Ralroads of the U. S.*, 1869–70—1885; F. C. Jewett, *Hist. and Geneal. of the Jewetts of America* (1908), vol. I; *Biog. Dir. Am. Cong.* (1928); *Augusta* (Ga.) *Chronicle*, Mar. 7, 1898.]

E. L. B.

JEWETT, JOHN PUNCHARD (Aug. 16, 1814–May 14, 1884), publisher, descended from Joseph Jewett of Bradford, Yorkshire, who came to Massachusetts in 1638 and settled at Rowley, was born at Lebanon, Me., the eldest son of the Rev. Paul Jewett and Eleanor M. Punchard. He was a brother of Charles Coffin Jewett [*q.v.*]. As a boy he worked in a bindery and bookstore at Salem, Mass. In 1847, when for some years he had been proprietor of a book and music store of his own, he moved his business to Boston and enlarged it to include publishing. His first offerings consisted of a series of school texts and graded readers.

Jewett supported the cause of abolition, and when he read the installments of Harriet Beecher Stowe's *Uncle Tom's Cabin,* then appearing as a serial in an abolitionist paper, the *National Era,* he made overtures to the author with a view to publishing the story in book form. On Mar. 13, 1852, an agreement was signed whereby Mrs. Stowe was to receive a royalty of ten per cent. Soon the unexampled sales began; the book was issued in two volumes on Mar. 20. "Ten thousand copies were sold in a few days." Mrs. Stowe afterwards wrote, "and over three hundred thousand within a year, and eight power-presses, running day and night, were barely able to keep pace with the demand for it" (Fields, *post,* p. 149). Jewett's profits may be estimated from the fact that as early as July 1852 Mrs. Stowe's royalties already amounted to $10,000. Jewett lost no time in pushing the book; he visited Washington, where in the approving company of Seward and Sumner, he brought it to the attention of many national leaders; he made plans for a translation into German; and he promptly issued Mrs. Stowe's *Key to Uncle Tom's Cabin.* His career was at its height about 1855, at which time he had a home office in Boston and a branch in Cleveland, Ohio. In that year the firm issued a catalogue of publications which listed, among other things, tracts on temperance and abolition, theological works by Professor Leonard Woods of Andover and by Lyman Beecher, a history of California, an encyclopedia of music, Maria S. Cummins' popular *Lamplighter,* and the augmented edition of Margaret Fuller's *Woman in the Nineteenth Century,* as well as one work against Roman Catholicism and one against the Rochester brand of Spiritualism.

The panic of 1857 weakened him; he published a few titles in the years preceding the outbreak of the Civil War, but the book trade was depressed, and he decided to give up both publishing and bookselling. After a visit to England in the late fifties he established a watch factory in Roxbury which he operated for several years. On Feb. 15, 1860, occurred the death of his first wife, Harriette Cobb, whom he had married in 1837, and on June 20, 1861, he married Helen Crane, who was to survive him. Attempting to establish himself in one business after another, he was in turn a purveyor of "Peruvian Syrup," an agent for a safety match company, and a negotiator of patents. In 1866 he left Boston for New York City, where he eventually relinquished his work in patents to return to bookselling in a quiet way. Though he came again to cherish the ambition of publishing, in this revived rôle he cut no figure of consequence. A writer in the *Orange Chronicle,* of Orange, N. J., noting his death which occurred there, justly observed that he was best known as "the man who published *Uncle Tom's Cabin.*"

[J. C. Derby, *Fifty Years among Authors, Books and Publishers* (1884); Annie Fields, *Life and Letters of Harriet Beecher Stowe* (1897); F. C. Jewett, *Hist. and Geneal. of the Jewetts of America* (2 vols., 1908); C. E. Stowe, *The Life of Harriet Beecher Stowe* (1889); S. M. Worcester, *A Tribute to the Memory of John Punchard* (1857); catalogues of John P. Jewett & Company, 1848 and 1855; City Directories for Salem, Boston, and New York; *Orange Chronicle,* May 16, 1884.]

F. M—d.

JEWETT, MILO PARKER (Apr. 27, 1808–June 9, 1882), educational pioneer, was born at St. Johnsbury, Vt., the son of Calvin and Sally (Parker) Jewett and a descendant of Joseph Jewett who emigrated to America in 1638. His father, a physician, sent him to the Academy at Bradford, Vt., and to Dartmouth College (B.A., 1828). The year following his graduation he was principal of Holmes Academy at Plymouth, N. H., and read law at the same time in the office of Josiah Quincy at Rumney. He then entered Andover Theological Seminary, spending his vacations in lecturing on the value of a common school system, believed to have been the first popular lectures of the sort. His fellow-student, J. O. Taylor, carried the movement to New York State. His increased interest in education led him on graduation from Andover in 1833 to accept a professorship at Marietta Collegiate Institute (later Marietta College) in Ohio. In the fall of the same year, on Sept. 17, 1833, he was married to Jane Augusta Russell of Plymouth, N. H. His early leaning toward promotion of educational ideas is shown in his campaign for funds for colleges among the Congregational Churches of New England at this time. Shortly after his appointment to Marietta, he served upon a committee of three professors to urge upon the state legislature the establishment of a common school system for Ohio. They were successful and an appropriation was made to send Professor Calvin E. Stowe to Europe to investigate the Prussian school system. Stowe's report then led to Horace Mann's mission. Jewett soon became a Baptist and, in 1838, resigned from Marietta College and established Judson Female Institute at Marion, Ala., which was one of the most successful schools in the South. In 1855 he returned to the North. In 1856 he purchased the Cottage Hill Seminary at Poughkeepsie, N. Y., which Matthew Vassar sold to him upon the death of his niece, Miss Lydia Booth, the former head. Vassar's interest in this school for girls and his ambition to emulate his supposed relative, Thomas Guy of London, in making some famous benefaction, was skilfully used by Jewett to realize his dream of a standard college for women. In his emphasis upon adequate apparatus and equipment, his proposals for Vassar were original. The curriculum which he devised and which never went into effect at Vassar seems to have been borrowed from the Southern practice dating back to Thomas Jefferson of a series of schools or study groups on a broad elective basis without texts or examinations. At Jewett's plea Vassar revoked his previous will in favor of a hospital and decided to equip and endow the Vassar Female College in his lifetime. For five years Jewett sustained Vassar's interest in the idea and in January 1861 the charter of Vassar College was granted and Jewett became the first president. Jewett's claim for Vassar that "there is not an endowed college for women in the world" is somewhat disingenuous, for he was fully aware of the Southern colleges, and Elmira College had been successfully running for several years and Jewett had investigated its curriculum. It is true that Vassar's venture was on a scale hitherto unknown. In 1862, Jewett at the request of the Vassar College trustees visited Europe and spent eight months studying university organization. His report on return added little of value to the study of the higher education of women, for there was none in Europe at the time.

The erection of the Main Building at Vassar College proceeded slowly through the years of the Civil War and Jewett's patience and Vassar's health wore out during the long strain. The contractor's bankruptcy and other worries incident to the slow completion of the design tempted Jewett to write an indiscreet letter referring to his benefactor as childish and, on the disclosure of the letter, he resigned. His behavior then and later was in every other way exemplary. In 1867 he removed to Milwaukee and speedily became one of the most valued citizens of the state in educational service. He was commissioner of public schools, chairman of the board of visitors of the state university, chairman of the Milwaukee board of health, and trustee of Milwaukee Female College, later Milwaukee-Downer College. He also acted in denominational affairs and was president of the State Temperance Society. He was at first a Whig, later a Republican. At Vassar College, Jewett Hall perpetuates his name. In temperament, he was the typical American pioneer: energetic, quick, lively, and benevolent. He was not a scholar, and his writings are highly rhetorical, but he undoubtedly deserves a place among early promoters of educational ideas in America.

[*Memorial of Milo Parker Jewett, LL.D.* (p.p. Milwaukee 1882); J. M. Taylor, *Before Vassar Opened* (1914); J. M. Taylor and E. H. Haight, *Vassar* (1915); manuscript memoir and letters in the Vassar Coll. Lib.]

H. N. M.

JEWETT, SARAH ORNE (Sept. 3, 1849–June 24, 1909), author, was a native of South Berwick, a village on the southern border of Maine. Her family was of old New England stock and on her father's side she was descended from Maximilian Jewett who emigrated from Yorkshire, England, in 1638, and in 1639 was one of the founders of Rowley, Mass. Her grandfather Jewett, the son of a New Hampshire landowner, having run away to sea as a boy, had settled in Portsmouth after the War of 1812 and become a ship-builder and wealthy merchant in the West Indian trade. Later he moved his family twelve miles up the Piscataqua River to the inland port of Berwick, where he bought the principal house in the village, a fine example of American architecture just prior to the Revolution. Sarah Jewett was born in this house, and made it her home throughout her life. Her father, Theodore Herman Jewett, took up the study of medicine following his graduation from Bowdoin and became the most distinguished doctor in the region. After his marriage to Caroline Frances Perry, a descendant of the Gilmans of Exeter with a touch of French blood in her veins, he settled to a wide country practice in all the neighboring fishing villages and upland farms. Through him, Sarah, the second of his three daughters, gained her first knowledge of the life she was later to recreate in her books. She was a delicate child, and, as she expressed it, subject to instant drooping whenever she was shut up in school. Consequently her education did not come so much from her somewhat irregular attendance at the Berwick Academy as from the well-stored shelves in the library at home, and from endless talks with her father as she rode with him on the trips through the countryside to see his patients. Although she did not realize it, she was being taught by his wise kindliness to observe every detail of her surroundings.

While she was still a child, she began to write down things she was thinking about, putting them into rhymes at first, for prose seemed more difficult. Somewhat later she began to write stories and sent the best of them off to the *Riverside,* a children's magazine of the day, shyly using a pseudonym, Alice C. Eliot, and pledging her older sister to complete secrecy. "The Shipwrecked Buttons" was accepted at once, and the very next month her first more elaborate story, "Mr. Bruce," was taken by the *Atlantic Monthly* when she was still only nineteen. It appeared in the issue of December 1869. Gradually what had started as a kind of game grew to occupy more and more of her attention. By the time the *Atlantic* had accepted a second story four years after the first, she had already instinctively found exactly the line she wished to follow. As a girl of fourteen her eyes had been opened to a keener perception of her village world by Harriet Beecher Stowe's account, in *The Pearl of Orr's Island,* of life along the Maine coast; and now she determined to record what she had learned of similar decaying shipless harbors and lonely farms. She immediately became aware of the magnitude of her father's influence, of how he had pointed things out to her, and had made her notice every sight and sound. At the very outset of her career she possessed an almost complete knowledge of her environment.

When a whole series of sketches about a village that she called Deephaven had appeared in the *Atlantic* over a period of two or three years, W. D. Howells, who was then editor, urged her to collect them. Under the title *Deephaven* (1877), the book enjoyed a distinct success and established her at the age of twenty-eight among the leading writers of New England. Notwithstanding the fact that the greater part of her life was passed in the country, she was at no time isolated or apart. As a girl she had made long visits with friends in New York and Philadelphia, and one summer she had gone as far west as Wisconsin. Following her first arrival in the *Atlantic* her relationship with Howells was of the most cordial friendliness, and through him she came to know the whole Boston circle. She was particularly devoted to Lowell and Whittier, and later to Thomas Bailey Aldrich. She also felt herself greatly indebted to the kind suggestions of Horace Scudder, the editor of the *Riverside,* and to old Professor Parsons, the Swedenborgian.

In 1878, the year after *Deephaven,* she encountered her first deep sorrow in the death of her father, whom she always considered the best and wisest man she had ever known. It was fortunate that her close intimacy with Annie Fields, the wife of the publisher, should have developed about this time. After Mr. Fields' death in 1881, the two women were constantly together, and were gradually absorbed into a union that lasted as long as their lives. Sarah Jewett had become a gracious and charming woman, with a quiet beauty in her slender figure and dark eyes and hair, but she seems never to have considered marriage except perhaps as a hindrance to the fulfilment of her dreams. However, her generous emotional nature demanded an outlet, which she found in her devotion to Annie Fields. This new relationship brought her an increasingly wide horizon both in Boston, and in several trips abroad where she formed valued contacts with Tennyson and Arnold, Du Maurier and Henry James. But she always returned to Berwick for long periods of work, and a steady succession of her books came from the press, several further volumes of sketches of country life, two or three novels, collections of children's stories, and a compact history of the Normans. At no point, however, did she allow herself to become hurried or careless, and she took pride in the fact that she "nibbled all round her stories like a mouse." Indeed, the discipline of her talent is possibly the most impressive quality in Miss Jewett's achievement. She might complain that she felt the lack of never having had any training in the logical ordering of her thoughts, or protest that she had never studied in her life, but she was in possession of a very broad culture.

She had read almost everything in the great literature of the past, and what was important for the development of her art, she was saturated not only with Jane Austen and Thackeray, but with Tolstoy and Flaubert as well. She kept two sentences from the Frenchman pinned on her desk as a constant challenge to perfection. She was fully aware that enduring literature is the product of a ripening personality, and she defined the reason for the gradual increase of her own power when she wrote: "The thing that teases the mind over and over for years, and at last gets itself put down rightly on paper—whether little or great, it belongs to Literature" (Preface to *The Best Stories, post,* p. ix). That process describes the difference between *Deephaven* and *The Country of the Pointed Firs* (1896). In both books Sarah Jewett was trying to catch the same essence, but the intervening twenty years had allowed her material time to mature in her imagination, and the result was no longer observation of life, but life itself.

She was at the top of her bent in this latter book. Her reputation had quietly grown until it was by no means confined to New England, and her stories appeared in the *Century* and *Harper's* almost as often as in the *Atlantic.* In 1901 she received the first Litt.D. that Bowdoin ever conferred upon a woman. Shortly after this she was thrown from her carriage and suffered a concussion of the spine. Although she had always had a passion for being outdoors, and an eagerness for riding and fishing, she had never been of very robust health and was unable to recover fully from this shock. She gained intervals of possession of herself, but she could not undertake the prolonged strain of writing during the last eight years of her life. However, her achievement was secure. She had given permanence to a disappearing order of New England, the remote provincial life which had lingered a few years after the dissolution of the West Indian trade before being engulfed by the new civilization of smoke and steam. Sarah Jewett had valued the separateness, the reserve, the sharp humor of those isolated fishermen and farmers as well as sympathizing with their drab loneliness; and because she possessed a style almost French in its clarity and precision, she wrote, in *The Country of the Pointed Firs,* what is destined to remain as a minor classic.

[F. O. Matthiessen, *Sarah Orne Jewett* (1929), contains a complete list of Miss Jewett's books. An autobiographical account of her childhood appeared in the *Youth's Companion,* Jan. 7, 1892. Mrs. Fields published *Letters of Sarah Orne Jewett* (1911). M. A. DeW. Howe, *Memories of a Hostess* (1922), contains a chapter on the relationship of Miss Jewett with Mrs. Fields. A brief appreciation of her work was written by Willa Cather as a preface to *The Best Stories of Sarah Orne Jewett* (1925). Other sources include: Edward Garnett, *Friday Nights* (1922), pp. 189–198; F. C. Jewett, *Hist. and Geneal. of the Jewetts of America* (2 vols., 1908); *N. Y. Times* and the *Boston Transcript,* June 25, 1909.]

F. O. M.

JEWETT, WILLIAM (Jan. 14, 1792–Mar. 24, 1874), painter, was born in East Haddam, Conn., one of the nine children of Nathan Hibbard and Mary (Griffin) Jewett. As a boy he worked on the farm of his grandfather. At sixteen he undertook the job of preparing paints for carriages for a coachmaker in New London. This early apprenticeship probably determined his future career, for while grinding paints for designs on coaches, he aspired to apply his knowledge of color mixing to some higher purpose than mere decoration. The second determining influence in his artistic life was his acquaintance with Samuel L. Waldo, the portrait painter. When young Jewett realized that Waldo was an artist, and not a poor artisan like himself, he offered to become his assistant. Thereupon a struggle ensued between the young apprentice and the master coachmaker who refused to release Jewett. Upon Waldo's departure for New York, nevertheless, Jewett followed, after signing a note with interest as indemnity for the loss of his services.

After three years of study and paint mixing, he began to assist Waldo in painting. In those days imported casts from antique sculptures were kept in the custom-house near Bowling Green, and there Jewett spent considerable time in drawing from casts. From the beginning Waldo took the young man into his home where he remained for eighteen years. Jewett performed routine studio work, and then he began to paint from nature. The two artists made journeys to the picturesque banks of the Hudson River and painted landscapes. After seven years Jewett was able to pay his debt to the exacting coachmaker, and within ten years he became Waldo's partner in the business of painting portraits. The two men worked jointly on the same portraits, and it is said that only experienced critics could distinguish the work of the one artist from that of the other. Isham (*post,* p. 141) says of their work that it was "so quiet and unaggressive that when its really considerable technical merit is revealed on close examination it comes as a surprise." That they must have been appreciated is evident from the number of commissions which they received. The New York Historical Society owns the portrait of Asher B. Durand (1796–1886), which was painted in 1825 and is credited to Jewett, and the portrait of John Pintard (1759–

1844), the founder of the Society, which was painted by Waldo and Jewett in 1832. The Metropolitan Museum of Art of New York possesses their portraits of Edward Kellogg, Mrs. Edward Kellogg, the Rev. Gardiner Spring, and Gen. Matthew Clarkson. Jewett was elected an associate of the National Academy of Design in 1847. He made his home in New York City until 1842, when he moved to Bergen Hill, N. J. He died in Jersey City.

[See Wm. Dunlap, *Hist. of the Rise and Progress of the Arts of Design in the U. S.* (1834); F. C. Jewett, *Hist. and Geneal. of the Jewetts of America* (2 vols., 1908); Samuel Isham, *The Hist. of Am. Painting* (ed. 1927); H. T. Tuckerman, *Book of the Artists* (1867); F. F. Sherman, "Samuel L. Waldo and Wm. Jewett, Portrait Painters," *Art in America*, Feb. 1930; H. C. Nelson, "The Jewetts: William and William S.," *Internat. Studio*, Jan. 1926. The date of Jewett's birth, given in the sketch, was taken from the Jewett genealogy. The date of death was taken from the death certificate.]

A. B. B.

JEWETT, WILLIAM CORNELL (Feb. 19, 1823–Oct. 27, 1893), publicist, peace advocate, was born in New York City, the son of Joseph and Matilda Cornell Jewett and a descendant of Maximilian Jewett, a native of Yorkshire, England, who emigrated to America in 1638 and in 1639 was one of the founders of Rowley, Mass. His early career is obscure, but it had a westward direction. In 1848 he was married in St. Louis to Almira Guion, who died within a few years. Meanwhile he had moved to San Francisco. Later he went to Colorado. His exact connection with the territory is disputed. He regarded himself as a public benefactor, but his opponents asserted that he was a holder of worthless claims and a procurer of money under false pretences. There remain only two definite records for these years: that of his marriage to Esther Garrison and his application for admission to a peace convention in 1861 as a delegate from Pike's Peak. The Civil War years found him in possession of funds and a will for peace. He was convinced that it could be obtained through European intervention. Consequently he made several visits to the continent, harried European potentates and premiers with his personal, telegraphic, and epistolary communications, and published in many pamphlets a narrative of his adventures. He had particular faith in "the mediation fidelity" of Napoleon III, "temporal and all powerful," and a particular bitterness for Abraham Lincoln, "a serpent tempter" and an obstacle to peace. His activities might have been dangerous if he had not been so obviously "an irresponsible . . . adventurer" (H. J. Raymond, *Life and Public Services of Abraham Lincoln*, 1865, p. 571). From time to time "Colorado Jewett" sailed to the North American continent to further his designs. Usually he preferred Canada, for there he could escape the arrest which he dreaded. Finally in January 1864 he issued from New York an appeal "to the American People and Church Universal" and began interviewing old and new acquaintances who, he hoped, were opposed to a continuance of the war.

By the summer he had fallen into the hands of George N. Sanders [*q.v.*], a foot-loose Confederate, who was voluntarily acting as a go-between for some of the Confederate commissioners who had been dispatched by Jefferson Davis to incite discontent and trouble in the Northern states. Sanders and Jewett, utilizing the latter's acquaintance with Horace Greeley, finally arranged a meeting between the editor of the *New York Tribune* and James P. Holcombe, one of the Confederate commissioners. John Hay was also present at the meeting, which took place at Niagara Falls on July 20. Both Greeley and Holcombe were somewhat unwillingly manipulated into this conference. At a critical time for Northern politics, it gave publicity to the pacificism of Greeley and to Lincoln's statement of peace terms in "To Whom It May Concern," which, by insisting upon reunion and abandonment of slavery as the fundamental terms of settlement, alienated some of the president's conservative supporters. By September, however, Jewett considered peace dead (*Buffalo Courier*, Sept. 24, 1864). His second wife having died, Jewett was married in 1867 to Charlotte Berna. The final years of his life were spent largely in Europe. He died at Geneva in 1893.

[E. C. Kirkland, *The Peacemakers of 1864* (1927); F. C. Jewett, *Hist. and Geneal. of the Jewetts of America* (2 vols., 1908); F. H. Severance, "The Peace Conference at Niagara Falls in 1864," *Buffalo Hist. Soc. Pubs.*, vol. XVIII (1914); W. R. Thayer, *Life and Letters of John Hay* (1915), I, 179 ff.; J. G. Nicolay and John Hay, *Abraham Lincoln: A Hist.* (1890), IX, 185 ff.; *N. Y. Daily Tribune, World* (N. Y.), July 29, 1864.]

E. C. K.

JOCELYN, NATHANIEL (Jan. 31, 1796–Jan. 13, 1881), painter and engraver, was born in New Haven, Conn., the son of Simeon and Lucina (Smith) Jocelyn. His father was a watchmaker, and Nathaniel, brought up to succeed to the business, received only an elementary education. At the age of fifteen, with his brother and a friend, he undertook a course of study in drawing, entirely without instruction. In 1817, after three years as apprentice to an engraver, he became a partner in a new enterprise, the Hartford Graphic & Bank Note Engraving Company; and later, with M. I. Danforth, he founded the National Bank Note Engraving Company. His share in the labor of the company, which was confined to the lettering, hardly afforded sufficient outlet for his talents, and at the age of twenty-five he began painting portraits, at first in Savannah, Ga., and later in New Haven. He had an unusual talent for securing a likeness, his brush-work was vigorous and his modeling strong and graceful, and there was an increasing demand for his work. He was thirty when several of his portraits, hung at the first exhibition of the National Academy, won favorable comment. In 1829 he went abroad, resided for a few weeks in London, and traveled in France and Italy with Samuel F. B. Morse [*q.v.*]. Upon his return, he established himself in a studio in New Haven and divided his time between business and his art.

For many years he was head of the art department of the American Bank Note Company, resigning in 1865. Investments in real estate and enthusiastic attempts to develop new sections of the city occupied his energy and drew him for a time out of his studio; but during the years of depression that followed the panic of 1837, he was in serious financial difficulties, and the burden he was carrying made it necessary for him to earn money with his brush. In 1844 he received the gold palette for the best portrait exhibited in Connecticut. In 1849, after a fire had destroyed his studio, he removed to New York; but he was soon back in New Haven, and most of his painting was done there. He taught many pupils, including Thomas Rossiter and William Oliver Stone [*qq.v.*]. August Street, who provided the original building of the Yale School of the Fine Arts, frequently stated that his gift was made largely as a result of Jocelyn's suggestions. The artist had his studio in Street Hall during the last fifteen years of his life, and some of his best work is now on exhibition in the gallery of the school. His celebrated portrait of Cinquè, leader of the *Amistad* Africans, hangs in the building of the New Haven Colony Historical Society, where there is also a portrait of Jocelyn painted by Harry Thompson.

Jocelyn was a member of the Connecticut Academy of Arts and an honorary member of the National Academy of Design. He declined an election to honorary membership in the Philadelphia Art Union because the society had offended his anti-slavery sentiments. He was always an ardent abolitionist. As early as 1831, he had made himself conspicuous at a town meeting by supporting a measure to establish a high school for negroes in New Haven. He was a wide reader and preserved a variety of interests down to the time of his death. In his old age, he left upon all who saw him the same impression of remarkable vitality that he had given in his prime—"a very handsome, lithe, graceful figure, with a brilliant complexion and mild blue eyes" (*Journal and Courier*, Jan. 17, 1881). His wife, Sarah Atwater Plant, daughter of Samuel Plant of New Haven, died seven months before his death.

[H. W. French, *Art and Artists in Conn.* (1879); Samuel Isham, *The Hist. of Am. Painting* (1905); E. L. Morse, *Samuel F. B. Morse: His Letters and Jours.* (1914); William Dunlap, *A Hist. of the Rise and Progress of the Arts of Design in the U. S.* (1834, 1918); D. M. Stauffer, *Am. Engravers upon Copper and Steel* (1907); S. E. Baldwin, "The Captives of the Amistad," *New Haven Colony Hist. Soc. Papers*, vol. IV (1888); *N. Y. Tribune*, Jan. 18, 1881; *N. Y. Jour. of Commerce*, Jan. 17, 1881; New Haven *Daily Morning Jour. and Courier*, Jan. 15, 17, 1881; *Commemorative Biog. Record of New Haven County* (1902).]

R. D. F.

JOGUES, ISAAC (Jan. 10, 1607–Oct. 18, 1646), missionary and martyr of New France, was a native of Orleans. He was of noble blood and lost his father while an infant, becoming the sole care of a pious mother, Françoise (de Saint-Mesmin) Jogues. He entered a Jesuit school at the age of ten; seven years later he became a Jesuit novice under the charge of Father Louis Lalemant, who had relatives in Canada. Jogues performed his novitiate both at Rouen and at Paris; in 1636 he was ordained to the priesthood and celebrated his first mass at his native city. He had already determined to enter the mission field, and sailed from Dieppe for Canada, where he arrived July 2, 1636.

The Jesuits had recently begun the mission for the Huron Indians on the far shores of Georgian Bay, south of Lake Huron. Thither young Jogues was sent within six weeks after his landing. The journey by canoe, over rapids and rocks, along wilderness coasts was so painful that the new missionary fell ill soon after reaching Huronia. Upon recovering he devoted himself to learning the Huron language and to building a new mission establishment on the River Wye, named Ste. Marie. In September 1641 Jogues with Raymbault accompanied a band of strange Indians northward for three hundred miles to the strait they named the Sault de Ste. Marie; here they instructed 2,000 savages and heard of Sioux Indians living beyond Lake Superior. Raymbault having fallen ill, Jogues obtained permission in 1642 to accompany him to the colony. On their return they were set upon by hostile Iroquois, and Jogues and his two donnés, René Goupil [*q.v.*] and Guillaume Couture, were captured. The missionary might have escaped but gave himself up in order to succor his companions. The Mohawk-Iroquois party carried the captives to central New York, on the way inflicting upon them horrible tortures, mutilating their hands, and loading them with burdens. Goupil was soon slain, Jogues was reserved for a more lingering martyrdom. For a year he was a slave in the Indian villages, using every opportunity to instruct his captors and to baptize all dying savages. Once, at great risk, he warned the governor of Canada of a projected attack. He was finally rescued by the Dutch at Fort Orange, taken to New Amsterdam (now New York City) and entertained by the Dutch dominie, Johannes Megapolensis [*q.v.*], in his house on the site of the present Cunard building.

Jogues reached Brittany on Christmas Day, 1643, and the Jesuit College at Rennes on Jan. 5, 1644. He was received with great joy, having been given up as lost. The queen regent granted him an audience and the pope permitted him to serve mass with his mutilated hands, saying, *"Indignam esset Christi martyrem, Christi non bibere sanguinem."* The same season the missionary returned to his labors in Canada. Two years later the governor sent him on an embassy to the Iroquois, during which he visited the scenes of his former torture. As an ambassador he was safe; upon his return to Canada, however, he asked and obtained leave to undertake a mission to the Mohawks. When he arrived at their village of Ossernenon, now Auriesville, N. Y., he was killed by the stroke of a tomahawk. In 1925 Pope Pius XI issued articles of beatification for Jogues and seven other missioners who were martyred in Canada. Jogues's character may be best given in the words of this document: "The Servant of God was by nature meek and timid, but by constant self-humiliation and the continuous practice of prayer he so strengthened his spirit that when commanded by his superiors he was ready to undertake most difficult things, and in facing dangers and torments he gave a truly marvelous example of Christian fortitude" (*Scott,* post, pp. 235–36).

[R. G. Thwaites, *The Jesuit Relations and Allied Documents* (73 vols., 1896–1901) are the chief source for his life and writings. Jogues wrote a description of New Netherland called *Novum Belgium,* translations of which appear in E. B. O'Callaghan, *Doc. Hist. of the State of N. Y.,* vol. IV (1851), and in J. F. Jameson, *Narratives of New Netherland, 1609–1664* (1909); see also T. J. Campbell, *Isaac Jogues, S. J., Discoverer of Lake George* (1911); J. J. Wynne, *The Jesuit Martyrs of North America* (1925); M. J. Scott, *Isaac Jogues, Missioner and Martyr* (1927); Felix Martin, *Le R. P. Isaac Jogues* (1873), tr. by J. G. Shea as *The Life of Father Isaac Jogues* (1885); J. G. Shea, in *Colls. of the N. Y. Hist. Soc.,* 2d series, vol. III (1857).]

L. P. K.

JOHNS, JOHN (July 10, 1796–Apr. 4, 1876), fourth bishop of the Protestant Episcopal Church in Virginia and president of the College of William and Mary, was born in New Castle, Del., son of Chief Justice Kensey Johns [*q.v.*] and Ann Van Dyke, daughter of Nicholas Van Dyke [*q.v.*], and brother of the younger Kensey Johns [*q.v.*]. It was said by a friend of Bishop Johns that his mother, by her example and guidance, "saved her family from falling into those dreadful social sins of sabbath visiting, card-playing, drinking, and theatrical amusements, which surrounded the Bishop in his early youth" (*Addresses, post,* p. 163). Another friend stated that "in his youth he was full of fun and frolic, bright in intellect and genial in disposition, passionately fond of hunting and a fine shot" (*Ibid.,* p. 164). He led his classes at the College of New Jersey. According to Dr. Charles Hodge, a classmate, "Johns was always first—first everywhere, first in everything (*Ibid.,* p. 164). After graduating in 1815, he remained at Princeton two years, studying theology.

He was ordained in 1819 and during the twenty-three years of his ministry he served only two churches—at Fredericktown (now Frederick), Md. (1819–28) and Christ Church, Baltimore (1828–42). He was unusually successful as a preacher and as a pastor, became leader of the "low church" party in the diocese, and, on at least two occasions, narrowly missed election as bishop of Maryland. When Bishop William Meade [*q.v.*] of Virginia requested the appointment of an assistant bishop, the Convention chose Johns. He was consecrated in Monumental Church, Richmond, Oct. 13, 1842. Richmond was his home for several years, but the greater part of his time was occupied in visitations throughout the diocese, which reached from the Ohio River to Hampton Roads. He worked diligently and well, and in perfect harmony with Bishop Meade. In 1849, with the consent of the church Convention, without pay Johns became president of the College of William and Mary, still continuing as assistant bishop. When he resigned the presidency in 1854, after a happy and successful administration, the number of students had more than doubled and new life had been breathed into the ancient institution.

He now built a home near Alexandria, where he lived during the remainder of his life, with the exception of the four years of the Civil War when he and his family were refugees. When Bishop Meade died on Mar. 14, 1862, Johns succeeded him and often ministered to the armies in the field and to Federal prisoners. In 1865 he returned to Alexandria. Here he taught two hours a week as professor of homiletics and pastoral theology in the Theological Seminary. When past seventy, he continued his visitations throughout Virginia and West Virginia. He had few equals as a public speaker, and possessed "a bright intellect, an emotional nature, natural earnestness, a melodious voice, and facility and felicity of speech" (Packard, *post,* p. 197). His sermons were carefully prepared, but were delivered without notes. Only a very few were published. These, together with his *Memoir of the Life of the Right Rev. William Meade, D.D.* (1867), are his only published works. He was married, first, in 1820, to Juliana Johnson of Fredericktown; second, to Jane Schaaf (or Scharf), and third, to a Mrs. Southgate. He died at midnight, Apr. 4, 1876, in his eightieth year.

[E. L. Goodwin, *The Colonial Ch. in Va.* (1927); Joseph Packard, *Recollections of a Long Life* (1902), ed. by T. J. Packard; C. I. Gibson, in *Addresses and Hist. Papers before the Centennial Council of the Protestant Episcopal Ch. in the Diocese of Va.* (1885); T. G. Dashiel, *A Digest of the Proc. of the Convention and Councils of the Diocese of Va.* (1883); *Evening Star* (Washington), Apr. 6, 7, 1876; *Richmond Enquirer,* Apr. 7, 1876; *The Churchman,* Apr. 15, 1876.]

R. L. M—n.

JOHNS, KENSEY (June 14, 1759–Dec. 20, 1848), Delaware jurist, was the son of Kensey and Susannah (Galloway) Johns of West River, Anne Arundel County, Md. He studied law, first with the noted Judge Samuel Chase [*q.v.*], and then moved to Delaware and completed his studies under George Read [*q.v.*]. Unusually successful in his practice, he soon accumulated a large estate, and in 1784, married Ann, the daughter of Governor Nicholas Van Dyke [*q.v.*]. Their sons Kensey Johns and John Johns [*qq.v.*] had distinguished careers. His first appearance in public life was as delegate from New Castle County to the constitutional convention of 1792, where he took a leading part in debate with such eminent men as John Dickinson, Richard Bassett, and Nicholas Ridgeley [*qq.v.*]. Upon the resignation of George Read from the United States Senate in 1794, Johns was appointed by Governor Joshua Clayton to fill the vacancy. Doubt was expressed as to the legality of this proceeding, however, since a session of the legislature had intervened between the occurrence of the vacancy and the appointment, so Johns never claimed the seat. By this time he had attained great success at the bar, but, probably upon the solicitation of Chief Justice Read, he relinquished his practice to accept the appointment of associate judge on the supreme court. Upon Read's death Johns succeeded him as chief justice, Jan. 3, 1799. In this capacity he served over thirty years.

He was an important transition figure in the judicial history of Delaware. The revolution from colony to state was still in process, and many questions, arising from the change of institutions and government, were unsettled. The statutes, which were collected, revised, and published by George Read in 1794, needed new constructions. As an associate of those men who had framed the constitution of 1776, and as an active member of the state convention of 1792, Johns had become thoroughly acquainted with the unwritten decisions upon the questions of law which arose during this period. He could therefore develop the law by interpretations based on the judgments of the state's founders. In April 1830 he was appointed chancellor, as successor to Nicholas Ridgeley. While chief justice he had acted as president of the court of errors and appeals in all chancery cases, which service had given him peculiar qualifications for his later position. Upon the adoption of the new constitution in 1832, he retired on account of his advanced age, and was succeeded by his son, Kensey Johns. The remaining years of his life were uneventful. His services have been summarized as follows: "Chief Justice Johns possessed a discriminating mind; and being thoroughly educated in the principles of his profession, he was generally able to lay hold of and accurately decide the important questions arising in a cause. His judgment was cautious, and his convictions, resulting always from a most careful examination, were so fixed as to be seldom shaken" (*Report of Cases, post,* 491).

[G. B. Rodney, in *Report of Cases . . . in the Court of Chancery, of the State of Del.,* I (1876), 490; H. C. Conrad, *Hist. of the State of Del.* (1908), vol. III; J. T. Scharf, *Hist. of Del.* (1888), vol. I; *Del. State Journal,* Dec. 22, 1848; *Del. Republican* (Wilmington), Mar. 30, 1857.]

C. W. G.

JOHNS, KENSEY (Dec. 10, 1791–Mar. 28, 1857), Delaware jurist, congressman, brother of John Johns [*q.v.*], was by birth and environment predestined for an eminent position in the judicial history of his state. Son of Chief Justice, afterwards Chancellor, Kensey Johns [*q.v.*], and grandson, through his mother, Ann, of Governor Nicholas Van Dyke [*q.v.*], he inherited high traditions of public service. He was born in New Castle, Del., and graduated from the College of New Jersey in the class of 1810 with James G. Birney, George M. Dallas, and others who later attained prominence. After studying law with his maternal uncle, Nicholas Van Dyke [*q.v.*], he completed a course in the law school at Litchfield, Conn., and was admitted to the Delaware bar in 1813. Shortly after, he was married to Maria McCallmont. While yet a young man he attained high standing as a sound and able lawyer. He possessed an analytical mind which enabled him to grasp the essentials in a case and refer every question to some basic legal principle. Fifteen years of law practice had established him securely as one of the leaders in the profession when he decided to enter public life. On Oct. 2, 1827, he was chosen to fill the unexpired term of Congressman Louis McLane [*q.v.*], who had been elected to the Senate, and at the expiration of the Twentieth Congress, Johns was elected for the following term. At its close, Dec. 3, 1831, he retired from national politics. Of his several speeches in Congress the one in favor of the tariff of 1828 was the most important. His chief argument was the sad plight of the manufacturers, and he handled the subject in a practical rather than a logical or statesmanlike manner (*Register of Debates,* 20 Cong., 1 Sess., p. 1940). After retiring from Congress he resumed the practice of law. In 1831 the constitutional convention reorganized the judiciary system. Although the chancery remained unchanged, his father, grown old in service, took this opportunity to resign; and the governor, at the suggestion of the bar, appointed the son chancellor, Jan. 18, 1832.

In this office, Johns carried out the ideals of legal study acquired in his youth. The process of grasping the leading principle in a case was carried a step further to a clearer enunciation, where needed, of those rules of equity hitherto imperfectly understood in Delaware law. Keen discrimination in selecting authorities and weighing principles, and thorough learning and research were his chief attributes. Though some of his decisions are now regarded as aberrant, his judgments were generally correct; and in most of the appeals from his decrees, his decisions were affirmed by the court of errors and appeals. After twenty-five years of active service, he died very suddenly at the close of a term in Sussex.

[*Gen. Cat. of Princeton Univ., 1746–1906* (1908); *Biog. Dir. Am. Cong.* (1928); G. B. Rodney, in *Reports of Cases . . . in Court of Chancery, of the State of Del.,* I (1876), 493; H. C. Conrad, *Hist. of the State of Del.* (1908), vol. III; J. T. Scharf, *Hist. of Del.* (1888), vol. I; certain information from Rev. Kensey Johns Hammond, through the courtesy of H. C. Conrad, Esq.] C. W. G.

JOHNSEN, ERIK KRISTIAN (Sept. 20, 1863–Jan. 21, 1923), Lutheran theologian, son of Erik Johnsen, a builder and contractor, and Else Kristine (Finkelsen) Johnsen, was born near Stavanger, Norway. From the Stavanger Latin school he went to the university of Christiania (Oslo), and after graduation in theology (1887) spent three years tutoring in Oslo. At this time he learned his favorite avocation, wood-carving. In 1892 he married Amunda Sörensen, a deaconess, and emigrated to America. He became professor of theology in Red Wing Seminary, supported by the Hauge's Synod at Red Wing, Minn., but owing to a theological controversy between two of his colleagues, resigned in 1897, was ordained, and became pastor of three congregations in and near Hudson, Wis., transferring his membership to the United Norwegian Lutheran Church. In 1900 he accepted the professorship of Old Testament exegesis in the seminary of his denomination at St. Paul. After the merging (1917) of his church with several other bodies in the Norwegian Lutheran Church of America, he continued as professor in the institution, now Luther Theological Seminary, until his death.

Johnsen was an excellent teacher, possessing sympathy, kindliness, and humor, and an amusing but wholesome directness of speech. From time to time he taught, in addition to Old Testament, the Pauline Epistles, homiletics, even dogmatics. Though he conversed in fluent English, he preferred to use his mother tongue in public; he spoke and wrote a beautiful Norwegian. For more than twenty years he was chief literary consultant of the Augsburg Publishing House, Minneapolis. His book reviews, numbered by the hundreds, were always fresh and discriminating. Every year he edited *Folke Kalender* and *Julebog for barn.* He also edited *Hoymes efterladte skrifter* (1904); two collections of sermons, *Fredstanker* (1901) and *Kors og Krone* (1909); and *Vor Herres Jesu Kristi Lidelses historie* (1909); and contributed to the periodicals *Ungdommens Ven* and *Lutheraneren.* His first notable theological contribution in the United States, *En kort udredning* (1895), an effort to shed light on the theological controversy at Red Wing, brought him ingratitude. His next contributions, written in popular style, were *Paulus* (1902), published in English as *Paul of Tarsus* (1919); and *Lykke i livet* (1911), in collaboration with his colleague, Dr. M. O. Böckman. In 1915 he toured Europe, and subsequently published *Paa Reise gjennem England, Norge, Danmark, Tyskland, Schweiz og Italien* (1918), which is filled with interesting observations and racy comments. In 1917 he was chief editor of *Fire hundredaarig Lutherdom,* a collection of twenty essays, by several authors of Norwegian antecedents, to which he contributed two clear and cogent essays: "Introduction," a survey of the Church until the Reformation, and "The Church in Norway 1814–1917." His least original work was *I Kirke* (1913), on ecclesiastical practices from the standpoint of liturgy. In it there breathes a spirit of Romanticism otherwise foreign to the author. His ablest work, *Brevet til Hebräerne* (1922), which was also his last, included an original translation in Norwegian of the Epistle to the Hebrews, accompanied by a searching commentary, calling attention to the difference between Paul's method of treating the atonement and that of the unknown author of the epistle. Both had, he declares, the same religion: "Religion is primarily not a system of doctrines or ethical precepts; it is life." His *Guds Rike i det Gamle Testamente* was published posthumously (1923) by N. N. Rónning.

Johnsen was for years a member of a committee negotiating with other church bodies for organic union. He favored mergings, but at heart cared little for the hair-splitting doctrinal formulations which were offered as bases for a merger. Deploring the poverty of the average American seminary library and the difficulties under which a theologian therefore had to labor, he did much to improve the condition. In his last year, while traveling on the Pacific Coast, he received an injury which left him with an affection of the heart; but he was about his labors as usual until his sudden death, in St. Paul, Jan. 21, 1923. His first wife had died in 1912, and in 1915 he had married Helen Nilsen, who, with three children of his first marriage, survived him.

[O. M. Norlie, *Norsk lutherske prester i Amerika* (1914); *Who's Who in America,* 1922–23; Rasmus Malmin, O. M. Norlie, O. A. Tingelstad, *Who's Who among Pastors in All the Norwegian Lutheran Synods of America, 1843–1927* (1928); P. Botten-Hansen, *Norske Studenter der har Absolveret Examen Artium ved Christiania Universitet* (1893–95); *St. Paul Pioneer Press,* Jan. 22, 1923.]

J. O. E.

JOHNSON [See also JOHNSTON].

JOHNSON, ALEXANDER BRYAN (May 29, 1786–Sept. 9, 1867), banker, writer, was born in Gosport, England. His schooling was unsystematic and ended when he was fourteen. Bryan Johnson, his father, emigrated to the United States in 1797, and in 1801 the family joined him in Utica, N. Y., where he was operating a store. The son worked in the store until he was twenty-one, when the elder Johnson retired from business. Alexander Johnson tried running a glass factory, spent two years in New York where he studied finance in general, then returned to Utica in 1812. There he interested himself in banking. Imitating Aaron Burr, who had secured from a hostile legislature a charter for a water company under which he conducted a banking business, Johnson secured a charter for an insurance company, incorporated in 1816 as the Utica Insurance Company, with the same intent. When the organization engaged in banking activities they were attacked through the courts and were obliged to drop that part of their business. Johnson retained his interest in banking and in 1819 was made president of the Utica branch of the Ontario Bank of Canandaigua. He also studied law and was admitted to the bar in 1822, but he never engaged in legal practice. He remained with the Ontario Bank until its charter expired in 1855. He helped to organize its successor and then retired from active business.

Johnson found time during his activities as a banker to write on a variety of subjects. *The Philosophy of Human Knowledge, or A Treatise on Language* (1828), *Religion in Its Relation to the Present Life* (1841), *The Meaning of Words* (1854), and *Deep Sea Soundings and Explorations of the Bottom; or, the Ultimate Analysis of Human Knowledge* (1861), reveal the philosophical bent of his mind. His writings on financial subjects include *An Inquiry into the Nature of Value and of Capital* (1813), *A Treatise on Banking* (1850), *The Advanced Value of Gold* (1862), and *Our Monetary Conditions* (n.d.). His reflections on American government and politics appear in *A Guide to the Right Understanding of Our American Union* (1857) and *The Union as It Was and the Constitution as It Is* (1862). In the former he argued that the federal constitution should be strictly construed; that slavery should be left to the states; that Texas should be annexed; that the second Bank of the United States should not be rechartered; that private enterprise is more efficient than government enterprise; that prohibition is not the best way to deal with the liquor traffic; and that savings banks are better than life insurance. Johnson was married in 1814 to Abigail Louisa Adams, a grand-daughter of President John Adams. His second wife was Lydia Masters of Madison County and the third, Mary Livingston of Columbia County. Alexander Smith Johnson [*q.v.*] was a son by the first marriage.

[There is a manuscript autobiography of Johnson in the possession of the family. Other sources include: M. M. Bagg, *The Pioneers of Utica* (1877) and *Memorial Hist. of Utica* (1892); F. A. Virkus, *The Abridged Compendium of Am. Geneal.,* vol. I (1925); and *Obituary Notices of Alexander Bryan Johnson* (Utica, 1868).]

J. D. M.

JOHNSON, ALEXANDER SMITH (July 30, 1817–Jan. 26, 1878), New York jurist, was born in Utica, N. Y. His father, Alexander B. Johnson [*q.v.*], one of the most influential citizens of that place, was the son of Bryan Johnson, who was prominent there when Utica was Old Fort Schuyler; his mother, Abigail Louisa Adams, was the daughter of the second son of President John Adams [*q.v.*]. Young Alexander was graduated from Yale College in 1835 and was admitted to the bar when he was twenty-one years old. He began practice in Utica but soon removed to New York City, where he had a comparatively short career as a lawyer.

In 1851, at an earlier age than any other person upon whom the honor had been conferred, he was elected to the court of appeals for the full term of eight years. He was chief judge in 1858 and 1859. His decisions were simple and precise expressions of a mind quick in the appreciation of facts and equipped with a varied and extensive knowledge of the law, and were absolutely impartial. In *Wynehamer* vs. *People* (13 *N. Y.*, 378, at p. 406) appears his opinion on the constitutionality of a statute to prevent intemperance, delivered in 1856, in which he held such a statute constitutional. At the expiration of his term the fortunes of politics retired him to private life and he returned to Utica to practise law. In July 1864, confirmed January 1865, President Lincoln appointed him a commissioner under the treaty of July 1, 1863, with Great Britain, for the settlement of the claims of the Hudson's Bay and Puget's Sound agricultural companies. For three or four years these duties occupied his attention. In January 1873 he was appointed a member of the commission on appeals and in December of that year, to the court of appeals, which appointment expired Dec. 31, 1874. An interesting opinion of this period was in *People* ex rel. *the Pacific Mail Steamship Co.* vs. *Commissioners of Taxes, etc., N. Y.* (58 *N. Y.*, 243), discussing the *situs* of sea-going vessels. He was appointed on a commission to revise the statutes of New York, but resigned when he was called to the federal bench in October 1875, from which time until his death he served as circuit judge of the Second Judicial Circuit. He died in Nassau, Bahama Islands, as a result of the strain of his judicial duties.

For some time he served as a regent of the University of the State of New York, and, according to the testimony of Judge E. C. Benedict, rendered invaluable service in building up the state library and the state cabinet of natural history. All his life he was a student of scientific subjects and an enthusiastic microscopist. His private life was quiet and unostentatious; he was fond both of hunting and fishing. He was modest and unassuming in manner, free from vanity or self-assertion, and his integrity and ability brought him general esteem, evidenced by the fact that during the period when he was not on the bench he was frequently sought as arbitrator in private disputes. In November 1852 he was married to Catherine Maria Crysler, by whom he had four children.

[F. A. Virkus, *The Abridged Compendium of Am. Geneal.*, vol. I (1925); *Obit. Record Grads. Yale Coll.*, 1878; "Proceedings of the Members of the Bar of the City of New York on the Death of the Hon. Alexander S. Johnson, Circuit Judge of the Second Circuit," 14 *Blatchford's Circuit Court Reports, N. Y.* (1879); Irving Browne, "The New York Court of Appeals," *Green Bag*, July 1890.]

A. S. M.

JOHNSON, ALLEN (Jan. 29, 1870–Jan. 18, 1931), teacher and writer of history, biographer, editor of this *Dictionary*, was the son of Moses Allen Johnson and Elmira Shattuck, and was born in Lowell, Mass., where his father was "agent" (manager) of the Lowell Felting Mills. His father, who died in 1874, was a native of Lynn, descended from Richard Johnson who came to Massachusetts in 1630. His mother was a lady of refinement and cultivation, studious—even of New Testament Greek—and of gentle and lovable character. Allen was the valedictorian of his high school class at Lowell in 1888, and one of the founders of a small society which read historical books, debated questions arising from them, and studied parliamentary law. A boyhood spent in a manufacturing city doubtless helped to give him an appreciation of industrial life, and he himself was persuaded that his boyish experience as an amateur printer was useful to him as an editor. From 1888 to 1892 he was a student in Amherst College, and was graduated as Bachelor of Arts in the latter year, rating high in scholarship and winning a prize in debate. His classmates uniformly depict him as a quiet, studious youth, not robust, in every way a gentleman; his favorite studies were history, political science, and literature; his recreation was tennis.

After graduation, Johnson was for two years, 1892–94, instructor in history and English in the Lawrenceville School, N. J. The next year he held a graduate fellowship at Amherst, reading philosophy and history and assisting in the teaching of the latter. Then for two years, 1895–97, he studied history in Europe, three semesters at Leipzig under Lamprecht and Marcks, and one at the École Libre des Sciences Politiques in Paris. Spending the next academic year in Columbia University, he received in

1899 its degree of doctor of philosophy, publishing a dissertation on *The Intendant as a Political Agent under Louis XIV* (1899). From 1898 to 1905 he was professor of history in Iowa (now Grinnell) College, at Grinnell, Iowa, eminently successful in teaching. The effects of his transplantation from New England to the Middle West, which were permanent, were to be immediately seen in his *Stephen A. Douglas: A Study in American Politics* (1908), a well-written book, obviously the work of a cultivated mind. The book was by intention more distinctly a contribution to Western and national political history than a product of biographical enthusiasm for one of the uncultivated, hard-fighting politicians of the forties and fifties. By the time of its publication Johnson was at Bowdoin College, where he served as professor of history and political science from 1905 to 1910. There he taught with vigor and skill, improving upon the commonplaces of historical instruction by introducing the maturer students to the critical study of sources and to philosophical consideration of the bases of historical statements. An especially fruitful innovation was his practice of dividing the more advanced classes into groups of four or five for intensive and personal conference, a practice costly to the teacher but in which the sagacious President Hyde discerned great promise (*Report of the President of Bowdoin College for the Academic Year, 1909–10*; *Nation,* Feb. 3, 1910). Never deficient in public spirit, Johnson while at Bowdoin prepared for the American Historical Association (*Annual Report . . . for the Year 1908*) a detailed report on the archives of the state of Maine.

In 1910 he was called to a professorship of American history in Yale University, where he remained till 1926. There his teaching, always marked by exceptional clearness, breadth of view, and sympathetic interest in adjoining subjects, was at its best with graduate students. Fruits of his teaching were his *Readings in American Constitutional History* (1912), later supplemented by *Readings in Recent American Constitutional History, 1876–1926* (1927), in which William A. Robinson collaborated; and, following a course in historical method given during his last years at Yale, *The Historian and Historical Evidence* (1926). The last-named book is a series of suggestive essays, not a complete and well-rounded treatise upon its subject, and would seem slight if put into comparison with the thorough-going work of the revered but heavy-handed Bernheim. But the intention was to provide a book of advice and suggestion which the not-too-patient American student would actually read, and it was so attractively written as to achieve that purpose. Another merit was its appreciation, natural to Johnson, of the value and use in historical thinking of modern philosophical studies, and especially of the recent acquisitions of experimental psychology. An earlier fruit of the Yale period was the second of the four volumes of the *Riverside History of the United States,* entitled *Union and Democracy* (1915), an orderly, systematic, and well-balanced narrative of the period from 1783 to 1829. But the principal work of this laborious scholar in these years, outside of his teaching, was his editing of the attractive series of fifty small volumes entitled *The Chronicles of America* (1918–21). The purpose with which Johnson undertook this formidable task was to provide the intelligent general reader with a history of the United States composed of volumes each having a certain unity, readable, yet conforming to high standards of scholarship. His own volume, *Jefferson and his Colleagues* (1921), delightful to the general reader yet satisfactory to the scholar, shows how he meant this difficult reconcilement to be achieved in the series. By unstinted labor on his own part, great editorial skill, and unsparing rigor in dealing with contributions, he kept the series well to the level which he had set. Soon after its completion, he spent the academic year 1924–25 in a journey around the world, varied by lecturing in educational institutions in Japan and China.

Along with his high reputation for scholarship in American history and his recognized ability as a writer, it was his editorial success with the *Chronicles of America,* and the vigor with which he kept them to his high standards, that caused the committee of management, in the spring of 1925, to invite him to become the editor of the *Dictionary of American Biography.* After thirty years of teaching, Johnson removed to Washington and at the beginning of February 1926 began the work which, from that day to the day of his death, was to engross all his remarkable powers. This is not the place in which to estimate the success of his labors upon this *Dictionary,* but it is permissible to dwell upon the breadth of view with which he took all sorts of men and women and all parts of the country into equal consideration, the pains he took to obtain the best advice as to persons to be included and writers to be engaged, his extraordinary ability as an organizer and capacity for administrative detail, his firm resistance to all pressure toward favoritism, ancestor-worship, and bias, the special measures he adopted to ensure accuracy, and the constant application of his keen critical judgment, ripe experience, and fine literary taste to the scrutiny of manuscripts. His rigor was disconcerting to some contributors, but it was salutary to the *Dictionary,* and his correspondence abounded in appreciation, sympathy, and helpfulness.

The death of Allen Johnson, struck by an automobile at evening in the streets of Washington, was as sudden as it was premature; but his sense of the pressure of his arduous editorial task upon a constitution never robust had caused the appointment of Dumas Malone as his colleague, a year and a half before; and this provision, the extraordinarily methodical care with which he kept his papers, and the forethought with which he had extended preparations into the later letters of the alphabet, made it possible for the work to go on without any interruption. Six volumes came out under his care, the sixth soon after his death; but, with every appreciation of the work of his successors, the whole series will in a sense be his monument. The articles which he himself wrote were those on Henry Adams, Francis Asbury, Jonathan Boucher, John Brown, George Claghorn, Myles Cooper, Stephen A. Douglas, Mary Baker Eddy, and Warren Felt Evans—a list which of itself shows the catholicity of his interests, though it was a cause of deep regret to him that his administrative tasks prevented him from writing more. He was married on June 20, 1900, at Germantown, Pa., to Helen K. Ross, daughter of Henry A. and Mary Ross. From the shock of her death in 1921 he never fully recovered. They had one son, Allen S. Johnson.

[Recollections of relatives, schoolmates, and college classmates; annual catalogues of the colleges mentioned; H. P. Gallinger, "The Career of Allen Johnson," in *Amherst Graduates' Quart.,* Aug. 1931; editorials in *N. Y. Times,* Jan. 20, 1931, *N. Y. Herald Tribune,* Jan. 21, 1931; personal knowledge.]

J. F. J.

JOHNSON, ANDREW (Dec. 29, 1808–July 31, 1875), seventeenth president of the United States, was born in Raleigh, N. C., the younger son of Jacob Johnson and Mary (or Polly) McDonough. Jacob Johnson, a bank porter and sexton in Raleigh, "an honest man, loved and respected by all who knew him" (Winston, *post,* p. 7), died in 1811, leaving his two sons in a condition of poverty not relieved by the second marriage of their mother. Apprenticed to a tailor and at one time advertised as a runaway, Andrew Johnson in 1826 moved, together with his mother and his stepfather, to Tennessee where, after some wandering, he finally settled at Greeneville. He married, May 17, 1827, Eliza McCardle, the daughter of a Scotch shoemaker, who assisted him in the improvement of his reading and writing, and whose gentle temper and unfailing courage were of deep importance to her husband throughout their long life together. They had five children, Martha, Charles, Mary, Robert, and Andrew. Even before he left North Carolina, Johnson, who was denied formal schooling, had begun to educate himself with the aid of *The American Speaker,* which contained specimens of the oratory of Pitt and Fox (Savage, *post,* p. 23). His eagerness to acquire knowledge and to argue was stimulated by individuals of greater culture who took an interest in the young tailor and by contacts with Greeneville College and Tusculum Academy which were near-by. Although he was not a student of either institution he did take part in their debates. In the course of time, by his thrift in the management of the tailor-shop which he established in Greeneville, he accumulated a small estate. Of medium size and height, dark-complexioned, with black eyes and hair, Johnson, as he progressed in his career, maintained a scrupulous neatness of appearance and, in ordinary conversation, a courtesy of manner. Powerful as a speaker, in his early years he was often crude both in his thought and in his diction. Like many other public men, he had to meet the charge of religious infidelity. He professed sympathy with the tenets of Christianity, but was not associated with any church.

His political career began with his election as alderman of his little town. This was brought about, one of his early biographers has said, by reason of his championing the cause of the working men of Greeneville against the aristocratic element of the town (Savage, p. 19). He was twice reëlected alderman and was then chosen mayor. In 1835 he was elected to the legislature of Tennessee from the district composed of Greene and Washington Counties. Defeated in 1837, he was reëlected in 1839. In 1840 he was a candidate as elector-at-large on the Democratic ticket, canvassing for Van Buren; and the next year he was elected to the state Senate. In 1843 Johnson was elected to the Twenty-eighth Congress as a representative of the first district of Tennessee. He served continuously in the House of Representatives for ten years. Then, gerrymandered out of his district by a Whig legislature, he ran for the governorship and was successful. He was reëlected governor in 1855. Two years later he was able to command election by the legislature to the United States Senate.

Although he attracted the favorable notice of men as different in their views as James K. Polk and John Quincy Adams, Johnson had climbed these many steps in the political ladder with little of the support that others had received from older or more prominent men: it was rather by his own demonstration of his political capacity than through any outside help that he made his ascent. In 1835, when he entered the legislature, the debates of that body, upon which lay the obligation to enact laws for carrying into effect the provisions of the new Tennessee constitution of 1834, were particularly educative for a new and untrained representative. After some hesitation and uncertainty, Johnson identified himself with the regular Jacksonian Democratic party. Throughout his early career he nearly always voted in strict regularity upon party questions, but he quarrelled with so many of the Democratic leaders (Winston, p. 50) that it is not strange that he lacked friends. To an earnest support of Democracy he added a point of view that was his own—a violent antipathy to any superiority claimed by right of birth or wealth. In this he was influenced, possibly, by baseless gossip which questioned whether Jacob Johnson was really his father. Perhaps he caught something from the various "workingmen's parties" of the day. At any rate, as the self-constituted friend of the working class, he again and again attacked those who seemed to speak or act in disparagement of the laboring man.

There soon came to be a general acceptance of the belief that his ideas were radical. East Tennessee, in which lay Johnson's home, was rather adapted for small farms than for extensive agriculture, and, in comparison with the other parts of the state, had few negro slaves. Hence Johnson advocated a change, within the state, to the "white basis" of representation, instead of the established count of five slaves as three whites. He supported the formation of East Tennessee, with perhaps those parts of the neighboring states where slavery was weak, into a new state. Yet he claimed to be orthodox on the subject of slavery, violently attacked John Quincy Adams, and reprehended the Abolitionists on all occasions. He suggested that the executive patronage should be apportioned by states, and urged amendments to the Constitution which should provide for the election instead of the appointment of federal judges, the election of senators by popular vote, and the abolition of the electoral college in the choosing of the president. He opposed governmental support of the Smithsonian Institution, and in general advocated retrenchment and economy, himself practising with extraordinary care the principles that he preached.

Of all the measures that came before Congress during this period, Johnson identified himself as the special advocate of one, the so-called "homestead" law, which looked to the granting of land, in limited quantity, to actual settlers, without price or at a nominal price (St. George L. Sioussat, in *Mississippi Valley Historical Review,* December 1918, pp. 253–87). In Tennessee, it should be noted, the United States had only a residuary title to the public lands and in the course of time parted with that; and there was, therefore, no opportunity for the operation, upon lands within the state, of a federal homestead law. Johnson managed skilfully to combine the promotion of a policy dear to the frontier states with an appeal to the interest of the laboring classes in the East. By the time that he retired from Congress in 1853 he had seen a homestead bill pass the House of Representatives, and had received a few votes as a presidential nominee at a session of the Industrial Congress, a body which expressed the radical ideas of the "land reformers" of the East (*New York Daily Tribune,* June 9, 1851).

His election as governor of Tennessee in 1853 clearly evinced his popularity outside his own district. During his first term he secured legislation providing for the levying of a tax in support of education, the first of the sort in the state, caused the establishment of a state board of agriculture and a state library, and, at the same time, he stood for sound finance. His reelection in 1855 over the candidate of the American or Know-Nothing party marked a triumph over the forces of religious and political intolerance.

He was not in Congress at the time of the passage of the Kansas-Nebraska Act, but that legislation he accepted; and in the campaign of 1856 he supported, as usual, the regular nominees, though Buchanan, whom he thought the weakest of the Democratic candidates, was his "last choice" (to A. O. P. Nicholson, June 27, 1856, New York Historical Society). In the Senate, he voted for Jefferson Davis's resolutions of Feb. 2, 1860, which declared against the power of either Congress or a territorial legislature to annul the right of citizens to take slaves into the common territory, and asserted it to be the duty of the federal government to afford to such property the needed protection (*Congressional Globe,* 36 Cong., 1 Sess., p. 658). His chief interest, however, was in the homestead bill and he resented the veto by President Buchanan of the partial measure passed by the Thirty-sixth Congress.

To the national convention of the Democratic

party which met in Charleston in April 1860, the Tennessee delegation, in accordance with the prior action of the state convention held at Nashville, presented the name of Johnson as a candidate for the presidential nomination. Although he had expressed bitter dislike of Douglas, there is evidence that Johnson would have been content to go upon the ticket of 1860 as candidate for vice-president with Douglas if the party had remained united (to Robert Johnson, Apr. 12, 1860, Johnson Manuscripts, Huntington Library); but after the schism of that year he supported, without enthusiasm, the candidacy of Breckinridge and Lane. His attitude was that of compromise, and on Dec. 13, 1860, with this end in view, he proposed amendments to the federal Constitution similar to those put forward by Crittenden.

On Dec. 18, 1860, however, at the very time when the secession convention of South Carolina was meeting in Charleston, addressing the Senate, he declared himself for the Union; and when the other Southern senators withdrew, he alone remained. The importance of Johnson's action was at once observed. The North welcomed a powerful ally and saw in him another Andrew Jackson devoted to the preservation of the Union. To the Southern extremists his course was that of a traitor. This speech Johnson followed up with others on Feb. 5 and Mar. 2, 1861, which, by reason of his vehement denunciation of his Southern critics and his sturdy insistence that the Union must be preserved, thrilled the North (Winston, pp. 173, 186, *New York Times,* Mar. 4, 1861). In the Congress which met in special session in July, Johnson introduced, July 24, an important resolution, which passed the Senate. By this the purposes of the war were declared to be, not conquest or subjugation, or interference with the rights or established institutions of the Southern states, but the defence and maintenance of the supremacy of the Constitution and the Union. This he supported in a powerful speech (*Congressional Globe,* 37 Cong., 1 Sess., pp. 243, 288–97). During the winter of 1861–62 he devoted much of his time to the work of the joint committee on the conduct of the war.

In March 1862, while still a senator, Johnson was appointed by President Lincoln military governor of Tennessee, with instructions to reestablish the authority of the Federal government in the state. During the adjournment of Congress in the spring of 1861, Johnson had spoken in behalf of the Union in East Tennessee but his efforts did not avail to save the state. It was the irony of fate that East Tennessee, strongly Unionist in sympathy, was overrun by the Confederates and placed under martial law. Both Johnson and William G. Brownlow [*q.v.*], who for years had been his Whig rival and bitter enemy, but whom the course of affairs was now forcing into cooperation with him, begged for military succor from the North; and their plea received Lincoln's warm-hearted support, the approval of General McClellan, and promises from General Buell. Yet East Tennessee remained under Confederate control until the summer of 1863. By Feb. 25, 1862, after the overwhelming success of Grant at Fort Henry and Fort Donelson, the flight of the Confederate state government to Memphis, and the complete overthrow of organized Confederate armies in the western part of the state, Buell, with the United States forces, was in Nashville. These facts explain why it was in the secessionist western part of the state, and not as had been hoped in Unionist East Tennessee, that Johnson, as military governor, began his attempt at the restoration of his state.

In the midst of a community which hated and despised him, forced by the nature of things to exercise arbitrary power that was dependent absolutely upon military force, Johnson faced yet other difficulties. The political purpose of his mission was at times entirely subordinated to those strategic principles which the higher military commanders on the ground felt should govern at the time, and Johnson was constantly at odds with the military authorities (Hall, *post,* pp. 50–87). There were successive waves of alarm lest the Confederates should repossess themselves of the capital and the state. Throughout these crises Johnson exhibited great intrepidity. At length, after the defeat of the Confederate armies, he found it possible to bring about, partly with the aid of the East Tennesseans, a restoration of civil government in the state. Tennessee was thus a sort of laboratory experiment for the reconstruction of the Union: Johnson's régime antedated Lincoln's emancipation proclamations of Sept. 22, 1862, and Jan. 1, 1863, in the latter of which Tennessee was not included, and also the President's plan of reconstruction set forth in the proclamation of Dec. 8, 1863. By January 1865, Johnson had the satisfaction of reporting to Lincoln the passing, by a constitutional convention that was, indeed, very irregular in its composition, of amendments that would bring about the abolition of slavery in the state. These were later ratified by popular vote. This restoration by state action foreshadowed the later policy of Johnson as president.

While Johnson was still engaged in his courageous efforts in Tennessee, Lincoln was renominated by the National Union Convention; and the same considerations which led that body to drop the party name Republican made Johnson a valuable asset as nominee for vice-president. His nomination was a recognition of the services of the militant Unionists of the South and helped to relieve the party of the purely sectional character which had at first attached to the Republicans. The strain of the campaign, superimposed upon that which he had long borne as the administrator of his state, exhausted Johnson. His health was impaired, and only Lincoln's urgent request hurried him to Washington in time for the inaugural ceremonies. The result was most unfortunate, for Johnson, when he took the oath of office, was under the influence of liquor (Oberholtzer, *post,* I, 4; Beale, *post,* pp. 12–17). No doubt the *faux pas* was due to illness and exhaustion, but it gave malice something to feed upon. On the morning of Apr. 15, 1865, the day after Lincoln's assassination, Johnson, who had paid a brief visit to Lincoln's bedside (Winston, p. 268), was officially informed by the cabinet of his accession to the presidency. In a simple ceremony, in which Johnson bore himself with dignity, the oath of office was administered by Chief Justice Chase. Later in the day Johnson announced that he would retain the cabinet as then constituted and would continue Lincoln's policies.

The assassination, coming as it did in such close sequence to the collapse of the Confederacy, produced in the North, in addition to the universal grief, a vindictive rage upon which it is impossible to look back without regret. Although no enemy now threatened, the surviving conspirators against Lincoln were tried by military commission, and four of them were hanged. The execution of Mrs. Surratt later gave rise to a violent controversy, in which Johnson maintained that he had been prevented from seeing the recommendation of mercy made by the court (Winston, pp. 283–91). Jefferson Davis and other eminent Southerners were charged with complicity in the murder of Lincoln, and imprisoned. Later Davis was indicted, not for any part in the plot but for treason; after two years he was released on bond. At first Johnson was as bitter as any. "Treason," he is reported to have said, "must be made infamous, and traitors must be impoverished" (G. W. Julian, *Political Recollections,* p. 257). The South viewed his accession with apprehension: the North approved. Johnson, however, soon freed himself from hysteria.

Among the first steps to bring back a return to the conditions of peace was the disbandment of as much as possible of the Federal army. In a series of proclamations, executive orders, and general orders, the external blockade was rescinded, and the trade of the Southern states was reopened. The most pressing problem, however, was the reëstablishment of government in the states that had seceded. Johnson did not have to invent a plan, for the work had already been started by Lincoln in the amnesty proclamation of Dec. 8, 1863. He had promised to recognize in any of the states, other than Virginia, such a government as should be established by persons, not less in number than one-tenth of the votes cast in the presidential election of 1860, who should take an oath of loyalty and who should be qualified voters under the state law. Against Lincoln's plan Congress had advanced the Wade-Davis bill of July 1864, to which Lincoln had given a "pocket veto," though he had accepted the scheme as possibly constituting an alternative plan. Lincoln had proceeded to promote the restoration of loyal governments in Louisiana and Arkansas; while Johnson himself had had in hand the reconstruction of Tennessee. In the Pierpont government, effective principally for the tearing of West Virginia from the Old Dominion, there was a tenuous basis for a government in Virginia. The executive order of May 9, 1865, which recognized Francis H. Pierpont as governor of Virginia, was the first important pronouncement of the new administration. Lincoln had dismissed the idea, which for a moment was in his mind, that the old Confederate state governments might be used; and Sherman's similar concession in his convention with Joseph E. Johnston had been promptly repudiated in the first days of the new President.

On May 29 Johnson set forth in two documents his continuation of Lincoln's plan. The first was a general proclamation of amnesty which, in contrast with Lincoln's simple paragraph, now listed fourteen classes of persons who must make special applications for pardon. Of these excepted classes, one included all persons the estimated value of whose taxable property was over $20,000. This was not so much reminiscent of Johnson's steady hostility to the aristocrats as an expression of his belief that the well-to-do had led the humbler classes of the South into secession. The second of the proclamations of May 29 had in view the establishment of a loyal government in North Carolina, and was followed by similar proclamations for the other states. In none of these was there any demand of a necessary proportion of loyal voters, such as Lincoln's one-tenth; in none was there any requirement of specific action by the conventions or legislatures to be established in the states. There was, however, a clear statement that it was the function of the state to determine who should vote and who should hold office.

During the summer and autumn of 1865, under the supervision of Johnson's provisional governors, elections were held for state conventions; upon the adoption of the new constitutions state governments were organized through the work of legislatures; and under stimulation from the President the ordinances of secession were repealed, slavery was abolished, the Thirteenth Amendment was ratified by all the Southern states but Mississippi, and the Confederate state debts were repudiated. Unfortunately the new governments failed to adopt Johnson's suggestion that the suffrage be extended to a few highly qualified negroes; and the police regulations intended to preserve order among the emancipated negroes were interpreted in the North as revealing an intention to restore slavery in fact. The organization of bodies of militia in the South was also viewed with suspicion and the reappearance in public life of many who had been active secessionists was bitterly resented. On the other hand, the Southerners disliked the presence of negro troops and complained of the interference of the Freedmen's Bureau. The North received the most conflicting reports as to what was going on in the South.

One must fairly conclude that, by the time the Thirty-ninth Congress met (Dec. 4, 1865), Johnson had accomplished much. The President's message, which was written by George Bancroft but expressed very definitely the ideas of Johnson himself (W. A. Dunning, in *American Historical Review,* April 1906, pp. 574 ff.; C. R. Fish, *Ibid.,* July 1906, pp. 951–52), was dignified and conciliatory in tone and won favorable comment on both sides of the Atlantic. The states and the Constitution, the President said, were mutually indispensable. The true theory was that all pretended acts of secession were, from the beginning, null and void. The states had been in a condition where their vitality was impaired, but not extinguished; their functions were suspended but not destroyed. The states should be invited to participate in the high office of amending the Constitution, and a ratification of the Thirteenth Amendment had been exacted as a pledge of perpetual loyalty and peace. It was for the Senate and the House each to judge of the elections, returns, and qualifications of its own members. As to the extension of suffrage to the negro, he said that was a power belonging exclusively to the states.

Although Congress was not openly aggressive, those who were to be its leaders had already resolved to block Johnson's plan. At the first meeting of the House the clerk passed over the names of the representatives of the new governments in the Southern states and the Senate likewise kept the Southerners waiting, despite the fact that Horace Maynard, one of the excluded representatives, had been a member of Congress from Tennessee until 1863 and the further fact that the President himself was a citizen of that state. Thaddeus Stevens [*q.v.*] of Pennsylvania, the author of the theory that the Southern states must come in as new states or remain conquered provinces, and one of the chief proponents of a policy of confiscation, moved and secured the establishment, with himself as chairman, of the famous joint-committee of fifteen, which as the "Central Directory" (*Diary of Gideon Welles,* II, 494) of the Radicals was to play a leading rôle throughout the period of reconstruction. The actions of Stevens, Sumner, Wade, and the other Radicals indeed merit the word "conspiracy" which Gideon Welles attached to them at the time (*Ibid.,* III, 314), and which the defenders of Johnson have continued to employ; and it is easy to sense the dramatic element in the conflict of strong and fearless men such as Johnson and his foes; but their struggle, which seems at first sight to have been so largely personal, is seen with more mature vision to have been the expression of mighty conflicting forces. The Civil War had brought about an enormous expansion of the executive, as distinct from the legislative, power, which already had aroused the resentment of Congress. When the war came to a close and the conquered South had to be restored, the situation was further complicated and confused by the sentimental appeal which the condition of the freedmen made to the spirit of altruism, and, unfortunately, by the human passion of revenge. Over and above all these factors reigned a more practical consideration. The result of emancipation, the Republican leaders clearly saw, would be to increase the representation of the white South in Congress, while the tendency of the return of peace would be to restore to leadership the same element that had dominated Southern politics in former years. That Lincoln, had he lived, would have been given free rein by Congress and by the emancipationists is most improbable. What actually happened in 1865 was that fate threw the control of the executive department of the government, with its vast patronage, into the hands of a Southerner and a Democrat of the state-rights school. To the determined group of which Thaddeus Stevens and Charles Sumner were the heads, the first consideration was the preservation of the rule of the Republican party; and this could only be assured, under the circumstances, by the use of the vote of the negroes in the Southern states, by writing into the Constitution new limitations on the power of the states, and by reducing to impotence, or, if that were impossible, by removing, a Democratic President.

Congress proceeded to pass an act for the extension of the Freedmen's Bureau, both as to duration and as to power. This received Johnson's disapproval, Feb. 19, and the veto was sustained. With characteristic tactlessness, Johnson permitted himself, in a speech made on Washington's birthday, to indulge in bitter personalities that could only stir up ill feeling in Congress and lose him the support of the more conservative Republicans. With his second veto, that of the Civil Rights Act, delivered Mar. 27, the breach between the President and Congress became more serious. The bill was passed over the veto Apr. 9. While Johnson has been criticized for not accepting this measure, it is clear that in accordance with his state-rights principles he could not conscientiously have done so; for the bill was intended to guarantee to the freedmen the preservation of their rights by the federal courts, against the infringement of these rights by state law. Before Congress adjourned the Fourteenth Amendment had been proposed to the states. This was intended to insure by constitutional change the maintenance of the principles of the Civil Rights Act. Congress also undertook through this amendment to enforce complete repudiation of the Confederate debt, and to prevent compensation for slave property. Moreover, while technically the Fourteenth Amendment did not force negro suffrage on the South, it established the alternatives of the enfranchisement of all male citizens or the reduction of representation in Congress. Tennessee had hastened, under the Brownlow régime, to ratify this amendment and was now admitted, but in grudging terms which drew a protest from Johnson. In June the joint-committee on reconstruction had made a very partisan report to Congress, embodying the results of an extensive investigation into conditions in the South.

That Congress and the radical Republicans were, for the time, in the ascendant, was made clear by the congressional elections which came towards the end of 1866. Disorders which arose in Memphis in May and in New Orleans in July reacted unfavorably upon Northern opinion. In July, Dennison, Speed, and Harlan, who had ceased to be willing to follow the President, resigned from the cabinet. In August an attempt to build up a Union party out of the loyal Democrats, the conservative Republicans, and the old Whigs seemed for a while promising; but Johnson's effort to win popular support on a tour through the eastern cities and the Middle West was robbed of whatever success it might have had by some of his own speeches, in which he made the mistake of slipping back into the political vernacular of his early Tennessee days, and of allowing himself to indulge in personal debate with members of the throngs that came to hear him. While this was bad enough, it was made far worse by the Republican newspapers, and the old charges of intemperance were assiduously though falsely revived (Schouler, *History of the United States,* VII, 1913, pp. 373–75). Though the President believed that he had aroused the people (*Diary of Gideon Welles,* II, p. 590), the event showed that the "swing around the circle" was a complete failure so far as its political purposes were concerned.

The original reconstruction law was vetoed by Johnson and passed over his veto on Mar. 2, 1867; it was supplemented by the acts of Mar. 23 and July 19, 1867, and Mar. 11, 1868. By this legislation military government was reëstablished in the Southern states, and the latter were required, if they would secure representation in Congress, to accept negro suffrage and to ratify the Fourteenth Amendment. In most of the Southern states the intended result was obtained, and the amendment was added to the Constitution. Upon those states which were recalcitrant and delayed their action was laid the additional requirement of ratifying the Fifteenth Amendment; but the story of this goes over into the administration of Grant.

The passage over Johnson's vetoes, by ample majorities, of one law after another, fully demonstrated that he was no longer able to interfere with the legislative power. It is vastly to his credit that he performed faithfully, though with strict construction of the law, every duty that Congress laid upon him. The president was shorn of power in other respects: Congress invaded the executive realm. Indignant at Johnson's extension of pardon to many prominent ex-Confederates, the Radicals attempted through the Fourteenth Amendment to limit the president's pardoning power, by excluding the leading Confederates from office until Congress should grant them amnesty. The army appropriation act of 1867 which Johnson signed, with a protest (March 2, Richardson, VI, p. 472), stripped him of much of his authority as commander-in-chief of the army. The Tenure of Office Act, passed over his veto Mar. 2, 1867, forbade the president to remove without the consent of the Senate an office holder appointed by and with the advice of the Senate. Cabinet officers were specifically included, but with the proviso, which was later to evoke violent controversy, that they should "hold their offices respectively for and during the term of the President by whom they may have been appointed and for one month thereafter, subject to removal" with the consent of the Senate (*Statutes at Large,* XIV, 430). Efforts to test in the courts the constitutionality of the various measures enacted by the Radicals were either denied by the Supreme Court itself on the ground that it would not interfere with political questions, or prevented through congressional action in regard to the appellate jurisdiction of the Supreme Court. As a necessary result, unless the President appealed to force, or the public turned to him and against Congress, his initiative and his usefulness as a constructive leader were at an end.

In August 1867, during one of the brief periods when Congress was not in session, Johnson took a step which made the Tenure of Office Act a vital issue. With unfortunate tolerance he had permitted the continuance in his cabinet of Edwin M. Stanton [*q.v.*], the secretary of war, who, although he for a time apparently had given cordial assent to Johnson's views and had expressed himself positively against the constitutionality of the Tenure of Office Act (*Diary of Gideon Welles,* III, 50–51), nevertheless had remained in the cabinet really for the purpose of serving as informer and adviser to the Radicals in Congress. At last Johnson asked Stanton to resign (Aug. 5), and when the latter refused to do so, suspended him (Aug. 12). Grant was commissioned secretary *ad interim.* On Dec. 12, Johnson submitted to the Senate his reasons for suspending Stanton, in which, on Jan. 13, 1868, the Senate refused to concur. The result was the reinstatement of Stanton, to whom Grant, in violation of the understanding which Johnson had with him, turned over the office. This caused an unseemly controversy between Grant and Johnson, in which the former appears to little advantage (Notes of Col. W. G. Moore, *American Historical Review,* October 1913, pp. 109–18). The effect was to drive Grant into the arms of the Radicals. On Feb. 21 Johnson formally removed Stanton, instructing him to turn the office over to Gen. Lorenzo Thomas, *ad interim.* This Stanton refused to do; and the Senate, supporting him, declined to confirm the nomination of Thomas. An attempt to secure a judicial test of the matter miscarried, and Stanton remained in possession of his office at the War department, protected by Radical sympathizers and supporters against any attempt which might be made to displace him by force.

On Feb. 25, 1868, with public excitement at a high point, Thaddeus Stevens and John A. Bingham appeared at the bar of the Senate and, in the name of the House of Representatives and of all the people of the United States, impeached the President of high crimes and misdemeanors in office. This was in fulfilment of a vote of the House of Representatives taken the day before. There had been talk of impeaching Johnson even before he sent in his first message; the first definite step had been taken in the short session of 1866–67; and in December 1867 a majority of the judiciary committee of the House of Representatives had recommended impeachment but had failed to carry the House. In February the matter had been transferred from the judiciary committee to Stevens' joint-committee on reconstruction. Johnson's removal of Stanton had now served to array with his foes many of the more conservative Republicans, who had been unable to accept the mass of irrelevant and in large degree fraudulent "testimony" which had been submitted to them up to this time. By Mar. 4 the seven managers appointed by the House, Bingham, G. S. Boutwell, J. F. Wilson, B. F. Butler, Thomas Williams, J. A. Logan, and Stevens, were ready to lay before the Senate eleven articles of impeachment. Of these, nine were concerned directly or indirectly with the Tenure of Office Act and the removal of Stanton; the tenth charged the President with attacking Congress in his speeches; the eleventh, designed "to catch the votes of doubtful Senators," reverted to the Tenure of Office Act, but added "a mass of indirect allegations" of illegal actions on the part of the President (DeWitt, *post,* pp. 386–87).

The following day, Mar. 5, Chief Justice Chase appeared in his judicial robes, and the Senate was organized as "a court of impeachment for the trial of the President of the United States" (*Proceedings in the Trial of Andrew Johnson,* etc., 1868). The trial really began on Friday, Mar. 13, when in the crowded Senate chamber, with galleries packed, Henry Stanbery, who had resigned his position as attorney general to assume the defense of Johnson, announced that the President entered his appearance, in answer to the summons of the Senate, by his counsel. With Stanbery were associated Benjamin R. Curtis, T. A. R. Nelson of Tennessee, William M. Evarts, and Jeremiah S. Black; but Black soon withdrew, after Johnson had refused to yield to a most improper pressure exerted upon him, at this critical time, to decide in the Alta Vela case in favor of Black's clients (DeWitt, pp. 397–400, 470–71). His place was taken by William S. Groesbeck.

It did not take long for Johnson's counsel to demonstrate that the only question of real importance legally involved in the articles of impeachment was that of the Tenure of Office Act; but the managers, of whom the notorious Butler played the leading part, assisted by the majority senators who frequently overruled the efforts of Chase to preserve the semblance of a trial, turned the impeachment proceedings into what the historian James Schouler aptly called "a solemn theatrical fiasco" (*History,* VII, 116). The effort to include the charge that Johnson was guilty of complicity in the murder of Lincoln had been abandoned; but there was little else that was not laid at his door. Upon those whose vote was considered doubtful there was brought varied, severe, and improper pressure. When, on May 16, a vote was taken on the eleventh article, and, on May 26, on the second and third articles, the result, 35 to 19, showed one less than the number necessary for conviction. Seven Republican senators had voted with the Democrats and the President stood acquitted. The other articles were not pressed.

After a warning from Stanbery as to the unwisdom of incautious utterance (*Diary of Gideon Welles,* III, 311), Johnson had maintained an admirable bearing throughout the period of the trial. Restless, at times he expressed the intention of appearing in person, but this he did not carry out. "The President," his private secretary wrote, "declares that the defence he desires to make in the impeachment trial is for the people —not merely for the Senate, and that he would care nothing for conviction by that body if he stands acquitted by the nation" (*American Historical Review,* Oct. 1913, p. 132). The impeachment trial was very shortly felt to have been a blunder and the failure of it fortunate for the country. As Dunning wrote, in a masterly analysis of the trial, "The single vote by which Andrew Johnson escaped conviction marks the narrow margin by which the Presidential element in our system escaped destruction" (*Essays on the Civil War and Reconstruction,* p. 303). In 1926 the Tenure of Office Act, which had been modified early in Grant's administration, and in large part repealed in 1887, was declared by the Supreme Court of the United States to have been unconstitutional (*Myers, Administratrix,* vs. *United States, 272 U. S. Reports,* 52–295).

From the adjournment of the impeachment trial to the end of Johnson's term as president was less than a year. While the trial was in its last days the National Union Republican convention had nominated for the presidency General Grant, whose personal popularity made him highly "available" to the Republicans. The Democratic convention finally nominated Horatio Seymour of New York. Johnson, though receptive, had made no effort to secure votes; he received 65 on the first ballot. Nearly all the measures by which Congress, in these last months of Johnson's term, continued to carry out its plan of reconstruction received his disapproval and were passed over his veto. Johnson duly proclaimed the ratification of the Fourteenth Amendment, but in his last annual message, that of Dec. 9, 1868, he presented a summary of his criticism of the policy of Congress. At the same time he offered once more his old recommendations that the Constitution should be amended in regard to the election of the president, the senators, and federal judges; and he added a plan to fix the succession to the presidency in the event of vacancies in both that office and the vice-presidency. By proclamations put forth on July 4 and on Christmas Day, 1868, he extended his previous grants of amnesty until, without limitation, all who had participated in the "rebellion" were included. As he retired from the White House he issued a valedictory address, violent in its indictment of the congressional policy.

The management of diplomatic and financial affairs during his presidency Johnson left to his secretaries, Seward and McCulloch, who, with Gideon Welles, secretary of the navy, remained loyally in his cabinet. In foreign relations the chief accomplishments were the retirement of the French from Mexico, the purchase of Alaska, the restraining of the Fenian movement, and the negotiation with Lord Clarendon by Reverdy Johnson [*q.v.*] of a convention which was rejected by the Senate, all but unanimously, in the first days of Grant's presidency. In the field of finance, the one important stand which Johnson took independently of his secretary was unfortunate. There was a widespread feeling that it was unjust that bondholders should be able to demand and receive gold for their bonds, while the poor man had to take greenbacks. Johnson went further, urging that, in view of the fact that purchasers of bonds had paid for them in paper notes worth in gold but half their face value, the payment of the interest for something over sixteen years ought to liquidate the principal.

Upon his return to his home in Tennessee, Johnson soon was drawn into the troubled currents of state politics. He tried to steer an independent course between the two extremes of the former Confederates and the radical Republicans of the Brownlow type. Although Tennessee had escaped congressional reconstruction, the problem of restoration was complex, involving not only the negroes but also the bitter animosities of the whites. In 1869 Johnson might have been elected to the Senate, had he not been deserted by one who had been his confidential private secretary. In 1872 he entered upon a campaign for election to Congress as representative-at-large from Tennessee, but was unsuccessful. In 1874, although weakened by an attack of yellow fever which he had suffered several months before, he became once more a candidate for election to the United States Senate. This time his effort was successful; and on Mar. 5, 1875, shortly after the Senate had met in special session in accordance with the call of President Grant, Andrew Johnson once more took his seat in the body which he had left in 1862. Death and the mutations of politics had removed many of his former enemies and of his faithful friends, but enough remained to give to the occasion of his return the dramatic element of a vindication. The low political ethics of the administrations of Grant had made Johnson's courageous honesty stand out in contrast; and soon after his election some of the leading newspapers contained expressions prophetic of the reversal of judgment upon him which was to come with the passing years (Stryker, pp. 808–11; Winston, p. 505). Before the session came to an end, Johnson delivered (Mar. 22) a speech in which he severely attacked the course which Grant had pursued in Louisiana, denounced Grant's aspirations for a third term, and closed with the plea "Let peace and prosperity be restored to the land. May God bless this people; may God save the Constitution." The Senate soon adjourned, and Johnson returned to his home in Tennessee. Several weeks later, while on a visit to his daughter, Mrs. Stover, near Carter Station, he suffered a paralytic attack. He died July 31, 1875.

[Representative of early biographies is John Savage's campaign sketch, published in *Our Living Representative Men* (1860), expanded in *The Life of Abraham Lincoln by H. J. Raymond; and the Life of Andrew Johnson by John Savage* (1864), and further enlarged as *The Life and Public Services of Andrew Johnson* (1866), the edition cited in this sketch. Some light is thrown on the earlier part of Johnson's career by D. L. Swain, *Early Times in Raleigh. Addresses Delivered . . . at the Dedication of Tucker Hall, and on the Occasion of the Completion of the Monument to Jacob Johnson* (1867). James S. Jones, *Life of Andrew Johnson* (1901), gave, though inadequately, an account of Johnson's whole career. Hugh McCulloch, *Men and Measures of Half a Century* (1888) was one of the first important works, by a contemporary of real significance, to give a favorable estimate of Johnson's presidency, which up to that time had been described for the most part by his enemies. W. A. Dunning, *Essays on the Civil War and Reconstruction* (1898), as the first examination of the reconstruction policies with the detached view of historical scholarship exerted a determining influence upon later writers. Influenced by Dunning is C. E. Chadsey, *The Struggle between Pres. Johnson and Congress over Reconstruction* (1896). C. H. McCarthy, *Lincoln's Plan of Reconstruction* (1901); J. W. Fertig, *Secession and Reconstruction of Tenn.* (1898); and J. R. Neal, *Disunion and Restoration in Tenn.* (1899), belong to the same period of writing.

D. M. DeWitt, for the preparation of his penetrating monograph, *The Impeachment and Trial of Andrew Johnson*, etc. (1903), examined some of the private papers of Johnson. In 1905 the Lib. of Cong. acquired the greater part of the Johnson papers. This collection, supplemented by that of Johnson's grandson, A. J. Patterson, also in the Lib. of Cong., and several of less importance in other repositories, now forms the indispensable basis for a study of Johnson's career. No adequate collection of his writings has yet been published. The Johnson papers in the Lib. of Cong. were promptly investigated by Dunning, who published interesting results in "More Light on Andrew Johnson," *Am. Hist. Rev.*, Apr. 1906, pp. 574 ff., and shortly wrote the valuable volume, "Reconstruction, Political and Economic" (1907) in the *American Nation* series. A flood of new light was thrown by the publication of John T. Morse, Jr., ed., *Diary of Gideon Welles* (3 vols., 1911), which had appeared before, in part, in the *Atlantic Monthly*. A timely word of caution as to the use of this has been given by H. K. Beale, in *Am. Hist. Rev.*, Apr. 1925, p. 547. The availability of the *Diary* and the Johnson papers enabled James Schouler in his *Hist. of the U. S.*, vol. VII (1913), to show the unfairness of some of the conclusions of James Ford Rhodes, in the latter's *Hist. of the U. S. from the Compromise of 1850*, vols. V, VI (1904–06). To be commended, as based on a careful research, is C. R. Hall, *Andrew Johnson, Mil. Gov. of Tenn.* (1916). Recent biographies are Robt. W. Winston, *Andrew Johnson, Plebeian and Patriot* (1928); L. P. Stryker, *Andrew Johnson: A Study in Courage* (1929); G. F. Milton, *The Age of Hate: Andrew Johnson and the Radicals* (1930). Each contains an extensive bibliography; that of Winston's book is particularly helpful as a guide to the voluminous periodical literature which has grown up about Johnson. For the presidential term of Johnson, E. P. Oberholtzer, *Hist. of the U. S. since the Civil War*, vol. I (1917), vol. II (1922), has the merit of an independent study. Other recent studies of value are H. K. Beale, *The Critical Year. A Study of Andrew Johnson and Reconstruction* (1930); C. G. Bowers, *The Tragic Era* (1929); R. H. White, *Development of the Tenn. State Educational Organization, 1796–1929* (1929); W. M. Caskey, "First Administration of Gov. Andrew Johnson," *Tenn. Hist. Society's Pubs.*, I (1929), pp. 43–59, and "Second Administration of Gov. Andrew Johnson, *Ibid.*, II (1930), pp. 34–54; Thos. P. Abernethy, *From Frontier to Plantation in Tenn.* (1932).

J. G. Blaine, *Twenty Years of Congress*, vol. I (1884); and S. S. Cox, *Union—Disunion—Reunion: Three Decades of Federal Legislation* (1885); are valuable but have to be handled with caution. Works purporting to throw reminiscent light on Johnson's career are Frank Cowan, *Andrew Johnson: Reminiscences of his Private Life and Character* (2 ed., 1894); and *Memoirs of the White House . . . Being Personal Recollections of Col. W. H. Crook*, etc. (1911), edited by Henry Rood. In his *Notable Men of Tenn.* (1912), O.

P. Temple, a younger contemporary of Johnson, has an interesting short account of the latter's life. See also J. D. Richardson, *A Compilation of the Messages and Papers of the Presidents,* vol. VI (1897); *Procs. in the Trial of Andrew Johnson, . . . before the Senate of the U. S.,* etc. (1868); B. B. Kendrick, *Jour. of the Joint Committee of Fifteen on Reconstruction* (1914); W. L. Fleming, *Documentary Hist. of Reconstruction* (2 vols., 1906–07).]
St. G. L. S.

JOHNSON, BENJAMIN PIERCE (Nov. 30, 1793–Apr. 12, 1869), agriculturist, was born in Canaan, N. Y., the son of William Johnson, a physician. His grandfather, William Johnstone, also a physician, emigrated from Scotland about the middle of the eighteenth century and settled in the province of Massachusetts Bay. As there was another physician of the same name in the vicinity, his grandfather changed his name from Johnstone to Johnson. Benjamin's father, after the Revolution, became a resident of Canaan, Columbia County, N. Y., where he managed a farm and also engaged in an extensive medical practice. He had six children, the youngest of whom was Benjamin Pierce Johnson. Benjamin's early life was spent at home upon the farm, his fondness for agriculture exhibiting itself strongly while he was still a boy. He was prepared for college in Lenox, Mass., entered Union College, Schenectady, N. Y., in 1810, and graduated in 1813. Having chosen law for his profession he first entered the office of his brother-in-law, John Foote, of Hamilton, and later studied with Elisha Williams. In 1816 his father moved to Oneida County, purchasing a small farm near Rome. The next year Benjamin followed his father and established himself in the practice of law in Rome. There he met and married, on Dec. 11, 1820, Anne McKinstry who died on Jan. 28, 1837. On Mar. 1, 1838, he married Mary Adams of Sherbourne, Chenango County. He became a favorite in his community, was elected to various public offices, and from 1827 to 1829 represented Oneida County in the New York Assembly. Returning to Rome at the close of his term, he resumed his law practice but also began to give more attention to agriculture. He became interested in the work of the New York State Agricultural Society and on its reorganization in 1841, he was elected one of the vice-presidents. In 1844 he was corresponding secretary and in 1845 president of the society. He led a busy life but he was unsuccessful in his money matters and in May 1846 found himself wholly unable to meet his obligations. Too proud to tell his friends, he sailed for Europe and was absent until November following, when he returned to Rome. His associates, having learned of his difficulties, had meanwhile arranged his affairs. While abroad he made a study of agricultural conditions in England and Wales. Although his departure to Europe was a serious mistake of judgment, it later turned out to his advantage. The experience he gained there and the contacts he made served him well in the position of corresponding secretary of the New York State Agricultural Society to which he was again elected in January 1847, soon after his return.

He moved to Albany with his family and made this his home for the remainder of his life. He gave up all other business and devoted himself wholly to the Society and to the development of the agricultural interests of New York state. Having been appointed by the governor of New York a commissioner to the London exhibition of 1851, to represent the interests of the state at the exhibition, he went to London in April 1850. He was placed on one of the most important of the juries, that of agricultural implements and machinery. His knowledge of the agricultural wants of England was particularly helpful in the trials of plows and American reapers, the success of which turned the tide of public opinion in favor of American inventions. In the summer of 1851, with a number of his associates, he visited France by invitation of the French Emperor. The National Agricultural Society of France honored him by the presentation of the society's medal of membership. During the Civil War he was appointed commissioner from the United States to the International Exhibition of 1862 in London and was again able to render valuable service to American exhibitors. He returned home in October 1862, to find his wife seriously ill. She died the following December and Johnson never fully recovered from the blow. He died Apr. 12, 1869, and was buried in Rome, N. Y. One son and a daughter survived him. His writings are contained for the most part in the *Transactions* and the *Monthly Journal* of the Society, the Albany *Cultivator,* and the *Central New York Farmer.* He was joint editor of the latter from 1842 to 1844. His report of the London exhibition, which appeared in the *Transactions* (vol. XI, 1852), was published separately under the title: *Report of Benjamin P. Johnson, Agent of the State of New York, Appointed to Attend the Exhibition of the Industry of all Nations* (1852).

[Marsena R. Patrick, *Memorial of Benj. P. Johnson* (1870), reprinted from the *Trans. N. Y. State Agric. Soc.,* vol. XXIX (1870); *Jour. N. Y. State Agric. Soc.,* Apr.–May 1869; *Cultivator and Country Gentleman.* Apr. 22, 1869; the *World* (N. Y.), Apr. 14, 1869.]
C. R. B.

JOHNSON, BRADLEY TYLER (Sept. 29, 1829–Oct. 5, 1903), politician, Confederate soldier, was born in Frederick, Md., the son of Charles Worthington and Eleanor Murdock (Tyler) Johnson, and grandson of Col. Baker Johnson of the Continental Army. He graduated at Princeton with honors in mathematics (A.B. 1849), studied law, and was admitted to the bar in 1851 in Frederick. On June 25, 1851, he was married to Jane Claudia Saunders of North Carolina. Entering politics, he was state's attorney, Democratic candidate for comptroller, state chairman of the Democratic Committee, and delegate to the national conventions of 1860. In the election of 1860 he supported Breckenridge.

After the outbreak of the Civil War he helped to organize the 1st Maryland Regiment, for the Confederate army, and served with it as major in J. E. Johnston's Valley campaign and at First Manassas. During 1862, having attained the rank of colonel, he ably commanded the 1st Maryland under Ewell and Jackson at Front Royal, Winchester, Harrisonburg, and the engagement at Gaines's Hill, before Richmond. Left without a command through the disbanding of his regiment by the Confederate war department, he commanded temporarily Gen. J. R. Jones's brigade at Second Manassas. Jackson recommended Johnson for promotion to the rank of brigadier-general, and meanwhile he was employed in several capacities, including another command of Jones's brigade, from July 2, at Gettysburg, to November 1863. Later he commanded Maryland cavalry under Wade Hampton, north of Richmond, where in February 1864 he checked Kilpatrick's raid, against a force far superior to his numerically. He was commissioned brigadier-general June 28, 1864, was given command of the cavalry brigade of Gen. William E. Jones, lately killed, and served under Early in the Valley and in Maryland. In McCausland's expedition of July 1864 to Chambersburg, Pa., Johnson executed Early's orders to burn the town. During the same raid he was disastrously surprised at Moorefield and barely avoided being captured. Later he participated in the campaign against Sheridan in the Valley. Heavy losses then made consolidation of commands necessary, and Johnson was displaced by officers senior in rank. He was sent to Salisbury, N. C., in November 1864, where, as commander of prisoners, he made strenuous efforts to restore order and relieve distress.

After the war, Johnson practised law in Richmond and represented railroad interests before the legislature. In the Virginia Senate (1875–79), he led in drafting the compromise measures designed to restore to order Virginia's tangled finances. From 1879 to 1890 he practised law in Baltimore, Md. His last years he spent in Amelia, Va. Besides articles on Virginia finances, he published: *Reports of Cases Decided by Chief Justice Chase 1865–69* (1876); *The Foundation of Maryland* (1883); *A Memoir of the Life and Public Service of Joseph E. Johnston* (1891); *General Washington* (1894); and the section on Maryland in Volume II of the *Confederate Military History* (1899), edited by C. A. Evans.

[*War of the Rebellion: Official Records (Army)*; *Who's Who in America*, 1901–02; *Battles and Leaders of the Civil War* (4 vols., 1887–88); W. W. Goldsborough, *The Md. Line in the Confed. Army* (1869); C. C. Pearson, *The Readjuster Movement in Va.* (1917); *The Biog. Cyc. of Representative Men of Md. and the District of Columbia* (1879); the *Sun* (Baltimore), Oct. 6, 1903.]

W. C. M.

JOHNSON, BUSHROD RUST (Oct. 7, 1817–Sept. 12, 1880), Confederate soldier, was born in Belmont County, Ohio, and after a common school education, entered West Point in 1836, graduating four years later in a class which included William Tecumseh Sherman. Grant was a fourth classman at the time. Assigned as second lieutenant to the 3rd Infantry, he was with a regiment that encountered much hardship and privation in the war with the Seminoles, and from 1843 to 1846, saw service in the West and Southwest. With the outbreak of war with Mexico, young Johnson participated in the battles of Palo Alto, Resaca de la Palma, Monterey, and the siege of Vera Cruz; and was on commissary duty in the latter city from Mar. 3 until Oct. 1, 1847, having been promoted first lieutenant, Feb. 29, 1844. He resigned from the army, Oct. 22, 1847, to become instructor in philosophy and chemistry at the Western Military Institute, Georgetown, Ky., and then, for four years more, superintendent of that institution (1851–55) and instructor in natural philosophy, mathematics, and engineering. When the school became part of the University of Nashville in 1855, Johnson became superintendent of the military college of the university, and professor of civil engineering. He held commissions in the militia of Kentucky as lieutenant-colonel (1849–51) and colonel (1851–54), and in the militia of Tennessee as colonel (1854–61). With the outbreak of the Civil War, he entered the Confederate army as a colonel of engineers, but was advanced to the rank of brigadier-general in January 1862. He commanded the garrison of Fort Henry when the latter fell before General Grant; and upon the fall of Fort Donelson, he succeeded in making his escape to the Confederate lines. He commanded a brigade at the battle of Shiloh (Apr. 6–7, 1862), where he was severely wounded, and took part in Bragg's invasion of Kentucky. He commanded a division at Chickamauga, and largely through his initiative the Federal right wing was swept from the field (*Battles and Leaders, post,* III, 655). He took part in the defense of Knoxville, and was soon after promoted major-general. He opposed Butler's assault on the Richmond railroad, near Petersburg (May 6–7, 1864), and took part in the engagement at Drewry's Bluff (May 16, 1864), where he captured the enemy's guns, but lost more than one-fourth of his division (*Ibid.,* IV, 202–03). He commanded South Carolina troops during the charge on the crater at Petersburg, and captured three stands of colors and 130 prisoners (*Ibid.,* 541, 567). With his division, he surrendered with Lee at Appomattox.

After the War, he returned to Tennessee, where in the year 1870 he became chancellor of the University of Nashville, and arranged to conduct a collegiate department of that institution with the Montgomery Bell Academy as a preparatory school. In June 1874, however, the school was compelled to close its doors for financial reasons. Broken in health, he passed his last years and died on a farm in Brighton, Macoupin County, Ill., his remains being interred in Miles Cemetery, where a monument marks his last resting-place (*Confederate Veteran,* December 1907, p. 551). His wife had died many years before, and his only son did not long survive his father.

[*Battles and Leaders of the Civil War* (4 vols., 1887–88), particularly III, 619–750, and IV, 196–565; *Twelfth Ann. Reunion Asso. Grads. U. S. Mil. Acad.* (1881); G. W. Cullum, *Biog. Reg. Officers and Grads. U. S. Mil. Acad.* (3rd ed., 1891, vol. II); J. H. McRae, "The Third Regiment of Infantry," *Jour. Mil. Service Inst. of the U. S.,* May 1895, repr. in T. F. Rodenbough, *The Army of the U. S.* (1896); H. M. Cist, *The Army of the Cumberland* (1882); A. A. Humphreys, *The Va. Campaign of '64 and '65* (1883).] C. D. R.

JOHNSON, BYRON BANCROFT (Jan. 6, 1864–Mar. 28, 1931), president of the American League of Professional Base Ball Clubs from 1900 to 1927, was one of three sons born to Alexander Byron and Eunice C. (Fox) Johnson at Norwalk, Ohio. As a youngster Ban Johnson, as he was later called, attended Oberlin and Marietta colleges but did not graduate from either institution. In later life (1897) he was given the degree of A.B. by Marietta College *honoris causa.* He attended a law school in Cincinnati but did not complete the course nor pursue the profession of law. When twenty-one years old he gave up his legal studies to become political and general reporter on the *Cincinnati Commercial Gazette.* A few years later he was made sports editor of that paper and thus came into contact with famous sporting figures, including ball players and owners of baseball clubs. One of these players, then manager of the Cincinnati team, was Charles A. Comiskey who, in 1893, persuaded the young reporter to accept the position of president of the Western League, a baseball organization that was just being revived after a financial collapse. For a year, while holding this office, he continued his newspaper work but in 1894 he abandoned it and cast his fortunes definitely with professional baseball.

The Western League at that time had teams in Kansas City, Detroit, Toledo, Indianapolis, Sioux City, Grand Rapids, Minneapolis, and Milwaukee. Young, ambitious, courageous, and with fine organizing ability, Johnson began to strengthen and improve the league, shifting the franchises and teams to larger cities with the idea of building up an organization to rival the National League, at that time the only major league of professional baseball. As the territory of the powerful National League was gradually invaded, a bitter baseball war developed in which "Big Ban" was victorious all along the line. After establishing itself in most of the big cities that formerly had been considered the exclusive baseball territory of the National League, the Western League changed its name to American League (1900) and three years later struck the National League a stunning blow by putting a club in New York, and thus rounding out a playing circuit on a par with that of its rival. With that blow the latter capitulated and accepted the American League as a major league organization on an equal footing. All this was due to the energy, skill, persistency, and financial shrewdness of Ban Johnson. Starting with clubs in small cities in the West, the American League, under Johnson, rose to a point where, at his death, the franchises and club properties of the circuit were estimated to be worth approximately $25,000,000; and the $2,500-a-year president of the Western League became the $40,000-a-year president of the American League.

Ban Johnson proposed and put through the scheme of holding a "World's Series" each autumn between the pennant-winning clubs of the two leagues. He drove rowdyism from the playing field and from the grandstand and bleachers, so that respectable people could witness baseball games with their families without being annoyed or insulted by the remarks or actions of any rough element. In 1920 there came the revelation that some Chicago White Sox players had been bribed to lose the World's Series of 1919 to the Cincinnati Club of the National League.

This scandal led the club owners to call in the federal judge, Kenesaw Mountain Landis, as commissioner of baseball with supreme authority. Though he had done much to help expose the scandal and to punish the wrongdoers, Johnson objected to the selection of any outsider to run baseball. He felt it a blow at his own dignity and authority. For this reason he bickered with Landis, and in the later years of his presidency precipitated one clash after another, gradually losing his authority and finally, in 1927, resigning his office. He was in poor health at the time and died in St. Louis, Mo., in March 1931. He is buried at Spencer, Ind. In 1894 he married Sarah Jane Laymon, who survived him. There were no children of this marriage. Huge in size, flamboyant, energetic, courageous, and ambitious, he did much to build up professional baseball to a high plane and for years was the most picturesque and powerful figure in the game.

[G. L. Moreland, *Balldom* (1914 and 1926); F. C. Richter, *Richter's Hist. and Records of Base Ball* (1914); *Spalding's Official Base Ball Guide*, 1901–32; *Saturday Evening Post*, Mar. 22, 1930; *Who's Who in America*, 1928–29; *Lit. Digest*, Mar. 27, 1926; *N. Y. Times, N. Y. Herald Tribune, World* (N. Y.), Mar. 29, 1931; personal acquaintance.]

J. K.

JOHNSON, CAVE (Jan. 11, 1793–Nov. 23, 1866), congressman and postmaster-general, was born near Springfield, Robertson County, Tenn., the son of Thomas and Mary (Noel) Johnson. His grandfather, Henry Johnson, removed from Pennsylvania to North Carolina during the Revolutionary War, in which struggle he served in the 10th Regiment of the North Carolina Continental Line. Thomas Johnson removed from North Carolina to the Tennessee country in 1789. He was a member of the first constitutional convention of Tennessee and of the first General Assembly, 1796; brigadier-general of militia, 1800; and led his brigade in the campaigns against the Creek Indians, 1813–14. Cave Johnson, commissioned a lieutenant, served as deputy quartermaster of his father's regiment in these campaigns of Gen. Andrew Jackson. He was educated at an academy and at Cumberland College, Nashville. He studied law under William W. Cooke, one-time supreme judge of Tennessee, and was elected prosecuting attorney in 1817. He was elected as a Democrat to represent his district in the Twenty-first and the three succeeding congresses (1829–37). As a Jacksonian, he met defeat by ninety votes in the political upheaval in Tennessee in 1836, but he was returned to the next three congresses (1839–45).

In the Polk-Clay contest for the presidency in 1844 Johnson was the confidential friend and adviser of Polk. He was of sound and vigorous though not brilliant parts and possessed of unusual sagacity and managerial skill in political affairs. He and Buchanan were the earliest selections by President Polk for cabinet places, Johnson being chosen for postmaster-general. He served as such throughout Polk's administration and did much to systematize the mail service, especially the service to foreign countries. On his recommendation postal rates were lowered and payment by the sender required. During his administration also the use of stamps, at first of denominations of five and ten cents, was introduced, the idea of a railway post-office was broached, and other steps were taken toward giving the government a monopoly in the carriage of the mails. Returning to the practice of law at his home in Clarksville, Tenn., he was appointed circuit judge in 1853. In 1854 he accepted the presidency of the State Bank of Tennessee and served for six years.

Johnson and Buchanan formed a close friendship while serving together in Polk's cabinet, and a correspondence covering many years resulted. Johnson was active in bringing Tennessee to the support of Buchanan for the presidency in 1856. On June 8, 1860, he was nominated by President Buchanan commissioner of the United States to settle disputed claims of citizens of the United States against the United States and Paraguay Navigation Company. In the decade before the Civil War he used his influence to stay sectional animosity, but when the conflict was on he adhered to the Southern Confederacy, in whose armies all of his sons enlisted. Shortly after the close of the war he was pardoned by President Johnson, an old congressional associate. In 1866 he was elected, without opposition, to the Tennessee Senate, but was not allowed to take his seat on the ground that he had given countenance to the Confederacy. Johnson was married to Elizabeth (Dortch) Brunson, Feb. 20, 1838. He died at Clarksville.

[The Buchanan-Johnson correspondence is to be found in the archives of the Pa. Hist. Soc.; the Polk-Johnson correspondence is with the Polk papers in the Lib. of Cong. Printed sources include: W. P. Titus, *Picturesque Clarksville, Past and Present* (1887); J. W. Caldwell, *Sketches of the Bench and Bar of Tenn.* (1898); Lucien B. Chase, *Hist. of the Polk Administration* (1850); St. George L. Souissat, "Tenn. and Nat. Pol. Parties," *Ann. Report, Am. Hist. Asso.*, 1914, vol. I, and *Letters of Jas. K. Polk to Cave Johnson, 1833–48* (n.d.), reprinted from the *Tenn. Hist. Mag.*, Sept. 1915; E. I. McCormac, *Jas. K. Polk* (1922).]

S. C. W.

JOHNSON, CHAPMAN (Mar. 12, 1779–July 12, 1849), Virginia lawyer and legislator, was born in Louisa County, Va., the son of

Thomas Johnson and his wife Jane Chapman. Despite the poverty of his youth, he was able to go to the College of William and Mary to study law, and in 1802 he was licensed to practise law in Richmond. On advice he removed to Staunton. His first years there were discouraging, but in 1805 he was admitted to the court of appeals and began "that career of forensic distinction which in a few years elevated him to the highest rank in his profession" (*Southern Literary Messenger,* November 1849, p. 676). In 1806 he married Mary Ann Nicholson of Richmond. In 1810 he was elected state senator from the Augusta district and, though frequently opposing the wishes of his constituents, he held this position for sixteen years. He was also active in the war of 1812 as captain of a company of horse and as aide to Gen. James Breckinridge. In 1824 his work forced him to return to Richmond. Thereafter he devoted his energies first to his appeals practice. He was admired for his professional zeal and high sense of duty and for his urbanity of manner. With Benjamin Watkins Leigh and Robert Stanard, his friends since college, he was one of "the great legal triumvirate, who swayed the Appellate Court of Virginia by their power and eloquence for a quarter of a century" (Dillon, *post,* I, 262). Among his many cases was the "long wrangle" over the wills of John Randolph of Roanoke.

Johnson was called by his old constituency across the Blue Ridge to serve in the memorable constitutional convention of 1829–30. Here he was one of the outstanding men in attendance. Representing the more democratic West he was a target for the vicious sarcasm of the aristocratic John Randolph, but from the convention he emerged unhurt, and his main principle—population as a basis for representation as against population *and* property—was adopted. He was devoted to the public welfare and was consulted continually on public measures. But with this devotion there was about him an independence that made him delight in joining minorities, and even at times a reluctance to be in the public eye at all. He held several minor political positions, however, and was recodifying the criminal laws of the state when his health broke. From 1819 to 1845 he was a member of the board of visitors of the University of Virginia, serving also, from 1836 to 1844, as rector.

[Esther C. M. Steele, "Chapman Johnson," *Va. Mag. of Hist. and Biog.,* Apr.–July 1927; *Proc. and Debates of the Va. State Convention of 1829–30* (1830); J. F. Dillon, *John Marshall: Life, Character, and Judicial Services* (1903), vol. I; P. A. Bruce, *Hist. of the Univ. of Va.,* vol. III (1921); J. L. Peyton, *Hist. of Augusta County* (1882); *Richmond Enquirer,* July 13, 1849.]

A. L. H.

JOHNSON, DAVID BANCROFT (Jan 10, 1856–Dec. 26, 1928), educator, was born at La Grange, Tenn., of both Puritan and Cavalier ancestry. His first American ancestor was a fellow-pioneer of John Winthrop. His father, David Bancroft Johnson, was born at Dresden, Me. After graduating at Bowdoin College he went south to teach and there met and married Margaret Emily White, a daughter of Col. John D. White, of Memphis, Tenn. He was called as president to La Grange College, Tennessee, but he died a year after the son David was born, and the mother returned to Memphis. The boy pursued his studies in the public schools of Memphis and of Nashville before entering at fifteen the preparatory department of the state university at Knoxville. Here he remained by self-help until he received in 1877 the degree of B.A. His appointment as assistant professor of mathematics, 1879–80, enabled him to complete his work for the master's degree. For the next two years (1880–82) he was superintendent of schools in Abbeville, S. C., and for one year in New Bern, N. C. In 1883 he returned to South Carolina to become the first superintendent of the schools of Columbia. Here he developed an organization which served as a model for other cities and towns of the state. Impressed with the need of well-trained teachers, and desiring to establish a training school for his own teachers, he went to Boston during the summer of 1886 and there through Robert C. Winthrop, chairman of the Peabody Board of Education, was granted for scholarships an annual appropriation of $1500, increased in 1888 to $2000. With this aid Johnson was able to open the Winthrop Training School in November 1886. Its first home was the chapel of the Columbia Theological Seminary, and its first enrolment was nineteen students taught by one teacher.

The school grew rapidly and state scholarships were awarded it even before it was launched as a state institution. In 1891 Johnson aroused the interest of Benjamin R. Tillman, then governor of the state, with whose aid the legislature was induced to make an appropriation for buildings and maintenance. Accordingly, in 1894, the corner-stone of the main building was laid at Rock Hill. In the fall of 1895 Winthrop College opened with twenty instructors and three hundred students. At the time of Johnson's death the plant had buildings and grounds worth considerably more than two million dollars, and a corps of a hundred and fifty officers and instructors ministering to nearly two thousand full-term students. The achievement itself is ample testimony of Johnson's abilities. In 1915–16 he was president of the National Education Association and in 1927 he received the first distinguished service medal awarded by the American Legion of South Carolina. He had married, in 1902, Mai Rutledge Smith, of Charleston, S. C., who with two sons and a daughter survived him.

[*Winthrop Jour.*, Memorial Number, Apr. 1929; Ralph E. Grier, *S. C. and Her Builders* (1930); J. C. Hemphill, *Men of Mark in S. C.*, vol. I (1907); *Jour. of Educ.*, Jan. 14, 1929; the *State* (Columbia, S. C.), Dec. 27, 28, 1928, Jan. 13, 1929; *Anderson Daily Mail*, Dec. 26, 1928; *Record* (Rock Hill) and *Herald* (Rock Hill), Dec. 27, 1928; *Proc. of the Trustees of the Peabody Educ. Fund*, 1886, 1888; private papers of Mrs. David Bancroft Johnson and Mrs. Paul Workman, Rock Hill, S. C.]
J. T. B.

JOHNSON, EASTMAN [See JOHNSON, JONATHAN EASTMAN, 1824–1906].

JOHNSON, EDWARD (September 1598–Apr. 23, 1672), colonial chronicler, was the son of William and Susan (Porredge) Johnson. His father was clerk of St. George's parish, Canterbury, where Edward was baptized Sept. 16 or 17, 1598. The son was brought up to the trade of a joiner, married Susan Munnter about 1618, and emigrated to Boston in 1630. He was licensed to trade with the Indians, admitted freeman in May 1631, and shortly after went back to England, returning with his family (wife, seven children and three servants) in 1636, in the midst of the Antinomian controversy, and settling in Charlestown, Mass. Johnson was somewhat unsettled by hearing that his venerated leaders were "under a covenant of Works," but after hearing a sermon of Thomas Shepard [*q.v.*] in Cambridge, his perplexities vanished and he became a defender of the standing order. One of the founders of Woburn in 1640, Johnson for thirty-two years was active in the affairs of that town as proprietor, clerk, selectman, militia captain, and deputy (1634–72, excepting 1647–48) to the General Court, which also employed him in the surveying of bounds, the inspection of arms and munitions, as commissioner to apprehend Samuel Gorton, and (with Richard Bellingham and Nathaniel Ward) on a committee "for perfecting the lawes." Johnson's title to fame, however, rests upon his authorship of the history of New England which he began to write about May 1650, and called *The Wonder-Working Providence of Sion's Saviour in New England.* Written with the avowed purpose to overwhelm the enemies of Massachusetts by evidence of divinely ordained success, and to hearten friends by stories of marvelous providences, Johnson's work is not an authority to be wholly relied upon in controversial matters, or for the events of the years when he was absent. But he gives many homely facts, such as the founding of new towns, the housing, food, and occupations of the people, which were ignored by more intellectual chroniclers like Bradford and Winthrop. Both the prose and the doggerel verse of *The Wonder-Working Providence* breathe "the very spirit and aroma of New England thought"; for Johnson was a representative man, a follower rather than a leader, one hundred per cent. loyal to the faith and the policy of the Puritan commonwealth. The keynote of his attitude is struck by one of his verses:

You that have seen these wondrous works by Sions Savior don,
Expect not miracle, lest means thereby you over-run;
The noble Acts Jehovah wrought, his Israel to redeem,
Surely this second work of his shall far more glorious seem.

[See M. C. Tyler, *A Hist. of Am. Lit.*, vol. I (1878); Samuel Sewall, *The Hist. of Woburn* (1868); *Records of the Gov. and Company of the Mass. Bay in New Eng.*, vols. I–IV (1853–54); Alfred Johnson, *Hist. and Geneal. of One Line of Descent from Capt. Edward Johnson* (1914), reprinted from the *New Eng. Hist. and Geneal. Reg.*, Apr. 1913; and J. Franklin Jameson's introduction to *Johnson's Wonder-Working Providence* (1910) in the Original Narratives of Early American History. The first edition was published anonymously at London in 1653 (dated 1654), with the title, *A Hist. of New Eng.* Another was edited by Wm. F. Poole (Andover, Mass., 1867).]
S. E. M.

JOHNSON, EDWARD (Apr. 16, 1816–Mar. 2, 1873), soldier, farmer, was born at Salisbury, near Midlothian, Chesterfield County, Va., the son of Dr. Edward Johnson, who later moved to Kentucky. After early schooling in the latter state, young Johnson received appointment to West Point July 1, 1833, graduating five years later. He served with his regiment, the 6th Infantry, in the Florida War, 1838–41, saw much frontier service in the Middle West, 1842–46, and served throughout the Mexican War, participating in the siege of Vera Cruz, and in the battles of Cerro Gordo, Churubusco, Molino del Rey, Chapultepec, and in the assault and capture of the City of Mexico. For his distinguished service in the Mexican War, the state of Virginia voted him a sword, as did also his fellow citizens of Chesterfield County. He was brevetted captain and major, respectively, for gallant and meritorious services at Molino del Rey and at Chapultepec, and was promoted first lieutenant in 1839, and captain in 1851, both commissions being in the 6th Infantry. On June 10, 1861, he resigned from the United States army to accept the colonelcy of the 12th Georgia Volunteers, Confederate army, and was promoted to brigadier-general, Dec. 11, 1861, and to major-general, Feb. 28, 1863. He was wounded at

McDowell, Va., May 8, 1862, where he commanded a brigade, and took part with Early's corps in engagements at Winchester and Martinsburg, and in the occupation of Carlisle, Pa. He commanded "Stonewall" Jackson's old division in the battle of Gettysburg and participated in the operations at Payne's Farm and in the battles of the Wilderness and Spottsylvania, where he was taken prisoner after gallantly resisting Hancock's onslaught at the Bloody Angle, May 12, 1864. After exchange as a prisoner of war, Johnson commanded a division in Lee's corps of Hood's army in the invasion of Tennessee and took part in the disastrous battles before Nashville—being again captured by the Federal army at Nashville, Tenn., Dec. 16, 1864.

After the war, Johnson engaged in farming at his old home in Chesterfield County, Va., and died in his fifty-seventh year at Ford's Hotel, Richmond. He had never married. Immediately on his death, the General Assembly of Virginia passed resolutions of eulogy and of regret, and adjourned out of respect for Johnson's memory. His body lay in state in the state Capitol—flags at half-staff—until the day of his funeral, Mar. 4, which took place from St. Paul's Protestant Episcopal Church, with interment at Hollywood Cemetery "in the presence of a large concourse of civil and military officers and friends."

[*Fourth Ann. Reunion, Asso. Grads., U. S. Mil. Acad.*, 1873; *Battles and Leaders of the Civil War* (4 vols., 1887–88); G. W. Cullum, *Biog. Reg. . . . U. S. Mil. Acad.* (3rd ed., 1891), vol. I; F. B. Heitman, *Hist. Reg. and Dict. of the U. S. Army* (1903), vol. I; *Horace* Porter, *Campaigning with Grant* (1897); the *Times-Dispatch* (Richmond), Nov. 26, 1905; the *Richmond Daily Whig* and the *Daily Dispatch* (Richmond), Mar. 4, 5, 1873.] C. D. R.

JOHNSON, EDWIN FERRY (May 23, 1803–Apr. 12, 1872), civil engineer, was born at Essex, Vt., the son of John and Rachel (Ferry) Johnson. When he was six, the family moved to Burlington, Vt., where Edwin studied Latin with the Unitarian minister, and was taught land surveying, his father's profession, by his father. In 1818 the father was a member of the northeastern boundary commission, and Edwin, though only fifteen, assisted him. After five years of surveying experience with his father, Johnson entered the American Literary, Scientific, and Military Academy at Middletown, Conn., the forerunner of Norwich University. There he was successively student and tutor, 1823–25, instructor in mathematics and assistant professor of natural history, 1825–26, and professor of mathematics and civil engineering, 1826–29. In his engineering courses he included discussions of railroad construction and railroad economics as early as 1825. In 1829, the institution was moved to Vermont, and after conducting a small school for a brief time at Middletown, Johnson gave up teaching. He was in charge of land surveys for the Erie Canal, 1829, the Champlain Canal, 1830–31, and the Morris Canal, 1831. Shortly thereafter he made his first active connection with railroad work as assistant engineer in charge of surveys for the Catskill & Canajoharie Railroad, 1831. His record from 1833 to 1861 is practically a review of the transportation facilities that were constructed during that period. He was engaged as chief engineer or principal assistant in the location of fourteen railroads, including the New York & Erie, the New York & Boston, the Chicago, St. Paul & Fond du Lac (now part of the Chicago & Northwestern), and of four canals, one of which was the Ontario & Hudson Ship Canal. He designed and directed the construction of three important bridges, and was for several years the president of the Stevens Association at Hoboken, N. J., which operated a railroad and steamship lines. He also supplied specifications and estimates to the federal government for the construction of a bridge over the Potomac River at Washington, 1832, designed a waterworks and sewerage system for Middletown, Conn., surveyed, and compiled a new city charter for that city. In 1861 his services were sought by the government in the prosecution of the Civil War. He declined a commission as brigadier-general and later declined the position of assistant secretary of war, but at the request of the War Department prepared a "Report . . . upon the Defences of Maine" (*Senate Executive Document 41*, 37 Cong., 2 Sess., 1862), and a *Report of a General Plan of Operations to the Secretary of War*, which he published as a pamphlet in 1863. In 1864 he conducted a cabinet and congressional party over the northeastern boundary. His successful railroad service and his numerous writings, established him as one of the foremost railroad engineers of his day. Starting with his *Review of the Project for a Great Western Railway* (1831), in which he advocated an extensive system of railroads to the Mississippi River, he continued to press the subject of great national railroads. In 1854 he wrote *The Railroad to the Pacific, Northern Route, Its General Character, Relative Merits, Etc.*, and on June 14, 1867, he was appointed chief engineer of the Northern Pacific Railroad. He held this position four years, after which he was consulting engineer to the road until his death. Gen. W. Milnor Roberts, who succeeded him as chief engineer, said, "The Northern Pacific Railroad and the American people . . . are indebted more to the intelligent forecast and untiring energy of Edwin F. Johnson than to any other individual" (Ellis, *post,* II, 151). The Northern Pacific is constructed upon practically the lines that he advocated in his work of 1854. In 1866 he published *The Navigation of the Lakes and Navigable Communications therefrom to the Seaboard.* He was the inventor of an improvement for canal locks, a screw-power press, a six-wheeled locomotive truck, and an eight-wheeled locomotive. He had wide business connections beyond the field of railroads and, though he refused many political offices, served two years as mayor of Middletown, 1856–57, and as a state senator in 1856. He married, Sept. 7, 1830, Charlotte Shaler of New York and Middletown, by whom he had eight children. He died in New York City.

[*Norwich University, 1819–1911, Her History, Her Graduates, Her Roll of Honor* (3 vols., 1911), ed. by Wm. A. Ellis; E. V. Smalley, *Hist. of the Northern Pacific R. R.* (1883); *Alumni Record of Wesleyan Univ.* (Centenary ed., 1931), p. viii; *Hist. of Middlesex County, Conn., with Biog. Sketches* (1884); *Railroad Gazette,* Apr. 20, 1872.] F. A. T.

JOHNSON, ELIAS HENRY (Oct. 15, 1841–Mar. 10, 1906), Baptist theologian, was the son of Elias Johnson, who had moved from Massachusetts to Troy, N. Y., where he became a prosperous manufacturer of stoves. The mother was Laura Gale, a Vermont woman. While both parents were religious, it was her influence which was especially penetrating and enduring. Elias early decided to enter the ministry and he began his preparatory work in the Troy high school, completing it at Essex, Conn. His college course was taken at the University of Rochester, where he ranked well as a student, receiving the degree of A.B. in 1862. Having applied himself too assiduously to his studies, he postponed his theological course for a year, averting idleness by studying law. His health broke again during his first year in Rochester Theological Seminary, and in April 1864 he entered the paymaster's service in the navy, having some sea service in the later months of the war; he did not retire until August 1866.

Going to the Northwest in the hope that the climate would prove beneficial, he was ordained to the Baptist ministry, Dec. 9, 1866, and served the church at Lesueur, Minn., for about two years. On Feb. 14, 1867, he married Mary Anna Lyon. Returning to Rochester in 1868, he pursued the three years' theological course there, graduating in 1871. His interest in music was always strong and he was active both as chorister and as composer. The condition of his health made immediate assumption of ministerial labors unwise, and with his wife he spent two years abroad, where he engaged in travel and study. Upon his return, after a short pastorate at Ballston Spa, N. Y. (November 1873–February 1875), he was called to Brown Street Baptist Church, Providence, R. I., continuing as pastor after it became the Union Baptist Church. Here he built up a reputation as a strong preacher, virile in thought and effective in expression. He declined the chair of church history at Rochester Theological Seminary, but in 1882 became professor of systematic theology at Crozier Theological Seminary, where his most distinctive work was done. His chief theological writings were *Outline of Systematic Theology* (1891, 1901); *Religious Use of Imagination* (1901); *The Holy Spirit, Then and Now* (1904); and the posthumously published *Christian Agnosticism as Related to Christian Knowledge: The Critical Principle in Theology* (1907). He edited a much-used hymn book, *Sursum Corda* (1898), and *Ezekiel Gilman Robinson, an Autobiography* (1896), and also contributed regularly to the religious press. His article, "The Idea of Law," in the *Baptist Review,* July 1888, he considered his most important contribution to theological thought. He was an ardent champion of freedom of speech and one of the most influential leaders in the organization of the Baptist Congress, which afforded a platform more open for the independent utterance of varying views than was to be found elsewhere even in such free organizations as his denomination provided. He was a man of intense nervous temperament, acutely sensitive to esthetic values, keen in logical power. His first wife died in December 1904, and on Sept. 2, 1905, about six months before his own death, he married Lillian Morgan.

[A biographical sketch and appreciation by H. C. Vedder, in Johnson's *Christian Agnosticism* (1907); G. E. Horr in *The Watchman* (Boston), Mar. 22, 1906; Rochester Theolog. Sem., *Gen. Cat. 1850–1910* (1910); *Who's Who in America,* 1906–07; *The Press,* and *Public Ledger* (Phila.), Mar. 11, 1906.] W. H. A.

JOHNSON, ELIJAH (*c.* 1780–Mar. 23, 1849), one of the founders of Liberia, was probably born in New Jersey. Nothing is known of his parentage. At any rate, he was in New Jersey in 1789 and there and in New York received some schooling. He took part in the War of 1812, serving in New Jersey, New York, and Massachusetts. For a while, he studied for the Methodist ministry. In February 1820 he joined the pioneer company of emigrants who left New York on the ship *Elizabeth* to establish an American negro settlement in Africa, a group consisting of eighty-eight colored persons and three white representatives of the United States government and the American Colonization Society.

Two commissioners of the Colonization Society had previously recommended the British colony of Sierra Leone as a place of settlement. The British Governor, however, would not permit the Americans to make permanent settlement there. They, therefore, went temporarily to the Island of Shebro, where many of them, including the three white men, died of fever. Elijah Johnson and another negro, Daniel Coker, took charge of the colony until the next year, when a second vessel arrived. The coast was explored and the present site of the capital of Liberia was finally chosen for settlement. The colonists landed first on Perseverance Island in the harbor below Cape Mesurado, but the place was low and unhealthy, the natives hostile, and there was difficulty with the white slave-traders. Eli Ayres, the white American in charge, was discouraged and wished to return to Sierra Leone. To this proposition Johnson was strongly opposed. He said: "Two years long have I wanted a home. Here I have found one, here I remain" (Johnston, *post,* I, 130). His stubborn determination decided the permanent settlement of Liberia.

Ayres returned to America, leaving Johnson in charge. Knowing that another rainy season passed on Perseverance Island would be fatal, in spite of native opposition he climbed the high Cape and cleared the site of Monrovia, future capital. The natives shot at the workers from the shelter of the forest and launched determined attacks upon them. A British gunboat appeared off the Cape and the commanders offered to punish the natives if Johnson would cede a piece of land to the British government and hoist the British flag. Johnson refused point-blank, remarking: "We want no flagstaff put up here; that will cost us more to get it down than it will to whip the natives" (Starr, *post,* p. 65).

Jehudi Ashmun, another white representative of the Colonization Society and by far the most efficient, arrived in August 1822. He found Johnson in charge, but the negotiations with the natives still unsettled. He put the colony under military law and made Johnson commissary of stores. In the years following, the colony, under the black men, Elijah Johnson and Lott Carey, and the white man, Jehudi Ashmun (who died in 1827), fought for existence against the natives and against the fever. The colonial troops in all cases were led by Elijah Johnson, and his energetic action gradually brought the neighborhood chiefs into submission and alliance. The colony grew and began to take definite shape. Johnson was a member of the conference which made solemn declaration of independence in July 1847. He died Mar. 23, 1849, having lived to see Liberia an independent state and a colored man elected as first president. His descendants to this day form one of the leading families in Liberia. His son, Hilary R. W. Johnson, served as president from 1884 to 1892.

[R. R. Gurley, *Life of Jehudi Ashmun* (1835); Sir Harry Johnston, *Liberia* (2 vols., London, 1906); Frederick Starr, *Liberia* (1913); T. H. B. Walker, *Liberia* (1921); Archibald Alexander, *A Hist. of Colonization on the Western Coast of Africa* (1846); *The African Repository and Colonial Journal* (Washington, D. C.), *passim,* esp. issue for Aug. 1849 which reprints obituary from the *Liberia Herald* (Monrovia), Apr. 27, 1849.]

W. E. B. D.

JOHNSON, ELLEN CHENEY (Dec. 20, 1829–June 28, 1899), educator, prison reformer, was born at Athol, Mass., the only child of Nathan and Rhoda (Holbrook) Cheney. Her father was a mill agent or manager, and her association with him brought to her much business experience. She attended school at Weare, N. H., and the Academy at Francestown; and taught school for a short time at Weare. At the age of eighteen she joined a temperance organization. When twenty she married Jesse Cram Johnson, a native of Unity, N. H., who became a business man in Boston. Their home, close by the State House, was a rendezvous for welfare workers. Mrs. Johnson was on the executive and finance committees of the New England branch of the United States Sanitary Commission; she canvassed widely for supplies, and herself taught women in a poor part of Boston to cut and sew, to cook and save. Such work took her into correctional institutions, and she was a leading promoter of the Temporary Asylum for Discharged Female Prisoners, opened in Dedham in 1864. She became one of a group which persistently urged the establishment of a separate prison for women, to be wholly under the care of women. In 1877 the Reformatory Prison for Women was opened at Sherborn, near Framingham. In 1879 when a state commission was created, with broad powers, for the establishment of a real prison system, Mrs. Johnson was appointed one of the five commissioners, and in 1884 she became superintendent of Sherborn. Throughout her fifteen years of service she proved herself a rare administrator. She not only developed industries within doors and on the farm but made recreation a means to higher interests and better living. She also developed a system of indenture for house service in families outside prison walls, under sympathetic supervision. The keynote of her administration was the conviction that every woman should have a fair start in a new life and that every effort should be made in that direction. She impressed upon her prisoners the validity of punishment, even when it was severe, but she believed equally in the efficacy of gentleness and patience with offenders. She stressed the need of finding methods of helping each woman to win self-control, and insisted that the first duty of the prison official was to familiarize himself or herself thoroughly with the physical, mental, and moral peculiarities of each prisoner. Many visitors came to observe and study the reformatory at Sherborn and it received the highest praise from prison experts. A bronze medal and diploma were awarded to Mrs. Johnson by the World's Columbian Exposition "for evidence of a model management in every detail." Her death occurred suddenly in London, England, after she had addressed the Women's International Congress, June 28, 1899. She left money to the City of Boston, in memory of her husband, for the erection of "a drinking fountain for man and beast."

[S. J. Barrows, *The Reformatory System in the U. S.* (1900); *Ann. Reports of the Commissioners of Prisons of Mass.*, 1884–99; *Charities Rev.*, July, Oct., Dec. 1899; C. H. Pope, *The Cheney Geneal.* (1897); *Boston Transcript*, June 28, 30, 1899; *Boston Herald*, July 3, 1899.]
J. R. B.

JOHNSON, FRANKLIN (Nov. 2, 1836–Oct. 9, 1916), Baptist clergyman, author, educator, was born at Frankfort, Ohio, the son of Rev. Hezekiah Johnson, of a Maryland family, and Eliza Shepherd (Harris) Johnson. His parents, Baptist missionaries on the frontier, were instrumental in founding Denison University at Granville. In 1845, prompted by Marcus Whitman and Ezra Fisher, they removed to Oregon City, Ore., where they established the first Baptist church on the Pacific Coast and helped found Oregon City (now McMinnville) College. Franklin Johnson peddled milk, taught school at The Dalles, and assisted in the printing office of the *Argus*. At the age of twenty-one he went east to Colgate Theological Seminary and while there he was delegated by the Republicans of Oregon, at the instance of his older brother, to represent them in the Chicago convention of 1860, where, after casting a first instructed ballot for W. H. Seward, he voted for Abraham Lincoln. Graduating from Colgate in 1861 and ordained in 1862, he served as a missionary in Bay City, Mich., 1861–63; then as pastor at Lambertville, N. J., 1864–66, and at the First Baptist Church, Passaic, N. J., 1866–72. Granted a leave of absence in 1869, he took a doctorate in divinity at the University of Jena. After a short pastorate at the Clinton Avenue Baptist Church, Newark, N. J., 1872–74, he went to the Old Cambridge (Mass.) Baptist Church. This period of his life, 1874–88, was exceedingly fertile in friendships (with Phillips Brooks, H. W. Longfellow, J. R. Lowell, William James, and others) and in authorship. With Dr. George Lorimer he served as co-editor of the *Watchman* from 1876 to 1880, contributing many editorials. He published three studies for Bible students in the International Sunday School Commentary: *The Gospel According to St. Matthew* (1873), *Moses and Israel* (1874), *Heroes and Judges from the Law-givers to the Kings* (1875), in which he adopted with caution the conclusions of his German critical teachers. An excellent English translation of *Dies Irae* appeared in 1880, to be followed in 1886 by *The Stabat Mater Speciosa and the Stabat Mater Dolorosa.* He also published: *True Womanhood: Hints on the Formation of Womanly Character* (1882); *A Romance in Song: Heine's Lyrical Interlude* (1884); *The New Psychic Studies in their Relation to Christian Thought* (1886). His contributions to symposia and encyclopedias were numerous and of solid merit (*e.g.*, his chapter on "The Atonement" in *Theology at the Dawn of the Twentieth Century*, 1901, edited by J. V. Morgan; sermon on "Our Duty to the Weaker Races of Man" in Vol. V of *Modern Sermons by World Scholars*, 1909, edited by Robert Scott and W. C. Stiles; introduction to *The New Testament Church*, 1898, by W. H. H. Marsh). He contributed articles and book reviews to periodicals, notably to the *Journal of Theology.* In 1888 he resigned his pulpit in Cambridge and traveled in Europe, spending the winter in Athens. The next year he was called to the presidency of Ottawa University, Kansas, which he left in 1892 to join the faculty of the University of Chicago as assistant professor of church history and homiletics. He became associate professor in 1894, professor in 1895, and professor emeritus in 1908. His chief theological work was produced in 1896: *The Quotations of the New Testament from the Old Considered in the Light of General Literature*; while his considerable pulpit and literary activity is evinced by such works as *The Home Missionaries* (1899); *Have We the Likeness of Christ?* (1901); *The Christian's Relation to Evolution* (1904). He served as trustee of the Newton Theological Seminary, 1883–91, and was a member of the executive committee of the Baptist Foreign Mission Society, 1885–88. After his retirement from the University, he visited Japan, China, India, and Palestine in his interest in missions, and thereafter made his home in Brookline, Mass., where he died.

He married Mary Alma Barton, in Buffalo, N. Y., Sept. 28, 1863, and after her death in 1882, married Persis Isabel Swett of Boston, June 29, 1886. Two children of his first marriage survived him. Johnson's scholarship was full and exact. In theological matters he was a liberal conservative, and though intellectually scrupulous and candid, he departed little from the beliefs in which he was reared.

[*Boston Transcript*, Oct. 9, 1916; *Watchman-Examiner*, Oct. 12, 1916; *Cambridge Chronicle*, Oct. 14, 1916; *Morning Oregonian* (Oregon City, Oregon), Oct. 26, 1916; *University Record* (Univ. of Chicago), Jan. 1917; *Who's Who in America*, 1916–17.]

C. H. L—e.

JOHNSON, GUY (*c.* 1740–Mar. 5, 1788), superintendent of Indian affairs, Loyalist, was born in Ireland, and may have been a nephew of Sir William Johnson [*q.v.*]. Coming to America at an early age, he was in the Mohawk Valley by 1756. He served throughout the French and Indian War, a part of the time as secretary to Sir William. He also held a commission as lieutenant in one of the New York independent companies and commanded a company of rangers under General Amherst in the campaign of 1759–60. Following the war, he was for a time colonel and adjutant general in the New York Militia. In 1762, he was appointed "Deputy for the Six Nations and Neighbouring Indians," under Sir William. As deputy agent he attended many Indian councils, serving occasionally as secretary to the Superintendent, and sometimes acting for him during his absence. Great confidence was reposed in him, both by Sir William and by the Indians themselves. In 1763 he was married to Sir William's daughter, Mary, and established his residence at Guy Park, near Amsterdam, N. Y. He was elected to the New York assembly for the term 1773–75. Upon the death of his father-in-law in 1774, he was directed by General Gage to assume the duties of superintendent of the northern department for the time being, the appointment being later confirmed from England.

Immediately upon the outbreak of revolutionary disturbances the following year, Johnson invited the cooperation of the Six Nations in the British cause and fortified Guy Hall, but in the latter part of May he retired to Lake Ontario, where he assembled a large number of Indians and secured their promises of assistance. In July 1775 he proceeded to Montreal, accompanied by some Indians and 220 rangers. He organized the Indians in that vicinity and for a time assisted in the defense of St. John's. In the following winter he visited England, but returned to America in the summer of 1776, arriving at Staten Island on July 29. It was his purpose to further military cooperation between the Indians and British on the New York frontier, but he was able to accomplish little.

In September 1778, he at last left New York for Quebec but, being obliged to winter at Halifax, did not reach his destination until July 1779. He then proceeded by way of Montreal to the upper country, and was with the British and Indians at the battle near Newtown, New York, in August 1779. During the ensuing two years he made his headquarters at Niagara, and incited the Indians to raiding expeditions along the back settlements. He was succeeded in his position as superintendent in 1782 by Sir John Johnson [*q.v.*]. After the Revolution Johnson, like many Loyalists, went to England, where he endeavored to secure compensation for the losses sustained by the confiscation of his estates. He died in London in 1788. A not too sympathetic contemporary observer described him as "a short, pursy man, of stern countenance and haughty demeanor," adding, "His voice was harsh, and his tongue bore evidence of his Irish extraction" (Stone, *Brant*, II, 67). He claimed credit for having inspired the raid which culminated in the Wyoming massacre.

[Lorenzo Sabine, *Biog. Sketches of Loyalists of the Am. Rev.* (1864), vol. I; *Dict. Nat. Biog.*; W. L. Stone, *Life of Joseph Brant* (2 vols., 1838) and *The Life and Times of Sir William Johnson* (2 vols., 1865); A. M. Davis, "The Indians and the Border Warfare of the Revolution," in Justin Winsor, *Narr. and Crit. Hist. of America*, vol. VI (1888); E. B. O'Callaghan, *Docs. Rel. to the Colonial Hist. of the State of N. Y.*, vols. VII, VIII (1856–57); *The Papers of Sir William Johnson* (7 vols. to date, 1921–31); R. E. Day, *Calendar of the Sir William Johnson MSS. in the N. Y. State Lib.* (1909); transcripts of Haldimand Papers, British Museum, in the Canadian Archives at Ottawa, calendared in *Report on Canadian Archives*, 1884–89 (1885–90); obituary in *Gentleman's Mag.*, Mar. 1788.]

W. E. S—s.

JOHNSON, HELEN LOUISE KENDRICK (Jan. 4, 1844–Jan. 3, 1917), author, daughter of Asahel Clark and Ann (Hopkins) Kendrick, was born at Hamilton, N. Y. Her father, professor of Greek in Madison University (later Colgate), in 1850 became professor of Greek in Rochester University. The following year Mrs. Kendrick died and for some years Helen lived either in a boarding house in Rochester, attending Miss Doolittle's School, or with her mother's sister at Clinton. From 1860 to 1863 she was not well, but from September 1863 to June 1864 she studied at Oread Institute at Worcester, Mass. Her school education was slight, but under the influence of a cultured father, she was always a great reader. Visiting the South, she wrote for a newspaper edited by Rossiter Johnson a story, "A Night in Atlanta." Soon after, in 1867, she met the young editor at her father's Rochester home and on May 20, 1869, they were married. They went to live at Concord, N. H., where Johnson was editor of the *New Hampshire Statesman.* Mrs. Johnson immediately began writing stories and Bible sketches for her husband's paper. Her first book, *Roddy's Romance,* for children, was not published until 1874. The Johnsons had four children, three of whom died in infancy; one daughter, Florence, survived her mother. In 1873 they removed to New York, where Mrs. Johnson undertook her most important literary work, *Our Familiar Songs and Those Who Made Them* (1881), a collection of over three hundred songs, with piano accompaniments and histories of the writers and songs. The family spent the summers in Europe, touring the West, on Staten Island, at Suffern, N. Y., Monmouth and Casco Bay, Me., Oak Ridge, N. J., and finally in their own summer home at Amagansett, Long Island. In New York Mrs. Johnson devoted much time to writing but was also active in club and social work. She was on the board of managers of the Henry Street Settlement and founded the Meridian Club and the Guidon Club, an anti-suffrage organization. For two years, 1894–96, she was editor of the *American Woman's Journal,* which covered art, literary, scientific, and household subjects. Through her editorship she became interested in the woman suffrage movement and was convinced that the suffrage was not wise for women. She wrote *Woman and the Republic* (1897), a discussion of the arguments of the advocates of suffrage, and many pamphlets and newspaper articles against the movement, besides speaking before legislative committees at Albany and Washington. A list of her published works includes: The Roddy Books (3 vols., 1874–76); *Tears for the Little Ones* (1878), quotations on the loss of children; *Illustrated Poems and Songs for Young People* (1884); The Nutshell Series (1884), six volumes of songs and epigrams from various sources; *Raleigh Westgate; or, Epimenides in Maine* (1889), her only novel; *A Dictionary of Terms, Phrases, and Quotations* (1895), edited in collaboration with the Rev. Henry Percy Smith; *Great Essays* (1900); and *Mythology and Folk-Lore of the North American Indian* (1908). She also contributed many articles to newspapers, magazines, and to *Appletons' Annual Cyclopaedia.* During years of hard work Mrs. Johnson found recreation at Amagansett. Here, in 1892, she and her daughter designed and built "Bluff Cottage." Later they built other cottages and Mrs. Johnson personally furnished them for tenants. The last cottage, "Thalatta," became their favorite summer home. In her last years Mrs. Johnson, always a Bible student, wrote "The Aryan Ancestry of Christ," and during her final illness completed "Woman's Place in Creation," neither of which was published. She died in New York City and was buried in Mount Hope Cemetery, Rochester.

[Rossiter Johnson, *Helen Kendrick Johnson (Mrs. Rossiter Johnson): the Story of her Varied Activities* (1917); *Who's Who in America,* 1916–17; obituaries in the *N. Y. Times* and *N. Y. Tribune,* Jan. 5, 1917.]

S. G. B.

JOHNSON, HENRY (June 25, 1855–Feb. 7, 1918), teacher, poet, translator, was born at Gardiner, Me., of old New England ancestry, the son of Richard Elliott and Louisa Abbie (Reed) Johnson. After attending local schools and Phillips Andover Academy, he went to Bowdoin College where he was graduated in the class of 1874 at the age of nineteen. At college he had the reputation of being very shy and reserved; he gave but little evidence of future distinction. Determining to devote his life to scholarship, from 1875 to 1877 he studied abroad at Göttingen and Paris; in 1884 he took his degree of Ph.D. at the University of Berlin. All his teaching was done at Bowdoin College. There he was instructor in modern languages from 1877 to 1881, and professor from 1881 until his death in 1918, holding the Longfellow Chair after 1882. He was also librarian from 1880 to 1885. As important as his professorship was his work as curator of the art collections of the college. The Walker Art Museum was built when he held this position and under his direction all the collections were placed and catalogued. On July 26, 1881, he married Frances M. Robinson, of Thomaston, Me., by whom he had two daughters. He died at Brunswick, Feb. 7, 1918, and was buried there.

As a teacher in a small college, Johnson not only gave the usual courses in the modern languages but also in his later years instruction in the history and appreciation of art. Like Charles Eliot Norton at Harvard, he not only taught the history of art and Dante but gave his students "a correct view of life." He was all his life interested in textual criticism. As a young man he edited *Schiller's Ballads* (1888) and *A Midsommer Nights Dreame* (1888). His *Macbeth,* a critical text, was published posthumously in 1921. He also published two volumes of selected verse, *"Where Beauty Is"* (1898) and *"The Seer"* (1910). His poems, though perhaps at times lacking in clarity, are classical in spirit, full of vivid phrases, and reflect a deeply spiritual nature. It is in his translations, however, that he made his most important contribution to American letters: *Les Trophées, José Maria de Heredia* (1910), from the French, is remarkable for its lyrical qualities and felicity of phrase; his *La Comedia di Dante Alighieri: The Divine Comedy* (1915) was almost literally the work of a lifetime. He also translated all the poems in the *Vita Nuova.* In the *Divine Comedy,* he used the medium of blank verse, and although he abandoned the rhyme of the original, he reproduced with remarkable success its music and rhythm. The translation swiftly won recognition as an achievement worthy to stand alongside of Longfellow's and gained warm commendation from European Dante scholars, the critic Pio Rajna declaring that it was closer to the original than any other translation in any language he had read.

[K. C. M. Sills, "Henry Johnson," *Bowdoin Coll. Bull.,* June 1918; L. C. Hatch, *The Hist. of Bowdoin Coll.* (1927); *Gen. Cat. of Bowdoin Coll.* (1912); *Who's Who in America,* 1916–17.] K. C. M. S.

JOHNSON, HERSCHEL VESPASIAN (Sept. 18, 1812–Aug. 16, 1880), jurist, Confederate senator, the son of Moses and Nancy (Palmer) Johnson, was born in Burke County, Ga. He was educated at the University of Georgia (B.A. 1834). Before his graduation he married, Dec. 19, 1833, Mrs. Ann (Polk) Walker, daughter of Judge William Polk of Maryland. After a few years of successful legal practice in Augusta, in Jefferson County, and in Milledgeville, he served one year of an unexpired term in the United States Senate (Feb. 14, 1848–Mar. 3, 1849). He was soon thereafter elected by the legislature to the judgeship of Ocmulgee Circuit, but continued to take an interest in the controversy resulting from the acquisition of territory in the Mexican War. He maintained that the North and the South should share equally in the benefits to be derived from the territories and that the people of each territory should decide for themselves the question of slavery. The compromise measures of 1850 did not meet with his approval but he was willing to accept them rather than to encourage the spirit of secession, although at this time he insisted that the rights of the South in the Union should be recognized.

He was elected by the Democrats to the governorship of Georgia and served two terms, 1853–57. While he deplored the resort to force in the territory of Kansas by both the advocates and opponents of slavery, he supported the Kansas-Nebraska Act of 1854. Writing to a group of influential Northern men in regard to the extension of slavery into the territories, he said: "The South does not desire to increase the slave power in the government for the purpose of aggrandizement. She rather desires to retain her power—preserve an equilibrium—to enable her to counteract aggression under the forms of legislation" (Flippin, *post,* p. 73). Johnson sincerely deplored the division within the Democratic party which occurred in the National Democratic Convention at Charleston in 1860, maintaining that the disruption of the Democratic party, the only truly national party, threatened the continuance of the Union, for the Republican party was a sectional party, committed to a policy which would antagonize the South to the point of secession. He pleaded earnestly but unsuccessfully for harmony in the Georgia Democratic convention of June 1860. In that month, at Baltimore, the national wing of the Democratic party nominated him for the vice-presidency on the ticket with Stephen A. Douglas. His acceptance of the nomination brought severe criticism upon him in Georgia, but he fearlessly argued that the best interests of the South depended upon the success of the National Democrats. Between the election of Lincoln and his inauguration Johnson maintained that the wisest and best policy of the South would be to postpone secession until Lincoln should have the opportunity of at least attempting to settle the sectional controversy. He strenuously opposed secession in the Georgia convention, January 1861, and offered resolutions calling for a convention of the slaveholding states at Atlanta which he hoped might result in the adoption of some line of action which would be acceded to by the non-slaveholding states. By a vote of 166 to 130, however, the convention decided to take Georgia out of the Union.

Although he acquiesced in secession once it had been voted, Johnson never expected the Confederacy to succeed. For the first year and a half of the war he remained at his home, but in the fall of 1862 he was elected to the Confederate Senate, in which he served to the end. His state-rights views remained constant; he opposed conscription as a violation of state rights, he introduced an amendment to the Confederate constitution permitting the peaceful secession of a state, he opposed the suspension of the writ of *habeas corpus,* and the establishment of a supreme court. His views regarding finances were usually sound, but did not prevail. Throughout the war he was loyal to President Jefferson Davis. In October 1865, he was president of the Georgia constitutional convention, and in the following year was elected to the United States Senate but was denied his seat. Throughout the period of Reconstruction he exhibited self-control and sound judgment. In 1873 he was appointed judge of the Middle Circuit and held this position until his death. His honesty and integrity were signally manifested in the struggle against misfortune due to financial losses resulting from the war.

[P. S. Flippin, *Herschel V. Johnson of Ga., State Rights Unionist* (1931), based on the Johnson papers; "From the Autobiography of Herschel V. Johnson," *Am. Hist. Rev.*, Jan. 1925; W. B. Collins, "Herschel V. Johnson in the Georgia Secession Convention," *Ga. Hist. Quart.*, Dec. 1927; sketch by J. K. Hines, in *Report . . . of the Ga. Bar Asso.*, 1924; *Biog. Dir. Am. Cong.* (1928); I. W. Avery, *The Hist. of the State of Ga. from 1851 to 1881* (1881); R. H. Shryock, *Ga. and the Union in 1850* (1926); *Atlanta Constitution* and *Savannah Morning News*, Aug. 18, 1880].

P. S. F.

JOHNSON, JAMES (Jan. 1, 1774–Aug. 13, 1826), soldier, congressman, was born in Orange County, Va. When he was six years of age, his father, Robert, and his mother, Jemima (Suggett) Johnson, migrated to Pennsylvania, where they remained one year before they moved to Kentucky and settled ultimately at Great Crossings, or Bryant's Station, near Lexington. In 1782 Bryant's Station was attacked by a large body of hostile Indians. The supply of water in the fort became exhausted and the women went to the spring for more, thinking that the Indians would be less likely to fire upon them than upon the men. It was Jemima Johnson who volunteered to lead the party and she accomplished the feat unmolested (*Register of Kentucky State Historical Society,* September 1905). Her husband also established his reputation in the new country. He acquired the title of colonel, was appointed in 1796 on the commission to determine the boundary between Kentucky and Virginia, and sat in the first and second constitutional conventions of his state.

James Johnson's fame rests exclusively upon his participation as lieutenant-colonel under command of his brother Richard Mentor Johnson [*q.v.*] in the battle of the Thames, Oct. 5, 1813. In this engagement the British left consisted of a force of regular troops; their right was made up of Indian allies under the famous Tecumseh [*q.v.*]. The regulars were drawn up in an open wood, while the natives were concealed in the edge of a swamp. Col. R. M. Johnson asked and received permission to begin the attack with his regiment of mounted riflemen. Seeing that there was not room for his whole force to maneuver in front of the British regulars, he led a part of his men off to attack in person the Indians concealed in the swamp and left his brother to lead the assault on the regular forces. Disposing his men in four columns of twos, James Johnson advanced slowly toward the enemy. A volley was fired upon him and several of the leaders fell. A second volley was fired before order could be restored. The horsemen then dashed forward. They rode through the British lines before muskets could be reloaded and, wheeling right and left, opened fire upon the enemy from the rear, thus disorganizing and defeating the force (B. J. Lossing, *The Pictorial Field-Book of the War of 1812,* 1868, pp. 551–57). It was a brilliant plan brilliantly executed, and it showed the frontier soldier at his best. During the battle James Johnson had under his command two of his sons, aged fifteen and seventeen years.

After this exploit, he returned to Great Crossings to live the life of a private citizen. In 1819 he undertook a contract to supply federal troops on the Missouri and Mississippi rivers. He was not successful as a business man, however. Because he trusted too much in the honesty of others, his affairs became seriously involved, and he was never able to extricate himself from the toils of debt (*Kentucky Reporter,* Aug. 21, 1826). In 1824 he was elected to Congress, but death overtook him before his term expired and his passing attracted little attention even in Kentucky.

[B. P. Poore, *The Political Register and the Congressional Directory* (1878); *Biog. Dir. Am. Cong.* (1928); *Argus of Western America* (Frankfort, Ky.), Aug 16, 1826; *Kentucky Reporter* (Lexington), Aug. 21, 1826.]

T. P. A.

JOHNSON, Sir JOHN (Nov. 5, 1742–Jan. 4, 1830), Loyalist, superintendent of Indian affairs in Canada, was born in the Mohawk Valley, the son of Sir William Johnson [*q.v.*]. His mother was probably Catharine Weisenberg, a German settler. His early education was better than that of the average frontiersman; in 1759 he was apparently attending an academy in Philadelphia, where he was "backward in writing and ciphering" (Captain Wraxall to Sir William, May 23, 1759, *Documentary History of the State of New York,* 8vo. ed., II, 1849, 785). As early as 1760, he was captain of a company of New York militia, and he served in the campaign for the suppression of Pontiac's Conspiracy. He attended numerous Indian conferences in the company of his father and was commissioned colonel of a regiment of horse in the New York militia. In the autumn of 1765 he accompanied Lord Adam Gordon on a visit to England, for the purpose of broadening his education, and there, on Nov. 22, was knighted. On June 30, 1773, he was married to Mary Watts, of a prominent New York family. Following the death of his father on July 11, 1774, he succeeded to the title of baronet and fell heir to the greater part of his father's estates, establishing his residence at Johnson Hall. In November he succeeded also to his father's post as major-general of militia.

It was inevitable that Sir John should sympathize with the Crown in the controversy with the colonies, and before long he was in correspondence with Governor Tryon of New York in regard to the possibility of organizing the settlers and Indians of the Mohawk region. In 1776, however, Johnson and some of his followers were disarmed and a *modus vivendi* was agreed upon, but when in the following May he learned that General Schuyler was sending a detachment to arrest him, he hastily fled with a small band of followers and ultimately reached Montreal. It is often charged that Johnson broke his "parole," but the question is a very technical one, the circumstances being extremely complex.

Upon reaching Montreal, he was commissioned lieutenant-colonel and authorized to raise a force which came to be known as the "Royal Greens." He accompanied St. Leger on his expedition against Fort Stanwix in 1777, and commanded a detachment at Oriskany on Aug. 6. Returning to Canada, he devoted himself to the relief of the Loyalists who were arriving in large numbers. In June 1778 he led a successful raid into the Mohawk Valley. In the autumn of 1779 he was at Niagara and Oswego, aiding friendly Indians and harassing those who were hostile to the British. In May 1780 he invaded the Lower Mohawk Valley at the head of a mixed force, in October he raided the Schoharie Valley with a command of about a thousand men, and then proceeded to the Mohawk. He thoroughly devastated the country and destroyed much grain.

In the autumn of 1781, Sir John left for England, and when he returned he bore with him a commission (dated Mar. 14, 1782) as "Superintendent General and Inspector General of the Six Nations Indians and those in the Province of Quebec." This was renewed in 1791. He also became a colonel in the British army. He had been attainted and his property confiscated by an act of the New York Assembly in 1779, and as compensation for his losses the British government granted him a large sum of money and a large tract of land in Canada, where he resided for the remainder of his life. For many years following the Revolution he exercised an important influence in Indian affairs and was active in relief measures on behalf of the Loyalists. He died in Montreal. Johnson's border warfare has been severely criticized, but the struggle in New York was in the nature of civil war and mutual recrimination was inevitable. It has been offered in his defense that he had been embittered by the treatment accorded his wife and children by the patriots, following his flight to Canada.

[Mabel G. Walker, "Sir John Johnson, Loyalist," *Miss. Valley Hist. Rev.*, Dec. 1916; W. L. Stone, *Life of Joseph Brant* (2 vols., 1838), and *The Life and Times of Sir William Johnson* (1865), vol. II, app. IX; P. H. Bryce, "Sir John Johnson, Baronet," *Quart. Jour. N. Y. State Hist. Asso.*, July 1928; A. M. Davis, "The Indians and the Border Warfare of the Revolution," in Justin Winsor, *Narr. and Crit. Hist. of America*, vol. VI (1888); *Orderly Book of Sir John Johnson During the Oriskany Campaign, 1776–1777* (1882), ed. by W. L. Stone, with an "Historical Introduction Illustrating the Life of Sir John Johnson, Bart.," by J. Watts De Peyster which is intensely prejudiced in Johnson's favor; S. G. C. Johnson, *Adventures of a Lady in the War of Independence in America* (1874); manuscript material in the Canadian Archives at Ottawa (see *Report on Canadian Archives*, 1883, 1885–90, and 1904); *The Papers of Sir William Johnson* (7 vols. to date, 1921–31); R. E. Day, *Calendar of Sir Wm. Johnson MSS. in the N. Y. State Lib.* (1909); Peter Force, *Am. Archives*, 4 ser., II–VI, (1837–46); E. B. O'Callaghan, *Docs. Rel. to the Colonial Hist. of the State of N. Y.*, vols. VII, VIII (1856–57); *Quebec Gazette*, Jan. 7, 8, 1830.]

W. E. S—s.

JOHNSON, JOHN ALBERT (July 28, 1861–Sept. 21, 1909), newspaper editor, governor of Minnesota, lecturer, was born near the frontier village of St. Peter, Minn. His parents were Swedish immigrants: Gustav Jenson, who became Johnson in America, and Caroline Christine (Haddén) Johnson. The struggles incident to John Johnson's early life of poverty probably influenced his mature character and temperament. Early in his boyhood the chief support of the family fell on the mother; and Johnson, the eldest son, worked outside of school hours calling for and delivering washing for his mother, and even helping her wash the clothes. At the age of thirteen he left school to work as clerk in a grocery at St. Peter, at a wage of ten dollars a month. In this period he read omnivorously—at first everything he could lay his hands on, and later books suggested by a discriminating older friend. At this time, too, he practised oratory and debating in that favorite school of politics, the country store. His early environment gave him the ability to judge his fellows and a lasting sympathy with the common man; and despite his hardships he preserved the sense of humor and buoyancy of spirit which enabled him to struggle on in the face of discouragement. He was later a clerk in a drug-store, and then in a general store in St. Peter. While he held this last position, his wages were raised enough so that he was able to assume the sole support of the family. He joined a debating club, was a member of fraternal organizations and the national guard, sang in a church choir, and was for some years secretary of the Nicollet County fair, thus entering fully into the life of his community. In the early eighties he became a registered pharmacist, but his health suffered under the confinement of indoor work, and he became a supply clerk, working for a firm of railway contractors in Iowa and Minnesota.

In February 1887 Johnson became editor and half-owner of the *St. Peter Herald,* at the instance of the other part-owner, and with funds supplied by townspeople interested in Johnson and convinced of his ability. Changing from a low-tariff Republican to a Democrat, to fit the policy of the *Herald,* Johnson flung himself eagerly into the conduct of a small-town newspaper. His lively interest in his fellowtownsmen and in broader national affairs, his sense of humor and keenness of judgment, stood him in good stead now. His share in the profits of the paper was such that after a year as editor he had repaid the money lent him to purchase his interest in the journal. Through the paper he began to be known beyond the limits of the town; his contact with other newspaper men in the Minnesota Editors' and Publishers' Association created for him a body of influential friends throughout the state. In 1891 he was elected secretary of the association, and in 1893 he became its president. On June 1, 1894, he was married at St. Peter to Elinore M. Preston, a teacher in a local parochial school.

Though his district was normally Republican, Johnson was elected to the state Senate in 1898, but he failed of reëlection in 1902 by a scant margin. In 1904 a split in the state Republican party gave the Democrats hope of winning the governorship, and at their state convention on Aug. 30, Johnson was nominated by acclamation. He threw himself into the campaign vigorously, made 103 speeches in 42 days, and was elected by a narrow margin, while the Republicans carried all the other offices. Two years later he was reëlected by a majority of 72,318 votes; and in 1908 he was elected for a third term by 27,139, while Taft carried the state over Bryan by 86,-442. As governor, he worked harmoniously with Republican legislatures and gave the state an intelligent and progressive administration. His message contained many recommendations for constructive legislation, some of which were enacted into laws. One of his most notable acts in office was his veto, in 1909, of a tonnage tax on iron ore, on the ground that such a measure would establish a double system of taxing a certain class of property, and that it would work too great hardship on one section of the state.

Johnson was a popular governor. His romantic rise endeared him to the public mind; his simple friendliness and unassuming bearing completed the conquest. He was dignified without being pompous; tall, erect, well-proportioned, with kindly gray-blue eyes and the magnetic gaiety of "the Johnson smile." During his years as governor, his talent as a public speaker attracted wide audiences, not merely in Minnesota, but elsewhere. In June 1907 he was Commencement orator at the University of Pennsylvania; in December 1907, at the annual Gridiron Club banquet in Washington, he was called upon unexpectedly to speak and proceeded to captivate probably the most critical audience in the country. It was after this speech that he first was mentioned as a presidential possibility, and in 1908 his name was presented by the Minnesota delegation to the Democratic convention which nominated Bryan for the third time. Meanwhile his lecturing increased; he spoke for a Chautauqua lyceum bureau in 1908 and 1909, with growing success. His untimely death in September 1909 plunged his state into sorrow, and has occasioned much speculation as to whether, had he lived, he might not have won the Democratic nomination which went to Woodrow Wilson in 1912.

[F. A. Day and T. M. Knappen, *Life of John Albert Johnson* (1910), a memorial biography; W. W. Folwell, *Hist. of Minn.*, vol. III (1926); J. H. Baker, *Lives of the Govs. of Minn.* (1908); the *Minneapolis Tribune* and the *St. Paul Dispatch,* Sept. 21, 1909; the *N. Y. Times,* Sept. 22, 1909.] S. J. B.

JOHNSON, JOHN BUTLER (June 11, 1850–June 23, 1902), civil engineer, was born on a farm near Marlboro, Stark County, Ohio, one of the seven children of Jesse and Martha (Butler) Johnson. Both his parents were descendants of Quakers who went to Ohio from Virginia in 1820. In 1866 the family moved to Kokomo, Ind., where after one year of high school John Johnson entered Howard College. After a short time there he went to the normal school conducted by Alfred Holbrook [*q.v.*] at Lebanon, Ohio, where he graduated about 1868. He taught for the next four years in elementary schools at various places in Indiana and Ohio, was principal of the New London (Ohio) high school and later of that at Kokomo, and in 1872 went to Indianapolis as secretary of the school board and instructor in the high school there. In 1874 he entered the University of Michigan, from which he was graduated as a civil engineer in 1878. On Nov. 12 of that year he was married to Phoebe E. Henby of Wabash, Ind. He was employed by the United States Great Lakes Survey for three years, and then for two years was an assistant engineer with the Mississippi River Commission. In this connection he made several suggestions for flood control on the Mississippi that were later used with some success (see his articles in *Journal of the Association of Engineering Societies,* Boston, February 1883 and July 1884, and the article, "Mississippi River," in *Johnson's Universal Cyclopædia,* vol. V, 1894, and *The Universal Cyclopædia,* vol. VIII, 1900). In 1883 he returned to teaching and joined the faculty of Washington University at St. Louis as professor of civil engineering. He remained there for sixteen years, and during this period published a number of books: *A Manual of the Theory and Practice of Topographical Surveying by Means of the Transit and Stadia* (1885); *The Theory and Practice of Surveying* (1886); *The Theory and Practice of Modern Framed Structures* (1893), with C. W. Bryan and F. E. Turneaure; *Engineering Contracts and Specifications* (1895); and *The Materials of Construction* (1897). These works, which are considered to be Johnson's greatest contribution to the engineering profession, are practical engineering reference books as well as textbooks, and were used extensively by practising engineers and students in both the United States and England. During the years 1892–95, for the Division of Forestry of the United States Department of Agriculture, he made in the laboratories of Washington University the earliest extensive and thorough investigations into the strength of timber. His series of tests established dependable values for the working strength of timber of all grades, thus, incidentally, permitting the marketing of many classes of timber previously considered worthless. In 1899 he was selected to fill the newly created position of dean of the College of Engineering of the University of Wisconsin, where for the short time remaining to him he enjoyed great success. He was largely responsible for the construction of an engineering building at the University, and the number of engineering students there was doubled during his term. He died suddenly in 1902 as the result of an accident at his summer home, Pier Cove, Mich. Johnson was largely instrumental in the formation of the Society for the Promotion of Engineering Education in 1893; he was secretary of the Society during its first two years and president in 1895. The work of the committee on industrial education, of which he was chairman, is considered one of the most important results of the formation of this society. In 1884 he originated, and for some years he carried on, the department of the index to engineering periodical literature for the *Journal of the Association of Engineering Societies,* the forerunner of *The Engineering Index* of the present day.

[*Trans. Am. Soc. Civil Engrs.*, vol. LI (1903); *Minutes of Proc. of the Inst. of Civil Engrs.* (London), vol. CLI (1903); *Trans. Wis. Acad. of Sci., Arts and Letters*, vol. XIV, pt. 2 (1903); *Proc. of Soc. for the Promotion of Engineering Educ.*, vol. X (1902); *Jour. Western Soc. of Engrs.* (Chicago), Oct. 1902; *Mich. Alumnus,* July 1902; *Engineering News,* supp. to issue of June 26, 1902, and regular issues of July 3 and 10, 1902; *Madison Democrat,* June 24, 1902.] F. A. T.

JOHNSON, JOHN GRAVER (Apr. 4, 1841–Apr. 14, 1917), lawyer, art collector, was born in Philadelphia, Pa. His father, who was a blacksmith, died when John was still a child and left the family in unfortunate financial circumstances. The son was able, however, to attend the public schools and graduated from the Philadelphia Central High School in 1857 and began the study of law upon entering the office of Benjamin and Murray Rush in Philadelphia as a scrivener. At the same time he became a student at the Law Academy and attended the law school of the University of Pennsylvania from which he was graduated with the degree of LL.B. in 1863. He was admitted to the Philadelphia bar in the same year and shortly afterward joined a company of volunteer artillery for service at the battle of Gettysburg, but after a very brief time in the field he returned to Philadelphia and began his legal practice in the office of William F. Judson. He discovered that few lawyers had a wide knowledge of corporation law and wisely decided to specialize in this branch of the profession. In a comparatively short time he became one of the best-known corporation lawyers in the United States. He took a leading part in many cases argued before the United States Supreme Court, appearing as counsel for the Northern Securities Company in *Northern Securities Company* vs. *United States* (1904—193 *U. S.,* 197) and in *Harriman* vs. *Northern Securities Company* (197 *U. S.,* 244) which followed the next year. In several important antitrust cases he represented the corporations as, for example, in the cases of *Standard Oil Company of New Jersey* vs. *United States* (1910—221 *U. S.,* 1) and *United States* vs. *American Tobacco Company* (1910—221 *U. S.,* 106). In 1908 he represented the railroad company in the case arising from the "commodities clause" of the Hepburn Act of 1906—*United States* vs. *Delaware and Hudson Railroad Company* (213 *U. S.*, 366). Shortly before his death he appeared before the Supreme Court to argue against the constitutionality of the Adamson eight-hour law (*Wilson* vs. *New* et al., 243 *U. S.*, 332). In later years he seldom appeared in court, devoting his time largely to consulting work, since it had become almost proverbial among financiers and others that his opinions were equivalent in value to judicial decisions. His strength before the courts was due not only to the vigorous power of his accurate reasoning, but still more to the fact that the courts felt absolute trust in the fidelity of his presentation of his cases. His relation to the bar was no less unusual. He cared nothing for public honors and twice refused a place on the bench of the United States Supreme Court, once offered by President Garfield and again by President Cleveland. He also refused the post of attorney-general in the cabinet of President McKinley.

Though his profession was absorbing to an unusual degree, Johnson had one great means of relaxation, and that was the enjoyment of art—particularly paintings. Over a period of forty years he built up one of the great private collections of America, which upon his death was left to the city of Philadelphia and became the nucleus of the collection later housed in the municipal art museum in Fairmount Park. His collection was thoroughly representative of the chief European schools of painting, especially of the Dutch, Flemish, and Italian. Rubens, Rembrandt, and some of the Dutch genre painters, such as Jan Steen and Adriaen Brouwer, were among his favorites. Among English painters, his collection by John Constable was outstanding, containing twenty-three examples of this artist. His group by Corot was also notable. Among more modern painters, Johnson's taste seemed to lean to French artists, particularly Théodore Rousseau, Degas, and Daubigny. He took an active interest in the Wilstach Museum in Fairmount Park, Philadelphia, and in the later years of his life was a director of the Metropolitan Museum of Art in New York. He took no interest in politics. In 1870 he had married the widow of Edward Morrell of Philadelphia, but they had no children. He died from heart failure after a brief illness in Philadelphia.

[*Report of the Twenty-third Ann. Meeting of the Pa. Bar Asso.* (1917); H. M. Allen, "John G. Johnson: Lawyer and Art Collector," *Bellman*, May 12, 1917; "A Great American and Great Art Connoisseur" and "Johnson as a Lawyer," *Literary Digest*, May 5, 1917; Bernhard Berenson and W. R. Valentiner, *Cat. of a Coll. of Paintings and Some Art Objects* (3 vols., 1913–14); *North American* (Phila.), Apr. 15–19; *Pub. Ledger, N. Y. Times*, Apr. 15, 1917.]

J. H. F.

JOHNSON, JONATHAN EASTMAN (July 29, 1824–Apr. 5, 1906), portrait and genre painter, the son of Philip C. and Mary K. Johnson, was born in Lovell, Me., whence he was taken to Fryeburg and later to Belfast, Me. His father was secretary of state for Maine and later held for some years with eminent credit a responsible office in the United States Treasury department. At an early age Eastman Johnson (as he was always called) began to make crayon portraits, his precocious aptitude as a draftsman giving him the ability to get an accurate likeness. When he was sixteen he went to Boston and found employment in Bufford's lithograph establishment, the same shop where, a few years later, Winslow Homer served his apprenticeship. In 1841 he was in Augusta, Me., again busy in drawing crayon portraits. For several years he carried on the same occupation there and in Cambridge, Mass., Newport, R. I., and Washington, D. C., where, in 1845, he made black-and-white likenesses of statesmen and government officials, in one of the Senate committee rooms at the Capitol.

In 1849 he went abroad to take up the study of painting, going first to Düsseldorf, where he worked for two years in the studio of Leutze, the historical painter. He then traveled in Italy and France, familiarizing himself with the works of the masters in the museums, and finally settled himself for a four years' sojourn at The Hague, where he met Mignot, made copies of the paintings in the Mauritshuis, took a studio, and painted his first genre pictures. His success was so pronounced that he was offered the position of court painter, which he declined. But the sound technical training that he derived from his long association with the Dutch school proved to be an invaluable asset. Returning to the United States shortly before the Civil War, he opened a studio in New York in 1858 and in a short time gained an enviable reputation as a painter of real merit, a reputation which increased steadily throughout his career. In 1860 he became a National Academician. He traveled in the South for the purpose of studying negro life at first hand, and several of his most successful genre pieces were delineations of such motives as his famous "Old Kentucky Home," belonging to the New York Public Library, which was exhibited at Paris in 1867 and at Philadelphia in 1876, and which contributed materially to his popularity. This he followed with a series of excellent genre pictures, such as the "Husking Bee," the "Old

Stage-Coach," and "Cranberry Pickers," in which the human interest was not more notable than the solid technical qualities of color, drawing, and composition. They bore the stamp of originality, sympathetic sentiment, and a quiet vein of humor.

As a portrait painter Johnson showed the same admirable qualities that are to be observed in his anecdotic work. He made the likenesses of many eminent Americans—John Quincy Adams, Daniel Webster, Henry Wadsworth Longfellow, Ralph Waldo Emerson, Presidents Arthur, Cleveland, and Harrison, William H. Vanderbilt, William M. Evarts, Edwin Booth, Dr. McCosh, and Bishop Potter, to name but a few. Of his heads of men it may be said in general that they are the work of a thoroughly competent and trustworthy hand. A good example is the well-known "Two Men," in the Metropolitan Museum, New York. Another interesting work in the same collection which combines portraiture with historical interest is the "Family Group" (1871) which depicts eleven children and their parents and grandparents in the library of a New York house—an authentic and valuable document of the period. As he advanced in years, Johnson made constant progress in his art, absorbing the best to be gleaned from the newer schools without losing his individuality. It has been said of him (Hartmann, *post,* p. 108) that "his self-portrait, painted in 1899, is technically superior to anything executed by him during the first fifty years of his life."

[See "The Field of Art," *Scribner's Mag.,* Aug. 1906; Sadakichi Hartmann, "Eastman Johnson: Am. Genre Painter," the *Studio,* Mar. 14, 1908; Samuel Isham, *The Hist. of Am. Painting* (1905); H. T. Tuckerman, *Book of the Artists* (1867); C. H. Caffin, *The Story of Am. Painting* (1907); Lorinda M. Bryant, *Am. Pictures and Their Painters* (1917); *Am. Art Ann.,* 1907–08; C. E. Clement and Laurence Hutton, *Artists of the Nineteenth Century* (1879); *The Metropolitan Museum of Art Cat. of Paintings* (1926); *The Pa. Acad. of the Fine Arts . . . Cat. of Thos. B. Clarke Coll. of Am. Pictures* (1891); *Cat. of Finished Pictures: Studies and Drawings by the Late Eastman Johnson* (1907); *Am. Art News,* Apr. 14, 1906; and the *N. Y. Times,* Apr. 7, 1906. Johnson's full name and that of his mother were supplied by the town clerk of Lovell, Me.]

W. H. D.

JOHNSON, JOSEPH (June 15, 1776–Oct. 6, 1862), physician and author, was born at Mount Pleasant, a suburb of Charleston, S. C., the fourth son of William and Sarah (Nightingale) Johnson, and the brother of William Johnson, 1771–1834 [*q.v.*], later associate justice of the Supreme Court of the United States. Prepared for college at a classical school in Charleston, Joseph was graduated from the College of Charleston in 1793, and at once entered the University of Pennsylvania Medical College. There he received the degree of M.D. in 1797, presenting as his thesis, *An Experimental Inquiry into the Properties of Carbonic Acid Gas, or Fixed Air* (1797). Entering immediately upon the practice of his profession in Charleston, where he spent the remainder of his life, he soon gained a wide and lasting reputation, not only as a successful and much beloved family physician, but as a medical scientist of high standing. In 1807 he was president of the South Carolina Medical Society. He wrote numerous articles for the *Charleston Medical Journal and Review,* two of the best known being, "Some Account of the Origin and Prevention of Yellow Fever in Charleston, S. C." (1849), and "The Alleged Connection between the Phases of the Moon and the Quantity of Rain" (July 1854). He also wrote many scientific articles of a popular character for the press, and in 1822 published *An Address to the Literary and Philosophical Society of South Carolina.*

Johnson's interest in history was scarcely less than his interest in medicine, and he dabbled in historical investigation for many years, publishing numerous sketches in newspapers. Many of these he incorporated in his best-known work, *Traditions and Reminiscences Chiefly of the American Revolution in the South* (1851). It is a highly valuable work, unscientific, of course, but preserving a wealth of information regarding the people and events of the Revolution that would otherwise have been lost, and so full of human interest that it had a wide popularity. He published also two excellent biographical studies in the *University of North Carolina Magazine*: "Biographical Sketch of Captain Johnston Blakeley" (February 1854) and "Memoir of Captain John Templer Shubrick, U. S. A." (June 1854).

For sixty-four years Johnson was a member of the South Carolina Society, an important educational, charitable, and social organization at that time. He served as steward for twenty-three years, and also as president, and he was president of the Apprentices' Literary Society. Possessed of large means, he developed important business interests and excellent business judgment, and from 1818 to 1825 he was president of the Charleston branch of the Bank of the United States. In 1826 he was intendant of Charleston. A firm believer in popular education, he served for years as commissioner of the public schools. He was actively and consistently interested in politics, and in 1832 was an active opponent of nullification and a leader of the Union party. In October 1802 he married Catherine, daughter of Francis and Hannah (Elfer)

Bonneau, by whom he had fifteen children. She died in 1859. He died at Pineville, S. C., to which place he had gone at the outbreak of the Civil War.

[H. A. Kelly and W. L. Burrage, *Am. Medic. Biogs.* (1920); *Cyc. of Eminent and Representative Men of the Carolinas* (1892), vol. I; *S. C. Hist. and Geneal. Mag.*, July 1909; *Charleston Daily Courier*, Oct. 8, 1862; MSS. in the possession of descendants.]

J. G. deR. H.

JOHNSON, JOSEPH FRENCH (Aug. 24, 1853–Jan. 22, 1925), educator, writer on finance, was born at Hardwick, Mass., the son of Gardner Nye and Eliza (French) Johnson, both of English extraction. His father was a country storekeeper. The family moved to Illinois in 1860 and finally settled in Aurora. After two years in the high school in Aurora, Joseph Johnson attended a Methodist academy in the town then called Clark Seminary. He was active in the debating society and all student activities. He graduated in 1872, then taught for a year in the Rockport Female Collegiate Institute. In 1873 he entered Northwestern University but transferred to Harvard the following year and graduated in 1878, having spent one year, 1875–76, at Halle, Germany, in company with Edmund J. James [*q.v.*]. After three years of teaching in the Harvard School in Chicago he traveled in Europe as tutor to Marshall Field, Jr. Turning next to journalism, he was on the *Springfield Republican*, under Samuel Bowles, from 1881 to 1884. On Aug. 4, 1884, he was married to Caroline Temperance Stolp of Aurora, Ill. His newspaper work was interrupted by a year as superintendent of schools in Yazoo City, Miss., and work with the Investors Agency in Chicago (a forerunner of the modern financial services). In March 1887 he became financial editor of the *Chicago Tribune*. Frank A. Vanderlip worked with him in the agency and on the *Tribune*. In 1890, with money furnished by H. H. Kohlsaat, Johnson went to Spokane, Wash., and founded the *Spokesman*. Three years later he sold the paper to become associate professor of business practice in the Wharton School of the University of Pennsylvania. Here he developed practical courses in finance and from 1895 to 1901 he was professor of journalism. From 1900 to 1903 he lectured on finance at Columbian University (later George Washington University). Meanwhile, in 1901, he went to the New York University School of Commerce, Accounts, and Finance, as professor of political economy, and from 1903 to 1925 he served as dean. During his deanship the enrolment of the school increased from less than a hundred students to over five thousand. He also worked out plans by which students might work during the day and take courses in the evening.

Johnson helped to organize the Alexander Hamilton Institute and was the editor of its publications. In addition to its reports, he wrote for the Institute *Business and the Man* (1917), designed to give the business man a philosophy of life, and *Economics, the Science of Business* (1924) a restatement for business men of the classical economic theory. His other writings include: *Money and Currency* (1906), a textbook which had wide use; *Organized Business Knowledge* (1923), treating the broader aspects of the scientific determination of business policy; and *We and Our Work* (1923), an elementary economics designed for adult education classes. He took an active part in financial reform. He was secretary of the special currency committee of the New York Chamber of Commerce in 1906; was appointed by the National Monetary Commission to investigate and write a report on the Canadian banking system, 1909; was a member of Mayor Gaynor's Commission on New Sources of Revenue for New York City, 1912; and a member of Van Tuyl Commission to Revise the Banking Law of the State of New York, 1913. He was influential in developing an opinion favorable to centralization in banking. In person he was genial and well-liked. His boyhood on the frontier, his education in the East and abroad, and his life in the Far West helped make him a keen judge of men. He had unusual ability to interpret academic concepts to business men and he made a great contribution to the development of a more practical training for business.

[See *Who's Who in America*, 1924–25; *Harvard Coll. Class of 1878, Fiftieth Anniversary Report, 1878–1928* (1928); *Dean Jos. French Johnson: Addresses Delivered at the Presentation of a Portrait Bust . . . to N. Y. Univ.* (1924); Lee Galloway, "Dean Johnson and the Transitional Period in Am. Education," *Ronald Forum*, Apr. 1925; *Jour. of Accountancy*, Mar. 1925; *World* (N. Y.), Feb. 5, 1925, p. 28; *N. Y. Herald Tribune* and *N. Y. Times*, Jan. 23, 1925. Johnson wrote an account of his connection with Frank A. Vanderlip in the *Caxton*, Apr. 1914. An appreciation of Johnson by Bruce Barton is to be found in the introduction to *Organized Business Knowledge* (1923).] J. D. M.

JOHNSON, LEVI (Apr. 25, 1786–Dec. 19, 1871), ship-builder and trader, was a native of Herkimer County, N. Y. Beyond the facts that his parents were farmers and left their son an orphan at an early age, nothing is known of his early boyhood. He lived with an uncle on a farm until the age of fourteen, when he entered a carpenter's shop as an apprentice. After four years he began working at his trade on his own account. From neighbors he heard stories of the new land of promise in the Western Reserve of

Ohio. In March 1809, he arrived in Cleveland. Though that settlement was as yet an unorganized village of only fifty inhabitants, he found immediate employment. During 1809 he built the first frame house in the town, in 1813, the old log courthouse and jail, located on the northwest corner of the square. While building a sawmill and a gristmill in Lorain County in 1810, he met Margaret Montier, of French parentage, and a native of Pennsylvania. A year later they were married and took up their residence in Cleveland.

The War of 1812 gave him the opportunity that changed the whole course of his life. The encampment of General Harrison's forces at Sandusky and after Commodore Perry's victory at Put-in-Bay the occupation of Detroit gave rise to an active trade in military supplies. The needs of transportation, in turn, started shipbuilding along the South Shore. Johnson and his brother-in-law loaded an abandoned flatboat with potatoes which they sold to the army at Put-in-Bay and followed up this profitable adventure with a load of supplies for the army at Detroit. Other expeditions followed. Johnson now undertook to build a ship of his own, a small, primitive affair with wooden pins in place of spikes and bolts. With this venture he initiated Cleveland's first industry of importance. His voyages were likewise the real beginning of lake navigation. He launched his first vessel, a schooner, in 1814, another in 1816, and a steamboat, the *Enterprise,* in 1824. After the War of 1812 he carried cargoes of merchandise from Buffalo to the small lake towns that flourished with the westward movement, and returned with cargoes of fur from the Northwest.

Johnson retired from the lake trade and shipbuilding about 1830, and during the remainder of his active life, 1830–58, he was a building contractor. Light-houses along the South Shore of Lake Erie, the first work on the government piers in Cleveland, and several important business buildings are monuments to his successful career. Profitable real estate investments completed the process by which he made one of Cleveland's early fortunes.

[Maurice Joblin, *Cleveland, Past and Present: Its Representative Men* (1869); J. H. Kennedy, *A Hist. of the City of Cleveland* (1896); S. P. Orth, *A Hist. of Cleveland, Ohio* (1910); G. V. R. Wickham, *The Pioneer Families of Cleveland* (1914); E. M. Avery, *A Hist. of Cleveland and Its Environs* (1918); *Cleveland Plain Dealer,* Dec. 20, 1871.]

E. J. B.

JOHNSON, MARMADUKE (d. Dec. 25, 1674), printer, was an Englishman who came to Massachusetts in 1660. He is credited with political pamphlets; but the Registers of the Stationers' Company list no imprint by him. There are some by his brother Thomas, one of which is *Ludgate, What It Is, Not What It Was, by M. Johnson, Typograph, a Late Prisoner There* (1659). This brochure, written from Ludgate Chapel, Nov. 7, 1659, is an account of the conditions within the prison. Since Samuel Green [*q.v.*], the only printer in Massachusetts, was untrained, and Eliot's Indian translation of the Bible was ready for printing, the Society for the Propagation of the Gospel in New England made a contract, Apr. 21, 1660, with Marmaduke Johnson, "Citizen and Stationer of London," whereby the latter agreed to go to Boston to serve the Society "in the Art of a Printer for . . . Three yeares" (*Records of the Colony of New Plymouth in New England,* vol. X, 1859, p. 447). The Commissioners of the New England Confederation informed the Society, Sept. 10, that "Mr. Johnson wilbee . . . acomodated . . . wee hope to content" (*Ibid.,* 243). If Johnson was content, however, others were not; for on Sept. 10, 1662, the Commissioners wrote the Society that he "hath Caryed heer very vnworthyly of which hee hath bine openly Convicted . . . hee hath proued very Idle an nought" (*Ibid.,* 276). His particular offense was trying to get Green's daughter to marry him in spite of her father. For this he was ordered to return to his wife in England, though he represented that she had died, but the banishment was deferred until he had completed his engagement with the Society. In 1663 Green and Johnson completed the printing of the Indian Bible, one of the outstanding productions of the colonial press, and the Society decided to continue Johnson's contract for another year because, according to Eliot, he was "an able and vsefull man in the presse" (*Ibid.,* 292). On Aug. 25, 1664, however, Eliot wrote, that Johnson was "now returning for Engld" (*Ibid.,* p. 385). He was in the colony in May 1665 with his own press and types, and the town of Boston permitted him to locate there; but the General Court interposed, May 27, with an order "that there shall be no printing presse allowed . . . but in Cambridge," and renewed the censorship (*Records of the Governor and Company of the Massachusetts Bay,* vol. IV, pt. 2, 1854, p. 141), which, first established Oct. 8, 1662, had been repealed on May 27, 1663. Johnson went to Cambridge, where there was not enough business for two printers and little cordiality between himself and Green, who wrote that Johnson "was so high that [he] . . . att last wrought me quite out of the Indian worke" (*Collections of the Massachusetts Historical Society,* 5 ser., vol. I, 1871,

p. 423). Yet they continued to issue joint imprints and probably occupied the same shop. The General Court finally heeded Johnson's petitions and permitted a Boston press, May 30, 1674, but he died soon after he moved into the city, so all his known imprints are Cambridge ones. Of these imprints Charles Evans (*American Bibliography,* vol. I, 1903) lists sixteen with Green in 1660–64, and thirty-five in 1665–74, twenty of them being with Green. Johnson married Ruth Cane of Cambridge, Apr. 28, 1670, and had a daughter who probably died young. A son left in England evidently never came to the colony to claim the estate.

[C. A. Duniway, *The Development of Freedom of the Press in Mass.* (1906), ch. iv., notes; L. R. Paige, *Hist. of Cambridge, Mass.* (1877), p. 593; *Mass. Hist. Soc. Proc.,* 1 ser. XX (1884), 265–68, 2 ser. XI (1897), 240–49; Isaiah Thomas, *Hist. of Printing in America* (2nd ed., 2 vols., 1874); John Strype's edition of John Stow, *A Survey of the Cities of London and Westminster, and the Borough of Southwark* (6th ed., 2 vols., 1754–55), II, 694–702; G. E. Littlefield, *The Early Mass. Press* (1907), vol. I; Wilberforce Eames, *Bibliog. Notes on Eliot's Indian Bible* (1890).] D. M. M.

JOHNSON, Sir NATHANIEL (*c.* 1645–1713), colonial governor, was the son of William and Margaret (Sherwood) Johnson of Kibblesworth, in the county of Durham, England. Before he migrated to the colonies he had served as a soldier, as a farmer of chimney taxes in the four northern counties, as member of Parliament for Newcastle-on-Tyne, and on Dec. 28, 1680, had been knighted. In 1686 he was appointed governor of the Leeward Islands, but when James II was driven from England, Johnson asked permission to retire, as he was unwilling to take the oaths of allegiance to William and Mary. Accordingly he made his plans to leave the islands. His family, including his wife and at least one child, Robert Johnson [*q.v.*], returned to England. They were taken prisoners by the French en route, and his wife died soon afterwards. Johnson himself sailed in July 1689 for South Carolina, where he already had the right to two baronies of 12,000 acres each through his appointment as a cacique by the Lords Proprietors, and now received an additional grant of 1,940 acres on the eastern branch of Cooper River. Here he experimented with the culture of silk, calling his plantation "Silk Hope." His efforts met with success, and he presented the proprietors with a sample of silk. He is recorded as deriving an income of three to four hundred pounds annually from this source. Ambitious and enterprising, he also attempted to manufacture salt and to grow grapes for the production of wine. In June 1702 he was appointed governor of the province, but did not begin active service until 1703. He personally administered South Carolina, appointing a deputy for North Carolina. This was the period of Queen Anne's war, and South Carolina, a British outpost, was in danger of attack from both France and Spain. Johnson was active in the defense of the colony, building fortifications and undertaking an offensive against the enemy's Indian allies at the suggestion of James Moore [*q.v.*], noted Indian trader and former governor. The Assembly consented to the move, but required the expedition to pay its own expenses. The attack was successful, and much booty and many Indian slaves were secured. Continuing his policy of weakening the French and Spaniards by crushing and alienating their Indian allies, Johnson made a treaty of friendship with the Creeks, a powerful tribe living on the border of Carolina and formerly hostile to the English. For his success in defending the colony, a fort was named in his honor and he was granted 1,200 acres of land.

The Indian trade was a leading economic interest in the colony and was largely controlled by the Assembly. Johnson approved a law regulating the trade by placing it under the management of a board of Indian commissioners and an Indian agent appointed and removed by the lower house. The Governor also gave up his right to have all presents from the Indians and received in return £200 outright and £100 yearly. In addition to his activity in behalf of the Indian trade, he introduced the domestic police system for the colony's protection against negro insurrection. This organization formed the basis of the military patrol which lasted until the Civil War. A strict High-Churchman, Johnson aided in the building of Pompion Hill Chapel, the first Anglican church in the province of Carolina outside of Charleston, and consistently supported the measure, passed in 1704, establishing the Church of England in Carolina. This law met with much opposition in the colony, but when the Assembly sought to repeal it, Johnson dissolved that body. He was superseded as governor in 1708, but lived in the colony until his death in 1713.

[*S. C. Hist. and Geneal. Mag.,* July 1911; B. R. Carroll, *Hist. Colls. of S. C.* (2 vols., 1836); Edward McCrady, *The Hist. of S. C. under the Proprietary Govt., 1670–1719* (1897); Alexander Hewat, *An Hist. Account of the Rise and Progress of the Colonies of S. C. and Ga.* (2 vols., 1779); W. J. Rivers, *A Sketch of the Hist. of S. C.* (1856); W. L. Saunders, *The Colonial Records of N. C.,* vols. I–III (1886); W. A. Shaw, *The Knights of England* (1906), II, 255; Robert Surtees, *The Hist. and Antiquities of the County Palatine of Durham,* II (1820), 218; *Calendar of State Papers, Col. Ser., America and West Indies, 1689–92* (1901), pp. xxviii, 43, 86–91.] H. B–C.

JOHNSON, OLIVER (Dec. 27, 1809–Dec. 10, 1889), anti-slavery leader, editor, was born at Peacham, Caledonia County, Vt., the son of Ziba Johnson, a Peacham pioneer in 1795, and Sally Lincoln. He was related on his mother's side to the Lincolns and Leonards of Massachusetts, and on his father's was descended from Isaac Johnson, who came to America in the late seventeenth century. Oliver grew up on a farm and attended the common school until he became an apprentice in the printing office of the *Vermont Watchman,* Montpelier. Here he came under the influence of William Lloyd Garrison [*q.v.*], whose paper, *Journal of the Times* (Bennington), he eagerly devoured. On Sept. 8, 1832, he married Mary Anne White, daughter of Rev. Broughton White of Putney, Vt. She was assistant matron of the female prison at Sing Sing, a promoter of prison reform, and later a lecturer on anatomy and physiology to women.

Going to Boston in 1831, he established the *Christian Soldier,* in opposition to the doctrine of Universalism. His office was in the same building with that of the *Liberator* and there soon sprang up between Johnson and Garrison an intimacy and an agreement on all phases of the slavery question which lasted throughout their lives. When in 1833 and 1840 Garrison went to England, he intrusted the editing of the *Liberator* in his absence to Johnson, and during the summers of 1837 and 1838 Garrison, because of ill health, turned his paper over to Johnson's care. In 1832 Johnson became one of the twelve founders of the New England Anti-Slavery Society and in 1836, its traveling agent. From this time forward he continuously engaged in the work of the anti-slavery crusade, lecturing under the auspices of several of the numerous anti-slavery societies, writing, and editing. He was Boston correspondent of the *New York Tribune,* 1842–44, and assistant to Horace Greeley, 1844–48. In 1849 he became editor of the *Anti-Slavery Bugle* (Salem, Mass.), somewhat later of the *Pennsylvania Freeman,* from which in 1853 the National Anti-Slavery Society transferred him to the associate editorship of the *National Anti-Slavery Standard* at New York. This post he held until the end of the Civil War. He was also connected with the *Republican* (Philadelphia), a Free-Soil paper, and the *Practical Christian* (Milford, Mass.). After the Civil War he was associate editor of the *Independent,* 1865–70; editor of the *New York Weekly Tribune,* 1870–73; managing editor of the *Christian Union,* 1873–76; editor of the *Journal* (Orange, N. J.); and associate editor of the New York *Evening Post* (1881–89). His wife died in June 1872, and on Aug. 27, 1873, he married Jane Abbott, daughter of John S. C. Abbott [*q.v.*], by whom he had one daughter. He died in Brooklyn, N. Y.

Johnson has been called "a wheel horse in every humanitarian movement for almost half a century, a man whose philosophy of life was quite simply to love his neighbor as himself" (*Henry Ward Beecher,* p. 238). As a reformer he was interested not only in abolition but in nearly all the progressive movements of his day. As early as 1838 his interest in women's rights was shown when he advocated full participation of women in anti-slavery societies. He was temporary secretary of the Peace Convention of 1838 at Boston and showed a consistent interest in the peace movement throughout his life. In politics he followed much the same course as Garrison until, in the election of 1872, he became an active worker in the reform campaign of Horace Greeley. He was a close friend of Henry Ward Beecher and of Theodore Tilton. As an editor he was able to use his pen in the interests of all those reforms which attracted him. His works include: *Consider This, Ye That Forget God* (1831); *Correspondence with George F. White* (1841); *What I Know of Horace Greeley* (campaign tract, 1872); *William Lloyd Garrison and His Times* (1880); *The Abolitionists Vindicated in a Review of Eli Thayer's Paper on the New England Emigrant Aid Society* (1887). In maturity he abandoned the Calvinism of his youth and became identified with a small group known as "Progressive Friends," whose center was at Kennett Square, Pa. Because of this affiliation, he was buried at Kennett Square.

[*William Lloyd Garrison, 1805–1879, The Story of his Life. Told by his Children* (4 vols., 1885–89); Paxton Hibben, *Henry Ward Beecher* (1927); *Independent,* Dec. 19, 1889; *N. Y. Herald,* Dec. 11, 1889; *Evening Post* (N. Y.), Dec. 11, 1889; *Nation,* Dec. 19, 1889; genealogical material from family records in the possession of Johnson's grand-niece, Miss F. F. Clark, Peacham, Vt.]

J. W. P—t.
A. G. T.

JOHNSON, REVERDY (May 21, 1796–Feb. 10, 1876), lawyer and diplomat, was a native of Annapolis, Md. His mother, Deborah Ghieselen, was a daughter of Reverdy Ghieselen, of Huguenot descent, who was for a time commissioner of the land office of Maryland. His father, John Johnson, whose ancestors had emigrated from England, served his state as a member of both houses of the legislature, as judge of the court of appeals, and as chancellor. The boy received his general education in St. John's College at Annapolis, graduating in 1811.

After reading law, first with his father and then with Judge Stephen, he was admitted to the bar in 1815. Four years later, on Nov. 16, he married Mary Mackall Bowie, whose mother's father was Gov. Robert Bowie [*q.v.*]. Johnson's law practice began in Upper Marlboro, Md., but in 1817 he removed to Baltimore, where for almost sixty years he continued active in his profession, becoming one of the greatest lawyers of his day. He had an unusual memory, which served him especially well in the latter half of his life, when he became partially blind. His mental alertness made him a rare cross-examiner. He possessed a deep, oratorical voice that immediately commanded attention and was an important professional asset, as were also his tact, good nature, and unusual courtesy. During his early law practice, in cooperation with Thomas Harris, clerk of the Maryland court of appeals, he compiled the reports of cases decided in that court (1–7 *Harris and Johnson Reports*, 1800–27).

His chief legal fame rested upon his ability as a constitutional lawyer. He appeared as counsel in a number of very important suits and had as associates or opponents many of the most famous men of his time. In 1854 he and Thaddeus Stevens obtained for Cyrus McCormick a decision upholding the validity of the reaper patent (*Seymour* vs. *McCormick*, 16 *Howard*, 480). Two years later, in a second suit between the same parties he was associated with Edward M. Dickerson in opposition to Edwin M. Stanton (19 *Howard*, 96). The most famous case with which he was connected was *Dred Scott* vs. *Sanford* (19 *Howard*, 393) in which he represented the defense and was credited by George Ticknor Curtis, one of Scott's attorneys, with being the major influence in bringing about the decision against the bondman (*Proceedings*, *post*, p. 12).

Johnson was an ardent Whig during the life of that party and later affiliated with the Democrats but never felt at home with them. In 1821 he was elected state senator from Baltimore and was returned to office in 1826 but resigned two years later because of the increasing demands of his profession. In 1845, when the Oregon and Texas questions were under discussion, he began his national career as a member of the United States Senate. On the Oregon question he attacked the administration and favored a boundary line following the forty-ninth parallel; in the matter of Texas, on the other hand, he deserted the Whigs to uphold Polk in prosecuting the war with Mexico. Yet he opposed the annexation of Mexican territory, for he feared that it would revive the whole problem of the extension of slavery. Although he thought that slavery was wrong, he believed that its expansion into the territories was a local concern, but, nevertheless, in order to avert the threatened disaster to the Union he urged compromise and suggested that the slavery question be submitted to the Supreme Court. In March 1849, he resigned from the Senate to become attorney-general under President Taylor, but his activities in this capacity were of little importance. He was soon under a cloud owing to an opinion he rendered on the Galphin claim in which Secretary of War Crawford had been attorney for the claimant. Before his death, Taylor was considering the dismissal of Johnson for his connection with the scandal, as well as that of Crawford, and of Meredith, the secretary of the treasury.

After Taylor's death Johnson resigned with the rest of the cabinet and soon became allied with the Democrats. He had much sympathy for the South, urged conciliation, and was a member of the futile peace congress held in Washington early in 1861. Secession, however, he looked on as treason and stood for the preservation of the Union. Hence he upheld Lincoln's suspension of the writ of *habeas corpus*, though he frequently urged leniency or acquittal for those charged with disloyalty. When he was chosen a member of the Maryland house of delegates in 1861 he worked hard to keep the state from seceding from the Union. The next year he was again elected United States senator but did not take his seat until 1863 because Lincoln soon sent him to New Orleans to investigate complaints of foreign consuls that General Benjamin Butler [*q.v.*] had seized their property. In the Senate he continued his moderate and conciliatory policy, championing the Constitution but occasionally giving way to expediency. He held that slaves who had enlisted in the army should be granted their freedom but was opposed to emancipating their families on this ground. In 1864 he supported McClellan for the presidency since he felt that the Emancipation Proclamation was unwise and resented Lincoln's interference in the Maryland and Kentucky elections. Though he had hoped that emancipation might come gradually, he voted for the Thirteenth Amendment.

In his attitude towards the South he stood out in strong opposition to Sumner's conquered-province theory, for he held the Union to be indestructible. He favored the Wade-Davis plan of reconstruction, which Lincoln vetoed and, after Lincoln's assassination, generally supported Johnson in his policy towards the South. He was a member of the committee of fifteen on reconstruction and also sat on the later joint congressional committee. He fought the bill creating the Freedmen's Bureau, chiefly on account of the provision for trial by courts martial, and repeatedly he used his eloquence against arbitrary imprisonment and other violations of personal liberty. While he opposed negro suffrage because he felt that the blacks were unprepared for the responsibility, he finally voted for the Fourteenth Amendment as a means of ending military domination in the South. Yet, later, he voted for the bill dividing that region into military districts. For his various inconsistencies he was called a "trimmer" by his opponents, a term that was not entirely undeserved, though some of his shifts can be explained by his open-mindedness and natural lack of strong prejudices. In the quarrel between Congress and President Johnson, he gave the executive considerable support and obtained an amendment to the Tenure of Office Act permitting the president to continue making recess appointments. In the impeachment of Johnson he was a member of the committee on rules for the Senate acting as a court, and filed an opinion that Johnson was not guilty. He seems to have been largely responsible for the acquittal through convincing a number of wavering senators that Johnson would enforce congressional reconstruction.

In 1868 he was appointed to succeed Charles Francis Adams as minister to Great Britain, where he was well received, for he was known to favor the maintenance of friendship with the British, but, at home, he was severely criticized for his cordiality towards individuals whose actions had not been friendly to the Union. There were three questions entrusted to Johnson for settlement, the alienability of allegiance, the jurisdiction over the San Juan islands in Puget Sound, and the claims for damages done by the *Alabama* and other vessels built in Great Britain for the Confederacy. Agreements were promptly signed whereby the British government recognized the right of expatriation for British subjects and pledged itself to submit the San Juan question to arbitration. Johnson also negotiated a treaty for the settlement, by means of arbitral commission, of all financial claims arising between the two countries after July 26, 1853. The most important of the American claims were those for damages done by the *Alabama* and similar vessels. None of these agreements was ratified, chiefly owing to the fact that they were the work of a supporter of Andrew Johnson, but they did form the bases for later treaties.

After the election of Grant, Reverdy Johnson returned to the United States in the summer of 1869, and resumed his law practice. He defended many Southerners charged with disloyalty to the Union and was attorney for Allen Crosby, Sherod Childers, and others in the Ku Klux trials of South Carolina (*Official Report of the Proceedings before the U. S. Circuit Court . . . Held at Columbia, S. C., November Term, 1871, 1872*). In 1875 with David Dudley Field he obtained the acquittal of Cruikshank (*United States* vs. *Cruikshank, 92 U. S.*, 542) who had been charged with fraud and violence in elections and indicted for conspiracy under the enforcement act of May 30, 1870. Still in active practice he died from an accidental fall while in Annapolis to argue a case before the court of appeals.

[Manuscript letters in Lib. of Cong.; B. C. Steiner, *Life of Reverdy Johnson* (copr. 1914); *Proc. of the Bench and Bar of the Supreme Court of the U. S. in Memoriam Reverdy Johnson* (1876); W. D. Lewis, *Great Am. Lawyers*, vol. IV (1908); H. W. Scott, *Distinguished Am. Lawyers* (1891); J. F. Essary, *Md. in National Politics* (copr. 1915); *Green Bag*, July 1891; *The Diary of Gideon Welles* (3 vols., 1911); Charles Warren, *The Supreme Court in U. S. Hist.* (3 vols., 1922), and *A Hist. of the Am. Bar* (1911); W. W. Bowie, *The Bowies and their Kindred* (1899); *Harper's Weekly*, Feb. 26, 1876; *Sun* (Baltimore), Feb. 11, 12, 1876.]

M. W. W.

JOHNSON, RICHARD MENTOR (1780–Nov. 19, 1850), ninth vice-president, brother of James Johnson [*q.v.*], was born, according to his own statement and that of his uncle (Meyer, *post*, p. 20; Cave Johnson, *post*, p. 209), at Beargrass, a frontier settlement on the site of the present Louisville, Ky. His father, Robert, and his mother, Jemima (Suggett) Johnson, had migrated from Virginia to the West shortly before his birth, and shortly afterward they moved to Bryant's Station near the present Lexington, Ky. Reared upon the frontier, young Richard had few educational advantages, but he was able to begin the study of Latin at the age of fifteen and thus equip himself for the study of law, which he pursued under George Nicholas and James Brown, professors in Transylvania University. He was admitted to the bar in 1802, and in 1804 was elected to the state legislature. Two years later he was elected to the United States House of Representatives, where he sat from 1807 until 1819.

In Congress Johnson supported President Jefferson and his embargo policy, and later favored the declaration of war against Great Britain. During the conflict which followed he left Washington to become colonel of a regiment of mounted Kentucky riflemen. Having a natural aptitude for military affairs, he worked out a theory of combat for such troops, which he was soon able to put into practice with remarkable success. With his regiment he marched under Governor Shelby to join General Harrison on the Canadian border, and here took part in the battle of the Thames. In this engagement his troops bore the brunt of the attack, and a part of them, commanded by his brother James, rode through the British lines to turn and attack the enemy from the rear. The Colonel, while charging the Indian allies of the British, was severely wounded, but his forces prevailed and he was borne from the field a hero (B. J. Lossing, *The Pictorial Field-Book of the War of 1812,* 1868, pp. 551–57). In the fighting he had killed an Indian chief, said by some to have been Tecumseh.

Johnson had not resigned his seat in Congress while engaged in military activities, and as soon as his wounds permitted he returned to Washington. As chairman of the committee on military affairs he was active in securing pension legislation. He opposed the establishment of the second United States Bank in 1816, but was in favor of protection and of internal improvements. In 1816 he proposed and secured the passage of a measure granting congressmen an annual salary of $1,500 instead of a *per diem* allowance. This, he believed, would encourage the members of that body to expedite their business, but the constituencies looked upon it as a "salary grab," and many members consequently lost their seats. Johnson retained his by bowing to the will of the people and working for the repeal of his own act. His willingness to recant is typical of his character. The next political storm in which he was involved arose in 1818 over the Seminole campaign of Andrew Jackson. When the question was before the House in 1819, Johnson alone of the committee on military affairs reported in favor of Jackson (James Parton, *Life of Andrew Jackson,* 1860, II, 534).

In 1819 a great financial panic struck the country. Johnson voluntarily retired from his seat in the House and was elected a member of the Kentucky legislature, which forthwith chose him to represent the state in the United States Senate. He has been given credit for the passage of the Kentucky law abolishing imprisonment for debt, and he later took a leading part in the agitation of similar legislation before Congress; it is, therefore, probable that his promotion at this time was due to his connection with the relief movement which was rampant in Kentucky. He retained his seat in the Senate from 1819 until 1829. In the presidential election of 1824 he favored Clay, but turned to Jackson when the forces of Clay united with those of Adams. Defeated for the Senate in 1829, he returned to the House of Representatives.

During Jackson's presidency, the relations between Johnson and the General were cordial, even intimate. Johnson signed the report condemning the Bank of the United States, not because he was convinced of its sins, but merely and frankly to accommodate the administration (Parton, *Jackson,* III, 405). He also supported the President in his tariff policies and opposition toward internal improvements, though his private views favored both (J. S. Bassett, *The Life of Andrew Jackson,* 1911, II, 487; W. G. Sumner, *Andrew Jackson,* 1882, pp. 376–78). Jackson used him as his personal agent on various occasions, notably (Parton, III, 303–08) when he was trying to force his cabinet to accept Peggy O'Neill, the wife of Secretary J. H. Eaton [*q.v.*]. The General decided that Johnson should be vice-president under Van Buren, and accomplished his nomination by the same kind of strong-handed action which secured that of the presidential candidate (J. B. McMaster, *A History of the People of the United States,* vol. VI, 1906, p. 361). During the campaign his partisans pressed his cause in a characteristic jingle: "Rumpsey, Dumpsey, Colonel Johnson killed Tecumseh" (H. A. Wise, *Seven Decades of the Union,* 1872, p. 175). Failing to secure a majority of the electoral vote, he became the only vice-president ever elected by the Senate. His career as vice-president was inconspicuous and in 1841 he retired to private life. In November 1850 he took his seat once more in the Kentucky legislature, but died less than a fortnight later, and his fame, in large measure, passed with him to the grave.

Johnson seems to have taken considerable interest in education. After the War of 1812 he introduced in Congress resolutions looking toward the establishment of military academies. He favored the establishment of a national seminary in the District of Columbia, and was one of the organizers of Columbian College (now George Washington University). He was a founder and trustee for some time of Georgetown College, Kentucky. He gave buildings on his land, supplied a teacher, and maintained general supervision of the Choctaw Academy, established under the treaty of Dancing Rabbit Creek (1825) for the education of the Indians. White boys also, among them his nephew, Robert Ward Johnson [*q.v.*], attended this institution, which flourished until after 1841. Johnson was never married, but had two daughters by Julia Chinn, a mulatto who came to him in the distribution of his father's estate (Meyer, *post,* pp.

317–21). He was possessed of the courage, dash, and military bearing of the best frontier type, and of the clear-cut, classic features which one associates with patrician blood. As a soldier he showed great promise, but as a politician, though not lacking in sagacity, he was lacking in purpose. History can give him no larger place than that of satellite to Andrew Jackson.

[L. R. Meyer, *The Life and Times of Col. Richard M. Johnson of Ky.* (1932), with bibliog.; Wm. Emmons, *Authentic Biog. of Col. Richard M. Johnson of Ky.* (1833); *A Biog. Sketch of Col. Richard M. Johnson of Ky.* (1843), "by a Kentuckian"; L. and R. H. Collins, *Hist. of Ky.* (1877); eulogy by J. C. Mather, *U. S. Mag. and Democratic Rev.*, Apr. 1851; reminiscences of Cave Johnson, *Reg. Ky. State Hist. Soc.*, May 1922; *Louisville Morning Courier*, Nov. 20, 21, 22, 1850.]
T. P. A.

JOHNSON, RICHARD W. (Feb. 7, 1827–Apr. 21, 1897), Union soldier, author, was born near Smithland, Livingston County, Ky., the son of Dr. James L. and Jane (Leeper) Johnson, who had moved to Kentucky from Prince Edward County, Va. His emigrant ancestor was Thomas Johnson, who came to America in 1700. Young Johnson's early schooling was primitive until the year 1844, when an elder brother, Dr. John Milton Johnson, later surgeon in the Confederate army, secured for him a cadetship at West Point. Graduating in 1849, and assigned to the 6th Infantry, he saw almost continuous frontier service at Fort Snelling, Minn., in Texas, and in Indian Territory, engaging in a skirmish with Comanche Indians on the Rio Concho, Tex., in 1856, and near Brady Creek, Tex., in 1858. With the outbreak of the Civil War, he participated in the action at Falling Waters, was appointed lieutenant-colonel, 3rd Kentucky Cavalry, Aug. 28, 1861, and brigadier-general of volunteers, Oct. 11 of the same year. On Aug. 21, 1862, he was made prisoner by Morgan near Gallatin, Tenn., and after exchange, commanded a brigade and division at Pittsburg Landing, Corinth, Stone's River, Tullahoma Gap, Liberty Gap, and Chickamauga, where he was brevetted lieutenant-colonel. Subsequently, he took part in the battle of Missionary Ridge, and was brevetted colonel, Nov. 24, 1863, for gallantry at Chattanooga. In the invasion of Georgia, March–June 1864, he took part in the battles at Dalton, Resaca, and New Hope Church, where he was severely wounded, and later took part in the battle of Nashville, being brevetted major-general of volunteers, brigadier-general and major-general, United States Army, for gallant and meritorious services. Retired, Oct. 12, 1867, with the rank of major-general, he became professor of military science at the University of Missouri, which gave him the degree of master of arts in 1868, and subsequently served in the same capacity at the University of Minnesota, making St. Paul his home until his death. In 1881 he was the unsuccessful candidate of the Democratic party for governor of Minnesota. He wrote manuals of Sharp's rifle and carbine and Colt's revolver for Thomas Worthington's *The Volunteer's Manual* (1861); an address published in the *Report of the First Meeting of the Society of the Army of the Cumberland* (1868); *A Memoir of Maj.-Gen. George H. Thomas* (1881), *A Soldier's Reminiscences in Peace and War* (1886), and "Fort Snelling from its Foundation to the Present Time" (*Collections of the Minnesota Historical Society,* vol. VIII, 1898). He was twice married, in 1855 to Rachael Elizabeth Steele of Fort Snelling, by whom he had three sons; and in 1894, to Julia Anne McFarland, prominent educator (*Who's Who in America,* 1922–23), by whom he had one son.

[*War of the Rebellion: Official Records (Army)*; *Battles and Leaders of the Civil War* (1887–88), vols. III, IV; G. W. Cullum, *Biog. Reg. Officers and Grads. U. S. Mil. Acad.* (3rd ed., 1891); F. B. Heitman, *Hist. Reg. of the U. S. Army* (1890); obituary in *Army and Navy Jour.*, May 1, 1897, repr. in *Twenty-eighth Ann. Reunion, Asso. Grads., U. S. Mil. Acad.* (1897); T. M. Newsom, *Pen Pictures of St. Paul, Minn.* (1886); *Daily Pioneer Press* (St. Paul), Apr. 22, 1897; information as to many important facts from Maj. Richard W. Johnson, U. S. A., Ret., who is authority for the statement that his father had no middle name—the "W" being merely a letter.]
C. D. R.

JOHNSON, ROBERT (*c.* 1676–May 3, 1735), colonial governor, first appeared in Carolina history in 1701, when he was accepted by the Board of Trade as surety for his father, Sir Nathaniel Johnson [*q.v.*], who was to be made governor of Carolina and who served in that capacity from 1702 to 1708. The son, a mercer, took oath as freeman of Newcastle-upon-Tyne, Jan. 19, 1702/3 (*The Register of Freemen of Newcastle upon Tyne,* 1923). In 1713 the Carolina proprietors expressed an intention of appointing him to succeed Governor Craven. In 1715 Johnson appeared with others before the Board of Trade to request in vain that the Crown aid in defending Carolina against the Yemassee Indians. The proprietors likewise failed to help, and the settlers had to carry on their struggle alone, but finally succeeded in turning back the Indians. Johnson was made governor in 1717, at a time when the colonists were petitioning that Carolina be made a royal province and rebellion against the proprietors was threatening. He arrived at Charleston to find the colony's coasts pillaged by pirates. After vain appeals to the proprietors for help, the colonists had sent out an expedition under Colonel Rhett, which defeated and captured the notorious Stede Bonnet, who later escaped and took part in pirate raids on Charleston harbor. Johnson, acting with courage and decision, organized a second expedition and in a pitched battle exterminated the buccaneers, recapturing Bonnet, who was sent to Charleston and hanged with twenty-two other pirate prisoners. Johnson's period as governor ended in 1719 when dissatisfaction with the weak and inefficient management of the proprietors reached a climax. The rebellion was immediately caused by the proprietors' disallowance of certain popular laws, including the regulation of elections to the legislature. Johnson's popularity was attested by the request of the revolutionary convention that he continue as governor in the King's name, an offer which he refused, remaining loyal to the proprietors. The revolutionists thereupon elected another governor and ultimately gained their ends when in 1729 a royal government was established in the colony, which was divided into two provinces, North and South Carolina.

Johnson in the meantime had gone to England. His efficiency and popularity were again recognized when he was selected as the first governor of South Carolina under the Crown, a position which he assumed in 1731. One of his instructions required fixing the line between his province and North Carolina, but this he did not accomplish. In 1732 he aided Governor Oglethorpe in founding the colony of Georgia, furnishing food and escort to the settlers. To safeguard the borders of his own province, he advocated further settlement through the erection of townships in which land would be granted to every actual settler, and also urged the giving of presents to the Indians and the stationing of an independent company on the frontier to maintain peace. He tried to promote his colony's growth by asking the Crown to help the Swiss and other foreigners emigrating there, and he welcomed Pierre Purry and his Swiss followers when they came to the lower Savannah and settled Purrysburg, which unfortunately did not prosper. Johnson ultimately disposed of all his property in England and thoroughly identified himself with colonial life. His will shows that at the time of his death he was a man of some wealth, the father of three sons and two daughters. His wife, Margaret, had died in 1732. The esteem and respect in which he was held are indicated by his title of "good Governor Robert Johnson." The Assembly erected a monument to him in Saint Philip's Church. His daughter Margaret married Henry Izard and became the mother of Ralph Izard [*q.v.*].

[Edward McCrady, *The Hist. of S. C. under the Proprietary Govt.* (1897), and *The Hist. of S. C. under the Royal Govt.* (1889); V. W. Crane, *The Southern Frontier, 1670–1732* (1929); *S. C. Hist. and Geneal. Mag.*, July 1901, Apr. 1904, July 1911; B. R. Carroll, *Hist. Colls. of S. C.* (1836); Alexander Hewat, *An Hist. Account of the Rise and Progress of the Colonies of S. C. and Ga.* (2 vols., 1779); Frederick Dalcho, *An Hist. Account of the Prot. Episc. Ch. in S. C.* (1820).]

H. B–C.

JOHNSON, ROBERT WARD (July 22, 1814–July 26, 1879), lawyer, congressman, was born in Scott County, Ky., the son of Benjamin and Matilda (Williams) Johnson. His father, a brother of James and Richard Mentor Johnson [*qq.v.*], sat on the bench for thirty-eight years, first as a state judge in Kentucky and then as a federal judge in the territory and state of Arkansas. Robert Ward Johnson received his academic training in the Choctaw Academy, which was established on the land of his uncle Richard M. Johnson, and at St. Joseph's College, Bardstown, Ky. After studying law, he opened an office in Little Rock, Ark., in 1835. Five years later he became prosecuting attorney for the district including Little Rock and thus, *ex officio,* attorney-general for the state. In 1846 he was elected to Congress as a Democrat, and was twice reëlected, but declined to be a candidate in 1852. The following year he was appointed to the Senate by Governor Conway to fill the vacancy caused by the resignation of Solon Borland, was elected by the legislature to fill out the term, and reëlected for a full term, serving from July 1853 to Mar. 3, 1861. He entered Congress in time to oppose the Wilmot Proviso and in 1850 he opposed Clay's plan of compromise, speaking and voting against the admission of California and voting against the compromise with Texas. He avoided committing himself on the territorial bill and the abolition of the slave trade in the District of Columbia, but supported the new fugitive-slave law. In the Senate, he supported Douglas' Kansas-Nebraska bill and the homestead bill, and during the latter half of his term was active on questions involving the public lands, securing large grants for railroads in Arkansas. He did not seek reëlection in 1860, but in the following year he stumped the state in favor of secession and was elected by the secession convention as a delegate to the Confederate Provisional Congress. Later he was elected to the Confederate Senate and served until the end of the war. He then planned flight to Mexico, but in Galveston he met an old friend in General Granger, who was in command of the United States forces there. Granger gave him a pass and advised him to go to Washington, where President Johnson, another old friend, gave him due protection. He then returned to his estate in Arkansas and tried to rebuild his fortune, but had to surrender it to his creditors. Going back to Washington he formed a law partnership with Albert Pike [*q.v.*], but Pike said that he never practised much (interview, *post*). His disabilities removed by act of Congress, he sought a seat in the Senate in 1878, but was defeated by J. D. Walker, and died the following year.

The "Johnson Family" was credited with ruling Arkansas from 1836 to 1860. R. W. Johnson's sister married Ambrose H. Sevier, the state's first senator, and a niece married T. J. Churchill, postmaster at Little Rock 1857–61, and later governor. In 1860 Richard H. Johnson, Robert's brother, was nominated for governor by questionable methods, but defeated by Henry W. Rector largely on the issue of the "Johnson Family." In 1862 the "Family" returned to power, but the close of the war broke up the dynasty, though Churchill was afterwards elected governor. R. W. Johnson himself was regarded as clean and incorruptible (*Arkansas Gazette*, July 29, 1879), and he served his state well—though some thought too well when he secured the passage of a bill to relieve the state of the obligation to improve the swamp lands. He was married in 1836 to Sarah Smith, daughter of Dr. George W. Smith of Louisville, Ky., and after her death in 1862 he married her sister, Laura. His first wife bore him three children. He was buried in Mount Holly Cemetery, Little Rock.

[*Cong. Globe*, 31 Cong., 1 Sess., App. 715–18, 33 Cong., 1 Sess., pp. 553–54, 555, 1125–26, 1661–62; John Hallum, *Biog. and Pictorial Hist. of Ark.* (1887); J. H. Shinn, *Pioneers and Makers of Ark.* (1908); Fay Hempstead, *A Pictorial Hist. of Ark.* (1890); D. Y. Thomas, *Ark. in War and Reconstruction, 1861–74* (1926); *Biog. Dir. Am. Cong.* (1928); interview with Albert Pike, *Washington Post*, July 28, 1879, repr. in *Daily Ark. Gazette*, Aug. 3, 1879; issues of the latter paper for July 27, 29, 31, 1879; *N. Y. Herald*, July 28, 1879.]
D. Y. T.

JOHNSON, SAMUEL (Oct. 14, 1696–Jan. 6, 1772), minister of the Church of England in colonial Connecticut, president of King's College, New York, was born at Guilford, Conn., the son of Samuel and Mary (Sage) Johnson. He appears to have been devoted to books and study even as a small child and at fourteen was ready to enter the Collegiate School, later Yale College, then located at Saybrook. After graduating he taught school at Guilford. In 1716 the Collegiate School was moved to New Haven and Johnson was made a tutor. Three years later, he resigned and on Mar. 20, 1720, was ordained pastor of the Congregational Church at West Haven, accepting that pastorate in part because of his desire to be near the library of the college. He read widely in theology and church history and soon, together with a small group of other intellectuals, including Timothy Cutler [*q.v.*], came to doubt the validity of the "Congregational Way." In September 1722 they made known their doubts at Commencement, and long official debates followed in the college library. Three of the protestants decided to join the Church of England and in the latter part of 1722 Johnson, Cutler, and Brown sailed from Boston for London. In England Johnson met many prominent people, visited Oxford and Cambridge, received holy orders in the English Church, and was appointed by the Society for the Propagation of the Gospel to be missionary at Stratford, Conn. Returning to the colonies, he landed at Piscataqua, Sept. 22, 1723, and traveled overland to Stratford. Here he had a small Anglican congregation and on Christmas Day, 1724, opened the first building dedicated to Church-of-England services in that colony, he himself being the only Connecticut clergyman of that faith. On Sept. 26, 1725, he married a widow, Charity Nicoll, daughter of Col. Richard Floyd of Brookhaven, L. I. This marriage allied him to some of the most prominent families in New York, and he became a close friend of Gov. William Burnet [*q.v.*]. His most famous friendship, however, was that with the English idealist philosopher, Dean Berkeley, who resided at Newport from 1729 to 1731, and whose gifts to Yale were made mainly on account of Johnson. Incidentally, Johnson became a convert to the Berkeleian philosophy.

The Church-of-England movement did not make great headway in New England and encountered much opposition. Johnson was the leader, and the whole history of the movement is reflected in his large correspondence. In 1743 he received the degree of D.D. from Oxford. During these middle years of his life he was constantly engaged in religious controversies in the colonies, and also in spreading the idealistic philosophy of Berkeley. In 1749 plans were matured for a college in Philadelphia, with the support of Franklin among others, and Johnson was asked to become its first president, a position which he declined. About this time, 1750, he also received a second call to Trinity Church, Newport, which he refused, since he felt he was needed for the fight against the established church of Connecticut. In 1753 a project for a college in New York was under way and it was indicated to Johnson that the plan would fail unless he became president. He finally accepted in the autumn of that year and, resigning his mission at Stratford, to which he had ministered for thirty-two years and to the interests of which, although a poor parish, he had been devoted, he moved to New York in April 1754, where he took up his duties as president of King's College, later to develop into Columbia University. He also served as lecturer at Trinity Church. His administration was successful but the first four years were marked by personal disaster. Two epidemics of smallpox interrupted the work of the college and Johnson lost his wife, a son, and a step-daughter. On June 18, 1761, he married Mrs. Sarah (Hull) Beach, widow of William Beach of Stratford, Conn., whose daughter his son, William Samuel Johnson [*q.v.*], had married. She died of smallpox in 1763 and Johnson resigned from the presidency of the college, resolved to live in retirement at Stratford. He took part in the agitation in favor of bishops in the colonies, published an English-Hebrew grammar, and kept in close correspondence with English friends during the growing political difficulties. He had again taken up the duties of rector at Stratford, which he carried on until his death.

He was a somewhat voluminous writer, mainly on philosophy, although only a few of his writings were published in his lifetime. In 1731 appeared his *Introduction to Philosophy,* a small and comparatively unimportant tract. In 1746 he published his much more valuable *Ethices Elementa, or the First Principles of Moral Philosophy,* and in 1752 Franklin reprinted this with a new section under the title of *Elementa Philosophica: Containing Chiefly, Noetica, or Things Relating to the Mind or Understanding; and Ethica, or Things Relating to the Moral Behaviour.* Owing partly to contemporary conditions in both England and America, Johnson did not receive the attention to which his thought and work entitle him and cannot be considered to have been of wide influence as a philosopher. He was, however, much more than a mere disciple of Berkeley. In distinguishing pure intellect from sensation he advanced beyond his master, as he did also in his analysis of intuitive evidence. He also did good and original work in harmonizing certain of the philosophical systems of the day. He ranks with Jonathan Edwards as one of the two most important exponents of idealistic philosophy in colonial America.

[T. B. Chandler, *The Life of Samuel Johnson, D.D.* (1805); W. B. Sprague, *Annals Am. Pulpit,* vol. V (1859); E. E. Beardsley, *Life and Correspondence of Samuel Johnson* (1874); I. W. Riley, *Am. Philosophy: the Early Schools* (1907), with bibliography; manuscripts in the Columbia College Library; the Fulham manuscripts, of which there are transcripts in the Library of Congress; Herbert and Carol Schneider, *Samuel Johnson, President of King's College: His Career and Writings* (4 vols., 1929).]

J. T. A.

JOHNSON, SAMUEL (Oct. 10, 1822–Feb. 19, 1882), independent liberal preacher, author, was born in Salem, Mass., a descendant of Timothy Johnson who was living in Andover, Mass., in 1674, and son of Dr. Samuel and Anna (Dodge) Johnson. His father was a prominent Salem physician, and Samuel grew up amid circumstances favorable to character and intellectual pursuits. At the age of sixteen he was ready for college, and four years later, 1842, ranking fourth in his class, he graduated from Harvard. He entered the Harvard Divinity School, graduating in 1846, his course having been somewhat interrupted by the condition of his health, for the benefit of which in 1844 he made a trip to Europe. One of his classmates was Samuel Longfellow [*q.v.*], and between the two a close and lasting friendship arose. The year their divinity course was completed they published *A Book of Hymns for Public and Private Devotion,* a *Supplement* to which appeared in 1848. Johnson began his ministry in the Unitarian church, Dorchester, Mass., where his views on the social and political questions of the day proved unacceptable, and he remained for only about a year. After preaching for some time to a society of liberals in Lynn, in 1853 he became their minister, a free church was organized, and Oxford Street Chapel was built, of which he continued in charge until 1870. He never married, and made his home at Salem until his father's death in 1876, after which he lived on an ancestral farm in North Andover. With Samuel Longfellow he visited Europe in 1860, remaining fifteen months, and during a portion of this time they worked on the compilation of *Hymns of the Spirit,* published in 1864. The hymns written by Johnson are of high excellence, some of the best known of which are "Father, in Thy mysterious presence kneeling," "Life of Ages richly poured," and "City of God, how broad, how far."

Although Unitarian in his associations, he was too radical an individualist ever to affiliate himself with any denominational body; strongly anti-slavery, and ardently humanitarian in sentiment, he joined none of the reform societies of his day, lest there be some interference with the freedom of his soul. He was a lover of nature, with an interest in geology, and long walks were his principal diversion. A mystic and poet, he was also a clear thinker and a patient student, enthusiastically devoted to discerning the truth behind appearances and bringing human life into harmony therewith. Philosophically, he was a thorough-going Transcendentalist, friendly to science, and an evolutionist, but insistent that spiritual verities cannot be ascertained by scientific methods. As a preacher, lecturer, and writer he was an exponent of natural religion, "its intimations of God and duty and immortality." Much of his life was given to an interpretation of Oriental religions, with a view to disclosing the unity of human experience and the development of the religious consciousness through the ages. The published results are to be found in three sizable works, *Oriental Religions and Their Relation to Universal Religion, India* (1872), *China* (1877), and *Persia,* left not quite completed at his death, and published in 1885 with an introduction by Octavius B. Frothingham [*q.v.*]. Selections from his manuscripts, *Lectures, Essays, and Sermons,* with a memoir by Samuel Longfellow, were published the year following Johnson's death.

[W. W. Johnson, *Records of the Descendants of John Johnson of Ipswich and Andover, Mass., with an Appendix Containing Records of Descendants of Timothy Johnson of Andover* (1892); S. A. Eliot, *Heralds of a Liberal Faith* (1910), vol. III; *Atlantic Mo.,* June 1883; *Christian Reg.,* Feb. 23, 1882, Mar. 2, 1882; John Julian, *A Dict. of Hymnology* (1891); *Boston Transcript,* Feb. 21, 1882.] H. E. S.

JOHNSON, SAMUEL WILLIAM (July 3, 1830–July 21, 1909), agricultural chemist, professor, experiment station director, and author, was born at Kingsboro, N. Y., the third son of Abner Adolphus and Annah Wells (Gilbert) Johnson, both of pure colonial descent. He spent his boyhood on his father's farm at Deer River, N. Y., and was educated at Lowville Academy, where he obtained his first instruction in chemistry. His youthful essay, "On Fixing Ammonia" (*Cultivator,* August 1847), gave promise of the man. He fitted up a laboratory on his father's farm in 1848, but gave up private experimenting late in this year to accept a position as instructor at Flushing Institute, L. I. In 1850, he entered Yale College where he was inspired by his teacher, John Pitkin Norton [*q.v.*], to make agricultural chemistry his life work. As a result of Norton's influence he went to Germany in 1853 to complete his chemical education under Erdmann at Leipzig and Liebig at Munich. After returning from his European studies he was appointed professor of analytical chemistry at the Yale Scientific School in 1856, and in the same year became chemist of the Connecticut State Agricultural Society. The subject of agricultural chemistry was added to his professorship in 1857. Seven books and 172 articles upon agriculture and agricultural chemistry are among the evidences of his industry. His lectures and publications upon soils, rotation of crops, fertilizers, methods of analysis, plant nutrition, food adulteration, and many other subjects exerted a great influence upon the development of scientific agriculture in America. By beginning in 1856 a systematic chemical examination of the commercial fertilizers which were sold in Connecticut, he became the founder of agricultural regulatory work in America. He was largely instrumental in securing the passage of the Connecticut law of 1869 which, although imperfect, was one of the first that required fertilizers to be labeled with a statement of composition. He was the first leader in the movement that led to the establishment of agricultural experiment stations in the United States, as a result of which Connecticut, in 1875, with private financial support, established at Middletown the first state institution of this kind, with W. O. Atwater [*q.v.*], a former pupil and assistant of Johnson, as director. In 1877, the experiment station was reorganized as a wholly independent state establishment in New Haven, with Johnson as director from 1877 to 1899. He was an excellent critic of agricultural chemical work and performed a lasting service in the two classic volumes *How Crops Grow* (1868) and *How Crops Feed* (1870), which have been translated into many foreign languages. He is also to be remembered for his well-known translations of the famous manuals of Fresenius by which many American chemists obtained their introduction to qualitative and quantitative analysis (*Manual of Qualitative Analysis,* 1864, 3rd ed., 1883; and *A System of Instruction in Quantitative Chemical Analysis,* 1870). On Oct. 13, 1858, Johnson married Elizabeth Erwin Blinn of Essex, N. Y. Although a man of modest and retiring disposition, he exerted a greater influence upon scientific agriculture in America than any one else of his generation. He was president of the American Chemical Society in 1878, president of the Association of Official Agricultural Chemists in 1885, president of the American Association of Agricultural Colleges and Experimental Stations in 1896, a member of the National Academy of Sciences from 1866, and an associate fellow of the American Academy of Arts and Sciences.

[*From the Letter-Files of S. W. Johnson* (1913), a biographical sketch by his daughter, Elizabeth A. Osborne, with selections from his correspondence and a complete bibliography of his writings; T. B. Osborne, "Samuel William Johnson," in *Nat. Acad. Sci. Biog. Memoirs,* vol. VII (1913), with bibliography; *Experiment Station Record,* Sept. 1909; *Science,* Sept. 24,

1909; *Am. Jour. of Sci.*, Oct. 1909; *Am. Chem. Jour.*, Nov. 1909; *Proc. Am. Chem. Soc.*, 1909; *New Haven Evening Register*, July 21, 1909.] C. A. B.

JOHNSON, SETH WHITMORE (May 3, 1811–Feb. 13, 1907), ship-builder, was, in effect, the successor of Levi Johnson [*q.v.*] as a pioneer in the Great Lakes ship-building industry, though the two Johnsons were in no way connected. He was a native of Middle Haddam, Conn., the second son and third child in a family of nine children born to Henry Johnson, a farmer, and his wife, Mary Whitmore. Seth left the farm at the age of fourteen to become an apprentice for seven years in a shipyard. At the end of his term, he set up in business for himself, repairing and building ships. Northern Ohio at this time was beginning to experience the beneficial effect of the Erie Canal and the Ohio canals. Attracted by the outlook, Johnson moved to Cleveland in the fall of 1834 and the following year entered upon his business as ship-builder. Ten years later he formed a partnership with Erastus Tisdale. For nineteen years they carried on what was then the chief industry of Cleveland. Their vessels were found on all the upper lakes: two were portages across the Sault to Lake Superior. Steamboats were built for the English coast trade. Johnson invested his profits in lake shipping until he became a large ship-owner as well as a builder. One of his vessels, loaded with staves, was among the first to pass through the Welland Canal and carry a lake cargo to European ports, inaugurating a direct service from Cleveland to Liverpool.

He married Augusta Sophia Norton of Middle Haddam, Conn., July 15, 1840. Such meager records as survive describe him as a man of genial, kindly ways, socially inclined.

[See *Cleveland Leader*, Feb. 15, 1907; *Annals of the Early Settlers' Asso.*, vol. V, no. IV (1907), p. 396; Maurice Joblin, *Cleveland, Past and Present* (1869), p. 161; S. P. Orth, *A Hist. of Cleveland, Ohio* (1910), I, 719; G. V. R. Wickham, *The Pioneer Families of Cleveland* (1914), II, 414; the vital records of East Hampton, Conn., give Johnson's middle name as Wetmore in the birth records and Whitmore in the marriage records.] E. J. B.

JOHNSON, THOMAS (Nov. 4, 1732–Oct. 26, 1819), member of the Continental Congress, first governor of the state of Maryland, and associate justice of the United States Supreme Court, was born in Calvert County, Md. He was one of twelve children of Thomas Johnson and Dorcas Sedgwick. The Johnsons had been prominent in England for many generations. His mother's parents were Puritans who had taken refuge in Calvert County. After receiving rudimentary education at home, he was sent to Annapolis, Md., where he secured clerical employment through the influence of Thomas Jennings, register of the Land Office. He studied law under Stephen Bordley, became a lawyer in Annapolis, and on Feb. 16, 1766, married Ann Jennings, daughter of his former employer. Meanwhile he had entered the Provincial Assembly as a delegate from Anne Arundel County in 1762. Following the passage of the Stamp Act, he was named on a committee to enunciate "the constitutional rights and privileges of the freemen of the province," and after Parliament passed the Acts of 1767, he was named on a committee (June 8, 1768) to draft a memorial to King George III. He was also one of the members selected to superintend the construction of the State House. He was a delegate to the Maryland convention of 1774, held in Annapolis, in which he was chosen one of the members to arrange for the Congress of the Colonies, and was authorized to represent Maryland at the Congress in Philadelphia.

Taking his seat in Congress on Sept. 6, 1774, he was one of the members appointed the following month to draft a petition to the Crown for a redress of grievances. In the second Continental Congress, when John Adams felt it would be tactful for a southerner to nominate George Washington for commander-in-chief of the Continental Army, and the delegates from Virginia felt a delicacy about nominating their own colleague, Johnson placed Washington in nomination for the supreme command on June 15, 1775 (*Journal of the Continental Congress*, vol. II, p. 91; Delaplaine, *The Life of Thomas Johnson*, p. 112). Returning to Annapolis to urge the people to assume the functions of government, he was one of the members who drafted the Association of the Freemen of Maryland—a declaration of rights for a new régime—signed by the deputies in the convention on Aug. 14, 1775. In the autumn of 1775 he took a lively interest in the debates on the floor of Congress: whereas John Adams had referred to him a year before as "a deliberating man, but not a shining orator" (C. F. Adams, *The Works of John Adams*, II, 1850, 395), he wrote some years later that Johnson was "the most frequent speaker" from Maryland; and while the hope for reconciliation led him, like Dickinson and Jay, "to retard many vigorous measures," Adams wrote that "ere long he and all his State came cordially into our system" (*Ibid.*, II, 506). Johnson was not in Philadelphia on the day the Declaration of Independence was adopted; but he voted in Annapolis, on July 6, 1776, for the Declaration of the Delegates of Maryland, declaring the separation of Maryland from the mother country. He was a member of the convention of 1776, which framed the declaration of rights and constitution of the state of Maryland. In the meantime he had been chosen as first brigadier-general of the Maryland militia; and, although urged to return to Congress, now went to Frederick to raise and equip recruits. Early in 1777 he led approximately 1,800 men from Frederick to the headquarters of General Washington in New Jersey.

Elected by the legislature in February as governor of Maryland, he accepted by letter from his camp at Basking Ridge, East Jersey, and was inaugurated on Mar. 21, 1777. Reëlected without opposition in November 1777, and again in November 1778, he served as the first chief executive of the state until Nov. 12, 1779. In 1780 and early in 1781, he served as a member of the lower house of the legislature, where he urged the adoption of the Articles of Confederation but not until after he felt convinced that the other states would surrender their claims to the western lands so that the territory beyond the Alleghanies would become the common property of the United States. After peace was restored, he and Washington revived the plan to extend navigation of the Potomac River and accordingly the "Patowmack" Company was organized in 1785 with Washington as president and Johnson as a member of the board of directors. Johnson served again in the legislature in 1786 and 1787, and in the state convention of 1788 which ratified the Federal Constitution. Warned by Washington that an adjournment of the Maryland convention "to a later period than the decision of the question" in Virginia would be "tantamount to the rejection of the Constitution" (Delaplaine, p. 442), Johnson worked and voted for its ratification. From April 1790 until October 1791 he served as chief judge of the General Court of Maryland. Meanwhile, on Aug. 5, 1791, he was appointed to the United States Supreme Court. On Nov. 7 the appointment was confirmed, and on Aug. 6, 1792, he took oath of office. He wrote the first opinion in the *Reports* of the United States Supreme Court, filed in the case of *State of Georgia* vs. *Brailsford* (*2 Dallas*, 402). He had also been appointed by the President in 1791 as a member of the board of commissioners of the Federal City, and in that year he and his associates, Daniel Carroll and Dr. David Stuart, wrote to Major L'Enfant that they had decided to call the Federal City the City of Washington. On account of his failing health, he resigned as associate justice in 1793 and as commissioner of the Federal City in 1794. In 1795 President Washington importuned him to accept the portfolio of secretary of state, but on account of growing physical infirmities Johnson declined this final appeal. He spent the latter years of his life in retirement near Frederick. His last public appearance was on Feb. 22, 1800, when he delivered a solemn panegyric in Frederick in memory of Washington. Johnson was somewhat of a philosopher and he knew how to live. His mind was sufficiently keen to enable him to transact business and to make his will in his eighty-sixth year. While he never sought political power, he admitted that one of his chief sources of happiness was the thought that he had served his country with honor and that his name would be revered by his descendants. His final years were cheered by the thought that he had gained "the friendship and confidence of Washington," that he had no enemies, and that he would meet Washington beyond the grave.

[Edward S. Delaplaine, *The Life of Thos. Johnson* (1927); J. T. Scharf, *Hist. of Western Md.* (1882), vol. I; T. J. C. Williams, *Hist. of Frederick County, Md.* (1910), vol. I; B. C. Steiner, "Maryland's Adoption of the Federal Constitution," *Am. Hist. Rev.*, Oct. 1899, Jan. 1900; F. B. Sawvel, *The Complete Anas of Thos. Jefferson* (1903); *Archives of Md.*, vols. XI (1892), XII (1893), XIII (1897), XXI (1901), and LXIII (1924); Washington MSS., Lib. of Cong.; manuscript letters and papers, Md. Hist. Soc.] E. S. D.

JOHNSON, TOM LOFTIN (July 18, 1854–Apr. 10, 1911), inventor, street-railroad operator, steel producer, member of Congress, mayor of Cleveland, Ohio, was born at Blue Spring, near Georgetown, Ky., the son of Albert Johnson and Helen Loftin. His elementary school education was interrupted by the Civil War in which his father served in the Confederate army. During the war the family moved from place to place and after the war, completely impoverished, settled in Staunton, Va., where Tom as a child assisted in the family support by establishing a newspaper monopoly through an arrangement with the conductor of the only train operating into the town. With money so made, the family moved to Louisville, Ky., where the boy did odd jobs until 1869, when he was employed in a rolling mill and later with the Louisville Street Railroad, which at that time belonged to Bidermann and A. V. Du Pont, grandsons of Pierre Samuel Du Pont, the founder of the family in this country.

Shortly after becoming connected with the street railroad, Johnson invented the first farebox for coins. Later he went to Indianapolis and with the backing of the Du Ponts, bought and rehabilitated the Indianapolis Street Railroad. From there he moved to Cleveland, Ohio, bought, built, and operated a street railroad, and became interested in similar properties in Detroit. With various members of the Du Pont family, Johnson became interested in the establishment of steel works—the Cambria Company at Johnstown, Pa., and the Lorain Steel Company at Lorain, Ohio. He invented and patented the so-called "trilby" rail and also the machine for rolling it. His younger brother, Albert W. Johnson, at one time associated in the Cleveland street-railroad enterprises, became interested in traction properties in Brooklyn and built the first traction line over the Brooklyn Bridge. At the time of the Johnstown flood (1889) Tom L. Johnson was appointed a member of the relief commission and showed great energy and intelligence in administering the relief fund of three million dollars contributed throughout the country for the sufferers. In the operation of his street-railroad properties in Cleveland, he came into conflict with a competing system dominated by Marcus A. Hanna. The opposition between these resolute and resourceful men continued until Johnson sold out his interest and retired from business to enter public life.

While still interested in Indianapolis and Cleveland street railroads, Johnson read *Progress and Poverty* by Henry George and became an advocate of free trade and the single tax. Later when he was elected to Congress on the Democratic ticket in 1890 and 1892, he boldly proclaimed his faith in free trade, although he was at that time interested in the heavily protected steel industry, and to the end of his life he advocated the single tax as expounded by Henry George, among whose adherents he came to be recognized as a leader. With other single-taxers, he built a home for Henry George near Ft. Hamilton, N. Y., where he himself had a residence, and took an aggressive part in the campaigns for the mayoralty of New York waged by Henry George in 1886 and particularly in 1897. In 1874 he had married a distant kinswoman of his own name, Margaret J. Johnson, a woman of striking beauty and culture. Around them constantly gathered the liberal-minded and progressive young and middle-aged men whom the American colleges, in the nineties, were sending out as missionaries in the cause of a higher social conscience in the economic and institutional development of the country.

In 1901 Johnson was elected mayor of Cleveland and was successively reëlected three times. During his mayoralty he transformed the city government and at the end of eight years had left a mark upon municipal government in America as perhaps the outstanding municipal executive so far produced in United States history. In accordance with his democratic theories, Johnson believed that the regeneration of city government could come only through an informed and interested electorate. The eight years of his mayoralty were, therefore, a continuous educational campaign. In order to carry his message to the people, he used a circus tent accommodating between four and five thousand persons. This tent he moved from place to place throughout the city and in it he held meetings for the discussion of public affairs in which the audience was invited to ask questions upon any subject relating to the city, its government, or its interests. His own method of public speech was informal, but he insisted that the least conspicuous member of the audience should be fairly dealt with both by the speakers and by the rest of the audience and he stimulated even shy men and women to inquire about city affairs. He required his subordinates to administer the ordinary housekeeping of the city with efficiency, integrity, and courtesy, devoting his own efforts primarily to secure municipal ownership and operation of the consolidated street-railroad services.

The slogan of his several campaigns was "Home rule; three cent fare; and just taxation." In order to secure municipal home rule and a revision of the tax laws of the state, he carried his fight into the state at large and as the result of his educational campaign, an amendment was added to the constitution of Ohio in 1910 which gave to Ohio municipalities large immunity from control by the state legislature in the management of their purely municipal and domestic concerns. The three-cent-fare movement resulted in an experimental leasing of the railroad for municipal operations, but the bitter contest between Johnson and the owners of the street-railroad property finally resulted in a receivership of the properties and their reorganization under a franchise drawn by Judge R. W. Tayler, district judge of the United States.

In 1909 Johnson was defeated for reëlection. His health had already begun to be seriously impaired but he assisted, during 1910, in the preparation of Tayler's Street Railroad Ordinance. Throughout his life he was a Democrat in politics and a democrat in the Jeffersonian sense. His advocacy of municipal ownership, public ownership of railroads, woman's suffrage, and other causes at the time deemed advanced, led him to be regarded as a radical, although many of his beliefs have since either been generally accepted or are tenets in the liberal creed. In many ways he was the most spectacular liberal in the public life of America from 1890 to 1910. Having accumulated a substantial fortune and having inherited the cultural traditions of a well-born and well-reared Southern boy, he was able by the charm of a magnetic personality to disarm, as to himself, much of the criticism then generally directed against radical opinion. By common consent he made Cleveland "the best governed city in America," and the impulse he gave to the establishment of good government upon the interest of an informed electorate has remained the foundation of muncipal progress.

[Tom L. Johnson, *My Story* (1911), written in collaboration with Elizabeth J. Hauser, is an intimate and detailed autobiography. See also: Carl Lorenz, *Tom L. Johnson* (1911); Lincoln Steffens, *The Shame of the Cities* (1904); S. P. Orth, *A Hist. of Cleveland, Ohio* (1910), vol. I; E. M. Avery, *A Hist. of Cleveland and Its Environs* (1918); *World's Work*, Feb. 1902, Jan. 1908; *Outlook*, Aug. 4, 1906, Nov. 16, 1907, July 24, Oct. 23, 1909, Apr. 22, 1911; *Nation* (N. Y.), Sept. 11, 1902, Sept. 3, 1903, Apr. 13, 1911; *Am. Rev. of Revs.*, May 1911; *Arena*, Nov. 1902, June, Aug., Nov. 1903, Dec. 1905, Apr. 1906, Dec. 1907, Apr., June 1908; *Gunton's Mag.*, Oct., Nov. 1903; *Cleveland Plain Dealer*, Apr. 11, 1911.] N. D. B.

JOHNSON, VIRGINIA WALES (Dec. 28, 1849–Jan. 16, 1916), author, daughter of M. Augustus and Sarah (Benson) Johnson, was born in Brooklyn, N. Y. Her parents were Bostonians, and she was a descendant of Judge Samuel Sewall [*q.v.*]. Her education was carried on at home and she began writing for her own amusement as a child. At fifteen she was writing her Kettle Club Series (1860–70), including *The Kettle's Birthday Party and Grandfather's Pocket-Book.* Her first novel, *Joseph the Jew* (1874), was published by Harper & Brothers in the Library of Select Novels and was taken for an English reprint. *A Sack of Gold* (1874), *The Calderwood Secret* (1875), and *Miss Nancy's Pilgrimage* (1876) were also published in that series. *The Catskill Fairies* (1876) was exhibited at the Centennial Exposition at Philadelphia as an example of American typography and was reprinted in England. In 1871 the four volumes of the Doll's Club Series had appeared: *Jack's Kite, Jo's Doll, Katy's Christmas,* and *Patty's Pranks.* In 1875 she went to Europe with her mother and sister for travel and study, and found a European existence so much to her taste that she spent the remainder of her life there, chiefly in Italy. Her later novels and stories include "The Image of San Donato," published in *Harper's Magazine,* January 1879; *A Foreign Marriage, or, Buying a Title* (1880), a story of modern Florentine life, published anonymously; *The Neptune Vase* (1881), a story of modern Siena and title-hunting American girls; *Two Old Cats* (1882), in which a châlet occupied by Queen Victoria at Mentone is the scene; *An English "Daisy Miller"* (1882), an attempt to show Henry James that not all indiscreet girls abroad are American; *The Fainalls of Tipton* (1884); *Tulip Place, a Story of New York* (1886); *The House of the Musician* (1887); *The Terra-Cotta Bust* (1887), first published in *Lippincott's Monthly Magazine*; *The Treasure Tower, a Story of Malta* (1892); *A Bermuda Lily* (1912); *A Lift on the Road* (1913). Most of her latest work took the form of books of travel and popular history: *The Lily of the Arno, or, Florence, Past and Present* (1891); *Genoa the Superb, the City of Columbus* (1892); *America's Godfather, the Florentine Gentleman* (1894), treating of Amerigo Vespucci; *A World's Shrine* (1902), of Como, Italy; *Many Years of a Florentine Balcony* (1911); *Summer Days at Vallombrosa* (1911); *Two Quaint Republics, Andorra and San Marino* (1913).

Beginning as a writer of children's books, she soon turned to fiction for adults. After 1875, her work shows intense love for Italy, both mediaeval and modern. Her knowledge of Italian history and literature and her familiarity with modern Italy, its fiestas, street life, sea and mountain resorts, are sufficient to make her books informative as well as readable.

[In addition to autobiographical material in the books mentioned above, see *Who's Who in America,* 1912–13, 1918–19; *Literary World,* June 3, 1882.] S. G. B.

JOHNSON, Sir WILLIAM (1715–July 11, 1774), superintendent of Indian affairs, was born at Smithtown, County Meath, Ireland, the son of Christopher and Anne (Warren) Johnson. He came to America probably late in 1737 or early in 1738, for by the latter year he had settled on the south side of the Mohawk River near the mouth of the Schoharie, assuming charge of an estate belonging to his uncle, Vice Admiral Sir Peter Warren. The valley of the lower Mohawk was being rapidly occupied, and its strategic location presented unusual opportunities for the conduct of the fur trade. Johnson set up a store and for several years combined trade with the Indians and neighboring settlers with his other interests. The year following his arrival he purchased a tract of his own on the north side of the Mohawk, near the present city of Amsterdam. Throughout his life, his eagerness to acquire land never waned, and when he died he was proprietor of one of the largest landed estates in the English colonies. About 1742 or 1743, he removed to the north of the river, his place of residence being called Mount Johnson.

Though it has been a matter for dispute, it would seem that about 1739 he married a German girl of the neighborhood, named Catharine Weisenberg, for he refers to her in his will as "my beloved wife" (Stone, *post,* II, 492). By her, he had a son and two daughters. During these early years, he laid the foundations of a large fortune and became intimately acquainted with the neighboring tribes of the Six Nations, particularly the Mohawks, who lived close by.

He first came into public prominence during King George's War. In 1745, when hostilities broke upon the New York frontier, it was feared that the Six Nations might go over to the French, and it was largely owing to Johnson's efforts that such a disaster was prevented. In 1746 he was made responsible for the supply of the English garrison at Oswego and in August of the same year was made colonel of the Six Nations by Governor Clinton, an appointment which also involved transferring to him the conduct of Indian affairs, which had formerly been in the hands of the Albany commissioners. He held innumerable councils with these tribes, secured extremely useful information, and organized and supplied war parties for operations against the French. In February 1748 he was placed in command of fourteen companies of New York militia raised for the defense of the frontiers. By a commission dated May 1, 1748, he was appointed colonel of a regiment of militia for the city and county of Albany. He also rendered valuable service upon the arrival of news of peace, persuading the Indians—who were in some instances reluctant—to bury the hatchet, and adjusting difficulties in regard to the exchange of Indian prisoners.

During the years of nominal peace, from 1748 to 1755, he resumed his activity in the fur trade and agriculture. His affairs were prospering and in 1749 he was engaged in constructing a stone house, which came to be called Fort Johnson, on his land north of the Mohawk. In 1751, he secured from the Onondaga tribe the grant of a valuable tract of land, the purchase being approved by the provincial Council two years later. By a royal commission dated Apr. 12, 1750, he was appointed a member of the Council of New York, an office which he held during the remainder of his life. Certain difficulties with the Assembly having arisen with respect to the payment of his accounts for the supply of the garrison at Oswego, he decided, late in 1750 or early in 1751, that he would no longer be responsible for the management of the affairs of the Six Nations. In spite of the protests of the tribes, he persisted in resigning, and control of Indian affairs was restored to the commissioners. Unofficially, however, he continued to render useful service and his residence became a sort of advanced "listening post."

By 1754, the French seemed determined to occupy the interior and it was evident that hostilities could not long be averted. Johnson ordered the militia to be in readiness and he was called upon in the crisis by Governors Clinton of New York and Shirley of Massachusetts for his views in regard to Indian affairs. In his capacity as a member of the Council of New York, he attended the famous Albany Congress, held in June and July of 1754, and assisted in drafting certain of the speeches which were delivered to the Indians. He also submitted a paper setting forth his views in regard to the measures necessary to thwart the designs of the French. The Indians renewed their request for his reappointment as agent and Johnson was willing to assume the responsibility providing his authority might proceed from the Crown, thus rendering him independent of any colony.

In April 1755, General Braddock, the new commander-in-chief of the British forces, held a council at Alexandria, Va., which was attended by several of the colonial governors. It was decided to launch expeditions against Fort Duquesne, Niagara, and Crown Point, and to Johnson was entrusted command of the force to be sent against the last-named stronghold. A commission from Braddock dated Apr. 15, 1755, gave him "sole Management & direction of the Affairs of the Six Nations of Indians & their Allies" (*Papers, post,* I, 465). He was also commissioned major-general by the governments supplying the troops for the enterprise, the colonies participating being New York, Massachusetts, New Hampshire, Connecticut, and Rhode Island. Albany was the point of concentration, and when Johnson's force reached Lake George, it numbered about two thousand colonial militia and some two or three hundred Indians. On Sept. 8, Johnson's main body was attacked by a force of French and Indians under Dieskau, and a pitched battle ensued in which the French were badly defeated, Dieskau himself being captured. What were left of the French fell back toward Lake Champlain. Johnson felt that his force was too weak to pursue them and contented himself with building a fort at the head of Lake George, which was named William Henry. A fort had previously been constructed at the carrying place to the southward and called Fort Edward. Leaving garrisons to hold these posts, Johnson broke camp late in November and disbanded his force. Though he had failed to capture Crown Point, he had warded off the French menace which threatened the northern colonies. This achievement was the more conspicuous because of the failure of the expeditions against Fort Duquesne and Niagara, and Johnson was acclaimed as a victor throughout the colonies. On Nov. 27, 1755, the King made him a baronet and on Feb. 17, 1756, issued a commission making him a colonel of the Six Nations and their confederates, and "Sole Agent and Superintendent of the said Indians and their Affairs" (*Ibid.*, II, 434). A superintendent was also appointed for the tribes south of the Ohio.

During the three years following the Crown Point expedition, Johnson devoted a large share of his time and energy to the protection of the northern frontiers. He held many councils and organized Indian war parties to cooperate with various military expeditions. By 1759 the tide had turned against the French, and, following the death of General Prideaux, it was Johnson's good fortune to command the force which captured Niagara on July 25 of that year. Leaving a garrison there, he returned to Oswego, where he was relieved of his command by General Gage. During the next few months he busied himself with Indian affairs and was also engaged in founding the settlement which became Johnstown, a few miles west of Fort Johnson. In 1760, he organized a force of several hundred Indians, joined Amherst at Oswego, and accompanied his successful expedition against Montreal.

With the downfall of French power in Canada a vast new territory and many strange tribes came under his jurisdiction. On July 5, 1761, he set out on a journey to Detroit at the request of Amherst, his objects being to secure information in regard to the territory which had been acquired by the British; to hold a council with the Indians; and to establish regulations concerning the fur trade of the interior. His mission seemed successful, and when in September he left Detroit, it was with the conviction that the Indians were well disposed toward the English and would not break the peace.

For several years, the conduct of Indian affairs had demanded an increasing share of Johnson's attention, and assistance had become necessary. In 1756, George Croghan [*q.v.*] had been made deputy superintendent for the tribes in Pennsylvania and the Ohio Valley; Daniel Claus was appointed deputy in 1760, with headquarters in Montreal, while Guy Johnson [*q.v.*], Sir William's former secretary, was designated in 1762 to assist him in his dealings with the Iroquois. Claus and Guy Johnson later became Sir William's sons-in-law. In the summer of 1763, the conspiracy of Pontiac necessitated much activity on Sir William's part. The uprising was at length crushed and by the summer of 1765 peace was reëstablished and the way prepared for English occupation of the interior.

During the period of Johnson's superintendency extending from the close of the French and Indian War to his death in 1774, he devoted himself to the difficult problems involved in the contact of races in the region north of the Ohio. He favored a centralized and independent Indian department, maintained by a separate fund. He also advocated centralized control of the fur trade, and believed that the activities of the traders should be limited to certain designated posts in the interior. His matured views are contained in his "Review of the Trade and Affairs of the Indians in the Northern District of America," dated Sept. 22, 1767 (*Illinois Historical Collections, post,* XVI, 24–66). In 1764, the Lords of Trade had drawn up a plan for the regulation of the Indian trade which embodied certain of Johnson's ideas in regard to centralized control, but this was only partially put into operation. In view of the chaotic state of British ministerial politics at this time, and a desire for economy, continuity of policy was impossible, and in 1768 responsibility for the regulation of the Indian trade was restored to the several colonies.

Constantly called upon to settle disputes arising out of the encroachments of white settlers upon the lands belonging to the Indians, Johnson for some years had favored the establishment of a boundary line which should separate the lands open to settlement from the hunting grounds reserved to the Indians. In the autumn of 1768 a great congress was held at Fort Stanwix which culminated on Nov. 5 in the signing of a treaty establishing an Indian boundary and opening up large tracts of land along the frontiers of New York, Pennsylvania, and Virginia. The interior was to be closed to settlement. Johnson was suspected in some quarters of endeavoring to further his own interests in the Treaty of Fort Stanwix, but the charges against him have never been proved.

During this same period, Johnson showed genuine interest in projects for civilizing the Indians through education and missionary activities. Though he had a considerable correspondence with members of the dissenting sects, as time went on he came to have especial sympathy with the efforts of the Anglicans. Much time and effort were also devoted to the preservation of peace among the various Indian tribes themselves, upon which the safety of the frontier and the security of the traders in the interior largely depended. His activities required many journeys, innumerable councils with the Indians in the department, the keeping of voluminous minutes of transactions, and the carrying on of a vast correspondence with all sorts of persons. He continued to show an active interest in the provincial militia, and in 1772 was given a commission as major-general. In 1774, when Lord Dunmore's war broke out upon the frontiers of Virginia, he was once more forced to exert himself to prevent the Six Nations from becoming involved. At a council held at Johnson Hall in July, the Indians complained of violations of the Treaty of Fort Stanwix and of the disorder into which the Indian trade had fallen since its management had been restored to the colonies. On July 11, a short while after delivering a long speech to the Indians, Johnson was taken violently ill and died. He had long suffered from a severe intestinal disorder and apparently the condition was aggravated by over exertion. He was succeeded as superintendent of Indian affairs by his son-in-law, Guy Johnson, and his son, Sir John Johnson [*q.v.*], inherited his title and estates.

Johnson's character is best revealed in his correspondence, from which it appears that he was a man of great energy and unusual versatility. He manifested considerable interest in literary and scientific matters, ordering books and periodicals, and occasionally even scientific instruments, from England. On Jan. 3, 1769, he accepted an election to the American Philosophical Society, and he was a member of the Society for the Promotion of Arts, which had as one of its objects the encouragement of agriculture. In a letter to Arthur Lee, dated Feb. 28, 1771, he presented an extremely valuable and interesting account of the language and customs of the Six Nations (Stone, II, 481–92). When Queen's College (later Rutgers) received its second charter, in 1770, his name appeared in the list of trustees. Although there is no doubt that he was ambitious, he seems to have had a genuine affection for the Indians with whom so much of his life was spent, and he often exerted himself to prevent them from being despoiled of their lands by unscrupulous whites. At the same time, however, his insatiable land hunger led him to secure large cessions from them for his own enrichment. Examples are the Kingsborough Patent, a tract of some sixty-six thousand acres ceded to him by the Mohawks, which came to be known as the Royal Grant, and a large tract secured from the Onondaga tribe, situated on the lake of the same name. He was also interested in land companies and was one of those concerned with the Grand Ohio Company, which was organized in 1769 and proposed to establish a colony to be called Vandalia (A. T. Volwiler, *George Croghan and the Westward Movement, 1741–1782*, 1926, p. 271). In the meantime the development of his estates in the Mohawk Valley went forward. Settlement was encouraged, agriculture developed, and live stock imported, thus transforming the frontier into a rich farming community.

In 1762, Johnson removed from Fort Johnson to a new residence, Johnson Hall, a short distance north of the settlement which became Johnstown. During his latter years he lived the life of a wealthy landed gentleman and man of affairs, his manner of existence bearing more the resemblance to that of a manorial lord than to that of a frontiersman. He had numerous slaves and servants and entertained freely, occasionally having distinguished Europeans as his guests. After the death of his wife, Catharine, he took an Indian woman named Caroline, niece of the Mohawk chief Hendrick [*q.v.*], into his home as housekeeper, and she bore him three children. She was succeeded by Molly Brant, another Mohawk woman, sister of the chief Joseph Brant [*q.v.*]. Molly Brant's position appears to have been one of dignity, and she and their eight children were provided for in Johnson's will. At least two authentic contemporary portraits of Johnson have survived (*Papers*, II, pp. ix–xii). According to the recollection of Mrs. Anne Grant (*Memoirs of an American Lady*, 1808, p. 194), "he was an uncommonly tall, well made man: with a fine countenance; which, however, had rather an expression of dignified sedateness, approaching to melancholy. He appeared to be taciturn, never wasting words on matters of no importance: but highly eloquent when the occasion called forth his powers." He was held in great affection by his Indian neighbors, who called him "Waraghiyaghey."

An imperialist whose sympathies were unquestionably with the Crown, Johnson had been much disturbed by signs of the approaching conflict. His death occurred at a critical time, but there is reason to suppose that his real work was done. The system for the control of Indian affairs of which he had dreamed and for which he had labored so long, could have been only temporary, at best. He did not foresee the rapidity with which conditions were to be changed by the westward march of the white settlers, but seems rather to have visualized a static condition, with a boundary line holding back the tide of settlement; he failed to appreciate the irresistible force of the white man's land hunger which is so clearly reflected in his own career. His real contribution to American development was threefold: he aided in opening up the Mohawk Valley to settlement; he rendered invaluable service in helping to drive the French power from North America; and following the conquest of Canada he did much to facilitate the difficult transition from French to English rule in the region north of the Ohio.

[Four biographies should be noted, A. C. Buell, *Sir William Johnson* (1903); W. E. Griffis, *Sir William Johnson and the Six Nations* (1891); W. L. Stone, Jr., *The Life and Times of Sir William Johnson, Bart.* (2 vols., 1865); and Arthur Pound and Richard E. Day, *Johnson of the Mohawks* (1930). The last two are much more valuable than the first two cited. The largest body of Johnson MSS. is in the N. Y. State Library, though the collection has been badly damaged by fire (see R. E. Day, *Calendar of the Sir William Johnson MSS. in the N. Y. State Lib.*, 1909). In the Public Archives at Ottawa are several volumes of records of Indian affairs including letter books of Sir William Johnson, minutes of councils, etc. Other depositories containing original papers are the Library of Congress, N. Y. Public Library, Harvard University Library, Dartmouth College Library, Bibliothèque Saint Sulpice, Montreal, W. L. Clements Library, Public Record Office and British Museum, London, and the American Antiquarian Society. Papers in the last-named depository are calendared in *Proc. Am. Antiq. Soc.*, n.s., XVIII (1907). The Illinois State Historical Library possesses transcripts of a large number of the Johnson papers at Albany, made before the fire. Published sources include E. B. O'Callaghan, *Docs. Rel. to the Colonial Hist. of the State of N. Y.* (15 vols., 1856–87), esp. vols. VI–VIII, X; E. B. O'Callaghan, *Doc. Hist. of the State of N. Y.* (4 vols., quarto ed., 1850–51); *Ill. State Hist. Lib. Colls.*, vols. X, XI, XVI (1915–21); *The Papers of Sir William Johnson* (7 vols. to date, 1921–31.)]

W. E. S—s.

JOHNSON, WILLIAM (Dec. 17, 1769–June 25, 1848), law reporter, was born in Middletown, Conn., the third son of Asahel and Eunice (Wetmore) Johnson. His ancestors were among the pioneer settlers of Connecticut. His maternal grandfather, Deacon Caleb Wetmore, a farmer of Middletown, was a descendant of Thomas Whitmore who came to America from England in 1635, acquired lands at Wethersfield, and was made a freeman at Hartford in 1652. From this record we may infer that he was orthodox and worth at least £200, the qualifications necessary for a freeman. William Johnson graduated from Yale College in 1788, studied law, and established his practice in New York City. At the Yale Commencement, 1793, he delivered an oration before the Phi Beta Kappa society on the "Political Situations and Prospects of the United States and the Nature and Effects of National Luxury and Vice." On June 17, 1809, in New York City, he married Maria, daughter of Oliver and Catherine Templeton, by whom he had four children.

In 1806 he was appointed reporter for the court of errors and for the supreme court of New York, succeeding the first reporter, George Caines [*q.v.*], who had been appointed in 1804. He served until 1823, and by the Act of Apr. 13, 1814, making the reporter of the supreme court the reporter of the court of chancery, he became reporter of the latter court also. He was such throughout the brilliant career of Chancellor Kent. At this time the courts of the United States were looking to England for decisions and principles on which to establish their rules of law. Johnson recognized that the American system of jurisprudence was based on that of England, yet so few of the court decisions at Westminster Hall were applicable to American cases that he considered it necessary to look to American decisions for the precedents which should have the binding force of authority and of law. He therefore made it his purpose to record not only the cases of his time, but also earlier decisions so far as he could obtain authentic materials. His publications include: *Report of Cases Argued and Determined in the Supreme Court of Judicature and in the Court for Trial of Impeachments and Correction of Errors, Feb. 1806–Feb. 1823* (20 vols.); *Cases Argued and Determined in the Court for the Trial of Impeachments and the Correction of Errors, 1799–1803* (3 vols., 1806–12); *Cases of the State Court of Chancery, March 1814–July 1823* (7 vols., 1816–24); *Digest of Cases in the Courts of New York, 1799–1836* (1838). He also translated from the French edition, and published in 1806, *Sistema Universale dei principii del diritto marittimo dell'Europa,* by D. A. Azuni. In dedicating his *Commentaries* to Johnson, Chancellor Kent paid tribute to the value of his friendship and of his services, and Judge Story in reviewing Johnson's reports said of him, "He loves the law with all his heart. . . . His reports are distinguished by the most scrupulous accuracy, good sense, and good taste. . . . No lawyer can ever express a better wish for his country's jurisprudence than that it may possess such a Chancellor and such a reporter." (*North American Review,* July 1820, pp. 164, 166.)

[B. W. Dwight, *The Hist. of the Descendants of Elder John Strong of Northampton, Mass.* (1871), vol. I; J. C. Wetmore, *The Wetmore Family of America* (1861); F. B. Dexter, *Biog. Sketches of the Grads. of Yale Coll., 1778–1792,* vol. IV (1907); Chester Alden, ed., *Legal and Judicial Hist. of N. Y.*, vol. II (1911); E. A. Werner, *Civil List and Constitutional Hist. of the Colony and State of N. Y.* (1888); James Kent, *Commentaries on American Law,* vol. IV (1830).]

D. V. S.

JOHNSON, WILLIAM (Dec. 27, 1771–Aug. 4, 1834), jurist, was born in Charleston, S. C., the son of William Johnson, a prominent Revolutionary leader in South Carolina, and of Sarah (Nightingale) Johnson. His brother was Joseph Johnson [*q.v.*]. After graduating with honors from Princeton in 1790, William studied law under Charles Cotesworth Pinckney and was licensed in 1793. On Mar. 20, 1794, he married Sarah, the sister of Gov. Thomas Bennett of South Carolina. From 1794 to 1798 he was a member of the lower house of the legislature and at his last session was speaker. In that year he was elected judge of the court of common pleas, on which he continued to sit until 1804 when Jefferson, with whom he was in close personal and political accord, appointed him associate justice of the Supreme Court of the United States.

As a judge Johnson's opinions showed a leaning toward Federalism, though he was opposed to the strong views of Marshall and Story. In particular he opposed Story's tendency to extend and enlarge admiralty jurisdiction. Some of Johnson's opinions, such as his dissent in the case of Bollman and Swartwout (4 *Cranch,* 99) and in *Fletcher* vs. *Peck* (6 *Cranch,* 142), were very able. In the latter there was some indication of the dissatisfaction with the doctrine of the Dartmouth College case that later became widespread. In many of his opinions, however, there were confusion and lack of precision, but they are all marked by individuality and a power of expressive phrase. When, in 1808, the collector of the port of Charleston, in obedience to executive instructions on the enforcement of the Embargo, refused to issue clearance to coasting vessels, Johnson, upon petition in the circuit court, granted a mandamus to compel the issuance of a clearance and in his opinion commented upon the illegality of the instructions (*Ex parte Gilchrist,* 5 *Hughes,* 5). Seeing in the decision a rebuke to Jefferson, the Federalists applauded Johnson and gave the case wide publicity. Jefferson, greatly surprised and somewhat disturbed at Johnson's remarks, referred the matter to Attorney-General Caesar A. Rodney, who prepared an opinion attacking the decision. Johnson replied by reiterating his conviction of the illegality of the President's orders to the collector and his satisfaction in his own course of action. Later, in the decision of another case, the Supreme Court affirmed the correctness of Rodney's opinion. The relations of Johnson and Jefferson, contrary to the usual account, remained friendly in spite of this disagreement. In 1824 Johnson became involved in another judicial controversy. In his opinion in a case in the circuit court for South Carolina, which involved the question of commerce in slaves, he upheld federal control of commerce in the broadest sense and opposed the doctrine of secession. The bitter resentment felt in South Carolina brought from Marshall the comment, "Our brother Johnson . . . has hung himself on a democratic snag in a hedge composed entirely of thorny State-Rights in South Carolina" (Warren, *post,* II, 86; Malone, *post,* p. 286). It was probably with these incidents in mind that Johnson, who was strongly opposed to nullification, removed to Pennsylvania in 1833. He died under an operation in Brooklyn a year later.

Johnson wrote *Sketches of the Life and Correspondence of Nathanael Greene* (1822) which called forth a good deal of criticism, especially in regard to certain reflections upon James Wilson of Pennsylvania, which, however, he immediately retracted when proof of his error was brought to his attention. In 1826 he published a *Eulogy of Thomas Jefferson,* and, as a member of the American Philosophical Society, wrote frequently for its meetings. He was modest and retiring, but utterly fearless and withal genial and warm-hearted. He scarcely deserved the characteristically acid comment of John Quincy Adams that he was "a restless, turbulent, hot-headed, politician caballing Judge" (Adams, *post,* V, 43) or that of Thomas Cooper that he was "a conceited man without talents."

[Charles Warren, *The Supreme Court in United States History* (3 vols., 1922); H. L. Carson, *The Supreme Court of the United States* (1891); *Memoirs of J. Q. Adams,* ed. by C. F. Adams, vols. IV–VII, XI (1875–76); *S. C. Hist. and Geneal. Mag.,* Apr. 1907, Apr. 1912, Oct. 1916, Apr. 1921; Dumas Malone, *The Public Life of Thos. Cooper, 1783–1839* (1926); *Am. Hist. Rev.,* Jan. 1898.]

J. G. deR. H.

JOHNSON, WILLIAM BULLEIN (June 13, 1782–Oct. 2, 1862), Baptist preacher, a pioneer educator in South Carolina, son of Joseph and Mary (Bullein) Johnson, was born in Beaufort County, S. C. His early education was defective, but by persistent personal effort he acquired considerable learning. Brown University recognized his attainments by conferring upon him in 1814 the honorary degree of A.M. He studied law, but never practised. In 1803 he married Henrietta Kelsall Hornby. The following year he was converted at Beaufort, was licensed to preach by the Beaufort church in January 1805, and ordained pastor of the Euhaw Baptist church in January 1806. For the most part, as a pastor he devoted himself to country and village churches, doing much itinerant evangelizing, both on his own initiative and as an appointee of organized bodies.

In 1809 he moved to Columbia to study in the

South Carolina College but was soon absorbed in preaching. He founded the First Baptist Church and erected its first house of worship, which was dedicated in 1811. From 1811 to 1815 he was pastor of the First Baptist Church, Savannah, Ga. He returned to Columbia but in 1822 removed to Greenville to become principal of the Greenville Female Academy, a position which he held until 1830. He led in founding the First Baptist Church and in the erection of its first house of worship, and acted as its first pastor till 1830. In the meantime he was actively interested in the larger movements of the denomination. He participated in the organization of the American Baptist Missionary Society in 1814, and was chosen its president in 1841. He was a leader in the formation of the South Carolina Baptist State Convention in 1821, assisted in drafting its constitution and by-laws, wrote the very able "Address" to the denomination, and traveled over the state explaining and defending this innovation. He was vice-president from 1821 to 1825 and president from 1825 till 1852, when he declined reëlection on account of ill health. When Furman Academy and Theological Institution, now Furman University, was projected, he was leader in the movement. He secured its charter, introduced it to the public, selected its first principal, and during the first uncertain twenty-five years of its history was its chief guide. He was long a trustee of the institution and most of its public documents of a non-legal character were written by him.

In 1830 he became pastor of the Edgefield Village Church, a position which, with the exception of the year 1845, he held until 1852. For at least a part of this time he was also principal of the Edgefield Female Academy. During the thirty years from 1822 to 1852 he was often moderator of the Saluda and Edgefield Associations, frequently preparing their public communications, and stimulating their benevolent and missionary undertakings. He was in hearty sympathy with the movement to organize the Southern Baptist Convention in 1845 and was president from 1845 to 1852. His name appears first among its incorporators and his voice was influential in the formulation of its constitution and by-laws. In 1848 at Anderson, S. C., he was instrumental in the founding of Johnson Female Seminary, the title of which was changed in 1852 to Johnson Female University, when a remarkable effort was made to establish a real university for the education of women. He now moved to Anderson to become chancellor of the University and president of its board. Failing health compelled him to resign in the late fifties, and he returned to Greenville to spend the remainder of his life. In 1860 he effected the organization of the Greenville Association on the basis of support for missions and education.

[Minutes of the S. C. Bapt. State Convention, the Southern Bapt. Convention, the Triennial Convention, and the Charleston, Edgefield, Saluda, and Greenville Associations; sermons and addresses (MSS.); files of the *Greenville Republican, The Mountaineer, The Baptist Courier*; Mrs. J. L. Mims, manuscript history of Edgefield Bapt. Ch.; W. J. McGlothlin, *Bapt. Beginnings in Educ., a Hist. of Furman Univ.* (1926).]

W. J. M.

JOHNSON, WILLIAM RANSOM (1782–Feb. 10, 1849), known as "The Napoleon of the Turf," was born in Warren County, N. C., the son of Marmaduke and Elizabeth (Ransom) Johnson. On his mother's side he was descended from ancestors established in Elizabeth City County, Va., as early as 1652. Reared in a region where horse-racing was the major sport of the planters, he early displayed an extraordinary aptitude for the training of thoroughbreds, and while he was still quite young undertook the management of his father's stables. About 1803 he married Mary Evans, daughter of Dr. George Evans of "Oakland," on the Appomattox River in Chesterfield County, near Petersburg, Va. When he was twenty-five he was elected to represent Warren County in the North Carolina House of Representatives and served from 1807 to 1814, with the exception of the year 1809. Meanwhile, he had established stables at "Oakland" and commenced his notable career on the Virginia turf. About 1816, influenced by his wife and his friend John Randolph of Roanoke, he moved his residence to Virginia and embarked upon a mercantile venture in Petersburg, but a few years later settled permanently at "Oakland." He sat in the Virginia House of Delegates from Petersburg, 1818–20, and from Chesterfield County, 1821–22, and was reëlected for the following term, but resigned his seat to enter the state Senate, where he served until 1826. He was in the House again, 1828–30, and from 1833 to 1837, when he resigned.

The vestiges of Johnson's training track at "Oakland" may still be seen. He bred horses to some extent, but his main interest was in training and running them. After successfully racing Sir Archy and Pacolet (between 1808 and 1813), he sold them at long prices to win greater renown in the stud than they had won on the track. In 1816, in a match race at Washington, D. C., he defeated Tuckahoe with Vanity and won $30,000. Match races were the order of the day, and in such contests the owners of the respective entries frequently had partners who shared the profits or losses. Johnson's fame as a manager of such affairs grew with the passing years; so that in 1823 when the long series of North and South matches began, he became by common consent the leader and manager for the South in the first race; and in practically all the thirty contests to 1834. In nearly all these contests Johnson was the largest stockholder on his side. The South won seventeen of the thirty races. In four of the five most famous North and South matches, of which the South won three, Johnson was manager for the South. In 1823 his entry, Henry, lost to American Eclipse. In 1825 he defeated Ariel with Flirtilla, owned by William Wynn of Virginia. In 1836 he defeated Post Boy with John Bascombe, owned by John Crowell of Alabama. In 1842 he lost with Boston, owned jointly by himself and James Long of Washington, D. C., in his race with Fashion. The Ariel-Flirtilla race was of three-mile heats; each of the other races of four-mile heats. The Post Boy-John Bascombe race was for a stake of $5,000; each of the other races, for $20,000. All four were run on the Union Course, Long Island, and were witnessed by vast multitudes assembled from both sections of the country.

The leading turfman of America for a generation, Johnson was noted for his "rare good sense," his executive ability, and his "great amiability of character." In later life, with his strong features and leonine shock of white hair, he was of striking appearance. His portrait was painted by Sully and by Inman. He died suddenly, of influenza, at Mobile, Ala., while racing, and was buried at "Oakland."

[*The Spirit of the Times*, July 27, Sept. 14, 1839, Feb. 24, 1849, and files, *passim*; files of the *Am. Turf Reg. and Sporting Mag.*, 1829–44, esp. issues of June and Sept. 1832; Balie Peyton's "Reminiscences of the Turf," *Rural Sun* (Nashville, Tenn.), 1872–73; H. W. Herbert, *Frank Forester's Horse and Horsemanship of the U. S.* (1857), I, 276, 292 and *passim*; C. E. Trevathan, *The Am. Thoroughbred* (1905); J. D. Anderson, *Making the Am. Thoroughbred* (1916); W. C. Bruce, *John Randolph of Roanoke* (2 vols., 1922); Mary N. Stanard, *Richmond: Its People and Its Story* (1923); Fairfax Harrison, *The Roanoke Stud* (1930); *Legislative Manual and Political Reg. of the State of N. C.*, 1874; E. G. Swem and J. W. Williams, *A Reg. of the Gen. Assembly of Va.* (1918); records in possession of Mrs. W. W. Morton of Richmond, Va.; information as to certain facts from Mrs. M. M. Baldwin of Birmingham, Ala., and from Fairfax Harrison, Esq.]
J. D. A.

JOHNSON, WILLIAM SAMUEL (Oct. 7, 1727–Nov. 14, 1819), statesman and jurist, was born in Stratford, Conn., where he lived during most of his life. His father was Samuel Johnson [*q.v.*], the well-known Anglican clergyman, Berkeleian philosopher, and first president of King's College, New York. His mother, Charity, the daughter of Col. Richard Floyd of Long Island and the widow of Benjamin Nicoll, brought to the Johnsons important New York connections. Under the skilful tuition of his father the younger Johnson was prepared for Yale, where he was graduated in 1744; three years later, he received the degree of A.M. from Harvard. His father hoped he would enter the ministry and for a time he served as a lay reader; but he finally turned to the law. Without formal training, he made effective use of the legal material then available and before long became a recognized leader at the bar, drawing clients from New York, as well as in his own state. Meantime he was also getting into public service. In 1753 he appears in the records of Connecticut as ensign in a Stratford company, and he was advanced in later years to higher grades in the militia. In 1761 and 1765 he represented Stratford in the House of Representatives, and in 1766 he became an Assistant, or member of the upper house, retaining his membership until the outbreak of the Revolution. Ezra Stiles, later president of Yale, observed (F. B. Dexter, *Extracts from the Itineraries . . . of Ezra Stiles*, 1916, p. 64) that Johnson was "the first Episcopalian ever bro't into the Council," a circumstance due, in part at least, to his pleasing personality and conciliatory temper. A few years before, he had advised his father to "stand perfectly neuter" in the controversy then raging between the New York Presbyterians and the Anglican promoters of King's College. Commenting on his son's advice, the old Doctor suggested that "even caution, one of the best things in the world, may be carried too far" (Beardsley, *Life and Correspondence of Samuel Johnson*, pp. 192–94).

To a man of Johnson's inheritance, temperament, and social position, the problems of the Revolutionary era were peculiarly difficult. His marriage, on Nov. 5, 1749, to Anne Beach, daughter of a prosperous Stratford citizen and niece of an Anglican clergyman who subsequently became an aggressive Loyalist, strengthened his association with the conservative elements in colonial society. One of his most intimate correspondents was Jared Ingersoll who served as collector under the Stamp Act of 1765. For a time, however, Johnson took an active part in the opposition to parliamentary taxation and went as a Connecticut delegate to the Stamp Act Congress. He was on the committee which drafted the address to the King and seems to have been on confidential terms with James Otis (Beardsley, *Life and Times of William Samuel Johnson*, p. 195). While his political attitude was popular at home, the honorary doctorate in law which he received from Oxford in 1766 indicated transatlantic connections of some importance, and in the same year he was appointed colonial agent in London. On this mission (1767–71), he had to defend the Connecticut title to the Mohegan lands, then in litigation before the Privy Council, and in cooperation with English lawyers he prepared the way for a favorable settlement. Another legal issue was that between Pennsylvania and the Susquehanna Company of Connecticut involving the territorial claims of the latter colony under its "sea-to-sea" charter. The company played an important rôle in Connecticut politics; but Johnson tried to keep the colony out of litigation in England, which might prove embarrassing at this time, and the issue remained unsettled until after the Revolution.

Connecticut was also concerned with other colonies in maintaining American claims against Parliamentary encroachments. Johnson's letters show that he was a moderate Whig, supporting the non-importation agreements in opposition to the Townshend Acts. He observed that Lord Hillsborough, the new colonial secretary, had "loose, mistaken notions"; but he was also skeptical about the opposition leaders. His contacts abroad were not exclusively legal or political. His father's reputation, as well as his own personal qualities, brought him into relations with influential churchmen and other outstanding personages. Among the English celebrities whom he met was Samuel Johnson, who subsequently wrote to his friend in Connecticut: "Of all those whom the various accidents of life have brought within my notice, there is scarce any one whose acquaintance I have more desired to cultivate than yours" (Beardsley, *William Samuel Johnson,* pp. 99–100). On the question of American bishops, ardently advocated by his father and other Anglican friends but strongly opposed by most of his Connecticut constituents, Johnson had a difficult course to steer. Personally sympathetic with the plan, he found little support for it among English politicians. In any case, he assured Governor Trumbull, an American bishop would not interfere with dissenters but would be confined to such purely ecclesiastical functions as ordination and confirmation. "More than this," wrote Johnson, "would be thought rather disadvantageous than beneficial, and *I assure you would be opposed by no man with more zeal than myself*" (Beardsley, *The History of the Episcopal Church in Connecticut,* I, 266).

On Johnson's return home, he was publicly thanked by the Assembly, reëlected to the Council and made a judge of the superior court. It was soon evident, however, that he was out of sympathy with the radical Whigs. While abroad, he had criticized the extremists on both sides and maintained that such men as his friend Ingersoll were entitled to official preferment, notwithstanding their unpopularity in America. In 1772 Johnson himself was an aspirant for office under the Crown. His letters show that he dreaded the consequences of political separation for America as well as for the mother country. On the other hand, his prominence in Connecticut politics led to his election (1774) as a delegate to the Continental Congress. He declined to serve, pleading a professional engagement; but there were other reasons also. He believed the Congress would "tend to widen the breach already much too great between the parent state and her colonies"; there would be little room "for moderate men or moderate measures" and "with no others," would he "be concerned" (Johnson to Latrobe, July 25, 1774, and Johnson to Jackson, Aug. 30, 1774, in the Johnson MSS., Connecticut Historical Society). He was sharply criticized for allowing a private engagement to interfere with a paramount public interest, and there was talk of dropping him from the Council, but he was continued for another year.

After the fighting at Lexington and Concord, the Connecticut Assembly decided (Apr. 26, 1775) to send Johnson, with Erastus Wolcott, to confer with General Gage about a possible suspension of hostilities. They met Gage but were afterward called to account by the Massachusetts Provincial Congress and on their return home found that the dominant radical party was in no mood to continue such negotiations. Johnson was now dropped from the Council and went into retirement at Stratford. In the summer of 1779, however, he was again brought into unwelcome prominence. Alarmed by British raids along the Connecticut coast, his Stratford neighbors asked him to intercede with the British commanders and though no communication was probably opened with the enemy, enough had been done to excite the suspicions of the American commanders. Johnson was placed under arrest, but he was fortunately permitted to confer with Governor Trumbull at Lebanon, where he presented a formal statement denying any attempt to correspond with the enemy, or any other proceedings, "in prejudice of the rights and liberties of this State"; he claimed, on the contrary, to have encouraged enlistments. After much debate and after he had taken the oath of fidelity to the state, he was released.

Evidently Johnson's conservatism did not wholly alienate even his political opponents. During the year 1779–80 he was suggested by

President Joseph Reed of Pennsylvania as a suitable head for the college at Philadelphia; and though the plan fell through, Johnson discussed it with President Stiles (February 1780). Stiles observed that Johnson seemed to find "no insuperable difficulty" in the renunciation of royal authority (F. B. Dexter, *The Literary Diary of Ezra Stiles,* 1901, II, 398, 401, 416). Two years later he was one of the Connecticut counsel before the congressional board of arbitration in the Susquehanna dispute with Pennsylvania. The case was decided unanimously in favor of Pennsylvania, December 1782; Joseph Reed, who had complimented Johnson as a good speaker and "a man of candour," considered his closing argument ineffective (W. B. Reed, *The Life and Correspondence of Joseph Reed,* 1847, II, 389–91). In 1784 Johnson was elected to the Confederation Congress, taking his seat in January 1785 and continuing his service in 1786 and 1787. Of his standing there S. P. Webb wrote to his friend Jeremiah Wadsworth in March 1785: "Dr. Johnson has, I believe, much more influence than either you or myself. . . . The Southern Delegates are vastly fond of him" (Charles Warren, *The Making of the Constitution,* 1929, p. 254, note).

The crowning event in Johnson's career was his work in the Federal Convention, of which he was one of the most generally respected members. He is best described by the Georgia delegate, William Pierce. "Johnson," writes Pierce, "possesses the manners of a Gentleman and engages the Hearts of Men by the sweetness of his temper, and that affectionate style of address with which he accosts his acquaintance." A distinguished lawyer, he was also reputed "one of the first classics in America." Pierce thought Johnson's oratory had been overrated but agreed that he was "eloquent and clear,—always abounding with information and instruction," of "a very strong and enlightened understanding" (Max Farrand, *Records of the Federal Convention,* 1911, III, 88). Johnson's diary shows that he did not miss a single day of the Convention from his first attendance (June 2) until the adjournment. A letter to his son (June 27) commends his colleagues for their "information and eloquence," also their "great temperance, candor, and moderation" (*Ibid.,* III, 49–50). Johnson's best-known contributions in the Convention are his part in the compromise on representation, and his service as member and spokesman of the important Committee of Style. His speeches on representation were certainly among the most important in the debate between the large and small states (*Ibid.,* I, 355–477, especially 461–62).

In general Johnson favored the extension of federal authority. He argued that the judicial power "ought to extend to equity as well as law" and the words "in law and equity" were adopted on his motion. He denied that there could be treason against a particular state even under the existing confederation, "the Sovereignty being in the Union." He also opposed the prohibition of *ex post facto* laws as "implying an improper suspicion of the National Legislature" (*Ibid.,* II, 346–47, 376, 428). He was one of the two Connecticut signers of the Constitution and worked effectively for ratification. In the state convention he emphasized the new sanction established in the federal system, which formed "one new nation out of the individual States. . . . The force, which is to be employed, is the energy of Law; and this force is to operate only upon individuals, who fail in their duty to their country" (B. C. Steiner, "Connecticut's Ratification of the Federal Constitution," *Proceedings of the American Antiquarian Society,* n.s., vol. XXV, 1915, p. 112). Johnson was one of the first two senators from Connecticut but retired in 1791 when the transfer of the capital to Philadelphia made this service hardly compatible with his duties to Columbia College. He took an active part in shaping the Judiciary Act of 1789, though he was not a member of the committee which reported it. Maclay, who distrusted lawyers and New Englanders, noted Johnson's enthusiasm for English jurisprudence, and his defense of the equity jurisdiction of the federal judiciary. Though he supported the chief Hamiltonian measures, he was one of the ten senators who voted against giving the president the power to remove a cabinet officer without senatorial concurrence.

As the first president of Columbia College (1787–1800), Johnson gave it the prestige of his distinguished public career, a reputation for scholarship, and a paternal interest in young men. By the close of his administration, the college was on a solid footing, with some new chairs including that in law, first held by James Kent. Though his election to the presidency was a departure from the traditional practice of choosing college presidents from the clergy, he was one of the outstanding laymen of the Anglican communion and a valued counselor in the organization of the church under its new American episcopate. As president, he maintained, though not in a sectarian spirit, the religious tradition of the old college. Retiring from the presidency on account of ill health, he returned to Stratford. His first wife having died in 1796, he married, Dec. 11, 1800, Mary (Brewster) Beach, a connection of his first wife. Surviving most of his pre-Revolutionary associates, he lived to a ripe old age. He was, wrote Asher Robbins, "in person, the *tout ensemble* of a perfect man, in face, form and proportion" (Wilkins Updike, *Memoirs of the Rhode Island Bar*, 1842, p. 209).

[E. E. Beardsley, *Life and Times of Wm. Samuel Johnson* (1876), was based largely on manuscript sources, is generally accurate, and contains some letters. It is, however, eulogistic, and inadequate as an interpretation of Johnson's political career. The briefer accounts are largely based on Beardsley. Useful also are: Beardsley's *Life and Correspondence of Samuel Johnson, D.D.* (1874), and his *History of the Episcopal Church in Conn.* (2 vols., 1866–68); Herbert and Carol Schneider, *Samuel Johnson, President of King's Coll.: His Career and Writings* (4 vols., 1929); L. H. Gipson, *Jared Ingersoll* (1920); W. G. Andrews, "Wm. Samuel Johnson and the Making of the Constitution," *Ann. Report of the Fairfield County Hist. Soc.*, 1889; and Evarts B. Greene, "Wm. Samuel Johnson and the Am. Revolution," *Columbia Univ. Quart.*, June 1930. Prime sources for his official career are *The Pub. Records of the Colony of Conn.*, vols. X–XV (1877–90) and *The Pub. Records of the State of Conn.* (3 vols., 1894–1922). Much material for the future biographer is still in manuscript in various depositories, including the libraries of Yale and Columbia Universities, the New York Public Library (Bancroft transcripts), the Connecticut Historical Society, and the Library of Congress. See Max Farrand, "The Papers of the Johnson Family of Conn.," *Proc. Am. Antiquarian Soc.*, n.s. vol. XXIII (1913). The chief printed collection of Johnson's letters is in "Trumbull Papers," *Mass. Hist. Soc. Colls.*, 5 ser., vol. IX (1885); next in importance is the selected correspondence of Jared Ingersoll in the *Papers of the New Haven Colony Hist. Soc.*, vol. IX (1918). A portrait of Johnson painted in 1793 by Gilbert Stuart was reproduced in the *Antiquarian*, Nov. 1929. Other copies are in the possession of Columbia University, Yale University, and Trinity College, Hartford.]

E. B. G.

JOHNSON, WILLIAM WOOLSEY (June 23, 1841–May 14, 1927), mathematician, the son of Charles Frederick Johnson, a lawyer and land owner at Owego, N. Y., and Sarah Dwight (Woolsey) Johnson, came of distinguished ancestry. He was a descendant of Jonathan Edwards, 1703–1758 [*q.v.*], and Sarah Pierpont, his wife; of Dr. Samuel Johnson, 1696–1772 [*q.v.*], the first president of King's College (now Columbia University), and of his son William Samuel Johnson, 1727–1819 [*q.v.*], one of the framers of the Constitution of the United States and the first president of the reorganized (1787) Columbia College. William Woolsey Johnson was graduated at Yale in 1862, at the age of twenty-one, and at once became connected with the United States Nautical Almanac office. After two years of service there he became an instructor in mathematics at the Naval Academy, Newport, R. I., and in 1865 moved with the school to Annapolis, where he remained until 1870, meantime (1868) receiving the degree of master of arts from his Alma Mater. On Aug. 12, 1869, he married Susannah Leverett Batcheller of Annapolis. After teaching at Kenyon College, Ohio (1870–72), and at St. John's College, Md. (1872–81), he returned to Annapolis as professor of mathematics, to remain there the rest of his active life. In 1913, through a special act of Congress, he was commissioned lieutenant in the navy, and in 1921 was retired with the rank of commodore. He was a founder member of the American Mathematical Society, and a member of the London Mathematical Society and various other learned organizations.

Johnson was one of the best-known of the expository mathematicians of his time, chiefly because of his numerous contributions to mathematical literature which helped to arouse interest in mathematical studies. He wrote a considerable number of textbooks, including *An Elementary Treatise on Analytical Geometry* (1869); *The Elements of Differential and Integral Calculus Founded on the Methods of Rates or Fluxions* (3 vols., 1874–76, with later revisions), in collaboration with J. Minot Rice; *An Elementary Treatise on the Integral Calculus Founded on the Method of Rates or Fluxions* (1881); *Curve Tracing in Cartesian Coordinates* (1884); *A Treatise of Ordinary and Partial Differential Equations* (1889); *The Theory of Errors and Method of Least Squares* (1890); and *An Elementary Treatise on Theoretical Mechanics* (2 pts., 1900–01; 1 vol. ed., 1901). He also wrote several monographs, including "Numeral transcendents, S_n and $s_n = S_n - 1$," in *Bulletin of the American Mathematical Society* (vol. XII, 1906, p. 477); "On Napier's Circular Parts" (*Messenger of Mathematics*, February 1919); "General Case of Circular Parts" (*Ibid.*, September 1920); "On Rules Derived by Composition from Cotes's Rules for Approximate Quadrature" (*Quarterly Journal of Pure and Applied Mathematics*, July 1912).

[*Yale University Obit. Record*, 1927; W. R. Cutter, *Geneal. and Family Hist. of the State of Conn.* (1911), vol. I; L. W. Kingman, *Owego: Some Account of the Early Settlement of the Village* (1907); *Who's Who in America*, 1920–21; *The Sun* (Baltimore), May 15, 1927; *N. Y. Times*, May 16, 1927; *Army and Navy Jour.*, May 21, 1927.]

D. E. S.

JOHNSON, WILLIS FLETCHER (Oct. 7, 1857–Mar. 28, 1931), editor, was born in New York City, the son of William Johnson, an architect of English birth who had come to the United States in 1830 and was associated with Richard Upjohn [*q.v.*] in the construction of Trinity Church; his mother was Althea (Coles) Johnson, a descendant of early New England settlers. After private education at his parents' home, "Firleigh Hall," near Summit, N. J., and at Pennington Seminary, he entered the University of the City of New York (now New York University) and took his degree with the class of 1879 (Records of New York University). In that same year he joined the *New York Daily Witness,* and in 1880 went to the *New York Tribune.* His service with the *Tribune* lasted till his death and exceeded in length that of any other editorial worker in the paper's history. In 1887 he became day editor, and in 1894, editorial writer, a position which he thereafter held continuously except for three years, 1917–20, when he was literary editor. He was noted for the encyclopedic range of his writing. Numerous papers by him appeared in the *North American Review,* of which he was contributing editor for some years beginning in 1914. When George Harvey [*q.v.*] founded the *North American Review's War Weekly* in 1918, later called *Harvey's Weekly,* Johnson was its principal writer, and a vehement critic of the Wilson administration.

Despite his assiduous journalistic work, he devoted much time to other interests. An ardent Republican, he made political speeches in fourteen national campaigns. He was actively interested in civil-service reform, and served as president of the New Jersey State Civil Service Commission from 1908 to 1912. This was his only public office, though during President Taft's administration he made a confidential survey of the United States Assay Office in New York, which resulted in a drastic reorganization. His attachment to New York University found expression in unstinted labors. He was a member of the University council from 1898 till his death, and of its executive committee from 1914 to 1926, serving also on various standing committees. He frequently lectured there and, beginning in 1913, held the post of honorary professor of American foreign relations. In 1901 he was biographical editor of *New York University,* in Chamberlain's *Universities and Their Sons.* For one year, 1923, he was an instructor in the Pulitzer School of Journalism.

He was a prolific writer. His first book was *History of the Johnstown Flood* (1889), of which more than 250,000 copies were sold in three months. He also produced popular biographies of James G. Blaine, William Tecumseh Sherman, and Henry M. Stanley, none of which he thought was of high importance. He was interested in lexicography, and proudly recalled that he was a collateral descendant of Dr. Samuel Johnson, but published nothing in that field. As products of his belief in expansion overseas, he produced *A Century of Expansion* (1903) and *Four Centuries of the Panama Canal* (1906). His most important work was *America's Foreign Relations* (1916), in two large volumes, which lacked analytical quality but showed independent research. Of his later publications, *America and the Great War* (1917) was frankly journalistic, but his *George Harvey* (1929) reflects his intimate friendship with the fellow editor and contains matter of permanent value on American political history. He was a religious man and for many years was a lay preacher in the Methodist Episcopal Church, though its prohibition policy became highly repugnant to him. In 1878 he had married Sue Rockhill, of Tuckerton, N. J.

[*N. Y. Herald Tribune,* Mar. 29, 1931, and editorial, *Ibid.,* Mar. 30, 1931; *Who's Who in America,* 1930–31; *N. Y. Univ.,* in *Universities and Their Sons,* mentioned above; proceedings of the Council of New York University, May 5, 1931.]

A. N.

JOHNSTON, ALBERT SIDNEY (Feb. 2, 1803–Apr. 6, 1862), soldier, youngest son of Dr. John and Abigail (Harris) Johnston, was born at Washington, Mason County, Ky. His grandfather, Archibald Johnston of Salisbury, Conn., was a captain in a New York regiment during the Revolution. Johnston studied under private tutors, and attended school in western Virginia and at Transylvania University, excelling in mathematics and Latin. His half-brother, Josiah, had him appointed to the United States Military Academy in 1822. There he was universally liked. He won mathematical honors and, as a first-classman, was corps adjutant. Upon graduation, he was brevetted second lieutenant, 2nd Infantry; and during 1826 he served at Sackett's Harbor, N. Y. He was later commissioned second lieutenant and joined the 6th Infantry at Jefferson Barracks, Mo., June 1, 1827. As regimental adjutant he participated in the Black Hawk War. On Jan. 20, 1829, he married Henrietta Preston. They had three children, one of whom died in infancy. Because of his wife's illness, Johnston resigned his commission, Apr. 24, 1834. After her death, Aug. 12, 1835, he tried farming near St. Louis but soon gave it up, went to Texas, and enlisted as a private in the Texan army. Over six feet tall, straight as an arrow, broad-shouldered, with massive chest, square jaws, and piercing eyes that bespoke his determination, he suited this frontier.

General Rusk, commander of the army of Texas, appointed him adjutant-general, Aug. 5, 1836, and, as senior brigadier-general, he assumed command of the army, Jan. 31, 1837. This appointment aroused the jealousy of Felix Huston, who challenged Johnston to a duel and seriously wounded him. Appointed on Dec. 22, 1838, as secretary of war for the Republic of Texas, he helped to free the Texan borders from Indian raids. Incidentally, his vigor against the Cherokees incurred Gen. Sam Houston's displeasure. He resigned Mar. 1, 1840, returned for a time to Kentucky, and, on Oct. 3, 1843, married Eliza Griffin, his first wife's cousin. Two of their children lived to maturity. He bought "China Grove" in Brazoria County, Tex., which caused him considerable financial distress. When the Mexican War started he was commissioned colonel, 1st Texas Rifle Volunteers, and served at Monterey under General Butler as inspector general. The next three years he farmed at "China Grove." On Dec. 2, 1849, he was commissioned paymaster, United States Army, and was detailed along the dangerous Texan frontier, where he served until appointed colonel of the 2nd Cavalry; he assumed command of the Department of Texas on Apr. 2, 1856. From 1858 to 1860, as brevet brigadier-general, he served in Utah, quelling a threatened Mormon uprising without resorting to force.

He sailed from New York, Dec. 21, 1860, for San Francisco, took command of the Department of the Pacific, and for three months creditably executed his duties. When Texas seceded he resigned his commission, Apr. 10, 1861, but continued in command until his successor, General Sumner, arrived, Apr. 25, 1861. Johnston's unimpeachable character was not comprehended in some quarters and a rumor had spread that he was plotting to deliver California to the Confederacy. When he heard this falsehood, Johnston was thoroughly enraged. He harbored no desire to incite civil strife, instead he sought seclusion at Los Angeles. Tardily realizing its error, the Federal government asked Johnston to reconsider, offering him command second only to Scott, but he refused.

Weary of the surveillance he was subjected to, Johnston committed his family to his brother-in-law, Dr. John S. Griffin, and, joining Alonso Ridley's company, journeyed overland, back to the South. He had had no communication or understanding with Confederate leaders prior to making this move. Joining Jefferson Davis in Richmond, he was appointed general in the Confederate army, and assigned to command the Western Department. He seized Bowling Green, Ky., called for troops, and began to form and drill an army. His greatest difficulty then, and afterward, was in securing enough troops; invariably his enemy outnumbered him, two to one. At Mill Spring, Jan. 19, 1862, through disobedience to his orders, part of Johnston's command was defeated by General Thomas. In rapid succession, other units lost Fort Henry, Feb. 6, 1862, and, on Feb. 16, 1862, Fort Donelson. Johnston now temporarily withdrew to the vicinity of Nashville. When Buell captured that city, Feb. 25, 1862, Johnston retreated to Murfreesborough, and thence to Corinth. After the loss of Henry and Donelson, Davis was implored to replace Johnston. He replied: "If Sidney Johnston is not a general, I have none" (*Battles and Leaders of the Civil War,* I, 550).

By Mar. 25, 1862, concentrations at Corinth were complete. Johnston planned to defeat Grant before Buell could join him. The Federals at Shiloh Church, near Pittsburg Landing, held a strong natural position with a numerically superior force. On Apr. 3, 1862, Johnston moved from Corinth, and on Sunday, Apr. 6, he struck. With Bragg, Hardee, Polk, and Breckinridge as corps commanders, Johnston drove everything before him, turning first one position then another, until the Federals, with both flanks turned and center broken, were driven back to the Tennessee River in complete rout. In his moment of triumph, Johnston was struck, an artery being severed in his leg, and he bled to death. With him went one of the greatest hopes of the Confederacy. Jefferson Davis spoke for the South when he said: "It may safely be asserted that our loss is irreparable and that among the shining hosts of the great and good who now cluster about the banner of our country, there exists no purer spirit, no more heroic soul, than that of the illustrious man whose death I join you in lamenting" (*Journal of the Congress of the Confederate States of America,* II, 1904, p. 136).

His body was carried to New Orleans and temporarily entombed. In January 1867, Texas claimed him and his remains were carried to Austin for burial. Stops were made at Galveston and Houston where his friends, prevented by General Sheridan's order from honoring him with a military funeral procession, showed their devotion to his memory by silently following his body as it was carried through the streets.

[Wm. P. Johnston, *The Life of Gen. Albert Sidney Johnston* (1878), and *The Johnstons of Salisbury* (1897); sketch by Frank Schaller in his translation of Marmont's *The Spirit of Military Institutions* (Columbia, S. C., 1864); *War of the Rebellion: Official Records (Army)*; F. B. Heitman, *Hist. Reg. of the U. S. Army* (1890); G. W. Cullum, *Biog. Reg. of the Officers and Grads. of the U. S. Mil. Acad.* (3rd ed., 1891); *Battles and Leaders of the Civil War* (4 vols., 1887–88); *Confed. Mil. Hist.* (1899), I, 642–44; *Sou. Hist. Soc. Papers,* Sept. 1878, June 1883; *Quart. of the Tex. State Hist. Asso.,* Apr. 1907.]
C. C. B.

JOHNSTON, ALEXANDER (Apr. 29, 1849–July 20, 1889), historian, was born in Brooklyn, N. Y., the son of Samuel G. Johnston, whose family emigrated to the United States from

County Antrim, Ireland. After the Civil War, in which he served, Samuel Johnston moved to Illinois, leaving Alexander in charge of his maternal uncle, John McAlan. In the Rutgers matriculation book young Johnston signed himself Alexander Johnson (no "t") and named his father as Samuel G. Johnson, of Pontiac, Livingston County, Ill. He studied at the Polytechnic Institute in Brooklyn, and was prepared for college under Prof. A. W. Palmer of Dartmouth. In 1870 he graduated from Rutgers College, valedictorian of his class. He showed special fondness for classical studies, an interest which he retained throughout his life, and he won college prizes in this field. After graduation he studied law and was admitted to the bar in New Jersey in 1875, but he returned from legal practice to the educational field. From 1876 to 1879 he taught in Rutgers College Grammar School and then founded a Latin School in Norwalk, Conn., of which he was principal until 1883. In November of that year he was called to the College of New Jersey (Princeton) as professor of jurisprudence and political economy, where he served until his death.

He was the author of the following works: *History of American Politics* (1879), which went through many editions; *The Genesis of a New England State (Connecticut)* (1883), published in the Johns Hopkins University Studies (No. XII); *A History of the United States for Schools* (1885); *Connecticut* (1887), in the American Commonwealth Series; the article on George Washington and the one on the United States, for the 9th edition of the *Encyclopaedia Britannica* (1887), the latter being reprinted as *The United States: Its History and Constitution* (1889); "The History of Political Parties," in Justin Winsor's *Narrative and Critical History of America,* vol. VII (1888); many articles on American history, politics, and government in J. J. Lalor's *Cyclopædia of Political Science, Political Economy, and of the Political History of the United States* (3 vols., 1881–84). These articles were later republished in two volumes (1905) entitled *American Political History,* edited by James A. Woodburn. Johnston also edited *Representative American Orations to Illustrate American Political History* (3 vols., 1884). He was an occasional contributor to the *Nation* (New York), and a frequent contributor to the "Topics of the Times" in the *Century Magazine.* He contributed to the *New Princeton Review* (July 1888) a notable article on "The American Party Convention." These historical and literary activities were crowded into ten years of his life. That he accomplished so much in such a brief span indicates a genius for study and writing, and gives evidence of great energy and intellectual fertility. His style was clear, compact, and simple. He was sound and forceful in his generalizations, though he gave little thought to any philosophy of history. He was as charming in conversation as with his pen. Socially and as a teacher he was singularly genial and attractive. "No instructor ever enjoyed a larger measure of affection and esteem from colleagues and pupils" (A. T. Ormond, *post*). He was married in Norwalk, Conn., Aug. 29, 1878, to Mary Louise Carter.

[W. H. S. Demarest, *A Hist. of Rutgers Coll.* (1924); *Nation* (N. Y.), July 25, 1889; the *Century Mag.,* Oct. 1889; A. T. Ormond in *Princeton Coll. Bull.,* Nov. 1889; J. H. Dougherty, *Alexander Johnston and His Contributions to Political Science* (1900); *N. Y. Times,* July 22, 1889.]

J. A. W.

JOHNSTON, ANNIE FELLOWS (May 15, 1863–Oct. 5, 1931), author of books for children, was born in Evansville, Ind., of pioneer stock. One of the grandparents of her mother, Mary Erskine, was a Maryland colonist who freed his slaves for conscience' sake and moved westward into the Ohio wilderness; another was a Scotch Covenanter who emigrated from Ireland to join the New Harmony Colony and eventually settled in the frontier hamlet of Evansville. Her father, Albion Fellows, a Methodist minister whose parents were early Illinois settlers from New Hampshire, died when Annie was two years old. She and her two sisters grew up in rural MacCutchanville, not far from Evansville. Here she lived a wholesome country life, listened to stories of pioneer endeavor and accomplishment, learned to work with a conscientious regard for duty, attended the district school, read the entire Sunday school library, the sentimental *Godey's Lady's Book, St. Nicholas,* and the *Youth's Companion,* and wrote stories and poems in imitation of those she read.

When she was seventeen she taught for one term in the district school which she had been attending. After a year of study at the University of Iowa, 1881–82, she taught in the public school of Evansville for three years and then, when teaching threatened her health, she worked in an office. She traveled for a few months in New England and in Europe. But whether in the school room or the office, in college or traveling she lived in the midst of cousins, whose number was legion and whose social environment and religious beliefs were similar to her own. It is therefore not surprising that she married a cousin, William L. Johnston, a widower with three young children (1888). He encouraged her to write, and during the three years of their married life she contributed occasional stories to the *Youth's Companion.* Her husband's death in 1892 and the necessity of supporting his children gave a forced impetus to her writing. Her first book, *Big Brother,* was published in 1893. After the completion of *Joel: A Boy of Galilee,* in 1895, Mrs. Johnston visited in the Pewee Valley, near Louisville, Ky., where her stepchildren had lived with relatives. A spirited little girl who resembled a colonel of the old school and the atmosphere of leisure and of aristocratic living which still lingered in the valley from the days of slavery so caught her fancy that when she returned to Evansville she depicted them in *The Little Colonel* (1895), the first of a series of twelve books.

Pewee Valley became the setting not only of many of her most popular books but of her own life. She moved there in 1898 and it remained home to her until her death more than thirty years later. From 1901 until her stepson died in 1910 she made a temporary home for him where the climate would benefit his health, first in Arizona, then in California, and, for eight years, in Texas. Her sojourn in the Southwest gave her the setting for several of her stories: *The Little Colonel in Arizona* (1904), *In the Desert of Waiting* (1905), *Mary Ware* (1908), and *Mary Ware in Texas* (1910). Without superior gifts of imagination, keen and balanced observation, or psychological acuteness, Mrs. Johnston entertained thousands of children and inspired many of them to emulate the integrity of her characters, who lived in a world where good intentions prevail and where simple virtues are glorified. By drawing upon her own idealized childhood and the scenes and people she loved, she created a glamour about her characters which charmed her youthful readers.

[Annie Fellows Johnston, *The Land of the Little Colonel: Reminiscence and Autobiog.* (1929); Albion Fellows Bacon, *Beauty for Ashes* (1914); Margaret W. Vandercook, "Annie Fellows Johnston, the Beloved Writer of Books for Young Folk," *St. Nicholas,* Dec. 1913; *Louisville Times,* Oct. 5, 1931.] V. L. S.

JOHNSTON, AUGUSTUS (*c.* 1730–*c.* 1790), lawyer, attorney-general for the colony of Rhode Island and for a brief period stamp-distributor, was born in Amboy, N. J., and educated in the colony of New York. Thence he removed as a young man to Newport, R. I., where he was admitted a voter on Apr. 30, 1751. He studied law with his step-father, Matthew Robinson, a lawyer of reputation and a wide reader, whose large private library was augmented by that of Johnston's maternal grandfather, a Huguenot named Lucas, who lived for a time in Newport. Johnston soon attracted notice by marked ability in his profession and an impressive self-confidence. He was appointed in 1754 and in 1756 to help in preparing bills for the General Assembly. In October 1756 he was made a first lieutenant in a regiment to be sent against Crown Point. In June 1757 he was appointed attorney-general, the candidate elected having died, and was reëlected each year until May 1766, serving practically nine years, though after the Stamp-Act riots of 1765 his name was omitted from a committee to revise the laws, and another attorney was appointed to join him in carrying on a suit brought by the colony against a late collector of customs. During his term of office, in 1760 he was one of four to revise the laws, and in 1763, one of four to draw up regulations for a hospital for smallpox inoculation and recommend a place to build it. The town of Johnston, separated from Providence in 1759, is said to have been named for the attorney-general.

On Aug. 27, 1765, Johnston, stamp-distributor, and two others who had supported the rights of Parliament were hanged in effigy; on Aug. 28, a reckless mob did serious damage to their houses and furniture. All three fled for their lives to the armed ship *Cygnet* in the harbor, and when Johnston came ashore next day he was forced to sign a paper agreeing not to execute his office of distributor without the consent of the colonists. In a letter to the collectors dated Nov. 22, 1765, he maintains that before the riots "no application was ever made to me by any one person to resign said office" (*Records,* VI, 477); but regard for life and property, he asserts, obliged him to deposit the stamped papers for safe keeping on the *Cygnet,* when they came, and hence he could not supply the collectors' demand for them. He was evasive when the Governor pressed him to answer whether he was or was not going to distribute stamps; but the Governor wrote to England that Johnston had resigned. The other two sufferers in the riots went to England and presented exaggerated accounts of their losses; Johnston also made an unwarranted estimate of his, at first. The matter called forth a prolonged correspondence between the Treasury and the General Assembly of Rhode Island, since it happened that the military disbursements of 1756 had never been repaid to the colony, and the Treasury refused payment until the three persecuted Loyalists were compensated. Although the claims were moderated, and the Assembly, after severe revision, allowed them, subject to payment of their own claim upon England, the matter was still under discussion in August 1773, and was never settled. Johnston remained unmolested in Newport, but on July 18, 1776, having refused the test of allegiance, he was ordered interned at South Kingstown. He held civil appointments at Newport during the British occupation, and left for New York when the town was evacuated in 1779. His property was confiscated, and, in spite of a pension from the British government, he died insolvent, to the distress of his step-father, who, having been Johnston's surety, was obliged in extreme old age to go to court and defend suits which were brought against him. Johnston left a widow and four children.

[Wilkins Updike, *Memoirs of the Rhode-Island Bar* (1842); *Records of the Colony of R. I. and Providence Plantations*, ed. by J. R. Bartlett, vols. V, VI, VII 1860–62; *Supplement to the R. I. Colonial Records* (1875); S. G. Arnold, *Hist. of the State of R. I., and Providence Plantations*, vol. II (1860).] E. M. S. B.

JOHNSTON, DAVID CLAYPOOLE (March 1799–Nov. 8, 1865), engraver, lithographer, and actor, was born in Philadelphia, where his father, William P. Johnston, served for some time as bookkeeper for David Claypoole, printer and publisher of *Claypoole's American Daily Advertiser*. His mother, Charlotte (Rowson) Johnston, was a sister-in-law of Susanna (Haswell) Rowson [*q.v.*], actress and dramatist, and had come to America with her brother and his wife in 1793 as a member of Wignell's theatrical company. Her stage career was not especially brilliant and does not seem to have extended beyond her marriage to William Johnston, which occurred in 1797. That year has sometimes been given as the year of David Johnston's birth, but he himself stated that he was born in March 1799 (Dunlap, *post*). Since as a school boy he displayed more interest in drawing than in his studies, his parents decided to place him under instruction. Though it was his ambition to be a painter, the family decreed that engraving offered more opportunity, and in 1815 he was apprenticed to Francis Kearny [*q.v.*], then a successful engraver in Philadelphia. At the conclusion of his apprenticeship, finding little business in the illustration of books, he began to produce social caricatures which he published himself. These amusing publications attracted a great deal of favorable interest but also aroused the ire of the military and others who were ridiculed. Some of those caricatured even demanded that Johnston's pictures be removed from the booksellers' windows, a threat which rang down the curtain on the young artist's enterprise.

At this juncture the lure of the stage caused him to apply to William B. Wood [*q.v.*], the actor-manager of the Walnut Street Theatre, and on Mar. 10, 1821, he made his first appearance, as Henry in *Speed the Plow*. For several years he was attached to the Philadelphia company, first as "walking gentleman" and later in minor comic rôles. In 1825 he went to Boston and joined the theatrical company in that city. While he was engaged as an actor, he continued occasionally to make caricatures and other prints, which he sold readily. Indeed, it was the desire to do more work with his etching needle that led him to Boston. He retired from the stage at the end of his first season there, and subsequently devoted himself to illustrating books and making drawings for comic prints.

His popularity increased rapidly, and he was in demand for drawing on wood, etching plates, and drawing on stone for the Pendletons, who had established the first important lithographic house in the United States. He quickly mastered the technique of crayon drawing on the stone, and his lithographs are equal, if not superior, to any in America at that time. He also managed to find time to paint pictures, and exhibited in the Boston Athenæum and in the National Academy of Design. Beginning in 1830, for a few years he issued annually a series of plates, each containing a number of comic sketches, under the general title of *Scraps*, evidently suggested by Cruikshank's *Scraps and Sketches*. In 1835 he published eight humorous and satirical plates to illustrate Fanny Kemble's *Journal*, which was issued that year. Joseph C. Neal's *Charcoal Sketches* (1838), with illustrations by Johnston, may be said to have established the reputation he had already earned as a book illustrator. Neal [*q.v.*] generously observed in his Preface: "Whether the letter-press be amusing, or not, the illustrations by Johnston are replete with humor and graphic skill. They who yawn in the perusal of our pages, can therefore turn for refreshment to the comicalities of the etcher, and excuse the dulness perpetrated by the pen, in laughing over the quaint characteristics embodied by our American Cruikshank." As late as 1863 Johnston issued a sheet of political satire on Jefferson Davis, *The House that Jeff Built* (Weitenkampf, *post*, p. 215).

Although Johnston was fertile in invention and quite original, the influence of Cruikshank is observable in almost everything he did, but in many instances his drawing was superior to that of his model. His dependence upon Cruikshank is revealed in the attitude he adopted in his observations of the life around him rather than in any servile imitation of the English caricaturist's style, although, like Cruikshank, he was capable of producing most delicate lines with the etching needle. He married Sarah Murphy of Boston in 1830, and they had eight children. One son, Thomas Murphy Johnston, inherited some of his father's talent. Johnston died at his home in Dorchester, Mass.

[Autobiographical letter in Wm. Dunlap, *Hist. of the Rise and Progress of the Arts of Design in the U. S.* (2 vols., 1834); G. O. Seilhamer, *Hist. of the Am. Theatre*, vol. III (1891); Elias Nason, *A Memoir of Mrs. Susanna Rowson* (1870); *New-Eng. Hist. and Geneal. Reg.*, Apr. 1866; D. M. Stauffer, *Am. Engravers upon Copper and Steel* (1907); J. T. Scharf and Thompson Wescott, *Hist. of Phila.* (3 vols., 1884); T. A. Brown, *Hist. of the Am. Stage* (1870), in which Johnston is called Johnson; Mantle Fielding, *Am. Engravers* (1917); Frank Weitenkampf, *Am. Graphic Art* (rev. ed., 1924).]

J. J.

JOHNSTON, GABRIEL (1699–July 17, 1752), royal governor of North Carolina, was born in Scotland, one of the Johnstons of Annandale. He is said to have attended the University of St. Andrews, pursuing at first a medical course, later taking up the study of Oriental languages and literature, and subsequently holding a minor instructorship; but he appears not to have taken a degree. About the year 1730 he joined Bolingbroke and William Pulteney, Earl of Bath, in editing *The Craftsman,* founded Dec. 5, 1726, a series of weekly papers of a literary and political nature, with a pronounced tinge of Jacobitism; though he later declared that he had never been a Jacobite (*Colonial Records,* IV, 918). During his career with *The Craftsman* he became acquainted with Lord Wilmington, who was influential in obtaining for him the post of royal governor of North Carolina, made vacant early in 1734 by the withdrawal of Governor Burrington.

Johnston arrived in the Cape Fear River in October 1734 and received the oath of office Nov. 2, amidst the applause and good will of the citizens assembled at Brunswick. Though he began his new office under exceedingly favorable circumstances, in less than three months he found himself in open collision with the General Assembly over the question of quit rents—Johnston insisting that quit rents, upon which his own salary depended, be paid in "proclamation money" instead of in commodities, and at four specified places in the colony. This dispute occasioned a political chaos in North Carolina for the next ten years (*Ibid.,* IV, xviii); Johnston convened and dissolved one Assembly after another without accomplishing one piece of legislation. Finally, in June 1746, the General Assembly declared that in view of the scarcity of silver and gold in the colony, the refusal of Governor Johnston to receive produce in payment of quit rent was "a very great grievance" (*Ibid.,* IV, 1746) and sent a remonstrance to the Governor, which he tactlessly ignored. The northern counties thereupon withdrew from the Assembly and refused to pay rent in any form, and their example was soon followed by some of the southern counties. In April 1749 Johnston was able to procure the passage of a quit-rent bill which satisfied him, but its actual results were slight, since by this time the whole colony was in practical rebellion against him. He died less than three years later, a broken and disappointed man.

Although Johnston's administration was marked chiefly by the quit-rent controversy, it can claim several accomplishments: free schools were opened; printing was established at New Bern in 1749; the boundary between North and South Carolina was partially settled. Johnston's "intentions doubtless were good, and his motives pure enough, but he was exceedingly arbitrary, not to say unscrupulous" (Saunders, in *Colonial Records,* IV, v). His papers reveal more of his personal quarrels than of the state of the province. Though he was headstrong, tactless, and often unnecessarily opposed to compromise, his failure was due not only to his own shortcomings, but in part to the unorganized condition of the colony and the weakness of his predecessors. He was twice married. His first wife, who had been married three times before, was Penelope (Golland) Pheney, daughter of John and Penelope Golland and step-daughter of Gov. Charles Eden [*q.v.*]; she died in 1741. His second wife, Frances, survived him and married, second, John Rutherford. By his first wife he left one child, Penelope, who married Col. John Dawson. His nephew, Samuel Johnston, 1733–1816 [*q.v.*], became a United States senator.

[W. L. Saunders, *The Colonial Records of N. C.,* vol. IV (1886); S. A. Ashe, *Hist. of N. C.* (1908), vol. I, and *Biog. Hist. of N. C.,* vol. V (1906); *N. C. Booklet,* Dec. 1903, p. 17; B. J. Lossing, *The Pictorial Fieldbook of the Revolution,* II (1852), 563; George Chalmers, *An Intro. to the Hist. of the Revolt of the Am. Colonies* (2 vols., 1845); H. L. Osgood, *The Am. Colonies in the Eighteenth Century,* IV (1924), ch. IX.]

E. L. W. H.

JOHNSTON, GEORGE BEN (July 25, 1853–Dec. 20, 1916), surgeon, was born in Tazewell, Va. His father, John Warfield Johnston, United States senator from Virginia, was a nephew of Gen. Joseph E. Johnston [*q.v.*]; his mother, Nicketti Buchanan Floyd, was the daughter of Dr. John Floyd [*q.v.*], a prominent physician and a governor of Virginia, and a sister of John Buchanan Floyd [*q.v.*], secretary of war under President Buchanan. Johnston's childhood was passed in the mountain country of southwestern Virginia, where he attended Abingdon Academy. Later he attended St. Vincent's Academy at Wheeling, W. Va., and entered the University of Virginia, where, following academic studies, he took one year of the medical course. In 1875 he went to the University of the City of New York from which he received his medical degree in 1876. Returning to Virginia, he associated himself with Dr. E. M. Campbell of Abingdon for the practice of his profession. After two years he moved to Richmond, which was his home for the remainder of his life. He early associated himself with the Medical College of Virginia, filling minor teaching positions until 1884, when he was appointed professor of anatomy. In 1893 he was made professor of didactic and clinical surgery, holding this position under various titles until 1914, when he resigned to become a member of the board of visitors of the college. Interested from his student days in surgery, he was the Virginia pioneer in antiseptic operations. He had an instinct for surgical diagnosis together with unusual operative skill and resourcefulness. These, united with an attractive personality and untiring energy, made him the outstanding surgeon of his section. He contributed much valuable information to the surgery of the kidney and spleen, and together with Dr. Murat Willis devised and reported the Johnston-Willis operation for ventral suspension of the uterus. Besides numerous journal articles relating to his specialty, he contributed to *American Practice of Surgery* (8 vols., 1906–11), edited by J. D. Bryant and A. H. Buck. He found Richmond greatly lacking in hospital accommodations and set himself to remedying the condition. He established the Old Dominion Hospital as an adjunct to the medical school and organized and built the Memorial Hospital, to which was later added a large annex for negro patients. With Dr. Murat Willis he built the Johnston-Willis Sanitorium for their private surgical practice and, as outgrowths of this hospital, founded the Abingdon Hospital at Abingdon, Va., and the Park View Hospital at Rocky Mount, N. C. Johnston also organized the hospital department for the City Home of Richmond. He was at various times president of the American Surgical Association, of the Southern Surgical and Gynecological Association, of the Medical Society of Virginia, and of the Richmond Academy of Medicine and Surgery. He was a fellow of the American College of Surgeons, a member of the International Surgical Society, and of the Society of the Cincinnati. For years he was one of the most active members of the state board of health and of the Richmond Civic Association.

Johnston was a tall, handsome man with a courtly manner and a gracious address which gave him leadership in any company in which he found himself. A brilliant conversationalist and raconteur, he was prevented from being a forceful public speaker by a shrill high-pitched voice. In 1911 he had an attack of angina pectoris, which recurred frequently until it carried him off suddenly in his home at Richmond in 1916. He was twice married: in 1881 to Mary McClung, who died the following year, and in 1892 to Helen Coles Rutherford of Rock Castle, Va., who with four daughters survived him.

[J. M. Hutcheson, in *Trans. Am. Therapeut. Soc., 1917* (1918); *Trans. Am. Surgic Asso.*, vol. XXXVI (1918); B. R. Tucker, in *Surgery, Gynecology and Obstetrics*, Aug. 1924; *Richmond Times-Dispatch*, Dec. 21, 1916.]

J. M. P—n.

JOHNSTON, HENRIETTA (d. March 1728/9), artist, in all probability the earliest woman painter in North America, was buried in St. Philip's Churchyard, Charleston, S. C., on Mar. 9, 1728/9, but of her parentage, lineage, and education very little is known (Willis, *post*). It seems that she never used any other medium than pastels, and that her pastel portraits (for she was a portraitist) never exceeded fourteen by sixteen inches in size. Those of her works that have been located were painted between 1707 and 1720; and the majority if not all of her sitters were grandees of South Carolina in the colonial days. Apparently she had no studio, but "became an inmate of the home of each of her patrons during the time required for the commissions given" (*Ibid.*). Only two of her portraits, so far as is known, belong to public institutions: that of Col. William Rhett (1711), rated as one of the best of her works, is in the Gibbes Memorial Art Gallery, Charleston; and a photograph of that of Col. Daniell, deputy for Governor Craven of South Carolina, is in the possession of the South Carolina Historical Society. She evidently led a busy life, painting the likenesses of the rich planters, colonial officials, military men, their wives and daughters, and the belles and beaux of the day in all their splendor of dress. Among her sitters were the aristocratic Mrs. Robert Brewton, who posed in "a surplice dress with elbow sleeves of Pompadour red, seemingly velvet," showing "a narrow line of lace at shoulders and elbow"; Anne, daughter of Lieut.-Gov. Thomas Broughton; his daughter-in-law, Mrs. Nathaniel Broughton; Judith, Anne, and Marie Du Bosc, the three lovely daughters of Jacques Du Bosc and his wife, Marie Du Gué, Huguenots who had sought asylum in America; Col. John Moore (1725) and his wife; and Frances Moore Bayard. Miss Johnston's work has nothing of genius in it, but it is ingenuous and of distinct historical interest. What Dr. Holmes wrote of the portrait of "Dorothy Q." may perhaps apply to her pastels:

> "Hard and dry it must be confessed,
> Flat as a rose that has long been pressed,"

yet there is something quaint and rare in these old works that one does not find equaled in the more accomplished and brilliant productions of contemporary painters.

[See Eola Willis, "The First Woman Painter in America," *International Studio,* July 1927; William Dunlap, *A Hist. of the Rise and Progress of the Arts of Design in the U. S.* (new ed., 1918), III, 311; Robert Wilson, "Art and Artists in Provincial South Carolina," *Year Book, 1899, City of Charleston, S. C.* (n.d.), App., pp. 138–39. The last two sources give her name as "Johnson."]
W. H. D.

JOHNSTON, HENRY PHELPS (Apr. 19, 1842–Feb. 28, 1923), educator, historian, was born in Trebizond, Turkey in Asia, son of Rev. Thomas Pinckney and Marianne Cassandra (Howe) Johnston, pioneer American missionaries to Turkey and Armenia. His father was descended from Robert Johnston, of Scottish origin, who settled in Iredell County, N. C. The outbreak of the Crimean War suggested the return of the missionaries to the United States, and Henry completed at the Hopkins Grammar School, New Haven, his preparation for Yale College, from which he was graduated in 1862. It was war time and he enlisted in August, in the newly formed 15th Connecticut Volunteers. He told his classmates (*The Twenty Years Record of the Yale Class of 1862,* 1884, p. 69) that for the next three years he "resided anywhere from the Potomac to the Neuse, in many a mudhole and swamp, in breastworks and forts, on picket lines and battle lines, and sometimes, too, in pleasant places." Late in the conflict he was transferred to the United States Signal Corps and ended his service in July 1865 on the staff of Gen. W. B. Hazen. This military experience served to lend color to his later teaching and writing of history, but it was not until 1879 that he settled down to a career of that sort. In the meantime one year at the Yale Law School had been followed by admission to the New York bar and a bit of office experience; then a try at school teaching, apparently without relish, and then several years connection with New York papers, including the *Sun, New York Times, New York Observer,* and *Christian Union.* He indulged his hobby for historical study in leisure hours, and the outcome was a monograph of recognized excellence, *The Campaign of 1776 around New York* (1878). On Jan. 1, 1879, he became a tutor in the College of the City of New York and four years later he succeeded Charles E. Anthon [*q.v.*] as professor of history. He was an inspiring teacher and an eloquent lecturer. His colleagues in the history department of the college became many as the institution expanded, and they testify to the keen interest he had in their success, to the open mind he always showed to the newer tendencies even though he himself adhered to the older school of historians, to his rich vein of quaint humor beneath a seeming austerity.

His passion for historical research was unceasing. The publication by E. F. de Lancey of the manuscript left by Judge Thomas Jones [*q.v.*], under the title *History of New York during the Revolutionary War* (2 vols., 1879), brought from Johnston's pen his *Observations on Judge Jones' Loyalist History of the American Revolution* (1880). His interest in Connecticut and his Alma Mater was shown by his *Yale and Her Honor Roll in the American Revolution* (1888), *The Record of Connecticut Men in the Military and Naval Service during the War of the Revolution* (1889), and *Nathan Hale, 1776: Biography and Memorials* (1901; revised 1914). Two monographs, *The Yorktown Campaign* (1881) and *The Battle of Harlem Heights* (1897); are witness to his continued interest in military history, while the *Correspondence and Public Papers of John Jay* (4 vols., 1890–93) shows his ability in quite a different field. He was the founder of the Museum of the College of the City of New York, now a large and valuable collection of historical manuscripts, maps, relics, and other interesting material. After his retirement in 1916 from active teaching he was continued as curator of the Museum. He married, Oct. 26, 1871, Elizabeth Kirtland Holmes of Lebanon, Conn. They had four sons.

[N. P. Mead, "Henry Phelps Johnston," in *City College Quart.,* Mar. 1917 (portr.); Yale classbook, *ante*; *Fifty Years' Meeting of the Yale Class of 1862* (1914); *Yale Univ. Obit. Record,* 1923; *N. Y. Times,* Mar. 3, 1923.]
A. E. P.

JOHNSTON, JOHN (Apr. 11, 1791–Nov. 24, 1880), agriculturist, was born in New Galloway, Scotland, and spent many of his early days on the hills tending his grandfather's sheep. He once said, "Whatever I know about farming I learned from my grandfather." A remark of the latter that "verily all the airth needs draining," made a deep impression on him and later resulted in his most important contribution to agriculture. He was married in 1818 and came to the United States in the spring of 1821. After looking about for a few months, he purchased a farm of 112 acres on the eastern shore of Seneca Lake, about three miles from Geneva, N. Y. When he bought it the farm was in badly run-down condition, but by hard work and good farming he gradually built it up and before many years had acquired an enviable reputation. Recollecting his grandfather's remarks about draining, he decided to drain his land. Remembering also that tiles were used for this purpose in Scotland, he sent to

Scotland for a pattern and had tiles made by hand. He commenced draining his land in 1835. Since underdraining was a new thing in those days he was the object of much ridicule. Some of his neighbors said, "John Johnston is gone crazy—he is burying *crockery* in the ground" (*American Agriculturist,* April 1874), but his draining soon showed results and his neighbors found that he was raising bigger crops than they did. In 1848 his friend John Delafield [*q.v.*] imported from England a Scraggs machine for making tiles, and from that time Johnston laid tiles as rapidly as he could get the work done. By 1851 he had laid sixteen miles of tile drain on his farm and by 1856 he had between fifty-one and fifty-two miles. The results which he attained were not due entirely to draining, however, but also to the methods of cultivation which he employed. "If not a pioneer in such practices as the use of lime and plaster, the surface application of manure, the purchase of oil meal for feeding cattle and sheep, the earlier cutting of hay" (*Cultivator and Country Gentleman,* Dec. 2, 1880), he was at least among the first. His fame spread and many of the foremost farmers of the country made pilgrimages to his farm to see his methods. He wrote comparatively little, but the occasional pithy statements which he contributed to farm journals had great weight. He was an original thinker and a sagacious observer. With determination and skill he made his farm produce large crops with few failures and from the farm he achieved a liberal competence. In appearance he was fine looking, tall and somewhat spare, with the bearing of a "gentleman of the old school." Respected and loved by all who knew him, he lived comfortably and brought up and educated a large family. He remained on his farm until 1877, when his increasing age led him to rent it and move to Geneva, where he died in his ninetieth year.

[L. H. Bailey, "John Johnston, the Father of American Tile-Draining," *Am. Gardening,* Mar. 1893; *Am. Agriculturist,* Apr. 1874, Aug. 23, 1924; *Cultivator and Country Gentleman,* Dec. 2, 1880; J. H. Klippart, *Principles and Practice of Land Drainage* (1861); *Fifteenth Ann. Report, Ohio State Board of Agric., 1860* (1861); *Country Gentleman,* Nov. 10, 17, 1859.] C. R. B.

JOHNSTON, JOHN TAYLOR (Apr. 8, 1820–Mar. 24, 1893), railroad executive, art collector, first president of the Metropolitan Museum of Art, was born in New York City, the son of John and Margaret (Taylor) Johnston. Both parents were of Scottish birth and enjoyed long visits periodically to the home land. John was with them on one of these visits and received an important part of his early education in the Edinburgh High School, being *"dux* of his class" most of the time. In 1839 he graduated from the University of the City of New York (New York University) of which his father was a founder and a Washington Square neighbor, and then he studied law, first at the Yale Law School, 1839–41, and later in the office of Daniel Lord in New York City. He was admitted to the New York bar in 1843, but the law had little appeal for him. After two years' travel abroad he became interested, through his father, in a little New Jersey railroad connecting Somerville and Elizabethtown, and in 1848, when twenty-eight years old, was elected its president. Extension of the road westward across New Jersey to Easton, Pa., was one of his first projects. Then came the acquisition of the Lehigh & Susquehanna, which gave the anthracite coal fields of Pennsylvania a direct rail connection with the seaboard. There had been a boat connection between Elizabethport and New York City by way of Kill van Kull, but Johnston foresaw the necessity for a terminal directly opposite the lower end of Manhattan Island. He began, therefore, quietly to acquire a right of way across the Jersey flats and to secure ample acreage for railroad yards at Jersey City, and then built the rail connection from Elizabeth which involved the construction of a long trestle with its drawbridge across Newark Bay. Passengers all took notice when a ferry boat of quality with no spittoons was ready to land them at the foot of Liberty Street. In this way the present Central Railroad of New Jersey had obtained a splendid start before the Civil War was over.

Johnston knew personally many of the patrons of his road, and bore them ever in mind. Their safety as well as convenience was his study. He saw to it that the grades were low, the alignment perfect, and the grade crossings as few as possible. Furthermore, himself a lover of things beautiful, he offered a prize annually to the station agent who should produce the most attractive grounds. Uniforms for trainmen were another innovation which he introduced after a trip to England. About thirty years of his life were given energetically to the railroad.

During these years he was acquiring in his own home a collection of pictures that had no parallel in New York and probably not in America. He wished to share his pictures with the public, and constructed two galleries attached to his house which he opened to visitors one day each week. When because of financial reverses he had to dispose of the main part of his collection in December 1876, New York City witnessed its first great art sale. The movement to establish a museum of art in the city found in him an enthusiastic supporter. A friend, writing of his characteristics, mentioned "his love of art, as well as his prominence and high standing in the community, his administrative ability, good judgment and sound common sense" (manuscript letter of W. L. Andrews to Mrs. R. M. de Forest, Aug. 24, 1908). In 1870 he was elected first president of the Metropolitan Museum of Art. Failing health compelled him to resign in 1889, but his devotion to the Museum, of which he remained honorary president, never flagged.

Another institution to which he gave a full measure of devotion was the University of the City of New York. Seven years after his graduation he was elected to succeed his father on the University Council, of which he became subsequently (1872–86) the president. He endowed a professorship in the Latin languages; the Law Library owes its start to his generosity; and he inaugurated the general endowment of the University in 1871. He died in his seventy-third year, survived by four of his five children. His wife, whom he married in 1850, was Frances Colles, daughter of James Colles.

["The Old New Jersey Central" in *Railroad Employee,* Mar. 1905 (portr.); "Worthy Member of a Great Class" in *N. Y. Univ. Alumnus,* Mar. 6, 1929; W. E. Howe, *A Hist. of the Metropolitan Museum of Art* (1913); *Hist. of N. Y. University* (1901), Vol. I; *Gen. Alumni Cat. of N. Y. U.* (1906); J. L. Chamberlain, *Universities and Their Sons: N. Y. Univ.* (1901), vol. I; *Evening Post* (N. Y.), Mar. 24, 1893, *Sun* (N. Y.), and *N. Y. Times,* Mar. 25, 1893; Johnston's manuscript journals and letters in the possession of the family; information from family.] A. E. P.

JOHNSTON, JOSEPH EGGLESTON (Feb. 3, 1807–Mar. 21, 1891), Confederate soldier, was born at "Cherry Grove," Prince Edward County, Va. His father, Peter Johnston [*q.v.*], who was descended from a Scottish family which emigrated to Virginia in 1727, served in the Revolution under Light Horse Harry Lee and later became a distinguished jurist; his mother, Mary, was a daughter of Col. Valentine Wood of Goochland County, Va., and a niece of Patrick Henry. Johnston's boyhood was spent near Abingdon, Va. He received his early education at the Abingdon Academy, which his father had helped to found. In 1825 he became a cadet at the Military Academy at West Point. Although he had weak eyes, he made a reputation in history, French, and astronomy. In 1829 he graduated No. 13 in a class of forty-six.

Appointed a second lieutenant, 4th Artillery, he resigned after eight years' service to become a civil engineer. In this capacity he joined Powell's expedition to Florida, which was routed by Indians, Jan. 15, 1838. Johnston took charge of the rear guard, and although twice wounded in the forehead he conducted the retreat so skilfully that he was recommissioned as first lieutenant, Topographical Engineers. On July 10, 1845, he married Lydia McLane, daughter of Louis McLane [*q.v.*] of Maryland. Promoted captain in 1846, he joined Scott's expedition to Mexico. In 1847 he was appointed lieutenant-colonel of Voltigeurs, and was twice wounded near Cerro Gordo. He led an assaulting column at Chapultepec, where he was wounded three times. At the end of the war he reverted to his old rank of captain, Topographical Engineers. In 1855, he became lieutenant-colonel, 1st Cavalry, and in 1860, quartermaster-general and brigadier-general.

Upon the secession of Virginia from the Union, Johnston resigned from the United States Army, Apr. 22, 1861. Going immediately to Richmond to offer his services to his native state, he was at once appointed a major-general of Virginia, and in May, brigadier-general, Confederate States Army, and assigned to Harper's Ferry. Here, with troops disabled by measles and mumps and lacking in arms, munitions, and transportation, he found himself confronted by a Federal force under Patterson, superior to his in strength.

When Beauregard's army near Bull Run was threatened by an advancing hostile force, Johnston quietly withdrew without attracting Patterson's attention, and by rail and marching joined Beauregard, arriving, himself, on July 20. He approved Beauregard's plans. The next day the battle of Manassas (Bull Run) was fought. At the beginning, Johnston was at the right of the line, pursuant to an intention to attack from that flank, but the Federals turned the Confederate left, and Johnston hastened thither, just in time to rally the first detachments which had been driven back. He showed excellent leadership in restoring the position, rearranging his troops, and organizing a counter-attack which drove the enemy back in a rout. He was then assigned to command in northern Virginia. In July he received a commission as general, Confederate States Army, which he accepted under protest because it placed him fourth in rank instead of at the head of the list of generals. President Davis, irritated, took no action on the protest, and the bad feeling thus begun between these two men lasted throughout the war.

When McClellan in March 1862 moved his army to Fort Monroe, Johnston was fully informed, and closely calculated McClellan's strength by counting transports as they steamed down the Potomac. He promptly transferred the bulk of his army to the Peninsula, east of Richmond. His authority was extended to include all of the new theatre of operations. After a personal examination of the lines about Yorktown, he recommended that they be abandoned and the army concentrated near Richmond. On the advice of Lee, President Davis directed that there be no withdrawal. Johnston temporarily complied with this order, but prepared to retreat, and did so on May 4, when McClellan was ready to assault with strong forces. Pursued, Johnston was forced to have his rear guard fight all day on May 5, near Williamsburg, to enable his army to march away. The rear guard successfully carried out its mission, and there was no further interruption in the march to Richmond.

For a time, Johnston remained passive, although urged by Lee, and the Richmond press, to attack. From May 28 to 30, discussions were held at Johnston's headquarters and it was decided to attack early on May 31. No written minutes were made, and subsequent events indicate that various generals present believed that their individual opinions had been approved by Johnston. The battle of Seven Pines (Fair Oaks) began May 31. Owing to useless marches by subordinates, the attack started, not at dawn, as planned, but after noon, and then with but a fraction of the troops which should have participated. Johnston was not with the force assigned to make the main attack, and he was not able to influence its action. Present on a flank, he was twice wounded toward the end of the battle. Though some success was gained it was local, and not decisive. Johnston insisted that his being wounded prevented a full accomplishment of his plans, but this is problematical. As he did secure some results, his explanation was, at the time, accepted, and his reputation increased as a result of this battle. His plan was excellent, but it miscarried owing to faulty issuing of orders and failure to supervise their execution.

In November 1862 he had sufficiently recovered from his wounds to report for duty and was assigned to command the Confederate forces consisting of the armies of Bragg in Tennessee and Pemberton in Mississippi. He soon requested relief, complaining that his authority was only nominal, that all he could do was to transfer troops from one army to another, that both armies were outnumbered by the enemy opposing them and never had any troops available to transfer; moreover, he contended, such a movement would require a month, much too long to meet an emergency. President Davis stated that there was nothing in Johnston's orders to limit his action, and that there had been no such intention. The orders bear out this statement, which has not been disputed. Johnston, however, disliked to interfere with army commanders and failed to give them orders.

No crisis occurred until May 1, 1863, when Grant crossed into Mississippi to attack Vicksburg. Pemberton wired asking for reënforcements. Johnston wired back orders to unite all forces to beat Grant. Johnston's private correspondence at this date indicates that he was not in good condition, physically or mentally. He took no further action until ordered by President Davis to proceed to Mississippi and assume chief command. He obeyed promptly, but arrived at Jackson, Miss., on May 13, too late to save the situation. He found Grant between himself and Pemberton. He had with him only a weak force, and sent word to Pemberton to come up on the rear of Grant at once, but Pemberton disobeyed the order, and Johnston was never able to join him. When Pemberton was defeated and fell back into Vicksburg, Johnston on May 17 directed the evacuation of that city, its garrison to march northeast to join him. Pemberton could have obeyed, but he failed to do so, and lost his army. Johnston should have relieved Pemberton and himself assumed command. He had been instructed to do so, but he maintained with some truth that he was unable to ride a horse long enough to go around Grant's army to reach Pemberton. Still he could have relieved Pemberton, and substituted some other general who would have obeyed orders. President Davis severely condemned Johnston for not concentrating troops in time to save Vicksburg.

In December 1863 Johnston was assigned to the Army of the Tennessee, then facing Chattanooga, with instructions to reorganize it and assume the offensive. He did effectively reorganize the army, but when suggestions were made that he attack, he showed irritation and refused on the ground of insufficient forces. He desired to be attacked in a prepared position, with a view to counter-attacking when the enemy was exhausted. In May 1864 the Federals advanced, and Johnston awaited them, all ready in line of battle. Unfortunately for his plan, however, the Federal general, Sherman, was too wise to waste troops in assaulting, and marched around the Confederates, forcing Johnston back in order to preserve his communications. Sherman only once departed from these tactics when on June 27 he attacked at Kenesaw Mountain. Badly beaten, he resumed his turning movements, and Johnston gradually fell back, until in July he was just in front of Atlanta. On July 17, he was relieved from command, on the stated ground that he had failed to arrest the advance of the enemy. In this, his most famous campaign, he was outnumbered, and that fact indeed was his excuse for never assuming the offensive. He saved his army intact for future use. The experience of his successor, John Bell Hood [*q.v.*], who later lost the major part of the army in unsuccessful attacks, seemed to justify Johnston's actions, but Johnston's strategy never would have stopped Sherman, who was delayed not so much by his opponent as by the necessity of repairing the railroad in his rear.

On Feb. 23, 1865, Johnston was reassigned to the Army of the Tennessee. During March and April he fought several engagements in North Carolina. On Apr. 13, at a conference at Greensboro, N. C., he proposed to President Davis that he, Johnston, should address a letter to Sherman asking for peace. Davis finally consented, and on Apr. 18, Sherman and Johnston signed an armistice, by which the Confederate armies were to be disbanded and civil government reëstablished. Johnston's troops at once commenced to desert, and when on Apr. 24 he was advised that the Federal government had disapproved the armistice, he was in no position to fight. Ordered by President Davis to move south to continue the war, he refused, and surrendered his command to Sherman on Apr. 26.

With the coming of peace, he established himself in Savannah, Ga., engaging in the insurance business. In 1877 he moved to Richmond, and in 1878 was elected a member of Congress, where he served one term. He then settled in Washington, D. C. In 1885 he was appointed commissioner of railroads. He published his *Narrative of Military Operations* in 1874; wrote an article, "My Negotiations with General Sherman," for the *North American Review* (August 1886); and contributed "Responsibilities of First Bull Run," "Manassas to Seven Pines," "Jefferson Davis and the Mississippi Campaign," and "Opposing Sherman's Advance to Atlanta" to *Battles and Leaders of the Civil War*. He died at his residence in Washington.

Johnston's reputation rests on the fact that he suffered no defeat throughout the war. He disliked risks. The only important attack he undertook was that at Seven Pines, and that was badly managed. In all his other campaigns he avoided the aggressive. He failed to accept the point of view of his government, and was at odds with its leader. He constantly foresaw difficulties, and was pessimistic. His one chance of beating Sherman in 1864 was by daring and rapid action, but for this type of warfare he was not suited.

[The main source for Johnston's campaigns is *War of the Rebellion: Official Records (Army)*, 1 ser. II (Manassas); XI, pts. 1–3 (Peninsula); XXIII, pts. 1, 2, and XXIV, pts. 1–3 (Vicksburg); XXXVIII, pts. 1–5 (Atlanta); XLVII, pts. 1–3 (North Carolina). Johnston's *Narrative of Military Operations* is accurate, obviously written from copies of original reports, and shows the author's side of disputed actions. R. M. Hughes, *General Johnston* (1893) follows the *Narrative* very closely. Joseph Longstreet, *From Manassas to Appomatox* (1896); Jefferson Davis, *The Rise and Fall of the Confederate Govt.* (1881); E. P. Alexander, *Military Memoirs of a Confederate* (1907); R. M. Johnston, *Bull Run* (1913), all contain important material. Interesting personal correspondence is in *Jour. Mil. Service Inst. of the U. S.*, May–June 1912. See also: *Battles and Leaders of the Civil War* (4 vols., 1887–88); B. T. Johnson, *A Memoir of the Life and Public Service of Jos. E. Johnston* (1891); G. W. Cullum, *Biog. Reg. Officers and Grads. U. S. Mil. Acad.* (3rd ed., 1891); E. A. Pollard, *Lee and His Lieutenants* (1867); *So. Hist. Soc. Papers*, vols. XVIII (1890), XIX (1891); *Confed. Mil. Hist.* (1899), I, 644–49; J. D. Cox, in the *Nation* (N. Y.), Mar. 26, 1891; *Washington Post*, Mar. 22, 1891.]

C. H. L—a.

JOHNSTON, JOSEPH FORNEY (Mar. 23, 1843–Aug. 8, 1913), governor of Alabama and senator, was born at "Mount Welcome" in Lincoln County, N. C., the son of William Johnston, a physician, and Nancy (Forney) Johnston. He was a descendant of Gilbert Johnston, who settled in North Carolina in 1745 and was a brother of Gabriel Johnston [*q.v*]. At the age of seventeen Joseph removed to Alabama, where he was in school when he enlisted as a private in the 18th Alabama Regiment on Apr. 21, 1861. He served through the war, rose to the rank of captain in the 12th North Carolina Regiment, and was wounded at Chickamauga, Spotsylvania Court House, New Market, and Petersburg. After the war he read law with his kinsman, William Henry Forney [*q.v.*], at Jacksonville, Ala., was admitted to the bar in 1866, and began practice at Selma, Ala. In August 1869 he married Theresa Virginia Hooper, of South Carolina, a great-grand-daughter of William Hooper [*q.v.*]. In 1884, when it was a town of only three thousand, he went to Birmingham to become president of the Alabama National Bank. There he identified himself with the growing financial and manufacturing interests and devoted his initiative and foresight to the development of the region. In 1887 he became first president of the Sloss Iron and Steel Company, which was the pioneer iron manufacturing company in the Birmingham district. For a number of years he was chairman of the state Democratic executive committee. He became an advocate of free silver and in 1896 was elected governor in order to unite the white voters of the state, who for years had been divided between the Democratic and Populist parties. He prided himself upon the efficiency of his administration in collecting taxes and economy in spending them, on the increased expenditures for the public-school system, and on the encouragement of outside capital to invest within the state. During his second term he lost prestige with his party because he, at first, approved a revision of the constitution to eliminate the negro from politics but, later, called a special session of the legislature to repeal the act providing for the constitutional convention. In 1899 he led a movement to sell to the Sloss Sheffield Company a large tract of the coal lands granted to the University of Alabama by the federal government. A bitter controversy ensued in which attacks were made against him due to his previous connection with the Sloss interests, but the record shows no evidence to substantiate the charges of corruption. The University trustees were seriously divided on the issue but finally refused to make the sale. Johnston returned to his law practice in Birmingham and made an unsuccessful campaign against John T. Morgan for a seat in the national Senate. On Aug. 6, 1907, at the death of Edmund W. Pettus, he became senator for the remainder of the latter's term. In 1909 he was elected for a full term during which he died at Washington.

[A. B. Moore, *Hist. of Ala. and her People* (1927), vol. I; T. M. Owen, *Hist. of Ala. and Dict. of Ala. Biog.* (1921), vol. III; *Memorial Record of Ala.* (1893), vol. II; *Joseph Forney Johnston, Memorial Addresses Delivered in the Senate and H. of R. of the U. S.* (1915); *Birmingham Age-Herald,* Aug. 9, 10, 11, 1913; *Trustees' Record, Univ. of Ala.,* 1899, 1900, 1901; information from Robison Brown, secretary of Board of Trustees, Univ. of Ala.] T. H. J.

JOHNSTON, JOSIAH STODDARD (Nov. 24, 1784–May 19, 1833), lawyer, statesman, son of John and Mary (Stoddard) Johnston, and a half-brother of Gen. Albert Sidney Johnston [*q.v.*], was born at Salisbury, Conn., where the Johnstons, who were of Scottish ancestry, possessed some property and local influence. His father, a physician, removed to Kentucky in 1788, and settled in Washington, where he lived until his death in 1831. When Josiah was twelve years of age, his father took him to New Haven, Conn., where he attended school for some years, but when ready for college he returned to Kentucky and entered Transylvania University at Lexington, graduating in 1802 (*A Catalogue of the Officers & Graduates of Transylvania University,* 1826). He then studied law with William T. Barry [*q.v.*] of Lexington, who was one of the leaders of the Kentucky bar.

In 1805, after completing his law studies, Johnston emigrated to the newly acquired territory of Louisiana and settled in Alexandria, then a frontier village. Here he opened a law office and rapidly gained wealth and distinction. He not only kept out of the numerous brawls which took place in that turbulent community, but by the application of honesty, fairness, and tact he was so successful in settling the disputes of others that he became known as "The Peacemaker." In 1814 he married Eliza Sibley, daughter of Dr. John Sibley of Natchitoches. He was elected to the first Louisiana territorial legislature and continued a member of that body until statehood was acquired in 1812. From 1812 to 1821 he was a Louisiana district judge. Toward the close of the War of 1812 he was elected commander of a regiment of volunteers, which he had aided in raising and helped to equip from his own means, and when Louisiana was invaded by the British they joined General Jackson at New Orleans, but too late to share in the victory of Jan. 8, 1815. In 1821 he was elected to the United States House of Representatives, and in 1823, when Senator James Brown [*q.v.*] of Louisiana resigned to accept an appointment as United States minister to France, Johnston was appointed to the vacancy. He was elected to the Senate in 1825, and reëlected in 1831, this time by a legislature opposed to him in political opinion. For several years he was chairman of the committee on commerce, and he was also a member of the committee on finance. He took advantage of every opportunity to press upon the government the duty of seeking the mitigation of the rules of maritime warfare, urging especially that neutral ships should protect the goods on board regardless of ownership, and that articles of contraband should be limited to the smallest possible number. He was a close friend of Henry Clay [*q.v.*], with whom he was in political affiliation, and, like the Kentucky statesman, he opposed the nullification movement of the early eighteen-thirties. According to all accounts, he was no orator although a clear and forceful speaker. He was killed on the morning of May 19, 1833, by an explosion of gunpowder which took place on the steamboat *Lioness,* on the Red River about forty miles above Alexandria, La., while he was on his way from New Orleans to Natchitoches.

[Wm. P. Johnston, *The Johnstons of Salisbury* (1897), and *Life of Gen. Albert Sidney Johnston* (1878); *Niles' Weekly Reg.* (Baltimore), June 15, 1833; remarks by Henry Clay, in *Reg. of Debates in Cong.,* 23 Cong., 1 Sess., cols. 11–12; J. T. Lloyd, *Lloyd's Steamboat Directory and Disasters on the Western Waters* (Cincinnati, 1856); *Biog. Dir. Am. Cong.* (1928).] M. J. W.

JOHNSTON, PETER (Jan. 6, 1763–Dec. 8, 1831), Revolutionary soldier, legislator, jurist, was born at Osborne's Landing on James River,

Virginia, the oldest son of a Scottish immigrant, Peter Johnston, and his wife, formerly the widow Martha (Butler) Rogers. Two years after his birth the family moved to Prince Edward County, where he was schooled by Scottish tutors before entering Hampden-Sidney College, newly established on land given by his father, to prepare for the ministry. Despite his father's royalist feelings, he soon became an ardent patriot, and shortly before his seventeenth birthday ran away from college with a classmate to enlist in the cavalry legion of Lieutenant-Colonel Henry Lee. Vigilant, enterprising, ambitious, and brave, within a year he had risen from the ranks to a lieutenancy and had become a favorite with his fellows and his commander. He fought with Lee's Legion throughout the Southern campaign, 1780–81, and bore himself most creditably at Guilford, Eutaw Springs, Wright's Bluff, and Ninety-six, resigning in 1782 to join as adjutant and captain the Light Corps formed by General Greene. Several years later the Virginia legislature fittingly commissioned him brigadier-general of militia. A soldier by instinct and heritage, passionately fond of riding, shooting, and hunting, he retained throughout life a predilection for the military profession, and, had he continued in it, he would doubtless have won more than local reputation.

After the war he returned to his father's home, devoted himself to the study of law, and built up a successful practice in Prince Edward and the adjoining counties. A man of impeccable character and vigorous, scholarly mind, of fine appearance, a forceful speaker, and a talented if infrequent writer, it was natural that he should soon have turned to politics. Aligning himself with the Jeffersonian school, he was elected to the legislature in 1792, and within the next eighteen years represented Prince Edward County a dozen times more, during the better part of two sessions (1805–06 and 1806–07) being speaker of the House of Delegates. His most conspicuous service in the Assembly was his strenuous advocacy, in committee and on the floor, of the famous Virginia Resolutions of 1798, protesting against the Alien and Sedition Acts and asserting the doctrine that the Union was a compact to which the states were parties. In 1802, with Gen. Joseph Martin and Creed Taylor, he represented Virginia on the commission appointed to settle the Tennessee boundary question. He was elected a judge of the Virginia general court, Feb. 1, 1811, and assigned to the Prince Edward district, but exchanged circuits with Judge William Brockenbrough, removed to "Panicello," near Abingdon, and until he resigned, a few months before his death, presided with distinguished ability over the superior court of the southwest Virginia circuit.

He married, June 23, 1788, Mary Wood, daughter of Valentine Wood of Goochland County and a niece of Patrick Henry [*q.v.*]; she died in 1825, and he married, second, Dec. 13, 1828, Anne Bernard of Buckingham County. There were ten children by his first marriage, among them, Joseph Eggleston Johnston [*q.v.*].

[R. M. Hughes, *General Johnston* (1893); *Fifteenth Ann. Report, Va. State Lib., 1916–17* (1917); Alexander Garden, *Anecdotes of the Revolutionary War* (1822), and *Anecdotes of the Am. Revolution, Second Series* (1828); E. A. Pollard, *Lee and His Lieutenants* (1867); *Debates in the House of Delegates of Va. . . . 1798* (1798; repr. 1829); *Gen. Cat. Officers and Students of Hampden-Sidney Coll., 1776–1906* (n.d.); *Richmond Enquirer*, Dec. 20, 1831.] A. C. G., Jr.

JOHNSTON, RICHARD MALCOLM (Mar. 8, 1822–Sept. 23, 1898), author, educator, was born on the family plantation, "Oak Grove," near Powelton, Ga. He was the son of Malcolm and Catherine (Davenport) Johnston, and the great-grandson of Thomas Johnston who emigrated from Scotland and settled in Pennsylvania, later moving to Charlotte County, Va.; his father was a planter and ordained Baptist preacher. After his graduation from Mercer University, Penfield (now at Macon), in 1841, Richard taught for a year in the village of Mount Zion, Hancock County. He then read law in the office of Henry Cumming, Augusta, was admitted to the bar, and became the partner of Eli W. Baxter of Sparta, Ga. In 1844 he was married to Mary Frances, daughter of Eli Mansfield, a native of New Haven, Conn. His law practice from 1844 to 1851 was interrupted by two periods of teaching; in the latter year he formed a partnership with Linton Stephens [*q.v.*], brother of Alexander H. Stephens. The opportunity was offered him in 1857 of accepting the judgeship of the northern circuit court of Georgia, the presidency of Mercer University, or the chair of rhetoric and belles-lettres in the University of Georgia. He chose the professorship and remained in Athens until 1861. From 1862 to 1867 he conducted a school for boys at Rockby, near Sparta, Ga., which became one of the most widely known and generously patronized in the state. Its discipline included distinct elements of the "honor system," with none of the espionage and flogging then so widespread. A victim of the Civil War and Reconstruction, he continued this school in Baltimore for several years under the name of Pen Lucy School. While a clerk in the bureau of education at Washington, 1896–98, he compiled at the request of Commissioner W. T. Harris what is probably the most complete record extant of the picturesque old field schools of his boyhood in Georgia ("Early Educational Life in Middle Georgia," *Report of the Commissioner of Education,* 1894–95, 1895–96).

He took up fiction writing almost by chance and largely because of the encouragement of Henry C. Turnbull, Jr., a Baltimore publisher, and Sidney Lanier, who was his most loyal friend and earliest critic. His first, most popular, and most characteristic volume of local-color fiction was *Dukesboro Tales* (1871). In this and in many similar volumes, Johnston, a voluntary exile from his native state, created anew the scenes of his early life. The stories are rich in humor and kindliness and are suffused with a passionate love for his native soil and its people; consequently major stress is laid upon character and setting and minor emphasis upon plot, with the result that many of the stories are weak in action and some of them almost without plot. His published works include: *The English Classics* (1860); with William Hand Browne, *English Literature* (1872) and *Life of Alexander H. Stephens* (1878); *Old Mark Langston* (1884); *Two Gray Tourists* (1885); *Ogeechee Cross-Firings* (1889); *Widow Guthrie* (1890); *The Primes and Their Neighbors* (1891); *Studies, Literary and Social,* first series (1891), second series (1892); *Mr. Billy Downs and His Likes* (1892); *Mr. Fortner's Marital Claims* (1892); *Little Ike Templin* (1894); *Old Times in Middle Georgia* (1897); *Pearce Amerson's Will* (1898); and *Autobiography of Col. Richard Malcolm Johnston* (1900).

In 1875 he was received into the Roman Catholic Church, in joining which his wife and younger children had preceded him. At his request, there was published posthumously his detailed statement of how and why he had embraced the Catholic faith, the reasons assigned being the historical precedence and infallible authority claimed by that church (*Truth,* Raleigh, N. C., April 1899). He delivered numerous lectures at St. Mary's Seminary and Notre Dame College, Baltimore, and St. Charles' College, Ellicott City, Md., and from 1895 to 1898 he was a member of the regular staff of lecturers at the Catholic Summer School, Plattsburg, N. Y. He was also a popular reader and lecturer in the eighties and nineties when the lyceum system flourished throughout the country. He lectured with several contemporary humorists—once, in 1889, with Mark Twain, who was the guest of the Johnstons in Baltimore. It is related that Twain, with characteristic generosity, refused to accept any of the receipts for the evening's lecture, leaving the entire proceeds to Johnston and his family, then in rather needy circumstances.

[Johnston's *Autobiography*; his letters, school records, contemporary newspaper accounts, and other documentary data; E. C. Stedman and S. B. Weeks, *Lit. Estimate and Bibliog.: Richard Malcolm Johnston* (1898); *Evening Star* (Washington), Sept. 23, 1898; the *Sun* (Baltimore), Sept. 24, 1898.] F. T. L.

JOHNSTON, ROBERT MATTESON (Apr. 11, 1867–Jan. 28, 1920), historian and educator, was born in Paris, France, the son of William Edward and Bertha (Matteson) Johnston. His father had served as correspondent for the *New York Times* in the Crimean War, and later settled in Paris where he practised medicine. Johnston was for the most part educated abroad, entered Pembroke College, Cambridge, in 1885 and received the degree of A.B. in 1889. He studied law, and was admitted to the Inner Temple, but practised virtually not at all. He was married in London, in 1895, to Emily Dawson. For a time he engaged in business in South Africa. After a period of study as a private scholar in Cambridge, he published, in 1901, the first of his historical works, *The Roman Theocracy and the Republic.* In that year he went to Naples, but in 1902 came to the United States and began his teaching career. He lectured at Harvard and at Mount Holyoke, having a permanent connection with the latter institution from 1904 to 1906. In the course of this period he published *The Napoleonic Empire in Southern Italy* (2 vols., 1904), *Napoleon, a Short Biography* (1904), *Memoirs of "Malakoff"* (2 vols., 1907), from the papers of his father; and prepared a series of historical sketches, *Leading American Soldiers* (1907). In 1907 he was called to Bryn Mawr, but after one year's teaching there became assistant professor at Harvard, with which institution he was identified for the rest of his life. He was a singularly gifted lecturer, with an original viewpoint, and though he occasionally verged on the bizarre, he never failed to be stimulating. He was particularly interested in the French Revolution, and did his best teaching work in this field. He published *The French Revolution* in 1909, *The Corsican,* a clever piecing together of Napoleon's recorded utterances to form a sort of biography, in 1910, and the *Mémoire de Marie Caroline, Reine de Naples* (Harvard Historical Studies, vol. XVI) in 1912. In this year appeared also his *Holy Christian Church,* a bold attempt to deal with the development of Catholic Christianity through the ages—an undertaking for which he was not thoroughly equipped, and to which he brought no really sympathetic insight. He had always been interested in military history, a taste perhaps acquired from his father, and he was a strong advocate of military preparedness, notably in his *Bull Run; Its Strategy and Tactics* (1913), excellent on the historical side, and in his *Arms and the Race* (1915). With Col. A. L. Conger he founded and edited the *Military Historian and Economist,* but the promising career of this journal was cut short by the World War. In April 1918, Johnston was commissioned a major in the army, and soon after became head of the Historical Section at General Headquarters. Gathering a group of younger historians around him, he began a series of studies on the military history of the war (see his *First Reflections on the Campaign of 1918,* 1920). Not many months after the armistice, however, his health broke, his staff was dispersed, and he himself subordinated to a regular army officer. He returned to the United States in ill health, and after a brief period of teaching, died in Cambridge, Mass.

Without special training, and beginning rather late, Johnston made a distinct position for himself among historical writers. If he sometimes fell short of the strictest canons of scholarship, he united keen insight and imagination with genuine gifts of style. If he sometimes generalized over-boldly, he at least avoided that cautious monotony of emphasis that frequently passes for scholarship.

[*The Book of Matriculations and Degrees in the University of Cambridge from 1851 to 1900* (1902); *Who's Who in America,* 1918–19; Ephraim Emerton in *Harvard Grads. Mag.,* Sept. 1920; F. S. Mead, *Harvard's Military Record in the World War* (1921); *N. Y. Times,* Jan. 29, 1920; personal information.] D. P.

JOHNSTON, SAMUEL (Dec. 15, 1733–Aug. 17, 1816), Revolutionary leader, United States senator, was born in Dundee, Scotland. While he was an infant, his parents, Samuel and Helen (Scrymoure) Johnston, emigrated to North Carolina, probably accompanying their brother, Gabriel Johnston [*q.v.*], who had become governor of the colony, and settled in Onslow County. Young Johnston attended school in New Haven, Conn., then in 1754 he went to Edenton, N. C., where he studied law and finally settled, residing after 1765 at "Hayes," a beautiful home on Albemarle Sound. In 1759, by election to the Assembly, he entered upon the most notable political career in the history of North Carolina. His service in the Assembly was uninterrupted until 1775. During part of that time he was clerk of the court of the Edenton district and deputy naval officer of the port. In 1773 he was a member of the Committee of Correspondence. He was also a delegate to the first four provincial congresses and was president of the third and fourth. In 1775 he became one of the colonial treasurers, a member at large of the provincial Council of Safety, the executive branch of the revolutionary government, and district paymaster of troops. He was defeated for the fifth provincial congress, but he was chosen by the body a member of the commission delegated to codify the laws then in force. In 1779, 1783, and 1784, he sat in the North Carolina Senate, a service interrupted in 1780 upon his election to the Continental Congress. In 1781 he declined the presidency of the Congress and the following year he retired. In 1785 he was named on the commission appointed to settle the boundary dispute between Massachusetts and New York. In 1787 he was elected governor and was twice reëlected, but in 1789 he resigned to become the first United States senator from North Carolina, filling that position until 1793. He was president of the North Carolina convention of 1788, which refused to ratify the federal constitution, and of that of 1789, which accepted it. He was the first trustee of the University of North Carolina and served for twelve years. His final public service was a superior court judgeship from 1800 to 1803, after which he spent the rest of his life in happy retirement. He married Frances Cathcart of Edenton.

Johnston was a man of imposing presence and of vigorous mental and physical strength. His intellect was highly cultivated, his vision clear, and his purposes, based always on deep conviction, unselfish. He was conservative and yet progressive; balanced and highly practical. He became a leader of the people, not through their affection, for he did not inspire it, but through his wisdom and force of character. He is chiefly important as the central figure in North Carolina during the Revolution and during the period of constitutional reorganization which followed it. From the beginning of the strife with England he was, though not an extremist, a member of the popular party. To him the point at issue was one of legality. He opposed the Stamp Act as unconstitutional just as he opposed the Regulation in North Carolina as an illegal movement, and while the assembly of 1770, under his leadership, passed many of the reforms demanded, he drafted the "Bloody Act," under which Governor Tryon suppressed the uprising by force. The first provincial congress recognized his leadership as second only to that of John Harvey, and when the latter died in 1775, Johnston took his place as the organizer of revolt. Independence declared, he was one of the committee of the fourth provincial congress appointed to prepare a constitution. He saw the problem clearly. It was to preserve the fundamental rights and privileges of English liberty without at the same time sacrificing law, order, and stability. It was soon evident that a wide divergence of view existed in the state concerning the character of the proposed government, and a division into radical and conservative groups followed. At the head of the former was Willie Jones of Halifax; Johnston led the latter.

By agreement, the adoption of a constitution was postponed until the next congress, and when the election came, a tremendous and united effort of the radicals resulted in Johnston's defeat. He was present in Halifax during the meetings of the congress, however, and exerted a powerful influence upon the character of the constitution adopted. He accepted the doctrine of the popular basis of government, but he could never believe that God employed the mass of the people for a mouthpiece. He believed firmly in constitutional protection of minority rights, and in annual elections to guard them further. He held that representatives should be accountable only to their constituents, but he was hostile to the idea of unrestricted manhood suffrage and advocated a property qualification as protection against "a set of men without reading, experience, or principle to govern them." Particularly did he desire life tenure for judges, and his influence probably secured it. He naturally became a Federalist, and his election as president of the convention of 1788 was a high tribute from his political opponents who controlled the body, but he was powerless to win them by his efforts in debate. In the Senate he was not fully in accord with his party, favoring Madison's rather than Hamilton's plan of funding the debt, and strongly opposing the assumption of the state debts, for which, however, he finally voted. But he won disfavor at home by declining to attend the sessions of the legislature to render an account of his stewardship, and he was denied a second election.

[R. D. W. Connor, "Gov. Samuel Johnston of North Carolina," *N. C. Booklet*, Apr. 1912, and *Revolutionary Leaders of N. C.* (1916); memoir of Johnston in *N. C. Univ. Mag.*, Aug. 1858; S. A. Ashe, *Biog. Hist. of N. C.*, vol. IV (1906); H. M. Wagstaff, "Federalism in North Carolina," *Jas. Sprunt Hist. Pubs.*, vol. IX, no. 2 (1910); G. J. McRee, *Life and Correspondence of Jas. Iredell* (2 vols., 1857–58); *Colonial Records of N. C.* and *State Records of N. C.* (26 vols., 1886–1907).]

J. G. deR. H.

JOHNSTON, SAMUEL (Feb. 9, 1835–Apr. 15, 1911), inventor, manufacturer, was born in Shelby, Orleans County, N. Y., the son of Henry and Nancy (Crippen) Johnston. His father was a farmer who, with his wife, was also engaged in the weaving of fine linen. Johnston attended the district school near his home and obtained an elementary education. At an early age he exhibited a marked interest in mechanics and throughout his career applied his talents chiefly to the improvement of farm machinery. At the age of twenty he perfected and patented a corn and bean planter, and very shortly thereafter turned his attention to harvesting machinery. The reaping machine as variously made by Bell, Hussey, McCormick, and Dorsey, had in 1860 reached the stage where it was satisfactory for fine standing grain but not for badly tangled crops of varying lengths. About this time, therefore, Johnston, then residing in Buffalo, N. Y., in an endeavor to correct this defect applied himself to the improvement of rakes and reels for harvesters. He obtained one patent on a rake in 1863; another on a harvester in January 1865; and on Feb. 7, 1865, was granted a patent for a combined rake and reel for a harvester (*House Executive Document No. 52,* 39 Cong., 1 Sess., I, 108; III, 82). This proved to be a revolutionary improvement in harvesting machinery, for practically every maker of reapers in the world altered his machine to use the Johnston system. In the great field trials of reaping machinery held in 1866 at Auburn, N. Y., William Wallace & Company of Syracuse entered a Hubbard machine with a Johnston rake attached, which won the gold medal (*Transactions of the New York State Agricultural Society,* 1866, pp. 371–72; *Cultivator and Country Gentleman,* Aug. 2, 1866, p. 81). The features of this patent consisted of a series of centrally located arms, each provided with teeth. The path which these arms described was under the full control of the driver. He was able to make the rake arms drop down in front of the cutters and pick up the lodged grain and he could cause any desired rake to sweep the platform and discharge the cut, thus making uniform bundles of grain no matter what was the condition of the crop. The patent was assigned to Johnston and R. L. Howard of Buffalo, in whose iron works Johnston's earlier patented corn planter and corn husker had been manufactured since 1858, and here the manufacture of his harvester rake was undertaken. In 1868 he established a manufactory for his machine on a larger scale at Syracuse, N. Y., which operated under the name of Johnston, Huntley & Company. Three years later this plant was abandoned and the Johnston Harvester Company was established at Brockport, N. Y., with which Johnston was actively associated until his retirement from the company in 1879. During the succeeding years he continued his inventive work on harvester rakes, grain binders, and on a complete grain-binding harvester. He also patented rotary and disc harrows. In connection with the construction of machinery to manufacture his improvements, he devised new metal-working processes and patented cold rolling mills, rolled forging mills, and casting machinery. He invented a metal process by which finished articles are produced in duplicate, and for a number of years prior to his death was at work on the design of a furnace using natural fuels for the production of extremely high temperatures. For this he devised and patented a fuel burner. He was married, June 8, 1856, to Arsula S. Vaughan of Fort Ann, Cattaraugus County, N. Y., and at his death, in Buffalo, was survived by a daughter.

[R. L. Ardrey, *Am. Agric. Implements* (1894); *The Implement Age,* Springfield, Ohio, Apr. 22, 1911; *Farm Implement News,* Oct. 1887, Apr. 20, 1911; *Who's Who in America,* 1908–09; *Buffalo Morning Express,* Apr. 17, 1911; Mar. 10, 1912; Pat. Off. records; U. S. National Museum correspondence.] C. W. M.

JOHNSTON, THOMAS (*c.* 1708–May 8, 1767), engraver, painter, was probably born in 1708. His tombstone, in King's Chapel, Boston, contains at present only his name and the year of his death, but in the printed reproduction of it kept by the Massachusetts Historical Society, "Aged 59 Years" is added in handwriting, and appearances make it seem probable that this line on the stone has been obliterated by the weather. Johnston has often been confused with an English mezzotint engraver named Johnson who was born in Boston, England and who seems to have engraved a portrait of Increase Mather (K. B. Murdock, *The Portraits of Increase Mather,* 1924). Johnston was admitted to the Brattle Street Church, Boston, Mass., in 1726. According to court records he married Rachel Thwing in 1730, and several children are attributed to this union, one of them, Thomas, an organist and japanner, often being confused with his father. There is a record of his purchase of a house and land on Brattle Street in 1742; and on Aug. 6, 1747, he married Bathsheba Thwing, a cousin of his first wife. By his second marriage he had three sons.

Except for the work he left, for references in contemporary newspapers, and for a few court records of suits against him and the administration of his will, little is known about him. His work which survives consists principally of engravings, and most of these are topographical. His charts, "The Canada River" and "The Kennebec and Sagadahoc Rivers," are little more than outline maps with an occasional fort or settlement indicated, and the same thing is true of most of his engravings. In his "Prospect of Yale College," however, the pictorial enters in, and in his "Battle of Lake George," beneath a map at the top of the page the English are shown encamped on the lake with the French and Indians attacking them through the woods. Besides this topographical and pictorial material, he also engraved music for Psalm tunes and the plates for the commissions issued by the Province of Massachusetts during the last eight years of his life.

There is a portrait attributed to him in the Boston Museum of Fine Arts, and another is owned by the Massachusetts Historical Society; while the fact that he was an heraldic painter is attested by a suit over a coat of arms in which his apprentice, John Greenwood, made an affidavit that is in the files of the Massachusetts supreme court under date of Mar. 16, 1749. In addition to engraving and painting, Johnston was also an organ builder, and an organ of his construction is still in the Old North Church of Boston where a marble tablet commemorates the fact that he made it in 1759. He was primarily a japanner, but in his personal estate, inventoried at about twelve pounds, there were an unfinished organ and part of another one, together with pictures to the value of about three pounds. His real estate was appraised as worth sixty-six pounds, thirteen shillings, and four pence. Though neither a painter nor an engraver of great merit, he kept up artistic activity under conditions that were not favorable. That he exerted some influence on painting is shown by the fact that his apprentice, John Greenwood, referred to above, and Johnston's son John both achieved some success as portrait and figure painters.

[Wm. Dunlap, *A Hist. of the Rise and Progress of the Arts of Design in the U. S.* (rev. ed., 1918), ed. by F. W. Bayley and C. E. Goodspeed; D. M. Stauffer, *Am. Engravers upon Copper and Steel* (1907); W. H. Whitmore, *Notes Concerning Peter Pelham* (1867); *Proc. Mass. Hist. Soc.,* VI (1863), 33, 37; IX (1867), 213; XII (1873), 324; XVII (1880), 2; *A Report of the Record Commissioners of the City of Boston Containing the Boston Marriages from 1700 to 1751* (1898).] S. G.

JOHNSTON, WILLIAM ANDREW (Jan. 26, 1871–Feb. 16, 1929), journalist and author, was born in Pittsburgh, Pa., the son of William Andrew and Agnes (Parry) Johnston. He graduated as bachelor of arts from the Western University of Pennsylvania (now the University of Pittsburgh) in 1891. After two years of reporting on local newspapers, he tried his hand at publishing, conducting in 1893–94 the Wilkinsburg (Pa.) *Independent;* but being neither successful nor happy in this rôle, he went to New York, where from 1894 to 1897 he served as a reporter on the *Morning Journal* and the *New York Press.* He then spent three years on the editorial staff of the *New York Herald.* In 1900 he became associated with the New York *World* and remained with that paper for twenty-seven years. Meanwhile, he wrote many books and magazine articles. His first book, *History Up to Date,* appeared in 1899. Drawing upon his experiences as a reporter, he wrote a number of mystery and "detective" novels. Among them were *The Innocent Murderers* (1910); *The Yellow Letter* (1911); *The House of Whispers* (1918); *The Apartment Next Door* (1919); *The Mystery in the Ritsmore* (1920); *The Tragedy at the Beach Club* (1922); *The Waddington Cipher* (1923). Politically, Johnston claimed to be a socialist, but he was by no means a malcontent. A big-bodied, jovial man, he was noted for his kindliness and keen sense of humor. Ray Long, editor of the *Cosmopolitan Magazine,* once wrote him up in that journal as "the happiest man I know." Johnston created much laughter with his monograph on *The Fun of Being a Fat Man,* published in 1922. In collaboration with H. T. Webster, the cartoonist, he produced *Webster's Bridge* in 1924. This was a humorous book, but he was really considered an authority on bridge, and for several years was associate editor of the *Auction Bridge Magazine.* In 1916, while he himself was on crutches as the result of an accident, he wrote his most appealing and popular book, *Limpy,* the story of a lame boy, published in 1917. It is claimed that more than one hundred thousand copies were sold. *These Women,* a series of magazine articles, issued in book form in 1925, was widely popular. Another series entitled variously, "If I Were a Clergyman," "If I Were a Doctor," "If I Were a Lawyer," "If I Were a Rich Man," "If I Were Out of a Job," etc., running in *Collier's,* in 1925–26, contained much pungent yet kindly philosophy. Johnston was chairman of the Parker Independent League, supporting Judge Parker's campaign for the presidency in 1904. He proposed the Fulton aerial flight, the first airplane flight of any considerable length, as a part of the Hudson-Fulton Celebration in New York in 1909, and in connection with which a prize of $10,000 was offered by the city. He was more proud of his civic and welfare work than of his writing. He was the founder of grammar-school field days in the New York public schools. For many years he was a campaigner for the elimination of danger from Fourth of July observances, and in recognition of his efforts in this direction, he was placed in charge of New York's "safe and sane" Fourth of July celebrations in 1910, 1911, and 1912, which resulted in a marked decrease in accidents. In 1927 he quit the newspaper business to take over the direction of publicity for the Dalberg enterprises and was made director and vice-president of the Celotex Company and vice-president of the Southern Sugar Company. He was married, first, Feb. 22, 1896, to Hazel Minnette Williams of Hampshire, England; and second, Apr. 12, 1910, to Hattie Belle McCollum of Lockport, N. Y. In 1927 he moved to Chicago, where he died.

[*Alumni Directory, Univ. of Pittsburgh* (1910); *Who's Who in America,* 1928–29; the *World* (N. Y.); *N. Y. Times,* Feb. 17, 1929; information from friends and associates.]

A. F. H.

JOHNSTON, WILLIAM PRESTON (Jan. 5, 1831–July 16, 1899), lawyer, soldier, educator, eldest son of Gen. Albert Sidney Johnston [*q.v.*] and Henrietta (Preston) Johnston, was born at Louisville, Ky. His mother died when he was four years old, his father soon after went to Texas, and he was brought up by maternal relatives—first by Mrs. Josephine Rogers, and after her death, by Gen. William Preston [*q.v.*]. His early education was obtained in the public schools of Louisville and at the academy of S. V. Womack, Shelbyville, Ky. He entered Centre College, Danville, Ky., in 1846, but remained only a short time; later he attended the Western Military Institute, Georgetown, Ky., which he had to leave in 1848 because of illness. In May 1851, after a desultory study of law, he entered the junior class of Yale University from which he graduated in 1852. Naturally studious, he stood high in scholarship, taking the Townsend prize for English composition, and the Clark prize for an essay on "Political Abstractionists."

After leaving Yale he entered the law school of the University of Louisville, graduating in the spring of 1853. On July 6 of that year he married, at New Haven, Conn., Rosa Elizabeth Duncan of New Orleans, and, except for a short interval when they lived in New York, they made their home in Louisville until the outbreak of the Civil War. Johnston then left his law practice and entered the Confederate service. He was first appointed major in the 2nd Kentucky Regiment, but was soon promoted to the rank of lieutenant-colonel in the 1st Kentucky. His health having broken because of typhoid-pneumonia and camp fever, and his regiment having been disbanded during his absence, he accepted in May 1862 the offer of President Jefferson Davis to become his aide-de-camp with the rank of colonel. He filled this position until the end of the war, his chief duties being those of an inspector and confidential staff officer for communicating with the generals in the field; and in these capacities he was present at many of the important battles. At the end of the war he was captured with President Davis, and for several months was imprisoned at Fort Delaware. After his release he spent a year of voluntary exile in Canada, and then returned to Louisville and his law practice.

His work as an educator did not begin until 1867, when Gen. Robert E. Lee, then president of Washington and Lee University, offered him the chair of history and English literature at that institution, which he accepted and held until 1877. In 1880 he was called to the presidency of the Louisiana State University, Baton Rouge, La. Paul Tulane made his first donation for the education of young white persons of New Orleans in 1882, and the following year the board of administrators of the Tulane Educational Fund requested Johnston to organize and take charge of the institution to be founded. In 1884 the administrators of the Fund became the administrators of the University of Louisiana, agreeing to devote their income to its development; and the name was changed to Tulane University of Louisiana. Johnston became its president, remaining as such until his death.

While at Washington and Lee he wrote a biography of his father, *The Life of Gen. Albert Sidney Johnston,* his best and most widely known work, published in 1878. In 1890 he published *Prototype of Hamlet and Other Shakespearian Problems* (1890), and in 1897 *The Johnstons of Salisbury,* a family record. Three volumes of poems came from his pen: *My Garden Walk* (1894), *Pictures of the Patriarchs and Other Poems* (1895), and *Seekers After God: Sonnets* (1898). He also wrote papers and essays on a wide range of subjects, and delivered numerous public lectures. He was a regent of the Smithsonian Institution, and a member of many learned societies. He was always handicapped by ill health, yet he reached an advanced age, dying at the home of his son-in-law, St. George Tucker, Lexington, Va. His body was taken to Louisville, where it was buried beside that of his first wife, who had died Oct. 19, 1885. He was survived by his second wife, formerly Margaret Avery, member of a prominent Louisiana family, whom he had married in April 1888, and by four of the six children by his first marriage. He was a typical gentleman of the old South: well-bred, courteous, kindly, and possessed of a beautiful and attractive character. He was democratic in his tastes, and bitterly opposed to all distinctions of caste and wealth. As an educator he was ever mindful of the poor student: free scholarships for such were his educational hobby.

[*Records of the Class of 1852, Yale Coll.* (1878); *Obit. Record Grads. Yale Univ.*, 1899; W. P. Johnston, *The Johnstons of Salisbury* (1897); *Biog. and Hist. Memoirs of La.* (1892), vol. I; E. W. Fay, *The Hist. of Education in La.* (1898); Henry Rightor, *Standard Hist. of New Orleans, La.* (1900); Jacob Cooper, *William Preston Johnston: A Character Sketch* (1899); *Memorial Services in Honor of William Preston Johnston* (1900); *Trinity Record,* vol. VI, no. 2; New Orleans *Daily Item,* July 16, 1899; New Orleans *Daily Picayune,* July 17, 1899; *The Olive and the Blue,* Oct. 4, 1899; *Evening Star* (Washington), July 17, 1899; *N. Y. Times,* July 17, 1899; *Harper's Weekly,* July 29, 1899.]

M. J. W.

JOHNSTON, ZACHARIAH (1742–January 1800), statesman, champion of religious liberty, Revolutionary soldier, was born near Staunton, Va. His father, William Johnston, an Ulster Scot, had lately come from Pennsylvania. The region around the Johnston cabin was still largely unbroken wilderness. The boy Zachariah had a typical frontier upbringing but gathered somewhat of an education from the log academy of John Brown several miles away. He married Ann Robertson, the daughter of a neighboring Scot family, and had settled down to the routine of a prosperous farmer when the outbreak of the Revolution introduced his ability to his country and state. In 1776 he was recommended for a captaincy in the Virginia militia and was duly commissioned. His company was unusually active in the frontier patrol against the Indians and in 1781 joined in the campaign that led to Cornwallis's surrender.

Johnston's civil service began while he was still active as a militia captain. In 1778 he was elected a representative from Augusta to the Virginia House of Delegates and continued to be elected without a break for the next fifteen years. When he moved from Augusta to Rockbridge in 1792 he was forthwith elected to represent the latter county. His greatest service to his state was rendered in 1785–86 when as chairman of the House of Delegates' important committee on religion and as an able colleague of James Madison he bore much of the brunt of the fight for Virginia's "Act for Establishing Religious Freedom" (1786). In addition to this he was an uncompromising opponent of paper money and an ardent champion of court reform and the payment of British debts in order that treaty faith might be kept. His greatest service to the nation was as a delegate to the Virginia Convention of 1788 when he carried the unanimous vote of his section with him for ratification. The importance of the part he played there is indicated by the fact that he made the closing speech for ratification. In this speech he summed up the reasons for the appeal of the new Constitution to his section in its provisions for equal representation, fair taxation, and a stronger government; its purported antagonism to slavery; and its denial of any jurisdiction in religion or matters of conscience. In the organization of the new federal government Johnston was the first elector for his section and later was urged to be a candidate for Congress but declined. He continued active in the state legislature until a few years before his death but his chief interest seems to have been in connecting the rivers of western Virginia with Washington's proposed system of Potomac navigation. He gave much of time and effort to this project.

An indication of the manner of man he was stands out in his refusal to accept a commission as a justice of the county court system tendered by Governor Jefferson in 1781, his reason being that he felt he should study law for a year or two first. His scrupulousness in all of his various activities is prominently evidenced in the rather copious collection of private papers that is preserved in the substantial house which he built for himself in Rockbridge County during his latter years.

[Archibald Alexander, "Zachariah Johnston," *Princeton Mag.*, I (1850), 367–69; Lyman Chalkley, *Chronicles of the Scotch-Irish Settlement of Va.* (3 vols., 1912); J. A. Waddell, *Annals of Augusta County, Va.* (1886); Augusta Court Martial Record Book; Minute and Order books of the upper Valley counties; David Robertson, *Debates and Other Proc. of the Convention of Va. . . . 1788* (1788); E. G. Swem, "A Bibliography of Virginia, Part II," *Bull. of the Va. State Lib.*, vol. X (1917); Johnston's private papers.]

F. H. H.

JOHNSTONE, JOB (June 7, 1793–Apr. 8, 1862), jurist, was born in Fairfield District, S. C., of Scotch-Irish ancestry. His father was John Johnstone and his mother was Mary Caldwell, of Londonderry County, Ireland. She had come originally from Scotland and was the daughter of a surgeon, Dr. Job Caldwell, for whom her son was named. The family was of rigid Presbyterian stock and Johnstone was a member of that denomination throughout his life. After attending schools in Chester, Winnsboro, and Newberry, he entered the South Carolina College in 1808 and was graduated from that institution in December 1810. He then began to read law, but in 1814 he turned to medicine, and after reading for a time in the office of a doctor in Columbia, he went to New York City in October 1815 and took a course in the College of Physicians and Surgeons. But his jealous mistress, the law, called him back to her side, and he renewed his legal studies in the office of John Belton O'Neall [*q.v.*], of Newberry. In 1818 he was admitted to the bar, and at once he became the partner of his preceptor, who himself later became chief justice of South Carolina. Subsequently the partners became alienated. O'Neall was an intense Union man, while Johnstone was equally intense in his devotion to state rights. The latter was a member of the nullification convention of 1832 and his name appears as one of the signers of the nullification ordinance. While he maintained, throughout life, unwavering loyalty in his belief as to the rights of the sovereign states, and while as a young man he courageously asserted those rights, even to the extent of voting to nullify an act of the Congress of the United States, when South Carolina seceded in 1860, he was opposed to the step on the ground that it was politically inexpedient. After the war began he supported the Confederacy.

Johnstone's political career began with his election as clerk of the Senate of South Carolina in 1826. He continued to hold this position until he was elected a chancellor of the state on Nov. 3, 1830. In 1847, following the death of William Harper, Johnstone became president of the equity court of appeals, and in 1859, when the new court of appeals was established, he became an associate justice. It was once said of him that "every appeal opinion in which he was overruled by the Appellate Court, and every appeal opinion in which he dissented from the majority of the chancellors" was "subsequently confirmed and made established law in South Carolina" (Brooks, *post*, I, 93). Johnstone was twice married. His first wife was Eliza Meek Johnstone, his cousin, whom he married on Nov. 14, 1816, and by whom he had four children. She died Jan. 23, 1843, and on Aug. 7, 1844, he was married to Amelia A. De Walt, by whom he had six children. He died at Newberry.

[See Maximilian LaBorde, *Hist. of the S. C. Coll.* (1859); J. B. Carwile, *Reminiscences of Newberry* (1890); J. B. O'Neall and J. A. Chapman, *The Annals of Newberry* (1892); U. R. Brooks, *S. C. Bench and Bar* (1908), vol. I; Yates Snowden, *Hist. of S. C.* (1920), vol. II; *Charleston Daily Courier*, Apr. 11, 1862; Chancery reports of S. C., 1830–66. Johnstone sometimes spelled his last name without the final *e*.]

J. N. F.

JOLINE, ADRIAN HOFFMAN (June 30, 1850–Oct. 15, 1912), lawyer, author, book-collector, was born at Sing Sing (now Ossining), N. Y., the oldest of the three children of Col. Charles Oliver Joline and Mary Evelyn Hoffman. His maternal lineage is traceable to Martin Hoffman, of Swedish origin, who came to Kingston, N. Y., in 1657. Adrian got his preparation for college partly at Mount Pleasant Academy, Sing Sing, and partly under the private tuition of Dr. James I. Helm. His father's military connections brought the lad in touch with courts martial during the Civil War, and this experience may have suggested to him a lawyer's calling. At least, after graduation from Princeton in 1870, he went to the Columbia Law School and was graduated in 1872. In his practice he specialized in cases relating to trusts, mortgages, and railroads. He was fortunate in possessing a remarkable memory and the faculty of expressing his thoughts clearly. He became counsel and chairman of the board of directors of the Missouri, Kansas & Texas Railroad Company and a director of a number of other corporations. When the Metropolitan Street Railway and New York City Railway companies went into bankruptcy in 1907, he was appointed one of the receivers. His success in restoring order from chaos won for him great praise, but his devotion to the task seriously undermined his health.

Joline's avocation was the collecting of autographs and rare books and his joy in this pursuit is reflected in his *Meditations of an Autograph Collector* (1902), *The Diversions of a Book-lover* (1903), *At the Library Table* (1910), and *Rambles in Autograph Land* (1913), edited by Mrs. Joline after his death. Many contemporary tendencies found in him an ardent antagonist: "The majority of railway accidents in this country are due to the relaxed discipline resulting from the labor-union tyranny," was a statement which he made before the New Jersey State Bar Association, June 15, 1907 (*New Jersey State Bar Association Year Book,* 1907–08, p. 55). This declaration was followed by another to the effect that the yellow press was "the yellow peril before which an oriental invasion fades into insignificance" (*Ibid.,* p. 56). When he told the directors of the Missouri, Kansas & Texas Railroad Company that "government ownership with politicians in control would result in the payment by the public of large dividends out of the pockets of the public" (Address, Apr. 4, 1907, quoted in *New York Herald,* Oct. 16, 1912), and classed William Jennings Bryan among those who did not appear to have given the subject "any intelligent attention," Woodrow Wilson, then president of Princeton, expressed by letter to him his entire agreement and added: "Would that we could do something, at once dignified and effective, to knock Mr. Bryan once for all into a cocked hat." Five years later, when Wilson and Bryan were fraternizing politically, Joline, whose fad never permitted him to destroy a letter, showed the epistle of 1907 to a friend. Then the newspaper reporter learned about it and the specter stalked through the land in the headlines of the press (*New York Times,* Jan. 8, 1912). After 1905 Joline was senior member of the firm of Joline, Larkin & Rathbone. He was married, in 1876, to Mary E. Larkin, daughter of Francis Larkin of New York.

[Obituaries in New York papers of Oct. 16, 1912 (portrait in *Herald*); *Publishers' Weekly,* Oct. 19, 1912; E. A. Hoffman, *Geneal. of the Hoffman Family: Descendants of Martin Hoffman* (1899); *N. Y. Times,* Jan. 7 and 8, 1912; *Who's Who in America,* 1912–13; Joline's own works and addresses as given above.]

A. E. P.

JOLLIET, LOUIS (September 1645–1700), explorer, was one of the earliest natives of Canada to distinguish himself. From the neighborhood of La Rochelle his father, Jehan Jollyet, emigrated to Canada as cartwright for the company of associates and married Marie d'Abancour *dite* La Caille. Although Jollyet's workshop was in the lower town of Quebec he had a concession near Beaupré in the parish of Château Richer, and there it is believed Louis was born. He was baptized Sept. 21, 1645, in Quebec. After his father's death, when the lad was five years old, his mother married again and lived on the Isle of Orleans but returned to Beaupré when the stepfather was drowned in 1665. Meanwhile Louis, who showed much talent for learning, had entered the Jesuit seminary at Quebec, where he proved himself an apt pupil, studied mathematics, the classics, rhetoric, and logic, became also a musician, and was a favorite with all his instructors. At the age of seventeen he took minor orders but, a few years later, abandoned the idea of becoming an ecclesiastic and, in 1667, went to Europe, under the patronage of Bishop Laval, to continue his scientific studies. The next year he returned to Canada and entered on the career of travel and exploration that brought him fame.

His first western voyage, in 1669, was in obedience to the request of Intendant Talon, who sent Jolliet to take supplies to Jean Peré, then searching for copper in Lake Superior. Jolliet also took trade goods and engagés, several of whom he sent to trade in Greenbay. He did not find Peré, but he met Father Jacques Marquette [*q.v.*] at Sault Ste. Marie and hastened back to Canada with an Iroquois prisoner, whom the Jesuits had rescued from the Ottawa. Guided by the Iroquois, this party was the first to pass down the Great Lakes by way of the Detroit River into Lake Erie. At the east end of this lake Jolliet met a party of Sulpician priests and told them of the new route to the West. Then pushing on to Quebec he arrived late in September 1669. The next year the explorer was sent with St.

Lusson's party and was present at the ceremony, on June 14, 1671, to annex the western country to the Crown of France.

Since by these voyages Jolliet, already an expert cartographer, had become more familiar with the Great Lakes region than any other Canadian, in 1672 he was chosen by the authorities of New France to find the great river of which so many rumors had been heard. Father Marquette, then at the Mackinac mission of St. Ignace, was chosen chaplain for the expedition. Jolliet arrived at St. Ignace late in 1672, and throughout the winter the two leaders collaborated in making plans and in drawing maps. On May 17, 1673, they left St. Ignace for the southwest in two canoes with five voyageurs. As far as the Mascouten village on the upper Fox River (near Berlin, Wis.) the route was already known. There they obtained guides who showed them the way to the portage. Although the Indians, magnifying the difficulties, besought them not to undertake the voyage, they pressed on, crossed the divide at the portage, fell into a westward flowing stream (the Wisconsin), and on June 17 sighted the Mississippi. They floated down the great river as far as the Arkansas; then, being certain it emptied into the Gulf of Mexico and dreading to find enemies on the lower course, they turned back. On the advice of the Indians they returned by way of the Illinois and Des Plaines rivers, and the portage at the site of Chicago, which, so far as is known, they were the first white men to visit. Jolliet appears to have spent the following winter exploring Lake Michigan. As early as feasible in 1674 he left the Sault Ste. Marie for Canada to report his discovery. At the rapids above Montreal his canoe was overturned, and he lost his maps, his journals, and all his souvenirs. He later made several maps from memory, to be presented to Governor Frontenac and to Minister of State Colbert.

Although Jolliet's discovery was much honored by the authorities, he was denied a share in exploiting the new land, probably because he belonged to the party of the Jesuits, who were then out of favor with the civil authorities. He was, however, granted several seigniories on the lower St. Lawrence, notably the island of Anticosti, where after his marriage to Claire Bissot in 1675 he established his home. He continued his explorations in the Gulf of St. Lawrence, along the coast of Labrador, and in 1694 visited Hudson Bay and reached a high latitude. In 1697 he was appointed royal hydrographer for Canada and made a number of useful maps. His death occurred after May 4 and before Oct. 18, 1700. His fame as a discoverer has been overshadowed by that of Marquette whose journals were preserved while Jolliet's were lost. In the wilderness he was at his best; he had an instinct for exploration, a talent for Indian languages, and the ability to control the savages. His services in opening the Great Lakes and the Mississippi Valley to civilization are his sure title to fame.

[R. G. Thwaites, *The Jesuit Relations,* vol. LIX (1900); Pierre Margry, *Découvertes et Établissements des Français,* vols. I, II (1876–77); Francis B. Steck, *The Jolliet-Marquette Expedition* (1927); L. P. Kellogg, *French Régime in Wis.* (1925); F. E. A. Gagnon, *Louis Jolliet* (1902); A. E. Gosselin, "Jean Jolliet et ses Enfants," *Proc. and Trans. of the Royal Soc. of Canada,* ser. 3, vol. XIV (1921).]

L. P. K.

JONES, ABNER (Apr. 28, 1772–May 29, 1841), leader in New England of the movement for undenominational Christianity, was born on a farm in Royalston, Mass. His parents were Deacon Asa Jones, a native of Sutton, Mass., and Dorcas Wade of Gloucester, R. I., both strict Baptists. In 1780 the family became the first settlers of Bridgewater, Vt., on the frontier. During his boyhood, Abner's soul was torn with conflicts between religious conviction and worldly ambition and oppressed with gloomy fears of his lost condition. At nineteen he began teaching, although his own schooling had not exceeded six weeks. At length his religious horizon cleared and he was baptized, June 9, 1793. While teaching he studied the Bible exhaustively, with medical study as a recreation. Gradually he gave up the Calvinistic system under the shadow of which he had grown up, and his views on the doctrines of the Trinity, the Atonement, and eternal punishment became very much modified, though he clung rigidly to his inherited doctrines of conversion, and baptism by immersion.

In 1796 he settled as a physician in Lyndon, Vt., and about this time married Damaris Pryor. Although successful in medicine, he was continually haunted by the call of the pulpit, and at length, under the influence of a revival, dropped his practice and began the work of an evangelist. In 1801, with about a dozen of his neighbors he founded a church in Lyndon, with no creed but the Bible and no denominational affiliation. The group called themselves simply "Christians." The movement thus begun in New England had its counterparts in other sections of the country, where the followers of James O'Kelly, Barton W. Stone, and Alexander Campbell [*qq.v.*] successively abandoned creeds and ecclesiastical centralization and reverted to "primitive Christianity." Out of these movements came the denominations known as the Disciples of Christ and the "Christian Connection," claiming the Bible as their only rule of faith and practice.

On Nov. 30, 1802, Jones was ordained by a Free Will Baptist council, not as a member of that denomination, but simply as a "Christian brother." He now began to labor with great zeal and success, traveling widely and constantly preaching and baptizing. In the fall of 1802 he founded a second church, in Hanover, N. H., and during the following winter another at Piermont. In the course of his career he was settled at different periods in Boston, Bradford, Salem, Assonet, and Upton, Mass., Portsmouth, Stratham, and Hopkinton, N. H., and Milan, N. Y. In founding the church at Portsmouth (1805) he was aided by Elias Smith [*q.v.*]. He presided over the United States Christian Conference held at Milan, N. Y., in 1832. In middle life he became a pioneer in the temperance movement. At the time of the anti-Masonic excitement, for conscientious reasons he abandoned the Masonic order, of which he had been a member. His education was almost wholly self-acquired, but he gained a reading knowledge of Hebrew, Greek, and Latin. He read extensively, especially in history and biography. Besides a few sermons and miscellaneous hymns and poems of no great merit, he published one book: *Memoirs of the Life and Experience, Travels and Preaching of Abner Jones* (1807). He died at Exeter, N. H., where he had recently settled. His first wife died in December 1836, and on Aug. 1, 1839, he married Mrs. Nancy F. Clark of Nantucket, who survived him.

[In addition to Jones's *Memoirs,* already mentioned, see: A. D. Jones, *Memoirs of Elder Abner Jones* (1842); E. W. Humphreys, *Memoirs of Deceased Christian Ministers* (1880); A. H. Morrill, "Abner Jones, Founder of the Christian Connection in New England," in *The Centennial of Religious Journalism* (1908); M. T. Morrill, *A Hist. of the Christian Denomination in America* (1912); W. E. Garrison, *Religion Follows the Frontier* (1931); *N. H. Gazette* (Portsmouth), June 1, 1841. A brief account of Elder Jones and the founding of his denomination is found in Vol. XII (1894) of the Am. Ch. Hist. Series, which erroneously gives the year 1800 as the date of the founding of the church in Lyndon.]

F. T. P.

JONES, ALEXANDER (*c.* 1802–Aug. 22, 1863), author, news reporter, physician, was the son of a North Carolina planter. Little is known of his life prior to his graduation, with the degree of M.D., at the Medical School of the University of Pennsylvania in 1822. About that time his father died, leaving a modest estate. Alexander relinquished his share in favor of his two sisters and went to Mississippi, where he practised his profession and at the same time became greatly interested in cotton culture. He also made improvements in the cotton gin. His repute as an authority on the Southern staple crop came to the notice of the British East India Company, which desired to retain him in building up an Indian cotton industry. Their negotiations came to a head about 1840. Jones went to London, but on reflection declined the company's offer, since it involved aid to a foreign country in rivalry with his own. He returned to the United States, settling in New York, and began writing regularly for the *Journal of Commerce,* using the signature "Sandy Hook." He also was correspondent for English newspapers.

After the first use of the electric telegraph between Washington and Baltimore, in 1844, several years elapsed before news could be transmitted on an important scale to and from New York. By the autumn of 1846, however, a telegraph line was in operation from New York to Washington, and under an arrangement between the newspapers of the two cities it fell to Jones to file the first news message by wire from the metropolis—an account of the launching of the United States sloop of war *Albany* at the Brooklyn Navy Yard. He related the incident in his *Historical Sketch of the Electric Telegraph,* published in 1852. Early in grasping the significance of the telegraph in news distribution, Jones was also a pioneer in organizing a practical cooperative press service among American cities. As first general agent of the New York Associated Press, which at that time included six newspapers (Jones, *post,* pp. 120–48), he was one of the earliest men to develop a scheme of market reporting by wire among the eastern cities. For the press service he devised a cipher system, which was employed as early as 1847. The prices of breadstuffs could be sent daily from Buffalo or Albany to New York in twenty words. Later the system was extended to Cincinnati, St. Louis, and New Orleans. After a few years Jones gave up the routine work as agent and from 1851 until his death served the *New York Herald* exclusively as commercial reporter. He seems to have continued the practice of medicine throughout his journalistic career. He was the author of *Cuba in 1851* (1851) and *The Cymry of '76; or Welshmen and Their Descendants of the American Revolution* (1855). He was a leading member of St. David's Society in New York. In addition to his other accomplishments he invented a street-sweeping machine, which the city of New York refused to adopt—possibly for political reasons.

[Jones's *Hist. Sketch of the Electric Telegraph* (1852); *N. Y. Herald,* Aug. 26, 1863; Victor Rosewater, *Hist. of Cooperative News Gathering in the U. S.* (1930), pp. 43, 70–73.]

W. B. S.

JONES, ALFRED (Apr. 7, 1819–Apr. 28, 1900), engraver, was born in Liverpool, England, the son of Samuel and Mary (Britten) Jones. He came to America when a very young man and was apprenticed as a bank-note engraver in the firm of Rawdon, Wright, Hatch & Edson, first in Albany, N. Y., and subsequently in New York City. He studied in every leisure moment at the National Academy of Design and received the first prize awarded by the Academy in 1839 for a drawing from a cast of Thorvaldsen's "Mercury." Bank-note companies furnished employment for the line engravers of that day. The vignettes on bank notes were engraved by Jones with good drawing and a certain boldness and richness of hue. He invented a process for successfully producing directly from a photograph a plate that could be printed with type, the popular "half-tone process" of a later day. He made his negative upon crown glass and produced the screen by ruling this negative in a ruling machine; from this ruled negative an electrotype was made. Consequently Jones's services were in demand by many publishers. In 1846 he went to Europe to study and spent a year in Paris in the life classes. He also visited England, working there under some of the best London masters. When he returned to New York, he engaged in business for himself, devoting his time almost exclusively to bank-note vignettes. Noteworthy are the two-cent, thirty-cent, and four- and five-dollar postage stamps of the Columbian series for the American Bank Note Company. He was elected an Associate of the National Academy of Design in 1841 and an Academician in 1851 and for many years was secretary and treasurer of the Academy. As a line engraver he had few, if any, superiors in the United States. Many of his engravings appeared in *Graham's Magazine* and *Godey's Lady's Book*. He engraved for the American Art Union "The Farmer's Nooning" (1843), after W. S. Mount, an especially admired plate, also "The Image Breaker" (1850), after the picture by E. Leutze, recognized as one of his best engravings. Other examples published by the Art Union were "Sparking" (1844) and "The New Scholar" (1850), after Francis Edmonds; "Mexican News" (1851), after W. C. Woodville; "One of Life's Happy Hours," after Lilly M. Spencer; "Poor Relations," after J. H. Beard; "Patrick Henry, Delivering his Celebrated Speech in the House of Burgesses, Virginia 1765," after P. F. Rothermel; and "Capture of Major André," after Durand. He engraved fine portraits of Washington, Asher B. Durand, and two portraits of Thomas Carlyle for the Grolier Club—all good examples of combination of line work and etching. Jones was a member of the Artists' Fund Society and the American Water Color Society; he was a painter in oils and water color as well as an engraver. He was one of the earliest members of the Century Association, being elected in 1847. He married, in May 1841, Louisa, daughter of Richard Major of Brooklyn, N. Y., and had three daughters. He died from injuries received when he was run over by a cab in New York City.

[Frank Weitenkampf, *Am. Graphic Art* (1912); W. S. Baker, *Am. Engravers and Their Works* (1875); D. McN. Stauffer, *Am. Engravers upon Copper and Steel* (1907); *Who's Who in America*, 1899–1900; *N. Y. Tribune*, Apr. 29, 1900.] H. W.

JONES, ALLEN (Dec. 24, 1739–Nov. 14, 1807), Revolutionary soldier and delegate to the Continental Congress, was born in what is now Halifax County, N. C., the son of Robert (Robin) Jones, attorney-general of North Carolina under the Crown, and of Sarah (Cobb) Jones. With his brother, Willie Jones [*q.v.*], he is said to have been educated at Eton College, England. On Jan. 21, 1762, he married Mary Haynes and, after her death, he married Rebecca Edwards on Sept. 3, 1768. Before the Revolution he attained local prominence as clerk of the superior court for Halifax district, and as member of the House of Commons from 1773 to 1775 for Northampton County. In 1771 he assisted Gov. William Tryon in the suppression of the Regulators.

His chief distinction was gained in the Revolution by able, devoted, and continuous labor in camp and council for the patriot cause. He was a member of the Committee of Safety for Halifax district in 1775 and represented Northampton County in the five Provincial Congresses from 1774 to 1776. He served on many important committees, especially those to provide military defense, to establish temporary forms of civil government, to empower the North Carolina delegates in Congress to concur with those of other colonies in declaring independence (Apr. 12, 1776), and to frame the state constitution of 1776. He was appointed brigadier-general of militia for Halifax district in 1776 and, until the end of the war, alternated between civil office and active military service in the two Carolinas. From 1777 to 1779 he was in the state Senate, of which he was speaker in 1778 and 1779, was a member of the Continental Congress from 1779 to 1780, in 1781 was on the Council Extraordinary that was charged with the conduct of the war, and was on the Council of State in 1782. On the grounds that there was no state law authorizing it and that the requisition of Congress was not binding, he protested, in 1778, against the sending of North Carolina militia to aid South Carolina. Yet his faith in the success of the patriot cause was as constant as his labors in its behalf; in 1777 he wrote: "No reverse of fortune can possibly damp my spirits or occasion any despondency, so thoroughly am I convinced that time and America must overcome all opposition" (*State Records,* xi, p. 561).

A large property owner himself, he was zealous for the rights of property, became an opponent of the proscriptive policy toward the Loyalists after the war, and a conservative in politics. In 1783, 1784, and 1787 he was a prominent member of the state Senate. Unlike his more famous brother, Willie, who was the anti-Federalist leader, he was a strong advocate of the federal Constitution but was defeated for a seat in the Hillsborough convention of 1788 and for the second federal convention, whose convocation was expected. In 1790 he was the owner of 177 slaves, the fourth largest slaveholding in the state. He was a friend of education and a promoter of plans to improve the transportation facilities of the Roanoke Valley and the Albemarle Sound region. He died at his seat, "Mount Gallant," in Northampton County.

[S. A. Ashe, *Biog. Hist. of N. C.,* vol. IV (1906); W. C. Allen, *Hist. of Halifax County* (copr. 1918); J. H. Wheeler, *Hist. Sketches of N. C.* (2 vols., 1851); G. J. McRee, *Life and Correspondence of James Iredell* (2 vols., 1857–58); *Colonial Records of N. C.* (10 vols., 1886–90); *State Records of N. C.* (16 vols., 1895–1906); E. C. Burnett, *Letters of Members of the Continental Cong.,* vols. IV, V (1928–31); Northampton County Court Minutes in the N. C. Historical Commission, Raleigh; Cadwallader Jones, *A Geneal. Hist.* (1900); *Raleigh Register and North-Carolina Gazette,* Nov. 26, 1807.]

A. R. N.

JONES, AMANDA THEODOSIA (Oct. 19, 1835–Mar. 31, 1914), author, inventor, was born in East Bloomfield, Ontario County, N. Y., fourth of the twelve children of Henry and Mary Alma (Mott) Jones. Her father was of Welsh-English and Scotch-Irish stock, long settled in western Massachusetts; her mother was of Huguenot, English, and "North River Dutch" descent. Amanda attended the district public schools and then the State Normal School at East Aurora, graduating about 1850. At an early age she began to write verse, though she published nothing until after she had begun to teach. Probably the first of her poems to appear in print was published in the *Methodist Ladies' Repository* of 1854. After this success she gave up teaching to devote her whole time to writing. Poems and dissertations on various subjects appeared thereafter in the *Repository* for fully ten years. A collection, *Ulah and Other Poems,* was issued in 1861 and six years later another volume, *Poems* (1867), appeared. Meantime, during the Civil War she wrote a series of war songs, published from 1861 to 1865 in *Frank Leslie's Illustrated Weekly.* Between 1869 and 1873 she was successively editor of the *Universe* (Chicago), a reform journal; literary editor of the *Western Rural* (Chicago); editor of the *Bright Side,* a juvenile periodical; and chief contributor to the juvenile department of the *Interior.* She later wrote for *Scribner's Monthly,* the *Continent,* the *Century,* the *Outlook,* and the *Youth's Companion.*

During the sixties, while living in western New York she became gradually more and more interested in Spiritualism as a result of her own psychic experiences. In the course of one of these, a visit from her "Dr. Andrews," in August 1869 (*Psychic Autobiography,* pp. 227–28), she was told that she was about to undertake a great work, but its nature was not then revealed to her. Four years later this work took shape in a patented process for preserving food in a vacuum without cooking, which process was applied also to canning foods in vacuo with cooking, and to desiccating foods in vacuo. In perfecting her invention she had the assistance of a cousin, L. C. Cooley of Albany, N. Y. On June 3, 1873, Cooley obtained a patent (No. 139,547), which he assigned to her, for an apparatus for preserving fruit. On the same day a second patent (No. 139,581) was issued jointly to Cooley and Jones for a method of preserving fruit, and two more patents (No. 139,580, June 3, 1873; No. 140,508, July 1, 1873) were granted to Miss Jones alone for an improved form of fruit jar, best adapted to use in her preserving process. On June 24, 1873, Cooley obtained a patent (No. 140,247) on an apparatus to exhaust air from fruit cans. This group of five patents constituted the Jones Preserving Process by which fruit was placed in a vessel, the air exhausted with an exhaust apparatus, and at the same time the vessel filled with fruit juices at a temperature of 100° to 120° Fahrenheit. Encouraged by her friends, Miss Jones, with extremely limited funds, labored for the succeeding five or six years to improve the process and to interest capital in her invention. Eventually there was organized in Chicago the U. S. Women's Pure Food Vacuum Preserving Company, in which as far as possible all of the officers and employees were women. Preserving of fruits and meats was begun in 1879. After a few years' operation, however, Miss Jones sold the rights in her patents to the packing interests and gave up active participation in the enterprise. In 1880 she perfected a liquid fuel burner (patent No. 225,839, Mar. 23, 1880) which, although designed especially for glass furnaces, was satisfactorily used under steam boilers, and she devised several types of valves and a can-opener, having, all told, six patents issued to her.

In the early eighties she settled in Junction City, Kan., and again took up her writing, publishing *A Prairie Idyl* (1882), *Flowers and a Weed* (1899), *Rubáiyát of Solomon and Other Poems* (1905), *Poems, 1854–1906* (1906), *A Mother of Pioneers* (1908), and *A Psychic Autobiography* (1910), which she dedicated to William James. To *Steam Engineering* (Chicago), beginning Aug. 10, 1903, she contributed a series of articles on the use of liquid fuel; and for the *Engineer* (Chicago), she prepared another series, which began in the issue of Mar. 1, 1904. Throughout much of her career she was driven by a philanthropic motive, her particular interest lying in the reform of unhappy women and the protection of girls. Early in her business life she was instrumental in founding near Buffalo one of the first homes for working women. She never married and resided in Junction City, Kan., at the time of her death.

[*A Psychic Autobiography* (1910); *Who's Who in America,* 1912–13, 1914–15; *Woman's Who's Who of America,* 1914–15; F. E. Willard and M. A. Livermore, *A Woman of the Century* (1893); *Specifications and Drawings of Patents Issued from the U. S. Patent Office,* June, July 1873, Mar. 1880; *Junction City Union,* Apr. 1, 1914.] C. W. M.

JONES, ANSON (Jan. 20, 1798–Jan. 9, 1858), last president of the Republic of Texas, was born in Great Barrington, Mass., thirteenth of fourteen children of whom four died in infancy. His parents, Solomon Jones, a harness maker, and Sarah (Strong) Jones, found difficulty in supporting their family, but the father was ambitious for the studious boy, and without any great zeal for the profession Anson Jones, at the age of nineteen, commenced the study of medicine. His studies were constantly interrupted by efforts to make a living. He taught school; he sold drugs; he spent two years in Venezuela, and after ten years, in March 1827, he received the degree of doctor of medicine from the medical department of Jefferson College, Canonsburg, Pa. Extreme poverty had left traces of bitterness which appear clearly in his reminiscences. For five years he kept an office in Philadelphia; but patients did not come. From Philadelphia, he drifted to New Orleans, where he had a serious illness, and where, he tells us, he was falling into habits of drinking and gambling. In the autumn of 1833, he landed at Brazoria, Texas, with seventeen dollars in his pocket. A trained physician was just what Brazoria wanted; Jones received an eager welcome, and he was soon established as a busy and highly respected member of a pioneer community.

In 1835, on the outbreak of difficulties with Mexico, he attended the so-called "Consultation," where he was not favorably impressed with some of his colleagues, especially James Bowie and Sam Houston [*qq.v.*]. Indeed, throughout his life he was perhaps apt to look on both himself and others with too critical an eye. He returned an open advocate of independence, and the next year served as a physician in Houston's little army, leaving his medicines to fight as a private soldier in the decisive engagement of San Jacinto. His brief career in the Texan Congress was interrupted when President Houston sent him as the Texan minister to Washington. After a few uneventful months, President Lamar recalled him; Jones returned to Texas, and, on May 17, 1839, was married to Mrs. Mary McCrory of Brazoria.

He was now elected to the Senate of Texas, of which he became presiding officer, and was known as a trenchant critic of the administration. During his vacations he practised medicine among his neighbors and took great interest in the organization of Masonic lodges. When late in 1841 Houston was reëlected president, he made Jones secretary of state. The two men were too unlike to become close friends. Jones was often irritated by the old chieftain's convivial habits; his feelings were hurt when Houston insisted on deciding important questions for himself; but Houston evidently trusted Jones and respected his superior education, without leaning too heavily on his judgment (*Diplomatic Correspondence,* II, 281).

On Sept. 2, 1844, Anson Jones, with the powerful support of Houston, was elected president of Texas for three years from Dec. 9. The chief subject under consideration at the time was a "diplomatic act," proposed by Lord Aberdeen, the British secretary of state for foreign affairs, which would secure peace for Texas by making it virtually a British protectorate. The proposal had been treated with caution by Smith, Houston, and Jones, Jones seeming to be more favorable to it than either of the other two. Strangely enough, however, on Sept. 23, Houston issued an executive order authorizing Jones to close with Aberdeen's offer, with the single proviso that Texas should extend to the Rio Grande. In spite of the order, Jones continued to pursue the same temporizing policy, and in the meantime, for reasons of his own, Aberdeen virtually withdrew his offer. In later years Jones made much of this incident to prove that he had saved Texas from the rash policy of Sam Houston and was the true father of annexation (*Niles' National Register,* Dec. 27, 1848, p. 413), but the order is quite out of line with Houston's cautious policy at the time as indicated by other documents. The probable explanation is that, according to custom, Houston was withdrawing from the seat of government and leaving affairs in the hands of the President-Elect, and was merely placing in Jones's hands authority which he might use as a diplomatic weapon in any emergency which arose. (For another explanation, see Ashbel Smith, *Reminiscences of the Texas Republic*, 1876, p. 64.)

Jones was now president of Texas in his own right. The election of Polk had made an offer of annexation by the United States virtually certain. Capt. Charles Elliot, the British chargé in Texas, believed that Jones was now opposed to annexation and in favor of continued independence. On Mar. 29, 1845, before the offer of the United States could be officially received, Jones authorized Elliot to go to Mexico and to bring pressure for an acknowledgment of independence. The people of Texas undoubtedly desired annexation on almost any terms. At great personal risk, Jones postponed consideration of the annexation offer until he had learned of the success of Elliot's mission. He was then able to proclaim peace with Mexico, and to lay before a convention, not one offer, but two. He was probably disappointed but not surprised when on July 4, 1845, the Texas convention voted for annexation.

On Feb. 19, 1846, the last president of Texas surrendered his authority to the newly elected governor of one of the United States, and retired to his plantation on the Brazos, which, in honor of his birthplace, he called "Barrington." He maintained an active interest in public affairs, taking a distinctly Southern position and on such questions as Oregon, Kansas, and the Know-Nothing movement coming out in bitter opposition to his old chief, Sam Houston. In 1857 he was disappointed in his hopes of election to the Senate of the United States, and early in the next year his many friends were shocked to learn that he had taken his own life in the old Capitol Hotel at Houston.

[The papers of Anson Jones, including an autobiography, were published in 1859, with little attention to arrangement, under the title, *Memoranda and Official Correspondence Relating to the Republic of Texas, Its Hist. and Annexation*. Much material for the life of Jones may be found in G. P. Garrison, "Diplomatic Correspondence of the Republic of Texas," *Ann. Report Am. Hist. Asso.*, for 1907 and 1908 (3 vols., 1908–11). See also J. S. Reeves, *Am. Diplomacy under Tyler and Polk* (1907); J. H. Smith, *The Annexation of Texas* (1911); L. E. Daniell, *Personnel of the Texas State Government* (1892); *Houston Telegraph*, Jan. 11, 1858; and especially E. D. Adams, *British Interests and Activities in Texas* (1910). The Anson Jones papers are in the possession of members of the family in San Antonio.]
R. G. C.

JONES, BENJAMIN FRANKLIN (Aug. 8, 1824–May 19, 1903), leader in the iron and steel industry, was born in Claysville, Washington County, Pa., the son of Jacob Aik Jones and Elizabeth (Goshorn) Jones. His family, coming from Wales, had settled in Philadelphia in 1682. At the age of thirteen Benjamin lived in New Brighton and studied in New Brighton Academy, but he left at nineteen to go to Pittsburgh. There he was employed, without salary at first, as receiving clerk with the Mechanics' Line, a transportation company operating between Pittsburgh and Baltimore, Philadelphia, and New York, chiefly by way of the Pennsylvania State Canal. Samuel M. Kier [*q.v.*], the owner, encouraged young Jones; in 1845 appointed him manager of the Mechanics' Line; and in 1847 took him into partnership. Jones continued to manage the Mechanics' Line and the younger Independent Line, founded by Kier in 1846, until 1854, when the Pennsylvania Railroad took complete possession of the field.

Jones's connection with iron and steel, which was eventually to occupy his full attention, began about 1846, when with Kier he bought an iron furnace and forge near Armagh, Pa. At this time practically no pig iron was produced in Pittsburgh. In 1850 Jones became interested in the American Iron Works begun that year by Bernard Lauth, and in 1851 the firm of Jones & Lauth was formed. In 1854 James Laughlin entered the firm, and in 1857 the name became Jones & Laughlin. That year the Falcon furnace at Youngstown was purchased, and in 1861 two blast furnaces were erected in Pittsburgh. With the entrance into the business of Laughlin's sons in 1861, the title was changed to Jones & Laughlins; the business was incorporated in 1883 as Jones & Laughlins, Limited, and in 1902 became the Jones & Laughlin Steel Company.

Jones was a man of great foresight and originality and it is possible to trace in his activities a number of ideas that have become fundamental in American industry. He had a clear conception of what is technically known today as "vertical combination"; that is, that a company should own its raw-material supply as well as all the intermediate steps in the producing of a finished product. To this end, he was among the first iron manufacturers to buy iron mines in the Lake Superior region and coal in the Connellsville region for conversion into coke. To him must also be credited the plan of the sliding scale of wages under which mill workers are paid at a stated rate per unit based on the selling price of the product. Pursuing a just and liberal policy in his treatment of employees, he enjoyed unbroken peace in a troublesome industry.

He was an ardent protectionist, and his article in the *North American Review* for April 1888 indicated his belief that a protective-tariff policy aided every one. He also offered some practical ideas on the financing of the Civil War. His interest in politics as well as his close friendship for James G. Blaine led the latter to appoint him chairman of the Republican National Committee in 1884.

Jones married Mary McMasters of Allegheny County, May 21, 1850, and became the father of four children. He died after a brief illness. A friend, writing just prior to his death, characterized him as "a man of rare mind, broadened and matured by close observation, a profound thinker, logical reasoner, and careful student," adding: "Anything he undertakes he carries forward to successful completion by his excellent judgment and tenacity of purpose. . . . He is genial, companionable, and although he has passed his seventy-eighth milestone in the journey of life, I cannot detect the least deterioration in his mental or physical vigor" (Reed, *post,* II, 5). When Andrew Carnegie learned of his death, he sent a cablegram which well sums up Jones' standing in industry: "Benjamin Franklin Jones, the Nestor in manufacturing has gone" (*Pittsburgh Post,* May 21, 1903). The *Iron Age* spoke of him as "the most highly respected man in the iron trade."

[Erasmus Wilson, *Standard Hist. of Pittsburg, Pa.* (1898); *Hist. of Allegheny County, Pa.* (1889), pt. II; G. T. Fleming, *Hist. of Pittsburgh and Environs* (1922), vol. III; G. I. Reed, *Century Cyc. of Hist. and Biog. of Pa.* (1904), vol. II; J. N. Boucher, *A Century and a Half of Pittsburg and Her People* (1908), vol. II; *Mag. of Western Hist.*, Oct. 1885; *Sunday Press Magazine* (Pittsburgh), Aug. 18, 1907; *Iron Age,* May 21, 1903; Pittsburgh newspapers, May 19, 20, 21, 22, 1903.]

A. I.

JONES, CALVIN (Apr. 2, 1775–Sept. 20, 1846), physician, fifth in descent from Thomas ap Jones, a Welsh emigrant to Weymouth, Mass., in 1651, was born in Great Barrington, Mass., the son of Ebenezer Jones, soldier in the War of the Revolution, and his wife, Susannah Blackmer. At the age of seventeen he passed an examination before the officers of the United Medical Society, a body of men of which hardly any records survive, and was licensed to practise medicine. His certificate was signed June 19, 1792. For about three years he practised with credit and profit in his home county and wrote a *Treatise on Scarlatina Anginosa* (1794) which was published at Catskill, N. Y., by the editors of the *Catskill Packet.* In 1795, for reasons quite unknown, he removed to Smithfield, Johnston County, N. C., and although but twenty years old, plunged into all the major activities of the new community, professional, political, military, educational, and social. In 1798 he was an officer in the Johnston Militia Company and in 1799 he organized the North Carolina Medical Society, was elected to the state legislature as representative of Johnston County, and took a prominent part in legislation, opposing the proposition to build a state penitentiary. He served again in 1802. The medical society, of which he was corresponding secretary, endured only until 1804, but during its brief life valuable papers were read before it, and material was collected for a botanical garden and museum of natural history. It is probable that when the society disbanded Dr. Jones remained in charge of these collections, and that they formed the nucleus of the material which he presented to the University of North Carolina in 1832 when he removed to Tennessee. In 1802 he was made a trustee of the University. In 1803 he removed to the state capital, Raleigh, and although by this move he lost his membership in the legislature, he was elected anew, in 1807, to represent Wake County. He was made chief of police of Raleigh and was a trustee of Raleigh Academy. In 1808 he adventured into journalism and with Thomas Henderson, Jr., founded a newspaper, the *Star,* retaining his connection until 1815, when he sold out to his partner. In 1808, also, a threat of war with France increased activity in militia circles, and Jones was made adjutant-general. After the outbreak of the War of 1812 he was commissioned a major-general of the North Carolina militia, 7th Division; and it was due to his vigilance and preparedness that a threatened British attack on the coast was abandoned. When he resigned from the army in 1814 he was quartermaster-general. Jones was eminently successful as a practitioner of medicine and performed many delicate surgical operations with success, even venturing into the field of ophthalmic surgery. He was the first in his part of the country to advocate vaccination against smallpox as a substitute for the older method of inoculation. He was a prominent Freemason. In 1832 he retired from practice and moved to his estate of 30,000 acres near Bolivar, Tenn. Here he built a mansion known as "Pontine" and lived the life of a planter until his death. In 1809 his fiancée, Ruina J. Williams, daughter of Maj. William Williams of Franklin County, N. C., died of tuberculosis; ten years later, in 1819, he married her sister, Temperance, widow of a colleague, Dr. Thomas C. Jones.

[M. DeL. Haywood, *Calvin Jones, Physician, Soldier, Freemason* (1919), repr. from *Proc. of the Grand*

Lodge, 1919, and condensed in H. A. Kelly and W. L. Burrage, *Am. Medic. Biogs.* (1920); *Encyc. of Mass., Biog.-Geneal.*, vol. IX (1920); A. M. Smith, *Three Blackmore Geneals.* (1930); *Weekly Raleigh Reg. and N. C. Gazette*, Oct. 16, 1846.] E. P.

JONES, CATESBY AP ROGER (Apr. 15, 1821–June 20, 1877), naval officer, was born at Fairfield, Va., the son of Mary Ann Mason (Page) Jones, niece of Light Horse Harry Lee, and Adjutant-General Roger Jones, United States Army, who was brevetted for services at Chippewa and Lundy's Lane, and made lieutenant-colonel for gallantry at Fort Erie in the War of 1812. Appointed a midshipman by President Jackson on June 18, 1836, young Jones first served under his uncle, Thomas ap Catesby Jones [*q.v.*], in the *Macedonian* and the *Relief*. Transferred to the frigate *Columbia*, East India Squadron, he became aide to Commodore George C. Read. At Callao, in March 1840, he joined the schooner *Shark*, Lieut. Abraham Bigelow, and the following year in the *Constitution*, flagship of the Pacific Squadron, Commodore Alexander Claxton, he returned to Hampton Roads. A passed midshipman since July 1, 1842, he served under Maury at the Depot of Charts and Instruments, Washington, in 1842 and 1843, also assisting in surveying Tampa Bay in the schooners *Flirt* and *Oregon*. He then made another cruise around the world; in the brig *Perry*, to Hong Kong, and thence in the *Brandywine*, by way of Valparaiso, to the United States (1843–45). During the Mexican War he was on the *Ohio*, Pacific Squadron, operating on the western coast of Mexico and South America, and thus was afforded no opportunity for active war experience. Made a lieutenant May 12, 1849, he was detached from the *St. Mary's* on Mar. 26, 1851, with leave for twelve months to visit Europe. This was extended because of serious wounds received in a street riot in Paris. Returning home, he was ordered, Feb. 28, 1853, to ordnance duty at the Washington Navy Yard, where he assisted Lieut. John A. Dahlgren [*q.v.*] in experiments leading to the perfection of the famous Dahlgren gun. On Feb. 5, 1856, at Dahlgren's request, he was sent to the *Merrimac* as the only other officer familiar with the new guns then on that ship. After ordnance duty on the *Plymouth*, *Caledonia*, and *Pawnee*, he was placed, May 19, 1860, on "waiting orders."

When Virginia seceded, Jones resigned his commission, and on Apr. 18, 1861, Governor Letcher appointed him captain in the Virginia navy. Early in June, he assisted in capturing the magazine at Norfolk with 300,000 pounds of powder and many shells. Becoming a lieutenant in the Confederate navy, June 10, 1861, he fortified Jamestown Island and on Nov. 11, went to Norfolk to prepare the battery for the ironclad *Virginia*, the reconstructed *Merrimac*. Then, as her executive officer under Capt. Franklin Buchanan [*q.v.*], he fought in the battle of Mar. 8, 1862, in which she sunk the *Cumberland* and burned the *Congress*. Buchanan having been wounded, Jones commanded her the next day in the renowned duel with the *Monitor*, an indecisive three hours' engagement. Josiah Tattnall relieving Buchanan, Jones remained executive officer of the ironclad, which after some repairs attempted vainly on Apr. 11 and May 8 to induce the *Monitor* to fight again. Jones was the last man to leave the *Virginia*, when the evacuation of Norfolk rendered her destruction necessary. Retiring with the crew to Drury's Bluff, he helped to defeat the Federal fleet there on May 15. After commanding the *Chattahoochee*, at Columbus, Ga., and the naval works at Charlotte, N. C., he was ordered on May 9, 1863, to command the important naval gun foundry and ordnance works at Selma, Ala. Meanwhile, he had become a commander, Apr. 29, 1863. At Selma, in spite of many obstacles, he manufactured cannon for Buchanan's squadron at Mobile and for Forts Morgan and Gaines as well as for the Confederate army.

After the war, Jones formed a partnership with John M. Brooke and Robert D. Minor to purchase American war supplies for foreign governments. The company was dissolved after a year or so, but not until Jones had made a trip to Peru early in 1866 for the firm. He then settled with his family at Selma, where he had married, Mar. 23, 1865, Gertrude T. Tartt. On June 19, 1877, he was shot in the lungs by J. A. Harral of Selma and died the next day. The two men were neighbors; both were leading citizens of the town and had been closely associated in religious and secular affairs. The difficulty that led to the tragedy seems to have originated in a quarrel between their children and the shooting occurred on Harral's premises (*Southern Argus*, Selma, June 22, 1877). Jones was survived by his wife, three sons, and three daughters.

[W. S. Mabry, *Brief Sketch of the Career of Capt. Catesby ap R. Jones* (1912); L. H. Jones, *Captain Roger Jones of London and Va.: Some of his Antecedents and Descendants* (1891); Navy Registers; *War of the Rebellion: Official Records (Navy)*, particularly 1 ser., vols. VII and XXI; *Battles and Leaders of the Civil War*, vol. I (1887); J. L. Worden, S. D. Greene, and H. A. Ramsay, *The Monitor and the Merrimac, Both Sides of the Story* (1912); William Tindall, *The True Story of the Virginia and the Monitor, the Account of an Eye Witness* (1923); Catesby ap R. Jones, "Services of the 'Virginia,'" *Sou. Hist. Soc. Papers*, XI (1883), 65–75; *Selma Times*, June 20, 21, 1877.]
C. L. L.

JONES, CHARLES COLCOCK (Oct. 28, 1831–July 19, 1893), historian, was born in Savannah and died in Augusta, Ga. He was a brother of Joseph Jones, 1833–1896 [*q.v.*]. Through both his father, Charles Colcock Jones, and his mother, born Mary Jones (Stacy, *post*, p. 150), he was the great-grandson of John Jones, who moved to Georgia from South Carolina shortly before the Revolution, and died, a major, at the battle of Savannah. Charles C. Jones, senior, a Presbyterian minister, at different times held positions as pastor in Savannah, professor of ecclesiastical history at the Columbia (S. C.) Theological Seminary, and secretary of the Presbyterian Board of Domestic Missions in Philadelphia; but between service in these positions and at the close of his life, he devoted himself, as a missionary, to an effort to evangelize the slaves of his own plantations, and he wrote a book describing his experiences in this undertaking. Young Charles grew up on the plantations, educated by private tutors. He attended South Carolina College, 1848–50, and in 1852 was graduated from the College of New Jersey, at Princeton. After reading law for a brief time in Philadelphia, he entered the Harvard Law School, from which he was graduated in 1855. That year he was admitted to the bar in Savannah. In 1859 he delivered an address before the Georgia Historical Society, published under the title *Indian Remains in Southern Georgia*; in 1860 he was elected mayor of Savannah; in 1861 he published *Monumental Remains of Georgia*; and about that time he delivered perhaps the first, and certainly one of the most ardent, of the pleas for secession made in Savannah. During the Civil War he was a colonel of artillery. In 1858, he had married Ruth Berrien Whitehead, and after her death he married in 1863 Eva Berrien Eve, niece and grand-niece, respectively, of John MacPherson Berrien [*q.v.*]. His second wife was also a niece of Paul F. Eve [*q.v.*]. In December 1865 Jones moved to New York and set up a law practice, but much of his time and interest must have been expended in historical research, for though he is said to have been a most rapid worker, no one could have formulated, without great effort, the vast number of historical speeches and papers that came from him. The enthusiastic reception of his substantial *Antiquities of the Southern Indians, Particularly of the Georgia Tribes* (1873) perhaps had its weight in persuading him that he had best take a small field for his researches and work that field thoroughly. In any case, most of his remaining studies seem to have been done on that principle. In 1877, he returned to Augusta, Ga., to continue an accelerated routine of delivering addresses and writing history. Among the most notable of his speeches are those he delivered from time to time before the Confederate Survivors' Association of Augusta, an organization which he formed and directed until his death. Among the most notable of his books—which were intelligent, careful, and, though rarely inspired, always solid and dignified—are the *The Dead Towns of Georgia* (1878); the *Memorial History of Augusta, Ga.* (1890), reaching only through the eighteenth century; and *History of Savannah, Ga.* (1890), covering the same period. The two-volume *History of Georgia* (1883), which, voluminous as it is, extends only through the Revolutionary epoch, is plainly the most ambitious and in general the most interesting of his works. He was referred to by the historian Bancroft as the "Macaulay of the South."

[Article on C. C. Jones by his son C. E. Jones in *Gulf States Hist. Mag.* (Montgomery, Ala.), Mar. 1903, offering an extended bibliography; *In Memoriam: Col. Charles C. Jones, Jr.* (1893), by the same author; W. J. Northen, *Men of Mark in Ga.*, vol. III (1911); M. L. Rutherford, *The South in Hist. and Lit.* (1907); *Gen. Cat. Princeton Univ.* (1908); *Quinquennial Cat. . . . Harvard Univ.* (1910); James Stacy, *Hist. of the Midway Congreg. Ch., Liberty County, Ga.* (1899), pp. 112–13, 150; *Report of the Eleventh Ann. Meeting, Ga. Bar Asso.* (1894); *Am. Anthropologist*, Oct. 1893; *Atlanta Constitution*, July 20, 1893.] J. D. W.

JONES, DAVID (May 12, 1736–Feb. 5, 1820), clergyman and army chaplain, was born in White Clay Creek Hundred, New Castle County, Del., the son of Morgan Jones, a native of Wales and a descendant of Morgan ap Rhyddarch. His mother was Eleanor, daughter of Roger Evans, who came with his parents to Philadelphia from Radnorshire, Wales, in 1695. David's early years were spent in agricultural life in a simple Welsh community. At the close of his twenty-first year he joined the Welsh Tract Baptist Church and very soon afterward went to Hopewell Academy, Hunterdon County, N. J., to study Latin and Greek under Rev. Isaac Eaton. In 1761, after being licensed to preach by his own church, he went to study under his cousin, the learned Abel Morgan, pastor of the Middletown, N. J., church. He was ordained at Freehold, Monmouth County, N. J., on Dec. 12, 1766, and became pastor of the church there. On Feb. 22, 1762, he had married Anne, daughter of Joseph and Sarah Stillwell of Middletown, by whom he had several children. Jones was a man of keen intellect and abounding energy. Though he was faithful and sincere in his ministry, his religious duties failed to consume the whole of his restless energy. His excess vitality found vent in a variety of activities. He remained farmer, minister, author, scholar, throughout his life and became at various times missionary and soldier. While at Freehold he conceived the idea of a visit to the Indians of the Ohio country, a conception born of missionary zeal not unmixed with more worldly "views of settling on the east bank of the river Ohio" (*Journal, post,* reprint, 1865, p. viii). His two missions, which consumed nearly a year (May 1772–April 1773), met with little success, and he abandoned his attempt with health and fortune impaired. In 1774, Rhode Island College, now Brown University, in testimony of his scholarly work in the pulpit, conferred upon him the honorary degree of master of arts.

As the American Revolution approached, Jones espoused the cause of the colonies and spoke his mind so boldly in the Loyalist community of Freehold that his life was endangered. In April 1775 he removed to become pastor of the Great Valley Baptist Church, Chester County, Pa., a post which he retained for the remainder of his life except for six years, 1786–92, spent at the Southampton Church, Bucks County, Pa., and several long leaves of absence while serving as army chaplain. In the fall of 1775 he preached to a group of Pennsylvania troops his noted sermon, *Defensive War in a Just Cause Sinless,* in which he took high ground for independence. This sermon was printed (1775) and exerted considerable influence in Pennsylvania. On Apr. 27, 1776, he was appointed chaplain of the 3rd and 4th Pennsylvania Battalions, the 4th being that of Col. Anthony Wayne. On Jan. 1, 1777, he was transferred to the 1st Brigade of Gen. Anthony Wayne's division of the Pennsylvania line, and Jan. 1, 1783, to the 3rd Pennsylvania Battalion. Chaplain Jones did not confine himself to religious duties. His influence in arousing patriotic zeal outside the ranks was considerable, especially in the Philadelphia district. General Wayne thought very highly of him and General Howe even offered a reward for his capture. At the close of the war he returned to his farm at Easton and to the Great Valley Church. From 1794 to 1796 he again saw service as an army chaplain at the request of General Wayne, who was sent with the Northern army to subdue the Indians of the Ohio country. So enormous was Jones's vitality, so ardent his patriotic zeal that when the War of 1812 came, though seventy-six years of age, he volunteered and served as chaplain throughout the war. The remainder of his long life was spent in attending to his parish duties and in writing numerous letters and articles for the press. He was buried at the Great Valley Church Cemetery.

His published works include, *A Journal of Two Visits Made to Some Nations of Indians on the West Side of the River Ohio, in the Years 1772 and 1773* (1774), reprint (1865); *The Doctrine of "Laying on of Hands," Examined & Vindicated* (1786); *A True History of Laying on of Hands upon Baptized Believers as Such: in Answer to a Hand-bill, Intitled, A Brief History of the Imposition of Hands on Baptized Persons; Published by Samuel Jones, D.D., Wherein his Mistakes Are Attempted to be Corrected* (1805); *Peter Edward's Candid Reasons Examined and Answered* (1811); *Review of Mr. John P. Campbell's Sermon . . . on the Subject and Mode of Baptism* (1811).

[The reprint of Jones's *Journal* contains a biographical sketch by his grandson, Horatio Gates Jones, Jr., who also published "The Bapt. Ch. in the Great Valley, Tredyffrin Township, Chester County, Pa.," in *The Cambrian*, Jan. 1884. See also C. J. Stillé, *Maj.-Gen. Anthony Wayne and the Pa. Line* (1893); *Pa. in the Revolution* (2 vols., 1880), ed. by J. B. Linn and W. H. Egle; W. B. Sprague, *Annals Am. Pulpit*, vol. VI (1860); *Poulson's Am. Daily Advertiser*, Feb. 10, 1820.]

J. W. P—t.
A. G. T.

JONES, DAVID RUMPH (Apr. 5, 1825–Jan. 15, 1863), Confederate soldier, was born in Orangeburg District, S. C. He was a descendant of Lewis Jones who emigrated from England and settled in Massachusetts about 1635. His father, Donald Bruce Jones, a native of Hartford, Conn., moved to South Carolina and later, to Georgia; his mother, Mary Elvira, was the daughter of Brigadier-General Jacob Rumph, a famous Revolutionary captain of South Carolina. After attending common schools, young Jones in 1842 became a cadet at the United States Military Academy, West Point, where he showed special ability in horsemanship and fencing. In 1846 he graduated, ranking forty-one in a class of fifty-nine, and was appointed second lieutenant, 2nd Infantry. He married Rebecca Taylor, niece of President Zachary Taylor, and cousin of Jefferson Davis's first wife. The year after he graduated he participated in the siege of Vera Cruz and was active in the campaign ending in the capture of the city of Mexico. For gallant and meritorious conduct he was brevetted first lieutenant. In 1853 he was transferred to the adjutant-general's department, and served on the Pacific coast and at St. Louis.

He resigned from the United States Army on Feb. 15, 1861, and, proceeding to South Carolina, was appointed major and chief of staff to General Beauregard, then besieging Fort Sumter. He visited Sumter, offered the terms of surrender, and is supposed to have hauled down the national colors. On June 17, he was commissioned brigadier-general, and assigned to a brigade which he led in the battle of Bull Run on

July 21. It had been intended to have Jones play a prominent part in this engagement, but owing to mismanagement for which he was not responsible the fortunes of the battle were decided before he attacked, late in the afternoon, only to be forced back by artillery fire. In March 1862 he was assigned to a division and on Apr. 5 he was appointed major-general, but the appointment was not confirmed until the following November. Temporarily commanding Magruder's division, he successfully withdrew it from the trenches at Yorktown. He was present during the Peninsular campaign but without having an active part therein until the Seven Days' Battles. On June 29, he attacked the retreating Federals near Savage Station, but because of lack of cooperation, failed to obtain any success. His command next formed part of Longstreet's corps in the second Bull Run campaign. By excellent judgment and activity, on Aug. 27, 1862, he seized Thoroughfare Gap, enabling Longstreet to arrive in time to assist Jackson in defeating the Federal army three days later. In this engagement, Jones had a leading rôle in the counter-attack ordered by General Lee. His division was prominent in the ensuing invasion of Maryland. Recalled in haste from Pennsylvania, he arrived on Sept. 14, at South Mountain Pass, in time to aid in repulsing the Federals. On Sept. 17, at the battle of Antietam, he was posted on the extreme right of the Confederate army, in front of Sharpsburg. No serious effort was made against him until about 1 P.M., when his advanced troops were forced from Burnside's bridge. After this initial success the enemy launched an overwhelming attack about 4 P.M., and Jones's division was driven into Sharpsburg. The critical situation which resulted, threatening the safety of Lee's entire army, was relieved by the opportune arrival of Gen. A. P. Hill, who, oriented by General Jones, assisted in a counter-attack, which turned the scales in favor of the Confederates. Soon after, Jones developed serious heart trouble, and after a brief illness died at Richmond.

[*War of the Rebellion: Official Records (Army)*, 1 ser. vols. II, XI (pts. 1–3), XII (pts. 1–3), XIX (pts. 1, 2); W. F. Northen, *Men of Mark in Ga.*, vol. III (1911); C. A. Evans, *Confed. Mil. Hist.* (1899), vol. V; *Battles and Leaders of the Civil War* (4 vols., 1887–88); F. B. Heitman, *Hist. Reg. U. S. Army* (1890); G. W. Cullum, *Biog. Reg. Officers and Grads. U. S. Mil. Acad.* (3rd ed., 1891, vol. II).] C. H. L—a.

JONES, ERNEST LESTER (Apr. 14, 1876–Apr. 9, 1929), director of the United States Coast and Geodetic Survey, commissioner of the International Boundary between the United States and Canada and Alaska and Canada, was born at East Orange, N. J., the son of Charles Hopkins Jones and his wife, Ada Lester. From the schools of Orange he went to the Newark Academy and prepared to enter Princeton University in the class of 1898, but, owing to ill health, soon sought the benefits of a country life, congenial to his general physical frailness as well as to his tastes. In September 1897 he married Virginia Brent Fox of Louisville, Ky., who with two daughters survived him.

President Wilson, soon after his first successful campaign, drew Jones from the rural pursuits of a Virginia farm near Culpeper by appointing him deputy commissioner in the United States Bureau of Fisheries. In this capacity he visited Alaska and, being there impressed with the dangers besetting navigation in those waters, he composed in an official report an appeal of convincing clearness for the prosecution of coast surveys and the production of mariners' charts to promote the security of shipping and to safeguard the lives of seamen (*Report of Alaska Investigations in 1914,* 1915). His striking words stamped him as one who could be used in creating sympathy for a branch of public work needed to serve the life of the nation, and in April 1915 he was appointed superintendent of the Coast and Geodetic Survey. During the World War, on furlough from his office, 1918–19, he served as lieutenant-colonel in the Signal Corps and later as colonel in the Division of Military Aeronautics in France.

When he died, at the early age of fifty-three years, he had held the directorship of the Coast and Geodetic Survey and membership in the International Boundary Commission for fourteen years without ever having claimed for himself any scientific distinction. That he was a most capable director is nevertheless evident from the history of the institution which he controlled. He took upon himself the cares of organization and supply, and left the chiefs of his scientific divisions unfettered freedom to pursue their technical work. He was the link between a service to science and the source of its support in the appropriations of the legislature, and he strengthened this relation by writing short and lucid primers, telling in simple terms the methods and purposes of various aspects of the surveying operations within his purview: *Elements of Chart Making* (1916); *Hypsometry* (1917); *Neglected Waters of the Pacific* (1918); *Safeguard the Gateways of Alaska* (1918); "The Evolution of the Nautical Chart" (*Military Engineer,* May–June 1924); *Earthquake Investigations in the United States* (1925); *Science and the Earthquake Perils* (1926); *Tide and Current Investigations of the Coast and Geodetic*

Survey (1926). It was a part of his philosophy of administration that the best work can be done only when men have the proper appliances for doing it, and so it was among his basic endeavors to supply suitable ships and modern instruments and equipment. In these efforts he was successful, and he supplemented them by securing legislation giving his organization more stability and greater financial competence. It is not an easy task to obtain increasing appropriations to support hydrographic and geodetic surveying on the scale to which he expanded these operations. His truthfulness to the legislators was met by their confidence, and his loyalty to the Coast and Geodetic Survey was met by the loyalty to him of its membership. Being unpretending and deferential, yet ready to assume responsibility, his modest deportment was rendered all the more becoming by a full measure of that self-respect which springs from the aim to do the greatest good that is practicable.

[*Ann. Report of the Supt., U. S. Coast and Geodetic Survey,* 1915–19; memoir by R. L. Faris, *Trans. Am. Soc. Civil Engineers,* vol. XCIV (1930); *Jour. Washington Acad. of Sci.,* May 4, 1929; *Popular Astronomy,* Aug. 1929; *Geog. Rev.* (N. Y.), July 1929; *Geog. Jour.* (London), July 1929; *Nature* (London), May 18, 1929; *Who's Who in America,* 1928–29; records of the Office of the Secretary of Princeton Univ.; *Evening Star* (Washington, D. C.), Apr. 9, 1929.] G. W. L.

JONES, EVAN WILLIAM (1852–Dec. 30, 1908), mechanical engineer, inventor of the mechanical underfeed stoker, was born in Monmouthshire, Wales, the son of Evan Jones, an ironworker. The father brought the family to America in 1854 and settled in Ironton, Ohio, where he obtained employment in the steel mills. Young Evan attended the public schools of Ironton until he was thirteen, when he entered the mills as an apprentice in the machine shops, thus beginning a lifetime of association with iron and machine works. After spending his early life in various plants in the region of Ironton and Portsmouth, Ohio, and Pittsburgh, Pa., he went to Portland, Ore., in the employ of the Union Iron Works, of which he was soon made manager and later president. In 1888 he became interested in the difficulties involved in burning Oregon fir, then the cheapest available fuel for the local industries. The high moisture content of the fir acted to deaden the fire each time a fresh supply was thrown into the furnace, with the result that constant high boiler pressures could be maintained only with great difficulty. Jones solved the problem by building a machine that would supply the wood to the furnace from below the fuel bed, in effect using the green fuel as grate bars to support the burning pieces. As a result, the fresh fuel was gradually dried out as it was pushed upward into the combustion zone of the fire bed and the fire was not harmed by the addition of new fuel. The first machine that Jones built was designed to force standard four-foot lengths of wood into the furnace and was operated by hand levers. This machine proved that the idea was practicable, and Jones added a steam ram to drive the wood and made several machines that were operated in 1889. He then turned his attention to the design of a stoker for use with bituminous coal. In 1892 he obtained permission to equip two boilers of the Portland Cable Railway Company with his coal stokers. These were without doubt the first power-driven mechanical underfeed stokers to be put into operation, and are the ones from which the modern underfeed stoker developed. Tests at the Portland Cable Railway Company in February and March 1892 showed a saving in fuel of 25.6 per cent. when the stokers were used instead of hand firing. The Under-Feed Stoker Company of America was formed to manufacture the Jones Stoker, and Jones obtained a block of stock for his invention and rights. The company became involved in litigation growing out of attempts to infringe the patents, and the stock fell in value. Jones then became a port engineer for the North West Commercial Company, in charge of their vessels and a small iron works at St. Michaels on the Yukon. He contracted pneumonia during a particularly trying season in the North and died at Portland at the age of fifty-six. He was married at Ironton, Ohio, to Margaret Helen Abrams, also of Welsh descent, and after her death at the age of thirty-two, he was married a second time, to a sister of C. W. Idleman of Portland. His second wife survived him.

["The Jones Underfeed Stoker," *Jour. of the Franklin Inst.,* Dec. 1904; G. C. Tewksbury, "The Under-Feed Stoker," *Trans. New Eng. Cotton Mfrs. Asso.,* no. 73 (1902); *Specifications and Drawings of Patents Issued from the U. S. Patent Office,* Aug. 1889, Mar. 1892, Oct. 1896; *Morning Oregonian* and *Oregon Daily Jour.* (both Portland), Jan. 2, 1909; correspondence with Mrs. Clarence H. Gilbert, a daughter of Jones.] F. A. T.

JONES, FRANK (Sept. 15, 1832–Oct. 2, 1902), brewer, capitalist, railroad executive, congressman, was born at Barrington, N. H., the fifth of seven children of Thomas and Mary (Priest) Jones. His grandfather, Peletiah Jones, had been brought from Wales as an infant. Frank lived on his parents' farm until he was about seventeen, then he went to Portsmouth, N. H., where he worked for his brother, selling stoves and hardware, for three years. He became his brother's partner in 1853. In 1861 he sold out his partnership and assumed the management of a brewery in which he had purchased an interest.

He soon became the sole owner of the brewery, to which he added a large malt house, considered at the time (1880) to be the largest and best equipped of its kind in America. Under the firm name of Jones, Johnson & Company, he extended his brewery operations to Boston. In the meantime he invested heavily in real estate in and around Portsmouth and became the owner of the Rockingham House, then the largest and handsomest tourist hotel in that section of New England. He also built and managed the Wentworth at Newcastle, N. H. He owned a large estate near Portsmouth known as "Gravelly Ridge," on which he maintained a racing stable.

In politics he was a Democrat, until the latter period of his life. He was four times nominated as the Democratic candidate for mayor of Portsmouth, and was elected twice, in 1868 and 1869, although the Republican party was in the majority at the time. Beginning in 1875, he served two terms in Congress. He refused a third nomination, but ran for governor as a Democrat in 1880 and was defeated, although he received the largest number of votes that ever had been given a Democrat for that office in New Hampshire. In 1896 he withdrew from the Democratic party and allied himself with the Republicans.

He first became interested in railroads as the chief promoter and first president of the Portsmouth & Dover Railroad. He was later interested in the old Eastern Railroad, which together with the Portsmouth & Dover was subsequently merged into the Boston & Maine system. He became a director of the Boston & Maine Railroad in 1889 and was elected president on Dec. 31 of the same year, serving in this capacity until Oct. 26, 1892, when he became vice-president and chairman of the board. He was again elected president in June 1893, but resigned in October following, and at the same time severed all relationship with the railroad.

On Sept. 15, 1861, he married Martha Sophia (Leavitt) Jones, the widow of his brother, Hiram Jones. He died in Portsmouth, N. H., at the age of seventy.

[*Granite Monthly*, Mar. 1881 and Nov. 1902; *Biog. Dir. Am. Cong.* (1928); Henry Hall, *America's Successful Men of Affairs*, vol. II (1896); *Manchester Union*, Oct. 3, 1902.]

A. M. S.

JONES, GABRIEL (May 17, 1724–Oct. 6, 1806), pioneer lawyer of the Valley of Virginia, adviser and executor for Lord Fairfax, was born near Williamsburg, Va., of English-Welsh parents, John and Elizabeth Jones. Following the father's death when Gabriel was still in his infancy the family returned to London. Here in an English boys' school he received his preparatory education, and subsequently served a law apprenticeship with one John Houghton. Before reaching manhood he had returned to Virginia and at the age of twenty-one had qualified as king's attorney for both of the newly organized frontier counties, Frederick and Augusta. For the thirty years between this time and the outbreak of the Revolution he rode the circuit of these and other Valley counties as a loyal representative of his king, and served almost continuously as a representative from some one of them in the Virginia House of Burgesses. It was in connection with this service that he "found" young George Washington and sponsored his entry (1758) into public life as a burgess from Frederick County (Barton, *post,* pp. 23–25). Jones is represented as having done yeoman service among the frontiersmen in behalf of the youthful political aspirant.

It is a tribute to the man and his integrity and an indication of the esteem and respect in which he was held that his lukewarmness and near antagonism to the Revolutionary movement seems to have enhanced rather than diminished his prestige. He was allowed to continue as the attorney for the state (if he so desired), but apparently did not continue, and a year or so later he became the prosecutor for the new county, Rockingham. Furthermore, in 1777 he was one of three commissioners designated by the Virginia Assembly to ascertain for the Continental Congress the reasons for disaffection around Fort Pitt. Twice in 1779 he was elected by the Assembly as a delegate to the Continental Congress but did not serve. Again in 1788 his state honored him by placing him at the head of the list of judges of the newly organized state court system, but he still refused to serve. His political activities after 1781 were confined to one session of the legislature (1783) and the convention of 1788 that ratified the new federal Constitution.

Gabriel Jones was the pioneer as well as in many senses the exemplar of the long line of frontier circuit-riding lawyers. He was to these what Daniel Boone was to the hunters and trail blazers, what Peter Cartwright was to the circuit riders for the churches. His eccentricities not only furnished tales and bywords but set the pace for frontier characteristics and idiosyncrasies. The outbursts of temper of the "peppery old gentleman" became classic; the Augusta County Records reveal that the county court once threatened a jail term for one Mr. Holmes if he "did not quit worrying Mr. Jones and making him curse and swear so" (Grigsby, *post,* II, 18). Much of the man and his motivation is portrayed in a pamphlet Jones issued a few years before his death. As a characteristically outspoken Federalist, he had attacked Jefferson soon after his inauguration as president. A friend of the latter then made a vicious attack on the character and practices of Jones. Jones's devastating reply, *A Refutation of the Charges Made by a Writer under the Signature of "Veritas" against the Character of Gabriel Jones* (1804), is a gem among the caustic political pamphlets of the time.

In 1749 he married Margaret (Strother) Morton, a widow, by whom he had four children. She was a daughter of a prominent Tidewater family and through her he became a close kinsman of the Lewis family of the Valley and of the Madisons. He died at the place that for more than half a century had been his home on the banks of the Shenandoah.

[For sketches see: R. T. Barton, "Gabriel Jones, the Lawyer," *W. Va. Mag. of Hist.*, Apr. 1902; H. B. Grigsby, *The Hist. of the Va. Federal Conv. of 1788* (2 vols., 1890–91), being *Va. Hist. Soc. Colls.*, n.s., IX, X; L. G. Tyler, *Encyc. of Va. Biog.* (1915), vol. I; T. K. Cartmell, *Shenandoah Valley Pioneers and Their Descendants* (1909); K. G. Greene, *Winchester, Va., and Its Beginnings* (1926); J. A. Waddell, *Annals of Augusta County, Va.* (2nd ed., 1902); J. W. Wayland, *Va. Valley Records* (1930); J. L. Peyton, *Hist. of Augusta County, Va.* (1882). Most of the data must be gathered from the Minute and Order books of the older Valley counties, from the *Journal of the House of Burgesses . . . of Va.*, 1748–64, the *Journal of the House of Delegates of the Commonwealth of Va.*, 1777–88, and from W. W. Hening, *The Statutes at Large; being a Collection of All the Laws of Va.*, particularly vol. IX (1821).] F. H. H.

JONES, GEORGE (July 30, 1800–Jan. 22, 1870), naval chaplain and author, was born on a farm near York, Pa., the son of Robert and Elizabeth (Dunnman) Jones. He graduated from Yale College in 1823, and was awarded the degree of A.M. in 1826. After teaching two years in a school he organized in Washington, he became secretary to Commodore Charles Morris [*q.v.*] commanding the *Brandywine*, and also teacher of navigation to the midshipmen, among whom was Matthew Fontaine Maury [*q.v.*]. After conveying Lafayette home from his visit to the United States, the *Brandywine* proceeded to the Mediterranean, where Jones was transferred to the *Constitution*, Capt. David T. Patterson [*q.v.*]. An account of the cruise of this frigate to important Mediterranean ports Jones wrote in the form of sixty-seven letters, entitled *Sketches of Naval Life* (2 vols., 1829). Returning to the United States in 1828, he was for two years a tutor at Yale, and then rector of the Episcopal Church, Middletown, Conn., for a year, after which poor health forced him to take employment in the open air in Indiana. In 1832 he was able to accept Commodore Patterson's invitation to become acting chaplain on the *United States*, flagship of the Mediterranean Squadron. In this frigate and the *Delaware*, to which he, with Patterson, was transferred in March 1834, he made a second Mediterranean cruise, an account of which he published after his arrival at Norfolk in February 1836, under the title, *Excursions to Cairo, Jerusalem, Damascus, and Balbec* (1836). Meanwhile, he was commissioned chaplain, Apr. 20, 1833. In 1837 he married Mary Amelia Silliman, daughter of Gold Selleck Silliman of Brooklyn, N. Y., and niece of the elder Benjamin Silliman [*q.v.*]. After four years at the Norfolk Navy Yard, he served for five years on the frigates *Macedonian, Columbus, Constitution,* and *Brandywine* in turn, doing effective temperance work among the crews and striving to bring about the establishment of a naval school by writing an appeal in the *Naval Magazine* (May 1836), by corresponding with various naval officers, and by interviewing Secretary of the Navy Upshur in Washington. On his return from a cruise to China in September 1845, Jones was, accordingly, ordered to the Naval School, recently organized at Annapolis. Here, as professor in charge of the department of English literature, sometimes assisting in mathematics, he remained until 1850. A chaplaincy having been established in the Naval School at its reorganization in October of that year, he became the first chaplain of the United States Naval Academy in February 1851. The following year, Commodore Matthew Calbraith Perry [*q.v.*] applied for his services, declaring he "could be useful to him" in the expedition to Japan. After this noted cruise came to a successful close, Jones was ordered by Perry to remain in New York and assist in preparing the official report of the expedition, his particular contribution being the observations of the zodiacal light in Volume III of the report (M. C. Perry, *Narrative of the Expedition of an American Squadron to the China Seas and Japan*, 3 vols., 1856). Then, obtaining leave of absence for a year, he went to Quito, Ecuador, where he spent seven months making observations to confirm his theory that this astronomical phenomenon comes from a nebulous ring round the earth. Returning home in the spring of 1857, he again became chaplain at the Naval Academy, for a period of four years. After a short tour of duty on the *Minnesota*, Commodore S. H. Stringham [*q.v.*], Atlantic Squadron, he was retired for age in July 1862. During the Civil War he did voluntary duty as chaplain and nurse in the army hospitals in Washington and at Gettysburg. His last two books were *Life-Scenes from the Four Gospels*

(1865), and *Life-Scenes from the Old Testament* (1868). His death occurred while he was stationed as chaplain at the United States Naval Asylum, Philadelphia.

[Autobiographical letter written by Jones, Feb. 5, 1864, to Librarian T. G. Ford, U. S. Naval Academy; Navy Registers; Park Benjamin, *Hist. of the U. S. Naval Academy* (1900); J. R. Soley, *Hist. Sketch of the U. S. Naval Acad.* (1876); *Phila. Enquirer*, Jan. 24, 1870.] C. L. L.

JONES, GEORGE (Aug. 16, 1811–Aug. 12, 1891), newspaper publisher, was born at Poultney, Vt., the son of John and Barbara Davis Jones, both immigrants from Wales. He went to country schools, worked in a country store, and at the age of twenty went into business in New York, marrying Sarah M. Gilbert of Troy in 1836. Horace Greeley, whom he had known as a boy in Poultney, asked him to become his partner in founding the *Tribune* in 1841, but Jones preferred a salaried position in the business office, where he formed a friendship with Henry J. Raymond [*q.v.*], Greeley's chief editorial assistant. The two were soon talking of starting a paper of their own, but the plan was not realized till 1851. Jones by that time was living in Albany, where he had prospered as a "free banker" dealing in the heterogeneous currency of the period; but a law which reduced the profits in note shaving persuaded him to give up his business and join Raymond in the establishment of the *New York Times.* Thanks in part to his direction, it had become an extremely valuable property when Raymond's sudden death in 1869 left it without a head.

A newspaper was still regarded as the organ of its editor; that the Civil War had finally made the news department more important than the editorial page was not yet appreciated. Jones, though the second heaviest stockholder in the *Times* and its business manager since 1856, had no editorial experience; he took command at first as a sort of regent for Raymond's son, who was still in college. But a brief and unfortunate experience with a hired editor soon compelled him to take over the direction of the editorial policy which was successively executed for him by Louis J. Jennings, John Foord, and Charles R. Miller. The successful fight against the "Tweed ring" which followed (1871) was due chiefly to Jones. Foord and Jennings did the work but he took the risk; the *Times* was subjected to legal attacks, suffered a considerable temporary loss in advertising, and might have been ruined if its campaign had failed. Tweed tried vainly to buy control of the paper, and finally Controller Connolly offered Jones five million dollars to give up the crusade. This story rests, to be sure, only on Jones's word, but Connolly was far more capable of making such a proposal than Jones of inventing it. Whatever contributions other men made to the fight, it was Jones's immovable determination that carried it through to victory.

The overthrow of Tweed was Jones's great public service, but he is important in the history of journalism as the first conspicuous instance of the modern business-office type of newspaper proprietor. As such, his relation to his editors was exemplary, from the editor's viewpoint. He always had the final word, as Jennings discovered when he challenged him on the issue of a third term for President Grant; but Jones selected editors in general agreement with his own opinions and showed due deference to theirs. In 1884 the *Times,* which had been Republican since the party was founded, bolted the presidential ticket. This was due to the initiative of Miller and Edward Cary, but Jones gave his assent and cheerfully bore the heavy financial loss which desertion of the party entailed. Four years later he privately preferred Harrison but permitted his editors to continue the paper's support of Cleveland. Personally he was quiet and retiring; outside his business he had no interests except his home, his church (he became an Episcopalian, but retained a Welsh Baptist delight in song), and the Union League Club. It was his pride that while he controlled the *Times* no man was ever asked to subscribe to it or to advertise in it. Such reticence became outmoded; but he died, rich and honored, before he found that out.

[Jones wrote almost nothing even for newspaper publication; and less was written about him, during or after his lifetime, than about any other newspaper proprietor of the period. See the obituaries in the New York papers (fullest in the *Herald*), Aug. 13, 1891, and editorial comments republished in the *Times* of the following days. Other sources include: Joseph Joslin, Barnes Frisbie, and Frederick Ruggles, *A Hist. of the Town of Poultney, Vt.* (1875); and Elmer Davis, *Hist. of the N. Y. Times* (1921), which draws on the recollections of his editors, Foord and Miller.] E. D.

JONES, GEORGE HEBER (Aug. 14, 1867–May 11, 1919), missionary, the son of Charles Edward and Susan (Cosser) Jones, was born at Mohawk, N. Y. His ancestry was a mixture of the three national stocks of Great Britain with the Welsh predominating. He was educated in the public schools of Utica, N. Y. As a youth of twenty, in 1887, only three years after the commencement of missionary work in that country, Jones went to Korea under the auspices of the Methodist Episcopal Church. His first five years in Korea he spent largely in educational work in Seoul in connection with the Pai Chai high school and college. In 1892 he received the B.A. degree from the American University at Harriman, Tenn., where he had been doing non-resident work for several years. In the same year he went to Chemulpo where he made his headquarters for the next ten years, being successively pastor and presiding elder. When he went to Chemulpo there were no Christians in all that region; ten years later there were forty-four organized churches and two thousand eight hundred Christians. Jones had the unusual honor of being the presiding elder of a district, every church of which he himself had organized and every church member of which he had baptized. From 1897 to 1899 and from 1907 to 1909 he was the superintendent of the Methodist Episcopal mission throughout Korea.

Jones was a careful student of the Korean language, and from 1902 to 1905 he was a member of the Board of Translators of the Bible into Korean. He was an editor of the *Korean Repository* from 1895 to 1898, and a founder and editor (1900–04) of the *Sin-hak Wol-po* (Theological Review). From its founding until he removed permanently from Korea he was vice-president of the Korea Branch of the Royal Asiatic Society. He was presented five times to the Emperor of Korea, and during the days of terror after the murder of the Queen in 1895 Jones took turns with a few other missionaries in staying with the King for the moral support that a foreigner could give him. With David W. Deshler, the financial promoter, he organized the Korean emigration movement to the Hawaiian Islands between 1903 and 1905, during which time eight thousand natives of the ancient Hermit Kingdom settled in the newly acquired American territory. He secured the support of the Korean government for the project and roused the enthusiasm of Koreans in his district, large numbers of whom were Christians.

In 1905 Jones lectured on missions at Morningside College, Sioux City, Iowa, and filled the same lectureship in De Pauw University in 1911 and in the Boston School of Theology (1915–18). In 1909 he returned permanently to the United States, and from 1913 to 1919 he was editorial secretary and associate secretary of the Board of Foreign Missions of the Methodist Episcopal Church. His literary work in Korean included a volume of studies in the Old Testament, a short history of the Christian church, a Korean Methodist hymnbook, and a Korean-English dictionary of scientific and technical terms. He wrote in English *Korea: the Land, People and Customs* (copyright 1907), and *Christianity and World Democracy* (1918). For a time he was Korea correspondent of the London *Times*. He was a contributing editor of the *Journal of Race Development,* and also a member of the American Society of International Law, the American Academy of Political and Social Science, the Board of International Hospitality and Conciliation, and of the Japan Society of New York. He possessed an unusually genial personality and made friends among all classes and peoples with whom he came into contact. That his worth and services were appreciated equally by the Korean and Japanese governments speaks well both for his impartiality and his friendly sympathy. On May 10, 1893, Jones was married in Seoul to Margaret Josephine Bengel of Pomeroy, Ohio. He died at Miami, Fla.

[The Missionary Research Library in New York City contains much interesting material, especially manuscripts, on the life and work of Jones. His voluminous journals are held privately. "A Journey Through Southern Korea in 1889, an Extract from the Journals of George Heber Jones, D.D.," ed. by Harold J. Noble, in the *Korea Mission Field* for Nov. 1928 and Jan. 1929, contains a brief sketch of his life. Other sources include: *Who's Who in America,* 1918–19; "A Partial Bibliography of Occidental Literature on Korea," *Trans. Korea Branch, Royal Asiatic Soc.,* vol. XX (1931); *Christian Advocate* (N.Y.), May 15, 1929; L. G. Paik, *The Hist. of Protestant Missions in Korea* (1929); *N. Y. Times,* May 13, 1919.] H. J. N.

JONES, GEORGE WALLACE (Apr. 12, 1804–July 22, 1896), pioneer miner, merchant, legislator, was a striking figure in the early history of Wisconsin and Iowa. He was born in Vincennes, Ind., the son of John Rice Jones, a Welshman, and Mary Barger of Pennsylvania. His early education was obtained in St. Louis and in 1825 he graduated from Transylvania University, Kentucky. While in college he was the protégé of Henry Clay and formed lasting friendships with Jefferson Davis and other Southerners who greatly influenced his later career. When the study of law impaired his health he migrated to Sinsinawa Mound, then in Michigan Territory, a frontier mining community. Here he acted as storekeeper and miner for ten years. He was married on Jan. 7, 1829, and in 1831 he took his young wife, Josephine Grégoire, daughter of an old French family, together with seven slaves, to Sinsinawa. He served as an aide to Gen. Henry Dodge in the Black Hawk War and was elected delegate to Congress from Michigan Territory in 1835. He secured the organization of the Territory of Wisconsin (1836), was delegate to Congress from that Territory, and procured the establishment of Iowa Territory. He failed of reëlection as delegate from Wisconsin (1838) largely because he had acted as a second in the fatal Cilley-Graves duel. Two years later he was appointed surveyor-general of Iowa and Wisconsin. He was removed from office in 1841 but in 1845 he was reappointed and established himself in Dubuque, where he settled permanently.

In 1848 Jones became one of the first senators from Iowa and represented the state twelve years. As a "Democrat in politics and a Southerner in all his instincts," he reflected the character of Iowa which was Southern in population and sympathies down to 1853–54. He was not an orator, but he was highly successful in securing legislation for public improvements because of his resourcefulness and wide acquaintanceship. In 1850 he got the Illinois Central Railroad Bill amended in such a way as to bring the Western terminus to Dubuque, Iowa, instead of Galena, Ill., and after repeated failures he procured land grants in 1856 for railway routes from Dubuque, Lyons, Davenport, and Burlington westward to points on the Missouri. In national legislation he had the approval of his state when he supported the compromise measures of 1850. It was not so in 1854, when, as member of the committee on territories, he approved the Kansas-Nebraska Bill. At this time Iowa was undergoing a marked political change and it was the first state to pass judgment on the bill. In a vigorous campaign in which he denounced "the Nebraska infamy," Grimes was elected governor and soon after Harlan, another anti-slavery candidate, succeeded Dodge as senator. When Jones voted for the Lecompton Constitution he was even deserted by his own party, which was loyal to Douglas, and he was not renominated in 1858. It was widely charged that Jones openly opposed Douglas in the famous senatorial campaign against Lincoln but Jones categorically denied this in a letter (Feb. 12, 1859) to Henry Clay Dean.

On Mar. 8, 1859, President Buchanan appointed Jones minister to New Granada, where his courtly manners and Catholic faith made him both acceptable and successful. On his return in December 1861, Secretary Seward ordered his arrest, charging him with treasonable correspondence with Jefferson Davis. While his letters were highly indiscreet, they were probably not treasonable since he was soon released by Lincoln's orders. On reaching Iowa, Jones made a public defense. He held that the Union could endure "part slave and part free" and that the conflict was not "irrepressible." In his judgment, the only obstacle to reasonable compromise was the "mad schemes" of the Abolitionists. This statement got little hearing; Iowa had changed while Jones had not, and his political career was ended. As time passed, however, bitterness subsided, and he gradually resumed his old friendships and associations. In 1892 he was granted a pension, and on his ninetieth birthday he was tendered a reception by the General Assembly in recognition of his great services to the commonwealth.

[J. C. Parish, *George Wallace Jones* (1912), contains, in addition to the biography, Jones's autobiography. Other sources include: E. H. Stiles, *Recollections and Sketches of Notable Lawyers and Pub. Men of Early Iowa* (1916); D. E. Clark, *Hist. of Senatorial Elections in Iowa* (1912); *Annals of Iowa*, Oct. 1897, Jan., Apr., and Oct. 1898; *Iowa Hist. Record*, Apr. 1887; *Dubuque Daily Herald*, July 23, 1896; Jones's correspondence in the Hist. Dept., Des Moines, Iowa.]

C. E. P.

JONES, HARRY CLARY (Nov. 11, 1865–Apr. 9, 1916), physical chemist, was born in New London, Md., the son of William and Johanna Clary Jones. He received his preparatory education in the county schools of western Maryland and entered Johns Hopkins University as an undergraduate in 1885. His work was characterized by such diligence and success that he was awarded two undergraduate scholarships. Upon receiving the degree of B.A. in 1889 he immediately entered the graduate school, pursuing work in the department of chemistry. Here he was the recipient of further academic honors, and was awarded the degree of Ph.D. in 1892. During these years he formed a lasting friendship with such masters as Ira Remsen and H. N. Morse, the two leading spirits in investigative chemistry in America at that time. Following his graduation, he went at once to Europe, where he worked with Ostwald at the University of Leipzig, Arrhenius in Stockholm, and Van't Hoff in Amsterdam, the three foremost physical chemists of the world at this time. It was in the laboratory of Arrhenius that he undertook the study of hydrates of sulfuric acid. The subject of hydrates in solution proved so fascinating to him that thereafter it determined the nature of the research which went on in his laboratory.

Returning to the United States, he was appointed instructor in physical chemistry at Johns Hopkins University, in 1895, and established there the first distinctive department of physical chemistry in America. In 1898 he was elected associate professor of physical chemistry, which position he held until his election to the professorship in 1903. In his research, which included a careful study of the conductivity and dissociation of electrolytes and their temperature coefficients in various solvents, he was able to show beyond doubt that the phenomenon of hydration in solutions is a rather general one. He further substantiated this belief by a detailed study of the absorption spectra of solutions. Through the generosity of the Carnegie Institution of Washington, he was enabled greatly to enlarge the scope of his researches in this field. He made numerous and important contributions to the chemical literature of his time, publishing *The Freezing Point, Boiling Point and Conductivity Methods* (1897); *The Modern Theory of Solution* (1899); *The Theory of Electrolytic Dissociation and Some of its Applications* (1900); *Outlines of Electrochemistry* (1901); *The Elements of Physical Chemistry* (1902), which went through four American editions and was translated into Italian and Russian; *Principles of Inorganic Chemistry* (1903); *Elements of Inorganic Chemistry* (1903); *The Electrical Nature of Matter and Radioactivity* (1906); *Introduction to Physical Chemistry* (1910); *A New Era in Chemistry* (1913); *The Nature of Solution* (1917), with a biographical sketch; *Practical Methods for Determining Molecular Weights* (1899), a translation of Heinrich Biltz's work. He was also joint author of ten monographs published by the Carnegie Institution of Washington, and contributed nearly a hundred articles to American, French, and German chemical journals. He was associate editor of *Zeitschrift für Physicalishe Chemie, Journal der Chemie-Physique,* and the *Journal of the Franklin Institute* of Philadelphia, and was a member of all the leading scientific and technical societies of the world. He was awarded the Longstreth medal of the Franklin Institute in 1913 for scientific discoveries.

He was a man of untiring energy and was dominated by a consuming passion for his work; he was also gifted as a teacher. In music and art he found his recreation. The son and grandson of farmers, he never lost his love for the country, and at his death he was one of the successful agriculturists of Maryland. On May 22, 1902, he was married to Harriet Brooks, the daughter of Henry Phelps Brooks, a prominent lawyer of Baltimore, and the grand-daughter of Chauncy Brooks, a well-known capitalist of that city.

[*Who's Who in America,* 1916–17; *Proc. Am. Chemical Soc.,* July 1916; *Baltimore American* and *Sun* (Baltimore), Apr. 10, 1916.] J. S. G.

JONES, HERSCHEL VESPASIAN (Aug. 30, 1861–May 24, 1928), journalist, bibliophile, was born in Jefferson, Schoharie County, N. Y., of mixed English, Scotch, and Welsh stock. His father, William S. Jones, a descendant of Welsh settlers of Massachusetts Bay Colony in 1663, kept a village store and cultivated a small farm. His mother, Helen (Merchant) Jones, was the daughter of a retired farmer of the village. Jones attended the Delaware Literary Institute, an academy of the old type, at Franklin, N. Y. His leanings toward journalism and books were both indicated early. There were only nine books in the family library, but at the age of ten he joined a subscription library. He earned the five-dollar fee by doing odd jobs. About the same time he began his first newspaper—a small sheet, printed with a lead pencil, limited to six or eight copies weekly and distributed to friends. Prevailing newspaper fashions of the day were followed by including in each issue an instalment of a "continued story" and several complete items composed by the youthful editor. At fifteen, his formal education stopped and he began to work on the staff of the *Jefferson Courier* at three dollars a week. At eighteen he bought the paper for $700. His grandfather gave him $250 and Jones gave notes for the rest. In 1883 he visited a group of western cities and selected Minneapolis as his future home. In 1885 he sold the *Jefferson Courier* at a profit of $700 and went to Minneapolis as a reporter on the *Minneapolis Journal,* with which he was continuously connected until his death. Convinced that the government forecasts of crops were unsatisfactory, in 1890 he started a market and crop report service in the *Journal.* Two notable predictions, one of heavy crops in 1900 and one of wheat-rust losses in 1904, gave him a national reputation. He traveled as much as 30,000 miles yearly gathering data for this service. In 1901 he founded the *Commercial West,* a financial and grain news weekly.

In 1908 Jones bought the *Minneapolis Journal* for $1,200,000 on an available personal fortune of $25,000. This tested to the utmost his lifelong theory that "credit, based on character and integrity" was more important than available cash. In his valedictory editorial in the *Jefferson Courier,* Feb. 25, 1885, he said: "To support a party is not always to be in accord with it." In his initial editorial as publisher of the *Minneapolis Journal* on Sept. 1, 1908, he stated: "The principles that should govern the publication of a newspaper are honesty and fairness." This independence was one of his chief characteristics as a journalist. He neither held nor sought political office of any kind. He was a director of the Associated Press and one of a group of American newspaper editors who toured the European battle-fields as guests of the British government.

Jones is perhaps even more widely known as a book-collector than as an editor. His first collection, comprising about six hundred volumes of first editions of modern authors, was one of the early first-edition collections. This was sold. His second collection, which included about 2,-

000 volumes of incunabula and early English poetry and drama, was sold at auction in New York in 1918–19 for about $400,000 at one of the notable sales of its kind. His personal library of about 3,000 volumes of standard works and his collection of early Americana are still intact. The latter, owned by his estate, is one of the most notable collections of its kind still in private ownership. His interest and taste in books and art were wide and discriminating. He collected chiefly as a means toward systematic self-culture. He was a trustee and benefactor of the Minneapolis Institute of Arts to which he gave a fine collection of prints. He bequeathed trust funds, of $25,000 each, to the Minnesota Historical Society and the library of the University of Minnesota. His rather reserved manner with mere acquaintances sometimes hid his real friendliness and wide sympathy, characteristically shown by his bequest for a fund for the relief of widowed mothers. Jones married Lydia A. Wilcox, of Jefferson, N. Y., Sept. 30, 1885. Their family included four sons and three daughters.

[J. H. McCullough, article in the *Am. Mag.*, Jan. 1924; E. C. Gale, memorial in *Minnesota Hist.*, Mar. 1929; the *Minneapolis Jour.*, May 24, 1928; and information as to certain facts from Jones's son, Jefferson Jones, and other members of his family and personal acquaintances.] F. K. W.

JONES, HUGH (*c.* 1670–Sept. 8, 1760), minister, mathematician, and historian, came to Virginia in 1716. He was probably one of the several graduates of Oxford by that name. In 1717 he was appointed to the chair of mathematics in the College of William and Mary upon the recommendation of the Bishop of London; during the next few years he served at the same time as chaplain to the House of Burgesses, minister of Jamestown, and "lecturer" in Bruton Church, Williamsburg. Meanwhile he found opportunity to support Governor Spotswood in his controversy with Commissary Blair and to compose an "Accidence to Christianity," an "Accidence to the Mathematicks," and *A Short English Grammar. An Accidence to the English Tongue,* the first English grammar written in America. Late in 1721 (W. S. Perry, *Papers Relating to the History of the Church in Virginia,* 1870, p. 249) he left the colony for England, and three years afterward brought out in London both *The Present State of Virginia* and the grammar. The former was intended to supplement existing histories of Virginia and to promote the colony's interests. Written largely out of the author's observation, in direct and sprightly style, it shows remarkable perspicacity, and has proved invaluable to subsequent local historians for its information concerning social, economic, and ecclesiastical matters in the colony during the early eighteenth century. It is further interesting for its advanced ideas upon education, including Jones's advocacy of a distinct chair of history and a school of administration at William and Mary.

Returning to America he resumed parochial work in St. Stephen's Parish, King and Queen County, Va., but early in 1726 removed with his family to Charles County, Md., where for five years he served as minister of William and Mary Parish, eking out his salary with school teaching. On Oct. 2, 1731, through Governor Calvert, he became rector of St. Stephen's (North Sassafras) Parish, Cecil County. Here he continued until his resignation a few months before his death, building up an estate, proving an efficient partisan of Lord Baltimore in the proprietary's contest with the heirs of William Penn, warring against Popery and Jesuitism, and guiding St. Stephen's to the highest degree of prosperity that it ever attained as an Episcopal parish. Learned, fearless, aristocratic, intellectually vigorous, he was a loyal Hanoverian and a most zealous churchman. The testimonials of his parishioners bear witness to his sober and exemplary life. Hardly less revealing is the desire, expressed in his will, to be buried with his feet to the westward. "He wished," he said, "to be facing his people as they arose from their graves. He was not ashamed of them."

[Rev. Hugh Jones has been repeatedly confused with two other colonial ministers of the same name, both rectors of Christ Church Parish, Calvert County, Md., as the *William and Mary Coll. Quart. Hist. Mag.*, Jan. 1902, points out. See Geo. Johnston, *Hist. of Cecil County, Md.* (1881); W. B. Sprague, *Annals of Am. Pulpit,* V (1859), 9–13; H. B. Adams, *The College of William and Mary* (1887); E. L. Goodwin, *The Colonial Church in Va.* (1927); *Archives of Md.*, VI (1888), 373, and IX (1890), 435; *Md. Hist. Mag.*, June 1923, Sept. 1924.] A. C. G., Jr.

JONES, HUGH BOLTON (Oct. 20, 1848–Sept. 24, 1927), landscape painter, born at Baltimore, Md., the son of Hugh B. and Laura Eliza Jones, began his art training at the Maryland Institute and later became a pupil of Horace W. Robbins. His first field work was done in the vicinity of his native city, and his earliest paintings were shown in Baltimore, but he sent pictures to the National Academy of Design as early as 1874. In 1876 he went to France. He made many outdoor sketches and studies in Brittany, with his headquarters at Pont-Aven, at that time a favorite resort of painters. In 1877 he made a sketching tour in Spain and North Africa. During the four years of his sojourn in Europe he exhibited several paintings at the Paris Salon and one at an international exposition in Paris. He returned to the United States in 1880 and established himself in New York, becoming a member of the Society of American Artists in 1881, and a National Academician in 1883. He was also a member of six or seven other artistic associations and three or four New York clubs. He was a regular contributor to the exhibitions of the National Academy for many years. He shared a studio with his younger brother, Francis C. Jones, a figure painter; but he spent a large part of his time in the country, finding many of his best subjects in New Jersey and New England.

His "Ferry Inn" was shown at the Centennial Exposition, Philadelphia, 1876. His "Tangiers" was purchased by W. T. Walters of Baltimore. Five of his works were in the Thomas B. Clarke collection which was sold in 1899. Medals were awarded to him at two international expositions in Paris and at the world's fairs in Chicago, 1893, St. Louis, 1904, and San Francisco, 1915. Both the Webb prize and the Shaw Fund prize were given him at the exhibition of the Society of American Artists in 1902. Two of his landscapes are in the Metropolitan Museum, New York; at the Corcoran Gallery, Washington, is his "Springtime"; other works are in the Pennsylvania Academy and the Brooklyn Institute. In his painting he held the mirror up to nature with the utmost fidelity, never adding any superfluous embroideries. His evident enjoyment of the beauty of spring foliage and skies was manifested in many ingenuous pages of fresh and delicate color. "Spring," given to the Metropolitan Museum by George I. Seney, and reproduced in Isham's *History of American Painting,* is a characteristic example. "The interest in all the minutiæ of nature which characterized the old Hudson River school is there," observes Isham (p. 444), "but the execution is surer and more artistic, and the coloring in its truthfulness and delicacy and in the absence of the brown studio tones shows the influence of the French open-air school." At the time of his death, which took place at his New York home, the artist was in his seventy-ninth year. He had never married.

[*Am. Art Annual,* 1927; Samuel Isham, *The Hist. of Am. Painting* (1905); *Who's Who in America,* 1926–27; *N. Y. Times,* Sept. 25, 1927; catalogue of the Thos. B. Clarke collection (1899); C. M. Kurtz, *Nat. Acad. Notes,* 1884, 1885.]

W. H. D.

JONES, JACOB (March 1768–Aug. 3, 1850), naval officer, was born near Smyrna, Del. His mother, *née* McDermott, died in the child's infancy, and his father, a well-to-do-farmer of Welsh-English stock, also named Jacob, died soon afterward. He had married again, and the boy was reared by his stepmother, a granddaughter of Judge Ryves Holt of the Delaware supreme court. He was educated in the academy at Lewes, Del., studied medicine for four years under Dr. James Sykes of Dover, and after further study at the University of Pennsylvania began practice in Kent County, Del. Finding progress as a physician slow, he became clerk of the Delaware supreme court. Then, after the death of his first wife, a sister of Dr. Sykes, and in the excitement of hostilities with France, on Apr. 10, 1799, at the age of thirty-one, he entered the navy as midshipman in the frigate *United States,* serving thus till the close of the war. Of a quiet, thoughtful nature, well beyond the average young officer in education and range of knowledge, he rose quickly to lieutenant, Feb. 22, 1801, and was second lieutenant in the *Philadelphia* when she grounded and was captured off Tripoli, Oct. 31, 1803. After twenty months' captivity, he was released at the end of the Tripolitan War and was in routine naval duties until the War of 1812, being promoted commander Apr. 20, 1810. In command of the sloop-of-war *Wasp,* he left Philadelphia, Oct. 13, 1812, and near midnight of the 17th, east of Hatteras, he ran into a British convoy protected by the brig *Frolic,* commanded by Capt. T. Whinyates. Having about equal broadsides, Jones attacked next day and forced the enemy's surrender after a hard-fought, close-range artillery duel of forty-three minutes, on converging courses in a heavy sea (J. F. Cooper, *History of the Navy of the United States of America,* 1839, I, 182–87). The *Wasp* was almost stripped of sails and rigging, but her own fire, delivered as she sank in the seas, was lower and more accurate, sweeping the enemy's decks and hull. When the *Wasp* closed and boarded there was no resistance. Of the 110 men in the *Frolic* not twenty remained uninjured, while the *Wasp* had but five wounded and five killed (*The Weekly Register,* Baltimore, Dec. 5, 1812; *Naval Chronicle,* London, January 1813). Unfortunately, both vessels were encountered that same day by the British 74-gun ship *Poictiers,* and being in no condition to escape were captured and taken to Bermuda; nevertheless, his victory brought Jones well-earned fame. Congress awarded him a gold medal, with $25,000 for officers and crew. Exchanged from Bermuda, he was made captain, Mar. 3, 1813, and given the frigate *Macedonian* in Decatur's squadron at New York. Owing to the British blockade, he was transferred in April 1814 to Lake Ontario, where he commanded the *Mohawk* till the close of the war. In 1815 he was again in the *Macedonian* in Decatur's squadron against Algiers. He commanded the Mediterranean Squadron, 1821–23, and, after a term as navy commissioner, the Pacific Squadron, 1826–29. Thereafter, he was on shore duty at the Baltimore station, 1829–39; at New York, 1842–45; and later in charge of the Philadelphia Naval Asylum until his death. By a second marriage he had a daughter and a son, Richard, who rose to commander in the navy, and by a third marriage, in 1821, to Ruth Lusby of Cecil County, Md., he had three daughters and a son. He was characterized in 1815 by Commodore John Rodgers as "a good officer . . . of far more than ordinary information," though—perhaps because of late entry into the service—he lacked "the particular kinds to qualify him" for the office of navy commissioner (C. O. Paullin, *Commodore John Rodgers,* 1910, p. 302).

[M. M. Cleaver, "The Life, Character and Public Services of Commodore Jacob Jones," *Papers of the Hist. Soc. of Del.*, no. XLVI (1906); Roland Ringwalt, "Commodore Jacob Jones," *Ibid.*, no. XLIV (1906); J. M. Clayton, *Address on the Life, Character and Services of Com. Jacob Jones* (Wilmington, 1851); Benjamin Folsom, *A Compilation of Biog. Sketches of Distinguished Officers in the Am. Navy* (1814); C. J. Peterson, *The Am. Navy* (1856); *Del. State Jour.*, Wilmington, Aug. 6, 1850.] A. W.

JONES, JAMES CHAMBERLAYNE (June 7, 1809–Oct. 29, 1859), governor and senator, the son of Peter and Catherine (Chappell) Jones, was born and reared near the line of Davidson and Wilson counties, Tenn., in the immediate neighborhood of Andrew Jackson's home, "The Hermitage." Losing his father in infancy, he spent his boyhood on the farm of his guardian, attending at intervals an old-field school. On Aug. 27, 1829, he was married to Sarah Watson Munford of Danville, Ky., and as a farmer settled near Lebanon, Tenn. His entrance into public life was as a member of the General Assembly of 1839. He demonstrated such ability as a stump speaker that he was chosen district elector on the Harrison ticket in 1840. To compass the defeat of James K. Polk in his second gubernatorial race in 1841, the Whigs chose Jones to be his opponent, as one fitted to carry over the enthusiasm of the "log-cabin campaign" of 1840. "Lean Jimmy," as he was dubbed by his admirers, was tall and swarthy, with a voice deep, flexible, and melodious. To match the methodical, logical, and well-trained Polk, the Whigs chose his opposite—one whose strong point was ability to fence, and, by the arts of a comedian, mimicry, raillery, and humorous thrusts, to divert the immense crowds that attended the joint debates in nearly every county of the state, Jones was elected by 3,243 votes—the first native of Tennessee to become governor of the state.

In 1843 Polk and Jones were nominated to renew the contest. Again Polk lost, by 3,837 votes. The most notable achievements of the two administrations of Jones were the commencement of the present state capitol, and the establishment of a school for the blind, at Nashville, and a school for deaf mutes, at Knoxville. In 1848 Jones was presidential elector for the state at large for Taylor and Fillmore. In 1850 he removed to Memphis and accepted the presidency of the projected Memphis & Charleston Railroad. In creating favorable sentiment and procuring subscriptions from towns and individuals he was successful; his order of ability fitted him for the task. That success aided in his election by a Whig legislature as United States senator, for the term 1851–57. He was the first senator chosen from that division of the state known as West Tennessee. Neither by his natural endowment nor by his training was he suited to a senatorial career; he was comparatively inconspicuous in that body. He was, however, seriously considered in 1852 for the vice-presidential nomination. So competent an observer as Salmon P. Chase, in February, thought "it pretty certain that Scott and Jones of Tennessee will be the nominees" (*Annual Report of the American Historical Association for the Year 1902,* II, 240). Jones in the national convention was influential in procuring the nomination of Scott over Fillmore.

Toward the close of Jones's term as senator, after the Whig party had disintegrated, Jones in a speech in the Senate (Aug. 9, 1856) announced his support of Buchanan for the presidency: "The Democratic party affords the best, if not last, hope of safety and security to the South." He canvassed Tennessee in behalf of Buchanan. Thereafter he worked for the advance of agriculture in the state, addressing the people at fairs, but he made no effort to reënter public life. Dying on his farm near Memphis at the comparatively early age of fifty, he was buried in Elmwood Cemetery in that city.

[J. M. Keating, *Hist. of the City of Memphis* (1888), I, 294; O. P. Temple, *Notable Men of Tenn.* (1912); M. W. Cluskey, *The Pol. Text-Book, or Encyc.* (1857); A. C. Cole, *The Whig Party in the South* (1913); S. G. Heiskell, *Andrew Jackson and Early Tenn. Hist.* (1918); P. E. Chappell, *A Geneal. Hist. of the Chappell, Dickie, and other Kindred Families of Va.* (1900); A. B. Fothergill, *Peter Jones and Richard Jones Geneals.* (1924); *Morning Bulletin* (Memphis, Tenn.), Oct. 30, 1859.] S. C. W.

JONES, JAMES KIMBROUGH (Sept. 29, 1829–June 1, 1908), senator from Arkansas, was the son of Nathaniel Jones and his wife Caroline Jane, daughter of Rev. Edmund Jones of Madison County, Tenn. His ancestors came from

Wales to Virginia in early colonial times, and the family later moved to North Carolina. His father and mother settled in Tennessee, but James was born in Marshall County, Miss., while his mother was visiting there. She died when her son was six years old, and three years later his father moved to Arkansas and settled on a farm in Dallas County. The boy's education was received from tutors and in private schools, which he attended irregularly because his health was frail. At the outbreak of the Civil War he enlisted in the 3rd Arkansas Cavalry (Confederate), but ill health made it impossible for him to give constant service, though he kept up his military connection until the end of the war. At its close, he engaged in farming, but was soon admitted to the bar and opened an office at Washington, Ark. In 1873 he was elected state senator as a Democrat and went to Little Rock to sustain the cause of Elisha Baxter [*q.v.*] in the Brooks-Baxter "war." He remained in the state Senate until 1879 and was president the last two years. In 1878 he was elected to the lower house of Congress, and in 1885 entered the United States Senate. The most noteworthy activity of his congressional career was his fight for tariff reform. In 1884, 1888, and 1890 he attracted national attention by the illuminating facts he presented and by the keen satire which he brought to bear on the tariff bills. In 1894 he was made chairman of a subcommittee in charge of the Wilson bill. He then took the bill to Senators Hill, Murphy, Smith, Brice, Gorman, Blanchard, and Caffrey to ascertain their minimum demands in the way of higher rates. For three weeks this work went on, and then the bill was laid before the Democratic caucus which, with Senator Hill absent, voted to accept it. After three weeks of debate it passed with 634 amendments. Before the vote was taken, President Cleveland had written to Jones, urging him, under all conditions, to get some sort of tariff bill passed. The amendments had been submitted to the President through Secretary Carlisle, and Cleveland had indicated to Jones during a personal interview that he would do almost anything to effect a compromise. While the House was discussing these amendments, a letter was read from the President expressing his keen dissatisfaction with the bill. This message was applauded in the House, but it only stimulated Gorman and others in the Senate to more stubborn resistance (Edward Stanwood, *American Tariff Controversies in the Nineteenth Century,* 1903, II, 336–55). Jones felt that the President's letter was a reflection upon himself and ceased to visit the White House. Later the President invited him to call, and explained that he did not mean to include him among the senators guilty of party perfidy, but he never made the apology public (Newberry, *post,* pp. 161–62). Jones received many commendations from various parts of the country and from members of both parties. The Dingley tariff bill he fought both in the Committee on Finance and in the Senate, but without avail. He early espoused the cause of free silver and took a prominent part in the Memphis convention (1895). Partly because of this advocacy of free silver, but largely because of his prominence in the Senate, a "boom" was started outside of Arkansas for his nomination for the presidency by the Democratic party, but he discouraged the movement and supported Richard Bland at Chicago until the nomination of Bryan. Both in this campaign and in 1900, when "imperialism" was the paramount issue, he served as chairman of the National Committee. He was interested in the Indians and sought to protect them in their rights. He also supported the Blair educational bill (1884–85), partly because it would bring better educational advantages to the negro (*Congressional Record,* 48 Cong., 1 Sess., App., pp. 332–38, *Ibid.,* 51 Cong., 1 Sess., p. 2081). After retiring from Congress he practised law in Washington until his death, though he always considered Arkansas his home. He was buried in Rock Creek Cemetery. On Jan. 16, 1863, he married Sue R. Eaton, who bore him two daughters; and after her death, he was married in 1866 to her cousin, Susan Somervell, who bore him three children.

[Farrar Newberry, *James K. Jones, The Plumed Knight of Arkansas* (1913), is the major account but contains numerous errors. See also J. W. Leonard, *Men of America* (1908); *Who's Who in America,* 1908–09; *Biog. Dir. Am. Cong.* (1928); *Journals of the Senate of Arkansas,* 1874–79; *Cong. Record,* 1881–1903; *Arkansas Gazette* (Little Rock), June 2, 1908.]

D. Y. T.

JONES, JEHU GLANCY (Oct. 7, 1811–Mar. 24, 1878), congressman, was descended from David Jones who in 1721, at the age of twelve, emigrated from Merionethshire, Wales, to join relatives in the "Welsh Tract," Radnor township, Delaware County, Pa. He later moved on to the Conestoga Valley, where, in Caernarvon Township, Berks County, his great-grandson, J. Glancy Jones, was born. His parents were Jehu Jones, a schoolmaster, and Sarah (Glancy) Jones. Destined by them for the Episcopal ministry, at sixteen he entered Kenyon College, Gambier, Ohio, and after preliminary work there, began the study of theology in Cincinnati. In 1832 he returned to Pennsylvania to marry Anna Rodman (June 23), who accompanied him back to Cincinnati, where he continued his studies until 1834. In the summer of that year he returned, with his family, to the home of his wife's parents in Bensalem Township, Bucks County, Pa., and in December was ordained deacon in the Protestant Episcopal Church by Bishop G. W. Doane [*q.v.*]. On Oct. 11, 1835, he was ordained to the priesthood in Christ Church, New Brunswick, N. J. For about three years he devoted his attention to the upbuilding of several parishes in New Jersey and then, in 1838, entered the mission field and established a church at Quincy, Gadsden County, Fla. Although he was successful in his ministry, he felt that a mistake had been made in the choice of his profession, and began the study of law. In 1841 he resigned his charge and completed his legal studies in Georgia, being admitted to the bar of that state the same year. He returned to Pennsylvania at once and was admitted to the bar at Easton, Pa., on Apr. 19, 1842. On the same day he delivered an address advocating a protective tariff before a meeting of "friends of American Industry." He took an active part in politics, being a Democrat by inheritance and a personal adherent of James Buchanan. On Dec. 31, 1844, he moved his residence to Reading, Pa., and on Jan. 7, 1845, was admitted to the Berks County bar. After holding a number of local offices, in April 1847 he was appointed district attorney for Berks County, and in May 1848 was a delegate to the National Democratic Convention and one of its vice-presidents. He was a delegate to the Democratic state conventions in 1848, 1849, and 1855, serving as president in 1855. In 1850 he was elected to the Thirty-second Congress (1851–53), but declined to become a candidate in 1852, desiring to return to his legal practice. His successor, however, died shortly after the opening of the Thirty-third Congress and Jones consented to fill the vacancy, taking his seat again on Feb. 13, 1854, and serving by successive elections until Oct. 30, 1858, when he resigned. He supported the Kansas-Nebraska bill and the Gadsden purchase, reported the bill to establish the United States court of claims, and was chairman of the committee on ways and means in the Thirty-fifth Congress. He was again a delegate to the National Democratic Convention in 1856, where he took an active part in securing the nomination of his friend Buchanan for the presidency of the United States. In the campaign which followed he was a leader of the Buchanan forces. After Buchanan's victory, he was considered for a place in the cabinet but owing to the opposition of a faction within the party he was not appointed. He was offered and declined the post of minister to Berlin. Unsuccessful as a candidate for reëlection to Congress in 1858, he resigned his seat to accept appointment as minister to Austria, in which capacity he served from Dec. 15, 1858, to Nov. 14, 1861. Returning to Reading, Pa., he withdrew from active participation in politics and resumed the practice of law for some ten years. Failing health then caused him to retire and he died in Reading after a long illness. Four of his nine children survived him.

[C. H. Jones, *The Life and Public Services of J. Glancy Jones* (2 vols., 1910), an uncritical biography by his son; E. M. Beale, *Geneal. of David Jones* (1903); *Biog. Dir. Am. Cong.* (1928); *The Twentieth Century Bench and Bar of Pa.* (1903), vol. I; *Record* (Phila.), Mar. 28, 1878.]

J. H. F.

JONES, JENKIN LLOYD (Nov. 14, 1843–Sept. 12, 1918), clergyman, editor, came in 1844 with his parents, Richard Lloyd and Mary (Thomas) Jones, from Wales, where his ancestors, Jenkin Jones and David Lloyd, were pioneer Arminian ministers. Sauk County, Wis., afforded him a meager schooling. Enlisting Aug. 14, 1862, in the 6th Battery, Wisconsin Artillery, in obedience to "conscience, not the government" (*An Artilleryman's Diary,* p. xiii), he took part in the battles of Corinth, Vicksburg, Chattanooga, and Missionary Ridge, and was mustered out July 18, 1865, a confirmed opponent of war. After teaching school in Wisconsin, 1865–66, he entered the Meadville Theological School, Meadville, Pa., from which he graduated in 1870. Married to Susan C. Barber and ordained to the Unitarian ministry the same year, he served at Winnetka, Ill., 1870–71, then at Janesville, Wis., 1871–80. With characteristic energy and originality he organized a mutual improvement society, embracing literary, scientific, civic, and philanthropic interests, that served as a pattern of many similar organizations ("Unity clubs") in Unitarian churches of the Middle West. In 1872 he began the publication of a series of Sunday School lessons for liberal churches, radically different from all contemporary courses because of their emphasis upon the evolution of man, the mythical analogies and ethical harmony of the great world religions, the flowering of Christianity into a universal religion of ethical theism (Erasmus to Emerson), and the credos in verse of great modern poets.

Into the work of the secretaryship of the Western Unitarian Conference which he filled from 1875 to 1884, he threw himself with pioneer zeal, that resulted at first in phenomenal progress but later, owing to his insistence upon ethical rather than theological unanimity as the basis of liberal fellowship and missionary work, in the withdrawal (1887–94) from the Conference of many of the conservative churches. The Conference, however, has never lost the gains and the catholic spirit of his secretaryship. In 1885 he undertook the full ministry of All Souls Church, Chicago, whose bond of union was his own work: "We join ourselves together in the interest of Morality and Religion as interpreted by the growing thought and purest lives of Humanity, hoping thereby to bear one another's burdens and to promote Truth, Righteousness and Love in the world." This church became the spiritual dynamo of the Abraham Lincoln Center, founded in 1905. Its name recalls the devotion to the Emancipator which led Jones, after a pilgrimage to the Lincoln birthplace in Hodgenville, Ky., 1904, to write in his paper, *Unity* (Mar. 24, 1904), an editorial on "The Neglected Shrine" which, through the interest of *Collier's Weekly,* led to the rehabilitation and dedication of cabin and farm as a national memorial. With William C. Gannett [*q.v.*] he wrote *The Faith That Makes Faithful* (copyright 1886). Other significant publications of his include: *Jess: Bits of Wayside Gospel* (1899); *A Search for an Infidel* (1901); *Love for the Battle-Torn Peoples* (1916).

His ideal of universal religion inspired not only his founding of the Tower Hill (Wis.) Summer School in 1889, but his general secretaryship of the World's Parliament of Religions, in connection with the World's Columbian Exposition, Chicago, 1893. As editor, 1880–1918, of *Unity,* a religious weekly dedicated to "Freedom, Fellowship and Character in Religion," he advocated most of the great social reforms of this period. He was an unrepentant member of the Ford Peace Ship Mission (December 1915–March 1916), while his editorial opposition to war in general and to the United States' participation in the World War led to the suspension of *Unity* in July and August 1918 by the postmaster-general.

He was a man of immense energy and striking appearance, stocky and sturdy, with a shaggy head of hair, full beard, and deep-set eyes. His first wife bore him a son and a daughter and died in 1911. He married Mrs. Edith Lackersteen in 1915.

[*An Artilleryman's Diary* (1914) covers Jones's boyhood and war experiences. For his later life see *Unity:* Sept. 19, 28, Oct. 10, 17, Nov. 28, Dec. 5, 12, 1918, Mar. 5, 1928. See also *A Chorus of Faith, Addresses of the Parliament of Religions* (Chicago, 1893); Wm. Kent in *American Mag.,* July 1910 and *Public,* Dec. 7, 1918; *Christian Register,* Sept. 26, 1918; *Chicago Daily Tribune,* and *Chicago Herald Examiner,* Sept. 13, 1918.]

C. H. L—e.

JONES, JOEL (Oct. 25, 1795–Feb. 3, 1860), lawyer, was born at Coventry, Conn., the son of Amasa and Elizabeth (Huntington) Jones. His father was a merchant and farmer and the first years of his life were spent on the farm. At the age of fifteen he entered the store of an uncle at Hebron, Conn., as a clerk. In his spare time he prepared himself for college, with the help of his pastor and the encouragement of his mother, and despite the opposition of his father and uncle, entered Yale College in 1813, taking rank from the first as a leader in his class. His family shortly met with financial reverses, and to support himself he tutored the sons of Judge Bristol of New Haven. At the same time, however, he maintained his academic standing and even pursued some medical studies outside of his course. Graduating with second rank in the class of 1817, he immediately entered the office of Judge Bristol and at the same time registered at the Litchfield Law School.

His family had removed to Wilkes-Barre, Pa., and as soon as his training was completed he joined them there and was admitted to the bar of Luzerne County, but subsequently moved to Easton, Pa., where he developed a large practice. He showed special ability in cases that required research into forgotten law. Perhaps his most famous case was that of *Barnet* vs. *Ihrie* (1 *Rawle's Pa. Reports,* 44, and 17 *Sergeant & Rawle's Reports,* 174), in which the remedy of assize of nuisance was revived. He took an active interest in educational affairs and was one of the founders of Lafayette College at Easton, Pa. In 1830 he was appointed one of the commissioners to revise the civil code of the state, and he wrote the report of the commission. In 1834 he moved to Philadelphia, and on Apr. 22 of the following year was elected associate judge in the district court of the city and county. Ten years later, Apr. 8, 1845, he became presiding judge of this court, but was forced by failing eyesight to resign in 1847. He was shortly elected (Dec. 15, 1847) as first president of Girard College, Philadelphia, founded under the will of Stephen Girard [*q.v.*], and he opened the institution on Jan. 1, 1848. Since, however, the duties of his office soon became irksome, and his educational ideas were not in accord with those of the board of directors, he served but eighteen months, resigning June 1, 1849. Immediately thereafter he was elected mayor of Philadelphia. Failing of reëlection the next year, he resumed his law practice, which he continued until his death.

Jones's knowledge of the law was considerable, although it was derived more from the ancient than the modern books and for this reason he sometimes found it difficult to apply his legal ideas to new problems. He regarded the law as a lofty science and its practice as the application of ethical principles in accordance with the rules of logic. A contributor to the *American Law Register* and to several English legal publications, he was also the compiler of *A Syllabus of the Law of Land Office Titles in Pennsylvania* (1850). A member of the American Philosophical Society and versed in seven languages, he was a thorough scholar in Hebrew and Greek, and a student of the Bible. He contributed to the magazines of his day on literary, philosophic, and religious subjects. For some time he edited *The Literalist,* a religious magazine in which he defended his belief in the literal fulfilment of scriptural prophecies. A volume, *Notes on Scripture* (1861), was published after his death. For some time he was a prominent leader in the Presbyterian Church. His wife was Eliza Perkins Sparhawk of Philadelphia, whom he married June 14, 1831. They had six children.

[Memoir in Jones's *Notes on Scripture* (1861); *Proc. Am. Phil. Soc.,* vol. VII (1861); W. B. Owen, *Hist. Sketches of Lafayette College* (1876); J. H. Martin, *Martin's Bench and Bar of Phila.* (1883); C. A. Herrick, *Hist. of Girard College* (1927); *Theol. and Lit. Jour.,* July 1860; *Obit. Record Grads. Yale Coll., 1859–60* (1860); *Morning Pennsylvanian* (Phila.), Feb. 4, 1860.] J. H. F.

JONES, JOHN (1729–June 23, 1791), surgeon, author of the first surgical textbook in the American colonies, was born in Jamaica, L. I., of Welsh Quaker stock, the son of Dr. Evan Jones and his wife, Mary Stephenson. His grandfather, Dr. Edward Jones, came to Pennsylvania in June 1682, and married Mary Wynne, daughter of Dr. Thomas Wynne who brought his family to Pennsylvania with William Penn on the *Welcome* later in the same year. After a course of study at a private school in New York, John Jones went to Philadelphia to begin medical studies under his uncle by marriage, Thomas Cadwalader [*q.v.*], but he received most of his education abroad, studying in London under William Hunter and Percival Pott, and in Paris under Petit and Le Dran. He also took courses at Edinburgh and Leyden (then a famous medical center), and finally obtained his degree in 1751 at the University of Rheims, where his graduation thesis (published in New York in 1765) bore the title *Observations on Wounds.* After graduation he settled in New York, where he soon became known as surgeon and obstetrician. He is said to have been the first American lithotomist, he was certainly a successful one, and his fame soon became diffused throughout the colonies. He never required over three minutes to complete the operation of lithotomy and performed it on occasion in half that time. At the outbreak of the French and Indian War he at once volunteered as surgeon, and served until the close of hostilities. In 1767, when the medical department of King's College, New York, was organized, he became professor of surgery and obstetrics. A little later, suffering from asthma, he made a long visit to London, where he improved the time by fraternizing with his former teachers and by attempting to obtain subscriptions for a hospital for New York.

In 1770, with Dr. Samuel Bard [*q.v.*] and others, he petitioned for a charter for the New York Hospital, and when the institution was opened he was made one of the attending physicians. The Revolution and the eventual destruction of the hospital by fire ended this enterprise. When New York was captured by the British he removed to Philadelphia. Although the frailty of his health kept him from being active in the field, he is given credit for an important share in organizing the medical department of the Continental Army (J. M. Toner, in *Transactions of the American Medical Association,* XXIX, 1878, p. 689). Perhaps a greater service to his country was the publication in 1775 of his *vade mecum* for the native surgeons under the title *Plain, Concise, Practical Remarks on the Treatment of Wounds and Fractures,* largely adapted from the teachings of Pott and Le Dran. Its value was increased the following year by binding with it the author's translation of Van Swieten's *Diseases Incident to Armies.* Having found the climate of Philadelphia favorable for his asthma, Jones definitely settled there in 1780, and was at once appointed attending physician to the Pennsylvania Hospital and elected president of the Humane Society. He was a personal friend of Washington, whom he attended professionally in 1790, and was the personal physician of Franklin, whom he attended in his last illness. He published "A Short Account of Dr. Franklin's Last Illness" in the *Pennsylvania Gazette* and the *Freeman's Journal,* both of Philadelphia, Apr. 21, 1790. When the College of Physicians of Philadelphia was formed in 1787, Jones was its first vice-president, and he contributed a paper, "A Case of Anthrax" (read posthumously), to the first volume of its *Transactions* (1793). A third edition of his book on wounds and fractures with the title, *The Surgical Works of the Late John Jones,* was brought out in 1795 by his friend Dr. James Mease.

[Memoir by Mease in the *Surgical Works* (1795) mentioned above; *Am. Medical and Philosophical Reg.*, Jan. 1813; *Trans. Coll. of Phys. of Phila.*, 3 ser., IX (1887); *Brooklyn Medic. Jour.*, June 1900; J. B. Beck, *An Hist. Sketch of the State of Am. Medicine before the Revolution* (1842); *A Reference Handbook of the Medic. Science* (3rd ed.), rev. by T. L. Stedman, VIII (1917), 46; *Gazette of the U. S.* (Phila.), June 25, 1791; *Pa. Gazette* (Phila.), June 29, 1791.] E. P.

JONES, JOHN B. (Dec. 22, 1834–July 19, 1881), soldier, was born in Fairfield District, S. C., the son of Henry and Nancy (Robertson) Jones. His father went to Texas in 1838, settling first in Travis County, later moving to Matagorda, and finally to Navarro. The boy attended school in Texas at Matagorda, Independence, and Rutersville, and completed his education at Mount Zion College, Winnsboro, S. C. Upon his return to Texas, he engaged successfully in farming and stock raising until the Civil War. Joining the Confederate forces, he served as private in Terry's Texas Rangers, but within a month he was made adjutant in the 15th Texas Infantry. In 1863 he was appointed adjutant-general of a brigade, with rank of captain, and the following year was recommended for the rank of major, but did not receive his commission before the war closed. Returning to Texas, at the request of friends, he went to search out a location for a colony, first in Mexico and later in Brazil, but found no place that he could recommend. In 1868 he was elected to the Texas legislature from Navarro, Hill, Kaufman, and Ellis counties, but was counted out by the Republican returning board.

His most distinguished service began on May 2, 1874, when Gov. Richard Coke appointed him major of the Frontier Battalion with instructions to clear the western border of Indians, and the interior of desperadoes. He organized six companies of Texas Rangers and established them on the Indian frontier from Red River to the Rio Grande. With a small escort he patrolled this line from one station to another, and in time developed the most competent corps of ranger captains that the service has ever known. His most notable Indian fight was that of Lost Valley, near Jacksboro, July 12, 1874. With twenty-eight men he attacked a band of a hundred or more Indians, thought to have been Kiowas, Comanches, and Apaches. Before the Indian trouble ceased, Jones turned his attention to the suppression of lawlessness among white men. The Horrell-Higgins feud was terrorizing the whole section around Lampasas. Indicative of his influence over the passions of rude men, on July 30, 1877, the Horrell faction wrote a letter to the Higginses proposing a cessation of the feud. The Higgins faction accepted the proposal. The letters are signed by the three leading members of the respective factions, and each letter was witnessed by "Jno. B. Jones, Maj. Frontier Battalion."

He knew how to use force, however. Sam Bass [*q.v.*], after robbing the Union Pacific in 1877, made his rendezvous in Denton County, Tex., and began a career of train robbing around Dallas. Finally, when Bass and his men entered Round Rock on July 19, 1878, Major Jones was there with a troop of Texas Rangers to receive him. Bass was mortally wounded and died two days later. In 1877 Jones was sent to El Paso to quell a mob that had arisen in connection with what is known as the Salt War. Here he found Americans surrounded by infuriated Mexicans, who threatened to kill them. With a Catholic priest, he went into the midst of the mob, placated it, and got the Americans free. After he left the trouble arose again, however, and the Americans were killed. A commission composed of two army officers appointed by the United States, and Major Jones, appointed by the governor of Texas, was asked to investigate the disturbance, which was international in character. Jones made a minority report in which he presented the case of the Americans. In January 1879, Gov. O. M. Roberts appointed him adjutant-general of Texas. In this office he continued to direct the activities of the Frontier Battalion until his death. On Feb. 25, 1879, he married Mrs. A. H. Anderson, widow of T. J. Anderson and daughter of Samuel Holliday. Jones is buried in Oakwood Cemetery, Austin, Tex.

[Numerous letters and official reports in office of the adjutant-general, Austin, Tex.; *Report of the Adjutant-General of the State of Tex.*, 1875–81; W. S. Speer and J. H. Brown, *Encyc. of the New West* (1881); *Biog. Encyc. of Tex.* (1880); *Biog. Souvenir of the State of Tex.* (1889); *Austin Daily Statesman*, July 19, 1881; "El Paso Troubles in Texas," *House Exec. Doc. No. 93*, 45 Cong., 2 Sess. (1878).] W. P. W.

JONES, JOHN BEAUCHAMP (Mar. 6, 1810–Feb. 4, 1866), journalist and author, was born in Baltimore, Md. Part of his boyhood was spent in Kentucky and the wilds of Missouri, out of which pioneer existence, crowded with vicissitude and adventure, grew several of his novels. Seemingly he early determined upon letters as his profession, for in 1841 Poe observed that Jones, who was then editing the *Baltimore Saturday Visiter* "with much judgment and general ability," had "been connected for many years past with the lighter literature of Baltimore" (*Autography,* Virginia Edition, 1902, XV, 235). Having failed to find a publisher for his first novel, *Wild Western Scenes,* Jones was printing it serially in the *Visiter* at the time of

Poe's encomium. When in 1841 he issued it in volume form at his own expense it proved popular, and in the next twenty years 100,000 copies were sold. Despite its sentimentality and an occasionally florid style, the book abounds in broad humor, vigorous incident, and local color, which, with some strong pieces of masculine character portrayal, have deservedly made it a minor classic of the frontier.

From the *Visiter* Jones, somewhat to his misfortune, passed to the *Madisonian,* organ of the Tyler administration, of which he was editor in 1842 when Congress, "to humiliate and mortify" the President (L. G. Tyler, *Letters and Times of the Tylers,* 3 vols., 1884–96, II, 311), took the executive printing from that periodical and let it out on contract. Beyond his marriage in 1840 to Frances T. Custis of Accomack County, Va., an offer of the chargéship to Naples during Polk's administration, and a few months of European travel, the rest of his life down to 1861 is largely the record of his publications, which include *Books of Visions* (1847) and a poem, *Rural Sports* (1849), *The Western Merchant* (1849), *The Rival Belles,* first published as *The Spanglers and Tingles* (1852), *Adventures of Colonel Gracchus Vanderbomb* (1852), *The Monarchist* (1853), *The Life and Adventures of a Country Merchant* (1854), *Freaks of Fortune, or the History of Ned Lorn* (1854), *The War Path* (1858), and *Wild Southern Scenes* (1859). Of these, only the last, an amusing and patriotically instructive narrative of the ills of disunion, promised to rival the popularity of his first book; but it was entombed by the stress of contemporary events, and republication two years later as *Secession, Coercion, and Civil War* failed to revivify it.

In 1857 he established in Philadelphia the weekly *Southern Monitor,* devoted to the interests of the South and intended to temper the rising spirit of sectionalism, and edited it until the sailing of the expedition for the relief of Sumter. He proceeded forthwith to Montgomery, Ala., to seek and obtain clerical work in the Confederate War Department which might afford him opportunity to write "a full and authentic Diary of the transactions of the government." The result, published in two volumes as *A Rebel War Clerk's Diary* (1866), was a valuable piece of journalism, terse, direct, and simply written for the most part, and sensible, if uninspired. Its historical worth is lessened by the author's prejudices and the vehemence of his impatience with Confederate authorities—there are also certain obvious later interpolations; nevertheless, it furnishes a fairly minute and extensive record of one important phase of the Confederacy's internal history, along with considerable light on the economic and social life of Richmond during 1864–65. Although Jones's industry and cheerfulness did not diminish, the deprivations of the war years, coupled with an enervating disease, had sapped his vitality, and he died at Burlington, N. J. (where he had resided while editing the *Southern Monitor*), while the *Diary* was in the press.

[There are few records bearing on Jones's life, other than the scattered autobiographical details in his books and prefaces, and an obituary notice, clipped from an unnamed New Jersey paper, now in possession of his daughter, Mrs. Fannie E. Ladd, of Los Angeles, Cal.; his strictures upon the Confederate leaders made him unpopular in the South, and he has consequently been neglected. Gamaliel Bradford, "A Confederate Pepys," *American Mercury,* Dec. 1925, discusses the *Diary* at length, but does not treat of him biographically.]

A. C. G., Jr.

JONES, JOHN PAUL (July 6, 1747–July 18, 1792), naval officer, known as John Paul until about 1773, was born in southwestern Scotland in the parish of Kirkbean, Kirkcudbrightshire. His father, John Paul, who was the gardener of William Craik, a member of the Scottish squirearchy and owner of the estate of "Arbigland" in Kirkbean, married Jean Macduff, the daughter of a small farmer in a neighboring parish. John, the fifth child of this marriage, was born in the gardener's cottage, a small one-story stone house, overlooking Solway Firth. After a brief period of education at the parish school in Kirkbean, he, at the age of twelve, crossed the Solway, which separated his native shire from Cumberland, England, and entered into the service of a shipowner of the port of Whitehaven as an apprentice. His first voyage, made in the *Friendship,* took him to Fredericksburg, Va., where his elder brother William was established as a tailor. During the stay of his ship at this port he lived with his brother and employed his spare time in studying navigation. Owing to reverses in the affairs of his employer, his apprenticeship was terminated and he obtained the berth of third mate on the slaver *King George.* At the age of nineteen he became first mate on the slaver *Two Friends.*

In 1769–70 he commanded the merchantman *John* of Dumfries and made two voyages in her to the West Indies. While at Tobago during the second voyage, he flogged Mungo Maxwell, carpenter of the *John,* for neglect of duty, and a few weeks later Maxwell died at sea. John Paul was charged by Maxwell's father with the murder of his son and was imprisoned in the tolbooth of Kirkcudbright. Procuring his release on bail, he subsequently obtained affidavits establishing his innocence. In 1773 he found himself again at Tobago, this time as master of the *Betsey* of London. Here his crew mutinied and in a fracas its ring-leader was killed, by rushing upon a sword in the hand of the master—according to John Paul's account. As the witnesses to the killing were hostile to the master, his friends advised him to go to America *incognito* and to remain there until a court martial could be assembled at the island. Accepting this advice, he proceeded to Fredericksburg, Va., and added "Jones" to his name, probably in order to conceal his identity. There is a tradition in the family of Willie Jones [*q.v.*], of North Carolina, and also in that of his brother Allen Jones [*q.v.*], that the name was derived from that family, but these traditions are unsupported by contemporary evidence.

The outbreak of the Revolution found Jones unemployed, living partly on the generosity of strangers. The hour of opportunity had struck and none was more likely to heed its stroke than this young Scottish adventurer. Going to Philadelphia before the Continental Congress had organized a navy, he established friendly relations with Joseph Hewes of North Carolina and Robert Morris of Pennsylvania, two influential members of Congress greatly interested in naval affairs. On Dec. 7, 1775, he was commissioned lieutenant. Before that date he had been employed in fitting out the *Alfred,* the first naval ship procured by Congress and the first to fly the Continental flag, when hoisted by Jones on Dec. 3. In the first navy list, Jones's name led the lieutenants and he was the ranking officer in that list chosen from the colonies south of Pennsylvania. In the first expedition of the Continental navy, early in 1776, resulting in the capture of New Providence and an engagement with the warship *Glasgow,* Jones, serving as the first lieutenant of the *Alfred,* had little chance to distinguish himself. It was quite otherwise when later in the year he was given command of the *Providence,* and still later of a small fleet, and was promoted captain. He soon established a reputation for professional success that was second to none in the navy. In a cruise in the *Providence,* he captured sixteen prizes and destroyed the fisheries at Canso and Isle Madame; and in a second cruise he took the transport *Mellish,* laden with a valuable cargo of soldiers' clothing, a privateer of ten guns, and several smaller vessels.

On Oct. 10, 1776, Congress determined the rank of the naval captains and placed Jones eighteenth in its list. He protested, giving excellent reasons in support of his claim to higher rank. As a newcomer in America who had entered the navy by way of the South, he was unpopular with many of its officers, mostly from the North, and his undisguised contempt of some of them aggravated his unpopularity. Congress, however, had come to place a high estimate on his professional abilities and was disposed to give him the best of the berths at its disposal. On June 14, 1777, it appointed him to command the sloop *Ranger.* Later the marine committee directed him to proceed to France with this ship and report to the American commissioners at Paris, and assured him that he should be given command of the frigate *Indien,* building on Continental account at Amsterdam—an attractive proposal to the rising young captain as it provided an unusual chance for acquiring distinction as well as an escape from the interference of politicians and political skippers. On arriving in France in December 1777, he suffered the severe disappointment of failing to receive the expected command, as the commissioners for political reasons transferred the *Indien* to the king of France.

While the *Ranger* was quite insufficient for Jones's larger schemes, he decided to make a cruise in her and accordingly on Apr. 10, 1778, sailed from Brest for the Irish Sea and the waters long familiar to him. First, he descended upon Whitehaven and after spiking the guns of its forts attempted to burn its shipping, but his plans miscarried. Next, he visited the Scottish coast for the purpose of seizing the Earl of Selkirk, whom he proposed to hold as a hostage for the proper treatment of American prisoners, but failed to find the earl at home. His crew, however, seized some of the family plate, which Jones later purchased from them and returned to the family. Lastly, he captured the British naval sloop *Drake* after a sharp action of a little more than an hour—the chief event of the cruise. The *Ranger,* which was of superior force, was better handled and fought than the *Drake.* Jones regained Brest on May 8, after an absence of twenty-eight days, with numerous prisoners, having taken seven prizes. From this cruise, which greatly alarmed the British coast, dates Jones's English reputation as a pirate or corsair. The enemy, always bitter toward him, was in the habit of saying that he fought "with a halter around his neck"—an allusion to his misfortunes at Tobago.

The cruise of the *Ranger* augmented Jones's reputation in Paris and in June he was called there for consultation. At Versailles he discussed with De Sartine, the French minister of marine, various plans for his employment. On

Feb. 4, 1779, De Sartine wrote to him that the King had placed under his command the French ship *Duras* of forty guns—a wornout East Indiaman which Jones renamed the *Bonhomme Richard* (*Poor Richard*) as a compliment to Franklin. A joint naval and military expedition against some of the larger English towns, in which the troops were to be commanded by Lafayette and the sea force by Jones, was planned by Franklin and the French government, but was finally abandoned. By the end of the summer a small squadron consisting of five naval vessels and two privateers had been fitted out and was at L'Orient ready to sail. The fleet, composed of diverse and discordant elements, had but one bond of union, its commander. It sailed under American colors, but its expense was borne by the French government.

Jones went to sea on Aug. 14 and sailing along the west coast of Ireland and around Scotland reached the east coast of Yorkshire, having taken seventeen ships and made an unsuccessful attempt to reach Leith and lay it under contribution. On Sept. 23 off Flamborough Head he fell in with the Baltic trade of forty-one sail, convoyed by his Majesty's ships *Serapis,* 44, Capt. Richard Pearson, and *Countess of Scarborough,* 20, Commander Thomas Piercy. Only three of Jones's ships took part in the engagement that ensued. The *Pallas* confined her attention to the *Countess of Scarborough,* which she forced to surrender. The *Alliance,* owing to her disgruntled commander, the eccentric Capt. Pierre Landais [*q.v.*], fired only a few shots, which damaged the *Richard* more than the *Serapis.* The *Richard,* essentially a twelve-pounder, one-decked vessel, engaged the *Serapis,* an eighteen-pounder, two-decked vessel. Thus outclassed, Jones's only hope of success lay in close action and the use of his musketry. By skilful maneuvering he placed the *Richard* alongside the *Serapis* and lashed the two ships together, stem to stern, with the muzzles of their guns touching. The engagement, which lasted more than three hours, ranks as one of the most desperate and sanguinary sea-fights in naval history. The *Richard* was so badly damaged that she was kept from sinking only by the steady use of her pumps. Both ships were set on fire in various places, and "the scene," Jones wrote, "was dreadful beyond the reach of language." The *Serapis* was compelled to strike her colors. "The achievement of the victory," in the words of A. S. Mackenzie, adopted by Admiral Mahan, "was wholly and solely due to the immovable courage of Paul Jones. The *Richard* was beaten more than once; but the spirit of Jones could not be overcome. . . . Pearson was a brave man . . . but, had . . . [he] been equally indomitable, the *Richard,* if not boarded from below, would, at last, have gone down with her colors still flying in defiance" (Mackenzie, *post,* I, 205–06; *Scribner's Magazine,* August 1898, p. 213).

On Oct. 3, 1779, Jones reached the Texel, Holland, with his squadron, but not with the *Richard,* for she was so badly injured that she sank the second day after the fight. Here he was beset with many difficulties, as Holland was at this time neutral. In compliance with the strict orders of George III, the British ambassador at The Hague requested the Dutch government to seize the ships and crews captured by the "pirate, Paul Jones, of Scotland, who is a rebel subject and a criminal of the state" (Sherburne, *post,* p. 135). Finally, the French government took possession of the prizes, the prisoners, and the fleet, with the exception of the *Alliance,* to which Jones transferred his flag. Ordered by the Dutch to leave, he sailed in December, and, eluding the British ships watching for him, cruised for a week or more off Cape Finisterre and to the southward in search of prizes before putting in to Corunna. Thence he sailed for L'Orient, where he arrived on Feb. 10, 1780. He began immediately to refit the *Alliance* preparatory to returning to America.

In April Jones went to Paris to expedite the sale of his prize, hoping to obtain money for his dissatisfied crew. His fame had preceded him and he found the French capital, always avid for a novelty, eager to lionize him. Fate had cast him for a part he was delighted to play. As the popular hero of the American Revolution, he was everywhere received with applause and adulation. The Masonic Lodge of the Nine Sisters gave a festival in his honor and ordered a bust of him to be executed by Houdon. The Queen presented him with a fob chain and seal, and the King, with a gold-hilted sword of fine workmanship, on which was engraved an inscription in Latin, which may be translated, "reward of Louis XVI to a strenuous defender of the rights of the sea." As a further reward the King sent to his minister in Philadelphia the cross of the Institution of Military Merit, with instructions to confer it on the naval hero after obtaining the consent of Congress. As a young bachelor, Jones tasted freely of the pleasures of Parisian society. From this period date his many friendships or flirtations with Parisian women, usually married and sometimes titled: with Countess La Vendahl, who painted the miniature of him now at the Naval Academy; with "Madame T," said to have been the natural daughter of Louis XV; and with "Delia," who wrote him impassioned letters, to which he replied in a much lower key. He often composed verse for his lady loves, which has been much admired by his panegyrists.

Detained longer than he should have been by the soft caresses of the Parisians, Jones returned to L'Orient where, soon after his arrival, while he was on shore, the command of the *Alliance* was seized by Landais, her former commander, supported by many of her officers and crew and by Arthur Lee, at one time American commissioner. Jones finally yielded rather than insist on his rights at the cost of bloodshed and the ship sailed for America without him. He next took command of the *Ariel,* loaned by the French government for the transportation of military supplies to America. Sailing in December, he captured the British ship *Triumph,* which however escaped by a discreditable ruse. A conspiracy among the Englishmen of the crew, he suppressed by placing the leaders in irons. On Feb. 18, 1781, he arrived at Philadelphia, having been absent from America three and a fourth years.

On Feb. 27 Congress, after expressing its "high sense of the distinguished bravery and military conduct" of Jones, consented to his acceptance of the cross of the Institution of Military Merit, and soon thereafter the French minister gave an entertainment attended by the principal residents of Philadelphia and conferred on the naval hero this decoration, which entitled him to be addressed as "Chevalier." On Apr. 14 Congress formally thanked him. While in Philadelphia he brought to the attention of Congress his early grievance in respect to naval rank and a committee of that body proposed to make him a rear-admiral. Some of the older officers remonstrated and prevented a resolution to that effect from passing. A compromise was agreed to and on June 26 Jones was unanimously elected to command the *America,* the first and only seventy-four in the Continental navy, then building at Portsmouth, N. H. It was at this time that the Board of Admiralty examined him respecting his European enterprises and elicited from him detailed replies, in every respect highly creditable to him. Before leaving Philadelphia he submitted his personal accounts showing that he had not received a dollar of pay for his five years of service. He is said to have advanced considerable sums on government account and in the end to have lost by his advances.

Reaching Portsmouth late in August 1781, Jones remained there more than a year engaged in the disheartening task of constructing one of the largest of naval vessels with insufficient means and inexperienced workmen. When at last the *America* was launched, and Congress had presented her to the French government, he returned to Philadelphia where his friend Robert Morris, now agent of marine, had tried in vain to procure for him a small squadron. Jones now succeeded in obtaining the permission of Congress to embark on board the French fleet of Marquis de Vaudreuil, then at Boston, for the purpose of improving himself in his profession, and more especially in the management of fleets. He was given quarters on the flagship *Triomphante.* The fleet cruised four months in the West Indies and doubtless afforded its observant guest many new ideas, although part of the time he was dangerously ill.

In 1783, as well as earlier, Jones gave the American government the benefit of his knowledge of naval organization and administration. His professional writings are well composed, for he had considerable facility with the pen, and they contain not a few original ideas and just reflections. He had studied naval history, and had observed closely naval practice. In the science as well as in the art of his profession he was much superior to most of the Continental captains. In his plans for the ships under his command he often disregarded his pecuniary interests and chose those enterprises that were best adapted to winning the war. He doubtless understood his own motives when he asserted that he fought for "glory." Few servants of the Republic have deserved better of it, and his achievements redound to its fame. While attached to America and devoted to her cause, he could however profess that he was a "citizen of the world" and that he had drawn his sword only "from principles of philanthropy" and in support of "the dignity of human nature" (Sherburne, *post,* pp. 59, 82).

Jones's excellences are apparent from his achievements—indomitable courage, unfaltering faith in himself, and ability to conceive daring schemes and to execute them with insufficient means. That the French and American governments were not remiss in paying him honors was largely due to his great skill in promoting his own interests. His defects, both of taste and character, sprang from his indifferent breeding and education. These he never completely overcame, although in his maturity he associated with superior persons and was a constant reader of books. His principal fault was vanity. Often obsequious to those above him, he sometimes forgot what was due to those below him and to his own character as an officer.

On Nov. 1, 1783, Congress, in response to an

application by Jones, no longer in the navy, which was discontinued at the close of the Revolution, passed a resolution recommending him to the American minister in Paris as agent to solicit, under the direction of the minister, the payment of monies due to America for the prizes taken in European waters by his ships. A few days later, after giving bond to Robert Morris, superintendent of finance, for the sum of two hundred thousand dollars, Jones sailed for France on the packet *Washington.* Soon after his arrival at Paris, Franklin empowered him to act as agent for the collection of prize monies. He was cordially received by Castries, minister of marine, who presented him to the King. The negotiations, which were with Castries, began on Feb. 1, 1784, and an agreement was reached in the following October, but on one pretext or another payment was long delayed. Jones's bill for his services was disputed by the American board of treasury, but was allowed by Congress in view of the difficulties of his mission.

As Jones had claims against Denmark in respect to some of his prizes, he set out from Paris in the spring of 1787 for Copenhagen, but at Brussels he decided to postpone his mission and return to America, where his private affairs demanded his attention. He therefore did not arrive at Copenhagen until March 1788. He was kindly received by the Danish minister of foreign affairs and was presented to the chief personages of the royal palace, but the minister refused to negotiate. Before Jones left Copenhagen, King Christian granted him an annual pension of fifteen hundred crowns, Danish money, as an appreciation of the regard which he had shown to the Danish flag during his cruises in European waters. From delicacy, he for a time declined to receive the pension. Three years later, however, when in need of money, he decided to avail himself of it, but found that the King's promises were an empty compliment.

During Jones's last visit to America, in the summer and fall of 1787, Congress on Oct. 16 resolved unanimously that a gold medal should be presented to him in commemoration of his valor and brilliant services, and that Thomas Jefferson, the American minister in Paris, should have it executed, with proper devices. Jones was the only officer of the Continental navy thus distinguished. On the same day Congress delivered to him a letter requesting the King of France to permit him to embark on the French fleets of evolution, as he was desirous of perfecting himself in his profession. Soon after he reached Paris in December, however, he received an offer from the Empress Catherine to enter the Russian navy and take part in her war with the Turks. Jones expressed his willingness to enter the Russian service, provided he was given the rank of rear-admiral. This was readily granted. While he eagerly embraced the new opportunity to acquire fresh fame, he wrote to Jefferson that he could "never renounce the glorious title of *a citizen of the United States*" (Sherburne, *post,* p. 298). On the failure of his mission at Copenhagen, he hastened to St. Petersburg where he was cordially received by the Empress, upon whom he made a good impression, and was warmly welcomed by all classes except the English. Proceeding to the Black Sea, he on May 26, 1788, raised his flag on the *Vladimir* and took command of the squadron of sailing ships. The flotilla of galleys was commanded by Prince Nassau-Siegen, a French adventurer, jealous of Jones. Both were responsible to Potemkin, a Russian prince, who favored the Frenchman and opposed the American. Under these circumstances, Jones's position from the first was an impossible one. He played an important part in several successful engagements with the Turkish fleet, but the credit was given to others. He was steadily undermined by the intrigues of his enemies and in October was deprived of his command. His only reward was the decoration of the cross of the Order of St. Anne. In the spring of 1789 his enemies circulated a story that he had violated the person of a young girl. His period of usefulness in Russia was at an end and he was given a furlough for two years, doubtless meant to be permanent. In September he left St. Petersburg for Paris, where he arrived in June 1790, having been sounded on the way in respect to his acceptance of a commission in the Swedish navy to fight Russia.

No longer a popular hero, Jones, a bachelor, spent the last two years of his life in Paris, in comfortable lodgings, with a few faithful friends. His health, long impaired, now slowly declined. His disappointment over his Russian experiences aggravated his bodily afflictions. He had a few good friends in America who did not forget him. On June 1, 1792, Jefferson, now secretary of state, wrote to him that President Washington had appointed him commissioner to treat with Algiers on the subjects of peace and the ransoming of prisoners. He died, however, before the letter reached Paris.

His will, in which he named Robert Morris executor, was drawn up a few hours before his death by Gouverneur Morris, the American minister. He left a respectable estate from which his heirs, after losing part of it, realized about

$40,000. Although he detested the French Revolution, the National Assembly, desirous of honoring the memory of a man who had "so well served the cause of liberty," sent a deputation of twelve of its members to his funeral. He was buried in the Protestant Cemetery in Paris, in a leaden coffin in order that his remains, in case the United States should claim them, might be the more easily removed.

Jones was homely, small, thin, and active. There was little or nothing about his appearance that attracted particular attention. His secretary or clerk, Midshipman Nathaniel Fanning, who was an excellent observer, described him as a "man of about five feet six inches high, well shaped below his head and shoulders, rather round shouldered, with a visage fierce and warlike, and wore the appearance of great application to study, which he was fond of" ("Fanning's Narrative," p. 117). Houdon in his statue (1780) of Jones, one of the finest works of that master, depicted a strong, seafaring face, prematurely aged, with an expression of decision and self will.

A movement for the return of Jones's remains to America began in 1845 when Col. John H. Sherburne of New York wrote to Secretary of the Navy George Bancroft requesting that they be brought home on one of the vessels of the Mediterranean Squadron. Although he received no reply, Sherburne continued his efforts and in 1851 obtained an order directing Capt. Joshua R. Sands of the *St. Lawrence* to receive the remains at Southampton. The relatives of Jones in Scotland interfered and Sherburne's plan was dropped. In 1899 Gen. Horace Porter [*q.v.*], the American ambassador in Paris, began an extensive and laborious search for the remains and six years later cabled the government at Washington that he had found them and that the identification was complete in every particular. In the summer of 1905 they were conveyed to Annapolis by a squadron of American naval vessels under the command of Rear-Admiral Charles D. Sigsbee, accompanied by a French cruiser. In the following year commemorative exercises were held in the armory of the Naval Academy in the presence of a distinguished audience, and with addresses by President Roosevelt, Ambassador Jusserand, and Gen. Porter. In 1913 the remains were placed in the crypt of the chapel of the Naval Academy, in one of the most ornamental and elaborate tombs in America, erected by Congress at a cost of $75,000. Porter's proof of identification, while not absolute, appears to have carried conviction to most minds. He was unfortunate however in the use that he made of the fictions of A. C. Buell's *Paul Jones* (1900). Park Benjamin [*q.v.*], a naval writer, Charles H. Hart [*q.v.*], an expert in portraiture, and other skeptics subjected the evidence to analysis and reached the verdict "not proven."

In 1912 a national monument to Jones, erected by the federal government, was unveiled in Potomac Park, Washington. This memorial and the one at Annapolis will long serve to remind his countrymen of his name and deeds. The writings of Cooper, Dumas, Melville, Churchill, and other novelists, who base some of their stories upon his romantic life, will help to keep alive his fame. One of the pithy sayings attributed to him—his reply to Captain Pearson's "Have you struck?"—may even attain immortality: "I've just begun to fight."

[J. H. Sherburne, *Life and Character of the Chevalier John Paul Jones* (1825); R. C. Sands, *Life and Correspondence of John Paul Jones* (1830); *Memoirs of Rear-Admiral Paul Jones* (2 vols., 1830); A. S. Mackenzie, *The Life of Paul Jones* (2 vols., 1841); Mrs. Reginald de Koven, *Life and Letters of John Paul Jones* (1913); J. F. Cooper, *Lives of Distinguished Am. Naval Officers* (1846), II, 5–112; C. H. Lincoln, *A Calendar of John Paul Jones MSS. in the Lib. of Cong.* (1903); *Jours. of Cont. Cong.*, 1775, 1777, 1781, 1783, 1787; A. T. Mahan, "John Paul Jones in the Revolution," *Scribner's Mag.*, July, Aug. 1898; D. C. Seitz, *Paul Jones* (1917), bibl., pp. 167–327; "Fanning's Narrative," *Pubs. of the Naval Hist. Soc.*, vol. II (1912); C. O. Paullin, *Diplomatic Negotiations of Am. Naval Officers* (1912), pp. 11–42; F. A. Golder, *John Paul Jones in Russia* (1927); "John Paul Jones Commemoration at Annapolis," *House Doc. No. 804*, 59 Cong., 1 Sess.; C. H. Hart and E. Biddle, *Memoirs of the Life and Works of Jean Antoine Houdon* (1911), pp. 125–54; Park Benjamin, "Is It Paul Jones's Body?" in N. Y. *Independent*, July 20, 1905; *Trans. and Jour. of Procs. of the Dumfriesshire and Galloway Natural Hist. and Antiquarian Soc., 1907–08* (1909), pp. 179–85.]

C. O. P.

JONES, JOHN PERCIVAL (Jan. 27, 1829–Nov. 27, 1912), senator from Nevada, was born in Herefordshire, England, of Welsh ancestry. He was the son of Thomas and Mary (Pugh) Jones who emigrated to the United States while he was still an infant and settled in Cleveland, Ohio, where the boy spent his youth and received his formal education in the public schools. From the Western Reserve with its invigorating pioneer atmosphere he turned to the gold mines of California in the first year of the gold rush. With several other young men he obtained a small vessel, in which they crossed the Great Lakes, sailed down the St. Lawrence, and around the Horn to San Francisco. In Trinity County, Cal., he engaged in farming as well as the new work of mining. Here also he served as sheriff when that was an arduous post, represented his county in the state legislature, and, later, ran unsuccessfully for the lieutenant-governorship. In 1867 he followed the tide of emigration to the

Washoe country in western Nevada, became superintendent of the famous Crown Point mine, and soon was part owner. When the stock of the company rose from two dollars to eighteen hundred dollars his fortune was assured so that he was in a position to use his qualities of leadership in the political life of the new state of Nevada. In 1873 he was elected by the state legislature as a Republican to succeed James W. Nye in the United States Senate, where he continued to sit for the next thirty years. He was an ardent advocate of free-silver theories from 1875 to the close of his life, but only once, in 1897, was he elected as a silver candidate. In 1900 he returned to the Republican party. In the Senate he achieved important results for the Western states as a member of the committee on post offices and post roads, but his most important service was in the sphere of mining legislation and on the problem of bimetallism. When, as a member of the committee on mines and mining, he was appointed chairman of the monetary commission, organized under a joint resolution of Congress on Aug. 15, 1876, he gave, as was his habit of life, his most careful attention. On two trips to Europe he had devoted himself to the question of a standard of money, and, after months of labor, his committee submitted an exhaustive report on the causes and effects of the change that had taken place in the relative value of gold and silver and advised the restoration of the double standard in this country ("Report and Accompanying Documents of the United States Monetary Commission," *Senate Report 703,* 44 Cong., 2 Sess., 2 vols., 1877–79). This report continues to be valuable for its compilation of data on the history of the precious metals and for its reflection of the economic thought of the period. When he was over eighty years of age he retired from active life to spend his declining years at the great house he had built in Santa Monica, where he had been an early land speculator and promoter.

In January 1861 he married Mrs. Cornelia (Conger) Greathouse, the daughter of Judge Thomas Conger of Sacramento, and some years later he married the daughter of Eugene A. Sullivan of San Francisco.

[Collection of pamphlets containing Jones's speeches in N. Y. Pub. Lib.; statements of Roy Jones, Mrs. R. K. Walton, and George Wharton James; L. A. Ingersoll, *Ingersoll's Century Hist., Santa Monica Bay Cities* (1908); Myron Angel, *Hist. of Nevada* (1881); H. H. Bancroft, *Hist. of Nev., Col., and Wyo.* (1890); *Los Angeles Times,* Nov. 28, 1912.]

J. E. W.

JONES, JOHN PETER (Sept. 4, 1847–Oct. 3, 1916), missionary, the youngest of the eight children of Peter and Sarah (Williams) Jones, was born at Wrexham, Denbighshire, Wales. There he secured his primary education, and there, also, at the age of twelve, he went to work in the coal mines. In 1865, he visited the United States for a year, where, after returning to Wales for a brief stay, he took up his residence. Toward the end of 1866 he went to work in the mines of Pennsylvania and later, in those of Ohio. At Shenandoah City, Pa., he identified himself with a Welsh congregation, and at Youngstown, Ohio, he often preached in his native tongue to the Welsh miners. He discovered thereby that he had the "gift" and decided to devote his life to the Christian ministry. Having saved over a thousand dollars from his wages, he entered the Western Reserve College, then located at Hudson, ranking third in his class. In the fall of the same year he entered Andover Theological Seminary, Andover, Mass., from which he graduated in 1878. On Aug. 13, 1878, at Hudson, he was married to Sarah Amy, daughter of one of the college professors, Henry B. Hosford. Four sons and two daughters were born to them. On Aug. 20 of the same year he was ordained to the Congregational ministry.

During his college days his attention had been turned toward India by the work there of a distant relative and notable missionary, Jacob Chamberlain [*q.v.*], and while at Andover he had applied to the American Board of Commissioners for Foreign Missions for appointment to that field. On Sept. 7, 1878, he and his wife sailed from New York and arrived at Madura, South India, on Dec. 16. From the autumn of 1879 until early in 1883 Jones was stationed in Manamadura, an important center in the native state of Sivaganga, Madura District. There he learned Tamil and had oversight of ten congregations, three of which were composed entirely of Christian communicants. In 1883 he was transferred to Pasumalai (near Madura), to take charge of the Seminary and its associated schools, but in June of that year, owing to the death of the Rev. John Russell, he was suddenly moved into Madura to take charge of the station and to serve as secretary-treasurer of the Mission. In 1884 he opened Madura's first Christian high school, and within two months three hundred pupils were enrolled, many of whom came of the best Hindu families. He continued energetically the station's program of evangelism in the town and among the outlying villages, instructing his evangelists, however, to preach without abusing the gods of Hinduism.

The last period of Jones's missionary career, from 1892 to 1914, was spent in Pasumalai, where a theological school had grown from one of the departments of the seminary and in 1892 had become an important institution. He served primarily as its principal, thus assuming charge of the training of pastors, teachers, and catechists for the entire Mission. He collaborated with Rev. J. C. Perkins in the introduction of annual harvest festivals throughout the Mission, and was chosen first president of the South India Christian Endeavor Union (organized, Pasumalai, 1897), in which capacity he traveled over India and Burma. The management of the Mission Press fell to his lot, and the editorship of the Mission periodical, *Satyavartamani*. He produced many books, including—in Tamil—an outline of Christian theology, a textbook on Christian evidences, and a life of Christ. Among his English writings are *India's Problem, Krishna or Christ* (1903), *India, its Life and Thought* (1908), *The Teaching of Jesus Our Lord* (1908), and *The Modern Missionary Challenge* (1910). He was decorated by the British Government with the Kaisar-i-Hind medal, and in 1909 he was one of twelve "apostles" selected from the fields of the American Board to conduct in America a "Together Campaign" on the Board's behalf. He retired from the Madura Mission in 1914 and spent the remaining two years of his life on the faculty of the Kennedy School of Missions, Hartford, Conn. He died in Hartford and was buried in Oberlin, Ohio.

[Files of the *Missionary Herald*, esp. Nov. 1916; alumni records of Western Reserve Univ.; *Congreg. Yearbook*, 1916; *Hartford Courant*, Oct. 4, 1916.]

J. C. A—h—r.

JONES, JOHN TAYLOR (July 16, 1802–Sept. 13, 1851), first American missionary to Siam, serving from 1833 until death, was born at New Ipswich, N. H., the son of Elisha and Persia (Taylor) Jones. At the academies of his native village and of Bradford he obtained his preparatory education. After a year at Brown University he transferred to Amherst College, where he graduated in 1825. He then spent three years in Andover Theological Seminary and one year at Newton Theological Institute. Upon completion of his studies he accepted appointment to the mission in Burma, just then notable because of the work of Adoniram Judson [*q.v.*]. He was married to Eliza Coltman Grew of Hartford, Conn., on July 14, 1830, and on July 28 he was ordained to the Baptist ministry. With his wife he sailed from Boston, Aug. 2, arriving at Moulmein, Feb. 17, 1831.

After a year and a half it was decided by the Burma mission that the two should go to Siam and establish a new mission. They reached Bangkok, after a six months' journey, on Mar. 25, 1833. Jones was well qualified to be a pioneer missionary both by native characteristics and academic attainments. He had the traits of self-reliance, patient endurance, clear-sightedness, capacity to labor in solitude, and an aptitude for languages. His first major task was the conquest of the language. By the aid of Chinese teachers who knew both Siamese and English he gained the fundamental principles. By diligence and persistence he not only acquired the structure of the language but, what is more difficult, the tonal pronunciation. For the benefit of English students he prepared an elementary grammar (*Brief Grammatical Notices of the Siamese Language,* 1842), and together with his wife constructed a vocabulary of several thousand words. "He was first, of American missionaries, to obtain a radical knowledge of the Siamese tongue. It rested on him in great measure to fix the Siamese usage of theological terms. . . . Portions of the Scriptures were also translated by Dr. Jones; and of some of them it may be stated, such is their accuracy and delicacy of finish, that not unfrequently they are recurred to by the most intelligent of nobles as among the choicest specimens of the Siamese literature" (*Missionary Magazine,* March 1852). Besides numerous religious tracts he published in 1834 a *Catechism on Geography and Astronomy.* This catechism was the beginning of that mode of approach for Christianity which undertook to remove mental obstacles by disclosing facts concerning nature previously unknown to the Siamese. His most notable literary work, however, was *The New Testament Translated from the Greek into Siamese,* the first version of which was published 1844, and a revised edition, in 1850. Rev. Carl Gutzlaff had previously made a translation by aid of interpreters, but it proved to be so imperfect that it was not printed. Jones combined his knowledge of the Greek with his familiarity with the colloquial Siamese and produced a translation which for the most part faithfully reproduced the thought of the original.

His first wife died of cholera in 1838, and during a visit to America in 1840 he married Judith Leavitt of Meredith, N. H., who died on a voyage homeward in 1846. He was married, a third time, to Sarah Sleeper of New Hampton, N. H., in 1847. He died at Bangkok.

[*Biog. Record of the Alumni of Amherst Coll. 1821–1871* (1883); S. F. Smith, *Missionary Sketches* (1879); *Memoir of Mrs. Eliza G. Jones* (1842); Howard Malcolm, *Travels in South-Eastern Asia* (2 vols., 1839); G. B. McFarland, *Hist. Sketch of Protestant Missions in Siam* (1928).]

G. H. F.

JONES, JOHN WILLIAM (Sept. 25, 1836–Mar. 17, 1909), Baptist clergyman, Confederate soldier, and author, was born at Louisa Court House, Va., son of Col. Francis William and Ann Pendleton (Ashby) Jones. After preliminary training in Louisa and Orange county academies he attended the University of Virginia, where he helped support himself by teaching school, and upon his graduation entered the Southern Baptist Theological Seminary. In 1860 he was ordained to the Baptist ministry, and on Dec. 20 of that year he married Judith Page Helm. Soon after his ordination he was appointed a missionary to China, but the political disturbances of the time delayed his departure and when Virginia seceded he enlisted as a private in A. P. Hill's 13th Virginia Regiment. He was with the Confederate troops from Harper's Ferry to the end of the war and won the sobriquet of "the fighting parson," serving in the ranks for a year, then as chaplain of the regiment, and after November 1863, as missionary chaplain to Hill's corps. The history of the famous revival services which swept through Lee's army during the winter of 1862–63, in which Jones played a major part, he has recorded fully in his valuable although somewhat discursive volumes, *Christ in the Camp* (1887), and the briefer "Morale of the Confederate Army," in C. A. Evans' *Confederate Military History* (1899), vol. XII.

After the war he became pastor of the Baptist church of Lexington, Va., where as one of the chaplains of Washington College he was thrown into frequent contact with Gen. Robert E. Lee. His admiration for his former chief subsequently led him to write two separate biographies, *Personal Reminiscences, Anecdotes, and Letters of Gen. Robert E. Lee* (1874), and *Life and Letters of Robert Edward Lee* (1906), which are important for their sympathetic portrayal of the Southern leader's character and for their detailed picture of his closing years. A few months after Lee's death Jones resigned his pastorate to become agent for the Southern Baptist Theological Seminary at Louisville; later he held various other church offices, filled pastorates in Ashland, Va., and Chapel Hill, N. C., did occasional teaching, and for four years represented his denomination as resident chaplain of the University of Virginia. In his latter years failing health compelled him to retire from the ministry, but until his death, while visiting in Columbus, Ga., he continued writing, lecturing, and laboring in various ways to keep alive interest in the history of the Confederacy.

An able, devoted, and eloquent servant of his church, he maintained at the same time as energetic an interest as any individual of his generation in preserving accurate historical data of the Civil War period and in perpetuating the ideals which the Confederacy represented. Appomattox left him a stanch though unembittered Confederate, and his sturdy figure and benevolent bearded face were long familiar to those who attended the annual conventions of the United Confederate Veterans, whose chaplain-general he was for almost nineteen years. From its organization in 1876 until July 1887, he was secretary of the Southern Historical Society, editing during that period fourteen volumes of its papers and helping to procure for the society a mass of invaluable source material on Confederate and Southern history. Besides the works already mentioned he published a *School History of the United States* (1896), which was widely adopted in the South; edited the *Army of Northern Virginia Memorial Volume* (1880) and *The Davis Memorial Volume* (1889); and was a frequent contributor to magazines and newspapers on subjects dealing with the Confederacy, various of his miscellaneous articles being of hardly less historical worth than his more exhaustive writings. He enjoyed a considerable sectional reputation as an author and as a lecturer on the Civil War, although his ability in exhausting known sources and uncovering fresh data was undoubtedly more pronounced than his purely creative gift.

[*Who's Who in America,* 1908–09; L G. Tyler, *Men of Mark in Va.,* vol. I (1906); obit. notices in Richmond, Va., newspapers, esp. the *Times-Dispatch,* Mar. 18, 1909; *Confederate Veteran,* May 1909.]

A. C. G., Jr.

JONES, JOHN WINSTON (Nov. 22, 1791–Jan. 29, 1848), congressman, was born in Amelia County, Va., eldest son of Alexander and Mary Ann (Winston) Jones. Upon his father's death in 1802, young Jones fell under the care of his uncle, Rev. David C. Jones; continued his education with his guardian and in the Hanover schools, and completed it by graduation from the law department of William and Mary College. For several years he taught school in Amelia and in Lynchburg, to help provide an education for his brother. In 1813 he was admitted to the bar and commenced the practice of law in Chesterfield County, settling, after his marriage to Harriet Boisseau of that region, at "Bellwood," near Petersburg.

His amenity, dignity, assiduity, and talents so helped him to win the confidence and affection of his neighbors that he advanced rapidly in his profession, and in 1818 he was appointed prosecuting attorney for the fifth Virginia judicial circuit, continuing in this office for seventeen years. In 1829, against his wishes, he was nominated for membership in the state constitutional convention and was returned senior member for his district, in competition with William B. Giles, Benjamin W. Leigh, Samuel W. Leigh, Samuel Taylor, and others. In that body he performed a faithful but modest and inconspicuous part. Returning to private life upon its adjournment, in 1834 he was elected as a Democrat to the House of Representatives. He was reëlected to the four succeeding Congresses; served creditably as chairman of the ways and means committee (1841–43) during a period of financial stress; and, even though his seat was then being contested, was elected speaker of the House in the Twenty-eighth Congress. He naturally asked to be relieved from naming the committee on elections: a motion that the appointment be given to the speaker *pro tempore,* instead of being left to the House, was carried; and the precedent thus established has since been followed in choosing committees in whose reports the speaker might have a personal interest. Although he "has been characterized as a clever politician who made but an indifferent presiding officer" (M. P. Follett, *The Speaker of the House of Representatives,* 1896, p. 90), and although John Quincy Adams refused to vote for the conventional thanks to the speaker on the ground that the testimony to Jones's impartiality "was too broad a lie for me to swallow" (*Ibid.,* p. 46), it is significant that not one of his decisions as speaker was reversed by the House.

Declining to stand for reëlection in 1844, he turned again to law and agriculture, but just a year after his retirement from Congress he was chosen "by the unanimous vote of the people of Chesterfield" to represent the county in the legislature. Early in the session of 1846–47 he succeeded W. O. Goode as speaker of the House of Delegates, and the following year was returned to the Assembly, but his health had failed so badly that he was unable to take his seat, and his death followed a few weeks after his resignation.

[A. B. Fothergill, *Peter Jones and Richard Jones Geneals.* (1924), p. 320; *Biog. Dir. Am. Cong.* (1927); *Jour. of the House of Delegates,* 1847–48; W. H. Smith, *Speakers of the House of Representatives of the U. S.* (1928); *Richmond Enquirer,* Feb. 4, 1848.]

A. C. G., Jr.

JONES, JOSEPH (1727–Oct. 26, 1805), Revolutionary statesman and jurist, was born in King George County, Va., of substantial Welsh and English stock, son of James Jones, "undertaker in architecture" and proprietor of an ordinary which his widow, Hester, continued to keep after his death. Where Joseph received his early education is unknown, but he was admitted to the Inner Temple on Dec. 7, 1749; to the Middle Temple, May 2, 1751; and on June 21, 1751, was called to the English bar (E. Alfred Jones, *American Members of the Inns of Court,* 1924, pp. 107–08). Soon afterwards he returned to northern Virginia and ultimately settled at Fredericksburg, devoting himself to the law—in 1754 he became deputy attorney for the king—and some time before 1758 marrying Mary, daughter of Col. John Taliaferro of Spotsylvania.

His career in the public service of Virginia began in 1772 with his election to the colonial House of Burgesses. From the outset of the differences with Great Britain he was active in the cause of the colonies, first as chairman of the Committee for King George County in 1774; subsequently, on the second Virginia Committee of Safety, in all the Virginia Revolutionary conventions, and in the House of Delegates. In the Convention of 1776 he was a member of the committee that framed the Virginia Declaration of Rights and the state constitution. Elected to the Continental Congress for 1777–78, he withdrew, Jan. 23, 1778, upon his appointment as judge of the Virginia general court, but less than two years later gave up this position to resume his service in Congress, representing Virginia during 1780–83 and declining to accept reëlection in 1786. On Nov. 19, 1789, he was reappointed judge of the general court and continued in this office until his death. A man of character and sensibility, an earnest and unselfish patriot, and an upright, praiseworthy judge, he was a figure of some eminence, although the one act with which his name is now associated was his leadership in preserving to the United States the Northwest Territory when the Virginia legislature considered revoking its cession. Modest and self-effacing, he was never a seeker of office, nor were his achievements of a spectacular sort; without lacking initiative, it was his lot to execute rather than to command. His judicious and far-seeing outlook, however, made him a valuable member of the legislative, state and federal, both in supporting the conduct of the war and in handling fiscal matters, for which he had considerable aptitude. As "confidential friend" of Washington, correspondent and partisan of Jefferson, and intimate colleague of Madison, he filled a not unimportant rôle; his influence over and solicitude for his nephew, James Monroe, is said to have been exceeded by that of no man (George Morgan, *The Life of James Monroe,* 1921, p. 14); while his numerous letters to these and other leading spirits give a valuable picture of public affairs, but especially of Virginia politics, during the period of his greatest activity.

[W. C. Ford, ed., *Letters of Joseph Jones* (1889); W. C. Rives, *Life and Times of James Madison* (3 vols., 1859–68); *Proc. Mass. Hist. Soc.*, 2 ser., vol. XIX (1906); *Calendar of Va. State Papers, Va. Mag. of Hist. and Biog.*, and *Wm. and Mary Coll. Hist. Quart.*, *passim*; *Va. Argus*, Nov. 2, 1805. Most accounts of Joseph Jones have confused him with Joseph Jones of Dinwiddie, member of the Virginia Convention of 1788 and major-general of militia.] A. C. G., Jr.

JONES, JOSEPH (Sept. 6, 1833–Feb. 17, 1896), physician and sanitarian, was born in Liberty County, Ga., the son of Rev. Charles Colcock Jones and Mary (Jones) Jones, and younger brother of the historian Charles Colcock Jones [*q.v.*]. His preliminary education was obtained by private tuition, and in 1853 he obtained the degree of A.B. at the College of New Jersey (Princeton). Three years later he was granted the degree of M.D. by the University of Pennsylvania. His teaching career began in 1858 with his appointment to the chair of chemistry in the Savannah Medical College. He was for a time professor of natural philosophy and natural theology in the University of Georgia at Athens and later professor of chemistry in the Medical College of Georgia at Augusta. With the outbreak of the Civil War he joined the Confederate army in the cavalry service, but after six months was transferred to the medical service, with which branch he was identified throughout the war, attaining the grade of surgeon-major. Following the close of the war he settled in New Orleans. In 1872 he was given the chair of chemistry and clinical medicine in the University of Louisiana, which he held until his death. He was also appointed president of the state board of health and served from 1880 to 1884. This was before the day of federal control of quarantine, and Jones found himself immediately the center of a feud with the harbor and railroad interests in his efforts to protect the city and state from contagious disease. A four-years' fight resulted in a court decision that the imposition of a quarantine was a legitimate exercise of police powers. Even with this victory his whole career was a thankless struggle for the sanitary improvement of New Orleans. He was keenly interested in the study of diseases of the Southern states and wrote a large number of papers in relation to them. Other papers reflect his interest in the prehistoric anthropology of the same region. His early work on physiological chemistry was reported in his doctoral dissertation, "Physical, Chemical and Physiological Investigations upon . . . the Solids and Fluids of Animals" (*American Journal of the Medical Sciences,* July 1856), "Digestion of Albumen and Flesh" (*Medical Examiner,* May 1856), and "Observations on Some of the Physical, Chemical, Physiological, and Pathological Phenomena of Malarial Fever" (*Transactions of the American Medical Association,* vol. XII, 1859). Later works include "Observations upon the Losses of the Confederate Armies from Battle Wounds and Disease" (*Richmond and Louisville Medical Journal,* October 1869–June 1870), *Outline of Observations on Hospital Gangrene . . . 1861–65* (1869), "Contributions to the Natural History of Specific Yellow Fever" (*New Orleans Medical and Surgical Journal,* January 1874), "Observations on the African Yaws and on Leprosy" (*Ibid.,* March 1878), "Explorations and Researches Concerning the Destruction of the Aboriginal Inhabitants of America by Various Diseases" (*Ibid.,* June 1878), "Contributions to Teratology" (*Transactions of the Louisiana Medical Society,* vol. X, 1888); part II of Volume II (1871) of the *Surgical Memoirs of the War of the Rebellion,* published by the United States Sanitary Commission, and *Medical and Surgical Memoirs, Containing Investigations of the Geographical Distribution, Causes, Nature, Relations and Treatment of Various Diseases* (3 vols. in 4, 1876–90).

His interest in everything pertaining to his section caused him to take a leading part in the organization and support of the Southern Historical Society. Besides being an active member of the Louisiana State Medical Society, he held membership in the Medical Society of Virginia and an associate fellowship in the College of Physicians of Philadelphia. He was married in 1858 to Caroline S. Davis of Augusta, Ga., who died in 1868. Two years later he married Susan Rayner Polk of New Orleans, daughter of the Bishop of Louisiana, who with five children survived him when he died, in New Orleans. His eldest son became a physician but preceded his father in death.

[*New Orleans Medic. and Surgic. Jour.,* 1896, with portrait; *Trans. Southern Medic. Soc.* (New Orleans), 1896; *Trans. . . . Medic. Soc. of Va.,* 1896; *Bull. Soc. of Medic. Hist. of Chicago,* Oct. 1920; *Times-Democrat* (New Orleans), Feb. 18, 1896; *Daily Picayune* (New Orleans), Feb. 18, 1896, with extensive list of Jones's writings.] J. M. P—n.

JONES, JOSEPH STEVENS (Sept. 28, 1809–Dec. 29, 1877), dramatist, actor, son of Abraham and Mary (Stevens) Jones, was born in Boston in a house on land now occupied by the Wilbur Theatre. His father was a sea captain, and his death at the hands of savages while on one of his voyages left the boy an orphan when he was ten years old. He received an elementary education in the Boston public schools, but was obliged to go to work at an early age, his interest in amateur theatricals leading him eventually into the profession that he served through many years as actor, manager, and dramatist. His début on the stage was made in Providence, R. I., at the age of eighteen, as Crack, a low-comedy character in Knight's once familiar play, *The Turnpike Gate.* He soon returned to Boston and almost immediately became influential in the theatrical life of that city, with which he was exclusively identified throughout his entire life. He acted a varied line of characters successively at the Tremont, the Warren, and the National theatres, also serving at the last-mentioned house as financial adviser, stage manager, and playwright.

During this entire period he was writing plays, mainly of an ephemeral nature. In 1839 he succeeded Thomas Barry as lessee and manager of the Tremont Theatre, but with such little financial success that at the close of the season of 1840–41 he relinquished his lease. For some years he had been studying medicine, and in pursuance of his plan to become a practising physician he retired from the stage, making his final appearance in the character of the Mock Duke in John Tobin's comedy, *The Honeymoon.* In 1843 he received the degree of M.D. from the Harvard Medical School. He continued to write plays, however, until shortly before his death: a conservative estimate credits him with one hundred and fifty. The historical drama especially interested him, but his plays were of all kinds, including comedies, melodramas, and farces. They were usually temporarily popular; some of them were constructed for special occasions and anniversaries; some were written to meet the immediate demands of a manager who had nothing in stock for his audiences; some were dramatizations of novels; and some were written in competition for prizes. His most famous play was *The Silver Spoon, or Our Own Folks,* the sub-title of which was later changed to *The Member from Cranberry Centre,* which was produced at the Boston Museum Feb. 16, 1852, and in which William Warren [*q.v.*] became famous as Jefferson Scattering Batkins, the representative in the Massachusetts General Court who was "agin the Boston click." It was revived season after season for many years, and its success there practically made Jones the unofficial dramatist of the Boston Museum. Among his early plays were *The Carpenter of Rouen, Moll Pitcher,* and *The Green Mountain Boy,* but the comedy that became most familiar to the American public outside of Boston was *The People's Lawyer,* in which John E. Owens starred for many years as Solon Shingle. His most popular occasional play was doubtless *Paul Revere and the Sons of Liberty* (1875), written to contribute to the local excitement attendant upon the centennial celebration of the famous ride. More than forty years previously he had written *Liberty Tree, or the Boston Boys* to appeal to a public then rejoicing over the fiftieth anniversary of the end of the Revolutionary War. The fame of Dr. Jones, as he was universally known, was transitory and largely local; yet *The Carpenter of Rouen* and others of his plays were acted throughout the United States and even in England. In 1871 he published a novel entitled *Life of Jefferson S. Batkins, Member from Cranberry Centre, Written by Himself, Assisted by the Author of The Silver Spoon.* In addition to his practice as a physician, he delivered lectures on anatomy and physiology. One of his three sons, Nathaniel D. Jones, was an actor.

[*A Vol. of Records . . . Containing Boston Marriages, 1752–1809* (1903); *The Boston Medic. and Surgic. Jour.,* Sept. 28, 1911; W. W. Clapp, *A Record of the Boston Stage* (1853); W. M. Leman, *Memories of an Old Actor* (1886); William Winter, *The Wallet of Time* (1913); A. H. Quinn, *A Hist. of the Am. Drama from the Beginning to the Civil War* (1923); J. B. Clapp, in *Boston Transcript,* Dec. 30, 1910; *Boston Transcript,* Dec. 31, 1877.]
E. F. E.

JONES, LEONARD AUGUSTUS (Jan. 13, 1832–Dec. 9, 1909), jurist, legal writer, was born in Templeton, Mass., the son of Augustus and Mary (Partridge) Jones. His family was established on American soil by Lewis Jones who was settled in Roxbury in 1640. In boyhood Leonard attended Lawrence Academy, Groton, Mass., combining his school studies with work in his father's chair factory and on his farm. He received the degree of bachelor of arts at Harvard in 1855, having won in his senior year the Bowdoin first prize for a dissertation on "The Nature and Limitations of Instinct." The following year he taught classics in the high school in St. Louis, Mo. After declining a position as tutor in Washington University, St. Louis, he entered the Harvard Law School in the fall of 1856, but after a year's attendance withdrew to pursue his studies in the office of C. W. Loring in Boston, and was admitted to practice at the Suffolk bar on Feb. 1, 1858. He reëntered the Law School in the spring term of that year and received the degree of LL.B. at the following Commencement. During this period he was awarded prizes for a dissertation on political economy, and a dissertation concerning property. In September 1858 he commenced the practice of law in Boston. The next few years were apparently uneventful, not even the crisis of the Civil War marring the even tenor of his life. He was drafted for military service but procured a substitute. In 1866 he went into a law partnership with Edwin Hale Abbott, which John Lathrop later joined. In 1876 the firm was dissolved, Jones continuing practice alone.

Two years later he commenced the publication of an exhaustive exposition of the law of securities, consisting of *A Treatise on the Law of Mortgages of Real Property* (1878), *A Treatise on the Law of Railroad and Other Corporate Securities, Including Municipal Aid Bonds* (1879), *A Treatise on the Law of Mortgages on Personal Property* (1881), *A Treatise on the Law of Collateral Securities and Pledges* (1883), and *A Treatise on the Law of Liens; Common Law, Statutory, Equitable and Maritime* (1888), each treatise containing references to the others. This task completed, he turned to the publication of a series of texts on certain aspects of real property, the first of which, *A Treatise on the Law of Real Property as Applied between Vendor and Purchaser in Modern Conveyancing*, appeared in 1896. *A Treatise on the Law of Easements* (1898) and *A Treatise on the Law of Landlord and Tenant* (1906) continued the subject. In addition Jones found time to compile *Forms in Conveyancing* (1886), expanded in later editions to include other forms; to publish *An Index to Legal Periodical Literature* (vol. I, 1888; II, 1899), covering Anglo-American legal journals of the period prior to 1899; and to contribute to magazines and law reviews, as well as to expand, revise, and reëdit his earlier treatises. He was associate editor of the *American Law Review* from 1884 to 1904, and editor from 1904 to 1907; he edited American notes for 19–25 *English Ruling Cases,* and supervised the publication of Conrad Reno's *Memoirs of the Judiciary and the Bar of New England, for the Nineteenth Century* (2 vols., 1900–01).

His mind may not have been that of a legal prophet and reformer, but the section of the law that he took as his field he covered thoroughly and well, as witnessed by the fact that many of his works are still considered standard. They show a wide erudition and a thorough understanding of the practical problems of the law, and were intended not so much for the student as for the practising lawyer who is confronted with concrete problems, solutions to which must be found. In this self-appointed task of clarifying the existing law he succeeded eminently. One edition of his works followed another both during his life and after his death. As recently as 1930 the eighth edition of his *Forms* appeared, of which the preface states, "Few, if any, law books have been more widely used and generally approved than the successive editions of Jones Legal Forms."

When in 1898, Massachusetts created a court of land registration (now called the land court) with jurisdiction to register titles to land and to pass on other questions relating to real estate, Governor Wolcott selected Jones as judge of this court. This function he performed faithfully and well until illness compelled him to resign in January 1909. He rendered further service to the commonwealth from 1891 to 1902, as member from Massachusetts of the Commission on Uniform State Laws. He was survived by his wife Josephine (Lee) Jones, whom he had married Dec. 14, 1867.

[W. B. Trask, *Some of the Descendants of Lewis and Ann Jones of Roxbury, Mass.* (1878); E. M. Bacon, *Men of Progress, . . . Mass.* (1896); C. E. Hurd, *Representative Citizens of the Commonwealth of Mass.* (1902); *The Report of the Secretary of the Class of 1855 of Harvard College* (1865); *Who's Who in America,* 1908–09; *Boston Transcript,* Dec. 10, 1909; *Am. Law Rev.,* Jan.–Feb. 1907, Jan.–Feb. 1910.] L. S.

JONES, MARY HARRIS (May 1, 1830–Nov. 30, 1930), "Mother Jones," labor leader, was born in Cork, Ireland, the daughter of Richard Harris. Her father emigrated to America in 1835 and after becoming a citizen of the United States sent for his family. His work as railroad construction laborer took him to Toronto, Canada, where Mary was brought up and attended high school and normal school. After teaching for a time in a convent in Monroe, Mich., she opened a dressmaking establishment in Chicago, but later returned to teaching in Memphis, Tenn. There she was married in 1861 to a member of the Iron Molders' Union and bore him four children. In 1867 her husband and children died in a yellow-fever epidemic in Memphis and in 1871 all her possessions were swept away by the Chicago fire. In the confusion following, she began attending meetings of the newly organized Knights of Labor. Gradually she sank her personal life wholly in the struggle for improved labor conditions and developed a talent for vigorous and moving speech, characterized by a picturesque vocabulary, a sharp and ready wit, and a strong sense of drama. For half a century she appeared wherever labor troubles were acute, a little old woman in a black bonnet, with a high falsetto voice and a handsome face framed in curly white hair and lighted by shrewd, kindly gray eyes which could flash defiance from behind their spectacles alike at distant capitalists and at near-by company guards and militia. She was in Pittsburgh during the labor riots of 1877, in Chicago at the time of the Haymarket tragedy of 1886, and in Birmingham during the American Railway Union strike of 1894. She worked in the cotton-mills of the South to gather material for a series of meetings against child labor, and while canvassing for the *Appeal to Reason* learned to know at first hand the labor and living conditions of the coal miners of Pennsylvania. During the coal-mine strikes of 1900 and 1902, as an organizer for the United Mine Workers, she attracted national attention by organizing marches of the wives of striking miners, armed with mops and brooms. Later she led a group of textile-mill children from Kensington, Pa., to Oyster Bay in an attempt to demonstrate to President Roosevelt the evils of child labor. In 1903 she was sent to Colorado by the United Mine Workers and, while posing as an itinerant peddler, secured information which led to a strike in the Colorado coal fields. When this strike was called off by President John Mitchell she violently denounced him and left the United Mine Workers. Deported from Trinidad, Colo., she went West, assisted the striking machinists of the Southern Pacific Railroad, was active in the defense of Moyer, Heywood, and Pettibone in Idaho (1906), and while in Arizona assisting the Western Federation of Miners in a copper-mine strike, she took up the cause of Mexican revolutionists imprisoned in the United States. She interviewed President Taft in the cause of the Mexicans and assisted in securing the appointment of a congressional investigating committee. By 1911 she was again an organizer for the United Mine Workers in West Virginia. During the strike of 1912–13 she spoke at a series of mass meetings in various cities. Later she was convicted, by a military court set up by the state militia, of conspiracy to murder, but shortly afterwards a senatorial investigating committee was appointed and ultimately her sentence to twenty years' imprisonment was set aside. Toward the end of 1913 she appeared again in southern Colorado where another coal-mine strike had broken out and was three times deported from Trinidad after varying terms of confinement. In 1914 she spoke at a series of mass meetings throughout the country, testified before the House Committee on Mines and Mining, and interviewed President Wilson in protest against conditions in the Colorado mines and against the "Ludlow massacre." During 1915–16 she was active in the garment and street-car strikes in New York City. Her last big struggle was the steel strike of 1919, but in 1921 she spoke at the meeting of the Pan-American Federation of Labor in Mexico City and as late as 1923, at ninety-three years of age, was still working among striking coal miners in West Virginia. On her one-hundredth birthday, May 1, 1930, she received many telegrams of congratulation from labor unions, friends, and acquaintances throughout the country, including one from John D. Rockefeller, Jr., held a reception on the lawn of a humble home at Silver Spring, Md., where friends were caring for her, and made a vigorous speech for talking-picture cameras. Six months later she died of old age and, after a requiem mass in Washington, D. C., was buried in the cemetery of the United Mine Workers at Mount Olive, Ill. She was sympathetic to socialist ideals though not a socialist, and was opposed to woman's suffrage and prohibition. By temperament a fiery agitator, she always preserved a sense of humor and a toleration and sympathy, even for her enemies, which, with a certain native dignity, made her beloved by thousands of rough working men and women and in the end won her general respect and admiration.

[*Autobiography of Mother Jones* (1925) cannot be wholly relied upon, especially for dates; other sources are her account of her life given as testimony before the U. S. Commission on Industrial Relations, *Senate Doc. No. 415*, 64 Cong., 1 Sess., vol. XI; her speeches at conventions of the United Mine Workers, usually published in their *Proceedings*; Elsie Glück, *John Mitchell, Miner* (1929); *N. Y. Times*, June 1, 1913, Dec. 1, 2, 1930; *Current Opinion*, July 1913; *New Republic*, Feb. 20, 1915; *Outlook*, Feb. 10, 1915; *Nation*, July 19, 1922; *United Mine Workers Jour.*, Dec. 15, 1930; *Labor* (Washington, D. C.), Dec. 9, 1930; *Labor's News*, Dec. 13, 1930; *Labor Age*, Jan. 1931; *Labor Clarion* (San Francisco), Dec. 5, 1930.] H. S. W.

JONES, NOBLE WYMBERLEY (*c.* 1724–Jan. 9, 1805), Revolutionary patriot, was born near London, England, the son of Noble Jones who moved to the Georgia colony very early in its existence and became a member of the council and the treasurer of the province. Young Jones grew up in Savannah, where he came under the patronage of Oglethorpe, who early made him a cadet in his regiment and, later, promoted him to be a first lieutenant. He was too young to take an active part in Oglethorpe's attack on St. Augustine in 1740, but, a decade later, he commanded a force of dragoons ready to meet a threatened uprising of the Cherokee. Following the profession of his father, he studied medicine and soon became virtually physician to the colony, prescribing for the prisoners in jail and for others dependent on the government. With a wife (Sarah Davis, daughter of John Davis of Georgia), six children, and twenty-seven slaves to care for he added, in 1771, eighteen hundred acres of land to the holdings he already possessed. Later he succeeded to his father's princely estate, the present "Wormsloe."

In 1755 he was elected to the commons house of Assembly, where he remained almost continuously until the outbreak of the Revolution. In 1768 he was unanimously elected speaker. The next year he was again unanimously elected. In 1771 his election was vetoed by the royal governor, and the following year, when the Assembly elected him again, the governor again vetoed his election. The Assembly, in a bellicose mood, immediately reëlected him only to receive another veto. A few months later, when the Assembly insisted on another reëlection, he refused to serve on account of professional duties. The royal displeasure had come from his outspoken opposition to the policies of the King. He had in 1765 been "a distinguished opposer of the stamp act," and by 1771 "he began to enjoy the honour of being hateful to tyrants" (*Georgia Republican and State Intelligencer,* Jan. 13, 1805). In 1768 he had signed a list of grievances to be sent to the King. Beginning in 1774 with his call for a meeting to protest against the King's treatment of Boston, his swing into rebellion was rapid. He was elected to the Second Continental Congress but, out of respect for his father, who remained loyal to Great Britain, he refused to go. At the outbreak of the Revolution, however, he became a member of the Council of Safety and of the various provincial congresses that were held. On May 11, 1775, with others, he broke open the powder magazine, which his father had helped to construct, and seized six hundred barrels of powder. He continued to be a powerful force in directing revolutionary affairs until the capture of Savannah in 1778, when he fled to Charleston. At the fall of the latter city he was seized and imprisoned in the old Spanish fort at St. Augustine. Being exchanged the next year he moved to Philadelphia, where he began to practise medicine. While there he was appointed by Georgia to serve in the Continental Congress. He returned to Georgia in 1782, was immediately elected to the Assembly, and made speaker.

He had professional interests in Charleston for the next five years, but by 1788 he had become definitely identified with Savannah. In 1791 he was chairman of the committee to welcome President Washington to Savannah; in 1795 he was made president of the state constitutional convention; and, the year before he died, he became the president of the Georgia Medical Society.

[*The Colonial Records of the State of Ga.*, ed. by A. D. Candler, vols. VII, IX–XIX (1906–11); *The Revolutionary Records of the State of Ga.*, ed. by A. D. Candler (1908), vols. I, III; W. B. Stevens, *A Hist. of Ga.*, vol. II (1859); C. C. Jones, Jr., *Biog. Sketches of the Delegates from Ga. to the Continental Cong.* (1891); Hugh McCall, *The Hist. of Ga.* reprinted in one vol. (1909); W. J. Northen, *Men of Mark in Ga.*, vol. I (1907); Wm. Harden, *Hist. of Savannah and South Ga.* (1913), vol. II; L. L. Knight, *Ga. Landmarks, Memorials and Legends* (2 vols. 1913–14); *Ga. Republican and State Intelligencer* (Savannah), Jan. 10, 13, 1805.]

E. M. C.

JONES, SAMUEL (July 26, 1734–Nov. 25, 1819), lawyer, was born at Fort Hill, Long Island, the son of William and Phoebe (Jackson) Jones. His grandfather, Major Thomas Jones of Strabane, County Tyrone, Ireland, in 1692 was in Jamaica, where he held a privateer's commission from James II. In that year also he appeared in Rhode Island, where he married Freelove Townshend. Three years later with his father-in-law, Captain Townshend, he bought approximately a thousand acres of land from the Indians at Oyster Bay, Long Island, and settled there. Samuel Jones, after a limited education at Hempstead, became a sailor in the merchant service and made several voyages to Europe. Tiring of the sea, he entered the office of Judge William Smith [*q.v.*] to study law. In 1765 he married Eleanor, daughter of Cornelius Turk, a merchant, and on her death he married in 1768 Cornelia Haring (also spelled Herring), whose grandfather was later a member of the Congress which adopted the Declaration of Independence. Jones's association with Judge Smith and his connections through marriage led him to espouse the cause of the colonists, though his father remained loyal to the Crown. In the days of agitation preceding the Revolution, he served as a member of the Committee of One Hundred, a provisional war committee whose object was to support the actions of the Continental Congress. He did not take up arms in the war, however, but spent most of his time at West Neck, Long Island, caring for his law practice. Conditions were described by John Morin Scott, in a letter dated Nov. 15, 1775: "Every office shut up almost but Sam Jones', who will work for 6/ a day and live accordingly" (C. B. Todd, *The Story of the City of New York,* 1888, p. 292). At the close of the war he rapidly gained repute as a real-estate lawyer.

In 1782 Jones and Richard Varick were appointed to collect and reduce into proper form for legislative enactment all such statutes of Great Britain as were continued in force under the constitution of 1777. The revision of Jones and Varick became authoritative and "may be regarded as the only comprehensive digest or revision of the laws of New York down to 1800" (J. G. Wilson, *The Memorial History of the*

City of New York, vol. II, 1892, p. 622). From 1786 to 1790 Jones represented Queens County in the New York Assembly, and he was in the Senate from 1791 to 1797. "His learning was vast. His principles . . . were ultra conservative. . . . He was the man above all others to adapt the system of laws to the new condition of things, . . . and on every subject of that description the Legislature followed him implicitly, while upon any subject connected with politics, they were sure to be on the other side, with entire unanimity" (*New York Legal Observer,* October 1853, p. 323). In 1788 he was a delegate to the state convention which ratified the new federal Constitution. At first opposed to the Constitution, he was won over by Hamilton (*Ibid.*), and he was influential in securing the assent of Governor Clinton and his party. He held the office of recorder of New York City from 1789 to 1796. He was appointed by Governor Jay to draft the law for establishing and regulating the office of comptroller, which office he filled from 1797 to 1800. In 1806 and 1807 he was unsuccessful as Federalist candidate for the state Senate.

Retiring from public life to his farm at Oyster Bay, he wrote for the New York Historical Society several critical and valuable letters on the early history of New York (*Collections of the New York Historical Society,* 1 ser. III, 1821). Though not so well known today as some of his more famous contemporaries he was an outstanding figure in the public life of his time. According to Chancellor Kent, "no one equalled him in his accurate knowledge of the technical rules and doctrines of real property, and in familiarity with the skillful and elaborate but now obsolete and mysterious black letter learning of the common law" (*Jones Family,* p. 109). His son Samuel Jones, 1770–1853 [*q.v.*], was also a distinguished member of the legal profession.

[E. A. Werner, *Civil List and Constitutional Hist. of the Colony and State of N. Y.* (1889); J. H. Jones, *Jones Family of Long Island* (1907); B. F. Thompson, *Hist. of Long Island* (1839; 3rd ed., 1918); F. B. Dexter, *Biog. Sketches Grads. Yale Coll.,* vol. II (1896); W. A. Duer, *Reminiscences of an Old New Yorker* (1867); J. W. Francis, *Old New York* (1866); N. Y. *Evening Post,* Nov. 26, 1819.]

D. V. S.

JONES, SAMUEL (May 26, 1770–Aug. 9, 1853), New York jurist, was the second son of Samuel Jones [*q.v.*], whose name lives in New York legal history in connection with the first revision of its laws. His mother was Cornelia, daughter of Elbert Haring (later spelled Herring), a prosperous descendant of an old Dutch family. Jones was born in the city of New York, where he spent practically his entire life. On June 17, 1770, he was baptized in the "Old Dutch Church" in Garden Street. His early education was obtained at Hempstead, Long Island, where, at the classical school of Rev. Leonard Cutting, he formed a life-long friendship with David B. Ogden [*q.v.*]. After nearly completing the course of studies at Columbia, he entered the senior class at Yale, where he graduated in 1790. Columbia bestowed upon him an *ad eundem* degree in 1793. He studied law in his father's office, where DeWitt Clinton [*q.v.*] was a fellow student. Admitted to the bar at the earliest possible age, he commenced a legal career which was unbroken, except for periods of judicial service, until two months before his death. He was particularly eminent in real-estate and maritime law and in chancery practice.

In February 1797 the legislature created a special justices' court in New York City to which he was one of the first appointees, but he sat for only a brief period. From 1809 to 1817 he served six terms as assistant alderman. He drafted the act which consolidated numerous laws relating to the city (*Revised Laws of 1813*). From 1812 to 1814 he was one of the representatives from the city in the state Assembly. Although early in his career he had been a Federalist, after the War of 1812 he supported Clinton on the policy of internal improvements, later voted for Jackson, and remained a Democrat. In 1823 he was appointed recorder of the City of New York and sat about a year. On Jan. 27, 1826, Governor Clinton nominated him as chancellor of the state; the Senate confirmed the nomination unanimously. He resigned Apr. 19, 1828, and was shortly thereafter appointed first chief-justice of the newly created superior court of the city of New York, which office he held until he was elected justice of the supreme court of the state under the constitution of 1846. He became an *ex-officio* member of the court of appeals, assisted in its organization, and sat there from 1847 to 1849, then returned for a few months to the circuit and term duties of the supreme court until his office expired, Dec. 31, 1849. Though eighty years old, upon retirement from the bench he resumed his practice. He died at the residence of his brother, Maj. William Jones, at Cold Springs, Long Island.

On Jan. 27, 1816, Jones was married to Catharine Schuyler, daughter of Philip J. Schuyler and grand-daughter of Maj.-General Schuyler of Revolutionary fame. Of his five children, his only son, Samuel, was a judge of the superior court of New York City and later reporter of the same court. Devoted to his country and to his church (he was a warden of the Church of the Annunciation from the forming of the parish), temperate in his habits, of unquestioned integrity, Jones was not rich in this world's goods but in the esteem of his professional brethren and of the community.

[*New York Legal Observer*, Sept.–Nov. 1853; F. B. Dexter, *Biog. Sketches Grads. Yale Coll.*, vol. III (1907); J. H. Jones, *The Jones Family of Long Island* (1907); *N. Y. Tribune*, Aug. 10, 1853.] A. S. M.

JONES, SAMUEL PORTER (Oct. 16, 1847–Oct. 15, 1906), evangelist, son of John J. and Nancy (Porter) Jones, was born in Chambers County, Ala. Both parents were of pioneer Methodist-preacher stock: one grandmother, who much impressed the child, had "read the Bible through thirty-seven times, on her knees" and ofttimes at church "gave vent to her feelings by shouting the praises of God" (*Life and Sayings*, p. 42). In 1856 the family moved to Cartersville, Ga., where, the mother having died, the father remarried and engaged in a successful but unregenerative practice of law until he entered the war as a captain. In the local schools the child Sam was deemed bright and fun-loving and clever at reciting pieces. Left head of the family in his father's absence, he began to drink (because of nervous indigestion, his wife asserts); and when the family fled the approaching armies, he somehow became separated from them and was swept into Kentucky. Here he met Laura McElwain, whom he married in November 1868 just after setting up as a lawyer in Cartersville. He began well as a lawyer; but the new and flattering associations increased his inebriety. He moved to Texas, then to Alabama, then (at his father's request) back to Cartersville. Here he lived in a cabin and, having abandoned the law, worked as a day laborer. Neither the descent of his wife from affluence to penury nor the coming of a child, whom he adored, could stop his drunkenness. In 1872, however, having promised his dying father to reform, he became an itinerant preacher of the North Georgia Conference of the Methodist Episcopal Church, South, equipped with "a wife and one child, a bobtail pony and eight dollars in cash" (*Ibid.*, p. 62). During eight years here he improved his economic condition little but kept sober and won a wide reputation because of the fire, force, and overflowing humor with which he attacked the inconsistencies of Christians. Then he was made agent of the Methodist North Georgia Orphans' Home and charged with raising funds, in which task he was eminently successful. Called, because of his Georgia reputation, to Memphis for evangelistic work in 1884, he succeeded so well that he was engaged by T. DeWitt Talmage [*q.v.*] for similar work in Brooklyn, in January 1885. In that year also came a "memorable meeting" (*Ibid.*, chs. XII, XIII) in Nashville. Thereafter until 1900 he was a national evangelist operating in almost all the large cities for from three to six weeks, speaking several times daily, often to ten thousand or more with many others unable to obtain seats. His success seems to have rested almost entirely on his mastery of audiences—a mastery so long and so often proved as to compel his recognition as perhaps the foremost American public speaker of his generation. The secret of his mastery seems to have been in part his physical and moral courage and in part his intuitive apprehension of the common man's dislike of sham and hypocrisy and delight in hearing them exposed and condemned in homely words and epigrammatic style. Though his exaggerations and his crudities always offended the sensitive and often made him a target for the secular press, the sentiment which he was able to evoke among the rank and file crushed all opposition and eventually compelled an almost unanimous approval from all classes. His preaching and lecturing, though never capitalized, are estimated to have brought him $750,000. After 1900 his evangelistic energies were given entirely, but unreservedly, to the South. His funeral in Georgia was an affair of state.

[*The Life and Sayings of Sam P. Jones* (1907), by his wife; *Sam Jones' Sermons* (2 vols., 1886); *Atlanta Journal*, Oct. 15, 16, 1906; Raleigh *News and Observer*, Oct. 16, 21, 1906.] C. C. P.

JONES, SYBIL (Feb. 28, 1808–Dec. 4, 1873), Quaker preacher, was born at Brunswick, Me., the third of the nine children of Ephraim and Susanna (Dudley) Jones, and the seventh in descent, on her mother's side, from Thomas Dudley [*q.v.*]. Her parents and grandparents were members of the Society of Friends. After attending the Friends' Institute at Providence, R. I., 1824–25, she taught for eight years in public schools and on June 26, 1833, married Eli Jones (1807–90), a Quaker preacher and teacher of China, Kennebec County, Me., by whom she had three sons and two daughters. Richard Mott Jones (1843–1917), headmaster of the William Penn Charter School in Philadelphia, was their third child. Soon after her marriage Sybil Jones was acknowledged by the Friends' churches as a gospel minister. In 1840 she was liberated to attend meetings and to do religious work in Nova Scotia and New Brunswick, thus beginning a career that was one of the principal factors in the great revival of her sect during the next four decades. She was a woman of deep religious sensibility, and there is abundant testimony to the extraordinary power that her simple, earnest preaching exercised over her hearers in the United States and in many countries of Europe. She visited the New England meetings in 1842, and in 1845 all the yearly meetings in Ohio, Indiana, Baltimore, and North Carolina. Her travels in the South aroused her solicitude for the spiritual welfare of the negroes, and in 1850 she felt summoned, in spite of her frail health, to preach to the blacks of Liberia. Accompanied by her husband, she sailed from Baltimore June 20, 1851, and returned to that port in December. She and her husband were kindly received by President Roberts at Monrovia, and she preached to many eager to hear her, but the chief effect of the mission was on her own inner life. A much more important mission was her visit to the meetings in Great Britain, Ireland, Norway, Germany, Switzerland, and France in 1852–54. She was in the South again in 1860 and during the Civil War was engaged in work among the sick and wounded in Union hospitals. In 1867 and again in 1868 she and her husband visited Syria and Palestine, where their meeting with Theophilus Waldmeier was especially significant for his future work. Mrs. Jones endeavored to explain the Quaker principle of the equality of the sexes to Moslem women; though she realized that her doctrine could not be put in practice, she had unwavering faith in the value of making it heard. Her most effectual work was accomplished, undoubtedly, in the United States, but she also did much to awaken interest in foreign missions. Her missionary zeal was a novel element in the Quakerism of her generation, and probably owed something to the influence on her, in her early years, of the Methodists of Maine. During her last years her strength failed gradually, and she died at her home on a farm near Augusta, Me.

[*Friends' Rev.* (Phila.), Twelfth Month 20, 1873, and First Month 17, 1874; *Biog. Cat. . . . London Friends' Institute* (1888); Dean Dudley, *Hist. of the Dudley Family* (11 pts., 1886–94); R. M. Jones, *Eli and Sybil Jones: Their Life and Work* (1889) and *The Later Periods of Quakerism* (2 vols., 1921).]

G. H. G.

JONES, THOMAS (Apr. 30, 1731–July 25, 1792), jurist, Loyalist, was born at Fort Neck, South Oyster Bay, Long Island, where his grandfather, Thomas, the first of the family in America, had acquired about six thousand acres of land. The younger Thomas, first cousin of Samuel Jones, 1734–1819 [*q.v.*], was the son of David and Anna (Willet) Jones. His father was a man of influence in the province, long member of the Assembly from Queens County, and justice of the supreme court. Thomas was graduated in 1750 from Yale College, an institution which he looked upon later as "a nursery of sedition, of faction, and republicanism" (*History, post,* I, 3). He probably studied law with his father and with Joseph Murray of New York City, and was appointed clerk of the court of common pleas of Queens County, Feb. 8, 1757. His contacts with various officials in 1778 as executor of the will of Joseph Murray, who bequeathed his library to King's College, later Columbia, led to his employment as attorney for that institution and later to membership on its board of governors. By his marriage, Dec. 9, 1762, to Anne de Lancey, daughter of Chief Justice James de Lancey [*q.v.*], he became connected with several influential families. Three years later he built a fine residence, "Mount Pitt," on the highest point in lower Manhattan. J. F. D. Smyth, in *A Tour in the United States of America* (London, 1784, II, 376), speaks of it as one of the three or four "uncommonly beautiful" seats on the island. Five years later his father built for him a magnificent country place at Fort Neck. From 1769 to 1773 he served as recorder for New York City. When in the latter year his father resigned as supreme court justice, Thomas was appointed to succeed him. He presided at the last court under the Crown at White Plains in 1776. "Extremely social and hospitable . . . polite in manner, dignified in bearing," he "naturally commanded respect" (*History,* vol. I, Introduction, p. lxxiii).

At this stage of his career he had attained to a position of honor and influence in his profession, his life was cast amid surroundings that for the time were luxurious, and his friends and associates were prominent in the affairs of the government. With the outbreak of the Revolution, however, his position in the service of the Crown and his other affiliations laid him open to the suspicions of the patriots and led to his arrest at Fort Neck, June 27, 1776. He was released upon parole to appear before the committee of the New York Provincial Congress upon reasonable notice. That body, on Aug. 11, voided such parole and the same day Jones was surprised, captured, and as a prisoner of the colonial army was soon sent to Connecticut. After four months he was paroled by Governor Trumbull and for about three years remained undisturbed at Fort Neck. During this period of inactivity he busied himself recording events with comments. This manuscript, edited by Edward F. de Lancey, was published over a hundred years later under the title, *History of New York during the Revolutionary War, and of the Leading Events of the other Colonies at the Period* (2 vols., 1879). It is the only history of the war from the standpoint of a Loyalist.

Jones's parole was again disregarded, Nov. 6, 1779, and he was stealthily conveyed to Newfield (now Bridgeport), Conn., and held there to serve as an exchange for Gen. G. S. Silliman who had been captured by the Loyalists. The exchange of the men, formerly fellow students at Yale, was not effected until April 1780. In 1781 Jones and his family sailed for Europe, and since he was named in the Act of Attainder which became effective at the close of the war, he was prevented from returning to the United States under penalty of death. Such of his American estates as were not entailed were confiscated. In compensation for these losses the British government paid him $5,447, probably less than half their value. He died at Hoddesdon, in Hertfordshire, England. The Judge and his wife had no children of their own but adopted Mrs. Jones's niece, Anne Charlotte de Lancey, who became the second wife of John Loudon McAdam, engineer and road-builder (see *Dictionary of National Biography*).

[Memoir by E. F. de Lancey in Jones's *Hist. of N. Y. during the Rev. War* mentioned above; H. P. Johnston, *Observations on Judge Jones' Loyalist Hist. of the Am. Rev.* (1880); Lorenzo Sabine, *Biog. Sketches of Loyalists of the Am. Rev.* (1864), vol. I; J. H. Jones, *The Jones Family of L. I.* (1907); B. F. Thompson, *Hist. of L. I.* (1839).]
A. E. P.

JONES, THOMAS AP CATESBY (Apr. 24, 1790–May 30, 1858), naval officer, second son of the seven children of Major Catesby and Lettice Corbin (Turberville) Jones, was born at his maternal grandfather's estate, "Hickory Hill," Westmoreland County, Va. He was of Welsh and English ancestry, a descendant of Capt. Roger Jones who emigrated from London to Virginia in 1680. Orphaned, he was taken by his uncle, Meriwether Jones of Richmond, and sent to school. Becoming a midshipman Nov. 22, 1805, he began his career under Hull and Decatur at Norfolk. Afterwards, at the New Orleans Station, he served for seven years under Captains Porter, Shaw, and Patterson, suppressing the slave trade, smuggling, and piracy, and enforcing neutrality laws. He became a lieutenant May 24, 1812. In an attack on the pirates at Barataria Sept. 16, 1814, according to Patterson's report, "Jones particularly distinguished himself by boarding one of the schooners which had been fired and extinguishing the fire after it had made great progress; a quantity of powder being left in her open cabin, evidently designed to blow her up." With five gunboats and two small schooners, he then opposed the entrance into Lake Borgne of Vice-Admiral Cochrane's fleet transporting General Pakenham's army against New Orleans. On Dec. 14, 1814, about a thousand British in forty barges, bearing forty-two cannon, attacked Jones's squadron, with its twenty-three guns and 175 men, and after a desperate engagement lasting two hours captured the gunboats, Jones being dangerously wounded. The British, however, lost ninety-four men; the Americans, only forty-one. For his gallantry, Jones received a sword from Virginia and high praise from a court of inquiry. Recovering his health, he spent three years in the Mediterranean Squadron under Chauncey and five years at the Washington Navy Yard and as inspector of ordnance. Meanwhile, he became master commandant Mar. 28, 1820, and married, July 1, 1823, Mary Walker Carter, daughter of Charles B. Carter of "Richmond Hill," Virginia. Commanding the Pacific Squadron in 1825, he visited in his flagship, the *Peacock,* the Sandwich (now Hawaiian) Islands to collect debts and look after deserters from American merchantmen. Here he supported the party led by American missionaries against the English consul's claim of British sovereignty over the islands. After five years as inspector of ordnance, Jones, a captain since Mar. 11, 1829, was appointed, June 28, 1836, to command the South Seas Surveying and Exploring Expedition. Unable to agree with Secretary of the Navy Dickerson as to the equipment and personnel of his ships, he resigned his command, Dec. 5, 1837, ill from worry and exasperation. After four years of inactive service, in 1842 he was again placed in command of the Pacific Squadron. The British frigate *Dublin* was maneuvering suspiciously off Callao, and Jones, thinking war had begun between the United States and Mexico, hastened north with two ships, Oct. 19, 1842, and took possession of Monterey. For this indiscretion he was relieved of his command, to conciliate Mexico, but was not censured by his government. Two years afterwards, he commanded the Pacific Squadron for the third time. After the Mexican War, he transported 300 refugees out of Lower California, paying the expenses from the military contributions levied at Mazatlan. For this the Secretary of the Navy commended him; but for later using this fund for "an improper and unauthorized" purpose, a general court martial in February 1850 suspended him from the service for five years with loss of pay for half that period. This suspension was remitted by President Fillmore, in 1853. Jones saw no further active service and was placed on the reserved list in 1855. On May 30, 1858, he died at Sharon, Fairfax County, Va., survived by four children.

[L. H. Jones, *Capt. Roger Jones of London and Va., Some of His Antecedents and Descendants* (1891); official papers in naval records and library of the Navy Department; Navy Register, 1806–58; reports of the Secretary of the Navy; J. F. Cooper, *The Hist. of the Navy of the U. S. A.* (1839), vol. II; *Daily National Intelligencer* (Washington, D. C.), June 1, 1858.]

C. L. L.

JONES, THOMAS GOODE (Nov. 26, 1844–Apr. 28, 1914), governor of Alabama, jurist, was the son of Samuel Goode and Martha Ward (Goode) Jones, first cousins, and a descendant of Maj. Peter Jones of Virginia who aided in punishing Indian depredations in 1676. He was born in Macon, Ga., but when he was still young the family moved to Montgomery, Ala. His father, a graduate of Williams College (1837), was a pioneer railroad constructor in the South, having built one of the first railroads in Georgia. Jones's early education was obtained in the schools of Montgomery and the academies of Charles Minor and Gessner Harrison in Virginia. When the Civil War opened, he was a cadet in the Virginia Military Institute. Leaving there to enter the Confederate army as a private in an Alabama regiment, he rose to the rank of major, served as an aide to Generals Early and Gordon, participated in many of the decisive battles in Virginia, and acted as bearer of a flag of truce at Appomattox.

At the conclusion of the war, Jones returned to Montgomery, engaged in agriculture, studied law, and was admitted to practice in 1868. From that time to his death he was almost constantly in public service and was generally engaged in sharp controversies. From June to November 1868 he edited the *Daily Picayune,* a Democratic paper published in Montgomery. He was connected with the municipal government for many years; was the reporter of the decisions of the Alabama supreme court from 1870 to 1880 (43–60 *Alabama Reports*); served in the lower house of the legislature and was the speaker of that body for two terms; and was colonel of the state troops from 1880 to 1890. In a bitter factional fight between the conservative democracy and the radical Farmers' Alliance group, he was elected governor in 1890. Renominated in 1892, he successfully withstood the vigorous attacks of the Farmers' Alliance men, now calling themselves Jeffersonians, under the leadership of his old political opponent, Reuben F. Kolb [*q.v.*]. This era constituted one of the stormiest periods in Alabama politics; there was much friction and recrimination, and Governor Jones was bitterly assailed in many quarters. He had large business capacity and his administration was notable for its constructive policies as well as for its vigor. In the Alabama constitutional convention of 1901 he played an important part and was instrumental in having placed in the new constitution a provision for the removal of sheriffs recreant to duty in the face of mobs. In the same year he was appointed by President Roosevelt a federal judge for the northern and middle district of Alabama. In his judicial capacity he was closely connected with the railroad rate fight in Alabama and in his decisions upheld the constitutional rights of corporations to appeal rate regulations to the federal court, when Gov. B. B. Comer [*q.v.*], elected on an anti-railroad platform, sought by state legislation to deny this right to common carriers. Many of his decisions struck at the system of peonage in the state. He was a man of great ability, forcefulness of character, and aggressiveness. As a controversialist, he was unsparing and singularly incisive. His career covered a transition period, and his long and bitter fight with Comer over railroad matters constituted an epoch in Alabama politics. He was married, Dec. 20, 1866, to Georgena Caroline Bird of Montgomery and was the father of thirteen children. He died in Montgomery shortly before his scheduled retirement from the federal bench.

[W. B. Jones, *John Burgwin, Carolinian, John Jones, Virginian* (1913); J. B. Gordon, *Reminiscences of the Civil War* (1903); A. B. Moore, *Hist. of Ala. and her People* (3 vols., 1927); T. M. Owen, *Hist. of Ala. and Dict. of Ala. Biog.* (4 vols., 1921); *Proc. . . . Ala. State Bar Asso.* (1914); *Who's Who in America,* 1914–15; material from the scrapbooks of Jones's son, Judge W. B. Jones, and files of the *Montgomery Advertiser, Birmingham Age-Herald,* and *Birmingham News,* in the last of which, May 31, 1914, appears a full-page sketch of Jones's career, by J. W. DuBose.]

T. H. J.

JONES, THOMAS P. (1774–Mar. 11, 1848), editor, was born in Herefordshire, England. Little is known of his early life except that he emigrated to the United States as a young man and settled in the South. Later he went to New York City, where he became associated with C. S. Williams in publishing the *American Mechanics' Magazine,* founded February 1825, of which he was editor. In August 1825 he became sole owner, and in December, he was appointed professor of mechanics and natural philosophy in the Franklin Institute for the Promotion of Mechanic Arts, Philadelphia, entering upon his duties Jan. 4, 1826. At the same time he was placed in charge of its journal, with which he merged his own periodical, the name becoming *The Franklin Journal and American Mechanics' Magazine* with the issue of January 1826. He undertook publication on his own account but with the assistance of the members of the Institute. This arrangement continued until the close of the year 1827, when the Institute assumed the sole responsibility for the continuance of the *Journal.* With the issue of January 1828 it became the *Journal of the Franklin Institute,* continuing as such with various subtitles, until the present time (1932). On Apr. 12, 1828, Jones was appointed superintendent of the United States Patent Office, in Washington, but at the meeting of the Franklin Institute held that month, a resolution was passed appointing him editor of the *Journal* during his life. The rest of his years were spent in Washington, where in addition to his official duties, he continued his editorial work. When the Patent Office was reorganized under the Act of July 4, 1836, he was appointed an examiner (July 4, 1837), from which position he resigned Dec. 22, 1838.

Under his editorship of twenty-two years, the *Journal of the Franklin Institute* became a valuable repository of information concerning scientific and engineering subjects. An important feature for many years (1826–59) was the list of patents, with descriptions, which had been filed in the government Patent Office. Jones's interest in the progress and development of inventive talent in the United States, as well as in the general improvement of the artisan classes, continued until his death. In his editorial capacity he was "always ready to recognize and warmly encourage genuine invention"; but "was equally watchful and uncompromising in showing the defects he believed to exist in any patented invention, especially in those cases in which the invention embodied no possible gain or advantage to the public" (Fowler, *post,* p. 5). He edited the eighth edition (1834), of the *Young Mill-Wright & Millers Guide* (1st ed., 1795), by Oliver Evans [*q.v.*]; and editions (1826 and 1831, respectively) of Mrs. Jane (Haldimand) Marcet's *Conversations on Natural Philosophy* and *New Conversations on Chemistry.* He died in Washington, D. C.

[F. Fowler, "Memoir of Thomas P. Jones," *Journal of the Franklin Institute,* July 1890; *Commemorative Exercises at the Fiftieth Anniversary of the Franklin Institute* (1874); F. L. Mott, *A Hist. of Am. Magazines* (1930); W. H. Wahl, *The Franklin Institute . . . A Sketch of Its Organization and History* (1895); *Daily National Intelligencer* (Washington), Mar. 13, 1848.] J. H. F.

JONES, WALTER (Oct. 7, 1776–Oct. 14, 1861), lawyer, a descendant of Capt. Roger Jones who came from England with Lord Culpeper in 1680, was born at "Hayfield," Northumberland County, Va. His mother's name was Alice Flood. His father, Dr. Walter Jones, an Edinburgh-trained physician of prominence in his day, was a delegate to the state constitutional convention of 1788 and a congressman from Virginia in 1797–99 and 1803–11. From a Scotch tutor named Thomas Ogilvie, Walter Jones received the classical education which characterized all his later work. He read law in Richmond under Bushrod Washington and was admitted to the bar of Virginia in May 1796, before he became of legal age. He practised first in the courts of Fairfax and Loudoun counties and in 1802 was appointed by President Jefferson, who was a friend of his father, as United States attorney for the District of Potomac, and in 1804, for the District of Columbia. In May 1808 he married Ann Lucinda Lee, daughter of Charles Lee, 1758–1815 [*q.v.*], attorney-general under Washington and Adams, by his first wife, Anne, daughter of Richard Henry Lee [*q.v.*], the Signer.

From the time of his marriage, which eventually resulted in three sons and eleven daughters, Jones made his home in Washington. He resigned his federal attorneyship in 1821, but until his last illness continued with distinguished success the practice of law before the United States Supreme Court as well as in the courts of Maryland and Virginia. In the famous case of *McCulloch* vs. *Maryland* (4 *Wheaton,* 316), argued in 1819, he was associated with Luther Martin and Joseph Hopkinson on behalf of Maryland, in opposition to William Pinkney, Daniel Webster, and William Wirt, who represented the Bank of the United States. Other important cases in which he participated actively were *Ogden* vs. *Saunders,* 1827 (12 *Wheaton,* 213), in which, with Edward Livingston, David B. Ogden, and William Sampson, he won the decision against Webster and Wheaton; *Binney* vs. *Chesapeake & Ohio Canal Company,* 1835 (8 *Peters,* 201), in which he was associated with Webster and Francis Scott Key; *Mayor of the City of New York* vs. *Miln,* 1837 (11 *Peters,* 102); and *Groves* vs. *Slaughter,* 1841 (15 *Peters,* 449), concerning the respective powers of the federal and state governments over the introduction of slaves within the border of a state, in which he was associated with Daniel Webster and Henry Clay against Henry D. Gilpin and Robert J. Walker. With Daniel Webster he was employed by the heirs to attempt to break the Girard Will (*Vidal et al.* vs. *Philadelphia,* 2 *Howard,* 127). Although he was unsuccessful in this case (1844), in which he was opposed by Horace Binney and John Sergeant, he won great praise from Rufus Choate for his "silver voice and infinite analytical ingenuity and resources" (*Addresses and Orations,* 1878, p. 228, quoted in L. H. Jones, *post*). He was of counsel for Myra Clark Gaines in much of the litigation over the will of her father, Daniel Clark [*q.v.*].

The law was not his only field of achievement. He took part in the battle of Bladensburg, in 1821 was commissioned by President Monroe as brigadier-general of militia, and at the time of his death was major-general of the militia of the District of Columbia. In 1835 he supervised the quelling of mob incendiarism and riot in Washington (*Daily National Intelligencer,* Aug. 13, 1835; *Daily Globe,* Aug. 14, 1835). Late in 1816, he was associated with Rev. Robert Finlay [*q.v.*], John Randolph, Bushrod Washington, Henry Clay, and others in founding the American Colonization Society "for the purpose of colonizing the free people of colour in the United States of America, in Africa, or elsewhere" (Alexander, *post,* p. 89), being a member of the committee to prepare a constitution and rules for the society and a member of the committee to present a memorial to Congress requesting support of the colonization proposal. He was also a founder of the Washington National Monument Society.

Small of stature and eccentric in dress, he was unimpressive in the court room. A contemporary newspaper-man wrote of him: "He speaks slowly and in a low tone, but with great purity of diction and clearness of thought. There is, however, a great want of force in his manner and few listen to him." "A rival of Pinkney, Wirt and Webster . . .," wrote the same correspondent, "as a common law counsellor he excelled them all in depth and variety of learning. . . . He is universally respected, and by those who know him, warmly beloved." (Quoted by Warren, *post,* II, 344.) He was possessed of such rare conversational powers and personal charm that he was socially in great demand, and he was generous and sympathetic to a fault. He died at Washington after an illness of eight or ten days. Although a Virginian by birth, he was devoted to the Union and held the secession movement in Virginia a double treason, first, to the United States, and second, to the Commonwealth of Virginia.

[L. H. Jones, *Capt. Roger Jones of London and Va.* (1891); F. L. Jones, "Walter Jones and His Times," *Records of the Columbia Hist. Soc.,* vol. V (1902); Charles Warren, *The Supreme Court in U. S. Hist.* (3 vols., 1922); *Va. Law Reg.,* Aug. 1901; W. B. Bryan, *A Hist. of the National Capital,* vol. II (1916); Archibald Alexander, *A Hist. of Colonization on the Western Coast of Africa* (1846); *Daily National Intelligencer* (Washington), Oct. 15–18, 1861.] H. F. W.

JONES, WILLIAM (Oct. 8, 1753–Apr. 9, 1822), Revolutionary soldier and Federalist governor of Rhode Island during the War of 1812, was born at Newport, R. I. His grandfather, Thomas Jones, came from Wales, and his father, William, was first lieutenant of the privateer *Duke of Marlborough* in the French and Indian War. William, senior, died in 1759, leaving a widow, Elizabeth (Pearce) Jones, and five children, of whom his namesake was the fourth. Not much is known of the son's early life; but he must have had a fair education and given evidence of character and ability, for he received a lieutenant's commission from the General Assembly in January 1776, and was made a captain about the time his regiment joined the main army in September. His brigade saw service in the battle of White Plains, the retreat to New Jersey, and the battle of Princeton. Jones left the army in February 1777. Just a year later he became captain of marines on the *Providence,* a frigate of twenty-eight guns built in Rhode Island, which sailed on Apr. 30, 1778, to carry the first dispatches to the commissioners in Paris after the conclusion of the treaty with France. On arrival near Nantes, Jones was chosen the messenger to Paris, and was probably the first officer to wear the American uniform there. His journal tells of seeing the sights and of dining with Adams, Lee, and Franklin. In 1779 the *Providence* made a successful cruise for prizes off Newfoundland, and later went to Charleston, S. C., where her crew and guns were landed to strengthen the batteries and were surrendered May 12, 1780. Jones returned to Rhode Island on parole and went into business in Providence.

He was a man of integrity and good sense, and his faithful performance of religious and other duties (he was a justice of the peace) won him the esteem of his townsmen. They made him a representative in the General Assembly, 1807–11; in 1808 he presented a petition from Providence against the Embargo, speaking forcibly of its dire effects upon the industrial and shipping interests of the town; in 1809 he became speaker of the Assembly, and in 1811 governor of Rhode Island on the Federalist ticket. He was reelected annually until 1817 by the opponents of the national government, while its supporters charged him with loving trade better than his country, and called him such names as "a haberdasher of British hardware" (Field, *post,* I, 295). Under his leadership Rhode Island, like Massachusetts and Connecticut, maintained a defiant attitude toward the national government throughout the War of 1812. The Governor's messages called the war unjust, asserted final authority in the use of the state militia, complained of defenseless coasts, and early in 1814 practically threatened secession. The making of peace meant ultimate loss of office, but his last campaign was a warm one, in which a prudent and economical administration was set against the "mourning and misery" brought on by twelve years of "misconduct" on the part of the government at Washington.

Jones was married on Feb. 28, 1787, to Anne Dunn of Providence, who, with an only daughter, survived him. He was a member of the Cincinnati, a president of the Peace Society and of the Rhode Island Bible Society, and a trustee of Brown University.

[W. J. Hoppin, "Memoir of Governor William Jones," *Proc. R. I. Hist. Soc. 1875–76* (1876); S. H. Allen, "The Federal Ascendency of 1812," *Narragansett Hist. Reg.*, Oct. 1889; Edward Field, *State of R. I. and Providence Plantations at the End of the Century*, vol. I (1902); *To the Freeman of the State of Rhode-Island, &c. &c.* (pamphlet, Mar. 6, 1817), by "a citizen"; *The Biog. Cyc. of Representative Men of R. I.* (1881); *Providence Gazette*, Apr. 10, 13, 1822; *R. I. American*, Apr. 12, 16, 1822.] E. M. S. B.

JONES, WILLIAM (1760–Sept. 6, 1831), congressman, cabinet officer, was born in Philadelphia. Little is known of his childhood except that at the age of sixteen he joined a company of volunteers and participated in the battles of Trenton, Dec. 26, 1776, and Princeton, Jan. 3, 1777. Later he served as a third lieutenant on the Pennsylvania private ship *St. James* under Captain (later Commodore) Thomas Truxtun [*q.v.*]. In 1781, he was promoted to first lieutenant for gallantry. During his service he was twice wounded and twice taken prisoner. Between 1790 and 1793 he served in the merchant marine, making his headquarters at Charleston, S. C. In 1793 he returned to Philadelphia, where he became a shipping merchant and, taking an active interest in politics, was elected as a (Democrat) Republican to the Seventh United States Congress (1801–03). He was elected a member of the American Philosophical Society on Jan. 18, 1805, and he read a number of papers before that body. On Jan. 12, 1813, he accepted the post of secretary of the navy in the cabinet of President Madison and served until Dec. 2, 1814, when he resigned in order to devote himself to business. He also served as acting secretary of the treasury from May 1813 to February 1814. In July 1816 he was elected as the first president of the second United States Bank, more for political reasons than because he possessed any particular ability as a banker. His administration of the bank's affairs was characterized by mismanagement, stock speculation, and fraud; and he was forced to resign the presidency in disgrace in January 1819. Investigation revealed, however, that he had been the tool of others in their efforts to manipulate the price of the bank's stock in the open market as well as in the adoption of an unsound system of branch-bank management; and he regained some of his lost prestige. In 1827 he was appointed collector of customs in Philadelphia, serving until 1829. He died in Bethlehem, Pa., and was buried in the Moravian Cemetery there.

Jones appears to have been hopelessly inefficient in positions of great authority. His administration of the Navy Department during the War of 1812 was open to criticism even though Madison, in a letter written in February 1827, refers to him as "the fittest minister who had ever been charged with the navy department," adding, "With a strong mind, well stored with the requisite knowledge, he possessed great energy of character and indefatigable application to business" (*Letters and Other Writings of James Madison*, 1865, III, 563). His work as acting secretary of the treasury between the resignation of Albert Gallatin [*q.v.*] and the appointment of George W. Campbell [*q.v.*] has also been severely criticized. Ignorance, however, was probably the chief factor in his mismanagement of the second United States Bank.

[J. T. Scharf and Thompson Westcott, *Hist. of Phila.* (1884), I, 585; E. P. Oberholtzer, *Phila.—A Hist. of the City and Its People* (n.d.), vol. II; W. W. Bronson, *The Inscriptions in St. Peter's Church Yard, Phila.* (1879); *Biog. Dir. Am. Cong.* (1928); *Writings of James Madison*, ed. by Gaillard Hunt, VIII (1908), 320n., IX (1910), 278–79n.; R. C. H. Catterall, *The Second Bank of the U. S.* (1903); D. R. Dewey, "The Second U. S. Bank," pub. as *Sen. Doc. 571*, 61st Cong., 2nd Sess., and as *Pubs. of the Nat. Monetary Commission*, vol. IV (1911); C. O. Paullin, "Naval Administration under Secretaries of the Navy Smith, Hamilton, and Jones, 1801–14," *Proc. U. S. Naval Inst.*, Dec. 1906; *Poulson's Am. Daily Advertiser*, Sept. 8, 1831.] J. H. F.

JONES, WILLIAM (Mar. 28, 1871–Mar. 29, 1909), Indian ethnologist, was born on the Sac and Fox Indian reservation in what is now Oklahoma. He inherited from his father, Henry Clay Jones, and his mother, Sarah (Penny) Jones, a mingling of English and Welsh blood with Fox. His mother died in his infancy and he was cared for by his Indian grandmother, who for nine years saw that he had a real Indian education. At ten he was placed in the Indian school at Newton, Kan., and later spent three years in the Friends' Indian boarding school at Wabash, Ind. Returning to Indian Territory he became a cowboy. In 1889 at the age of eighteen he went to Hampton Institute, proving himself a prize pupil; thence to Phillips Academy at Andover, Mass., where through the advice of Prof. F. W. Putnam [*q.v.*] he entered Harvard in 1896. In the ensuing year he spent the summer season collecting data among the Sauk and Fox Indians near Tama, Iowa. Life at Harvard had rewards for Jones. He wrote for the *Harvard Monthly* and became editor. Graduating A.B.

in 1900, he pursued graduate work at Columbia, and during this period, under the auspices of the Bureau of American Ethnology and the American Museum of Natural History, carried on exploratory work among the Sauk and Fox Indians. Receiving the degree of Ph.D. in 1904, he commenced investigations among the northern Algonquian tribes. The Field Columbian Museum of Chicago utilized his services in 1906, and among the assignments offered him he chose that of investigating the uncivilized tribes of the Philippines, where three years later, in the savage jungle, he was fatally wounded by the Ilongots.

Jones's contributions to science were almost exclusively on Algonquian language and lore, particularly on the Fox branch from which he sprang and to whose secrets his Indian connection gave him full access. His chief papers were: "Episodes in the Culture-Hero Myth of the Sauks and Foxes" (*Journal of American Folk-Lore,* October–December 1901); "Some Principles of Algonquian Word-Formation" (*American Anthropologist,* n.s., vol. VI, no. 3, Supplement, 1904), his doctor's thesis; "The Algonkin Manitou" (*Journal of American Folk-Lore,* July–September 1905); "Central Algonquin" (*Annual Archæological Report,* Ottawa, Canada, 1905); "An Algonquin Syllabary" (*Boas Anniversary Volume,* 1906); "Mortuary Observances and the Adoption Rites of the Algonkin Foxes of Iowa" (*Congrès International des Américanistes, Quebec, 1906,* 1907); "Fox Texts" (*Publications of the American Ethnological Society,* vol. 1, 1907); "Notes on the Fox Indians" (*Journal of American Folk-Lore,* April–June 1911); *Algonquian (Fox), an Illustrative Sketch* (Bulletin 40, pt. 1, Bureau of American Ethnology, 1911). Dr. Franz Boas said of his "Fox Texts": "This collection is the first considerable body of Algonquian lore published in accurate and reliable form in the native tongue, with translation rendering faithfully the style and contents of the original. In form, and so far as philological accuracy is concerned, these texts are probably among the best North American texts that have ever been published" (*American Anthropologist,* January–March 1909, p. 138). In addition to the technical papers listed above, which were intended only for specialists, Jones wrote magazine articles of lighter cast, and popular lectures.

Possessing in a high degree the reserve of the Indian, he nevertheless made many friends, and was held in high regard by his co-workers in anthropology. He was of medium height, with brown eyes and hair. In appearance he took after his Indian forebears rather than his white ancestors. He never married.

[H. M. Rideout, *William Jones* (1912); *Harvard Grads. Mag.,* June 1909; Harvard College, Class of 1900, *Twenty-fifth Anniversary Report* (1925); *Am. Anthropologist,* Jan.–Mar. 1909.]
W. H.

JONES, WILLIAM ALFRED (June 26, 1817–May 6, 1900), author, was born in New York City, the son of Judge David Samuel Jones and his first wife, Margaret, daughter of Dr. Thomas Jones of New York and grand-daughter of Philip Livingston [*q.v.*]. He graduated from Columbia in 1836, and studied law with Daniel Lord, but finding this profession uncongenial, he soon gave it up for a literary career. For some years he contributed frequent essays and literary criticisms to New York periodicals, notably the *American Monthly Magazine, Arcturus, Broadway Journal, United States Democratic Review,* and *American Whig Review.* He was for a time associated with Rev. Francis Lister Hawks in the editorship of the *Church Record,* with Charles Fenno Hoffman in the *Literary World,* and with his brother-in-law, Rev. Samuel Seabury, in *The Churchman.* He was a friend and correspondent of Irving, Bryant, Halleck, Dana, and many other literary men of his day. In 1840 he published *The Analyst;* in 1847, *Literary Studies;* and in 1849, *Essays upon Authors and Books.* These volumes consisted almost wholly of essays and reviews reprinted from periodicals. His *Characters and Criticisms* (2 vols., 1857) was a reprint of most of the material in his previous volumes, with a few additions. These writings, distinctly eighteenth-century in flavor, received high praise from Irving and Poe (S. A. Allibone, *A Critical Dictionary of English Literature,* vol. I, 1858, p. 995).

Jones was appointed librarian of Columbia College in 1851, succeeding Dr. Lefroy Ravenhill. He held this position until 1865 and, with the exception of Nathaniel Fish Moore [*q.v.*], was the most active and efficient librarian the college had had up to that time. As librarian, he published a "Statement" in the volume of investigations into the affairs of the college, 1857 (*Statements, Opinions and Testimony Taken by the Committee of Inquiry,* 1857); an article, "The Library of Columbia College" (*University Quarterly,* January 1861); and a *Report* in 1862. His sketch, "The First Century of Columbia College" (*Knickerbocker,* February 1863), calls attention to many interesting little-known alumni. Jones took great pride in his ancestry, and published a genealogy of his family in his *Memorial of the Late Hon. David S. Jones* (1849). In 1860 he published a catalogue of his personal library, and in 1863 an address, *Long Island,* delivered before the Long Island Historical Society. In 1867 he retired to Norwich Town, Conn., the home of his first wife, Mary Elizabeth Bill, where he spent the remainder of his life. His wife died in 1872, and the following year he married Mary Judith Davidson, who survived him. He had no children. A small oil portrait of him, painted at one sitting, Oct. 3, 1853, by William Sidney Mount, and exhibited at the National Academy in 1854, is now in the Library of Columbia University. He was small in stature; and in manner, brisk and animated.

Jones was a man of great disappointment. His early life had been full of promise, and he had some hope of becoming an important literary figure. He had also entertained hopes of inheriting a large fortune from one of his relatives, but he was ignored in that relative's will, and thereafter was a broken man. He was not bitter, but his disappointment was so severe that he had no energy to open new fields for himself, and for over thirty years he lived a retired, eccentric, idle life, keeping much to himself, and completely out of touch with the times, an interesting man, but without interests.

[J. H. Jones, *The Jones Family of Long Island* (1907); James Grant Wilson in *N. Y. Geneal. & Biog. Record,* July 1900; *Norwich Bulletin* and *Norwich Record,* May 7, 1900; F. L. Mott, *A Hist. of Am. Mags.* (1930); manuscript minutes of the trustees of Columbia, and of the meetings of the library committee, 1851–65; personal recollections of Henry Watson Kent.]
M. H. T.

JONES, WILLIAM PALMER (Oct. 17, 1819–Sept. 25, 1897), physician, psychiatrist, was born in Adair County, Ky. He was a great-grandson of David Jones, who emigrated from Wales to Maryland, and the son of William Jones, who fought with Jackson at New Orleans. His mother was Mary, daughter of Maj. Robert Powell, a Virginian who fought in the Revolutionary War. The death of her husband left her with nine children to rear. Young Jones grew up on the farm and at the age of twenty began to study medicine at the Louisville Medical Institute. He took his degree in 1840 from the Medical College of Ohio (Cincinnati), and later received another degree from the Memphis Medical College. He began practice at once in Edmonton, Ky., but within a year removed to Bowling Green in the same state and in 1849 removed permanently to Nashville, Tenn. In 1851 he was married to Jane Elizabeth Currey, by whom he had nine children. In addition to his medical practice, Jones founded, in 1852, and conducted for some years a popular journal, the *Parlor Visitor.* During the period 1853–56, he was also co-editor of the *Southern Journal of the Medical and Physical Sciences,* and edited the *Tennessee School Journal.* In 1858 he was a co-founder of the Shelby Medical College, where he held the chair of materia medica. At the outbreak of the Civil War, he chose to support the Union, and was placed in charge of the Academy Hospital, the first Federal hospital to be established in Nashville. From 1862 to 1869 he was superintendent of the Tennessee Hospital for the Insane, and in this capacity was instrumental in getting an appropriation for erecting near Nashville a special institution, the Central Hospital for the Insane, for colored patients. In 1876 he was made president of the faculty of the Nashville Medical College, which three years later became the medical department of the University of Tennessee. He was president of the medical faculty for twenty years, or nearly to the time of his death, and held also the chair of medicine and the chair of psychology and mental hygiene. He was prominent in the local political life, was postmaster of Nashville for many years, and was on the city council and board of education. In 1873 he was elected a state senator and worked especially for the enactment of a public-school law which sought to end racial discrimination, and to secure normal schools and additional insane asylums. Jones was but little known to the general medical public, and the three series of the *Index Catalogue* of the Surgeon-General's Library contain no mention of any work from his pen nor of any biographical sketch or portrait—the sole reference to him being a mention of his editorship of the *Southern Journal of the Medical and Physical Sciences.* He was, however, a member of the American Medical Association, the American Association for the Advancement of Science, and the Association of Medical Superintendents of American Institutions for the Insane.

[H. A. Kelly and W. L. Burrage, *Am. Medic. Biogs.* (1920); *Jour. Am. Medic. Asso.,* Oct. 2, 1897; W. B. Atkinson, *The Physicians and Surgeons of the U. S.* (1878); H. M. Hurd, *The Institutional Care of the Insane in the U. S. and Canada,* IV (1917), 432; *Nashville American,* Sept. 26, 1897.]
E. P.

JONES, WILLIAM PATTERSON (Apr. 23, 1831–Aug. 3, 1886), educator and United States consul, was a native of Philadelphia, the second son of William Patterson and Ursula (Linderman) Jones, his ancestors having come from England with the first group of Lord Baltimore's colonists. His father, who was building contractor for Girard College, was forced by the panic of 1837 to remove to the West, where he continued as a builder both in St. Louis and Alton, Ill., and interested himself in the newly established McKendree College at Lebanon, Ill. The son graduated at Rock River Seminary, Mount Morris, Ill., in 1849, and from Allegheny College, Meadville, Pa., in 1853. He immediately became an enthusiastic supporter of the higher education of women, and determined to establish a college "where," to use his own words, "all that was taught at Yale and Harvard should be placed within the reach of womanhood" (Ward, *post,* p. 59). In order to popularize his plan, he went about the country speaking wherever opportunity offered. To finance these journeys, he and his brother exhibited daguerreotypes of the Far West, enlarged by means of a pantoscope. On one of these tours, he met Matthew Vassar, who urged him to join him in his plans for Vassar College, and Henry Fowle Durant, later the founder of Wellesley College, with whom he discussed his theories.

In 1855, with gold obtained through the Californian mining adventures of his brother, J. Wesley Jones, he bought land in Evanston, Ill., then a hamlet in the wilderness, where Northwestern University was about to be established, and with the help of his father and two young brothers, he erected a building which was dedicated Jan. 1, 1856. Under the name Northwestern Female College, the institution had opened in October 1855 with eighty-three girls in attendance. As was the case with many colleges in the West at the time, the preparatory department contained the greater number of pupils; the college classes were always small. Jones's educational methods, however, were considered at the time little less than revolutionary. Inspired with the idea that the school must be adapted to the pupil, he made development through individual instruction the basis of his method. The young women practised student self government and the honor system and, in order to cultivate self expression, even published a tiny newspaper. As a result, many self-reliant, individualistic women of the mid-nineteenth century are numbered among the graduates of the college, the most notable being Frances E. Willard [*q.v.*], who used Jones's methods in her own teaching experience, and May Wright Sewall [*q.v.*]. In 1869 he transferred the college to a group of women, by whom it was operated under the name of Evanston College for Ladies, in conjunction with Northwestern University, by which institution it was finally absorbed.

In 1862 Jones was appointed United States consul at Macao, later at Amoy and then at Canton. Returning to the United States in 1868, he lectured in many parts of the country with the hope of bringing about a better understanding of conditions in China. He also took an active part in promoting the plan, originated by the United States minister, Anson Burlingame, but never adopted, to use the surplus of the Chinese Indemnity Fund of 1856–57 to establish an American University for the Chinese at Peking (*House Report No. 113,* 45 Cong., 3 Sess.). Jones was an enthusiastic student of Indian lore and produced two epic poems based on Indian legends, one of which, *The Myth of Stone Idol,* was published in 1876. He was coauthor with R. P. Porter and Henry Gannett of *The West: from the Census of 1880* (1882). He also wrote extensively for the Chicago newspapers on education. On Feb. 22, 1857, he married Mary Elizabeth Hayes, who was his earliest assistant at Northwestern Female College. His death occurred at Fullerton, Nebr. For the last two years of his life (1884–86) he had been president of the normal school at Fremont, in that state.

[Published material includes F. E. Willard, *A Classic Town: the Story of Evanston* (1892), *Glimpses of Fifty Years* (1889), and *Nineteen Beautiful Years* (1864); E. F. Ward, *The Story of Northwestern Univ.* (1924); A. H. Wilde, *Northwestern Univ., A Hist. 1855–1905* (1905), vol. II; *The Canton Indemnity Fund* (1871); A. D. Field, *Memorials of Methodism in the Bounds of the Rock River Conference* (1886); *Daily Inter Ocean* (Chicago), Aug. 5, 7, 1886; a biography of Jones by Lydia J. Trowbridge is in course of preparation.]

E. F. W.

JONES, WILLIAM RICHARD (Feb. 23, 1839–Sept. 28, 1889), engineer, steelman, was the son of the Rev. John G. Jones who came to the United States from Wales in 1832. The father's calling took the family from Pittsburgh to Scranton, Wilkes-Barre, and finally Hazleton, Pa., where William was born. Owing to his father's poor health, the boy began to work at the age of ten as an apprentice to the molder's trade at the Crane Iron Company in Catasauqua, Pa. Passing from foundry to machine shop, he was receiving at the age of fourteen the customary wages of a journeyman machinist. Upon learning the trade, he left Catasauqua and entered the employ of James Nelson at Janesville. The years preceding the panic of 1857 being very unfavorable to manufacturing, he went from place to place and job to job—to Philadelphia and the machine shop of J. P. Morris & Company, to Tyrone, working as a lumberman, as raftsman, and as farmhand. In 1859 he was employed at the Cambria Iron Company in Johnstown, Pa. The following year, as master mechanic, he went to Chattanooga, Tenn., to erect a blast furnace, but the menace of secession caused his return to Johnstown. On July 31, 1862, he enlisted as a private in Company A, 133rd Pennsylvania Volunteers, even though he had married on Apr. 14 of the previous year. His wife was Harriet Lloyd and four children were born to them.

During the nine months for which he was enlisted, he became a sergeant and took part in the campaigns at Fredericksburg and Chancellorsville, serving with distinction and refusing to leave the regiment, though he was badly wounded at the crossing of the Rapidan. His term of enlistment having expired, he returned to Johnstown, but reënlisted during the Gettysburg campaign. He raised Company F, 194th Pennsylvania Regiment of Emergency Men, and became its captain July 31, 1864. He was finally mustered out June 17, 1865. His commanding officer, Gen. Lew Wallace, said of him that he had one of the best-disciplined and best-drilled companies in the service. With the close of the war, Jones returned to Johnstown and in 1872 became assistant to the general superintendent of the plant. When the superintendent died, he went to Pittsburgh as a master mechanic for the Edgar Thomson Steel Company and helped in the erection of the steelplant and rolling-mills at Bessemer. In 1875 he was made the general superintendent of this company at Braddock, Pa., a position which he held until his death. In 1888 he became consulting engineer to Carnegie, Phipps & Company.

Characterized as "probably the greatest mechanical genius that ever entered the Carnegie shops" (Bridge, *post,* p. 79), he was quick to discard a tool or a method as soon as he learned of something better. Among the devices and processes he himself patented were: a method of operating ladles in the Bessemer process; improvements in hose-couplings; designs for Bessemer converters; washers for ingot molds; hot beds for bending rolls; apparatus for compressing ingots while casting ingot molds; feeding appliance for rolling-mills; the making of railroad bars; apparatus for handling, setting, and removing rolls; and, most important of all, the Jones mixer (1889), for mixing molten iron from the blast furnaces for the converter. His royalties each year amounted to some fifteen thousand dollars, and, coupled with the "thundering big salary" of thirty-five thousand dollars which he chose in preference to an interest in the company, made his income tremendous for those days. It has been said that he gave ten thousand dollars a year to charity. He was a member of the leading technological societies and contributed frequently to their publications, but would never read a paper at a meeting nor accept an office. His fame led the owner of the great Krupp steel works at Essen to invite him to inspect the factory; he was the first American to be so honored.

Jones's preëminence as a steel-mill superintendent was due in part to his inventive genius and engineering skill, but primarily to his ability as a manager of men. Himself a master of all the details in the steel-making process, he was quick to recognize exceptional work. His experience enabled him to see the difficulties between employer and employed from the points of view of both, and his reports to the officers of the company contained discerning analyses of the human as well as the engineering problems of the mills. During the great strike at Braddock, it is said that he attended a meeting of the men and after reading his proposition to them, said: "There it is for you now, you can do what you please with it. I am going to Pittsburgh to the ball game." His high regard for others and his qualities of leadership were notably manifested during the Johnstown Flood, which caused the death of over three thousand people. At the first news of the flood, which followed the breaking of a dam ten miles from the city, Jones loaded and delivered three box cars of provisions. In addition he gathered three hundred men and took them to Johnstown to aid in the rescue work. Later, when hundreds of other volunteers arrived, he assumed the task of feeding them and directing their activities. His work won for him a lasting name in Johnstown and the city held a memorial meeting after his death. He was fatally injured, in September 1889, by the explosion of a furnace which he was helping his men to repair, and two days later he died in the Homeopathic Hospital at Pittsburgh. On the day of his funeral the great mill at Braddock was shut down; all the stores and the schools, both public and parochial, were closed; and the whole city was draped in mourning. An unusual tribute was paid him in the resolutions of the Carnegie Company to the effect that never had it lost "an officer whose services were more valuable, or to whom it was more deeply indebted for the success which has attended its operations."

[*Trans. Am. Inst. Mining Engineers,* vol. XVIII (1890); *Trans. Am. Soc. Mech. Engineers,* vol. X (1890); *Mil. Order of the Loyal Legion of the U. S., Commandery of the State of Pa., Circular No. 1, Ser. of 1890*; F. Connelly and G. C. Jenks, *Official Hist. of the Johnstown Flood* (1889); *Hist. of Allegheny County, Pa.* (1889); *A Biog. Album of Prominent Pennsylvanians,* 3 ser. (1890); D. S. Goddard, *Eminent Engineers* (1906); *Jour. Iron and Steel Inst.* (London), 1890; *Bull. Am. Iron and Steel Asso.,* Oct. 2, 1889; *Iron Age,* Oct. 3, 1889; J. H. Bridge, *The Hist. of the Carnegie Steel Co.* (1903); *Specifications and Drawings of Patents Issued from the U. S. Patent Office,* Dec. 1876, Apr., June, Aug., Nov. 1877, Sept., Oct. 1878, July 1881, Oct. 1883, Sept. 1885, Apr., May, Oct. 1886,

May, June, Aug. 1888, Jan., June 1889; *Pittsburgh Dispatch* and *Pittsburgh Press*, Sept. 27–30, 1889.]

A. I.

JONES, WILLIE (*c.* 1741–June 18, 1801), Revolutionary leader, was born in Northampton County, N. C. His Christian name is pronounced Wylie. His great-grandfather, Robert or Robin Jones, emigrated to Virginia from Wales in the middle of the seventeenth century, and his father, the third Robert or Robin ap Jones, went to North Carolina as attorney and agent for Lord Granville. His mother was Sarah, the daughter of Robert Cobb of Virginia. With his older brother, Allen Jones [*q.v.*], he was sent to England to be educated, and both spent some years at Eton. He traveled on the Continent for a time and returned to North Carolina in the early sixties. He loved society, hunting, racing, and cards, and he built in the town of Halifax a handsome house, "The Grove," which became a center of lavish entertainment and, later, of political discussion and council. There, on June 27, 1776, he took his beautiful and charming bride, Mary Montfort, sister of Eliza Montfort who married John Baptista Ashe [*q.v.*]. According to a well-established family tradition, unsupported, however, by contemporary documentary evidence, it was out of gratitude for hospitality at "The Grove" and at the home of Allen Jones across Roanoke River, that John Paul assumed the name of Jones (see John Paul Jones). Willie Jones prospered as a planter and business man and acquired what was in that day a large fortune. He became increasingly well known in the province and, long before he held office, was a man of wide influence. He was an aide to Governor Tryon in the Alamance campaign against the Regulators.

From the beginning of the quarrel with the mother country he was an ardent supporter of colonial rights, and nothing else, probably, could have drawn him into politics. For that cause he labored untiringly and unceasingly. In 1774 he was recommended by the Board of Trade for a place on the colonial council but naturally was not appointed, serving instead as chairman of the Halifax Committee of Safety. He threw his influence in favor of the call of the first Provincial Congress in 1774, and, from either the borough or the county of Halifax, was elected a member of each of the five provincial congresses, but he could not attend the fourth because the Continental Congress had appointed him superintendent of Indian affairs for the southern colonies. Yet he exerted a great influence in that Congress, which was attempting to draft a constitution. His group was in a majority but postponed action in the hope of a compromise that would reconcile the conservative element led by Samuel Johnston [*q.v.*]. At the fifth Congress, again with a liberal majority, Jones served on the committee to draft the constitution, which was a compromise satisfactory to all but the conservative extremists. He was influential in determining its form and character, and by many has been credited with its authorship.

For the next dozen years Jones was politically the most powerful man in the state, the undisputed leader of the democratic element, which was in the ascendant; yet no man ever used power more moderately. He was a member of the House of Commons from the borough of Halifax in 1777 and 1778, and from the county in 1779 and 1780. He was senator in 1782, 1784, and 1788. In 1781 and 1787 he was a member of the Council of State. In 1780 he was elected to the Continental Congress and served a year. He was elected a delegate to the federal convention but declined to accept, and, when the Constitution was submitted, he led the opposition to its ratification. A close and devoted friend of Jefferson, he agreed enthusiastically to his suggestion that four states should decline to ratify until a bill of rights was obtained, but, when Jefferson changed and favored unanimous ratification, Jones, if aware of the change, did not follow him. His objections to the Constitution were fundamental; Jefferson's only incidental. He was a delegate to the convention of 1788, and behind him was a majority of one hundred against ratification. He favored a vote without debate but yielded to the desire of his opponents for a full discussion. He spoke seldom and briefly, exerting his influence off the floor and talking to the members in terms of popular understanding. When the debate was over the convention by a majority of one hundred refused to ratify, recommended twenty-six amendments and adjourned.

Jones favored a delay of some years in ratification, but the tide set the other way. He was elected to the convention of 1789 but did not attend. His public life was over. He was a member of the first board of trustees of the University of North Carolina, and was one of the commission which located the capital and provided for building a statehouse. A county and a street in Raleigh bear his name. He built a home in Raleigh and, dying there after a long illness, was buried there in a grave, by his own request unmarked.

He was a man of superior ability and was a political organizer of genius. As a leader he was cool-headed and temperate and, in those respects, a striking contrast to his political opponents, who hated him as the Federalists later hated Jefferson and for the same reasons, and who covered him with the same scandalous abuse. While an aristocrat in social life, he had a genuine passion for political democracy. From the first he saw in the struggle with Great Britain a democratic movement and was determined to embody its ideals into the resulting government. His opposition to the Constitution was not, as his opponents described it, due to wrongheadedness nor yet to mere particularism, but was inspired by his fear of checking the development of liberal government. Personally he was a man of culture and great charm, warm-hearted and affectionate, a devoted husband and father. In religion he was a free-thinker and in his will (recorded in Halifax County, N. C.) directed that "no priest or any other person is to insult my corpse by uttering any impious observations over it."

[*Colonial Records of N. C.*, esp. vols. IX, X (1890); *State Records of N. C.*, esp. vols. XII, XVII, XIX, XXV (1895–1906); G. J. McRee, *Life and Correspondence of James Iredell* (2 vols., 1857–58); J. S. Jones, *A Defence of the Revolutionary Hist. of the State of N. C.* (1834); W. C. Allen, *Hist. of Halifax County* (copr. 1918); R. D. W. Connor, "The Colonial and Revolutionary Periods," *Hist. of N. C.*, vol. I (1919); J. H. Wheeler, *Hist. Sketches of N. C.* (2 vols., 1851); Cadwallader Jones, *A Geneal. Hist.* (1900); S. A. Ashe, *Hist. of N. C.*, vol. II (1925); D. H. Gilpatrick, *Jeffersonian Democracy in N. C.* (1931); *South Atlantic Quart.*, Oct. 1905, Jan. 1906.]

J. G. deR. H.

JORDAN, DAVID STARR (Jan. 19, 1851–Sept. 19, 1931), naturalist, teacher, university president, peace advocate, was born on a farm near Gainesville, N. Y., and died at his home, "Serra House," Stanford University, Cal. His parents were Hiram Jordan (1809–88) and Hulda Lake Hawley (1812–99). The Jordans came to America from Devon, England, and the Hawleys, also originally from England, were among the early settlers in Connecticut. The name of the latter family had been Holly, but in the time of Jordan's grandfather one line changed it (*Days of a Man*, I, 5). The ancestry on both sides was made up largely of farmers, teachers, lawyers, and preachers of New England stock. Jordan's early education was received at home and in the local ungraded school. When fourteen years old he was one of two boys who were enrolled for a time in the Gainesville Female Seminary, where he studied algebra and geometry, and learned to read French about as readily as English. When only seventeen years old he taught the unruly village school at South Warsaw, a few miles distant from his home, and managed to hold the position until the close of the term in March 1869, when, having won through competitive examination a scholarship in Cornell University, he entered that institution.

During his boyhood on the farm he began to make lists of the species of plants he found and to study not only their structural resemblances and differences but their ecological relations also; when he was only a junior at Cornell his knowledge of botany was such that he was appointed an instructor in that department. His interest in zoölogy and in animal breeding also was great. His first papers were one on "Hoofrot in Sheep," published in the *Prairie Farmer* in 1871, and another on "The Flora of Wyoming County," never published, which was his graduating thesis for the degree of master of science at Cornell in 1872. Following his graduation at Cornell, he went to Lombard University (now College), Galesburg, Ill., as professor of natural science. His duties included classes in half a dozen branches of science, political economy, evidences of Christianity, and, incidentally, German and Spanish. He was given charge of the weekly "literary exercises," had a class in Sunday School, and served as pitcher of the student ball team.

At the end of one year he resigned and went at once to Penikese, in Buzzard's Bay, where he joined the summer school of science that was established by the elder Agassiz [*q.v.*] the summer before his death. Jordan spent also the summer of 1874 at Penikese. In the meantime, he had spent one year (1873–74) as principal and teacher of science and modern languages in the Collegiate Institute and Scientific School at Appleton, Wis. While there, he prepared and published, with Balfour Van Vleck, *A Popular Key to the Birds, Reptiles, Batrachians and Fishes of the Northern United States, East of the Mississippi River* (1874); of this, as Dr. Elliott Coues remarked (*Days of a Man*, I, 131), "the less said the better," except that it prepared the way for the excellent *Manual of the Vertebrates of the Northern United States* (1876). Many editions of the *Manual* appeared, under slightly varying titles, and it is doubtful if any other work has had so great an influence in the study of the species of vertebrate animals of America. In the fall of 1874, Jordan went to Indianapolis as a teacher of science in the high school of that city. The next year he received the degree of M.D. from Indiana Medical College. It was "scarcely earned," he says, but he had done some medical study for the sake of teaching physiology (*Days of a Man*, I, 145–46). On Mar. 10, 1875, he married Susan Bowen of Peru, Mass., whom he had met at Penikese and who was assistant professor of botany at Mount Holyoke Female Seminary. She died Nov. 15, 1885, and on Aug. 10, 1887, Jordan married Jessie L. Knight of Worcester, Mass., sister of Austin M. Knight [*q.v.*], later a rear-admiral in the navy. From the Indianapolis High School, Jordan went in 1875, as professor of natural history, to Northwestern Christian University (now Butler College), where he remained four years. In the fall of 1879 he went to Indiana University, where he succeeded Richard Owen as head of the department of natural science. On Jan. 1, 1885, he became president of Indiana University; in this position he remained until 1891, when he went to California as the first president of the recently established Leland Stanford Junior University. After twenty-two years as president of Stanford (1891–1913) he was relieved of administrative duties and made chancellor of the university; he was chancellor emeritus from 1916 until his death.

David Starr Jordan was, first of all, a naturalist and explorer. In his boyhood days he began, in the proper and natural way, to study the kinds of animals and plants he found about him, and their structural and ecological relations, with the result that he soon became a systematic botanist, then a systematic vertebrate zoölogist, and finally, the greatest living authority in ichthyology, using that term in its broadest sense. Ever eager to see Nature under different aspects, he became a traveler and an ardent student of the problems of geographic distribution of animal and plant species. His wide observation and study of Nature in her varied forms and in many lands, together with his breadth of scholarship, made him more than a zoölogist or botanist; he became a philosophical biologist in the broadest sense. As a teacher he owed much to Agassiz; for, as Darwin had "walked with Henslow" at Cambridge, so Jordan "walked with Agassiz" at Penikese and learned how to "know Nature when he met her in the woods and fields." His strength as a teacher lay in his first-hand knowledge of the subject, his constant and intelligent use of specimens for the students to examine, his simplicity and earnestness of expression, and his felicity of illustration. His readiness to have his special students share with him the investigation of research problems and the authorship of the resulting papers was a stimulus of the greatest inspiration to them.

Until 1885 Jordan's interest lay chiefly in scientific research and in teaching, though an ever-increasing number of executive duties came to him. His election to the presidency of Indiana University was an outcome as undesired by him as unexpected. He accepted the responsibility temporarily, at the same time filing a letter of resignation to take effect, if desired, at the close of the academic year. His great abilities as an organizer and executive soon became apparent. A more or less apathetic legislature was induced to increase the income of the university and to make a special appropriation for a new building. Very popular as a public speaker, he carried the message of higher education into every county in the state, and the attendance at the university began to increase rapidly. Important changes were effected whereby the curriculum was made more elastic so that the special aptitudes of the students could be met; subjects elementary in their nature were relegated to the first two years, and each third-year student was required to choose, with the advice and consent of his major professor, a specialty or "major subject."

The selection of David Starr Jordan for the presidency of Leland Stanford Junior University was largely due to his old teacher, Andrew D. White, whom Governor and Mrs. Stanford had consulted regarding the matter (*Autobiography of Andrew D. White,* 1905, II, 447–48; *Days of a Man,* I, 354). His acceptance of the offer, in March 1891, was a momentous decision, profoundly affecting the remainder of his life. Stanford University was formally opened Oct. 1, 1891. Jordan announced, as "Circular No. 3," certain guiding principles to be observed (*Days of a Man,* I, 357–58). The statement of these, he felt, marked an epoch in his own experience, if not in the history of higher education in America. He set as his first object the selection and retention of a faculty of talented teachers, also successful in original investigation. Applied science was to be stressed, along with pure science and the humanities. No fixed curriculum was contemplated, but large freedom of election was to be permitted. The professorship rather than the department was to be the unit of faculty organization. The "major-professor" system, which had been in successful operation at Indiana University for five years but was still generally regarded as an innovation, was to be introduced. The choice of a major subject was originally made at Stanford at the beginning of the first year, though it was later changed to the third year, as at Indiana.

In forming a faculty, Jordan found it difficult to attract to the Far West men of established reputation in the East, and, drawing considerably upon the institutions with which he himself had been associated, he commonly selected younger men, trusting his own judgment as to their future development (*Ibid.,* I, 396–97). The death of Leland Stanford in 1893 left the university in desperate financial straits. The settlement of the estate was delayed because of business conditions and a suit brought by the federal government to recover Stanford's share of the loan to the Central Pacific Railway Company, which was not decided in favor of the university until 1896. Furthermore, because of a technical defect in the enabling act, the trustees were unable to receive endowments until an amendment to the state constitution was passed in 1900 (*Ibid.*, I, 493–510). In 1906, the year of the California earthquake, Jordan declined the secretaryship of the Smithsonian Institution, feeling that he could not leave the university at such a time. He turned to the heavy task of physical reconstruction, realizing that he must abandon certain "intensive educational schemes" he had hoped to develop and devote the rest of his administration chiefly to the solidifying of what already had been accomplished (*Ibid.*, II, 174, 177).

Despite his heavy executive duties at Indiana and to a much greater extent at Stanford, Jordan responded to many calls from the federal government and various organizations to serve on important special commissions. In particular he studied and reported on fisheries from the Atlantic to the Pacific, in Alaska, the Hawaiian Islands, and Samoa, and thus rendered valuable service to his government and to science. He doubtless knew more kinds of fishes at sight and intimately than any other man ever knew. Among his notable publications in the field of ichthyology may be cited the following: *Guide to the Study of Fishes* (1905); *Fishes* (1907, 1925); and, with Barton W. Evermann, *The Fishes of North and Middle America* (4 vols., 1896–1900) and *American Food and Game Fishes* (1902). The factors and principles determining the geographic distribution of animals and plants had a strong appeal to him and he was always eager to study different species in their physical and biological environment. One of his most valuable contributions to the subject of geographic distribution of species, called "Jordan's Law" by Dr. J. A. Allen, is as follows: "The nearest relative of any given form is usually not found in exactly the same region, nor at a distance, but just on the other side of some barrier to distribution" (*Days of a Man*, I, 329).

Early in 1898 Jordan made his first public address on international arbitration as a means of adjusting differences among different countries, and during the remaining years of his life this was almost a religion to him and he became an indefatigable crusader for international peace. At times the cause seemed hopeless and there was considerable ridicule of his efforts, but, never losing hope as to the final outcome, he fought only the harder and more continuously. He delivered addresses on international relations and world peace in practically every state of the union and in many foreign countries (see *For International Peace: List of Books, Reviews, and other Articles in the Interest of Peace, Friendship, and Understanding between Nations, by David Starr Jordan, 1898 to 1927*). In his public addresses and in his published books, especially in *The Human Harvest* (1907), he stressed the biological effects of war, but when the United States entered the World War he said: "I would not change one word I have spoken against war. But that is no longer the issue. We must now stand together in the hope that our entrance into Europe may in some way advance the cause of Democracy and hasten the coming of lasting peace" (*Days of a Man*, II, 735). In 1925 Jordan received the Raphael Herman prize of $25,000 (award made Dec. 7, 1924) for the best working plan to create and maintain international peace (*A Plan of Education to Develop International Justice and Friendship*, 1925).

Jordan was an imposing figure; more than six feet three inches tall and well built in proportion, he was athletic in a rather ponderous way. He had a marvelous memory for names, places, and dates. His knowledge of the classics as well as of modern languages was remarkable. His style was simple and direct, often epigrammatic; with a keen sense of humor and a rich mellow voice he was an attractive speaker. He was a versatile and prolific writer; a complete bibliography of his books and other publications has not yet been completed but the number of titles will exceed one thousand. In addition to the works already named, the following may be cited as typical: in science, with Vernon L. Kellogg, *Evolution and Animal Life* (1907); and on educational and social topics, *The Care and Culture of Men* (1896), *The Voice of the Scholar* (1903), *Life's Enthusiasms* (1906), and *The Higher Foolishness* (1925). In 1922 he published his autobiographical work, *The Days of a Man*. In this he said (I, vii) that for half a century he had been a "very busy man, living meanwhile three more or less independent lives; first, and for the love of it, that of naturalist and explorer; second, also for the love of it, that of teacher; and third, from a sense of duty, that of minor prophet of Democracy." He added that, if he had his life to live over, he would again choose all of the three.

[The principal source is Jordan, *The Days of a Man; Being Memories of a Naturalist, Teacher, and Minor Prophet of Democracy* (2 vols., 1922). This was reviewed by Vernon L. Kellogg in *Science*, Mar. 23, 1923. See also Isaac Russell, "David Starr Jordan," in *World's Work*, Apr. 1914; *San Francisco Examiner*,

Sept. 20, 1931; *N. Y. Times, San Francisco Chronicle*, Sept. 20, 21, 1931; *Science*, Oct. 2, 1931; *Who's Who in America*, 1930–31. G. T. Clark, *Leland Stanford, War Gov. of Cal., Railroad Builder and Founder of Stanford Univ.* (1931), contains little that is new about Jordan but much about the plans of the university.]

B. W. E.

JORDAN, EBEN DYER (Nov. 7, 1857–Aug. 1, 1916), merchant, patron of music, a descendant of Rev. Robert Jordan who came from England to the coast of Maine about 1641, was the son of Eben Dyer and Julia M. (Clark) Jordan. His father, country born and bred, had established through strenuous efforts the Boston drygoods firm of Jordan, Marsh & Company. Eben, junior, was born in Boston in the year of the panic which ruined many merchants but which his father weathered successfully and with enhanced prestige. After attending Boston public schools he was sent to Adams Academy, Quincy, where he was prepared for Harvard College. He entered in 1876 with the class of 1880, but trouble with his eyes compelled him to leave college in his freshman year. After a journey to California he entered his father's store.

The impress of the younger Jordan's personality on Jordan, Marsh & Company was soon evident. A less picturesque figure than his father, concerning whom many stories and legends persist in Boston, he was not less effectual and far-seeing. He started in a humble job, packing and unpacking as a "lumper." Having earned promotion into the retail department, he went to Europe as a buyer. Thereafter for several years he made two trips overseas annually, gaining an expert knowledge of British and Continental manufacture and methods of merchandising. On Feb. 1, 1880, he was admitted to partnership. During several years prior to his father's death, which occurred Nov. 15, 1895, he carried most of the operating responsibility of the store. As president, after 1895, he continued to give close attention to the expansion of the business, destined to become, after his death, the foremost unit of a great department-store chain.

Jordan was married, Nov. 22, 1883, to Mary Sheppard of Philadelphia, by whom he had two children. His tastes, like hers, were strongly domestic. At their Boston home they built up gradually and unostentatiously a considerable collection of American and European paintings and other works of art. They maintained for many years a summer residence surrounded by a large landed estate at Chiltonville, near Plymouth. Here were reared the fine carriage horses and race horses with which Jordan captured many ribbons and other prizes at American horse shows. In 1909 the Jordans leased for a summer Inverary Castle, in Argyllshire, Scotland. The family so greatly enjoyed their experiences on a Scottish estate that for several successive seasons they leased Drummond Castle, Perthshire, one of the show places of Great Britain.

Jordan's active interest in musical projects was due both to personal inclination and public spirit. As a young man he had lessons in singing, and he developed so good a voice that but for his wealth and many responsibilities he might have sung professionally. His father was long a trustee and principal supporter of the New England Conservatory of Music, founded by Dr. Eben Tourjée in Boston in 1867. After the elder Jordan's death the son was urged to take a place on the Conservatory board. He acceded, at first reluctantly, but he presently found the problems of the school absorbingly interesting. During the period of uncertainty following Dr. Tourjée's death in 1891, Jordan personally had visited the studio of George W. Chadwick and secured him as director. Jordan was later among those responsible for placing the Conservatory's business management in the capable hands of Ralph L. Flanders. He aided materially in removing the school from Franklin Square to a better location at Huntington Avenue and Gainsborough Street, near Symphony Hall, and he made it possible to include in the new building a fine concert auditorium, which was named Jordan Hall in his honor. In 1903 he was elected president of the Conservatory trustees and he served until his death.

His special fondness for vocal music made it natural for him to support a project, initiated in 1909, to establish opera in Boston. Mainly through his aid was erected, at cost of about $1,000,000, the present Boston Opera House, in which the Boston Opera Company gave its first performance, a superb presentation of *La Gioconda,* on Nov. 8, 1909. For several seasons, until the World War made it impossible to secure singers and the Boston company was disbanded, Jordan valiantly made good its deficits. He died at West Manchester, Mass., from a paralytic stroke, and after impressive services at Trinity Church, was buried at Forest Hills Cemetery.

[Sketch by John Woodbury, secretary of the Class of 1880, in *Harvard Grads. Mag.*, Sept. 1916; *Harvard Coll. Class of 1880, Fortieth Anniv. Report* (1920); obituary and editorial in *New Eng. Conservatory Mag.-Rev.*, Sept.–Oct. 1916; obituary by W. H. Luce, in *Musical America*, Aug. 12, 1916; *Boston Transcript*, Nov. 9, 1909, Aug. 2, 1916; *Boston Daily Globe*, Aug. 2, 1916; *Memorial Tributes to Eben D. Jordan, Oct. 13, 1822–Nov. 15, 1895* (1896); T. F. Jordan, *The Jordan Memorial* (1882); H. M. Dunham, *The Life of a Musician Woven into a Strand of History of the New Eng. Conservatory of Music* (1931).] F. W. C.

JORDAN, JOHN WOOLF (Sept. 14, 1840–June 11, 1921), librarian, editor, antiquary, was a descendant of Frederick Jordan of Kent, England, who settled in New Jersey in the second half of the eighteenth century, and the eldest son of Francis and Emily (Woolf) Jordan. He was born in Philadelphia, where his father was a prominent merchant, a member of the grocery and chemical house of Jordan & Brother. After preliminary education in private schools of his native city, John was sent to Nazareth Hall Military Academy near Bethlehem, Pa., where he graduated in 1856. After leaving school he was taken into his father's office to learn the business, and when he had reached his majority, was made a member of the firm. In 1863, when Pennsylvania was invaded by the Confederates, he served as quartermaster-sergeant in Starr's battery, attached to the 32nd Regular Pennsylvania Militia. He retired from business later, and in 1885 became assistant librarian of the Historical Society of Pennsylvania. In 1903 he was elected librarian, and retained that office until his death.

His most significant work was done as editor of the Society's quarterly magazine, the *Pennsylvania Magazine of History and Biography,* which he conducted from 1887 until his death. For its pages he edited many important manuscript sources, including a number of Revolutionary orderly books, "Narrative of John Heckewelder's Journey to the Wabash in 1792" (January, April, July 1888), "Notes of Travel of . . . John Heckewelder . . . to Gnadenhuetten on the Muskingum . . . 1797" (July 1886), and "Spangenburg's Notes of Travel to Onondaga in 1745" (1878, 1879). He was the author of a number of historical papers, published in the *Magazine,* among them being "Bethlehem during the Revolution" (January–April 1889), "The Military Hospitals at Bethlehem and Lititz during the Revolution" (July 1896), and "Franklin as a Genealogist" (April 1899). He edited W. C. Reichel's *Friedensthal and Its Stockaded Mill, 1749–67* (1877) and *A Red Rose from the Olden Time* (1883), and did most of the work of editing *Extracts from the Diary of Jacob Hiltzheimer* (1893), issued by Jacob Cox Parsons. His name appeared as chief editor of *Historic Homes and Institutions and Genealogical and Personal Memorials of the Lehigh Valley, Pa.* (1905), and from 1914 until his death, as chief editor of the *Encyclopedia of Pennsylvania Biography* (vols. I–XIII, 1914–21); with these works, however, he had comparatively little to do. He edited and contributed to *Colonial Families of Philadelphia* (2 vols., 1911), and *Colonial and Revolutionary Families of Pennsylvania* (3 vols., 1911). To his editorial work he brought learning and sure knowledge of Pennsylvania history, particularly of the Revolutionary period, and of the Moravian settlements, in both of which fields he was regarded as an authority. He was well informed on American history generally, and was held in high regard by historical writers who consulted him, but as a historian he made no positive impression.

In 1888 Jordan was one of the founders of the Pennsylvania Society of the Sons of the Revolution, of which he was registrar until his death. He was vice-president of the Colonial Society of Pennsylvania; vice-president of the Swedish Colonial Society; honorary member of the Pennsylvania Society of the Cincinnati; founder and first president of the Pennsylvania Federation of Historical Societies; secretary of the Valley Forge Park Commission; a member of the Commission for the Preservation of Public Records of Pennsylvania; a member of the state commission in charge of preparing the history of Pennsylvania's part in the World War; and a member of the Baronial Order of Runnymede. Lafayette College, in 1902, gave him the degree of LL.D. He was married on May 19, 1883, to Anne Page, daughter of Alfred and Rebecca Page, and had issue, two sons and a daughter.

[Strangely enough, the *Pa. Mag. of Hist. and Biog.* published no obituary. See *New Eng. Hist. and Geneal. Reg.,* Apr. 1923, supp.; *Encyc. of Pa. Biog.,* vol. II (1914); *Who's Who in Pa.* (1904); *Who's Who in America,* 1918–19; *Public Ledger* and *North American,* both of Phila., June 13, 1921.] J. J.

JORDAN, KATE (Dec. 23, 1862–June 20, 1926), novelist, playwright, was born in Dublin, Ireland, the daughter of Michael James and Katherine Jordan. Her father was a professor, and his people, who traced their descent from an artist in the Court of Henry VIII, were nearly all artists, singers, writers, or professors. She came with her family to New York in childhood and was educated at home by tutors. True stories of her childhood are related in her book *Trouble-the-House.* When she was only twelve her first story was published and this success made her determine to be a writer. She continued to contribute stories and poems to magazines and gradually won many readers. One of her most popular tales was "The Kiss of Gold," published in *Lippincott's Monthly Magazine* in October 1892. In 1897 she married Frederic M. Vermilye, a broker, of New York City, who died some time before her own death. She had no children. After her marriage she continued to write under her maiden name, and soon began to compose plays as well as stories. She traveled all over the world and lived for long periods in England and France. In London she was a member of the Pen and Brush Club, the Lyceum, and the Writers' Club, and in the United States, of the Society of American Dramatists and the Authors' League of America. Her published novels include *The Other House* (1892); *A Circle in the Sand* (1898); *Time the Comedian* (1905); *The Creeping Tides* (1913); *Against the Winds* (1919); *The Next Corner* (1921); *Trouble-the-House* (1921). Her most popular plays were *A Luncheon at Nick's* (1903); *The Pompadour's Protégé* (1903); *Mrs. Dakon* (1909); and *The Right Road* (1911).

She was a woman of vivid personality who won the admiration and devotion of friends. She understood human, especially feminine, moods and suffering, and she interpreted character with a measure of skill. Her plots are sophisticated and have abundant incident; her backgrounds are varied, as far apart as Paris and "Bates Crossing" or "Lanetown." In her plays she showed an understanding of dramatic technique and of popular demand. She was in failing health for several years, suffering from insomnia and worrying because she was unable to finish a novel on which she was at work. In the spring of 1926 she left her home in New York and spent some months with a niece at Mountain Lakes, N. J. Here, one Sunday morning, in the woods near her niece's home, she committed suicide by taking poison. Her body was cremated and her ashes were buried in Sleepy Hollow Cemetery.

[*Who's Who in America*, 1922–23; *Bookman*, June 1913; *Publishers' Weekly*, June 26, 1926; *N. Y. Times*, June 24, 1926; *N. Y. Herald Tribune*, June 22, 1926; information as to certain facts from Mrs. Vermilye's niece, Mrs. George A. Reeder, Mountain Lakes, N. J.]

S. G. B.

JORDAN, THOMAS (Sept. 30, 1819–Nov. 27, 1895), soldier, journalist, son of Gabriel and Elizabeth Ann (Sibert) Jordan, was born at Luray, Va. A maternal grand-uncle, a Withers of South Carolina, served on General Sumter's staff in the Revolution, and it was a family tradition that the Jordans and the Washingtons were kinsmen in England. After a common-school education, young Jordan entered the United States Military Academy in 1836, and graduated four years later in a class which included William Tecumseh Sherman (his roommate) and George H. Thomas. Commissioned as a lieutenant in the 3rd Infantry, he served in the Florida war and took part in the surprise and capture of the Seminole chieftain, Tiger Tail, near Cedar Keys, in November 1842. He was promoted first lieutenant, June 18, 1846, and distinguished himself at Palo Alto and Resaca de La Palma in the war with Mexico, his battalion being the first to cross the Rio Grande in advance of General Taylor's army. He was later appointed captain and quartermaster and at Vera Cruz had charge of the final withdrawal from Mexico by land and sea of some 35,000 men of Scott's army. For this service he was commended by General Twiggs. He served as a staff quartermaster during the second uprising of the Seminoles, 1848–50 and then on the Pacific Coast, notably during operations against hostile Indians in what is now the state of Washington. While stationed at Fort Dalles, Ore., 1856–60, he is said to have introduced steam navigation on the Columbia River above that point, and also to have initiated a successful irrigation project (Marrin, *post*).

On May 21, 1861, under a sense of loyalty to his native state, he resigned his commission and entered the Confederate army, first as a lieutenant-colonel of Virginia troops, and later as adjutant-general of the forces which fought the first battle of Bull Run, July 21, 1861. As Beauregard's chief of staff, he took part in the battle of Shiloh, being promoted brigadier-general for gallantry on the field; and subsequently participated in the Corinth campaign. Later, he served as Beauregard's chief of staff in the operations around Charleston, S. C., until the end of the war.

On leave of absence, 1860–61, he had written *The South, Its Products, Commerce, and Resources* (1861), and at the close of the war he returned to writing, publishing in *Harper's Magazine* (October 1865) an article on Jefferson Davis which aroused wide-spread interest and comment. It was markedly censorious of the Southern leader, depicting him as imperious, narrow, and so lacking in the gift of organization and in statesmanship as to have been unfitted for the administration of the Confederacy. Soon after the appearance of this article Jordan became editor of the *Memphis Appeal* (1866). With J. B. Pryor he published *The Campaigns of Lieutenant-General N. B. Forrest* in 1868.

In the year 1869 he became chief of staff and later commander of the Cuban insurgents, and in January 1870 he met and defeated a superior Spanish force at Guaimaro, Cuba. At this time, Spain is said to have placed a price of $100,000 on his head. Recognizing the impracticability of reorganizing the Cuban army, and with his war supplies becoming exhausted, he resigned his command in February 1870 and returned to the United States and to his literary pursuits. In the same year he became the founder as well as editor of the *Financial and Mining Record* of

New York, a journal devoted to the interests of the free coinage of silver, which he conducted until ill health forced him to abandon the undertaking in 1892. He contributed "Notes of a Confederate Staff Officer at Shiloh" to *Battles and Leaders of the Civil War* (vol. I, 1887). As a soldier, Jordan's most conspicuous quality was his organizing ability, for which General Beauregard gave him high praise. As a writer and journalist, his work was marked by clearness of diction as well as vigorous style. He was married to the daughter of Edmund Kearny, of Keyport, N. J., who had been a captain in the British navy; his wife died in the year 1884. A son and a daughter were born to them.

[Jordan's Civil War career is well covered by numerous references in *Battles and Leaders of the Civil War* (vols. I and IV, 1887–88), while many details of his private life are related by his friend and counsel, W. J. Marrin, in *Ann. Reunion Asso. Grads. U. S. Mil. Acad.*, 1896. See also C. A. Evans, *Confed. Mil. Hist.* (1899), vol. III; L. G. Tyler, *Encyc. of Va. Biog.* (1915), vol. V; *Frank Leslie's Illustrated Newspaper*, Feb. 26, 1870; *N. Y. Times*, Nov. 28, 1895.] C. D. R.

JORDAN, WILLIAM GEORGE (Mar. 6, 1864–Apr. 20, 1928), editor and author, was born in New York City, a son of Henry and Mary Moat Murdock Jordan. His higher schooling was obtained in the College of the City of New York, but he did not graduate. In 1886–87 he was the editor of *Book Chat* and later of *Current Literature* and of the *Saturday Evening Post* (1898–99). Meanwhile he had developed a keen interest in educational reform and for a time withdrew from editorial work to lecture on "Mental Training by Analysis, Law, and Analogy." In 1905–06 he was editor of the *Search-Light* and, observing the need of greater uniformity in state legislation, he proposed the organization of the state executives into a House of Governors to work for that object (see his brochure, *The House of Governors,* 1907). At the conference of governors on conservation called by President Roosevelt in May 1908, a committee was named to arrange for a permanent organization and the first meeting of the actual House of Governors was held two years later. The project, as it was actually worked out, however, was described by the *Nation* (May 21, 1908) as "merely one of those devices to collect and express public opinion and to forward good causes, in which American political genius has always been fruitful."

Jordan wrote and published a series of homilies that attained a greater popularity than is usually the lot of essays on such hackneyed topics—*The Kingship of Self-Control* (1899), *The Power of Truth* (1902), *The Crown of Individuality* (1909), *Little Problems of Married Life* (1910), *The Trusteeship of Life* (1921), *The Vision of High Ideals* (1926). His treatment of these and kindred themes was characterized by simplicity and clarity of statement, often by humor. All his books had a good sale for years. In 1919 he brought out a pamphlet summarizing objections to America's joining the League of Nations (*What Every American Should Know About the League of Nations*). He retained to the last his convictions, formed early in life, as to the essential inconsistency and wastefulness of the American educational system and contributed to the *Forum* March-June 1923) four articles that summed up his thought on the subject. His attacks on the evils of cramming with indigestible facts and the ignoring of true intellectual discipline were supported by not a few educationists; but he lacked a program that appealed to school administrators as constructively practical. On May 6, 1922, he married Nell Mitchell of New York, who survived him.

[*Who's Who in America,* 1926–27; *Who's Who in N. Y.,* 1924; *N. Y. Times,* Apr. 21, 1928.] W. B. S.

JOSEFFY, RAFAEL (July 3, 1852–June 25, 1915), concert pianist, teacher, and editor, was born in Hunfalu, Hungary, but in early childhood was taken by his parents to Miskolcz, not far from Budapest. He was the only child of Vilmos and Cecilia (Lang) Joseffy, both Hungarian Jews. The father was a learned rabbi, a man of culture, and a teacher of Oriental and European languages. He early recognized his son's talent for music, and while the boy was in no sense a prodigy his early efforts at the piano were indicative of sufficient talent to gain for him thorough training. When he was eight years old his father took him to Budapest and placed him under Brauer, who had been the teacher of Stephen Heller, and when he was fourteen he entered the Leipzig Conservatorium. Here he became a student of E. F. Wenzel, though he also had some lessons from Moscheles. He remained in Leipzig for two years, after which, in 1868, he went to Berlin for further study under Tausig. The last-named teacher was by far the most potent influence in shaping the young pianist's ideas and in developing his brilliant technique. While he spent two summers (1870 and 1871) at Weimar with Liszt, who doubtless developed his artistic side, Liszt's influence upon him was by no means as great as was that of Tausig. How highly Liszt estimated the youth's abilities is evidenced by the fact that among Joseffy's many autograph letters of Liszt, there is one in which the master speaks of him as "my successor and heir."

He made his début in Berlin in 1872 and won

immediate recognition. There followed concerts in Vienna and other large music centers with similar success. He was at once recognized as a virtuoso with a remarkable technique. Hanslick acclaimed him as being an unusually brilliant performer, whose technique, quality of tone, and clean-cut phrasing showed clearly the influence of Tausig, though he had not as yet developed the poetic side of his genius. Another critic spoke of the "elegance and sparkle" of his runs, and added "such brilliant delicacy, such elegant fluency . . . has not been heard since the time of Tausig and Liszt" (quoted in Mathews, *post,* p. 126). He made concert tours through Holland, Germany, Italy, Denmark, Sweden, Norway, and Russia, everywhere meeting with marked success. After several years spent in touring Europe, he came to America in 1879, making his first appearance in New York soon after his arrival with an orchestra conducted by Dr. Leopold Damrosch [*q.v.*]. He was immediately hailed as one of the greatest concert pianists. Soon afterward he played with the Philharmonic Orchestra and subsequently appeared in New York and elsewhere with the Theodore Thomas Orchestra. Notwithstanding his sensational success, Joseffy withdrew from the concert stage and for five years studied intensively to discover the deeper meaning of his art and to make his splendid technique the vehicle for the expression of the poetic, imaginative content of music. When he returned to the concert platform there appeared a mature Joseffy, his old superb technical skill now enriched with a new depth and warmth of tone-quality. While he excelled as a player of Bach and Mozart, he was equally impressive in presenting the impassioned works of Beethoven, Schumann, Chopin, Liszt, and Brahms. He was a pioneer in America in making known the works of Brahms; indeed, he was one of the first to give frequent renditions of the Brahms "Concerto No. 2."

At the height of his success, weary of constant travel, he withdrew entirely from public performance and devoted himself thenceforth to teaching and writing, living much of the time at his summer home at Tarrytown, N. Y. From 1888 to 1906 he was professor of piano at the National Conservatory in New York. His ideas on piano technique and interpretation, drawn from his experience as teacher and virtuoso, are embodied in two comprehensive and elaborate works: *School of Advanced Piano Playing* (1902), which was translated into German, and *First Studies* (1913), a work of even larger scope. He edited many standard works (some pieces by Liszt and a collection of the works of Brahms), but his largest editorial contribution was his *Complete Works of Chopin* (1915), in fifteen volumes. Unlike most virtuosi, he was a deep student and possessed in a marked degree the ability of self-analysis, which enabled him to bring his own great technical and interpretative powers to the service of his pupils' needs. His influence as a pedagog was far-reaching. He was a graceful figure at the piano and exacted from his students similar grace and simplicity. While conscious of his own value as a teacher, he was generous in acknowledging good work done by others. In his youth he wrote some salon pieces, but his work as composer is not significant. He was married in September 1890 to Marie Gumere, who had been his housekeeper. He died at his home in New York City and his body was cremated at Union Hill, N. J.

["Rafael Joseffy's Contribution to Piano Technic," *Musical Quart.,* July 1916, by Edwin Hughes, a former student; certain personal information from Mr. Hughes and from Joseffy's friend and student, Sigmund Herzog, Esq.; James Huneker, "The Rare Art of Rafael Joseffy," *N. Y. Times,* July 4, 1915, pt. IV, p. 14; "Rafael Joseffy," *Musical Observer,* Aug. 1915; W. S. B. Mathews, *A Hundred Years of Music in America* (1889); *Freund's Music and Drama,* Dec. 25, 1890; *N. Y. Times,* June 26, 1915; personal recollections of Joseffy's pianism.]

F. L. G. C.

JOSEPH (*c.* 1840–Sept. 21, 1904), a Nez Percé chief, generally regarded as the greatest of Indian strategists, was born probably in the Wallowa Valley, Ore. His Indian name, Hinmaton-Yalaktit, means "thunder coming from the water up over the land." His mother was a Nez Percé and his father a Cayuse, also known as Joseph. On his father's death, in 1873, young Joseph became chief of the "non-treaty" Nez Percés, who refused to recognize the agreement of 1863 ceding three important regions to the government and confining the tribe to the Lapwai reservation in Idaho. In 1876 the government, after thirteen years' delay, determined to enforce the treaty. Gen. O. O. Howard, commander of the district, sought to prevent war by negotiations with Joseph. The difficulty of the situation was increased, however, by the fact that the squatters had committed repeated outrages upon the Indians, and on June 13, 1877, the favorable progress of Howard's negotiations was stopped by the outbreak of a small band of Indians who terrorized the countryside and killed twenty whites. Reluctantly Joseph was drawn into the hostilities, in which he displayed signal ability. Realizing, however, that he could not cope with the military, he resolved to escape to Canada. Gathering fewer than two hundred warriors, burdened with three times as many women and children, he began his brilliant retreat, which occupies a unique place in the annals of Indian warfare. With Gen. John Gibbon at Fort Shaw in front of him, General Howard behind him, and numerous detachments summoned by the white man's telegraph to menace his flank, he eluded Howard, defeated Gibbon in a desperate battle at Big Hole (Wisdom) River, Mont., on Aug. 9, and fled for more than a thousand miles through southwestern Montana, a corner of Idaho, the Yellowstone Park, and along Clark's Fork to the Yellowstone River. On the north side of the river he pushed aside Gen. S. D. Sturgis and gained the Bear Paw Mountains, only thirty miles from the safety of the Canadian boundary. There, believing that he had outdistanced his pursuers, he rested. On Sept. 30, however, Gen. Nelson A. Miles, who had made a cross-country dash from Fort Keogh, threatened him, and Joseph had only the choice of escaping by abandoning his wounded and helpless, accepting capture, or giving battle. With the military genius which is highly praised by those most competent to judge, he intrenched himself in a way that suggested the work of a professional engineer and from the shelter of the rifle pits faced his enemy. After five days of siege he surrendered on Oct. 5. With his band, comprising eighty-seven warriors (forty of whom were wounded) and their women and children—a total of 431—he was taken to Fort Leavenworth, Kan. In July 1878 they were transferred to the Indian Territory, where many of them sickened and died. Subsequently about half of the remainder were returned to Lapwai. Joseph, however, with about one hundred and fifty of his followers, was sent to the Colville reservation, in Washington. He stoically accepted his lot, keeping the vow made at the time of his surrender, never again to take arms against the whites, giving his best efforts to the work of educating the children, fostering industry, and discouraging drunkenness and gambling. In 1903 he visited the President and General Miles in Washington. He died at Nespelim, on the Colville reservation, far away from the beautiful valley of his youth.

Joseph was six feet tall, of erect carriage, and with handsome and impressive features. His expression was serious, even somber, and he seldom smiled. He was noted for his humaneness in warfare. Although some outrages were committed by members of his band, he did not countenance them; he bought supplies which he might have confiscated, saved property which he might have destroyed, and spared hundreds of lives which most other Indians would have taken.

[*Ann. Report of Commissioner of Indian Affairs,* 1859, pp. 415ff.; *Ibid.,* 1873, pp. 158ff., 245; *Ibid.,* 1875, pp. 72, 260–61; *Ibid.,* 1877, pp. 9ff., 13, 81, 211–17; *Ibid.,* 1878, pp. xxxiv, xxxv, 33; *Ann. Report of the Secretary of War,* 1877, pp. 119ff., 576ff.; O. O. Howard, *Nez Percé Joseph* (1881); Nelson A. Miles, *Personal Recollections* (1896); *14 Ann. Report, Bureau of Am. Ethnology,* pt. II (1896); *Century,* May 1884; C. T. Brady, *Northwestern Fights and Fighters* (1907); G. O. Shields, *The Battle of the Big Hole* (1889).]

W. J. G.

JOSSELYN, JOHN (fl. 1638–1675), traveler and writer, published two volumes dealing with New England, based on his observations made during two visits to that region. His first, *New-Englands Rarities Discovered,* was licensed for publication, at London, on June 24, 1672 (Edward Arber, *The Term Catalogues,* vol. I, 1903, p. 112). It contained a wealth of information relating to the animals and plants of the country, being the first systematic account of the botanical species of this portion of English America (*Publications of the Colonial Society of Massachusetts,* vol. III, 1896, p. 184). Josselyn's book was immediately noticed with approval in the pages of *Philosophical Transactions* (issue for July 15, 1672), the organ of the Royal Society. Thus encouraged, Josselyn turned to his desk and wrote *An Account of Two Voyages to New-England,* which was published first in 1674 and again in 1675. Though this work was dedicated to the Fellows of the Royal Society, no official notice of it was taken. Both volumes were considered worthy of inclusion, however, in the library then being gathered by the Plantation Office at London (*New-England Historical and Genealogical Register,* July 1884, p. 262). The *Two Voyages* is the more ambitious work: it is a rather strange compound of scientific lore, suggestions for settlers, bits of local history, and much general observation. Its tone, by and large, is fair, but scattered through it are to be found some statements that are slyly hostile to the inhabitants of Massachusetts Bay. This occasionally unfriendly attitude is most probably explained by the circumstance that the author's brother, Henry Josselyn, was for many years a principal representative in eastern New England of the interests of the Mason and Gorges heirs, which were endangered by the Bay Colony's expansion into Maine. Of John Josselyn but little is known. He was a bachelor, the second son of Sir Thomas Josselyn, Knight, of Torrell's Hall in Willingale-Doe, Essex, and his second wife, Theodora (Cooke) Bere, of a Kentish family (*Ibid.,* July 1917, p. 248). His writings furnish ample evidence that his was an educated mind, and that he was not without a degree of curiosity in matters scientific, as he was likewise not without an element of occasional credulity in judging of them. One infers that he had been trained as a surgeon and physician. He first came to New England in the summer of 1638, and after visiting John Cotton and John Winthrop in Boston and staying some months at his brother's place in Black Point (now Scarborough, Me.), he departed in October 1639. His second visit extended from July 1663 till August 1671. He appears to have spent these years as a student and observer rather than as a gentleman-planter, and was again with his brother in the eastern country. His writings show him as a jovial companion, fond of good cheer, and it is not a surprise to learn that while in Maine he was twice presented by the grand jury for not being a regular attendant at divine service (*Province and Court Records of Maine,* I, 237, 334). After his return to England he perhaps came to enjoy a royal pension, if we may accept literally a statement in the *Two Voyages* (edition of 1865, p. 117). The rest is silence. Excerpts from his second work were slightly revised, and, with a map by Seller, hydrographer-royal, were published as *A Description of New-England* at some time between 1680 and 1682.

[*New Englands Rarities* was reprinted wth notes by Edward Tuckerman in *Trans. Am. Antiq. Soc.,* vol. IV (1860), and, with revised notes, was issued separately in 1865. *An Account of Two Voyages* was reprinted in *Mass. Hist. Soc. Colls.,* 3 ser. III (1833) and separately in 1865. See also, in addition to authorities mentioned above, J. P. Baxter, *Doc. Hist. of the State of Me.,* III (1884), 140; *Province and Court Records of Me.,* vols. I, II (1928–32), ed. by C. T. Libby; Fulmer Mood, "Notes on John Josselyn, Gent.," to be published in *Colonial Soc. of Mass. Pubs.,* probably in vol. XXX; H. W. Felter, *The Genesis of the Am. Materia Medica, Including a Biog. Sketch of "John Josselyn, Gent."* (1927).]
F. M—d.

JOUBERT DE LA MURAILLE, JAMES HECTOR MARIE NICHOLAS (Sept. 6, 1777–Nov. 5, 1843), Roman Catholic priest, member of the Society of Saint Sulpice, and founder of the Oblate Sisters of Providence, was born of noble lineage at Saint Jean d'Angely on the western coast of France. The destruction of church and family records which accompanied the revolutionary outbursts in the French provinces have left no documentary trace of his parentage. Orphaned at an early age he found shelter with kind-hearted relatives in Beauvais. As a youth he was enrolled in the school of Reboisen-Brie to prepare for a military career, but later he abandoned his studies in order to take up a position in the French tax department. Sent overseas in 1800, he was assigned similar duties in the French West Indian island of Santo Domingo, where a paternal uncle, C. Joubert de Maine, was engaged in business. In September 1804 an uprising of slaves took place in which some of his relatives were massacred. Both uncle and nephew escaped, and eventually reached Baltimore, Md. De Maine became a teacher and De la Muraille, under the guidance of his fellow countrymen, the priests of Saint Sulpice, entered St. Mary's Seminary, Baltimore, as a student for the priesthood.

Joubert completed his ecclesiastical studies and was ordained priest by Archbishop Carroll in 1810. The same year he was admitted by his teachers as a member of their Society and as such consecrated his life to the education and training of the clergy. He was appointed teacher of French and of geography at St. Mary's College, established by the Fathers of St. Sulpice with the hope that it would both develop candidates for the Church and aid materially in the sustenance of the ecclesiastical Seminary of St. Mary's. It became, however, a select school to which were sent the children of prominent non-Catholic families from Maryland, from distant states of the Union, and from the French and Spanish West Indies. Father Joubert became successively disciplinarian and vice-president. All the former experiences of his life united to make him an efficient teacher, a popular and kind, yet firm, head-master, and a successful administrator.

In 1827 he began work among the French West Indian negroes who had followed their masters in exile to Baltimore. They had settled around the seminary, worshipped in its chapel and, speaking only French, were ministered to by the Fathers of the seminary. Father Joubert was given the charge of catechizing them. Pitying their ignorance, he thought of establishing a school where the little ones could at least be taught to read and write and receive religious instruction. He lacked, however, all means, nor could he look forward to any future help. His ecclesiastical superiors approved his plans but could offer no material aid. Eventually he discovered two Catholic negro women of West Indian birth, Elizabeth Lange and Marie Magdalen Balas, who were conducting a little school for negro children. They were capable and willing, but were about to close the school for lack of funds. Father Joubert then conceived the idea of founding a religious society of colored women for the education of children of their race. With the moral support of the Archbishop of Baltimore in 1828 he established the new community, which consisted of four, in a little rented house on George Street. Later with the scant but whole-hearted aid of a few lay Catholic men and women he moved them to a larger one on Richmond Street. He drew up a rule of life for the prospective Religious which was approved by Archbishop Whitfield of Baltimore in 1829, and the Sacred Congregation of the Propaganda in

Rome gave confirmation to the new society, the Oblate Sisters of Providence, by a rescript under date of Oct. 2, 1831. The society now (1932) counts fifteen different establishments in the United States, besides the academy and an orphanage at the mother-house in Baltimore. In 1838 Father Joubert began to fail in health, but, as best he could from his room in the Seminary, he continued to encourage and care for his spiritual children till his death.

[Father Joubert's journal (MS.); Nécrologie des Messieurs de Saint Sulpice (MS.); Register of St. Mary's College (MS.); C. G. Herbermann, *The Sulpicians in the U. S.* (1916); H. J. Duffy, "The Centenary of the Oblate Sisters of Providence" (dissertation for the degree of M.A., 1925), in library of St. Mary's Seminary, Baltimore; Grace H. Sherwood, *The Oblates' Hundred and One Years* (1931); *The Metropolitan Cath. Almanac,* 1844; the *Sun* (Balitmore) and the *Baltimore Clipper,* Nov. 8, 1843.] H. B.

JOUETT, JAMES EDWARD (Feb. 7, 1826–Sept. 30, 1902), naval officer, was the son of the painter, Matthew Harris Jouett [*q.v.*], and Margaret Henderson Allen. He was born near Lexington, Ky., and was appointed a midshipman in the United States Navy on Sept. 10, 1841. In the so-called "Berribee War" on the coast of Liberia in 1843 he served on the *Decatur* in the squadron under Matthew C. Perry [*q.v.*]; in the Mexican War he was on the *John Adams* on the east coast of Mexico, being one of those landed to defend Point Isabel. After about a year at the new Naval School at Annapolis, he was made a passed midshipman and sent to the Mediterranean in the *St. Lawrence.* During the early fifties he cruised in the Pacific on the *Lexington* and the *St. Mary's.* In 1858–59 he served as a lieutenant on the steamer *M. W. Chapin* in the Paraguay expedition.

At Pensacola at the beginning of the Civil War he was captured by the Confederates, but was given a document stating that he had given his "parole of honor not to bear arms against the state of Florida," and permitted to leave. He disavowed the statement, escaped North, and was sent to the Galveston blockade. Here he distinguished himself on Nov. 7–8, 1861, by heading a boat party from the *Santee* which captured the armed schooner *Royal Yacht,* guarding the harbor entrance at Galveston. Though wounded several times, Jouett brought off the crew as prisoners and set fire to the vessel. For this achievement he was given command, first of the *Montgomery* (December 1861), and then of the fast steamer *R. R. Cuyler* off Mobile (April 1863). In his blockading work he attracted the favorable attention of Farragut and in September 1863 was put in command of the *Metacomet,* the fastest gunboat in the squadron.

In the battle of Mobile Bay (August 1864), the *Hartford* and the *Metacomet* were lashed together. At the critical moment, Farragut in the port shrouds of the *Hartford* gave the historic command to Jouett on the starboard wheelhouse of the *Metacomet:* "Damn the torpedoes! Four bells! Captain Drayton, go ahead! Jouett, full speed!" A little later the *Metacomet* was sent after the Confederate gunboats, and by a fast pursuit and hazardous navigation in shoal water Jouett riddled the *Gaines* and captured the *Selma.* His dashing exploits secured high commendation from Farragut but no special reward except nearly a hundred thousand dollars prize money from blockade runners captured (Clark, *post,* p. 98). In 1880 Jouett's efforts to secure promotion over the heads of sixteen of his seniors created much ill feeling. His most important command did not come till 1884, when he was put in charge of the North Atlantic Squadron. Here he is credited with inaugurating the custom of all hands saluting the colors when they are raised or lowered. In 1885 he commanded the American naval force of eight ships and 2,648 men which was sent to Aspinwall (now Colón) to reopen transit across the Isthmus of Panama, lately interrupted by a revolt against Colombia. By vigorous measures he established free passage for the trains of the Panama Railroad and thus brought about the failure of the insurrection.

Jouett was retired in 1890 with the rank of rear admiral, and by an act of Congress, Mar. 3, 1893, was allowed full pay for life. His closing years, except for a short period in Orlando, Fla., were spent at "The Anchorage," his home near Sandy Spring, Md. In his later days he was a great lover of fox hunting and a racy raconteur of his naval experiences. In 1852 he had married Galena Stockett of Howard County, Md., who survived him. He was buried in the National Cemetery at Arlington.

[See sketch by Alfred Pirtle, in *United Service,* Dec. 1896, Jan. 1897; *War of the Rebellion: Official Records (Navy),* 1 ser. IV, 59 ff., XVI, 755–62, XXI, 442 ff.; *Army and Navy Jour.,* Mar. 6, 13, 20, 27, June 12, 19, 1880, Oct. 4, 1902; J. M. Morgan, "Jim Jouett," in C. E. Clark, *Prince and Boatswain* (1915); George Baber, in *Ky. State Hist. Soc. Reg.,* May 1914; Loyall Farragut, *The Life of David Glasgow Farragut* (1879); *Evening Star* (Washington), Oct. 1, 1902. The date of Jouett's birth in the Navy Department record is Feb. 27, 1828, but the family Bible as cited by Pirtle shows Feb. 7, 1826, and the date 1826 is on Jouett's tombstone at Arlington.] W. B. N.

JOUETT, JOHN (Dec. 7, 1754–Mar. 1, 1822), Revolutionary patriot, was born in Albemarle County, Va., a descendant of Daniel de Jouet who settled in Rhode Island in 1686, and the second son of Capt. John Jouett, later proprietor of the Swan Tavern in Charlottesville, and his wife, Mourning Harris. Little is recoverable concerning his early manhood save that he was a dead shot and, despite his gigantic stature—he stood six feet four inches and weighed over two hundred pounds—an expert rider, fond of the chase; that he was one of a group of Albemarle citizens who signed an oath of allegiance to the commonwealth in 1779; and that he held a captain's commission in the Virginia militia. Although his name is closely associated with the beginnings of Kentucky's statehood, his chief claim to remembrance lies in his daring and dramatic ride of more than forty miles to save Governor Jefferson and the Virginia legislature from capture.

On June 3, 1781, Cornwallis detached two hundred and fifty splendidly mounted horse under his "hunting leopard," Tarleton, to cover in twenty-four hours the seventy miles between his position in Hanover County and Charlottesville, whither the legislature had fled from Richmond, with the aims of seizing Jefferson, dispersing the Assembly, and destroying certain stores. Jouett was at Cuckoo Tavern, some miles beyond Louisa, when Tarleton's troopers swept along the main road shortly before midnight. Divining their purpose, he skirted the enemy's bivouac, rode through the night across the countryside or over circuitous, disused byways and footpaths, and reached "Monticello" before sunrise. After warning Jefferson he hastened on to spread the alarm, so that when Tarleton, who had been purposely delayed at the home of Dr. Thomas Walker, reached Charlottesville two hours later he found his quarry flown. Several members of the Assembly were taken, and only a further ruse of Jouett's saved Gen. Edward Stevens; but those most sought by the British—Richard Henry Lee, Benjamin Harrison, Nelson, Henry, and Jefferson—were safely beyond reach. The legislature, reconvening in Staunton, promptly voted Jouett "an elegant sword and pair of pistols" in appreciation of his activity and enterprise, even though they neglected to deliver the sword to him until 1803.

The year following his history-making ride Jouett moved to Mercer County (now in Kentucky); married, Aug. 20, 1784, Sallie Robards; entered actively into local affairs, and rose rapidly to prominence. Hospitable, attractive, and high-spirited, he entertained lavishly and made friends readily, numbering among his intimates Clay, Jackson, the Breckinridges, and the Marshalls. He represented Lincoln (1786–87) and Mercer (1787–88, 1790) counties in the Virginia Assembly; took a leading part in the Danville Convention, and was strongly influential in organizing Kentucky as a separate state; represented Mercer in the Kentucky legislature for one term, and, after moving to Woodford County about 1793, thrice served as its representative, winning reputation the while as an able and progressive statesman of the Jeffersonian school. His advocacy, in later life, of importing fine breeds of foreign cattle is said to have been largely instrumental in enabling Kentucky to become a great stock-raising center. One of his sons, Matthew Harris Jouett [*q.v.*], attained distinction as a portrait painter, and a grandson, James Edward Jouett [*q.v.*], was one of Farragut's officers at the battle of Mobile Bay.

[The fullest account of Jouett is by Virginius Dabney, "Jouett Outrides Tarleton," *Scribner's Mag.*, June 1928; other valuable material is contained in the unpublished address (based on family records and MSS.) by E. S. Jouett of Louisville, delivered at the unveiling of a tablet to Jouett at Cuckoo, Va., Sept. 6, 1926. Most early notices of Jouett's ride, apparently confusing identities of name and military rank, attribute it to John Jouett, Sr., but recent researches indicate conclusively that the credit belongs to "Young Jack" and not to his father. See also John Burk, Skelton Jones, and L. H. Girardin, *The Hist. of Va.*, vol. IV (1816); H. S. Randall, *The Life of Thomas Jefferson* (1858); P. L. Ford, *The Writings of Thomas Jefferson* (1897), VIII, 363 ff.; Edgar Woods, *Albemarle County in Va.* (1901); W. C. Ford, ed., *Letters of Joseph Jones* (1889), p. 82; S. W. Price, *Old Masters of the Bluegrass* (1902); *Jour. of the House of Delegates,* passim.]

A. C. G., Jr.

JOUETT, MATTHEW HARRIS (Apr. 22, 1787–Aug. 10, 1827), painter, father of James Edward Jouett [*q.v.*], was born near Harrodsburg, Mercer County, Ky., the second son of John [*q.v.*] and Sallie (Robards) Jouett. As a young boy, "before he could count one hundred or repeat the Lord's Prayer" (Price, *post,* p. 12), Matthew drew likenesses which astonished his family. Art, however, was not thought of as a possible profession at that time. Captain Jouett, a practical farmer, one day called together his several sons and announced that he would try to make one of them a gentleman. Matthew was chosen for this honor. In 1804 he was entered at Transylvania University, from which he was graduated four years later with honors. In accordance with his parents' wishes he then studied law with Judge George M. Bibb of the Kentucky appellate court. He had begun to practise when the War of 1812 stirred patriotic fervor in his state. Enlisting in the 3rd Mounted Regiment of Kentucky Volunteers he was presently appointed by President Madison first lieutenant and paymaster of the 28th United States Infantry. On July 13, 1814, he became captain, resigning Jan. 20, 1815.

On his return from the army Jouett decided not to follow the law but to become a portrait painter, and he established himself at Lexington. This choice of occupation disgusted his father who said: "I sent Matthew to college to make a gentleman of him and he has turned out to be nothing but a d—d sign painter" (*Ibid.*, p. 21). Jouett's profession was not a bad business venture, however, since he began at once to paint on an average three portraits a week at twenty-five dollars each, a good income for the town and the time. He had married in 1812 Margaret Henderson Allen, daughter of William Allen of Fayette County. In 1816 Jouett set out on horseback for the Atlantic coast, intending to study in Europe, but his journey extended only to Boston, where from July to October he studied with Gilbert Stuart [*q.v.*]. He made a favorable impression on the veteran artist, who called him familiarly "Kentucky" and advised against his going abroad. Jouett accordingly returned to Lexington where, calling himself a pupil of Stuart, he doubled his prices. When work was slack in Kentucky he painted at New Orleans, Natchez, and other Southern cities. He executed with graceful, facile technique at least 334 portraits (catalogued by Price, *post*). The most celebrated of these, though not artistically the most successful, is the likeness of Lafayette now at the capitol, Frankfort. He painted Henry Clay at least three times and left records of nearly all the other celebrities of the region. His portraits of children were particularly pleasing. Contemporary artists held his work in high esteem; John Neagle [*q.v.*] once traveled to Lexington thinking to settle there but was surprised to find in Jouett "a good and well instructed artist" with whom he could not hope to compete.

Jouett's social graces qualified him for a successful career as a portrait painter. He was tall and handsome, gifted in music, and well grounded in literature. He was also deeply religious, a good husband and father, and was adored by his eight children. As he reached his fortieth birthday he seemed to have many years of creative activity before him, but he succumbed a few months later to an illness contracted on a painting trip. While his portraits have long been treasured in Southern homes, he was not nationally known until, in 1892, C. H. Hart (*post*), as organizer of a retrospective American exhibition for the Chicago Exposition, "discovered" Jouett's likenesses of Gen. Charles Scott and John Grimes. The latter canvas is now at the Metropolitan Museum, New York.

[*Ky. Reporter* (Lexington), Aug. 15, 1827; William Dunlap, *A Hist. of the Rise and Progress of the Arts of Design in the U. S.* (1918), ed. by F. W. Bayley and C. E. Goodspeed; H. T. Tuckerman, *Book of the Artists* (1867); C. H. Hart, "Kentucky's Master-Painter," *Harper's Mag.*, May 1899, and "Jouett's Kentucky Children," *Ibid.*, June 1900; S. W. Price, *The Old Masters of the Bluegrass* (1902), Filson Club Pubs. no. 17; I. M. Cline, *Art and Artists in New Orleans during the Last Century* (1922).] F. W. C.

JOUTEL, HENRI (*c.* 1645–after 1723), was a native of Rouen, a contemporary of La Salle [*q.v.*], and the journalist of his last expedition to America and of his last days and death. Joutel's father was a gardener for an uncle of La Salle. Henri had a fair education for his time and served for sixteen or seventeen years in the French army. He was at home in Rouen when in 1684 La Salle visited there while arranging for an expedition to form a settlement at the mouth of the Mississippi. Joutel was easily persuaded to join the party and become La Salle's confidential subordinate—"*intendant*" he called himself. They sailed from La Rochelle in July 1684 with four ships, carrying a contingent of colonists and plentiful supplies. After a stormy passage of over four months in which one vessel was taken by Spanish corsairs, the flotilla entered the Gulf of Mexico, but by mistaken reckoning passed the Mississippi mouth and landed on the coast of Texas in Matagorda Bay. There a colony was begun on a site on Lavaca Bay.

After the commander of the largest ship had sailed for France, La Salle discovered his mistake and made several efforts to find the Mississippi. During these journeys, Joutel was frequently left in charge of the camp and with great difficulty controlled the growing dissatisfaction of the colonists. Twice they plotted to kill him and seize the control, but the conspiracy was found out and thwarted. Finally La Salle determined to abandon the place and make a final effort to reach the Mississippi. They left Jan. 12, 1687, and journeyed northeasterly until on Mar. 19, after crossing the Brazos River, near the present city of Navasota, Tex., La Salle was set upon by conspirators and foully murdered. Joutel was absent from camp at the time, and when he returned and learned the facts he expected to meet a like fate; but he and a brother and nephew of La Salle were spared and allowed to escape. With a little company of six he crossed what is now Arkansas and at Arkansas Post found two of Tonty's men in charge of a hunting station. They escorted the retreating party to the Mississippi, where friendly Indians agreed to take them to Tonty's fort on the Illinois River. When Joutel and Jean Cavelier (La Salle's brother) reached Fort St. Louis on the Illinois in August, Tonty was absent on a war expedition. When he returned in October the adventurers for several reasons concealed from him the fact of La Salle's death. They passed the winter at the Illinois post, leaving in May for Quebec via the Great Lakes and Ottawa River route. From Quebec Joutel late in 1688 sailed for France and thereafter lived at Rouen until his death.

While on his arduous and adventurous journey he took notes of all that passed and on his return to France cast his notes into the form of a narrative, which was published in 1713 and appeared the next year at London as *A Journal of the Last Voyage Perform'd by Monsr. de la Sale to the Gulph of Mexico to Find out the Mouth of the Missisipi River.* Joutel complained that his published journal was changed from the original. It was prepared by one Michel, probably Jean Michel, who in 1687 was at Lachine, Canada. Charlevoix met Joutel at Rouen in 1723 and spoke of his straightforward nature—"a very upright man" (Stiles, *post,* p. 30). Joutel's narrative is like his character. He was simple, loyal, practical, resourceful, and prudent. For fullness of detail and exactness of statement his is the best description of La Salle's last expedition, while his journey from Texas to Quebec as an exploit has seldom been surpassed.

[Joutel's full narrative is published in Pierre Margry, *Découvertes et Établissements des Français dans l'Ouest et dans le Sud de l'Amérique Septentrionale* (1878); his journal was reprinted in facsimile by the Caxton Club (1896). H. R. Stiles edited a reprint (1906). Joutel's journal is also printed in I. J. Cox, *The Journeys of René Robert Cavelier Sieur de la Salle* (1905), vol. II. The latest authority is Baron Marc de Villiers, *L'Expedition de Cavelier de la Salle dans le Golfe du Mexique* (Paris, 1931). On the sites of La Salle's Texas colony and the place of his murder see H. E. Bolton in *Miss. Valley Hist. Rev.*, Sept. 1915.]

L. P. K.

JOY, AGNES ELIZA [See SALM SALM, AGNES ELIZA JOY, PRINCESS, 1840–1912].

JOY, JAMES FREDERICK (Dec. 2, 1810–Sept. 24, 1896), lawyer, railroad builder, was born at Durham, N. H., son of James and Sarah (Pickering) Joy, and a descendant of Thomas Joy [*q.v.*]. He received his early education in his native town, and after a couple of years as clerk in a store, graduated from Dartmouth College in 1833 at the head of his class. He then entered the Harvard Law School. He was compelled to interrupt his studies to teach school, but in 1836 he completed his course and was admitted to the bar. The same year he moved to Detroit, and the following year formed a partnership with George F. Porter.

The year 1837 was a momentous one in the history of Michigan, for it witnessed the authorization of a loan of $5,000,000 for the construction of three railroads across the state. Of these the state constructed only a few miles of the Michigan Southern Railroad and that part of the Michigan Central Railroad between Detroit and Kalamazoo. The panic of 1837 made it impossible for the state to borrow enough to complete them, and Joy urged their sale to a private company. In conjunction with John W. Brooks, superintendent of the Auburn & Rochester Railroad, he interested a group of New York and Boston capitalists, headed by John Murray Forbes [*q.v.*], in the purchase of the Michigan Central Railroad from the state, and in 1846 drew up the charter under which the sale was made. The new company paid $2,000,000 and made Forbes the first president. The road was now extended toward Chicago, but in order to obtain an entrance into that city made an arrangement with the Illinois Central for the use of its tracks. Joy had charge of the litigation involved, and Abraham Lincoln, employed first by Joy in 1850, assisted him at Springfield.

The next problem which was presented was that of extensions west of Chicago. For this purpose the Chicago & Aurora branch railroad was purchased in 1852, of which the following year Joy was made president. In 1856 he combined it with the Central Military Tract Railroad, of which he was president also, and gave them the name of the Chicago, Burlington & Quincy. In this same year the Burlington & Missouri River Railroad, stretching west from Burlington, received a federal land grant of 350,000 acres, and after the panic of 1857 Joy was able to purchase this road at a low figure. By the outbreak of the Civil War he had built the road as far as Ottumwa; in 1866 he was elected president and by 1869 had pushed it on to Council Bluffs on the Missouri. A charter and a federal land grant were obtained for the extension of the road across Nebraska and in 1873 it reached Fort Kearny, where a junction was effected with the Union Pacific. Meanwhile, Joy had acquired the Hannibal & St. Joseph Railroad, which gave control of southern Iowa and northern Missouri. The termini of the two lines were connected by building the Kansas City, St. Joseph & Council Bluffs Railroad, of which Joy was president from 1870 to 1874, and branches were constructed to Atchison and Kansas City. Having in mind a possible route to the Gulf, Joy with the aid of his Boston backers, bought the Kansas & Neosho Valley Railroad. This he reorganized under the name of the Missouri River, Fort Scott & Gulf. By 1870 it was completed to the southern boundary of Kansas. He also acquired the Leavenworth, Lawrence & Galveston, which he built only as far south as Coffeyville, near the southern boundary of the state, obtaining thereby a part of the Kansas land grant. The "Joy system" was the first important western railroad combination. Sale of control of the Hannibal & St. Joseph, the "key link," to Jay Gould by Boston interests in 1870, upset Joy's plans for a line to the Pacific over part of the Santa Fé route. The remainder of the roads in the "Joy system" in Kansas were disposed of to other interests or absorbed by the Burlington.

In organizing and carrying out these plans Joy was inevitably led into many positions of power and responsibility. In 1852 he became the counsel general for the Michigan Central and in 1853 for the Illinois Central, serving the latter for only one year. He became president of the former road in 1867 and practically rebuilt it; later he took over the Wabash, St. Louis & Pacific, of which he was president from 1884 to 1887, and arranged an eastern connection for it. He was one of the incorporators of the St. Mary's Falls Ship Canal Company, which, under contract with the state of Michigan, built the first ship canal at Sault Ste. Marie (1853–55). For a short time he was president of the Detroit *Post and Tribune* (1881–84), and was long a director of the Detroit National Bank. He was a member of the Michigan legislature in 1861–62, and was floor-leader of the House. A Whig in his early politics, Joy later became a Republican, assisting in the election of Lincoln and vigorously defending his policies as president. He was twice married, first, Aug. 12, 1841, to Martha Alger Reed of Yarmouth, Mass., by whom he had four children; and second, Dec. 12, 1860, to Mary Bourne of Hartford, Conn., by whom he had three children. He died at his home in Detroit.

[J. R. Joy, *Thomas Joy and His Descendants* (1900); *Colls. and Researches of the Mich. Pioneer and Hist. Soc.*, vols. XXII (1894), XXX (1906); Otto Fowle, *Sault Ste. Marie and Its Great Waterway* (1925); R. E. Riegel, *The Story of the Western Railroads* (1926); H. G. Pearson, *An Am. Railroad Builder: John Murray Forbes* (1911); H. V. Poor, *Manual of the Railroads of the U. S.*, 1868–69 to 1887; *Detroit Free Press* and *Detroit Tribune*, Sept. 25, 1896; letter from Henry B. Joy Historical Research, Detroit, Mich.] E. L. B.

JOY, THOMAS (*c.* 1610–Oct. 21, 1678), architect, builder, was born in England, although the probability that his native place was the village of Hingham in Norfolk has not been made a certainty by definite evidence. His name first appears in the records of the town of Boston in New England on Feb. 20, 1636, o.s., when he received leave to purchase land of Robert Turner, and "to have it upon the usuall Condition of inoffensive Carryage." In 1637 he married Joan Gallop, daughter of John Gallop, a shipmaster and trader whose name is still borne by one of the islands in Boston Harbor. Joy's occupation seems to have brought him early prosperity, and his name appears in the list of Boston property holders, although he was not yet a freeman. In 1646, however, he took part in the agitation for the extension of the suffrage, and his fortunes suffered as a consequence. Only members of Puritan congregations could vote, and a petition to Governor Winthrop to remedy this condition being rejected, Joy was active in securing signatures to an appeal to the British Parliament. He was arrested and kept in irons for his contumacy, and though he recanted and was released, he removed to Hingham, twelve miles from Boston, where he seems to have maintained himself and his family with some difficulty for about ten years, chiefly from his interest in a grist and saw mill. By 1656 he had again become prominent in Boston, his early radicalism having been either forgiven or forgotten; and in 1657 he received the contract for the erection of the most pretentious building yet undertaken in the colony. Capt. Robert Keayne left three hundred pounds in his will for a structure to house the markets, courts, town council, and other public bodies, and the bequest was more than doubled by public subscriptions. Joy designed the building, although for its construction he had an associate, Bartholomew Bernad, in the contract. It was on the site now occupied by the "Old State House," a Georgian building of brick; but this "pine statehouse," as Emerson calls it in his "Boston Hymn," was of wood and pronouncedly Tudor in character. It was sixty-one feet long, thirty-six feet wide, and set upon twenty-one pillars ten feet from pedestal to capital. The building projected three feet beyond the pillars, on all sides. It was of three stories, with three dormer windows on the north and south sides of the upper one, and a "walke upon the Top fourteen or 15 foot wide with two turrets, & turned Balasters and railes round about the walke" (Joy, *post*, p. 22). Completed in 1658, it was burned in 1711, but was an outstanding architectual feature of the colony while it stood. Joy became very active in the town's development, and no doubt exerted considerable influence on its early architecture; but he was perhaps equally remarkable for his liberal political opinions and the courage to profess them at a time when both were rather rare. Of his ten children five survived him, and through them his descendants are very numerous.

[J. R. Joy, *Thomas Joy and His Descendants* (1900); C. C. Joy Dyer, *A Brief Hist. of the Joy Family* (1876); *Second Report of the Record Commissioners of the City of Boston . . . 1634–1660, and the Book of Possessions* (1902); *Re-dedication of the Old State House, Boston* (1893).] S. G.

JOYCE, ISAAC WILSON (Oct. 11, 1836–July 28, 1905), bishop of the Methodist Episcopal Church, was born in Colerain Township, Hamilton County, Ohio, the son of James Wilson and Mary Ann Joyce. His father's ancestors were Irish, and his mother's, German. Until 1863 he spelled the family name "Joice." When he was thirteen years old his parents migrated to Tippecanoe County, Ind., and settled north of Lafayette. They were poor, struggling people, with only a two-room log house for a home, and Isaac worked on the farm summers and attended the district school winters. The determining event of his youth occurred while he was on a coon hunt. Separated from his companions in the woods, he was drawn by the sound of singing to a schoolhouse on the road. Entering, he found a revival conducted by a United Brethren preacher in progress, and was converted. Later he was baptized through a hole cut in the ice on the Wabash River. There followed a desire for an education and the work of the ministry, two years in Hartsville College, a United Brethren school in Bartholomew County, where he supported himself by the humblest forms of labor, and then his licensure as a local preacher. In 1858, while he was teaching in Rensselaer, Ind., Rev. Granville Moody persuaded him that the Methodist Church offered him greater opportunity for usefulness, and he joined that denomination. This same year the Northwest Indiana Conference gave him work as a "supply," on the Rolling Prairie Circuit.

Equipped with a horse and two dollars and twenty-five cents, the gift of his father, and with a few clothes, Bible, Discipline, and hymnal in his saddlebags, he set out for his field of labor one hundred and fifty miles away, beginning a ministry destined to be world-wide in extent. His rise to influence and prominence was rapid. By assiduous study he added much to his education. In 1859 he was admitted to the Conference on trial, ordained deacon in 1861, and elder in 1863. On Mar. 20, 1861, he married Caroline Walker Bosserman of La Porte, Ind. After strenuous circuit work, in 1866 when he was but thirty, he was appointed to the Ninth Street Church, Lafayette. In this city he remained ten years, serving also as presiding elder of the district, and as pastor of Trinity Church. Poor health caused him to take a supernumerary relation in 1876–77, during which time, however, he supplied Bethany Church, Baltimore. From 1877 to 1880 he was pastor of Roberts Chapel, Greencastle, the seat of Indiana Asbury University (De Pauw). In the latter year he was a delegate to the General Conference. Transferred to the Cincinnati Conference in 1880, he was stationed eight years in that city as pastor of St. Paul's and Trinity. In 1886 he was fraternal delegate to the Methodist Church of Canada, and two years later was elected bishop. His first episcopal residence was at Chattanooga, Tenn. (1888–96). For five years during this period, as chancellor, he guided U. S. Grant University through a critical period of its history. From 1896 until his death his residence was at Minneapolis.

His influence and renown came primarily from his abilities as a preacher and pastor. The Irish in him displayed itself in his fervor, sense of humor, quick sympathies, and generous impulses. Using the language of the common people and speaking with abandon and evangelistic zeal, he sometimes held great audiences for the space of two hours. Religious awakenings invariably attended his ministry. To the board of bishops he brought capacity for hard work, sound judgment, and well-balanced character and powers; and his associates delegated to him some of their most important duties. In 1892 he presided over the conferences in Europe; in 1894 supervised Methodist work in Mexico; spent two years (1896–98) with the churches in China, Japan, and India, giving a great stimulus to missionary activity; and in 1903 and 1904 made episcopal tours in South America. From 1900 to 1904 he also presided over the Epworth League. While preaching at a camp meeting at Red Rock, Minn., in July 1905, his activity was brought to a close by a cerebral hemorrhage, and he died a few weeks later.

[W. F. Sheridan, *The Life of Isaac Wilson Joyce* (1907); *Meth. Rev.*, Jan. 1907; *Minneapolis Tribune*, July 28, 30, and Aug. 1, 1905; *Zion's Herald, Northwestern Christian Advocate, Western Christian Advocate*, Aug. 2, 1905; *Christian Advocate* (N. Y.), *Northern Christian Advocate*, Aug. 3, 1905; *Who's Who in America*, 1903–05.]
H. E. S.

JOYNES, EDWARD SOUTHEY (Mar. 2, 1834–June 18, 1917), Southern educator and writer, was born in Accomac County, Va., a son of Thomas Robinson and Ann Bell (Satchell) Joynes, and a grandson of Maj. Levin Joynes of the Continental Army, whose ancestors were among the earliest English settlers of Virginia. His father was an able and successful attorney. After preparatory training at Delaware College and at Concord Academy, Fredericksburg, Va., Edward entered the University of Virginia in 1850. He received the degree of B.A. in 1852 and that of M.A. the following year. Upon his graduation he was appointed assistant professor of ancient languages, a position which he filled until 1856. He then went to Berlin for two years' study at the University, where his instructors were the most noted scholars then living, Haupt, Bopp, and Benary. Of this period of his life he wrote most interestingly ("Old Letters of a Student in Germany," *Magnolia,* Richmond, 1863–64, reprinted 1916, as a bulletin of the University of South Carolina). While in Berlin he was elected professor of Greek and German at the College of William and Mary. He held this position for three years, in 1859 marrying Eliza Waller Vest, of Williamsburg.

When the Civil War began, Joynes became chief clerk in the Confederate War Department, Richmond, serving in this capacity until 1864. In 1864 and 1865 he taught English at Hollins Institute, Va., and in 1866 continued the same work at Washington College, Lexington, Va., under Gen. Robert E. Lee. Later, in 1875, he became a member of the faculty of Vanderbilt University; in 1878 of the faculty of the University of East Tennessee. After four years he was made professor of modern languages and English in South Carolina College, Columbia. He taught there until 1908 when, after fifty-five years in educational work, he was made professor emeritus and received a retiring allowance from the Carnegie Foundation for "unusual and distinguished service as a professor of Modern Languages."

Throughout his life Joynes devoted himself to the upbuilding of the schools and the colleges of the South and of the teaching profession. His vigorous addresses before the Tennessee Assembly were a potent factor in the organization of the University of Tennessee. His *Concerning the University of South Carolina* (1905), addressed to the state legislature, performed a similar service in that state. He directed, in 1880, the first teachers' institute ever held in South Carolina. He helped to organize and later became a member of the board of trustees of the state normal and industrial school for women, now Winthrop College, Rock Hill, S. C. He zealously advocated better training for teachers, more public schools, new methods of teaching in Virginia, Tennessee, and South Carolina. The long series of textbooks which he wrote and edited put his principles into practice. His publishers thought his ideas too radical but his judgment has been vindicated by the fact that many of his texts in German and French are still in use. Among the best known of these are an edition of Schiller's *Maria Stuart* (1880), *A German Grammar for Schools and Colleges Based on the Public School German Grammar of A. L. Meissner* (1887), and *Minimum French Grammar and Reader* (1892). Many of the negro schools in South Carolina today are directly traceable to the enthusiasm with which he sponsored education for all classes.

[*Lib. of Southern Lit.* (16 vols., 1909), vol. VII, which contains bibliog. to 1909; *A Tribute to Dr. Edward Southey Joynes on His Eightieth Birthday,* Bull. of the Univ. of S. C., 1914; *The State* (Columbia, S. C.), June 19, 1917.]

H. S., Jr.

JUDAH, SAMUEL (July 10, 1798–Apr. 24, 1869), lawyer, was born in New York City, of a Hebrew family, the son of Dr. Samuel Bernard Judah, and a grandson of Samuel Judah who emigrated to America from London about 1760 and was active in the American Revolution. His mother, Catherine Hart Judah, was the daughter of Aaron Hart who accompanied Amherst to Canada in 1760, served as commissary general on Haldimand's staff, and settled in Three Rivers. Young Samuel graduated from Rutgers College in 1816, was admitted to the bar, and in 1818 moved to Indiana and established himself in Vincennes, where he practised his profession until his death. His father visited him in 1872 and kept a journal, which was published in the *Indiana Magazine of History,* December 1921 ("A Journal of Travel from New York to Indiana in 1827"). Judah participated in politics and was a member of the state House of Representatives in 1827–29 and 1837–41, being elected speaker in 1840. He was originally a Democrat and was one of the committee that wrote the address of the Jackson convention in 1824. For some time he was United States attorney, but he lost his position in 1833 and the following year was opposing Jackson. In 1839 he presided over the Whig legislative caucus. In local politics he was a leader in the internal improvements party, was chairman of the canal committee of the Assembly, and reported in favor of canals, but the bill for their construction was defeated.

It was as a lawyer, however, that he was best known; he was considered one of the ablest in Indiana, and his practice extended beyond state lines and to the Supreme Court of the United States. To a deep knowledge of the law he joined great cleverness in the management of his cases. His most notable case was undertaken in 1842 in behalf of Vincennes University, the question at issue being the right of that institution to certain lands granted by act of Congress in 1804 but later taken by the state and in part sold. Judah procured the passage of a bill through the legislature granting the institution the right to bring suit against the state for the recovery of the property. Suit was brought in the Marion County court, and the university obtained a judgment for $30,099.96 and interest amounting to $5,-

428.87. The supreme court of Indiana reversed the decision, but the Supreme Court of the United States upheld the university's claim. Ultimately, in 1855, the state legislature passed a bill providing for the payment to the university of $66,585, out of which Judah retained for fees and expenses $26,728.23. The board of trustees of the school brought suit to compel him to make an accounting, and in his answer, among other things, he stated that he had used $4,500 in procuring the passage of the act of 1855. The trustees opposed this item, alleging that the money had been fraudulently and corruptly expended "in hiring persons to aid him in influencing members of the legislature and in bribing members to procure the passage of said act." The courts, however, sustained Judah's claim. Echoes of the case continued to be heard for half a century, and in 1909 the state paid the university another large sum to satisfy its claim.

Judah was learned outside the law and during his long career maintained a love for science and the classics. His proficiency in Greek and Latin was well known and he possessed an interesting general library. In 1825 he married Harriet Brandon of a prominent family in Corydon, Ind. Six of their children reached maturity.

[*A Biog. Hist. of Eminent and Self-Made Men of the State of Ind.*, vol. I (1880); *A Hist. of Vincennes Univ.* (1928); J. P. Dunn, *Indiana and Indianans* (5 vols., 1919); Logan Esarey, *A Hist. of Ind.*, vol. I (1915); *Compilation of Laws, Records, and Hist. Matter Relative to Claim of Vincennes Univ. against State of Ind.* (Indianapolis, 1909); *Am. Jewish Hist. Soc. Pubs.*, I (1892), 117, XIX (1910), 34, XXVII (1928), 490; J. A. Woodburn, *Higher Education in Ind.* (1891); A. A. Leonard, "Personal Politics in Ind., 1816 to 1840," *Ind. Mag. of Hist.*, Mar., June, Sept. 1923.] P. L. H.

JUDAH, SAMUEL BENJAMIN HELBERT (*c.* 1799–July 21, 1876), author, playwright, was born in New York City, the son of Benjamin S. and Elizabeth Judah. He was a descendant of an old colonial Jewish family that had settled in New York early in the eighteenth century. His father was a prominent merchant who was ruined by the War of 1812. Samuel attended the New York schools and acquired some knowledge of the classical languages and French. As a very young man he showed great interest in the theatre, and with more ambition than dramatic ability he wrote three plays that were accepted by the producers of his day. *The Mountain Torrent* (1820) was first performed at the Park Theatre on Mar. 1, 1820. Odell, in his *Annals of the New York Stage* (II, 557), characterizes it as "but an attempt to pour sour European wine into American bottles." A wholly worthless production, it met with no success. His next piece, *The Rose of Arragon; or, the Vigil of St. Mark* (1822), was produced at the Park Theatre on Apr. 18, 1822. The author boasts that he wrote this play in "about two days," and the reader has no reason to doubt him. Like *The Mountain Torrent,* it is a highly inflated piece of writing which has a strong flavor of French melodrama. In his third and last play to be performed Judah tried his hand upon a native theme, an event of the Revolution. This was *A Tale of Lexington* (1823), first performed at the Park Theatre on July 4, 1822. Since the author tells us that he spent but four days in its composition, we cannot be surprised at the verdict of Odell, who calls it "the most ridiculous thing conceivable" (*Ibid.*, III, 29). In 1822, Judah published *Odofriede, the Outcast,* a lugubrious dramatic poem of eighty-nine pages, a copy of which he sent to Thomas Jefferson. Probably embittered by his failure as a dramatist, he published in 1823 *Gotham and the Gothamites,* a book of versified satire of a highly libelous character, in which he attacked over a hundred people more or less prominent in New York City. The work was devoid of any literary merit and was written to vent his spleen. For this publication he became involved in a libel suit. He was found guilty, fined $400, and sent to prison, where he spent almost five weeks before he was pardoned by the governor because of ill health. Not sufficiently chastened by this experience, he published *The Buccaneers, a Romance of our Own Country* (1827), under the pseudonym of Terentius Phlogobombos. This contains a preface from which certain libelous passages were cut after the book had been printed; it is stated that no copy is known which preserves these missing pages. Judah's last publication was *The Maid of Midian* (1833), a dramatic poem in four acts.

In 1825, he was admitted to the bar as an attorney and counsellor of the supreme court, and for many years he practised law. Commenting upon Judah's later years, Judge Charles P. Daly says, "As an attorney, a gentleman who had much to do with him in the transaction of business described him to me as acute, cunning, technical, and not very reliable; notwithstanding which he was able to obtain what, in those days when imprisonment for debt was allowed, was called a collecting business, by which he was able to secure an ample competency, on which he lived for the rest of his life" (*post,* pp. 144–45). Judah, it appears, was a vain and shallow man. He never married, and he died in New York City.

[Details of the life of Judah are meager, and no account is entirely accurate. The *Jewish Encyclopedia* contains a brief biography and a few misstatements of facts; the longest and most revealing account is found in C. P. Daly, *The Settlement of the Jews in North*

America (1893). A criticism of Judah's plays is found in A. H. Quinn, *A Hist. of the Am. Drama from the Beginning to the Civil War* (1923), and in G. C. D. Odell, *Annals of the N. Y. Stage*, vols. II (1927), III (1928). A complete list of his writings is found in the *Am. Jewish Hist. Soc. Pubs.*, no. 30 (1926). The date of his death and the spelling of his third name are taken from the records of the congregation Shearith Israel, N. Y. City.]
H. W. S—r.

JUDAH, THEODORE DEHONE (Mar. 4, 1826–Nov. 2, 1863), engineer, railroad builder, was born in Bridgeport, Conn., the son of an Episcopal clergyman, Henry R. Judah. He studied at the Rensselaer Polytechnic Institute, Troy, N. Y., and on May 10, 1847, married Anna Ferona Pierce, daughter of a local merchant in Greenfield, Mass. After leaving the Institute he was employed by the New Haven, Hartford & Springfield Railroad, the Connecticut River Railway, and the Erie Canal. He also erected a large bridge at Vergennes, Vt., planned and built the Niagara Gorge Railroad, and was for a time in charge of construction on the line of the Buffalo & New York Railway, now a part of the Erie system. In 1854 he was called to the Pacific Coast as chief engineer of the Sacramento Valley Railroad, a local project completed in 1856 from Sacramento east to the town of Folsom. Leaving the employ of this road shortly before the line reached Folsom, he engaged for a time in engineering and construction work for other railroad companies. During these years he was frequently in the California mountains, and considered plans for a railroad which should run from California eastward to an ultimate junction with the railroad systems of the Mississippi Valley states. The desirability of such an enterprise was recognized upon the Pacific Coast, and the location of its western terminus, the general character of the route to be followed, and the extent to which the federal government might be induced to provide funds for its completion were subjects discussed in the state legislature, in the press, and in conventions called for this specific purpose in 1853 and in 1859. Judah published a pamphlet in 1857 upon the subject of a transcontinental railroad that was circulated among members of Congress at Washington. He was a prominent figure in the Pacific Railroad Convention of 1859 and was its accredited agent at the national capital in 1859 and 1860. In the latter year, after his return to California, he announced that he had discovered a practicable railroad route across the Sierras, and solicited private subscriptions to enable him to perfect the organization of a company which should undertake the work. The following year he was able to persuade Collis P. Huntington, Leland Stanford [*qq.v.*], and certain of their friends to join him in the organization of the Central Pacific Railroad Company, and to contribute to the expenses of an instrumental survey across the mountains. The survey proved satisfactory, Judah was again sent to Washington to seek national support, and after the passage of the federal act of July 1, 1862, he returned to California to direct construction.

Judah, rather than Huntington, Stanford, Hopkins, or Crocker is to be credited with the initiation and successful promotion of the first realized plan for the construction of a railroad across the Sierra Nevada mountains. He did not, unfortunately, survive to see the completion of his undertaking, and it is possible that he would not have remained with the Central Pacific even if he had lived. Friction between Judah and the Huntington group appears to have led the "Big Four" to buy the former out in 1863 for the sum of $100,000, at the same time that they gave him an option to purchase their respective shares for a similar amount each. Judah sailed for the East to seek other financial support, but contracted typhoid fever while crossing the Isthmus, and died soon after his arrival at New York. His record gives evidence of imagination and capacity for sustained enthusiasm, and also of a high degree of technical ability. Though he never had opportunity to display administrative talent in the management of a large enterprise, he is properly credited with a leading part in the early stages of a great railroad project which other men brought to a successful conclusion.

[C. I. Wheat, "A Sketch of the Life of Theodore D. Judah," *Cal. Hist. Soc. Quart.*, Sept. 1925; W. E. Curtis, in *Los Angeles Times*, Nov. 19, 1909; Stuart Daggett, *Chapters on the Hist. of the Southern Pacific* (1922); T. H. Hittell, *Hist. of Cal.*, vol. IV (1897); H. H. Bancroft, *Hist. of Cal.*, vol. VII (1890); C. C. Goodwin, *As I Remember Them* (1913). The Bancroft Library at the Univ. of Cal. contains a manuscript letter by Mrs. Judah and a considerable body of pamphlet material bearing upon Judah's activities upon the Pacific Coast.]
S. D.

JUDD, GERRIT PARMELE (Apr. 23, 1803–July 12, 1873), Hawaiian statesman, was born at Paris, Oneida County, N. Y., the eldest son of Dr. Elnathan Judd, Jr., and Betsey Hastings Judd, and a descendant of Thomas Judd who was living in Cambridge, Mass., in 1634. At an early age he began the study of medicine in his father's office and afterwards attended a medical school at Fairfield, Herkimer County, graduating in 1825. Converted in 1826, he decided to become a missionary, and in the fall of 1827 was appointed physician to the Sandwich Islands Mission of the American Board of Commissioners for Foreign Missions. On the eve of his departure for his distant field of labor he was married to Laura Fish, a young woman of good education and much strength of character. They had nine children.

Judd's service in the Mission extended over a period of fourteen years. In his professional capacity he was constantly brought into contact with the King and chiefs, won their implicit confidence, and gained an accurate insight into the Hawaiian character. Having a perfect command of the language, he was, from about 1833, drawn gradually into the councils of the nation by acting as interpreter and translator, and was on many occasions called upon for advice on matters of state. In 1842 the affairs of the kingdom came to a crisis—the native race seemed doomed to extinction and the independence of the island government was in jeopardy. Before this time Judd had assisted in introducing system into the business of the government; he now separated himself from the Mission and took service under the King, first as a member of the treasury board, then as recorder and translator, and finally, in 1843, as secretary of state for foreign affairs, while still holding his former offices. He was the trusted adviser of the King, and under his guidance a policy was devised whose underlying principle was a union of natives and foreigners as subjects and supporters of the independent native monarchy, which should be organized on a constitutional basis, so as to gain for the nation the benefits of foreign intercourse without allowing the native race to be overwhelmed by a flood of aliens. This policy drew into the government, as ministers or subordinate officials, a number of the best-qualified foreigners, in order that the administrative and judicial procedure might conform to the standards of civilized governments. The plan was effective in saving the nation, but the policy and many of the details of its working out brought Judd and other members of the government into collision with certain of the foreign residents who disliked the idea intensely. During a large part of his official career, Judd was a subject of violent criticism. A man of positive convictions, he acted with decision in critical moments and did not shirk the responsibility for his acts. He was minister of foreign affairs, 1843–45; minister of the interior, 1845–46; minister of finance, 1846–53; and during all this time he was the prime minister in fact if not in name. In 1849 he undertook a diplomatic mission abroad with the objects of obtaining reparation from France for acts of the French consul and French admiral at Honolulu in August 1849, and of making new treaties with the United States, Great Britain, and France. The first object was not accomplished, but toward securing the treaties some progress was made. Judd represented the King (Kamehameha III) on the committee which drew up the liberal constitution of 1852. In the following year he was forced out of the government by opposition which threatened the overthrow of the monarchy.

During the remaining twenty years of his life he devoted himself to his profession and to the agricultural development of the islands, but he always took a lively interest in politics and in the moral and religious welfare of the nation. He was a member of the legislature of 1858 and of the constitutional convention of 1864; during the sessions of the convention he strongly opposed the efforts of Kamehameha V to increase the power and prerogatives of the crown. He was one of the original members (1863) of the board of the Hawaiian Evangelical Association and served on that board until his death.

[Printed sources include: Laura Fish Judd, *Honolulu . . . from 1828 to 1861* (1880, reprinted 1928); *Fragments: Records of the House of Judd* (5 vols., printed for private circulation, 1903–30); G. R. Carter, *A Record of the Descendants of Dr. Gerrit P. Judd of Hawaii* (1922); Sylvester Judd, *Thomas Judd and His Descendants* (1856); reports of the Hawaiian minister of foreign relations, 1845–55, of finance, 1846–54, of the interior, 1845–46; *The Story of Hawaii and Its Builders* (1925); ed. by G. F. Nellist; Honolulu *Polynesian*, Apr. 12, 1845; *Pacific Commercial Advertiser*, July 19, 1873; *The Friend*, Aug. 1873; A. G. M. Robertson, in *Centenary Service Commemorating the Landing . . . of the Third Company Sent to the Sandwich Islands Mission by the A.B.C.F.M.* (1928). Criticism of Judd is most fully set forth in unpublished dispatches of the American commissioner and British consul general in Hawaii during the years 1844–53; A. Häolé (G. W. Bates), *Sandwich Island Notes* (1854), prints some documents bearing on Judd's retirement from the government; in preparing the present sketch, use has also been made of Honolulu newspapers and of unpublished materials in the Archives of Hawaii.] R. S. K.

JUDD, NORMAN BUEL (Jan. 10, 1815–Nov. 11, 1878), lawyer, congressman, diplomat, was born to Norman and Catherine (Van der Heyden) Judd at Rome, N. Y. The father, a descendant of Thomas Judd who was living in Cambridge, Mass., in 1634, was a potter by trade and an early settler of Oneida County, while the mother was a member of an old Dutch family settled at Troy. Norman, after a high-school education at Rome, made successive and unsuccessful efforts to find a niche as a merchant, a newspaperman, and a medico. The law finally claimed him and he was admitted to the New York bar, but, attracted by the possibilities of the new West, he migrated to Chicago in 1836. He arrived in time to draft the city's first charter, using that of Buffalo as a model, and this service was rewarded by his choice as first attorney of Chicago in 1837 and 1838. He was elected to the board of aldermen (1842) and in 1844, as a Democrat, began sixteen years of service in the state Senate. In 1844 also he married Adeline Rossiter.

The subsequent years found him increasingly identified with railroad operation and litigation, a connection in which his political position was doubtless no drawback. Between 1848 and 1860 he served as president, attorney, or director with the following railroad enterprises: Peoria & Bureau Valley, Railroad Bridge Company of Rock Island, Michigan Southern & Northern Indiana, Pittsburgh, Fort Wayne & Chicago, Mississippi, Missouri & Chicago, Milwaukee & St. Paul. He was prominent in the legal manipulations by which several of these roads were consolidated into the Rock Island system and became first attorney for the new organization.

His railroad interests whetted his enthusiasm for politics, and in May 1856 he was one of the Anti-Nebraska delegates to the Bloomington convention at which Illinois Republicanism was launched. The new party chose him as first chairman of its state central committee, a position which he held until 1860. He helped to make the arrangements leading to the Lincoln-Douglas debates, was Lincoln's manager in the campaign for the nomination in 1860, and led the Illinois forces in the election race. He had hoped and expected to be the choice of his party for the governorship, but was sidetracked in favor of Richard Yates, who, it was thought, could draw more votes from certain of the central counties and thus secure at once the success of Lincoln and the election of a legislature which would return Lyman Trumbull to the Senate. A personal and political feud of long standing with "Long John" Wentworth of Chicago, a rival Republican leader, likewise hurt his chances.

Following the election, after some unsuccessful angling for a cabinet position, he was chosen by Lincoln as minister to Prussia, a post which he filled capably but without particular distinction from 1861 to 1865. After Lincoln's reëlection he re-rented his house for four years and ordered new furniture on the supposition that his berth would be continued—an expectation which was sadly disappointed by Johnson's request for his resignation. Writing to Trumbull, June 12, 1865, of this circumstance, he commented: "A certain writer who usually signs himself 'J. W.' [Wentworth] has rather prompt revenge . . ." (Trumbull Papers). Wentworth was then in Congress. Judd returned to Chicago, and in 1866 was able to supplant his old rival in the Fortieth Congress. He served in this and the succeeding Congress (1867–71), interesting himself in the local needs of his city and in various legislative projects the desirability of which had become evident to him during his diplomatic service. He was pensioned by the Grant administration in the post of collector of customs at Chicago (July 17, 1872), a position which he occupied until failing health, leading finally to his fatal illness, forced his retirement in 1876.

[Scattered letters from and concerning Judd in the Lyman Trumbull Papers, Lib. of Cong.; Sylvester Judd, *Thomas Judd and His Descendants* (1856); A. T. Andreas, *Hist. of Chicago*, vol. II (1885); *The Biog. Encyc. of Ill. in the Nineteenth Century* (1875); Arthur Edwards, *Sketch of the Life of Norman B. Judd* (n.d.); L. O. Leonard in *Rock Island Mag.*, May 1926; *Chicago Daily Tribune*, Nov. 12, 1878; files of the *Tribune* and of the Springfield *Daily Register*.]

L. E. E.

JUDD, ORANGE (July 26, 1822–Dec. 27, 1892), agricultural editor and publisher, was born near Niagara Falls, N. Y., one of the ten children of Ozias and Rheuama (Wright) Judd, and a descendant of Thomas Judd who settled at Cambridge, Mass., about 1634. The boy's inherited bent for education took him, after attaining self-support, to Wesleyan University at Middletown, Conn., where he graduated in 1847. He became a teacher at Wilbraham Academy in western Massachusetts, but shortly developed an interest in agricultural chemistry and pursued that subject as a graduate student from 1850 to 1853 at Yale. His persistence in his researches at a time when the relation of chemistry to farming had received little or no attention in America seems to entitle Judd to rank among the pioneers, even in the absence of any single discovery placed to his credit.

In 1853 he removed to New York City to become joint editor of the *American Agriculturist* with Anthony Benezet Allen [*q.v.*], thus making a definite transition from a career of scholarship to one of active journalism, which was to end only with his death, forty years later. At first he did all the office work on the *Agriculturist* and wrapped and addressed by hand the entire edition. Within three years he was owner and publisher, as well as editor, and between 1856 and 1864 he raised the circulation of the journal (changed from a weekly to a monthly) from less than 1,000 to more than 100,000. He was also the agricultural editor of the *New York Times* from 1855 to 1863. His articles were brief, practical, and addressed to definite farm problems. Before the Department of Agriculture had begun to publish extensively and before the land-grant colleges were operating, the farm journal was almost the sole medium for providing the farmer with a sound scientific knowledge of his calling. Belonging to the once disparaged group of "book farmers," Judd always had the needs of the "dirt farmer" in mind and was one of the few agricultural writers of his time who had a first-hand acquaintance with both the farm and the laboratory.

The Civil War interrupted his editorial labors. He was with the United Christian Commission at Gettysburg, and with the Sanitary Commission followed the fortunes of the Army of the Potomac from the Rapidan to Petersburg. After the war his publishing interests in New York rapidly expanded. Besides the *Agriculturist* he controlled *Hearth and Home* from the end of its second year (1870–73), and owned the copyrights of many agricultural books. He devised the crop-reporting percentage system later adopted by nearly all nations.

As he gained wealth his thoughts turned to the possibilities of establishing scientific instruction at Wesleyan University. In 1871 his ideals were partially embodied in the Orange Judd Hall of Natural Science, which he gave to the University. His interest in his alma mater was also shown in the alumni catalogue, *Wesleyan University, Middletown, Conn., Alumni Record, 1833–1869* (1869), which he laboriously compiled. Meanwhile he had become internationally known through his crop-reporting system and the *Agriculturist* had acquired a substantial circulation among farmers in the Middle West. By his tender of $1,000 the establishment of the first of the State Agricultural Experiment Stations at Wesleyan University, serving the State of Connecticut, was made possible (A. C. True in *Year Book of the Department of Agriculture, 1899,* 1900, p. 516). Years before, in 1857–58, he had imported sorghum seed into the United States and distributed it gratis, thus helping to initiate a new industry.

He was president of a railroad built to connect Flushing, L. I., with New York City, and his losses in the venture, coupled with unfortunate real-estate speculations, brought about his failure in 1883. Retiring from the *Agriculturist* he went to Chicago and there edited the *Prairie Farmer* from 1884 to 1888. In the latter year he bought the St. Paul *Farmer,* and moved it to Chicago where, as both editor and business manager, he conducted it as the *Orange Judd Farmer* until his death. For many years thereafter his name was carried at the head of various farm papers.

On Oct. 10, 1847, Judd married Sarah L. Ford, who died in 1854; and on May 1, 1855, he took as a second wife Harriet Stewart. Two sons were associated with his publishing enterprises. As one of his side occupations he early busied himself with a series of weekly Sunday-school lessons, *Lessons for Every Sunday in the Year* (4 vols., 1862–65), which served as a pattern for the famous International Lessons.

[Sylvester Judd, *Thomas Judd and His Descendants* (1856); *Am. Agriculturist,* Feb. 1893; *Harper's Weekly,* Jan. 7, 1893; *Orange Judd Farmer,* Jan. 7, 1893; F. L. Mott, *A Hist. of Am. Magazines, 1741–1850* (1930); *Wesleyan Univ., Middletown, Conn., Alumni Record* (3rd ed., 1883); *N. Y. Times, N. Y. Tribune,* and *Chicago Daily Tribune,* of Dec. 28, 1892.]

W. B. S.

JUDD, SYLVESTER (July 23, 1813–Jan. 26, 1853), Unitarian clergyman, author, was born in Westhampton, Mass., the son of Sylvester and Apphia (Hall) Judd, and a descendant of Thomas Judd who came to Cambridge, Mass., from England about 1634, moved to Hartford, Conn., in 1636, and later was one of the first settlers of Farmington, Conn. Sylvester grew up in his native town and in Northampton, Mass., where in 1822 his father, a man of antiquarian tastes who achieved some reputation as a local historian, became editor of the *Hampshire Gazette.* His schooling was interrupted when he was about sixteen years old and he worked for a time as clerk in Greenfield and Hartford stores. He then prepared for college at Hopkins Academy, Hadley, Mass., graduated from Yale in 1836, and later taught a private school in Templeton, Mass. In 1837, having become a Unitarian, he entered the Harvard Divinity School, graduating in 1840. During the second year of his course he wrote for the *Christian Register* a series of letters upon the change in his religious views under the title "Familiar Sketches," which the American Unitarian Association published as Tract No. 128, *A Young Man's Account of his Conversion from Calvinism.* On Oct. 1, 1840, he was ordained in Augusta, Me., as pastor of the church and society known as East Parish, and the following year, Aug. 31, he married Jane Elizabeth, daughter of Hon. Reuel Williams [*q.v.*], then United States senator from Maine.

His early death limited his professional career to less than twelve years, during all of which period his home was in Augusta. The influence he exerted as preacher and pastor was extended by his activities as a Lyceum lecturer and writer. An idealist, sometimes more visionary than practical, he devoted himself ardently and unselfishly to bettering human relations. He worked for the adoption of his idea of the "birthright church," maintaining that family, church, and state are divine institutions in which all individuals by birth become members; and he outlined an ecclesiastical year with a unique array of monthly festivals. His opposition to war and his advocacy of non-resistance cost him in 1842 his position as chaplain to the Maine legislature. He deplored slavery, but did not sympathize with the belligerent attitude of the abolitionists; he supported the temperance movement, but had no faith in the Maine Law as a remedy for the evils it was intended to suppress; and he condemned capital punishment as both unchristian and inexpedient. His religious and social views are set forth in two novels, *Margaret* (1845) and *Richard Edney and the Governor's Family* (1850); and in a didactic poem, *Philo, an Evangeliad* (1850). The novels attracted considerable attention, and received both praise and ridicule. They are lacking in literary form and are full of eccentricities, but delineate certain aspects of New England life faithfully and effectively, and contain descriptive passages of rare excellence. James Russell Lowell in *A Fable for Critics* refers to *Margaret* as "the first Yankee book with the *soul* of Down East in't." A revised edition in two volumes was issued in 1851. After his death, *The Church in a Series of Discourses* (1854) was published, and he left in manuscript a five-act drama, "The White Hills, an American Tragedy."

[Sylvester Judd, *Thomas Judd and His Descendants* (1856); *Hist. and Biog. Record of the Class of 1836 in Yale Coll.* (1882); F. B. Dexter, *Biog. Notices of Grads. of Yale Coll.* (1913); Arethusa Hall, *Life and Character of Rev. Sylvester Judd* (1854); W. B. Sprague, *Annals Am. Unitarian Pulpit* (1865); *No. Am. Rev.*, Jan. 1846, Apr. 1850, Apr. 1851, Apr. 1855; *Christian Examiner*, Jan. 1855; *Fraser's Mag.*, July 1867.]
H. E. S.

JUDGE, WILLIAM QUAN (Apr. 13, 1851–Mar. 21, 1896), theosophist, was born in Dublin, Ireland, one of the seven children of Frederick H. Judge, a prominent Freemason, and Alice (Quan) Judge. He developed normally until his seventh year when, after a serious illness, he began to show signs of "queerness" and very early plunged into a precocious study of mesmerism, magic, and Rosicrucianism. In 1864, Frederick Judge, after the death of his wife, brought his large family to America and settled in Brooklyn, N. Y. William Judge studied law in the office of George P. Andrews, later justice of the New York supreme court, and was admitted to the bar in 1872. He entered into partnership with Henry Steel Olcott [*q.v.*] in the firm of Olcott, Gonzalez & Judge. As a lawyer he was noted for his industry, thoroughness, and pertinacity. In 1874 he was married to Ella Smith of Brooklyn. Introduced by Olcott to Mme. H. P. Blavatsky [*q.v.*], he became a charter member of their Theosophical Society in September 1875. In 1878 he acted as legal counsel for Mme. Blavatsky in her divorce from M. C. Betanelly. After the departure of Olcott and Mme. Blavatsky for India in the latter year, the New York branch of the Theosophical Society went to pieces, but it was reorganized by Judge in 1883 as the Aryan Theosophical Society, with himself as president. At first his organization enjoyed but a precarious existence. Sometimes the only member present, he would nevertheless formally open the meeting, read a chapter of the Bhagavad-Gita, and enter the minutes. His faith was eventually rewarded. Despite the exposure of Mme. Blavatsky by the London Society for Psychical Research in 1885, the theosophic movement began to spread in America, and during the next few years Judge, appointed vice-president by Olcott, succeeded in establishing branches in every large city of the country. In 1886 he began the publication of *The Path*, a theosophical monthly which he edited until his death. In 1889 he crushed the formidable revolt of Elliott Coues [*q.v.*], against whom, together with the New York *Sun*, he brought a libel suit in July 1890 on behalf of Mme. Blavatsky which was terminated two years later by the *Sun's* abject apology (*Sun*, Sept. 26, 1892). In 1893 he gave up his legal practice in order to devote all his time to the work of the Society. In the following year, however, he was formally charged by Mrs. Annie Besant with having fabricated letters in his own praise supposed to have been "precipitated" from the Mahatmas of the Himalayas. There is evidence that he had come to believe he was himself "the Mahatma K. H." (Alice Cleather, *H. P. Blavatsky: Her Life and Work for Humanity*, Calcutta, 1922, pp. 121–22). The affair caused an ugly scandal (Edmund Garrett, "Isis Very Much Unveiled," *Westminster Gazette*, Oct. 29–Nov. 8, 1894). As a result of the controversy, the American section withdrew from the Theosophical Society and formed itself into an independent organization, Judge being elected president. At the time of his death, a year later, this organization was estimated to have 400,000 members.

Judge was the author of *The Yoga Aphorisms of Patanjali; an Interpretation* (1889, reprinted 1912), *Echoes from the Orient* (1890), *The Ocean of Theosophy* (1893), *Notes on the Bhagavad-Gita* (published posthumously, 1918). He was one of the few who remained loyal to Mme. Blavatsky. It was he who went to India on her behalf in 1884 and destroyed her tell-tale shrine before it could be inspected by the representative of the Society for Psychical Research, and it was he who assisted in establishing the Esoteric Section which restored her influence in 1888. Although apparently not averse to trickery, he was of genuinely mystical temperament and believed thoroughly in the occult teachings of theosophy. His personal kindness, gentleness, and earnestness of purpose aroused intense devotion among his followers.

[The record of Judge's activities as a theosophist is scattered through the pages of the *Theosophist, Lucifer, The Path,* and other theosophical magazines; the anonymous history entitled *The Theosophical Movement 1875–1925* (1925) is largely devoted to an account and vindication of him; there is a laudatory biographical sketch by Julia Keightley in *Letters that Have Helped Me,* compiled by Jasper Niemand (vol. II, 1918); obituaries appeared in the *Irish Theosophist,* the *Sphinx,* and the *Lamp* for Apr. 1896, the N. Y. *Sun, N. Y. Tribune* (portr.) for Mar. 22, 1896, the *N. Y. Times,* Mar. 23, 1896.] E. S. B.

JUDSON, ADONIRAM (Aug. 9, 1788–Apr. 12, 1850), Baptist missionary, son of Adoniram and Abigail (Brown) Judson, was descended in the fifth generation from Joseph Judson who with his father, William, emigrated from Yorkshire, England, to America, settling at Concord, Mass. The elder Adoniram Judson was a Congregational minister. Born at Malden, Mass., young Judson lived in turn in Wenham, Braintree, and Plymouth, where his father held successive pastorates. With the ordinary schooling of these small communities, he entered Brown University as sophomore at the age of sixteen and was graduated as valedictorian of his class in 1807. He had developed skeptical tendencies, but after a year of teaching at Plymouth, during which he published two textbooks, *Elements of English Grammar* and *The Young Lady's Arithmetic* (both 1808), he entered the second-year class at Andover Theological Seminary. It was several weeks before he considered himself definitely a Christian and dedicated himself to the ministry. He became associated with the Williams College group, by this time at Andover, and soon was a leader in the movement resulting in the organization of the American Board of Commissioners for Foreign Missions. He drew up the petition presented to the General Association at Bradford and was selected as messenger to England to consult with the London Missionary Society. On the voyage the vessel was captured by a French privateer and he was held a prisoner at Bayonne for a short time. When he reached London, although he was cordially received, he found opinion adverse to joint control of the missionary enterprise. Returning to America, he was appointed on Sept. 19, 1811, as one of four missionaries to Burma or other fields which might open. He was already betrothed to Ann Hasseltine (see Ann Hasseltine Judson) and on Feb. 5, 1812, they were married. The following day he was ordained to the Congregational ministry at Salem and on Feb. 19 the Judsons, with Samuel Newell and his wife, embarked there for Calcutta.

During the voyage, since he expected to meet English Baptist missionaries and might need to justify his own views and practices, Judson studied the question of baptism, and by the time they reached Calcutta, both Judson and Mrs. Judson were in serious doubt as to pedobaptism, though Judson had advanced nearer to the Baptist position than had his wife. After further study, late in August he wrote to the English missionaries requesting baptism, and on Sept. 6, 1812, both the Judsons received believers' immersion at the hands of Rev. William Ward. This change in views cut them off from treasured early associations and from their financial support. Judson at once communicated with the American Board and with Thomas Baldwin of Boston and Lucius Bolles of Salem, to whom he had already suggested the organization of a Baptist foreign mission society. These two men were subsequently leaders in the organization of the Baptist Triennial Convention which in 1814 assumed the support of what had become a Baptist missionary enterprise. The officials of the East India Company ordered the Judsons to America, but after days of anxiety, they finally received a pass permitting them to board a ship bound for the Isle of France. After a further voyage of six weeks they reached Port Louis and there learned of the death of Mrs. Newell. Four months later they sailed to Madras, hoping to go from there to some suitable location in the Straits of Malacca. They found a vessel about to sail for Rangoon, and embarking, finally reached the land which had been most specifically their desired destination.

Judson set about the task of learning Burmese in order to preach to the natives and to translate the Scriptures into their tongue. Both his chief biographers give full particulars of his method of evangelization and the discouragingly slow progress that was made. His linguistic ability was extraordinary, however, and his translations and his construction of an English-Burmese dictionary are recognized as monuments of highest scholarship. From Aug. 21, 1821, till Dec. 13, 1823, while Mrs. Judson was absent on her only return to the homeland, he applied himself assiduously to the translation of the Bible (completed in 1834), though he also took advantage of every opportunity for evangelistic work. Upon his wife's return, they transferred their station to Ava. Almost immediately the war with England began and Judson and others were seized on June 8, 1824. For eleven terrible months he was confined at the Ava prison, and then for six months which were possibly even worse, at the prison pen of Oung-pen-la. The horrors of the experience, hardly touched upon by Judson in his writings, have been described explicitly by some of his fellow prisoners, and most thrillingly by Mrs. Judson in a letter to her brother. Release came when the progress of British arms made negotiations for peace necessary and Judson and his colleague, Dr. Price, were desired as interpreters.

After the establishment of peace, Judson declined a relatively large salary offered him if he would continue as interpreter. Resuming his missionary work, he removed to Amherst where there was British protection. Later, encouraged by Mrs. Judson and hoping to secure liberty for religious work in Burma, he accompanied a British embassy to Ava. While on this mission the tidings reached him of the death of his beloved wife (Oct. 24, 1826). The infant daughter, born during her father's imprisonment at Ava, survived her mother only six months. Their first child had died, after seven months of life, in 1816. Despite the poignancy of his grief, Judson hardly faltered. He soon transferred his work to Maulmain, which was to become for some time the center of American Baptist activities in Burma and the chief stage of his later career. During this period he showed a tendency toward asceticism and also, under the influence of the writings of Madame Guyon, toward mysticism. In 1829, he renounced the degree of doctor of divinity which Brown University had conferred upon him six years before.

On Apr. 10, 1834, he married Sarah Hall Boardman (see Sarah Hall Boardman Judson), widow of George Dana Boardman, another missionary in Burma. There followed a marital association of over eleven years, quite as remarkable in its intellectual and spiritual compatibility as the first marriage had been. Eight children, including Adoniram Brown Judson and Edward Judson [*qq.v.*], were born of this marriage, but three died in infancy. The condition of Mrs. Judson's health compelled them to start for America in 1845, with the three older children. They were encouraged by a temporary improvement, but Mrs. Judson died on Sept. 1, just after reaching St. Helena. Judson continued the voyage, reaching Boston Oct. 15, 1845. He was shown much attention and traveled to many places to give missionary addresses, although the frailty of his health and the condition of his voice made it usually necessary to have another speaker convey his words to the audience. In America he met and was attracted to a young writer, Emily Chubbuck, whom he married, June 2, 1846 (see Emily Chubbuck Judson). On July 11, following, they embarked at Boston, reaching Maulmain Nov. 30; a daughter was born there in December 1847. Judson resumed his missionary work and in January 1849 had completed his *Dictionary, English and Burmese,* published that same year. The Burmese-English part, which he left unfinished, was completed by his colleague, Edward A. Stevens, and appeared as *A Dictionary, Burmese and English* in 1852. Burdened by recurring sickness in his home, Judson's own health soon gave way. In April 1850 he undertook a sea voyage, which seemed the only chance for his recovery; but four days after the vessel sailed he died, and his body was buried at sea.

[There are two fairly adequate biographies: Francis Wayland, *Memoir of the Life and Labors of the Rev. Adoniram Judson* (2 vols., 1853), and Edward Judson, *Life of Adoniram Judson by His Son* (1883). See also Wm. Cothren, *Hist. of Ancient Woodbury, Conn.* (1854); *How Judson Became a Baptist Missionary* (1913), by his son Adoniram Brown Judson and the obituary in *Missionary Mag.*, Oct. 1850. There are numerous popularly written biographies, and the story of Judson's earlier Burman years until his second marriage is presented in a historical novel, *The Splendor of God* (1929), by Honoré Willsie Morrow.] W. H. A.

JUDSON, ADONIRAM BROWN (Apr. 7, 1837–Sept. 20, 1916), surgeon, brother of Edward Judson [*q.v.*], was born in Maulmain, Burma, a son of the well-known missionary, Adoniram Judson, and his second wife, Sarah (Hall) Boardman Judson [*qq.v.*]. His early years were spent in Burma, but in 1845 he was taken to the United States, where he was educated. He received a degree in arts from Brown University in 1859 and had begun the study of medicine at Harvard when the outbreak of the Civil War led him to apply for appointment as assistant surgeon in the United States navy. Despite the fact that he was an undergraduate, he passed the required examination and in 1864 was promoted to passed assistant surgeon. In 1865 he took his first degree in medicine from Jefferson Medical College, Philadelphia, and in 1868 a second, *ad eundem,* from the College of Physicians and Surgeons, New York. He then resigned from the navy and settled in the metropolis. He was an inspector on the board of health of New York City from 1869 to 1877, when he resigned to take the post of pension examining surgeon. In 1873 he published papers on the epizoötic in horses and on the epidemic of cholera in the Mississippi Valley, but at a later period he decided to devote himself to the then new specialty of orthopedic surgery, and thenceforth the great majority of his papers dealt with that subject. Although he never secured a position on any of the medical-college faculties nor in the special orthopedic hospitals, he made good use of the orthopedic class of the New York Hospital Out-patient Department, of which he was the head from 1878 to 1908. In 1887 he was instrumental in the formation of the American Orthopedic Association and in 1891 became its president. He was always active in having its papers published not only in American but in European journals, and thus was instrumental in making American orthopedics well-known abroad. Although Judson was a prolific writer—he published more than fifty papers—he wrote no books and his name was never associated with any new operation or surgical device. His practice was not so large as to monopolize his best hours, for in 1901 he secured the post of medical examiner of the New York State Civil Service Commission and in the same year was again appointed pension examining surgeon. He gradually withdrew from the work of the American Orthopedic Association and concentrated on that of the section of orthopedics of the New York Academy of Medicine, of which he was for many years the chairman. Here, as in his earlier office, he was instrumental in having the work of members published at home and abroad. Greatly interested in the Academy of Medicine, he was its statistical secretary from 1886 until the time of his death, and prepared memoirs of all its numerous fellows. He was nearly eighty when he died of diabetes, from which he had suffered for many years. Judson was a friendly, companionable man of unusual modesty. For many years he was an active member of the Judson Memorial, the Baptist church of which his brother Edward was pastor. He was married, Nov. 19, 1868, to Anna Margaret Haughwout of New York.

[*N. Y. Medic. Jour.*, Oct. 14, 1916; *Medic. Record*, Sept. 23, 1916; *Jour. Am. Medic. Asso.*, Oct. 7, 1916; *Who's Who in America*, 1916–17; H. A. Kelly and W. L. Burrage, *Am. Medic. Biogs.* (1920), *N. Y. Times*, Sept. 21, 1916; personal acquaintance.] E. P.

JUDSON, ANN HASSELTINE (Dec. 22, 1789–Oct. 24, 1826), missionary to Burma, daughter of John and Rebecca (Barton or Burton) Hasseltine, was born at Bradford, Mass. She was named Nancy but later changed her name to Ann. Educated at the well-known academy in Bradford, for a short time she taught in nearby towns. Her own account of her early religious experience (Knowles, *post*) reads like a continuation of the Great Awakening. In this religious experience one can discern that missionary spirit which found its opportunity in her marriage, Feb. 5, 1812, to Adoniram Judson [*q.v.*], who was about to embark as a pioneer American missionary to Burma. Although her personal qualities would have carried her far in a social career, she chose the life of a missionary and she was the first woman dedicated to the evangelization of the heathen to leave America. With exceptional courage and devotion she made her husband's tasks her own, supplementing his great talents in many ways. Her experiences were full of pain and difficulty: the severing of old associations caused by conversion to the Baptist faith; perils of travel; perils of childbirth without medical attendance; the death of her infant son; and her own impaired health. In 1822–23 she returned for her only visit to America, and while here published her *Account of the American Baptist Mission to the Burman Empire* (1823). She rejoined her husband only to undergo a series of terrible experiences during his seventeen months of imprisonment with other foreigners at Ava and Oung-pen-la. It was especially while he was a prisoner and she herself completely isolated from the civilized world that Mrs. Judson showed in its perfection that blend of worldly tact and other-worldly spirit which is discernible throughout her life. When relief at last came and the missionaries took up again their task in a new field at Amherst, in Burma, she did not have the reserve of strength to resist the ravages of a severe tropical fever, and she died during the absence of her husband, leaving an infant daughter who survived her but six months.

[J. D. Knowles brought together some of the letters of Mrs. Judson and portions of her journals (though many of her papers she had destroyed at Ava) in his *Memoir of Ann H. Judson, Missionary to Burmah* (1829); most later biographies depend primarily upon this material, supplemented by the biographies of Judson. A sketch by Arabella W. Stuart appears in *The Lives of Mrs. Ann H. Judson and Mrs. Sarah B. Judson, with a Biog. Sketch of Mrs. Emily C. Judson, Missionaries to Burmah* (1851). For genealogy see W. B. Lapham, *Geneal. Sketches of John Hazelton and Some of His Descendants* (1892). The story of Mrs. Judson's life appears in popular form in W. N. Wyeth, *Ann H. Judson: a Memorial* (1888); in E. D. Hubbard, *Ann of Ava* (1913); and in the historical novel, *The Splendor of God* (1929), by Honoré Willsie Morrow.]

W. H. A.

JUDSON, EDWARD (Dec. 27, 1844–Oct. 23, 1914), Baptist clergyman, brother of Adoniram Brown Judson [*q.v.*], was born of missionary parents, Adoniram Judson and Sarah (Hall) Boardman Judson [*qq.v.*], in Maulmain, Burma. Left motherless when only a few months old, he was cared for temporarily in the home of Edward A. Stevens, one of his father's colleagues, and then by his stepmother, Emily Chubbuck Judson [*q.v.*]. Upon the death of his father in 1850 the family went to America, where Edward, not quite seven, saw for the first time two older brothers and a sister. Most of the remaining years of his boyhood were spent in Hamilton, N. Y. After his stepmother's death, he lived for some time in the home of Dr. Ebenezer Dodge [*q.v.*], while preparing for college in the academy at Hamilton. He spent one year at Madison (now Colgate) University, then transferred to Brown University, where he was graduated in 1865, ranking high in scholarship. Having served two years as principal of Leland and Gray Seminary at Townshend, Vt., he returned to Madison University, first as instructor in languages and from 1868 to 1874 as professor of Latin and modern languages. In 1871, he married Ellen Antoinette Barstow, daughter of the Congregational minister at Lebanon, N. Y. Following a year of study and travel abroad with his wife, in 1875 he became pastor of the North Orange Baptist Church, Orange, N. J. Here he found a most congenial field, in a community of wealth and refinement, where he could expect considerate treatment and great opportunity for the enjoyment of the quiet tastes of his mind and his spirit.

He was much impressed, however, by the religious needs of great cities, being particularly aware of the necessity for readjustment in the relations of the down-town city church with its immediate community. Because of his interest in this problem he accepted, in 1881, the call of the Berean Baptist Church in New York, at a salary of only $1,000, far less than he was receiving at Orange. This sacrificial act, which attracted attention and brought some financial support to the enterprise, was only the beginning of the continued self-sacrifice, loyally shared by his wife, through which alone the work was maintained for the remaining thirty-three years of his life. In 1890 the church moved into the Judson Memorial, on Washington Square, one of the first institutional church buildings in the country. The principles of adjustment to the field which he elaborated in *The Institutional Church* (1899) came to be widely adopted as a practical basis for the work of city churches. He made his own church a laboratory and in part a clinic for religious workers. For about ten years the senior class from Colgate Theological Seminary spent its winter term in New York under his instruction. Though other important institutions for social amelioration developed, he continued to believe that upon the local church must remain the primary responsibility for meeting the needs of individuals and of groups in its own community. He contributed a monograph, "The Church in its Social Aspect," to the *Annals of the American Academy of Political and Social Science,* November 1907.

Gifted as a teacher—he lectured on pastoral theology at the University of Chicago, 1904–06, and on Baptist principles and polity at Union Theological Seminary, 1906–08—he was offered several professorships; with a wide knowledge of the best in literature and a memory rich in its store of poetry, he was sought constantly as a preacher and pastor. He was importuned by both universities in which he had been a student to become president. He had committed himself, however, to the church in Washington Square, built as a memorial to his father; and it became as well a memorial to the son whose life went into its upbuilding and maintenance. In 1883 he published a biography of his father, *The Life of Adoniram Judson,* and in 1892, with C. S. Robinson, he edited *The New Laudes Domini.* A man of quiet demeanor, with humor now sparkling and now subtle, he was a charming personality; association with him was both delightful and memorable.

[C. H. Sears, *Edward Judson, Interpreter of God* (1917); *Who's Who in America,* 1914–15; *Watchman-Examiner,* Oct. 29, Nov. 12, 1914; *N. Y. Times,* Oct. 24, 1914.] W. H. A.

JUDSON, EDWARD ZANE CARROLL (Mar. 20, 1823–July 16, 1886), writer, adventurer, known also by his pen-name of Ned Buntline, was born at Stamford, Delaware County, N. Y., the son of Levi Carroll Judson and the great-grandson of Samuel Judson, a scion of the Fairfield, Conn., family, who was one of the founders of Stamford in 1789. His father was a schoolmaster at Bethany, Wayne County, Pa., 1826–36; was admitted Oct. 22, 1836, to the Philadelphia bar; and compiled several volumes on patriotic, moral, and Masonic themes. Edward, while still a youngster, ran away to sea as a cabin boy; became an apprentice in the navy; and, for heroism displayed when a boat capsized in the East River, was rewarded Feb. 10, 1838, with a midshipman's commission. As in strength, activity, and capacity for mischief he was already the equivalent of his weight in wild cats, his nautical career was correspondingly eventful. An account of one escapade he published, over the signature of Ned Buntline, as *The Captain's Pig* (no copy known), which attracted the attention of Lewis Gaylord Clark [*q.v.*] and later gained him entrée to the *Knickerbocker Magazine.* On June 8, 1842, he resigned from the navy. During the next two years he is supposed to have soldiered in the Seminole War and then to have gone to the Yellowstone region as an employee of a fur company. In spare hours he was writing fiction. At Cincinnati, in 1844, he began *Ned Buntline's Magazine* but speedily gave it up. With the trustful, altruistic Lucius A. Hine for a partner, he edited six numbers

(November 1844–April 1845) of the *Western Literary Journal and Monthly Magazine* and then decamped, leaving Hine to pay the bills. At Eddyville, Ky., in November, he set out alone in pursuit of three men wanted for murder and captured two of them, thereby securing a bounty of $600. Next, he started a sensation sheet, *Ned Buntline's Own,* at Nashville, Tenn. On Mar. 14, 1846, he shot and fatally wounded Robert Porterfield, with whose wife he was alleged to be carrying on an intrigue. While he was being arraigned in the courthouse, Porterfield's brother opened fire on him. Judson bolted through a window and was pursued, amid a hail of pistol shots, to the third story of the City Hotel, whence he leaped to the ground. He was then jailed. That night a mob hanged him in the square, but some one cut the rope and smuggled him back to the jail, his neck still unbroken. The grand jury failing to indict him, Judson removed to New York, where he was welcomed by the group of congenial souls that centered around William Trotter Porter [*q.v.*] of the *Spirit of the Times.*

In New York Judson revived *Ned Buntline's Own,* taking Marcus Cicero Stanley of the *National Police Gazette* as his assistant, and made his paper the organ of a rowdy, jingoistic, nativistic patriotism. He was out of the city for a short time during the Mexican War, in which he claimed to have participated. In 1848 he explored a cavern, a half mile in length, extending beneath Eddyville, Ky. Applying native American principles to dramatic criticism, he became a partisan of Edwin Forrest and on the night of the Astor Place riot (May 10, 1849) led the mob that showered the theatre with cobblestones. In September of that year he was convicted of inciting and fomenting the outbreak and was sentenced to a year's imprisonment on Blackwell's Island and to a fine of $250. On his release he was escorted home in a parade and banqueted by various patriotic and political organizations. He was next heard from in St. Louis, where in the spring of 1852 he was indicted for causing an election riot in which several citizens were slain, two houses burned to the ground, and much other property destroyed. He escaped by jumping his bail. By this time he was one of the chief organizers of the Know-Nothing party, and he is credited with devising the tactics that gave it its name (Scisco, *post*). Unfortunately, because of his criminal record, he was himself unable to run for office. His personal popularity was very great. After the collapse of the Know Nothings, in 1856, he bought some land in the Adirondacks and devoted his leisure to hunting and fishing.

Ever since 1846 he had been engaged constantly in writing cheap sensational fiction. He was in fact the first of the dime novelists, having invented the technique and brought it to perfection some twelve years before the firm of Beadle & Adams, with their editor Orville J. Victor [*q.v.*], popularized the form. Typical Ned Buntline Stories were: *The Mysteries and Miseries of New York* (1848); *The Bhoys of New York*; *The Gals of New York*; *War Eagle, or Ossiniwa the Indian Brave*; *Ned Buntline's Life Yarn* (1848); *Navigator Ned*; *Cruisings Afloat and Ashore from the Log of Ned Buntline*; *Stella Delorme, or The Comanche's Dream* (1860). Of many of his earlier stories he was his own hero; later he took to exploiting various more or less authentic Westerners; but he also produced a great variety of other tales of adventure —400 in all—innumerable articles on hunting and fishing, much miscellaneous journalism, some plays, the rituals of various patriotic secret orders, temperance lectures and tracts, a number of poems, and at least one hymn. He was well paid for his work, lived affluently, and was generous to needy friends. For a time he sported a steam yacht on the Hudson. On Sept. 25, 1862, he enlisted in the 1st New York Mounted Rifles, became a sergeant of Company K, was reduced to the ranks and transferred to the 22nd Veterans' Reserve Corps, and was finally discharged Aug. 23, 1864, on War Department Special Orders 268, Aug. 12, 1864, his record being thoroughly discreditable. On his return to New York, he gave out that he had been "Chief of the Indian Scouts with the rank of Colonel," and as Colonel Judson he was thereafter known.

In 1869 he went to Fort McPherson, Nebr., made the acquaintance of William Frederick Cody [*q.v.*], and, conferring on him the name "Buffalo Bill," began a series of dime novels in which Cody was the ostensibly historic hero. Three years later he persuaded Cody and J. B. Omohundro ("Texas Jack") to come to Chicago and go on the stage as the heroes of his play, *The Scouts of the Plains,* which was later renamed *Scouts of the Prairies.* The play opened in Chicago Dec. 16, 1872, reached Niblo's Garden, New York, via St. Louis Mar. 31, 1873, and was a huge success. Cody was dissatisfied, however, with $6,000 as his share of the season's profits, and broke with his exploiter. Thereafter Prentiss Ingraham [*q.v.*] was Cody's authorized biographer, and Judson took up other subjects. In 1871 he returned to Stamford, N. Y., built a comfortable house, and lived there, a busy, respected citizen, until his death. He was married four times: in 1845 to a Southern woman, "Seberina," who died at Clarksville, Tenn., a few weeks before the killing of Porterfield; in the winter of 1848–49 to Annie Bennett of New York, who divorced him in 1849 and secured the custody of their child; about 1857 to Marie Gardiner, who had been his housekeeper in the Adirondacks and who died shortly after; and in 1871 to Anna Fuller of Stamford, N. Y., who bore him two children, survived him, and married his journalistic partner, E. Locke Mason. During his last years he suffered from the numerous wounds received in campaigns and gun scrapes, from several unextracted bullets, sciatica, and heart trouble, but he remained personally cheerful, even genial, and wrote steadily until his death. He died at his home and was buried at Stamford.

[See T. H. S. Hamersly, *Gen. Reg. of the U. S. Navy and Marine Corps* (1882); *Ann. Report of the Adj.-Gen. of the State of N. Y.*, 1895, p. 667; W. H. Venable, *Beginnings of Literary Culture in the Ohio Valley* (1891); *The Knickerbocker, or New-York Monthly Magazine*, XXIV (1844), 102, 582–83; XXVII (1846), 277, 376–77, 466–67; L. D. Scisco, *Political Nativism in New York State* (1901), p. 88; Lewis and R. H. Collins, *Hist. of Ky.* (1874), II, 490–91; *N. Y. Herald*, Sept. 20–Oct. 3, 1849, July 18, 1886; *Hist. of Delaware County, N. Y.* (1880), ed. by C. D. Lathrop, pp. 294–97, 363; F. E. Pond, *Life and Adventures of "Ned Buntline"* (1919); R. J. Walsh, *The Making of Buffalo Bill* (1928); *N. Y. Times*, Apr. 1, 1873; *St. Louis Globe*, Dec. 27, 28, 1872; *The Extraordinary Public Proceedings of E. Z. C. Judson, alias Ned Buntline, against Thomas V. Paterson for an Alledged Libel*, etc. (1849); *Republican Banner* (Nashville), Mar. 18, 1846; *Tri-Weekly Nashville Union*, Mar. 17, 19, Apr. 9, 1846; *Republican Banner and Nashville Whig*, Oct. 13, 1849. Several minor sources have also been used.]

G. H. G.

JUDSON, EGBERT PUTNAM (Aug. 9, 1812–Jan. 9, 1893), inventor and manufacturer of explosives, was born at Syracuse, N. Y., the son of William and Charlotte (Putnam) Judson. Very little is known of his early life beyond the facts that he was educated as a civil engineer and joined the rush to the California gold fields in 1850. He is said to have founded the first assay works in San Francisco in 1852, and about 1867 was one of the organizers of the San Francisco Chemical Works (Judson & Sheppard). In August 1867 three pounds of dynamite were made at this plant and used in a trial blast of boulders. This is considered to be the first instance of the manufacture and use of dynamite in the United States after the invention of that explosive by Alfred Nobel in 1866. The trial was successful and led to the formation of the Giant Powder Company in the same month. Judson, a director of the Giant company, continued to operate the San Francisco Chemical Works which supplied acid to the Giant company, and shortly afterwards formed the Judson Powder Company at Kenvil, N. J. On June 3, 1873, he patented his "Giant Powder, No. 2" (patent no. 139,468), which was manufactured successfully by both companies. This powder consisted of forty parts nitroglycerine, forty parts sodium nitrate, six parts sulphur, six parts rosin, and eight parts kieselguhr, and was essentially a blasting powder. "Giant powder" was for a long time a synonym for dynamite in the United States.

Judson was the first to meet the need for an explosive which, though powerful, would be more "gentle" in action than a blasting powder, producing a heaving rather than a shattering effect. The first such explosive was patented by him on Oct. 31, 1876 (patent no. 183,764, reissued 4, 568). As it was particularly well suited for moving banks of rock and earth in railroad construction, it was marketed as railroad powder or "Judson's RRP," in various grades designated by number. Railroad powder as a class developed from this invention.

Judson was interested in many successful mining enterprises, including the Alaska Treadwell Gold Mining Company and the Anaconda Mining Company; and he founded the Judson Fuse Works, Judson Iron Works, Judson Candle Works, and Butterworth & Judson Chemical Works. He was a man of aggressive character and great business ability. At the age of seventy-eight, as a final gesture, he sold his interest in the Giant Powder Company when that company stopped buying acid from his chemical works, and promoted the Judson Dynamite & Powder Company, a $2,000,000 concern, which competed successfully with the Giant company. At the time of his death, which occurred in San Francisco, he was president of the Judson Manufacturing Company and the California Paper Company. He never married.

[See A. P. Van Gelder and Hugo Schlatter, *Hist. of the Explosives Industry in America* (1927); *Specifications and Drawings of Patents Issued from the U. S. Patent Office*, June 1873, Oct. 1876; J. C. Trautwine, *The Civil Engineer's Pocket-Book*, 9th ed. (1885) and subsequent editions; Arthur Marshall, *A Short Account of Explosives* (London, 1917); *San Francisco Morning Call*, Jan. 10, 1893. Mrs. Frank (Pearl Judson) Somers supplied the names of Judson's parents.]

F. A. T.

JUDSON, EMILY CHUBBUCK (Aug. 22, 1817–June 1, 1854), writer, missionary, daughter of Charles and Lavinia (Richards) Chubbuck, was born at Eaton, near Hamilton, N. Y., where her parents, coming from New Hampshire, had settled in 1816. She was descended from John Chubbuck, who emigrated to America from Wales about 1700. Charles Chubbuck and his wife, always poor, were people of character and intelligence. Emily, their fifth child, was frail from birth, and the circumstances of her early years did not aid her chance of health. The family lived in many poor homes near and in Hamilton, and the mother and daughters performed all sorts of drudgery, including the collecting of firewood from snowy fields, while the father attempted to earn a living in various ways. Emily combined different occupations with attendance at district schools, at one time working in a woolen factory, at another assisting her mother in taking boarders. The family were Baptists and Emily, having read of the work of Rev. Adoniram Judson in Burma, decided to be a missionary; but under the influence of a teacher who was a student of Voltaire and Tom Paine, her faith in the Bible was shaken. Later she set herself to learn refutations for infidel arguments, in preparation for a missionary life. From 1832 to 1840 she taught at Nelson Corners, Morrisville, Smithfield, Brookfield, Syracuse, Hamilton, and Prattsville, carrying on her own studies all this time. Though she had always been abnormally religious, she underwent conversion in 1834. In 1840 the Misses Sheldon, of Utica Female Seminary, assisted her to enter their school for advanced study. Here she overworked, attaining high scholarship and writing sketches and verses for a Hamilton paper in order to help her parents. In 1841 she became teacher of English at the Utica Seminary and published a Sunday-school book, *Charles Linn, or How to Observe the Golden Rule.* Other books of the same type followed: *The Great Secret, or How to be Happy* (1842), *Allen Lucas, or the Self-Made Man* (1842), *John Frink* (1843). With $400 from her meager earnings she bought a house for her parents in Hamilton. In 1844 she wrote a humorous letter to N. P. Willis, editor of the *New York Mirror,* asking for literary work, and thus became a regular contributor, under the name of Fanny Forester. She used personal experiences in her sketches, which are conversational and quietly humorous. Many of them were published in two volumes: *Trippings in Author-Land* (1846) and *Alderbrook: a Collection of Fanny Forester's Village Sketches, Poems &c* (1847).

The winter of 1845–46 she spent in Philadelphia and there met the hero of her girlhood, Rev. Adoniram Judson [*q.v.*], home temporarily from Burma. Though he disapproved of her writing on frivolous subjects, he proposed marriage to her soon after their first meeting and also asked her to write a memoir of his second wife, Sarah Hall Boardman Judson [*q.v.*], who had just died. On June 2, 1846, Judson and Emily Chubbuck were married; they sailed for Burma July 11, and reached Maulmain in November. In February 1847 they went to Rangoon, where living conditions were so wretched and the natives so hostile that they remained only seven months, returning to Maulmain, where in December a daughter was born. The *Memoir of Sarah B. Judson, Member of the American Mission to Burmah* was published in 1848. The record of Mrs. Judson's next two years is one of continuous illness, and in April 1850, her husband died. Her second child, a boy, was born ten days after his father's death and died almost immediately. Her own health entirely broken, she left India with her child and two step-children on Jan. 22, 1851. Arriving in Boston, she made arrangements for the three elder Judson children already in America and began preparations for a memoir of her husband. In May 1852 she purchased a house in Hamilton, N. Y., which was her home during the two years of life remaining to her. Hemorrhages from her lungs warned her that her condition was serious, and she hastened to finish some writing and to make financial arrangements for her parents, her own child, and Judson's children. She published *An Olio of Domestic Verses* (1852), *The Kathayan Slave, and Other Papers Connected with Missionary Life* (1853), and *My Two Sisters* (1854). Early in 1854 she attempted an abridged memoir of her husband but was unable to finish it. She died at Hamilton in June.

[A. C. Kendrick, *The Life and Letters of Mrs. Emily C. Judson* (1860); Arabella W. Stuart, *The Lives of Mrs. Ann. H. Judson and Mrs. Sarah B. Judson, with a Biog. Sketch of Mrs. Emily C. Judson* (1851); W. N. Wyeth, *Emily C. Judson: a Memorial* (1890); Edward Judson, *The Life of Adoniram Judson* (1883); Francis Wayland, *A Memoir of the Life and Labors of the Rev. Adoniram Judson* (2 vols., 1853).] S. G. B.

JUDSON, FREDERICK NEWTON (Oct. 7, 1845–Oct. 18, 1919), lawyer, legal writer, throughout his formative years was a resident of New England. His birthplace was St. Mary's, Ga., where his father, Frederick Joseph Judson, with a medical training from Yale, had gone to practise, and where his mother, Catherine, the daughter of Isaac N. Chapelle, lived before her marriage; but in 1846 the family moved to Bridgeport, Conn., where Dr. Judson became prominent both in the medical profession and in leadership for the educational advancement of the community. The son was tutored for college in part by his father and in part by the Rev. Henry Jones of Bridgeport. A few months of teaching in the district school and a little taste of journalism on a local paper added to his preparation. He entered Yale in 1862, early won scholarships and honors, and received the bachelor's degree in 1866. For the next few years he was a teacher of classics and other subjects successively in the Hopkins Grammar School of New Haven, Conn., the city high school of Nashville, Tenn., and the Montgomery Bell Academy of the University of Nashville. During these years he made occasional contributions to newspapers and did some reading in the field of law. In 1871, after a year in residence, he completed the work for the degree of LL.B. in the St. Louis Law School (now a part of Washington University). For two years after his graduation he served as the private secretary of Gov. B. Gratz Brown of Missouri. On Feb. 8, 1872, he married Jennie W. Eakin of Nashville, Tenn.

Early in 1873 he began the practice of law in St. Louis, and gradually achieved a reputation and a place of distinction which brought him national recognition. While his practice was general in its range, it was as corporation attorney that he was most successful. Important cases and large fees were for him the normal lot. Yet, in spite of his connection with the big corporations, in 1903 he won the everlasting goodwill of labor, as well as a national renown, through his skilful and victorious defense of the strikers in the injunction case of *The Wabash Railroad Company* vs. *John J. Hannahan et al.* in the circuit court of the United States for the Eastern District of Missouri.

His interest in education continued throughout his life. As member and president of the board of education of St. Louis he was a constructive leader for the four years 1878–82 and again in 1887–89. From 1892 to 1910 he was a lecturer in the law school of Washington University. In 1913 he delivered the William L. Storrs lectures at Yale University. While he sought no public office and was largely independent and unpartisan in politics (although by affiliation and doctrine a Democrat), as a private citizen he responded graciously and with dignified generosity to the many calls made upon him by the government during the last two decades of his life. In 1905 and in 1910 he served as special counsel of the United States in important railway rebate and rate cases. In 1910 he was a member of President Taft's commission to investigate the power of regulating the issue of railway securities. In 1912 he served on a special railway arbitration board. During the World War he served on President Wilson's Labor Board as the alternate of William Howard Taft. He was the chairman of the State Tax Commission of Missouri in 1906, a member of the Missouri Code Commission in 1914, and a member of the Charter Commission of St. Louis in 1913. He was also connected with an impressive list of unofficial reform associations and learned and professional societies. He was a stanch supporter of the policies and proposals of President Wilson and made his last public appearance in behalf of the League of Nations.

Aside from a variety of printed addresses, Judson's writings consist of a number of legal treatises, primarily descriptive and analytic but in a few instances also critical and constructive. In 1900 appeared *A Treatise upon the Law and Practice of Taxation in Missouri*; in 1903 came the more comprehensive and standard *Treatise on the Power of Taxation, State and Federal, in the United States* (revised in 1917); in 1905, *The Law of Interstate Commerce and Its Federal Regulation* (revised in 1906, 1912, and 1916). His annotated edition of the *Federal Rate Bill and Negligence Act of 1906* was published in 1907. In 1913, the Storrs lectures were published under the title of *The Judiciary and the People*. The day after Judson's death in St. Louis, the *New York Times* referred to him as "one of the most prominent attorneys and legal authors in the country."

[Obituary notices and editorial comments in the *St. Louis Globe-Democrat,* Oct. 19, *St. Louis Post Dispatch,* Oct. 18 and 19, 1919; *The Bench and Bar of St. Louis . . . and Other Missouri Cities* (1884); J. W. Leonard, *The Book of St. Louisans* (1912); *Who's Who in America,* 1901–19; *Yale Univ. Obit. Record,* 1920; references in the text above.]
A. J. L.

JUDSON, HARRY PRATT (Dec. 20, 1849–Mar. 4, 1927), educator, was born at Jamestown, N. Y., the second son of Lyman Parsons Judson and Abigail Cook Pratt. His father was a descendant of William Judson, a Yorkshireman, who came to Massachusetts with his wife and son soon after its founding, and settled at Concord; his mother was also descended from early New England ancestors. His schooling was gained at the Classical and Union School at Geneva, N. Y., and at the Lansingburg Academy. He was a student at Williams College in the later years of Mark Hopkins' presidency. Having graduated from college in 1870, he was for fifteen years a teacher and principal of the Troy, New York, high school. From Troy he went to the University of Minnesota (1885), where he served for seven years as professor of history.

When William Rainey Harper [*q.v.*] was at work upon the foundations of the University of Chicago, he found need for the assistance of a man of experience with capacity for organization and a respect for methodical detail. This man he found in Judson, who was appointed in January 1892 dean of the colleges and professor of history in the new university. The two men admirably supplemented each other. Judson was essentially practical and judicious, but by no means incapable of appreciating the enthusiasm and vision of the President. He at once took upon his shoulders a very large portion of the preliminary administrative labors. Till the death of President Harper in 1906, this happy and fortunate relationship continued, with results beneficial to the University. Soon after his appointment, Judson's title was changed to professor of political science and head dean of the colleges, and this title sufficiently indicates his position and work till he became acting president in 1906. Till he retired from all active service in 1923, he continued in charge of the department of political science, devoting his teaching especially to international law, a subject in which he took great interest.

After a year of service as acting president he was installed in the permanent position. One of the pressing tasks awaiting him was so to manage affairs that the University could and would live within its income. This task he almost immediately accomplished. It was necessary to concentrate the institution's energies. This was done. The years of his presidency are usually and justly called conservative; but the word should not connote an absence of progress. The development of the University went on in many substantial ways. The President never lost sight of the importance of research or the demand for effective teaching. Funds for healthy expansion came into the treasury, never empty but always yearning; students increased in numbers. Unquestionably a part of this development is attributable to the wisdom and good sense of the administration. As an executive officer, Judson was not characterized by creative imagination; but he disposed of administrative questions quickly and with understanding; he was straightforward as well as sympathetic in dealing with the problems of faculties and individual professors; he clung tenaciously to the ideals of frankness and freedom and to the development of the intellectual interests of the University, which gained much from his steadying hand and his sagacious judgment.

Interest in public affairs inevitably led to Judson's being summoned to service beyond college walls. From 1906 till his death he was a member of the General Education Board; from 1913 to 1924 a member of the Rockefeller Foundation. As chairman of the China medical commission he went to China in 1914 to report upon conditions. In 1918 he visited the Near East as director of the American-Persian relief commission and to report on conditions for the American commission to negotiate peace. He was decorated by various foreign governments and received in 1920 the gold medal of the National Institute of Social Sciences. Among his published works are *Europe in the Nineteenth Century* (1894, 1901); *The Growth of the American Nation* (1895); *Our Federal Republic* (1925). From 1895 to 1902 he was one of the editors of the *American Historical Review.* A member of the Baptist Church and of deep religious faith, in this matter as in others he was free from ostentation and broad in his intellectual sympathies. In manner he was reserved, but not self-effacing; those who knew him best often spoke of his unselfish interest in others and his devotion to his friends. His death came suddenly and unexpectedly, Mar. 4, 1927. He was survived by his daughter and by his wife, Rebecca A. Gilbert, whom he had married in 1879 and who had been of great assistance to him in carrying the social responsibilities of his position.

[This sketch is written on the basis of personal knowledge, supplemented by manuscript material. Published sources include T. W. Goodspeed, *A Hist. of the Univ. of Chicago—The First Quarter-Century* (1916); *Univ. of Chicago Mag.*, Apr. 1927; *Who's Who in America*, 1926–27; C. B. Whittelsey, *The Ancestry and the Descendants of John Pratt of Hartford, Conn.* (1900); *Chicago Daily Tribune*, Mar. 5, 1927. The work of the presidency is disclosed in the annual reports to the trustees.]

A. C. McL.

JUDSON, SARAH HALL BOARDMAN (Nov. 4, 1803–Sept. 1, 1845), missionary to Burma, was the eldest of thirteen children of Ralph and Abiah O. (Hall) Hall. Born at Alstead, N. H., she spent her girlhood at Salem, Mass., where household duties and meager resources hindered her education. Intellectually ambitious, however, she used various means of self-improvement and cultivated her not inconsiderable poetic talent. Her religious experience united from the first with interest in foreign missions. A poem she wrote upon the death of James Colman, a young missionary to Burma, attracted the attention of George Dana Boardman, who had volunteered to take Colman's place in this field, and led to their marriage, July 4, 1825, after an engagement somewhat prolonged in order that Boardman might have additional preparation for his work. Sailing from Philadelphia on July 16, 1825, they reached Calcutta, Dec. 2. Held here for over a year by the war in Burma, they began the study of Burmese under native teachers. Here their first child was born. In the spring of 1827 they were able to proceed to lower Burma, and soon transferred from Amherst to Maulmain, a new and thriving city. The first four years in Burma were filled with tragic circumstances: robbery of most of their valuables, a state of siege in Tavoy, whither they had moved in 1828, with peril from gunfire and impending massacre; recurring tropical sickness assailing all members of the family; the birth of a very frail son (George Dana Boardman, Jr., who became an eminent minister in Philadelphia); the death of the first-born and the birth of another son, who lived less than a year; Boardman's frequent absences on evangelizing tours, and his failing health. On his death, Feb. 11, 1831, Mrs. Boardman remained at her post to continue the missionary task, notwithstanding urgent reasons for returning to America. Her missionary method was largely the founding of small village schools, which became models for the government schools later established. On Apr. 10, 1834, she was married to Adoniram Judson [*q.v.*], and with him soon took up her work in Maulmain. Eight children were born of this marriage; one dying immediately and two others in infancy; two sons, Adoniram Brown Judson and Edward Judson [*qq.v.*], lived to attain distinction, one as a surgeon, the other as a minister. In spite of her frail health and many domestic duties, Mrs. Judson was of great assistance to her husband, especially through her knowledge of the Burmese language. She herself translated *The Pilgrim's Progress* into Burmese and several tracts into Burmese or Peguan. Sailing for America in search of health in May 1845, she was accompanied by her husband and the three older children. At Mauritius her improvement encouraged him to think that he might return to Burma, but a relapse caused Judson to continue with her, and she died while the vessel was anchored in harbor at St. Helena. She was buried on that island.

[Emily C. Judson, *Memoir of Sarah B. Judson* (1848); Arabella W. Stuart, *The Lives of Mrs. Ann H. Judson and Mrs. Sarah B. Judson, with a Biog. Sketch of Mrs. Emily C. Judson* (1851); D. B. Hall, *The Halls of New England* (1883); W. N. Wyeth, *Sarah B. Judson, a Memorial* (1889); *Missionary Mag.*, Nov. 1845.]
W. H. A.

JUENGLING, FREDERICK (Oct. 18, 1846–Dec. 31, 1889), wood-engraver, was born in Leipzig, Saxony, and attended the common schools there. He was apprenticed to a printer but abandoned that trade for wood-engraving. In 1866 he came to New York, where he worked first for Frank Leslie [*q.v.*] but later opened an engraving shop with several employees, making cuts for the *American Agriculturist*, the *Fireside Companion*, and other publications. An attempt to combine a printing office with his engraving establishment failed disastrously in the late seventies, and he thenceforth gave his attention wholly to his own work, becoming "one of the most impassioned advocates of individualism in wood-engraving" (Koehler, *post*, p. 2). In 1877, with the publication in *Scribner's Monthly* of his cuts after drawings by James E. Kelly, he took his place as a leader of the "new school" of American wood-engravers whose effort was to reproduce, rather than to "interpret," the work of the artist. It was this school, condemned at first by such conservatives as W. J. Linton [*q.v.*], which under the sponsorship of *Scribner's Monthly, The Century,* and *Harper's,* elevated American wood-engraving to the high level which it reached between 1876 and 1896.

In 1879 Juengling entered the Art Students' League, where his impetuosity and enthusiasm made him a favorite. He wanted his name pronounced "Youngling," but his intimates preferred the metallic sound of the first syllable and one day on entering the League room he found a large placard: "Look out for the engine at the *Juengling* of the bells." He afterward became president of the League. His paintings and watercolors appeared in exhibitions, but were few because of his devotion to engraving. He also produced some excellent etchings. He was the first American wood-engraver to be recognized in the Paris Salon, where he received honorable mention in 1881, and in 1883 he was awarded a gold medal by King Ludwig of Bavaria for his contribution to the International Exhibition at Munich.

For Juengling to be at his best he needed subjects congenial to his own plain, rugged nature, such as the peasant scenes of Jean François Millet or the negro subjects of his friend Alfred Kappes. Prettiness in art did not appeal to him. A butcher in his shop, a girl ironing clothes, a farmer with his pipe, an immigrant, these were subjects that he liked. A few of the best of his engravings are: "The 'Longshoreman's Noon," by J. G. Brown; "Edison in His Workshop," by H. Muhrman; "John Brown Going to Execution," by Thomas Hovenden; "Poe's Raven," by G. Doré; "Good Morning," by Walter Shirlaw; "Poe's Cottage at Fordham," drawn by Juengling himself; landscapes by Charles H. Miller, A. H. Wyant, George Inness, and Bruce Crane.

He fretted more than most engravers over the petty insistences of critics. Many of his blocks were greatly weakened by recutting due to such criticisms. His first proofs often contained more of the true nature of the original than the finished result. In beauty and exactness of line he could not compete with Cole, King, and some others, but his line had a peculiar charm and his beautiful stipple was purely his own. His devotion to his work was absorbing. Life outside of his art meant little to him. It was difficult for his wife to drag him to an entertainment or even to meals. At the dining table he sometimes had a block propped up where he could study it. His nervous temperament and tendency to overwork lessened his resistance to the disease, diabetes, which caused his death. After a vain trip to Carlsbad for treatment in the fall of 1887, he made a tour through Europe with his wife, and, returning to New York late in 1889, succumbed to a cold on the last day of the year. He left no children.

[S. R. Koehler, *Frederick Juengling* (1890); G. H. Whittle, "Frederick Juengling," *Printing Art*, Oct. 1917; Boston Museum of Fine Arts, *Exhibition of the Soc. of Am. Wood-Engravers* (1890); W. J. Linton, *The Hist. of Wood-Engraving in America* (1882); G. E. Woodberry, *A Hist. of Wood-Engraving* (1883); Frank Weitenkampf, *Am. Graphic Art* (1912); *N. Y. Times*, Jan. 2, 1890; *N. Y. Herald*, Jan. 1, 2, 1890; personal acquaintance.] C. W. C.

JUILLIARD, AUGUSTUS D. (Apr. 19, 1836–Apr. 25, 1919), merchant, capitalist, patron of music, was a son of Jean Nicolas and Anna (Burlette) Juilliard. He was born at sea while his parents, French Protestants, were on the three-months voyage in a sailing vessel to America from Burgundy. In Stark County, Ohio, the children were reared in the Lutheran faith. Augustus left home at an early age, got work, and while still a youth made his way to the city of New York and found employment in a textile house, where in due time he was advanced to a place of trust and responsibility. The financial crash of 1873 threw the business into bankruptcy. Juilliard was made receiver. In that capacity his management of affairs was skilful and successful in conserving the firm's assets. After the revival of trade he was able to organize his own dry-goods commission company, the beginning of a prosperous business that made for him a lifelong career. Later he became heavily interested in the manufacture of woolens, silk, and cotton, particularly in the Atlantic Mills at Providence, R. I., the Standard Silk Company, Phillipsburg, N. J., cotton mills at Aragon, Ga., and Brookford, N. C., and the New York Mills Corporation.

Meanwhile he gradually became an outstanding figure in the New York banking and investment field. At his death he was a director in the Guaranty Trust Company, the Bank of America, the Mercantile Insurance Company of America, and other financial institutions. He was also a trustee of the Central Trust Company, the Title Guaranty & Trust Company, the New York Life Insurance & Trust Company, and the Mutual Life Insurance Company. At the same time he held a directorship in the Atchison, Topeka & Santa Fé Railroad. In politics he was never especially active except in the sound-money campaign of 1896, when he supported McKinley. He was always a high-protectionist.

From the early years of the Metropolitan Opera House in New York, Juilliard was an active supporter of that enterprise. When he died, he was president of the Metropolitan Opera & Real Estate Company, the holding corporation. He was a regular attendant at the performances; in fact, he had been present at the opera early in the evening of Apr. 19, 1919, on which he came down with the attack of pneumonia that caused his death, less than six days later. His will provided that the bulk of his great fortune should go to a fund to establish musical departments in American colleges, provide musical education at home or abroad for promising students, encourage musical composition, and produce operas of merit. The Juilliard Foundation maintains a school of music in New York and a number of fellowships in other institutions, and has contributed to the support of the Metropolitan Opera Company and the summer Stadium concerts.

In 1877, Juilliard married Helen Marcelus Cossitt (Nov. 16, 1847–Apr. 2, 1916), daughter of Frederick H. and Catherine (Andrus) Cossitt of New York. She was for many years a member of the managing board of the Lincoln Hospital and Home for colored persons. She endowed St. John's Guild, which in summer transported mothers and children from the New York tenements to Coney Island for rest and refreshment; gave the Guild its first boat, the *Helen C. Juilliard*, and later, with her husband, gave the Guild a hospital ship. For Colorado College she built the Frederick H. Cossitt Memorial, designed to serve as a center of social and athletic life for the men of the college. She also made a bequest of $50,000 to the American Museum of Natural History, of which her husband was a trustee for over twenty years and to which he left $100,000 by his will in addition to numerous gifts in his lifetime.

[Information as to certain facts from Mrs. Wilda W. Krabill of Louisville, Stark County, Ohio (a niece of Augustus D. Juilliard); John Danner, *Old Landmarks of Canton and Stark County, Ohio* (1904); *Textile World Jour.*, May 3, 1919; *Who's Who in America*, 1918–19; obituary of Mrs. Juilliard in *N. Y. Times*, Apr. 3, 1916; Pearl S. Cossitt, *The Cossitt Family* (1925); editorial, *N. Y. Times*, June 28, 1919; *Musical America*, July 5, 1919; *Musical Courier*, Aug. 7, 1924; *Inst. of Musical Art of the Juilliard School of Music, Calendar*, 1931–32.] W. B. S.

JULIA, Sister (Feb. 13, 1827–Nov. 12, 1901), educator, a daughter of Neil and Catherine (Bonner) McGroarty, small respectable farmers, was born at Inver, County Donegal, Ireland, and christened Susan. In 1831 her family emigrated by way of Quebec to Cincinnati where Mrs. McGroarty's brother, Hugh Bonner, was a successful medical practitioner. Buying land at Fayetteville, Neil McGroarty farmed, but soon engaged in turnpike and railroad contracting. Moving to Cincinnati, he was succeeding in business when in 1838 he fell a victim to pneumonia, leaving a widow with ten children who were dependent on the Bonners for support. Susan's early training in a Protestant private school and a Catholic academy had been so wretched that at eleven years she was unable to read. Encouraged by Bishop Purcell [*q.v.*], however, she displayed more interest in her studies at the newly established Sixth Street academy of the nuns of Notre Dame de Namur, whom the bishop had brought from Belgium; but at best her education was only fragmentary when she became a postulant, Jan. 1, 1846. A few months later, she took the habit and on Aug. 3, 1848, she was professed as Sister Julia, in the meantime teaching the infant school.

In charge of the academy's day school, she displayed an aptitude for teaching and won the full confidence of Sister Superior Louise. Six years later, she was assigned as mistress of boarders to the Academy of Notre Dame, Roxbury, Mass., where she stayed until 1860, when she was made superior of a new convent and academy in Philadelphia. During the Civil War her happiness was shadowed by the deaths of three brothers in the service. As the community she was serving grew, she built a school on Rittenhouse Square (1867), where the patient nuns silenced the opposition of exclusive neighbors who disapproved of a convent in their midst. In 1868–69 she made the first of many visits to Namur. She had the art of winning friends in all stations, numbering among them Archbishops Wood and Ryan and society women like Katherine Drexel, who was interested in her free school for negroes (1877–82). In 1885, she somewhat regretfully left Philadelphia to become assistant to the aged Superior in Cincinnati, whom she succeeded two years later.

As superior, Sister Julia was a kind, if firm, mother of the community. In 1888 she assisted in the election of the mother-general at Namur, and visited the European convents in an effort to improve her own academies. She built an imposing novitiate at Waltham, Mass., in 1889, a large convent and school at The Summit, Grandin Road, Cincinnati, and at least thirteen other foundations. She visited the Notre Dame schools on the Pacific Coast which were placed under her management in 1892, and with the aid of Judge M. P. O'Connor she founded an institute for orphans at San José, Cal. She improved the parochial schools taught by her sisters, who numbered 1,500, and standardized their thirty academies by preparing an outline of studies and general examinations whose results were sent to the provincial-house.

Her most arduous labor, however, was the establishment of a college for higher education of Catholic women in the vicinity of the Catholic University of America—a move which was not favored by the mother-general and was openly condemned by some Catholic leaders on the grounds that the school, at the very gate of the university, was really a venture in coeducation. Supported by Cardinal Gibbons, by the rector of the university, and by Apostolic Delegate Martinelli, she persisted nevertheless, and built Trinity College (1899–1900)—though not without direct papal approbation. Today this college is her monument, but the worry occasioned by the undertaking no doubt hastened her death, which occurred at the Notre Dame convent in Peabody, Mass. Her remains were brought back to the provincial-house in Cincinnati from which she was buried with a requiem mass by Archbishop Elder in the community chapel at The Summit.

[Sister Helen Louise, *Sister Julia* (1928), a full and satisfactory biography; *An Hist. Sketch of Trinity Coll., Washington, D. C.* (1925), by a Sister of Notre Dame; *Catholic World*, June 1904; *Trinity College, for the Higher Education of Women* (brochure, 1898); *Boston Transcript*, Nov. 13, 1901; *Cincinnati Enquirer*, Nov. 14, 18, 1901.]

R. J. P.

JULIAN, GEORGE WASHINGTON (May 5, 1817–July 7, 1899), abolitionist leader, son of Isaac and Rebecca (Hoover) Julian, was born in a log cabin a mile and a half south of Centerville, Wayne County, Ind. His father, descended from René St. Julien, a Huguenot who came to America about the end of the seventeenth century, was a soldier in the War of 1812 and at one time a member of the Indiana legislature. His mother, of German descent, was a Quaker, whose paternal ancestors were also those of Herbert Hoover. Isaac Julian died when George was only six years old, but by hard work and frugality the widowed mother managed to bring up the family of children. George attended the common schools, at eighteen taught a district school, presently studied law, and in 1840 was admitted to the bar, practising successively in Newcastle, Greenfield, and Centerville. In 1845 he was elected to the state legislature as a Whig, but voted with the Democrats against the repudiation of the Wabash and Erie Canal bonds. About the same time he began to write newspaper articles attacking slavery. Defeated in 1847 in an attempt to secure the Whig nomination for state senator, he presently joined the Free-Soil party and the next year attended the Buffalo convention that nominated Van Buren. His activities as an abolitionist had caused him to be ostracized by many former friends and associates and had even brought about the dissolution of a law partnership with his brother, but the political tide presently turned in his favor and in 1848, having been nominated for Congress by the Free-Soilers, he was elected, with the assistance of many Democratic votes. As a member of the little group of anti-slavery men in Congress he vigorously opposed the compromise measures of 1850. Beaten for reëlection in that year, he resumed the practice of law but continued his advocacy of abolition both in speeches and in the press. In 1852 he was nominated for the vice-presidency by the Free-Soil party and took an active part in the campaign.

Julian's real opportunity came with the rise of the Republican party, of which the Free-Soil party had been a forerunner. In 1856 he participated in the Pittsburgh convention that formally organized the new party, and was chosen one of the vice-presidents and chairman of the committee on organization. His earnest fight for human freedom brought reward at last when in 1860 he was elected to Congress. Four times reëlected, he speedily won a prominent place in legislative deliberations, and among the committees on which he served was the very important committee on the conduct of the war. He early began to urge the emancipation of slaves as a war measure, advancing the argument of John Quincy Adams, that such a step would be within the war powers of the president and Congress. As chairman of the committee on public lands he had an important part in the passage of the celebrated Homestead Act, a measure he had urged in 1851. Though he thought Lincoln too slow in some respects and opposed his reconstruction plan, Julian refused to join in the attempt in 1864 to nominate Chase in Lincoln's stead. Julian favored punishing Confederate leaders and confiscating their lands and early advocated the granting of the suffrage to the freedmen. He stood, therefore, with the Radicals in their battles with President Johnson, and in 1867 was one of the committee of seven appointed by the House to prepare the articles of impeachment against the President. In 1868 he proposed an amendment to the Constitution conferring the right of suffrage upon women, a reform he continued to champion to the end of his life.

Failing of renomination in 1870, he devoted much of his time to recuperating his broken health and to compiling a volume of *Speeches on Political Questions,* published in 1872. He had come to be out of sympathy with the influences that dominated the Republican party nationally and in Indiana, and joined the Liberal Republican movement, presiding during parts of two days over the Cincinnati convention (1872) that nominated Horace Greeley. The next year he removed to Irvington, a suburb of Indianapolis, and for some years was occupied with writing and championing reform measures. He supported Tilden in the campaign of 1876, and two million copies of his speech, *The Gospel of Reform,* were distributed by the Democratic National Committee. In the years that followed he contributed notable articles on politics, the public lands, and other subjects to the *North American Review* and other periodicals. Meanwhile he was writing his *Political Recollections 1840–1872,* published in 1884. After the election of Cleveland in that year he was appointed surveyor general of New Mexico, a post for which he was particularly fitted. During his administration (July 1885–September 1889) he brought to light many flagrant frauds in connection with public land grants. In 1889 he published a volume, *Later Speeches on Political Questions with Select Controversial Papers,* edited by his daughter. His last important literary work was *The Life of Joshua R. Giddings* (1892). In 1896 he supported the Gold Democrats. He died at his home in Irvington in the summer of 1899.

Julian was twice married. His first wife was Anne Elizabeth Finch of Centerville, who died in November 1860, a few days after his election to Congress. His second wife, whom he married Dec. 31, 1863, was Laura Giddings, daughter of Joshua R. Giddings [*q.v.*]. She died in 1884.

[Consult Julian's own *Political Recollections* (1884); *George W. Julian* (1923), by his daughter, Grace Julian Clarke; and *Indianapolis Sentinel,* July 7, 1899. Julian also left an unpublished diary, containing much interesting and important historical material, which is in the possession of his daughter, Grace Julian Clarke, Indianapolis.]

P. L. H.

JUMEL, STEPHEN (*c.* 1754–May 22, 1832), wine-merchant, known chiefly as the husband of the charming but unscrupulous Mme. Jumel who later became Mrs. Aaron Burr, came from a family of Bordeaux merchants. He first appears in American history in 1795 when he landed in New York, having come by way of St. Helena from Haiti, where he had been driven from his coffee plantation by the insurrection of the blacks. Just before leaving he had shipped a cargo of coffee to New York, and with the proceeds of its sale he laid the foundations of a highly successful wine business. He was soon naturalized and went into partnership with Jacques Desobry. His commercial correspondence reveals the cunning mind which piled up a considerable fortune in the years during which American commerce was interrupted. While the Embargo was in force, for instance, he doled out his wine in small quantities, knowing that the price would continue to rise, but as soon as word came of its repeal, he rushed a cargo to New Orleans, instructing the captain to go up the river alone to dispose of the cargo before the crew could spread the news which would lower its value. During the period of non-intercourse with France, he had wine carried overland from Bordeaux to San Sebastian, taking care that Spanish labels were substituted for the French. His agents in the Spanish port were told that when a ship flying his house flag appeared, they were to fly a white flag if the coast was clear, but a red-and-white flag if the officials were making seizures, and all his captains were provided with safe "dummy" instructions in addition to the real ones.

Jumel has been described as a "handsome, graceful giant" with a generous and impulsive nature. The fortune which he amassed was ultimately lost through his marriage on Apr. 7, 1804, with Eliza Brown, otherwise known as Betsey Bowen, "a beautiful blonde with a superb figure and graceful carriage" with whom he had been living for several years. In 1810 he purchased for her the Roger Morris house, at one time Washington's headquarters, now preserved as a museum. After a vain attempt to force his wife upon New York society, he sailed with her to France in 1815 and is said to have offered to bring Napoleon to America after Waterloo. The Jumels were more successful socially in Paris than in New York, but in 1826, Mme. Jumel returned to the latter city bearing a power of attorney with which she gained control over most of the property of her husband, who returned two years later in reduced circumstances. Joseph Bonaparte and Louis Napoleon were friends of the Jumels at this period. Jumel died as the result of a fall from a wagon in 1832 and on July 1, 1833, his widow married Aaron Burr.

[Meade Minnigerode, *Lives and Times* (1925), an impressionistic sketch; Wm. H. Shelton, *The Jumel Mansion* (1916); J. C. Pumpelly, "The Old Morris House, Afterwards the Jumel Mansion: Its History and Traditions," *N. Y. Geneal. and Biog. Record*, Apr. 1903; J. A. Scoville, *The Old Merchants of N. Y. City*, vol. I (1863); letter book of Jumel & Desobry in the manuscript collections of the N. Y. Pub. Lib.; papers of the brig *Eugenia* in the collection of High Court of Admiralty, Prize Cases, N. Y. Ships, vol. I, in the same library; *N. Y. Standard*, May 24, 1832; obituary of Mme. Jumel in *N. Y. Times*, July 18, 1865.] R. G. A.

JUNE, JENNIE [See CROLY, JANE CUNNINGHAM, 1829–1901].

JUNEAU, SOLOMON LAURENT (Aug. 9, 1793–Nov. 14, 1856), founder of the city of Milwaukee, was a native of L'Assomption, Canada, near Montreal, whither his parents, François and Thérèse Galerneau Juneau *dit* La Tulipe, had come from Alsace four years earlier. The family had had representatives in Canada since the seventeenth century. Solomon, who was the second son, was well educated for his day and when he entered the fur trade he was articled as a clerk (*commi*), not as a voyageur. He arrived in Mackinac in 1816 where he engaged with Jacques Vieau a trader from Green Bay, who had several posts along the western shore of Lake Michigan. In 1818 Juneau began operations at Milwaukee, where Vieau had long traded, and after marrying his principal's daughter, Josette, he built a house at Milwaukee and became the agent there of the American Fur Company. He was tall—six feet, four inches—with dark curly hair, fine features, and an engaging, courteous manner. He was very popular with the Indians among whom he traded, who called him "Solomo," and with whom he was allied through his wife, whose grandmother was an Indian.

In 1831 Juneau took out papers of naturalization and began to learn English. Two years later he entered into partnership with Morgan L. Martin, an American of Green Bay, to plat a town on the Milwaukee River. This was accomplished in 1835 when Juneau entered his claim as a preëmption and began to sell lots in the new town. He was its first postmaster, and the first president of the village. As settlers came in he aided them by every means in his power. As resident partner, he with Martin gave a square for a court house and land for a lighthouse, and later Juneau gave lots for the Catholic cathedral and for the Protestant Milwaukee Female College. At one time he was reputed to be worth at least a hundred thousand dollars, but the panic of 1837 and his personal generosity reduced his fortune. None the less, he was recognized as a leading citizen by the Easterners who flocked to Milwaukee. He built the first store, the first inn, and when the city was incorporated in 1846, became its first mayor. He retained his interest in the Indians and after the treaty of 1849 entered his wife and children as halfbreeds of the Menominee nation.

In 1852, at his wife's instance, Juneau retired from Milwaukee and went to live on a plat of ground in Dodge County where he founded the village of Theresa, named for his mother. There Mrs. Juneau died in 1855. The next year Juneau served as delegate to the Democratic convention that nominated James Buchanan. Before Buchanan took his seat Juneau had died on the Menominee Indian reservation, whither he had gone to a "payment." When he was buried, at Milwaukee, six Menominee chiefs acted as pall-bearers. "He was always the same unselfish, confiding, open-hearted, genial, honest and polite gentleman" (*Wisconsin Historical Collections,* XI, 1888, 405–07), wrote his former partner, who testified that he was the soul of honor, and that their accounts, though kept verbally, were settled without difficulty (Buck, *post,* I, 40–41). Milwaukee contains many memorials of Juneau in the names of streets, a park, and a fine statue presented in 1887 to the city and placed in Juneau Park on the lake front. In the mayor's office is an original portrait by Samuel M. Brooks, ordered by the city and painted from life. He left a large family of whom there are many descendants.

[Joseph Tassé, *Les Canadiens de l'Ouest* (Montreal, 1878), I, 213–23; J. S. Buck, *Pioneer Hist. of Milwaukee,* vol. I (1876); Isabella Fox, *Solomon Juneau; a Biog., with Sketches of the Juneau Family* (copr. 1916); *Unveiling of the Juneau Monument, July 6th, 1887* (1887); *Daily Milwaukee News,* Nov. 18, 1856.]

L. P. K.

JUNGMAN, JOHN GEORGE (Apr. 19, 1720–July 17, 1808), Moravian missionary, was born at Hockenheim in Baden, a descendant of French Protestants. His mother's death when he was less than five affected him deeply, making him unnaturally serious. His father, a cooper by trade, was probably that Johann Dietrich Jungmann who landed in Philadelphia May 15, 1732 (I. D. Rupp, *A Collection of . . . Names of German . . . Immigrants in Pennsylvania,* 1876, p. 71). He taught his son the rudiments of arithmetic and "singing from notes," and encouraged characteristics of piety and diligence. When Jungman was eleven years old the family undertook to emigrate to Pennsylvania, landing in Rhode Island after twenty-five weeks at sea. His stepmother and three sisters succumbed to the extreme privations of the journey; the survivors were fed by Indians, who thus won from the boy a gratitude which resulted in a lifelong devotion to their race. When the Jungmans at last arrived in Philadelphia, friends cared for their needs until they were settled on their own land in Oley. The lad soon carried the responsibility of the farm while the father practised his trade. In 1742 the young man first came in contact with the Moravians, and was, as he tells us, "awakened" to a new religious life. After trying in vain to reconcile his father to his plan, he decided to join the community at Bethlehem. In 1743 he took his first Holy Communion, and two years later was appointed teacher in the children's school. In the latter year (Aug. 24, 1745) he married Anna Margaret (Bechtel) Büttner, daughter of Rev. John Bechtel and widow of Rev. Gottlob Büttner. From that time until her death forty-eight years later she was his companion in all his missionary enterprises.

For a year after his marriage Jungman kept a school at Falkner's swamp, but in 1746 he began his labors at Gnadenhütten on the Mahoning, a community established by the Moravians for the Christian Indians. In 1754 he was transferred to Pachgatgoch, a similar community near the present town of Kent in Connecticut. During the French and Indian War, as in the period of the Revolution, the work of the Moravians was hindered because their pacifism caused both parties to suspect them of treachery. In 1758 the Jungmans left Connecticut, and after short periods of service at Christiansbrunn, Wyalusing, and Lanuntutenmunk on the Beaver River, they entered a new field at Schönbrunn on the Muskingum in Ohio. In 1777, because of the confusion due to Indian uprisings, they returned to Bethlehem, but in 1781 they were back on the Muskingum. In that same year they with other missionaries and their Indian converts were captured by the Hurons under English direction, and were driven into the wilderness of the Upper Sandusky. In the following year, although the leaders had satisfactorily answered the charges brought against them, the missionaries were all ordered to Detroit. Under the patronage of the Detroit commander, they attempted to establish their mission on the Clinton River. In 1785, however, the Jungmans returned to Bethlehem and retired from active service. Anna Jungman died on Nov. 22, 1793, and her husband, July 17, 1808. They had suffered both the hardships of the pioneer and the trials of the missionary. The account of Jungman's teaching, preaching, and labor among the Indians is told with characteristic humility in his autobiography.

[Sources include: "The Narrative of the Life of John George Jungman" from his own MS., in *Periodical Accounts Relating to the Missions of the Church of the United Brethren,* vol. VI (1814); *Diary of David Zeisberger* (2 vols., 1885), ed. by E. F. Bliss; John Heckewelder, *A Narrative of the Missions of the United Brethren among the Delaware and Mohegan Indians* (1820); *Trans. Moravian Hist. Soc.,* I (1876), 356 and V (1899), 129, 161; *Poulson's Am. Daily Advertiser* (Phila.), Aug. 2, 1808. The name is spelled Jungman in the *Periodical Accounts* and Jungmann in Zeisberger's *Diary* and the *Transactions.*]

D. M. C.

JUNKIN, GEORGE (Nov. 1, 1790–May 20, 1868), Presbyterian clergyman, educator, was a descendant of Scotch Covenanters who fled to Ireland under the persecution of the Stuarts. His grandfather, Joseph, emigrated from Antrim, Ireland, about 1735, and acquired five hundred acres of land in what is now Cumberland County,

Pa. Here George was born, the son of Joseph and Eleanor (Cochran) Junkin, and the sixth of their fourteen children. He received such instruction as the log schoolhouses of the frontier afforded until 1806, when the family moved westward and settled in Mercer County. For the next three years he was farmer, lumberman, carpenter, cabinetmaker, miller, and wool-carder. In 1809, however, he entered the grammar school of Jefferson College, and in 1813 graduated from that college, with the reputation of being a grave, reserved youth, intent upon study. He developed into an austere, unyielding man, a strict disciplinarian, one who held to any course upon which he entered with Scotch-Irish tenacity. Immediately after his graduation he went to New York where he studied theology in the seminary established by Rev. John Mitchell Mason [*q.v.*], and in September 1816 he was licensed to preach by the Associate Reformed Presbytery of Monongahela. For three years he was engaged in missionary work, being in the meantime ordained, June 29, 1818, by the Associate Reformed Presbytery of Philadelphia. On June 1, 1819, he married, at Philadelphia, Julia Rush Miller, daughter of John and Margaret Miller.

His first and only pastorate was at Milton, Pa., where he was installed on Oct. 17, 1819. Here for eleven years he devoted himself zealously to the interest of religion, did pioneer work in behalf of temperance, and became increasingly interested in problems of education. Through his exertions Milton Academy was established. He also started and edited a fortnightly paper, *The Religious Farmer,* which was issued from Jan. 1, 1828 to Jan. 1, 1830. In 1826 the General Synod of the Associate Reformed Church having united with the General Assembly of the Presbyterian Church a few years earlier, he was sent as a commissioner to that body, and thereafter became prominent in the councils and controversies of his denomination. He resigned his church at Milton in 1830, and began a long career as head of educational institutions by becoming principal of the Manual Labor Academy of Pennsylvania at Germantown. He remained in this position but two years, and then became the first president of Lafayette College, Easton, Pa. The institution had been chartered in 1826, but had no property or funds. The trustees hired a farm; the manual-labor system, of which President Junkin was an earnest advocate, was adopted; and former pupils at Germantown constituted the student body. Through his untiring efforts money was secured, a permanent site obtained, and the first building completed in May 1834. For nine years he devoted himself to the upbuilding of the college, resigning in 1841 to become president of Miami University, Ohio. In the meantime, during the strife which resulted in the division of the Presbyterian Church in 1837–38 he had been one of the uncompromising leaders of the Old School party, and had instigated the trial of Albert Barnes [*q.v.*] for heresy. He was also a vigorous opponent of abolitionism, although opposed to slavery and an advocate of compensated emancipation. These facts together with some local difficulties interfered with his success at Miami, and in 1844 he again became the head of Lafayette College, continuing as such until 1848, when he assumed the presidency of Washington College, Lexington, Va. This position his loyalty to the Union compelled him to resign in 1861. Thereafter he resided in Philadelphia. In 1863 he published *Political Fallacies: An Examination of the False Assumptions and Refutation of the Sophistical Reasonings Which Have Brought on the Civil War.* A week before his death he completed *A Commentary upon the Epistle to the Hebrews* (1873). Among his other publications are *The Vindication, Containing a History of the Trial of the Rev. Albert Barnes . . .* (1836); *The Integrity of American National Union vs. Abolitionism . . .* (1843); *A Treatise on Justification* (1849); *A Treatise on Sanctification* (1864); *The Tabernacle, or the Gospel According to Moses* (1865); *Sabbatismos* (1866). One of his daughters, Eleanor, was the first wife of Gen. Thomas J. Jackson [*q.v.*], and another, Margaret Junkin Preston [*q.v.*], became widely known as a writer of poetry.

[D. X. Junkin, *The Reverend George Junkin, D.D., LL.D.* (1871); Alfred Nevin, *Encyc. of the Presbyt. Ch. in the U. S. of America* (1884); W. L. Tobey and W. O. Thompson, *The Diamond Anniversary Volume Miami Univ., 1824–1899* (n.d.); *Lafayette College, Some Pages of its Past, Pictures of its Present, and Forecast of its Future* (n.d.); *Public Ledger* (Phila.), May 21, 1868.]

H. E. S.

KAFER, JOHN CHRISTIAN (Dec. 27, 1842–Mar. 30, 1906), engineer, educator, was born in Trenton, N. J., and was appointed from his native state as a third assistant engineer in the United States Navy on Jan. 16, 1863. From that time until the close of the Civil War he was constantly at the front, taking part in the James River campaign and the first attack on Fort Fisher. He was warranted second assistant engineer May 28, 1864. Following the war he was assigned to sea duty on the *Kearsarge,* then on the *Susquehanna,* and in 1868 became an instructor in steam engineering at the Naval Academy. He was engaged in this duty twice (1868–74, 1876–82), an aggregate of nearly ten years. Every class but one of the separate course for engineers came at some time under his tuition. He was a successful teacher, adding to his technical proficiency a great interest in young men. His pupils continued his friends through life. He taught before the development of the great engineering schools, at a time when much of the instruction had to be the original work of the instructor, and he was generally considered the ablest of them all. In 1885 he declined a professorship of engineering at Cornell University. For a time he was assigned to the practice ship *Despatch,* and later, to the Bureau of Steam Engineering, where he was principal assistant to Engineer-in-Chief C. H. Loring and also, for a short time, to Engineer-in-Chief G. W. Melville [*qq.v.*]. He had just previously been Melville's chief aid in the design of new machinery. Kafer suffered for years from varicose veins, and in 1888 he was retired for physical disability. After his retirement he was general manager and vice-president of the Morgan Iron Works (John Roach & Sons) in New York and later vice-president of the Quintard Iron Works. A few weeks before his death he formed with two of his old pupils the firm of Kafer, Mattice & Warren, consulting engineers. He died at Trenton in his sixty-fourth year.

Kafer's service in the navy covered the period when the "Line and Staff" controversy was at its worst. His ability and professional pride marked him out as one of the leaders of the Staff. Among the broad-gauge men of both sides, however, this dispute was not personal, and Kafer counted some of his warmest friends among his opponents. It is gratifying to record that he lived to see the end of the strife and the dawn of increased efficiency as a result of the amalgamation of the line and the engineer corps in 1899, brought about largely by the ability of the younger men whom he had trained. He was active as a member of the American Society of Mechanical Engineers and also of the Society of Naval Architects and Marine Engineers, and was senior American member of the Institute of Naval Architects of Great Britain. He was for a time a manager and vice-president of the first of these societies and was a member of council of the second from its organization. He took an active part in the discussion of professional papers. He was also one of the most valued and useful members of the Engineers' Club of New York, was for many years a governor and for three years (1901–04), president. He was instrumental in the first removal of the Club from West Twenty-ninth Street to Fifth Avenue, and furthermore, realizing that the organization should have its own home, he secured at his own risk options on the Fortieth-Street site of the present edifice, which is the gift of Andrew Carnegie to his fellow members. Kafer was treasurer of the building fund for the Club and also for the United Engineering Building on Thirty-ninth Street, another gift from Carnegie. In a sense the club building is a monument to Kafer, although he died not long before its completion. He was never robust, but was an indefatigable worker, and immensely popular in every relation.

[W. M. McFarland in *Jour. Am. Soc. Naval Engineers,* May 1906; *Trans. Am. Soc. Mech. Engineers,* vol. XXVII (1906); *Army and Navy Jour., Army and Navy Reg.,* Apr. 7, 1906; Navy Registers, 1864–1906; *N. Y. Times,* Apr. 1, 1906; *True American* (Trenton), Apr. 2, 1906.]

W. M. M.

KAH-GE-GA-GAH-BOWH [See Copway, George, 1818–*c.* 1863.]

KAHN, JULIUS (Feb. 28, 1861–Dec. 18, 1924), congressman, was born in Kuppenheim, Baden, Germany. His parents, Herman and Jeannette (Weil) Kahn, emigrated to America when he was five years old, settling first in Calaveras County, Cal., and afterwards moving to San Francisco. There he attended the public schools until reaching the age of sixteen. After two years' work in a clerical capacity, he went on the stage, and for about ten years followed the theatrical profession, playing in companies with Joseph Jefferson, Edwin Booth, Tomasso Salvini, and other hardly less well-known stars. His last rôle was that of Baron Stein in *Diplomacy.* While still active on the stage, he commenced the study of law, but before completing his legal studies he was elected to the California Assembly (1892). He served one term in that body, and at the end declined a nomination for the state Senate. In 1894, he was admitted to the bar and began the practice of law in San Francisco, where he soon became a member of the firm of Foote & Coogan. In 1898, he was elected as a Republican to the national House of Representatives. Reëlected in 1900, he was defeated two years later, but in 1904 he won back his seat, which he retained until his death in 1924. He served twelve terms in all, a longer period than any other representative from the Pacific Coast up to that time, and was elected for a thirteenth the month before he died. In his later elections, he ran without opposition, and sometimes even had the Democratic indorsement.

Appointed a member of the committee on military affairs in 1905, twice its chairman, Kahn was ranking minority member at the commencement of the World War. Long an advocate of military preparedness, he had helped to organize the National Defense League in 1913, and later became its chairman. Convinced of the unpreparedness of the country, he labored in season and out, and against heavy odds, to impress the committee with the need of planning for the emergency which might arise. The National Defense Act of 1916 was one result of his efforts. By this measure, at least a skeleton organization for defense was outlined. When finally the United States entered the War, it fell to Kahn, owing to the lack of Democratic support for President Wilson's program, to formulate and carry out the military policy of the government. The outstanding piece of legislation with which his name soon became identified, was the Selective Draft Act (1917), carried in the face of very strong opposition which included the Democratic speaker, the floor leader, and even the chairman of the committee on military affairs. Kahn also took an important part in the amendment of the Army Emergency Increase Act (August 1918), providing for a reservoir of men not included in the Selective Draft Act. He was likewise keenly interested in the development of aviation, in both the army and the navy. His last big piece of legislation was the National Defense Act (1920), which reorganized the whole military establishment.

Kahn displayed exceptional ability to secure legislation favorable to San Francisco and the state of California, such as large appropriations for development projects, and laws for the protection of fruit and other agricultural products from the ravages of insect pests. He was instrumental in preventing the closing of the San Francisco mint, and in the Sixty-first Congress (1909–11), he successfully led the campaign to hold the Panama-Pacific International Exposition at San Francisco in 1915. Other measures of more distinct national interest with which his name was prominently associated include the insertion in the Panama Canal Act of the clause providing free tolls for American ships—the repeal of which he afterwards vigorously opposed—and the extension of the federal publicity statutes, applicable to campaign funds, to cover primaries as well as elections.

In 1899, Kahn married Florence Prag, who, upon his death, was almost immediately elected to succeed him in the House. Two sons also survived him. He was of the Jewish faith, and a member of numerous fraternal organizations. Amiable, genial, open-hearted, he was one of the best-loved figures on the political stage of the past generation.

[The main facts of Kahn's career have been obtained in part from his widow, and in part from extended articles in the *San Francisco Chronicle* and the *San Francisco Examiner* for Dec. 19, 1924. The *Congressional Record* for the Congresses in which he was a member (56–57, 59–68 Cong.), gives some idea of his work in that body. See also *Biog. Dir. Am. Cong.* (1928); *Who's Who in America,* 1922–23; "Memorial Address Delivered in the House of Representatives in Memory of Julius Kahn," *House Doc. No. 672,* 68 Cong., 2 Sess.; *Manual and Review of the National Defense League* (1917?); *Outlook,* Dec. 31, 1924.] P. O. R.

KAISER, ALOIS (Nov. 10, 1840–Jan. 5, 1908), synagogue cantor and composer, was born in Szobotist, Hungary, the son of David Loeb Kaiser. He received his education in the Realschule, the Jewish Teachers' Seminary, and the Conservatory of Music in Vienna. At ten years of age he entered the synagogue choir of the renowned cantor, Solomon Sulzer, in which for some time he was leading soprano. After eight years in that choir, having gained a thorough familiarity with Sulzer's cantillation and choral music and having developed a rich baritone voice, he was chosen in 1859 as assistant cantor to the Fünfhaus synagogue, in the outskirts of Vienna. In 1862 he married Caroline Fould. He served as cantor in the Neusynagogue in Prague from 1863 until 1866, when he came to America to be cantor of the Oheb Shalom synagogue in Baltimore, a position which he filled until his death. In America, he was the leading cantor of the school of Sulzer, a school in which Jewish musical tradition was modified by the standards of Teutonic oratorio, operatic, and choral music. For several years he was president of the Society of American Cantors. An unusual compliment was paid to his character and scholarly musicianship when in 1895 he was elected an honorary member of the Central Conference of American Rabbis. For nineteen years before his death, as president of the Hebrew Education Society of Baltimore, he won the affection of his congregants and the respect of all who knew him.

Among his published works, besides a cantata, many hymns, and music for special services, is *A Collection of the Principal Melodies of the Synagogue, from the Earliest Times to the Present* (1893), which he compiled with William Sparger as a souvenir of the Jewish Women's Congress held under the auspices of the World's Parliament of Religions at Chicago. This useful collection contains fifty traditional synagogue melodies with accompaniments and English texts, sixteen modern compositions, and a prefatory historical survey of synagogue music. Between 1871 and 1886 Kaiser, together with others, issued *Zimrath Yah,* a more ambitious, but less valuable collection of synagogue music. These four volumes contain little that is traditionally Jewish, the bulk of the material being either compositions by the editors or by Christian composers, marked by an intricate or a German melodic style. Kaiser edited *The Union Hymnal* (1897) for the Central Conference of American Rabbis, contributing about forty hymns, the majority of the rest being adaptations from Christian composers.

This hymnal is characteristic of the dual character of Kaiser's work. On the one hand, he freely introduced into the Synagogue sacred and secular music of non-Jewish character; on the other, he pleaded for the retention of traditional Jewish music in American Reform Jewish temples. In their reaction from the historical traditions of the synagogue service the Reform congregations tended strongly to dispense with the cantor and thereby with most of the traditional synagogue music; thus Kaiser could truthfully say of American Reform temples that they had borrowed so much from the church, the opera, and the concert stage that in some Jewish houses of worship Jewish melodies had almost entirely disappeared. When he pleaded for the retention of the old music, however, he was of opinion that themes reduced to the fixed rhythm of hymns and anthems were all that could be preserved. For the rest, he believed that the traditional modal chanting of the Synagogue with its uniquely Jewish character and amazing melismatic richness of coloratura and free improvisation, which is so vigorously alive and developing today, was already in his time a thing of the past.

[Adolph Guttmacher in *Year Book of the Central Conference of American Rabbis,* vol. XVIII (1909); *American Jewish Year Book,* 1903–04; *A Third of a Century in the Service of God and the Oheb Shalom Congregation of Baltimore* (1899); A. Z. Idelsohn, *Jewish Music in Its Historical Development* (1929); *The Jewish Encyc.,* vol. VII (1925); *Jewish Comment* (Baltimore), Jan. 10, 17, 1908; *Sun* (Baltimore), Jan. 6, 1908.]

D. deS. P.

KALANIANAOLE, JONAH KUHIO (Mar. 26, 1871–Jan. 7, 1922), delegate to Congress from Hawaii, was born at Kauai, a descendant of the last independent king of that island. His father was High Chief David Kahalepouli Piikoi; his mother, Princess Kinoiki Kekaulike. He was a cousin of King Kalakaua and a nephew by marriage and was created a prince by royal proclamation in 1883. He was educated in the best public and private schools of Honolulu, at St. Matthew's School in California, and at the Royal Agricultural College in England, finishing with a business course. Before the overthrow of the monarchy in 1893 he held some minor offices in the government. In 1895 he was arrested, convicted, and served a prison sentence for complicity in the royalist uprising against the Republic of Hawaii. The following year he was married to Elizabeth Kahanu Kaauwai, a young woman of rank. The abrogation of the monarchy and subsequent annexation of Hawaii to the United States cut off the career to which the young prince had been looking forward. Some years of uncertainty followed, during which he traveled abroad, hunted big game in South Africa and accompanied the British army as a kind of observer during the Boer War. He thought for a time of residing permanently away from his native country, but finally returned to Hawaii at the end of 1901, frankly accepted the new order of things, and began to take his part in public affairs as a loyal American citizen.

His first political affiliation was with the Home Rule party, but he soon became dissatisfied with the narrow racial policies and undemocratic practices of that party. In the summer of 1902 he led a revolt of younger Hawaiians against the party management, in the interest of governmental efficiency and a sincere acceptance of American citizenship, and in the fall of that year joined the Republican party. He was named as the party candidate for delegate to Congress and was triumphantly elected. Although frequently at variance with his party leaders on questions of policy and faced with strong opposition at the polls, he was reëlected at each succeeding election until his death. Beginning with more than the ordinary handicaps of a new member of Congress, Prince Kuhio (as he was usually called) gradually made a place for himself which enabled him to accomplish important results for the Territory. The crowning achievement of his career was his successful fight for the adoption of the Hawaiian Homes Commission Act (1921), the object of which was the rehabilitation of the native race by putting the Hawaiians back on the soil as homesteaders. He was the first member appointed on the commission and before his death had begun to see the plans for the project taking shape.

Kuhio was an all-round athlete and sportsman and had in high degree the genial personality and natural dignity characteristic of his race. His example and influence were of great weight in reconciling the Hawaiians to their loss of independence as a nation.

[See *Jonah Kuhio Kalanianaole: Memorial Address Delivered in the House of Representatives . . . Jan. 7, 1923* (1924); *The Story of Hawaii and Its Builders* (1925), ed. by G. F. Nellist; *Biog. Dir. Am. Cong.* (1928); *Who's Who in America,* 1920–21; obituary articles by A. P. Taylor in *Honolulu Advertiser,* Jan. 7 and 16, 1922; other articles in same paper and in *Honolulu Star-Bulletin,* Jan. 7–16, 1922; *Paradise of the Pacific,* Feb. 1922. Honolulu newspapers during summer and fall of 1902 furnish data for Kalanianaole's political activity and conversion to Republican party.] R. S. K.

KALB, JOHANN (June 29, 1721–Aug. 19, 1780), Revolutionary general, known as "Baron de Kalb," was born in Hüttendorf, Germany, the son of Johann Leonhard and Margarethe (Putz, *née* Seitz) Kalb, peasants. He received his early schooling at Kriegenbronn, became a waiter, and at the age of sixteen left home. After six years, of which the records are silent, he is found serving under the name of Jean de Kalb as a lieutenant in Count Loewendal's regiment of French infantry. This assumption of a title to which he had no legal right made possible and facilitated his military career. He shared, though somewhat humbly, in the brilliant victories of Marshal Saxe and served throughout the War of the Austrian Succession. He was assiduous in the study of modern languages, mathematics, and troop organization. In 1747 he became captain and adjutant and was made "officer of detail," a post which combined the offices of general manager and judge of the regiment. He submitted in 1754 elaborate plans for the organization of a marine infantry for sudden attacks upon the English coast and colonies. He went to Paris to prosecute his venture, but since he was unschooled in court intrigue and lacked necessary influence his plans failed. In 1756 he became a major and served with distinction in the Seven Years' War. At the end of the war he expected promotion, but his office was abolished and he was given the position of captain with the rank of lieutenant-colonel. On Apr. 10, 1764, he married Anna Elizabeth Emilie Van Robais, the daughter of a wealthy and retired cloth manufacturer. Possessed, now, of a comfortable fortune, he retired from the army and settled near Paris, but his insatiable thirst for glory and his longing for activity urged him to resume his military career; and in 1765 he unsuccessfully attempted to enter the Portuguese service, hoping, after a few successful campaigns, to return to France a general. In April 1767 the Duc de Choiseul requested him to undertake a secret mission to America to report on the affairs of the British colonies. Arriving in Philadelphia in January 1768, he traveled in the colonies about four months. His numerous and detailed reports were the observations of a shrewd and impartial investigator. The interception of his reports caused him to return to France, where toward the close of the year Choiseul's interest in the colonies languished and Kalb was unceremoniously dismissed. After two years of rural retirement he received two invitations to serve in Poland, which he declined. With the accession of Louis XVI and the return to influence of the brothers Broglie, who had earlier been Kalb's patrons, the paths to promotion were again opened: he was made brigadier-general for the islands on Nov. 6, 1776. Having determined to serve in America, he was engaged as a major-general by Silas Deane [*q.v.*]. It was through Kalb that his protégé Lafayette [*q.v.*] met Deane and engaged to serve in America with Kalb and his companions. After numerous delays they sailed in April 1777, Kalb bringing with him the extraordinary offer of De Broglie to become the benevolent dictator of the revolting colonies.

They landed on the coast of South Carolina June 13, and at the end of July arrived in Philadelphia, where they discovered that Congress had refused to ratify the contracts and appointments made by Deane. Having repudiated Deane's arrangements, Congress received Lafayette as a major-general. Kalb was indignant and wrote bitterly to the president of Congress, threatening civil suit to enforce his contract with Deane. Having despaired of favorable action, he was about to embark for France, when he was notified that Congress had elected him to a newly created major-generalship, a post which he accepted after much consideration. He joined the army early in November and commanded a division of New England regiments. He took part in the last operations before Philadelphia and spent the winter in the bleak encampment at Valley Forge. At times he wished to return to the French army, to become the French envoy to America, or to represent France in Geneva, but these were idle hopes. In 1778 he was Lafayette's second in command in the Canadian expedition that arose from the Conway cabal, but at Albany the expedition was abandoned and they returned in time to celebrate the announcement of the French alliance, an event which Kalb thought would quickly terminate the war. Until the spring of 1780 he was constantly with the army, though without the conspicuous distinction for which he hoped. On Apr. 3, 1780, he was ordered to the relief of Charleston, S. C., then besieged by the British. Lack of men and supplies retarded his advance. At Deep River, N. C., he was joined by General Gates, recently appointed to command in the South, who, despite Kalb's advice, rashly determined to march to Camden to attack the British. Near Saunders' Creek they suddenly encountered the army of Lord Cornwallis. The first attack of the British scattered the Virginia and North Carolina militia, who, with Gates, fled. Kalb, in command of the right wing, three times charged the enemy. In the hand-to-hand fighting the issue of the battle was long in doubt. When the American position became hopeless Kalb, sword in hand, again led his few men to the attack. Mortally wounded and bleeding from eleven wounds, he fell and his surviving soldiers retreated. Three days later, on Aug. 19, he died at Camden.

[Friedrich Kapp, *Leben des Amerikanischen Generals Johann Kalb* (Stuttgart, 1862), translated as *The Life of John Kalb* (privately printed 1870, published 1884); Ludovic de Colleville, *Les Missions Secrètes du Général-Major Baron de Kalb et son Rôle dans la Guerre de l'Indépendance Américaine* (Paris, 1885); Charlemagne Tower, *The Marquis de La Fayette in the Am. Rev.* (2 vols., 1895); G. W. Greene, *The German Element in the War of American Independence* (1876); B. F. Stevens, *Facsimiles . . . Relating to America, 1773–1783* (25 vols., London, 1889–98); "The Deane Papers," *N. Y. Hist. Soc. Colls., Pub. Fund Ser.*, vols. XIX–XXIII (1887–91); manuscript letters in Vol. 164 of the Papers of the Continental Congress, in the Lib. of Cong.]

F. M—n.

KALISCH, ISIDOR (Nov. 15, 1816–May 11, 1886), reform rabbi, was born to Burnham and Sarah Tobias Kalisch in Krotoschin, Posen, Prussia. Kalisch's published attitude toward the Prussian government was too far advanced for the Germany of his day; several articles from his pen were condemned as seditious, and in 1848 he found it impossible to remain in Prussia. After a few months in England, he came to the United States, landing in New York in 1849. In America the scholarship which he had imbibed at the universities of Berlin, Breslau, and Prague, and in Jewish institutions of learning, gave distinction to the pulpits which he occupied, but a certain aggressive restlessness in his disposition, combined with the uncongenial immaturity of many reform Jewish communities, especially in the Middle West, caused him to pass through a series of short pastorates in Cleveland (1850–56), Cincinnati (1856–57), Milwaukee (1857–60), Indianapolis for two years, Detroit (1864–66), Leavenworth (1866–68), Newark, N. J. (1870–72), and Nashville (1872–75). At Cleveland (1850–56) he led a schism and formed a new congregation. Twice during these years he gave up a fixed rabbinate to serve as a public lecturer on Jewish themes, and in 1869 he opened a school in New York City, which did not prove a successful venture. In 1875 he returned from Nashville to Newark, giving himself thereafter to lecturing and to volunteer services as a rabbi.

Kalisch was an industrious writer. His most ambitious work is his *Wegweiser für Rationelle Forschungen in den Biblischen Schriften* (Cleveland, 1853), translated by M. Mayer as *A Guide for Rational Enquiries into the Biblical Writings, Being an Examination of the Doctrinal Difference between Judaism and Primitive Christianity, Based upon a Critical Exposition of the Book of Matthew* (1857). He also translated a number of works into English, notably Lessing's *Nathan der Weise,* 1869, the *Sefer Yezirah,* 1877, and Salomon Munk's *Philosophie et Écrivains Philosophes des Juifes,* 1881, and published a volume of original poems entitled *Die Töne des Morgenlandes* (1865).

His importance lies less in his literary work, which for the most part bears the ephemeral impress of the style and the interests of his day, than in his contributions towards moulding reform Judaism in America. He was a leading spirit at the Conference of Reform Rabbis held at Cleveland in 1855, a conference which he opened. He was one of the three editors of the *Minhag America,* the forerunner of the Union Prayer Book, the standard prayer book of reform Judaism. Kalisch conducted the lustily vehement polemics of his day with radical reform Judaism, which he considered as leading to atheism, and with orthodox Judaism, which he denounced as superstitious bigotry. He believed that a modernized Judaism would engender freedom of conscience. With a conviction as profound as in retrospect it appears pathetic, he held that outward political and inward spiritual emancipation of Jewry marked the dawn of a golden age of universal brotherhood. It is not to his discredit that history has so far mocked the lifelong dream of one whom Oliver Wendell Holmes characterized as "an admirable man and enlightened scholar." He died in his seventieth year, in Newark, N. J. His first wife, Charlotte Bankman, whom he married in 1843, died in 1856; she was the mother of Samuel Kalisch [*q.v.*], justice of the supreme court of New Jersey. In 1864 he married Adelaide Baer, who survived him.

[Samuel Kalisch, *In Memoriam: Rev. Dr. Isidor Kalisch* (1886), enlarged in the memoir accompanying *Studies in Ancient and Modern Judaism . . . Selected Writings of Rabbi Isidor Kalisch* (1928), ed. and compiled by Samuel Kalisch; *Pubs. Am. Jewish Hist. Soc.*, XVII (1909), 116, 147; F. B. Lee, *Geneal. and Memorial Hist. of the State of N. J.* (1910), III, 1067–69.]

D. de S. P.

KALISCH, SAMUEL (Apr. 18, 1851–Apr. 29, 1930), jurist, was born at Cleveland, Ohio, the third son of Rabbi Isidor [*q.v.*] and Charlotte (Bankman) Kalisch. His childhood and youth were spent in Cleveland, Cincinnati, Milwaukee, Indianapolis, Detroit, Leavenworth, and New York, as his father took positions in these cities. In 1870 the father accepted a pastorate in Newark, N. J., which, with an interruption of three years, was henceforward to be Samuel Kalisch's home. He was educated in the public schools of Detroit and Leavenworth, and received the degree of LL.B. from Columbia Law School in 1870. On Apr. 26, 1877, he married Caroline Elizabeth Baldwin of Newark. As a young man he became active in Democratic politics. He was city attorney of Newark in 1875, and was the Democratic nominee for the New Jersey Assembly in 1879 and for the state Senate in 1899 and in 1902, but was not elected to either body.

Admitted to the New Jersey bar in 1871, he began at once to develop a considerable law practice in Newark. His clientele consisted largely of members of labor organizations, and it is said that he declined many retainers offered by corporations. In both his civil and criminal practice he was remarkably successful before juries and upon appeal. He is said to have been the first attorney in New Jersey to obtain the release of a convict from the state prison on a writ of *habeas corpus*. He often established legal precedents, and his energy and legal acumen are evidenced in the many cases in which he figured as counsel, recorded in 37–81 *New Jersey Reports* and in the state *Equity Reports*. In 1911 he was appointed by Gov. Woodrow Wilson as a justice of the supreme court of New Jersey, and at the expiration of his term in 1918 he was reappointed by Governor Edge (Republican), and again in 1925 by Governor Silzer. In all, he served nineteen years on the supreme bench, and at his death he was the oldest judge of that tribunal. His decisions as judge usually stood the test of appeal, and his opinions in the appellate courts were conspicuous for a terse clearness expressive of a logical legal mind.

His judicial circuits brought him to Atlantic County, which had been for a quarter of a century notorious for graft, election frauds, and open gambling under protection of political bosses. Grand juries selected by servile sheriffs had repeatedly failed to bring indictments. In 1922, Kalisch astonished the state by disqualifying the sheriff from selecting the special grand jury. Resorting to a century-old statute, he appointed elisors (electors) for that function. As a result, an independent grand jury indicted the sheriff and many others. As a further result, elisors were also named in investigations in Morris and Hudson counties.

Kalisch inherited some of his father's literary ability, and wrote poems and essays. In 1886 he published *In Memoriam: Rev. Dr. Isidor Kalisch,* a biographical sketch of his father. In 1928, he elaborated this sketch and incorporated it in a volume wherein he reprinted several of his father's writings, under the title *Studies in Ancient and Modern Judaism . . . Selected Writings of Rabbi Isidor Kalisch*. His articles on "Legal Abuse," published in a Newark newspaper in 1872, had a widespread effect in remedying certain defects in the judiciary. As a hobby he collected books and autographs. He was a Scottish Rite Mason and a member of numerous professional organizations. In 1909–10 he was president of the New Jersey State Bar Association. He had a dignified presence and an attractive personality. However hot and pressing a legal argument might be, he always maintained his equanimity, and pursued his course with calm, convincing, persuasive reasoning.

[*Who's Who in America,* 1928–29; *Who's Who in American Jewry,* 1928; *Green Bag,* May 1914; *N. J. State Bar Asso. Year Book,* 1930–31; *N. Y. Times,* Apr. 30, 1930; *Temple Tidings* (published by Temple B'nai Jeshurun of Newark), May 9, 1930; *Newark Evening News,* Apr. 29, 1930.] D. de S. P.

KAMAIAKAN (*c.* 1800–*c.* 1880), Yakima chief, was the eldest child of Jayayaheha, a Nez Percé, and Kaemoxnith, the daughter of Weowicht, chief of the Pishwanwapum or Yakima. He was born near the present town of Lewiston, Idaho, but, when he was about ten years old, his mother took him back across the Columbia to the Yakima Valley. There he acquired wealth in the traditional form of horses, but he also planted a garden after the manner of the white man's agriculture, imported and maintained a herd of cattle within the tribe, and, about 1847, obtained the establishment of a mission by two Oblate Fathers. Absorbed in the pursuits of peace, he lent his influence to keep other tribes from going to war with the whites. Nevertheless, he watched with growing concern the degeneration of neighboring Indians in contact with white settlements, and when the American government sought Yakima lands, he tried, in vain, to prevent the cessions of the treaty of 1855. Before the treaty was ratified or provision made for the removal of the Indians, the country began to fill up with eager miners and settlers; friction developed; and in September war broke out. Kamaiakan avowed his determination to drive all white settlers out of the upper country, moved up and down the region rousing the Indians with the eloquence of his oratory, notable even in the great tradition of Indian speech, and gathered to himself most of the northwest tribes. Two thousand warriors turned out to meet the white troops. In January 1856 the attack of a thousand Indians under Leschi was repulsed with difficulty by the new town of Seattle. In September 1858 the defeat of the main body of Indians under Kamaiakan himself brought the outbreak to an end. He found refuge across the border in British Columbia and among the Crow Indians until his wife's homesickness made him invite the peril of a return to his native land. Among his kindred, the Paloos, he found a home, where, as his life lengthened year by year, he continued to tend his little farm and to ignore the five-hundred-dollar annuity promised him by the white government.

[Files and ledgers of the Office of Indian Affairs; information from the General Accounting Office; A. J. Splawn, *Ka-mi-akin* (1917); Hazard Stevens, *The Life of Isaac Ingalls Stevens* (1900), vol. II; C. A. Snowden, *Hist. of Wash.* (1900), vols. III, IV; H. H. Bancroft, *Hist. of Wash., Idaho, and Mont.* (1890); *House Exec. Doc. No. 93,* 34 Cong., 1 Sess. (1856).] K. E. C.

KANE, ELISHA KENT (Feb. 3, 1820–Feb. 16, 1857), naval officer, physician, explorer and pioneer of the American route to the North Pole, was born in Philadelphia of distinguished parentage. His father, John Kintzing Kane [*q.v.*], was a lawyer of ability and culture; his mother, Jane Duval Leiper, an accomplished beauty. Elisha was the eldest of five sons and one daughter. In youth he disliked study and was incessantly active. When a student at the University of Virginia (September 1838–November 1839), he contracted rheumatic fever which left his heart permanently impaired. Graduated on Mar. 19, 1842, from the medical department of the University of Pennsylvania, he passed examinations and became assistant surgeon in the United States Navy. He was appointed physician to the China Mission under Caleb Cushing [*q.v.*] and spent eighteen months in the Orient, Africa, and Europe, fervidly seeking adventure. He was long ill in China. At the outset of the Mexican War he was ordered to the African Squadron but was invalided home with coast fever. Later he secured orders for Mexico where he achieved some fame in a casual encounter with the enemy. From Mexico he was again invalided home, recovering from wounds and a virulent typhus.

In 1850 he was attached to the United States Coast Survey. In this year a government expedition, using ships supplied by Henry Grinnell [*q.v.*], was organized under Lieut. Edwin J. DeHaven, U. S. N. [*q.v.*] to search the Arctic for Sir John Franklin, missing since 1845. Kane sought and obtained the post of senior medical officer with this expedition, which provided him with a rugged polar novitiate. He told its story in a stirring narrative, *The U. S. Grinnell Expedition in Search of Sir John Franklin* (1853), which in abridged form was reprinted in 1915 under the title, *Adrift in the Arctic Ice Pack.*

Upon his return to New York, in September 1851, he immediately launched plans for a new expedition. Popular belief and many first-rank scientists, including M. F. Maury [*q.v.*], posited an open polar sea. On the shores of such a sea some remnant of Franklin's men might yet be alive; the route to that sea might lie through Smith Sound; no one had yet sailed beyond its northern portals. Kane determined to do so. John P. Kennedy [*q.v.*], secretary of the navy, gave enthusiastic personal support, and Henry Grinnell donated the brig *Advance.* Private subscription financed the enterprise.

The Second Grinnell Expedition sailed from New York May 31, 1853, with Passed Assistant Surgeon Kane, assigned to special duty, in command. Passing through Smith Sound the brig entered unknown waters now called Kane Basin. The way north was icebound. The only water passage hugged the shore, bearing toward the northeast. Against the recommendations of his officers, Kane forced the brig up this hazardous waterway. The expedition wintered at Rensselaer Bay. The first winter brought to light serious deficiencies of equipment. Scurvy appeared; the dogs died, but Kane indomitably held to his plans. The first spring sledging party broke down and was rescued only by that superhuman energy which served Kane in extremity. Two men died; but the commander, himself scurvy-ridden and at times near death, steadily sustained his campaign. In May, Isaac I. Hayes [*q.v.*], surgeon of the expedition, crossed Kane Basin reaching Ellesmere Land. In June, William Morton reached Cape Constitution, 80° 10′ N., "Farthest North" for the western hemisphere. Morton saw Kennedy Channel ice-free, tumbling in sunshine. Kane reported the evidence as further attesting the open polar sea theory, yet reserved opinion that it might well be another "illusory discovery."

No trace of Franklin's party was found by the expedition, but the coasts of Kane Basin were charted and Kennedy Channel was discovered, later to be the route of Hayes, Charles F. Hall [*q.v.*], A. W. Greely, and fifty-four years afterward, of Robert E. Peary [*q.v.*]. Meteorological, magnetic, astronomical, and tidal observations, botanical, glacial, and geological surveys, studies of animal and Eskimo life, established sound foundations for the scientific study of the Arctic. In August 1854 Hayes and eight men, protesting the commander's resolve to remain a second winter, announced their determination to hazard the journey to the South Greenland settlements. Kane, sanctioning the withdrawal, equipped them from limited supplies. In December they returned to the vessel, broken in body and morale. Kane became doctor, nurse, and cook to a shipful of bedridden men. With indomitable courage he planned and then executed their escape. The *Advance,* still frozen in, was abandoned May 20, 1855. With the loss of one man, the party, carrying the invalids, reached

Upernivik in eighty-three days, a retreat which stands in the annals of Arctic exploration as archetype of victory in defeat.

A government relief expedition under Lieut. H. J. Hartstene found them in South Greenland, and landed them in New York, on Oct. 11, 1855. Kane wrote his book, *Arctic Explorations: The Second Grinnell Expedition in Search of Sir John Franklin, in the Years 1853, '54, '55* (2 vols., 1856), told his publisher, whose fortune it made, "The book, poor as it is, has been my coffin," sailed for England, met Lady Franklin, left for Havana, and died there Feb. 16, 1857, just after his thirty-seventh birthday. The funeral journey was a pageant of national mourning. The body lay in state in New Orleans, Louisville, Columbus, Baltimore, and finally in Independence Hall. Military, civic, masonic processions were organized; poems, editorials, sermons were composed. *Arctic Explorations* lay for a decade with the Bible on almost literally every parlor table in America.

Between his two expeditions Kane met Margaret Fox [*q.v*], the Spiritualist medium. They were often seen together and it is known that he tried unsuccessfully to sever her connections with Spiritualism. After the Civil War an anonymous book appeared, entitled *The Love-Life of Dr. Kane* (1866), claiming to be his letters to Margaret and asserting that there had been a common-law marriage. The letters bear evidence of being at least in part genuine. The editing is vulgar and untrustworthy.

[See Kane's books mentioned above, his "Physical Observations" published in *Smithsonian Contributions to Knowledge*, vols. X–XIII (1858–60) and as *Smithsonian Inst. Pubs. No. 198* (1859–60), and his paper "Access to an Open Polar Sea," in *Bull. Am. Geog. and Statistical Soc.*, Jan. 1853; memorial proceedings, *Ibid.*, vol. II (1857); William Elder, *Biog. of Elisha Kent Kane* (1857); W. M. Kerr, "Elisha Kent Kane," in *Annals of Medic. Hist.*, vol. VI (1924); I. I. Hayes, *An Arctic Boat Journey in the Autumn of 1854* (1860); A. W. Greely, *Explorers and Travellers* (1893); journal of the brig *Advance,* in the library of the Hist. Soc. of Pa., Philadelphia; *N. Y. Tribune,* Feb. 18, 24, 26, 1857. A biography of Kane based on new source material is now in preparation by Margaret Elder Dow.]

M. E. D.

KANE, JOHN KINTZING (May 16, 1795–Feb. 21, 1858), jurist, was born at Albany, N. Y. His grandfather, John Kane (originally O'Kane), came to New York from Ireland shortly after 1750 and married Sybil, daughter of the Rev. Elisha Kent. A Loyalist, he went to England after the Revolution, and his family went to Nova Scotia. His sons returned to New York, however, where one of them, Elisha, a merchant, married Alida Van Rensselaer. They were the parents of John Kintzing Kane. He was baptized John, but later took his middle name in honor, it is said, of his stepmother. About 1801 the family moved to Philadelphia, where the boy attended local schools. He also studied at a tutoring school in New Haven, and graduated from Yale College in 1814. He studied law in the office of Joseph Hopkinson [*q.v.*] in Philadelphia and on Apr. 8, 1817, was admitted to the bar. Winning a reputation as an able lawyer, he built up a substantial practice.

Although he was at first a Federalist in politics, he vigorously supported Andrew Jackson in the presidential campaign of 1828, and was thereafter identified with the Democrats. He was appointed city solicitor of Philadelphia and held that office 1829–30. Reappointed in 1832, he resigned to serve, 1832–36, as one of the commissioners to settle claims under the convention of July 4, 1831, with France. In 1836 he published *Notes on Some of the Questions Decided by the Board of Commissioners under the Convention with France, of 4th July, 1831.* He assisted President Jackson in the preparation of certain letters and state papers, particularly in the crusade against the Bank of the United States. His activities in this cause are said to have occasioned his social ostracism, for a time, in Philadelphia. In December 1838 he was a leader of the Democrats of the state in the political struggle known as the "Buckshot War." In January 1845 he was appointed attorney general of Pennsylvania, but he resigned in June of the following year to accept appointment as judge of the United States district court for the eastern district of Pennsylvania, which office he held until his death. As a judge his decisions, especially in admiralty and patent cases, were able and commanded respect, but in 1856 his action in committing an abolitionist to jail for contempt of court in refusing to produce certain fugitive slaves, aroused much hostile feeling.

In 1825 he became a member of the American Philosophical Society and was its secretary from 1828 until 1848, its vice-president from 1849 until 1857, and its president from Jan. 2, 1857, until his death. He was also a member of the first board of trustees of Girard College and was vice-president of the Institution for the Instruction of the Blind, vice-provost of the Law Academy, and a member of various lodges and societies. President of the board of trustees of the Second Presbyterian Church of Philadelphia and a member of the board of trustees of the General Assembly, he sided with the Old School at the time of the division of the denomination in 1837. He was also connected with the promotion or direction of the Girard Bank, the Franklin Fire Insurance Company, the Sunbury

& Erie Railroad, the Delaware & Chesapeake Canal, and the Mutual Assurance Company. Prominent as a citizen and talented as a speaker, he was chosen to deliver many occasional addresses. Although he produced little original writing, he was an accomplished literary scholar, edited several works in law, medicine, and divinity for various friends, and was the author of a number of technical and legislative reports on various aspects of internal improvements.

On Apr. 20, 1819, he married Jane Duval Leiper, said to have been one of the most beautiful women of her time. They had seven children, two of whom, Elisha Kent Kane and Thomas Leiper Kane [*qq.v.*], attained distinction. Kane died of typhoid pneumonia, in Philadelphia.

[J. H. Martin, *Martin's Bench and Bar of Phila.* (1883); E. P. Oberholtzer, *Phila.—A Hist. of the City and Its People* (n.d.), vols. II, III; F. B. Dexter, *Biog. Sketches Grads. Yale Coll.*, vol. VI (1912); Henry Simpson, *The Lives of Eminent Philadelphians* (1859); *Proc. Am. Philosophical Soc.*, vol. VI (1859); Nathan Crosby, *Annual Obit. Notices . . . 1858* (1859); J. T. Scharff and Thompson Westcott, *Hist. of Phila.* (1884), vols. I, II; L. V. Briggs, *Geneals. of the Different Families Bearing the Name of Kent* (1898); *Daily News* and *Pennsylvanian* (both of Phila.), Feb. 23, 1858.]

J. H. F.

KANE, THOMAS LEIPER (Jan. 27, 1822–Dec. 26, 1883), soldier, born in Philadelphia, Pa., was the son of John Kintzing [*q.v.*] and Jane Duval (Leiper) Kane, and the brother of Elisha Kent Kane [*q.v.*]. He attended school in Philadelphia until he was seventeen then visited England and France, remaining some years in Paris. Upon his return to Philadelphia he studied law with his father and was admitted to the bar in 1846 but rarely practised. He did, however, hold the position of clerk under his father who was judge of the United States district court for the eastern district of Pennsylvania. He also served as one of the United States commissioners in this district. At heart he was an abolitionist and contributed many articles on this and other subjects to the press of the day. In 1848 he became chairman of the Free Soil State Central Committee, and upon the passage of the Fugitive-slave Law of 1850, found that the duties of a United States commissioner were in conflict with the dictates of his conscience and resigned the office. His father construed his letter of resignation as contempt of court and he was committed. This action, however, was overruled by the supreme bench and he was set free, becoming an active agent of the Underground Railroad. Having become interested in the activities of the Mormons, he took part in securing the assistance of the government in their westward migration and accompanied them in their wanderings for a considerable time. In this way he became a friend of Brigham Young and won his confidence to such an extent that in 1858, when Young had called upon his people to resist the entrance of United States troops into Utah, and a proclamation had been issued declaring the territory to be in a state of rebellion, Kane was able to convince the Mormon leader that such an action would be useless and so brought about an amicable settlement of the affair. In later years he continued his interest in the Mormon church, though there is no evidence that he ever became a member.

Shortly after his return to Philadelphia he removed to the northwestern part of Pennsylvania and founded the town of Kane. It was here that he organized at the outbreak of the Civil War a regiment of woodsmen and hunters known as the "Bucktails." He was elected colonel of this regiment on June 12, 1861, but shortly resigned in favor of the Mexican War veteran, Charles J. Biddle. He was immediately elected lieutenant-colonel and continued to serve with the regiment. He was wounded at Dranesville and captured at Harrisonburg. On Sept. 7, 1862, he was appointed brigadier-general for gallant services and commanded the 2nd Brigade, 2nd Division, XII Army Corps, at Chancellorsville. He contracted pneumonia and was in the hospital at Baltimore just before the battle of Gettysburg when he was entrusted with a message to General Meade that the Confederates were in possession of the Union cipher. He delivered the message after considerable difficulty and resumed command of his brigade on the second day of fighting, although still too weak to sit his horse. He was compelled to resign Nov. 7, 1863, being brevetted major-general for "gallant and meritorious services at Gettysburg" on Mar. 13, 1865. Upon retiring from the army he resided at his home in Kane and also in Philadelphia, taking an active interest in charitable matters and serving as the first president of the Pennsylvania Board of State Charities. He was a member of the American Philosophical Society and other organizations and was a director in various enterprises. He was the author of three privately printed books: *The Mormons* (1850); *Alaska* (1868), and *Coahuila* (1877). He had married, on Apr. 21, 1853, Elizabeth Dennistoun Wood, who afterward became a doctor of medicine. He died of lobar pneumonia in Philadelphia.

[S. P. Bates, *Hist. of Pa. Volunteers,* vol. I (1869); *War of the Rebellion: Official Records (Army)*; O. R. H. Thomson and W. H. Rauch, *Hist. of the Bucktails* (1906); E. P. Oberholtzer, *Phila.: A Hist. of the City and Its People* (n.d.), vol. II; F. J. Cannon and G. L.

Knapp, *Brigham Young and His Mormon Empire* (1913); T. B. H. Stenhouse, *The Rocky Mountain Saints* (1873); the *Press* (Phila.), Dec. 27, 1883.]

J. H. F.

KAPP, FRIEDRICH (Apr. 13, 1824–Oct. 27, 1884), publicist and historian, was born at Hamm, Westphalia, where his father, Dr. Friedrich Kapp, was the distinguished director of the Gymnasium. At Easter 1842, young Friedrich entered the University of Heidelberg as a law student, undertaking at the same time studies in philosophy and philology. He went to the University of Berlin in the summer of 1844; after his year of military service he was admitted to the practice of law at Hamm on Apr. 7, 1845. With the outbreak of the revolution he left Hamm in March 1848 and became a newspaper correspondent, first in Frankfurt, later in Brussels and Paris. He returned to Germany in 1849 to participate in the new revolution, but actual contact with the movement revealed its stupidity and he again went to Paris. In July 1849 he moved on to Geneva, and there was associated with a group of German and Italian revolutionists, whose futile plottings wearied him and caused him to abandon the movement.

In March 1850 he came to New York and there, with two dollars, began his American career. His recent bride, Louise Engels, joined him in the summer. He became a member of the law firm of Zitz, Kapp & Froebel; yet, despite his early success, he had no liking for the law. He began to write for many newspapers and periodicals, including the early numbers of the *Nation,* and in 1850 he became the editor of the *New-Yorker Abendzeitung.* From 1861 to 1865 he was the American correspondent for the *Kölnische Zeitung* and with his return to Berlin in 1870 he became the regular correspondent of the New York *Nation.* His political notions were idealistic and he entertained an optimistic belief in the capacity of the people for leadership. Once in America he became associated with the Whigs, because he thought that with them the arts and knowledge were among the highest things in life. He became a powerful influence among the German population of New York; no German project was launched without his advice and assistance. He and his friends became interested in the slavery question and his writings and political agitation brought him into the front ranks of the newly founded Republican party, for which his labors were incessant and fruitful. No German did more, with the exception of Carl Schurz [*q.v.*], to unite the German-Americans in support of the Union during the Civil War. From 1867 to 1870 he was an active member of the New York Board of Immigration, where he successfully introduced various reforms.

Kapp was a man of extensive culture: his home in New York was the center of a literary and political circle. It is he who is portrayed as "the citizen of two worlds" in Bertold Auerbach's *Das Landhaus am Rein* (translated as *The Villa on the Rhine,* 1869). Neither the extent nor the value of his historical writings has yet been sufficiently appreciated. His first writings appeared at a time when the general state of historical writing in America was low; his researches were based chiefly upon manuscript sources, he possessed a fresh and vigorous style, and his writings were characterized by their realism and humor. His *Leben des Amerikanischen Generals Friedrich Wilhelm von Steuben,* published in New York and Berlin in 1858, was privately printed in English in 1870 and published in 1884. His most valuable biographical work, *Leben des Americanischen Generals Johann Kalb* (Stuttgart, 1862), was translated in 1884. The *Geschichte der deutschen Einwanderung in Amerika* (New York, 1867) has frequently been republished under various titles. A third important study of eighteenth-century American history was his *Friedrich der Grosse und die Vereinigten Staaten von Nord-Amerika,* published at Leipzig in 1871. His *Aus und über Amerika* (Berlin, 1876), two brilliant volumes on the United States, was another important title in a lengthy bibliography (see *Deutsch-Amerikanisches Magazin,* I, 371, 73). Written after he had definitely returned to Germany in 1870, it was unfavorably received in America because of its realism and candid opinions. The last years of his life were devoted to his literary and political activities. Naturalized as a Prussian in 1870, he was elected to the Reichstag as a National Liberal in 1871 and served 1871–78 and again 1881–84. He was also a member of the Prussian Landtag, 1874–77. Admiring Bismarck as the bringer of German unity, he found it difficult to accept his domestic policies. He died of diabetes in Berlin while engaged upon a monumental history of the German book trade, of which the first volume, *Geschichte des deutschen Buchhandels bis in das siebenzehnte Jahrhundert,* was published posthumously at Leipzig in 1886.

[*Nation* (N. Y.), Oct. 30, Nov. 6, 13, 1884; Ernest Bruncken, *German Political Refugees in the U. S. . . . 1815–1860* (reprinted from *Deutsch-Amerikanische Geschichtsblätter,* 1904); A. B. Faust, *The German Element in the U. S.* (2 vols., 1909); Simon Sterne, *Memorial Resolutions . . . of the Medico-Legal Society of N. Y.* (1884); H. von Holst, in *Preussiche Jahrbücher,* vol. LV (1885); H. A. Rattermann, in *Deutsch-Amerikanisches Magazin,* vol. I (issues of Oct. 1886,

Jan., Apr. 1887); N. Y. *Evening Post*, Oct. 28, 1884; information from Heinz Singer of Berlin.] F. M—n.

KASSON, JOHN ADAM (Jan. 11, 1822–May 18, 1910), diplomat, son of John Steele and Nancy (Blackman) Kasson, was descended from a Scotch-Irish immigrant, Adam Kasson, who came to America in 1722. Born at Charlotte, Vt., he was educated at an academy in Burlington, and at the University of Vermont, where he graduated second in his class in 1842. He studied law in the office of his brother in Burlington, and then at Worcester, Mass., and after being admitted to the bar devoted himself to mercantile and maritime practice. On May 1, 1850, he married Caroline Eliot (G. M. Kasson, *Genealogy of a Part of the Kasson Family*, 1882; although *Who's Who in America*, 1899, gives his status as "unmarried"). In 1850 he moved to the West, settling first at St. Louis, where he became associated in his law practice with B. Gratz Brown. In 1857 he established himself at Des Moines, Iowa. As early as 1848 he had shown an interest in the slavery question and had gone as a delegate to the Free-Soil convention in Buffalo. He now became an active Republican and chairman of the Republican state committee. He was a delegate to the Republican National Convention of 1860, and as a member of the drafting committee shared with Horace Greeley the chief responsibility for the platform finally adopted.

On Lincoln's election to the presidency, Kasson, through the good will of political friends in Missouri, became first assistant postmaster-general. This might easily have been a routine job, with patronage-peddling as its principal activity. Kasson made it of high importance. He secured the codification of the postal laws and devised a plan for securing uniformity in postal intercourse between the United States and foreign nations. At his suggestion the President called a postal conference which met in Paris in 1863, and to which Kasson was sent as a delegate. In this conference the way was prepared for the foundation of the International Postal Union. Later in 1867, Kasson acted as United States commissioner in the negotiation of six postal conventions.

In 1862 he was elected to Congress, after a close contest for the nomination in which his control of patronage materially aided him. In the post-bellum controversy over reconstruction he clearly belonged to the moderate wing of his party, but, to judge from his frequent abstentions from voting, he lacked the courage vigorously to oppose the radicals, and he withdrew from Congress in 1866. He was elected to the state legislature, serving from 1868 to 1872 and taking a leading part in the successful fight for a new state capitol. In 1872 he was again a candidate for Congress, and served from 1873 to 1877. He voted for resumption of specie payments, and for the Civil Rights Bill, but against the Force Bill of 1875. In 1877 he was appointed by President Hayes as minister to Austria-Hungary, and in that post gained great popularity. Returning to the United States, he again entered the House, serving from 1881 to 1884. A member of the committee which drafted the Civil Service Act of 1883, he piloted it through the debates to final passage. In 1884 he was sent to Berlin as envoy extraordinary and minister plenipotentiary, and he served as the American representative in the international conference to regulate the status of the Congo. He here performed important services, helping to secure the acceptance by the conference of liberal treaty provisions for the protection of the natives and for freedom of trade, and promoting the agreement to respect the neutrality of the region. In 1889 he was one of the American representatives at the Berlin conference held to regulate the status of Samoa. Under the McKinley administration he served as a member of the British-American Joint High Commission of 1898 which made an unsuccessful effort to solve the Alaskan boundary question, and as special commissioner to negotiate reciprocity agreements with foreign countries under the Dingley Act. Though he was successful in negotiating a number of such conventions, his work failed to receive the approval of the Senate, and after having once offered his resignation and seen it declined, Kasson laid down his post in 1901. He died at Washington in May 1910.

Kasson was not a great political leader, but he had genuine abilities, and some pretensions to scholarship. In 1887 he was president of the Centennial Commission which directed the celebration of the one-hundredth anniversary of the drafting of the Constitution, and for this occasion prepared his "History of the Formation of the Constitution," published in the first volume of the *History of the Celebration . . .* (2 vols., 1889). It was later republished in *The Evolution of the Constitution of the United States of America and History of the Monroe Doctrine* (1904). He wrote on the tariff, revealing himself as a firm but not always logical protectionist, with a bent toward reciprocity (*Information Respecting Reciprocity and the Existing Treaties*, 1901). In 1890 he gave a course of lectures before the Lowell Institute on the Historical Evolution of Diplomacy, following these with similar courses at Johns Hopkins. His "History of the Monroe Doctrine" is a summary of judicious quality. One of his most interesting contributions was a speech to the Naval War College, published with the title, *International Arbitration* (1896). In this address Kasson brings forward the fruitful idea, of classifying certain types of disputes as peculiarly susceptible of submission to arbitration. In international matters, indeed, he showed much breadth of view, a willingness to enter into closer relations with other nations, an interest in the protection of weaker peoples, and a genuine desire to promote the cause of peace. Not an imposing figure, he deserves an honorable place amongst American diplomats. In personal bearing he was cool, and suave, without great personal magnetism.

[Perhaps the best account of Kasson's life is in E. H. Stiles, *Recollections and Sketches of Notable Lawyers and Public Men of Early Iowa* (1916). See also B. F. Gue, *Hist. of Iowa* (4 vols., 1903); "John A. Kasson: An Autobiography," *Annals of Iowa*, July 1920; *Ibid.*, July 1899, Jan. 1900, July 1911; J. L. Laughlin and H. P. Willis, *Reciprocity* (1903); A. B. Keith, *The Belgian Congo and the Berlin Act* (1919); *Pioneer Lawmakers' Asso. of Iowa, Reunion of 1911* (1913); *Who's Who in America*, 1910–11; obituaries in *Washington Post, Sioux City Journal*, and *Register and Leader* (Des Moines), May 19, 1910. Kasson's activities in Congress are naturally to be traced in the *Cong. Globe, Cong. Record*, and his diplomatic career in the archives of the State Department.] D. P.

KATTE, WALTER (Nov. 14, 1830–Mar. 4, 1917), civil engineer, was born in London, England, the son of Edwin and Isabella (James) Katte and a descendant of Edwin Katte, a political refugee from Prussia in the reign of Frederick the Great. He attended Kings College School, London, and served a three-year apprenticeship in the office of a civil engineer. In 1849 he came to America and obtained employment as a clerk and draftsman in the office of the chief engineer of the Central Railroad of New Jersey during the construction of the line from Whitehouse to Easton, Pa. He then (1851) went as a rodman to the Belvidere & Delaware Railroad, with which company he rose, in three years, to the position of division engineer. He was employed for a short time by a land company engaged in laying out the town of Dearman (now Irvington-on-Hudson), N. Y., and then became chief assistant to the engineer of the western division of the Pennsylvania Railroad. In 1857 he was resident engineer of the state canals of Pennsylvania; in 1858–59 served the Pittsburgh, Fort Wayne & Chicago Railroad, and in 1859–61, the Pittsburgh & Steubenville Railroad. In 1861 he was made a colonel in the United States Army in charge of wartime bridge and railroad construction in the vicinity of Washington, D. C. Among the other duties of this important military assignment, he directed the construction of the highway bridge ("Long Bridge") over the Potomac River between Washington and Virginia. He left the military service in 1863. (For a complete chronological record of his subsequent connections see *The Biographical Directory of the Railway Officials of America*, 1906.)

In 1875 Katte closed a ten-year connection with the Keystone Bridge Company of Pittsburgh as superintending engineer for the erection of the Eads steel-arch bridge over the Mississippi River at St. Louis, and the next year he served as engineer of the city of St. Louis. He then went to New York City as chief engineer of the New York Elevated Company and built the first sections of the Third Avenue and Ninth Avenue elevated structures, 1877–80. From 1886 to 1899 he was chief engineer, and after that, consulting engineer, with the New York Central & Hudson River Railroad. During his connection with this road he constructed the four-track, depressed right of way in New York City north of the Harlem River, the four-track steel viaduct in Park Avenue, and the Harlem River drawbridge, all major railroad constructions. The Harlem River bridge was the largest drawbridge then built and few surpass it in size today.

At the time of his retirement in 1905 Katte was considered one of the foremost railroad construction engineers of the world. Several of his inventions, including the "three-tie" rail joint, have been widely used. He contributed several papers on subjects of railroad construction to the *Transactions* of the American Society of Civil Engineers, was a founder of the Western Society of Civil Engineers and was a director of the American Society of Civil Engineers in 1885 and 1889. He married Margaret Jack at Greensburg, Pa., in 1859. She died in 1864, and on Nov. 22, 1870, he married Elizabeth Pendleton Britton at St. Louis. He died at his home in New York City, survived by his wife and three children.

[*Proc. Am. Soc. Civil Engineers*, vol. XLIII (1917); *Trans. Am. Soc. Civil Engineers*, vol. LXXXI (1917); *Who's Who in America*, 1916–17; *N. Y. Times*, Mar. 5, 1917.] F. A. T.

KATZER, FREDERIC XAVIER (Feb. 7, 1844–July 20, 1903), Roman Catholic prelate, was born at Ebensee, Upper Austria, the son of Charles and Barbara (Reinhartsgruber) Katzer. He received his preparatory training at Gmunden, Austria, and continued his studies at Linz, the capital of Upper Austria, under the direction of the Jesuit Fathers, from 1857 to 1864 when he graduated. In the latter year Father Francis Pierz visited Austria to appeal to the priests and seminarians in his native land to join him in his missionary labors among the Indians in Minnesota. Katzer was one of the fifteen students who answered his appeal. Coming to America filled with zeal and a desire to serve God in difficult fields, he finished his course at St. Francis Seminary, Milwaukee, Wis., and was ordained a priest, Dec. 21, 1866, at St. Francis, Wis., by Bishop Henni [*q.v.*]. After his ordination he remained at the Seminary, teaching mathematics and later philosophy and dogmatic theology until 1875, when he became secretary to Bishop Krautbauer. Upon the death of the latter in 1885, Katzer was appointed administrator of the diocese, and in that capacity took part in the deliberations of the First Provincial Council of Milwaukee, which opened its sessions May 23, 1886, at St. John's Cathedral. In the following week (May 31) he was chosen bishop of Green Bay, and was consecrated in St. Francis Xavier's cathedral, on Sept 21 of the same year by Archbishop Michael Heiss [*q.v.*]. Under his efficient administration of the diocese churches flourished and harmony prevailed.

The most significant thing in Bishop Katzer's life to those outside of the Church was the part he took in the campaign against the Bennett law, a law passed during the administration of W. D. Hoard [*q.v.*] as governor of Wisconsin making it compulsory to use the English language in all public, private, and parochial schools. This law —which was introduced by a Roman Catholic public-school teacher—had passed without much opposition; but it was soon conceived to be a blow at parochial schools and the German language, and a vigorous opposition was developed, especially among Catholics and Lutherans. The law was vigorously opposed by Archbishop Heiss of Milwaukee, Bishop Flasch of La Crosse, and Bishop Katzer of Green Bay as unnecessary, harmful, and unjust. Both Heiss and Flasch soon died, and the burden of the closing stages of the campaign fell to Katzer. The Bennett law became the political issue in the election of 1890, and Governor Hoard was defeated by a majority of twenty-eight thousand. The effect upon the Republican party was disastrous. The new legislature promptly repealed the law, and the state Republican convention of 1892 declared that it regarded the "education issue of 1890 as permanently settled in this state, not to be renewed in any of its phases by the Republican party or under its auspices."

In December 1890, after the death of Archbishop Heiss, Katzer was appointed to the archepiscopal dignity as third archbishop of Milwaukee. He remained some months at Green Bay, however, and did not assume his new duties until June 30, 1891. Cardinal Gibbons, in his address at Archbishop Katzer's reception of the pallium, spoke of the "loyalty, reverence and filial affection" which had "marked his career as a priest, a professor and a bishop of the Church of God." His administration of the archdiocese was characterized by a uniform regard for justice and strict adherence to the laws of the Church. He was a man of profound learning and an excellent theologian. His most significant pastoral letter was probably that issued on June 20, 1895, on secret societies. He was interested in poetry and manifested some poetical talent in his allegorical drama, entitled *Der Kampf der Gegenwart* (The Combat of the Present Age), published in 1873. He died at Fond du Lac, and was buried in the little cemetery near the "chapel in the woods" at St. Francis.

[*Cath. Encyc.*, vol. X (1911); *Milwaukee Sentinel*, Mar. 13, 1890; H. H. Heming, *The Cath. Ch. in Wis.* (1895–98); *Milwaukee Journal*, July 21, 1903.]

E. A. F.

KAUFFMAN, CALVIN HENRY (Mar. 10, 1869–June 14, 1931), botanist, was born on a farm in Lebanon County, Pa., the son of John Henry and Mary Ann (Light) Kauffman. His early life was spent on the farm, with such preparatory training as the country schools of the vicinity afforded. He attended Palatinate College, Myerstown, Pa., 1890–92, and from that institution went to Harvard University, where he graduated in 1896 with the degree of A.B., having specialized in Greek and Latin. In September 1895 he married Elizabeth Catherine Wolf. From 1896 to 1898 he was principal of a preparatory school at Lebanon, Pa., and then taught science in a high school at Decatur, Ind., and at Bushnell Normal College, Bushnell, Ill. In the fall of 1901 he entered the University of Wisconsin, specializing in chemistry and botany. At this institution his interest in mycology was definitely aroused through the influence of Professor R. A. Harper. His mycological studies were continued, 1902–04, at Cornell University, where he served as a graduate assistant to Professor G. F. Atkinson [*q.v.*]. Atkinson not only stimulated and developed Kauffman's interest in the mushrooms or *Agaricaceae* but exercised a marked influence on his entire scientific career.

An instructorship in the botanical department of the University of Michigan, tendered him in 1904, permitted him to carry on his graduate studies. He received the degree of Ph.D. from this institution in 1907, submitting a dissertation entitled "A Contribution to the Physiology of the *Saprolegniaceae* with Special Reference to the Variations of the Sexual Organs." The direction of his career was now firmly established, and during the succeeding years he developed courses and directed research with the lower plants, including the mosses and algae, with the fungi always as his primary interest. He became assistant professor in 1911 and associate professor in 1919. From 1912 to 1921 he was curator of the Cryptogamic Herbarium and in the latter year was made director of the University Herbarium. From 1923 until his death he was professor of botany. The period of the World War (1917–19) saw him stationed in Washington, D. C., on leave of absence, as pathological inspector with the Federal Horticultural Board of the United States Department of Agriculture.

During his professional career Kauffman published approximately forty papers of major importance. His outstanding work, *The Agaricaceae of Michigan,* issued in two volumes in 1918, is not only a scholarly and original treatise on the mushrooms of Michigan but serves as a standard reference for the species described. He also published monographic studies of various genera of the *Agaricaceae,* including *Cortinarius, Inocybe, Lepiota, Clitocybe, Armillaria, Flammula,* and *Paxillus.* His work on the *Agaricaceae* reflects not only the early influence of Atkinson but also that of Elias Fries, of whom he was a profound admirer. A period of study in the Fries herbarium at Upsala, Sweden, and field work in the surrounding region in 1908 intensified this influence. His researches, however, were by no means confined to the mushrooms, but included papers on other groups—the *Phycomycetes, Thelephoraceae,* and *Polyporaceae* in particular—as well as a series of mycological floras of the several regions of the United States in which he carried on summer field work. Among these may be noted an extensive series of reports on the fungi of Michigan, and others covering his field studies in Tennessee, Kentucky, Colorado, the Siskiyou Mountain region of Oregon, Mount Hood, and the North Elba region of New York. He also contributed a number of publications in the field of plant pathology.

[E. B. Mains, "Calvin Henry Kauffman, 1869–1931," with bibliography, in *Phytopathology,* Apr. 1932, and article in *Science,* Sept. 4, 1931; *Who's Who in America,* 1930–31; J. M. and Jacques Cattell, *Am. Men of Sci.,* 1927; C. G. Lloyd, in *Mycological Notes,* Feb. 1917; *Harvard College Class of 1896* (1921); *Detroit Free Press, News* (Detroit), and *N. Y. Times,* June 15, 1931.] J. A. S.

KAUTZ, AUGUST VALENTINE (Jan. 5, 1828–Sept. 4, 1895), soldier, was born in Ispringen, Baden, Germany, the son of George and Doratha (Lalwing) Kautz. His brother, Albert Kautz (1839–1907), became an admiral in the United States Navy. The same year in which the elder son was born, the parents emigrated, and after a stop in Baltimore, settled in 1832 in Brown County, Ohio, where Kautz attended public school in Georgetown. On June 8, 1846, he enlisted in the 1st Ohio Infantry, and served through the Mexican War. In 1848, he entered the United States Military Academy, graduating four years later and being assigned to the 4th Infantry at Vancouver Barracks, Wash. Here, with almost constant field service against Puget Sound Indians, he was wounded in a skirmish Oct. 25, 1855, in the Rogue River Expedition, and again wounded, Mar. 1, 1856, in an action at White River. Becoming a first lieutenant during this period, with the beginning of the Civil War he was made a captain in the newly organized 6th Cavalry, and participated in the Peninsular campaign (March–August 1862), most of the time being in command of his regiment. On Sept. 10, he was promoted to colonel, 2nd Ohio Cavalry, and after some months in command of Camp Chase, Ohio, commanded the 1st Cavalry Brigade in the action at Monticello, Ky., June 9, 1863, and took part in the subsequent pursuit and capture of Morgan and his raiders. Appointed chief of cavalry of the XXIII Army Corps, Kautz took part in the East Tennessee campaign, including the siege of Knoxville; and was made a brigadier-general of volunteers, May 7, 1864, becoming for a time, chief of cavalry for the Department of Virginia, and from April 1864 to March 1865, commanding a cavalry division with the Army of the James. As division commander he participated in important operations against the Petersburg & Weldon, the Richmond & Danville, and the Petersburg & Lynchburg railroads, culminating in an assault on Petersburg, June 9, 1864. Subsequently he led the advance of Wilson's raid south of Richmond, with actions at Roanoke Bridge, June 25, and at Reams's Station, Va., June 29, 1864. On Oct. 7 following, while covering the left flank of the Army of the James, he suffered severe casualties at Darbytown. He received, for gallantry, the successive brevets of major, lieutenant-colonel, colonel, brigadier-general and major-general in the Regular Army, and major-general of volunteers. On Apr. 3, 1865, as commander of the 1st Division, XXV Corps (colored), he entered the city of Richmond with his troops.

In May and June 1865 Kautz was a member of the military commission which tried the conspirators in the assassination of President Lincoln. He was mustered out of the volunteer service, Jan. 15, 1866. In the army reorganization of this year, he became lieutenant-colonel, 34th Infantry. By the army consolidation of 1869, he was assigned to the 15th Infantry in New Mexico, and successfully brought back to their reservation the Mescalero Apaches. He was promoted colonel, 8th Infantry, June 7, 1874, and after various stations in the West and Southwest, was appointed a brigadier-general, Apr. 20, 1891, and commanded the Department of the Columbia until retirement, Jan. 5, 1892—making his home in Seattle, Wash., where he died, highly honored by the community.

Kautz was a great student, methodical, industrious, possessed of unusual energy and powers of endurance. His published literary work includes *The Company Clerk* (1863), *Customs of Service for Non-Commissioned Officers* (1864), *Customs of Service for Officers of the Army* (1866), and "The Operations South of the James River," in *Battles and Leaders of the Civil War* (IV, 533). He was twice married: in September 1865, to Charlotte, daughter of Gov. David Tod [*q.v.*] of Ohio, and in 1872, to Fannie Markbreit of Cincinnati, Ohio. A son and two daughters were born of his second marriage.

[*Annual Asso. Grads. U. S. Mil. Acad.*, 1896; G. W. Cullum, *Biog. Reg.* (3rd ed., 1891), vol. II; *Battles and Leaders of the Civil War* (4 vols., 1887–88), esp. vol. IV; *War of the Rebellion: Official Records (Army)*; *Hist. of Brown County, Ohio* (1883); "Diary of Gen. A. V. Kautz," *Washington Historian*, Apr.-Oct. 1900; C. A. Snowden, *Hist. of Wash.* (1909), vols. III, IV; *Army and Navy Jour.*, Sept. 7, 1895; *Seattle Post-Intelligencer*, Sept. 5, 1895.] C. D. R.

KAVANAGH, EDWARD (Apr. 27, 1795–Jan. 21, 1844), governor and diplomat, was born at Damariscotta Mills, in the District of Maine. His mother, Sarah, daughter of Andrew Jackson, though of Puritan stock, was an early convert to Catholicism. His father, James, an Irish immigrant to Boston about 1780, erected mills and a store on the Damariscotta River in 1790 and became a wealthy landowner, ship-builder, and merchant. At his home Father John Louis de Cheverus and Bishop John Carroll [*qq.v*], were entertained in the course of visits to Maine. In 1798 James helped to build a chapel and in 1808 was one of the builders of St. Patrick's Church, probably the oldest Catholic church still standing in New England. Failing in his effort to divert his ministerial tax to his chapel, he carried the issue to the supreme court of Massachusetts, which ruled (1801) that the constitution obliged every one to support Protestant ministers, and reminded Kavanagh that Papists must expect nothing more than toleration.

Edward studied in Boston, at St. Mary's College, Baltimore, and at Georgetown College near Washington; then spent two years in Europe, becoming an accomplished linguist. He gained admission to the bar, but never practised. In 1819 a college essay of his was used anonymously in committee in the Maine constitutional convention to defeat a clause debarring Catholics from office-holding (Collins, *post*).

Kavanagh himself held public office almost continuously. After several years in the state legislature, he served from 1831 to 1835 in Congress, where he loyally supported the Jackson administration. He even defended Jackson's removal of deposits while his constituents were complaining that it had ruined business. His opposition to the Bank and protection cost him his seat, but Jackson rewarded him by appointing him chargé d'affaires in Portugal, where during six years' service his tact and patience secured a favorable commercial treaty, signed in 1840, and he paved the way for recognition (1851) of spoliation claims of Napoleon's day. Returning to the state Senate he became chairman of the joint select committee on the Maine boundary and one of four Maine commissioners sent to negotiate with Webster and Ashburton. His rôle as boundary commissioner was difficult. Maine expected concessions which Ashburton's instructions did not permit. To break off negotiations would have been unwise. The commissioners secured all that was possible under trying circumstances—indeed, Kavanagh believed they forced Ashburton to stretch his legitimate powers—but Kavanagh had difficulty making the unpopular settlement palatable to Maine. He was governor from Fairfield's resignation on Mar. 7, 1843, until Jan. 1, 1844, twenty days before his death. As governor he conducted with vigor a controversy with the federal government over its failure to protect Maine under the treaty.

Kavanagh's education, background of foreign travel, linguistic equipment, and urbanity were unusual in a frontier state. His modesty and natural charm made him universally liked. He was no speaker, but worked effectively in committee and conference. Possessed of executive ability, unusual tact, a keen sense of justice, and high integrity, he had courage of conviction that led him to oppose the views of his constituents when he knew such action meant defeat and to veto a popular "town court bill" while governor.

[Brief, usually inadequate accounts of Kavanagh are found in *Me. Hist. Soc. Colls.*, vol. VI (1859), 74–75; L. C. Hatch, *Maine, A Hist.* (1919), I, 278–81, II, 315–18; *Sprague's Jour. of Me. Hist.*, May 1914, June 1917, July–Sept. 1922, Jan.–Mar. 1923; *Me. Hist. and Geneal. Recorder*, July 1898. Kavanagh's papers, which have disappeared, were used by Father C. W. Collins in preparing a valuable sketch subsequently published in the Boston *Pilot* and in the U. S. Cath. Hist. Soc. *Hist. Records and Studies*, vol. V, pt. 2 (Apr. 1909). Other

sources are Collins' brief article in the *Cath. Encyc.*, VIII, 612; H. S. Burrage, *Maine in the Northeastern Boundary Controversy* (1919); *Biog. Dir. Am. Cong.* (1928); files of the Portland *Press* and the *Eastern Argus* (Portland), the Kavanagh family Bible and some papers and scrapbooks in the possession of Miss Blanche Bryant of Damariscotta Mills.]
H. K. B—e.

KAY, EDGAR BOYD (Jan. 15, 1860–Apr. 20, 1931), teacher, sanitary engineer, was born at Warriors Mark, Pa., the son of Isaac Franklin Kay, a physician, and Catherine (Bell) Kay. His ancestor, John Kay (sometimes spelled Key), whose parents came from England in the ship *Welcome* with William Penn in 1682, was the first child of English parentage born in Philadelphia. In recognition of this fact William Penn gave him a grant to a tract of land in Philadelphia, which patent is still on record. Edgar Boyd Kay received his early education in Bellwood and Birmingham, Pa., where he prepared for Rensselaer Polytechnic Institute, from which he graduated in civil engineering in the class of 1883. For two years he was an instructor in civil engineering at Rensselaer and then for some ten years was engaged in professional work, first as a contractor and later in consulting practice. Between 1896 and 1912 he returned to teaching, being an instructor at Union University, Schenectady, N. Y., 1897–98, instructor in engineering at Cornell University, 1898–1903, and professor of engineering and first dean of the College of Civil Engineering at the University of Alabama, 1903–12. Here under his direction and supervision Comer Hall was built to house the College of Engineering.

While he was in Alabama he was also very busy in his profession—serving as consultant for the Alabama Railroad Commission (1903–15), for the state convict bureau, and for various power companies. His work during this period included the construction of many water works, sewer and lighting systems, and steam and electric railways. On Sept. 26, 1900, he was married to Florence Edna Means, daughter of Lyman North Means, a banker and plantation owner of Wapakoneta, Ohio. They had no children.

In 1918, as a leader in the field of sanitation he became chief of the hydraulic and sanitary section of the Quartermaster-General's Office of the United States Army and under his direction sanitation measures for the large army cantonments were studied comprehensively and outlined. In this connection Kay developed an incinerator which was adopted by the War Department as its standard. While Kay, as inventor, was granted patents upon the device, he gave the Department the right to use it, retaining only the commercial rights for himself. His invention, the United States Standard Incinerator, has been widely adopted by municipalities, and large plants following Kay's designs have been installed in various American cities. Kay's later years were most active in the field of sanitation and incineration, in which he became a leader, his studies and investigations including conditions in Europe as well as in America. His ability as an inventor was evidenced also in other ways. At Cornell he designed and built an automatic machine for testing the time and rate of the setting of cement. He had a keen sense of humor and a deep appreciation of the beautiful. While in Alabama he was the promoter of Pinehurst, one of the subdivisions of Tuscaloosa, where he established a home that became a notable social center. He had a wide membership in professional societies and clubs, and was a Thirty-second Degree Mason. During the last years of his life he resided in Washington, D. C., where he died.

[Information supplied by Mrs. Edgar Boyd Kay; *Who's Who in Engineering,* 1925; *Engineering News-Record,* Apr. 30, 1931; *Evening Star* (Washington) and *N. Y. Times,* Apr. 21, 1931.]
H. K. B—s.

KAYE, FREDERICK BENJAMIN (Apr. 20, 1892–Feb. 28, 1930), scholar, author, was born in New York City, the son of Julius Gustav Kugelman and Carrie Stern Kugelman. After preparation at Columbia Grammar School, Hotchkiss School, and Phillips Academy, Andover, he entered, in the fall of 1909, Yale University, where he received successively the degrees of bachelor of arts (1914), master of arts (1916), and doctor of philosophy (1917). In the fall of 1917 he became an instructor in English in Northwestern University, where he proceeded through the various ranks to a professorship in 1929. His connection with Northwestern, which continued until his death, was interrupted only by his service in the United States Naval Reserve Force, which he entered in May 1918, retiring from active service a year later with the rank of ensign. His name was changed to Kaye in September 1919, as he had found that the Teutonic sound of Kugelman was a considerable handicap to his scholarly work in Europe during the post-war period.

In the ten years that followed the completion of his formal education Kaye, whose special interest was English literature of the neo-classical period, achieved an international reputation for sound and brilliant scholarship. He was a member of the Commission on Literary History of the International Historical Congress, and a member of the Authors' Club of London. The several protracted illnesses from which he suffered from his early years did not overcome his keen and witty mind or his generous and enthusiastic disposition. His remarkable capacity for work was, however, impaired during the last three years of his life by the progress of the disease of which he eventually died (chromophobe adenoa of the pituitary gland). His death took place in Peter Bent Brigham Hospital, Boston, in February 1930, following an operation for pituitary tumor. He was unmarried.

Many of Kaye's stories and essays contributed to college publications in his undergraduate days were written in a grotesquely humorous vein which he neglected to develop after leaving Yale. He wrote and published with increasing frequency, however, on topics of general and of scholarly interest. Two of his publications are of special importance. *A Census of British Newspapers and Periodicals, 1620–1800* (1927), compiled in collaboration with Ronald S. Crane, is one of the most valuable existing tools of scholarship in the period with which it deals. A revised and expanded edition was in progress at the time of Kaye's death. His edition of Bernard Mandeville's *The Fable of the Bees* (1924) has a three-fold importance. It rescues from comparative obscurity one of the most interesting and significant thinkers of the eighteenth century, elucidates his philosophy, and traces both the roots of that philosophy and its subsequent influence. At the same time Kaye's introduction and notes, which stand as a model of scholarly method, provide the best existing account of a hitherto neglected current of seventeenth- and eighteenth-century thought, to which he gave the name "anti-rationalism." Kaye's residuary legatee presented to Northwestern University Kaye's fine collection of books dealing with deistic philosophy, and to Yale University a large part of his collection of drawings and etchings.

[The chief sources of this article are the records of Yale and Northwestern universities, and the personal knowledge of the author. Obituaries were printed in the *N. Y. Times,* Mar. 1, 1930, and in the *Obit. Record of Grads. of Yale Univ. Deceased During the Year 1929–30* (1930). For a list of reviews of his edition of *The Fable of the Bees,* see the *Philological Quart.*, Apr. 1927.] A. E. C.

KEAGY, JOHN MILLER (Aug. 31, 1792–Jan. 13, 1837), physician and educator, the sixth child of Abraham Keagy and Barbara Boehm, was born in Strasburg, Lancaster County, Pa. He was of Swiss descent, a great-grandson of Johannes Keagy who came to America about 1715. Of his early years little can be said save that, being delicate and studiously inclined, he was "designed in early life for some one of the learned professions." He was trained in medicine and practised for a few years, but his imagination was caught by the common-school agitation, the Lancasterian and Pestalozzian enthusiasms of the day, and the notion of professional preparation of teachers. Accordingly, he assumed the rôle of schoolmaster. His brief career was marked by success in teaching, at Asbury College, Baltimore, 1818, at the Classical Academy, Harrisburg, 1826, and at the Penn Charter School, Philadelphia, 1830–35. He was an accomplished linguist, having a thorough knowledge of French, German, and Hebrew as well as Latin and Greek; but his major interest was science. He was a trustee of Dickinson College, 1833–35, and at the time of his death had just been called to the chair of natural science.

It was, however, as a contributor to the movement toward professionalizing education that Keagy's influence was felt in the state. As the chairman of a committee of the Philadelphia Association of Teachers, he prepared an address, "To Teachers and Friends of Education throughout the State of Pennsylvania" (1831), stressing the importance of investigating "those principles appertaining to the philosophy of mind, its faculties, their arrangement . . . and the best methods of development." Four years later he led in calling the State Educational Convention at West Chester, which effected a permanent organization, of which he was made vice-president, having as its stated purpose the "advancement of education throughout the State, especially through the medium of schools and lyceums, and to cooperate with other lyceums in the diffusion of useful knowledge." To promote the same end, Keagy assisted in founding and contributed to the *Monthly Journal of Education* (January 1835) which became the *Schoolmaster and Advocate of Education* in 1836.

His most noteworthy contributions to educational literature were articles in the Baltimore *Chronicle,* 1819, published as *An Essay on English Education* (1824); and the *Pestalozzian Primer* (1827), one of the earliest examples of Pestalozzian influence in American textbooks. Though the *Primer's* motto was "to teach a child to think," the author carried the Pestalozzian principle of A B C of Observation to an absurdity. He gave twenty-six lessons on the alphabet, passed then to nonsense syllables of three letters, devoted seventy-eight pages to monosyllables, and, after 104 pages, brought the pupil to words of more than two syllables. Keagy was a man of practical piety, a worker in the American Sunday School Union, and a devout Methodist. He married Helen M. Hulings, by whom he had three children. His death, caused by pulmonary consumption, occurred in his forty-fifth year.

[Franklin Keagy, *A Hist. of the Kägy Relationship* (1899); Henry Barnard's *Am. Jour. of Educ.*, XXII (1871), 649–50; Penn Charter School Minutes (MS.), 1830–35; J. P. Wickersham, *Hist. of Educ. in Pa.* (1885); Poulson's *Am. Daily Advertiser* (Phila.), Jan. 14, 1837; *Alumni Record of Dickinson College*, 1886 and 1905; brief references in Paul Monroe, *A Cyc. of Educ.*, vol. III (1912); Keagy's publications, the most important of which are mentioned above.] T. W.

KEANE, JAMES JOHN (Aug. 26, 1857–Aug. 2, 1929), Roman Catholic prelate, was born in Joliet, Ill., one of the five children of John and Margaret (O'Connor) Keane, immigrants from Ireland. His parents soon moved to a frontier farm near Rochester, Minn., and although in humble circumstances managed to send their son to St. John's Seminary, Collegeville, Minn., and to the College of St. Francis Xavier, New York City. Deciding to enter the priesthood, young Keane was assigned to the Grand Seminary at Montreal, where he completed his theological studies under the Sulpicians and was ordained by Archbishop E. C. Fabre, Dec. 23, 1882. He served as a curate at St. Mary's and as pastor of St. Joseph's Church, St. Paul, 1882–85. Transferred to St. Thomas College as instructor and bursar, he was appointed rector in 1888 by Archbishop Ireland [*q.v.*], who thought highly of his executive and financial ability. In 1892, he was given the rectorship of the Church of the Immaculate Conception, the leading parish of Minneapolis, where he won the love of his congregation as a forceful preacher, as a democratic, candid man, and as a builder. Influenced by his archbishop, he played a leading citizen's part in civic affairs, and no small share in the beginning of the Basilica of St. Mary's can be ascribed to his skill as a collector. With sincere grief mingled with joy, his congregation witnessed his selection as the third bishop of Cheyenne, Wyo.

Consecrated at the St. Paul Cathedral by Archbishop Ireland, Oct. 28, 1902, Keane commenced the arduous labors of the missionary bishop of a huge, sparsely settled area with 7,000 scattered communicants and only a few priests. Wyoming grew slowly, but under his rule the number of Catholic communicants almost doubled, missions gave way to churches, new stations were established, and funds were gathered for the erection of St. Mary's Cathedral. On Aug. 11, 1911, Keane was translated to the archepiscopal See of Dubuque, a compact, prosperous diocese. Again, he proved an invigorating leader of priests and people rather than a ruler. Liberal in his views, he lived as simply as a curate and despite ill health carried the burdens of his office. He fostered the *Catholic Tribune Weekly*, founded in 1899, and the *Daily American Tribune*, founded in 1920; established a diocesan organ, *The Witness*, in 1921; built about thirteen churches; reorganized Columbia College, collecting an endowment of a million dollars and erecting nine halls; and created a diocesan bureau of missions and a bureau of education in the hope of standardizing the eight academies and a hundred parochial schools; supported Clarke College for women; established St. Therese's Home for Foundlings; and displayed unusual interest in the charitable institutions and the eleven hospitals with which the diocese was provided. Almost a purely diocesan figure, he attracted little national attention: though in 1908 he gave the opening prayer at the Democratic National Convention; in 1920, he was a member of the Peace Commission on Ireland; and in 1926, he was a speaker at the eleventh annual meeting on the World Alliance for International Friendship, held in Pittsburgh. He was known for his patriotic support of the government in the World War, as a believer in the League of Nations who so deprecated American failure to join that he publicly announced that he would be forced to leave the Republican party (*Daily American Tribune*, Sept. 20, 1922), an opponent of socialism, and a bitter foe of intemperance. Aside from an occasional lecture or a sermon, he left no literary remains for he made no pretence of erudition. He was made an assistant at the pontifical throne in connection with the celebration of his episcopal jubilee. Long in precarious health, he died suddenly of apoplexy and was buried from St. Raphael's Cathedral in Mount Olivet Cemetery.

[Annual Catholic directories; *Who's Who in America*, 1928–29; *Catholic Who's Who* (1911); *Minneapolis Tribune*, Oct. 29, 1902; *St. Paul Globe*, Oct. 29, 1902; *Cheyenne State Leader*, Aug. 10, 1911; *Acta et Dicta*, July 1914; *Daily American Tribune* and *Telegraph-Herald* (Dubuque), Oct. 27, 1927, Aug. 3–8, 1929; *The Witness*, Aug. 8, 1929; personal knowledge and materials supplied by Keane's associates.] R. J. P.

KEANE, JOHN JOSEPH (Sept. 12, 1839–June 22, 1918), Roman Catholic prelate, was born in Ballyshannon, County Donegal, Ireland, the son of Hugh and Fannie Keane. There were two other sons and two daughters in the family, but the four died at an early age. At the time of the famine in Ireland in 1846 Keane was brought to Baltimore by his parents. His early education was obtained at the schools of the Christian Brothers there. At seventeen, against the advice of his parents, who desired that he enter college, he became a clerk in a drygoods store where he remained for three years. During that period he spent much of his leisure time studying Latin, Greek, and history. At twenty he entered St. Charles' College, Ellicott City, Md., where he completed the six years' course in half time; in 1862 he entered St. Mary's Seminary, Baltimore, and was ordained to the priesthood in 1866.

He was immediately appointed curate at St. Patrick's Church in Washington, where he served until 1878 when he was appointed bishop of Richmond, Va. At one time he thought of entering the community of Paulist Fathers, but was dissuaded by Archbishop Spalding of Baltimore. An active figure at the Third Plenary Council of Baltimore in 1884 he did much there to promote the project of a Catholic University and was made a member of the board charged with preliminary steps to that end. When the University was founded at Washington in 1889, he was named its first rector, for an indefinite term, and was made titular bishop of Jasso. In 1896, when the policy of limiting the term of the rectorship was introduced, Pope Leo XIII offered him appointment to an archbishopric in the United States or to two powerful Congregations in Rome, those of Propaganda and of Studies. He went to Rome in 1897 and was made Archbishop of Damascus, Canon of St. John Lateran, and was placed on the two Congregations named. He remained in Rome for two years, during which time he declined to consider appointment as archbishop of Portland, Ore. At the invitation of the trustees of the Catholic University he returned to the United States in 1899 to work for its endowment. He was appointed archbishop of Dubuque in July 1900, and remained in active service there until 1911 when he resigned his See on account of failing health, although he served as vicar general under his successor. Throughout his entire active career he was intimately associated with Cardinal Gibbons and Archbishop Ireland.

As a young man Keane was far from robust. In spite of very poor vision which made sustained reading a severe effort, he was a man of varied and superior erudition. His alert mind, constant industry, remarkable powers of assimilation, philosophic temper, and broad sympathies gave him singular competence and distinction, while his charm of personality, spirit of self-effacement, practical charity, and spiritual concept of personal and social life gave him universal appeal. His interests ranged from the scholarly interpretation of the Catholic Church to the American mind—as illustrated by his lectures at Yale and Harvard—to education, civic welfare, the suppression of the saloon, and the enlightenment of the negro. He was an active figure in the Parliament of Religions at the World's Columbian Exposition, Chicago, in 1893.

Distinguished appearance, simplicity of style, directness, lucid exposition, fluency, and imagination gave him extraordinary power as an orator. He was as effective in French as in English. An address in French at the International Scientific Congress of Catholics in Brussels in 1894 was noted widely in the European press as an example of finished oratory. Few of his addresses were put into permanent form. He contributed articles to the *American Catholic Quarterly Review* (April 1888, April, July 1890, July 1891) and to the *Catholic University Bulletin* (July 1896). Maurice Francis Egan compiled a volume of extracts from his sermons and addresses under the title *Onward and Upward* (1902). Keane published one volume of spiritual reflections, *Emmanuel* (1915), but it was written when his powers were failing and is not in his best style. His papers, *The Providential Mission of Pius IX* (1878), and *The Providential Mission of Leo XIII* (1888), are more nearly representative of his style and scholarship.

[Sources include: *Cath. Univ. Bull.*, Jan. 1895, Oct. 1896, Nov. 8, 1918; *Revue Catholique de Bordeaux*, Oct. 10, 1894; *N. Y. Herald*, Mar. 29, 1878; *N. Y. Times*, June 23, 1918; *Dubuque Times-Journal*, June 22–23, 1918; *Who's Who in America*, 1918–19; *Souvenir of the Installation . . . of the Most Rev. John J. Keane* (Dubuque, 1901); unpublished letters. There are some minor discrepancies among the sources indicated. The details of Keane's earlier life are derived from his own statements.] W. J. K.

KEARNEY, DENIS (Feb. 1, 1847–Apr. 24, 1907), labor agitator, was born at Oakmount, County Cork, Ireland, the second son in a family of seven. Going to sea at the age of eleven, he sailed for some years under the American flag, finally attaining the rank of first officer on a coasting steamer. In 1870, two years after reaching San Francisco, he married Mary Ann Leary. Four children were born to them. By his temperance and industry he was able to buy a draying business in 1872 and abandon his seafaring life. His business prospered long enough for him to acquire some property and become a taxpayer. In 1876 he became a naturalized citizen, and the next year represented the Draymen and Teamsters' Union in presenting the grievances of organized labor to United States Senator Sargent. In the meantime he had regularly attended a lyceum for self-culture where, as in trade-union meetings, he overcame a natural awkwardness of expression and developed into a voluble speaker. An eager reader, greatly interested in history and in the works of Darwin and Spencer, he picked up considerable information from these sources and from newspapers and political pamphlets. Through his connection with popular open-air mass meetings he developed a reputation as an agitator. His speeches dealing with current grievances, delivered in a powerful voice, were direct, trenchant, and somewhat epigrammatic; and, despite their numerous rough and violent expressions, read surprisingly well. Practically no violence resulted from his diatribes against railroad magnates, bank officials, local politicians, and particularly the Chinese; a fact tending to justify Kearney's claim that his speeches were garbled by an unfriendly press. He repeatedly warned his followers against acts of violence; and in answer to those who called him a socialist and communist, he disclaimed any desire to attack the institution of private property. Nevertheless, he was repeatedly arrested for "incendiary" utterances or upon related charges, but in each instance he was acquitted by a jury or the charges were dismissed.

In the organization of the Workingmen's Party of California, in October 1877, he took a leading part, soon becoming its president, chief promoter, and a director of the party organ, the *Open Letter*. The Kearney movement, as the Party is often called, was the workingman's protest against widespread unemployment, dishonest banking, inequitable taxation, land monopoly, railroad domination, Chinese labor competition, and other economic and political evils of the day. As party leader, Kearney addressed his followers in almost nightly speeches, many of which were delivered on the "sand lot," now the civic center of San Francisco, and in Oakland. He constantly and vehemently stressed the necessity of stopping Chinese immigration, and afterwards claimed that his agitation had made the Chinese question a national issue and hastened the enactment of the exclusion act of 1882.

Several attempts were made to undermine his leadership. Against insurgents, dissenters, and lukewarm subordinates he employed highly drastic methods, and was roundly assailed as a "dictator" and a "Cæsar." He seems to have been devoid of any selfish political ambition, however, and fought to keep the party free from control by self-seeking politicians.

Fifty-one Workingmen delegates were elected to the constitutional convention of 1878, where, in combination with a small group of Grangers, they constituted a majority on several issues. They lacked ability and experience, however, and appear to have left little direct impress upon the new constitution. By the time of the presidential campaign of 1880, the party had so dwindled that Kearney supported General Weaver, the Greenback candidate; shortly thereafter he retired from public view. As he stated, "I was poor, with a helpless family, and I went to work to provide for their support." He died at Alameda, Apr. 24, 1907. He was of nervous, active temperament, naturally forceful, earnest and audacious, possessed of a talent for organization, and endowed with Celtic shrewdness, quickness of repartee, and vigorous, abounding energy. He was primarily an agitator and not an original or constructive thinker.

[The newspapers are the most valuable source: The *San Francisco Evening Post*, and, for a time, the *San Francisco Chronicle* looked with favor upon the Kearney movement. Opposed to it were the *Daily Alta California*, the *Bulletin*, and especially the *San Francisco Call*. Of contemporary pamphlets, J. C. Stedman and R. A. Leonard, *The Workingmen's Party of California* (1878), deserves special mention. The authors were members of the party, and trace its development down to the election of delegates to the constitutional convention. Henry George gave dispassionate contemporary estimate of Kearney and his movement in "The Kearney Agitation in California," *Pop. Sci. Mo.*, Aug. 1880. Of less value are two anonymous pamphlets, appearing probably in 1878, entitled, *Denis Kearney, His Relations to the Workingmen's Party of California* (n.d.), and *The Labor Agitator, or the Battle for Bread* (n.d.). The most discriminating secondary sources are J. P. Young, *San Francisco—A History of the Pacific Coast Metropolis* (n.d.), vol. II, chs. XLVII, L–LI; and James Bryce, *The Am. Commonwealth* (4th ed., 1910), vol. II, ch. XC. Next to be recommended are H. H. Bancroft, *Popular Tribunals* (1887), vol. II, ch. XL; T. H. Hittell, *Hist. of Cal.*, vol. IV (1897), chs. X–XI; and, based upon the two preceding works, Z. S. Eldredge, *Hist. of Cal.* (n.d.), vol. IV, chs. VII–VIII; and H. H. Bancroft, *Hist. of Cal.* (1890), vol. VII, chs. XIV–XV.]

P. O. R.

KEARNY, FRANCIS (July 23, 1785–Sept. 1, 1837), engraver in line and aquatint, the sixth son of Michael and Elizabeth (Lawrence) Kearny and brother of Lawrence Kearny [*q.v.*], was born in Perth Amboy, N. J. His father was a New York merchant and his mother was a sister of Capt. James Lawrence [*q.v.*] of the United States Navy. Young Kearny studied drawing with Alexander and Archibald Robertson in their Columbian Academy of Painting, New York City, and at eighteen was placed with Peter R. Maverick [*q.v.*] of New York, to receive training in the art of engraving. Maverick was paid $250 to take him as apprentice, but it is generally observed that Kearny succeeded in spite of his master, studying "principally by the aid of books" (Dunlap, *post*). As soon as he had become of age, Kearny opened an engraving studio of his own, in New York, his card describing him as "historical engraver." He engraved a bookplate for Dr. Henry M'Murtrie, the translator of Cuvier's *Animal Kingdom,* and another for Hector Coffin, and made a few plates for John Pinkerton's *General Collection of the Best and Most Interesting Voyages and Travels* (1810–12). He went to Philadelphia in 1810, and the remainder of his professional career was passed in that city. For half a dozen years he pursued his profession alone, and during this period he had a number of apprentices among whom were David C. Johnston [*q.v.*], George B. Ellis, and William E. Tucker. Kearny engraved some of the plates for the *Analectic Magazine*, and for that publication (December 1813), he engraved as a remarque, under Edwin's portrait of Capt. James Lawrence, a view of the battle between the *Chesapeake* and the *Shannon*, in which the gallant naval commander lost his life.

In 1817, Kearny associated himself with Benjamin Tanner and Cornelius Tiebout, under the style of Tanner, Kearny & Tiebout, engaged principally in banknote engraving. The following year the firm was Tanner, Vallance, Kearny & Company, while, in 1819, the business was conducted as before. Kearny is said to have lost heavily by this venture. In 1829, when John Pendleton went to Philadelphia to establish a commercial lithograph house in that city in conjunction with Cephas Grier Childs [*q.v.*], Kearny became a member of the firm, which was known as Pendleton, Kearny & Childs. The partnership was short-lived, however, Kearny and Pendleton retiring from it within a year. At this juncture, Kearny turned his attention to engraving plates for annuals and religious books, in which field he was successful; and in 1830, began his largest and most important engraving, a large plate of "The Last Supper," after Leonardo da Vinci, from Raphael Morghen's plate of the same subject. Called to Perth Amboy in June 1833 to assist in settling his father's estate, he took the unfinished plate with him, and completed it there. The plate was sold to a publisher, who, when Dunlap's *History . . . of the Arts of Design* was published in 1834, had "already sold 1500 impressions at $5 each" (Dunlap, *post*, II, 212).

During his residence in Philadelphia Kearny engraved many title-pages to books and magazines. His work may be found in the volumes of the *Analectic*, the *Casket*, and Godey's *Lady's Book*. He also made some plates for Collins' *Quarto Bible* (1814), and engraved in aquatint a large plate of West's "Our Saviour Healing the Sick." He died in Perth Amboy, and was buried in the churchyard of St. Peter's Church in that place. In 1928 he was represented in the exhibition of one hundred notable American engravers, held in the New York Public Library.

[W. N. Jones, *The Hist. of St. Peter's Church in Perth Amboy, N. J.* (copr. 1924); Wm. Dunlap, *Hist. of the Rise and Progress of the Arts of Design in the U. S.* (1834), vol. II; W. S. Baker, *Am. Engravers and Their Works* (1875); D. M. Stauffer, *Am. Engravers upon Copper and Steel* (1907), vol. I; Mantle Fielding, *Am. Engravers upon Copper and Steel* (1917); C. D. Allen, *Am. Book Plates* (1894); *Catalogue of an Exhibition of Early Am. Engraving upon Copper* (Grolier Club, 1908); *One Hundred Notable Am. Engravers* (N. Y. Pub. Lib., 1928); Phila. directories; *Newark Daily Advertiser*, Sept. 2, 1837.]

J. J.

KEARNY, LAWRENCE (Nov. 30, 1789–Nov. 29, 1868), naval officer, son of Michael and Elizabeth (Lawrence) Kearny and brother of Francis Kearny [*q.v.*], was born in Perth Amboy, N. J., where his great-grandfather, Michael Kearny, coming from Ireland about 1704, had settled in 1720. From this ancestry also came the distinguished soldiers, Stephen Watts Kearny (first cousin of Lawrence Kearny) and Philip Kearny [*qq.v.*]. Elizabeth (Lawrence) Kearny, half-sister of Capt. James Lawrence [*q.v.*], established a local reputation as a poet, besides rearing eight sons.

Kearny was appointed a midshipman in the navy July 24, 1807, and for a number of years was assigned to vessels engaged in cruising up and down the coast to protect American shipping. Commissioned lieutenant Mar. 6, 1813, he commanded successively the schooners *Caroline, Ferret*, and *Nonsuch*, and then a flotilla of galleys and barges. On Jan. 29, 1815, he captured the tender belonging to the British ship *Hebrus*, and thirty-six men (*Niles' Weekly Register*, Feb. 11, 1815, p. 382). While in command of the *Enterprise* (1821), he captured several piratical boats off southern Cuba, and destroyed a pirate rendezvous at Cape Antonio, Cuba (*Ibid.*, Dec. 21, 1822). Promoted to rank of master commandant Mar. 3, 1825, he was given the *Warren* and ordered to the Mediterranean. At this time the Greeks, no longer controlled by the Turks, were making depredations on ships of all nations. Cruising almost constantly (1827–29), he convoyed American ships to Smyrna and patrolled the waters about the Cyclades. In a little over two months after his arrival he had taken seven boats belonging to the pirates and recovered much stolen property. He was promoted to captain Dec. 27, 1832.

In 1840 he was given command of the East India Squadron and instructed to protect American interests in China. Going to Canton at the conclusion of the Opium War, he made a highly favorable impression by announcing (Mar. 31, 1842) that the United States "does not sanction 'the smuggling of opium' on this coast under the American flag, in violation of the laws of China"

(Kearny correspondence, *post*, p. 7). American merchants, at this time carrying on extensive trade at Canton, had suffered losses due to mob violence. Kearny arranged for the prompt payment of reparations; but ruling against excessive claims, he further impressed the Chinese by his fairness. When he heard that China had signed a treaty with Great Britain opening five ports to her merchants, he recognized the opportunity for America, and dispatched his report to Washington by special messengers, one copy by sea and two copies by the overland route. At the same time he addressed the Governor of Canton, the Chinese High Commissioner, urging that American citizens "be placed upon the same footing as the merchants of the nation most favored" (*Ibid.*, p. 21). This brought a prompt reply to the effect that the interests of American merchants should be considered (*Ibid.*, p. 22). On Aug. 1, 1843, the American consular agent at Canton was informed that the right to trade at the five ports had been granted to all foreign nations, and in the letter containing this announcement, reference was made to Kearny's request of ten months previous. Here was the beginning of the Open Door Policy in China. The successful negotiation of the first treaty (July 3, 1844) between the United States and China was in no small measure due to the influence of Kearny, who promoted friendly feeling during the critical period, urged equal rights for America while the details of the British treaty were being elaborated, and by timely representations at Washington prompted the sending of the commission that negotiated the treaty. His correspondence was called for by the Senate and was printed in full. On his return trip Kearny visited Hawaii, lending his influence towards maintaining the sovereignty and independence of the islands, which was being seriously threatened by the excitable and erratic Lord George Paulet.

His subsequent career was comparatively uneventful: he was president of the board to examine midshipmen (1846), commandant of the Norfolk Navy Yard (1847), general superintendent of ocean mail steamships at New York (1852), commandant of the New York Navy Yard (1857). He was retired Nov. 14, 1861, and commissioned commodore on the retired list Apr. 4, 1867.

Kearny was married to Josephine C. Hall, Jan. 2, 1834, and had two sons. Returning often to Perth Amboy, he was mayor of the city, 1848–49, and vestryman of St. Peter's Church (Protestant Episcopal), 1851–55. He died at Perth Amboy in the house in which he was born.

[*U. S. Mag. and Democratic Rev.*, Mar. 1851; *N. Y. Tribune*, Nov. 30, 1868; W. N. Jones, *The Hist. of St. Peter's Church in Perth Amboy, N. J.* (copr. 1924); W. J. Mills, *Historic Houses of N. J.* (1902); Kearny's official reports and letters in the Office of Naval Records and Library, Navy Dept., and in the archives of the State Dept.; private letters, letter books, and log books in the collection of J. Lawrence Boggs, Newark, N. J.; Kearny correspondence, *Sen. Doc. No. 139*, 29 Cong., 1 Sess.; Cushing correspondence, *Sen. Doc. No. 67*, 28 Cong., 2 Sess.; *Papers Relating to the Foreign Relations of the U. S. . . . 1894* (1895), App. II; Tyler Dennett, *Americans in Eastern Asia* (1922); C. O. Paullin, *Diplomatic Negotiations of Am. Naval Officers, 1778–1883* (1912); J. W. Foster, *Am. Diplomacy in the Orient* (1903); Thomas Kearny, "Commodore Lawrence Kearny," in *Proc. N. J. Hist. Soc.*, vol. L, no. 2 (Apr. 1932), and "The Tsiang Documents" in *Chinese Social and Political Science Review*, Apr. 1932; T. F. Tsiang, in the same journal, Oct. 1931.]

C. S. A.

KEARNY, PHILIP (June 1, 1814–Sept. 1, 1862), soldier, son of Philip and Susan (Watts) Kearny and nephew of Stephen Watts Kearny [*q.v.*], was born in New York City to great wealth and distinguished social position. His mother died in 1823, and during much of his boyhood and youth he made his home with his maternal grandfather, John Watts, Jr. A succession of boarding schools, including the Round Hill School conducted by Joseph G. Cogswell and George Bancroft [*qq.v.*], furnished his elementary education. Family opposition kept him from entering the United States Military Academy, and he enrolled at Columbia College as a sophomore in 1830. His grandfather, who had lost all his sons, sought to divert him from the military career on which his heart was set by offering him $1,500 a year if he would study for the ministry. To this proposition Philip could not agree, but he compromised by taking a law course. Nevertheless, during the European trip which followed his graduation from Columbia in 1833 his whole attention was given to military maneuvers, and when his grandfather died in 1836, leaving him a fortune of about a million, he at once applied for a commission in the army. Keenly fond of horses and a fearless rider from boyhood, he naturally turned to the cavalry branch of the service and secured (Mar. 8, 1837) a second lieutenancy in the 1st United States Dragoons, commanded by his uncle, Stephen Watts Kearny. After two years' service on the frontier he was sent to France by the secretary of war to study cavalry tactics in the cavalry school at Saumur, and in 1840 saw service with the Chasseurs d'Afrique in Algiers (see his *Service with the French Troops in Africa*, 1844, reprinted in *Magazine of History*, Extra No. 22, 1913). Upon his return to the United States he acted as aide-de-camp to Gen. Alexander Macomb, commander in chief of the army, and to his successor, Gen. Winfield Scott. On June 24, 1841, he married Diana Moore Bullitt of Louisville, Ky., grandniece of William and George Rogers Clark [*qq.v.*]. They had five children. Kearny saw further service on the frontier, but early in 1846 resigned his commission.

A month later, however, on the outbreak of the Mexican War, he was reinstated, recruited his squadron to war footing in the Middle West, and became General Scott's bodyguard on the advance to the city of Mexico. His dragoons were mounted on uniform dapple-gray horses, selected by Kearny and procured at his expense, "the hoofs of all striking simultaneously . . . as if they were galloping to set music" (Reid, *post*). While leading a charge on the retreating Mexicans at Churubusco his left arm was shattered so badly as to require amputation. He was promoted to the rank of major for his courage in action.

After leading an expedition in California against the Rogue River Indians, he resigned from the army in 1851 and took a trip around the world. Upon his return he settled for a few years in New Jersey, employing himself in extensive improvements on his recently acquired country estate, "Belle Grove," near Newark, N. J., in a section now named Kearny. In 1859, however, he returned to France and was attached to the staff of General Morris, commander of the cavalry of the Imperial Guard under Napoleon III. He was present at the battles of Magenta and Solferino, and is said to have participated in every charge of the cavalry. The Cross of the Legion of Honor was awarded to him by the French Emperor for his military services.

Upon the outbreak of the Civil War he hurried from Paris to Washington hoping to secure a general's commission, and was appointed brigadier-general of volunteers in command of the 1st New Jersey Brigade. Throughout the Virginia campaigns he had ample opportunity, at first on the Peninsula under McClellan, later as major-general under Pope, to show his mettle. He participated in at least twelve engagements. The dash and spirit which he had come to symbolize are expressed in E. C. Stedman's poem, "Kearny at Seven Pines." The men of his division each wore on his uniform a bit of scarlet cloth known as the "Kearny patch." "You are marked men," Kearny said to them on one occasion, "you must be ever in the front . . ." (*War of the Rebellion: Official Records,* 1 ser. II, pt. 3, pp. 215–16). It is said that his troopers cheered him every time he rode down their lines.

Following his custom, when ordered to a new position, of riding through the country learning the roads, he unwittingly entered the enemy's lines at Chantilly, Sept. 1, 1862, and met his death. General Lee, who had known Kearny in the Mexican War, forwarded the body under a flag of truce to General Pope, and subsequently, at the request of Kearny's widow, he delivered to her the General's sword, horse, and saddle. Kearny won not only the devotion of his men, but the sincere respect of his fellow officers: "Tall and lithe in figure, with a most expressive and mobile countenance, and a manner which inspired confidence and zeal in all under his command, no one could fail to admire his chivalric bearing and his supreme courage," wrote General Pope. "He seemed to think that it was his mission to make up the shortcomings of others, and in proportion as these shortcomings were made plain, his exertions and exposure were multiplied" (*Battles and Leaders,* II, 492). General Scott called him "the bravest man I ever knew, and a perfect soldier" (De Peyster, *post,* p. 495). In 1912 his body was removed from the Watts vault in Trinity Churchyard, New York, to the National Cemetery at Arlington, Va., where the state of New Jersey has erected an equestrian statue in his honor.

[J. W de Peyster, *Personal and Military Hist. of Philip Kearny* (1869); Cortlandt Parker, *Philip Kearny* (1868); W. N. Jones, *The Hist of St. Peter's Church in Perth Amboy, N. J.* (copr. 1924); *N. Y. Herald,* Sept. 3, *N. Y. Tribune,* Sept. 3, 4, and *Evening Post* (N. Y.), Sept. 5, 1862; *War of the Rebellion: Official Records (Army),* 1 ser. XI (pt. 3), XII (pt. 2), XIX (pt. 2); Mayne Reid, "A Dashing Dragoon," in *Onward,* Jan. 1869, repr. in *Mag. of Hist.,* Extra No. 22 (1913).]

A. E. P.

KEARNY, STEPHEN WATTS (Aug. 30, 1794–Oct. 31, 1848), soldier, was the fifteenth and last child of Philip and Susanna (Watts) Kearny and a first cousin of Lawrence Kearny [*q.v.*]. On his mother's side he was connected with the De Lancey, Van Cortlandt, Nicoll, Van Rensselaer, and Schuyler families. His earliest American ancestor on the father's side was Michael Kearny, who came from Ireland about 1704 and about 1720 settled in Perth Amboy, N. J. Michael's grandson, Stephen's father, was a prosperous wine merchant and landholder, but suffered the confiscation of his estates because of his Loyalist activities during the Revolution. Later he lived in New York City, and thereafter in Newark, where Stephen was born. The boy, after attending common school in Newark, entered Columbia College in 1811, but on the approach of the War of 1812 joined the army, beginning his long military career as a first lieutenant in the 13th Infantry, Mar. 12, 1812. At the battle of Queenston Heights (Oct. 13), wherein he showed conspicuous gallantry, he was wounded and captured, but was shortly afterward exchanged, and on Apr. 1, 1813, was made a captain. From 1819, except for an occasional detail in the East, his service was on the western frontier. In the fall of that year he accompanied Col. Henry Atkinson to the site north of the present Omaha, where Camp Missouri (later Fort Atkinson), the farthest outpost of the army, was established. In the summer of 1820 he accompanied Capt. Matthew J. Magee's expedition from Camp Missouri through a then unknown region to Camp Cold Water (later Fort Snelling), near the present St. Paul; and on the march kept a journal which was published eighty-eight years later. On Apr. 1, 1823, he was brevetted a major for ten years' faithful service in one grade.

In 1825 he took part in General Atkinson's expedition to the mouth of the Yellowstone. In August 1828 he assumed command of Fort Crawford (Prairie du Chien). He was appointed a major in May 1829, and in July, after selecting the site of a new Fort Crawford and energetically beginning the work, he was transferred to Jefferson Barracks, Mo. At St. Louis, Sept. 5, 1830, he was married to Mary Radford, the stepdaughter of Gen. William Clark [*q.v.*]. Toward the end of the year he reoccupied the site of the destroyed Fort Towson, in the present Oklahoma, and rebuilt the structure. Made lieutenant-colonel of the newly organized dragoons (Mar. 4, 1833), he led an expedition in September into the present Iowa, where he began the building of the first Fort Des Moines. On July 4, 1836, he became colonel of the dragoons, with headquarters at Fort Leavenworth, where in 1842 he assumed command of the Third Military Department, being later transferred, as head of the department, to St. Louis. In 1845 he led an expedition to South Pass, and in May of the following year, accompanied by General Brooke, began the building of the first Fort Kearny (Nebraska City, Nebr.), a post abandoned, two years later, on the establishment of the famous post on the Platte which after his death was named for him.

In May 1846 he was placed in command of the Army of the West, and on June 30 was made a brigadier-general. Leaving Fort Leavenworth with about 1,660 men, he entered Santa Fé without opposition on Aug. 18. From Aug. 18 to Sept. 22 he was military governor of New Mexico. After organizing a civil government, he set out for the Pacific Coast on Sept. 25, with 300 dragoons, 200 of whom, on his receipt of information that California had been conquered, were sent back. On Dec. 6, at the Indian village of San Pasqual, he attacked a superior force of Californians, suffering casualties of a third of his command and being twice wounded. The next day he moved forward, only to find his way blocked, but a relief force sent by Commodore Robert Field Stockton [*q.v.*] enabled him to reach San Diego. The combined forces of Stockton and Kearny, about 600 strong, started for Los Angeles on Dec. 29. Two so-called battles, in which the Americans lost but one man killed, were fought (Jan. 8 and 9, 1847); on Jan. 10 the town was occupied, and on Jan. 13 the Californians surrendered to a separate force under Lieut.-Col. John Charles Frémont [*q.v.*]. Almost immediately a quarrel arose between Kearny and Stockton as to the chief command, and Frémont, who had been appointed civil governor by Stockton, refused to obey Kearny's orders. On the departure of Stockton for Mexico and the arrival of orders from Washington sustaining Kearny's authority, Frémont was deposed from his office, subjected to many indignities by Kearny and his under-officers, and in June ordered to follow Kearny's escort on its return overland to the east. At Fort Leavenworth Frémont was ordered to proceed, under arrest, to Washington, where he was court-martialed, and on being found guilty of insubordination he indignantly resigned from the army.

Kearny next proceeded to Mexico. He was for a time (May–June) civil governor of Vera Cruz, and for a brief period held a like post in the city of Mexico. In August, against the determined opposition of Senator Benton, Frémont's father-in-law, he was brevetted a major-general. Late in the summer he was back at Jefferson Barracks. A tropical disease contracted at Vera Cruz had shattered his health. He was conveyed to a quiet place in the country and later to the home of Maj. Meriwether Lewis Clark, in St. Louis, where he died.

Of the courage, energy, and ability of Kearny there has never been dispute, and during his period of nearly thirty years on the frontier he rendered the nation a devoted and inestimable service. He published a *Carbine Manual* in 1837, and in 1846 a code of laws drawn up under his supervision for the government of New Mexico. A rigid disciplinarian, he was stern in manner and inflexible in will. His conduct in the Frémont episode has been often condemned, even by writers unfriendly to the Pathfinder—Justin H. Smith characterizing him as "grasping, jealous, domineering and harsh." It may be that some regret for this action troubled his last hours, for on his deathbed, according to Mrs. Frémont, he sent a request for her to come to see him, which she resentfully declined.

[Selected bibliography: W. N. Jones, *The Hist. of St. Peter's Church in Perth Amboy, N. J.* (copr. 1924); F. B. Heitman, *Hist. Reg. and Dict. U. S. Army* (1903); *Nebr. State Hist. Soc. Pubs.*, vol. XX (1922); B. E. Mahan, *Old Fort Crawford and the Frontier* (1926); Grant Foreman, *Pioneer Days in the Early Southwest* (1926); J. H. Smith, *The War with Mexico* (1919); Allan Nevins, *Frémont* (1928); Cardinal Goodwin, *John Charles Frémont* (1930); F. S. Dellenbaugh, *Frémont and '49* (1914); military service record of Kearny, compiled by the Adjutant-General, Nov. 17, 1928; Thomas Kearny, "The Mexican War and the Conquest of California," *Cal. Hist. Soc. Quart.*, Sept. 1929, and "Kearny and 'Kit' Carson," *N. Mex. Hist. Rev.*, Jan. 1930; V. M. Porter, "General Stephen W. Kearny and the Conquest of California," *Ann. Pubs. Hist. Soc. So. Cal.*, vol. VIII (1911); information from Thomas Kearny, Esq., New York City; Kearny's journal of the Magee expedition, annotated by V. M. Porter, in *Mo. Hist. Soc. Colls.*, vol. III (1908); record of the Frémont court martial in *Sen. Ex. Doc. 33*, 30 Cong., 1 Sess.]

W. J. G.

KEARSLEY, JOHN (June 4, 1684–Jan. 11, 1772), physician, architect, teacher, was born and baptized at Greatham, Durham County, England, emigrated to America in 1711, and settled in Philadelphia in 1717. He was a son of the Rev. John Kearsley, vicar of Greatham, a Cambridge man (proceeded B.A. 1675–76). Since civic leadership, owing to Quaker influence, did not then so frequently fall to clergymen and lawyers he became not only an active figure in the medical profession of Pennsylvania, but a representative for several terms in the House of Assembly. His medical office has been called "the first college" in the Province, wherein were trained under a seven-year term of tutelage such men as Lloyd Zachary, John Redman, Thomas Cadwalader, William Shippen, Thomas Bond, Phineas Bond, Cadwalader Evans, John Bard, and John Kearsley, Jr. (a nephew). He sowed fruitful seed, for these men became directly or indirectly founders of the Pennsylvania Hospital, the first medical schools of Philadelphia and New York, and the College of Physicians of Philadelphia.

Kearsley's contributions to the literature of medicine comprised at least two: one on yellow fever, and one on smallpox, malaria, pneumonia, and various fevers "incidental to the Province." He was interested in astronomy, and observations (February 1736/7) on a comet and an eclipse of the sun, which he sent to Peter Collinson, were printed in the *Transactions of the Royal Society* for the years 1737–38 (vol. XL, 1741). He also designed, financed, and built Christ Church, Philadelphia, which he served as vestryman and warden throughout his active career. The building, begun in 1727, equaled anything of the kind in the Colonies, and stands today a singularly beautiful and graceful structure. In addition to Christ Church, he designed St. Peter's, a chapel of ease to Christ Church, architecturally of great charm and still eloquently expressive of the eighteenth century and its designer's powers. He was one of a committee of three appointed in 1729 to plan and build a State House for Pennsylvania in which the Assembly, the Governor's Council, and the supreme court could meet, out of which plan grew Independence Hall; but the completion of this task ultimately fell to Andrew Hamilton. The so-called Christ Church Hospital, another memorial to Kearsley, was founded and endowed by him for the support of clergymen's widows and poor women of the communion of the Church of England. He was married twice: first to Anne Magdalene, *née* Fauconnier, widow of Theophilus Caillé, and second, Nov. 24, 1748, to Margaret Brand. The one child of his first marriage died in infancy; by his second marriage there was no issue.

[*Medical Times*, Feb. 1923; W. S. Middleton, in *Annals of Medic. Hist.*, Dec. 1921 (with portrait); Frederick Henry, *Standard Hist. of the Medic. Profession of Phila.* (1897); James Thacher, *Am. Medic. Biog.* (1828); J. F. Watson, *Annals of Phila.* (rev. and enl., 1898), vol. III; E. L. White, *The Descendants of Jonathan Kearsley* (1900); A. E. Helffenstein, *Pierre Fauconnier and His Descendants* (1911); H. D. Eberlein, in *Arch. Rev.* (London), Dec. 1920, and *The Architecture of Colonial America* (1915); L. C. Washburn, *Christ Church* (1925); *Pa. Gazette* (Phila.), Jan. 16, 1772; certain information from Miss May Atherton Leach (Geneal. Soc. of Pa.), Miss Emily L. Cashel, genealogist, London, England; Dr. J. Madison Taylor, and Horace Wells Sellers, Esq., of Philadelphia.]

A. C. J.

KEATING, JOHN McLEOD (June 12, 1830–Aug. 15, 1906), journalist, author, was born in Kings County, Ireland, of Scotch-Irish parentage. Educated in Scotland until his ninth year, he completed his school education in Dublin at thirteen, and was apprenticed to the printer's trade. At eighteen he was foreman of the printing office of the Dublin *World* and a prominent member of the Young Ireland Club. Following the revolution of that body in 1848, he emigrated to America, settled in New York, and again became foreman in a newspaper plant. He went to New Orleans in 1854, whence, after a short experience in the printing business, he moved to Baton Rouge and later to Nashville, Tenn., where he was made foreman of the composing room of what is now the Methodist Publishing House. From Nashville he went back to Baton Rouge and became superintendent of state printing, later returning to Nashville to become managing editor of the *Daily News.* In 1859 he settled in Memphis, and was there employed as commercial and city editor of the *Daily Morning Bulletin.* At the outbreak of the Civil War he was for a short time a private secretary on the staff of Gen. Leonidas Polk.

After the capture of Memphis and until the end of the war he served as city editor of the *Memphis Daily Argus,* which was then the only Democratic newspaper in that place. In 1865 he established the *Memphis Daily Commercial,* and a year later combined it with the *Argus,* publishing the two as the *Commercial and Argus* until 1867. A close personal friend of President Andrew Johnson, he spent the winter of 1867–68 in Washington as one of the President's political counselors. Later he was nominated as postmaster of Memphis by President Johnson, but the Senate rejected the nomination. He returned to Memphis in 1868 to purchase a half interest in the *Memphis Appeal,* which he edited for twenty-one years. As an editor he was active in attacking Carpet-baggers, and in securing the enfranchisement of former Confederate soldiers, the education of the emancipated negroes, and the adoption of the present constitution of Tennessee. He also advocated the political equality of women. In the decade following the Civil War he took part in enterprises to tunnel or bridge the Mississippi at Memphis, to construct railroad lines out from that city, and to erect elevators there. He escaped the yellow-fever epidemics which the city suffered from time to time and continued to publish the *Appeal* regularly, even though the force of the paper was sometimes reduced to himself and one other man. During the epidemic of 1878 he acted as editorial writer, business manager, reportorial force, and compositor, and, in addition, served as a member of the executive committee that practically governed the city. His vivid daily accounts of the epidemic in the *Appeal* have been compared to Defoe's *Journal of the Plague Year,* in their portrayal of grotesque horrors. His *History of the Yellow Fever,* published in 1879, was followed by a campaign to do away with the unsanitary conditions around Memphis, a campaign in which he played a conspicuous part. In 1889 he became editor of the *Commercial,* continuing as editor until 1891 when he left Memphis for Washington, D. C.

Keating was the author of *The Southern Question* (1889); *Dirt, Disease and Degradation* (1890?); *History of the City of Memphis and Shelby County, Tennessee* (3 vols., 1888); and a portion of *The Military Annals of Tennessee* (1886), edited by J. B. Lindsley. He was a stanch Democrat, but was opposed to slavery and did much to soften the feelings of bitterness created in the hearts of the Southern people by the Civil War. Once he left newspaper work, but although he found dealing in cotton, groceries, and insurance profitable, he soon returned to the newspaper office. He began to study for the ministry of the Protestant Episcopal Church in 1859 and was prepared to take orders in 1862, but without antagonism toward the Church he gave up his idea of becoming a clergyman when he felt he could not accept the Church's creed. He was married in 1856 in Nashville to Josephine Esselman Smith. They had two children. He died in Gloucester, Mass., at the home of his daughter.

[Wm. S. Speer, *Sketches of Prominent Tennesseans* (1888); J. M. Keating, *Hist. of the City of Memphis* (1888), vols. II, III; *Who's Who in America,* 1906–07; *Commercial Appeal* (Memphis), Aug. 18, 1906; private information.] W. W.

KEATING, JOHN MARIE (Apr. 30, 1852–Nov. 17, 1893), physician, author, editor, was the eldest son of Dr. William Valentine Keating, a professor of obstetrics in the Jefferson Medical College, and Susan (LaRoche) Keating, daughter of the eminent Philadelphia physician, René LaRoche [*q.v.*]. John and his parents were born in Philadelphia. They came from Irish and French ancestry; William V. Keating was a nephew of William Hypolitus Keating [*q.v.*], and John's great-grandfathers on the paternal side had been officers in the Irish Brigade of the French army during the reign of the Bourbons. Great-grandfather René LaRoche (of the same name and profession as Keating's grandfather) practised in the Island of Santo Domingo until the insurrection, when he came to Philadelphia.

John Marie Keating received his early education at Roth Academy in Philadelphia and Seton Hall in South Orange, N. J. Afterwards he attended the Polytechnic College in Philadelphia, and then entered the medical department of the University of Pennsylvania, from which he was graduated with honor in 1873. After an interneship in the Philadelphia Hospital, he was appointed a visiting physician, attending the obstetric and children's departments for many years. He lectured on diseases of children in the University until his resignation in 1880; and for a time was professor of medicine in the Woman's Medical College of Philadelphia. He was also gynecologist to the St. Joseph's and St. Agnes hospitals, assistant physician to the Children's Hospital, and physician-in-charge of the children's departments of the Howard Hospital and St. Joseph's Female Orphan Asylum. He was elected medical director of the Penn Mutual Life Insurance Company in 1881, which position he held for ten years. In 1879 he was one of

General Grant's party that visited India, Burma, the Malay Peninsula, Siam, and China, and on his return he wrote an interesting account of the journey, entitled *With Grant in the East* (1879).

Throughout his short professional life (he died at forty-one years) he was an enthusiastic and productive worker. He took an active part in various medical societies: he was elected a fellow of the College of Physicians of Philadelphia in 1887; was a member of the American and the British Gynecological societies, the Association of Life Insurance Medical Directors, and a president of the American Pediatric Society. His best-known work was the *Cyclopedia of Diseases of Children,* which contained various articles by leading authorities in the English-speaking world. Published in five volumes, 1889–99, it was hailed as the most advanced and complete work on the subject. Keating himself contributed articles to William Pepper's *System of Practical Medicine* (5 vols., 1885–86), A. H. Buck's *Reference Handbook of the Medical Sciences* (9 vols., 1885–93), and the *Annual and Analytical Cyclopædia of Practical Medicine,* edited (1899–1901) by C. E. de M. Sajous. Alone or in collaboration with others he wrote: *Mother's Guide in the Management and Feeding of Infants* (1881), *Maternity, Infancy, and Childhood* (1887), *Diseases of the Heart and Circulation in Infancy and Adolescence* (1888), *How to Examine for Life Insurance* (1890), *A New Pronouncing Dictionary of Medicine* (1892), *Mother and Child* (1893). He founded the *International Clinics,* of which he was an editor from 1891 until his death. He was also editor of the *Archives of Pediatrics.*

In 1890 his failing health was found to be due to tuberculosis and he moved to Colorado where, according to his friend, Dr. Judson Daland, the invigorating climate soon produced a happy effect, and in about a year he was able to resume the work of his beloved profession. He made brief visits to his native city but it soon became evident that he was waging a battle for life. He died at Colorado Springs, survived by his wife who was Edith McCall, daughter of Peter McCall of Philadelphia, three daughters, and a son.

[J. K. Mitchell, "Memoir of John M. Keating, M.D.," *Trans. Coll. of Physicians of Phila.,* 3 ser. XVI (1894), xxxv; Judson Daland, "In Memoriam," *International Clinics,* 3 ser. IV (1894), xi; H. A. Kelly and W. L. Burrage, *Am. Medic. Biogs.* (1920); *Trans. Am. Pediatric Soc.,* vol. VI (1894); *Archives of Pediatrics,* Apr. 1893; E. P. Davis, in *Trans. Am. Gynecol. Soc.,* vol. XIX (1894); *Encyc. of Pa. Biog.,* vol. XV (1924); L. W. Murray, *The Story of Some French Refugees* (1903); *Rocky Mountain News* (Denver), and *Phila. Inquirer,* Nov. 18, 1893.]

E. H. F.

KEATING, WILLIAM HYPOLITUS (Aug. 11, 1799–May 17, 1840), mineralogical chemist, was born in Wilmington, Del., the son of Baron John and Eulalia (Deschapelles) Keating. His father, of Irish extraction, formerly a colonel in the Irish Brigade of the Frerch army, had resigned his commission and settled in Delaware. Later the family moved to Philadelphia where young Keating received his early education. Entering the University of Pennsylvania in 1813, he graduated in 1816 with the degree of A.B. He then continued the study of chemistry and mineralogy in polytechnic schools in France and Switzerland, and received the degree of A.M. from the University of Pennsylvania. In 1821 he published *Considerations upon the Art of Mining . . . and Advantages Which Would Result from an Introduction of this Art into the United States.* The following year he was appointed professor of mineralogy and chemistry at the University of Pennsylvania, which position he held until 1828, when he resigned. In his first year at the University he announced the discovery of a new mineral which he named Jeffersonite, but later it was definitely proved that Jeffersonite was only a variety of pyroxene. In 1822 also, Keating was responsible for the tests which proved that a supposed new mineral announced from Columbia County, N. Y., was nothing but an artificial zinc oxide. In later years, as a result of studies made near Franklin, N. J., he was largely responsible for the discovery of eight or ten new minerals, including red zinc ore, franklinite, dysulsite, and zinc carbonate.

In 1823 he served as geologist and historiographer of the expedition under Maj. Stephen H. Long [*q.v.*], sent out by the Secretary of War to explore the region about the headwaters of the Mississippi River. Upon his return he compiled two volumes of the notes made by himself and the other members of the expedition, publishing them under the title, *Narrative of an Expedition to the Source of St. Peter's River, Lake Winnepeek, Lake of the Woods, etc.* (Philadelphia, 1824; London, 1825). He was also editor of an American edition of *Conversations on Chemistry, Etc.,* published in 1824. In that year, together with Samuel V. Merrick [*q.v.*], he had an important share in awakening sufficient public interest to ensure the satisfactory inauguration of the Franklin Institute of Pennsylvania. He was one of its first managers and was also elected professor of chemistry. Since 1822 he had been a member of the American Philosophical Society, which he served as a secretary for a time.

He was a man of great scientific attainments, but also took an interest in the law, in business affairs, and in politics. He read law and was admitted to the Philadelphia bar, May 3, 1834, and served in the Pennsylvania House of Representatives in that same year. He was one of the founders of the Philadelphia & Reading Railroad and was responsible for the successful negotiation of its first mortgage loan in England. He died in London while on a business trip. He had been married to Elizabeth Bollman.

[Univ. of Pa., *Biog. Cat. of the Matriculates of the College, 1749–1893* (1894); J. H. Campbell, *Hist. of the Hibernian Soc.* (1892); L. W. Murray, *The Story of Some French Refugees* (1903); *Encyc. of Pa. Biog.*, vol. XV (1924); *The Book Issued to Commemorate The Centenary of the Franklin Inst. of Pa.* (1924); E. P. Oberholtzer, *Philadelphia, A Hist. of the City and Its People* (n.d.), vol. II; E. F. Smith, *Chemistry in Old Phila.* (1919); the *Times* (London), May 20, 1840.]

J. H. F.

KEDZIE, ROBERT CLARK (Jan. 28, 1823–Nov. 7, 1902), physician, chemist, sanitarian, was born in Delhi, Delaware County, N. Y., the son of William Kedzie. When Robert was very young his parents took up a tract of land near Monroe, Mich., where the boy was reared. Having decided upon a college career he worked toward that end and paid his own way—in part at least—through Oberlin, receiving his degree in 1847. After graduation he taught for two years at the Rochester Academy, Michigan, and then entered the new medical department of the University of Michigan at Ann Arbor, graduating with the earliest class in 1851. He had married, in 1850, Harriet Fairchild of Ohio. He practised for a while at Kalamazoo but later removed to Vermontville, Mich. On the outbreak of the Civil War he was made surgeon to the 12th Michigan Infantry. Taken prisoner at the battle of Shiloh he was found on his release to be unfit for service and was invalided home. As soon as he recovered he resumed the practice of medicine at Lansing and in 1863 began to teach chemistry at the Agricultural College of the State of Michigan, becoming full professor in 1867. In 1874 he was chosen president of the Michigan State Medical Society, in 1876 he was chairman of the section of public hygiene and state medicine of the American Medical Association, and in the following year he became president of the State Board of Health, remaining active in that body for many years. He retained his connection with the Agricultural College for thirty-six years and at his death was emeritus professor.

Kedzie was a prolific contributor to periodical literature but published no major work. It is said that he wrote thirty-two papers on sanitation and public health alone. In the field of accident prevention, which was also a major interest with him, he wrote on the resuscitation of the drowned, lightning prevention, and kerosene explosions. He showed that the frequency of kerosene explosions was due to improper testing for the explosive point and devised an oil tester to guard against the possibility of such accidents. He taught farmers to put up their own lightning rods. Under the head of ordinary sanitary precautions he wrote articles on drinking water and incidentally exploded the notion that the well waters of the state had magnetic properties, thus saving the public from exploitation by charlatans. Other subjects which he treated included the ventilation of railway cars, the dangers of arsenical poisoning from wall papers, and the ill effects of deforestation. He was greatly interested in the climatology and meteorology of the state. In the realm of agricultural chemistry proper his services were also notable. He was the founder of the local farmers' institute which became popular over the country and in that way fostered the spread of a knowledge of chemistry among farmers. He showed that a certain kind of wheat was best suited to the soil and climate of the state and had much to do with introducing the beet-sugar industry into the country. Finally he revolutionized the sale of fertilizers by securing legislation which made it compulsory for agents to be licensed and to publish on the labels of their products the analyses of the preparations for sale.

[L. S. Munson, "A Memoir of the Late R. C. Kedzie," *Bulletin*, no. 73 (1903), of the U. S. Dept. of Agriculture, Bureau of Chemistry; W. J. Beal, *Hist. of the Mich. Agric. Coll. and Biog. Sketches* (1915); *Medic. Record*, Nov. 15, 1902; H. A. Kelly and W. L. Burrage, *Am. Medic. Biogs.* (1920); *Detroit Free Press*, Nov. 8, 1902.]

E. P.

KEEFE, DANIEL JOSEPH (Sept. 27, 1852–Jan. 2, 1929), labor leader, industrial arbitrator, and United States commissioner-general of immigration, was born at Willowsprings, Ill., near Chicago, the son of John and Catherine Keefe. When he was ten his mother died and shortly afterward he left school with a fourth-grade education. At twelve he began driving for his father, who was a teamster in Chicago, but two years later his father's death left him to make his own way. A strong, good-looking boy, at eighteen he was a lumber handler and longshoreman. Later, developing his Irish knack for leadership, he contracted with shipping companies to furnish men, largely recent immigrants, to load and unload vessels, and in 1882 was elected president of the Lumber Unloaders' Association. When the National (now International) Longshoremen's Association was formed in 1892 he promptly became the dominant figure in that organization, serving as its president, except for three years, from 1893 until 1908. He was also from 1897 to 1901 a member of the Illinois State Board of Arbitration. Like a brother who became a capitalist, Keefe was a shrewd business man who knew how to deal successfully with employers and under his leadership the longshoremen developed a system of cooperative contracts, taken directly by the union for specific pieces of work, which soon became general on the Great Lakes. Though he was a conservative, the practical needs of the situation which he confronted in the international union led him to favor an industrial rather than a craft form of organization, and he built up a powerful industrial federation which claimed in 1905 some 100,000 members and included all workers connected with water transportation except seamen. He took an active part in the organization and early history of the National Civic Federation and was intimately associated with the development of Roosevelt's plan for the use of his Nobel Peace Prize money to establish the Foundation for the Promotion of Industrial Peace. He was also a member of the executive council of the American Federation of Labor from 1903 to 1908, first as seventh and later as sixth vice-president. But when, in 1908, the Federation came out for Bryan for president, Keefe, who had always voted with the Republican party on national issues, broke away from the Gompers policy and campaigned for Taft. On Dec. 1, 1908, he was appointed by President Roosevelt commissioner-general of immigration. In that office he soon found himself merely an instrument for the administration of an act which he considered entirely inadequate as interpreted by the solicitor of the Department of Commerce and Labor. In defense against criticisms of his administration by former associates in the labor movement he could only recommend in his annual reports methods of strengthening the law—recommendations which fell with Taft's veto of the bill imposing a literacy test. Shortly after leaving office on May 31, 1913, he made a tour of the Orient and Europe studying labor conditions and organizations. During the World War he was a conciliation commissioner for the United States Department of Labor, and from August 1921 until his retirement in April 1925, he was engaged in the prevention and settlement of labor disputes for the United States Shipping Board Merchant Fleet Corporation. His last years were spent at Elmhurst, a suburb of Chicago, where he died. In 1878 he married Ellen E. Conners and in 1904, after her death, took as his second wife Emma L. Walker who died in 1925. Genial, self-reliant and adaptable, Keefe built his entire career on his experiences as a boy with the work and the workers of the Chicago waterfront.

[Biographical material is scattered through reports and proceedings of the organizations with which Keefe was connected: the convention proceedings of the Internat. Longshoremen's Asso. and of the Am. Federation of Labor, and the reports of the Ill. State Board of Arbitration, the U. S. Commissioner-Gen. of Immigration, and the Secretary of Labor. The sketch published in *Who's Who in America,* 1916–17, and that published in the *New Internat. Encyc.* contain several errors which have been corrected by his sons, who have also furnished additional facts, from data in their possession. References to Keefe's work are found in several books such as John R. Commons, *Labor and Administration* (1913), and Samuel Gompers, *Seventy Years of Life and Labor* (1925), vol. II, and in newspaper files covering the periods of his most conspicuous activity. Brief obituary notices were published in the *N. Y. Times,* the *Chicago Tribune,* the *Chicago News,* and other papers.] H. S. W.

KEELER, JAMES EDWARD (Sept. 10, 1857–Aug. 12, 1900), astronomer, was descended from Ralph Keeler who settled in Hartford, Conn., in 1635. His father, William F. Keeler, took part as an officer in the engagement between the *Monitor* and the *Merrimac.* His mother, Anna E. Dutton, was a daughter of Henry Dutton [*q.v.*]. He was born in La Salle, Ill., where he received his early education in the public schools. When the family moved to Mayport, Fla., in 1869, he continued his studies at home. His fondness for astronomy and his mechanical ability here found dignified expression in the building and equipping of the "Mayport Astronomical Observatory" in the years 1875–77. The observatory apparently contained a clock, a quadrant, a 2-inch telescope, and a meridian-circle. The first "was a small kitchen affair, and kept execrable time," the last was a home-made, but well-constructed instrument with which Keeler determined positions of stars and the latitude of his observatory.

Keeler entered Johns Hopkins University in 1877 and graduated with the degree of B.A. in 1881. He defrayed a considerable portion of his expenses by assisting in the lectures and in the laboratory work. At the end of his freshman year he accompanied the expedition from the Naval Observatory to Central City, Colo., to observe the eclipse of July 29, 1878. After graduation he went to the Allegheny Observatory as assistant to Langley. His association with Langley at the time when the latter was perfecting the bolometer for the measurement of heat radiation from the heavenly bodies must have been a source of inspiration. From May 1883 to June 1884 he was abroad, chiefly at Heidelberg and

Berlin, as a student under Quincke, Bunsen, Helmholtz, Kayser, and Runge. After two more years at Allegheny he was called to the Lick Observatory in 1886. He devised many improvements about the observatory, including a magnetic control for the 36-inch telescope, and designed the visual spectroscope for the telescope. While awaiting the completion of the latter he made a beautiful series of drawings at the telescope of Mars, Jupiter, and Saturn, and of the satellites of Jupiter. Of his many spectroscopic studies at this time, the most striking and important is his observation of the radial velocities of the Orion nebula and of thirteen planetary nebulae, definitely showing that these nebulae, like stars, are in motion.

Keeler succeeded Langley as director at Allegheny in 1891 and at once built an instrument with which to photograph spectra of the heavenly bodies. With this instrument he took the plates which furnished that striking confirmation of the theory of Clerk Maxwell that the rings of Saturn are composed of small bodies, each following its own orbit. In 1898 he was elected director of the Lick Observatory. He devoted his research to the taming of the Crossley reflector which had proved very refractory to previous handlers. He made one change after another and in five months began to show the fine results of which the instrument was capable. He began a series of photographs of nebulae which showed at once that nebulae were exceedingly numerous and that a large proportion of them are spiral in form. Keeler was married to Cora S. Matthews at Oakley Plantation, La., on June 16, 1891. He received the Rumford and the Henry Draper medals. He was a member of the National Academy of Sciences, fellow of the Royal Astronomical Society, served as president of the Astronomical Society of the Pacific, and was affiliated with other learned societies.

[Memoir, with bibliography, in *Nat. Acad. Sci. Biog. Memoirs,* vol. V (1905); W. W. Campbell, "Jas. Edward Keeler," *Pubs. of the Astronomical Soc. of the Pacific,* Oct. 1, 1900; *Pop. Astronomy,* Oct., Nov. 1900; *Science,* Sept. 7, 1900.] R. S. D.

KEELER, RALPH OLMSTEAD (Aug. 29, 1840–Dec. 17, 1873), journalist, the son of Ralph and Amelia (Brown) Keeler and grandson of Colman J. Keeler, a major of militia in the War of 1812, was born on a farm in Northern Ohio where the town of Custar is now situated. At eight he was left an orphan and was sent to live with an uncle at Buffalo, N. Y. Here he lived and attended school for three years until the too constant canings by his uncle made him revolt and run away. For a time he served as cabin-boy on various Great Lakes steamers. By saving money he was able to attend school for brief periods during the winter months when the boats were laid up. He quit school finally to perfect himself in playing the banjo and in clog-dancing so that he might join a minstrel troupe. When he finally found a minstrel company willing to accept him he became a leading attraction as a child phenomenon, dancing, and playing female parts. His last minstrel connection was with the show-boat, *The Floating Palace.* On leaving this show troupe Keeler entered St. Vincent's College, a Jesuit school, at Cape Girardeau, Mo., which he attended from Feb. 21, 1856, until June 1, 1857. He spent the succeeding year at Toledo, Ohio, and then entered Kenyon College in September 1858 as a freshman, leaving without a degree in June 1861. At college he had the reputation of being somewhat of a poet. He returned to Toledo and got a position in the post-office. After saving $181, he sailed for Europe and entered Karl-Rupert University at Heidelberg. He stayed here two years, left without a degree, and returned to America. Settling in San Francisco he spent another two years lecturing, teaching English to foreigners, and writing for the *Alta California,* the *Golden Era,* and the *Californian.* In 1868 he returned to the East to act as correspondent for the *Alta California.* He spent this year lecturing in various towns, and published at his own expense a novel, *Gloverson and His Silent Partners* (1869), which, as W. D. Howells put it, "failed instantly and decisively."

Soon after July 1869 Keeler became, through the influence of Howells, a proof-reader on the *Atlantic Monthly.* In 1870 appeared his best work, *Vagabond Adventures,* an autobiographical account of his life for the most part made up of material published in the *Atlantic Monthly* and *Old and New.* In the same year he contributed to *Every Saturday* "The Marquis de Villemer," from the French of George Sand, which was later published in book form, and in 1871, as correspondent for the same magazine, he toured the Mississippi Valley, contributing a series of descriptive articles which appeared almost consecutively from Apr. 29 to Dec. 9. Five months of the year 1871 he spent at Geneva, Switzerland, reporting the proceedings of the high court of arbitration then settling the *Alabama* claims. On Nov. 25, 1873, he sailed from New York to Cuba as special correspondent for the *New York Tribune,* and a number of his articles on the situation in the island appeared in that newspaper. On the night of Dec. 17, he either fell or was thrown overboard from the boat on which he was traveling from Santiago to Havana on his return to New York.

[Sources include: W. D. Howells, "Ralph Keeler," *Atlantic Monthly*, Mar. 1874, and "Some Literary Memories of Cambridge," *Harper's Mag.*, Nov. 1900; *Mark Twain's Autobiog.* (1924), vol. I; A. B. Paine, *Mark Twain, A Biog.* (1912), vol. I; W. D. Howells, *My Mark Twain* (1910); *Life and Letters of Wm. Dean Howells* (2 vols., 1928), ed. by Mildred Howells; Ferris Greenslet, *Thos. Bailey Aldrich* (1908); Keeler's autobiographical magazine articles, the *N. Y. Tribune* (semi-weekly), Dec. 30, 1873, Jan. 2, 1874, Jan. 9, 1874; and information as to certain facts from a nephew of Keeler.]

J. M. P—l.

KEELEY, LESLIE E. (1832–Feb. 21, 1900), physician, who exploited commercially an institutional cure of chronic alcoholism and drug addiction, was born in St. Lawrence County, N. Y. He took a degree in medicine at Rush Medical College, Chicago, in 1864, then joined the army as acting assistant surgeon, serving until the close of the Civil War. After the war he settled in Dwight, Ill., where for many years he practised medicine along conventional lines. He claims to have begun his treatment of alcoholism and drug addiction in 1879. In the following year he published a small pamphlet on the opium habit and its treatment. Little was heard from him until he brought out in 1890 a pamphlet entitled *A Popular Treatise on Drunkenness and the Opium Habit, and Their Successful Treatment with the Double Chloride of Gold, the Only Cure.* At the same time he opened his original sanitarium at Dwight and after temporary suspension reopened it as the Leslie E. Keeley Company. There was a rapid extension of branches throughout the United States and in some foreign countries. Keeley retained a half interest in the enterprise and accumulated over a million dollars in less than ten years. In 1895 he claimed a total of 250,000 cures. By that year there had been organized 359 chapters of the Keeley League with a total of 30,000 members. All of the men members were cured patients but in the women's auxiliary leagues many of the members were temperance workers.

In 1891 the Keeley Company began the publication of a weekly paper, the *Banner of Gold.* Despite its charlatanistic aspects, the Keeley movement received the sanction of the church and temperance workers and was used in soldiers' homes, in one or more of the army posts, and among the Indians of the reservations. Keeley never sought to antagonize his profession and employed only regular graduate physicians. The cost of treatment was not exorbitant —twenty-five dollars a week with a minimum period of treatment of four weeks. Patients had rooms but were required to board out. They had free access to the best brands of liquors, but they "lost all desire after two days of treatment." Keeley attributed his success wholly to the hypodermic injections given, which were chiefly of the double chloride of gold, and denied that suggestion played a rôle, alleging that only five per cent. of his cures were followed by relapse. He published several pamphlets upholding the view that drunkenness is a disease and not a vice. His sole major work, *The Non-Heredity of Inebriety,* appeared in 1896. The medical profession objected to his commercial methods and denied that the good results were due to gold, ascribing them in the main to suggestion. The sudden disrelish of the patient for his whiskey was attributed to injections of apomorphin and to injections of strychnia and other alkaloids. Relapses were said to be frequent. Toward 1900 Keeley's health failed and he moved to Los Angeles where he died of heart disease. At the time of his death he was under the care of mental-treatment cultists—a fact which points to his belief in suggestion. The Keeley institutes flourished after his death but suffered a decline, attributable probably to the fact that sanitarium treatment could give the same results without the disagreeable publicity of a Keeley cure.

[*The Keeley Insts. of the U. S., Canada, and Other Countries* (1896); *Report of the Keeley League, Second Gen. Convention,* 1892; *Medic. Record,* Mar. 3, 1900; *Los Angeles Times, N. Y. Times,* Feb. 22, 1900.]

E. P.

KEELY, JOHN ERNST WORRELL (Sept. 3, 1827–Nov. 18, 1898), inventor and impostor, grew up in Philadelphia, Pa., where his career was run. Both his parents died while he was an infant and he is not known to have had any schooling after the age of twelve. He had been for a time leader of a small orchestra and in certain more or less apocryphal stories he figured as a circus performer. In 1872 he was a journeyman carpenter, but in the following year, when he announced the discovery of a new physical force, he seems to have ceased that occupation for the rest of his days, and for a quarter of a century he was a public character, maintained by the contributions of those who believed in the future of the inventions based on his discovery. The supposed new force was explained by Keely as resulting from the intermolecular vibrations of ether. His problem was to construct a machine to respond to the vibrations and in that way produce power. In 1874 he had advanced far enough in the fabrication of such a machine, or engine, to permit exhibitions at his workshop. Such results as he could show amazed the general public, but physicists and engineers declared that the same results could be obtained by employing known forces, and until Keely would prove the exclusion of such known forces from his experiments they would refuse to believe in his discovery. Nevertheless, the Keely Motor Company was incorporated and the stock was taken in large amounts throughout the country.

As time passed without the perfection of Keely's motor or the securing of patents, the stockholders grew impatient and by 1880 payments to the inventor virtually ceased and the bills he had incurred remained unpaid. When bankruptcy was facing him a wealthy Philadelphia woman, Mrs. Clara S. J. Bloomfield-Moore, came to the rescue and financed his operations for many years. Meanwhile the Keely Motor Company brought suit to compel a disclosure of the secret and Keely's refusal to answer questions led to his imprisonment for contempt of court. A compromise was reached, however, without the divulging of the secret, and Keely was released. In 1887 experiments were conducted for the United States government at Fort Lafayette. The Keely Motor Company retained its faith in the inventor and continued to market stocks.

In 1895 Professor Lascelles-Scott, the English physicist, spent a month in Philadelphia for the purpose of investigating Keely's work, at the request of Mrs. Bloomfield-Moore. His report was never published, but after his return to London Keely's patroness withdrew her assistance. Keely was now an old man, afflicted with Bright's disease. At his death, on Nov. 18, 1898, the Keely Motor Company had more than 3,000 shareholders. In their interest the company's officers arranged with the widow, Anna M. Keely, to have a thorough examination made of all the apparatus left in Keely's workshop. The ensuing investigation, friendly in motive, resulted in the uncovering of tubes in the form of hollow wires by which compressed air had been applied to the machinery claimed to have been operated by the mysterious new force. In some instances compressed air had been used to start clockwork, but more generally hydraulic power, derived from a water motor. The exposure was complete and unanswerable. A Philadelphia newspaper suggested that the "motor" be exhibited to the public, but no one had the heart to act on the suggestion. Keely's secret was out at last. But nothing short of his death kept the public from trusting him.

[E. A. Scott, "The Keely Motor," *Proc. Engineers' Club of Phila.*, vol. XIV (1897); Julius Moritzen, "The Extraordinary Story of John Worrell Keely," *Cosmopolitan Mag.*, Apr. 1899; Chas. Fort, *Wild Talents* (1932); *Appletons' Ann. Cyc.*, 1887, 1898; *Pub. Ledger* (Phila.), Nov. 19, 1898, and editorial, Jan. 30, 1899; Clara S. J. Bloomfield-Moore, *Keely and His Discoveries* (1893), and articles supporting Keely's claims in *Lippincott's Mag.*, July 1890, Dec. 1892, and in the *New Sci. Rev.*, July 1894, Apr., July, Oct. 1895, Jan. 1896.]

W. B. S.

KEEN, MORRIS LONGSTRETH (May 24, 1820–Nov. 2, 1883), inventor, was born in Philadelphia, Pa., the son of Joseph Swift and Ann (Longstreth) Keen. He was descended from Jöran Kyn, a soldier who accompanied Gov. Johann Printz from Sweden to the Swedish colony on the Delaware River near Chester, Pa., in 1643. Keen received his early education in private schools in Philadelphia and subsequently entered the shops of the Norris Locomotive Works there as an apprentice machinist. He also learned pattern making and iron foundry work, and shortly after he completed his apprenticeship he organized with his brother Joseph a manufacturing business, specializing in the making of flat-irons. The design of these irons was based upon an invention which Keen patented in the early fifties.

More interested in the development of new ideas than in business, he turned his attention toward improvements in paper manufacture. Many attempts to produce a pulp out of the softer kinds of wood had been made and many patents had been issued for such processes, both in Europe and in America. It was not until 1854, however, that a practicable chemical wood-pulp patent was secured by Watt and Burgess of London. The process, in a crude form, was the soda pulp process still extensively used. For three or four years Keen conducted experiments in the design of wood-pulp boilers. He continued this work at Royers' Ford, outside of Philadelphia, where Hugh Burgess, one of the co-patentees of the soda process in London, settled in 1855. By 1858 Keen had advanced with his experiments so far that he believed he possessed improvements over the Watt and Burgess basic invention, and after securing the financial aid of William F. Ladd he obtained an assignment of the Watt and Burgess patent. With the American rights to this basic patent he then continued his experimental work and on Sept. 13, 1859, secured his first paper-making patent, on a boiler for making paper pulp from poplar wood. Burgess then joined Keen, and the two began to make wood-pulp paper at Royer's Ford. In 1863 they formed the American Wood Paper Company at Manayunk, Pa., near Philadelphia, and in the succeeding years produced a considerable quantity of pulp. In 1863 also Keen obtained an improvement on his pulp boiler, and in 1865 he was granted with Burgess a joint patent for an apparatus to evaporate and calcine alkaline solutions. About 1870 Keen transferred his work to Jersey City, N. J. There between 1870 and 1873 he secured three patents on the manufacture of paper stock, which were assigned to Samuel A. Walsh of Jersey City. Subsequently, Keen went to Stroudsburg, Pa., and on a site between Stroudsburg and the Delaware Water Gap established what he called "The Experiment Mills." Here he continued his research work in paper manufacture and obtained several additional patents. One of these, a reissue on the process and apparatus for evaporating and calcining alkaline solutions, was granted Jan. 30, 1877, and assigned to the American Wood Paper Company. His last patent on paper making, No. 240,318, was obtained Apr. 19, 1881, two years before his death. He died at "Highland Grove" near Stroudsburg, Pa., and was buried there. He was unmarried.

[E. H. Knight, *Knight's Am. Mech. Dict.*, vol. III (1876); *Pa. Mag. of Hist. and Biog.*, vol. VI, no. 1 (1882); G. B. Keen, *The Descendants of Jöran Kyn of New Sweden* (1913); E. W. Byrn, *Progress of Am. Invention* (1895); C. M. Depew, *One Hundred Years of American Commerce* (1895), vol. I; *Paper Trade Jour.*, Dec. 1, 1883; *Pub. Ledger* (Phila.), Nov. 3, 1883; Patent Office records.] C. W. M.

KEENAN, JAMES FRANCIS (Apr. 8, 1858–Feb. 24, 1929), actor, better known as Frank Keenan, was born in Dubuque, Iowa, a son of Owen Keenan, an Irish immigrant, and his wife, born Frances Kelly in Maine. His father failed in business in Dubuque, removed to Boston, where he worked for three years as a bookkeeper, then bought a farm in Iowa, where Frank first tried to plow at the age of eleven. His father took over a large railroad grading contract, but through the absconding of an official, he again faced bankruptcy and once more returned to Boston. Here Frank had a piecemeal schooling, interspersed with periods of work. He was sent out as a traveling salesman at the age of seventeen and two years later set up his own cigar store, but this was not successful. He had joined the Young Men's Catholic Association of Boston College and the McCullough & Kean Dramatic Association and was more interested in the latter than in business. The manager of a small professional stock company saw him act one evening and made him an offer, with the result that Keenan made his professional début with that company as Archibald Carlyle in *East Lynne* at Richmond, Me., in 1880. The company soon disbanded, and Keenan then spent some time playing various rôles with the Boston Museum Stock Company. After several years of ups and downs, he gained valuable experience under James A. Herne and made his first noteworthy success in Herne's *Hearts of Oak*. He played leads in *McKenna's Flirtations, A Texas Steer,* and many other comedies in the eighties and nineties, and succeeded Sol Smith Russell in the leading rôles in *A Poor Relation, Peaceful Valley,* and *The Honorable John Grigsby*. He played Garretson in *The Capitol* in 1895, and when *The Christian* was produced in 1898, he staged the mob scene and played the part of Brother Paul, later taking over the male lead, John Storm. He devoted considerable time to directing about this period, staging *The King's Musketeers, Such a Little Queen,* and other productions. Early in 1905 he experimented with the Parisian idea of three one-act plays in one evening, but the novelty did not seem to appeal to American audiences.

Keenan's rugged, deeply lined face as he reached middle life lent itself particularly well to character parts, and of these he played a great number and variety. He was tremendously successful as Jack Rance, the gambler, in Belasco's notable play, *The Girl of the Golden West,* opening in 1905, and as General Warren in *The Warrens of Virginia,* 1907. He appeared in *On the Eve,* 1909; in *The Heights,* 1910, and as Cassius with Faversham in *Julius Caesar,* 1912. In 1914 he was cast for the leading part in *Yosemite,* and in 1920–21 he played the title rôle in St. John Ervine's *John Ferguson,* which opened in Chicago. Afterward he toured the country with it. He was particularly popular as a "road star," being known in every town of consequence between the two oceans. He played the lead in *Rip Van Winkle* in San Francisco in 1921, and in *Peter Weston,* opening in New York in 1923. But meanwhile the multiple-reel motion pictures had come into being and in 1915 Keenan was attracted to the films, his first appearance being in the part of a Southern gentleman in a Civil War drama, *The Coward.* During the last thirteen years of his life he devoted most of his time to motion pictures, with occasional incursions into vaudeville and brief returns to the legitimate stage. His first wife, Katherine Agnes Long, of St. John, New Brunswick, was an actress in the Boston Museum Stock Company in Keenan's youth, and he married her while they were playing together there. Of the two daughters born of this union, one married the comedian, Ed Wynn. Keenan's second wife was Margaret White, from whom he was divorced in 1927; his third was Leah May, who survived him.

[*Who's Who in America,* 1926–27; *Who's Who in the Theatre,* 1925; the Keenan scrap book in the Robinson Locke dramatic collection, N. Y. Pub. Lib.; Frank Keenan, "My Beginnings," in the *Theatre,* Mar. 1908; T. A. Brown, *A Hist. of the N. Y. Stage* (1903), vols. II and III; interviews in *Motion Picture Classic,* Aug. 1919, the *Theatre,* Dec. 1914, and the *N. Y. Dramatic Mirror,* Nov. 30, 1910; numerous other articles and comments on his plays in the *Dramatic Mirror* and newspapers; obituary notices in the *Boston Herald, Los Angeles Times,* and *N. Y. Times,* Feb. 25, 1929.]

A. F. H.

KEENE, JAMES ROBERT (1838–Jan. 3, 1913), speculator and turfman, was born at Chester, near Liverpool, England. Little is known of his parentage. He once described his father as an "Irish gentleman." The boy had good opportunities in English schools, but when about fourteen he accompanied his father to America. They lived for a short time at Lynchburg, Va., but early in the fifties they both set out for California. In Shasta County James engaged in a variety of occupations—selling milk, teaching school, studying law, editing newspapers, caring for horses, working in a mill, mining, freighting, and stock-raising. After the Civil War the discovery of the Comstock silver lode in Nevada gave him an opportunity for speculation from which he quickly realized $10,000. With that capital he began a career as stock manipulator on the San Francisco Exchange which lasted ten years and involved the winning and losing of fortunes. At first he was only a street broker handling the orders of active speculators. In 1869 Charles N. Felton, assistant treasurer of the United States, made him a loan and within a year Keene repaid the loan and cleared $400,000 on the market. At the height of his success he married Sara Jay Daingerfield, sister of Judge William P. Daingerfield, of an old Virginia family. Within a few months he lost by speculation all that he had won and even his household goods were attached for debt. But bold and skilful trading in Nevada mining stocks soon retrieved his losses. Within five years he was reputed to be worth $5,000,000. In 1875 he was made president of the Stock and Exchange Board and in the same year had a part in rehabilitating the Bank of California after the suicide of its president.

In 1876 Keene crossed the continent from San Francisco with a voyage to Europe in prospect. He stopped in New York and became greatly interested in Wall Street and its mechanism—particularly in the operations of Jay Gould. When he joined Gould in a pool formed with the avowed purpose of putting down Western Union stock, Gould unscrupulously sold him out. Keene found that Wall Street was not so easily controlled as the San Francisco market, but the challenge only put him on his mettle. In other pools that he formed he was successful. At the top of the wild speculation that set in during 1879 Keene's profits may have reached $9,000,000. But in corn and wheat trading he did not fare so well. After a few years of prosperity he over-extended his credits and bought recklessly. The climax was reached in 1884 when Keene tried to manipulate wheat, pushing the price up to $1.30 a bushel. Here he overplayed and when it fell to $.90 his failure was announced. Recovery from this defeat was long-delayed. Keene tasted poverty for the second time since his early days of affluence. Trading in National Cordage, sugar, and tobacco at last put him on his feet again. In the early nineties he engineered movements in sugar stock for the Havemeyers and his share of the profits was estimated at $4,500,000. In 1901, when the new issue of the United States Steel Company's stock had to be marketed, Pierpont Morgan, Sr., was willing to put the undertaking in Keene's hands. J. J. Hill and the Great Northern interests also employed Keene to buy $15,000,000 of Northern Pacific stock to insure control against Harriman.

All his life Keene had been a lover of horses. Soon after going to New York he began to buy thoroughbreds. In 1881 his horse Foxhall won the Grand Prix at Paris. Thereafter for more than a quarter of a century Keene's horses won many of the most famous sweepstakes in England, France, and America. Domino, Cap-and-Bell, and Sysonby were among his favorites. For the ten years from 1898 his total turf winnings were believed to exceed $2,000,000. At his death, in 1913, he was again a millionaire.

[Edwin Le Fevre, "James R. Keene, Manipulator of Stocks," *World's Work,* July 1901; M. M. Reynolds, "The Hocking Pool and James R. Keene," *Moody's Mag.,* Feb. 1910; J. L. King, *Hist. of the San Francisco Stock and Exchange Board* (1910); Henry Clews, *Fifty Years in Wall Street* (1915); E. J. Dies, *The Plunger* (1929); *Blackwood's Edinburgh Mag.,* July 1844; C. A. Collman, *Our Mysterious Panics* (1931); R. I. Warshaw, *The Story of Wall Street* (1929); Geo. Kennan, *E. H. Harriman: A Biog.* (1922), vol. I; the *Sun* (N. Y.), Jan. 3, 1913; *N. Y. Times,* Jan. 4, 1913; *Argonaut* (San Francisco), Jan. 18, 1913; F. G. Griswold, *Race Horses and Racing* (1925); W. S. Vosburgh, *Racing in America* (1922); C. E. Trevathan, *The Am. Thoroughbred* (1905); O'Niel Sevier, "The Race-Horse of 1905," *Munsey's Mag.,* Nov. 1905.]

W. B. S.

KEENE, LAURA (*c.* 1826–Nov. 4, 1873), actress, has suffered an unmerited oblivion. The date of her birth in England is uncertain; her real name is unknown. Her family seems to have been of high respectability and considerable culture, for she was widely read. In her youth she had some connection with the world of art; as a child she had haunted Turner's studio. Throughout her career she used a trained pictorial sense in dramatic production. Rachel's voice, floating through the windows of a theatre, stirred her ambition to become an actress, and she joined the company of the great light *comédienne* and manager of the time, Madame Vestris, from whom she acquired a rich taste in stage production. In 1852, at the invitation of James W. Wallack, she came to New York as leading lady at his new theatre, where she achieved a brilliant success. She was beautiful, with chestnut hair and eyes, an exquisite pallor, and a fine carriage. Slight and graceful, she had "the water-color touch," and did not so much draw details of character and action as suggest them. She could play Rosalind with spirit and delicacy, a milkmaid with lusty vigor.

In 1853, at the apex of her fame, she left Wallack's without notice and went to Baltimore for a brief period of management at the Charles Street Theatre. In the spring of 1854 she went to San Francisco, where she became a star at the Metropolitan Theatre under the gifted Catherine Sinclair. Within a few months she left for Australia as abruptly as she had left Wallack's. Her tour, partly with young Edwin Booth, proved unsuccessful. Undaunted, she returned to San Francisco and began a highly original interlude of management at the Union and later at the American Theatre, gathering about her the most vivid talent in the region and wiping out the poor impression she had made by her sudden departure. Comedy had had a great vogue among the mining audiences, and the time was ripe for her adventure into extravaganza, a novelty there as elsewhere in the country. Her productions of the gay, wild pieces always had a poetic turn. She gave a notable *Midsummer Night's Dream* among the Shakespearian productions. Returning to New York in 1855, she opened Laura Keene's Varieties and became doubly a pioneer, the first woman manager in New York of scope or power, and the first producer to give dignity and charm to the lighter side of the theatre. In 1856 she moved to Laura Keene's Theatre, built for her by Trimble, where for seven years she was both manager and leading actress, sustaining a high achievement against the odds of competition by many gifted comedians, including Wallack, and with the handicap in 1857 of the general panic. Young, talented actors like Jefferson and Sothern were drawn to her company, as were the experienced Boucicault and Blake.

As a manager Miss Keene was imperious; many amusing stories were told of her tiffs with actors. But her own humor was unfailing, her integrity unmistakable. She made costumes, painted scenery, could prompt any actor, and herself took the feminine leads, gaining an enthusiastic personal following. *Our American Cousin* was her most conspicuous success, but she had many others on the lighter side of comedy. She habitually encouraged American playwrights. Her position as a woman manager remained difficult; in 1863 she decided that it was considered "not quite respectable," and moreover that she was "ever sinking the actress in the manager." She relinquished her theatre, and thenceforward her career was broken. Perhaps she had made a wrong turning, but the form of comedy to which she was deeply attracted, extravaganza, had not yet come into vigorous growth; and social comedy, in which she played with unusual finish, had entered a dreary phase. The English plays had grown stale; American social comedy was not yet written.

She was next seen in the event which has given her a modicum of fame, playing in *Our American Cousin* at Ford's Theatre in Washington on the night when President Lincoln was assassinated. In 1869 she took the Chestnut Street Theatre in Philadelphia, but her materials were old and the venture was a failure. She became a wandering star, acting in forlorn small theatres in the West, keeping an irrepressible humor both on and off stage. She embarked upon the grandiose project of editing a magazine called the *Fine Arts,* and lost money. She wrote plays, lectured, and acted until the end. Overworked, she failed suddenly, dying Nov. 4, 1873. She had married John Taylor in England, to whom she had borne two daughters, but the marriage was unhappy. She had brought the children to America and later married John Lutz. Little is known of her personal life. The few faint glimpses reveal a distinguished and complex character.

[John Creahan, *The Life of Laura Keene* (1897); *The Autobiog. of Jos. Jefferson* (1890); Lester Wallack, *Memories of Fifty Years* (1889); C. T. Copeland, *Edwin Booth* (1901); T. A. Brown, *A Hist. of the N. Y. Stage* (3 vols., 1903); G. C. D. Odell, *Annals of the N. Y. Stage,* vols. VI and VII (1931); files of the *Alta California* and the Sacramento *Daily Union* in the Cal. State Lib.; clippings and programs in the Harvard Theatre Collection; files of the New York *Clipper*; programs and clippings in the Robinson Locke Collection in the N. Y. Pub. Lib.; *N. Y. Tribune,* Nov. 7, 1873.]

C. R.

KEENE, THOMAS WALLACE (Oct. 26, 1840–June 1, 1898), actor, whose real name was Thomas R. Eagleson, was born in New York City. He was the son of a journalist named Eagleson, who died while Thomas was a child. Like so many New York boys of the time, he attended the old Bowery Theatre and very early got a chance to appear in small parts, becoming a professional actor while still in his teens. His first important part, however, he recorded in later life, was with James Henry Hackett, who engaged him to come to Albany to play Henry IV in 1862. He studied the rôle on the train. He played Robert to John E. Owens' Solon Shingle, was juvenile at Wood's Theatre, made a tour of the West, and a trip to England, and in the early seventies supported, at various times, Booth, Charlotte Cushman, E. L. Davenport, and Clara Morris. In 1875 he was engaged for the famous California Theatre Stock Company in San Francisco, remaining with this organization five years, and greatly increasing his reputation, especially by his support of Booth when that actor played a long guest engagement with the company. In 1880 he returned to the East, acting Coupeau in *Drink* with much success in Boston, and then going to Chicago as a star. This experiment succeeded so well that he embarked on a tour of the country in a repertory which included Richard III (long his most popular rôle), Hamlet, Louis XI, Othello, Romeo, Richelieu, and occasionally other similar parts. This tour was annually repeated, and Keene prospered, though as time went on he was more welcome in the smaller cities than in the large centers, where he often played in popular-priced houses such as the Grand Opera House in Boston. Early in his career he married Margaret Creighton of New York, and later in life he bought an old tavern at Castleton Corners, Staten Island, where the family made their home, and where he was greatly beloved by his neighbors. In 1898, while on a tour of Canada, he was stricken with appendicitis, was brought home, and died.

Keene's pictures suggest a man oddly resembling, in face and figure, William Jennings Bryan, though his hair was curly and his nose more aquiline. His acting, certainly, was of the florid, robust school. A Boston critic spoke of his "full voiced, demonstrative tragedy." He himself often declared that what he called "the majestic method" was alone fitted to project tragic rôles. "Emotional stilts" was another term he used to describe his ideal. In 1895 he told an interviewer that every seven years a new generation of dramatic students grew up who wanted to hear him in Shakespeare, which explained the success of his tours. For modern plays, as for the modern method of acting them, he had little sympathy. But he was aware that his fame was not equal to that of Booth or Barrett, and it sometimes saddened him. Doubtless his skill was not so great as theirs, nor his methods so refined, but he lived on after their passing, into the era of Ibsen, Pinero, and Jones, and his popularity would have waned in the larger cities had he been a finer representative than he was of the old school. Among his professional workers, he was noted for his kindliness, and his private life was happy and blameless.

[T. A. Brown, *A Hist. of the N. Y. Stage* (1903), vols. I and III; *N. Y. Dramatic Mirror,* June 11, 1898; *N. Y. Clipper,* June 11, 1898; *N. Y. Times,* June 2, 1898; Theatre Collection Harvard Coll. Lib.; Robinson Locke Collection, N. Y. Pub. Lib.] W. P. E.

KEENER, WILLIAM ALBERT (Mar. 10, 1856–Apr. 22, 1913), lawyer, educator, author, the son of Henry and Isabella Keener, was born in Augusta, Ga. His parents died when he was very young and he was brought up in the home of a married sister. The public schools of Augusta gave him the preparation necessary to enter Emory College in Oxford, Ga. Matriculating at fourteen, he was a bachelor of arts with distinction at eighteen (1874). After working in a law office in Augusta for some months he entered the Harvard Law School. In 1877 he received the law degree, but he went on with a post-graduate course for another year. On July 16, 1878, he married Frances McLeod Smith of Somerville, Mass.

After a brief initiation into the practice of law in New York, 1879–83, he entered the profession of teaching and made in it a notable career for close upon twenty years. For five years he was an assistant professor of law at Harvard. In 1888 he was promoted to the distinguished Story Professorship. In 1890 he was appointed to a professorship of law in Columbia College as a preliminary step to his elevation to the deanship of the Columbia Law School in 1891. The next year he was further honored with the Kent Professorship of law. Aside from his classroom instruction and his authoritative lectures, he did much to reorganize the methods of teaching law along the newer lines of the case-system. His publications added measurably to his prestige and standing. Two volumes, *A Selection of Cases on the Law of Quasi-Contracts,* appeared in 1888 and 1889. In 1893 he published *A Treatise on the Law of Quasi-Contracts.* During the years from 1894 to 1896 he completed *A Selection of Cases on Equity Jurisdiction,* in three volumes; and in 1896, *Selections on the Elements of Jurisprudence.* In 1898 appeared *A Selection of Cases on the Law of Contracts,* in two volumes, and the next year, *A Selection of Cases on the Law of Private Corporations,* alsc in two volumes. The eminently scholarly, systematic, and exhaustive work done in the preparation of these standard volumes stands out conspicuously because at the time they were published modern case-book production was as yet in its early stages.

In the autumn of 1901, Keener gave up his office as dean, and the following year resigned his professorship to accept appointment to the supreme court of New York, to complete the unexpired term of Justice Beach, deceased. In the next election he was one of the unsuccessful candidates for the full term. Thus his career as a judge was brief and on the whole uneventful. He returned now to the private practice of law which he had left twenty years before and continued in it, with only inconspicuous success, through the remaining years of his life. He died in New York in 1913, survived by his wife and his son. At the time of his death he was a member of the American Bar Association and of various clubs.

[*N. Y. Herald,* and *Sun* (N. Y.), Apr. 23, 1913; *The Asso. of the Bar of the City of N. Y., Year Book,* 1914; *Who's Who in America,* 1912–13; information from personal acquaintances.] A. J. L.

KEEP, HENRY (June 22, 1818–July 30, 1869), financier, was born at Adams, Jefferson County, N. Y., the son of Heman Chandler and Dorothy (Kent) Keep. He was descended from John Keep who was living in Longmeadow, Mass., in 1660. Heman Keep died in 1835, leaving the family in such poverty that they sought shelter in the county poor house. Henry was bound out to a farmer, who in taking him agreed to send him to the public school, but the farmer did not carry out the agreement and in later life Keep used to boast that he "graduated at the poor house." Tiring of farm work and the harsh treatment which he received, he ran away from his master and eventually made his way to Honeoye Falls, near Rochester, N. Y., where he obtained employment as a teamster on the Erie Canal. He later became a hackman in Rochester. Having managed to save some money, he invested in depreciated currency during the financial crisis of 1837. With the return of normal monetary conditions he found his small capital nearly quadrupled by the appreciation of his holdings. His next speculation was concerned with Canadian bank notes, of which there were a considerable number in circulation on the American border. Since they were not legal tender in the United States, the holders were glad to dispose of them at a fair discount. He journeyed about buying all he could find, paying for them with state notes which were generally also at a discount, and then, as soon as he had accumulated enough to warrant the expense, went over to various towns in Canada and cashed the notes at par. This itinerant brokerage business was an innovation, and he made a good profit from it. After a time he accumulated enough capital to open an exchange and banking office at Watertown, New York. Here he met and married Emma A. Woodruff, by whom he had one child. He soon established several other country banks, and about 1850 the scope of his speculative operations became so great that he moved to New York and started operating in Wall Street. He became widely known as one of the boldest and most successful operators in railroad stocks, winning the nickname "William the Silent" because one of the strong points in his character as a financier was his reticence about everything relating to his investments. He dealt extensively in the stock of the Michigan Southern & Northern Indiana Railroad Company, commonly nicknamed "Old Southern," and served as treasurer of this company from 1861 to 1863. In 1866, in the face of considerable opposition, he was elected president of the New York Central Railroad, holding the position for six months, after which he resigned and Commodore Vanderbilt assumed control. At the time of his death he was president of the Chicago & Northwestern Railway, of which, with the aid of Rufus Hatch [*q.v.*], he had secured financial control. At this time he also controlled the Northern Indiana and Cleveland & Toledo railroads, serving as president of the latter. He was essentially a financier, not a railroad man in the true sense of the word, and his positions as a railroad executive were assumed purely for financial reasons. He is credited with having left an estate of over four million dollars, a remarkable achievement considering that he started without a cent and that his success was due entirely to his own unaided efforts. He died at his residence in New York City.

[F. E. Best, *John Keep of Longmeadow, Mass.* (1899); Henry Hall, *America's Successful Men of Affairs,* vol. I (1895); W. W. Fowler, *Ten Years in Wall St.* (1873); M. H. Smith, *Twenty Years among the Bulls and Bears of Wall St.* (1870); *N. Y. Herald,* July 31, 1869.] J. H. F.

KEEP, ROBERT PORTER (Apr. 26, 1844–June 3, 1904), educator, had a scholarly inheritance. He was born in Farmington, Conn., the son of Rev. John Robinson Keep, for more than a quarter of a century a teacher in the American Asylum for the Deaf and Dumb at Hartford. Robert's mother was Rebecca (Porter) Keep, daughter of Rev. Noah Porter of Farmington, and sister of President Noah Porter [*q.v.*] of Yale College. The Keeps were descended from John Keep who was settled in Longmeadow, Mass., in 1660. In 1852, Robert's family moved to Hartford, where the boy attended the public schools, later entering Yale College, from which he graduated in 1865. Although slow to mature, he was one of the leading scholars of his class. After post-graduate study in New Haven, he spent two years as teacher in the Post School for children of officers at the United States Military Academy, West Point. For the next two years he was tutor in Greek at Yale, where President Woolsey said, "I consider him to be one of the most faithful and upright young men I know." He received the degree of doctor of philosophy from Yale in 1869.

Keep was now appointed United States consul at the Piræus, the port of Athens, but resigned in 1871 and devoted the next three years to researches in Germany and Italy, living for some months in Berlin with Curtius, the historian of Greece. From 1876 to 1885 he taught Greek in Williston Seminary, Easthampton, Mass., and in July 1885 became principal of the Free Academy in Norwich, Conn., which under his direction developed into what Daniel Coit Gilman characterized as "an example of a true university of secondary education."

At Norwich, Keep broadened and enriched the curriculum by organizing a department of manual training; starting courses in book-binding, pottery, printing, and cooking; forming a valuable collection of plaster casts; establishing the Norwich Art School—which had in its day a national reputation; and creating the Norwich Normal School, which flourished for six years until the state provided a similar institution in the near-by city of Willimantic. He resigned, Dec. 19, 1902, after having been appointed by his aunt, Miss Sarah Porter, as trustee of Miss Porter's School for Girls, at Farmington; and a few months later he moved there to take charge of her estate. He died in Farmington at the age of sixty, after a brief illness from double pneumonia.

Keep was married on Dec. 23, 1879, to Margaret Vryling Haines, daughter of Richard Townley and Francina (Wilder) Haines of Elizabeth, N. J. They had three sons and one daughter, of whom one son and the daughter survived their father. After Mrs. Keep's death in 1893, he married, July 6, 1897, Elizabeth V. Hale of Elizabeth, N. J., who died Mar. 28, 1917.

Keep was slender, erect, and alert in his movements, with a rather austere expression except when he smiled. He had a wide variety of interests, including music and the visual arts. His forceful character, scrupulous integrity, and personal charm won him a wide and enduring influence among his pupils and friends. A careful and profound student of the Greek classics, he published in 1877 a translation of G. G. P. Autenrieth's *Homeric Dictionary for Schools and Colleges,* and edited *Stories from Herodotus* (1879). He was the author of *The Essential Uses of the Moods in Greek and Latin* (1879 and subsequent editions) and *Greek Lessons* (1885), as well as of numerous articles on educational topics.

[F. E. Best, *John Keep of Longmeadow, Mass.* (1899); *Obit. Record Grads. Yale Univ.,* 1904; *Hartford Daily Courant,* June 4, 1904; information as to certain facts from Ella A. Fanning, Norwich, Conn., and Keep's son, Robert Porter Keep, Farmington, Conn., who also allowed the use of unpublished letters.]

C. M. F.

KEHEW, MARY MORTON KIMBALL (Sept. 8, 1859–Feb. 13, 1918), leader in constructive social movements, especially for women in industry, was the daughter of a Boston merchant and banker, Moses Day Kimball, and his wife, Susan Tillinghast Morton, whose father was Gov. Marcus Morton [*q.v.*] of Massachusetts. Educated in private schools and abroad, she early devoted herself to the practical study of social science. On Jan. 8, 1880, she married William B. Kehew, a Boston manufacturer who, though not himself active in public life, supported her in her interest in the progressive movements to which she largely devoted her private fortune. She is best known as the moving spirit of the Women's Educational and Industrial Union during the quarter-century 1892–1918 and served as its third president. As early as 1886 she was active in the affairs of the Union, and in 1892, while yet trades-unionism for men was an economic heresy, she saw the need of organizing women in industry. Securing the services of a young Chicago bookbinder, Mary Kenney, afterward Mrs. O'Sullivan, as missionary to the factories, she drew working-girls into friendly gatherings where the doctrine of unionism could be preached. When the need for protection for women workers became pressing, and there were no facts on which to base reform measures, she organized at the Union the research department for the training of women capable of securing adequate industrial data which could be used for securing legislative action. This department furnished the basis for the creation of the Massachusetts Department of Labor and Industry and served as a model for courses and methods in universities and women's colleges. Mrs. Kehew was a pioneer in laboratory methods of teaching as exemplified in every department of the Educational and Industrial Union. She fostered its appointment bureau, which was the prototype of seven other bureaus of occupation for trained women, and she promoted the trade school for girls and the school of salesmanship. In 1903 she was elected first president of the National Women's Trades Union League.

In Massachusetts Mrs. Kehew was active in establishing the state branch of the Association for Labor Legislation, was one of the founders of Denison House, and of the Public School Association, a member of the State Commission for Industrial Education, and a member of the executive committee of the Massachusetts Child Labor Commission. She did much toward founding organizations for infant welfare, including day nurseries. In the field of higher education she lent her support to the establishment and growth of Simmons College. Her service to the blind was also important. Out of a committee which she formed at the Union there developed, in 1903, the Massachusetts Association for Promoting the Interest of the Adult Blind. Three years later the state took over the work of the organization. She then turned to the promotion of a Loan and Aid Association for the Blind, the founding of Woolson House, a settlement for blind women, and the establishment of a magazine devoted to the interests of the sightless, *The Outlook for the Blind.* Mrs. Kehew was a woman of creative originality and was also a born administrator. Her plans for the Union, broadly grounded, remained sound and workable after her death.

[Sources include an unpublished memorial in the possession of the Women's Industrial and Educational Union; L. A. Morrison and S. P. Sharples, *Hist. of the Kimball Family in America* (1897), I, 27–28, 511–12; *Life and Labor,* Apr. 1918; *Boston Transcript,* Feb. 13, 1918, editorial and obituary.] M. B. H.

KEIMER, SAMUEL (Feb. 11, 1688–*c.* 1739), printer, was born in St. Thomas' parish, Southwark, London. He was admitted Sept. 11, 1699, to Merchant Taylors' School and was later apprenticed to Robert Tookey, printer, of Christopher's Court, Threadneedle St. In 1707, with his mother and sister Mary, he joined the French Prophets, a small, noisy sect of cataleptics, exhibitionists, and their dupes, led by Sir Richard Bulkeley and John Lacy [*qq.v.* in the *Dictionary of National Biography*]. He married and opened a printing office in 1713 but went bankrupt in 1715 and was committed to the Fleet for an unknown period. In 1717 he spent fifteen weeks in the Gatehouse for some objectionable matter in the *Weekly Journal,* of which he was the printer. He now turned author with *A Brand Pluck'd from the Burning: Exemplify'd in the Unparallel'd Case of Samuel Keimer* (1718), a lachrymose exposure of the French Prophets, somewhat in the manner of Daniel Defoe, for whom Keimer had done printing. *The Platonick Courtship* (1718) narrates in doggerel the wooing of a "virgin soul" by personifications of thirteen sects, denominations, and religions. The author designated himself on the title-page as Keimer Samuel and explained in the preface that he did so for conscience' sake, Keimer being the first name given him by his parents. *A Search after Religion among the Many Modern Pretenders to It* (1718), listed in the *British Museum Catalogue,* is on the same subject and may be the same book. Although he cherished a certain affinity for Quakers, Keimer's own religious observances consisted solely of wearing his beard untrimmed (eventually it attained a prodigious length) and of keeping the Sabbath instead of Sunday. Set at large in 1721, he deserted his wife and embarked for Pennsylvania.

On his arrival at Philadelphia in February 1722, he advertised in Andrew Bradford's *American Weekly Mercury* that he was willing to teach male negroes to read the Holy Scriptures without charge to their masters. In the summer of 1723 he obtained a font of worn type and a broken press and set up as a printer with Benjamin Franklin as his factotum. Keimer's first Philadelphia imprint was his own *Elegy on the Much Lamented Death of the Ingenious and Well-Beloved Aquila Rose* (1723), which Franklin saw him compose in a double sense. On Sept. 29, 1723, the Philadelphia Monthly Meeting of Friends disowned him for publishing a *Parable* (1723), in which Keimer, probably with some aid from Franklin, attempted to counterfeit the language of Friends. A little later, however, the Friends gave him the contract to print an edition of Sewel's *History of the People called Quakers* and advanced him some money. Keimer sent to London for paper and equipment and filled his house with five incompetent and superfluous apprentices. Franklin, returning from London, worked for him again, enabling him among other things to print some paper money (1727 or 1728) for the province of West Jersey. Keimer also got out a spurious edition of Jacob Taylor's Almanac for 1726 and in the following year had some trouble with William Bradford [*q.v.*] over an edition of Titan Leeds' Almanac. Getting wind of Franklin's proposal to start a magazine, he published Dec. 24, 1728, the first number of the *Universal Instructor in all Arts and Sciences and Pennsylvania Gazette,* which he disposed of to Franklin and Meredith after its thirty-ninth issue, Sept. 25, 1729. By this time the double competition of Franklin and of Andrew Bradford had reduced him to bankruptcy. He went to Bridgetown, Barbados, worked at his trade, and in 1731 started the *Barbados Gazette,* the first newspaper in the Caribbean, which he conducted in spite of many difficulties until the end of 1738. He is supposed to have died about this time. Keimer was a negligible person, maundering, frowzy, and incompetent, half fool, half knave, and wholly pitiable; but the racy account of him in Franklin's *Autobiography* has kept his memory alive.

[C. J. Robinson, *Reg. of the Scholars Admitted into Merchant Taylors' School, 1562–1874*, vol. I (1882); J. F. Fisher, "Some Account of the Early Poets and Poetry of Pa.," *Memoirs Hist. Soc. Pa.*, II, ii (1830), 61–65; Nathan Kite, "Antiquarian Researches among the Early Printers and Publishers of Friends' Books," *The Friend*, XVII (Seventh-Day, Eleventh Month 4, 1843), 44–45; Isaiah Thomas, *Hist. of Printing in America* (rev. ed., 1874); C. R. Hildeburn, *A Century of Printing: The Issues of the Press in Pa., 1685–1784* (2 vols., 1885–86); H. R. Tedder, article on Keimer, *Dict. Nat. Biog.*, vol. XXX (1892); Stephen Bloore, "Samuel Keimer," *Pa. Mag. Hist. and Biog.*, July 1930; Thomas Wright, *The Life of Daniel Defoe* (bicentenary ed., London, 1931); James Crossley, *Notes and Queries*, Oct. 11, 1851, p. 283. The elegy on Aquila Rose is reprinted in Samuel Hazard, *Reg. of Pa.*, Nov. 1828, and in E. A. and G. L. Duyckinck, *Cyc. of Am. Lit.* (rev. ed., 1875), vol. I.] G. H. G.

KEITH, BENJAMIN FRANKLIN (Jan. 26, 1846–Mar. 26, 1914), theatre owner and theatrical manager, was born at Hillsboro Bridge, N. H., the youngest of the eight children of Samuel C. and Rhoda (Gerould) Keith. His father was of Scotch descent, his mother of French extraction. At seven he began to work on a Western Massachusetts farm. Here he remained eleven years attending the district school and the village academy during the winter months. At seventeen he was greatly attracted by a country circus which he attended and soon thereafter he removed to New York, obtaining employment with Bunnell's Museum. He next became connected with P. T. Barnum and later with the Forepaugh circus. He continued in the circus business, both as employer and proprietor, until 1885. In the meantime, however, he added to his theatrical experience by taking small shows on the road, "on three consecutive occasions returning home with his finances completely exhausted." His career as a vaudeville proprietor and promoter began in 1883, when in partnership with Col. William Austin he opened a popular-priced show in Boston. In this venture he was successful. As part owner of the Gaiety Theatre, Boston, he began the first "continuous performance" shows in America. He conceived the idea of operating a chain of popular-priced vaudeville theatres throughout the country which would furnish refined entertainment to the public and at the same time raise the standard of vaudeville from the coarse and vulgar type which had characterized this form of public amusement in America for many years. He induced stars from the legitimate stage to appear in vaudeville and during his years as a manager the salaries of performers increased tremendously. The number of theatres under his control grew rapidly and he was enabled to concentrate his organization into the Keith's Circuit, and later the United Booking Offices, with headquarters in New York. In 1906 he joined with F. F. Proctor in organizing the Keith & Proctor Amusement Company, which became almost a synonym for American vaudeville. At the time of his death in 1914 it was estimated that about four hundred theatres bore his name.

Toward the end of his career he associated with himself in his business his general manager, E. F. Albee, and his only son. During the last five years of his life owing partly to ill health he withdrew from active participation in his theatrical ventures, and at the time of his death at Palm Beach, Fla., his business affairs were given over to his son to whom he willed his entire estate. He was twice married. His first wife was Mary Catherine Branley, daughter of Charles Branley of Providence, R. I., whom he married in 1873. She died in 1910, leaving one son, Andrew Paul Keith. He married again on Oct. 29, 1913, Ethel Bird Chase, daughter of Plympton B. Chase of Akron, Ohio, and Washington, D. C. He maintained his residence in Brookline, Mass., where he was an active patron of the art and musical institutions in the neighboring city of Boston.

[*Who's Who in America*, 1912–13; *The Green Room Book*, 1909; *N. Y. Dramatic Mirror*, Apr. 1, 1914; *Variety*, Apr. 3, 1914; *Billboard*, Apr. 4, 1914; the *Am. Mag.*, May 1914; S. L. Gerould, *The Geneal. of the Family of Gamaliel Gerould* (1885); *Boston Transcript, N. Y. Times*, Mar. 27, 1914.] A. M. S.

KEITH, GEORGE (*c.* 1638–Mar. 27, 1716), founder of the "Christian Quakers," schoolmaster, Anglican missionary, was born at Peterhead, Aberdeenshire, Scotland, about the year 1638, though the exact date cannot be determined. Only a short part of his life and his public career directly touches America, but that contact is of much importance in the history of American Quakerism. He was educated at Marischal College in Aberdeen and received the degree of Master of Arts at Aberdeen University in 1658. He was a scholar of marked ability, especially in mathematics and Oriental studies. He intended to enter the ministry of the Church of Scotland but became a convinced Quaker under the ministry of the Quaker apostle, William Dewsbury, in 1664. He quickly became one of the foremost interpreters of the central principles of the Quaker faith for which he suffered severe persecution, including a long imprisonment in the Tolboth. He exercised a profound influence on Robert Barclay, the author of the *Apology,* the first great interpretation of the faith of the Quakers. In his own line of interpretation Keith produced important books, the best of which are: *Immediate Revelation not Ceased* (1668) and *The Universall Free Grace of the Gospell Asserted* (1671). He married Elizabeth Johnston of Aberdeen and both he and his wife, who became a Quaker, traveled in 1677 with George Fox, William Penn, and Robert Barclay on a momentous missionary expedition through Holland and Germany. Shortly after his return from the Continent Keith established a boarding school in Middlesex. About 1685 he was appointed surveyor-general of New Jersey to run the boundary line between East and West Jersey (*Archives of the State of New Jersey,* 1 ser., vol. I, 1880, pp. 480, 571). In 1689 he settled in Philadelphia where he became head master of the famous school which William Penn was founding in that city, now called the William Penn Charter School.

Before going to America Keith had become influenced by the teaching of Francis Mercurius van Helmont and had become a mild advocate of the transmigration of souls. In one of his early publications in Philadelphia, *The Presbyterian . . . Churches in New England . . . Brought to the Test* (1689), he expressed sympathy with the use of the Lord's Supper as an agape, or love meal, as portrayed in the New Testament. He further denied the sufficiency of the inner Light and criticized the Philadelphia preachers for their tendency to slight the importance of the Christ of history. He also attempted to correct slackness in the administration of Quaker Discipline. After the death of Fox (1691) and Barclay (1690) Keith quite plainly aspired to be the recognized Quaker leader and authority. For these reasons, and owing to his somewhat contentious disposition, he came into sharp collision with the Quaker leaders in Pennsylvania, especially with Thomas Lloyd, the deputy-governor of the province, and with William Stockdale, a prominent Quaker preacher. The controversy became extremely bitter and ended in the formation of a separatist party known as the "Christian Quakers," popularly known as "Keithians." The defection was serious from the point of view of the main body of the Quakers, as it profoundly affected sixteen out of the thirty-two Meetings of Philadelphia Yearly Meeting. Earnest efforts were made for a reconciliation and when these efforts failed a vigorous declaration of disunity was issued against Keith by the Meeting of Ministers and Elders in Philadelphia, and the action was approved by Philadelphia Yearly Meeting held at Burlington, N. J., July 4–7, 1692. Three years later he was "disowned" by London Yearly Meeting, the complaint being his "unbearable temper and carriage" and because he refused to withdraw intemperate charges against Friends in Philadelphia.

Keith thereupon rented a hall in London where, while still wearing the Quaker garb, he preached and administered baptism and the Lord's Supper, issuing vigorous pamphlets against prominent Friends, especially against William Penn. (See *The Deism of William Penn and his Brethren,* 1699.) In 1700 he entered the Anglican Church and was ordained by the Bishop of London, preaching his first sermon at St. George's Church, May 12, 1700. He returned to America in 1702 as the agent of the Society for the Propagation of the Gospel in Foreign Parts. He did much to expand and establish the Episcopal Church in New Jersey and he spent two years traveling widely throughout the colonies, everywhere attacking the Quakers and drawing away many of their members to the Episcopal Church (*A Journal of Travels from New Hampshire to Caratuck,* 1706). One counter effect of the work of Keith was to push the Society of Friends in Philadelphia over to a much more positive formulation of orthodoxy. The "Keithians" gradually joined the Episcopal Church or in some cases drifted into the Baptist societies, or, as frequently happened, returned to their original home in the Society of Friends. Keith returned to England in 1704 and died in March 1716.

[Alexander Gordon's article in *The Dict. of Nat. Biog.* contains a fuller account of Keith's English career. See also: *Fasti Academiae Mariscallanae Aberdonensis,* vol. II (1898); George Fox, *Journal* (1901); William Sewel, *The Hist. of the . . . Quakers* (3rd ed., 1728); Robt. Barclay, *The Inner Life of the Religious Societies of the Commonwealth* (1876); Francis Bugg, *Pilgrim's Progress from Quakerism to Christianity* (1698); H. M. Lippincott, "The Keithian Separation," in *Bull. of Friends' Hist. Asso.,* Autumn Number, 1927; R. M. Jones, *The Quakers in the Am. Colonies* (1911); Jos. Smith, *A Descriptive Cat. of Friends' Books* (1867), II, 18–50; Minutes of the Society of Friends for Philadelphia Yearly Meeting and for London Yearly Meeting, covering the controversial period.]

R. M. J.

KEITH, JAMES (Sept. 7, 1839–Jan. 2, 1918), jurist, was born near Warrenton, Fauquier County, Va., of aristocratic Virginian stock, son of Isham and Juliet Chilton Keith. His early education, enriched by extensive reading under his mother's guidance, was acquired under private tutors, after which he studied law under Professor John B. Minor at the University of Virginia, and on July 31, 1860, he was admitted to the bar. The day before Virginia seceded he enlisted as a private in the Black Horse Troop (subsequently Company H, 4th Virginia Cavalry); from December 1863, served as adjutant of the regiment; and fought through the day of Lee's surrender. Always of large frame and striking appearance, in the army he developed from an inactive and delicate youth into a man of powerful bodily vigor. Resuming his legal studies, he soon formed a partnership with the celebrated cavalry leader, John S. Mosby, which continued until 1869 when Keith was elected to the state legislature. His abilities and character so impressed his colleagues that before the end of his first session the Assembly made him judge of the eleventh judicial circuit. He continued in this office, earning recognition as a competent and impartial jurist, disposing of a great mass of litigation, and winning the respectful confidence and esteem of the bar, until Jan. 1, 1895, when he became a member of the Virginia supreme court of appeals. Shortly before this he had performed valuable, if unheralded, service as unofficial member of the Olcott Committee, formed to settle the state debt. When the court organized, Keith was elected its president and so remained until he retired in June 1916. A year later he published his only volume, *Addresses on Several Occasions.*

During his long tenure in the appellate court Keith delivered the court's opinion in a surprisingly large number of cases, a summary of the most conspicuous of which opinions has been published (*Virginia Law Register,* January 1916, pp. 641–73). Independent in his legal convictions, he was fearless and strict in enforcing the law: while vigilant to guard and preserve the rights of the accused, he permitted neither technicalities nor sentiment to impede or defeat justice, recognizing that the pardoning power belongs to the executive and not to the judiciary. His vigorous mind possessed much of the same sound discretion in the application of theoretical principles that characterized his kinsman, John Marshall. His calm consideration of facts, patient hearing, and integrity of purpose combined with his mental gifts to make him, for almost fifty years, so positive and beneficial an influence upon the legal history of the commonwealth that a successor on the supreme bench commented not too extravagantly that "not one of the great Virginia judges that preceded him contributed more to the wealth of the jurisprudence of the state than did he" (Stafford G. Whittle, *Remarks,* etc., 1918). Keith married, first, in 1873, Lillias Gordon Morson, daughter of Arthur Alexander Morson, of Richmond. After her death he married, in 1887, her sister, Frances Barksdale Morson.

[Katherine I. Keith, "Jas. Keith of Fauquier," Fauquier Hist. Soc. *Bulletin,* June 1923; Sallie E. Marshall Hardy, "Some Virginia Lawyers of the Past and Present," the *Green Bag,* Apr. 1898; Eppa Hunton, Jr., "Judge Jas. Keith," *Report of the Twenty-ninth Ann. Meeting of the Va. State Bar Asso.,* 1918; *Richmond Times-Dispatch,* Jan. 3, 1918.] A. C. G., Jr.

KEITH, MINOR COOPER (Jan. 19, 1848–June 14, 1929), capitalist, railroad builder, and a founder of the United Fruit Company, was born in Brooklyn, N. Y., the son of Minor Hubbell Keith, a successful lumber merchant. His mother, Emily Meiggs, was a sister of Henry Meiggs [*q.v.*], who built the famous Callao, Lima & Oroya Railroad in Peru. The boy was educated in private schools until sixteen years of age, when he started to earn his own living at various employments. His real career began when in 1871 he went to help his elder brother, Henry, who through Meiggs had received a contract from the Costa Rican government to build a railroad from the Caribbean to San José. When Henry died in 1874, Minor Keith, then twenty-six years old, was left in charge of the undertaking. By 1882, against almost unbelievable difficulties, he carried construction to the Rio Sucio, seventy miles inland. He was obliged to spend the next three years in London to find financial backing to complete his road, Costa Rica having gone bankrupt and defaulted in her promised payments. With the aid of a loan of £1,200,000 he completed the line to San José in 1890.

Meanwhile, Keith had become completely identified with the country. In 1883 he married Cristina, daughter of José Mario Castro, former president of Costa Rica. Banana plantations, which he had set out near Limon in 1873 as an experiment, prospered and expanded so rapidly that by 1890 they surpassed his completed railroad in value and furnished most of its freight. While in London he organized the Tropical Trading & Transport Company to take over these banana interests, to provide transportation for the increasing shipments to the United States, and to manage the chain of stores which he had established up and down the coast, at which merchandise was traded for native products of the region. He also acquired control of the expanding banana plantations around Santa Marta, Colombia, by an arrangement with the Colombian Land Company. Soon a similar deal with the Snyder Banana Company of Panama gave him large interests there. By 1899 he dominated the banana business of Central America, and in that year he engineered a consolidation of his interests with those of his chief rival, the Boston Fruit Company—whose plantations were all in the West Indies—to form the United Fruit Company. He left the management of this powerful corporation in the hands of Andrew W. Preston, accepting only the vice-presidency, and turned to new interests.

As his banana developments had created an economic empire with its own peculiar civilization in the eastern lowlands of Central America, Keith now began a period of railroad building which was to influence the old Spanish civilizations of the plateaus as well. By 1908 he completed a railroad from Puerto Barrios on the Caribbean to Guatemala City, the United Fruit Company following his line in the Guatemalan lowlands with their banana plantations. His purchase of the Western Guatemala Railroad, between Guatemala City and the Pacific, gave him an inter-coastal system, and he increased the value of this by extending a branch which in 1911 reached the Mexican frontier and connected with Mexican lines. In 1912 he organized the International Railways of Central America, of which he remained president until 1928. This corporation took over his Guatemala lines and also a line in Salvador which he was building from the port of La Unión toward the capital, San Salvador. After surmounting innumerable political and financial complications he completed in 1929 a long and difficult connecting line between the Guatemalan and Salvador railroads, thus uniting a system totaling 800 miles in length and valued at $80,000,000. His dream of continuing the railroad south to the Panama Canal was interrupted only by his death. Keith had a great many other interests in the region and at his death was the best-known North American in Central America. He was more cordially welcomed than most North Americans because he was a creator, rather than an accumulator, of wealth. His estate at his death was valued at only $3,336,507. His unrivaled collection of Aztec gold images and ornaments and a large collection of Central American pottery were bequeathed to the American Museum of Natural History in New York.

[F. U. Adams, *Conquest of the Tropics* (1914), and Samuel Crowther, *The Romance and Rise of the Am. Tropics* (1929), are popular accounts of the United Fruit Company and its history, and each devotes a chapter to Keith. Additional facts may be found in W. R. Long, *Railways of Central America and the West Indies* (1925), U. S. Bureau of Foreign and Domestic Commerce, Trade Promotion Series, No. 5; Wallace Thompson, *Rainbow Countries of Central America* (1926); *Who's Who in America*, 1928–29; the *Pan-American Mag.*, June 1929; the *Nation*, July 3, 1929; obituaries in the *N. Y. Times* and *N. Y. Herald Tribune*, June 15, 1929. The same newspapers carry items on his will, June 15, 1929, and the appraisal of his estate, Mar. 27, 1930.] O. W. H.

KEITH, Sir WILLIAM (1680–Nov. 18, 1749), royal customs official in the colonies, governor of Pennsylvania and Delaware, traces his lineage to the eminent Scotch feudal family of Keith whose head was earl marischal to the Scotch king. More directly the future governor was one of the Keiths of Ludquhairn, descendants of Andrew Keith who received that estate in 1492 from his father, Sir Gilbert, lord of Inverugie. Keith was baptized Feb. 16, 1680, probably at Peterhead within the barony of Inverugie. His mother was Jean, daughter and heiress of Smith of Rapness, and his wife was Ann Newbury (or Newberry), widow of Robert Diggs. He succeeded to the baronetcy on the death of his father, Sir William, probably in 1720. He had spent his youth at the court of St. Germain where the exiled Stuarts lived under the patronage of Louis XIV, and he hoped to hold office in Scotland on the restoration of the Stuarts. Indeed he was implicated in an abortive Scotch plot to restore the Stuarts and was imprisoned on a charge of treason, but released in February 1704.

In 1714 he was appointed surveyor-general of customs for the southern colonies and during his short tenure of less than two years, he served the royal office well. During 1714–15 he inspected the customs service, making a tour first from Virginia to Pennsylvania, thence to Jamaica, and back to Carolina. Deprived of office, he visited Philadelphia, a fortunate turn for one dependent upon his wit and the pickings of public employment for support. The provincial leaders, displeased with the administration of Governor Gookin, saw in Keith a better man for the post. Armed with this support, Keith went to England to plead his case and returned as governor, bringing his wife, three sons, a step-daughter, and another son born at sea. He took oath of office May 31, 1717. His gracious manners and fine appearance pleased both parties: the Assembly as the representative of popular interests; the Council as the stronghold of proprietary concerns. It was a difficult rôle to play. Keith finally cast his lot with the Assembly, for the fortunes of the Penn family were at ebb tide and the Assembly strong in its control of the purse strings. As tribune of the people, Keith was masterly in his management of the Assembly, scornful of the Council and proprietary orders. Proprietary power exerted itself and Keith was dismissed from his post in 1726. Aspiring to continue as popular leader by plebiscite, he won a seat in the Assembly but failed to secure the speakership. In May 1728 he sailed quietly for England, resolved "speedily to return." His family remained; Keith never returned.

Keith's administration was not without merit. Whatever his motives, his espousal of popular interests harmonized with the liberal tendencies bedded in colonial life. He dealt fairly with the Indians and visited the Six Nations in New York in the interest of the province. Although a Churchman, he respected the Quaker principles on the affirmation. He encouraged the thrifty Germans to settle in the colony and assisted in founding a sound medium of paper currency to meet the expanding commercial needs of the province.

In London he was occasionally called to advise the Board of Trade on Indian Affairs, naval stores, and other items of colonial concern. He assisted in the negotiation of the notable treaty of 1730 made with a delegation of Cherokee Indians then in London. His famous "Report on the Progress of the French Nation," drafted in 1719, helped to focus the attention of English authorities on the dangers of French encirclement of the colonies. His "Discourse" of 1728 on colonial settlement, trade, and industry, although conceived in orthodox mercantilistic thought, displayed a good knowledge of the colonies and a vision imperialistic in scope. He proposed a stamp tax on the colonies by act of Parliament to maintain a standing army on the frontier and to support royal officials and indeed in various proposals on colonial affairs anticipated the British policy of 1763–65. In 1740 he published a *Collection of Papers and Other Tracts Written Occasionally on Various Subjects* embracing his reports on colonial matters. He eked out a precarious existence in London, for he was plagued with debt. He borrowed and failed to pay the interest. In 1734 the doors of Fleet Street Prison closed on him for debt. He died in the Old Bailey in November 1749.

[See C. P. Keith, "Sir William Keith," *Pa. Mag. of Hist. and Biog.*, Apr. 1888, for an account of Keith's genealogy. Other sources include the Penn Papers in the library of the Pa. Hist. Soc.; the Board of Trade Journals and the Papers, Plantations General (transcripts in the Library of the Pa. Hist. Soc.); Robert Proud, *The Hist. of Pa.* (2 vols., 1797–98); "Biographical Sketch of Sir William Keith," *Memoirs of the Hist. Soc. of Pa.*, vol. I (1826); *Gentleman's Mag.*, Nov. 1749; W. R. Shepherd, *Hist. of Proprietary Government in Pa.* (1896); H. L. Osgood, *The Am. Colonies in the Eighteenth Century* (1924), II, 330–36, 530–53; V. W. Crane, *The Southern Frontier* (1928); Gilbert Burnet, *Bishop Burnet's Hist. of His Own Time* (ed. 1823), V, 122–29.] W. T. R.

KEITH, WILLIAM (Nov. 21, 1839–Apr. 13, 1911), painter, engraver, was born in Old Meldrum, Aberdeenshire, Scotland, the son of William Keith and Elizabeth Bruce. On his father's side he is said to have descended from the earls marischal of Scotland. In his boyhood he emigrated to America with his parents and began his artistic career as an engraver for the Harper publications. In 1859 he went to California, becoming fascinated with the mountains, the Pacific, and the slopes to the sea. He first made sketches in black and white and then began to paint landscapes. He was employed for a time by the Northern Pacific Railroad to paint some of the characteristic scenes along its route. His pictures found ready sale and by 1869 he had saved enough money to go abroad for study, spending some time in Düsseldorf. He returned to California in 1871. For a period in the eighties he lived in New Orleans. In 1893 he studied in Munich and later visited Spain, where he became "enamored of the Spanish painters." In California he became one of that famous trio of nature lovers, which included John Burroughs and John Muir. Together they tramped the hills. It was said of Keith that there was "scarcely a mountain in three-fourths of California" on which he had not "kept vigil for days at a time, studying every detail of color, flower, rock, forge, shadow and sunshine" (George Wharton James, in the *Craftsman,* December 1904, pp. 300–03). His landscapes are painted with a wealth of color in sunsets and morning skies. His redwood pictures are especially beautiful, giving vivid impressions of California scenery. The visit of George Inness to California in 1890 brought together two men who had much in common, through their art, though their methods were radically different. Inness went west for his health and for many weeks he made Keith's studio over the old California Street Market his headquarters. His influence thereafter was apparent in Keith's painting.

Keith was California's most industrious painter as well as the most representative. Even in his old age and in ill health he made his annual trip to the Yosemite. His home in Berkeley was the center of intellectual sociability, a meeting place for professors of the university and distinguished writers and artists. His studio adjoined the campus, with its live oaks which so often appeared in his canvases. His work recalls, in composition, the manner of the painters of the Barbizon School—Diaz, Corot, and Dupré—but he was absolutely original and he interpreted the beauty of the country with poetic understanding. His "Glory of the Heavens" sold at auction in San Francisco for $12,000. A sale of thirty canvases at the Anderson Galleries in New York in 1916 brought $30,800. Keith's first wife was Elizabeth Emerson, an artist, whom he married in 1865. His second wife was Mary McHenry, daughter of Judge William McHenry, a jurist of New Orleans. She was the first woman graduate of the Hastings College of Law. He is represented in the Corcoran Gallery of Art, the National Gallery in Washington, in the Chicago Art Institute, in the Brooklyn Institute, and in many private galleries. A large collection of his pictures was exhibited at the Panama-Pacific International Exposition in 1915.

[*Who's Who in America,* 1910–11; E. P. B. Hay, *Wm. Keith as Prophet Painter* (1916); *Biog. Sketches of Am. Artists* (1924), pub. by the Mich. State Lib.; I. M. Cline, *Art and Artists in New Orleans During the Last Century* (1922); *Internat. Studio,* Nov. 1907; *Arts and Decoration,* Sept. 1913; Art Inst. of Chicago, *Exhibition of Paintings by the Late Wm. Keith . . . Apr. 22 to May 6, 1913* (n.d.); *Am. Art News,* Apr. 22, 1911; the *Craftsman,* Aug. 1911; *Art and Progress,* June 1911; *San Francisco Chronicle* and *San Francisco Call,* Apr. 14, 1911.] H. W.

KEITT, LAWRENCE MASSILLON (Oct. 4, 1824–June 2, 1864), congressman, soldier, was born in Orangeburg District, S. C., the son of George and Mary (Wannamaker) Keitt. He was graduated from the South Carolina College in 1843, was admitted to the bar in 1845, and practised at Orangeburg Courthouse. In 1848 he began a service of four years in the state House of Representatives and immediately thrust himself to the front among the radical slavery leaders. When the Nashville Convention of 1850 failed to recommend secession, he advocated the secession of South Carolina alone. In 1852 he was elected to Congress and, with the exception of twenty days, served until the secession of his state. His intense individualism and his devotion to Jeffersonian principles of simplicity in government made him an independent Democrat—"a constitutional Democrat" he called himself—but in all important matters he was a loyal Southern member of the party. In the debates on the Kansas-Nebraska bill and the bill for admitting Kansas as a free state he freely prophesied secession if the anti-slavery party should win. He was not frequently on the floor, but was ready with objection and effective reply. He was well versed in the classics, contemporary history, and economic philosophy, and he had the firm religious faith of the orthodox South. Though sometimes bombastic, his lengthy speeches were usually of great force, telling in phrase, and eloquent with a burning conviction. With his unusual capacity for wrath, occasional explosions were inevitable (see, for instance, *Congressional Globe,* 35 Cong., 1 Sess., p. 1702; Reuben Davis, *Recollections of Mississippi and Mississippians,* 1889, p. 372). Learning that his friend, Representative Preston Smith Brooks [*q.v.*], was determined to beat Senator Charles Sumner, he went to the Senate chamber and, when the assault occurred, attempted to prevent interference. The House expressed its disapprobation of his conduct, and the next day, July 16, 1856, he resigned his seat. He was promptly reëlected, however, and returned to his place Aug. 6.

Keitt sat in the South Carolina secession convention, and rejoiced in the separation. In the Confederate Provisional Congress and Convention in Montgomery he took part in organizing the new government and in drafting the constitution. He opposed the election of Davis as president, believing that for the salvation of the Confederacy the common sense of Howell Cobb was needed (*Diary from Dixie,* p. 68). In January 1862 he raised the 20th Regiment of South Carolina Volunteers, and was elected its colonel. The regiment was at once ordered to Charleston, where it served for more than two years. During most of this time Keitt was in command of the forces on Sullivan's Island. For the gallantry and skill with which he defended and evacuated Battery Wagner on Morris Island, he was praised by Generals Ripley and Beauregard (*Official Records,* 1 ser., vol. XXVIII, pt. 1, pp. 91, 390, 404). In May 1864 his regiment was ordered to Virginia, and he himself was mortally wounded at Cold Harbor on June 1, dying the next day (*Tri-Weekly South Carolinian,* June 7, 1864).

"Old tempestuous Keitt breakfasted with us yesterday," wrote Mrs. Chesnut in Richmond two months before his death: "I wish I could remember half the brilliant things he said" (*Diary from Dixie,* p. 258). He was a man of genial manners and was exceedingly fond of society. He married Susanna Sparks of Bennettsville, S. C. Of their two daughters, their only children, one died in infancy and the other never married.

[Data concerning the family from Mrs. Thomas W. Keitt of Newberry, S. C., and J. E. Wannamaker, Esq., of St. Matthews; Ada Sterling, *A Belle of the Fifties* (1905); *A Diary from Dixie* (1905), ed. by I. D. Martin and M. L. Avary; Edward Mayes, *Lucius Q. C. Lamar* (1896); *Jour. of the House of Representatives of the State of S. C.,* 1848, p. 95, 1849, p. 240; 1850, pp. 46–48, 216; 1851, pp. 68–69; *Cong. Globe,* 33 Cong., 1 Sess., App., pp. 130–33, 463–68; 34 Cong., 1 Sess., App., pp. 442–46, 3 Sess., p. 100, App., pp. 140–45; *War of the Rebellion: Official Records (Army),* 1 ser. XXVIII (pt. 1) and XL (pt. 3); *Biog. Dir. Am. Cong.* (1928); *Charleston Mercury,* June 3, 6, 1864.] R. L. M—r.

KELLER, ARTHUR IGNATIUS (July 4, 1867–Dec. 2, 1924), painter, illustrator, was born in New York, the son of Adam and Matilda (Spohr) Keller. His paternal forebears belonged to Cassel, Germany, where his great-grandfather was burgomeister. On his mother's side he was collaterally descended from the great violinist, Ludwig Spohr. He began his career as a lithographer, but realizing his lack of fundamental art training, he entered, at seventeen, the National Academy of Design, where for three years he studied under Professor Wilmarth. Later he followed the rush of American art students to Munich, becoming the pupil of Ludwig Löfftz. He captured the first Hallgarten composition prize, and his canvas, "At Mass," was purchased for the Munich Academy. When in the late eighties or early nineties he returned to New York, it was as a painter in oils and watercolors, in which mediums he won a long series of awards, including the prize for watercolors of the Philadelphia Art Club, 1899; silver medal, Paris Exposition, 1900; bronze medal for drawings, Pan-American Exposition, 1901; Evans Prize of American Water Color Society, 1902; gold medal and silver medals, St. Louis Exposition, 1904; and gold medal, Panama-Pacific Exposition, 1915. His first adventure into the field of illustration was with the *New York Herald.* Soon however, he forsook newspapers for book and magazine illustrating, for which work he was in constant demand, taking his place beside Abbey, Rinehart, Smedley, Pyle, Remington, and other figures of the golden age of American illustration. He became the favorite illustrator of S. Weir Mitchell and F. Hopkinson Smith, and illustrated special editions of Bret Harte, Longfellow, Irving, and Locke. "Circumstances diverted him into illustration," wrote Royal Cortissoz (*post*), "but the change of base was more apparent than real. . . . He was essentially a painter." To masterful technique, to admirable drawing and design, however, he added the fidelity to his author and the dramatic insight belonging to the true illustrator. He delighted in getting his local color or historical settings accurate to the minutest detail, and accumulated for the purpose a considerable library and a notable collection of period costumes and properties. He was a tireless student of types—physical, racial, professional—and he made countless graphic notes, two volumes of which have been published (*Figure Studies from Life,* 1920, with an introduction by James B. Carrington). "These superb studies in chalk or crayon, done with a flying hand . . . may hold comparison with Watteau," wrote W. J. Duncan (*post*). He used the model conscientiously for the figure, and obtained his facial expression by posing his model before a mirror and conjuring up the mood. A charter member of the Society of American Illustrators, he was elected its president in 1903, and in 1925 the Society paid him the tribute of a memorial exhibition.

Keller was twice married: on June 20, 1894, to Myra A. C. Hayes, and on June 3, 1908, to Edith Livingston Mason. Six children and his second wife survived him. He died of pneumonia in New York, at the height of his powers, his death drawing from the critic Cortissoz the comment, "Whenever the best of American illustrators are recalled his name will be held in honor among them."

[*N. Y. Times,* Dec. 3, 1924; Royal Cortissoz, in *N. Y. Herald Tribune,* May 17, 1925; W. J. Duncan, in *Arthur I. Keller Memorial Exhibition* (1925); *Bull. of the Art Center, N. Y.,* May 1925; *Soc. of Illustrators, 1901–1906* (1928); *Bookman,* Apr. 1900; *Who's Who in America,* 1922–23; F. R. Southard, in *Am. Art Student and Commercial Artist,* Jan. 31, 1926.]

M. B. H.

KELLER, MATHIAS (Mar. 20, 1813–Oct. 12, 1875), composer, was born in Ulm, Württemberg, Germany. His education in music was begun in Stuttgart and continued at Vienna. At the age of sixteen he was first violinist in the Royal Chapel, where he was engaged for five years, and then he became bandmaster of the Third Royal Brigade, leading it for seven years. In time he became somewhat unpopular with the officers of the army, because of his republicanism, and on his thirty-third birthday he started for America. Through the help of a friend in Philadelphia, he obtained a position in the Walnut Street Theatre as a player of the viol, and later at the Chestnut Street Theatre be became leader for Jean Davenport. Before leaving Germany he had become interested in the making of violins by watching the process carried on by some of his neighbors, and in Philadelphia he procured from an old building that was being demolished some old and well-seasoned lumber from which he fashioned an instrument alone. Later he secured an assistant, and in 1857 he advertised his factory as "Keller's Patent Steam Violin Manufactory." From Philadelphia he moved to New York where he saw the announcement of a prize of five hundred dollars for an American hymn, and he determined to try for it. His contribution won the prize. Both the words and the music were his composition, and the hymn is perhaps best recalled by its first line, "Speed our republic, O Father on high." His effort to introduce it to the people in a grand public concert resulted in failure, and almost financial ruin, for the expenses were six hundred dollars, and the total receipts only forty-two dollars. In Boston the music was played by the bands, and when the flags that had been carried through the Civil War were deposited in the State House in 1865, this tune was played by Gilmore's band at the special request of Governor Andrew.

At the beginning of the Civil War Keller set to music and dedicated to the Massachusetts regiments a song written by W. W. Story, beginning "Up with the flag of the Stripes and the Stars." At the close of the war he wrote "Our Banner's Constellation." At the Peace Jubilee given in Boston in 1869 "The Hymn of Peace," written by Oliver Wendell Holmes, was sung to the music of Keller's American Hymn on the first day. At the Second Peace Jubilee in 1872 one of Keller's compositions, his "German Union Hymn," was sung on the third day of the festival under the direction of its author. A comment by a newspaper of that day characterized it as an effective composition, "constructed on the true model of a national hymn, being broad, simple and imposing." He wrote over one hundred songs. Among them may be mentioned "The Girls of dear New England," "Good Night, Little Blossom," "The King and the Miller," "Mother, O Sing me to Rest," and "Angels, Let her Still Dream On." He wrote the music for a Christmas carol in 1869. His "Ravel Polka" was composed during his voyage to America when he met a family by the name of Ravel on the boat. For many of his songs he wrote the words as well as the music and in 1874 he published many of his verses in *A Collection of Poems*. After the death of his wife Keller lived with a married daughter in Boston; and in that city he died and was buried.

[Geo. Birdseye, "Mathias Keller," *Potter's Am. Monthly*, Mar. 1879; F. J. Metcalf, *Am. Writers and Compilers of Sacred Music* (1925); *Boston Globe, Boston Advertiser,* and *Boston Evening Jour.*, Oct. 14, 1875; vital records in the City Hall, Boston, and in the State House.]

F. J. M.

KELLEY, ALFRED (Nov. 7, 1789–Dec. 2, 1859), community builder, was born in Middlefield, Conn., the second son of Daniel and Jemima (Stow) Kelley and great-grandson of Joseph Kelley who was one of the early settlers of Norwich. When Alfred was ten years of age, the family moved to Lowville, N. Y. Daniel Kelley flourished on the fast-growing frontier, and soon became a large property owner and judge of the court of common pleas. Alfred was educated in the common schools of Lowville and the Academy at Fairfield, N. Y. From 1807 to 1810 he read law in an office in Whitesboro, N. Y. An uncle, Joshua Stow, was a member of the Connecticut Land Company and had been one of the surveying party led by Moses Cleaveland [*q.v.*] to the Western Reserve in 1796. In company with this uncle and a young medical student, Jared P. Kirtland [*q.v.*], Kelley set out for Cleveland, Ohio, in May 1810, traveling on horseback. His parents and five brothers soon joined him in Cleveland. He was admitted to the bar in the fall of 1810, becoming thereby Cleveland's first lawyer, and was almost immediately appointed county prosecuting attorney (1810–22). In 1814, Cleveland became an organized village, and at the following election Kelley was chosen the village president, an office in which his father succeeded him (1816–19). Alfred's brother, Irad, held the local postmastership from 1816 to 1830. A bank was organized in 1816, the Commercial Bank of Lake Erie, and Alfred Kelley became its president. With his father and two brothers, Datus and Irad, he was among the incorporators of the Cleveland Pier Company in that same year.

It was the larger field of state affairs, however, which claimed Alfred Kelley's best endeavors. He was elected a representative in the state Assembly in 1814, and served in the House or Senate through twelve sessions between 1814 and 1857. His energetic and well-informed espousal of a state system of canals led to his appointment in 1822 as a canal commissioner, charged with securing surveys, and after the passage of the Canal Act in 1825, he became acting canal commissioner (1825–34), an office which made him one of the executive officers responsible for the construction of the Ohio canal system. He abandoned his law practice in Cleveland for this office, which paid him three dollars a day and gave him an opportunity for a coveted public service. In 1830 he removed his family to Columbus, Ohio, his home for the remainder of his life. When Ohio became involved in the mad policy of lending its credit to promote private canals, railroads, and turnpikes, Kelley raised a voice of warning. When the state faced bankruptcy and repudiation he was appointed a canal fund commissioner (1841–43) and served his state effectively in reëstablishing its credit. While his greatest public service is connected with canal affairs, the legislation which reformed the state banking system (Act of 1845) and the general property tax system (Act of 1846) was the result of his labors.

Kelley had a leading part, also, in the second era in the history of transportation in Ohio. He became one of the railroad builders of the prosperous years after the Mexican War. He was the president of the Columbus & Xenia Railroad, opened to traffic in 1850, and of the Cleveland, Columbus & Cincinnati Railroad, opened in 1851. He was also president of the Cleveland, Painesville & Ashtabula Railroad, 1851–54, and waged the conflict with the city of Erie over the extension of the line through northwestern Pennsylvania to connect with the Buffalo & Erie. It is doubtful whether the enterprises of any other man so deeply affected the material welfare of Ohio and of Cleveland in particular as did those of Alfred Kelley.

On Aug. 25, 1817, Kelley married Mary Seymour Welles of Lowville, N. Y., daughter of Maj. Melancthon W. Welles. They had eleven children. Exposure during the canal-building days broke his health and limited his activities during the latter years of his life. In bearing he was dignified and commanding; Henry Clay said of him that he "had too much cast-iron in his composition to be popular" (quoted in Bates, *post,* p. 210). Vision, courage and resourcefulness made him a leader under all circumstances. He may justly be called the founder of his state's canal system, the preserver of its public credit, and the author of its system of banking and taxation.

[J. L. Bates (a son-in-law), *Alfred Kelley, His Life and Work* (1888); H. A. Kelley, *A Geneal. Hist. of the Kelley Family* (1897); Alfred Yaple, *Reminiscences of Alfred Kelley* (1875); W. A. and A. C. Taylor, *Ohio Statesmen and Annals of Progress* (2 vols., 1899); *Daily Ohio Statesman* (Columbus), Dec. 3, 1859; MSS. in Western Reserve Hist. Soc. (MS. 166; MSS. Folio 22, bk. 9; MSS. Folio 21, bk. 2), biographical sketches by associates.] E. J. B.

KELLEY, HALL JACKSON (Feb. 24, 1790–Jan. 20, 1874), propagandist, was born at Northwood, N. H., a son of Dr. Benjamin Kelley (or Kelly) and Mary Gile. He was descended from John Kelly, who died in Newbury, Mass., in 1644. In 1801 his father moved to Gilmanton, N. H., where Kelley received his schooling in the Academy. He began teaching at sixteen and graduated from the college at Middlebury, Vt., in 1813. In 1818 he took charge of one of the Boston public schools. He soon published several educational books and a Sunday-school lesson book, and helped to establish the Sunday school. In 1823 the Boston school board "dispensed" with his further services, thus closing his teaching career.

Kelley was a mathematician of parts and he now devoted himself to surveying. In 1828 he became engineer for the Three Rivers Manufacturing Company, Palmer, Mass., in which he invested heavily. Its failure in 1829 dissipated most of his fortune. By that time, however, he was obsessed with a plan for colonizing Oregon. He organized the American Society for Encouraging the Settlement of the Oregon Territory which was incorporated under the laws of Massachusetts in 1831. He enlisted some recruits, notably Nathaniel J. Wyeth of Cambridge, petitioned Congress for aid, and, awaiting congressional action, repeatedly postponed the date for beginning the emigrants' march to Oregon, which was finally fixed for the spring of 1832. His theoretical arguments were ridiculed by keen newspaper critics, especially W. J. Snelling, editor of the *Boston Journal,* and Kelley suffered the mortification of seeing his companies of prospective emigrants disintegrate. Only Wyeth made the trip and he severed his connection with Kelley entirely.

Leaving his family to be cared for by relatives, Kelley now raised some money, traveled overland to New Orleans, shipped to Vera Cruz, crossed Mexico to the Pacific, and visited California. There he encountered the trader Ewing Young, under whose guidance he made his way, most of the time a very sick man, to the land of his dreams, reaching the Columbia (Fort Vancouver) Oct. 27, 1834. Despite evil reports about his emigrant enterprise sent up from California by sea, Dr. John McLoughlin [*q.v.*] of the Hudson's Bay Company cared for him at Fort Vancouver during the winter and in spring gave him a passage in the company's ship *Dryad* to the Sandwich Islands, whence he sailed to Boston, arriving early in the year 1836, sadder but not perceptibly wiser than before his mad adventure. His best and only significant writing on the Oregon question, the so-called "Memoir," was supplied to Caleb Cushing in 1839 and was printed with Cushing's report on Oregon (*House Report No. 101,* 25 Cong., 3 Sess., App.). It summarizes Kelley's personal study of western geography. Kelley continued for many years to write petitions praying reimbursement for his losses, accounts of the hard usage he had received from the Hudson's Bay Company and others, and *Letters from an Afflicted Husband to an Astranged Wife* (1851).

He had been married May 4, 1815, to Mary Baldwin of Boston who died the following year, leaving a son; on Apr. 17, 1822, he married Mary Perry of Boston, who bore him three sons. His wife became "astranged" when he insisted on breaking up the home in order to go to Oregon, and she remained separated from him thereafter. Kelley followed engineering occasionally but lived a hermit's life at Three Rivers for a whole generation, afflicted by poverty, blindness, and "queerness," fed and befriended by charitable neighbors. He was an impressive fanatic, possessed some real ability, and exerted an appreciable influence on the popular and official mind in favor of the American occupation of Oregon. This is his sole title to fame.

[F. W. Powell published an exhaustive bibliography of Kelley in *Ore. Hist. Soc. Quart.,* Dec. 1907; in the same journal, Mar.–Dec. 1917, he published an equally exhaustive series of biographical papers containing much material from Kelley's writings, including the "Memoir" entire, a manuscript map, and extensive quotations of autobiographical matter from his *Hist. of the Settlement of Oregon* (1868). E. G. Bourne, in *Ore. Hist. Soc. Quart.*, Sept. 1905, deflates popular exaggerations of Kelley's influence upon Oregon colonization. For family history see G. M. Kelly, *A Geneal. Account of the Descendants of John Kelly of Newbury, Mass., U. S. A.* (1886).] J. S—r.

KELLEY, JAMES DOUGLAS JERROLD (Dec. 25, 1847–Apr. 30, 1922), naval officer, writer, great-grand-nephew of Commodore John Barry [*q.v.*], was born in New York City, the son of Manus and Annie (Barry) Kelley. He graduated from Seton Hall College, N. J., and entered the Naval Academy Oct. 5, 1864, the last midshipman appointed by President Lincoln. At the Academy he was an excellent student, graduating fifth in his class, an organizer of the first baseball team, and author, then or somewhat later, of the naval song "God Bless Sweethearts and Wives." As described by a classmate, "Jimmy" was "lively as quicksilver," full of witty sayings, with an Irish command of language and a wit sometimes biting, "a competent naval officer but always more of a literary man than an executive one." After graduation he was on the European station, 1868–70; in the Pacific, 1870–72; and during the next twenty-five years on many routine sea and shore assignments, rising to lieutenant, 1872, lieutenant commander, 1893, and commander, 1899. During the Spanish-American War he was member and for a time chairman of the Board on Auxiliary Vessels. He commanded the *Resolute* in the West Indies, October-December 1899, and was inspector of merchant vessels in New York from June 1900 until his retirement for incapacity incident to service, Apr. 1, 1901.

His distinction as a writer began with his winning of the gold medal of the United States Naval Institute in 1882 for an essay on the revival of the merchant marine (*Proceedings*, vol. VIII, 1882), expanded as *The Question of Ships* (1884). He produced several volumes elaborately illustrated with water-color plates by F. S. Cozzens, notably *American Yachts; Their Clubs and Races* (1884), *Typical American Yachts* (1886), and *Our Navy* (1892). The prose part of these books is not mere hack-work, but is marked, like Kelley's other writing, by finish of style and unusual historical accuracy. A student by taste, he was also an enthusiastic yachtsman, for many years member of the New York Yacht Club, and one of its fleet-commanders. His other books include a novel, *A Desperate Chance* (1886); a book of sketches, *The Ship's Company* (1897); *The Navy of the United States, 1775–1899* (1900); and, with Col. A. L. Wagner, *Our Country's Defensive Forces in War and Peace* (1899). After his retirement he was editor of naval news for the *New York Herald*, becoming a member of the board of control and later one of the three managing directors until the sale of the paper to Munsey in 1920. He was also greatly interested in wireless telegraphy, was a director in the original Marconi Company, and was in charge of the erection of the first station at Nantucket. During the World War he returned to active duty, serving as censor of wireless and in the Office of Naval Intelligence. He died of arteriosclerosis at his home in New York City, survived by his wife, Isabel dePuga Morrell, daughter of Thomas Morrell of New York, whom he married Feb. 9, 1884, and by three married daughters. His grave is in Woodlawn Cemetery.

[Information derived chiefly from family sources and naval records; N. J. K. Cook, *Thomas Halsey and His Descendants in America* (1932); *Who's Who in America*, 1922–23; obituary notices in *Army and Navy Jour.*, May 6, 1922, *N. Y. Times*, May 1, 1922, and *N. Y. Herald*, May 1, 3, 4, 1922.] A. W.

KELLEY, OLIVER HUDSON (Jan. 7, 1826–Jan. 20, 1913), founder of the Grange, great-grandson of Thomas Kelley who came to America in 1755, was the fifth child of William Robinson Kelley, a tailor, and Nancy (Hancock) Kelley. He was born in Boston and educated in the schools of that city. After experiences as a drug clerk and a newspaper reporter in Illinois and as a telegraph operator in Iowa, he went to Minnesota in 1849, took up land at Itasca, near the site of Elk River, in which is now Sherburne County, and engaged in trade with the Indians near there. His first wife, Lucy Earle, to whom he was married in 1849, died in 1851. He was married in 1852 to Temperance Baldwin Lane of Boston, who was teaching in Minnesota. They had four daughters.

Kelley was an early and enthusiastic advertiser of Minnesota, writing letters to Eastern papers to attract settlers to the new region. In 1863 he contributed an article on Minnesota to the report of the United States commissioner of agriculture (*House Executive Document No. 91*, 38 Cong., 1 Sess., pp. 31–41). In 1864, though still operating his Minnesota farm, he went to Washington as a clerk in the Bureau of Agriculture. Meantime he wrote to friends, as correspondent of the *National Republican* of Washington, for "*reliable* information" on Minnesota that he might use to encourage prospective settlers. In 1865 he made a trip through Minnesota to survey agricultural conditions for the Bureau of Agriculture, and in 1866 he was sent to the South on a similar mission. It was on this trip that he conceived the idea of organizing the farmers into a fraternal association.

For the next decade, Kelley was a man of one idea—"an engine with too much steam on all the time," a friend called him—and he worked against tremendous odds with incredible energy. In the winter of 1867, with six others, he organized the National Grange of the Patrons of Husbandry, of which he was made secretary. In the spring of 1868 he started for the West, dispensing charters for local granges to pay his expenses. At Madison, Wis., he had to borrow money to take him to his home in Minnesota. From there, undaunted, he continued the organization work.

The farmers hesitated at first to join an unknown organization of somewhat vague purposes, but Kelley kept the idea before them by writing and getting others to write communications to the agricultural press and by appointing interested individuals as organizers in the different states. Kelley emphasized the social, intellectual, and fraternal benefits of the order, but others pointed out the possibility of using it as a weapon with which to attack the monopolies that were thought to be oppressing the farmers; and this argument, coupled with the agricultural depression of the seventies, led to a rapid growth. By the fall of 1874 there were over twenty thousand granges, with the main strength in the Middle West and the South, but the decline of the order in the last half of the decade was almost as spectacular as its rise.

In 1870 Kelley established the secretary's office in Washington, but in 1875 he moved it and his family to Louisville, Ky. Soon thereafter he became the leading spirit in an extensive land speculation in northern Florida and there founded the town of Carrabelle, which became his home. In 1878 he resigned as secretary of the Grange and turned his whole attention to his land business. This enterprise does not appear to have been startlingly successful; at any rate, Kelley returned to Washington to spend his last years, and was pensioned by the National Grange in 1905. He died in January 1913, and a monument to him in Rock Creek Cemetery, Washington, was dedicated by officers of the Patrons of Husbandry in 1926. His book on the Grange, *Origin and Progress of the Order of the Patrons of Husbandry* (1875), is still readable and interesting, not more for the subject matter than for its revelation of the author, at once naïve and shrewd, fanatic and humorous, and always undismayed.

[See Kelley's own book; T. C. Atkeson, *Semicentennial Hist. of the Patrons of Husbandry* (1916); W. H. Kelley, *Geneal. Gleanings Relating to the Kelleys of Brentwood, N. H.* (1892); S. J. Buck, *Granger Movement* (1913); *Evening Star* (Washington), Jan. 21, 1913. The J. H. Stevens Papers of the Minn. Hist. Soc. throw light on Kelley's land speculation.]

S. J. B.

KELLEY, WILLIAM DARRAH (Apr. 12, 1814–Jan. 9, 1890), congressman, was born in Philadelphia. One group of his ancestors came from Ireland and settled on the Delaware in 1662; another group, of French Huguenot extraction, were early settlers in New Jersey. Both his grandfathers fought in the American Revolution. William Darrah was the youngest of four children and the only son of David and Hannah (Darrah) Kelley. His father, a leading watchmaker and jeweler of Philadelphia, was financially wrecked during the crisis following the War of 1812, and died in 1816.

Kelley attended the congregational school of the Second Presbyterian Church until he was eleven, when he found employment in a lottery office at a salary of a dollar a week. He worked for a time with an umbrella maker, and shortly after became copy-reader in the printing office of Jesper Harding [*q.v.*]. At the age of thirteen he became a jeweler's apprentice. His indenture expired in 1834 when employment was scarce in Philadelphia, so he proceeded to Boston where he worked at enameling. He employed his leisure hours in study; contributing also to the periodical press and winning a reputation as a lecturer and debater. He suffered an injury in 1838 and returned to Philadelphia where he read law. He was admitted to the bar in 1841, was appointed prosecutor of the pleas for Philadelphia in 1845 and, in 1847, was appointed judge of the court of common pleas, oyer and terminer, and quarter sessions. When the latter office was made elective in 1851 Kelley was recommissioned for ten years. As judge he showed evidence of sound legal mind as well as genuine interest in public welfare.

Kelley always opposed slavery and, with the repeal of the Missouri Compromise, abandoned the Democratic party to become one of the founders of the Republican organization. He resigned the judgeship in 1856 to run for Congress; was defeated, and resumed legal practice until 1860 when he was elected to Congress from the Fourth Pennsylvania District. He was reelected fourteen times and served for twenty years on the committee on ways and means, of which he was chairman in 1881–83.

Although exempt from military service, he answered the emergency call of September 1862, and joined an artillery company just before the battle of Antietam, but never took part in an engagement. He favored a vigorous prosecution of the war, and boldly criticized the dilatory practices of General McClellan; he favored conscription and urged Congress to use negro soldiers. He supported all measures for the abolition of slavery and extension of suffrage to the freedmen; he believed in the "state suicide" theory and in military reconstruction.

After the war he advocated the reduction of internal taxes and became an extreme advocate of protection for American industries. He had once been a free trader, but impressions made on him by English laboring conditions and the business depression of 1857 led to the abandonment of this position and, by 1866, he was recognized as the leader of high protectionists in Congress. For over twenty years, in speeches, pamphlets, and books, he endeavored to refute the "abstract generalities" of free trade and vigorously maintained that protection was needed to attract immigrants, to keep out the "pauper labor" goods of Europe, to develop and diversify American industry, and to make the United States independent of England. He religiously believed in protecting all American industries and gloried in the creation of new ones, plate-glass, beet sugar, and tin-plate being his hobbies. Though he had no iron or steel holdings, he labored so assiduously for high duties, especially on iron and steel, that his colleagues called him "Pig Iron."

He held the unique position of being the chief mouthpiece for the inflationists as well as the protectionists. He opposed the resumption of specie payments until the exportation of precious metals could be checked by a protective tariff. In the depression following the panic of 1873 he adopted theories which bordered closely on repudiation. He believed that more money was needed for the development of the South and West; that it was essential for labor; and he was certain that contraction was a "double-quick march to bankruptcy." His own remedy for the financial situation was the $3.65% bond bill.

He traveled widely in America and Europe, and wrote a number of books based on his travels and on other subjects, publishing *Speeches, Addresses, and Letters on Industrial and Financial Questions* (1872); *Lincoln and Stanton* (1885); *The Old South and the New* (1888), and other smaller works. His interest in the West led him to be inveigled into receiving a small amount of Crédit Mobilier money, but he escaped the censure of Congress. Fiery, humanitarian, and honest, apt at repartee, he was considered the best orator on the Republican side of the House. He was twice married and had four children. His first wife was Isabella Tennant of Baltimore; his second, Caroline Bartram Bonsall of Philadelphia. He died in Washington, D. C., after suffering ill health for many years.

[*Biog. Album of Prominent Pennsylvanians,* 1 ser. (1888); L. P. Brockett, *Men of Our Day* (1872); *Biog. Dir. Am. Cong.* (1928); "Memorial Addresses on the Life and Character of William D. Kelley," *House Misc. Doc. No. 229,* 51 Cong., 1 Sess.; T. C. Smith, *The Life and Letters of James Abram Garfield* (2 vols., 1925); R. C. Caldwell, *James A. Garfield* (1931); *Evening Star* (Washington), Jan. 10, 11, 1890; letters in the possession of the family.]

H. T. L.

KELLOGG, ALBERT (Dec. 6, 1813–Mar. 31, 1887), physician, botanist, the son of Isaac and Aurilla (Barney) Kellogg, was born at New Hartford, Conn. His parents were well-to-do farming people, his father a descendant of Joseph Kellogg of Great Leighs, Essex, England, who was settled in Farmington, Conn., in 1651. At an early age Albert developed a liking for gathering the native simples, and accordingly, while he was still a youth, his family placed him with a physician at Middletown to study medicine. Failing in health, he was sent to South Carolina, but he continued his medical studies and later received his degree of doctor of medicine at Transylvania University in Kentucky. He traveled widely through the Southern states and the Mississippi Valley, gratifying his taste for natural history, and on one occasion fell in with John James Audubon [*q.v.*], and accepted his invitation to accompany him on a journey to Texas. Once more he returned to his native village, but only to join soon a band of Argonauts bound in a sailing vessel for California and the gold fields by way of the Straits of Magellan. The little vessel landed the party at Sacramento, near the placer diggings, Aug. 8, 1849. After a few years in the mining district, Kellogg went to San Francisco to practise his profession.

As the first botanist resident in California, he found a rich and novel silva awaiting his discriminating eye. Even the astounding Big Tree had not yet been discovered. Branches and cones of this wonder came into Kellogg's possession before June 1852 and he began its study; but no ways of publication were at that time open to him. Always a true and unselfish scientist, he showed the specimens to William Lobb, collector for the London Horticultural Society, who immediately secured material and left California quickly for England. The subsequent publication of the Big Tree by John Lindley, the English botanist (*Gardeners' Chronicle,* London, Dec. 24, 1853), antedates that of Kellogg and his coworkers (*Proceedings of the California Academy of Natural Sciences,* May 7, 1855), but Kellogg continued to study the tree in the Sierran groves, and his descriptions of it, because first hand, are still the best of all the early accounts.

In 1867, under the auspices of the Coast and Geodetic Survey, he joined as surgeon and botanist the first expedition sent by the United States government to Bering Sea, and was enabled on this voyage to examine the northern extension of the Pacific Coast forest area. By 1882 the results of over three decades of his study of arboreous species were organized and printed in a brochure of 148 pages, under the title *Forest Trees of California,* being included the same year in the *Report* of the State Mining Bureau. This was the first botanical account of one of the most remarkable silvas of the earth's vegetation.

From the days of his first arrival, Kellogg sought to bring together the few pioneers who were interested in natural history. In consequence he was one of seven that met Apr. 4, 1853, on Montgomery Street in San Francisco and formed the California Academy of Sciences. Devoting himself largely to the flowering herbs and shrubs, he made known to science some sixty new species and genera. His writing was careful and conscientious; in general it represents an odd mixture of Biblical allusions, tender appreciation of the beauties of flowers and the grandeur of Sequoias, and accurately stated botanical facts. For nearly forty years it was his privilege to study the rich and varied flora that made California for him an earthly paradise. He was of singularly unworldly temperament, deeply religious, and childlike in his simplicity. Of methodical habits, he carefully entered in his book all sums due him by his patients but he was never known to present a bill. Protected by loving friends from the hard side of the world, he ended his days happily at Alameda. The genus Kelloggia, founded by John Torrey [*q.v.*], commemorates him. It consists of a single species—a modest and delicate herb of the Sierran woodlands.

[In *Pittonia,* vol. I (1887–89), E. L. Greene writes a sympathetic and understanding sketch of the gentle Kellogg. The brief notice in *Zoe,* Apr. 1893, carries a portrait. See also *Annals of Botany,* 1887–88; *Am. Jour. Sci.,* Mar. 1888; *Proc. Cal. Acad. of Sci.,* 2 ser., vol. I (1889); H. A. Kelly and W. L. Burrage, *Am. Medic. Biogs.* (1920); Timothy Hopkins, *The Kelloggs in the Old World and the New* (1903), vol. I; *San Francisco Chronicle,* Apr. 1, 2, 1887.] W. L. J—n.

KELLOGG, CLARA LOUISE (July 12, 1842–May 13, 1916), dramatic soprano, daughter of George Kellogg and Jane Elizabeth Crosby, was born in Sumterville, S. C. She was a niece of Albert Kellogg [*q.v.*]. Her mother was musically gifted; her father an inventor. From 1846 to 1855 he manufactured surgical instruments and other devices of his own invention in Birmingham, Conn., and during his later years was active in photographic experiment in New York.

Clara Louise accompanied her parents to New York in 1857. She received her education at the Ashland Seminary, Catskill, and studied singing in New York City. After a concert tour in which she sang selections from the part of Linda in Donizetti's *Linda di Chamounix,* she made her New York début in 1861, as Gilda in Verdi's *Rigoletto,* at the Academy of Music. She sang in *Sonnambula* in Boston before Civil War conditions ended the season. In 1863 she appeared in Gounod's *Faust* as Marguerite. After its first New York presentation (Academy of Music, Nov. 25, 1863), *Faust* became one of the major attractions offered by rival operatic companies during the next three decades (Mattfeld, *post*). It was nearly always sung in Italian, and Clara Louise Kellogg was outstandingly identified with the rôle of its heroine. In this rôle she made her London début in 1867. From 1868 to 1873 she toured the United States in Italian opera and concert, and appeared in London as Linda. In 1873 she organized her own company and attempted to popularize Italian and French opera in English in the United States, even extending her supervision of detail to the translation of the libretti, to the stage settings, and to the training of principals and chorus. During the winter season of 1874–75 she sang no less than 125 nights. Thereafter she divided her time between Europe and America, singing in London, in Italian opera in Vienna, and in St. Petersburg. Her repertory included more than forty rôles. In 1887 she married her impresario, Carl Strakosch, and thereafter appeared less frequently in public, finally retiring and establishing herself in her home, "Elpstone," New Hartford, Conn., where she died. In 1913 she published her autobiography, *Memoirs of an American Prima Donna.*

As a singer she was equally at home both in dramatic and in more purely lyric rôles. Her voice was a pure, sweet soprano of penetrating quality and extraordinary range. In the course of her long and successful career she established a deserved reputation for her readiness to respond to charitable appeals, especially in connection with musical objects, and for her generosity in encouraging and financing struggling aspirants to musical fame. She had the usual prima-donna complex regarding her musical superiority, as her autobiography reveals, but in this characteristic she was only true to type. Her abiding service is that for some twenty years she maintained the best traditions of Italian and French operatic singing in the United States, and by means of her artistic gifts and popularity as a native prima donna advanced the cause of opera sung in English.

[The chief source of information regarding Clara Louise Kellogg remains her *Memoirs*. See also Julius Mattfeld, *A Hundred Years of Grand Opera in New York* (1927); *Musical America*, May 20, 1916; *Musical Courier*, May 18, 1916; *Ev'ry Month*, Feb. 1900; *N. Y. Times*, May 14, 1916.] F. H. M.

KELLOGG, EDWARD (Oct. 18, 1790–Apr. 29, 1858), author of books on financial reform, was born in Norwalk, Conn., a descendant of Daniel Kellogg who was settled there in 1656, and the son of James Kellogg, a substantial farmer, and Lydia (Nash) Kellogg. In 1793 the family moved to Dutchess County, N. Y., where Kellogg received the little early education that was his. In 1802 the family moved again, to Northfield, Conn., where in 1817 Kellogg married Esther Fenn Warner. He had engaged in business in Norwalk soon after coming of age and in 1820 he removed to New York City and established the firm of Edward Kellogg & Company, acting as a wholesale drygoods merchant. In the financial panic of 1837 he was unable to make collections and though his assets were ample he was forced to suspend business. This failure caused him to turn his attention to the evils resulting from the existing monetary system and he became convinced that money, being a public medium of exchange, should not be under the control of private corporations, but should be issued by the government. He was particularly indignant at the extortions of usurers. In 1838 he removed to Brooklyn where he became interested in real estate and about 1843 he accumulated enough property to retire from active business and devote himself to the study of finance, retaining an office in New York. He was assisted in his writings by his daughter. He published in 1843 at his own expense, in newspaper form, *Currency, the Evil and the Remedy,* which was circulated by the aid of Horace Greeley and the *New York Tribune.* This appeared in 1849, after much further work, as *Labor and Other Capital: The Rights of Each Secured and the Wrongs of Both Eradicated,* copies of which Kellogg sent to Proudhon and the prominent members of the French Assembly and other statesmen in foreign countries, but his book failed to attract much notice at that time. He urged the abolition of interest by means of government notes issued on the security of land or other "real values" and loaned at one per cent. interest. These notes could be exchanged for government bonds bearing also one per cent. interest. When, during the Civil War, the government actually issued bonds at 3.65 per cent., in order that they might serve as money, his scheme, known as the "interconvertible bond plan of financial reform," had actually come into practice.

Kellogg died in Brooklyn, New York, in 1858, being at work on a new edition of his book till the end. Pamphlet editions of his original work, brought out during the sixties by his daughter, Mary Kellogg Putnam, under the title *A New Monetary System,* achieved wide circulation and entitle the author to be called the father of Greenbackism, a doctrine which appealed to laborers, farmers, and small business men because it was supposed to bring about a lower rate of interest even if it did not entirely abolish it. Kellogg's theory had many adherents in the National Labor Union and was important in the effort to establish a Labor party which ended with the campaign of 1872. His *New Monetary System* makes him the American contemporary and counterpart, during the decade of the forties, of the anarchist and communist philosophers of Europe. Each of these doctrines was formulated in that decade on the same labor theory of value, and each was caught up in the sixties on a similar movement. Although more fanciful than its European contemporaries, Greenbackism was more successful, for it left its permanent contribution to American political economy in the legal-tender paper currency. Greenbackism as proposed by Kellogg, however, was more than currency—it was industrial revolution.

[Biographical sketch by Mary Kellogg Putnam, in Edward Kellogg, *Labor and Capital: A New Monetary System* (edition of 1883); Timothy Hopkins, *The Kelloggs in the Old World and the New* (1903), vol. I; references on Kellogg and the proceedings of the National Labor Union in *A Doc. Hist. of Am. Industrial Soc.*, vol. IX (1910), ed. by J. R. Commons and J. B. Andrews; *N. Y. Daily Tribune*, Apr. 30, 1858.]

J. R. C.

KELLOGG, ELIJAH (May 20, 1813–Mar. 17, 1901), Congregational clergyman and author, was born in Portland, Me., a descendant of Joseph Kellogg who was living in Farmington, Conn., in 1651, and the son of Rev. Elijah and Eunice (McLellan) Kellogg. His early boyhood was spent in Portland, but before he entered Bowdoin College in 1836 he had been "indentured" on a farm for one year and had followed the sea for three years. While in college, from which he was graduated in 1840, he made friends with the farming and sea-faring folk of the neighboring town of Harpswell; and after three years at Andover Theological Seminary, he became pastor of the Congregational church there, being ordained June 18, 1844. His virility, his devoutness, and his methods of using scythe and hoe, seine and boat, in preaching the Gospel won for him the affection of his parishioners. He would swim, sail, farm, and fish with the boys in his parish and then, at an unexpected moment, kneel down in their boat, or in the field by the side of a cock of hay or a shock of corn, and pray with them. His love of boys and his skill in handling them enabled him to help Bowdoin College meet some of its difficulties; for the faculty often sent down to stay with him for a few weeks backward or unruly students whom they thought best to "rusticate." On June 3, 1855, he married Hannah Pearson Pomeroy of Syracuse, N. Y., and by this marriage had a son and a daughter.

From 1855 to 1867 he was pastor of the Mariners' Church and chaplain of the Sailors' Home in Boston, and then for eighteen years gave himself to authorship. While in the seminary he had written as a class exercise the declamation, "Spartacus to the Gladiators," first published in the *School Reader* (1846) of Epes Sargent [*q.v.*], and later he wrote several other declamations which delighted the hearts of schoolboys, such as "Regulus to the Carthaginians," "Hannibal at the Altar," and "Pericles to the People," but his first long tale, *Good Old Times,* appeared in 1867. It was published that year in *Our Young Folks,* and issued in book form in 1878. The story of his great-grandfather's struggle at the beginning of the eighteenth century to cut a home out of the forest wilderness of Maine, it at once became popular. After that, from his pen the books came thick and fast, so that by 1883 there were twenty-nine in all. Of these perhaps the best liked are *Lion Ben* (1869), *The Young Ship-Builders of Elm Island* (1870), *The Sophomores of Radcliffe* (1872), *The Mission of Black Rifle* (1876), and *A Strong Arm and a Mother's Blessing* (1881). His stories deal with the doings and adventures of folk along the shores of Casco Bay in Maine, of Scotch-Irish settlers on the western frontier of Pennsylvania, and of the students of Bowdoin College during or just before his own college days. His boys are not pirates or savages, neither are they plaster saints. They are courageous country boys, "able to cut their own fodder." The stories teach the virtues of neighborliness, virility, and fair dealing. While they do not depreciate book-learning, they place a high value upon the ability to do all kinds of manual work. Although the language in which they are told sometimes shows signs of haste and often seems homely, it is quaint and idiomatic, and the tales give unmistakable evidence that the author knew well both the speech and the life of the people about whom he wrote. In 1885 he returned to Harpswell, to his old church, and for the rest of his life he preached there or in the neighboring town of Topsham, much admired and beloved by Bowdoin men and by the country people round about.

[W. B. Mitchell, *Elijah Kellogg: The Man and His Work* (1903), giving a complete list of his books and their dates of publication; Timothy Hopkins, *The Kelloggs in the Old World and the New* (1903), vol. I; *Tales of Bowdoin* (1901), comp. by J. C. Minot and D. F. Snow; Isabel T. Ray, in *New England Mag.,* June 1902; *Daily Eastern Argus* (Portland), Mar. 18, 1901; *Congregationalist,* Mar. 23, 30, 1901.] W. B. M—l.

KELLOGG, MARTIN (Mar. 15, 1828–Aug. 26, 1903), Congregational clergyman, seventh president of the University of California, was born at Vernon, Conn., and died at Berkeley, Cal. He was a descendant in the eighth generation of Martin Kellogg (born Nov. 23, 1595) of Braintree, Essex, England, through his son Daniel who was living in Norwalk, Conn., in 1656. The younger Martin's great-grandfather, Ebenezer Kellogg (Yale 1757), was for half a century pastor at North Bolton (later Vernon), Conn. His father was deacon Allyn Kellogg, a farmer; his mother, Eliza White, was descended from Elder John White, who in 1636 went with Rev. Thomas Hooker to settle at Hartford. From Williston Seminary, Easthampton, Kellogg entered Yale College, where he received the degree of A.B. in 1850, delivering the valedictory oration at his Commencement. After teaching for a time in the high school at Woodbury, Conn., he studied theology at the Union Theological Seminary (gaining its degree in 1854), at Andover, and at New Haven. Ordained in 1855, he soon went as a home missionary to California, serving about four years in that capacity at Shasta City and Grass Valley. One of his letters (1856), cited by W. W. Ferrier in the *Origin and Development of the University of California* (1930), shows that Kellogg found in his missionary work "a higher exhilaration than the noblest worldly enterprise can give" (p. 190).

The College of California was incorporated Apr. 13, 1855, but the trustees deferred opening the institution until the necessary funds could be secured. Time was also needed for students to be suitably prepared for admission. Finally, on Aug. 13, 1859, the trustees met for the election of the faculty of the College. As a result,

Henry Durant [*q.v.*] became professor of Latin and Greek and Martin Kellogg professor of mathematics. In 1860 the College began its formal work. Kellogg spent that year in the East in quest of endowments, and upon his return transferred his attention to Latin, teaching it until 1869 when the College, by action of the trustees and of the state legislature, was converted into the University of California. Kellogg was married, Sept. 3, 1863, in Ellington, Conn., to Louisa Wells Brockway. Two children were born but died in infancy. An adopted daughter, Annie, died in young womanhood.

In September 1869 the University of California opened, with Kellogg as professor of Latin and Greek. When Daniel C. Gilman became president in 1874, he found Kellogg one of his wisest and most loyal supporters. In addition to his teaching duties and research Kellogg was dean of the College of Letters and Science from the beginning to 1885. In 1876 the classics were divided into two departments and he became professor of the Latin language and literature. After serving as acting president, 1890–93, he was made president of the University in 1893 and continued in that office until 1899. Throughout all the years of his connection with the University, he was "its unceasing builder and its devoted servant" (Howison, *post*, p. 214). After his death President Wheeler wrote: "He was a much beloved man. For forty-three years —that is, from the very beginning of the University in the form of the little college in Oakland— he was more intimately connected with the full life of the institution than any other man . . . I believe, taking all things into consideration, there is no man whose service can be matched against that of Dr. Kellogg" (*San Francisco Call.*, Aug. 27, 1903, p. 4). In 1899–1900, accompanied by his wife, he made a journey round the world, and upon his return, though at the time in emeritus status, voluntarily taught Latin at the University until shortly before his death. He was an accomplished speaker and one of his most notable addresses was delivered at Berkeley, May 2, 1902, before the Phi Beta Kappa Society on the theme of "Language and Literature."

As an editor of classical texts he published *Ars Oratoria* (1872), selections from Cicero and Quintilian. His edition of the *Brutus* of Cicero (1889) was well received on both sides of the Atlantic and gave him high rank as a scholar.

[Addresses by W. B. Rising, G. H. Howison, and others in the *Univ. Chronicle* (Univ. of Cal.), Nov. 1903; W. W. Ferrier, *Origin and Development of the Univ. of Cal.* (1930); *Obit. Record Grads. Yale Univ.*, 1903; *Biog. Record of the Class of 1850 of Yale College* (1861); Timothy Hopkins, *The Kelloggs in the Old World and the New* (1903), vol. I.]
L. J. R.

KELLOGG, SAMUEL HENRY (Sept. 6, 1839–May 3, 1899), Presbyterian clergyman, missionary to India, was born at Quogue, Long Island, N. Y. Descended from Daniel Kellogg who was living in Norwalk, Conn., in 1656, he was the son of Rev. Samuel and Mary Pierce (Henry) Kellogg. He was a frail and precocious lad and prepared for college mostly under the tuition of his parents. He matriculated at Williams College in 1856, but on account of ill health withdrew after a single term, but entered Princeton College in 1858 and graduated in 1861 with high honors. The following fall he enrolled in Princeton Seminary to prepare himself for the Presbyterian ministry. He received his theological degree in 1864, having served during the last two years of his course as instructor in mathematics in the college. While he was a student in the Seminary his attention was turned toward India by the Rev. H. M. Scudder, and on Apr. 20, 1864, he was ordained by the Hudson (N. Y.) Presbytery as a missionary. On May 3, in Montrose, Pa., he married Antoinette Whiting Hartwell, daughter of Philander Hartwell of Greenville, N. Y.

Kellogg and his wife embarked at Boston on Dec. 20, 1864, aboard a merchant vessel bound for Ceylon. Several days out of Boston the ship's captain was washed overboard in a storm and the command fell to the incompetent first mate. Kellogg was prevailed upon to act as mate and navigator throughout the voyage—to Ceylon and thence to Calcutta. He landed in Calcutta in May 1865, and proceeded to Barhpur, near Fategarh, North India, to join the Farukhabad Mission of his church. Making immediate progress in the study of Hindi, he soon shared in the conduct of the weekly religious services in that tongue, and engaged in evangelism in and about his station. In 1871 ill health compelled his withdrawal from India, but he rejoined his mission after less than two years' absence in America and took up work in Allahabad at the newly established Theological School of the India Synod of his church. Along with his teaching he engaged in evangelism and authorship. By December 1875 he had completed his monumental *Grammar of the Hindi Language* (2nd ed., 1893).

In 1876 the death of his wife, leaving four small children, compelled him to return to America. He resigned his missionary commission, and was soon called to the pastorate of the Third Presbyterian Church of Pittsburgh, where he was installed July 15, 1877. From 1877 until

1885 he was professor of systematic theology in the Allegheny (Pa.) Theological Seminary. From May 20, 1886, until Sept. 7, 1892, he acted as pastor of the St. James Square Presbyterian Church of Toronto, Canada. During the whole period of fifteen years he retained his interest in missions and in Oriental scholarship, and in 1889 took part in the International Congress of Orientalists held in Stockholm. On May 20, 1879, he was married to Sara Constance Macrum, daughter of James M. Macrum of Pittsburgh. Two sons and two daughters were born of this union.

Kellogg was recalled to India in 1892 to aid in the work of revising the Hindi Old Testament. In the following spring he joined the Revision Committee in Landour, a station in the Himalayas, where he thereafter spent seven or eight months of each year. At irregular intervals he visited the scenes of his earlier missionary labors, delivering sermons and lectures both in Hindi and in English. He looked forward to the completion of the Old Testament revision in 1899 and his subsequent return to America by 1900, but on the eve of the work's completion he died in Landour as the result of a fall from his bicycle.

Kellogg's writings, in addition to his Hindi *Grammar,* include: *A Living Christ* (a tract published when he was in college); *The Jews, or, Prediction and Fulfilment* (1883); *From Death to Resurrection* (1885); *The Light of Asia and the Light of the World* (1885); *The Book of Leviticus* (1891), an exposition; *The Genesis and Growth of Religion* (1892), and *A Handbook of Comparative Religion* (1899).

[*Missionary Review of the World,* Aug. 1899; H. H. Holcomb, *Men of Might in India Missions* (1901); *Necrological Report, Princeton Theol. Sem.,* 1900; *Harvest Field,* XIX (1899), 201, 320; J. J. Lucas, biog. memoir in S. H. Kellogg, *Are Premillennialists Right?* (new ed., 1923); Timothy Hopkins, *The Kelloggs in the Old World and the New* (1903), vol. III; *N. Y. Tribune,* May 5, 1899.] J. C. A—h—r.

KELLOGG, WILLIAM PITT (Dec. 8, 1830–Aug. 10, 1918), senator and governor of Louisiana, descended from Joseph Kellogg who settled at Farmington, Conn., about 1651, and the son of the Rev. Sherman and Rebecca (Eaton) Kellogg, was born in Orwell, Vt. He secured his formal education at Norwich Military Institute, and after his removal to Illinois in 1848, read law several winters while teaching a district school. Upon being admitted to the bar in 1853, he began practice in Canton, Ill. Like many other young Western lawyers, he early won a place in local politics, and in 1856 became a delegate to the state convention in Bloomington at which the Republican party of Illinois was organized. Four years later he was chosen a presidential elector on the Lincoln ticket. In March 1861, President Lincoln named him chief justice of Nebraska Territory, but he resigned at the outbreak of war to raise a regiment of cavalry in Illinois. After serving for less than a year in the Missouri campaign under Pope and winning promotion to the rank of brigadier-general, he was compelled by ill health to resign.

One of President Lincoln's last official acts was to commission Kellogg collector of the port of New Orleans, where he promptly became conspicuous as a Carpet-bag politician. The legislature of Louisiana elected him in 1868 to the United States Senate, but his nomination by the Republican or "Radical" party for the governorship of his adopted state led to his resignation in 1872. His entire administration was torn with dissensions. The announcement of his election was followed by a battle of injunctions. Two returning boards were organized to canvass the ballots, two rival legislatures convened, and two governors duly inaugurated. When the failure of Congress to decide between the contesting state governments threw action upon the administration, President Grant recognized Kellogg as the legitimate governor (May 22, 1873). The trials of his term included a riot, during which the conservatives by seizure of the state buildings drove the "usurper" Kellogg to the customhouse for refuge until he was restored by a presidential proclamation. A second threat of civil conflict led to a compromise which left Kellogg in office for the remainder of his term. In violation of the spirit of the compromise, he was impeached by the lower house, but the state Senate wisely dismissed the case. The Louisiana election of 1876 resulted again in dual governments and it was to the Republican faction that Kellogg owed his second election as United States senator. Notwithstanding the questionable legality of the election, the national Senate by a close party vote seated Kellogg rather than his contesting rival, although the Democratic legislature was ultimately recognized by President Hayes. Declining to be a candidate for reelection to the Senate, where he had in no way distinguished himself, he was elected to the House of Representatives for one term, 1883–85. Thereafter, except for his appearance as a delegate at the Republican national conventions until 1896, he dropped out of politics, living in retirement at Washington, D. C., until his death. He was married June 6, 1865, to Mary Emily Wills at Canton, Ill.

While there can be no doubt that Kellogg undertook to serve Louisiana under grave difficulties, falling heir to the bitter hatred which had been accumulating against Carpet-baggers and which vented itself in several attempts upon his life, he indubitably lacked the force demanded by the troublous times, and his administration augmented rather than mitigated the odium which attached to Carpet-bag rule.

[In addition to the usual sources for the Reconstruction period of Louisiana history including the state newspapers—the *New Orleans Bee*, the *National Republican*, and the *Daily Picayune*—see W. D. Foulke, *Life of Oliver P. Morton* (2 vols., 1899); Timothy Hopkins, *The Kelloggs in the Old World and the New* (1903), vol. I; W. L. Fleming, *Doc. Hist. of Reconstruction*, vol. II (1907); Ella Lonn, *Reconstruction in La. after 1868* (1918); G. S. Merriam, *The Life and Times of Samuel Bowles* (1885), vol. II; Charles Nordhoff, *The Cotton States* (1876); *Biog. Dir. Am. Cong.* (1928); *Evening Star* (Washington, D. C.), Aug. 10, 1918; *Washington Post*, Aug. 11, 1918; *Nation*, Nov. 11, 1915.] E. L.

KELLY, ALOYSIUS OLIVER JOSEPH (June 13, 1870–Feb. 23, 1911), physician, teacher, author, was born in Philadelphia, Pa., the son of Dr. Joseph V. and Emma Jane (Ferguson) Kelly. As a boy he was a quiet and industrious student. At eighteen he received the degree of A.B. from LaSalle College in Philadelphia and three years later, in 1891, he obtained his degree as doctor of medicine from the University of Pennsylvania. A few weeks after graduation from the medical school, he became a resident physician at St. Agnes' Hospital, Philadelphia, and entered upon his medical career. In 1892 he went abroad where he worked assiduously for two years, spending part of his time in London, Dublin, Prague, and Heidelberg, but chiefly in Vienna. It was in these clinics and laboratories that he laid the foundation for the work that he later produced. Here also his ability won him both the interest and friendship of Franz Chvostek, Anton Weichselbaum, and many others. His career as a teacher began with his return to Philadelphia in 1894, when he was appointed recorder in the medical dispensary of the hospital of the University of Pennsylvania. From that time on his promotion in that institution was consistent and rapid. He was made instructor in physical diagnosis in 1896 and by 1906 had become assistant professor of medicine, occupying that position until the time of his death. He had married, on Oct. 30, 1897, Elizabeth Morrison McKnight of Philadelphia.

As a clinical teacher in the University Kelly became closely associated with Dr. John H. Musser, for many years acting as his chief of clinic and, when occasion required, serving as his substitute. Kelly's teaching was not confined to one institution. In 1900 he was appointed professor of the theory and practice of medicine in the University of Vermont where he performed a constructive service in introducing modern methods of clinical teaching in medicine and in helping to formulate the policies of the medical school. In 1906 he was appointed to the chair of pathology in the Woman's Medical College of Pennsylvania. His chief scientific interest lay in pathology, and it was in this field that some of his most enduring original work was done. In 1894 he became pathologist to St. Agnes' Hospital and the following year director of the laboratories of the Philadelphia Polyclinic. In a few years he relinquished these positions to become pathologist to the German Hospital. Here, in association with the surgical clinic of Dr. John B. Deaver, he had the opportunity to study an enormous amount of pathological material, especially in relation to diseases of the appendix, the liver, and the gall bladder. It was in this laboratory that he collected the data that enabled him to prepare several of his contributions: his Mutter Lecture, "Infections of the Biliary Tract," delivered before the College of Physicians of Philadelphia in 1905; his article on the "Nature and Lesions of Cirrhosis of the Liver," published in the *American Journal of the Medical Sciences* (December 1905); and the chapter on diseases of the liver, gall bladder, and bile ducts which he contributed to William Osler's *Modern Medicine* (vol. V, 1908).

From the beginning of his medical career, Kelly took a deep interest in the literary aspects of medicine. He wrote with facility and developed a convincing yet graceful literary style. As early as 1895 he began to contribute to medical journals and during his life wrote many articles all of which bore the mark of painstaking preparation. From 1903 to 1907 he edited *International Clinics* and in the latter year he became editor of the *American Journal of the Medical Sciences.* Shortly before his death he completed a text-book, *Practice of Medicine* (1910) based upon his own wide clinical experience and extensive pathological observations. At the time of his death he had completed, in association with Dr. Musser, two volumes of a composite four-volume work entitled *A Handbook of Practical Treatment* (1911–17). Few American physicians have occupied a more influential or distinguished position in the field of medical literature than did Kelly. He never sought a large private practice. His interests centered chiefly about the library, the laboratory, and the clinic. At the time of his death he had been physician to St. Agnes' Hospital since 1897 and assistant physician to the University hospital since 1899. Those who came in contact with him as his patients became aware of his rare medical judgment and therapeutic skill. His premature death, coming at a time when his intellectual powers and professional attainments were reaching their height, deprived the medical profession of a truly great physician and teacher.

[*Who's Who in America*, 1910–11; *Trans. Coll. of Physicians of Phila.*, XXXIV (1912), p. lxii; *Am. Jour. of the Medic. Sci.*, Mar. 1911; H. A. Kelly and W. L. Burrage, *Am. Medic. Biogs.* (1920); Phila. *Press* and *Phila. Inquirer*, Feb. 24, 1911.] G. M. P.

KELLY, EDMOND (Mar. 28, 1851–Oct. 4, 1909), lawyer, political reformer, sociologist, was born at Blagnac, near Toulouse, France, of American parents, Robert Edmond and Sarah Kelly. After his early schooling at King's School, in Sherborne, Dorsetshire, England, he came to New York with his parents, in 1868, and studied at Columbia College, graduating in 1870. Then followed a science course at St. John's College, Cambridge University, in England (A.B. 1875), and finally a regular law course at Columbia, where he obtained the degree of LL.B. in 1877. His professional career began in the office of Coudert Brothers, New York City, for which firm he went to Paris several years later as its representative. In 1883 he obtained his License en Droit from the École de Droit and opened an office of his own, continuing his practice there until 1891. During this period, and again, from 1899 to 1907, he represented a number of well-known American corporations, among them the American Contracting & Dredging Company, which worked the east coast of the Panama Canal, and the Equitable Life Assurance Society. He was also counsel for the United States Embassy.

As a lawyer Edmond Kelly ranked high, but it was not his professional achievements which distinguished him from among his contemporaries. There was in him a subdued, yet tense, strain of emotionalism which responded sharply to the human aspects of the maladjustments of our social order. It was as a champion of the powerless and a crusader against the political evils of his time, that he stood out from the rank and file. In the autumn of 1892, Kelly met George Haven Putnam and asked to be brought into personal contact with some of the "cranks" of New York. Putnam himself was already known as one of the severer critics of the corrupt political machine that ruled the city, but he lacked the optimism to begin the battle. This optimism Kelly supplied. Also, Kelly possessed the gift of wit and persuasive speech; his, too, was the plan of campaign. Very much as he first proposed it, it was later carried into effect; good government clubs organized, one in every assembly district, centralized in a general association whose permanent headquarters served as a clearing house for the local clubs.

Judged from a close viewpoint, in the matter of time, Kelly's movement seemed a dismal failure. He apparently felt this most keenly himself. Beyond contributing to the overturn of Tammany in 1894 and bringing about the election of half a dozen aldermen of a higher type, the movement accomplished nothing immediate. The general mass of the citizens remained indifferent. The press was mildly sympathetic, or cold. Yet the central association survived as the City Club. Kelly wrote extensively, ever showing a growing tendency in the direction of Socialism, whose main principles, at least, he finally accepted. He wrote as a seeker and a questioner, rather than as a teacher, and his works were appreciated by those who were thinking along parallel lines. His published writings include: *Evolution and Effort* (1895); *Government, or Human Evolution* (2 vols., 1900–01); *A Practical Programme for Working Men* (1906); *The Elimination of the Tramp* (1908); and *Twentieth Century Socialism* (1910). In 1884 he married Frances Bacon Barto. She died in 1891, and in 1905 he married Edith Thuresson. He died on his farm, near Nyack, N. Y.

[Sources include: *Columbia Univ. Quart.*, Dec. 1909; *Columbia Alumni News*, Oct. 11, 1909; G. H. Putnam, *Memories of a Publisher, 1865–1915* (1915); *The Triumph of Reform* (1895); *N. Y. Times*, Oct. 5, 1909; information as to certain facts from Kelly's son, Shaun Kelly.] A. S.

KELLY, EUGENE (Nov. 25, 1808–Dec. 19, 1894), banker and philanthropist, was born in County Tyrone, Ireland, of an ancient rebel family. As an active participant in the Rebellion of 1798, his father, Thomas Boye O'Kelly of Mullaghmore, was ruined in fortune and sought safety in the common name of Kelly which made legal identification more difficult. Eugene was trained in a local hedge school and apprenticed to the draper's business. With interest he watched the growing exodus of Ulsterites to America whither his brother John (1805–1866) had gone in 1825. The latter, a distinguished priest of New York and Albany, volunteered for the negro missions in Liberia (1845–48), and on his return was settled as rector of St. Peter's Church in Jersey City where he became a force in the civic and religious life of the community. With £100 in his pocket, Eugene emigrated to New York in the thirties and found employment with Donnelly & Company, then the city's leading dry-goods concern. Soon he married the proprietor's sister and amassed a small fortune in the dry-goods business in Maysville, Ky. Selling his merchandise, he traveled to St. Louis which was becoming a Mecca for Irish immigrants attracted by steamboating, fur trading, and overland freighting. Here again, he was doing well when he contracted the gold fever and set forth for California with a train of mules under the guidance of Aubrey, "White Cloud of the Prairies." He arrived in San Francisco in 1850 and thus much to his later regret missed being a "Forty-niner."

In San Francisco Kelly founded, along with Adam Grant, Joseph A. Donohoe, and Daniel T. Murphy, Murphy, Grant & Company, which later became the chief dry-goods firm on the coast, and Donohoe, Ralston & Company, a banking house which after 1864 was known as Donohoe, Kelly & Company. Eugene Kelly & Company, founded in 1856, was its New York branch. In 1891 the San Francisco house became a joint-stock company under the firm name of Donohoe-Kelly Banking Company. Kelly's first wife had died in 1848 and in 1857 he was married to Margaret Hughes, niece of Archbishop John Hughes [*q.v.*]. Thereafter he made his home in New York. His private banking and brokerage house made him a multi-millionaire. He was influential in ecclesiastical, Irish, and Democratic circles. In Reconstruction days, he was heavily interested in the rehabilitation of Southern railroads and was a founder of the Southern Bank of Georgia in Savannah. He was also a director of the Bank of New York, the Emigrant Savings Bank, the National Park Bank, and of the Equitable Life Assurance Society. In civic affairs, he was known as chairman of the Electoral Committee of the State of New York (1884), a member of the Board of Education for thirteen years, a trustee and patron of the Metropolitan Museum of Art, and an active member of the committees on the Washington Arch and Bartholdi Statue. A sturdy Irish nationalist and friend of John Dillon, he served as treasurer of the Irish Parliamentary Fund and as president of the National Federation of America. He contributed to Catholic charities, to St. Patrick's Cathedral in New York, and to Seton Hall College, of which he was a trustee, and is regarded as one of the founders and benefactors of the Catholic University of America in Washington which he served as treasurer and financial consultant from its establishment (1887) until his death. As a reward for his philanthropies his intimate associate Archbishop Corrigan obtained for him a papal honor, Chamberlain of the Cape and Sword, which because of his inability to go to Rome was transferred to his eldest son in 1894.

[*Cath. Univ. Bull.*, Jan. 1895, Apr. 1899; *Records of the Am. Cath. Hist. Soc.*, Mar. 1900; *Sadlier's Cath. Directory* (1867), p. 47; the *Sun* (N. Y.), and the *N. Y. Herald*, Dec. 20, 1894.] R. J. P.

KELLY, JOHN (Apr. 20, 1822–June 1, 1886), Tammany politician and congressman, was born in New York City, the son of Hugh and Sarah (Donnelly) Kelly. His father had emigrated from Ireland in 1816. John attended the parochial school attached to St. Patrick's Cathedral, then, after his father's death, became an office boy on the *New York Herald*. At thirteen he was apprenticed to a grate-setter and soap-stone cutter. He was industrious, intelligent, and thrifty, so that he was able about 1843 to go into business for himself. Democratic politics was the breath of life to young Irishmen of the fourteenth ward, where Kelly lived, and he entered the game early. He fought Tammany as a young man and was beaten in his two candidacies for office during this period. In the reorganization of Tammany in 1853, however, he was admitted to the Society, and at once received its support in the fall elections. He was elected alderman in November 1853, congressman in 1854, and reëlected to Congress in 1856. In Washington he made a favorable impression. He was conspicuous for his attacks on the Know-Nothing party, and for a speech on religious toleration. In 1857 he was chosen sheriff of New York County and resigned his seat in Congress to take this office. He was reëlected sheriff in 1865. In 1868 he was nominated for mayor, against A. Oakey Hall, but he withdrew, on the plea of ill health, and went abroad. These were years of deep personal grief. The death of his wife (née McIlhargy) was followed by the deaths of his son and two daughters, leaving him without family.

Returning from Europe, he now entered upon his career as dictator in Tammany Hall. The infamies of the "Tweed ring" had thoroughly discredited Tammany and Kelly was called upon to reorganize the Society. He plunged into this work with intense energy. Elected Grand Sachem of Tammany Hall, he began an iron-hand rule that saved the organization as a political force but committed him personally to one bitter quarrel after another. He is credited with the thorough organization of the assessment of candidates and office holders for the support of the Tammany machine and the profit of the leaders. In 1881 he was confronted with a revolt in Tammany itself, but he remained the head of the Society until ill health caused his retirement in

1882. He was succeeded by his friend and protégé, Richard Croker. During his leadership of Tammany, he was appointed comptroller by Mayor Wickham in 1876. Three years later he opposed the reëlection of Gov. Lucius Robinson and presented himself as a candidate for the governorship. His bolt, which brought about the election of the Republican candidate, Alonzo B. Cornell, was probably the reason for Mayor Cooper's refusal to reappoint him as comptroller in 1880. Kelly was responsible for the nomination of Grace for mayor in 1880 and for that of Edson in 1882. In 1884 he played a conspicuous part in preventing the reëlection of Tammany members of the Board of Aldermen who had been bribed to grant the Broadway Railway franchise. He was a burly, square-set man of great physical strength. His roughness and his domineering ways had, after his experience in Congress, given way to suavity and diplomacy masking the same inflexible will and autocratic rule. In 1876 he married Teresa Mullen, a niece of Cardinal McCloskey [*q.v.*]. His widow and two infant children survived him upon his death.

[J. F. McLaughlin, *The Life and Times of John Kelly* (1885); Stephen Fiske, *Off-hand Portraits of Prominent New Yorkers* (1884); M. R. Werner, *Tammany Hall* (1928); Gustavus Myers, *The Hist. of Tammany Hall* (1901); M. P. Breen, *Thirty Years of N. Y. Politics* (1899); *N. Y. Times, N. Y. Tribune, N. Y. Herald,* June 2, 1886.] L. H. H.

KELLY, LUTHER SAGE (July 27, 1849–Dec. 17, 1928), army scout, known as "Yellowstone Kelly," traced his ancestry to John Kelly who died at Newbury, Mass., in 1644. His father, Luther Kelly, crossed from New Hampshire into New York state and married Jeannette Eliza Sage of Chittenango. The couple settled in Geneva, and it was there that Luther Sage was born. He entered the Genesee Wesleyan Seminary at Lima, N. Y., from the Geneva Union School. In March 1865, claiming to be over eighteen, he enlisted in Company G, 10th Infantry, at Rochester. At the conclusion of the war he was ordered West, having unwittingly joined the regulars, a misunderstanding which shaped his career. Upon receiving his discharge in 1868, he left Fort Ransom, Dakota Territory, and roamed the Yellowstone region as hunter and trapper, learning the trails of Wyoming and Montana. Later as dispatch bearer he made round trips monthly from Fort Union to Devil's Lake. His knowledge of the Sioux language made him a valuable guide to Gen. George A. Forsyth on his expedition to the upper Missouri and Yellowstone and the information which he gained on that expedition proved invaluable in the war against the Sioux three years later. As chief army scout for Gen. Nelson A. Miles from 1876 to 1878, Kelly served in many campaigns, his three most important being those against Sitting Bull, the Sioux tribe, and later against the Sioux and Cheyennes along the Tongue River. Two years later, in 1880, he again acted as scout for the regular army, this time in the Ute country in Colorado.

During a flying trip east and after a brief courtship Kelly married Alice May Morrison at Detroit in 1885. Later he entered the general service of the War Department, serving as clerk at Chicago, Governors Island, and in the Pension Bureau at Washington, D. C. In 1898 he was chosen by Capt. Edwin Forbes Glenn, who was heading an exploring expedition to Alaska, to act as guide. Kelly wrote a sub-report recommending a practical railroad route from Portage Bay to Kirk Arm. The following year, 1899, he was in Alaska as guide to the Harriman expedition. Later, as captain of a company of volunteers he went to the Philippines, saw active service, and was made commander of Post Dapitán, Mindanao. In 1903 while treasurer of the province of Surigao he led the inhabitants in a defense against attack and siege of the town by escaped convicts and outlaws. For his conduct in this affair he received special praise from President Roosevelt. Returning to the United States in 1904 Kelly became Indian agent at the San Carlos Reservation in Arizona, retaining this position until 1908. He then undertook to supervise a gold mine near Lida, Nev., but was unsuccessful in this and other mining ventures. In 1915 he started a fruit ranch at Paradise, Cal., where he lived his remaining years. In 1926 he published his reminiscences in *"Yellowstone Kelly": The Memoirs of Luther S. Kelly,* and at the time of his death he had in manuscript a work on Alaska and the Philippines. He died in 1928 and was buried at Kelly Mountain, Billings, Mont. His great service was that of helping to prepare the West for the advance of civilization.

[In addition to Kelly's memoirs see E. F. Glenn and W. R. Abercrombie, *Reports of Explorations in the Territory of Alaska* (1899), and Kelly's sub-report, "From Cabin Creek to the Valley of the Yula, Alaska," both reprinted in *Compilation of Narratives of Explorations in Alaska* (1900); *Personal Recollections and Observations of Gen. Nelson A. Miles* (1896); "Report of the Philippine Commission," 1903, which is found in vols. V–VIII of the annual report of the War Dept. for 1903; G. M. Kelly, *A Geneal. Account of the Descendants of John Kelly of Newbury, Mass.* (1886), and the *Bismarck Tribune* and *N. Y. Times,* Dec. 18, 1928. Certain information was supplied for this sketch by relatives of Kelly.] F. W. S.

KELLY, MICHAEL J. (Dec. 31, 1857–Nov. 8, 1894), baseball player, otherwise known as

"King Kelly" and the "Ten Thousand Dollar Beauty," was born in Troy, N. Y. His parents were probably Michael Kelly, a paper-maker, and his wife, Catherine, both natives of Ireland. His early professional career was with the Olympics of Paterson, N. J., and the Buckeyes of Columbus, Ohio. In 1879 he was with the Cincinnati team of the National League, playing right field and change catcher. During a post-season series in California, 1879–80, Adrian Anson [*q.v.*] secured his services for the Chicago White Stockings with which he remained until 1887. He soon became a popular idol. He played right field, caught, and in the season of 1882 filled in at short stop. The White Stockings won five championships while he was with them, to which achievement he contributed his full share, for he always played for the victory of the team, and never for personal aggrandizement. "When we marched on the field," Kelly once boasted in a newspaper interview, "with our big six-footers out in front it used to be a case of 'eat 'em up Jake.' We had most of 'em whipped before we threw a ball. They were scared to death." Kelly himself was about six feet tall, but was awkward and had a shambling gait. He was a big, bulgy, jovial Irishman. His success as a player was not due to exceptional skill or dexterity. He had an unfortunate tendency to fall down at critical moments, without apparent cause, his feet becoming panicky when he was about to catch a ball; neither was he a dependable catcher, thrower, or infielder. His greatness was due to nerve, mental agility, and mastery of the game. He seemed to have an intuitive sense of what an opposing player was going to do, and he generally out-witted him. His ability to divine what was in the pitcher's mind made him a good batter, and in 1886 he led the league. Once on the bases it was almost impossible to get him out; he slid with cleverness and abandon, becoming the hero of the popular song, "Slide, Kelly, slide!" and if a run were needed to win a game he was almost certain to get it. His good-natured badinage with spectators contributed to his popularity as did his arguments with umpires, for as a "kicker" he outclassed every one in his profession.

His sale to the Boston team in 1887 for $10,000 created a furor and gave him the title of "Ten Thousand Dollar Beauty." The willingness of the Chicago management to let him go was largely due to the fact that "he was of a highly convivial nature, extremely fascinating and witty, and his example was demoralizing to discipline" (A. G. Spalding, *America's National Game,* 1911, p. 516). When the Brotherhood War broke out in 1890, Kelly signed with the Boston Players League Club, and admirers presented him with a farm in Hingham. A. G. Spalding offered him $10,000 and a three-year contract at his own figure to desert the Brotherhood, and he won the former's respect by refusing "to go back on the boys" (*Ibid.,* pp. 295–97). After the collapse of the Players League, he took charge of the Cincinnati American Association Club, and in 1892 returned to Boston. He was loaned to New York in 1893, and upon his return at the close of the season was released. His death, occasioned by an attack of pneumonia, occurred in the Emergency Hospital, Boston, to which city he had come to appear at the Palace Theatre with the London Gaiety Girls, in the rôle of "Casey at the Bat." Just before he died he slipped off a stretcher, and remarked, "This is my last slide." He was the author of a little book entitled, *"Play Ball"; Stories of the Diamond Field* (Boston, Emery & Hughes, 1888).

[Francis C. Richter, *Hist. and Records of Base Ball* (1914); *Baseball Mag.,* June 1914; Elwood A. Roff, *Base Ball and Base Ball Players* (1912); U. S. Census of 1860, Rensselaer County, N. Y., I, 67; Boston, New York, and Chicago papers, Nov. 9, 1894.] H. E. S.

KELLY, MYRA (Aug. 26, 1875–Mar. 30, 1910), author, was born in Dublin, Ireland, of Irish parents, Dr. James Edward and Annie (Morrogh) Kelly. When she was a child the family came to New York City, where Dr. Kelly developed a large practice on the East Side. Myra was educated at the Mt. Saint Vincent and Sacred Heart convents, the Horace Mann School, and Teachers College, Columbia University, where, in 1899, she received a diploma as a teacher of manual training. Her familiarity with the East Side and interest in its denizens made her choose that as her first field of work. She taught for two years at No. 147 public school, east of the Bowery, where her pupils were of many nationalities, speaking many tongues. Here she rapidly gathered literary material. She was critic teacher at the Speyer School, Teachers College, 1902–03, and during this time began to put her East Side experiences into stories. Her first story, "A Christmas Present for a Lady," was sent to two magazines, with the idea that both would probably reject it. Both accepted it and some complications in adjustment followed. This successful beginning proved an omen for her future literary career, and she told friends long afterward that no manuscript of hers had ever been rejected. Her first volume appeared in 1904, *Little Citizens; the Humours of School Life,* stories which are almost entirely accounts of her own experiences as a teacher in No. 147. There she had learned not only the physical and mental characteristics of her pupils but their dialect expressions and tricks of behavior, which enabled her to write genuine realism. As a teacher, she had also visited the homes of the children and become acquainted with the mothers, always less American than the children, but welcoming her because of her delicate, sweet personality and her sympathy which never appeared like curiosity. Other volumes of stories followed: *The Isle of Dreams* (1907); *Wards of Liberty* (1907); *Rosnah* (1908); *The Golden Season* (1909); *Little Aliens* (1910); *New Faces* (1910); *Her Little Young Ladyship* (1911). In 1909 she wrote for publication by the American Association for International Conciliation a pamphlet, *The American Public School as a Factor in International Conciliation.*

Myra Kelly's stories, almost all about children, have interested people of all ages. Each narrates some human episode and illustrates some characteristic of the immigrant New Yorkers who were the models for her characters. She had mastery of both pathos and humor and her short story technique was admirable. Her collection *Little Citizens* aroused the interest of Allan Macnaughtan, president of the Standard Coach Horse Company. He sought an acquaintance, and in August 1905 they were married. They had one child, a boy, who died in infancy. At one time they were associated with a project for establishing a literary colony at Oldchester Village, Orange Mountain, N. J., and lived there for a while. Never very robust, Myra Kelly's health became impaired, tuberculosis developed, and, in the hope of a cure, she went to Torquay, on the English Channel, where she died and was buried.

[*Who's Who in America,* 1910–11; obituaries in the *N. Y. Times* and the *N. Y. Tribune,* Apr. 1, 1910; "The President and Myra Kelly," *Bookman,* Nov. 1907; information as to certain facts from Mrs. Clara H. Macnaughtan, Los Angeles, Cal.] S. G. B.

KELLY, WILLIAM (Aug. 21, 1811–Feb. 11, 1888), original inventor of the "air-boiling process," or what later was known as the Bessemer process, of steel making, was the son of John and Elizabeth (Fitzsimons) Kelly. He was born in Pittsburgh, Pa., and educated in the public schools of that city. His father was a well-to-do landowner who is said to have built the first two brick houses in Pittsburgh. Though inventive and fond of metallurgy, at thirty-five years of age Kelly found himself in the dry-goods business in Philadelphia, being junior member of the firm McShane & Kelly. Having been sent out to collect debts for the firm, he arrived in Nashville, Tenn., where, casually attending graduation exercises at a girls' school, he became acquainted with Mildred A. Gracy, a young lady from Eddyville, Ky., whom he married shortly after. Securing from friends letters of introduction to merchants of that town, he visited Eddyville, cultivated particularly the acquaintance of the young lady's father, a wealthy tobacco merchant, settled there, and with his brother purchased iron-ore lands adjacent and a furnace known as the Cobb furnace. Developing the Suwanee Iron Works & Union Forge, Kelly manufactured sugar kettles, which were much in demand among the farmers thereabouts. The manufacture of wrought iron from pig iron for these kettles, by burning out of the excess carbon, required much charcoal; and Kelly soon found his local supply of fuel running low. While worrying over his higher costs, he one day noticed that though the air-blast in his "finery fire" furnace was blowing on molten iron with no charcoal covering, yet the iron became white hot. Experimenting, he found that contrary to all iron-makers' beliefs, molten iron containing sufficient carbon became much hotter when air was blown on it; in other words, that the three to five per cent. carbon contained in molten cast iron can be burned out by air-blast, this carbon itself acting as fuel and making the molten mass very much hotter.

So obsessed was Kelly with his new discovery that his wife, thinking her husband mentally unbalanced in his talk of making steel "without fuel," dispatched her daughter to Mr. Gracy (her father and Kelly's partner) and a Dr. Higgins. Fortunately the latter recognized the possibility of Kelly's discovery and believed him of sound mind. His customers, however, could not be convinced of the fact that the iron he made by this cheaper process was thoroughly good, and Kelly had to revert to the use of charcoal. Meantime, with two iron makers, he started building secretly an experimental converter three miles back in the secluded forest. It was a four-foot high brick kettle in which air was blown through holes in the bottom into and through molten pig iron. Because of insufficient blast pressure, only partial success resulted. This was the first of seven experimental converters built secretly between 1851 and 1856. In the latter year, hearing that Henry Bessemer of England had been granted a United States patent on the same process, Kelly applied for a patent, and, convincing the patent officials of his priority, on June 23, 1857, was granted United States patent No. 17,628 and declared to be the original inventor (*Scientific American*, Oct. 18, 1856, July 4, 1857). On June 15, 1871, Kelly's patent was renewed for seven years, while Bessemer was refused renewal (*Decisions of the Commissioner of Patents for the Year 1871*, pp. 186–87).

The panic of 1857 bankrupted Kelly, and to secure ready money he sold his patent for $1,000 to his father who bequeathed it to his daughters. They, thinking Kelly incompetent in business matters, would not return it to him, though in later years it came to his children. He then went to Johnstown, Pa., where Daniel J. Morrell of the Cambria Iron Works listened to his story and encouraged him to work out his new process in that plant. Here he built his eighth converter, the first of the tilting type, which is preserved as a valued exhibit in the office of the Cambria plant, now a part of the Bethlehem Steel Company. The first trial was a failure, due to too strong a blast, and, for years, "Kelly's fireworks" were a standing joke. The second trial, however, was a success, and Morrell's financial backers purchased a controlling interest in the process, which, with a slight modification, necessary also in Bessemer's process, made soft steel for the first time cheaply, and in the large quantities necessary for rails, bars, structural shapes, etc., in the great "Steel Age" which was just beginning. Acclaimed a genius and no more a crank, Kelly remained for five years at Johnstown, and then returned to Louisville where he founded an axe-manufacturing business later carried on by his sons in Charles Town, W. Va. He retired from active business at the age of seventy and remained in Louisville, where he died and was buried.

Steel under the Kelly patent was first blown commercially in the fall of 1864 at the Wyandotte Iron Works near Detroit, Mich., constructed by W. F. Durfee [*q.v.*] for Capt. E. B. Ward of Detroit, a large owner in the Cambria Iron Works (see article by Durfee in *Transactions of the American Society of Mechanical Engineers*, vol. VI, 1884–85). Ward and his partner, Z. S. Durfee [*q.v.*], a cousin of W. F. Durfee, had purchased control of Kelly's patent and the American rights to Mushet's addition of carbon and manganese, which was a necessity for both the Bessemer and Kelly processes. They later took Morrell and others into the corporation, which was called the Kelly Pneumatic Process Company. In 1865, manufacturing under Bessemer's American patent was begun by Alexander Lyman Holley [*q.v.*] at Troy, N. Y. He was not very successful for Mushet had sold the entire American rights to his recarburizing process to Durfee. Bessemer, however, had patented in America the machinery for handling the converter and Holley controlled the right to its use. In the face of this situation, which made each company a violator of patent rights owned by the other, with threat of considerable litigation, the two companies consolidated. Just why those astute steel men, Ward, Durfee, and Morrell, who controlled the most important of the patents, accepted only three-tenths of the stock of the new company, with Holley and his associates holding seven-tenths, has never been satisfactorily explained. Kelly never was satisfied, but since his patents were controlled by Ward, Morrell, and others, he had little voice. Even Bessemer's name thereafter was used in connection with the process in this country, probably chiefly because of the reputation which imported English Bessemer rails had acquired. Kelly received altogether only about $450,000 from his epoch-making invention while Bessemer received approximately $10,000,000 in royalties and was knighted. On Oct. 5, 1925, a bronze tablet to Kelly's memory was erected by the American Society for Steel Treating, at the site of the Wyandotte Iron Works.

[H. N. Casson, *The Romance of Steel: the Story of a Thousand Millionaires* (1907), first published in *Munsey's Mag.*, Apr. 1906; J. N. Boucher, *Wm. Kelly: A True Hist. of the Bessemer Process* (1924); L. W. Spring, *Non-Technical Chats on Iron and Steel* (1927); "The Dedication of Bronze Tablet to the Memory of Wm. Kelly," *Trans. Am. Soc. for Steel Treating*, III (1922), 162; obituary in *Courier-Journal* (Louisville, Ky.), Feb. 13, 1888.]

LaV. W. S.

KELPIUS, JOHANN (1673–1708), mystic, was born near Schässburg in Transylvania (Siebenbürgen), probably at Halwegen, where his father, Georg Kelp, who died Feb. 25, 1685, as pastor at Denndorf in the same district, was then the incumbent. He was educated at the expense of three friends of his father and attended the University of Altdorf, in Bavaria, where he received his master's degree in 1689 and published a thesis on natural theology. He next published an *Inquisitio an Ethicus Ethnicus Aptus sit Christianae Juventutis Hodegus*, etc. (Nürnberg, 1690), and, in collaboration with Prof. Johannes Fabricius, *Scylla Theologica, Aliquot Exemplis Patrum et Doctorum Ecclesiae Qui cum Alios Refutare Laborarent . . . in Contrarios Errores Misere Inciderunt, Ostensa*, etc. (Altdorf, 1690). He had little right to fling this stone, for his own orthodoxy was overlain, in the most sumptuous rococo manner, with cabalism, chiliasm, Pietism, and Rosicrucianism. He was deeply versed in the writings of Jacob Boehme and became an intimate of Johann Jacob

Zimmermann, the deposed deacon of Britigheim in Württemberg. Zimmermann, a mathematician, astronomer, and author as well as a theologian, had determined by exact calculations that the Millennium would begin in the autumn of 1694 and was raising a company of about forty adherents, male and female, who were to voyage to Pennsylvania and await its arrival in the solitude of the primeval forest. Kelpius joined the expedition and succeeded to the leadership when Zimmermann died at Rotterdam on the eve of their sailing.

After a perilous voyage they disembarked June 22, 1694, at Bohemia Landing, Md., and proceeded to Germantown, Pa., where they settled on the wooded ridge overlooking Wissahickon Creek. "Hermit Spring" and "Hermit Lane" in Fairmount Park commemorate their occupancy of this tract. Even after the failure of Zimmermann's prediction, the community patiently awaited the Millennium, meanwhile devoting itself to prayer and meditation, the cultivation of medicinal plants, and religious instruction among the Germans of the vicinity. Among the abler members of the group were Johann Gottfried Seelig, Daniel Falckner [*q.v.*], and Heinrich Bernhard Köster, a man at once so learned and so eccentric that Johann Christoph Adelung included a biography of him in his *Geschichte der Menschlichen Narrheit* (vol. VII, Leipzig, 1789). Köster, after creating much stir as a preacher, returned to Germany in 1699. About 1700 Reinier Jansen [*q.v.*] may have published a tract by Kelpius entitled *Kurtzer Begriff oder Leichtes Mittel zu Beten oder mit Gott zu Reden,* of which no copy is known to be extant. Christopher Witt's translation of it was published as a *Short, Easy, and Comprehensive Method of Prayer* (Philadelphia, Henry Miller, 1761; Germantown, Christopher Sower, 1763). Kelpius' other literary remains are a diary of the voyage to America, some miscellaneous letters, and a book of original hymns with musical scores. He was on friendly terms with Andreas Rudman, Eric Tobias Biörck, and Jonas Auren, the Swedish Lutheran clergymen on the Delaware, and apparently possessed a wide reputation as a sage and saint. Of his saintliness there has never been any doubt. Exposure and privation undermined his health, tuberculosis set in, and finally he had to relinquish the hope of escaping bodily death. The touching story of his end was preserved by Henry Melchior Mühlenberg (*Hallesche Nachrichten, Vierzehente Fortsetzung,* Halle, 1774, pp. 1265–66.) Seelig became the leader of the community, which continued to exist for some years after Kelpius' death.

[Kelpius' journal of the voyage to America has been translated by J. F. Sachse, *Proc. and Addresses Pa.-German Soc.,* vol. XXV (1917); his hymn book has been reproduced photographically in *Church Music and Musical Life in Pa. in the 18th Century,* vol. I (1926), being *Pubs. of the Pa. Soc. Colonial Dames of America,* vol. IV. For his life see Oswald Seidensticker, *Bilder aus der Deutsch-pennsylvanischen Geschichte* (1885), and J. F. Sachse, *The German Pietists of Provincial Pa.* (1895).]

G. H. G.

KELSEY, FRANCIS WILLEY (May 23, 1858–May 14, 1927), classicist, archeologist, was born at Ogden, N. Y., the son of Henry and Olive Cornelia (Trowbridge) Kelsey. The family is traced to William Kelsey who was at Cambridge, Mass., in 1632. A New England tradition of simplicity, austerity, and piety received a touch of fervor from the part of New York State which was Kelsey's birthplace. The boy attended the Union School of Lockport, and then the University of Rochester (A.B., 1880). The next two years he spent as instructor in classics at Lake Forest University, Lake Forest, Ill. With leave of absence he studied in Europe (1883, 1884–85) and meanwhile (1884) received his professorship. Five years later (1889) he was called to a position of the same rank at Michigan, and within six months became the successor of Henry S. Frieze [*q.v.*] as head of the Latin department, which position he held until his death, thirty-eight years later.

Kelsey was no narrow philologist. His teaching was enriched by the archeologist's ability to recreate the classic life of antiquity, but he was prevented by his heritage and his times from being a romanticist. His first publications, following the fashion of that day, were textbooks: Cicero's *De Senectute* and *De Amicitia* in one volume, 1882, Lucretius' *De Rerum Natura* in 1884, Cæsar's *Gallic War* in 1886, *Xenophon's Anabasis* (1889), *Selections from Ovid* (1891), *Select Orations and Letters of Cicero* (1892). Most of these passed through several or many editions: the Cæsar, through twenty-one. He had an unusual interest in Lucretius, but, while printing the complete text, found it intolerable to discuss or annotate more than books I, III, and V. Following the example of Frieze and his own tastes, he sponsored the University Musical Society and its associated activities to the end of his life. Kelsey had a perennial interest in his pupils, and a passion for bringing together the worker and the work.

In the later nineties he turned to more important publication, editing with Percy Gardner a series of Handbooks of Archæology and Antiquities to which he contributed *Pompeii, Its Life and Art* (1899), translated from the work of August Mau. He was occupied now with his teaching, editing, and revising, and a vast correspondence covering innumerable enterprises. He belonged to the American Philological Association (president, 1906–07), the American Historical Association, and the Archæological Institute of America (president, 1907–12), under which he was director of the American School of Classical Studies in Rome (1900–01). In the nineties he originated the Classical Conference. In the following decade he fought at Michigan and at large for the classics, then threatened with extinction; and published a symposium, *Latin and Greek in American Education* (1911). While the World War was in progress he undertook (1918) for the Carnegie Peace Foundation, with the help of others, a translation of Grotius' *De Jure Belli et Pacis,* and completed his share of the work, which was published in 1925. The great German *Thesaurus Totius Latinitatis* was at this time saved from extinction by funds contributed through him.

Although Kelsey published various philological and archeological articles which amply prove his ability as an investigator, his energy naturally flowed into the conduct of learned enterprises. His greatest achievements were the publication of the University of Michigan Studies: Humanistic Series, and the organization of the University of Michigan expeditions to the Near East. The Humanistic Series (which he edited with Henry A. Sanders) was begun in 1904, and by 1932 numbered twenty-four volumes. Not only Latin and Greek, but Biblical, Orientalistic, musical, and other studies are represented: for Kelsey had a sympathy and understanding even larger than his interest. He spent thousands of hours in the drudgery of editing and printing. His taste was exquisite. The expeditions to the Near East began in 1920 and one of them is still (1932) at work. They have excavated at Antioch of Pisidia, Carthage, and Karanis (Egypt); and have brought back papyri and manuscripts, photographs and varied archeological material. These enterprises were financed by men of affairs who saw Kelsey as one of themselves and made his concerns their own.

Imposing in appearance, especiallly as he grew older, Kelsey loved work, and never learned the purposes of play. Great intelligence protected him where most men require a keener sense of humor. A seasoned traveler, his cosmopolitanism was one of understanding and toleration rather than of taste. He had little regard for distinction, and accepted only two honorary degrees (Ph.D., 1886, LL.D., 1910, Rochester). In later years he became a member of the American Association for the Advancement of Science, the Classical Association of Great Britain, the Deutsches Archäologisches Institut, and the Académie des Inscriptions et Belles-Lettres. He dignified his unchanging orthodoxy with a personal example of unselfishness, self-control, and disregard of affront. His unaccountable power over men might have carried him to the highest positions in politics or finance, or academic administration, had he been interested in these things. His habit of having his way and accomplishing his unfathomable purposes sometimes aroused resentment. He died surrounded by his books and correspondence. His wife, who before her marriage was Isabella Badger, survived him, as did two daughters and a son.

[Kelsey left no materials for the writing of his biography. His voluminous letter files and diaries, as far as known, contain only the record of his undertakings, and never anything personal. This article is based on personal knowledge and acquaintance, and on information collected in the community. Published information may be found in B. A. Hinsdale and I. N. Demmon, *Hist. of the Univ. of Mich.* (1906); notice by H. A. Sanders in *Classical Philology,* July 1927; *The President's Report for the Year 1926–27* (Univ. of Mich., 1928); *Who's Who in America,* 1926–27; E. A. Claypool and others, *A Geneal. of the Descendants of Wm. Kelsey,* vol. I (1928); *Detroit Free Press,* May 15, 1927.] W. H. W.

KELTON, JOHN CUNNINGHAM (June 24, 1828–July 15, 1893), soldier, was born in Delaware County, Pa., of Irish-Scotch ancestry, a great-grandson of James Kelton who came from Scotland to Chester County, Pa., in 1735, and the son of Robert and Margaretta Ross (Cunningham) Kelton. His father became a leading iron-master of Lancaster County, and later, an influential citizen of Philadelphia. After an academic education, young Kelton entered the United States Military Academy at the age of nineteen, and graduated in 1851 with a commission in the 6th Infantry. After a period of frontier duty, during which he was promoted first lieutenant, May 9, 1855, he became assistant instructor in infantry tactics as well as in the use of small arms and in gymnastics, at the Military Academy, Mar. 6, 1857–Apr. 14, 1861 (Cullum, *post,* p. 459).

With the outbreak of the Civil War, Kelton was for a short time purchasing commissary at St. Louis, commanded a brigade of Pope's division, and served as assistant adjutant general under General Lyon until Sept. 19, 1861, when he received appointment as colonel, 9th Missouri Volunteers. Upon General Halleck's urgent request, Kelton reluctantly gave up command of combatant troops, and returned to duty as assistant adjutant general, Department of Missouri, accompanying Halleck to Mississippi and participating in the advance upon, siege, and occupation of Corinth (Apr. 19–July 17, 1862), serving for some four months also, as Halleck's aide-de-camp. He accompanied General Halleck to Washington and served as an intimate member of his staff while Halleck was general in chief and chief of staff of the army, and in command of the Military Division of the James (July 11, 1862–July 1, 1865). On Mar. 13, 1865, he was awarded the brevets of lieutenant-colonel, colonel, and brigadier-general, for most valuable and arduous services during the war; and became chief of the appointment bureau of the Adjutant General's Office at Washington (July 1, 1865–July 26, 1870), having been promoted lieutenant-colonel, Mar. 23, 1866. From Aug. 3, 1870, to Sept. 26, 1885, he served at San Francisco on the staff of Generals Schofield, McDowell, and Pope; and on Oct. 13, 1885, went to Washington as principal assistant to the adjutant general. He became adjutant general, June 7, 1889, and served as such until his retirement by operation of law, June 24, 1892. He was then appointed governor of the United States Soldiers' Home at Washington, where he died the following year, and where, after simple military services, his body was interred. A monument, erected by old soldiers, bears the inscription, "The Soldiers' Friend."

During his life, Kelton invented many improvements for the service rifle and revolver, and while adjutant general, initiated many measures for the benefit of the enlisted men of the army. On Apr. 30, 1870, he was married to Josephine Parmly Campbell, daughter of William S. Campbell, for many years United States consul at Dresden, Germany. She, with three sons and four daughters, survived his death. His published writings include: *New Manual of the Bayonet* (1861), *A New Treatise on Fencing with Foils* (1882), *Pigeons as Couriers* (1882), *Information for Riflemen* (1884), *Select Songs for Special Occasions* (1884). He was the editor of John Grace's *System of Horse Training* (1884).

[Gen. Samuel Breck's biographical sketch in the *Annual Reunion, Asso. Grads. U. S. Mil. Acad.*, 1894, has been largely drawn upon, with material facts checked in G. W. Cullum, *Biog. Reg. . . . U. S. Mil. Acad.* (3rd ed., 1891), vol. II, and in F. B. Heitman, *Hist. Reg. and Dict. U. S. Army* (1903). Obituaries appeared in *Army and Navy Jour.*, July 22, 1893, and *Evening Star* (Washington), July 17, 1893. Certain essential details have been furnished by members of General Kelton's family.] C. D. R.

KEMBLE, FRANCES ANNE (Nov. 27, 1809–Jan. 15, 1893), actress, reader, author, was born in London, England, the eldest daughter of Charles Kemble and his wife, Maria Theresa De Camp, also an actress. She was thus the niece of John Philip Kemble and of Sarah Siddons, the blood royal in the English theatre. But a greater part of her life was intimately and vividly bound up with the life of the young American republic, and she is often remembered today as the grandmother of Owen Wister. Educated as a girl in France, she made her début on Oct. 5, 1829, at Covent Garden, where her father was a proprietor, playing Juliet to his Mercutio. In her *Records of a Girlhood* (1878) that début is described with extraordinary vividness. It was at once evident that she had the family *flair* for acting, to a high degree, and the sinking fortunes of the theatre were temporarily retrieved by her success. In 1832 she and her father came to America and began their tour acting with the Park Theatre Company in New York. Charles Kemble appeared as Hamlet on Sept. 17, and Fanny as Bianca in *Fazio* on the 18th. Her success was immediate and decisive. Presently she played Juliet to her father's Romeo—a strange arrangement, for Charles Kemble was fifty-seven. Fanny continued to act in America, from New York to New Orleans, for two seasons, winning the utmost acclaim everywhere, especially as Julia in *The Hunchback*. Her last appearance was at the Park, June 20, 1834. Two weeks before she had married Pierce Butler of Germantown, Pa., heir to a large Georgia plantation, and she now retired from the stage, the more gladly as she acutely disliked the profession of acting, despite her success in it.

In May 1835 she published, in two volumes, *Journal of a Residence in America*, which was a record of her tour, and freely though good-naturedly she criticized various American customs. The young republic was touchy, however, and for a time she was roundly abused. The winter of 1838–39 she spent with her husband on his Georgia plantation where for the first time she saw the inside workings of slavery and realized the source of her husband's income. She was deeply revolted and again kept a journal, but she refused to publish it until the Civil War, when she issued it to influence British opinion (*Journal of a Residence on a Georgian Plantation*, 1863). Her visit to Georgia deepened the gap which tastes and temperament had already made between her and her husband. She passed many of her summers in Lenox, Mass.; in 1841 she went alone to England; and in 1846 she left her husband entirely and returned to the stage in London. The next year she spent in Italy, writing *A Year of Consolation* (1847) as a result. In 1848 her husband sued for divorce, alleging abandonment. The case was long a famous one, especially as she was defended by Rufus Choate. The divorce was granted in 1849, after Fanny had returned to America and discovered a way to employ her talents successfully without appearing on the stage. She gave public readings from Shakespeare, and so great was the demand to hear them, in England as well as America, that she was able to purchase a cottage in her beloved Lenox, in the Berkshire Hills, where she made her summer home for the next few years. Her last public reading was given in 1869. Pierce Butler died in 1867, and the two daughters of their marriage had now grown up and married. After 1869, Fanny alternated much of her time between them—one the wife of a clergyman in England, the other of Dr. Owen J. Wister of Germantown, Pa. Fanny Kemble died in London, Jan. 15, 1893.

Even as a young woman, she was never beautiful in the conventional sense, but yet she managed often to seem so, and quite evidently radiated a kind of imperious charm. Wendell Phillips records that when he was in the Harvard Law School the students saved all their money to see her act, and Phillips, finding Judge Story equally infatuated, asked him how he reconciled his admiration with his inherited Puritanism. "I don't try to," the Judge answered, "I only thank God I'm alive in the same era with such a woman" (Bobbé, *post*, p. 87). Praise from a Puritan could hardly go farther! Later, in spite of her book about America, and the notoriety of a divorce case (to be sure, it was entirely *non criminis*), her popularity on the reading platform was equally pronounced. Longfellow wrote a sonnet to her. Statesmen admired. She, more than any one else, was responsible for the fame of Lenox first as a summer literary colony and then as a resort of fashion, though her unconventional ways and independent demeanor somewhat shocked the natives. She must have remarkably combined high artistic talent, intellectual alertness, and social charm and distinction. She was more than a flashing, independent, outspoken character—she was somewhat of a genius as a woman.

Perhaps no one ever attained such eminence on the stage with less liking for it. She had in high degree the sensitiveness of the true actor, but almost a loathing for exhibiting herself in public in an assumed character. For this reason, not from indolence, she never studied the technique of acting, and her impersonations, accordingly, varied from night to night, and from scene to scene of the play, depending upon how far she forgot herself. She speaks of this at length in her autobiographical books. She hated the rôle of Lady Macbeth, because of her aunt's fame in it, and once said, "I played like the clever girl I am, but I was about as much like Lady Macbeth as the Great Mogul." Tom Moore found her acting "clever but not touching." It could be touching—but only when she was inspired to forgetfulness. On the reading platform, however, she could interpret Shakespeare without playing what she thought a childish game, and here her performances were, apparently, uniformly good and deeply moving.

She wrote two plays early in life, *Francis the First* and *The Star of Seville,* and three more later. None was of consequence. In 1844 she published a volume of poems, once popular, and wrote more poetry later. In addition to the works already mentioned she published *Records of Later Life* (1882); *Notes Upon Some of Shakespeare's Plays* (1882); *Far Away and Long Ago* (1889), a rambling novel of the Berkshires; and *Further Records* (1891). The autobiographical books reveal her keen intelligence with vividness and vivacity and are among the most delightful records of our early stage and the earlier years of American life. They show a woman whose inner resources were too great to be conquered by any exterior circumstances and explain the willing subjection of most people to her spell.

[In addition to the autobiographical works see: Dorothie Bobbé, *Fanny Kemble* (1931); Brander Matthews and Laurence Hutton, *Actors and Actresses of Great Britain and the U. S.* (1886), vol. III; G. C. D. Odell, *Annals of the N. Y. Stage,* vol. III (1928); Henry Lee, "Frances Anne Kemble," *Atlantic Monthly,* May 1893; *Letters of Edward Fitzgerald to Fanny Kemble* (1895); *Life and Letters of Catharine M. Sedgwick* (1871), ed. by Mary E. Dewey; Julian Hawthorne, *Nathaniel Hawthorne and His Wife* (1885), vol. I; Samuel Longfellow, *Life of Henry Wadsworth Longfellow* (3 vols., 1891); R. deW. Mallary, *Lenox and the Berkshire Highlands* (1902); the *Mail* (London), Jan. 18, 1893.]

W. P. E.

KEMBLE, GOUVERNEUR (Jan. 25, 1786–Sept. 16, 1875), manufacturer, was the eldest son of Peter and Gertrude (Gouverneur) Kemble and came from a family of business men. He was born in New York, N. Y., and attended Columbia College, from which he graduated in 1803. In the years before the War of 1812 he followed inclinations of his family toward a mercantile life and in the same period he became a member of the brilliant coterie of young men who surrounded Washington Irving in the New York of that day and who often assembled at a mansion of the Kembles on the Passaic in New Jersey, celebrated in *Salmagundi* as Cockloft Hall. "Who would have thought," Irving remarked to Kemble years later, referring to the pranks and revels of those times, "that we should ever have lived to be two such respectable old gentlemen!" (*The Life and Letters of Washington Irving*, I, 166).

In Monroe's administration Kemble went as consul to Cadiz, and here he took the trouble to study the Spanish methods of casting cannon. In 1817 he visited the Mediterranean ports to procure supplies for the United States navy during the Tripolitan War. When he returned to the United States he "turned Vulcan," as Irving expressed it, and began "forging thunderbolts" at Cold Spring, N. Y., opposite West Point on the Hudson River. His factory, chartered in 1818, was known as the West Point Foundry Association. It produced the first fairly perfect cannon ever cast in the United States and became so successful in the manufacture of ordnance as to receive the special patronage of the government. For many years it was the leading industry of Cold Spring. "It feeds all, clothes all, and supports all," wrote W. J. Blake in 1849 (*post*, p. 245).

Kemble now set up his home, as Irving writes, "in the very heart of the Highlands, with magnificent scenery all around him; mountains clothed with forests to their very summit, and the noble Hudson moving along quietly and majestically at their feet" (*Life and Letters*, IV, 173). He served two terms as Democratic representative in Congress during Van Buren's administration, from 1837 to 1841. In 1840 he published a pamphlet, *Letter from Gouverneur Kemble . . . In Answer to Certain Inquiries*, justifying his conduct while in office which had been impugned by several residents of his congressional district, but he refused to let himself be nominated for another term. Four years later he was a delegate to the Democratic national convention which nominated Polk, and in 1846 he was delegate to the state constitutional convention of that year. Again, he was a delegate to the futile schismatic Democratic national convention of 1860, just before the outbreak of the Civil War.

Kemble was ever a convivial man, and at his home in Cold Spring he continued the hospitality begun at "Cockloft Hall." Every Saturday night to the end of his life he gave a dinner to which all the professors and principal officers of the West Point Military Academy across the river had a standing invitation, together with such other notables as happened to be in the vicinity at the time. Irving, after he had seen Kemble for the last time, was profoundly affected, wept, and exclaimed, "That is my friend of early life—always unchanged, always like a brother; one of the noblest beings that ever was created" (*Life and Letters*, IV, 290). Kemble died at Cold Spring. He was never married.

[*Biog. Dir. Am. Cong.* (1928); W. J. Blake, *The Hist. of Putnam County, N. Y.* (1849); W. S. Pelletreau, *Hist. of Putnam County, N. Y.* (1886), pp. 559–61, 615–17, *et passim*; G. S. Hellman, *Washington Irving Esquire* (1925); Pierre M. Irving, *The Life and Letters of Washington Irving* (4 vols., 1862–64); E. F. De Lancey, *The Kembles of N. Y. and N. J.* (n.d.), reprinted from *N. Y. Hist. Soc. Colls.*, Pub. Fund Ser., vol. XVII (1885); *N. Y. Times*, Sept. 17, 1875.]

E. P. S.

KEMEYS, EDWARD (Jan. 31, 1843–May 11, 1907), sculptor, was born in Savannah, Ga., the son of William Kemeys, a native of Scarborough, N. Y., and Abby Greene, of Providence, R. I. His paternal ancestry was Welsh, and to that inheritance he attributed his intuitive qualities. When he was very young his parents returned to the North, where he went to public school at first in Scarborough and later in New York City. At thirteen he spent a vacation in Illinois and there he saw for the first time the fauna of the frontier. His boyish love for wild animals was quickened to an absorbing interest. On Mar. 31, 1862, he enlisted in the 65th Regiment, New York, and except for a brief discharge he served throughout the Civil War. He then tried farming in Dwight, Ill., but he was a dreamer and hunter more than a farmer. Drifting to New York City, he found employment as an axeman in an engineer corps working in Central Park, where his chief joy was to visit the zoo. One day, seeing a modeler making a head of a wolf, he felt the urge to become a sculptor of wild animals. He bought wax and began to model. Within a year he had produced his heroic group, "Wolves," which in 1872 was bought for Fairmount Park in Philadelphia. With money thus earned, he went West to study animals. With a gun and banjo he covered the plains and the mountains. When he found himself penniless in the buffalo country, his banjo won him entrée to a hunting-party out for big game. All the finest specimens of wild animals were his to dissect and to model—antelope, buffalo, wolf, elk, and bear. He also came to know the Indians and their lore. Later his interest found permanent expression in his bronze statue, "Prayer for Rain" (Champaign, Ill.), an Indian flanked by animals.

In 1877 Kemeys went abroad to exhibit in London and Paris. His second large group, "Deer and Panther," was sold in London, while his third, "Bison and Wolves," was well received at the Paris Salon of 1878. He studied the methods of the consummate French sculptor Barye, perhaps without fully comprehending Barye's greatness. He was intolerably homesick in Paris. To one who had hunted the bison "under the wolf-skin," Indian fashion, the caged creatures of the Jardin des Plantes meant little. His first notable work after his return to New York was the heroic bronze crouching cougar, called "Still Hunt" (1883), placed high on a rock-like pedestal in Central Park. Sometimes, as in his "Jaguar Lovers" and in "Bear Eating Grapes," he portrayed the whimsical, even genial, aspects of formidable beasts. In all of his work he showed an almost uncanny insight into animal psychology. In 1887 he finished his colossal "Bison Head" for the Union Pacific bridge at Omaha; in 1893 he had completed his groups for the Columbian Exposition, and in 1895, his "Lions" for the entrance to the Chicago Art Institute building. For several years he kept a Chicago studio, from which he made frequent trips into the wilds. Many of his small works of intimate appeal were studied from nature in an Arizona shack. Collections of these pieces are in Chicago, Philadelphia, and in the National Gallery of Art in Washington. During his final years, undaunted by failing health, he worked in Washington. Kemeys was the first American to specialize in animal sculpture. Moreover, just what he did can never be done again in our country, because already civilization has obliterated the lairs of the wild. His works are therefore historic records. He called himself self-taught, and his consequent limitations are revealed in his Indian heads which are ethnographic rather than artistic. His mastery in animal subjects is shown by a certain "impressionistic realism." For niceties of technique he cared little. Kemeys was married, in 1885, to Laura Swing of New Jersey, an artist who sympathized with his aims. He died at Georgetown, D. C., and was buried with military honors in the National Cemetery at Arlington.

[Julian Hawthorne, "American Wild Animals in Art," *Century Mag.*, June 1884; Hamlin Garland, "Edward Kemeys," *McClure's Mag.*, July 1895; E. L. Cary, "Animal Sculptures by Edward Kemeys," the *Scrip*, Feb. 1908; Leila Mechlin, "Edward Kemeys: An Appreciation," *Internat. Studio*, Oct. 1905; Lorado Taft, *The Hist. of Am. Sculpture* (1924); C. H. Caffin, *Am. Masters of Sculpture* (1903); *Who's Who in America*, 1906–07; Mich. State Lib., *Biog. Sketches of Am. Artists* (1924); *Washington Post*, May 12, 1907; *N. Y. Times*, Jan. 12, 1908.]
A. A.

KEMP, JAMES (May 20, 1764–Oct. 28, 1827), second bishop of the Protestant Episcopal Diocese of Maryland, was born in the parish of Keith Hall, Aberdeenshire, Scotland, the son of Donald and Isabel Kemp. After preparation at a local school, he entered Marischal College, Aberdeen, where he graduated in 1786. In April of the following year he came to America. As he had been an excellent student and was disposed towards a teacher's life, he obtained a position as tutor in a family on the Eastern Shore of Maryland. Although brought up in the Presbyterian faith, in his new environment he became interested in the Protestant Episcopal Church. It was at that time working to organize its scattered parishes into an efficient national and diocesan system. He threw in his lot with that church and read for holy orders under the supervision of the Rev. John Bowie, rector of Great Choptank Parish. On Dec. 26, 1789, at Philadelphia, he was ordered deacon and the next day presbyter, by the Rt. Rev. William White, bishop of Pennsylvania. There was then no bishop in Maryland. He returned to Great Choptank to become assistant to the rector, whom he succeeded in 1790. In 1802 he received the degree of D.D. from Columbia College. Kemp remained at his first parish until 1813, when he became associate rector of St. Paul's Parish, Baltimore, the most important in the state. In the next year he was elected assistant bishop to the Rt. Rev. Thomas J. Claggett, of Maryland. It was understood at the time that he should succeed the diocesan. His jurisdiction, meanwhile, was to be the Eastern Shore, where he was well known and which included one third of the parishes of the state. He was consecrated bishop Sept. 1, 1814, by Bishop White of Pennsylvania, Bishop John Henry Hobart of New York, and Bishop Richard Channing Moore of Virginia.

The election of Kemp was the occasion for a short-lived schism in the Protestant Episcopal Church in Maryland, under the lead of the Rev. Daniel Dashiell. "The Evangelical Episcopal Church," however, never numbered more than four or five clergymen. Kemp succeeded to the episcopate of Maryland on the death of Bishop Claggett, Aug. 2, 1816. By his tact and moderation he was able to heal the schism in his diocese. His episcopate was a critical period in the diocese of Maryland. The Church had greatly declined before the Revolution and had as yet made little headway. It was due to Bishop Kemp that the diocese shared in the general revival which had begun in New York under Bishop Hobart and in Virginia under Bishop Moore [*qq.v.*]. Kemp's writings were few: *A Tract upon Conversion* (1807), one or two other tracts, and occasional sermons separately published. After his death, *The Monument: A Small Selection from the Sermons of the Late Right Rev. James Kemp, D.D.* (1833), was issued, with a funeral sermon by Dr. W. E. Wyatt and a biographical sketch. In 1790 Kemp married

Elizabeth, the daughter of Capt. Edward Noel of Castlehaven, Dorchester County, Md., by whom he had three children. He died as the result of an accident at New Castle, Del. He had been in Philadelphia, participating in the consecration of Henry U. Onderdonk as assistant bishop of Pennsylvania; on the return journey his coach was overturned and he was so seriously injured internally that he died within three days.

[W. B. Sprague, *Annals Am. Pulpit*, vol. V (1859); *Fasti Academiae Mariscallanae Aberdonensis: Selections from the Records of Marischal Coll. and Univ.*, vol. II (1898); Fred. Hitchin-Kemp, *A Gen. Hist. of the Kemp and Kempe Families of Gr. Britain and Her Colonies* (n.d., pref. 1902); F. L. Hawks, *Contributions to the Ecclesiastical Hist. of the U. S.*, vol. II (1839); journals of the Diocese of Maryland and journals of the General Convention of the Protestant Episcopal Church; *Church Magazine*, Nov. 24, 1827.]

J. C. Ay—r.

KEMP, JAMES FURMAN (Aug. 14, 1859–Nov. 17, 1926), geologist and mining engineer, son of James Alexander and Caroline Anna (Furman) Kemp, was born in New York City, of Scotch ancestry, his great-grandfather, Joseph Alexander Kemp, having come from Perth, Scotland, in 1797 and established himself as a flour and grain merchant in Albany, N. Y. As a boy, young Kemp was a vigorous, wholesome-minded youth, fond of nature and outdoor sports, a characteristic he retained to the last. He received his early training in Lockwood and Adelphi Academies, and was graduated from Amherst College in 1881 with the degree of A.B., and received the degree of E.M. from Columbia College in 1884. Later he studied in the universities of Munich and Leipzig, in Germany. On returning to America in 1886, he became instructor and later adjunct professor of geology and mineralogy in Cornell University. In 1891 he accepted a call to Columbia, where, in the following year, he was made full professor of geology, a position he continued to fill until his death in 1926.

As with several of his contemporaries, Kemp's early tendencies were along lines of petrographic investigation and in 1896 he became author of a *Handbook of Rocks, for Use without the Microscope,* designed especially for his students. It was not long, however, before he was drawn into the consideration of economic problems. As early as 1887 he was engaged in an investigation of the processes of deposition and concentration of the lead and zinc ores of southeastern Missouri, and in 1893, he published his *Ore Deposits of the United States* (third edition revised and enlarged, 1900, under the title, *Ore Deposits of the United States and Canada*), the second work of its kind from the pen of an American author.

During the period 1890–1902, when not occupied by his professional duties, he was engaged in studies of the geology of the Adirondack region of New York, under the joint auspices of the federal and state surveys, but as the years passed by he devoted himself more and more to the subjects of ore deposition and alteration. His bibliography on these subjects is long and his publications are of a high order. He was in demand as an expert in mining problems and was noted for the fair, unbiased character of his testimony. He served as consulting geologist to the Board of Water Supply of New York City in connection with the Croton Dam and the Catskill Aqueduct. He was one of the promoters and associate editors as well as a regular correspondent of the magazine *Economic Geology,* founded in 1905. He was a member of numerous scientific bodies, including the National Academy of Sciences, the American Association for the Advancement of Science, and the American Philosophical Society, and was at various times president of the American Institute of Mining Engineers, the Mining and Metallurgical Society, the New York Academy of Science, and the Society of Economic Geologists. He married Kate Taylor of Kingston, R. I., in 1889. They had three children, two sons and one daughter.

Preëminently, Kemp was a teacher: one gifted with the happy faculty of making his subject interesting and attractive to his pupils, of holding and inspiring them through his magnetic personality. He delighted in the title of "Uncle Jimmie," bestowed upon him by his students, but with his faculty of being hail-fellow-well-met he combined a dignity of character that warded off rude or undue familiarity. He was a ready speaker, overflowing when occasion offered with droll extravagances, and was frequently called upon to represent his colleagues in social and official capacities. Only thirty-six hours before his death he attended a meeting of the American Institute of Mining Engineers and gave an interesting account of visits to mines in Spain the previous summer. He died of heart failure as he was about to take a train at Great Neck, L. I., for New York City.

[Personal recollections; correspondence with members of the family; *Who's Who in America*, 1926–27; editorial by W. Lindgren in *Economic Geology*, Jan.–Feb. 1927; *Mining and Metallurgy*, Dec. 1926; article by C. P. Berkey in *Engineering and Mining Journal*, Nov. 27, 1926; *N. Y. Times*, Nov. 18, 1926.]

G. P. M.

KEMP, JOHN (Apr. 10, 1763–Nov. 15, 1812), professor in Columbia College, was born at

Auchlossan, Aberdeenshire, Scotland. He matriculated at Marischal College, Aberdeen, in 1779 as "Joannes Kempt, f[ilius] Joannis in Coull" and graduated (M.A.) in 1783. In 1782 he won in competition a Gray mathematical bursary, and, leaving the college with an excellent reputation for scholarship, he came immediately to America, where he was in charge of the academy at Dumfries, Va., for two years. In April 1785 he was appointed to teach mathematics for one year at Columbia College in New York City. At the end of that time there was a public examination of his class, in which each student was required to draw a number out of a box and demonstrate without further assistance the problem or theorem in Euclid to which it referred. The examination was unusually successful, and this convincing exhibition of Kemp's mastery of his subject and his ability to teach it led to his appointment as professor of mathematics and natural philosophy in 1786 at the age of twenty-three. In 1795 he accepted the additional charge of the professorship of geography. Meanwhile honors had come to him from abroad: the degree of LL.D. from King's College, Aberdeen, in 1787 (upon the recommendation of Gen. Arthur St. Clair, and Col. William Grayson of Dumfries, Va.), and a foreign fellowship in the Royal Society of Edinburgh in 1792. His courses, which are described in *The Present State of Learning in the College of New York* (1794), ranged from arithmetic to the higher branches of algebra, and over the whole field of "natural philosophy," and provision was made for the attendance of the general public upon some of his lectures.

Kemp's zeal and patient labor were never relaxed during nearly three decades of faithful service to the college. His courses required constant modification, from the discoveries and improvements continually being made in the physical sciences, and undoubtedly his intense industry, unaccompanied by suitable precautions for his health, led to his comparatively early death, which occurred at New York in his fiftieth year. He was twice married, and left a daughter by his first wife. The tablet erected to his memory in Trinity Church by the Peithologian Society of the college, is transcribed in Timothy Alden's *Collection of American Epitaphs* (1814, IV, 259). His portrait, now in the possession of Columbia University, is that of a chubby little man with a look of geniality and keen intelligence.

Kemp's instruction made a deep impression upon DeWitt Clinton, one of his early pupils, and his confidence in the feasibility of a canal across New York State, increased after a tour along the proposed route in 1810, was of great assistance to Clinton in his efforts that resulted in the building of the Erie Canal, although the two men had been estranged since 1799, when Kemp became a Federalist.

[*New York Gazette,* Nov. 16, 17, 18, 1812; *Am. Medic. and Philosophical Reg.,* Jan. 1813; James Hardie's *New York Magazine,* May 1814; *Fasti Academiae Mariscallanae Aberdonensis: Selections from the Records of Marischal Coll. and Univ.,* II (1898), 355; *Officers and Grads. of Univ. and King's Coll., Aberdeen* (1893), p. 112; James Renwick, *Discourse on . . . De Witt Clinton* (1829), *passim*; David Hosack, *Memoir of De Witt Clinton* (1829), pp. 96–97; Fred Hitchin-Kemp, *A Gen. Hist. of the Kemp and Kempe Families of Great Britain and Her Colonies* (n.d., pref. 1902); minutes (MS.) of the Trustees of Columbia College.]

M. H. T.

KEMP, ROBERT H. (June 6, 1820–May 15, 1897), shoe-dealer, director of "Old Folks' Concerts," was born in Wellfleet, Mass., the son of Nathan and Hannah (Wharf) Kemp. Brought up in a community where most of the wage-earners followed the sea, he spent three years on a fishing boat. At the age of twenty he became a shoe-dealer in Boston as junior member of the firm of Mansfield & Kemp. For a short time about 1843 he was a member of the Boston Fire Department. Soon after his marriage he purchased a farm in Reading, and established his home in that suburban town. From 1854 to 1870 he was occupied as conductor of the Reading Old Folks' Musical Society.

The development of this unique institution, by which "Father" Kemp will be remembered, was a natural growth of the times in which he lived. The absence of public entertainments called for a substitute in the home and community. Robert Kemp's pleasure in singing the old songs of the church suggested to him that he might gather the singers from around his home in Reading and spend the evenings in reviving the music of their fathers. From these neighborhood gatherings the Reading Old Folks' Musical Society sprang. So much enthusiasm was aroused by the rehearsals that it was determined to give a public concert to please the many friends who were accustomed to crowd into and around the house when the "Old Folks" sang. On a December evening in the early fifties an entertainment was held in the Lyceum Hall in Reading. The hall was packed and many were unable to gain admission, but listened from the outside. Concerts in Lynn and Boston followed. Next a short trip was taken extending as far south as Washington, and in New York more than six thousand persons attended one of the concerts in the Academy of Music, the proceeds of which were devoted to charity. The following season a seven months' tour was made into the West. In 1861 thirty members left Boston for a tour in England. Liverpool, London, and Chester heard their entertainments, but the proceeds were not paying expenses, and at Brighton the conductor decided to return home. After his return, Kemp went back to selling shoes in Boston. The next season a series of "Monday Popular Concerts" was projected for Tremont Temple in Boston, and these were repeated in many cities in other parts of the United States. In 1868 Kemp published *Father Kemp and His Old Folks: A History of the Old Folks' Concerts, Comprising an Autobiography of the Author.*

Perhaps the book of songs most used in the earlier Old Folks' Concerts was the *Billings and Holden Collection of Ancient Psalmody* (1836), one of a long line of collections of ancient music. Some contributions were made by Father Kemp to the *Continental Harmony* (1857), which was especially intended for Old Folks' Concerts. In 1874 he sponsored *Father Kemp's Old Folks Concert Music,* published that year. During the Temperance agitation, *The Faneuil Hall Temperance Song Book* (1876) was compiled by Mother Kemp. The strangest fact in Kemp's career is indicated in the last sentence of his autobiography: "Although I have swung my baton before a large choir in upwards of six thousand concerts, my word upon it, I never knew a note of music, and cannot distinguish a 'minim' from a 'demisemiquaver.' I flatter myself, however, that I can beat time with the most accomplished impressario." As old age came on, he became an inmate of the Old Men's Home in Charlestown, where he died in his seventy-seventh year.

[Sources include Kemp's autobiography; *Boston Transcript,* May 15, and *Boston Daily Advertiser,* May 17, 1897; and death certificate for date of death and parents' names. The copyright records and his signature in the copy of his autobiography at the Lib. of Cong. give his name as Robert H. Kemp; the preface to the *Continental Harmony* refers to him as R. C. Kemp. The record of his death gives no middle initial.]

F. J. M.

KEMPER, JACKSON (Dec. 24, 1789–May 24, 1870), first missionary bishop of the Protestant Episcopal Church, was the son of Daniel and Elizabeth (Marius) Kemper. He was born at Pleasant Valley, Dutchess County, N. Y., near the place where his grandfather, Jacob, formerly an officer in the army of the Palatine, had settled soon after 1741. He was christened David Jackson in honor of David Jackson [*q.v.*] of Philadelphia, who had married his father's sister, but dropped his first name in early life. Daniel Kemper, a soldier in the Revolution, was at one time customs receiver for New York City. With Napoleon's continental blockade and the American embargo, financial disaster began to threaten the family. Fortunately Jackson Kemper was well advanced in his education before the days of adversity. He graduated from Columbia College in 1809 as valedictorian of his class, and began the study of theology, being ordained deacon in 1811 and presbyter in 1814. His first charge was in Philadelphia. Very early he developed an interest in the West, making missionary journeys into the wilds of Pennsylvania, Virginia, and Ohio. In 1816, he married Jerusha Lyman of Philadelphia who died two years later. He was married a second time, in 1821, to Ann Relf, also of a Philadelphia family. Three children were born of this marriage. In 1831, he moved to Norwalk, Conn., where his second wife died in 1832.

His first missionary journey to the farther West was made in 1834 when he visited the Indian Mission near Green Bay, Wis. Though he was not at all of the pioneer type, his courteous and sympathetic methods were peculiarly successful with frontiersmen. In 1835, he was elected first missionary bishop of the church, with definite jurisdiction over Missouri and Indiana. His field was almost immediately renamed "the Northwest." Annual visitations throughout a constantly shifting jurisdiction absorbed much of his time. In 1837, he traveled as far west as Fort Leavenworth. In the winter of 1838, he journeyed on horseback across the unsettled prairies of southwestern Missouri to visit the Seneca Indians just beyond the state boundaries. Reading his Greek Testament in the bar rooms of the Wabash river towns, exchanging anecdotes with trappers along the Missouri, or making kindly contacts with all sorts and conditions of men on the Western roads and rivers, he became a familiar and beloved figure in the Northwest between 1835 and 1859. He declined an election to the Maryland episcopate in 1838, refusing to desert the missionary field. Missouri, Indiana, and Iowa in turn became independent dioceses, but new areas inevitably developed. From the first, Wisconsin had been a favorite part of his see. In 1854, he became its diocesan, retaining the missionary office as well, and in 1859 he retired from the strenuous labor of keeping abreast of western settlement and devoted himself exclusively to the diocese of Wisconsin.

Bishop Kemper's experience with clergymen who migrated westward was discouraging. It was seldom that the Eastern clergy could adjust themselves to the West, and it seemed necessary, therefore, to provide training for Western men. Kemper College, Missouri, the first attempt to fill this need, ran afoul of financial difficulties in the forties, was torn by faculty animosities which even the tactful and kindly policy of the bishop could not heal, and closed its doors in 1845. Nashotah House in Wisconsin and later Racine College (1852) were more successful. In church politics Kemper was a high churchman, though never an acrimonious partisan, and under his direction, Nashotah and Racine became prominent for ritualistic observances. From secular politics he held aloof as a religious duty. In his seventy-ninth year (1868) he ventured upon a journey to England to the Council of Bishops. Here he was honored with the degree of LL.D. by Cambridge University. He died two years later at his home in Delafield, Wis. He had established seven dioceses, founded three colleges, opened numerous schools and academies, and planted the Episcopal church in the Northwest.

[The best material on Bishop Kemper is found in his diaries, letters, etc., collected in Wis. MSS., Ser. G, State Hist. Soc. of Wis., Madison. Brief extracts from these have been published in *Wis. Hist. Colls.*, vol. XIV (1898) and in the *Nashotah Scholiast*, Dec. 1883–July 1884, Oct. 1884–June 1885. See also G. L. Nute, in *Minn. Hist.*, Sept. 1926; W. S. Perry, *The Bishops of the Am. Church* (1897); Greenough White, *An Apostle of the Western Church: A Memoir of the Rt. Rev. Jackson Kemper* (1900); G. C. Tanner, *Fifty Years of Church Work in the Diocese of Minn.* (1909); M. T. Gardner, *Conquerors of the Continent* (copr. 1911); *Wis. State Jour.* (Madison), May 25, 1870.] K. J. G.

KEMPER, JAMES LAWSON (June 11, 1823–Apr. 7, 1895), Confederate soldier, governor of Virginia, was born in the piedmont Virginia county of Madison. He came of good colonial stock, his father, William, being descended from John Kemper of Spotswood's Germania settlement and his mother, Maria Elizabeth (Allison) Kemper, from Col. J. J. Stadler of Washington's staff. Having received the degree of B.A. (1842) from Washington College and a grounding in military drill at the Virginia Military Institute, the youth read law under George W. Summers [*q.v.*] and settled for its practice in Madison. Commissioned captain of volunteers in the Mexican War, he reached Taylor's army too late for active service. Back at the law, in 1853 he married Cremora Conway Cave and went to the House of Delegates for the first of five terms. He was chairman of the committee on military affairs, president of the board of visitors of the Virginia Military Institute, and speaker of the House from December 1861 to March 1862. Though not an "original secessionist," he volunteered promptly for the war and was commissioned colonel on May 2, 1861. Having fought with the 7th Virginia Regiment from Bull Run to Williamsburg, where he led a charge under the eye of A. P. Hill [*q.v.*], he was made brigadier-general; in this capacity he served faithfully and creditably until Gettysburg. Here he led in person the right wing of Pickett's charge, was desperately wounded, captured, and imprisoned. Exchanged but incapacitated for active service, he was made major-general and put in command of the Conscript Bureau. Soldiers loved him for his fine bearing, fearlessness, dash, and impassioned eloquence; officers prized his good sense and high conception of duty.

After the war, returning to the law in Madison, Kemper met much success, particularly as an advocate. In politics he favored a conciliatory course (though he did not recant as to secession or apply for pardon) with a view particularly to the state's economic rehabilitation. Accordingly he vigorously supported with tongue and pen the Conservative party in 1869 and in 1872 canvassed the state as elector on the Greeley ticket. Living in the center of the state's white population and acceptable to them because of his record as a soldier, his striking appearance, and his stirring eloquence, Kemper also enjoyed the confidence of Gen. William Mahone [*q.v.*], the powerful president of the Atlantic, Mississippi & Ohio Railroad. Consequently, in 1873 he won the party nomination for governor over Col. R. E. Withers, who was anti-Mahone and deemed Bourbonish; and he was elected over R. W. Hughes [*q.v.*], whose liberalism had led him into the Republican party. Governor Kemper's administration (1874–77) was marked by his independence. An offer of a federal senatorship (which could probably have been made good) he declined, saying that Virginia had already given him her highest honor. He urged full recognition of civil rights for the negroes, a sympathetic encouragement of them, and their protection against the unscrupulous. A bill putting the government of Petersburg under a commission he vetoed as contrary to the principles of local self-government, though he professed sympathy with the city's desire to escape negro rule. Against federal interference in elections he protested formally and vigorously. He asked that Congress share the burden of state education of the negroes and assume the state's debt, both as incidents of the war. To the disgust of the financial world, he insisted on a conference with the state's creditors, designed to secure equality of creditors and reduction of the debt burden; when the conference failed, he joined the "Debt-payers" to the indignation of "Readjusters." Constantly in pain from his old wound, he sometimes appeared unduly irascible and arbitrary. None, however, doubted his integrity; and the cultured highly prized the literary quality of his papers and addresses. Returning again to the practice of law, he died in Orange County. Five children survived him. Frederic Kemper Freeman [*q.v.*] was his nephew.

[Walter Harrison, *Pickett's Men* (1870); R. E. Withers, *Autobiography* (1907); C. C. Pearson, *Readjuster Movement in Va.* (1917); F. A. Virkus, *The Abridged Compendium of Am. Geneal.*, III (1928), 451; *Richmond Dispatch* and *Times* (Richmond), Apr. 9, 1895.] C. C. P.

KEMPER, REUBEN (d. Jan. 28, 1827), a controversial figure on the West Florida border, was the son of a Baptist clergyman and was probably born in Loudoun or Fauquier county, Va. An early resident of Cincinnati, he there formed a connection with John Smith [*q.v.*], prominent merchant and land speculator, who from 1800 on associated Reuben and his two brothers with himself in a colonization enterprise near Baton Rouge. A controversy having arisen with Smith over their joint accounts, Kemper believed himself wronged both by his partner and by the Spanish authorities, for the latter expelled him and his brothers from their land holdings. Resentful over this treatment and abetted by Daniel Clark [*q.v.*] and other speculators who had hoped to see West Florida included in the Louisiana transfer, Reuben Kemper was persuaded to strike a blow in behalf of "Floridian Freedom." On Aug. 7, 1804, supported by a small group of border malcontents, his two brothers, Nathan and Samuel, duly instructed by Reuben from New Orleans, sallied from Mississippi Territory and attempted to surprise and capture Baton Rouge. Foiled in this attempt they straightway retreated into Mississippi, from which point of vantage the three continued to embroil the whole border (Cox, *post,* pp. 152–63).

In July 1805 Reuben acquired property in the town of Pinckneyville (Land Record A, Williamson County, Miss.). On the night of Sept. 3, while he was visiting his two brothers, who lived still nearer the border, a masked party seized the turbulent trio and delivered them below the line to a Spanish patrol, "casually" encountered there. In the course of the next day, however, captives and captors were apprehended on the Mississippi, and the Kempers, under bond to keep the peace, returned to their American asylum. The incident, greatly distorted in press and in official report, became an international *cause célèbre* (*American State Papers, Foreign Relations,* vol. II, 1832, pp. 683–89; Cox, pp. 165–68). Reuben Kemper proceeded to take both legal and personal vengeance on his enemies. One died of disease, contracted while hiding from him; another had his ears cropped after being beaten into insensibility; while two brothers, the chief leaders in seizing Kemper, were forced to meet a judgment of $7,000 in his favor (Land Record A, Williamson County; Pickett, *post,* p. 486).

In 1810 this irrepressible borderer, under commission from the insurgents at Baton Rouge, attempted to subvert the Spanish government at Mobile and Pensacola. The settlers from the nearby American communities, already exasperated against the Spaniards, afforded him some recruits, and with this dubious crew he sought to compel the surrender of Mobile. Defiantly raising his "lone star" flag on Sunday, Nov. 25, at a suitable bluff rechristened Bunker Hill, he maintained for some weeks a "moving camp" on the east side of Mobile Bay. From this varying point he vainly tried to negotiate with the Spanish commandant. When his force inevitably began to melt away, he transferred it to the other side of the bay and went across the border for more recruits. He was promptly arrested and while the American authorities forcibly detained him, the Spaniards surprised and dispersed the remnant of his irregular levies, killing and wounding a few and taking seven or eight prisoners. Kemper's ill-advised foray simply strengthened the Spanish hold on Mobile (Cox, pp. 457–85).

Kemper later figured in land transactions both in Mississippi and Louisiana. Twice he journeyed to Washington in behalf of his captured followers, who were imprisoned at Havana. He is generally credited with serving in the Gutierrez-Magee expedition into Texas (1812–13), but it was his brother Samuel (d. 1814) who thus kept up the family tradition. He himself died while on a business trip to Natchez.

[Kemper's name appears occasionally in the county records at Woodville, Miss., and in the parish records at St. Francisville and Baton Rouge, La., but most of the details given above are derived from *Papeles procedentes . . . de la Isla de Cuba,* a section of MSS. in the Archivo General de Indias, at Seville, and from the West Florida Papers in the MSS. Division of the Library of Congress. Definite references will be found in I. J. Cox, *The West Florida Controversy* (1918). For more favorable accounts of the Kempers consult J. F. H. Claiborne, *Mississippi as a Province, Territory and State* (1880), I, 260–62, 307–11; A. J. Pickett, *Hist. of Ala.* (1851), II, 209–10, 236–39; and a letter of J. F. Watson to George W. Morgan dated at Philadelphia, Aug. 20, 1807, and published as a broadside in New Orleans some months later (copy in Ky. Hist. Soc., Frankfort). An obituary appeared in *The Ariel* (Natchez), Feb. 9, 1827.] I. J. C.

KEMPFF, LOUIS (Oct. 11, 1841–July 29, 1920), naval officer, was born near Belleville, Ill., the son of Friedrich and Henrietta Kempff.

He entered the Naval Academy in 1857, was detached in April 1861, and was ordered to the *Vandalia* on the Charleston blockade. After taking a captured schooner to New York he was sent to the *Wabash,* took part in the attack on the forts at Port Royal, and commanded a howitzer in the boat attacks on Port Royal Ferry and Fernandina, Fla.—all before he was warranted as a midshipman in 1862. In that year he was sent to the *Susquehanna,* was present at the recapture of Norfolk, and engaged in blockade duty off Mobile. In 1863 he served on the gunboat *Sonoma* off the Sabine River and in the next year was on the *Connecticut* off Wilmington. The close of the war found him on the gunboat *Suwanee* in the Pacific, the region in which, except for a short period at the War College, he served the rest of his career. This service involved duty as executive officer on the *Portsmouth, Independence, Mohican, Saranac,* and *California,* various posts at the Mare Island Navy Yard, and command of the *Alert,* 1881–82, of the *Adams,* 1885–88, and of the *Monterey,* 1893–95.

In 1899 Kempff was made a rear admiral and assigned to duty as second in command of the Asiatic Squadron. In 1900, during the Boxer troubles, he was the senior American naval officer off Taku, where an international fleet was assembled to protect the lives of foreigners in northern China. Under his orders sailors and marines were landed, but when the other foreign admirals demanded of the Chinese the surrender of the Taku forts, fearing that the Boxers would seize them and thus be able to interrupt communication with Tien Tsin and Peking, Kempff declined to join in the demand. His decision was based on his belief that the Chinese imperial authorities had not as yet committed any act of war and was in accordance with his instructions from Washington and the general policy of the United States toward China. In the bombardment that followed on June 17, the American gunboat *Monocacy,* on which a number of foreign women and children had taken refuge, was hit by a stray shot from the forts but did not return the fire.

News of the attack reached Peking that same day and was probably responsible for the opposition offered by Chinese imperial troops to the advance of the allied relief column toward Peking; but it is doubtful whether the conflict could have been much longer delayed. Kempff cooperated with the other foreign commanders in later operations and was commended by the Navy Department for his refusal to join in the attack on the forts. When he returned to the United States, he was given a complimentary banquet in San Francisco by friends of China, at which the Chinese minister, Wu Ting Fang, was a speaker; and his friends even introduced a resolution of thanks into Congress, but it never came to a vote.

After this cruise Kempff served as commandant of the Pacific Naval District until he was retired in 1903. He died in Santa Barbara, Cal., and was buried there. In 1873 at Fair Oaks, Cal., he had married Cornelia Reese, adopted daughter of Thomas H. Selby. His wife survived him.

[For the Taku incident see J. D. Long, *The New Am. Navy* (1903), II, 129–38; G. N. Steiger, *China and the Occident* (1927), pp. 224–34; P. H. Clements, *The Boxer Rebellion* (1915), pp. 128–32; Kempff's dispatches in *House Doc. No. 645,* 57 Cong., 1 Sess., and in *Army and Navy Jour.,* July 28, 1900. For biographical details see *Who's Who in America,* 1920–21, and obituaries in *N. Y. Times,* July 30, 1920 and *Army and Navy Jour.,* July 31, 1920.] W. B. N.

KEMPSTER, WALTER (May 25, 1841–Aug. 22, 1918), physician, psychiatrist, son of Christopher and Charlotte (Treble) Kempster, was born in London, England. His parents emigrated to the United States about 1849 and settled in Syracuse, N. Y. Here he received his preliminary education and then entered the Long Island College Hospital at Brooklyn. On the outbreak of the Civil War he enlisted in the 12th New York Infantry and was mustered into the United States service for a three months' term, May 13, 1861, remaining until the expiration of his original enlistment. Mustered out of service in October 1861, he reënlisted in November in the 10th New York Cavalry. He was appointed hospital steward and detailed to hospital duty in Baltimore, Md., where he assisted in organizing the Patterson Park Hospital in April 1862. In the following January, at his own request, he was relieved of this duty and rejoined his regiment in the field, and on June 9, 1863, he was promoted to first lieutenant for gallantry on the field at Brandy Station. Owing to injuries received at Mine Run he resigned his commission in December 1863. During his convalescence he completed his medical studies and graduated from the Long Island College Hospital in June 1864. He then reëntered the service as acting assistant surgeon and served in this capacity until the close of the war.

After leaving the service Kempster made a special study of nervous and mental diseases, and in 1866 he was appointed assistant superintendent of the State Asylum for the Feeble-Minded at Syracuse, N. Y. In 1867 he was appointed assistant physician at the State Lunatic Asylum at Utica, N. Y., where he remained until 1873. During his service at Utica he acted as assistant editor of the *American Journal of Insanity,* a position he held for ten years, and in collaboration with the superintendent, John P. Gray [*q.v.*], developed a method for photographing and projecting on a screen gross and microscopic preparations of the brain. In 1873 he was appointed superintendent of the Northern Hospital for the Insane, at Oshkosh, Wis. Here he remained until 1884, when he resigned his position and removed to Milwaukee. During his service at Oshkosh he continued his study of the minute structure of the brain and also studied the effects of chloral, hyoscyamus, and other drugs.

Appointed in 1891 a member of the congressional commission to investigate conditions of emigration, he visited Europe under instructions to report on emigration from Russia. The commission, however, met opposition, and the report was not allowed to be circulated in Russia. The following year Kempster was a member of a congressional commission on epidemics, and on visiting Turkey, Palestine, and Persia, found that no quarantine regulations were enforced. In 1894 he was health commissioner of Milwaukee and had opposition in his attempt to enforce rules regarding smallpox. Eventually the matter was brought into court and he and his regulations were fully sustained. On account of his reputation as a specialist in the treatment of insanity Kempster was frequently called to serve as an expert witness in civil and criminal cases and was one of the witnesses for the prosecution in the celebrated case of Guiteau, slayer of President Garfield. He contributed numerous papers to the standard publications on insanity, mental hygiene, and jurisprudence and published a volume on *The International Dissemination of Cholera and Other Infectious Diseases, with Plan for Effectual Quarantine* (1893). A shorter paper, "The Early Days of our Cavalry in the Army of the Potomac," he published in the *War Papers* (vol. III, 1903) of the Wisconsin Commandery of the Loyal Legion. Kempster was married to J. L. J. Poessell on June 28, 1913. He died at Milwaukee in his seventy-eighth year.

[*Memoirs of Milwaukee County* (2 vols., 1909), ed. by J. A. Watrous; *Am. Jour. of Insanity,* Jan. 1919; H. A. Kelly and W. L. Burrage, *Am. Medic. Biogs.* (1920); *Milwaukee Sentinel, N. Y. Times,* Aug. 23, 1918.] W. S. M.

KENDALL, AMOS (Aug. 16, 1789–Nov. 12, 1869), journalist, postmaster-general, writing at the age of forty-five to a boyhood friend, delineated a distinctive aspect of his entire life, "I seem to have lived in several different worlds and to have been the associate of many races of human beings" (Letter to Caleb Butler, May 13, 1835, Manuscript Division, Library of Congress). The first of these worlds was New England, where his boyhood, youth, and early manhood were spent. Born in Dunstable, Mass., he was the son of Zebedee Kendall and of Molly (Dakin) Kendall and a descendant in the fifth generation of Francis Kendall, who was at Woburn, Mass., as early as 1640. As a boy, though never sturdy, Amos shared in the hard labor of his father's farm in Dunstable, whose acres lay upon both sides of the boundary between Massachusetts and New Hampshire. Despite meager educational opportunities he entered Dartmouth College at eighteen. Fragments of a diary reveal him as an exceptionally diligent and serious-minded student, though not wholly aloof from the rough college life of the day. Following the custom then prevalent, he spent a considerable portion of each college year teaching country schools. On graduation in 1811 he stood at the head of his class. Ill health and uncertainty delayed his choice of a profession. Finally, deciding to become a lawyer, he studied at Groton, Mass., for about two years in the office of William Merchant Richardson [*q.v.*]. New England birth and training exerted a deep and abiding influence upon Kendall's personality.

In 1814 Kendall was caught up in the flood of migration from New England to the West. Chance took him to Kentucky, where he remained until 1829. His first year was spent in the family of Henry Clay, as a tutor; his second at Georgetown, as lawyer, postmaster, and editor of two struggling newspapers. In October 1816 he moved to Frankfort, the capital of the state, to take charge of the *Argus of Western America,* an established paper of a good deal of influence. Here Kendall found his opportunity. His keen analysis, trenchant style, and aptitude in controversy speedily won for his paper additional prestige. At first a supporter of Henry Clay, Kendall broke with him in 1826 and soon developed the intense devotion to Andrew Jackson that marked the remainder of his life. For this change Kendall was often accused of ingratitude and self seeking. These charges he always vigorously denied. An examination of his earlier opinions makes it seem clear that Kendall was destined to follow Jackson rather than Clay. That Jackson carried Kentucky in 1828, a triumph which gave him great delight, was undoubtedly due in large measure to Kendall. For this service he was chosen to carry the electoral vote to Washington. With his arrival there his life entered into its best-known phase.

For the next twelve years Kendall was closely identified with the Jackson régime as carried on by Jackson and Van Buren. Officially he served for the first six years as fourth auditor of the treasury; then for five years as postmaster-general; during the last year, as editor of the *Extra Globe,* he fought for the reëlection of Van Buren and the continuation of the régime. For eight years he belonged to the group of Jackson's closest associates and influential advisers popularly known as the "Kitchen Cabinet." Although the functioning of the group has not been studied in a way to disclose the precise influence exerted by individual members, it is clear that Kendall was among the most potent; that his influence steadily increased, especially after 1831; and that in the war on the Bank of the United States his influence was the most powerful.

As an administrator Kendall was the most capable and successful of the Jackson appointees. At the beginning of the régime, as fourth auditor, he discovered corruption on the part of his predecessor and instituted reforms. This enabled the Jackson men, in appearance at least, to make good their campaign assertions and promises. Six years later, when Jackson's popularity was seriously endangered by gross corruption among several of his appointees and when the post-office department had admittedly fallen into bad condition, Kendall was appointed postmaster-general for the purpose of bringing about drastic reforms. He speedily corrected the flagrant abuses, paid off the debt of the department, and gave it a new organization that remained in operation without material change for many years. His action in condoning the illegal exclusion of abolitionist propaganda from the mails by southern postmasters was bitterly criticised by active anti-slavery men, but it seems to have met popular approval even in the North.

As a writer Kendall rendered Jackson service of the highest importance, though its extent and character were often exaggerated at the time by rumor and by hostile critics. In many instances the form and much of the substance of Jackson's state papers were due to Kendall. Comparison of Jackson's messages to Congress with manuscripts in Kendall's handwriting, preserved among the Jackson papers now in the Library of Congress, shows clearly that Kendall had a large share in the preparation of at least five of the annual messages; that he was the principal author of the message of July 10, 1832, vetoing the bill to recharter the Bank of the United States; and that he wrote Jackson's well-known letter of June 26, 1833, to Duane foreshadowing the removal of the deposits. Kendall also wrote many of the replies to the addresses presented to Jackson and had a hand in much that appeared in the newspapers in Jackson's behalf. He was largely instrumental in bringing Francis P. Blair, Sr. [*q.v.*], to Washington to establish the *Globe* as the organ of the administration, and he wrote extensively for it.

In the spring of 1840 Kendall returned to journalism. Continuing at Washington he there tried, during the next four years, several journalistic experiments. One or two started well but none of them succeeded. Financial embarrassment and ill health made these years the most trying of his life. As a means of livelihood, in 1843 he reluctantly became an agent for the collection of claims against the government. The immediate results were inconsiderable, but one in behalf of the Cherokee Indians brought him a large fee many years later. For the sake of his health he purchased on credit a farm of one hundred acres about a mile north of the capitol. Working upon this farm improved his health; at a later date its increased value brought him a large financial return; but for the moment its possession increased his perplexities. His burdens were further increased by prolonged litigation growing out of controversies with mail contractors, which had begun while he was postmaster-general. As a consequence of this litigation he was for a considerable period technically a prisoner for debt at large on his own recognizance but restricted in his movements to the District of Columbia. A favorable decision by the Supreme Court in one case and a special appropriation by Congress finally relieved him of his liability in the matter.

In 1845 Kendall entered upon an entirely new phase of his career, as the business agent of S. F. B. Morse, the inventor of the telegraph. Knowing his own lack of business talent, Morse engaged Kendall to act as his agent on a percentage basis. In this capacity Kendall looked after the defense of Morse's interests in dozens of lawsuits involving patent rights. He sold or let out on royalty the right to use the patents to many companies operating in different parts of the country. He organized several companies and took a hand in their operation. He was also the most active promoter of the early efforts to consolidate the numerous small companies into a few large systems. For some years Kendall's labors, though prodigious for a man of his age, brought only small and uncertain returns. By 1859 the initial difficulties had been so far conquered that both Morse and Kendall had become rich men, as wealth was reckoned at that time.

On the eve of the Civil War Kendall was

again drawn into the political arena. Shortly before the election of Lincoln he vigorously denied the right of secession in a public correspondence with James L. Orr. Soon after the election in his "Letter on Secession" (contained in *Secession Letters of Amos Kendall: also his Letters to Col. Orr and Prest. Buchanan,* 1861), addressed particularly to the South, he elaborated and reinforced his arguments. It seems highly probable that Kendall was the author of "The Diary of a Public Man," published anonymously in the *North American Review* from August to November in 1879, perhaps the most vivid contemporaneous picture of the secession winter at Washington. During the war, though opposing Lincoln's administration on some points, Kendall at all times advocated vigorous measures for the prosecution of the war. Remaining a Democrat, he steadily opposed the efforts of the Vallandigham wing to control the Democratic party.

The closing years of Kendall's life were devoted chiefly to religion and philanthropy. By large donations he made possible the erection of the original and of the present Calvary Baptist Church in Washington. He also gave money liberally and participated actively in the Sunday school and mission work of that church. He was the leading spirit in the foundation of the Columbia Institution for the Deaf and Dumb, now Gallaudet College. As president of its board of trustees, he piloted it in its early and most difficult years, donated a portion of Kendall Green for its campus, and used his influence to get appropriations for it from Congress. His last appearance in politics was in the campaign of 1868, for which he wrote his "Letter to Rutherford," perhaps the keenest criticism of the Republican reconstruction policy that was ever written.

Kendall's appearance and manner were always striking. As a young man he was usually described as homely and awkward. By middle age he had greatly improved in looks and bearing. Harriet Martineau, seeing him at Washington in 1834, pronounced him a great genius. She was struck by his talent for silence, his splendid audacity, the extreme sallowness of his complexion, and by his very white hair, as well as by his countenance, which she thought would not help the superstitious to escape their dread of him. As an old man he was still an arresting figure. John W. Forney, who greatly admired him for his effective campaign writing, found it hard to believe that so soft-spoken a man could have written those nervous editorials, which aroused so much Whig resentment and Democratic enthusiasm in the Jackson era. Few men in American public life ever met the amount of bitter denunciation, violent hatred, and unsparing ridicule that fell to the lot of Kendall. He was denounced by his enemies as dishonest, selfish, and treacherous. Yet in fact, he was scrupulously honest, self sacrificing, and of the highest loyalty. In his later years his true character was widely but not universally recognized. His first marriage was to Mary B. Woolfolk, of Jefferson County, Ky., in October 1818. After her death in 1823, he married, on Jan. 5, 1826, Jane Kyle, of Georgetown, Ky., who was twenty years his junior.

[S. F. B. Morse Papers, Jackson Papers, Giddings-Julian Collection, Miscellaneous MSS. of Kendall in Lib. of Cong.; *Autobiog. of Amos Kendall,* ed. by Wm. Stickney (1872); J. W. Forney, *Anecdotes of Public Men,* vol. II (copr. 1881); C. G. Bowers, *The Party Battles of the Jackson Period* (1922); James Schouler, *Hist. of the U. S.,* vol. IV (1889); *Evening Star* (Washington, D. C.), Nov. 12, 1869.] F. M. A.

KENDALL, GEORGE WILKINS (Aug. 22, 1809–Oct. 21, 1867), journalist, son of Thaddeus and Abigail Wilkins Kendall, was born at Mount Vernon, near Amherst, N. H. His father was of early New England stock; his mother was derived from an ancestor who came to New England in 1628. Having acquired the printer's craft at Burlington, Vt., he was employed in Washington and by Greeley in New York, and, fond of anecdotes and epigrams, he early acquired a reputation for wit. About 1832 he went south, spending a year with the *Alabama Register* in Mobile, and then proceeding to New Orleans. With Francis Lumsden he founded the first cheap daily in that city, naming it the *Picayune* from the small coin so called. The first number appeared in January 1837, a four-page folio of ten by fifteen inches. The audacious little sheet, reflecting the personality of its editor, both entertained and irritated the public by its light banter. Kendall possessed both the instinct of the press man for news and the ardor of the soldier of fortune for adventure. His paper well established, in 1841 he joined the Santa Fé expedition, now sponsored by General Lamar, the president of the independent state of Texas, who by proclamation offered protection to the people of Santa Fé, then under Mexican rule, avowing his purpose in any event to open commercial relations. The badly equipped expedition ended in disaster. Governor Armijo of New Mexico marched the surviving members to the City of Mexico. One of their nights Kendall described as "spent in another Black Hole of Calcutta." He was kept some time in a prison for lepers. Influential friends obtained his release, and on his return he wrote his *Narrative of the Texan Santa Fé Expedition* (2 vols., 1844), which was widely read.

During the next three years Kendall in the *Picayune* maintained the necessity of going to war with Mexico, and when hostilities began he started at once for the Rio Grande. There he rode with the Rangers, witnessed most of Taylor's battles, and himself captured a cavalry flag. When the Scott expedition was organized he attached himself as a voluntary aide to the staff of General Worth and saw nearly all the fighting from Vera Cruz to Chapultepec. He was mentioned in dispatches and received a wound in the knee in the storming of the last fortress.

This war was the first ever to be reported comprehensively in the daily press. The correspondents, of whom New Orleans alone sent a score, were war reporters of the modern type. Rivalry was keen. New Orleans became a clearing house of war news for the nation. Kendall and his associates several times out-sped the government dispatches by the system of couriers and boats which they established. American officers entrusted their own letters to "Mr. Kendall's express." The *Picayune* became famous for its war news and its reports were extensively copied. Kendall now spent several years in Europe, partly devoted to the preparation of *The War between the United States and Mexico* (1851) with the well-known illustrations by Nebel. In Paris he married Mlle. Adeline de Valcourt. He then removed to Texas to reside on a ranch in the county now bearing his name, continuing his interest in the *Picayune,* however, until his death.

[Waddy Thompson, *Recollections of Mexico* (1846); *The Diary of James K. Polk* (4 vols., 1910), ed. by M. M. Quaife; J. F. H. Claiborne, *Life and Correspondence of John A. Quitman* (2 vols., 1860); J. S. Kendall, "Geo. Wilkins Kendall and the Founding of the New Orleans 'Picayune,'" *La. Hist. Quart.,* Apr. 1928; *An Artillery Officer in the Mexican War . . . Letters of Robert Anderson* (1911), ed. by E. A. Lawton; F. Lauriston Bullard, *Famous War Correspondents* (1914); *Niles' Nat. Reg.,* for the years 1846 and 1847; newspapers of New Orleans, Baltimore, and New York; information as to certain facts from the office of the *Picayune* and from Kendall's family.]

F. L. B.

KENDRICK, ASAHEL CLARK (Dec. 7, 1809–Oct. 21, 1895), scholar, classicist, was descended from New England stock on both paternal and maternal sides. He was born at Poultney, Vt., the second of the eight children of the Rev. Clark Kendrick, a Baptist minister, and Esther (Thompson) Kendrick. He spent a year at an academy in Granville, N. Y., then attended Hamilton College at Clinton, N. Y., graduating in 1831. He immediately accepted an appointment as professor of ancient and modern languages in Madison (now Colgate) University. In 1850 he severed his connection with Madison and with five other professors of the same faculty, "the coach load of professors," removed to Rochester, N. Y., where at the time both the University of Rochester and the Rochester Theological Seminary were being established. He was elected to the professorship of Greek language and literature at the university and although he retired from active teaching in 1888, he held the chair until his death in 1895. He was acting president on two occasions, for a time in 1863 and again during the year 1877–78. He also served as acting professor of Biblical literature and New Testament exegesis at the theological seminary, 1865–69, 1875–77. He was president of the American Philological Association for 1872–73 and a member of the American New Testament Revision Committee from 1872 to 1880. He was twice married: in 1838 to Ann Elizabeth Hopkins of Clinton, N. Y., who died in 1851; and in 1857 to Helen Morris Hooker.

As a scholar in the field of the Greek language and its literature, which he taught for almost sixty years, Kendrick had few equals in his day. He was one of the first of American professors to visit Greece and to spend many months in study and travel there. His books: *The Child's Book in Greek* (1847); *An Introduction to the Greek Language* (1841); *Greek Ollendorff* (1851); and *The Anabasis of Xenophon* (1873), with notes and vocabulary, uncovered a new method for the study of the language. His own knowledge of the Greek poets, philosophers, and historians was exact and extensive, and he had a ready memory for quoting passages from Homer and Plato. He contributed the *Commentary on the Epistle to the Hebrews* (copyright 1889) in the American Commentary series edited by Alvah Hovey; edited and revised Olshausen's Commentary which he published under the title *Biblical Commentary on the New Testament* (6 vols., 1856–58), and supplied the preface and supplementary notes to the *Critical and Exegetical Hand-book to the Gospel of John* (1884), translated from the German of H. A. W. Meyer. His numerous contributions in the *Baptist Quarterly Review* and in other journals, and his occasional addresses before educational conventions and at college and seminary gatherings show the breadth of his scholarship. In the field of biography he wrote *The Life and Letters of Mrs. Emily C. Judson* (1860) and *Martin B. Anderson* (1895). He also published in a series of three volumes *Our Poetical Fa-*

vorites (1871, 1876, 1881), an anthology of selections from English and American poets, and *Echoes* (1855), a volume of his own translations of German and French poems. He was widely loved and appeared to best advantage in the classroom among his students and in unconventional intercourse with his friends.

[*An Am. Scholar* (1913), a tribute to Kendrick, was written by his daughter, Florence K. Cooper. See also: *The Baptist Encyc.*; Jos. Joslin and others, *A Hist. of the Town of Poultney, Vt.* (1875); *Rochester Theol. Seminary: Gen. Cat.* (1910); *A Gen. Cat. of Colgate Univ.* (1913); *Gen. Cat. of the Univ. of Rochester* (1900); J. L. Rosenberger, *Rochester: The Making of a Univ.* (1927); *N. Y. Times*, Oct. 23, 1895.]
A. J. R.

KENDRICK, JOHN (*c.* 1740–Dec. 12, 1794), navigator and trader, was the son of Solomon and Elizabeth (Atkins) Kenwrick and the grandson of Edward Kenwrick, who by 1704 had settled in Harwich on the southern shore of Cape Cod. There John Kendrick, as he later preferred to designate himself, was born. He early took to the sea and at twenty went a-whaling to the St. Lawrence. His adventurous spirit led him into the French and Indian War, but after one campaign he returned to the sea and entered the coasting trade. In December 1767 he was married to Huldah Pease of Edgartown, Martha's Vineyard. During the Revolutionary War he commanded privateers: in 1777, the *Fanny*; in 1778, the *Count D'Estaing*; and in 1780, the *Marianne*. He was a pioneer in the maritime fur-trade, commanding the expedition of the *Columbia* and the *Washington* (or *Lady Washington*) which left Boston in September 1787 and arrived at Nootka a year later. There his diplomatic skill saved his vessels from seizure by the Spaniards. In July 1789 he transferred the *Columbia* to his associate, Capt. Robert Gray [*q.v.*], and traded in the little sloop, *Washington*, along the coast from Nootka to Queen Charlotte Islands. In the autumn of 1789 he sailed for China, by way of the Hawaiian Islands, and while there had a vision of opening a trade in pearls and sandalwood. For that purpose he left three men to collect these commodities, but the effort proved a failure as the men tired of the task.

Arriving in China Kendrick spent fourteen months in disposing of his cargo and in rerigging the *Washington* as a brig. In March 1791 he sailed thence for the Northwest Coast. On his way he visited Japan—the first to fly the stars and stripes in Nippon—but the country offered no market for sea-otter skins. At Queen Charlotte Islands—then a fur-trader's paradise—the Indians attempted to capture the *Washington*. Kendrick's courage enheartened his crew who drove the assailants off with heavy loss. During this voyage he purchased large areas of land from the natives of Vancouver Island, but the speculation was a complete failure. In the spring of 1793 he sailed again from China and traded on the Northwest Coast in the seasons of 1793 and 1794. Late in 1794 on his route to China, he revisited the Hawaiian Islands and took part in an inter-island war. His faction being successful, he, while at anchor in Honolulu Harbor, in December 1794, requested a fellow trader, Captain Brown of the *Jackal*, to salute him. By some negligence one of the guns had not been unshotted. Its ball pierced the side of the *Washington*, killing him as he sat at his table. Kendrick was a man of large stature, great strength, and unbounded courage. He could see possibilities of riches in untried schemes, but he lacked the perseverance necessary to transmute dreams into realities.

[For printed sources see: Josiah Paine, *Edward Kenwrick, the Ancestor of the Kenricks or Kendricks . . . and His Descendants* (1915); Amasa Delano, *A Narrative of Voyages and Travels, in the Northern and Southern Hemispheres* (1817); F. W. Howay, "Captains Gray and Kendrick: The Barrell Letters," *Wash. Hist. Quart.*, Oct. 1921, and "John Kendrick and His Sons," *Quart. of the Ore. Hist. Soc.*, Dec. 1922; and G. W. Allen, *Mass. Privateers of the Revolution* (1927). Manuscript sources include Robt. Haswell's log of the first voyage of the *Columbia*, in the Bancroft Library, Berkeley, Cal., John Hoskins' manuscript narrative in the library of the Mass. Hist. Soc., and John Boits' "Journal of a Voyage Round the World," in the same library, which gives date of death.]
F. W. H.

KENEDY, PATRICK JOHN (Sept. 4, 1843–Jan. 4, 1906), Catholic book-seller and publisher, was born in New York City, the only child of John and Ellen (Smith) Kenedy. His father, an emigrant from Ireland, had established a printing, publishing, and book-selling concern in Baltimore in 1826 which he transferred to Mott Street in New York City in 1838. Patrick was trained in the Christian Brothers' School in Canal Street and in his father's business with which he became actively associated in 1860. Despite the war, the business grew under their joint direction with the increasing Catholic population and its social improvement. In 1866, on his father's death, Kenedy assumed sole control and remained in that position until 1904, when the business was incorporated under the name of P. J. Kenedy and Sons, with Arthur and Louis Kenedy in active management of the organization. In 1873 the publishing house was removed to Barclay Street where within twenty years the business required a five-story building. As the publishers of the original *Key of Heaven* (1867), the first *Manual of the Children of Mary* (1868), *A General Catechism of the Christian Doctrine*

(1872) as enjoined by the Third Plenary Council of Baltimore, of works by Catholic authors who could find no place in the lists of secular publishing houses, of novels dealing with Catholic life, of ascetical and apologetic works, of historical books especially on Ireland, of a complete series of text-books in the parochial school field, and of the quasi-official, annual Catholic Directories, the Kenedys won for their firm an assured place as one of the chief publishing houses in the English-speaking Catholic world and gained special favor by maintaining popular prices. In reward for his services and as a testimonial to his integrity, Patrick John Kenedy at the suggestion of Archbishop Corrigan was designated by the Sacred Congregation of Propaganda in 1895 as a "publisher to the Holy See." On Aug. 12, 1874, Kenedy married Elizabeth Teresa Weiser by whom he had three sons and four daughters. His son Eugene became a Jesuit priest. He was an exceptionally well read and cultured man, an active Catholic who did not hold aloof from parochial affairs and religious associations, and an unassuming contributor to various charities.

[*Cath. News* (N. Y.), Jan. 6, 1906; *Jour. of Am.-Irish Hist. Soc.*, VI (1906), 116; death notes in the *Sun* (N. Y.) and *N. Y. Herald*, Jan. 5, 1906; information as to certain facts from Kenedy's son, Arthur Kenedy.]

R. J. P.

KENNA, JOHN EDWARD (Apr. 10, 1848–Jan. 11, 1893), congressman and senator, was born in Kanawha County, Va. (now W. Va.), and was for the greater part of his life identified with the progress of the Kanawha Valley. His father, Edward Kenna, was an Irish immigrant who after entering into various enterprises in the Mississippi and Ohio valleys began the study and practice of law in Cincinnati, and in 1847, upon his marriage to Margery Lewis, member of a prominent Virginia family, removed to Valcoulon, Kanawha County. His death in 1856 left the family in such straitened circumstances that the mother and three children went to live with her brother in southern Missouri where pioneer conditions provided little opportunity for even an elementary education. Here in 1864, at the age of sixteen, Kenna joined General Shelby's brigade of the Confederate army. Despite his youth he acquitted himself with distinction in the year's campaigning, being severely wounded in the shoulder before his regiment surrendered at Shreveport. At the close of the war he returned to West Virginia where the benevolence of friends enabled him to study for three years at St. Vincent's College in Wheeling. In 1870, after two years in a Charleston law office, he was admitted to the bar.

Immediately Kenna revealed political ambitions, in which he was considerably aided by the rising tide of Democratic strength in West Virginia. Tall, handsome, impressive in bearing, a glamourous figure because of his war experiences, he found instant favor in the Democratic party. A ready and versatile tongue made him valuable to the organization, and in 1872 he was a successful candidate for the office of prosecuting attorney of Kanawha County. In 1875 he was designated by the bar as justice *pro tempore* of the circuit court of his district. The next year he was elected to represent the southeastern district of West Virginia in the national House of Representatives. Here he was aided somewhat by the interest which the House usually displays in its youngest member and even more by the Democratic desire to hold West Virginia. His most favorable committee assignment was on commerce, where his association with John Henninger Reagan [*q.v.*], who was chairman, made Kenna a constant champion of railroad legislation in the years leading up to the act of 1887.

Kenna's greatest legislative care, however, was federal aid for slack-water navigation on the Kanawha, a task to which he gave his full energy. His successful agitation for the project of a navigable river which would tap the rich resources of coal, timber, and salt in southern West Virginia, won for him such widespread popularity in his state that in 1883, before his fourth term in Congress had begun, he was elected to the Senate. In the upper house he continued his work for improved navigation along the Kanawha and its tributaries, became one of the leading advocates of Reagan's proposed railroad regulation, and gradually won his place as a prominent leader of the Democratic minority. In the controversy between Cleveland and the Senate over the refusal of the former to detail his reasons for the dismissal of certain officials appointed with the advice and consent of the Senate, Kenna emerged as spokesman for the minority in a brilliant and persuasive argument for the independence of the executive (*Congressional Record,* 49 Cong., 1 Sess., pp. 2328–37). His abilities as a controversialist were also utilized by the minority to defend Cleveland's message in 1888 against the barbed shafts of Sherman and to indict the opposition for the failure of tariff reform. His sudden death, at the age of forty-five, cut short a promising career. Kenna was married in September 1870 to Rosa Quigg. She died four years later and in November 1876 he was married to Anna Benninghaus.

[For biographical details see: G. W. Atkinson, *Prominent Men of W. Va.* (1890); *Men of W. Va.* (1903), II, 411–15; M. P. Shawkey, *West Virginia* (1928), II, 372; "Memorial Addresses on the Life and Character of John Edward Kenna," *Senate Miscellaneous Doc. 66*, 52 Cong., 2 Sess.; *Wheeling Daily Reg.*, Nov. 22, 1876, Jan. 12, 1893. For Kenna's efforts to secure federal aid for slack-water navigation on the Kanawha, see the *Cong. Record*, 46 Cong., 1 Sess., p. 1334, 46 Cong., 3 Sess., App. pp. 145–46, 47 Cong., 2 Sess., p. 3446, 49 Cong., 1 Sess., pp. 4236, 4258, 4261, 6556, 7032.] W. S. S.

KENNAN, GEORGE (Feb. 16, 1845–May 10, 1924), explorer, journalist, and author, son of John and Mary Ann (Morse) Kennan, was born at Norwalk, Ohio, of New England-Scotch forebears. His father, a lawyer, was more interested in mechanical inventions than in legal lore and became entranced with S. F. B. Morse's development of the electric telegraph. The result was that while still a boy Kennan developed expert proficiency as a telegrapher. During the Civil War, prevented by physical limitations from going to the front, he served as military telegrapher in Cincinnati. He proved so efficient that the Western Union Telegraph Company selected him at twenty years of age as a member of its Siberian expedition for the purpose of surveying a possible route for the extension of the telegraph system from America to Europe by way of Alaska and Bering Strait and across Siberia and Russia. For two years he lived under the almost arctic conditions of northeastern Siberia, often enduring a temperature of 50° and 60° below zero. This adventure, which laid the foundation for his subsequent career, was brought to an abrupt conclusion by the news of the successful laying of the Atlantic cable. Making a perilous journey of five thousand miles by dog sledge Kennan finally reached St. Petersburg and so returned home. The results of his experiences he embodied in a book entitled *Tent Life in Siberia* (1870) which arrested public attention.

Kennan returned to the Russian Caucasus in 1870 and spent a year in a study of its people and manners. For the next few years he held minor business positions in Medina, N. Y., and New York City, then he was called to Washington to be the assistant manager (1877–85) of the Associated Press. His reputation for honor and accuracy was such that when President Garfield was shot in 1881 Kennan was called to the White House where he remained night and day in charge of all the telegraphic reports of the President's condition until the latter was removed to Elberon, N. J., where he died.

Kennan became widely and favorably known both in England and the United States as a popular lecturer on the Russian Orient. In 1885 he was commissioned by Roswell Smith, president of the Century Company, to visit Russia and make a study of the horrors of the prisons in Siberia. Accompanied by an American artist, George A. Frost, he went to Siberia somewhat prejudiced against the revolutionaries and sympathetic with the Czar's efforts to maintain law and order and a stable government, for he was a conservative by nature and temperament. But the year which he spent, meeting and talking with Russian patriots in exile and sharing their hardships, changed his point of view. His book, *Siberia and the Exile System* (2 vols., 1891) was the first revelation outside of the bounds of Russia of the medieval and cruel character of the Romanoff government, and its publication had much to do with the overthrow of the Romanoff régime in Russia. No future history of the fall of imperial autocracy and the rise of popular government in Russia can be written without a careful examination of the papers and records accumulated and written by Kennan. Many of these time-worn pages, penned in the prison cells of Yakutsk or in the attics of Paris, have a wider appeal as moving human documents.

Kennan became an accomplished Russian scholar and spoke and read Russian fluently. His study of Russian affairs and his contributions to world knowledge on the subject constituted his greatest achievement, but he also obtained a wide recognition as a correspondent in Cuba during the Spanish-American War; in Japan during the Russo-Japanese War; and in his studies of American political conditions. As a journalist he was an important if not vital factor in the exposure and downfall of the notorious John Edward O'Sullivan Addicks [*q.v.*] in Delaware. He wrote innumerable magazine and newspaper articles in a copperplate handwriting which was as legible as typewriting. In addition to the books named above, he published: *Campaigning in Cuba* (1899); *Folk-tales of Napoleon* (1902), based on his translation of Russian folk legends about Napoleon's march to Moscow; *The Tragedy of Pelée* (1902), a first-hand account of the eruption on the Island of Martinique in 1902; *A Russian Comedy of Errors* (1915); and *E. H. Harriman: A Biography* (2 vols., 1922). Kennan was not a college graduate, having been called to the Siberian telegraph enterprise just at the time when he was fitting himself to enter college. Once, when asked in what institution he had obtained his academic education, he replied, "Russia." He was an amateur in the study of natural history and one of his hobbies was the study of both domestic and exotic flora and fauna. He possessed great physical endurance, an extraordinarily fascinating intellect, and an unusual capacity for warm and delightful friendship. He married, Sept. 25, 1879, Emeline Rathbone Weld of Medina, N. Y.

[The biography is based largely upon the contributor's long and intimate personal acquaintance with Kennan and upon his diaries and journals. For printed sources see: *Who's Who in America*, 1924–25; W. W. Ellsworth, *A Golden Age of Authors* (1919); R. U. Johnson, *Remembered Yesterdays* (1923); Catherine Breshkovsky, *The Little Grandmother of the Russian Revolution* (1917); David Fairchild, article in *Jour. of Heredity*, Oct. 1924; Edmund A. Walsh, *The Fall of the Russian Empire* (1928); articles in the *Outlook*, June 4, 1898, July 19, 1916, May 21, 1924; T. L. Kennan, *Geneal. of the Kennan Family* (1907); *N. Y. Times*, May 11, 1924; *Evening Star* (Washington, D. C.), May 12, 1924. Many of his records and papers are in the Lib. of Cong. and in the N. Y. Pub. Lib.]

L. F. A.

KENNEDY, ARCHIBALD (1685–June 14, 1763), British colonial official, son of Alexander Kennedy of Craigoch, was a descendant of a younger line of the Cassillis peerage of Scotland. He emigrated as a young man to New York, where he was granted the freedom of the city on July 25, 1710. Of his first dozen years in America little is known; he may have been an officer of the regular troops stationed in the province. He was appointed collector of customs and receiver-general of the province Aug. 8, 1722, and was sworn of the Council, Apr. 13, 1727. In this official capacity, maintained for half a century, he appears to have been punctilious and diligent, cannily refraining from excess of initiative, and consistently "regular" in his political attitudes. Like other colonial officials he participated in land speculations. He bought Bedlow's Island in New York harbor for one hundred pounds in 1746 and in 1758 sold it to New York City for one thousand pounds, the island being required for quarantine purposes. Another transaction was his purchase of the premises at numbers one and three Broadway, upon the former of which he erected in 1760 the "spacious and famous mansion" which became a landmark among the city's residences. In December 1736 he married Mary (Walter) Schuyler, widow of Arent Schuyler of New Jersey, thereby making an alliance of great advantage both for wealth and for family connection with the local aristocracy. This was apparently his second marriage. His son and heir, Capt. Archibald Kennedy, R. N., who succeeded as eleventh Earl of Cassillis in 1792, was the offspring of an earlier marriage (G. E. Cockayne, *Complete Peerage*, II, 1889, 177).

Kennedy had an active mind and he exploited the opportunities afforded by his position for observation of the workings of British economic policy. This is evidenced by three pamphlets from his pen, *Observations on the Importance of the Northern Colonies under Proper Regulations* (1750), *The Importance of Gaining and Preserving the Friendship of the Indians to the British Interest Considered* (1752), and *Serious Considerations on the Present State of the Affairs of the Northern Colonies* (1754). It is clear that he was in full sympathy with the mercantilist aims of the policy of the empire but dissented from the methods employed to give them effect. He foresaw the possibility of trouble for the empire unless changes were made, maintaining that the Americans could not be kept dependent by keeping them poor. And he quotes with approval a "Mr. Trenchard" who had remarked: "nor will any Country continue their Subjection to another, only because their Great Grand Mothers were acquainted!" (*Observations on the Importance of the Northern Colonies*, p. 32). The pamphlet on Indian policy was the result of his prolonged experience as a member of the New York Council and was addressed both to the imperial authorities and to the American provincial assemblies. In 1761 he asked to be relieved from service on the Council because of the infirmities of age, and he died within two years of his retirement from that body.

[Biographical sources include: E. B. O'Callaghan, *Docs. Relative to the Colonial Hist. . . . of N. Y.*, vols. V and VI (1855–56), and vol. XI (1861); *N. Y. Hist. Soc. Colls.*, Public Fund Ser., vol. XVIII (1886), and vol. XXX (1898); G. W. Schuyler, *Colonial N. Y.* (1885), vol. II; I. N. P. Stokes, *The Iconography of Manhattan Island*, vol. IV (1922); N. Y. State Lib., *Calendar of Council Minutes* (1902); the *Scots Mag.*, July 1763. A copy of the pamphlet on Indian policy is at the John Carter Brown Library, Brown Univ.; the other two are to be found at the N. Y. Pub. Lib.]

C. W. S.

KENNEDY, JOHN DOBY (Jan. 5, 1840–Apr. 14, 1896), soldier and political leader, was the son of Anthony M. and Sarah (Doby) Kennedy of Camden, S. C. His mother was the grand-daughter of Abraham Belton, a pioneer settler of Camden and soldier during the Revolution. His father was born in Scotland and emigrated to the United States in 1834. Kennedy received his preparatory education in the schools of Camden and entered South Carolina College in 1855. Here he remained until the fall of 1857 when he entered the law office of W. Z. Leitner. He was admitted to the bar in January 1861. At the outbreak of the Civil War he enlisted as captain of Company E, 2nd South Carolina Regiment, under the command of Col. J. B. Kershaw. When Kershaw was made brigadier-general in 1862, Kennedy succeeded him as colonel of the 2nd Regiment, and two years later, when the former succeeded McLaws as commander of the 1st Division of Longstreet's corps, Kennedy became brigadier-general. He was present at the bombardment of Fort Sumter at the beginning of the war and remained in active service until the surrender of Johnston in April 1865, participating in the battles of Bull Run, Savage Station, Sharpsburg, Fredericksburg, Chancellorsville, Gettysburg, Chickamauga, Knoxville, the Wilderness, Spotsylvania, Petersburg and Cedar Creek. After the fall of Atlanta, Governor Magrath of South Carolina requested that Kennedy's brigade be detached to oppose the invasion. Kennedy now joined Johnston's army and his command vainly disputed Sherman's progress at Averysboro and Bentonville.

The war over, Kennedy returned to Camden and reëntered the legal profession. In December 1865 he was elected to Congress but did not take his seat because of his refusal to take the "iron clad oath." He took a prominent part in the redemption of his state from carpetbag domination. After white supremacy had been reestablished, he was prominent in the counsels of the Democratic party. As a member of the National Democratic Convention which met at St. Louis in 1876, he cast his vote for Tilden and Hendricks. He was a member of the state executive committee of the Democratic party in that year, and the chairman of the committee two years later. He served two terms in the lower house of the state legislature (1878, 1879). In 1880 he was elected lieutenant-governor of South Carolina and was prominently mentioned for governor in 1882, but he was defeated in convention by Col. Hugh Thompson. In 1884 he was presidential elector-at-large on the Democratic ticket. From 1885 to 1889 he was consul-general at Shanghai, China, by appointment of President Cleveland. Kennedy was active in fraternal organizations and was popular with Confederate veterans' organizations, taking an active interest in the establishment of Camp Kirkland. He was twice married. His first wife, whom he married in 1857, was Elizabeth Cunningham. She died in 1876 and in 1882 he was married to Harriet A. Boykin. His sudden death at his home in Camden resulted from a stroke of apoplexy.

[T. J. Kirkland and R. M. Kennedy, *Hist. Camden. Part Two: Nineteenth Century* (1926); Yates Snowden, *Hist. of S. C.* (1920), vol. II; *Cyc. of Eminent and Representative Men of the Carolinas of the Nineteenth Century* (1892), vol. I; *War of the Rebellion: Official Records (Army)*; *News and Courier* (Charleston), Apr. 15, 1896; newspaper clippings in the possession of Mrs. Harriette Kershaw Leiding, Charleston, S. C.] J. G. V–D.

KENNEDY, JOHN PENDLETON (Oct. 25, 1795–Aug. 18, 1870), author and statesman, was the son of John Kennedy, a native of north Ireland of Scotch descent, and his wife, Nancy Clayton Pendleton, a Virginian whose forebears were English. Kennedy was born in Baltimore, Md., where his father was at the time a prosperous merchant. He received his general education at what became Sinclair's academy and at Baltimore College in his native city, graduating from the latter in 1812. During the war with England which broke out in that year he participated in the battles of Bladensburg and North Point. After studying in the law offices of an uncle and of Walter Dorsey in Baltimore he was admitted to the bar and began practising in that city in 1816. In 1824 he married Mary Tennant, daughter of a Baltimore merchant, but she died within a year, and in 1829 Elizabeth Gray of Ellicott Mills, Md., became his wife. Kennedy did not like the law, and a legacy from an uncle who died at about this time made him less dependent upon it. Therefore he gradually withdrew from his practice and began to live more in accordance with his natural inclinations. In the early years of his greater leisure the qualities distinguishing him during the remainder of his life reached maturity. He was broad, tolerant, and cheerful, had a genial humor, and a deep love for his fellow men. He was greatly interested in local affairs and served on various civic committees. For some years he was provost of the University of Maryland. He was also president of the board of trustees of the Institute founded in Baltimore, largely in accordance with his advice, by George Peabody in 1866.

The last forty years of Kennedy's life were chiefly devoted to creative writing and to politics. He had begun scribbling as a schoolboy but published nothing of importance until 1832, when under the pseudonym Mark Littleton he published *Swallow Barn,* a series of sketches of life in Virginia shortly after the Revolution. This was well received and was followed in 1835 by "Littleton's" *Horse-Shoe Robinson,* a novel dealing with the battle of King's Mountain. Three years later came *Rob of the Bowl,* a novel of early colonial Maryland, which was less popular. But a humorous political satire published in 1840, under the title *Quodlibet: Containing Some Annals thereof . . . by Solomon Second-thoughts, Schoolmaster,* delighted many, especially the Whigs, of whom the author was one. His last major work, *Memoirs of the Life of William Wirt,* appeared in two volumes in 1842. Kennedy's works of fiction were classed by some contemporary critics with those of

Cooper and Irving. Among his minor writings were pamphlets and articles for the press, notably for the *National Intelligencer,* discussing political questions. The first of these having influence was a pamphlet issued in 1830 (under the pseudonym Mephistopheles) which reviewed the report on commerce by C. C. Cambreleng of the national House of Representatives. The views presented caused Kennedy to be regarded as a leading exponent of protection. Already he had begun to fill public office, through election in 1820 to the Maryland House of Delegates. During these years he was an ardent supporter of John Quincy Adams. Early in 1838 he was elected as a Whig to fill a vacancy in the House of Representatives caused by the death of Isaac McKim. He failed of reëlection in November of that year but was successful in 1840 and 1842. In Congress he was chairman of the committee of commerce for a time. He strongly opposed the annexation of Texas and held that its admission by joint resolution was unconstitutional. Largely through his influence an appropriation of $30,000 was voted for a test of Samuel Morse's electro-magnetic telegraph.

Following the death of President Harrison Kennedy wrote the manifesto entitled *A Defense of the Whigs* (1844), denouncing the political defection of Tyler. In the congressional election of 1844 he was defeated, but two years later he was chosen to the Maryland House of Delegates, was made speaker, and served one term. In July 1852 he accepted the secretaryship of the navy under President Fillmore and while filling that office organized four important naval expeditions, including that sent to Japan under Matthew C. Perry. When he left office in March 1853, following the inauguration of President Pierce, his public career ended, but his interest in politics continued. In 1860 he voted for Bell and Everett and strove, by writing and speaking, to prevent secession. When this proved futile, he supported the Union cause in the war, voting for Lincoln in 1864. But after the conflict ended he favored "amnesty and forgiveness to the weak and foolish who have erred, charity for their faults and brotherly assistance to all who repent." Kennedy died at Newport, R. I., after a long illness.

[The Kennedy manuscripts in the library of the Peabody Institute include extensive correspondence, a diary, and an uncompleted autobiography. For printed sources see H. T. Tuckerman, *The Life of John Pendleton Kennedy* (1871); E. M. Gwathmey, *John Pendleton Kennedy* (1931); *Biog. Dir. Am. Cong.* (1928); *Ann. Report of the Secretary of the Navy,* 1852; V. L. Parrington, *The Romantic Revolution in America* (1927); *The Cambridge Hist. of Am. Lit.,* vol. I (1917); E. A. and G. L. Duyckinck, *Cyc. of Am. Lit.* (2 vols., 1875).]

M. W. W.

KENNEDY, JOHN STEWART (Jan. 4, 1830–Oct. 31, 1909), capitalist and philanthropist, was born at Blantyre, Lanarkshire, Scotland, the fifth son of John and Isabella (Stewart) Kennedy. He had the discipline of the Glasgow public schools from his sixth to his thirteenth year, but at the end of that period he went to work in a shipping office. At seventeen he connected himself with an iron and coal concern and continuing in that business traveled in the United States for a London firm in 1850, having headquarters at New York until July 1, 1852. He then returned to Glasgow, but in 1857 he came again to America and entered into a partnership in the banking business with Morris K. Jesup [*q.v.*]. Spending a year at Chicago in starting a branch office, Kennedy retained his membership in the firm for ten years, withdrawing in 1867 to found (one year later) the banking house of J. S. Kennedy & Company. In the next fifteen years, as active head of the business, Kennedy formed connections and developed interests which eventually made him an important factor, especially in Western railroad building. His appointment by Congress as one of the Union Pacific Railroad incorporators gave him prominence and subsequently he became a director of the Chicago, Burlington & Quincy, the Pittsburgh, Fort Wayne & Chicago, the New York, Chicago & St. Louis, the Cleveland & Pittsburgh, and other railroads. He was a member of the syndicate that built the Canadian Pacific Railway. He represented the Dutch committee of bondholders of the bankrupt St. Paul & Pacific Railroad and advised the acceptance of the offer to them by James J. Hill, thus making possible the creation of the Great Northern system.

When Kennedy resigned the control of the banking house in 1883 to his nephew, J. Kennedy Tod, he had acquired interests that demanded his diligent attention for the remaining twenty-six years of his life. Besides the great railroad properties in which he was concerned (at his death he was owner of stock to the value of $10,000,000 in the Northern Pacific and of $7,000,000 in the Great Northern), he was on the directing boards of various institutions, to which he devoted his personal attention as well as liberal gifts of money. Among these were the Presbyterian Hospital of New York, Robert College of Constantinople, Columbia University, the Metropolitan Museum of Art, the New York Public Library, and the American Museum of Natural History. Probably his most distinctive service to New York was his active support of organized charity. By erecting a centrally situated building for the use of societies active in welfare work for the city's unfortunate, he brought such organizations into closer relations with one another, thus promoting the central objects for which they were all striving. He founded and maintained the School of Philanthropy, which was always national in its scope, and his services were known to social workers everywhere. He was a member of the New York Committee of Fifteen which investigated and reported on prostitution in 1901–02.

To the end of his life Kennedy never wholly lost his Scotch brogue, nor did his sense of humor fail him. He was an enthusiastic angler, delighting especially in salmon-fishing on Canadian streams. One of his most intimate business associates was James J. Hill, builder of the Great Northern Railroad. He had an active part in the formation of the Northern Securities Company which was dissolved by the United States Court. Kennedy was married, on Oct. 14, 1858, to Emma Baker of Elizabeth, N. J., who survived him. There were no children. His will, made seven months before his death, gave large sums to the institutions in which he had been interested. All of the bequests were without restrictions of any kind.

[G. A. Morrison, Jr., "John Stewart Kennedy," *N. Y. Geneal. and Biog. Record,* July 1910; R. H. Graves, "J. S. Kennedy, a Quiet Giver," *Evening Post* (N. Y.), Feb. 6, 1909; Edward T. Devine, "Mr. Kennedy's Will," *Survey,* Nov. 13, 1909, reprinted in *Social Forces* (1910); memoir in the *Survey,* Nov. 27, 1909; J. G. Pyle, *The Life of Jas. J. Hill* (1917), vol. I; *N. Y. Times,* Nov. 1, 1909.] W. B. S.

KENNEDY, JOSEPH CAMP GRIFFITH (Apr. 1, 1813–July 13, 1887), statistician, and superintendent of the Seventh and Eighth censuses, was born in Meadville, Pa., the son of Thomas Ruston and Jane Judith (Ellicott) Kennedy. He was the grandson of Samuel Kennedy, surgeon of the 4th Pennsylvania Battalion in the Revolutionary War, and of Andrew Ellicott [*q.v.*]. Kennedy entered Allegheny College in Meadville in 1829 but left before graduating. On Oct. 21, 1834, he married Catharine Morrison, by whom he had four children. While still a young man he purchased and edited the Crawford, Pa., *Messenger,* said to be the third newspaper published in the United States north and west of Pittsburgh. When this undertaking proved financially unsuccessful in the course of a few years, he moved to his farm on the outskirts of Meadville and remained there until called to Washington in May 1849 to serve as secretary of a board engaged in the preparation of a plan for taking the Seventh and subsequent censuses. Shortly afterward he was appointed superintending clerk of the Census of 1850.

With the inauguration of a Democratic president in March 1853, Kennedy, who was an ardent Whig, was succeeded by a Democrat. When Buchanan, a Pennsylvania Democrat, entered the White House, Kennedy was asked to prepare a digest of manufactures, ordered in 1858. Upon the completion of the report in December of the next year, he remained as superintending clerk of the Eighth Census. His formal association with census statistics ended June 7, 1865, when the secretary of the interior, who directed the Census Office, transferred the completion of the enumeration to the commissioner of the General Land Office, owing to the failure of the appropriation. Two volumes of the projected four had been distributed and the remaining two were in semi-finished form when the transfer occurred. The third volume, on manufactures, soon appeared without Kennedy's name as compiler or his carefully written preface. He petitioned Congress for redress from such "unlawful" procedure by the committee on printing returned an unfavorable verdict inasmuch as the secretary had acted within his authority.

In the summer of 1851 Kennedy was authorized to go abroad in the interests of census work and to examine the systems of statistics in other countries. He visited England, France, Belgium, Austria, and Prussia, studied official statistics, informed himself as to methods of census-taking, and had conferences with public officials. He endeavored to interest foreign statisticians in the adoption of a uniform classification system to make comparable census statistics of different countries. He was cordially received by representatives of foreign governments and was asked to give several addresses and statements, notably one before the section on statistics of the British Association for the Advancement of Science. Kennedy was chiefly responsible for the organization of the First International Statistical Congress which met in Brussels in 1853 and was a member of the Second and Fourth congresses of 1855 and 1860. He was secretary of the United States commission to the world's fair in London in 1851 and a commissioner for the international exhibition there a few years later. His innovations and thoroughness in treating official statistics won substantial praise for him both at home and abroad. After his retirement from public service in 1865 he was a bank attorney and a real-estate dealer in Washington, D. C. He was brutally murdered in the summer of 1887 by a fanatic whose property he had purchased.

[C. W. Evans, *Biog. and Hist. Accounts of the Fox, Ellicott, and Evans Families* (1882); *Pa. Mag. of Hist.*

and Biog., Mar. 1884; E. A. Smith, *Allegheny: A Century of Education* (1916); copy of Kennedy's diary (for 1851) in the possession of W. F. Willcox, Ithaca, N. Y.; *Report of the Secretary of the Interior*, 1851, p. 512; *House Report 50*, 39 Cong., 1 Sess.; *Daily Constitutional Union* (Washington, D. C.), Oct. 21, 1865; *Washington Post* and *Evening Star* (Washington), July 14, 1887; information as to certain facts from Kennedy's nephew, John E. Reynolds, Meadville, Pa.]

W. R. L.

KENNEDY, ROBERT PATTERSON (Jan. 23, 1840–May 6, 1918), Ohio soldier, lawyer, congressman, was born in Bellefontaine, Ohio, the son of William G. Kennedy, a native of Maryland, and Mary (Patterson) Kennedy. He attended the local schools and Geneva College, then at Northwood, Ohio. At the beginning of the Civil War he joined the first company from Logan County, Ohio, which started for camp at Columbus on the Tuesday succeeding the firing upon Fort Sumter. The company went into three months' service but later joined the 23rd Ohio—the first three years' regiment from the state. Entering the service as a second lieutenant, Kennedy served as assistant adjutant-general, being promoted captain on Oct. 7, 1862, and major on Nov. 16, 1864. He resigned on Apr. 8, 1865, but was recommissioned six days later as colonel of the 196th Ohio Infantry. He had been brevetted on Mar. 13, 1865, lieutenant-colonel of volunteers for gallant and meritorious service during the campaign in West Virginia and in the Shenandoah Valley, and brigadier-general of volunteers for distinguished gallantry during the war. He was mustered out of service on Sept. 11, 1865. At the battle of Antietam in 1862, by the fortunes of war, he was in temporary command of a portion of the left wing of the army, and upon the review of that army by President Lincoln on the battlefield, he was called to the front and presented as "the youngest commander of the Army of the Potomac."

After leaving the army Kennedy returned to Bellefontaine where he studied law and was admitted to the bar in 1866. He then entered a law partnership, West, Walker & Kennedy, and continued in the firm until 1878. In that year he was appointed collector of internal revenue for the fourth district of Ohio by President Hayes and served until 1883. Two years later he was a candidate for governor on the Republican ticket but was defeated for the nomination by Joseph B. Foraker. The convention then by acclamation nominated him for lieutenant-governor. He was elected and while serving in that capacity acquired by reason of his sturdy rulings the appellation of "King Bob." He resigned his office on Mar. 3, 1887, having been elected to the United States House of Representatives in the fall of 1886. He served in the Fiftieth and Fifty-first congresses (Mar. 4, 1887–Mar. 3, 1891) but was not a candidate for renomination in 1890. In 1899, following the Spanish-American War, he was appointed by President William McKinley a member of the Insular Commission to visit Cuba and Porto Rico to investigate and report upon conditions existing in these countries and to formulate a code of laws for Porto Rico. He became president of the commission. After the Civil War he was active in every presidential campaign in nearly every state from Maine to Kansas. In 1903 he published *Historical Review of Logan County, Ohio*. On Dec. 29, 1862, Kennedy was married to Mary Lewis Gardner of Bellefontaine. After her death he was married, on Sept. 4, 1894, to Emma (Cowgill) Mendenhall of Wabash, Ind. He spent practically all of his life in his native city of Bellefontaine, Ohio, but died in Columbus, Ohio.

[In addition to Kennedy's book, mentioned above, see: John C. Hover and others, *Memoirs of the Miami Valley*, vol. I (1919); *Biog. Dir. Am. Cong.* (1928). F. B. Heitman, *Hist. Reg. and Dict. of the U. S. Army* (1903), vol. I; W. M. Glasgow, *The Geneva Book* (1908); *Who's Who in America*, 1916–17; and the *Ohio State Jour.* (Columbus), May 7, 1918. Information as to certain facts was supplied for this sketch by Kennedy's son, W. C. Kennedy, Columbus, Ohio.]

H. L.

KENNEDY, WILLIAM SLOANE (Sept. 26, 1850–Aug. 4, 1929), biographer and anthologist, was born at Brecksville, Ohio, not far from Cleveland, the son of the Rev. William Sloane Kennedy and Sarah Eliza (Woodruff) Kennedy. His father was a Presbyterian minister. His mother was a daughter of the Rev. Simeon Woodruff, a graduate of Yale (A.B. 1809) and of Andover Theological Seminary and the first pastor of the Congregational church at Tallmadge, Ohio. William attended the preparatory and collegiate departments of Miami University, then entered Yale as a junior in 1873. After graduating in 1875 he remained at Yale for private study in 1875–76 and then taught for two years. During the school year 1877–78 he combined teaching in Meadville, Pa., with study in the Meadville Theological Seminary and completed his theological training by two years' study at the Divinity School at Harvard University. He left in 1880 without graduating. Instead of following the family tradition and seeking ordination to the ministry, he decided to devote himself to literary work and became a member of the staff of the *American* in Philadelphia, which he served for one year. In 1882 he published biographies of Longfellow and of Whittier and in 1883 a life of Oliver Wendell

Holmes. These were followed by *Wonders and Curiosities of the Railway* (1884), *Art and Life, a Ruskin Anthology* (1886), and *John G. Whittier, the Poet of Freedom* (1892). From 1892 to 1895 he was a proof-reader for the *Boston Transcript* and a special contributor to the *New York Critic,* the *Boston Herald,* the *Boston Index,* and the *Literary World.* At this time his home was in Belmont, Mass.

While in Philadelphia Kennedy had become a friend of Walt Whitman and was on intimate terms with the poet until Whitman's death in 1892. This friendship is reflected in his *Reminiscences of Walt Whitman* (1896) and his edition of *Walt Whitman's Diary in Canada,* published in 1904. Kennedy regarded as his most important book *The Fight of a Book for the World, A Companion Volume to Leaves of Grass* (1926), a history of Whitman's volume with a variety of critical and bibliographical helps for readers. He compiled *Breezes from the Field* (1886), a small anthology of poems, *In Portia's Gardens* (1897), a collection of his own essays on nature lore, and *Autolycus Pack or What You Will* (1927), a collection of literary and critical essays. He published in translation *Psychic Mysterious Forces* (1907), from the original of Camille Flammarion, and *After Death—What?* (1909), from Cesare Lombroso. Most of his original verse is included in a pamphlet, published in 1926, entitled *Poems of the Weird and Mystical.* From 1909 to 1920 his dominant interest was Italy and the Italian language and literature, and in 1927 he published *Italy in Chains—A Nation Under the Microscope.* Kennedy was married, in June 1883, to Adeline Ella Lincoln, daughter of Cyrus and Abigail Lincoln of Cambridge, Mass. After her death in 1923 he made his home in West Yarmouth, Mass., frequently spending the winter in Rome or in California. He was abroad in 1924–25 and in 1926–27. During the summer he lived alone at West Yarmouth. He was drowned in August of his seventy-ninth year, while swimming in Lewis Bay near his home, and was buried in Mt. Auburn Cemetery, Boston. His books and a legacy were bequeathed to Rollins College.

[*Who's Who in America,* 1928–29; *Yale Univ. Obit. Record,* 1930; *N. Y. Times, Boston Transcript,* Aug. 5, 1929; unpublished reminiscences of Kennedy's sister, Mrs. Charles Devillo Foote, Cleveland, Ohio.]

J. C. F.

KENNER, DUNCAN FARRAR (Feb. 11, 1813–July 3, 1887), Confederate agent, sugar planter, youngest son of William and Mary (Minor) Kenner, was born in New Orleans. His father, a prosperous New Orleans merchant, had emigrated to Louisiana from Caroline County, Va., soon after the purchase; his mother was the daughter of Major Stephen Minor, commandant at Natchez, Miss., during the Spanish régime in Louisiana. He received his early education from private tutors and in the public schools of New Orleans, and then entered Miami University, Oxford, Ohio, where he graduated in 1831. After four years of travel and study in Europe, mostly spent in England and France, he read law for a time with John Slidell, but instead of practising, he settled upon "Ashland" plantation, Ascension Parish, La., where he became a sugar planter and horse breeder. He had a private track for training purposes, and became widely known among turf followers throughout the country, his thoroughbreds winning consistently at the New Orleans, Saratoga, and other tracks. On June 1, 1839, he married Anne Guillelmine Nanine Bringier, member of an old and influential French family of Louisiana.

In 1836 Kenner was elected to the Louisiana House of Representatives from Ascension Parish, and subsequently served several terms in the state legislature, first in the House and then in the Senate. He was a member of the state constitutional convention in 1844, and president of the state constitutional convention in 1852. He was one of seven delegates from Louisiana to the provisional Congress of the Confederacy at Montgomery, Ala., in 1861, and after the Southern capital was removed to Richmond, Va., he continued to represent his state in the Confederate House of Representatives, where he was chairman of the committee on ways and means. As the war went on, he became more and more convinced of the impossibility of Confederate success without European recognition and that slavery stood in the way, and in 1864, when the Southern cause looked desperate, he urged upon his friend, Judah P. Benjamin, secretary of state, the sending of a special commission to Europe to offer England and France the abolition of slavery in return for recognition. President Davis reluctantly agreed to the plan, and, realizing the need of secrecy, accepted the responsibility without appealing to Congress, but instead of a commission he followed the advice of Benjamin and appointed Kenner sole envoy with the rank of minister plenipotentiary. In disguise Kenner made his way overland to New York, and sailed from that port Feb. 11, 1865, on the steamer *America.* He arrived safely in Europe, but Sherman's campaign had destroyed all confidence in the chances of Confederate success, and the mission, aptly characterized as grasping at a straw, was a failure.

The war over, Kenner returned to a plantation in ruins, for "Ashland" had been raided by Union troops in 1862. The house had not been burned, but his valuable horses had been seized, his overseers captured, and his slaves freed. At fifty-two he had to begin life over again, but, undaunted, he went to work, and by close application and the exercise of great business skill he built up an estate which was larger and more valuable at the time of his death than it had been before the war. He is said to have been the first in the state to introduce and use the portable railroad to carry cane from fields to mill, the Rillieux double-effect pans, and the McDonald hydraulic pressure regulator. He played a leading part in organizing the Louisiana Sugar Planter's Association in 1877, and the Sugar Experiment Station in 1885, and served as first president of each.

Kenner was also active politically and otherwise during these post-war years. During 1866–67 he represented Ascension in the state Senate, and in 1877 he was elected to the same body from New Orleans, where he then lived. He was prominent in all efforts to wrest the state from Republican control during Reconstruction days. In the winter of 1876–77 he was in Washington, D. C., in the interests of the Democratic party during the Hayes-Tilden election contest. Two years later he was a candidate for the United States Senate, but failed of election. In 1882 he was appointed a member of the United States Tariff Commission by President Arthur. He was chairman of the building committee for the Cotton Exposition held in New Orleans during 1884–85 and for a number of years he was a member of the Louisiana Levee Board. When the Louisiana Jockey Club was formed he became its president and held the position until his death. He died suddenly, at his home in New Orleans.

[The principal account is G. D. Price, "The Secret Mission of Duncan F. Kenner, Confederate Minister Plenipotentiary to Europe in 1865" (M.A. thesis in the library of Tulane Univ.). It is based partly upon material furnished by Mrs. Thomas Sloo of New Orleans, a grand-daughter of Kenner, documents in the possession of Mrs. William Stubbs of New Orleans, and the Kenner papers at the Cabildo, New Orleans. See also John Bigelow, "The Confederate Diplomatists," *Century Mag.*, May 1891; J. M. Callahan, *The Diplomatic Hist. of the Southern Confederacy* (1901); J. H. Latane, *A Hist. of Am. Foreign Policy* (1927); F. L. Owsley, *King Cotton Diplomacy* (1931); S. C. Arthur and G. C. H. de Kernion, *Old Families of La.* (1931); obituary notices in *Times-Democrat* and *Daily Picayune*, both of New Orleans, July 4, 1887; and article on the Kenner family in *Times-Democrat*, Oct. 23, 1892.]

M. J. W.

KENNICOTT, ROBERT (Nov. 13, 1835–May 13, 1866), naturalist, explorer, was born in New Orleans, La., second of the seven children of Dr. John Albert and Mary Shutts (Ransom) Kennicott. While he was an infant, his parents moved to Northfield, Ill., a small town some eighteen miles northwest of Chicago. Robert's father, a physician who eventually relinquished his medical practice and devoted his energies to horticultural pursuits, began at an early date to train his son's mind in the study of nature. In childhood the lad was rather delicate and was not able to pursue his education in the classroom, but this handicap was overcome later by his association with such men as J. P. Kirtland [*q.v.*] of Cleveland, Spencer F. Baird [*q.v.*], of the Smithsonian Institution, P. R. Hoy, of Racine, Wis., and others, under whom he was able to carry on studies in natural history. At the age of eighteen he was making extensive collections of natural-history material. In 1855 he made a comprehensive natural-history survey of southern Illinois for the Illinois Central Railroad Company, and some of his earliest scientific papers were devoted to the description of this material.

In 1856, at the age of twenty-one, he united with others in the founding of the Chicago Academy of Sciences. The progress of this institution was one of the main objects of his life, and chiefly to his energies and ability was due the important place which it came to fill in the science of that day. In 1857 he began building up a museum for Northwestern University. To supplement its collections he made a trip to the Red River of the North and later spent part of a winter in the Smithsonian Institution, studying and identifying the material obtained. He was at the Smithsonian during the winter of 1858–59 also, studying collections made in California by Lieut. W. P. Trowbridge [*q.v.*], which under the expert hand of Kennicott were labeled and divided between the Smithsonian Institution and the University of Michigan.

In 1859 he made his first expedition to British and Arctic America, aided by the Smithsonian Institution and friends in Chicago who provided the necessary funds. Three years were spent on this expedition, during which the central area of British America as far north as Fort Yukon, including that part of the country known as Keewatin (now Manitoba and western Ontario in part), was carefully explored and collections were made of the fauna. Kennicott's journal, which is replete with observations on the animal life, the inhabitants, and the country in general, shows an unusual breadth of perspective and an unusual ability to interpret the first-hand facts of observation. During the winter of 1862–63 he was again at the Smithsonian, studying the material he had obtained, which included many animals new to science. The magnitude of Kennicott's collections and his reputation as an explorer stimulated a movement to bring a part of his material to Chicago. Accordingly the Chicago Academy of Sciences was reorganized and properly endowed, and Kennicott was made its curator (later director) and a trustee. The year 1864 was spent in transporting his collection from the Smithsonian to Chicago and arranging it in the hall of the Academy.

In 1865 the Western Union Telegraph Company sent an expedition to northwestern America for the purpose of surveying a route for an overland telegraph line to the Old World, and because of Kennicott's previous experience in this region he was chosen as leader of one party which was to survey Alaska and the Yukon River. In addition to the work of the survey his party was to secure specimens of the natural history of the region traversed, to be divided between the Chicago Academy of Sciences and the Smithsonian Institution. Before his work was completed, however, he died of heart disease at Fort Nulato, Alaska. He was found in the early morning on the beach whither he had gone for exercise and observation. Robert Ridgway [*q.v.*] called Kennicott "Illinois's first and most gifted naturalist." His writings were characterized by keen insight into the relationships of animals, their habits, and distribution. His published papers, about a dozen in number, relate mostly to the vertebrates of North America, but also include several valuable Indian vocabularies.

[*Trans. Chicago Acad. Sci.*, vol. I (1869); *Western Monthly*, Mar. 1870; *Am. Jour. Sci.*, Nov. 1866; *Am. Jour. of Conchology*, Apr. 4, 1867; W. C. Ransom, *Hist. Outline of the Ransom Family of America* (1903); *N. Y. Times*, Oct. 14, 29, 1866; private information from F. Kennicott Reilly, Esq.] F. C. B—r.

KENRICK, FRANCIS PATRICK (Dec. 3, 1796–July 8, 1863), Roman Catholic prelate, brother of Peter Richard Kenrick [*q.v.*] and son of Thomas and Jean (Eustace) Kenrick, was born in the Liberties of Dublin, where his father kept a scrivener's office. Educated in local schools and under an uncle, Rev. Richard Kenrick, he was sent in 1814 to the Propaganda at Rome, where he made a brilliant course in scriptures, Greek, Hebrew, and modern languages, and learned from Pius VII how to endure persecution and yet firmly uphold the liberties of the Church. Ordained in Rome (Apr. 7, 1821), he was called by Bishop Flaget [*q.v.*] to the chair of theology in St. Thomas Seminary, Bardstown, Ky., and a lectureship in Greek and history at St. Joseph's College. As pastor of the local congregation and preacher of the Jubilee Year throughout the diocese, he won recognition as a pulpit orator whose sermons were finished productions and as a controversialist willing to enter the lists with local Protestant divines (*The Letters of Omega and Omicron on Transubstantiation,* 1828). As a theologian, he attended the First Provincial Council of Baltimore (1829), for which he acted as a secretary. In its solution of the difficulties in the mismanaged diocese of Philadelphia, the Council petitioned the Holy See to name Kenrick coadjutor of the enfeebled Bishop Henry Conwell [*q.v.*], with full power of administration. This was done, and Kenrick as titular bishop of Arath was consecrated at Bardstown (June 6, 1830) by Bishop Flaget assisted by Bishops Conwell and David [*q.v.*].

Arriving at Philadelphia a month later, he took over the diocese (*Metropolitan,* August 1853), though his patience was sorely tried by the truculent old bishop, who misunderstood his authority and misinterpreted his kindly consideration. He ended trusteeism in the diocese by placing an interdict (1831) on St. Mary's Church until its trustees surrendered in accordance with the will of a majority of the congregation, and by ordering that the bishop's name be substituted for that of the trustees in future donations to the Church. During the cholera epidemic (1832), he won general approbation because of his personal services, of the ministrations of his priests and Sisters of Charity, and of the assignment of St. Augustine's school as a hospital. Though he was keenly concerned about poor relief, temperance, and immigrant aid, his ardent Americanism prevented the enthusiastic support of O'Connell and the Irish movement for repeal of the Act of Union which the Irish-Americans demanded of a hero. The moderation of his diocesan paper, the *Catholic Herald,* founded in 1833 with the aid of Michael Hurley, O. S. A., and of his secretary, John Joseph Hughes [*q.v.*], did not escape criticism. His success lay in being bishop of all his people, and Catholicity in Pennsylvania was representative of diverse races. A strict canonist, he forbade the Masonic funeral of Stephen Girard from Holy Trinity Church but permitted Christian burial on the score that Girard's sudden illness had prevented reconciliation with the Church. In 1832, he held a diocesan synod which was attended by thirty priests representing about 100,000 Catholics, and thereafter he held frequent councils and conducted scrutinizing visitations. He not only supported parochial schools, the Augustinian College of Villanova (1842), the Jesuit College of St. Joseph (1851), and the various convents, academies, and asylums, but he successfully forced the issue with the controllers of public schools in Philadelphia against compulsory attendance of pupils at instructions based on the King James version of the Bible (1842). In 1844, with firmness and patience, he faced the nativist riots which resulted in the firing of Catholic properties including St. Michael's and St. Augustine's churches (*Catholic Herald,* May–July 1844, *passim*). He counseled moderation, prevented retaliation by his embittered people, temporarily closed the churches, and placed the burden of protection upon civil authorities by turning over the keys of church properties. Criticized as a negative character by aggressive followers, Kenrick, nevertheless, by the tactics he pursued, paved the way for better relations, and in the reaction against lawless bigotry received a number of noted converts into the Church. A year later the situation was sufficiently in hand so that he could journey to Rome in the interest of his diocese. An era of building followed, as the Catholic population increased with immigration, so that on his translation to the archepiscopal See of Baltimore (brief of Aug. 3, 1851), Kenrick left his successor a corps of 146 priests and seminarians and 102 churches and chapels.

Named apostolic delegate, he presided over the First Plenary Council in 1852. The following year, at the request of the pope, he collected the views of the American episcopate on the doctrine of the Immaculate Conception, which he heard promulgated in Rome in 1854. In 1858 he introduced the Forty Hours' devotion into the United States. As in Philadelphia, he actively concerned himself with the foundation and support of schools and charitable institutions, giving full patronage to the Sulpicians and Loyola College. A Unionist, he found Baltimore less pleasant during the Civil War. His address on "Christian Patriotism" in which he hinted that national loyalty should supersede state patriotism was not well received, and at times he was irritated by the pro-Southern editorial views of the *Catholic Mirror.* His death was hurried by the reports of the slaughter at Gettysburg.

Kenrick was a thorough scholar, and aside from diaries, pastoral letters, magazine articles, and a voluminous correspondence with prelates and Catholic scholars at home and abroad, left the following theological studies which are in current use: *A Letter on Christian Union* (1836); *Adnotationes in Tractatum X* (n.d.); *Theologia Moralis* (3 vols., 1841–43); *Theologia Dogmaticae* (4 vols., 1839–40); *The Catholic Doctrine of Justification* (1841); *A Treatise on Baptism* (1843); *The Four Gospels* (1849); *The Acts of the Apostles, The Epistles of St. Paul, the Catholic Epistles and the Apocalypse* (1851); *A Treatise on Baptism and Confirmation* (1852); *Form of Consecration of a Bishop of the Roman Catholic Church* (4th ed., 1850); *A Vindication of the Catholic Church in a Series of Letters* (1855), addressed to Protestant Episcopal bishop of Vermont, John Henry Hopkins [*q.v.*]; *The Psalms, Books of Wisdom, and the Canticle of Canticles* (1857); *The Book of Job and the Prophets* (1859); *The Historical Books of the Old Testament* (1860); *The Pentateuch* (1860); and *The New Testament* (1862).

[M. O'Connor, *Archbishop Kenrick and his Work* (pamphlet, 1867); J. J. O'Shea, *The Two Kenricks* (1904); *The Philadelphia Theological Seminary of St. Charles Borromeo* (1917); J. L. J. Kirlin, *Catholicity in Philadelphia* (1909); *The Life and Letters of Eliza Allen Starr* (1905), ed. by J. J. McGovern; M. J. Riordan, *Cathedral Records* (Baltimore, 1906); *Am. Cath. Hist. Researches* (1884–1912), see index volume; *Records Am. Cath. Hist. Soc.*, Sept. 1920; *Am. Cath. Quart. Rev.*, Apr. 1892, Oct. 1900; *Diary and Visitation Record of Rt. Rev. Francis Patrick Kenrick* (1916), ed. by F. E. Tourscher; *The Kenrick-Frenaye Correspondence* (1920).]

R. J. P.

KENRICK, PETER RICHARD (Aug. 17, 1806–Mar. 4, 1896), Roman Catholic prelate, son of Thomas and Jean (Eustace) Kenrick, was born in Dublin, Ireland. He attended St. Patrick's College, Maynooth, and was raised to the priesthood, Mar. 6, 1832. In the following year he joined his elder brother, Francis Patrick Kenrick [*q.v.*], then bishop of Philadelphia, and was appointed pastor of the Cathedral, president of the Seminary, and vicar general of the diocese. In addition to his official duties, he assumed the editorship of the diocesan organ, the *Catholic Herald,* and wrote three books of permanent value: *The New Month of Mary* (1840), *The Validity of Anglican Ordinations* (1841), and *The Holy House of Loretto* (1842).

In Philadelphia he met Bishop Rosati of St. Louis, who was so deeply impressed with the sterling qualities of the young priest that he asked for his appointment as coadjutor in St. Louis. After his consecration, Nov. 30, 1841, Kenrick, with the title of Bishop of Drasa, started for St. Louis; whilst Bishop Rosati journeyed to Rome and thence, as legate, to Haiti. St. Louis at this time was a small, straggling frontier town, with about 20,000 inhabitants—French, English, Irish, and German—and only one Catholic church. After the death of Bishop

Rosati at Rome, Sept. 25, 1843, his coadjutor took the title of bishop of St. Louis; and on Jan. 30, 1847, when St. Louis was raised to the dignity of an archdiocese, he became archbishop.

The rapid growth of the Catholic population required many new buildings in city and country. To open new resources, the Archbishop entered upon a banking venture that proved highly beneficial to the parishes and institutions of St. Louis. When he closed his bank, he had neither debts nor superfluous funds; all the money had gone into the upbuilding of the Church. In the course of his administration a large number of separate dioceses were erected, so that the diocese of St. Louis at last was reduced to the Eastern half of Missouri, but the Catholic population in the restricted territory had outstripped by far the numbers Bishop Kenrick found in the vast territory of his early days. As archbishop he held one synod, and one provincial council. He was a leading figure in the various Councils of Baltimore. In the Ecumenical Council of the Vatican he took a prominent part as an opponent of the dogmatization of infallibility, holding, that as the pope's decisions had been always accepted by the Church as final, his infallibility was practically assured, and that there was no need of an official declaration. When, however, the Council by a large majority decreed the dogma that the pope, when speaking *ex cathedra* in matters of faith and morals, was infallible, he accepted the decree as final. The crowning glory of Kenrick's life was the celebration in 1891 of the fiftieth anniversary of his consecration as a bishop. After that event his health rapidly declined and his place was taken by Archbishop Kain, while he received the title of archbishop of Marcianopolis. He died in his ninetieth year, recognized, in the capacities of preacher and scholar, administrator and organizer, as one of the notable Catholic churchmen of his day.

[J. J. O'Shea, *The Two Kenricks* (1904); *The Kenrick-Frenaye Correspondence* (1920); letters selected from the Cathedral Archives, Phila., in *Records Am. Cath. Hist. Soc.*, Dec. 1919; letters in Archives of St. Louis Hist. Soc. and of Notre Dame Univ.; J. E. Rothensteiner, *Hist. of the Archdiocese of St. Louis* (2 vols., 1928), with additional references.]

J. E. R.

KENRICK, WILLIAM (Dec. 24, 1789–Feb. 14, 1872), nurseryman, was born in Newton, Mass., the elder son of John Kenrick (1755–1833) and Mehitable Meriam, daughter of Rev. Jonas Meriam. His father, one of the pioneer nurserymen in America, established a nursery in 1790 on Nonantum Hill, near the town line between Newton and Brighton. By 1823, William had become associated with his father in the enterprise, and for half a century he was one of a small group of nurserymen who laid the foundation of the fruit industry of the present day. He was one of the original members (1829) of the Massachusetts Horticultural Society, and a member of its council, 1829–41. By 1832, if not before, he had established a nursery independent of his father's, for in that year he issued his own catalogue of fruit and hardy ornamental trees and shrubs, which were for sale at his nursery "located near the nursery commenced 35 years ago by the elder Kenrick." In this catalogue there were listed 148 varieties of apples, about twenty-five of which are well-known sorts of the present day; 155 varieties of pears; ninety-nine of peaches; forty-seven of plums; forty-eight of cherries. In 1833, upon his father's death, he inherited the original establishment, and by 1838 the list of apple varieties appearing in his catalogue had increased to 228; pears to 317; with fewer additions to the stone fruits.

He gave much attention to variety-testing, his activity in this work being evinced and his memory best perpetuated by his book, *The New American Orchardist,* first published in 1833. In all, seven editions appeared, the last being in 1844. In the early forties the author visited France and England where he gathered much information on varieties, which he incorporated in the seventh edition of his book. In 1835 the Massachusetts Horticultural Society made a special award to Kenrick in recognition of "his successful efforts in procuring scions of new fruits from Europe, and for his valuable treatise on fruit trees" (Benson, *post,* p. 55). He is credited with the importation of the purple beeches still characteristic of Newton.

His interests were not entirely centered in nursery and fruit enterprises. At one period he gave considerable attention to silk culture. In 1835 there appeared under his authorship *The American Silk Grower's Guide,* which included a discussion of the growing of the mulberry. A second edition was printed in 1839. In a communication to the *Cultivator* (March 1837, p. 21) he expressed "sanguine hopes that the sugar beet culture will succeed and flourish with us, as it now does in France," and he elsewhere stated the conviction that agriculture, commerce, and manufactures must all flourish together. In 1845 he gave a public park to the town of Newton. He retired from strenuously active participation in affairs about 1856, but until the end of his life he watched with interest "the progress of his favorite pursuit" (*Country Gentleman,* July 31, 1856).

On May 13, 1824, he married a widow, Har-riot (Russell) Jackson. They had no children. He died at Newton in his eighty-third year.

[L. H. Bailey, *Cyc. of Am. Horticulture,* II (1900), 856, and *The Standard Cyc. of Am. Horticulture,* III (1915), 1582; A. E. Benson, *Hist. of the Mass. Horticultural Soc.* (1929); *New England Farmer,* Oct. 4, and 11, 1823; *Cultivator,* Mar. 1837, Dec. 1841, July 1844; *Country Gentleman,* July 31, 1856; nursery catalogues, 1832, 1838–39, and others; Newton *Journal,* Feb. 17, 1872; certain information from members of the family, from Rev. G. H. Ewing of Wellesley, and from the librarian of the Mass. Horticultural Society.]

H. P. G.

KENSETT, JOHN FREDERICK (Mar. 22, 1816–Dec. 14, 1872), landscape painter and engraver, born in Cheshire, Conn., was the son of an English engraver, Thomas Kensett, who came to America in 1812 from Hampton Court, and the following year married Elizabeth Daggett, a grand-daughter of Naphtali Daggett [*q.v.*], president of Yale College. John Kensett, the second of six children, followed in his father's footsteps, taking his first lessons in engraving from his father, and continuing his training later under his uncle, Alfred Daggett of New Haven. He then went to New York and for a little over two years worked for the American Bank Note Company. Here he made the acquaintance of A. B. Durand, John William Casilear, and Thomas P. Rossiter [*qq.v.*]; and in 1840 he went to Europe with these artists for the purpose of studying the great art collections and for practical experience in painting. Kensett remained abroad about seven years—from the age of twenty-two to that of twenty-nine. He was in Paris in 1841, where he shared a studio with Benjamin Champney [*q.v.*] of Boston, in the *rue de l'Université,* and made sketching excursions with him to the Forest of Fontainebleau. Kensett went from Paris to England to receive a small legacy, expecting to stay only a short time, but there were some legal complications, and his sojourn was prolonged for two years. His time was not wasted, for he continued to paint landscapes from nature and did some engraving. "My real life commenced there," he wrote, "in the study of the stately woods of Windsor and the famous beeches of Burnham and the lovely and fascinating landscape that surrounds them" (Tuckerman, *post,* p. 510). At length he returned to Paris, and, after a few more weeks of sketching in the suburbs, he and his friend Champney, with two others, started on a long walking tour, sketching as they went, up the Rhine, through Switzerland, and over the Simplon to the Italian Lakes. Thence Kensett went on to Rome where he took rooms with Thomas Hicks near the Piazza di Spagna. This was in November 1845. The following summer, 1846, he and Hicks, with other art students, went on a sketching tour through southern Italy and the Abruzzi mountains, returning to Rome in October. A part of another summer was passed at Palermo and along the coast of the Bay of Naples. Kensett continued his studies in Rome until August 1847, when he went to Venice for a month. Thence, in company with George William Curtis [*q.v.*], he traveled through Germany, finally returning to America in the autumn and establishing himself in New York, where he was destined to enjoy a great success. He was made a National Academician in 1849.

During his extended stay abroad he had sent many landscapes to the New York exhibitions, and he found his reputation already won. His "View of Windsor Castle," exhibited in London, in 1850, was warmly praised. He did not give up his habit of wandering after his return to New York, for among his pictures we find subjects from the Adirondacks, Lake George and Lake Champlain, the Genesee River, the White and the Catskill mountains, Newport, Narragansett, Beverly, the Connecticut shores of Long Island Sound, the Hudson, Niagara, and even the Middle West. His work became more and more popular, as it deserved to be. His landscapes were sweet and likable; their sentiment, though not deep, was authentic. Like most of the American landscape work of the period, they were undeniably thin: if in atmospheric delicacy they contained a faint promise of Corot's ethereal refinements, they had no trace of Corot's sense of composition; nor were they remarkable for solidity of construction. On the other hand, however, they were imbued with the sincerest love of nature, and the skies and distances were often of an airy beauty which went far to atone for the insignificance of the foregrounds.

Kensett was a kindly, generous, sympathetic character. He had, says Isham, "the gift of forming deep and lasting friendships." He was habitually reserved, but "even his silence diffused an atmosphere of friendliness about him." In his youth, he was a romantic-looking figure, with long dark hair, a straggling beard, high forehead, straight nose, and sensitive expression, somewhat dreamy. He was never married. In 1859 he was appointed a member of a commission to supervise the decoration of the Capitol at Washington, but it does not appear that this body ever accomplished anything. Soon after his death in 1872 the pictures and studies left in his studio were sold for the great sum of $150,000. Thirty-eight of his works, some of them unfinished, belong to the Metropolitan Museum of Art, New York. More than half of these, painted at Darien, Conn., during his last summer, were given to the museum by his brother, Thomas Kensett. The Corcoran Gallery, Washington, has two good examples of his work, "Lake George" and a view of the Genesee River.

[H. W. French, *Art and Artists in Connecticut* (1879); C. E. Fairman, *Art and Artists of the Capitol of the U. S. A.* (1927); S. B. Doggett, *A Hist. of the Doggett-Daggett Family* (1894); Benjamin Champney, *Sixty Years' Memories of Art and Artists* (1900); Samuel Isham, *The Hist. of Am. Painting* (1905); H. T. Tuckerman, *Book of the Artists* (1867); *Harper's New Monthly Mag.*, Apr. 1876; *Commemorative Exhibition by Members of the Nat. Acad. of Design, 1825–1925* (1925); *N. Y. Times*, Dec. 15, 1872; *N. Y. Tribune*, Dec. 16, 1872.] W. H. D.

KENT, CHARLES FOSTER (Aug. 13, 1867–May 2, 1925), Biblical scholar, educator, author, was born at Palmyra, N. Y., the only child of William Hotchkiss Kent and Helen Maria Foster. His ancestors on both sides settled on Long Island before the middle of the seventeenth century, but soon moved to western New York. In the full and varied life of a country home, notwithstanding the Puritan ancestry of the parents, he was given an unusual degree of freedom. In the excellent Palmyra Union Classical School he prepared for college. From the very first he showed himself a good student. At seventeen he entered the Sheffield Scientific School in New Haven, Conn., but at the end of his freshman year he decided to transfer to Yale College, although this involved mastering both French and Greek during the intervening summer. Though studious, he played a part in athletics; and, as an editor of the *Yale Daily News*, he exercised and developed a native talent for writing. He graduated with the class of 1889.

It had been his original intention to study law. Inspired, however, by the enthusiasm of William Rainey Harper, the first Woolsey professor of Biblical literature in Yale College, he determined to work in that field. Accordingly he entered the Yale Graduate School where, in 1891, he received the Ph.D. degree in Semitic languages and philosophy. During the following year he continued his studies at the University of Berlin, besides making a four months' trip to Palestine and the Near East. At a later period (1896–97) he devoted an additional year to research at Breslau, Germany. From 1892 to 1895 he taught Biblical literature at the University of Chicago. On July 9, 1895, he married, at Palmyra, Elizabeth Middleton Sherrill, daughter of the Rev. Samuel Bartlett Sherrill and Louise Bloodgood Root. This year he removed to Providence, R. I., where he was associate professor of Biblical literature and history in Brown University until 1898, and professor from 1898 to 1901. He was then called back to Yale as Woolsey professor of Biblical literature, a position which he held until his death.

The founding of the National Council on Religion in Higher Education, designed to facilitate the training of choice men for college teaching or administration in the field of religion, was one of his notable achievements. To provide the necessary fellowships he secured pledges of $20,000 a year. His other outstanding service, through which he became widely known, consisted in the publication of a series of thirty-five or more volumes, principally on Biblical subjects. From among these special mention should be made of *The Student's Old Testament* (6 vols., 1904–27); *The Historical Bible* (6 vols., 1908–16); and *The Shorter Bible* (2 vols., 1918–21), a superior selection and translation of the more significant portions of Scripture, made in collaboration with several other scholars. It is probably no exaggeration to say that, through his readable books, Kent did more than any other American scholar of his day to make accessible to the public the significant results of modern Biblical study.

[The *Obituary Record of Yale Grads.*, 1924–25, pp. 1380–83, furnishes a detailed account of Kent's activities and publications. See also *Yale College, Yale Univ. Class of '89 Vicennial* (1910); *Who's Who in America*, 1924–25; *Jour. of Biblical Lit.*, vol. XLV (1926), p. v; *N. Y. Times*, May 4, 1925.] G. D.

KENT, EDWARD (Jan. 8, 1802–May 19, 1877), lawyer, governor of Maine, jurist, was born in Concord, N. H., the son of William Austin and Charlotte (Mellen) Kent. His father was a native of Charlestown, and his mother, of Sterling, Mass. He was one of a family of eight children. He graduated from Harvard College in the class of 1821, at the age of nineteen, with Phi Beta Kappa honors. Among his classmates were Josiah Quincy and Ralph Waldo Emerson. After reading law under Benjamin Orr and Chancellor Kent he opened a law office in 1825 in Bangor, Me., where he maintained his legal residence from that date until his death fifty-two years later. His first law partner was Jonathan P. Rogers, attorney-general of Maine; later for eighteen years he was a member of the firm of Kent & Cushing; and from 1853 to 1859 he was associated with his brother, George Kent. His interest in public affairs, his commanding personality, and his agreeable manner soon secured for him election to numerous local offices, including that of moderator of the town meeting, member of the superintending school committee (1829–31), and mayor of Bangor (1836–38). He first attained state office upon his election to the lower house of the state legislature in which he represented the Bangor district in 1828–29.

In 1827 Kent was admitted to practice in the supreme judicial court. He was appointed the same year chief justice of the court of sessions of Penobscot County which office he filled for two years. His legal success and political prominence won for him the Whig nomination for governor in 1836, but he was defeated by the Democratic nominee, Robert P. Dunlap of Brunswick. Nominated again in 1837 he was opposed by his fellow townsman Gorham Parks. His election was contested by the Democrats in the legislature on the ground of "informalities" in the election proceedings in several towns. The state supreme court ruled, however, that the legislature was not competent to "go behind the returns" from those communities. After the Democrats had won under the leadership of John Fairfield in the next two elections Kent was again chosen governor in 1840, but this time by the legislature since no candidate received a clear majority at the polls. Despite the fact that he received only a slight plurality at the polls, it was proclaimed in song and story that Maine "went hell-bent for Governor Kent."

During his two terms Kent by his vigorous attitude probably stirred the national government to action in bringing the Northeastern boundary question to a final settlement. In 1842 he was appointed by the legislature on a commission to confer with the secretary of state, Daniel Webster, during the Webster-Ashburton negotiations, in support of Maine's claims. Although his stand for the so-called "territorial integrity of the state" was disregarded, he finally joined his colleagues in approving the agreement. Following his support of President Taylor in the nominating convention of 1848 he was appointed consul to Rio de Janeiro and served from 1849 to 1853. In 1859 he was appointed by Governor Morrill a justice of the supreme judicial court which position he filled with ability for fourteen years. He afterward continued his law practice in Bangor until his death in 1877. His last public service was to act as chairman of a commission of ten appointed in 1875 by Governor Dingley "to consider and frame" amendments to the constitution of Maine. Kent was married on July 26, 1827, to Sarah Johnston of Hillsboro, N. H. She died in 1853 and in 1855 he was married to Abby A. Rockwood, daughter of the Rev. Otis Rockwood of Lynn, Mass.

[L. C. Hatch, *Maine: A Hist.* (1919), vol. I; John E. Godfrey, memoir of Kent in the *Me. Hist. Soc. Colls.*, vol. VIII (1881); *Me. Hist. and Geneal. Recorder,* Oct. 1893; *Docs. Printed by the Order of the Leg. . . . of Me. . . . 1841* (1841); the *Green Bag,* Feb. 1896; L. V. Briggs, *Geneals. of the Different Families Bearing the Name of Kent* (1898); *Hist. of Penobscot County, Me.* (1882); *Daily Kennebec Jour.* (Augusta), May 21, 22, 1877.]

O. C. H.

KENT, JAMES (July 31, 1763–Dec. 12, 1847), jurist, legal commentator, was the eldest son of Moss and Hannah (Rogers) Kent, who were married in 1760. His mother was the daughter of Dr. Uriah Rogers of Norwalk, Conn.; his father was the son of the Rev. Elisha Kent, a Presbyterian minister who preached first at Newtown, Conn., and later in Fredericksburgh (now Southeast, Putnam County), then a part of Dutchess County, N. Y. Here Moss Kent practised his profession of lawyer, and here James Kent was born. The latter was prepared by private tutors and in schools at Norwalk, Pawling, and Danbury, to enter Yale College in September 1777, where he received his degree of B.A. on Sept. 12, 1781. His college course was several times interrupted by the events of the Revolutionary War. During one of these intervals, while living in the country, he came across a copy of *Blackstone's Commentaries.* He read the four volumes which, he said, "inspired me, at the age of fifteen, with awe, and I fondly determined to be a lawyer." In November 1781, he began a three years' legal apprenticeship in the law office of Attorney-Gen. Egbert Benson, at Poughkeepsie. At the age of twenty-one, in January 1785, he was admitted to the New York supreme court bar, and in the same year married Elizabeth Bailey, sixteen years old, the daughter of Col. John Bailey, of Poughkeepsie. In April 1785, Kent entered into a law partnership with Gilbert Livingston, which continued until April 1793, when he moved to New York City.

Kent's years in Poughkeepsie were not overburdened with legal practice, but the use to which his leisure was put had a great influence on his life. His political affiliations were fixed by association with Federalist leaders who came to Poughkeepsie to attend the constitutional convention of 1788, and particularly by admiration for Alexander Hamilton, who was already a national figure. He supported Jay in the contested gubernatorial election awarded to Clinton and thus aroused the opposition of the adherents of the latter, among whom was his brother-in-law, Theodorus Bailey. In 1793 he ran for Congress but was defeated by Bailey. This political check, and the unpleasant personal relations which were incident to it, determined him to move to New York. The rest of his political career may be briefly sketched. He was three times elected to the New York Assembly, but his political influence was thereafter exerted as an incident to judicial office. His appointment to the New York supreme court, and afterward to the chancellorship, made him *ex officio* a member of the council of revision charged with examining bills from the legislature and vetoing them at discretion. His stout conservatism made him enemies, while other members were accused of political bias. As a consequence, in the constitutional convention of 1821, the Democratic majority abolished the council. In this same convention, Kent's political principles were well illustrated when he opposed the abolition of the property qualification for the suffrage. Throughout his career he fought always, says Fox, "for the rights of the individual as distinguished from those of the people."

When Kent moved to New York, he owned real property worth £200, had £100 in cash, and possessed a small library. Legal business did not come to him and for a time he was in financial straits. He had, however, the reputation of being a scholar and a well-read lawyer, and through the influence of prominent Federalist friends was appointed professor of law in Columbia College. The appointment was dated Dec. 24, 1793, and his first course of twenty-six lectures was delivered from Nov. 17, 1794, to Feb. 27, 1795, two a week, to "seven students and thirty-six gentlemen, chiefly lawyers and law students who did not belong to the college." His subsequent courses did not attract students. Beginning in November 1795, he read, in his office, thirty-one lectures to two students and a few law clerks. The announcement of his third course attracted no students; and after the conclusion of his lectures to six students in the winter of 1797–98, he presented his resignation to take effect in April. This was the end of the first professorship in law in Columbia University. In the meantime, Kent had been active in state politics and had been thrice honored by Governor Jay. In February 1796 the latter gave him the lucrative appointment of master in Chancery, an office which he retained after he became recorder of the City of New York in March 1797. These two offices he resigned on his appointment, on Feb. 6, 1798, to be a judge of the New York supreme court. He moved to Poughkeepsie, but after one year, took up a residence in Albany which lasted twenty-four years. In 1804 he became chief judge of the court, and on Feb. 24, 1814, he was appointed chancellor of the New York court of Chancery.

The record of Kent's achievement as a judicial officer is to be found in three sets of law reports: Johnson's *Cases Argued and Determined in the Court for the Trial of Impeachments and the Correction of Errors, 1799–1803* (3 vols.), his *Report of Cases Argued and Determined in the Supreme Court of Judicature and in the Court for Trial of Impeachments and the Correction of Errors, February 1806–February 1823* (20 vols.), and his *Cases of the State Court of Chancery, March 1814–July 1823* (7 vols). It was through Kent's influence that the practice of handing down written opinions in the New York supreme court was instituted; and, as chief justice, he appointed William Johnson [*q.v.*] official reporter under the act of 1804. In 1814 Johnson followed Kent to the court of Chancery. It was the fortunate association of these two men through a period of twenty-five years which developed and preserved a line of decisions in law and equity fundamental in American jurisprudence. Even the opinions reported as *per curiam* were nearly all written by Kent. Before he became chancellor, the court of Chancery had had no great influence. He was therefore loath to accept the appointment, but afterward he found in it his greatest judicial opportunity. "I took the court," he wrote, "as if it had been a new institution, and never before known in the United States. I had nothing to guide me, and was left at liberty to assume all such English Chancery powers and jurisdiction as I thought applicable under our Constitution. This gave me grand scope, and I was checked only by the revision of the Senate, or Court of Errors" (Kent, *Memoirs, post,* p. 158). He thus became practically the creator of equity jurisdiction in the United States. When English law and legal institutions were regarded with distrust, he preserved their best features and by his own personal conduct set an example of dignity and intellectual eminence, dominated by a high sense of judicial responsibility.

The constitutional convention of 1821 had provided that judges should be retired on reaching the age of sixty. This brought Kent's judicial career to a close on July 31, 1823, "in the full meridian" of his faculties and fame, while yet in perfect mental and bodily health. He resented this enforced retirement and moved to New York City on Oct. 29, 1823, with no other prospect than that of writing opinions as chamber counsel. In the following month, however, he was offered and accepted a reappointment to the law professorship in Columbia College, which had remained vacant since his resignation in 1798. His introductory lecture, delivered Feb. 2, 1824, in the College Hall, was published by the trustees. Two of the courses of lectures which followed, from Feb. 6, 1824, to May 18, 1825, were attended by more auditors than students. The third course, from October 1825 to Apr. 22, 1826, was taken by thirteen students and no auditors. The largest number of lectures given in a single course was fifty. Kent disliked both the preparation and the delivery of lectures. "They give me a good deal of trouble and anxiety," he wrote. "I am compelled to study and write all the time, as if I was under the whip and spur." "Having got heartily tired of lecturing, I abandoned it."

Thus came to an end, without enthusiasm or conspicuous success, Kent's second essay as law teacher. The lectures were not prepared with a view to publication, and except for the urgent solicitation of his son William, nothing more would have been done with them. On so slight a chance hung the preparation of his *Commentaries on American Law,* a work on which his permanent reputation rests no less firmly than on his judicial decisions. In the two occupations of legal writer and of judge he found an opportunity friendly to his genius. In both he devoted himself, under little pressure, to the dignified development and exposition of the law, with results which he could not produce through teaching.

At the age of sixty-three, he began the rewriting, expansion, and extension of his lectures for the purpose of publication. Volume I was published in 1826, at his own expense, at a cost, in sheets, of $1,076.27. The original plan was to complete the work in two volumes, but the preface to Volume II, published in 1827, promised a third volume. When this volume appeared in 1828, it announced that a fourth volume would be devoted to the doctrine of real estates. This volume was written with difficulty. The "subjects are very abstruse and perplexing," he wrote in January 1830, "and I move very slowly and warily through the mazes of contingent remainders, executory devises, uses, trusts, and powers, and the modifications which they have received by our Revised Statutes" (*Memoirs,* pp. 195–96). The volume, published in 1830, contained a dedication of the complete work to William Johnson.

By December 1830, every complete set of the *Commentaries* had been sold, and Kent began the preparation of a second edition. This edition of 1832 was followed by the third, fourth, fifth, and sixth editions, in 1836, 1840, 1844, and 1848 respectively, all prepared by him. Eight editions have been issued since his death. Part I, of Volume I, on International Law, has been twice separately printed, in 1866 and in 1878, edited by John T. Abdy; and Part II of the same volume, on the Constitution of the United States, was translated into German (Heidelberg, 1836), and into Spanish (Mexico City, 1878). The portion on Commercial and Maritime Law was published in Edinburgh in 1837. The treatise on International Law is the first general American work on that subject, being ten years earlier than Wheaton's *Elements of International Law.* The fact that Kent based his discussion on the decisions of American and English courts, made his work, says Chamberlain, "superior to any previous treatise on this subject, and a landmark in the history of international law." His greatest contribution was in his treatment of the subject of neutral commerce in time of war. The treatise on the United States Constitution possessed less novelty, but even today, says Powell, one who "desires a brief review of the foundation stones of our constitutional jurisprudence can go nowhere else with such profit and pleasure as to this second part of the *Commentaries.*" "In his constitutional principles," says the same writer, "he foreshadowed Marshall, and his opinions are worthy of a place beside those of the great Chief Justice." The whole work is in six parts devoted respectively (1) to the law of nations, (2) to the government and constitutional jurisprudence of the United States, (3) to the sources of the municipal law of the several states, (4) to the rights of persons, (5) to personal property, and (6) to real property. He had no American model for his work, and he did not copy Blackstone. His entire first volume has no counterpart in the English *Commentaries,* and he omitted separate treatment of the law of crimes, which is the subject of Blackstone's fourth volume. Strangely enough for one who made his judicial reputation as chancellor of New York, he has no separate part devoted to equity. Law and equity are discussed side by side throughout the four volumes under the various topics. During Kent's lifetime, the work was almost extravagantly praised, but the eulogies were not without foundation, for the work still remains the foremost American institutional legal treatise.

Only two other legal works are associated with Kent's name—a revision of New York Laws, prepared with Jacob Radcliff (2 vols., 1801), and an annotated edition of the charter of New York City, 1836. Of non-legal writing he did little, and that little only to prepare addresses for particular occasions. He was, however, a man of wide learning and literary taste, the result of a lifetime of systematic reading and study. Undoubtedly this habit broadened his thinking, and gave to his opinions and his *Commentaries* a grace which increased their effectiveness. "I know not how it is," wrote Joseph Story, in 1831, "but you carry me a voluntary captive in all your labors, whether in law or in literature. You throw over everything which you touch a fresh and mellow coloring, which elevates while it warms, and convinces us that the picture is truth and the artist a master." His reading habits were formed during the comparative leisure of the first years of practice in Poughkeepsie. He was influenced to take up the study of the classics by the example of Edward Livingston, and he gave up reading Greek only when in old age his eyesight was failing. He divided his day between his profession, the languages, and belles-lettres. Gradually the small, well-chosen library which he owned in 1793 when he moved to New York City, grew into a large and valuable collection. "My library has at present," he wrote in 1807, "prodigious charms and incomprehensible interest." In 1828, his 3,000 volumes included nearly every work, authority, or document referred to in the three volumes already published of his *Commentaries.* "Next to my wife, my library has been the source of my greatest pleasure and devoted attachment," he wrote in 1828; and in his eightieth year, he said that his ardor for reading was as alive as ever, and that he remained fully sensitive to the charms of nature, of literature, and society. Nearly every volume in his library shows evidence of use, and of his habit of reading pen in hand. In many volumes, letters are inserted relating to the author, or the donor; and on fly-leaves he jotted down not only criticisms and observations on the books, on the authors of them, and on persons and events mentioned in them, but items concerning the intimate affairs of his own professional and family life. This devoted attachment to reading far and wide gave him a life-time of pleasure but also was professionally helpful. His reading in foreign law furnishes an example in point. "I made much use of the *Corpus Juris,*" he said of his experience on the bench, "and as the Judges (Livingston excepted) knew nothing of French or civil law, I had an immense advantage over them. I could generally put my brethren to rout and carry my point by my mysterious wand of French and civil law" (*Southern Law Review, post,* pp. 387–88). On account of his phenomenal memory, combined with his omnivorous reading, he was reputed by the members of the New York Bar to know all about everything he had ever studied, and to have studied almost everything. It was said that he literally forgot nothing.

Kent's last years were happily occupied in reading, preparing new editions of his *Commentaries,* and in writing occasional opinions. He spent his last summers at a cottage in Essex County, N. J., and his winters in New York City. Until the time of his death he suffered no serious illness, and he died in New York, on Dec. 12, 1847, at the age of eighty-four. He was small of stature, with a head large in proportion to his body. His forehead was high and his eyes widely separated, giving to the upper half of his countenance a mild and thoughtful expression. His mouth was large and his lower lip set forward so that, seen in profile, it gave him a look almost of pugnacity. It indicated, however, determination and steadfastness rather than combativeness. He was firm in the maintenance of his own rights as an individual even when he did not care to exercise those rights. When a temperance committee urged him to sanction their aims and set an example by pledging himself not to use intoxicating liquors, he replied, "Gentlemen, I refuse to sign any pledge. I never have been drunk, and, by the blessing of God, I never will get drunk, but I have a constitutional privilege to get drunk, and that privilege I will not sign away" (*Memoirs,* p. 165). He rigidly regulated his own life, but resented any other kind of personal control. His best work both as judge and writer was done while he worked alone. He gave heed to this trait when, after retiring from the chancellorship, he declined to serve on a committee to revise the New York laws, but was willing, although the offer was not accepted, to undertake the task alone.

[The chief sources are an autobiographical sketch published in the *Southern Law Rev.,* July 1872, and in the *Am. Law School Rev.,* Spring 1911; Wm. Kent, *Memoirs and Letters of Jas. Kent, LL.D.* (1898); John Duer, *A Discourse on the Life, Character and Pub. Services of Jas. Kent* (1848); Wm. J. Curtis, *Jas. Kent, the Father of Am. Jurisprudence* (1900); Macgrane Coxe, *Chancellor Kent at Yale, 1777–81* (1909); Frederick C. Hicks, "Jas. Kent and his Commentaries," in *Men and Books Famous in the Law* (1921), pp. 136–58, and "A Man of Law as a Man of Letters," *N. Y. Times Book Rev.,* May 27, 1923; a series of articles in the *Columbia Alumni News,* Apr. 27, 1923, by Harlan F. Stone, Dixon R. Fox, Frederick C. Hicks, Jos. P. Chamberlain, and Thos R. Powell; Chas. Evans Hughes, "Address at the Kent Centennial Celebration, Columbia Univ.," *Columbia Alumni News,* July 1923; F. B. Dexter, *Biog. Sketches of the Grads. of Yale Coll.,* vol. IV (1907), and *The Lit. Diary of Ezra Stiles, D.D., LL.D.* (1901), vol. II; L. V. Briggs, *Geneals. of the Different Families Bearing the Name of Kent* (1898); *N. Y. Daily Tribune,* Dec. 13, 14, 1847. There are 15 volumes of Kent MSS., including diaries, diplomas, and commissions, in the Lib. of Cong. Part of his legal collection was presented in 1911 to the Columbia University Law Library.] F. C. H.

KENT, JOSEPH (Jan. 14, 1779–Nov. 24, 1837), congressman, governor, senator, was born in Calvert County, Md., the son of Daniel Kent. His education must have included the study of medicine, for he was licensed as a physician in 1799. He was the partner of Dr. Parran of Lower Marlboro for a time, but in 1801 he established an independent practice at Bladensburg, Md., where he also engaged in agriculture. He entered the militia as surgeon and rose to be colonel of cavalry. He was interested in public affairs and in 1811 entered the national House of Representatives. With the exception of the years 1815–19 he served until 1826. Although he was first elected as a Federalist, he voted for the War of 1812 and later became a Republican, serving as a Monroe elector in 1816. He opposed the tariff bills of 1820 and 1824, voted for the bill providing for the general survey for roads and canals (1824), and favored other internal improvement measures. In the discussion over the admission of Missouri, he supported the compromise measures. During the presidential election of 1824, he took no part in the caucus, and in the House voted for Adams, with four of the nine Maryland representatives.

In 1826 Kent resigned from the House to become governor of Maryland (Jan. 9, 1826–Jan. 15, 1829). He won his first election by a vote of fifty-nine to thirty; his two reëlections were almost unanimous. His messages were said to have established "a new era" in that he "added the expression of opinions and recommendation of measures, and an assumption of that responsibility which justly belongs and should always appertain to this branch of the government" (*Niles' Weekly Register,* Jan. 6, 1827). Having been a director of the Chesapeake & Ohio Canal, he was greatly interested in internal improvements by both federal and state aid. He urged state support both for the canal and for the Baltimore & Ohio Railroad, deprecating the idea of antagonism between the two projects. He also supported the resolution of a previous legislature for a popular presidential vote by districts, but he insisted upon state equality in the election by the House. In matters of social importance he favored prison reform and aid to schools and colleges.

Having become closely identified with the National Republicans, Kent in 1831 was a member and a vice-president of the Baltimore convention which nominated Henry Clay for the presidency and was himself later elected to the Senate, taking his seat on Dec. 2, 1833. Here he was a friend and faithful follower of Clay, supporting the censure on Jackson's removal of deposits, and opposing Jackson's attitude toward France, the land distribution bill, and the surplus distribution bill. He favored some non-partisan measures, including the bills providing for the repeal of the four-year term of officials, forbidding interference with anti-slavery mail, and those granting aid to the Chesapeake & Ohio Canal and to the Baltimore & Ohio Railroad. He also favored a reform in the method of electing the president and a reduction of the vote necessary to override a presidential veto. Although he seldom spoke in debate, when he did, according to Clay, it was always to good purpose. His death occurred at his home, "Rosemount," near Bladensburg, following a fall from his horse. His eulogy was pronounced by Clay. He had married twice. His first wife was Eleanor Lee Wallace, who died in 1826. His second wife was Alice Lee Contee.

[H. E. Buchholz, *Govs. of Md.* (1908); *Biog. Dir. Am. Cong.* (1928); *Remarks of Mr. Kent of Md. in Relation to the Removal of the Pub. Deposites (sic)* (1834); *Niles' Weekly Reg.,* Jan. 10, 1829; *Cong. Globe,* 25 Cong., 2 Sess., p. 8; *Daily Nat. Intelligencer* (Washington, D. C.), Nov. 25, 27, 1837.] W. C. M.

KENT, WILLIAM (Mar. 5, 1851–Sept. 18, 1918), mechanical engineer, editor, was born in Philadelphia, Pa., the son of James Kent and his second wife Janet Scott, who came to America from Bothwell, Scotland, in 1848. William attended the public schools of Philadelphia and graduated from Central High School at seventeen. After his graduation he had part-time employment with the Jersey City (N. J.) Gas Company and later with the Ringwood Iron Works, Hewitt, N. J., and attended classes at Cooper Union in New York City. In 1874 he entered the junior class of Stevens Institute of Technology, Hoboken, N. J., and in June 1875 became an assistant to Dr. Robert L. Thurston, professor of mechanical engineering at Stevens, with whom he conducted (1875–77) studies of the properties of copper-tin and copper-zinc alloys for the United States Iron and Steel Testing Board. At the same time he continued his class work and was graduated with the degree of M.E. in 1876. From 1877 to 1882 he was in turn editor of the *American Manufacturer and Iron World,* Pittsburgh, and mechanical engineer and open-hearth superintendent for Schoenberger & Company, Pittsburgh. In 1882 he became manager of the Pittsburgh office of the Babcock & Wilcox Company, manufacturers of water-tube boilers, and at the same time, with William F. Zimmerman, formed the Pittsburgh Testing Laboratory. This business, which was the pioneer commercial physical testing laboratory, was sold to Alfred E. Hunt [*q.v.*] of Hunt & Clapp, and Kent went to New York City as superintendent of sales and engineer of tests for the Babcock & Wilcox Company. In this position he carried on a series of investigations in the proper combustion of fuel and the design of steam boilers, the results of which are the basis of many of the present methods of computing in the design of combustion equipment. He obtained many patents in this field and invented among others the wing-wall furnace and a gas producer of the Dowson type.

In 1887 Kent left the boiler company to become

general manager of the United States Torsion Balance and Scale Company. After holding this position for four years he established a private consulting engineering practice in New York City which he continued except for one or two interruptions throughout his life. At about this time, too, he began his serious editorial work and writing. He became associate editor of *Engineering News* in 1895 and served in this capacity for eight years, resigning then to become dean of the L. C. Smith College of Applied Science at Syracuse University, Syracuse, N. Y. In 1908 he left this position to become manager of the Sandusky Foundry and Machine Company at Sandusky, Ohio. Two years later he resumed his consulting practice in New York, and at the same time, from 1910 to 1914, served as editor of *Industrial Engineering*. In 1895 he had published the first edition of his *Mechanical Engineers' Pocket-Book*. This was the first mechanical engineer's handbook of the modern type and was a carefully authenticated compilation of the engineering data which he had collected and used during the years of his practice. The book stood alone for about twenty years and at the time of his death the ninth edition had been published. Kent will probably be remembered longest for this reference work, but he was a leading authority on all phases of fuel combustion, steam-boiler practice, and shop planning and management. He was also the author of *Steam Boiler Economy* (1901), *Report of Syracuse Chamber of Commerce Committee on Education* (1908), *Investigating an Industry* (1914), and *Book-keeping and Cost Accounting for Factories* (1918). He was an organizing member and vice-president (1888–90) of the American Society of Mechanical Engineers, contributing several papers to their *Transactions,* and was president (1905) of the American Society of Heating and Ventilating Engineers. Kent's wife was Marion Weild Smith whom he married on Feb. 25, 1879. He died suddenly in Gananoque, Ontario, Canada, and was buried from his brother's home in Passaic, N. J.

[*Trans. Am. Soc. Mech. Engineers,* vol. XL (1918); *Who's Who in America,* 1918–19; L. V. Briggs, *Geneals. of the Different Families Bearing the Name of Kent* (1898); *N. Y. Times,* Sept. 19, 1918; Patent office records.] C. W. M.

KENTON, SIMON (Apr. 3, 1755–Apr. 29, 1836), frontiersman, Indian fighter, was the son of Mark and Mary (Miller) Kenton and was born in Virginia, probably in Fauquier County. His father was an emigrant from Ireland, and his mother was of a Scotch-Welsh family that had settled in Virginia at an early day. As a boy he worked on his father's farm and had no opportunities for schooling. He never learned to read or write and signed his name only with great difficulty. He was about six feet one in height, of a full but not corpulent form, and in his prime weighed about one hundred and ninety pounds. When he had just turned sixteen he fought a savage combat with a rival in a love affair, and, believing that he had killed his antagonist, he fled westward. Assuming the name of Simon Butler, he voyaged with two companions down the Ohio probably as far as the site of Maysville. For more than two years, sometimes alone and usually in imminent danger from roving bands of Shawnees, he hunted along the Ohio and along the Great and the Little Kanawha. In 1774 he served as a scout in Dunmore's War. Near the future Maysville, in the spring of 1775, he built a cabin and planted corn, but in the autumn, learning of the settlement at Boonesborough, he moved there. Appointed a scout by Boone, he took a leading part in all the local encounters with Indians, in one of which he saved Boone's life. In 1778, as a scout, he accompanied General Clark's little army to Kaskaskia, and, on being sent back with dispatches, joined Boone in a raid against the Indian town at Chillicothe. Later in the year he scouted for Colonel Bowman on the Little Miami but was pursued to the Ohio and captured. Eight times compelled to run the gauntlet and three times tied to the stake for burning, he was successively reprieved. Taken to Detroit he was held by the British under close surveillance but, on the night of June 3, 1779, escaped. In 1780 and again in 1782 he scouted for General Clark in Ohio. Learning that his boyhood rival was living, he resumed his own name and, in 1785, established himself at Maysville, where, on Feb. 15, 1787, he married Martha Dowden. He acquired large tracts of land and, for a few years, enjoyed a period of quiet and prosperity, although he continued to bear the burden of constant vigilance against the Indians, and in 1794 he served as a major in Wayne's expedition. After his first wife died, he married her cousin, Elizabeth Jarboe, on Mar. 27, 1798. At the end of that year he left Kentucky, the next spring settled near the present Springfield, Ohio, and, two or three years later, moved to Urbana. In 1805 he was made a brigadier-general of militia. In the War of 1812 he joined General Shelby's Kentuckians and took part in the battle of the Thames. About 1820 he moved to the vicinity of Zanesfield in Logan County. Owing to defective titles to some of his land, improvidence, and open-handed generosity, his later years were spent in poverty, relieved by a government pension of twenty dollars a month. He died near

Zanesfield and was buried there. In 1865 the remains were reinterred at Urbana and, in 1884, marked by a monument erected by the state of Ohio.

[Kenton Papers, Clark Papers, Kentucky Papers, and Draper Notes in the Draper MSS. of the State Hist. Soc. of Wis.; Edna Kenton, *Simon Kenton* (copr. 1930); R. W. McFarland, "Simon Kenton," *Ohio Archaeol. and Hist. Quart.*, Jan. 1904; W. D. McKinney, "Simon Kenton," *Ibid.*, Jan. 1925; J. A. McClung, *Sketches of Western Adventure* (1832); John McDonald, *Biog. Sketches* (1838).] W. J. G.

KEOKUK (fl. 1790–1848), a Sauk war leader, was born of the Fox clan in the great Sauk village on Rock River, Ill., near the present city of Rock Island. His mother, Lalotte, was part French. He himself betrayed his white blood in his small hands and feet, his flat cheek bones, and his blue eyes. As a horseman he early won distinction against the swift-riding Sioux, the hereditary foes of his nation, and was thereupon accorded the privilege of appearing mounted on all public occasions. His astuteness obtained for him admission to the Sauk tribal council, and his eloquence made for his advancement. His voice was resonant, his bearing lofty, his thoughts framed themselves in striking imagery. Although not of the ruling clan, he became a chief through the support of the United States government in return for his unfaltering aid to its plans. In 1812 when Black Hawk [*q.v.*] left the Sauk village to join the British against the Americans on the Canadian frontier, Keokuk seized the opportunity to push himself into Black Hawk's place. His supremacy was assured by the latter's defeat in the so-called Black Hawk War of 1832. Keokuk was given charge of his rival, and, by the treaty of Sept. 21, 1832, in which the Sauk and Fox ceded their lands in eastern Iowa to the United States, his faction was accorded a reservation of four hundred square miles on the lower reaches of the Iowa River. Moreover, to him fell the right to dispense the twenty-thousand-dollar annuity that was pledged to the Sauk and the Fox by this treaty. In 1833 by direction of the United States government he took Black Hawk on a sight-seeing tour of eastern America. In 1837 the tour was repeated, principally for the sake of a conference at Washington between the Sauk and Fox and the Sioux in order to adjust their differences over the "neutral line," fixed in 1825 by the United States government in the region now the state of Iowa. Here Keokuk so eloquently set forth the Sauk and Fox claim that the *Niles' National Register* on Oct. 7, 1837, spoke of "the celebrated *Keo-Kuck,* one of the most sagacious Indians on our frontier . . . the Thersites of the Day." In 1845, having receded to the United States the reservation on the Iowa, he removed with the Sauk and Fox to Kansas. Here his intemperance and his love of money brought him trouble and disgrace. He died, probably in the spring of 1848, at the Sauk Agency in Franklin County.

[*Life of Black Hawk,* ed. by M. M. Quaife (1916); Benjamin Drake, *Life and Adventures of Black Hawk* (1839); Perry A. Armstrong, *The Sauks and the Black Hawk War* (1887); Frank E. Stevens, *The Black Hawk War* (1903); Jacob Van der Zee, "The Black Hawk War and the Treaty of 1832," *Iowa Jour. of Hist. and Politics,* July 1915; I. B. Richman, *John Brown Among the Quakers and other Sketches* (1894); F. R. Aumann, "The Watchful Fox," *The Palimpsest,* April 1928.] I. B. R.

KEPHART, EZEKIEL BORING (Nov. 6, 1834–Jan. 24, 1906), college president, bishop of the United Brethren Church, was born in Decatur Township, Clearfield County, Pa., the son of Henry and Sarah (Goss) Kephart, of Swiss and Pennsylvania German ancestry. He was the fifth of thirteen children. In his youth he was subjected to the rigors of pioneer life and had little opportunity for reading or schooling. In early boyhood he responded to religious appeals and made a public profession of faith. On a cold winter day when the snow was deep, his father, at the boy's request, baptized him in a running stream. He spent a few months each winter in a log schoolhouse and later took a partial course in Dickinson Seminary, Williamsport, Pa. In 1857, with his brother Isaiah [*q.v.*], he entered Mount Pleasant College, a United Brethren institution. This same year the college was merged with Otterbein University, Westerville, Ohio, and he continued his studies there. Leaving Otterbein in 1858, in January of the following year, with his brother, he was received as a member of the Allegheny Conference and assigned to the Troutville mission. During the next three years he served churches in Johnstown, Pa., Altoona, and Greensburg. In 1864 he returned to complete his course at Otterbein University and graduated the following year. He then served for a year as president of Collegiate Institute, Leoni, Mich., and was afterward pastor at Mount Pleasant, Pa.

In 1868 he was elected president of Western College (later Leander Clark College), at Western, Iowa, where he served until 1881. Whether as college teacher and president, as pastor, or as bishop he always stood sturdily for high standards of church education. During his presidency at Western College he was elected to the state Senate of Iowa, serving from 1872 to 1876. Here he was chairman of the committee on Temperance, and, in 1874, of the committee to investigate the Iowa State Agricultural College. He was always interested in legislation for the improvement of schools. The Republican party offered him nomination for the governorship.

The largest service he rendered, however, was as bishop of the United Brethren church. He was first elected in 1881. About this time he was invited to the presidency of Iowa Agricultural College, but he preferred to remain in the bishopric at a much lower salary. After serving as active bishop for twenty-four years, from 1881 to 1905, he was elected bishop emeritus. In 1890–91 and again in 1892–93 he made visitations to the missions abroad. On Jan. 24, 1906, while assisting in the promotion of Indiana Central College, a new institution in Indianapolis, he died very suddenly. His dignified, stately bearing, his majestic appearance, his reserve of manner, coupled with a strong religious faith and a deep sense of fairness, made him a strong leader, a wise executive, and a dependable churchman. Among his published writings are: *A Manual of Church Discipline* (1895), *Apologetics; or a Treatise on Christian Evidences* (1901), and *A Brief Treatise on the Atonement* (1902). He was married Nov. 4, 1860, at Johnstown, Pa., to Susan J. Trefts; there were four children of this marriage.

[L. F. John, *The Life of Ezekiel Boring Kephart* (1907); A. W. Drury, *Hist. of the Ch. of The United Brethren in Christ* (1924); the *Religious Telescope*, Jan. 31, 1906; *Watchword*, Feb. 6, 1906; *Indianapolis News*, Jan. 25, 1906; *Who's Who in America*, 1906–07.]

W. G. C.

KEPHART, ISAIAH LAFAYETTE (Dec. 10, 1832–Oct. 28, 1908), United Brethren clergyman, editor, was born in Decatur Township, Clearfield County, Pa., the son of Henry and Sarah (Goss) Kephart, and brother of Bishop Ezekiel Boring Kephart [*q.v.*]. He was reared in a log cabin with a large family of children, subject to the simplicities and deprivations of such a life. His first schooling was in a log schoolhouse under very inadequate teaching and it was not till his twenty-third year that he studied geography and grammar. In his boyhood days and early manhood, he spent most of his time at logging and rafting, with many thrilling experiences. In 1856 he attended Dickinson Seminary at Williamsport, Pa., and in 1857 entered Mount Pleasant College, which was merged that year with Otterbein University. He soon left, however, to earn money and was for a time a traveling assistant pastor. In 1859 he enrolled at Otterbein University and the same year was admitted to the Allegheny Conference and assigned to the Mahoning Circuit. In 1863 he was ordained.

His public services were varied. From 1859 to 1867 he was engaged in pastoral work; he was principal of public schools in Jefferson, Iowa, 1867–69, and superintendent of schools, Greene County, Iowa, 1869–71; professor of natural science at Western College (now Leander Clark College), 1871–76; actuary of the United Brethren Mutual Aid Society, 1876–83; professor in San Joaquin College, 1883–85, professor in Westfield College, 1885–89; and editor of the *Religious Telescope* from 1887 until the time of his death. He was made a fellow of the Society of Science, Letters, and Art of London (1888) in recognition of a scholarly paper on "Soul Culture" which he wrote and submitted at that time. During two years of the Civil War (1863–65) he served as chaplain of the 21st Pennsylvania Cavalry. His service as editor stands out most conspicuously, and his term of service in this connection was longer than in any other relationship. Although calm and reserved, he was positive in his own convictions and in his statement of them. Temperamentally he was conservative but not dogmatic. He had a fine sense of the rights of other people, and an exalted appreciation of piety, honesty, and integrity. He was fearless and courageous as an advocate of temperance and other aspects of social reform, and his editorials reveal a strong grasp on subjects of public as well as of church interest. Among his published writings are *A Compendium for the Agents of the United Brethren Mutual Aid Society of Pennsylvania* (1877), *An Essay on the Evils of the Use of Tobacco by Christians* (1882), and *The Holy Spirit in the Devout Life* (1904). He married in 1861 Mary Elizabeth Sowers; they had two children.

[C. J. Kephart and W. R. Funk, *Life of Isaiah L. Kephart* (1909); A. W. Drury, *Hist. of the Ch. of the United Brethren in Christ* (1924); L. F. John, *The Life of Ezekiel Boring Kephart* (1907); the *Religious Telescope*, Nov. 4, 1908; *Watchword*, Nov. 14, 1908; *Who's Who in America*, 1906–07.]

W. G. C.

KEPPEL, FREDERICK (Mar. 22, 1845–Mar. 7, 1912), print-dealer, art-critic, was the fourth son of John and Ellen (Hadden) Keppel. He was born in Tullow, Ireland, his ancestors on both sides having lived for centuries in County Carlow. His mother's family was mainly Welsh, whereas John Keppel was of Dutch descent. Frederick's father, a stern theologian, was a flour-miller in County Carlow. He sent his son to a Dublin boarding-school, then to Wesley College. When the boy was fifteen the elder Keppel removed to Liverpool where he established a grocery, but in 1862 he emigrated to Canada, settling first in Guelph, Ontario, as a grocer, then on a farm. Frederick liked farming, but he was incapacitated for it when he fell from a wagon and the prongs of a hay-fork accidentally pierced his lungs. In 1864 he went to Utica, N. Y., to work in a store, but in time he went to New York and became a book-seller. While he was engaged in this business an accident turned his attention to prints. Out of pity for an Old London print-seller, stranded in New York, he paid one hundred dollars for a portfolio of prints which he was not eager to buy. Through his friend George Gebbie, a publisher in Philadelphia, he was introduced to Philadelphia collectors who gave him a knowledge of the value of prints. When he returned to New York with money from those he had sold he determined on print-selling for a livelihood. In 1868, after he had collected in Europe, he set up shop at 66 Beekman Street. This shop, and its successors at 243 Broadway and on Sixteenth and Thirty-ninth Streets, became centers for connoisseurs and exhibition rooms for foreign etchers whose work he introduced to New York, and for many an American beginner in graphic art. He became one of the leading authorities in America on etching and engraving and was valued not only for his technical acumen, but for his personal qualities as well. He was a delightful talker, widely read, and had a genius for friendship. His annual journeys to London and Paris during forty years brought him into contact with celebrities of the print world, and his anecdotes of print-makers, dealers, and collectors at home and abroad were keen and witty. He had an unusual fondness for animals and wild birds. A feature of the shop at 20 East Sixteenth Street, not always popular with women, was a tame raccoon which roamed the place. His garden at Quogue, L. I., was haunted by pet ravens, crows, and magpies. He was an accomplished lecturer on art topics and wrote many critical articles for American and English periodicals. He also published *Christmas in Art* (1909); *The Golden Age of Engraving* (1910), *The Gentle Art of Resenting Injuries* (1904), which records a quarrel with Whistler, and pamphlet sketches of engravers put out by Keppel & Company. He married, in 1875, Fannie M. Vickery, of County Cork, Ireland.

[There is an introductory autobiographical chapter in *The Golden Age of Engraving*. See also: *Who's Who in America*, 1910–11; the *Bookman*, July 1913; *Outlook*, Mar. 16, 1912; *N. Y. Times*, Mar. 8, 1912.]

M. B. H.

KEPPLER, JOSEPH (Feb. 1, 1838–Feb. 19, 1894), caricaturist, founder of *Puck*, was born in Vienna, Austria, the son of a confectioner, John Keppler, and his Hungarian wife, Josepha Pellwein. His youth was restricted more by his lack of money than by his lack of wits. Possessing talent for both acting and drawing, he vacillated for many years between the two professions. In an attempt to get to Italy where he wished to study art, he twice joined strolling theatrical companies, once traveling through Styria and the Tyrol, and once into Hungary, but in neither case reaching his destination. In 1856 he enrolled at the Akademie der Bildenden Künste in Vienna, where he acquired a good technical foundation in drawing. Several of his humorous sketches were accepted by *Kikeriki*. His father had emigrated to New Frankfort, Salina County, Mo., after the Revolution of 1848, where he farmed and kept the general store. In 1867 young Keppler followed him. Shortly after his arrival he went to St. Louis with the intention of studying medicine, but he was drawn once more into acting, at which he was successful, and from that into managing, at which he was not. On Aug. 28, 1869, the first number of his first humorous weekly appeared. This was *Die Vehme, Illustriertes Wochenblatt für Scherz und Ernst*. After a year it failed, and in March 1871 Keppler began to publish *Puck, Illustrierte Wochenschrift*, which lasted until February 1872. Shortly thereafter, with his wife, Pauline Pfau of St. Louis, whom he had married in July 1870, he went to New York. There he was employed by Frank Leslie and by 1875 was preparing nearly all of the cover cartoons for *Frank Leslie's Illustrated Newspaper*, specializing in attacks upon Grant and party graft. He still desired a paper of his own, however, and in 1876 he and Adolph Schwarzmann broke away from the Leslie publications and founded another *Puck, Humoristisches Wochenblatt*. Schwarzmann supplied the financial and business support, and permitted Keppler complete editorial freedom. The German *Puck* was so successful that in March 1877 an English edition was inaugurated which survived until 1918, twenty-two years longer than its German predecessor.

Previous humorous weeklies had had but one large cartoon. *Puck* had three. Formerly cartoons had been cut in wood. *Puck's* were lithographed, at first in black and white, later with two colors produced by woodblocks, and finally with several colors lithographically produced. Its main contribution to comic art, however, was not mechanical. Keppler brought with him from Austria the German conception of cartooning, in which caricature played a large part. He also brought with him a sense of satire unrepressed by the primness of nineteenth-century America. As a result, particularly in the early numbers when Keppler was drawing all the cartoons and some of the advertisements, *Puck* had a foreign and exuberant flavor quite different from its rivals. Eventually the magazine attracted the contributions of several good American cartoonists, and a number of artists were imported from Vienna, but until Keppler's death, his own personality was to some degree reflected in its pages. From the beginning it espoused the causes of the national Democratic party and lampooned both Tammany and the Republicans. At no time, however, were its jibes purely partisan. Monopolies, labor unions, woman's suffrage, Catholicism, camp meetings, and all forms of graft, extravagance, and injustice were at some time ridiculed. Keppler's cartoons were usually large, with many figures illustrating the parable. They were always composed with a certain sweep of design, and delicately finished. Characteristic examples appearing in *Puck* are: "Consolidated," Jan. 26, 1881; "The Carol of the 'Waits,'" Dec. 23, 1885; "The Mephistopholes of Today—Honest Labor's Temptation," Oct. 20, 1886; "At Last," Jan. 18, 1888, and "It Isn't the Cowl That Makes the Monk," Aug. 28, 1889. In 1893 Keppler overtaxed his strength in the management of the *World's Fair Puck,* and early in the following year he died at his home in New York City.

[See H. C. Bunner, *A Selection of Cartoons from Puck by Jos. Keppler* (1893); A. B. Maurice and F. T. Cooper, *The Hist. of the Nineteenth Century in Caricature* (1904); Frank Weitenkampf, *Am. Graphic Art* (1912); Alfred Trumble, article in the *Epoch* (N. Y.), June 13, 1890; *Appletons' Ann. Cyc.*, 1894; *Puck*, Feb. 28, 1894; A. B. Faust, *The German Element in the U. S.*, II (1909), 363–64; J. B. Bishop, *Our Political Drama* (1904); the *Illustrated American*, Mar. 10, 1894; *N. Y. Times*, July 20, 1890, p. 3; *N. Y. Herald*, *N. Y. Tribune* and *World* (N. Y.), Feb. 20, 1894. Information as to certain facts was supplied for this sketch by Keppler's son, Joseph Keppler, Woodland, N. Y.]

C. P. M.

KERENS, RICHARD C. (Nov. 12, 1842–Sept. 4, 1916), railroad builder and politician, was born in Kilberry, County Meath, Ireland, the son of Thomas and Elizabeth (Gugerty) Kerens. His parents emigrated to the United States when he was an infant and settled in Iowa. Here he received an ordinary public-school education and at the age of nineteen entered the United States army as chief mule driver for the Army of the Potomac. In 1863 he was placed in charge of transportation for the Army of the Frontier in Arkansas and Indian Territory. At the close of the war he settled at the frontier Indian trading post, Fort Smith, and became the proprietor of a livery stable. He soon took a contract for carrying the Southern overland mail by pony express. He prospered, and on June 2, 1867, he was married to Frances Jane Jones. In 1874 he moved to San Diego, Cal., where he continued to prosper with his mail business. But while he was in California a foregleam of the immense possibilities in railroad construction came to him, and he moved to St. Louis in 1876 in order to be better situated for taking part in the activities he pictured in that field of work. In time he became closely connected with railroad developments and played a prominent part in the building of the Cotton Belt & Northern Railway, the West Virginia Central & Pittsburgh, the St. Louis & North Arkansas, the San Pedro, Los Angeles & Salt Lake, and the St. Louis, Iron Mountain & Southern. He also became a heavy stockholder and a leading director in several of the same railway systems. In association with Henry Gassaway Davis and Senator Stephen Benton Elkins [*qq.v.*] he helped to develop the lumber and mining industries of West Virginia. These investments produced most of his wealth.

In spite of the fact that Kerens was neither an able writer nor a forceful speaker, he held a position of outstanding influence in Missouri politics for almost forty years. There were two chief reasons for his power. In the first place, he generously donated large sums of money to the Republican campaign funds; and, secondly, he displayed superior ability in the direction and control of many faithful political lieutenants. He was Republican national committeeman for three consecutive terms (1884–1900) and was the leader in dispensing federal patronage in Missouri during that period. Three times he was given the complimentary vote of the Republican minority in the state legislature for United States senator. But when his party had its inning in 1905 with the selection of Maj. William Warner [*q.v.*] as a compromise candidate, because of the deadlock over Thomas K. Niedringhaus, the caucus nominee, and Kerens, the latter was bitterly disappointed at being denied the election. In 1891 he had been appointed by President Harrison one of the three members from the United States on the Continental Railway Commission. He served ten years on this board and assisted in completing a railway survey through fifteen South American republics. For his faithfulness and liberal financial contributions to the party Harrison offered him the ambassadorship to Italy, and later McKinley urged him to take his choice of diplomatic posts excepting only London, Paris, and Berlin. All these he declined, but President Taft finally obtained his acceptance of the post at Vienna in 1909. Like many another man whose ambassadorship has come as a reward for political services, Kerens had no training and possessed no special qualifications for such a position. Except for the social activities of the post, in which his wife ably aided him, his four years in Austria-Hungary were marked by an ordinary colorless routine. He was a devout and influential Catholic and in 1904 received the Laetare Medal from the University of Notre Dame, awarded to prominent Catholic laymen. He died at Merion, Pa.

[Sources include *Who's Who in America,* 1916–17; *The Book of St. Louisans* (1906), ed. by J. W. Leonard; *St. Louis Republic,* Dec. 21, 1909, Sept. 5, 1916; *St. Louis Globe-Democrat,* Feb. 13, Mar. 19, 1905, Sept. 5, 1916; *Kansas City Star,* Sept. 4, 1916; and Kerens' reports to the State Dept. The middle initial in Kerens' name probably does not stand for a name.]

H. E. N.

KERFOOT, JOHN BARRETT (Mar. 1, 1816–July 10, 1881), first Bishop of the Protestant Episcopal Diocese of Pittsburgh, was born in Dublin, Ireland, the son of Richard Kerfoot and his wife Christiana Barrett, both of Scotch-Irish extraction. The family removed in 1819 to Lancaster, Pa., where the father died early. The training the boy received was largely due to the care of William Augustus Muhlenberg [*q.v.*], rector of the parish and his lifelong friend. Young Kerfoot afterward removed to Flushing, L. I., to attend the Collegiate Institute which Muhlenberg had established there. Here he graduated and became an instructor, and studied theology under Samuel Seabury and Samuel Roosevelt Johnson. In 1837 he was ordered deacon by the Rt. Rev. H. U. Onderdonk of New York and returned to work as a teacher with Muhlenberg until 1842. In the meanwhile, in 1840, he was ordained presbyter. In 1842 he married Eliza M. Anderson of New York and removed to Washington County, Md., where he became the head of St. James' Hall, afterward the College of St. James. This institution had been founded by Bishop W. R. Whittingham of Maryland. Kerfoot was profoundly influenced in his character and as a teacher by Muhlenberg, and in his theology by Whittingham. The new school flourished and served as the model for St. Paul's School, Concord, N. H., and others. In 1843 Kerfoot visited England and was greatly impressed by the services in the cathedrals, his training under Muhlenberg having led him to appreciate the esthetic side of religion. He also studied the Oxford Movement, then at its height. But, although a High-Churchman of the Seabury, Hobart, Whittingham type, he declined the lead of Pusey and the other Tractarians.

The Civil War ruined the college. Kerfoot was opposed to secessionism and many of the students were from the South. In a raid in 1864 Kerfoot was captured by Gen. Jubal Early to be taken to Richmond and held as a hostage. Fortunately he was exchanged and in the same year became president of Trinity College, Hartford, Conn. In 1865 the Diocese of Pittsburgh was organized and Kerfoot was elected its first bishop. It comprised twenty-four counties in western Pennsylvania. In a population of possibly 700,000 there were about 1,700 communicants; but half of the parishes were self-supporting. Kerfoot was consecrated bishop, Jan. 25, 1866, by the presiding bishop, John Henry Hopkins, assisted by Bishops McIlvaine, Whittingham, Williams, Talbot, Coxe, and Clarkson. In the administration of his diocese Kerfoot was so efficient that at his death in 1881 the number of communicants was 5,838, and of the self-supporting parishes, 58. He was determined in his resistance to the advance of Ritualism, for, though he was a High-Churchman, he believed that it was quite out of place in the conditions prevailing in his diocese. In 1867 he attended the first Lambeth Conference and received the degree of LL.D. from Cambridge University. In 1874 he attended the Old Catholic conferences at Freiburg and at Bonn, and the second Lambeth Conference in 1878. He died at his summer home, Meyersdale, Somerset County, Pa. Except for a lecture on the "Inspiration of the Holy Scriptures" in a series of lectures on the *Evidences of Christianity* (1855), edited by Alonzo Potter, Kerfoot left no publications beyond the usual occasional sermons and addresses and Convention charges. Of these a partial list is given in Hall Harrison's life of Kerfoot.

[Hall Harrison, *Life of the Right Rev. John Barrett Kerfoot, D.D., LL.D., First Bishop of Pittsburgh, With Selections from his Diaries and Correspondence* (2 vols., 1886); Anne Ayers, *Life and Work of W. A. Muhlenberg* (1880); the *Churchman,* July 16, 1881; *Pittsburgh Dispatch,* July 11, 1881; and the Journals of the Diocese of Pittsburgh.]

J. C. Ay—r.

KERLIN, ISAAC NEWTON (May 27, 1834–Oct. 25, 1893), pioneer psychiatrist, who made the first important contributions toward the understanding and care of mentally deficient children and adults, was born at Burlington, N. J., the son of Joseph and Sarah (Ware) Kerlin. He was educated in the Burlington public schools, the John Collins Academy, and at the University of Pennsylvania, where he studied medicine under Dr. Joseph Parrish. He graduated in 1856 and after one year as resident at the Wills Eye Hospital in Philadelphia, he became assistant superintendent of the Pennsylvania Training School for Feeble-minded Children at Elwyn, near Media (1858–62). In 1862 he enlisted in the army but was soon detailed as medical officer in an impoverished hospital at Hagerstown, Md. In 1863 he served with the United States Sanitary Commission in the Army of the Potomac. The following year he left the service to become superintendent of the Pennsylvania Training School. Conditions were difficult, the work discouraging. He soon realized the necessity of closer contact and coöperation with heads of similar institutions. Through his efforts a national Association of Superintendents of Institutions for the Feeble-minded was formed at a meeting held at Elwyn in 1876, with O. Edouard Seguin as president and Kerlin as secretary. Kerlin remained secretary until his death and became largely responsible for the gradual extension of the association until it included almost all psychiatrists interested in mental deficiency. The Elwyn institution was his life work. Here he conducted a series of autopsies and laid some foundation for the psychopathology of the future. He held advanced ideas for his time, insisting that all mental deficients were wards of the state. He planned separate small buildings for their care, the first of which, holding 112 children, was opened in 1883. At his death, he had a central building, providing schoolrooms and accommodations for 400 teachable deficient children, and four detached buildings for 400 custodial and unteachable patients. His management was thorough and economical, but achieved at the cost of constant strain. In 1865 he married Harriet C. Dix, a Massachusetts woman, who predeceased him by a few months, leaving four sons.

About 1888 cardiac and renal symptoms began to make Kerlin's work difficult, but he was only happy when busy. His trustees offered him ample leaves of absence, and he made protracted visits to Europe (1889 and 1891), during which he was enthusiastically welcomed at all prominent institutions for the feeble-minded in Great Britain, Norway, and Denmark. But he would not give up his work. He died in the fall of 1893 and is buried in a grove on the Elwyn grounds. During his life he had little time for extensive literary production. His numerous short articles on subjects related to his work are able and instructive. He published two books, *Mind Unveiled* (1858), based on his early experiences with mental deficients, and *The Manual of Elwyn* (1891), and framed the draft of a bill, passed by the legislature, to provide institutions similar to that at Elwyn in the western part of Pennsylvania.

[*Trans. Medic. Soc. of the State of Pa.*, vol. XXV (1894); H. A. Kelly and W. L. Burrage, *Am. Medic. Biogs.* (1920); W. B. Atkinson, *The Physicians and Surgeons of the U. S.* (1879); H. M. Hurd, *Institutional Care of the Insane in the U. S. and Canada*, vol. IV (1917); *Medic. and Surgic. Reporter*, Nov. 25, 1893; the Phila. *Press*, Oct. 28, 1893.] J.R.O.

KERN, JOHN WORTH (Dec. 20, 1849–Aug. 17, 1917), statesman, was the son of Dr. Jacob Harrison Kern and Nancy (Ligget) Kern, and was born at Alto, Howard County, Ind. He was a descendant of Adam Kern, an emigrant from Germany who settled in Frederick County, Va., about the middle of the eighteenth century. In 1854 the family removed from Indiana to Warren County, Iowa, and remained there nine years but after the death of Mrs. Kern they returned to Alto. John attended the district schools and the normal college at Kokomo, Ind.; he became a teacher in the school of his home village when fifteen, and subsequently in the Dyar school, a few miles distant. In this period he displayed much interest in debating, and thereby helped to fit himself for his future career. He entered the law school of the University of Michigan in 1867, graduated in 1869, and entered practice in Kokomo. Being a ready speaker and resourceful in debate, he speedily won clients and showed himself able to hold his own against even such lawyers as Hendricks and Voorhees.

An ardent Democrat from boyhood, Kern soon became a local leader in his party. The county and city were prevailingly Republican but, though defeated as a candidate for the legislature in 1870, he became city attorney in 1871 and served in this office until 1884. His political activities won him recognition by the state Democracy and in 1884 he was nominated for reporter of the Indiana supreme court and was elected. Upon the expiration of his term of office in 1889 he remained in Indianapolis, whither he had moved four years before, and continued the practice of law. Elected to the state Senate in 1892, he served there from 1893 to 1897 and played a prominent part in legislative affairs, being especially active in behalf of union labor. Though opposed to free silver, he remained with his party in 1896 and supported Bryan, with whom he ever afterward remained on terms of intimacy. In 1900 and again in 1904 he was the Democratic candidate for governor but each time was beaten. In 1908 the Democratic National Convention at Denver nominated him by acclamation for the vice-presidency, and he made extended speaking tours but went down to defeat with his ticket. In Indiana, however, the Democrats won the legislature; Kern confidently expected to be elected senator, but was beaten, as he afterward said, by the activities of the "brewery crowd" (Bowers, *post*, p. 196). In 1910 he was indorsed for the Senate by the state convention and, when the Democrats carried Indiana that year, he was elected over Albert J. Beveridge, the Republican candidate.

From the outset he took a prominent part in the Senate, being regarded as a leader of the progressive Democrats. As a member of the committee on privileges and elections, he helped to investigate the notorious election of Senator Lorimer of Illinois, who was later unseated. As a result of the election of 1912 the Democrats gained control of the Senate, and Kern was chosen Democratic floor leader, a post to which no one with so short a period of service had before been elevated. During the remainder of his term he cooperated with President Wilson and played an active part in connection with the important legislation of that period. He was especially interested in child-labor legislation and other measures for social justice, and he secured a federal investigation of the notorious labor conditions that existed in West Virginia.

Beaten for reëlection by a small majority in 1916, Kern retired to private life. He died of tuberculosis the following year at Asheville, N. C. During most of his life Kern wore a beard, of which he wrote after his election to the Senate that it "has been attached to me so long it would be an act of base ingratitude to desert it now." Though a strong partisan, he was highly regarded by even his political opponents, and his honesty was never seriously questioned. He was married, in 1870, to Anna Hazzard of Kokomo. She died in 1884, and in December 1885, he married Araminta A. Cooper, also of Kokomo, who survived him.

[C. G. Bowers, *The Life of John Worth Kern* (1918); "John Worth Kern" by "Tattler," *Nation*, Dec. 9, 1915; *Indianapolis News, N. Y. Times,* Aug. 18, 1917.] P. L. H.

KERNAN, FRANCIS (Jan. 14, 1816–Sept. 7, 1892), lawyer and Democratic politician, was born on a farm in Wayne, Steuben County (now Tyrone, Schuyler County), N. Y. He was the son of William and Rose (Stubbs) Kernan, both natives of Ireland. After graduating from Georgetown College, Washington, D. C., in 1836, Francis took up the study of law with his brother-in-law in Watkins, N. Y. In 1839 he moved to Utica to continue his study in the office of Joshua A. Spencer. In 1840 he was admitted to the bar and also into partnership with Spencer. On May 23, 1843, he was married to Hannah Devereux of Utica. His family grew to include six sons and two daughters. Before 1848 Kernan had not been politically conspicuous, having served only a term as alderman and as school commissioner. In that year, however, he entered state politics by taking the stump for the Free Soil candidates. The sheer brilliancy of his speeches in this campaign gained him a statewide reputation. After the bitterness of the Free Soil fight had passed, he was appointed in 1854 reporter of the court of appeals and served for three years. His work was distinguished by accuracy and good judgment. These *Reports* were published in four volumes (Albany 1855–57). In 1860 he was elected a member of the Assembly, and in 1862 he won a seat in Congress over Roscoe Conkling. In the election of 1864 he was defeated by Conkling by a small margin, and he returned to his law practice.

In 1867 he was named a member of the constitutional convention, and later of the constitutional commission. In 1871 he was brought into action against the "Tweed ring" by Tilden, who believed him to be the leader best able to break the ring's hold on the state organization. This led to his nomination in 1872 as the Liberal Democratic candidate for governor. He was defeated, probably because many Protestant Democrats abstained from voting for him on account of his religion, but in 1874, when the Democrats gained control of the legislature, he was elected to the United States Senate to succeed Fenton. Probably John Kelly, the Tammany leader, had as much as any one to do with making Kernan's election possible, but his choice was universally approved throughout the state. Kernan was the first Democratic senator from New York in twenty-four years. In the 1876 Democratic convention at St. Louis, Kernan put Tilden in nomination and took an active part in the succeeding campaign. In 1880 the Republicans carried New York state, and the legislature chose Thomas C. Platt to succeed Kernan. The following year, when Platt and Conkling resigned from the Senate, Kernan was the Democratic choice for the Senate, but the Republicans combined to elect Warner Miller. After his retirement from the Senate, Kernan devoted his whole attention to his law practice in Utica. He was prominent also in educational matters, serving for over twenty years as school commissioner in Utica, and from 1870 until his death as a member of the Board of Regents of the State of New York. He was a man of decided convictions, brilliant intellect, persuasive speech, and great industry. Though at times he suffered from the religious prejudices of others, he himself was among the most tolerant of men. He retained the dress and courtly manners of an older generation and endeared himself to his fellows by his honesty and sincerity.

[W. H. Watson, *Address in Memory of Hon. Francis Kernan, LL.D., 1816–1892* (1893); H. J. Cookinham, *Hist. of Oneida County, N. Y.* (1912), vol. I; C. E. Fitch, *Encyc. of Biog. of N. Y.* (1916), vol. I; *The Writings and Speeches of Samuel J. Tilden* (2 vols., 1885), ed. by John Bigelow; *Biog. Dir. Am. Cong.* (1928); *N. Y. Herald, N. Y. Tribune, N. Y. Times,* Sept. 8, 1892.] L. H. H.

KERR, JOHN GLASGOW (Nov. 30, 1824–Aug. 10, 1901), missionary physician in China, was born on the "Old Kerr Farm," one mile east of Duncansville, Adams County, Ohio, the son of Joseph and Jane Loughridge Kerr, both of them children of Scotch-Irish immigrants. Kerr's father died in 1830 and the boy spent a number of years with an uncle in Lexington, Va., and there began the study of Latin and Greek. From 1840 to 1842 inclusive he attended what is now Denison University. In the autumn of 1842 he began the study of medicine with Doctors Sharpe and Duke in Maysville, Ky., and had a course of medical lectures in Transylvania University. He next studied in Jefferson Medical College, Philadelphia (1846–47), receiving the degree of M.D. in 1847. For several years he practised medicine in Brown and Adams counties, Ohio. Then, hearing a lecture by a Chinese portraying the physical suffering in China which might be relieved by Western medicine, he decided overnight to go as a medical missionary to that country. He applied to the Board of Foreign Missions of the Presbyterian Church, was appointed to Canton, and arrived on the scene of his future labors in May 1854. Almost immediately there was transferred to him the medical work which another member of his mission, Andrew P. Happer [*q.v.*], had begun. The following year he was placed in charge of the famous hospital of the Medical Missionary Society in China which had been founded two decades before by Peter Parker and which was financed by foreign residents in China. For over forty years he continued to head the institution. This appointment and his own energy and ability quickly made him the leading foreign physician in the city, a position which he held for nearly half a century. Most of his time was, naturally, given to medical practice. In his hospital and, for years, in one or more dispensaries in Canton and neighboring cities, he and his assistants and associates treated over three-quarters of a million patients. He developed much skill as a surgeon, especially for urinary calculus, and is said to have performed successfully over twelve hundred operations for that disorder.

At least as early as 1869 Kerr was also beginning medical education in connection with his hospital, and during his superintendency approximately two hundred Chinese were there trained in Western medicine. Moreover, Kerr gave much time to preparing literature in Chinese on Western medicine and related subjects and in English on medical matters and on the Canton dialect. The list of his works in Chinese includes a materia medica—in which he helped to lead the way in providing a Chinese nomenclature of Western medical terms—and treatises on vaccination, on symptomatology, on affections of the skin, and on diseases of the eye. It was natural that when, in 1886, the Medical Missionary Association of China was founded, Kerr should be made its first president. His crowning work was the founding, in Canton, of the first hospital in China for the treatment of the insane. For years he dreamed of such an institution, but his mission board found it impossible—or outside the scope of its proper activities—to provide the funds. Kerr accordingly obtained the necessary money from friends and from his own limited resources. In 1892 he was able to purchase land and, after six years of waiting, in 1897 to erect buildings. In 1898 he resigned the headship of the Canton Medical Missionary Society's hospital and thenceforward, until his death, Aug. 10, 1901, he gave the major portion of his time to the new enterprise. Kerr not only took a leading part in introducing Western medicine to China; he was also genuinely interested in the religious side of his task, saw that Christian instruction was given his patients, and regularly preached, conducted services, and distributed Christian literature. To a remarkable extent he won the confidence and the affection of the Chinese and received substantial recognition of this in gifts for his hospital. He was married three times: on Sept. 20, 1853, to Abby L. Kingsbury, who died Aug. 24, 1855; on July 4, 1858, to Isabella Jane Moseley, who died Apr. 1, 1885; and on June 9, 1886, to Martha Noyes, who survived him.

[Sources include: *Ann. Reports of the Board of Foreign Missions of the Presbyt. Ch. in the U. S. A.,* 1855–1902; manuscript records of the Board of Foreign Missions; a brief manuscript autobiography of Kerr in the possession of his family; the *Chinese Recorder,* Nov. 1871, May–June 1876, Sept. 1901; Harriet N. Noyes, *Hist. of the South China Mission of the Am. Presbyt. Ch.* (Shanghai, 1927); *A Century of Protestant Missions in China* (1907), ed. by D. MacGillivray; the *China Mission Year Book,* 1915, pp. 544–49.] K. S. L.

KERR, WALTER CRAIG (Nov. 8, 1858–May 8, 1910), engineer, son of Aaron Hervey and Elizabeth (Craig) Kerr, was born at St. Peter, Minn. His father was a home missionary of the Presbyterian Church and chaplain of the 9th Minnesota Regiment throughout the Civil

War. His mother was fond of mathematics, especially as applied to astronomy. Walter grew up in St. Peter, then a small frontier town, but the schools were good for the time and place and were ably supplemented by training in the Kerr home. As a boy he loved nature study and was also interested in all things mechanical. With the help of his mother he completed his preparation for college and entered the course in mechanic arts at Cornell University in September 1875. He made a record as a student that resulted in his appointment to an instructorship at graduation in 1879, and in 1880 he was made an assistant professor, serving two years. But life in calm, academic shades lacked the zest which his nature demanded, and he resigned to enter engineering practice in New York City in 1882. His first engagement was with a sales' agency for Westinghouse engines. Thus he was brought into touch with engineers and financiers who were undertaking the building and equipping of large complex plants for power development, manufacturing, and transportation. Contracts for the construction of such plants were let, at that time, to a number of independent bidders, each doing a portion of the work, with resulting discussion of the limits of responsibility. This plan brought confusion, delays, and increased expense. Kerr foresaw the coming industrial development and was convinced that one competent organization should undertake entire contracts, and with the approval and financial backing of George and H. H. Westinghouse, he became the moving spirit in the upbuilding of such a firm, organized as Westinghouse, Church, Kerr, & Company.

The company's first large contract on the new plan was to complete, ready for operation, all the mechanical equipment of the South Station in Boston. The immediate success in operation of this system of engineering elements was promptly recognized, and Kerr's plan came into quite general use for construction of large engineering properties. This was, indeed, his most important contribution to the engineering practice of his time. In 1907 he became a director of the Merchants' Association of New York City, which at the time was considering the menace to public safety of the surface railroad tracks on the West Side. A committee was appointed by the association, with Kerr as chairman, to study the problem and to suggest a solution. The resulting report (*Disposal of West Side Railroad Tracks,* 1908) was entirely Kerr's work, and the plan was carried out with only minor modifications. This was one of his last projects; he died in 1910. He had married, on Dec. 27, 1883, Lucy Lyon, a daughter of Judge Marcus Lyon of Ithaca, N. Y. He retained always his interest in education and for twenty years was a member of the board of trustees of Cornell University, giving counsel on university problems, especially those relating to Sibley College of Engineering. His boyhood love of nature lasted throughout his life. After he made his home on Staten Island, in his leisure time he studied the local flora and fauna and became one of the most active members of the Staten Island Association of Arts and Sciences, the presidency of which he held for eight years. He was also a lover of literature, especially of poetry. He found recreation in yachting and was an enthusiastic member of the Seawanhaka-Corinthian and the New York yacht clubs.

[See: Albert W. Smith, *A Biog. of Walter Craig Kerr* (1927), containing quotations from his letters and extracts from his addresses; *Trans. Am. Soc. Mech. Engineers,* vol. XXXII (1911); *Cornell Alumni News,* May 11, 1910; *N. Y. Tribune, N. Y. Times,* May 9, 1910. Kerr's paper, "The Mechanical Equipment of the New South Station, Boston," *Trans. Am. Soc. Mech. Engineers,* vol. XXI (1900), gives a full account of this project.] A. W. S.

KERR, WASHINGTON CARUTHERS (May 24, 1827–Aug. 9, 1885), geologist, was born in the Alamance region of Guilford County, N. C., the son of William M. and Euphence (Doak) Kerr. When he was quite young his parents died and he was adopted by the Rev. Washington Caruthers, a Presbyterian minister after whom he had been named and under whose guidance he received his early education. In 1847 he entered the University of North Carolina at Chapel Hill and in 1850 he graduated with high honors. His first employment after graduation was as a school teacher in the nearby town of Williamston, a position he shortly resigned to accept a professorship in Marshall University, in Texas. In 1852 he became one of the computers in the Nautical Almanac office in Cambridge, Mass. Here he came into contact with some of the most noted scientific men of the day. Rapidly developing a love for geology, mathematics, and engineering, he entered the Lawrence Scientific School and remained until 1856, when he accepted the professorship of chemistry and geology at Davidson College in North Carolina. He retained this position until 1865, although in 1862 he was granted leave of absence to become chemist and superintendent in the Mecklenburg Salt Works at Mt. Pleasant, S. C. When the fortunes of war brought about the destruction and abandonment of the works he returned to North Carolina where he was shortly appointed state geologist " 'nominally, and without pay and with especial instructions to look after certain chemical and mineral manufactures in which this state might be vitally interested' " (Holmes, *post,* p. 7). The confused condition of affairs incidental to this closing year of the war naturally precluded systematic work, and the organization, if such it can be called, for he had no regular assistants, seems to have died a natural death. In April 1866, however, Kerr was reappointed by Governor Worth and continued to hold the position without interruption, though through many difficulties, until 1882, when he became connected with the United States Geological Survey with headquarters in Washington. Declining health, however, compelled his final retirement in 1883.

Kerr was a hard worker, energetic and efficient, though wholly untrained along any special lines of his profession. The state, despite previous work by Olmsted and Emmons, was still largely unknown territory, and there were no maps sufficiently accurate for plotting geological details. Under these circumstances, Kerr set himself to remedy the deficiencies. In a rough, in part mountainous, country, notorious for its poor roads, he was compelled to travel long distances on horseback and on foot. The one great result of this survey was a map of the state published in 1882, sufficiently and accurately detailed to serve as a base map for future work. His most striking geological observation was that in both of the Carolinas the eastward flowing rivers always presented high banks and bluffs on the south side and low plains and swamps on the north, a fact he attributed to the coördinate action of the flowing streams and the earth's revolution. He is also one of the first to call prominently to attention the phenomena of "soil creep" on inclined surfaces due to the joint action of gravity and frost. His observations relative to indications of possible glaciation within the state were not generally accepted. The value of his work was real: he advertised the resources of North Carolina as no one before him had done, and he worked whole-heartedly for the good of the state, but the times were evil, and for several years he shared the common fate of many public officials in the South. "His motives were misrepresented, his character assailed, his abilities questioned, his work maligned" (Holmes, *post,* p. 20). Kerr was a man of slight, rather delicate frame, of a nervous, sensitive temperament, but hospitable and generous in the extreme. In 1853 he married Emma Hall, of Iredell County, N. C. He died at Asheville.

[J. A. Holmes, "A Sketch of Prof. Washington Caruthers Kerr" (with bibliography), *Jour. of the Elisha Mitchell Sci. Soc.,* 1887, pt. 2; G. P. Merrill, *The First One Hundred Years of Am. Geol.* (1924); *Am. Jour. Sci.,* Sept. 1885.]

G. P. M.

KERSHAW, JOSEPH BREVARD (Jan. 5, 1822–Apr. 13, 1894), soldier, jurist, was born at Camden, S. C., the son of Col. John Kershaw and of Harriette Du Bose, of distinguished ancestry. His grandfather, Joseph Kershaw, who emigrated from England in 1748, became prominent in the affairs of his state and took an active part in the War of the Revolution. His father, several times mayor of Camden, was a judge of the County of Kershaw, a member of the South Carolina House of Representatives, and a member of Congress for one term. Joseph Brevard Kershaw received his early schooling in and near his birthplace, studied law in the office of Hon. John M. De Saussure, and was admitted to the bar in the year 1843. He entered the Mexican War as a lieutenant in the Palmetto Regiment of his state Feb. 6, 1843, but after seeing considerable field service, was forced by a protracted illness to return to his home the following June, when he resigned from the army and resumed the practice of law. He was elected to the state legislature in 1852 and again in 1854. In 1860 he was a member of the secession convention which met at Charleston, and in April 1861 he entered the Confederate army as colonel, 2nd South Carolina Volunteers, which regiment he had recruited. His command was at Morris Island during the bombardment of Fort Sumter and formed a part of Bonham's brigade in the first battle of Bull Run. He was commissioned brigadier-general, Feb. 13, 1862, and thereafter his command became well known as "Kershaw's Brigade" of McLaws' division, Longstreet's corps, Army of Northern Virginia. He took a prominent part in the Peninsular campaign, and in the battles of Second Bull Run, South Mountain, and Antietam (*Battles and Leaders of the Civil War,* II, 195–393, 596, 613). His brigade distinguished itself at the battle of Fredericksburg, where it held the sunken road below Marye's Heights, at Chancellorsville, and at Gettysburg, where he led the attack of Longstreet's corps and lost over half his command (*Ibid.,* III, 78–95, 325–38). Transferred westward, his brigade took part at Chickamauga in the famous charge which crushed the Federal right wing and in all the engagements of the Tennessee campaign. Rejoining the Army of Northern Virginia and promoted major-general, May 18, 1864, he commanded a division of Longstreet's corps in the battles of the Wilderness, Spotsylvania, Cold Harbor, and Petersburg. At Sailor's Creek his division was a part of Ewell's corps which surrendered Apr. 6, 1865 (*Ibid.,* IV, 124–246, 543).

Kershaw was confined for several months as

prisoner of war at Fort Warren, Boston. After his release he resumed the practice of law in Camden and entered politics. He became a member of the state Senate in 1865 and for one year was its president. In 1870, as a member of the Union Reform party convention, he prepared the resolutions recognizing the Reconstruction acts. In 1877 he was elected judge of the fifth circuit court of his state, which office he held until failing health required his retirement sixteen years later. When he left the bench, in 1893, he was made postmaster of Camden, but he died the following year. Interment was in the Quaker burial ground. Kershaw's wife, whom he married in 1844, was Lucretia Douglas. He had one son and four daughters. He was prominent in Masonry and at one time was grand master of the state of South Carolina. He prepared for *Battles and Leaders of the Civil War* "Kershaw's Brigade at Fredericksburg" and "Kershaw's Brigade at Gettysburg" (vol. III, pp. 95 and 331).

[U. R. Brooks, *S. C. Bench and Bar*, vol. I (1908); Jefferson Davis, *The Rise and Fall of the Confed. Government* (1881), vol. II; Jas. Longstreet, *From Manassas to Appomattox* (1896); *Battles and Leaders of the Civil War*, vols. II–IV (1887–88); J. S. Reynolds, *Reconstruction in S. C.* (1905); Yates Snowden, *Hist. of S. C.* (1920), vol. II; the *S. C. Hist. and Geneal. Mag.*, Jan. 1924; *News and Courier* (Charleston), Apr. 14, 1894; notes supplied by Kershaw's grand-daughter, Mrs. Harriette Kershaw Leiding, Camden, S. C.]

C. D. R.

KESTER, VAUGHAN (Sept. 12, 1869–July 4, 1911), journalist and novelist, the son of Franklin Cooley and Harriett Watkins Kester, was born at New Brunswick, N. J., and died at his home, "Gunston Hall," in Fairfax County, Va. He was educated in the public schools of Mt. Vernon, Ohio, and by a private tutor in Cleveland, where his mother established a school of art. As a young man, he traveled much in the South and West, spending some time on a ranch in Colorado; the influence of these experiences is discoverable in most of his work. On Aug. 31, 1898, he was married to Jessie B. Jennings, of Mt. Vernon, Ohio. After having lived in Florida, New York City, and England, Kester finally settled at "Gunston Hall," the former home of George Mason which he bought in 1908. During his residence in New York City, he served on the staff of the *Cosmopolitan Magazine* and assisted his brother, Paul Kester, in promoting special performances of Ibsen's *Ghosts* and other modern plays. His ambition to write was awakened by his association with William Dean Howells, his mother's cousin, who continued to give encouragement, counsel, and practical assistance throughout the literary career of his protégé.

Kester began his career in literature by writing short stories for the magazines. His episodic tale, "The Bad Man of Las Vegas," which appeared in *Munsey's Magazine*, January 1900, reveals his *flair* for melodramatic situation and the portrayal of indigenous types of character. In his first novel, *The Manager of the B & A* (1901), which was accepted by Harper & Brothers through the influence of Howells, there is a sensational plot, which includes such materials as a workers' strike, a political campaign, a forest fire, and a murder; but there is also realistic description of a small town in the lumber region of Michigan, where the scene of the action is laid, and the dialogue is genuine and racy. *John o' Jamestown* (1907), published appropriately when the celebration of the tercentenary of the first settlement in Virginia was in progress, is a historical novel based upon the career of Captain John Smith. Like Kester's other work, it is marked by vivid description, stirring incident, and sincerity of purpose. Published only a short time before his death, but not too late for Kester to know that his book had been received enthusiastically by both the critics and the reading public, *The Prodigal Judge* (1911) was not only his most popular novel but his finest achievement. The book is weak structurally, and many of its incidents are melodramatic; but the picture of a frontier settlement in western Tennessee has a compelling authenticity. A fourth book by Kester, a group of short stories, collected from various magazines, was published posthumously under the title, *The Hand of the Mighty* (1913). Two stories in this volume, "Mr. Feeny's Social Experiment" and the title story, "The Hand of the Mighty," are of particular interest for their somewhat socialistic criticisms of capitalism.

Kester is a significant figure in the history of early twentieth-century American fiction. His portraits of native types of character associated with the primitive life of the frontier, particularly his sketches of itinerant wastrels, are remarkable for their shrewdness and humor. At least two characters in *The Prodigal Judge*, Slocum Price, the judge, and Cavendish, the "man of title," deserve to be remembered. No one since Mark Twain, perhaps, has caught better the idiom of the American backwoodsman.

[*Who's Who in America*, 1910–11; the *N. Y. Times*, July 6, 1911; Paul Kester, "Biographical Sketch of Vaughan Kester," in *The Hand of the Mighty*.]

R. S.

KETTELL, SAMUEL (Aug. 5, 1800–Dec. 3, 1855), editor, was born in Newburyport, Mass., the son of Jonathan and Mary (Noyes) Kettell. His father was an officer in the custom house.

After teaching for three or four years in Mr. Thayer's school in Chauncy Place, Boston, Kettell became an amanuensis and hack writer for Samuel Griswold Goodrich [*q.v.*]. He was a simple, guileless, mild-eyed man, a life-long haunter of libraries, with a fund of droll humor, a faculty for acquiring languages, of which he is said to have learned fourteen, and a baneful incapacity for making money. After publishing two translations from the Spanish, the *Personal Narrative of the First Voyage of Columbus* (1827) and *Records of the Spanish Inquisition* (1828), he edited *Specimens of American Poetry* (1829), the first comprehensive anthology of native verse. The three duodecimo volumes contain an introduction descriptive of early New England verse, selections from 189 writers from Cotton Mather to J. G. Whittier, and a catalogue of American poetry arranged chronologically from the Bay Psalm Book (1640) to volumes issued in 1829. The work was projected by Goodrich and originally undertaken by a Boston journalist, Frederic S. Hill, and was conceived as a refutation of Sydney Smith and other calumniators of American genius. To make the refutation sufficiently crushing, Kettell went into the highways and hedges in search of eligible bards with the result that his collection throws a brilliant light on the state of literary culture in the period covered. The reviewers [*e.g.*, S. A. Eliot, *North American Review,* October 1829] fell foul of its indiscriminate inclusiveness and of several editorial shortcomings; Goodrich, in consequence, lost $1,500 on the venture and felt that insult was added to injury when he discovered that the *Specimens* were commonly referred to as "Goodrich's *Kettle* of Poetry." While living with Thomas Nuttall [*q.v.*] in the Craigie House in Cambridge, Kettell contributed four pleasant papers on "Our Birds" to the first volumes of the *New-England Magazine.* In 1832 he went to Europe, having Ralph Waldo Emerson, it is said, for a companion on the voyage. During the wearisome days at sea he amused himself by turning a Peter Parley book into modern Greek. He visited Malta and Sicily, lived in Naples, Florence, Paris, and London, contributed articles to English periodicals, and returned to Boston and to Goodrich's employ in 1835. After Kettell's death the *Boston Courier* claimed that he had been "the veritable Peter Parley." Goodrich denied the allegation and issued a detailed statement of the work that Kettell had done for him. The honesty and essential accuracy of this statement need not be doubted. Kettell wrote much for the *Courier,* being noted for humorous and satirical articles that he contributed over the signatures of "Peeping Tom," "Timothy Titterwell," and "Sampson Short-and-Fat." Some of these articles were so popular that they were later published separately. On June 25, 1848, he succeeded Joseph Tinker Buckingham [*q.v.*] as editor. Like many a shy and gentle person, he could ramp when he had a pen in his hand, and his vigorous editorials were relished by the Whigs. In 1851–52 he was a representative in the General Court. He died at his home in Malden after an illness of a year and a half. His wife and his mother survived him.

[*New-Eng. Hist. and Geneal. Reg.*, Jan. 1856, p. 99; H. E. Noyes, *Geneal. Record of Some of the Noyes Descendants,* vol. I (1904); *Boston Courier,* Dec. 5, 8, 1855; *Boston Transcript,* Dec. 4, 5, 8, 10, 1855; *Daily Herald* (Newburyport), Dec. 7, 8, 11, 1855; *N. Y. Times,* Dec. 31, 1855; S. G. Goodrich, *Recollections of a Lifetime* (1856); J. T. Buckingham, *Personal Memoirs* (1852), II, 76, 214–15.] G. H. G.

KEY, DAVID McKENDREE (Jan. 27, 1824–Feb. 3, 1900), lawyer, soldier, senator, judge, was born in Greene County, Tenn., the son of John and Margaret (Armitage) Key, both natives of the same county. He was descended from Moses Key who emigrated from England in 1700 and settled in Chester County, Pa. In 1826 John Key removed to Monroe County, where David received his early education in the rather primitive schools of the county. Later he attended Hiwassee College, then recently established, and was one of the first graduates in 1850. While at college he also read law and was admitted to the bar in the same year that he graduated. In 1853 he removed to Chattanooga, Tenn., where he made his home until his death and where, except while serving as a soldier, he practised law until 1870. On July 1, 1857, he was married to Elizabeth Lenoir. In 1861 he was made adjutant-general on General Caswell's staff in the Confederate army, later becoming lieutenant-colonel of the 43rd Regiment, Tennessee Infantry. He was wounded and captured at Vicksburg.

Prior to the Civil War, Key had been an elector on the Buchanan ticket in 1856 and on the Breckenridge ticket in 1860. From 1870 to 1894 his public service was unbroken. In 1870 he was a member of the convention which framed a new constitution for Tennessee, and in the same year he was elected chancellor of the third district of Tennessee. Five years later he was appointed United States senator to succeed former President Andrew Johnson. Resigning the office of chancellor, he served in the Senate until the legislature met in 1877, when he was a candidate for the unexpired term but was defeated by James E. Bailey. In the Senate his efforts and speeches were directed toward a restoration of good feeling between North and South. This led President Hayes to tender him, though Key was a Democrat, a place in the cabinet, and he became postmaster-general in May 1877. He held this office until May 1880 when he resigned to accept, at the hands of President Hayes, the office of United States district judge for the eastern and middle districts of Tennessee. He presided over the courts of these districts until 1894. Then, having reached the retiring age, he resigned and retired to his home in Chattanooga.

Of his twenty-four years of public life, Key spent twenty years on the bench, either as a state or federal judge. Large of frame, dignified but modest and gentle in bearing, he looked the part of a just and, in his later years, a patriarchal judge. He was distinguished as a jurist for being much more concerned with doing justice than with following precedent or seeking approval. He was particularly at home in the field of equity jurisprudence. In his opinions he made no effort to display great learning but preferred to deal simply and justly with the issue at hand. During his fifteen years on the federal bench, he tried many cases involving violations of the Internal Revenue laws in the illicit manufacture of liquor, especially by the mountaineers of East Tennessee. He understood these people and their view that they had a natural right to market their corn by making it into whiskey, and he dealt kindly with them. Time and again he withheld sentence, after conviction, and permitted an offender to finish making a crop, upon his promise to return at the next term for sentence. And he was fond of saying that not one of them had ever broken faith with him.

[J. W. Caldwell, *Sketches of the Bench and Bar of Tenn.* (1898); *Biog. Dir. Am. Cong.* (1928); *East Tenn.: Hist. and Biog.* (1893); *Tenn.: The Volunteer State* (1923), vol. II; Mrs. Julian C. Lane, *Key and Allied Families* (1931); the *Chattanooga Sunday Times*, Feb. 4, 1900; information as to certain facts from Key's son, Commodore Albert L. Key, Chattanooga, Tenn.]

W. L. F.

KEY, FRANCIS SCOTT (Aug. 1, 1779–Jan. 11, 1843), author of "The Star Spangled Banner," lawyer, was born on the family estate, "Terra Rubra," then in Frederick but now in Carroll County, Md. He was the great-grandson of an Englishman, Philip Key, who came to Maryland about 1720, and son of John Ross Key, who married Ann Phoebe Charlton. He attended St. John's College, Annapolis, 1789–96, living with his grandmother Ann Ross Key at "Belvoir" on the Severn River, and with her sister Mrs. Upton Scott in Annapolis. After graduation he studied law under Judge J. T. Chase in Annapolis, and in 1801 he opened practice in Frederick, whither he was accompanied by a fellow student, Roger B. Taney, later chief justice, who married his only sister. On Jan. 19, 1802, in the beautiful "Chase House" in Annapolis, then owned by Col. Edward Lloyd, he married the colonel's daughter, Mary Tayloe Lloyd, by whom he had six sons and five daughters. Shortly after his marriage the family moved from Frederick to Bridge Street, Georgetown, D. C., where Key was at first associated in practice with his uncle, Philip Barton Key [*q.v.*]. It was as an influential young Washington attorney that Key was called in 1814 upon the mission that occasioned "The Star Spangled Banner." During the British retreat from Washington a prominent physician, Dr. William Beanes, of Upper Marlboro, Md., was seized and confined aboard the British fleet. Key was asked to undertake his release. Accompanied by Col. J. S. Skinner, government agent for exchange of prisoners, he went down the Chesapeake from Baltimore on Sept. 5, visited Admiral Cockburn, and secured Beanes's liberation, but he was detained pending the projected attack on Baltimore and was off the city in an American vessel during the attack. Through the night bombardment of Sept. 13–14 he remained on deck in agonized suspense but at daybreak was overjoyed to see the flag still flying over Fort McHenry. In intense emotional excitement he then composed the poem.

According to an account by Chief Justice Taney in the 1857 edition of Key's poems, the verses were first set down from memory on an envelope on the way ashore that morning and were rewritten in a hotel that night. Next morning he showed them at the home of Judge Joseph Hopper Nicholson, who had married his wife's sister. The judge was enthusiastic, and according to a fairly authentic story, his wife at once took the poem to a printer, who struck off handbills for circulation through the city. It was published in the *Baltimore American*, Sept. 21, sung in Baltimore taverns and theatres, and soon gained nation-wide popularity. Probably Key himself had in mind the well-known English tune "To Anacreon in Heaven" in writing the poem, though its adoption has also been credited to Judge Nicholson and to the first singer of the poem, the actor Ferdinand Durang. The tune had been previously used for a song of the American Revolution, "Adams and Liberty." Key's manuscript fair copy was preserved in Annapolis by Mrs. Nicholson until her death in 1847 and is now in the Walters Gallery, Baltimore. Neither before nor after writing his famous song did Key take his muse at all seriously. The slender collection of his poetry published posthumously (*Poems of the Late Francis S. Key, Esq.*, 1857) contains obituary, religious, amatory, and mildly facetious verse, respectable in meter but of slight consequence, save perhaps the hymn, "Lord, with Glowing Heart I'd Praise Thee," still included in hymnals. Key was of a warmly religious nature, in 1814 seriously considered entering the clergy, was delegate to the general conventions of the Episcopal Church, 1814–26, and for many years was lay reader in St. John's Church, Georgetown. An effective speaker, as suggested by several of his addresses preserved in print, with a quick, logical mind, he had an extensive practice in the federal courts. He was United States attorney for the District of Columbia, 1833–41, and in October 1833 he was sent by President Jackson to Alabama, where he negotiated a settlement between the state and federal governments over the Creek Indian Lands (T. C. McCorvey, "The Mission of Francis Scott Key to Alabama in 1833," *Alabama Historical Society Transactions,* vol. IV, 1904). About 1830 he changed his residence from Georgetown to Washington. Until his death he remained slender, erect, fond of riding, with dark blue eyes and thin, mobile features, expressive of his ardent, generous nature. He died of pleurisy at the home of his daughter, Mrs. Charles Howard, Mt. Vernon Place, Baltimore. His body was placed first in the Howard vault, St. Paul's Cemetery, Baltimore, then transferred in 1866 to Mt. Olivet Cemetery, Frederick. He has monuments there, at Fort McHenry, and at Eutaw Place in Baltimore, and in Golden Gate Park, San Francisco.

[Francis Scott Key Smith, *Francis Scott Key, Author of the Star Spangled Banner* (1911), and "The Star-Spangled Banner," *Current Hist.*, May 1930; P. H. Magruder, "The Original Manuscript of the Final Text of the 'Star-Spangled Banner,'" *Proc. U. S. Naval Inst.*, June 1927; O. G. T. Sonneck, *Report on the Star-Spangled Banner* (1909); Anne Key Barstow, "Recollections of Francis Scott Key," *Modern Culture,* Nov. 1900; H. D. Richardson, *Sidelights on Md. Hist.* (1913), vol. II; T. J. C. Williams, *Hist. of Frederick County, Md.* (1910), vol. I; *Md. Hist. Mag.*, June 1907, June 1909, June 1910; Mrs. Julian C. Lane, *Key and Allied Families* (1931); the *Sun* (Baltimore), Jan. 13, 1843.]

A. W.

KEY, PHILIP BARTON (Apr. 12, 1757–July 28, 1815), congressman, was born near Charlestown, Cecil County, Md., the son of Francis and Anne Arnold (Ross) Key, both of prominent Maryland families. His grandfather, Philip Key, coming from England about 1720, had been sheriff, delegate, and councilor, and his uncle, Edmund Key, had been provincial attorney-general. Francis Scott Key [*q.v.*], the author of "The Star Spangled Banner," was his nephew. His early education was apparently private, and in 1775 he began to study law in Annapolis. He is said to have participated in the early Revolutionary movement, but he refused to follow his brother, Lieut. John Ross Key, with Price's Maryland Rifle Company, to the siege of Boston. In December 1777 he joined the British forces in Philadelphia and was commissioned captain in Chalmers' regiment of Maryland Loyalists (April 1778). During 1778 he was with the regiment near New York and is said to have been in the battle of Monmouth. In 1779 the regiment went to Florida. Key participated in the attempt to recapture Mobile from the Spanish and led the defeated troops back to Pensacola, where they were besieged and finally forced to surrender (1781).

Paroled in Havana, Key went to England, where he was admitted to the Middle Temple, Feb. 2, 1784. Returning to Maryland the following year he was admitted to the bar and practised in Leonardtown (1787) and Annapolis (1790). On July 4, 1790, he married Ann, daughter of Gov. George Plater: they had two sons and six daughters. In 1794 Key was elected from Annapolis to the House of Delegates, where he became a leader, serving on important committees and commissions. In November 1796, as chairman of the committee on the reply to the governor's address, he drafted resolutions that showed the Federalists' support of President Washington and their abhorrence of "the intrigues of foreign emissaries" and of Republican agitation. Narrowly defeated in 1800 (and unfairly, he thought), Key was appointed chief justice of the fourth United States circuit court and established his residence near Georgetown, D. C. In 1802, when his office was abolished, he resumed practice in Montgomery County, Md., and was in 1805 of counsel for Justice Samuel Chase in his trial before the Senate. His speech was a vindication of Chase's impartiality in the Callender trial. In 1806 he resigned his British half-pay, built a summer home in Montgomery County, and stood as the Federalist candidate for the third congressional district of Maryland. He was elected, and, after a contest over his British service and residence in the District, was seated. Twice reëlected, he was throughout a consistent Federalist, opposing the Embargo, non-intercourse, war with Great Britain, the seizure of West Florida, and other Republican measures. He supported the Navigation Bill (1810) and the recharter of the United States Bank (1811). He was also interested in District of Columbia affairs and brought about the establishment of a standing District committee. His death occurred in Georgetown, D. C.

[*Biog. Dir. Am. Cong.* (1928); *The Royal Commission on the Losses and Services of Am. Loyalists, 1783 to 1785* (1915), ed. by H. E. Egerton; *Orderly Book of the "Maryland Loyalists Regiment"* (1891), ed. by P. L. Ford; Chas. Evans, *Report of the Trial of the Hon. Samuel Chase* (1805); Mrs. Julian C. Lane, *Key and Allied Families* (1931); *Md. Hist. Mag.*, June 1908, June 1910; Lorenzo Sabine, *Biog. Sketches of Loyalists of the Am. Revolution* (1864), vol. I; Bernard C. Steiner, *The Life and Correspondence of Jas. McHenry* (1907); E. A. Jones, *Am. Members of the Inns of Court* (1924); letter from Key to Ephraim K. Wilson, Oct. 12, 1800, in the Manuscript Division, Lib. of Cong.]
W. C. M.

KEYES, EDWARD LAWRENCE (Aug. 28, 1843–Jan. 24, 1924), surgeon and one of the pioneers in America in male genito-urinary surgery, was born in Fort Moultrie, Charleston, S. C., the son of Gen. Erasmus Darwin Keyes [*q.v.*] and Caroline M., daughter of Dr. James B. Clarke of New York City. He was privately educated and doubtless spent much time with his father at various military posts. In 1859 he entered Yale, graduated in 1863, and then joined the Federal army as a member of his father's staff with the rank of captain. At the close of the war he began the study of medicine—influenced somewhat by the fact that both grandfathers and one great-grandfather had been successful physicians—and received the degree of M.D. from the medical department of the University of New York in 1866. His preceptor, Dr. William H. Van Buren [*q.v.*], mapped out for him a course of study in Paris, with special emphasis on dermatology, syphilis, and male genito-urinary diseases, and upon his return he entered practice as Van Buren's associate, later becoming his partner, the relationship lasting until Van Buren's death in 1883.

He began as a general practitioner and so great was his hold upon his patients that he remained the family physician to some of them long after he had narrowed his practice to specialties. In 1868 he had a class in the Bellevue out-patient department and was one of the demonstrators of anatomy in the Bellevue Hospital Medical College. In 1870 he was made a lecturer on dermatology in the same institution and delivered the first course of lectures on this subject in the United States. In this year he married Sarah M. Loughborough of Georgetown, D. C. For some years ending in 1875 he was visiting surgeon to Charity Hospital, Blackwell's Island, and in the latter year was made professor of dermatology, associate professor of surgery, and visiting surgeon at Bellevue. In association with Van Buren he had published in the previous year *A Practical Treatise on the Surgical Diseases of the Genito-Urinary Organs Including Syphilis.* In 1876 he was appointed a delegate to the International Medical Congress at Philadelphia. In January of that year he had published in the *American Journal of the Medical Sciences* a remarkable paper with blood count determinations in which he showed that mercury in small doses is not a poison but a tonic ("The Effect of Small Doses of Mercury in Modifying the Number of the Red Corpuscles in Syphilis"). This was followed in 1877 by another entitled *The Tonic Treatment of Syphilis* with a description of a new technique, which was of international importance. A later edition was issued in 1896, but the method having served a good purpose was superseded in time by hypodermic and intramuscular injections of mercury. In 1880 appeared a monograph, *Venereal Diseases,* followed ten years later by another edition, in which Dr. C. H. Chetwood was junior collaborator. In 1886 he contributed articles on genito-urinary surgery to Ashhurst's *International Encyclopedia of Surgery.* In 1888 after the death of Van Buren there was published a new edition of the Van Buren-Keyes textbook under the authorship of Keyes alone, which received a Spanish translation. In 1905 with his son, Edward Loughborough Keyes, he published a second edition and in 1908 appeared *Syphilis; a Treatise for Practitioners.* A new work, *Diseases of the Genito-Urinary Organs,* came out in 1910, second edition, 1912; and in 1917, a final effort, *Urology,* second edition, 1923. A non-technical work *The Fear of Death* was privately printed in 1910 for circulation among his friends. In addition to the preceding he contributed many important papers on his special work to medical periodicals. He was the founder and first president of the American Association of Genito-Urinary Surgeons and may be said to have founded a small school of genito-urinary surgeons, for his son, E. L. Keyes, a nephew, C. H. Chetwood, and a third junior associate, E. M. Fuller, all became eminent in this field.

Keyes was a man of remarkable personality. With younger men he had an abrupt and military way and was a strict disciplinarian but few men equaled him in tact and *savoir faire* in the sickroom and in social life. Early in his career he became affiliated with the Roman Catholic Church and Pope Pius X conferred on him knighthood in the Order of St. Gregory; and he was medical adviser to high ecclesiastical dignitaries. His death was due to pneumonia some years after he had retired from active practice.

[*Archives of Dermatology and Syphilology,* May 1924; *Trans. of the Am. Asso. of Genito-Urinary Surgeons,* vol. XVIII (1925); *Medic. Jour. and Record,* Feb. 6, 1924; *Surgery, Gynecology and Obstetrics,* May 1928; *N. Y. Times,* Jan. 25, 1924.]
E. P.

KEYES, ELISHA WILLIAMS (Jan. 23, 1828–Nov. 29, 1910), lawyer, politician, widely known as the Bismarck of Western politics, was born in Northfield, Vt., third son of Capt. Joseph Keyes, a skilled millwright and machinist, and an inventor, and Olive Williams. In 1836 Joseph opened a pioneer farm in Jefferson County, Wisconsin Territory, and in 1837, being joined by his family, he founded the village of Lake Mills where he soon built a gristmill and a sawmill. Elisha worked on the farm, drove a team for the mill, and attended the district school. He also enjoyed several winters' instruction in Beloit Academy. In December 1850 he began the systematic study of law in Madison, was admitted to the bar a year later, and opened an office there. President Fillmore granted him a solicitorship in the Post Office Department which gave him a wide acquaintanceship in the state. In 1853 he joined a law firm which had a large general practice. Had he not been tempted to subordinate law to politics, he might have gained distinction in the profession.

He was district attorney from 1859 to 1861. In the latter year Lincoln appointed him postmaster at Madison, a position he held for twenty-one consecutive years. Then in 1898, after an interval of sixteen years, he was appointed to the same office by McKinley and held it till his death twelve years later. He was mayor of Madison three terms, assemblyman one term, and university regent twelve years. In 1872, 1876, and 1884 he was chairman of the Wisconsin delegation to the Republican National Convention. But his most important political service was as chairman of the Republican state central committee from 1867 to 1877. Keyes was an autocrat who ruled the party with a rod of iron. He dictated nominations for state and national offices and to some extent for local offices also. His political ethics were those of his day. C. C. Washburn, his political opponent, charged him with being an agent and beneficiary of the whiskey ring in Wisconsin (letter of Washburn to President Hayes, Apr. 16, 1877; copy in Washburn Collection of the state Library of Wisconsin). He used every "honorable" device to control votes, induced employers of labor to line up their men for the straight ticket, sent out heelers where they seemed to be needed, and drew heavily upon the railroads for free transportation. His success was due less to subtle strategy than to sleepless vigilance in supervising details of campaigns, insight in choosing aides, and inexorableness in visiting punishment upon shirking, refractory, or treasonable partisans.

His greatest disappointment came in 1879 when, as candidate for the United States senatorship, he succumbed to Matthew Hale Carpenter's witching popularity. In January 1881 he tried again and went down before Philetus Sawyer, candidate representing a working alliance between lumber kings and the railroads which lasted till overthrown by La Follette twenty years later. Keyes was no more fortunate two months later when the death of Carpenter created a vacancy which was filled by the election of Cameron. He made a last ineffectual attempt in 1882 as an independent "reform" candidate for Congress against George C. Hazelton, regular nominee, but succeeded only in electing a deserving Democrat and in eliminating himself definitively from state politics. His stocky, long-coated, high-hatted figure was familiar to Madisonians for half a century. Rough, irascible, and often profane, he was kind-hearted, affectionate to family and friends, and sometimes magnanimous to opponents. He married first Caroline Stevens; second, Mrs. Louise Sholes; third, Mrs. Eliza M. Reeves.

[The best sketch, edited by Keyes himself, is in his *Hist. of Dane County* (1906). The best sources for his political career are the voluminous Keyes MSS., the diaries of George B. Smith and of Willett S. Main, all in the State Hist. Lib., Madison, Wis. Other sources include: John Gregory, *Centennial Proc. and Hist. Incidents of the Early Settlers of Northfield, Vt.* (1878); Asa Keyes, *Geneal.: Solomon Keyes of Newbury . . . and His Descendants* (1880); E. B. Usher, *Wisconsin: Its Story and Biog.* (1914), vol. IV; *Biog. Rev. of Dane County, Wis.* (1893); *Proc. State Hist. Soc. of Wis.*, 1911; *Wis. Hist. Colls.*, vol. XI (1888); State Hist. Soc. of Wis., *Bull. of Information No. 81*, Mar. 1916; *Madison Democrat*, Nov. 29, 30, 1910.] J. S—r.

KEYES, ERASMUS DARWIN (May 29, 1810–Oct. 14, 1895), soldier, business man, was born at Brimfield, Mass., the son of Justus Keyes, a prominent physician, and of Elizabeth (Corey) Keyes. His English ancestry went back to Solomon Keyes, who emigrated to Massachusetts Bay Colony; and to Giles Corey, said to have been killed for witchcraft. When the son was still a youth, the Keyes family moved to Kennebec County, Me., from which state he secured appointment to West Point, graduating in the year 1832 as brevet second lieutenant. For a time he was at Fort Monroe, Va., then he was at Charleston, S. C., during the nullification troubles. On Aug. 31, 1833, he was commissioned second lieutenant, 3rd Artillery. He was aide-de-camp to Gen. Winfield Scott, 1837–38, and after a brief service in the West and South again served as aide, 1838–41. He received promotion to captain, 3rd Artillery, Nov. 30, 1841, and from 1842 to 1844 he was in garrison at New Orleans Barracks and at Fort Moultrie, S. C. In the latter year he became a member of the board of visitors to the Military Academy, immediately thereafter serving as instructor at the Academy in field artillery and cavalry, 1844–48. From 1851 to 1860 he was for the most part on the Pacific Coast, during which period he saw service against the Indians in Washington in 1855 and participated in the Spokane Expedition in the year 1858. He was commended in official reports for services in the combat at Four Lakes, Washington, Sept. 5, 1858, and was present at a skirmish with Indians on Spokane River, Sept. 8. On Oct. 12, 1858, he received promotion to major, 1st Artillery, and from Jan. 1, 1860, to Apr. 19, 1861, served as military secretary to General Scott, with the rank of lieutenant-colonel. On May 14, 1861, he became colonel, 11th Infantry, and on May 17, brigadier-general of volunteers, commanding a brigade in General Tyler's division at Bull Run (*Battles and Leaders of the Civil War,* I, 175–215), for his conduct of which he received commendation.

He commanded the IV Army Corps in McClellan's Peninsular campaign, participating in many battles and engagements, and received promotion to major-general of volunteers, May 5, 1862. His corps performed important rear-guard service in the transfer of McClellan's base from the York to the James River. For gallant and meritorious conduct at Fair Oaks, Va., he was brevetted brigadier-general, United States Army, May 31, 1862. The IV Corps remained on the Peninsula, 1862–63, and in a controversy with General Dix over participation in expeditions against White House and West Point, Va. (Jan. 7, and May 7, 1863), Keyes asked for an official investigation which was refused him. He served on an army retiring board, July 15, 1863, to May 6, 1864, when he resigned from the army and moved to the city of San Francisco. In the West he became president of the Maxwell Gold Mining Company (1867–69), vice-president of the California Vine-Culture Society for Napa County, and of the Humboldt Savings and Loan Society (1868–70). Keyes had married, on Nov. 8, 1837, Caroline M. Clarke, who became the mother of five children, one of whom was Edward Lawrence Keyes [*q.v.*]. She died in 1853 and on Nov. 22, 1862, he was married to Mary (Loughborough) Bissell, by whom he had five children. His death occurred at Nice, France, but final interment was at West Point, Nov. 19, 1895, where his portrait in oils hangs in Cullum Memorial Hall. His *Fifty Years' Observation of Men and Events* (1884), and "The Rear-Guard at Malvern Hill" (*Battles and Leaders of the Civil War,* II, 434), are among his published writings.

[Keyes's autobiography, while giving intimate descriptions of Scott, Sherman, Lee, Grant, McClellan, Thomas, and others, furnishes little regarding himself. Valuable details are to be found in the *Twenty-seventh Ann. Reunion, Asso. Grads., U. S. Mil. Acad.,* 1896; G. W. Cullum, *Biog. Reg. . . . U. S. Mil. Acad.,* vol. I (ed. 1891); *Battles and Leaders of the Civil War* (4 vols., 1887–88); F. B. Heitman, *Hist. Reg. and Dict. of the U. S. Army* (1903), vol. I; Asa Keyes, *Geneal.: Solomon Keyes of Newbury . . . and His Descendants* (1880); *N. Y. Tribune, Examiner* (San Francisco), Oct. 15, 1895.]

C. D. R.

KEYT, ALONZO THRASHER (Jan. 10, 1827–Nov. 9, 1885), physician, physiologist, was born at Higginsport, Ohio, the son of Nathan and Mary (Thrasher) Keyt. He was of Dutch extraction on his father's side, and a descendant of Edward Penn of Pennsylvania on his mother's side. His boyhood was spent at Moscow, Ohio, and after attending Parker's Academy in Felicity, Ohio, he began the study of medicine first with Dr. William Johnston and then at the Medical College of Ohio at Cincinnati, taking his degree of M.D. from the latter school in 1848. He began practice at Moscow but in 1850 moved to Cincinnati, where he remained in active practice till his death from heart disease at the age of fifty-eight. His principal interest was in diseases of the circulation, and to perfect methods of diagnosis of pathological states of the heart and circulation, he devised a means of simultaneously recording graphically and accurately the heart beat and the pulse. In 1873 he began work in this direction using the sphygmograph of Étienne Jules Marey of Paris, then recently invented. Finding this instrument insufficient for his purpose, he devised an ingenious and accurate instrument, the best of its kind, in which the following important improvements over any previous similar instrument were made: the medium used to transmit the pulse or heart impulse to the recording device was water, not air; simultaneous records were obtained of two or more pulses, or of the heart beat and pulse; and a chronograph registered fifths of seconds and recorded beneath the pulse curve. The chronograph was afterward adopted by Marey.

Keyt's perfected instrument was called a multigraph sphygmometer and cardiograph, or the compound sphygmograph. He applied the instrument to normal and diseased men, and he made an artificial circulation scheme by which he could produce various lesions like those occurring in disease. Using these observations he made many contributions to the knowledge of the circulation and also greatly perfected the clinical methods of diagnosis of diseased conditions of the circulation. He made the first accurate determination of the velocity of the pulse wave and proved its dependence upon the character of the arterial wall and the condition of the heart valves. He also described the delay following aortic regurgitation. His work was published in a series of articles in American medical journals. Although he was widely known in France and England by those working in his field, he seems to have been relatively unknown and unrecognized by American physiologists and has suffered accordingly an unmerited neglect. His papers, collected and rearranged after his death, were published by his colleagues and assistants, A. B. Isham and M. H. Keyt, under the title: *Sphygmography and Cardiography, Physiological and Clinical* (1887). The volume places him in the list of great American pioneers in physiology and medicine. Keyt was married in 1848 to Susannah D. Hamlin of Cincinnati. They had seven children.

[See Preface to *Sphygmography and Cardiography*; H. A. Kelly and W. L. Burrage, *Am. Medic. Biogs.* (1920); *Philadelphia Monthly Medic. Jour.*, Dec. 1899; *Jour. Am. Medic. Asso.*, Aug. 11, 25, Oct. 20, Dec. 1, 15, 1883; *Cincinnati Enquirer*, Nov. 10, 1885.]

A. P. M.

KICKING BIRD (d. May 3, 1875), Kiowa chief, also called Tené-angpóte, was the grandson of a captive Crow who had been adopted by the Kiowa. He early won a reputation as a warrior of skill and resourcefulness. When, in later life, his policy of peace was jeopardized by taunts of cowardice, he took a small band of warriors on a raiding expedition through Texas, defeated the troops sent against him, and returned to dominate once more his own tribe, now reassured as to his warlike abilities. At the end of the Civil War he seems to have been convinced of the uselessness of opposition to the white government, and he accepted reservation in what is now the state of Oklahoma. In 1872 he persuaded Thomas C. Battey to open the first school for the Kiowa. In 1873 he kept the tribe from going to war because the government of Texas refused to release two Kiowa chiefs as the federal government had promised. When the last great combination of the southern plain Indians was formed, the next year, he found himself in a difficult position. Broken treaty promises, white aggression, and ruthless thefts of Indian horses and cattle were pushing the Kiowa to war. Kicking Bird began to doubt the good faith of the white government, and he was cut to the quick by his own people's distrust of his motives. For a time he hesitated but in the end set himself to winning adherents for peace. By virtue of his tact and intelligence he was so far successful that two-thirds of the Kiowa refused to follow Lone Wolf to war. Shortly after the defeat of the war party he was taken suddenly ill and died expressing his satisfaction that he had chosen to follow the way of the white man.

[Files of the Office of Indian Affairs; *Seventeenth Ann. Report of the Bureau of Am. Ethnology*, pt. I (1898); T. C. Battey, *The Life and Adventures of a Quaker Among the Indians* (1875); A. L. Vail, *A Memorial of Jas. M. Haworth* (1886); *Ann. Report of the Commissioner of Indian Affairs . . . 1875* (1876).]

K. E. C.

KIDD, WILLIAM (*c.* 1645–May 23, 1701), "Captain Kidd," the most celebrated pirate in English literature, born at Greenock, Scotland, was, according to tradition, the son of a Calvinist minister. By 1690 he had established himself as a ship-owner and sea-captain in New York. With the outbreak of war between France and England, following the accession of William of Orange, the English colonies were harassed by French privateers. Kidd had brought his ship into the king's service and was sent by General Codrington to join Capt. Thomas Hewetson, with whom he fought in two engagements against the French; Hewetson later testified that Kidd was a "mighty man" in the West Indies. He had also rendered the colony useful services during the insurrection of Leisler and Milborne so that the Provincial Council, on Apr. 18, 1691, appointed a committee to inform the House of Representatives of his many good services and to consider a suitable reward; on May 14 they voted him the sum of £150. Two days later Kidd secured a license to wed Mrs. Sarah Oort, the widow of John Oort, a sea-captain. She was the daughter of Capt. Samuel Bradley, a man of property, and had first married William Cox, who died and left her his estate. Kidd and his wife owned considerable property in New York, including a large, luxurious home at what is now the corner of Pearl and Hanover streets, and a country estate at Haarlem. On May 25 Captains Kidd and Walkington were dispatched in pursuit of the French; later in the year the colony of Massachusetts commissioned Kidd to chase an enemy privateer from the coast.

The East India Company in 1695 petitioned William III to send a man-of-war against the pirates in the Red Sea and the Indian Ocean, but, because of the war with France, none was available. The King determined that the necessary ship might be fitted out as a private undertaking and at the same time appointed Richard Coote, Earl of Bellomont, governor of New England (commissioned 1697), with special instructions to suppress piracy. In London Bellomont consulted Robert Livingston [*q.v.*], prominent in New York affairs, about the undertaking against the pirates. Livingston then met

Kidd who had been in London since August 1695, when he had given evidence before the Lords of Trade in a colonial election case, and introduced him to Bellomont. Articles of agreement were signed on Oct. 10. Bellomont agreed to raise four-fifths of the necessary £6,000 and to secure the necessary royal authorization; he was to receive four-fifths of the net profits, and if there were none was to be reimbursed to the amount of the original sum. Livingston agreed to post several bonds and Kidd accepted command of the expedition. In raising his share Bellomont secured as partners Edmund Harrison, Sir John Somers, the Earls of Orford and Romney, and the Duke of Shrewsbury; the names of the latter four were carefully concealed from public knowledge.

By the end of November Kidd had disposed of his brigantine, the *Antegoa,* and had secured the *Adventure Galley,* of 287 tons and thirty-four guns, which was launched in December. After several delays he sailed from Plymouth Apr. 23, 1696, for New York. During the voyage Kidd captured a small French vessel; from this prize he secured £350, used in buying supplies. In New York he was forced to complete his crew; "many flockt to him from all parts, men of desperate fortunes and necessitous in expectation of getting vast treasure . . . 'twill not be in Kidd's power to govern such a hord of men under no pay" (*Documents Relative to the Colonial History of the State of New York,* IV, 275). He sailed from New York on Sept. 6, 1696, and by the middle of December was rounding the Cape of Good Hope. Kidd had told Bellomont that "he knew the pyrats hants so well, that he could sail directly to 'em" (*Ibid.,* IV, 815), but now he avoided the eastern coast of Madagascar, infested by pirates, and headed for the western coast. By February he had reached the Comoro Islands, where one-third of his crew died of cholera and the *Adventure Galley* began to leak. It was almost a year since they had left London and not a penny had been earned, for the agreement was: no prizes, no pay, for either Kidd or his crew. It was now that Kidd, threatened by a mutinous crew, crossed the line of demarcation between a privateer and a pirate and determined to plunder the ships that he had been sent to protect. He unsuccessfully attacked the Mocha fleet in August, but did succeed in taking several small ships during September. His refusal to attack a Dutch ship the following month provoked a small mutiny, which later resulted in Kidd's striking one of his gunners with a bucket. From that injury the gunner died and Kidd definitely was embarked upon a career of crime. On Jan. 30, 1698, Kidd captured his richest prize, the *Quedagh Merchant,* an Armenian merchantman of between 400 and 500 tons, and sailed with her to Madagascar, where he arrived in May. Kidd then scuttled his own unseaworthy ship and took the *Quedagh Merchant.* He divided the booty among his crew, some of whom deserted to join Culliford, a notorious pirate. Kidd met and entered into friendly relations with both Culliford and Kelly, the very pirates that he had been sent to apprehend. In September 1698 he sailed from Madagascar, his ship richly laden with loot; at the end of April 1699 he anchored off Anguilla, in the West Indies, and discovered that he and his crew had been proclaimed pirates. From the time that Kidd had first sailed from London the depredations of the pirates upon English shipping had increased, and in August 1698 news came to London that Kidd had himself turned pirate. This caused wild rumors and a storm of protest against the lords who had subscribed funds for the enterprise. A general alarm was broadcast and a squadron sent in pursuit of Kidd. He determined to return to New England; he left the *Quedagh Merchant* at Hispaniola and sailed in the *Antonio,* which he had recently purchased. Early in June he anchored in Oyster Bay and sent for Emmot, an old lawyer friend, through whom he communicated with Bellomont. He protested his innocence and offered to surrender himself if granted a pardon; after long negotiations Bellomont "wheedled" him into coming ashore by the promise of a pardon. Kidd landed in Boston July 2 and the following day appeared before Bellomont and the council; after several opportunities and several failures to produce a satisfactory record of his voyage he was imprisoned. He and his men were later shipped to London as prisoners.

Kidd was privately examined by the Board of Admiralty on Apr. 14, 1700, and was then sent to Newgate. The House of Commons, fearing the successful intervention of the powerful lords who had underwritten the expedition, had insisted that he should not be tried before the next session of Parliament. He languished in Newgate until Mar. 27, 1701, before he was brought into the House of Commons and examined. Had he given evidence against the lords who had contributed to the venture, he might have been pardoned, but he proclaimed his innocence, was truculent, and, some accounts add, drunk. It was voted that he be given an ordinary trial. On May 8 he was tried for the murder of William Moore, his gunner. The judge was patient and scrupulously fair; Kidd was found guilty upon clear and weighty evidence. The other indictments charged him with piracy against five separate vessels; in respect to two of these, Kidd said that he had been deprived of French passes which he had taken from them at the moment of capture. This was true; the prosecution concealed them and denied their existence, but, had they been produced, they could not have cleared him. This concealing of evidence was regrettable, but did not result in a miscarriage of justice (*Trial of Captain Kidd,* pp. 43–47). The evidence against Kidd was eloquent and abundant and he was found guilty in the three trials for piracy. When, on May 9, he was sentenced to be hanged, Kidd replied: "My Lord, it is a very hard sentence. For my part I am the innocentest person of them all . . ." (*Ibid.,* p. 187). During the next two weeks the Rev. Paul Lorrain exhorted him to repentance and confession, but Kidd was adamant. On May 23 he was led to the gallows at Execution Dock, saw Darby Mullins hanged, and then, having addressed the crowd, was himself turned off. The rope broke and Kidd fell to the ground with the halter around his neck. He was finally hanged from a tree, for the gallows had broken down. His property and effects, forfeited to the Crown, brought only £6,471. The value of the jewels, gold, and goods recovered by the authorities was near £10,000. Contemporary opinion was satisfied that the *Quedagh Merchant* had been seized by Boulton and his crew, and the cargo, consisting mostly of perishable bale goods and valued at between £40,000 and £50,000, sold. But with time there came new stories of hidden treasure, of jewels and pieces-of-eight—all to the undoing of innumerable and sanguine seekers of fortune. Kidd's widow later married a Christopher Rousby; his daughter had died before the trial and his only son was killed in a battle near Sterling in 1715.

[*The Trial of Capt. Kidd* (Edinburgh, 1930), ed. by Graham Brooks, publishes in full the trial documents and contains an excellent introduction. The article on Kidd in *Dict. Nat. Biog.,* often unreliable, contains useful bibliographical suggestions. Sir Cornelius Neale Dalton, *The Real Capt. Kidd* (1911); Ralph D. Paine, *The Book of Buried Treasure* (1911), pp. 26–129; and Homer H. Cooper, in *The Am. Mercury,* Nov. 1924, are extravagant vindications. References in colonial documents are numerous, see especially: *Calendar of N. Y. Hist. MSS., Pt. 2, English* (1866); *Docs. Relative to the Colonial Hist. of the State of N. Y.,* vol. IV (1854); *Calendar of State Papers, Colonial Ser., America and West Indies,* 1689–92 (1901), pp. 122, 326–27. See also Chas. Johnson, *The Hist. of the Pyrates,* vol. II (n.d.); F. de Peyster, *The Life and Administration of Richard, Earl of Bellomont* (1879); J. F. Jameson, *Privateering and Piracy in the Colonial Period* (1923); I. N. P. Stokes, *The Iconography of Manhattan Island, 1490–1909* (6 vols., 1915–28); Lord Birkenhead, *Famous Trials of History* (1926); Alfred Sternbeck, *Filibusters and Buccaneers* (1930); *New York's Land-Holding Sea Rover: Capt. Kidd* (N. Y., privately printed, 1901); and Franklin Harvey Head, *Studies in Early Am. Hist.: A Notable Lawsuit* (Chicago, privately printed, 1898).]

F. M—n.

KIDDER, DANIEL PARISH (Oct. 18, 1815–July 29, 1891), Methodist clergyman and educator, was born of early New England stock at South Pembroke, now Darien, Genesee County, N. Y., to Selvey and Mehetabel (Parish) Kidder. His boyhood was passed in an uncle's family in Randolph, Vt. From the age of fourteen he taught school, attended country academies, read books, and earned his living. From Genesee Wesleyan Seminary at Lima, N. Y., he entered Hamilton College in 1833 as a sophomore. Though his father was opposed to the Methodist doctrine, the son was converted at Lima and brought under the conviction that he should be a minister. In pursuance of this object he transferred to Wesleyan University, where he was graduated in 1836. That year he taught French, mathematics, and ancient languages in the Amenia (N. Y.) Seminary and began to preach. He was eager to go to China as a missionary, but the way was closed and he joined the Genesee Conference and received a charge in Rochester, N. Y., whence he was drafted in 1837 for a new Methodist mission in Brazil. From Rio de Janeiro he traveled extensively, distributing the Scriptures and Portuguese tracts, and preaching wherever a Protestant could command a hearing.

In 1840, on the death of his wife, Kidder returned to the United States. Joining New Jersey Conference, he served churches in Paterson and Trenton. In 1844 his denomination elected him, when barely twenty-eight years old, secretary of its Sunday School Union and editor of the literature of its Sunday schools. He gave himself with enthusiasm to this work, then quite unorganized. He made the Catechism an available textbook for Sunday schools, provided a Sunday-school hymnal, developed the system of raising funds for the extension work of the Sunday School Union, and systematized the method of gathering the statistics of the Sunday school. He was also a pioneer in Sunday-school normal conventions and institute work. He edited the *Sunday School Advocate* and supervised hundreds of publications for the church libraries. After twelve years in this office (1844–56) he entered the service of theological education. He taught practical theology in Garrett Biblical Institute, Evanston, Ill., 1856–71, and in Drew Theological Seminary, Madison, N. J., 1871–81. Not an extraordinary preacher himself, he had the gift of teaching others the art of preaching. In 1880 he was elected secretary of the Board of Education of his Church. He filled this office with distinction until the failure of his health in 1887 forced him to retire. He then went to reside at Evanston, Ill., where he died four years later. Kidder was a thorough workman rather than an innovator, and the remarkable developments in the field of religious education which his successors introduced were largely due to the solid educational foundations which he had prepared. Of his many books, one of the most popular was *Sketches of Residence and Travel in Brazil* (1845). Another, *Brazil and the Brazilians* (1857), on which he collaborated with J. G. Fletcher, was long a standard work. His other writings include: *Mormonism and the Mormons* (1842); *Clerical Celibacy* (1844), translated from the original of Diogo Antonio Feijo; *A Treatise on Homiletics* (1864); and *The Christian Pastorate* (1871). He was a delegate to the General Conference of his denomination in 1852 and 1868. He was twice married: in 1836 to Cynthia H. Russell, of Salisbury, Conn., who died in Brazil; and in 1842 to Harriette Smith, Principal of Worthington (Ohio) Female Seminary, who survived him.

[G. E. Strobridge, *Biog. of the Rev. Daniel Parish Kidder, D.D., LL.D.* (1894); *Alumni Record of Drew Theol. Sem. . . . 1867–1925* (1926); *Minutes of the Ann. Conferences of the M. E. Ch., Spring Conferences of 1892* (1892); F. E. Kidder, *A Hist. of the Kidder Family* (1886); the *Christian Advocate* (N. Y.), Aug. 6, 1891; *Chicago Tribune*, July 30, 1891.] J. R. J.

KIDDER, FREDERIC (Apr. 16, 1804–Dec. 19, 1885), author, son of Isaiah and Hepsey (Jones) Kidder, was born in New Ipswich, N. H. Although his father, who had been successively teacher, store-keeper, farmer, and manufacturer, died in 1811, the family managed to send the boy to the town school and academy. From 1819 to 1821 he attended in Hanover the preparatory school to Dartmouth College. Being the eldest son, he was compelled to forego college to aid in the support of the family. In November 1826, after four and one-half years as a grocery clerk in Boston, he went to Wilmington, N. C., for his health. He left with his younger brother Edward in a schooner which he had purchased and loaded with goods with which to engage in trade. Edward spent the remainder of his life there but Frederic returned to Boston after eight years. Except for intervals, he was in business, sometimes alone and sometimes in partnership, on India Street, Boston, from 1836 to 1868, dealing primarily in southern goods, such as cotton and naval stores. The profits from his business enterprises, which also included an investment in Maine lands, enabled him, in spite of setbacks during the financial depression of 1857 and the Civil War, to spend much time, especially in the intervals between his engagements in business, in indulging his antiquarian tastes. Encouraged by his fellow-members of the New-England Historic Genealogical Society, he published in collaboration with A. A. Gould a history of his native town, *The History of New Ipswich* (1852). After the Civil War, turning again to research, he published in 1867 *Military Operations in Eastern Maine and Nova Scotia During the Revolution.* Neither in this volume nor in his *History of the Boston Massacre* (1870) did Kidder show especial ability for narrative writing but he did display a capacity for painstaking, laborious, and minute research. Many shorter articles from his pen appeared in the *New-England Historical and Genealogical Register,* the *Historical Magazine,* the *Continental Monthly,* the *Boston Transcript,* and the *Boston Journal.* His interest in the career of his great-grandfather, Capt. Ephraim Jones, who was active in the last French and Indian War, led him to collect a great deal of material on the Acadians, but he published nothing on the subject. He had married, on Jan. 12, 1841, Harriet Maria Hagar. She was taken sick in December 1870, and, after long suffering, died in December 1875. From this blow he never recovered. In failing health he lingered on at his home in Melrose, where he had lived since 1869.

[See J. W. Dean, "Memoir of Frederic Kidder," *New-Eng. Hist. and Geneal. Reg.*, Apr. 1887; F. E. Kidder, *A Hist. of the Kidder Family* (1886); and the *Boston Daily Advertiser*, Dec. 21, 1885. The New-Eng. Hist. Geneal. Soc. possesses Kidder's "Memorial of the Jones Family from 1648 to 1876," which contains an autobiography. For a list of Kidder's writings see E. H. Goss, *Bibliog. of Melrose* (1889), or the same author's *Hist. of Melrose* (1902).] R. E. M.

KIEFT, WILLEM (September 1597–Sept. 27, 1647), fifth governor of New Netherland, was the oldest son of Gerrit Willemszoon Kieft, a merchant living on the Oude Zyde, Voorburgwal, Amsterdam, and of Machteld Huydecoper, daughter of Jan Jacobszoon Bal *alias* Huydecoper, the well-known magistrate of Amsterdam (J. E. Elias, *De Vroedschap van Amsterdam, 1578–1795* vol. 1, 1903, 187, 188). He appears to have been born between Sept. 6 and Sept. 13, 1597, and was baptized on the latter date (Birth Registers of the Oude Kerk at Amsterdam, vol. III). He was brought up to be a merchant and removed to La Rochelle, France. Before long his business failed and he is said to have gone to the Ottoman Empire to ransom some Christians, but he set free only those for whom the least had been paid, hoping to get more money for the prisoners he left behind. His relatives in Amsterdam helped him to secure a post in New Netherland. In May 1637 the Dutch West India Company secured permission from the States-General in The Hague to dismiss Van Twiller and appoint Willem Kieft in his place as director of New Netherland. On Sept. 2, 1637, Kieft appeared in The Hague and took the oath of office. He left Holland on the *Harinck,* which set sail at the end of September 1637 but did not reach New Amsterdam until Mar. 28, 1638.

Upon his arrival in New Amsterdam, Kieft found the city in a dilapidated condition, with the fort practically useless and all the ships except one unserviceable. He immediately assumed absolute control of the colony, and although he permitted the existence of a council, he himself dominated it. He ordered a number of reforms to be made in the civil administration, the police system, and the military force. His administration is principally noted, however, for the cruel massacre of the Indians and the serious results it entailed. In 1641 he levied contributions on the Indians living near New Amsterdam. The Raritans revenged themselves by destroying one of the outlying colonies, while many other settlements were similarly wiped out during the following four years. Some of these were English colonies within the borders of New Netherland, such as those of Anne Hutchinson and of the Rev. Francis Doughty. Between 1639 and 1644 there were only five months of peace. The climax came on Feb. 25 and 26, 1643, when, at the instigation of Kieft, eighty Indians were murdered. In 1642 Kieft had dissolved the Board of Twelve Men and had prohibited public meetings without his consent. When the people began to place all the blame of the Indian massacre upon him, he finally asked them to meet, whereupon they elected a Board of Eight Men to consider conditions in the benighted colony. Kieft was still held guilty of hypocrisy, impudence, and self-aggrandizement. Complaints were sent to the States-General in Holland. Then (1645) Stuyvesant, director of the Dutch West Indies, who happened to reside in the Netherlands, was appointed to displace Kieft, who had in the meantime been attacked by Bogardus, the Dutch preacher at New Amsterdam (Brodhead, *post,* 309–465).

On Aug. 16, 1647, Kieft left America in the *Princes,* carrying with him a store of various minerals which he had collected in the Dutch colony. Bogardus and seventy-nine others were also on the ship. As it neared the British Isles, it was wrecked on the Welsh coast (Sept. 27, 1647). Only twenty passengers were saved. Kieft was among the dead. In New Netherland the news of his death caused little regret, and in New England it was viewed as a judgment of God (John Winthrop, *A History of New England,* 1825, II, 316). It should be observed, however, that Kieft's faults are generally exaggerated by American historians. The impartial critic can say no more than that he was imprudent in his treatment of the Indians, represented the autocratic tendencies prevailing in Dutch municipal governments, and therefore was confronted by popular indignation in America which he misunderstood. He resorted to abusive language in defending his policies and was consequently an unsatisfactory governor, causing great financial loss to his superiors in Holland and innumerable hardships to his subjects.

[The records of Kieft's administration are now in the State Library at Albany. They form the first volumes in a set of 103 volumes entitled "Historical Manuscripts." The first volume was burned in the fire of 1911, but a translation by O'Callaghan has been preserved. The English translation of the Dutch volumes (1638–64), which were referred to as the "Albany Records," are lost. In addition to these there were the "Holland Documents," also destroyed by the fire of 1911, consisting of copies made by Brodhead in European archives. The first eight volumes of this series were printed in *Docs. Relative to the Colonial Hist. of the State of N. Y.,* ed. by E. B. O'Callaghan, vol. I: "Holland Documents," 1603–56 (1856). Other printed sources are: *N. Y. Hist. Soc. Colls.,* 2 ser. I (1841), 2 ser. III (1857); D. P. de Vries, *Korte Historiael ende Journaels Aenteyckeninge van verscheyden Voyagiens* (1655), reprinted in: *Werken uitgegeven door de Linschoten-Vereeniging,* vol. III (1911), ed. by H. T. Colenbrander. An excellent treatment of Kieft's administration is J. R. Brodhead, *Hist. of the State of N. Y.,* vol. I (1853). Another useful work is E. B. O'Callaghan, *Hist. of New Netherland,* vol. I (1846). Valuable source-material is found in: *Ecclesiastical Records, State of N. Y.,* vol. I (1901), and in *N. Y. State Lib. Van Rensselaer Bowier MSS.* (1908), ed. by A. J. F. van Laer.] **A. H.**

KIENTPOOS [See CAPTAIN JACK, 1837?–1873].

KIER, SAMUEL M. (1813–Oct. 6, 1874), industrialist, pioneer oil refiner, was born somewhere between Saltsburg and Livermore along the Conemaugh River, Indiana County, Pa., where his father, Thomas Kier, of Scotch-Irish descent, was engaged in the manufacture of salt from brine. After receiving a common-school education Kier left home and went to Pittsburgh where he soon found employment with a forwarding merchant. This business, the forerunner of the modern railway express enterprises, apparently appealed to him and in it he progressed, in due time entering into partnership and successfully operating under the firm name of Hewitt & Kier. The business thrived until 1837 when it went down in the general shipwreck of commerce and trade of that year. Although ruined financially, Kier had established a reputation which enabled him to organize in 1838 the firm of Kier, Royer & Company, owners and operators of canal boats plying over the Pennsylvania State Canal from Pittsburgh to Philadelphia with a branch line to tidewater at Havre de Grace, Md. Kier was even more successful in this field of transportation than in his earlier activities and paid off his earlier debts although freed of them by the bankrupt laws. He continued the active direction of the affairs of his "Mechanics' Line" of boats for more than ten years, taking as partner in 1847, after Royer dropped out, Benjamin Franklin Jones, the iron manufacturer. Aware of the pending establishment of a private railway system from Philadelphia to Pittsburgh, Kier established the "Independent Line" of section boats in 1846. James Buchanan, prior to his election to the presidency of the United States, was a partner in this enterprise. The boats of the "Independent Line" were more or less amphibious canal boats which were hauled over the railroad where that transportation medium existed and pulled through the canal in sections where the railroad did not exist. After 1854, when the invasion of the transportation field by the Pennsylvania Railroad became complete, the boat lines were dropped.

While transportation constituted the major part of his work, Kier was also a pioneer in the manufacture of firebrick, having established four works in Western Pennsylvania. Here he also established a pottery and in his later years was engaged in the coal mining and steel business. During this time his father had continued in the salt producing business, aided financially by his son. Around 1846 oil began to flow from their salt wells at Tarentum, Pa. Kier, knowing that seepage oil had been used for years as a panacea for human ills, undertook to bottle and distribute his oil through the medium of the "medicine road show." Again he was partly successful, and as a steady market was established, "Kier's Rock Oil" was sold directly to druggists. This market, however, did not consume all of the crude oil yield of the wells and Kier as early as 1850 began experiments with it as an illuminant. He had burned the oil at the wells but its offensive smoke and odor made it unsuited for household use in the existing whale oil and camphene lamps. He was advised by a chemist to refine the oil by distillation, and after much experimenting he succeeded in developing finally a five-barrel still with which a rather clear oil, but retaining its repugnant odor, was obtained. By slight changes in the existing camphene lamp Kier's refined oil burned without smoke. The demand for this product was immediate for Kier sold it cheaper than the established illuminants. Subsequently he perfected but did not patent a four-pronged burner lamp which produced a steady flame with his oil. For these contributions he has come to be regarded as America's first oil refiner and industrialist. Kier married Nancy Eicher of Greensburg, Pa., who with four children survived him. He died in Pittsburgh.

[J. T. Henry, *The Early and Later Hist. of Petroleum* (1873); J. D. Henry, *Hist. and Romance of the Petroleum Industry*, vol. I (1914); G. I. Reed, ed., *Century Cyc. of Hist. and Biog. of Pa.* (1904), vol. II; *Hist. of Allegheny County, Pa.* (1889); the *Pittsburgh Commercial*, Oct. 7, 1874.]
C. W. M.

KILBOURNE, JAMES (Oct. 19, 1770–Apr. 9, 1850), surveyor, minister, congressman, was born at New Britain, Conn., the son of Josiah and Anna (Neal) Kilbourne. Because of family losses occasioned by the Revolutionary War, his father advised him at the age of sixteen years to begin life for himself. Realizing that he must have an education he secured employment with a Mr. Griswold and studied Greek, Latin, English, and mathematics under his direction. On Nov. 19, 1789, when he was nineteen, he married Lucy Fitch, daughter of John Fitch [*q.v.*]. At the age of thirty he convinced his friends of the practicability of organizing a company to establish a colony in the Northwestern Territory as soon as it should be determined that the new state of Ohio would be free from slavery. Early in 1802 he formed a company which accepted his plans and asked him to explore the country and select enough land for forty families. He made a careful survey of the state of Ohio, while his associates purchased the land and completed the organization of the Scioto Company. Their community was established a few miles north of the present city of Columbus at Worthington. A church was at once organized, the first Episcopal church in Ohio, with Kilbourne as rector. He retired from the ministry in 1804.

Kilbourne became a captain of the frontier militia in 1804, was later elected major of a frontier regiment, then lieutenant-colonel. Finally, against his will, he was elected colonel, but he declined the rank. In 1805 he was appointed surveyor of public lands by Albert Gallatin, secretary of the treasury, and in 1812 he was appointed by the president of the United States a commissioner to settle the boundary line between the public lands and the great Virginia reservation. He was one of the first trustees of Ohio University at Athens, and a member of the commission appointed to select the seat of Miami University. When Worthington Academy was chartered in 1817, he was elected president of the corporation. He was elected to Congress in 1812 and was reëlected two years later. While in Congress he introduced the first Homestead bill in 1814. He was a member of the Ohio General Assembly in 1824 and again in 1838. He early identified himself with the Whig party and presided at the famous Whig Convention which nominated William Henry Harrison for the presidency. In 1811 he and a few friends started the *Western Intelligencer*, the first newspaper in central Ohio. He died at his home in Worthington at the age of eighty years. His first wife had died not long after his removal to Ohio, and in 1808 he was married to Cynthia Goodale.

[C. B. Galbreath, "Col. James Kilbourne," *Ohio Arch. and Hist. Quart.*, Jan. 1922; A. A. Graham, "An Early Abolition Colony and Its Founder," *Ohio Arch. and Hist. Soc. Pubs.*, vol. IV (1895); Emma Jones, *A State in Its Making: Correspondence of the Late Jas. Kilbourne* (1913); P. K. Kilbourne, *The Hist. and Antiquities of the Name and Family of Kilbourn* (1856); A. E. Lee, *Hist. of the City of Columbus, Capital of Ohio* (1892), vol. I; W. A. Taylor, *Ohio in Cong. from 1803 to 1901* (1900); letters and MSS. in the Ohio State Archæological and Historical Society Library, Columbus, Ohio.] H. L.

KILDAHL, JOHAN NATHAN (Jan. 4, 1857–Sept. 25, 1920), Lutheran clergyman, was born in Beitstaden, Norway, the son of Johan and Nicolina A. (Buvarp) Kildahl. In 1866 the family emigrated to America, the father serving as parochial teacher in the congregations of the Rev. B. J. Muus in Goodhue County, Minn., until invalided by ill health in 1870. Muus sent Johan Nathan to Luther College, Decorah, Iowa, in 1873, and in 1879 the boy received the degree of A.B. from that school. After three years of theological study at Luther Seminary, Madison, Wis., he was called to Vang and Urland congregations in Goodhue County, Minn., where his pastorate of seven years was interrupted by a year's leave of absence to serve as president of Red Wing Seminary, Red Wing, Minn. (1885–86). After serving as pastor in Chicago for ten years with distinction, he was called to fill the difficult position as president of St. Olaf College, Northfield, Minn., at the reorganization of the school in 1899. He still found time to serve St. John's congregation, Northfield, Minn., from 1899 to 1903, in 1906–07, and again from 1911 to 1913. In 1914 he was elected professor of dogmatics at the United Norwegian Lutheran Church Seminary, St. Paul, Minn. In this position he remained until his death. He had married, in 1882, Bertha Soine of Holden, Minn.

Kildahl took a conspicuous part in the predestination controversy that raged within the Norwegian Synod from 1880 to 1887, but he was the last to leave that body and join the Anti-Missourian Brotherhood. As secretary of the Brotherhood, he worked for the formation of the United Norwegian Lutheran Church of America out of the Brotherhood, the Norwegian-Danish Conference, and the Norwegian-Danish Augustana Synod. At the formation of the United Church in 1890, he was elected secretary of the new body and served for five years. In 1912 he became vice-president of the organization and served until it entered a union in 1917 with the Norwegian Synod and the Hauge's Synod. Again he took a prominent part and became the vice-president of the Norwegian Lutheran Church of America, as the new body was called. Incidentally, he served as mission secretary of the United Church (1895–99), as member of the committee on union (1906–12), and as collector of the Jubel Fund (1912). In 1905 he was made a knight of the first class of the order of St. Olav, and in 1912 he was given the degree of D.D. by the Minnesota Conference of the Augustana Synod. His writings include: *Barnedaaben* (1906), translated as *Infant Baptism* (1908); *Naar Jesus kommer ind i huset* (1906), translated as *When Jesus Enters the Home* (1917); *Synd og Naade* (1912, Sin and Grace); *Helliggjörelsen* (1919, Sanctification); *Misforstaaelse av den Helligaands ord og gjerning* (1919), translated as *Misconceptions of the Word and Work of the Holy Spirit* (1927); and *The Doctrinal Teachings of Christian Science* (1915, 1920).

[The chief bibliographical materials on the life of Kildahl are: *Dr. John Nathan Kildahl, En Mindebok* (Minneapolis, 1921), ed. by Rasmus Malmin; O. M. Norlie, *Lutherske Prester i Amerika 1843–1913* (Minneapolis, 1914) translated and revised by Rasmus Malmin, O. M. Norlie, and O. A. Tingelstad as *Who's Who Among the Pastors in All the Norwegian Lutheran Synods of America, 1843–1927* (1928); *Who's Who in America*, 1918–19; *Minneapolis Tribune*, Sept. 26, 1920]. J. M. R.

KILMER, ALFRED JOYCE (Dec. 6, 1886–July 30, 1918), poet, critic, soldier, better known simply as Joyce Kilmer, was the son of Frederick Barnett Kilmer, a professional chemist, and Annie (Kilburn) Kilmer. The family ancestry appears to have been predominatingly German and English. Born in New Brunswick, N. J., he attended Rutgers College (1904–06) and later went to Columbia University (A. B., 1908). In June 1908 he married Aline Murray, step-daughter of Henry Mills Alden, and during the following year taught Latin in the high school at Morristown, N. J. He then moved to New York City, where he at first found random employment. Soon he joined the staff of the *Standard Dictionary* (1909–12) and did considerable occasional writing for the magazines. After serving for a year as literary editor of the *Churchman,* an organ of the Episcopal Church of which he was a member at the time, he secured in 1913 an appointment to the staff of the *New York Times* Sunday *Magazine Section* and *Review of Books.* During the autumn of the same year he and his wife entered the Roman Catholic Church and thereafter he took a fervent interest in Catholic literature and affairs. Sometime previously the family had moved to Mahwah, N. J.

Kilmer began to supplement his work on the *Times* with various other activities. He conducted poetry departments for the *Literary Digest* and *Current Literature,* wrote prefaces to books (among them Hilaire Belloc's *Verses,* 1916, and Thomas Hardy's *Mayor of Casterbridge,* 1917), and lectured extensively on current letters. Poetry had definitely become his chief concern. *Summer of Love* (1911) contained verse for the most part derivative in character, showing the influence of Yeats and the Celtic Revival. *Trees and Other Poems* (1914) constituted a notable advance. During the years preceding, Kilmer had read Coventry Patmore studiously. He seems to have adopted the metrical principles of this poet, adding the best characteristics of American newspaper verse and an inspiration distinctly his own. The title-poem, published in *Poetry: A Magazine of Verse* in August 1913, attained world-wide popularity. *Main Street and Other Poems* (1917) is a mellow book which contains some of Kilmer's most appealing lyrics. His other books are: *The Circus, and Other Essays* (1916); *Literature in the Making* (1917), a series of interviews with literary personages; and *Dreams and Images* (1917), an anthology of modern English and American Catholic poetry. As a critic Kilmer was bright, never pedantic, but sometimes swayed a little by enthusiasms. He is described as a man "stockily built," of medium height and reddish-brown hair, whose eyes gave the impression that the "brain behind them was working intensely and perhaps even feverishly," and whose person reflected the dignity of a sensitive spirit conscious of having become, in a measure, a man of the world. His attitude to the War, during its earlier stages, is not accurately reflected in "The White Ships and the Red," a poem written to order for the *New York Times* on the occasion of the sinking of the *Lusitania* (1915). But when the United States joined the Allies against Germany, Kilmer entered the Columbia Officers' Training Corps, then enlisted as a private in the 7th Regiment, New York National Guard, and finally transferred to the 165th Regiment. He had four children, and another was born just before he sailed for France.

Though his motives in enlisting are possibly difficult to understand, they were in keeping with his character and high sense of honor. In France he transferred to the intelligence department of his regiment, won the rank of sergeant, and wrote poems (notably "Rouge Bouquet") in which something of the French Catholic attitude toward the War is reflected. This verse is sad, but his letters show hardly any trace of diminished enthusiasm. During the final days of July 1918, the 165th attacked the hills above the Ourcq. On July 30 Kilmer was found dead, an enemy bullet through his brain, some distance from the town of Seringes. He had volunteered to assist Col. W. J. Donovan in place of Lieut. Oliver Ames, who had just been killed. His bravery was rewarded by burial with the officers at a spot near which he fell, by mention in the official dispatches, and by the *Croix de Guerre* (posthumous). In one of his last letters he wrote: "You will find me less a bookman when you see me next, and more, I hope, a man." At any rate he became for Americans less a writer than a symbol of soldierly courage and poetic idealism. At the time of his death he was writing a historical account of the 165th Regiment which Francis P. Duffy appended to *Father Duffy's Story* (1919). Kilmer's selected works and letters were published by Robert C. Holliday in a volume entitled *Joyce Kilmer: Poems, Essays and Letters* (1918).

[There is a memoir of Kilmer by R. C. Holliday in *Joyce Kilmer: Poems, Essays and Letters.* See also: Annie Kilburn Kilmer, *Memories of My Son Sergeant Joyce Kilmer* (1920); Katherine M. C. Brégy, *Poets and Pilgrims* (1925); John Bunker, "Joyce Kilmer, the Man," *America,* Aug. 31, 1918; Richard Le Gallienne, "Joyce Kilmer," *Bookman,* Oct. 1918; *N. Y. Times,* Aug. 18, 22, 25, 1918.]

G. N. S.

KILPATRICK, HUGH JUDSON (Jan. 14, 1836–Dec. 2, 1881), soldier, diplomat, was the son of a farmer who lived near Deckertown, N. J. After a common-school education he entered West Point in 1856 as Judson Kilpatrick, graduating May 6, 1861—a month earlier than usual—as second lieutenant, 1st Artillery. He is said to have possessed more than ordinary ability—graduating seventeenth in a class of forty-five members. On the day of his graduation he married Alice Nailer of New York, and three days later he secured appointment as a captain, 5th New York Volunteers (Duryée's Zouaves). He left with his regiment for Fort Monroe, Va., in time to participate in the battle of Big Bethel, June 10, 1861, in which he was severely wounded. His gallant service won for him appointment as lieutenant-colonel, 2nd New York Cavalry, and thereafter until the end of the Civil War he had almost continuous field-service with cavalry, with unusual participation in actions, engagements, and battles. When General McClellan transferred the Army of the Potomac to the James River, Kilpatrick assisted in covering the defenses of Washington with his cavalry, and for two years he took an active part in cavalry operations of the Army of the Potomac: in the Department of the Rappahannock (March–July 1862); in the Northern Virginia campaign (August–September 1862), where he was constantly and gallantly fighting Stuart's cavalry; and in the Rappahannock campaign (January–June 1863). At Beverly Ford he commanded a brigade and participated in the ill-fated Stoneman's raid where he destroyed immense quantities of enemy's stores and penetrated to within two miles of Richmond. He was promoted brigadier-general of volunteers (June 13, 1863) and shortly afterward commanded a cavalry division in the engagements of Aldie, Middleburg, and Upperville, Va. For gallant and meritorious services at Aldie he was brevetted major in the regular army. He took an active and successful part at the battle of Gettysburg in cavalry assaults upon the Confederate right flank, and in pursuit of the defeated enemy. In subsequent operations in Central Virginia (August–November 1863), he initiated the Kilpatrick raid on Richmond, with the object of releasing Federal prisoners in Libby Prison—an operation ably executed but barren of results. Thereafter he was transferred to command of the 3rd Cavalry Division, Army of the Cumberland, assembling in northern Georgia for the campaign against Atlanta, and for conspicuous services at the battle of Resaca, where he was again severely wounded, he was brevetted colonel in the regular army. He joined Sherman's march to the sea while still unable to ride a horse, and in the invasion of the Carolinas which followed, his cavalry division performed valuable service. He was brevetted (Mar. 13, 1865) brigadier-general and major-general respectively for gallant and meritorious services in the capture of Fayetteville, N. C., and in the campaign in the Carolinas.

After the war, Kilpatrick resigned from the army and entered politics, receiving appointment as United States minister to Chile (1865–68). But after Grant's second campaign for the presidency, Kilpatrick was recalled and joined the Democratic party in supporting Horace Greeley. In the year 1876 he again became a Republican and in 1880, while a director of the Union Pacific Railroad, was nominated for Congress from his native state but was defeated. In the same year he was a delegate to the Republican National Convention and in March 1881 was reappointed by President Garfield United States minister to Chile. While involved in a diplomatic controversy with Stephen A. Hurlbut, United States minister to Peru—Chile and Peru being then at war—he died at Santiago of kidney trouble. His first wife had died during the Civil War. He was later married to a Chilean, who survived him. As a cavalry commander he was a brilliant leader, having originated the saying that "cavalry can fight anywhere except at sea." In political life he was an eloquent, magnetic, and forceful public speaker.

[G. W. Cullum, *Biog. Reg. . . . U. S. Mil. Acad.* (ed. 1891), vol. II, contains a sketch by Kilpatrick's classmate, Gen. James H. Wilson. See also: *Thirteenth Ann. Reunion, Asso. Grads. U. S. Mil. Acad.*, 1882; *War of the Rebellion, Official Records (Army)*; *Foreign Relations of the U. S.*, 1867–68, 1881–82; *N. Y. Tribune*, May 19, Nov. 18, Dec. 7, 22, 1881.] C. D. R.

KILTY, WILLIAM (1757–Oct. 10, 1821), army surgeon and jurist, was born in London, England, the son of John Kilty and Ellen Ahearn. The names are suggestive of Celtic origins. He was educated in the College of St. Omer in France and was brought to America by his parents shortly before the outbreak of the Revolutionary War, the family settling in Annapolis, Md. Here he studied medicine under Dr. Edward Johnson and in April 1778 he was appointed surgeon's mate of the 4th Maryland Regiment which he joined at Wilmington, Del. In April 1780, upon the resignation of Michael Wallace, surgeon of the regiment, he was appointed to the vacancy. He was taken prisoner at the battle of Camden and after futile efforts to effect an exchange, he was paroled and compelled to await at Annapolis the end of the war. He appears at this time to have abandoned the profession of medicine for that of law and in 1798 he was authorized by an act of the legislature to compile the statutes of the state. The result was *The Laws of Maryland* (1799–1800) published in two volumes. In 1818 he collaborated with Thomas Harris and John N. Watkins in the issue of a four-volume continuation of the same work. In 1800 he moved to Washington and in April of the following year President Adams appointed him chief justice of the circuit court of the District of Columbia. He occupied this position until Jan. 25, 1806, when he resigned to accept an appointment by the governor of Maryland as chancellor of the state. He held this post until his death in Annapolis in 1821.

Supplemental to his earlier work he compiled *A Report on All Such English Statutes as Existed at the Time of the First Emigration of the People of Maryland, and Which by Experience Have Been Found Applicable to their Local and Other Circumstances* (1811). Not all of his writings were on legal matters, nor in so serious a vein. There exists a manuscript volume by Kilty entitled *A Burlesque Translation of Homer's Iliad, with Notes. The Second Part.* The title is the same as that of a work by Thomas Bridges, published in England in 1764. Kilty offered his poem as a sequel to the earlier production and thus explained his beginning with the thirteenth book. It is probable that the poem was not an original translation, but an adaptation from that of Pope or of Cowper. Without disclaiming a knowledge of Greek, he gives the impression that he had scant skill in the language. He is also credited with the authorship of a satirical historic poem, *The Vision of Don Crocker,* published in Baltimore in 1813. Except for his service with the Revolutionary army there is no evidence that he made any use of his medical knowledge. His claims to remembrance rest upon his career in the law and his legal literary work. He is described as a judge whose opinions show industry and a close familiarity with English equity jurisprudence. An obituary describes him as "an honest, upright and enlightened man, and highly esteemed by all that had had business to do with him, either in his public or private character. *His death, we believe, has deprived Maryland of the only person that exactly knew what is the constitution of the state*" (*Niles' Register,* Oct. 13, 1821, p. 97). He was of a quiet unassuming character, happy in his judicial and professional work, but vitally interested in the welfare of his state and country. In the troubled times preceding the War of 1812 he was active in demanding redress from England and in calling upon the people to support the President in his policies of defense. He was a member of a resolution committee appointed at a meeting in Annapolis, Feb. 4, 1809, for the purpose of expressing approval of the course of the President toward Great Britain and France. He was one of the founders of the Society of the Cincinnati. For diversion he wrote verse and tried his hand at music. He married Elizabeth Middleton of Calvert County, Md. They had no children.

[See: W. L. Marbury, "The High Court of Chancery and the Chancellors of Maryland," *Proc. Tenth Ann. Meeting of the Md. Bar Asso.* (1905); *Old Maryland,* May 1906; *Md. Hist. Mag.,* June 1918; H. A. Kelly and W. L. Burrage, *Am. Medic. Biogs.* (1920); the *Md. Republican,* Oct. 13, 1821. The manuscript of Kilty's *Burlesque Translation of Homer's Iliad* is in the Harris Collection of American poetry in the library of Brown University.] J. M. P—n.

KIMBALL, GILMAN (Dec. 8, 1804–July 27, 1892), surgeon, was born in New Chester (now Hill), N. H., the son of Ebenezer and Polly (Aiken) Kimball. He was descended from Richard Kimball who emigrated to America in 1634 and settled eventually in Ipswich, Mass. Kimball was graduated, M.D., from the Medical Department of Dartmouth College in 1827. During his four years' medical course he spent part of his time in Boston at the office of Edward Reynolds [*q.v.*], at the Massachusetts General Hospital, and at the Harvard Medical School. He served for a time as resident physician at the United States Marine Hospital in Boston. After two years of general practice in Chicopee, Mass., he spent a year in Paris studying surgery with Guillaume Dupuytren, the best teacher of the time. Returning, he settled in 1830 in Lowell, Mass., where he remained for the rest of his life. First as a mill surgeon and later as surgeon to the Lowell Corporation Hospital, established in 1839, he was a pioneer in difficult, and at that time almost unknown, operations in gynecology. One of his earliest operations was the successful removal of a tumor of the uterus on Sept. 1, 1853, by abdominal incision (*Boston Medical and Surgical Journal,* May 3, 1855), and on Mar. 1, 1854, he operated, also with success, upon a patient with an ovarian tumor (*Ibid.,* May 10, 1855). He performed both operations with the use of chloroform and without the benefit of asepsis. Kimball also performed excellent traumatic surgery, including an excision of the elbow joint, amputation of the hip joint, and successful ligation of some of the larger external arteries. In 1870 he joined Ephraim Cutter [*q.v.*] in the treatment of uterine tumors by electrolysis (*Ibid.,* Jan. 29, 1874). He performed over three hundred major operations in a period of about forty years. Many of them were unknown at the time and even condemned by the medical profession as unjustifiable. Living in a comparatively small town, he achieved a reputation as one of the foremost surgeons in America, and his courage and skill contributed in no small degree to the progress of medicine in the United States.

Kindly, firm, and substantial, Kimball was a splendid figure of a progressive, pioneer surgeon. In addition to his extensive surgical practice, he taught in the Berkshire Medical Institution and at a number of other local medical schools, served during the Civil War as brigade surgeon, and visited Europe several times to make a survey of the practice of ovariotomy. He served as vice-president of the Massachusetts Medical Society in 1878 and as president of the American Gynecological Association in 1882–83. He married twice: first Mary, daughter of Henry Dewar, a physician of Edinburgh, Scotland, and, secondly, Isabella, daughter of Henry I. Defries of Nantucket, Mass. He was survived by his second wife and a son.

[The chief reference to Kimball is the article by F. H. Davenport in the *Am. Jour. of Obstetrics,* Oct. 1892. See also: H. A. Kelly and W. L. Burrage, *Am. Medic. Biogs.* (1920); *Boston Medic. and Surgic. Jour.,* Aug. 4, 1892; *Boston Evening Transcript, Boston Herald,* and *Evening Star* (Lowell), July 28, 1892.] H. R. V.

KIMBALL, HEBER CHASE (June 14, 1801–June 22, 1868), apostle of the Latter-day Saints, was born in Sheldon, Vt., the son of Solomon Farnham and Anna (Spaulding) Kimball. He moved with his family in 1811 to West Bloomfield, N. Y., where he completed his desultory schooling and learned from his father the blacksmith's trade. When Solomon Kimball suffered financial ruin following the War of 1812, Heber was thrown upon his own resources and, after experiencing some hardships, learned the potter's trade from an elder brother, with whom he later moved to Mendon, N. Y. On Nov. 7, 1822, he took as a bride of sixteen, Vilate Murray, of Victor, N. Y. The turning point in his hitherto undistinguished career came in the spring of 1832, when, after having met some itinerant elders of the Church of Jesus Christ of the Latter-day Saints, he rejected a newly made alliance with the Baptists and became a Mormon. His wife was also a ready convert. By the fall of the year 1832 he had been ordained to the ministry and within another year, with his friend Brigham Young, he had decided to join Joseph Smith at Kirtland, Ohio. He became a guileless follower of the founder of the church, and, possessing now a strong religious fervor and a ready belief in the existence of miracles, visions, and his own gift of prophecy, he was destined to take a favored place in the hierarchy of the church.

On Feb. 14, 1835, Kimball was ordained one of the twelve apostles who, in the early days of the church organization, stood next to Joseph Smith in rank and authority. Shortly afterward he was directed to engage in missionary service. He toured New York and New England for two summers and on one occasion, while traveling with some Swiss emigrants, he believed that he spoke to them in their own language (*Life of Heber C. Kimball,* pp. 109–10). In the spring of 1837 he was named head of the first mission to England. His immediate astonishment at the thought of undertaking the task gave way to his eagerness to promote the interests of the church, and with four associates he sailed for Liverpool in July. He arrived destitute but undaunted. He began to preach in and about Preston and in less than a year is said to have baptized some fifteen hundred persons. After his return to Kirtland in 1838, he joined the migration to Jackson County, Mo. The unhappy sojourn there ended with the expulsion of the Mormons from the state, and he moved his family to Commerce (later Nauvoo), Ill., in the summer of 1839. In September he was again on his way to England, to preach and baptize, and to encourage converts to join the Mormons in America. He returned two years later to continue his missionary tours in the United States and in 1844 was on a mission to urge the candidacy of Joseph Smith as president of the United States when his campaign was cut short by the prophet's death.

Kimball and one of his wives joined the first Mormon migration to the Salt Lake Valley in the spring of 1847. He returned to "Winter Quarters" in the fall but joined the great trek of the following year and settled permanently in the West. His final promotion in the church had come in December 1847, when, with Willard Richards, he became one of Brigham Young's chief counselors. The three formed the "first presidency" and represented the executive head of the church. Fortified by his position, he exerted a forceful influence in the affairs of the community. He was elected chief justice and lieutenant-governor upon the organization of the State of Deseret and later became a member of the legislature. Under the territorial government of Utah he served as a member of the Council until 1858 (president, 1855–58), and as lieutenant-governor until his death.

Kimball was a man of large build and tremendous vigor. Known to the Saints as Brother Heber, he stood well in the affections of his people. His theology was his own naïve interpretation of the Bible and the Book of Mormon, and he discoursed with a fluency of speech which derived emphasis from his moral zeal and native sturdiness. He believed in the divine authority of Joseph Smith and Brigham Young and accepted their teachings as infallible. Though he suffered some mental anguish on first receiving the doctrine of plural marriage, he in time accepted it wholeheartedly and practised it fully, attaining to forty-five wives and sixty-five children. Forty-one of his children survived him.

[Orson F. Whitney, *Life of Heber C. Kimball, An Apostle* (1888), is a eulogistic biography written by Kimball's grandson. The *Jour. of Heber C. Kimball*

(1840) was reprinted in slightly different form under the title: *President Heber C. Kimball's Jour.* (1882). Other sources include: *Latter-Day Saint Biog. Encyc.*, vol. I (1901); L. A. Morrison and S. P. Sharples, *Hist. of the Kimball Family in America* (1897), I, 314, 585; H. H. Bancroft, *Hist. of Utah* (1890); Jules Remy, *A Journey to Great-Salt-Lake City* (2 vols., 1861); Frederick Piercy, *Route from Liverpool to Great Salt Lake Valley* (1855); E. W. Tullidge, *The Women of Mormondom* (1877); Ruth and Reginald Wright Kauffman, *The Latter-Day Saints* (1912); "Among the Mormons," *Atlantic Monthly*, Apr. 1864; *Latter-Day Saints' Millennial Star*, July 25, 1868.] M. B. P.

KIMBALL, NATHAN (Nov. 22, 1823?–Jan. 21, 1898), soldier, the son of Nathaniel, a small merchant, and of Nancy (Furgeson) Kimball, was born in Fredericksburg, Washington County, Ind. He matriculated at Asbury College (now DePauw University) in 1839 but did not graduate. In 1841, soon after leaving college, he began to teach school at Independence, Mo., later tried his hand at farming, and, in 1843, undertook the study of medicine with Dr. Alexander McPheeters, whose sister, Martha Ann McPheeters, he married on Sept. 23, 1845. He practised medicine until the Mexican War, when he raised a company and served as a captain in the 2nd Indiana Regiment. At the battle of Buena Vista the cowardice of the colonel caused the regiment to retreat in disorder, but Kimball was able to rally his company to continue fighting. He was mustered out in 1847 at New Orleans and returned to Indiana, where he was practising medicine at Loogootee when the Civil War broke out. He was commissioned captain by Governor Morton, helped to raise the 14th Indiana Regiment, and became its colonel. In 1861 he and his regiment saw action at Cheat Mountain and at Greenbrier. On Mar. 22, 1862, near Winchester in the Shenandoah Valley, where Gen. James Shields was wounded in a skirmish, he assumed command of Shields's division, a part of the V Corps of the Army of the Potomac. Next day he fought and defeated "Stonewall" Jackson at the battle of Kernstown. The Union losses were less than six hundred, while those of the Confederates were more than seven hundred. For this distinguished service Kimball was made a brigadier-general. In September his brigade fought gloriously at Antietam and in the disastrous assault on Fredericksburg his brigade again distinguished itself, but he was badly wounded. On his recovery, the next spring, he commanded a division of the XVI Corps in the siege of Vicksburg. After the capture of that place he served for a time in Arkansas against Price, made a journey to Washington with important dispatches to the government, and returned to Arkansas for the reorganization of the state government. In the spring of 1864 he joined Sherman's army in its advance on Atlanta, being attached to the 1st Division of the IV Army Corps. For services in the battle of Peachtree Creek he was given command of the division. Soon after the fall of Atlanta he was recalled to southern Indiana to help in suppressing the activities of the "Knights of the Golden Circle." Successful in these efforts he returned to the front in time to participate in the battles of Franklin and Nashville, and to aid in the almost total destruction of Hood's army. On Feb. 1, 1865, he was brevetted major-general and was mustered out of the service in the following August. In political and in civil life he continued to be respected and trusted by Governor Morton and by the people of the state. In 1864 he had been offered the Republican nomination for Lieutenant-Governor but considered it his patriotic duty to remain with the army. Soon after the war ended he helped to organize the Grand Army of the Republic in Indiana and became its state commander. He contributed the article "Fighting Jackson at Kernstown" to *Battles and Leaders of the Civil War*, vol. II (1884), pp. 302–313. In 1866 and, again, in 1868 he was elected state treasurer and in 1872 was elected to the state legislature, where he served on the committee of ways and means. Appointed surveyor general of Utah by Grant in the next year he went there and ultimately settled in Ogden, where he became postmaster under Hayes, and was serving in that capacity at the time of his death.

[*War of the Rebellion: Official Records (Army)*, espec. ser. 1, vols. V, XII, XIX, XXI, XXII, XXIV, XXXVIII (1881–91); F. B. Heitman, *Hist. Reg. and Dict. of the U. S. Army*, vol. I (1902); *Battles and Leaders of the Civil War*, vols. II, III, IV (1884–87); F. A. Walker, *Hist. of the Second Army Corps* (1886); *What Others Say of the Gen. Nathan Kimball and Later of Gen. S. S. Carroll Brigade* (n.d.); L. A. Morrison and S. P. Sharples, *Hist. of the Kimball Family in Am.* (1897), vol. II; *Indianapolis News*, Jan. 22, 1898; *Indianapolis Journal*, Jan. 23, 1898.] P. L. H.

KIMBALL, RICHARD BURLEIGH (Oct. 11, 1816–Dec. 28, 1892), author, lawyer, the son of Richard and Mary (Marsh) Kimball, was born in Plainfield, Sullivan County, N. H., the youngest of four children. His paternal and maternal ancestors were identified with many of the pioneer improvements in New England. He was seventh in descent from Richard Kimball, of Suffolk County, England, who landed at Boston in 1634. He passed his early childhood in Lebanon, N. H., where the Kimballs had settled in 1802. At the age of eleven he had passed his examination for admission to Dartmouth College, but because of his youth, the college authorities refused to accept him until two years later. He was graduated from Dartmouth in 1834 at the age of seventeen, with the degree of A.B., one of the first six in his class and a member of Phi Beta Kappa. After leaving Dartmouth he studied law and was admitted to the bar in Waterford, N. Y., in 1836. In that year he went to Paris to continue his studies. On his return he began to practise at Waterford under the patronage of William A. Beach. He had read law with Judge Doe, of Waterford, and the elder Dupin, of Paris, France. Shortly before he attained his majority he was made a master in chancery. He moved from Waterford to Troy, N. Y., in 1840, where he lived for a short time, in the same year going to New York City to enter the office of his brother, Elijah H. Kimball, at 30 Wall Street. Some months later he opened an office of his own and continued in active practice until 1854. Possessing much of the pioneer instinct of his ancestors he became interested in the Southwest and early in the fifties founded the town of Kimball, Tex. He also built part of the first railroad in that state. Known as the Galveston, Houston & Henderson Railroad, it ran from Galveston to Houston and beyond. He served as its president from 1854 to 1860.

After Kimball relinquished the practice of law, he devoted much of his time to literature, becoming an author of established reputation in his day. For the most part his writings were the result of his experiences in travel and in business, and in the course of his journeys he became acquainted with many of the prominent authors and statesmen of the nineteenth century. He knew Dickens intimately and had met Lamartine, Thackeray, Lord Palmerston, and the elder Peel, and among prominent Americans knew Washington Irving, Webster, and Clay. His brief sketches of these men appeared in the *New York Times* during the last two years of his life. He became a constant contributor to the old *Knickerbocker* magazine, in which appeared, in 1849–50, his metaphysical novel, "St. Leger; or, The Threads of Life." This was his first literary work to attract attention and was immediately translated into the French and Dutch languages. Among the works that followed this successful novel are: *Cuba and the Cubans* (1850); *Romance of Student Life Abroad* (1853); *Undercurrents of Wall Street* (1862); *Was He Successful?* (1864); *Henry Powers, Banker* (1868); and *To-day in New York* (1870). He edited and published *In the Tropics* (1863), and *The Prince of Kashua* (1866), a West Indian story. Many of his books have been translated into Dutch, French, and German, and some were published in both London and Leipzig. On Apr. 17, 1844, Kimball was married to Julia Caroline, daughter of Dr. David and Cornelia (Adams) Tomlinson. To them were born five children. He died at St. Luke's Hospital in New York City.

[Geo. T. Chapman, *Sketches of the Alumni of Dartmouth Coll.* (1867); L. A. Morrison and S. P. Sharples, *Hist. of the Kimball Family in America* (1897), vol. I; Samuel Orcutt, *Henry Tomlinson, and His Descendants in America* (1891); the *N. Y. Times* and *Sun* (N. Y.), Dec. 29, 1892.] A. L. B.

KIMBALL, SUMNER INCREASE (Sept. 2, 1834–June 21, 1923), organizer of the United States life-saving service, was born at Lebanon, Me., the son of Increase Sumner and Miriam White Bodwell Kimball. He was descended from Richard Kimball and from William White, both of whom were early settlers at Ipswich, Mass. He was graduated from Bowdoin College in 1855, was admitted to the bar in 1858, and in 1859 was a member of the Maine legislature. On Oct. 12, 1858, he was married to Ellen Frothingham Fenno. After a year in Boston, he went to Washington in 1861 and began his career there in the service of the federal government as a clerk in the office of the second auditor of the Treasury, where he rose to the grade of chief clerk. In 1871 he was made chief of the revenue marine, later revenue-cutter service, in which position he served until his appointment as general superintendent of the United States life-saving service in 1878 by President Hayes. He won the distinction at this time of receiving the immediate and unanimous confirmation of the Senate, without the usual reference to a committee. He occupied this post from 1878 to 1915, when the life-saving service and the revenue-cutter service were combined into the United States coast guard. For seven years prior to the establishment of the life-saving service, from 1871 to 1878, he was at the head of the life-saving system of the country. Wherever governments or individuals have organized kindred institutions, Kimball's work has been carefully studied and highly commended. It was a unique achievement because the United States life-saving service was one of the first, if not the first, institution of its kind supported wholly by the state.

The confidence reposed in Kimball during his official career in Washington is shown by the frequency with which he was designated temporarily to perform the duties of other high officials during their absence or disability. In April 1872 he was appointed by President Grant a member of the board of examiners for appointments and promotions in the Treasury Department. In 1889 he was appointed by President Cleveland to the diplomatic position of delegate on the part of the United States to the International Marine Conference convened at Washington, and composed of leading representatives of the principal maritime nations of the world. In 1892 he was appointed by President Harrison acting first comptroller of the Treasury. In the same year he received from the President a like designation as acting register of the Treasury. In 1900 President McKinley appointed him acting comptroller of the Treasury and in the same year he was appointed acting solicitor of the Treasury. The most important of his public services, however, was the creation and development of the life-saving service. He witnessed it grow to acknowledged supremacy, through his personal industry and efforts, and he never failed to give credit to the officers and men of the service who had aided him. Under the provisions of the act creating the coast guard, Kimball was retired from active service as general superintendent on Jan. 15, 1916. He died in Washington, D. C. His published writings include *Organization and Methods of the United States Life-Saving Service* (1889), and *Joshua James—Life-Saver* (1909).

[*Who's Who in America,* 1922–23; Edwin Emery, *The Hist. of Sanford, Me.* (1901), pp. 473–81; L. A. Morrison and S. P. Sharples, *Hist. of the Kimball Family in America* (2 vols., 1897); *Am. Mag.,* Aug. 1913; D. H. Smith and F. W. Powell, *The Coast Guard; Its Hist., Activities, and Organization* (1919); *Evening Star* (Washington, D. C.), June 21, 22, 1923.]

F. C. B—d.

KIMBALL, WILLIAM WIRT (Jan. 9, 1848–Jan. 26, 1930), naval officer, was born at Paris, Me., son of Brig.-Gen. William King and Frances Freeland (Rawson) Kimball. He was descended from Richard Kimball who emigrated to America in 1634. Appointed to the Naval Academy as an officer's son, he graduated in 1869 and following a sea cruise was in the first group of officers who studied at the torpedo station in Newport, 1870–71. Three years later, after serving in the *Shawmut* of the North Atlantic Fleet, he was torpedo officer in the *Intrepid* and *Alarm,* the two first torpedo boats of the United States navy. After promotion to lieutenant, 1874, and an Asiatic cruise in the *Alert,* 1875–79, he was on ordnance duty, 1879–82, and again, 1886–90, engaged in the development of magazine and machine guns. According to his statement he "designed, constructed, and operated the first armed cars used by United States forces" (*Who's Who in America,* 1928–29). These must have been used by the landing force which guarded rail transit in Panama, April-May 1885, in which Kimball served. In that year he also prepared a special intelligence report of progress on the Panama Canal (*House Miscellaneous Document 395,* 49 Cong., 1 Sess.). During this period he was especially interested in submarines, and in 1885 tried vainly to arrange that the inventor John P. Holland [*q.v.*] should be employed by the Navy Bureau of Ordnance, the government to own his designs. He drew up the specifications when the government first called for bids on submarines in 1886–87. His friendship for Holland extended over many years. A series of extant letters from Holland to Kimball, 1886–1910, testify to the latter's unwavering support of the inventor's ideas, and to his suggestions for their military adaptation in detail. The inventor offered Kimball a financial share in his discovery, but apparently the offer was not accepted. In 1889 Holland assured Kimball that the submarine was "a subject that you must have the credit of putting into practical shape and introducing."

After further sea duty Kimball was head of the Office of Naval Intelligence, 1894–97, and, promoted to lieutenant-commander, in 1897 took command of the first American torpedo boat flotilla, which he held till the close of the Spanish-American War. Torpedo combat was still experimental, and during the war the flotilla did not operate as a unit, but Kimball was in the Santiago campaign in the *Du Pont* and offered to try sinking Cervera's ships with a Holland submarine, if the government would buy it. He was at the Washington Navy Yard, 1900–01; commanding the *Alert,* 1901–03; inspector of the Eighth Light House District, 1904–05; then commander of the *New Jersey;* and, with the rank of rear admiral (1908), was given command of the Nicaragua Expeditionary Squadron in December 1909. Though retired for age in January 1910, he remained with the squadron until it was withdrawn in the following April. Recalled to active duty during the World War, he served as president of the board for examining officers and was in charge of the historical section, office of operations, of the Navy Department. In later years he spent his winters in Washington and summers in Paris, Me., writing occasionally on naval topics, notably a pamphlet on *Our Question of Questions: Arm or Disarm* (1917). Of strong mechanical bent, he was always an enthusiast for progressive development in submarines and aeronautics. He was of slight but active physique, quick, aggressive, with keen wit and most genial, kindly manner. It was said that "he never commanded an unhappy ship nor an inefficient one" (*Army and Navy Register,*

Feb. 1, 1930, p. 111). In 1925 he was elected president of the Maine Three-Quarter Century Club. He was also secretary of his naval academy class and was chiefly instrumental in promoting its annual reunions, covering sixty years. His wife was Esther Smith Spencer of Maryland, whom he married July 18, 1882, and who died Feb. 12, 1930. He had no children.

[In addition to references cited in the biography, see: L. R. Hamersly, *The Records of Living Officers of the U. S. Navy and Marine Corps* (7th ed., 1902); F. T. Cable, *The Birth and Development of the Am. Submarine* (1924); W. W. Kimball, "Submarine Torpedo-Boats," *Harper's New Monthly Mag.*, Sept. 1900; L. A. Morrison and S. P. Sharples, *Hist. of the Kimball Family in America* (1897), vol. II; *Washington Post*, Jan. 27, 1930. Information as to certain facts was supplied by Mr. John R. McMahon, Little Falls, N. J.] A. W.

KING, ALBERT FREEMAN AFRICANUS (Jan. 18, 1841–Dec. 13, 1914), physician, was born in Oxfordshire, England, to Dr. Edward and Louisa (Freeman) King. He owed his name Africanus to his father's interest in the colonization of Africa. His early schooling was obtained in Bichester, near Oxford. With his father, brother and sister he arrived in America, in 1851, members of a colony of immigrants for northern Virginia. He studied medicine at the National Medical College, now the Medical Department of the George Washington University in Washington, where he graduated in 1861. Selecting Haymarket, Va., as the place to begin his practice, he was hardly settled before the Civil War broke and the battle of Bull Run was fought almost at his door. He assisted in the care of the wounded after the battle and later was assigned to the staff of the Lincoln Hospital, on the site of the present Lincoln Park, in Washington.

In 1865 he obtained his degree in medicine from the University of Pennsylvania and returned to Washington to practise. In the same year he was appointed lecturer on toxicology in the National Medical College. In 1870 he was made an assistant in obstetrics and the following year he became professor of obstetrics and diseases of women and children. He held this chair until 1904, when the teaching of gynecology and pediatrics was divorced from that of obstetrics, and he was continued in the chair of the latter subject until his death. He thus taught obstetrics for forty-five years at the same school through its many changes of name. He was dean of the faculty from 1879 to 1894. For many years he conducted an "intensive" spring course in obstetrics at the University of Vermont. His whole teaching career was marked by unvarying routine and method. He was an interesting, forceful speaker, exceedingly dramatic, but with a fund of good nature and a good sense of humor. He brought out his *Manual of Obstetrics* in 1882. Such was its popularity that he was engaged upon the twelfth edition at the time of his death. He was one-time president of the Medical Society of the District of Columbia and of the Washington Obstetrical and Gynecological Society.

A bibliography of King's papers shows eighty-two titles including a number of biographical sketches of medical men. Without question the most notable of his papers was "The Prevention of Malarial Diseases, Illustrating *inter alia* the Conservative Function of Ague," read before the Philosophical Society of Washington on Feb. 10, 1882, and published in abbreviated form in the *Popular Science Monthly* of September 1883. In this paper he made a clear and direct statement of his belief in the transmission of malaria by the mosquito and supported his belief by a list of nineteen well-considered and well-presented reasons. He also listed the means of prevention of the mosquito dissemination of the disease, including screening of houses, drainage of swamps and pools, planting of trees, and the destruction of the insects by traps and the burning of pyrethrum. The reading of this notable paper produced little impression upon an audience which was skeptical and unconcerned. L. O. Howard, the distinguished entomologist, who furnished King with the life history of the mosquito, took no stock in the malaria theory, and Dr. J. S. Billings, who heard the paper, could see in the mosquito transmission of the disease nothing more than the chance of a possible accidental inoculation. It was more than a decade before Ross confirmed King's theory, made possible by the discovery of the malarial parasite by Lavaran. It is only fair to state that King's implication of the mosquito in the transmission of malaria had been antedated by that of Josiah Nott in 1848, and Nott credits Sir Henry Holland with putting forward a similar idea at an earlier date. Never, however, had the case been presented so fully in accordance with the subsequent confirmation. King's credit in this matter would have been better if he had not put forward a number of other scientific hypotheses, usually fantastic, one on the origin of cancer being especially so. He apparently took much to heart the scant hearing accorded to his theories by the local medical societies. He was taken ill in his classroom in Washington and died two days later. He had married, on Oct. 17, 1894, Ellen A. Dexter of Boston, Mass.

[*Trans. Am. Gynecol. Soc.*, vol. XL (1915); *Album of the Fellows of the Am. Gynecol. Soc.* (1930); *Wash-*

ington Medic. Annals, Mar. 1915; H. A. Kelly and W. L. Burrage, *Am. Medic. Biogs.* (1920); the *Evening Star* (Washington), and *Washington Post,* Dec. 15, 1914.] J. M. P—n.

KING, AUSTIN AUGUSTUS (Sept. 21, 1802–Apr. 22, 1870), judge, congressman, governor, was born in Sullivan County, Tenn. His father was Walter King, an owner of iron mines; his mother was the daughter of John Sevier, the Tennessee military and political leader. His brief formal education was obtained under frontier conditions; he then studied law and practised several years in Jackson. In 1830 he moved to Missouri and settled in Columbia, where he entered immediately the civic and political life of central Missouri. An ardent Jacksonian Democrat, he was elected in 1834 and in 1836 to the legislature from Boone, a Whig county. Here he became a leader in the opposition to the use of state credit to finance internal improvements. In 1837 he was appointed by Governor Boggs to a circuit judgeship in northwestern Missouri. He served in this frontier judicial post for eleven years, riding the circuit and administering justice with common sense and good judgment. He presided in 1838 at the trial of the Mormon leaders, who accused him of bias and unfairness (William A. Linn, *Story of the Mormons,* 1902, p. 214).

King's judicial duties did not prevent him from continuing his active interest in Democratic politics. He was an admirer and supporter of Senator Benton, submitting without question to the political absolutism of the Missouri leader, the most powerful figure in state politics. The state Democracy since the early forties had been torn by internal dissension, but the Benton faction was able to nominate King for governor in 1848. His views on national and state issues were those of a "pure and consistent Democrat" (*Jefferson Inquirer,* Apr. 1, 1848, p. 2), that is, he represented the Jacksonian rather than the Calhoun element. King was elected and entered the governorship just as the state was emerging from the pioneer stage and when the railroad question was foremost. The governor fully recognized this problem and was eager to proceed to its solution (*Messages and Proclamations,* II, 276–79, 307–11). Unfortunately for King, the Benton and the anti-Benton factions in 1849 came to a definite parting of the ways. King, a lifelong slave-owner, was a strong advocate of the non-intervention doctrine for the territories (*Ibid.,* II, 321). The legislature, owing to factional warfare which demoralized several sessions, neglected the pressing economic problems; but finally, at the end of his term, he was able by skilful leadership to secure legislation incorporating several railroads and granting them indirect state aid. Important policies were inaugurated concerning education and corporate economic enterprises.

In 1852 and in 1854 King was defeated as a Benton Democrat in contests for Congress and for the legislature. He supported Douglas in 1860 and was instrumental in securing for him the vote of Missouri. As the storm approached, King, sympathetic toward the South, favored compromise and opposed armed force. He decided for the Union in 1861, however, and supported the provisional government in Missouri. The following year as a Union or War Democrat he was elected, after a turbulent canvass, to the Thirty-eighth Congress. His chief concern was to support, against his Radical colleagues, the conservative régime in the state. He was one of the eleven Democrats who voted for the submission of the Thirteenth Amendment, two weeks after slavery in Missouri had been abolished (*Congressional Globe,* 38 Cong., 2 Sess., p. 531). Because of his moderate views, King failed to be reëlected in 1864 and the triumph of the Radical Republicans eliminated him from politics. He was active in the reorganization of the Democratic party in 1868 and favored a temporary alliance in 1870 with the Liberal Republicans. His successful practice of law was terminated by death, in St. Louis, in 1870.

[King's earlier career can best be traced in the files of the *Missouri Statesman* and the *Jefferson Inquirer.* His official papers and a biographical sketch are contained in *The Messages and Proclamations of the Govs. of the State of Mo.,* vol. II (1922), ed. by Buel Leopard and F. C. Shoemaker. P. O. Ray, *The Repeal of the Mo. Compromise* (1909) and S. B. Harding, "Missouri Party Struggles in the Civil War Period," *Am. Hist. Asso. Ann. Report,* 1900, vol. I, are useful for Missouri party history. See also *Appletons' Ann. Cyc.,* 1870, and the *Biog. Dir. Am. Cong.* (1928).] T. S. B.

KING, BASIL [See KING, WILLIAM BENJAMIN BASIL, 1859–1928].

KING, CHARLES (Mar. 16, 1789–Sept. 27, 1867), merchant, editor, and ninth president of Columbia College, was born in New York City, the second son of Rufus King, 1755–1827 [*q.v.*] and Mary, daughter of John Alsop of New York. When Rufus King went to England as United States minister in 1796, he took his family with him, and Charles and his brother, John Alsop King [*q.v.*], were placed in a school near London, whence they went to Harrow in 1799. Charles remained there from December 1799 until December 1804 (School records), and after a few months at a school in Paris he became a clerk in the banking house of Hope & Company in Amsterdam. In 1806 he returned to New York and entered the mercantile house of Archibald Gracie. On Mar. 16, 1810, he married Gracie's daughter, Eliza, and the same year became a partner in the firm. The War of 1812 found him captain of a regiment of militia in New York City, and though he was actually in service, he consistently opposed the war, especially during his term (1814) in the New York Assembly. Late in 1814 business took him to England, and the following April, when the shooting of some mutinous American prisoners occurred at Dartmoor, he was asked, at the suggestion of Henry Clay and Albert Gallatin, to serve on a commission to investigate the affair. On Apr. 26, 1815, less than three weeks after the massacre, King and Francis Seymour Larpent, the English commissioner, submitted their report (*American State Papers, Foreign Relations,* vol. IV, 1834). While this did not exonerate the English, it was considered too magnanimous in the United States, and was later used against King and his father by politicians.

In 1823, the Gracie firm failed, and King became proprietor and editor of the *New York American;* the same year his wife died, and on Oct. 20, 1826, he married Henrietta Liston Low, daughter of Nicholas Low of New York. King was a scholarly editor and a finished writer, but he lacked sufficient enterprise to make a successful newspaper, and after a long struggle with the penny press, the *American* was united in 1845 with the *Courier and Enquirer,* and King became associate editor with James Watson Webb and Henry J. Raymond [*qq.v.*]. He resigned in 1848, and retired to "Cherry Lawn," his estate at Elizabethtown, N. J. At the time of his retirement, he was one of the most distinguished citizens of New York. He was a valued director of the Bank of New York, a prominent officer of the Chamber of Commerce, a frequent speaker at public ceremonies, and an important figure in the delightful society which Philip Hone has recorded. He was a very handsome man, and his dignity and the perfection of his manners and dress earned him the nickname of "Charles the Pink."

On Nov. 5, 1849, he was elected president of Columbia College, succeeding Nathaniel Fish Moore [*q.v.*]. He was not an "educator," nor was he master of any branch of learning, yet his administration at Columbia was notable. In the spring of 1857 the college was removed from Park Place to Madison Avenue and Forty-ninth Street; the same year, after an extensive investigation, the college curriculum was enlarged and diversified, and a "university course of study," which marked the conscious beginning of Columbia University, was entered upon. The Law School was begun in 1858, the College of Physicians and Surgeons was united with Columbia in 1859, and in 1863 beginnings were made for the School of Mines. During King's presidency the faculty numbered about a dozen and the student body did not greatly exceed a hundred; there was much personal contact between the president and "his boys," and he was greatly beloved for his kindness, sympathy, and unfailing sense of justice. At the age of seventy-five, he resigned, and after a year at Oyster Bay, went abroad with his family and settled in Rome, where his son, Gen. Rufus King [*q.v.*], was United States minister. In the spring of 1867, he had a severe attack of his chronic malady, the gout, and was taken to Frascati, where he died. He wrote and published: *A Memoir of the Construction . . . of the Croton Aqueduct* (1843); "History of the New York Chamber of Commerce," in *Collections of the New York Historical Society* (2 ser., II, 1849); memoirs of John Quincy Adams, James Gore King, and Samuel Ward. He also contributed to the *Outline of a Course of English Reading, Based on That Prepared . . . by the Late Chancellor Kent, with Additions by Charles King . . . Edited with Further Additions and Notes by Henry A. Oakley* (1853). An anonymous volume, *Abridged Tactics for the School of the Soldier and of the Company* (1826) is ascribed to him at the New York Historical Society.

[J. H. Van Amringe in *Columbia Univ. Quart.,* Mar. 1904; Gertrude (King) Schuyler, "A Gentleman of the Old School," *Scribner's Mag.,* May 1914; *N. Y. Times,* Sept. 30, 1867; files of the *New York American;* manuscript minutes of the trustees of Columbia; *Addresses at the Inauguration of Mr. Charles King as President of Columbia Coll.* (1849); W. W. Spooner, *Historic Families of America* (n.d.); C. R. King, *The Life and Correspondence of Rufus King* (6 vols., 1894–1900), *passim;* D. R. Fox, *The Decline of Aristocracy in the Politics of N. Y.* (1918), pp. 180 *et passim;* Bayard Tuckerman, *The Diary of Philip Hone* (2 vols., 1889), *passim.*]
M. H. T.

KING, CHARLES WILLIAM (*c.* 1809–Sept. 27, 1845), merchant in Canton, China, was the third of eight children of Samuel and Harriet (Vernon) King. His father, a son of Samuel King [*q.v.*], was the senior partner of the New York firm of King & Talbot, engaged in the East India trade; his mother was a daughter of Samuel Vernon of Newport, R. I. Charles, the eldest son, studied at Brown University in 1823–25 and went to China in 1826 as an employee of Talbot, Olyphant & Company. With the exception of the years 1839–42, when he was living in New York (New York Directories), his active life was spent in China. For many years he was a partner in the firm of Olyphant & Company (see sketch of D. W. C. Olyphant)

—a firm which had no dealings in opium and which heartily supported Protestant missionary work. He married Charlotte Elizabeth Mathews, daughter of Rev. James McFarlane Mathews, first chancellor of the University of the City of New York, and had two sons and a daughter.

King's broad conception of the place of trade in modern life is shown clearly in an address which he delivered before the Mercantile Library Association in New York City, in which he described commerce as the nurse and companion of freedom, the civilizer and refiner of nations, the disseminator of science and literature, and the herald of religion ("Commerce as a Liberal Pursuit," *Hunt's Merchants' Magazine,* January 1840). His contributions to the *Chinese Repository* during the years 1832–40 give evidence of wide reading and analytical thought. These papers deal with Central and Southeastern Asia, the Philippines and Japan, and analyze in a masterly manner Anglo-Chinese relations prior to the treaty of Nanking. It is doubtful whether any other American of the period visualized as clearly as did King the significance of Eastern Asia.

In the summer of 1837 he attempted to open Japan to intercourse with Americans. Seven shipwrecked Japanese at Macao gave excuse for the expedition. The Olyphant ship *Morrison,* unarmed, carried King and his wife, S. Wells Williams, Peter Parker [*qq.v.*], Charles Gutzlaff, and seven Japanese to Uraga in July. Refused intercourse and having been fired upon, they proceeded to Kagoshima, where they received similar treatment. They then abandoned the enterprise and retired to China. In his "Notes of the Voyage of the *Morrison* from China to Japan" (published in New York, 1839, as volume I of *The Claim of Japan and Malaysia upon Christendom*) King protested against the insult to the United States flag and argued the need for vigorous but friendly action by the United States government in opening Japan to foreign intercourse.

On Mar. 10, 1839, Imperial Commissioner Lin Tse-su arrived in Canton for the purpose of ending the opium traffic. From Mar. 25 to May 4, the foreign merchants were held in the factories pending the settlement of the question. On Mar. 25, King addressed a communication to Lin assuring the latter that he had "never bought, sold, received, or delivered, one catty of opium or one tael of sycee silver," and that he had "used his best efforts to dissuade all men from the injurious traffic" (*Chinese Repository,* April 1839, p. 637). He begged that his business be allowed to proceed undisturbed. Lin replied that he had "heard that the said foreigner King never trafficked in opium; of all he is the most praiseworthy" (*Ibid.*); but that it was impossible to change his "great plans" for the sake of one person. At Chenkow, on June 17, King and his wife and the Rev. Dr. Elijah C. Bridgman [*q.v.*] witnessed the destruction of part of the surrendered opium. Later in the day, despite his refusal to perform the *kotow,* King was received in audience by Lin. Seizing the opportunity to act as a mediator, he urged on Lin a program including the opening to foreign nationals of three ports to the north of Canton, the granting by the imperial government of permission for ministers plenipotentiary to reside in Peking, and the trial of foreign criminal offenders by foreign consuls of the offender's nationality acting jointly with the local native commissioner of justice (*Ibid.,* June 1839, p. 76). The principles motivating King may be summarized as follows: The West has a right to trade freely with the East, but Western policy should be pacific. Consulates should be established; a show of force should be made only as a last resort. Merchants should have nothing to do with opium; missionaries should be aided, since they are the "more appropriate agency which may be relied on, to give the blessings of civil and religious liberty to the whole eastern world." The views here expressed are traceable in the China policy of the United States through the nineteenth century.

In the summer of 1845, broken in health, King left China. He died Sept. 27, on board the *Bentinck,* not far from Aden, and was buried in the Red Sea.

[A pamphlet by King, *British Intercourse with China by a Resident in China* (London, 1836), was noted in the *Chinese Repository,* Oct. 1836, pp. 253–59. *A Gen. Index of Subjects Contained in the Twenty Vols. of the Chinese Repository* (1851) lists the articles by King and contains a comment upon him by the editors, E. C. Bridgman and S. W. Williams. See also H. B. Morse, *International Relations of the Chinese Empire,* vol. I (1910); W. C. Hunter, *The 'Fan Kwae' at Canton before Treaty Days* (London, 1882); K. S. Latourette, "The History of Early Relations between the United States and China," *Trans. Conn. Acad. Arts and Sci.,* vol. XXII (1917); *Chinese Repository,* Nov. 1839, July 1846, July 1851; F. W. Williams, *Life and Letters of Samuel Wells Williams* (1889); G. B. Stevens, *Life, Letters and Journals of the Rev. and Hon. Peter Parker* (1896); *Hist. Cat. of Brown Univ., 1764–1904* (1905); Rufus King, *Pedigree of King, of Lynn, Essex County, Mass.* (1891); G. A. Morrison, Jr., "The King Families of New England" (MS. in Geneal. Div., N. Y. Pub. Lib.), I, 83, under heading "Daniel King Branch of Lynn, Mass."]
H. F. M.

KING, CLARENCE (Jan. 6, 1842–Dec. 24, 1901), geologist, mining engineer, and administrator, was born in Newport, R. I., the only son of James Rives—a brother of Charles William King [*q.v.*]—and his wife Florence (Little)

King. His earliest American ancestor on his father's side was one Daniel King, who came to Lynn, Mass., in 1637 and who in his turn was a younger son of Ralphe Kinge of Watford, Hertfordshire, England. Clarence received his elementary education at the Hopkins Grammar School in Hartford, Conn., but when still young was taken by his widowed mother to New Haven, where, in 1859, he entered the Yale Scientific School. He is described at this time as having the same bright face, winning smile, and agile movement that characterized his later life. At Yale he came under the influence of Prof. J. D. Dana, George J. Brush [*qq.v.*] and others, and graduated in 1862 with the degree of B.S.

From early boyhood he had shown a taste for the sciences which his associations at New Haven could but have increased. In May 1863, in company with James T. Gardiner [*q.v.*], a geologist, he started on a horseback trip across the continent, joining at St. Joseph an emigrant family with which they continued as far as the noted Comstock Lode in Nevada. Here they remained to study the mine, their stay being unintentionally prolonged by a fire which caused the loss of their entire equipment, thus compelling them to seek employment at the mine until they had accumulated sufficient capital to continue their journey. They crossed the Sierras on foot, and went down the Sacramento by boat to San Francisco. While on this trip, King formed the acquaintance of W. H. Brewer [*q.v.*], an assistant of the geological survey of California under J. D. Whitney [*q.v.*]. This resulted in his volunteering his own services with the same organization, and remaining with it for nearly three years, his duties being largely exploratory. During the winter of 1865–66 he also was engaged as a scientific assistant or aid, under General McDowell, in an exploration of the desert region of Southern California. In the autumn of 1866, after his return east, King brought to maturity a plan he had been brooding for a survey entirely across the Cordilleran ranges from eastern Colorado to the Californian boundary. So favorably did he impress Congress with his plan that the necessary appropriations were granted, and King placed in charge, subject only to the administrative control of Gen. A. A. Humphreys [*q.v.*]. Upon this work, with a corps of geologists, King was engaged until 1877, although the field work was for the most part completed in 1873. It comprised an area about a hundred miles in width, extending from eastern Colorado along the line of the fortieth parallel to the California line. The published results of the survey, filling seven large quarto volumes, reached perhaps the highest standard yet attained by governmental publications (*Report of the Geological Exploration of the Fortieth Parallel,* 1870–80). The sixth volume includes a description by F. Zirkel of Leipzig of the microscopic structure of the igneous rocks, thus introducing into American literature the newly evolved science of micropetrology. The third volume, "Mining Industry," by J. D. Hague [*q.v.*], is still considered a classic in its line, and has served as a model for others. The popularity of western surveys had now become so great that four independent parties, each under governmental auspices, were in the field. More or less rivalry and overlapping was inevitable, and in 1878 a complete readjustment by Congress resulted in the establishment of a single organization, the United States Geological Survey, with Clarence King at its head. Having accepted the position with the understanding that he would remain only to appoint the staff and start the activity, he resigned in 1881 to enter private practice as a mining engineer.

King's services to geology lay as much in his far-sighted administrative ability as in the technical quality of his writings. His standards of work were of the highest and he was the first to introduce into mapping the system of denoting topography by contour lines worked out by Hoffmann. His "Systematic Geology," the first volume of the series of reports, was masterly, and no more thrilling picture of the growth of the Cordilleran country has ever been written than is there given. He was among the first, moreover, to make extensive use of the laboratory in the solution of geophysical problems. Among his latest publications is a paper on the age of the earth (*Smithsonian Institution: Annual Report for 1893;* and *American Journal of Science,* January 1893), based upon the rate of cooling of molten magmas as determined in a laboratory he had fitted with the essential details for the work at his own expense.

His writings are not numerous. Aside from the report mentioned, a considerable portion of which was prepared by others under his direction, his "Catastrophism and Evolution" (*American Naturalist,* August 1877), and "The Age of the Earth" (*supra*) are the most important of his scientific contributions. The fact should not be overlooked, however, that from early youth King had shown literary qualities of a high order, and it has always been a source of regret among his friends that he left so little evidence of it. A most delightful conversationalist and raconteur, he seemed averse to putting his thoughts on paper. A series of sketches appearing first in the *Atlantic Monthly* and afterward in book form, under the caption of *Mountaineering in the Sierra Nevada* (1872), and his "Helmet of Mambrino" in the form of a letter to his friend "Don Horacio" (Horace F. Cutter) in San Francisco, published in the *Century Magazine,* May 1886, serve but to show his latent capability.

King was not a large man, but was remarkably robust and capable of great endurance when occasion demanded. Notwithstanding this fact, he was subject to sudden and serious breakdowns. An injury to his spine caused, it is thought, by a kick from his saddle animal, gave him much trouble. He lost heavily in the business depression of 1893, had an attack of nervous prostration, and was for some months in 1893–94 mentally incapacitated and confined in Bloomingdale Asylum. In 1901 he suffered an attack of pneumonia and tuberculosis ensued. Though one of the most companionable and charming of men, with scores of friends, among whom may be mentioned Henry Adams, John Hay, John La Farge, William Dean Howells, and more of his own professional calling, he steadfastly refused to allow them to be inconvenienced by his illness and died almost alone in far-off Arizona. He never married. Honors came to him, though in no way commensurate with his merits. He was remarkably unobtrusive and never sought them. He was a member of the National Academy of Sciences, the American Institute of Mining Engineers, and the Geological Society of London, but rarely attended or took part in their meetings.

[Rufus King, *Pedigree of King, of Lynn, Essex County, Mass. 1602–1891* (copr. 1891); *Clarence King Memoirs. The Helmet of Mambrino* (1904), by the King Memorial Committee of the Century Asso., N. Y.; S. F. Emmons, "Clarence King, A Memorial," *Engineering & Mining Jour.*, Jan. 4, 1902, and *Am. Jour. of Sci.*, Mar. 1902; *Nat. Acad. Sci. Biog. Memoirs*, vol. VI (1909); Henry Adams, *The Education of Henry Adams* (1918), *passim;* Worthington C. Ford, *The Letters of Henry Adams* (1930), *passim;* W. R. Thayer, *The Life and Letters of John Hay* (1915), *passim.*]

G. P. M.

KING, DAN (Jan. 27, 1791–Nov. 13, 1864), physician, pamphleteer, was born in Mansfield, Conn., the son of John and Jane (Knight) King. As a youth, and against his father's will, he entered the family of Dr. Adams of Mansfield as a medical student. Matriculating at the Yale Medical School in 1814, and receiving his license in the following year, he began practice at Brewster's Neck, Conn. In 1816 he married Cynthia Pride, by whom he had eleven children. Early in his career he removed to Charlestown, R. I., where he eked out his professional income by manufacturing "nigger cloth" at King's Mill. Owing to fire and financial ruin he removed in 1841 to Woonsocket, R. I., where he practised till 1848, then he proceeded to Taunton, Mass. In 1852 the Berkshire Medical Institution conferred upon him an honorary degree of M.D. In 1859 he retired to Pawtuxet, R. I., but during the Civil War he carried on his son's practice.

For a time King was representative from Charlestown in the General Assembly and, as such, in 1833, with Benjamin B. Thurston, presented an important paper on the Narraganset Indians. He took a prominent and aggressive part in the Suffrage movement and in 1837 was nominated, with Thomas Wilson Dorr, for Congress as standard-bearer of the party. His first medical papers were contributed chiefly to the *Boston Medical and Surgical Journal,* but his main interest lay in the exposition of ethical subjects in that and other publications. He was fearless and uncompromising in his opinions, whether spoken or written, never sacrificing strong conviction to timid expediency. "While all his life long he had the esteem of the community and the high respect of his professional fellows, he never was successful as a man of business, either within the limits of his profession or without" (*Biographical Sketches of Dan King and His Sons,* p. 6).

He was a prolific writer. In 1857 he published *Spiritualism: An Address, to the Bristol County Medical Society,* and the following year he wrote *Quackery Unmasked,* which, while in the main an indictment of homeopathy, was also an eloquent plea for higher standards of medical education. *Tobacco, What It Is, and What It Does* (1861) was a tirade against a "useless and pernicious habit," under whose "depressing influence the scale of intellect has fallen, and all the proud traits of honor, benevolence, and self-sacrificing heroism have been lost" (p. 155). His most important literary work was *The Life and Times of Thomas Wilson Dorr* (1859), which preserves the history of the struggle and progress of the Suffrage movement in Rhode Island, as seen and understood by a participant. He was a stanch Unionist and anti-slavery man, but he opposed conscription and is credited with having written *The Draft, or Conscription Reviewed by the People* (1863). Naturally the activities and opinions of so implacable a protagonist often ran counter to public sentiment, but he never forfeited the respect and affection of the community in which he lived. When, for example, during the Dorr War, he was arrested and brought into prison, the officer in charge immediately released him. Frequently he suffered the trials and tribulations of a man of ideal principle who is obliged, in the pursuit of that ideal to have contact in politics with the practical man of affairs.

[E. P. and Henry King, *Biog. Sketches of Dr. Dan King and His Sons* (1892); B. H. Chace, *A Discourse Commemorative of the Life and Services of the Late Dr. Dan King, . . . Nov. 14, 1864* (1865); *Representative Men and Old Families of R. I.* (1908), vol. III.]

G. A. B—r.

KING, EDWARD SKINNER (May 31, 1861–Sept. 10, 1931), astronomer, was born in Liverpool, N. Y., the son of Nathaniel and Cornelia C. (Skinner) King. From his paternal ancestors he inherited a scholarly tradition. In 1887 he received the degree of B.A. from Hamilton College, having distinguished himself in mathematics during his college days. Dr. C. H. F. Peters, then professor of astronomy at Hamilton College, realizing the quality of his student, sent him in 1887 to Professor Pickering, director of the Harvard Observatory. Pickering found in the diffident young man a person who could undertake responsibility, and within two years King was in charge of the Harvard observing station near the summit of Mount Wilson, California. In 1890, on his return from the Mount Wilson station, he was married to Kate Irene Colson, of Batchellerville, N. Y., and with her he shared the remainder of his days. The first few years of his married life were clouded by his failing sight, but in 1893 he was able to return to his temporarily suspended duties at the Harvard Observatory.

Under King's hands, two extensive programs of work were undertaken in the early nineties, the standard testing of all photographic plates used, and the photographic photometry of astronomical objects on a uniform scale. The standard testing of photographic plates was carried on continuously for forty years. In addition to providing valuable specific information about the plates used, this work made King master of a wealth of knowledge about photographic method. Some of the fruits of the experience of forty years are stored in his *Manual of Celestial Photography* (1931), following some years after his *Photographic Photometry* (1912). King's work abounds in ingenious methods, some of them leading to important results. He was the first to photograph the spectrum of the aurora borealis, and his photographic device for the observation of occultations is remarkable in its simplicity. He was also an independent discoverer of the Hartmann-Cornu formula, although he did not publish his results until long after Hartmann had done so. Better known perhaps are his determinations of the apparent magnitudes of the sun, moon, and earth. His determinations of the brightness of the lucid stars will long be standard, though they were among the first contributions to a branch of astronomy notoriously difficult of conquest.

The lifetime of scientific work did not go unrecognized. King was successively observer (1887–1913), assistant profesor (1913–26), and Phillips Professor (1926–31) at the Harvard Observatory. He practically lived out his life in office, surviving his resignation but ten days. He was a fellow of the American Academy of Arts and Sciences, a member of the American Astronomical Society and the Société Astronomique de France, an honorary member of the Maria Mitchell Association, and a member of Phi Beta Kappa. Among his colleagues King moved as a very individual figure, profoundly faithful to his work, and intensely loyal to the Observatory. As an avocation, he delighted in old books, of which he had an interesting collection. The discovery of a common interest in such matters caused him to drop his more usual diffident manner, and to appear as a delightful raconteur. The greater part of his contributions to science are to be found in the annals, circulars, and bulletins of the Harvard Observatory, where he published a large number of papers of a fundamental nature. He also did great service by his popular writing, published usually in the more ephemeral periodicals, but always distinguished by the fine style and punctilious care that were characteristic of all his work.

[*Who's Who in America*, 1928–29; S. I. Bailey, *The Hist. and Work of Harvard Observatory* (1931); the *Boston Transcript* and *N. Y. Times*, Sept. 11, 1931; *Science*, Oct. 16, 1931; personal acquaintance and information as to certain facts from Mrs. Edward Skinner King.]

C. H. P.

KING, EDWARD SMITH (Sept. 8, 1848–Mar. 27, 1896), journalist, and author, was born at Middlefield, Mass., the son of Edward and Lorinda (Smith) King. When he was about three years old his father, a Methodist minister, disappeared while on a sea trip to recover his health. His mother then taught school until about 1860 when she moved to Huntington, Mass., and there married Samuel W. Fisher, a clergyman who abandoned the ministry and became a teacher and paper-mill worker. After being educated by his step-father, King began work in a factory, but at sixteen he left home, went to Springfield, and became a reporter on the *Springfield Daily Union.* Two years later he joined the staff of the *Springfield Republican* which he served until 1870 as reporter, subeditor, and editorial writer. He was sent to the Paris exposition in 1867 and while there gathered materials for his first book, *My Paris* (1868), an account of Parisian life seen through youthful and romantic eyes. When he went to the *Boston Morning Journal* in 1870, he returned to France to cover the Franco-Prussian War and the events of the Commune. He was adventurous, was twice arrested as a spy by the Germans, served as an emergency nurse to the wounded at Frankfort, and claimed and cared for the bodies of Americans killed in the street fighting of the Commune. These experiences were exploited in his first novel, *Kentucky's Love* (1873), which involved a group of war correspondents, and later in *Under the Red Flag* (1895), a story for boys laid in Paris in the days of the Commune.

After Dr. J. G. Holland, of the *Springfield Republican,* became editor of *Scribner's Monthly,* he invited King to travel through the southern states and gather materials for a series of articles on the effects of the Civil War, the economic promise of the South, and interesting features of its landscape and social life. This tour extended into 1874, and the articles published in *Scribner's,* illustrated by J. Wells Champney, appeared in book form as *The Great South* (1875). This was twice reprinted in the same year in England as *The Southern States of North America.* In New Orleans he met George W. Cable and read some of his short stories. Through King's interest Cable's stories began to appear in *Scribner's,* and an enduring friendship grew up between them (L. L. C. Bikle, *George W. Cable,* 1928, 45–47). In 1875 he returned to Europe as correspondent to the *Boston Morning Journal,* with his headquarters at Paris, but made visits to America for the Philadelphia world's fair in 1876 and the opening of the Northern Pacific Railroad in 1883. He went to Spain to report the Carlist Wars and to the Balkans for the Russo-Turkish War of 1877–78. In 1876 appeared his *French Political Leaders,* with an introduction explaining the make-up of the National Assembly. His first volume of verse, *Echoes from the Orient* (1880), included poetical sketches of Balkan scenes and people, with some lyrics. This was followed by a novel, *The Gentle Savage* (1883), in which an Oklahoma Indian is placed against a background of European sophistication. Utilizing many of his newspaper articles, he pieced together a large book, *Europe in Storm and Calm* (1885), which described European life and events to the untraveled American. King was popular in American circles in Paris, where he founded the Stanley Club and was secretary of the *Société de Gens de Lettres.* After 1885 he became involved in a disastrous business venture, which burdened him with heavy debts. In 1886 *The Golden Spike* was published, a feeble novel in which the opening of the Northern Pacific Railroad and the scenery of the Northwest supply the background and chief interest. He then returned to poetry in *A Venetian Lover* (1887), a narrative in decorous blank verse interspersed with many pleasing lyrics.

Still harassed by business troubles, he returned to America in 1888 and served as editorial writer on the New York *Morning Journal* and on *Collier's Once a Week.* In 1893 he went to Chicago to write articles on the world's fair. In the same year appeared his best novel, *Joseph Zalmonah,* which exposed the conditions of the masses in the slums and sweatshops of New York. In addition to articles and correspondence, he published many stories and poems in his newspapers. He also compiled *Cassell's Complete Pocket Guide to Europe* (1891 and later editions), contributed four chapters to an elegant travel book, *On the Rhine* (1881), and wrote a biographical and critical introduction to M. French Sheldon's *Salammbô of Gustave Flaubert* (1885). Although all of his books were written primarily for money, he was ambitious to write good poetry. At his death he left in manuscript a number of poems which his friends praised as his best work. King never married. He lived with his half-sister and her husband, John McGhie, in Brooklyn. After a short illness, he died Mar. 27, 1896, and was buried at Bridgeport, Conn. He was described as a simple, dignified man, with a restrained and gentle manner.

[*Evening Post* (N. Y.), Mar. 28, 1896; *Springfield Republican, Morning Jour.* (N. Y.), and *N. Y. Times,* Mar. 29, 1896; E. C. and P. M. Smith, *A Hist. of the Town of Middlefield, Mass.* (1924); *Vital Records of Middlefield, Mass., to the Year 1850* (1907).]

R. W. B.

KING, FRANKLIN HIRAM (June 8, 1848–Aug. 4, 1911), agricultural scientist, was the son of Edmund King and Deborah (Loomer) King. His paternal ancestors were Green Mountain folk, and from them he inherited great physical energy and strength of mind. His mother, a Nova Scotian, gave him his love of the out-of-doors and an ability to express his thoughts in pure and simple English. Born on a farm near Whitewater, Wis., in the days when the state was frontier land, the boy grew up in an environment which developed his natural seriousness of purpose and a thoroughness in whatever he did. From the time he was seven until he was nineteen, his education was obtained chiefly from experience on the farm. Then he attended Whitewater Normal School, at that time a newly opened institution, where he was instructed by Thomas C. Chamberlin [*q.v.*], who later became president of the University of Wisconsin. Under his personal guidance, King's real interest in science began.

The years 1873 to 1876 were spent in teaching science in high school at Berlin, Wis. There he published *A Scheme for Plant Analysis* (1875), which was afterwards incorporated in Wood's botanies. At Berlin he married in 1880 Carrie H. Baker. To her untiring devotion and interest in his work much of his later scientific success was due, and he never failed to acknowledge this debt.

Under Chamberlain, King had worked for a time on the state geological survey. During this period, he also made a study of the economics of bird life in the northern woods. This led to two years' study at Cornell University, where he worked under the well-known entomologist, Comstock. At Cornell, he examined the stomachs of more than 2,000 birds, determining what insects formed part of their diet. He also spent a great deal of time in the study of physics, chemistry, biology, and geology. Returning to Wisconsin in 1878, he taught science for ten years in the River Falls Normal School, his summers being used for further study. It was during this period that he and his wife prepared relief models and maps of the continents to be used for instruction in physiography and meteorology. In this work King was a pioneer. In 1888, he was called to the Wisconsin College of Agriculture to occupy the chair of agricultural physics, the first to be established in the United States. In this field, his contributions to agriculture were varied and valuable. His most important contributions to farm life were the construction of the round silo, a new method of barn ventilation, and his studies of soil solution. Other important studies which he made included the water requirement of crops, the protection of sandy soils from wind erosion, and original work in irrigation and drainage. His books present the results of his researches in an interesting and a permanent way. *The Soil* was written in 1895, *Irrigation and Drainage* in 1899, *A Textbook of the Physics of Agriculture* in 1900, and *Ventilation for Dwellings, Rural Schools and Stables,* in 1908. His findings are also recorded in bulletins of the Wisconsin Experiment Station, in publications of the United States Department of Agriculture and the United States Geological Survey, and in encyclopedia and periodical articles. *The Soil* has been translated into Chinese and is widely read in China. His interest in birds led him to give considerable attention to popular nature study. He wrote many articles for educational journals under the headings, "Our Observations on Birds," "By the Wayside," and others. The results of his bird study were also published under the title, "Economic Relations of Wisconsin Birds," in *Geology of Wisconsin: Survey of 1873–79* (vol. I, pt. 2, 1883).

From 1901 to 1904, he was chief of the division of soil management of the United States Bureau of Soils. Then he retired from this office to write and to travel. As a result of his journeys in China, Korea, and Japan, he wrote *Farmers of Forty Centuries* (1911), which came from the press just after his death. This book is his outstanding work, for it is the most detailed and accurate account of soil management and methods of maintaining soil fertility in the Orient which has yet been written. His most remarkable mental characteristics were his scientific honesty and accuracy, his open-minded search for truth, his keen powers of observation, and his ability to apply science to the practical problems of agriculture.

[L. S. Ivins and A. E. Winship, *Fifty Famous Farmers* (1924); R. G. Thwaites, *The Univ. of Wis.* (1900); *Wis. Alumni Mag.*, Nov. 1901; *Who's Who in America,* 1908–09; *Madison Democrat,* Aug. 6, 1911; information from Mrs. King and from acquaintances.]

W. A. S.

KING, GRACE ELIZABETH (Nov. 29, 1851–Jan. 14, 1932), author, was the third child and eldest daughter of William Woodson and Sarah Ann (Miller) King, the former a successful New Orleans lawyer, the latter, "a charming *raconteuse,*" the daughter of a lawyer, Branch Walthus Miller. Though not a Creole, her parents being English, Scotch, and Irish, with one Huguenot ancestress on the mother's side, Grace King was born in New Orleans and received her education there. After the age of governesses and the home instruction of the four war years passed on a plantation, she attended the old French *Institut St. Louis* described in her "Monsieur Motte." She then became a pupil of the Misses Cenas, and to the instruction of Miss Héloise Cenas she attributed her success as a writer. Excellent tutors followed, and to French and English, languages in use at home, she added German and Spanish. She read widely, and her first appearance in print, in 1885, was as the author of an essay on "Heroines of Fiction," German, French, English, and American.

Her first story, "Monsieur Motte," appeared in the *New Princeton Review* for January 1886. Written in consequence of a remark by Richard Watson Gilder to the effect that readers dissatisfied with the Creole stories of George W. Cable should attempt to better them, it endeavored to correct what its author believed to be a false impression of her fellow citizens, both white and black. This story and three others were published as *Monsieur Motte* in 1888. About the same time *Lippincott's Monthly Magazine* accepted a novelette, "Earthlings," and *Harper's* and the *Century Magazine* the first of many short stories. The books that followed were *Tales of a Time and Place* (1892), New Orleans after the war; *Jean Baptiste le Moyne, Sieur de Bienville* (1892), in the Makers of America Series; *Balcony Stories* (1893), first published in the *Century Magazine; A History of Louisiana* (1893), a school book written in collaboration with John R. Ficklen; *New Orleans, the Place and the People* (1895); *De Soto and His Men in the Land of Florida* (1898); *Stories from Louisiana History* (1905), with J. R. Ficklen; *The Pleasant Ways of St. Médard* (1916), a novel of reconstruction days in New Orleans; *Creole Families of New Orleans* (1921); *Madame Girard, an Old French Teacher of New Orleans* (1922), reprinted from the *Yale Review; La Dame de Sainte Hermine* (1924), a novel; and *The History of Mt. Vernon on the Potomac* (1929). Her *Memories of a Southern Woman of Letters* was prepared for publication just before her death.

Besides writing the books mentioned and also much that has not been reprinted, Miss King served for many years as secretary of the Louisiana Historical Society and as one of the editors of its *Quarterly*. She was also active in many social, cultural, and philanthropic organizations. At home she discoursed wittily and with humor, and endeared herself to each new generation of writers by her appreciation of their accomplishments and her understanding of their problems. To the people of New Orleans she became a symbol of their culture, the best representative of their city's charm and hospitality. Her literary work, never extravagantly praised, received commendation for its sincerity, its sensitive observation, and a quality of style, more French than English, which was at once an expression of personality and appropriate to the matters described. The recipient of many tokens of admiration and affection from her own people, she was also a fellow of the Royal Society of Arts and Letters (1913) and an *Officier de l'Instruction Publique* (1915).

[Biographical information was obtained from *Memories of a Southern Woman of Letters* (1932) and from members of the King family. Printed sources include: *Who's Who in America*, 1930–31; C. W. Coleman, Jr., "The Recent Movement in Southern Literature," *Harper's New Monthly Mag.*, May 1887; T. Bentzon, "Les Romanciers du Sud en Amerique," *Revue des Deux Mondes*, Apr. 1893; D. A. Dondore, *The Prairie and the Making of Middle America* (1926); Edward Garnett, "A Gossip on Criticism," *Atlantic Monthly*, Feb. 1916; F. L. Pattee, *The Development of the Am. Short Story* (1923), and *Century Readings in the Am. Short Story* (1927); *Lib. of Southern Lit.*, vol. VII (1909); *La. Hist. Quart.*, July 1923, Apr. 1932; the *Bookman*, Aug. 1932; the *Times-Picayune*, Jan. 15, 1932.]

R. R. K.

KING, HENRY (May 11, 1842–Mar. 15, 1915), journalist, was born in Salem, Ohio, the son of Selah W. and Eliza (Aleshire) King. In childhood he went with his parents to Illinois, where he learned the printer's trade. His father was a delegate to the Bloomington convention of 1856, at which Lincoln delivered his famous "lost speech." Young Henry accompanied his father on that occasion and was permanently impressed by Lincoln's sincerity. For a time he edited and published a weekly newspaper in his home town, Laharpe. At the outbreak of the Civil War he went from town to town in Illinois exhorting the citizens to enlist in the Union cause, becoming known locally as "the boy orator." He himself served four years in the Union army, attaining the rank of captain, a title which he always bore. After the war he engaged in business and studied law, but soon joined the staff of a Quincy, Ill., newspaper, of which he became editor. In 1869 he went to Topeka, Kan., where he edited in turn the *Kansas State Record*, the *Weekly Commonwealth*, and the *Topeka Daily Capital*. While with the *Capital*, he contributed historical and literary articles to the *Century* and other leading monthlies, writing, among other things, reminiscences of the Lincoln campaigns. He was for a time editor of the *Kansas Magazine*, a periodical devoted to the literature of the West, particularly of the young state of Kansas. In 1883 he joined the staff of the *St. Louis Globe-Democrat* as editorial writer and became its editor in 1897. He declined an appointment as United States senator from Missouri offered him by the Republican governor of the state, declaring that a newspaper editor should not sacrifice his influence with the public or limit his independence by becoming an office holder. He made the *Globe-Democrat* a great conservative force in American journalism, attracting to it also some of the most brilliant Western writers. Its Sunday edition had an especially high literary character. Personally one of the most lovable of men, he was constantly on the alert to help younger folk. The door of the *Globe-Democrat's* editorial room was literally open at all times to youthful, aspiring journalists. Once, in Topeka, he wrote editorials for the editor of a rival paper who was ill, some of them bitter attacks on his own paper. He was much interested in education for journalism and delivered the first lecture in a series preparatory to the establishment of a school of journalism at the University of Missouri. He remained editor of the *Globe-Democrat* until three weeks before his death, which was due to chronic bronchitis. He was buried at Laharpe, Ill., beside his wife, Maria Louise Lane, whom he married Nov. 17, 1861. They had two children. He was first president of the Missouri Republican Editorial Association, and head of the World's Press Parliament at the Louisiana Purchase Centennial Exposition. Among his writings are: *American Journalism* (1871), an address delivered before the Editors' and Publishers' Association of Kansas, and "The Story of Kansas and Kansas Newspapers," contributed to the *History of Kansas Newspapers* (1916), published by the Kansas State Historical Society.

[J. W. Leonard, *The Book of St. Louisans* (1906); *Who's Who in America,* 1914–15; biog. sketch in *Hist. of Kansas Newspapers* (1916); *St. Louis Globe-Democrat,* Mar. 16, 1915; *St. Louis Republic,* Mar. 16, 1915; *St. Louis Post-Despatch,* Feb. 27, Mar. 16, 1915; *Kansas City Times,* Mar. 16, 1915; *Kansas City Jour.,* Mar. 16, 1915.]

W. W.

KING, HENRY MELVILLE (Sept. 3, 1838–June 16, 1919), Baptist clergyman, was born in Oxford, Me., the son of Samuel Hall and Eliza (Shaw) King. Through his mother he was a descendant in the eighth generation from John Alden of Plymouth, and through another maternal line, a descendant of Francis Eaton, also of the Mayflower group. He was graduated from Bowdoin College in 1859 and from Newton Theological Institution in 1862. Called to an instructorship in Hebrew in the latter, he was ordained to the Baptist ministry, Aug. 28, 1862, and on Sept. 2 of that year married Susan Ellen Fogg of Portland, who lived until Oct. 21, 1901. Before the end of his first year as instructor, he began, Apr. 1, 1863, a pastorate of almost nineteen years at the Dudley Street Church, Roxbury, a town annexed to Boston in 1868, declining calls to important educational and missionary tasks. From Jan. 1, 1882, to June 1891, he served the Emmanuel Baptist Church, Albany, N. Y. For the rest of his life he was pastor of the First Baptist Church, Providence, R. I., becoming *emeritus* in 1906. Through most of this time, he held a position of eminence in his denomination. He was for many years on the boards of control of the three oldest Baptist seminaries in the North (Colgate, Newton, Rochester), and also trustee of Brown University, Vassar College, and other educational institutions. His interest in foreign missions was strong and persistent; he was long a member of the executive committee of the American Baptist Missionary Union and served as chairman of its board of managers.

During his pastorates, he gave many addresses at important religious meetings and he contributed voluminously to the religious press. His literary work, including articles in the *Christian Era* under the pseudonym "Ephraim Plaintalk," was largely ethical and theological in interest until he commenced his pastorate in Providence. Here he began those historical studies which are likely to be the most enduring part of his literary production. In his theological writings and preaching he expressed strong convictions and was reckoned among the dogmatists. He never intentionally misstated, but was sometimes the advocate rather than the judge in appreciation and emphasis. He was assiduous in search for materials, but failed to see the bearing of some evidence, and he had a tendency to swing the argument from silence to serve the desired end. Much of his interpretation, however, must be taken into account until more positive evidence appears. The history of his own church in Providence received his primary attention, and closely connected with that, the status of Roger Williams. Perhaps his most constructive historical study is *A Summer Visit of Three Rhode Islanders to the Massachusetts Bay in 1651* (1896). Other important historical writings are *The Mother Church* (1896); *The Baptism of Roger Williams; A Review of Dr. Whitsitt's Inference* (1897); and a biographical sketch, *Sir Henry Vane, Jr.* (1909).

[*Who's Who in America,* 1918–19; *Providence Daily Jour.,* June 17, 1919; sketch by the necrologist of Newton Theological Institution for 1919 (M. F. Johnson) and scrapbooks compiled by King, all in the library of the Newton Theological Institution; data provided by a grandson, Osborne Earle, Cambridge, Mass.]

W. H. A.

KING, HORATIO (June 21, 1811–May 20, 1897), editor, lawyer, postmaster-general, was born at Paris, Me., a descendant of Philip King, who had emigrated from England before 1680, settling first at Braintree, and then at Raynham, Mass. A farmer's boy, the seventh of the eleven children of Samuel and Sally (Hall) King, Horatio received a common school education and at eighteen became printer's devil on the weekly *Jeffersonian* of which, in the following year (1830) with his friend, Hannibal Hamlin, he became part owner. Horatio and Hannibal turned the press while the village schoolmaster for twelve York shillings a week assisted in the editing. In another six months King became sole proprietor. His paper reflected his stanch advocacy of Jacksonian Democracy. Removing his press to Portland in 1833 he continued to edit the *Jeffersonian* until 1838, when he sold out to the *Standard* (later merged with the *Eastern Argus*). In 1839 he received from Amos Kendall a clerkship at $1,000 a year in the Post Office Department at Washington.

For twenty-two years, under Democratic and Whig administrations, from Van Buren to Lincoln, he served in the Post Office Department and by ability and courtesy advanced in successive promotions until he achieved the distinction of rising from clerk to head of department. In charge of mail contracts in New England (1841) he became superintendent (1850) of the foreign mail service, and was instrumental in improving the existing postal conventions with Bremen and Great Britain, and extending the service to the West Indies, South American countries, France, Prussia, Hamburg, and Belgium. The convention with Bremen (1853) inaugurated cheap transatlantic postage. As first assistant postmaster-general (Mar. 28, 1854–Jan. 1, 1861) under Pierce and Buchanan, he satisfactorily filled a position which required infinite political tact. He became acting postmaster-general (January 1861), when Joseph Holt was transferred to the War Department, and served as postmaster-general in Buchanan's cabinet from Feb. 1 to Mar. 8, 1861.

"For the Union without reservations, equally against disunionists at the South and abolitionists at the North" (*Turning on the Light,* p. 51), King made earnest efforts during the last days of Buchanan's administration to arouse influential men on both sides to avert the impending struggle. In what has been termed the first official denial of the right of secession, he warned Representative J. D. Ashmore of South Carolina (Jan. 28, 1861) that his continued use of the franking privilege was evidence that both he and his state were still in the Union. "For God's sake," he implored Attorney-General Black (Dec. 14, 1860), "let us see the Government placed squarely and unequivocally on the side of the Union!" (*Ibid.,* p. 34). To John A. Dix, later through his efforts made secretary of the treasury, he wrote (Dec. 17, 1860): "I am determined to sustain the Union until not a hope of its continuance remains" (*Ibid.,* p. 35). He remained a loyal Union Democrat throughout the war and served on President Lincoln's commission which determined compensation for slaves emancipated within the District of Columbia.

King's law practice before the executive departments, war claims, and international commissions at Washington won him wealth and a considerable reputation. One of Washington's foremost citizens for thirty-five years, he was secretary of the Washington Monument society, a leader of the Saturday Evening Literary Club which met at his home, and a frequent contributor to newspapers and magazines on political, historical, and literary subjects. His tours of Europe (1867, 1875–76) resulted in his *Sketches of Travel* (1878), and his letters in rhyme delighted a wide circle of friends. Late in life he published *Turning on the Light* (1895), a defense of Buchanan's administration. He was ever active in postal affairs, drafting the law requiring prepayment on transient printed matter, and devoting seven years of "vexatious, gratuitous labor" until, by the act of July 5, 1884, the economical and efficient device of the official "penalty envelope" was adopted. King was married, on May 25, 1835, to Anne Collins of Portland. She died in 1869 and on Feb. 8, 1875, he was married to Isabella G. Osborne, of Auburn, N. Y. He died in Washington in his eighty-fifth year.

[In addition to King's books mentioned in the biography, see Horatio C. King, *Horatio King* (n.d.); *Centennial Lit. Reunion at the Residence of Horatio King* (Washington, 1884); Enoch Sanford, *Geneal. of the Families of Kings* (1866); *Evening Star* (Washington), May 20, 1897. The Horatio King Papers are in the Manuscript Division of the Lib. of Cong.]

B. M.

KING, JAMES GORE (May 8, 1791–Oct. 3, 1853), financier, the third son of Rufus King, 1755–1827 [*q.v.*], and Mary (Alsop) King, and brother of Charles and John Alsop King [*qq.v.*], was born in New York City. Several years of his boyhood were passed in London while his father was minister to the Court of St. James's. Between the ages of seven and ten he was a student in a London boarding school. One of his masters at this period called him a "prodigy in learning" (*Life and Correspondence of Rufus King, post,* vol. III, p. 50). For three years he was in a Paris school, chiefly for the purpose of acquiring the French language. Returning to America, he was tutored for Harvard by the Rev. Dr. J. S. J. Gardiner, rector of Trinity Church, Boston. He was graduated from Harvard in 1810 at the age of nineteen and began reading law with the well-known jurist, Peter Van Schaick, of Kinderhook, N. Y., continuing his studies at the famous Litchfield, Conn., school under Tapping Reeve and James Gould.

In the War of 1812 he left the legal profession to serve as assistant adjutant-general of militia. At the end of the war he opened a commission house in New York, which he conducted with moderate success for three years. In 1818 he established in Liverpool the house of King & Gracie and remained as senior partner in that enterprise until 1824. He was then asked by John Jacob Astor to become manager of the American Fur Company, but declined. He accepted, however, a partnership in the New York banking house of Prime, Ward & Sands, beginning thus a long and successful career as a banker. His interests and activities extended beyond Wall Street. In 1835 he was made president of the New York & Erie Railroad and served until 1839. The road was then making its first surveys westward from the Hudson River to Lake Erie. The first construction work on the line was done in King's administration, but was stopped by the financial stringency that began in 1836 and continued for over two years. King's business reputation helped to get needed support for the enterprise. In the panic of 1837, when specie payments were suspended, he was able to render an unusual service to the financial interests, not of New York only but of the country at large. Going to London, he persuaded the officials of the Bank of England to loan £1,000,000 sterling (with the guaranty of Baring Brothers) to be distributed among the New York banks. The consignment was made to Prime, Ward & King and the responsibility for handling the money fell chiefly to the junior partner. So wisely was the apportionment made that the operation was a complete success, resulting in the resumption of specie payments in May 1838, with prompt repayment of the loan to the Bank of England. King's repeated election as president of the New York Chamber of Commerce is some indication of his standing in the business community during that period, and the frequent references to him in Philip Hone's diary represent him as a leading spirit in the select social circles that foregathered on Manhattan Island in the early nineteenth century.

Meanwhile, King, with his brothers, had become interested in Whig politics, and having established a residence in New Jersey, where he had a home on the heights of Weehawken, he was elected to Congress in 1848. He served only one term, as a minority member of the House, his brother John holding a New York seat at the same time. He voted against the fugitive slave bill and the other compromise measures of 1850, and did what he could to uphold the Taylor administration. On Feb. 4, 1813, he married Sarah Rogers Gracie, daughter of Archibald Gracie, and sister of Eliza, his brother Charles's wife. She with four daughters and three sons survived him.

[W. W. Spooner, *Historic Families of America* (n.d.); E. H. Mott, *Between the Ocean and the Lakes, The Story of the Erie* (1899); Chas. King, "James Gore King," in *Hunt's Merchants' Mag.*, Jan. 1854, reprinted in Freeman Hunt, *Lives of Am. Merchants* (1858), vol. I; J. A. Scoville, *The Old Merchants of N. Y.*, vols. I–III (1863–65); *The Life and Correspondence of Rufus King* (6 vols., 1894–1900), ed. by C. R. King; George Wilson, *Portrait Gallery of the Chamber of Commerce of the State of N. Y.* (1890); Bayard Tuckerman, *The Diary of Philip Hone* (2 vols., 1889); *N. Y. Tribune*, Oct. 5, 1853.]
W. B. S.

KING, JOHN (Jan. 1, 1813–June 19, 1893), physician, leader of the reform in American medical therapeutics, and one of the founders of the eclectic school of medicine, was born in New York City. His father was Harman King; his mother was Marguerite La Porte, the daughter of Marquis La Porte who came to America with Lafayette. Early in his college life his bent toward science appeared and in 1835, at twenty-two, he lectured before the Mechanics Institute of New York City on magnetism and its relation to geology, astronomy, and to physiology, and repeated the lectures later in New Bedford, Mass. He was throughout his life an indefatigable student, a clear, pleasant expositor, with a sense of language and of accurate statement. As a medical student in the Reformed Medical College of the City of New York he came under the influence of Wooster Beach, a leading physician who was working to secure a reform in therapeutics to less drastic methods. King graduated from the college in 1838 and after teaching at the school settled first in New Bedford but in 1845 moved to Sharpsburg, Ky., and later to Owingsville. In 1848 he was secretary of the first national convention of Reform Medical Practitioners, which was held in Cincinnati. At this convention the name "Eclectic" was officially adopted. King moved to Cincinnati, whither the Worthington Reform Medical College, after its failure in Worthington, Ohio, had been transferred and reëstablished under the name of the Eclectic Medical Institute. He went the next year (1849) to Memphis, Tenn., as professor of materia medica, and therapeutics, but in 1851 he returned to Cincinnati to become professor of obstetrics in the Eclectic Medical Institute. With the exception of a few years he remained there until his death. He was president of the National Eclectic Medical Association in 1878 and first president of the Ohio State Eclectic Medical Association.

As a pharmacologist King introduced into general use the resin of mandrake, podophyllin, that of macrotys, and the oleo-resin of iris, the first and perhaps the best of the resin class of drugs. He also introduced hydrastis and sanguinaria. He prepared these and other drugs himself, and a collection of his apparatus, together with samples of these and other drugs, is to be found in the Smithsonian Institution at Washington. He had a wide knowledge of botany and discovered many of the active principles of native plants. His most notable work, *The American Dispensatory* (1852), during his lifetime passed through eighteen editions. In this he preserved the knowledge of the therapeutic principles of American plants and crystallized the therapeutics of the eclectic school. It is one of the most important American contributions to materia medica. There followed in rapid succession *American Obstetrics* (1853); *Women: Their Diseases and Treatment* (1858); *The Microscopist's Companion* (1859); *The American Family Physician* (1860); *Chronic Diseases* (1866); *The Urological Dictionary* (1878); and *The Coming Freeman* (1886). The last was written in behalf of laboring men. King was an early Abolitionist, did much to help poor children, championed the cause of labor, and fought attempts to license and restrict medical practitioners. He believed in the greatest possible amount of personal freedom. As a medical pioneer he had to stand much obloquy but he was always courteous toward those who regarded him as a charlatan. His mind was extraordinarily active, sympathetic, and kindly. He was twice married. His first wife was Charlotte M. Armington whom he married in 1833. She died in 1847 and in 1853 he married Phebe (Rodman) Platt. He died at North Bend, Ohio.

[*Trans. Nat. Eclectic Medic. Asso.*, vol. XXI (1894); *Bull. of the Lloyd Lib.*, no. 12, 1910; Otto Juettner, *Daniel Drake and His Followers* (1909); H. A. Kelly and W. L. Burrage, *Am. Medic. Biogs.* (1920); *Eclectic Medic. Jour.*, June 1891; *Cincinnati Times-Star*, June 23, 1893.] A. P. M.

KING, JOHN ALSOP (Jan. 3, 1788–July 7, 1867), congressman, governor of New York, was the eldest son of Rufus, 1755–1827 [*q.v.*], and Mary (Alsop) King and brother of Charles and James Gore King [*qq.v.*]. He was born in New York City, but a good part of his boyhood was passed, with his brothers, in England, while the father was United States minister to that country. He attended Harrow School under the head mastership of Dr. Joseph Drury, while Lord Byron and Robert Peel were pupils there. The discipline was a rare experience for American boys. At that time, the opening years of the nineteenth century, the curriculum was rigidly confined to Latin and Greek. From Harrow the King brothers were sent to a branch of the École Polytechnique in Paris for drill in the use of the French language. Their father, having been relieved of the English mission by the Jefferson administration, had returned to America. In Paris the boys took prizes and were schoolfellows of several of the Empress Josephine's young relations. When they rejoined their parents the family was settled at Jamaica, Long Island. John's later studies were chiefly confined to the law. Although admitted to the bar, he had hardly begun practice when the War of 1812 interrupted his plans, and he was commissioned a lieutenant of cavalry at New York.

After the peace, King, who had married Mary Ray, Jan. 3, 1810, cultivated a farm on Long Island not far from his father's estate. At this time his interest in agriculture became dominant. His other absorbing interest was politics. Schooled in Federalism, his earlier alliances in New York were with anti-Clintonian Democrats, or Republicans. He was a member of the state Assembly in 1819–21 and of the state Senate in 1823–25, resigning his seat to go to London as secretary of legation with his father, who was appointed minister to the Court of St. James's by President John Quincy Adams. After his return to America King was in turn allied with the anti-Masons, the National Republicans, and the Whigs, harboring also antislavery sentiments. He was sent at intervals by his district to the state Assembly (1832, 1838, 1840), suffering several defeats for the same office, however. He was a delegate to the Whig national convention of 1839 and ten years later was sent to Congress as a Whig representative, his brother James having a seat for a New Jersey district in the same House. In Congress King opposed the Clay compromise measures, particularly the Fugitive-slave Bill, and urged the admission of California as a free state. He was a delegate to the Whig national convention of 1852, but two years later he presided at the New York state anti-Nebraska convention and in the New York Whig convention of 1855 he moved the adoption of the name "Republican." He was a delegate to the first Republican National Convention in 1856. In the state convention of that year he was named for governor on the second ballot and was elected in November by a large plurality. His term of office was uneventful, the perennial New York issues of education and canal enlargement receiving the usual emphasis in his messages to the legislature. New York's attitude on the question of slavery extension was also set forth at length. The private life to which King retired at the age of seventy-one was only once interrupted, when he was appointed a member of the New York delegation to the Peace Conference of 1861 at Washington. He was stricken by paralysis while making a Fourth of July address to his Long Island neighbors in 1867 and died three days later in the homestead that had been his since his father's death in 1827. He had seven children, one of whom, Charles Ray King, M.D., edited *The Life and Correspondence of Rufus King.*

[W. W. Spooner, *Historic Families of America* (n.d.); *The Life and Correspondence of Rufus King* (6 vols., 1894–1900), ed. by C. R. King; D. S. Alexander, *A Pol. Hist. of the State of N. Y.*, vol. II (1906); "Eulogium on the Late Gov. John A. King," *Trans. N. Y. State Agric. Soc.*, pt. I, vol. XXVII (1868); *Union League Club of N. Y. Proc. in Reference to the Death of John A. King, July 11th, 1867* (1867); Bayard Tuckerman, *The Diary of Philip Hone* (2 vols., 1889); J. A. Scoville, *The Old Merchants of N. Y.*, vols. I–III (1863–65); *N. Y. Tribune*, July 8, 1867.]

W. B. S.

KING, JOHN PENDLETON (Apr. 3, 1799–Mar. 19, 1888), lawyer, railroad president, senator, was born near Glasgow, Ky. His father was Francis King, a native of Hanover County, Va.; his mother was, before her marriage, Mary Patrick, of Pendleton District, S. C. When he was quite young his parents moved to Bedford County, Tenn., where he received his first schooling. At sixteen, with money and a horse given him by his father, he set out for Columbia County, Ga., to visit an uncle. Becoming strongly attached to Georgia, in 1817 he entered the Academy of Richmond County at Augusta, not far away, to complete his formal education. He soon became acquainted with Freeman Walker, a Georgian of note, and under his guidance began the study of law. Though under the prescribed age, he was admitted to the bar in 1819 and immediately succeeded to a lucrative practice upon Walker's election to the United States Senate in December of that year. After three years at the bar, he decided to visit Europe for study and general culture. He remained two years.

By 1829 King's fortune had become so large and his business interests so exacting that he gave up the law. Though not politically ambitious and not characteristically a politician, he entered the two state constitutional conventions of 1830 and 1833, acting with the Jacksonian Democrats. The year following the first convention, he was appointed a judge of the court of common pleas, a position which he soon abandoned. So insistent was his adopted state on honoring him that he received the appointment to the United States Senate in 1833 to fill out the unexpired term of George M. Troup, who had resigned. The next year he was reëlected for the full term, but he resigned in 1837 when he found himself the object of considerable criticism in Georgia because of his refusal to support the policies of President Van Buren in their entirety. Returning to private life, he became one of the constructive industrial leaders in the ante-bellum South. In 1841 he assumed the presidency of the Georgia Railroad & Banking Company and through his private fortune rescued it from bankruptcy. He remained at the head of this road until 1878. During the Civil War he used his resources in furthering the Confederacy and for his pains, suffered damages at the hands of Sherman's army to the amount of $3,000,000. He was also the chief promoter and president of the Atlanta & West Point Railroad, one of the most profitable short lines in the South. He entered into the cotton manufacturing business in Augusta early, and it was through his vision and efforts that the Augusta Canal, a water-power development, was constructed on the Savannah River. King married in 1842 the only daughter of J. M. Woodward of New York City. Four children were born to them. He died in Summerville, Chattooga County, Ga., and was buried in St. Paul's Churchyard, Augusta.

[A. D. Candler and C. A. Evans, eds., *Georgia* (1906), vol. II; L. L. Knight, *Georgia's Landmarks, Memorials and Legends*, vol. II (1914); W. J. Northen, ed., *Men of Mark in Ga.*, vol. III (1911); *War of the Rebellion: Official Records (Army)*, 4 ser. II, pp. 273, 274; *Biog. Dir. Am. Cong.* (1928); *Appletons' Ann. Cyc.*, 1888; *Atlanta Constitution*, Mar. 20, 1888.]

E. M. C.

KING, JONAS (July 29, 1792–May 22, 1869), missionary, consular officer, was the son of Jonas and Abigail (Leonard) King. His grandfather, Thomas King, was an early settler and a leader in the political and religious life of Hawley, Mass.; his father lived a more retired life on his little farm near the town, carrying on the strict Puritan tradition in his home. After a fragmentary but eagerly acquired elementary education he graduated from Williams College in 1816, and from Andover Theological Seminary in 1819. He spent six months in mission work among the negroes and seamen in Charleston, S. C., where he was ordained as an evangelist by the South Carolina Congregational Association on Dec. 17, 1819, and returned to Andover for a year of graduate work in 1820–21. Precarious health, which more than once broke under the strain, and slender resources, replenished by intervals of teaching and preaching, only intensified his struggle for an education. He determined to study Arabic under the noted Orientalist De Sacy in Paris, with a view to future missionary work, and spent nearly a year there.

Receiving an appeal from his seminary mate, Pliny Fisk, to join him in the Palestine mission of the American Board of Commissioners for Foreign Missions, he accepted the call and himself raised the money for his support. After three active years in the mission he left behind him his famous *Farewell Letter* (1825), in which he set forth his reasons for not joining the Roman Catholic Church. This work, written originally in Arabic, was translated into several languages and exercised a wide influence. On his way home he lingered several months in Smyrna, in the home of a Greek family named Mengous, where he exchanged English lessons for lessons in modern Greek, and where he became acquainted with Annetta Aspasia Mengous, whom he married in 1829. In 1828 he was persuaded by "The Ladies' Greek Committee of New York City," a group of American Philhellenes, to take charge of a shipload of food and clothing collected for the relief of Greek sufferers in the war against Turkish rule, and to remain in Greece as a missionary. In 1830 he returned permanently to the service of the American Board. Moving to Athens while the city was still demoralized by wartime conditions, he purchased some land near the Acropolis, which he named "Philadelphia," and began the construction of a home, school, and church. Part of this property was later seized for public use by the government, which denied compensation for many years.

Puritan ancestry and home influence, an innate kindliness, a passion for learning, a flaming evangelistic spirit, a profound conviction of his calling, and an unshakable faith in his credo were factors which combined to make a life singularly consistent in its devotion to the missionary vocation. His long service was crowded with activity. Besides translating a number of English works into modern Greek, he published in addition to the *Farewell Letter* already mentioned: *Defence* (1845), in Greek; *Exposition of an Apostolic Church* (1851); *Speech before the Areopagus* (1847), in Greek; *Hermeneutics of the Sacred Scriptures* (1857), in Greek; *Sermons* (2 vols., 1859), in Greek; *Synoptical View of Palestine and Syria, with Additions,* in French, translated into Greek, 1859; *Miscellaneous Works* (1859), in Greek; *Answer to a Pamphlet Entitled "The Two Clergymen," by the Bishop of Karystia, Macarius, Kaliarchus* (1863). He planned with his pupil, Dr. Kalopothakes, a distinctively Greek Protestant Church, which was afterward realized in a permanent organization. Several times he acted as an unofficial agent between the United States and the Greek government, and on Mar. 15, 1851, he was appointed United States consular agent at Athens, and served until Aug. 18, 1857. Six weeks later he was appointed acting consul, his term lasting until the following March. In 1868 he served for a few weeks as vice-consul at Piraeus. Among a people whose established religion was as dear to them as was the Greeks', it is not strange that his evangelical ardor, his positive and uncompromising theology, and his controversial books aroused opposition which at times amounted to persecution. He was the object of libelous articles in the press and was threatened with mob violence. He was tried in the Athens courts in 1852 on the charge of reviling the Greek Church, and sentenced to fifteen days' imprisonment followed by exile. Only one day of his prison sentence was served, and the sentence of exile was later reversed. An investigation of his case by George P. Marsh, United States minister at Constantinople, in 1852 and 1853, established the injustice of his trial and the justice of his land claims. The land claims were settled in 1855 through Roger A. Pryor. In 1863 King was anathematized by the Holy Synod of Athens and one of his books burned. Not long before his death, however, a reconciliation was effected between him and the Metropolitan Bishop of Athens. His burial place is in Athens.

[The letters of King are in the possession of the Am. Bd. of Commissioners for Foreign Missions and are deposited in the Andover-Harvard Theolog. Lib. Consular letters are preserved in the U. S. State Dept. archives, and Marsh's report is published as *Sen. Ex. Doc. No. 67,* 33 Cong., 2 Sess. Long extracts are quoted from King's letters in the *Missionary Herald,* vols. XIX–LXV (1823–69). F. E. H. Haines, *Jonas King: Missionary to Syria and Greece* (1879), is the only complete biography. H. M. Baird, *Modern Greece* (1856), gives an eye-witness account of King's trial. See also H. H. Jessup, *Fifty-three Years in Syria* (1910); Thomas Laurie, *The Ely Volume, or The Contributions of Our Foreign Missions to Science and Human Well-Being* (1881); *Congregationalist and Boston Recorder,* June 24, 1869; W. G. Atkins, *Hist. of the Town of Hawley, Franklin County, Mass.* (1887).]

I. L. T.

KING, PRESTON (Oct. 14, 1806–Nov. 13, 1865), politician, was born in Ogdensburg, N. Y., the son of John King and Margaret Galloway. His elementary education obtained in Ogdensburg was followed by a classical course in Union College where he graduated with honors in 1827. He passed the bar after a study of the law in Silas Wright's office. In 1830 he established the *St. Lawrence Republican.* He was a Democrat from principle and became a dogged, uncompromising Jacksonian. Through Wright's influence he served as postmaster at Ogdensburg from 1831 to 1834 at which time he was elected to the Assembly. He was hostile toward the movement to finance internal improvements at government expense and thought Whiggery was an extension of Federalism, neither of which had accomplished any good. He won the confidence and respect of his party before he became involved in the Canadian Rebellion of 1837–38.

The imprisonment of some of his friends whom he had urged to participate in that war temporarily unbalanced his mind and he entered an asylum in Hartford, Conn., after his fourth term in the Assembly. He recovered rapidly, however, returned to politics, and entered Congress in 1843. Having long opposed the extension of slavery, he broke with the majority of his party in 1846, when he advised Wilmot to introduce his Proviso and then gave it his powerful support. He participated in the Free Soil convention at Buffalo in 1848 and supported Van Buren. He was not a candidate for election to the Thirtieth Congress, but he was elected in 1848 as a Free Soiler and was reëlected in 1850. He was strong in his opposition to the Fugitive-slave Law. In 1852 he supported Pierce for President but later turned against him and the party, because of the Kansas-Nebraska Act, and allied himself with its opponents. He urged the nomination of Frémont and was himself considered for the vice-presidential nomination by the Philadelphia convention in 1856. In 1857 he entered the Senate where he severely denounced Buchanan as being "false to his high trust" (*Congressional Globe,* 35 Cong., 1 Sess., p. 1134). He proposed to establish agricultural land grant colleges in every state, but he failed to secure the passage of such a bill. The idea of secession was repugnant to him, although he advocated state rights in preference to extreme centralization. He refused to support any proposed compromises with the South in 1860, and he ardently supported Lincoln in his war policies. At the expiration of his term in 1863 he returned to his law practice. He acted as chairman of the National Committee of the Republican party from 1860 to 1864 and served as a delegate in the Republican Convention at Baltimore where he urged the nomination of Johnson for vice-president. After the latter became president, he appointed King collector of customs in New York City (Aug. 15, 1865). King accepted the office, for which he believed himself wholly unfitted, only upon the earnest insistence of Weed. An invasion of office-seekers and the fear that he might fail to perform his duties satisfactorily caused another mental aberration. He tied a bag of shot about his body and slipped off a Hoboken ferry-boat. His remains were buried near the graves of his father and mother at Ogdensburg, N. Y., in May 1866. He had never married.

[D. S. Alexander, *A Pol. Hist. of the State of N. Y.*, vol. II (1906); *Autobiog. of Thurlow Weed* (1884), ed. by Harriet A. Weed; C. B. Going, *David Wilmot, Free Soiler* (1924); H. D. A. Donovan, *The Barnburners* (1925); *Diary of Gideon Welles* (3 vols., 1911); S. W. Durant and H. B. Pierce, *Hist. of St. Lawrence County, N. Y.* (1878); obituary notices in the *World* (N. Y.), Nov. 15, 16, 1865, and the *N. Y. Tribune,* Nov. 15, 1865.]

W. E. S—h.

KING, RICHARD (July 10, 1825–Apr. 14, 1885), steamboat captain and founder of a great ranch, was born in Orange County, N. Y. His parents, whose names have not been preserved, were evidently poor, and at the age of eight the boy was apprenticed to a jeweler. Being harshly treated, he ran away and slipped aboard a steamship bound for Mobile, Ala. There he became a cabin boy. One of his employers, Capt. Joe Holland, took quite a fancy to the lad and sent him to Connecticut for eight months in school, which made up the whole of his formal education. Returning to Mobile, he continued with Captain Holland, served for a brief period as a volunteer in the Seminole War, and was then engaged on various steamers on the Chattahoochee River. In 1847 he was attracted to Texas by the Mexican War and served as a pilot on a government steamer on the Rio Grande. He made the acquaintance of his commander, Capt. Mifflin Kenedy, and the two remained close friends. When the war was over, King bought a small steamer and engaged in trade on the Rio Grande, and, in 1850, joined Kenedy in organizing Kenedy & Company. Between 1850 and the close of the Civil War, the company built or purchased twenty-two vessels. During the war, King was engaged in exchanging cotton for supplies from Mexico for the use of the Confederate forces. He and his partner are described as "too well known to render it necessary to speak of their ability to comply with this contract" (*War of the Rebellion: Official Records, Army,* 1 Ser. XV, p. 1074).

King had already conceived the plan of creating a great ranch in the region between the Nueces and the Rio Grande. In 1852 he purchased a tract of 75,000 acres known as the Santa Gertrudis ranch situated in Nueces County southwest of Corpus Christi. On Dec. 10, 1854, he was married to Henrietta M. Chamberlain, the daughter of a Presbyterian minister. The young couple established themselves on the ranch, where King was soon the virtual ruler of a great sweep of country. Firm, bold, and prompt in his decisions and actions, he did not hesitate to hold the lawless characters of the frontier in check with an iron hand. His enemies said he was sometimes unscrupulous in his methods of acquiring land, but even they gave him credit for open-handed generosity. The ranch was soon famous for its hospitality. Before the Northern markets were opened, King erected rendering establishments on his ranch and shipped tallow and hides to market by water. Later thousands of his cattle were driven over the long trail to Kansas and the Northern ranges. From 1876 to 1880 he was engaged in building a railroad from Corpus Christi to Laredo. At one time his livestock holdings included 100,000 cattle, 20,000 sheep, and 10,000 horses. At the time of his death he owned outright more than half a million acres in flourishing condition, and the original "longhorns" were being rapidly replaced by improved breeds which he imported. The town of Kingsville has been built on land which formerly was a part of the ranch.

[J. H. Brown, *Indian Wars and Pioneers of Tex.* (n.d.); J. M. Hunter, *The Trail Drivers of Tex.* (2nd ed., 1924); *Harper's Weekly*, Aug. 18, 1906; *Kingsville Record*, Apr. 1, 1925; Jas. Cox, *Cattle Industry of Tex.* (1895); *Southwestern Hist. Quart.*, Apr. 1916; information as to certain facts from King's daughter, Mrs. R. J. Kleberg, Kingsville, Tex.] R. G. C.

KING, RUFUS (Mar. 24, 1755–Apr. 29, 1827), Federalist statesman and minister to Great Britain, was born in Scarboro, Me. (then part of Massachusetts), the eldest son of Captain Richard King, a successful merchant, and his first wife, Isabella (Bragdon) King. At the age of twelve he was sent to Dummer Academy, South Byfield, Mass., under Master Samuel Moody, and then entered Harvard, graduating in the class of 1777. He studied law at Newburyport, Mass., under Theophilus Parsons [*q.v.*], incidentally acquiring some military experience as aide to General Glover during General Sullivan's brief and ill-fated expedition to Rhode Island. Admitted to the bar in 1780, he opened an office in Newburyport. As a delegate to the Massachusetts General Court from that town in 1783, 1784, and 1785, he showed himself to be "a man of business, a ready debater, and a pleasing orator" (J. B. McMaster, *A History of the People of the United States*, I, 1883, p. 359), and won a place of leadership by favoring a bill granting a five per cent. impost to the Continental Congress.

For three successive years, from 1784 to 1786, he was elected by the legislature as a delegate to Congress, then sitting in Trenton, N. J. As a member, he moved, Mar. 16, 1785, a resolution providing that there should be neither "slavery nor involuntary servitude" in the section to be known as the Northwest Territory. The phrase employed by King was later incorporated in the Ordinance of 1787, which was drafted in part by him but introduced in Congress by his colleague, Nathan Dane, while King was serving in the Constitutional Convention at Philadelphia. As chairman of a committee on finances, he offered a report (Feb. 15, 1786) urging all the states to contribute toward federal expenses, and he was sent, with James Monroe, on an unsuccessful mission to persuade the Pennsylvania legislature to emulate Massachusetts in granting Congress a five per cent. impost. Although he was already recognized as a brilliant speaker, he broke down in the midst of his prepared address and had to ask Monroe to take his place. An hour later, however, he rose and delivered extemporaneously what he always declared to be the best speech he ever made. During this period also King sat upon a commission to adjust the boundary between Massachusetts and New York.

In the Constitutional Convention, which opened May 14, 1787, King was probably the most eloquent orator. Although he had at first been fearful of the dangers which might arise from such an assembly and had been opposed to any radical action in altering the Articles of Confederation, his opinions underwent a change, and he was found during the debates arguing in favor of a vigorous central government. He was on the committee which revised the style and arranged the order of the final draft of the Constitution, and he was one of its signers. In the Massachusetts convention for ratification, as a delegate from Newburyport, he courageously pleaded for its adoption, and his logic and fervor, as well as his familiarity with the provisions of the document, were of vital assistance in securing the approval of his state.

Before the federal government was organized, King, having married, Mar. 30, 1786, Mary Alsop, only daughter of a wealthy New York merchant, had moved to New York City and abandoned the practice of law. Shortly after his arrival, he was elected to the New York Assembly and was soon chosen by the legislature, July 16, 1789, as United States senator from that state, his colleague being Gen. Philip Schuyler. King, who was fortunate enough to draw the long term, became perhaps the ablest Federalist in the Senate, upholding Alexander Hamilton in all his financial measures. Of the Jay Treaty, negotiated in 1794 with England, he was an earnest advocate, and he joined with Hamilton and Jay in publishing, under the signature of "Camillus," a series of papers explaining its details, King's share being a discussion of commercial matters and maritime law, on which he was an authority. He was elected in 1791 as a director of the Bank of the United States, which he had labored assiduously to create. He was chosen for a second senatorial term, Jan. 27, 1795, by a small majority in each branch of the legislature.

Washington, after some hesitation, named

King as minister plenipotentiary to Great Britain, succeeding Thomas Pinckney, in 1796. In recommending him to the President, Hamilton described him as "a remarkably well informed man, a very judicious one, a man of address, a man of fortune and economy, whose situation affords just ground of confidence" (*The Life and Correspondence of Rufus King,* VI, p. 680). King completely justified the hopes of his sponsors and is said to have been "one of the most effective representatives the United States ever had at London" (Edward Channing, *A History of the United States,* IV, 1917, 353). Arriving in London, July 23, 1796, at a moment when issues of a critical nature were arising almost daily between the two nations, King, by firm yet tactful diplomacy, averted any open breach. He concluded in 1803 two important conventions with the Addington ministry, and he even felt, probably too optimistically, that, if he could have remained a few months longer, he might have persuaded Great Britain to abandon her policy of impressment. He was, however, relieved at his own request in 1803 and returned to the United States. In the autumn of 1804 he was by general agreement the Federalist candidate for vice-president with Charles C. Pinckney as the presidential nominee, but they received only fourteen electoral votes—from Connecticut, Delaware, and Maryland—and were overwhelmed by Jefferson and Clinton. Being out of sympathy with the Jefferson administration he settled on an estate in Jamaica, Long Island, where he interested himself in agriculture, imported a herd of Devon cattle, and kept up an extensive correspondence. In 1808 Pinckney and King were again nominated and were given forty-seven electoral votes—all New England, except Vermont, going for the Federalist nominees.

Like a true Federalist, King did not approve of the War of 1812, and when he was again elected in 1813 to the United States Senate from New York, he became the leader of the nine opposition members in that body. He made a fiery speech against the abandonment of the city of Washington after the British had burned the Capitol in 1814; and, when it became evident that the war had become one of defense, he sanctioned measures for its vigorous prosecution, thus winning the respect of his opponents for his patriotic attitude. He was suggested frequently by Republican newspapers as a possible secretary of state, the hope being that he might persuade his Federalist followers to join him in standing by the administration. In the presidential election in 1816, he won the votes of all the Federalist electors, representing Massachusetts, Connecticut, and Delaware, and thus received 34 votes to Monroe's 183. He had joined Webster, then in the House of Representatives, in opposing the establishment of the second Bank of the United States; and he was the author of the Navigation Act of 1818. He studied carefully the problem of the public lands and carried through a measure providing that they should be sold for cash, at a lower price than before. In 1820 he was reëlected by the New York legislature, although the majority of the members differed with him politically. The following year he was a member of the New York constitutional convention.

During his last term in the Senate he took a decisive stand on negro slavery. He resisted the admission of Missouri as a state, with slavery, and opposed the Missouri Compromise of 1820 on the ground that it merely prolonged the controversy and postponed its adjustment. He argued that further extension of slavery would be unfair to the free states and fatal to their welfare. For the abolition of slavery he proposed applying the proceeds of the sale of the public lands toward the emancipation of negroes and toward their removal to some territory outside of the national borders. Upon the expiration of his term King declined a reëlection. He had suffered badly from the gout. But his desire to resume private life was overcome by the insistence of President John Quincy Adams that he should once more accept the ministry to the Court of St. James's. Shortly after his arrival in Liverpool, June 26, 1825, he was taken ill and was obliged to return to America the following summer. Within a year he died, worn out by the exhausting demands of a long and creditable career in the service of his country. He was buried in the cemetery of Grace Church, in Jamaica.

In the estimation of one who knew him well, King "had the appearance of one who was a gentleman by nature and had improved all her gifts" (William Sullivan, *Familiar Letters on Public Characters and Public Events,* 2nd ed., 1834, p. 21), but he was sometimes thought to be haughty and austere in manner. The existing portraits of him by John Trumbull, Gilbert Stuart, and Charles W. Peale would indicate that he was handsome. The testimony as to his ability is ample. Jeremiah Mason, King's colleague in the Senate, thought him to be "the most able man and the greatest orator" he had ever met (*Memoir, Autobiography and Correspondence of Jeremiah Mason,* 1917, p. 57). Webster wrote of him, Feb. 5, 1814, to his brother Ezekiel:

"You never heard such a speaker. In strength, and dignity, and fire; in ease, in natural effect, and gesture as well as in matter, he is unequalled" (*The Writings and Speeches of Daniel Webster,* National Edition, 1903, XVII, 241). During a long and stormy political career, he never had a serious quarrel nor was there the slightest imputation against his public or private life. He reared a notable family of children of whom several attained distinction, among them being John Alsop, Charles, and James Gore King [*qq.v.*].

[The standard authority on Rufus King is *The Life and Correspondence of Rufus King* (6 vols., 1894–1900), edited by his grandson, Charles R. King. Other sources include: C. E. Fitch, *Encyc. of Biog. of N. Y.* (1916), I, 34–37; W. W. Spooner, *Hist. Families of America* (n.d.); *Autobiog. of Martin Van Buren* (1920), published as Vol. II of the annual reports of the Am. Hist. Asso. for the year 1918; D. S. Alexander, *A Pol. Hist. of the State of N. Y.*, vol. I (1906); Max Farrand, *The Records of the Fed. Convention of 1787* (3 vols., 1911); D. R. Fox, *The Decline of Aristocracy in the Politics of N. Y.* (1919); E. H. Brush, *Rufus King and His Times* (1926).] C. M. F.

KING, RUFUS (Jan. 26, 1814–Oct. 13, 1876), soldier, editor, diplomat, was born in New York City, the son of Charles [*q.v.*] and Eliza (Gracie) King, and grandson of Rufus King [*q.v.*]. He attended the preparatory department of Columbia College, entered the United States Military Academy, West Point, July 1, 1829, graduated in 1833, and was commissioned in the corps of engineers. Resigning, Sept. 30, 1836, because he felt that the army in peace time offered little opportunity for a career, he became assistant engineer in surveying for the New York & Erie Railroad, of which his uncle, James Gore King [*q.v.*], was president. In 1839 he went to Albany and was editor of the *Albany Daily Advertiser* until 1841, after which year till 1845 he was associated with Thurlow Weed in editing the *Albany Evening Journal.* From 1839 to 1843 he was adjutant-general of New York under Gov. William H. Seward and commanded the troops called out to suppress the anti-rent disturbances.

Removing to Milwaukee in 1845, he became part owner and editor of the *Milwaukee Sentinel and Gazette* (later the *Milwaukee Sentinel*). In 1857 he sold his share but remained as editor until 1861. He made the paper one of the leading journals of the Northwest. He himself engaged actively in many public affairs. He was a leader in the fight to defeat the first constitution proposed for Wisconsin (1846), and was an influential member of the second convention which framed the constitution adopted in 1848. Especially interested in education, he served for years as superintendent of schools of Milwaukee without the title or compensation, and was formally superintendent, 1859–60. He was an earnest proponent of "free instruction in all the institutions of the state, from the primary schools to the university," and was one of the first regents of the University of Wisconsin (1848–54).

His old friend, Secretary Seward, secured his appointment, Mar. 22, 1861, as minister to the Papal States, but as he was about to sail for Rome, Fort Sumter was fired upon. He returned to Washington and on May 17, 1861, was commissioned a brigadier-general, organized the famous "Iron Brigade," and served in the defenses of Washington until March 1862, when he was given a division. On Aug. 28, 1862, near Gainesville, his division, a part of Pope's army, was unexpectedly attacked by Stonewall Jackson with a large force. King held his ground until nightfall, then retreated. Next day Jackson and Lee united and defeated Pope in the battle of Manassas. After this disastrous engagement the false impression got abroad that King, when he retreated, disobeyed Pope's orders, and that he was therefore responsible for the junction of Jackson with Lee. "For long years he had to bear the stigma," says his son, Gen. Charles King (*post,* p. 380), "and it ruined his health and broke his heart." He continued in the army until October 20, 1863, when ill health—he was a victim of epilepsy—forced him to resign.

He had, on Oct. 7, been reappointed minister to Rome. While there he apprehended John H. Surratt, implicated in the conspiracy to assassinate Lincoln and Seward, who had fled to Italy. In 1867 Congress failed to appropriate funds for continuing the mission at the Papal Court on what King called "the alleged but erroneous grounds that the Pope refuses to permit Protestant worship within the walls of Rome" (*Papers Relating to Foreign Affairs,* 1867, pt. 1, p. 708). King protested, but Congress at its next session having again made no appropriation for the continuance of the mission, he resigned Jan. 1, 1868. He served as deputy collector of customs for the port of New York until 1869, when ill health compelled his retirement from public life. In 1836 he married Ellen Eliot, who died in 1838; in 1843 he married her sister Susan, by whom he had a son and a daughter.

[W. W. Spooner, *Historic Families of America* (n.d.); Charles King, in *Wis. Mag. of Hist.*, June 1921; *Wis. Hist. Soc. Colls.*, vol. XXVIII (1920), vol. XXIX (1928); files of the *Milwaukee Sentinel,* 1845–61; G. W. Cullum, *Biog. Reg. Officers and Grads. U. S. Mil. Acad.*, vol. I (3rd ed., 1891); *War of the Rebellion, Official Records (Army)*, 1 ser. XII, pt. 1; *Papers Relating to Foreign Affairs,* 1866, pt. 2, pp. 127ff., 1867, pt. 1, pp. 695ff.; *Milwaukee Sentinel,* Oct. 14, 1876; information from Gen. Charles King.] W. E. M.

KING, SAMUEL (Jan. 24, 1748–Dec. 30, 1819), portrait painter and maker of nautical instruments, was a son of Benjamin and Mary (Haggar) King, of Newport, R. I. The father, described as "a gentleman of very respectable character," was born at Salem, Mass., a descendant of Daniel King, the emigrant, who settled in Lynn, Mass., before 1644. The mother was of a Rhode Island family. The senior King made and repaired instruments for navigators in a shop bearing a quadrant as its sign at the corner of Thames and Pelham streets and here Samuel learned his principal means of livelihood. He was sent to Boston to study house-painting and perhaps other forms of applied art, according to a plausible tradition. On his return to Newport he is said to have painted a portrait of a local gentleman which he exhibited in his father's shop window. It was so lifelike that the sitter's negro factotum, mistaking it for reality, bowed low before it. It has also been said (Bolton, *post,* p. 92) that King received the encouragement of Cosmo Alexander, the visiting Scottish painter, who also befriended Stuart. King married, Aug. 26, 1770, Amey Vernon, daughter of Samuel Vernon, a prominent Newport merchant. She died Feb. 14, 1792, and in November 1795 he married Sarah Ward, also of Newport.

Although he was an able portraitist, as shown by his likeness of Benjamin Mumford (Newport Historical Society) and other examples, King appears to have been unable to live from his art but continued to follow his father's business after the latter's death. Washington Allston (Flagg, *post,* p. 9) speaks of Samuel King as one "who made quadrants and compasses, and occasionally painted portraits," and depicts him as a friendly man to whom "sometimes I would take . . . a drawing, and was sure to get a kind word of encouragement." King also instructed Edward Malbone, Gilbert Stuart, Anne Hall, who became a miniaturist, and Charles B. King, prolific painter of portraits at Washington, D. C., and benefactor of the Redwood Library, Newport. A fine portrait of Mrs. Richard Derby may have been painted by King at Salem while he visited his father's relatives. In August 1770 Ezra Stiles sat for a portrait in Newport. In the same month he married King and Miss Vernon.

In May 1783 King designed and displayed in front of the Rhode Island State House, Newport, a patriotic transparency which disclosed, among other execrated personages, Benedict Arnold suspended from a gallows. His name does not thereafter appear very frequently in the local records. His son Samuel King, Jr., father of Charles William King [*q.v.*], became an opulent East India merchant in New York, of the firm of King & Talbot, and another son, William Vernon King, a graduate of Brown University, successfully practised law in Rhode Island. The artist was buried at Newport.

[Rufus King, *Pedigree of King, of Lynn, Essex County, Mass.* (1891); *New-Eng. Hist. and Geneal. Reg.*, July 1879, for the Vernon Family; Maud Howe Elliott, "Some Recollections of Newport Artists," *Bull. of the Newport Hist. Soc.*, Jan. 1921; Theodore Bolton, *Early Am. Portrait Painters in Miniature* (1921); Wm. Dunlap, *A Hist. of the Rise and Progress of the Arts of Design in the U. S.* (1918), vol. II; J. B. Flagg, *The Life and Letters of Washington Allston* (1892); F. B. Dexter, *The Lit. Diary of Ezra Stiles, D.D., LL.D.* (1901), vol. I; Hannah R. London, *Portraits of Jews by Gilbert Stuart and Other Early Am. Artists* (1927); J. N. Arnold, *Vital Records of R. I., 1636–1850*, vol. VIII (1896), vol. XVIII (1909); *Newport Mercury*, Nov. 27, 1786; *Rhode-Island Republican* (Newport), Jan. 5, 1820.]

F. W. C.

KING, SAMUEL ARCHER (Apr. 9, 1828–Nov. 3, 1914), aeronaut, was born at Tinicum, Pa., the son of Dr. Isaac B. King. Early in life he became interested in aeronautics, and on Sept. 25, 1851, he made his first balloon ascent at Philadelphia. In the course of his life he made several hundred ascensions, for the most part in the vicinity of Philadelphia and Boston. Fourth of July celebrations and state fairs figured largely in his life because the flight of a balloon carrying one or more men was an attraction that could be depended upon to draw crowds, and those taking part were accordingly liberally paid. In the early eighties King became convinced that the balloon offered a means of crossing the Atlantic, and he did much of his later work with this end in view. At this time he got in touch with the United States Signal Service and offered to carry an observer on some of the preliminary voyages from inland cities like Minneapolis and Chicago to the Atlantic seaboard. On Sept. 13, 1881, with Prof. Winslow Upton as representative of the Signal Service, he made a preliminary ascent at Minneapolis. The weather was unfavorable and nothing definite came of the effort. King hoped by this and later ascents to prove that a balloon could be constructed of such material that a sufficient volume of hydrogen gas could be kept within it for three or more days. He himself devised a fabric, a kind of rubber cloth, for this purpose. He also hoped to prove that either by one long voyage, lasting four or five days, or by a succession of shorter ones, he could go in one general direction.

King estimated that a balloon of 300,000 cubic feet capacity, with supplies and outfits for three persons, would cost about $14,000. He proposed to build such a balloon and attempt to cross the Atlantic under official sanction but the suggestion was rejected. In an article in the *Century Magazine* (October 1901) he gave at some length his views on the practicability of the experiment. He placed much reliance upon his drag-rope method of controlling the balloon. He also suggested the employment of water anchors, made of stout canvas, which when lowered to the ocean would serve as anchors and retard progress in the wrong direction. In 1885 W. H. Hammon, representing the Signal Service of the army, made four voyages with King in order to obtain data concerning winds and temperatures at moderate elevations. The balloon was the *Eagle Eyrie,* the use of which, as well as his own services, King gave without charge. Moreover he agreed to start on telegraphic notice from Washington. The campaign was successfully carried out, and flights were made under different weather conditions on Jan. 19, Mar. 13, Mar. 27, and Apr. 16, 1885. A detailed account of the observations made are recorded in a paper by Hammon in the *Proceedings of the American Association for the Advancement of Science, 1890* (1891). King did not live to the time when the Atlantic Ocean was crossed by dirigible balloons. Though it is doubtful whether he would have succeeded in making the journey he must nevertheless be credited with a positive faith in the feasibility of such an undertaking, and if means had been provided, he would doubtless have made the attempt. He lived to old age, a marked exception to the fate of most of the early aeronauts. Prof. Cleveland Abbe regarded King as the most cautious, wisest, and safest balloonist of his age. He died in Philadelphia, survived by his wife, Margaret Roberts, and two sons.

[Fulton T. Chalmers article in *Fly,* Feb. 1909; W. H. Hammon, article in *Am. Meteorol. Jour.,* Feb. 1891; *The Balloon: Noteworthy Aerial Voyages from the Discovery of the Balloon to the Present Time, with a Narrative of the Aeronautic Experiences of Mr. Samuel A. King and a Full Description of His Great Captive Balloons and Their Apparatus* (1879), pub. by the American Aeronautic Society of New York; the *Press* (Phila.), *Philadelphia Inquirer,* and *Pub. Ledger,* Nov. 4, 1914; information as to certain facts from Mr. W. N. Jennings.] A. M.

KING, SAMUEL WARD (May 23, 1786–Jan. 21, 1851), physician and governor, was born in Johnston, R. I., the son of William Borden and Welthian (Walton) King. Although he entered Brown University in 1802 and attended for four years, he did not graduate with his class. Instead he studied medicine and received a diploma in Providence in 1807. In the course of the War of 1812, he married Catherine Latham Angell (May 20, 1813), and employed his talents as a surgeon, first on a privateer and later on the *Hornet.* After the war he became interested in business and politics. Elected in 1839 as first assistant, he served as acting governor in default of the election of a governor and lieutenant-governor, then served as governor in his own right, upon his election to the office in the Whig year of 1840. He was reëlected in 1841 and 1842. During his administration a vigorous attempt was made to supersede the charter of 1663 with a new constitution. The governor's relation to this episode, known as the Dorr War, is his only claim to importance. The old charter, in an era of Jacksonian democracy, seemed to many Rhode Islanders a distasteful anachronism. Agitation against its provisions had occurred from time to time but new vitality was breathed into the movement by the formation in 1840 of the Rhode Island Suffrage Association. This organization, adopting the high ground of "natural rights," proceeded to choose a "people's convention," draw up a "people's constitution," ratify that document and elect officers under its provisions. The governor chosen, Thomas W. Dorr [*q.v.*], was inaugurated May 3, 1842, and affected to regard himself as the lawful executive of the state.

In dealing with this movement, the King administration proceeded with caution. While busying itself with arrangements for drawing up a counter constitution, conciliatory in tone, it apparently hoped to obliterate the Dorr menace with the aid of the national government. In early April Governor King made an appeal to President Tyler for federal assistance on the ground that Rhode Island was "threatened with domestic violence." The President preferred to await an overt act. In later May and June, King lived under the fear of "an incursion" headed by Dorr from neighboring states, and he so informed Tyler on two separate occasions. The President, however, could not be persuaded that federal intervention was warranted. Consequently when Dorr entered the state at the end of June, to place himself at the head of a few of his followers, the state authorities had to deal with the situation. On June 26 King proclaimed martial law under an authorization of the legislature, and Dorr's army dispersed before the arrival of the state militia. Before King left office in 1843, the franchise movement had been practically allayed by a more liberal constitution. King does not seem to have played a decisive part in these proceedings. The governor's power, for one thing, was severely limited by the charter. In the second place, he was aided throughout the crisis by a special board of councilors, appointed by the legislature at his own request. He retired from the governorship having played a comparatively colorless rôle, and died a few years later.

[A. M. Mowry, *The Dorr War* (1901); *House Report 546*, 28 Cong., 1 Sess.; *Representative Men and Old Families of R. I.* (1908), vol. I; G. A. Morrison, Jr., *King Geneal.: Clement King, of Marshfield, Mass., 1668, and His Descendants* (1898); *Providence Daily Jour.*, Jan. 23, 1851; Dorr MSS., Brown Univ.]

E. C. K.

KING, THOMAS BUTLER (Aug. 27, 1800–May 10, 1864), lawyer, planter, congressman, diplomat, was of English ancestry in both branches of his family. His great-grandfather came from Suffolk County, England, and settled in Massachusetts. His father was Daniel King, who became a captain in the Revolution; his mother was Hannah Lord, of New London, Conn. Thomas Butler King was born in Palmer, Mass., one of nine sons. He attended Westfield Academy, but both his father and mother died before 1816, and he was placed under the care of his uncle, Zebulon Butler [*q.v.*], who made it possible for him to study law in Philadelphia. Here he was admitted to the bar in 1822. The next year he decided to visit a brother in Waynesville, Ga., and so well did he like his new surroundings that he began the practice of law there. On Dec. 2, 1824, he was married to Anna Matilda, the only daughter of William Page, who was a large cotton planter on St. Simon's Island. In due time King succeeded to this estate, called "Retreat," and thereby combined with other interests the pleasures of a great planter. He was soon in politics, serving as state senator in 1832, 1834, 1835, and 1837. True to his station in life, he developed into a stanch Whig and entered upon a national career. He was elected to the Twenty-sixth and Twenty-seventh congresses (1839–43), failed of election to the Twenty-eighth, but was victorious in the next three campaigns. He was a positive figure in Congress. As chairman of the committee on naval affairs, he became greatly interested in navigation and in the merchant marine. He promoted the founding of the National Observatory in Washington and the appointment of Matthew F. Maury to direct it. He also used his influence to help American shipping through mail subsidies granted to the Collins and other lines. He accompanied Henry Clay on his Southern campaign in 1844, and in 1849 when President Taylor needed a personal adviser on the situation in California with regard to statehood, King was selected to make the investigation. He resigned from Congress to make the trip. Following the death of Taylor, he was appointed in 1851 by President Fillmore collector for the port of San Francisco. He was soon in the race for the senatorship from California but lost by a slight margin on a strictly party vote. In 1852 he resigned from his San Francisco post and returned to Georgia.

King was almost as important a figure in the economic world as in the political. His activities as a planter led him to become greatly interested in transportation. He was a delegate to the railroad convention held in Macon in 1836, and in 1840 he became president of the Brunswick Railroad & Canal Company. He was among the earliest to dream of a transcontinental railroad. In 1859 he was elected to the state Senate again and in 1860 he was sent as a delegate to the Democratic Convention held in Charleston. He was opposed to secession, but when the movement had run its course he worked loyally for the Confederacy. Immediately after Georgia left the Union but before the Confederacy had been organized, Gov. Joseph E. Brown appointed him a commissioner to England, France, and Belgium to explain the state's new position, to gain recognition of her independence, and especially to establish direct steamboat connections between Savannah and European ports. The success of his negotiations was prevented by the blockade of the South. He returned to Georgia early in 1862. Two years later he died of pneumonia at Waresboro, in Ware County, and was buried on St. Simon's Island. He had six sons and four daughters. Four of his sons achieved distinction in the military service of the Confederacy.

[A. D. Candler and C. A. Evans, eds., *Georgia* (1906), vol. II; W. J. Northen, ed., *Men of Mark in Ga.*, vol. II (1910); I. W. Avery, *The Hist. of the State of Ga. from 1850 to 1881* (1881); A. D. Candler, *The Confed. Records of the State of Ga.*, vol. II (1909); L. L. Knight, *Georgia's Landmarks, Memorials, and Legends*, vol. I (1913); "The Diary and Correspondence of Salmon P. Chase," *Ann. Report, Am. Hist. Asso.*, 1902, vol. II, and "The Correspondence of Robert Toombs, Alexander H. Stephens, and Howell Cobb," *Ibid.*, 1913, vol. II; *Appletons' Ann. Cyc.*, 1864; *War of the Rebellion: Official Records (Army)*; *Biog. Dir. Am. Cong.* (1928); H. G. Wheeler, *Hist. of Cong.* (N. Y., 1848), II, 9–63; *De Bow's Commercial Rev. of the South and West*, June 1850.]

E. M. C.

KING, THOMAS STARR (Dec. 17, 1824–Mar. 4, 1864), Unitarian clergyman, lecturer, and writer, was of German, French, and English descent. His mother's father, Thomas Starr, was a native of the Rhineland, but was brought by his father to America in the latter part of the eighteenth century, where he married a woman of French extraction, Mary Lavinus. Starr King, as he was commonly called, was the oldest child of their daughter Susan and Rev. Thomas Farrington King, a Universalist minister, of English ancestry. The boy was born in New

York while his mother was on a visit to her parents. His father, then in charge of a circuit in Connecticut, was living in Norwalk, but soon settled in Hudson, N. Y. In 1828 he removed to Portsmouth, N. H., and seven years later became pastor of the Universalist society in Charlestown, Mass. In Portsmouth and Charlestown Thomas had all the formal schooling which he ever received. Before he was fifteen years old and while he was preparing for college, the physical breakdown and subsequent death of his father compelled him to help support the family, which now included five younger children. He first worked as clerk and bookkeeper in a dry-goods store, but in December 1840, although barely sixteen, he was appointed assistant teacher in the Bunker Hill Grammar School, Charlestown. Two years later he became principal of the West Grammar School, Medford. Because of the larger compensation offered and the prospect of more leisure time, in 1843 he accepted the position of bookkeeper in the Charlestown Navy Yard.

The responsibilities laid upon his youthful shoulders interrupted his schooling but not his education. He gathered knowledge from every side with the spontaneity and delight of a child at play. Having an agile and retentive mind, he absorbed the contents of books with great rapidity. He gathered his acquaintances together for reading, debate, and dramatics, and attended lectures in Boston and Cambridge. At seventeen he was deep in metaphysics, and astonished older men by his quick understanding of abstruse problems. Edwin H. Chapin, the younger Hosea Ballou, and Theodore Parker [*qq.v.*] became his advisers and friends. Meeting him in Medford, Parker wrote in his diary under date of Apr. 13, 1843: "Saw Schoolmaster Thomas Starr King,—capital fellow, only nineteen. Taught school three years. Supports his mother. . . . Reads French, Spanish, Latin, Italian, a little Greek, and begins German. He is a good listener." (Quoted by Frothingham, *post.*) From his earliest years onward, he captivated all who met him. "Slight of build, golden haired, with a homely mouth which everyone thought beautiful on account of the beaming eyes, the winning smile, and the earnest desire of always wanting to do what was best and right," is the portrait drawn by one of his schoolmasters (Simonds, *post,* p. 4). A generous disposition, sunny temperament, and almost rollicking mirthfulness were also a part of his attractiveness. Soon he began to preach, for from boyhood he had considered no calling but the ministry, and people were held by his clear thought, electric delivery, and rich, resounding voice. "He has the grace of God in his heart and the gift of tongues," wrote Parker (*Ibid.,* p. 6). Later the rough settlers of California were equally charmed. "I say, Jim, stand on your toes and get a sight of him!" exclaimed an old miner to a companion as on the edge of a crowd they listened to one of his speeches in support of the Union: "Why, the boy is taking every trick" (Wendte, *post,* p. 196).

His first pastorate began in 1846 at the Universalist church, Charlestown, which his father had formerly served. Two years later he was installed over the Hollis Street Church, Unitarian, Boston; and on Dec. 17, 1848, he married Julia Wiggin of East Boston. During his eleven years' stay he became one of the leading preachers of the city and one of the most popular Lyceum lecturers in the country, rivaling Beecher in his ability to draw large audiences. An enthusiastic lover of natural scenery, he did much to make the beauties of New Hampshire widely known through the publication in 1860 of an elaborate descriptive work, *The White Hills, Their Legends, Landscapes, and Poetry.* This same year he accepted a call to the struggling Unitarian parish in San Francisco. "We are unfaithful," he wrote to a friend, "in huddling so closely around the cosy stove of civilization in this blessed Boston, and I, for one, am ready to go out into the cold and see if I am good for anything" (*Ibid.,* p. 69). People flocked to hear him preach and lecture. He soon freed his parish of a $20,000 debt and built a new church costing $90,000, to which amount he contributed $5,000 from the proceeds of his lectures. An enthusiastic explorer and mountain climber, he introduced the East to the beauties of the Pacific Coast through vivid letters to the *Boston Transcript.* When the Civil War came and with it the danger of California's secession from the Union and the formation of a Pacific republic, his arguments and patriotic appeals were a powerful factor in keeping the state loyal. He was the mainstay of the United States Sanitary Commission in California. According to a recent writer, "It was the eloquence of Starr King that saved the Commission's work from financial ruin. Of the total of $4,800,000 cash received from the country California alone supplied upwards of $1,234,000." (Rockwell D. Hunt and Nellie Van de Grift Sánchez, *A Short History of California,* copyrighted 1929, p. 526.) Unfortunately, his career was cut short in his fortieth year by an attack of diphtheria followed by pneumonia. In four years he had become one of the best known and most beloved men on the Pacific

Coast. At the news of his death, places of business, the United States Mint, government offices, and the courts were closed. The state legislature adjourned for three days. In the East, Whittier, and in the West, Bret Harte, commemorated him in poems. His portrait was hung in the State House at Sacramento, and in resolutions passed by the legislature he is described as "the man whose matchless oratory saved California to the Union." A monument was erected to him in Golden Gate Park, San Francisco; a peak in the White Mountains and one in the Yosemite National Park are named for him; and in 1931 a statue, the gift of the state of California, was unveiled in the Capitol at Washington. A number of his sermons and addresses were published during his lifetime, and after his death there were issued *Christianity and Humanity, A Series of Sermons* (1877) and *Substance and Show and Other Lectures* (1877), both edited by Edwin P. Whipple, the former with a memoir.

[Richard Frothingham, *A Tribute to Thomas Starr King* (1865); C. D. Bradlee, *The Life, Writings, and Character of Rev. Thomas Starr King* (1870); H. W. Bellows, *In Memory of Thomas Starr King* (1864); Elbert Hubbard, *Little Journeys to the Homes of Eminent Orators* (1903); S. A. Eliot, *Heralds of a Liberal Faith* (1910), vol. III; C. W. Wendte, *Thomas Starr King, Patriot and Preacher* (1921); W. D. Simonds, *Starr King in California* (1917); *Christian Register*, Mar. 12, Apr. 9, 1864; *Unitarian Rev.*, Dec. 1877; *Boston Transcript*, Mar. 5, 1864; *Bulletin* (San Francisco), Mar. 4, 1864; *San Francisco Chronicle*, Mar. 1, 1931.]

H. E. S.

KING, WILLIAM (Feb. 9, 1768–June 17, 1852), ship-owner, first governor of Maine, the seventh child of Richard King, a wealthy lumber exporter, and his second wife, Mary (Black), was born in Scarboro, Me., then a part of Massachusetts. When William was seven years old, his father died, leaving the bulk of his wealth in unproductive lands, thus depriving the boy of the educational advantages which his half-brother, Rufus, 1755–1827 [*q.v.*], and his brother, Cyrus, received. After a short stay at Phillips Academy, Andover, Mass., at the age of thirteen, he worked in sawmills in Saco, and in Topsham, where he later formed a mercantile partnership with his brother-in-law, Dr. Benjamin Porter. In 1800 he moved to Bath, where he spent the remainder of his life as merchant and ship-builder and owner, amassing a large fortune and becoming at the height of his career the largest ship-owner in Maine. He was organizer and president of Bath's first bank, one of the principal owners of the first cotton-mill in Maine, at Brunswick (1809), and an extensive owner of real estate, including the township of Kingfield, Franklin County.

He entered politics as the representative of Topsham in the Massachusetts General Court for 1795 and 1799. He represented Bath from 1804 to 1806, and was Lincoln County's senator, 1807 to 1811, and 1818 to 1819. In the legislature he successfully championed the "Betterment Act" (1808), which obliged owners of wild lands to sell them at appraised original value to settlers or pay for the improvements made. He was one of the chief spirits behind the "Toleration Act" (1811), doing away with the law which obliged towns to support a minister. He was twice the defeated candidate for the office of lieutenant-governor of Massachusetts.

The Embargo Act and the War of 1812 seriously affected his business enterprises but he gave freely of his time and money in carrying out measures for the protection of the coast in his capacity as major-general of militia, and in recruiting soldiers as colonel in the United States army. Subsequently, he was accused by his political enemies (see Benjamin Ames and J. F. Wingate, *The Disclosure—No. 1. Documents Relating to Violations and Evasions of the Laws*, etc., 1824), of violating the Embargo and of trading with the enemy during the war. King's defense (*Mr. King's Reply to a Pamphlet Published at Bath, Me.*, etc., 1825), in which he showed the unreliability of the witnesses against him and charged his accusers of violating the same laws, is a vigorous and powerful, though, as other evidence indicates, not a conclusive vindication.

King's greatest work was done in his leadership of the movement for the separation of Maine from Massachusetts. For seven years until the successful result in 1820, he was the moving force behind the Democracy of Maine. He wrote letters and petitions; organized clubs, caucuses, and conventions; argued, threatened, and cajoled, with such recognized skill and success that he was made president of the constitutional convention of 1819 and elected Maine's first governor with a vote of 21,083 in a total of 22,014. As governor, he was non-partisan in his appointments, and by his moderate policy did much to quiet the fears of the opponents of separation. Failing to put through some cherished plans, and perhaps because he was ambitious for a position in national affairs, he resigned the governorship in 1821 to become a commissioner (1821–24) to put into effect the treaty with Spain. Never a Jacksonian, he failed to be reappointed collector of the customs at Bath, a position which he had occupied from 1830 to 1834. In 1835, as the Whig candidate for the governorship, he was overwhelmingly defeated. Even in his home town, where he was known as the "Sultan," his political power was gone. He was a trustee of Waterville (now Colby) College, 1821–48, overseer of Bowdoin, 1797–1821, and trustee, 1821–49.

Naturally commanding, forceful rather than persuasive, he rode rough-shod over all opposition. His lack of education was seriously felt; his opponents made sport of his blunders in grammar and spelling. Yet in thought he was original, and in reason, sometimes profound. Many who knew both Rufus and William King considered William the intellectual superior. Financial and family troubles darkened his old age; his mental powers failed; "his sun went down in great darkness" (Willis, *post*, p. 504). The state of Maine has recognized his services by placing his statue by Franklin Simmons [*q.v.*] in the Capitol's statuary hall. In 1802 he married Ann Frazier of Boston, by whom he had two children.

[See William Willis, *A Hist. of the Law, the Courts, and the Lawyers of Me.* (1863); H. C. Williams, *Biog. Encyc. of Me. of the Nineteenth Century* (1885); A. F. Moulton, *Memorials of Me.* (1916), *Me. Hist. Sketches* (1929); Deane Dudley, "Recollections of Gen. King, First Gov. of Me.," in *Me. Hist. and Geneal. Recorder,* vol. I (1884); P. M. Reed, *Hist. of Bath and Environs* (1894); G. A. and H. W. Wheeler, *Hist. of Brunswick, Topsham, and Harpswell, Me.* (1878); G. T. Eaton, "William King," in *Phillips Bull.* (Andover, Mass.), Jan. 1926; *Kennebec Jour.* (Augusta, Me.), June 24, 1852. The William King Papers are owned by the Me. Hist. Soc.] R. E. M.

KING, WILLIAM BENJAMIN BASIL (Feb. 26, 1859–June 22, 1928), Episcopal clergyman, novelist, and spiritualist, best known by his pen name, Basil King, was born at Charlottetown, Prince Edward Island, Canada, and died at Cambridge, Mass. His parents were William and Mary Anne Lucretia King. He attended St. Peter's School in Charlottetown, and the University of King's College in Windsor, Nova Scotia, where he was graduated in 1881. He married Esther (Manton) Foote, at Dublin, N. H., June 28, 1893. From 1884 to 1892 he served as curate and rector of St. Luke's Pro-Cathedral in Halifax, Nova Scotia, and from 1892 to 1900, as rector of Christ Church, Cambridge, Mass. Because of ill health, accompanied by failing eyesight, he abandoned his ecclesiastical career in 1900, and devoted the rest of his life to writing. Although continuing to reside in Cambridge, he spent much of his time in Europe.

During his literary career King wrote twenty novels. The following books may be taken as representative of their author's talent in this genre: *Let Not Man Put Asunder* (1901), *The Steps of Honor* (1904), *The Inner Shrine* (1909), *The Street Called Straight* (1912), *The Side of the Angels* (1916), and *The Happy Isles* (1923). The first novel to win a wide popularity was *The Inner Shrine,* which was published anonymously. His subsequent stories were almost invariably "best sellers." It cannot be claimed that his novels achieve a high distinction. His prose style is undistinguished; his plots are little more than ingenious mechanisms; his characters rarely come to life. Written with a frankly moral purpose, his fiction is too often ponderously didactic or mawkishly sentimental. He was particularly anxious to demonstrate the sanctity of marriage and the evils of agnosticism. It is not likely that his novels will be read in the future, except perhaps by students of popular literary taste.

During the last decade of his life, King wrote eight "serious" books, dealing with psychological, religious, and spiritualistic subjects from the point of view of his own personal experience. Two of these, *The Abolishing of Death* (1919), and *The Conquest of Fear* (1921), are of particular interest. During the World War, his attention was attracted to spiritualistic phenomena, and in *The Abolishing of Death* he gave an account of messages received from a great chemist, fictitiously named Henry Talbot, through the mediumistic agency of a young girl called Jennifer, who was in reality King's daughter Penelope. *The Conquest of Fear* is largely a record of his own courageous struggle, prolonged over a period of nearly thirty years, against physical infirmities—failing eyesight and a disease of the thyroid gland. The continued popularity of this book is attested by the fact that thirty thousand copies were sold in 1930. It is possible that in the modern neurasthenic world this authentic record of a personal experience may continue to attract many who will find in Basil King's life and counsel an aid in the conquest of fear.

[*Who's Who in America,* 1928–29; *N. Y. Times,* June 23, 1928; *Christian Century,* July 19, 1928; information from Mrs. Esther Manton King.] R. S.

KING, WILLIAM RUFUS DEVANE (Apr. 7, 1786–Apr. 18, 1853), congressman, minister to France, vice-president of the United States, was born in Sampson County, N. C., the son of William and Margaret (Devane) King. His ancestors came of North of Ireland and also of Huguenot stock, and his father was a Patriot planter of means. He graduated from the University of North Carolina in 1803 and after law study under William Duffy of Fayetteville was admitted to the bar in 1806. He served in the state legislature and was elected to Congress in 1810. From 1811 to 1816 he acted with the "War

Hawks" and then resigned to accompany William Pinkney to Naples and St. Petersburg as secretary of legation. Returning in 1818 he moved to Alabama, settling in Dallas County where he maintained his residence for the rest of his life. He became immediately active in politics, served in the first constitutional convention and became one of Alabama's first senators. During his senatorship his principal interest was in public lands. For a time he served as chairman of that committee in the Senate and in his early years was active in doing away with the credit system of land purchase. With the advent of Jackson he became his faithful supporter and participated in the various moves of attack and defense for which the Senate from 1829 to 1837 was famous. From 1836 to 1841 he was president *pro tempore* of the Senate, an office which was of more than usual importance while the inefficient Richard Mentor Johnson occupied the vice-presidency. When the Texas question arose he was eager for annexation and his ardor in that cause transferred him to a new scene of action.

In April 1844, fearing that Great Britain and France were going to act in concert to oppose the annexation of Texas, President Tyler appointed King minister to France, after the nomination of Henry A. Wise had been rejected by the Senate. So threatening was the situation that the new minister left Washington for France without delay. At first he was assured by Louis Philippe and Guizot that they would take no such action but during the winter he became suspicious and was on the verge of offering a formal protest against French interference in Texas. He refrained, however, and in October 1845 could report that France had acquiesced in annexation. Upon his return to the United States in 1846 he sought to reënter the Senate. He sided with the Union faction of his party and the state-rights wing succeeded in defeating him and electing his chief rival, Dixon H. Lewis. When Bagby resigned in 1848, the governor appointed King as his successor in the Senate and the legislature later elected him. His second senatorial term was chiefly marked by his activity in behalf of the compromise measures of 1850 and the Clayton-Bulwer treaty. As chairman of the committee on foreign relations he labored strenuously to secure the ratification of the treaty. When Fillmore became president, King was elected to preside over the Senate.

During these later years he had been active in supporting James Buchanan for the presidency; and when at the convention of 1852 the latter's hopes were blasted, King was given second place on the Democratic ticket to placate Buchanan's friends. Pierce and King were easily elected but King was so weakened by tuberculosis that he resigned from the Senate to find strength in Cuba. When it became apparent that he could not attend the inauguration a special act was passed to permit him to take the oath in Cuba. Shortly thereafter he determined to come home and died the day after he reached his plantation, "King's Bend." He had never married. His friends in the Senate who sought to eulogize him could point to little more than the extraordinary length of his service in the Senate, nearly twenty-nine years.

[The best short sketch of King is in T. M. Owen, *Hist. of Ala. and Dict. of Ala. Biog.* (1921), vol. III. A few of his letters are in the Buchanan MSS. in the Historical Society of Pennsylvania. His diplomatic career is best noticed in the sketches of John C. Calhoun and James Buchanan in *The Am. Secretaries of State and Their Diplomacy,* vol. V (1928), ed. by S. F. Bemis. See also: *Biog. Dir. Am. Cong.* (1928); *Obit. Addresses on the Occasion of the Death of Wm. R. King . . . Delivered in the Senate and the House of Representatives* (1854); *Mobile Daily Advertiser,* Apr. 20, 1853.] R. F. N.

KING OF WILLIAM, JAMES (Jan. 28, 1822–May 20, 1856), editor, was born at Georgetown, D. C., and there he received his education. He adopted the suffix "of William" (his father's name) in order to distinguish himself from other James Kings. When about fifteen he left home to earn his living, going first to Pittsburgh, where for a year he was clerk in a store. Then, after a brief stay in Berrien and St. Joseph, Mich., ill health caused his return to Georgetown (1838), where he became a post-office clerk. Between 1840 and 1848 he was connected with *Kendall's Expositor,* a Democratic campaign paper, with the Washington *Daily Globe,* and with the banking house of Corcoran & Riggs of Washington.

Letters from an elder brother, Henry, a member of Colonel Frémont's exploring expeditions (1846–48), led him to set out for the Pacific Coast, May 24, 1848, by way of Panama and Valparaiso. At the latter place he learned of the discovery of gold in California and started thither. After reaching San Francisco, Nov. 10, 1848, he had a brief but successful experience in digging gold at Hangtown (Placerville). Shortly thereafter he was in business in Sacramento. Seeing the possibilities of profitable banking in the new country, he went East, secured capital, and opened a bank in San Francisco, Dec. 5, 1849. As a banker, he carried on an extensive and lucrative business. He was reported in 1853 to be worth $250,000. The dishonesty of a trusted agent, however, brought the institution to the verge of bankruptcy, and King used up his private fortune in paying creditors and depositors. In June 1854, he became cashier for the express and banking firm of Adams & Company.

When that firm failed in February 1855, he turned to newspaper work. On borrowed capital, he started a small newspaper, the *Daily Evening Bulletin.* The first issue appeared Oct. 8, 1855, with King in full control. In his editorial position, he gave free rein to the instincts of a militant reformer. He had been a member of the first Vigilante in San Francisco (1851), and one of its executive committee. In 1853 he had been foreman of a grand jury which, in the face of murderous threats, returned an indictment against the city treasurer. He viewed the flagrant immorality and unblushing public corruption of the day with implacable hatred. From its first appearance, the *Evening Bulletin* fairly bristled with scourging attacks upon every person, firm, institution, judge, and law-maker—all called by name—that he regarded as guilty of dishonesty, corruption, wickedness, or fraud. His paper met with instant success and soon became the forum in which all kinds of public questions were discussed by correspondents. At the same time, its attacks infuriated the corrupt and criminal element. Finally, James P. Casey, the owner of the *Sunday Times,* a politician with a Sing Sing record, whose character had been incidentally assailed, shot King, openly and without warning, on the streets of San Francisco, May 14, 1856. He lingered for several days, dying on May 20. Two days later he was buried in Lone Mountain cemetery. Meantime, Casey had surrendered to the authorities. So low was public confidence in their integrity, however, that it was generally believed justice would be thwarted. In less than a week, therefore, the Vigilante had been revived, had compelled the sheriff to surrender the prisoner, and had tried and convicted him. His execution occurred at the very hour of King's funeral.

In 1843 King married Charlotte M. Libbey of Georgetown. In 1851 she and their four children joined her husband in San Francisco. They and two other children survived him. So great was the popular sympathy for the family, that a public subscription of nearly $32,000 was raised and presented to the widow and children.

[The most complete accounts of King's editorial career and the popular uprising which followed his murder are in H. H. Bancroft, *Popular Tribunals* (2 vols., 1887), and T. H. Hittell, *Hist. of Cal.* (4 vols., 1885–97). Briefer narratives appear in O. T. Shuck, *Representative and Leading Men of the Pacific* (1870); Z. S. Eldredge, *Hist. of Cal.* (5 vols., copr. 1915); Alonzo Phelps, *Contemporary Biog. of Cal.'s Representative Men* (1881), and G. W. James, *Heroes of Cal.* (1910). See also files of the *Daily Evening Bull.*, San Francisco, especially the issues of May 14–22, 1856; and two contemporary pamphlets, C. Rivers, *A Full and Authentic Account of the Murder of James King of William* (1857); and *A True and Minute Hist. of the Assassination of James King of William at San Francisco* (1856).]

P. O. R.

KINGSBURY, JOHN (May 26, 1801–Dec. 21, 1874), educator, was born in South Coventry, Conn., son of a farmer, John Kingsbury, and Dorothy Leavens, daughter of Benjamin Leavens of Killingly, R. I. On his father's side he was descended from Henry Kingsbury who, with his wife, Susan, emigrated to Massachusetts in 1630. Until he was twenty years old he worked on the farm, attending winter sessions of the district school as pupil to the age of fifteen, and then for four years serving as teacher in his own or a neighboring district. Having prepared himself in the classics under Rev. Chauncey Booth of South Coventry, Conn., he entered Brown University in 1822, still teaching part of the year to pay expenses; in 1826 he graduated, ranking second in his class.

Before graduation he had joined G. A. Dewitt in conducting the Providence high school (a private venture), and two years later he opened a department for girls, which soon became a separate young ladies' high school, startlingly novel in every feature. Its room had papered walls, carpeted floor, comfortable chairs, desks covered with broadcloth; instead of six annual holidays it had a four-weeks' vacation; tuition was fifty dollars a year; pupils were courteously treated, corrected for faults in manners, dismissed with curtsies on the one side and bows on the other. There softness ended, however: a weekly certificate of scholarship and behavior and a system of honors and rewards secured regular attendance, punctuality, and a wholesome rivalry in excellence; and the curriculum included no "showy and superficial accomplishments," but thorough drill in Latin, algebra, geometry, several natural sciences, and "the higher English branches." Doubt and ridicule had no effect upon Kingsbury's reasoned proceedings; shouts of "There goes the man who is teaching the girls Latin" left him unperturbed. The school was soon full, drew visitors from near and far, and in time could easily have doubled its size; it never received more than forty-three, even after occupying a fine new building in 1848. During its thirty years under Kingsbury, it educated more than five hundred young women, some of them from distant places.

Kingsbury helped to originate and direct public movements for better education. In 1830 he was among the founders of the American Institute of Instruction, and was for many years an officer and councilor, serving as president from 1855 to 1857. His *Lecture on Failures in Teaching* (1848), an address delivered before the Institute, at Bangor, Me., in August 1848, is a singularly clear and sane analysis of what goes to make a good school and a good teacher. The degree of illiteracy and of prejudice against free public schools, especially in rural parts of Rhode Island, was a subject of serious concern. The Rhode Island Institute of Instruction, founded 1845, undertook to secure cooperation in every community for putting into force a new system of public instruction just authorized by the state. Kingsbury was its most active founder and for the first eleven years its president. Upon him fell the task of raising funds and securing speakers to win popular approval of the schools. His year of service as commissioner of public instruction (1857–58) was a fitting culmination of these labors; his tour of inspection included every school; he investigated, consulted, made practical suggestions, and bade the workers go on "with steady courage and cheerful hearts." "The welfare of children," he said, "should never be weighed in the scales of pecuniary gain or loss. There is something infinitely higher and better than money—and *that* is character" (E. M. Stone, *post*, p. 42). His constant insistence upon high moral character in teachers, and his own rare firmness, patience, and self-control were altogether in keeping with this article of faith.

In many kindred ways Kingsbury served his generation: as teacher of a young men's Bible class, beginning when Sunday schools were a novelty; mover for a new church (the Central Congregational) in a growing part of Providence and collector of funds to build it; member of the American Board of Commissioners for Foreign Missions; distributor of Bibles to the poor of Rhode Island; raiser of endowment to finance President Wayland's "New System" of education at Brown University; officer of the Rhode Island Alpha of Phi Beta Kappa for seventeen years; president of the Franklin Society; trustee for twenty years of the Butler Hospital for the Insane; trustee, fellow, and secretary of the corporation of Brown University. For the last fifteen years of his life, he was president of the Washington Insurance Company in Providence. His wife, Mary Mackie Burgess, whom he married Aug. 19, 1834, died before him; three daughters survived.

[F. J. Kingsbury, *The Geneal. of the Descendants of Henry Kingsbury of Ipswich and Haverhill, Mass.* (1905); Henry Barnard, *Am. Jour. of Educ.*, June 1858; E. M. Stone, *Manual of Educ.: A Brief Hist. of the R. I. Institute of Instruction* (1874); *Providence Jour.*, Dec. 22, 1874; "Necrology of Brown Univ.," in *Providence Jour.*, June 16, 1875.]

E. M. S. B.

KINGSFORD, THOMAS (Sept. 29, 1799–Nov. 28, 1869), inventor, manufacturer, was born in Wickham, Kent County, England, the son of George and Mary (Love) Kingsford. He attended school until he was seventeen years old when the death of his father compelled him to find employment to help support his widowed mother. For five years he was a baker in London. He then found employment in a chemical plant where he developed a marked ability for chemical research and acquired a practical working knowledge of chemistry. Ill health, however, compelled him to give up this occupation after a few years and he again turned baker, working at his trade in various parts of England. At Kensington in addition to his baking business he maintained a general store. About 1830, when financial reverses ruined his business, he went to Headcorn in Kent County and with the assistance of his wife started a school. The following year he determined to seek his fortune in America, and leaving his wife in charge of the school, he emigrated to New York City, landing on Dec. 12, 1831. He was able to send for his family in 1833. After working at his trade for a few months he found employment in the starch factory of William Colgate & Company at Harsimus, Bergen County, N. J., then the largest firm engaged in the manufacture of this commodity, and by his energy and resourcefulness soon rose to be superintendent. Starch was then made from wheat and there were many objectionable features in both the methods of manufacture and in the product. As early as 1833 Kingsford began to study means of improving the methods in use and became convinced that in ripe Indian corn lay a source of obtaining starch. For seven or eight years he continued this study without any encouragement from his employers and followed it in 1841 by a series of experiments. After many discouraging trials, upon determining that the starch in corn could not be extracted as in wheat, Kingsford accidentally placed some lime-treated corn in a receptacle containing corn treated with lye which a few days later yielded a thoroughly separated starch. Almost a year had transpired before this successful accident occurred, and very quickly thereafter, in 1842, Kingsford perfected his process and produced a quantity of marketable starch. A business engagement quickly followed between Kingsford and William Colgate & Company whereby Kingsford was to superintend all of the operations, devise the manufacturing machinery, and at the same time retain knowledge of the process for himself. Four years later, in 1846, Kingsford organized his own company with his son Thomson, erected a small factory at Bergen, N. J., and there began the manufacture of Kingsford starch. Two years later he founded the Oswego Starch Factory and erected a large plant at Oswego, N. Y., where he carried on a successful business until his death. In 1850, after a series of experiments, Kingsford successfully produced cornstarch for food purposes, which quickly came into public favor. Aside from his manufacturing interests, he was active in banking circles in Oswego and also prominent in the establishment of the Oswego water works. Kingsford's first wife, Ann Thomson, whom he married in 1818, died in 1834, and in 1839 he married Mrs. Elizabeth Austen. At the time of his death in Oswego his sole survivor was his son Thomson.

[Chauncey Depew, *1795–1895: One Hundred Years of Am. Commerce* (1895); Crisfield Johnson, *History of Oswego County, N. Y.* (1877); John C. Churchill, *Landmarks of Oswego County, N. Y.* (1895).]

C. W. M.

KINGSLEY, CALVIN (Sept. 8, 1812–Apr. 6, 1870), bishop of the Methodist Episcopal Church, was born in Annsville, Oneida County, N. Y., the oldest of twelve children. His father, Oran Kingsley, Jr., was a native of Connecticut, and his mother, of the north of Ireland. When Calvin was about twelve years old the family moved to Ellington, Chautauqua County. His parents were not actively affiliated with any church, but here the boy came under Methodist influence, was converted, and made up his mind to get an education. He worked on the farm summers, attended school winters, and at the end of three years was employed by the trustees to teach the school. Later he taught at Randolph, Cattaraugus County. It was not until he was twenty-four that he found opportunity to go to college. With no means of support other than his hands and brains, he entered Allegheny College in 1836, eking out a bare living, first by acting as janitor, and then by cutting wood, which he found more remunerative. Twice his course was interrupted by periods of teaching. He had a keen, logical mind, and showed especial aptitude for mathematics and such science as was then taught. During his senior year he was made instructor in mathematics and after his graduation in 1841 he continued to teach at Allegheny, becoming in 1843 professor of mathematics and civil engineering. The year he graduated he was admitted to the Erie Conference of the Methodist Episcopal Church on trial and married Delia Scudder. Except for the period 1843 to 1846, when the withdrawal of state aid necessitated the closing of the college, he was connected with the institution until 1856. Ordained deacon in 1843 and elder in 1845, he held preaching appointments at Saegerstown, Pa. (1841), Meadville (1842), and Erie (1844–46). In these earlier years he became known as an able controversialist and defender of the doctrines and polity of the Methodist Episcopal Church. In 1843, first at Salem, N. Y., and later at Jamestown, he met in debate Luther Lee [*q.v.*], one of the organizers of the Wesleyan Methodist Connection, the question being whether the Methodist Episcopal Church justified slavery, and in government was arbitrary and unscriptural. In Erie he took a tilt at the Universalists; in Meadville, at the Unitarians; and in 1847, having read *Anastasis* by George Bush [*q.v.*], he published *The Resurrection of the Dead: a Vindication of the Literal Resurrection of the Human Body: in Opposition to the Work of Prof. Bush,* which went through several editions.

He was a delegate from the Erie Conference to the General Conference of 1852, and had by this time become well enough known and highly enough esteemed to receive a respectable number of votes for bishop. At the succeeding General Conference (1856), he was elected editor of the *Western Christian Advocate,* Cincinnati. The question of slavery was causing strife and division in the Church, and Kingsley made the *Advocate* aggressively anti-slavery. He was chairman of the committee on slavery at the General Conference of 1860, and presented and ably supported the substituted chapter in the *Discipline,* which admonished the membership of the Church to seek the "extirpation" of slavery "by all lawful and Christian means." Throughout the Civil War the *Advocate* gave strong support to the Union cause. At the General Conference of 1864 he was elected bishop. Although he was a comparatively young man, his service was brief. He made his home in Cleveland, but his duties carried him far. In 1865 and 1866 he presided at Conferences on the Pacific Coast, and the following year attended the mission Conference in Switzerland and Germany. In 1869 he was again on the Pacific Coast, and from there went to India and China and then again to Switzerland and Germany. While on a trip to the Holy Land he died suddenly of heart disease at Beirut, where he was buried. A monument erected by American Methodists marks his grave. His account of some of his travels, *Round the World: A Series of Letters,* in two volumes, with a biographical sketch, was published in 1870.

[Samuel Gregg, *The Hist. of Methodism Within the Bounds of the Erie Ann. Conference of the M. E. Ch.,* vol. II (1873); J. N. Fradenburg, *Hist. of Erie Conference* (1907), vol. II; *Minutes of the Ann. Conferences of the M. E. Ch. for the Year 1870*; *Western Christian Advocate*, Apr. 13, 20, 1870; E. A. Smith, *Allegheny—A Century of Education, 1815–1915* (1916); John McClintock and James Strong, *Cyc. of Biblical, Theol. and Eccl. Lit.*, vol. V (1873); J. P. Downs and F. Y. Hedley, *Hist. of Chautauqua County, N. Y., and Its People* (3 vols., 1921); *Autobiog. of the Rev. Luther Lee* (1882); *Ladies' Repository*, May 1865.]

H. E. S.

KINGSLEY, ELBRIDGE (Sept. 17, 1842–Aug. 28, 1918), engraver, painter, was born in Carthage, Ohio, son of Moses W. and Rachel W. (Curtis) Kingsley and grandson of Seth Kingsley of Hatfield, Mass. His parents returned from Ohio to Hatfield in 1843, where they lived on a farm and reared a family of six boys. Elbridge studied at the Hopkins Academy in Hadley, Mass., for two years and then entered the office of the *Hampshire Gazette* at Northampton. He used his spare time in drawing, taking his subjects from the Bible and Indian stories. When his apprenticeship was over, he studied painting at the Cooper Union in New York and in the establishment of J. W. Orr, where he acquired the rudiments of wood-engraving. He was employed as engraver by the Century Company and about 1880 started a school to inspire students to become creative artists rather than mechanical engravers. In 1882 he made a notable original picture and engraving of the Hatfield woods, "In a New England Forest." He was particularly successful in presenting the rich foliage of Rousseau, Diaz, and Corot, and the misty works of Tryon. He engraved fifteen illustrations directly from nature for Whittier's *Poems of Nature* (1886). He also illustrated an article by John Burroughs entitled "Signs and Seasons" (*Century Magazine,* March 1883). "White Birches" earned for him a gold medal at the Paris Exposition, 1889. In 1884 he became a member of the Grolier Club of New York and of the Society of American Wood-engravers, serving on the exhibition committee in Paris, where he was awarded a gold medal by the international jury.

At a meeting of the members of the Grolier Club in May 1915 a paper of Kingsley's was read in which he described his travels in his "sketching car." In order that he might be out of doors to enjoy the scenery of Hadley he had a gipsy car constructed in which he could live. It contained two sleeping berths at one end, a desk for his work, and a kitchen in the rear. A farmer's horse was always available when he desired to change his location. His descriptions of the dawns, the cool mists, and the glory of New England in its autumn coloring, are as poetic as his sketches. He entertained many painters, engravers, and poets in his unique touring car. After 1890 he devoted himself to his original engravings from nature and reproductions from prominent painters, mainly large work for Japan proof, representing Daubigny, Inness, Ryder, and others. Kingsley was twice married: to Emma Brown, who died within a year after their marriage, and on Oct. 14, 1869, to Elizabeth W. Cook of Hadley. He died at the home of his daughter in Brooklyn, N. Y. He was awarded, besides the Paris gold medal, a medal at the Columbian Exposition at Chicago, 1893, a gold medal at the California Midwinter International Exposition, 1894, and he received honors in Vienna and Berlin. A complete collection of his engravings is contained in a room entirely devoted to his work in the Dwight Memorial Art Building, Mt. Holyoke College, known as the "Clara Leigh Dwight Collection."

[*Cat. of the Works of Elbridge Kingsley, Consisting of a Life Sketch, Complete List of Book and Mag. Engraving* . . . (1901); *Am. Art Ann.*, 1918; *Who's Who in America*, 1916–17; *Scribner's Mag.*, July 1895; *Springfield Republican*, Aug. 30, 1918; A. V. S. Anthony, Timothy Cole, and Elbridge Kingsley, *Wood-Engraving* (1916), pub. by the Grolier Club.]

H. W.

KINGSLEY, JAMES LUCE (Aug. 28, 1778–Aug. 31, 1852), educator, was born at Scotland, Windham County, Conn., the son of Jonathan Kingsley and Zillah (Cary) Kingsley, widow of James Luce. He was a descendant of John Kingsley of Hampshire, England, who emigrated to Plymouth, Mass., in 1630 and died in 1678. James's father was a man of some prominence in the community, fond of reading, and a founder of a local society for the circulation of books. Young Kingsley early manifested an unusual interest in study. Prepared at Plainfield Academy and under clergymen of neighboring towns, he entered Williams College in 1795 and completed the freshman year. After a period at home due to ill health, he joined the sophomore class at Yale in May 1797 and graduated with the degree of B.A. in 1799. The next year he taught school in Wethersfield, Conn., and spent the following year at home giving private instruction. In 1801 he was appointed tutor in Yale College, and from 1801 to 1812 he performed the arduous task of giving instruction to a group in all the required studies up to the end of junior year. In 1805 he was appointed professor of the Hebrew, Greek, and Latin languages and of ecclesiastical history, being the first professor of languages at Yale. The title of professor of ecclesiastical history was merely nominal and was dropped after 1817. He gave up the teaching of Greek in 1831, and of Hebrew in 1835, and from that time until his retirement in 1851 he devoted himself exclusively to Latin, which had always been his major interest. In addition to his duties as professor he acted as librarian from 1805 to 1824. He married, Sept. 23, 1811, Lydia, daughter of Daniel Lathrop and Elizabeth (Bill) Coit of Norwich, Conn. They had three sons and one daughter.

Kingsley was distinguished in his generation for breadth of intellectual interest and accuracy of scholarship. The original trend of his mind was toward mathematics, and he always maintained an activity in that field, particularly in astronomical calculations. The study of science, then in its infancy, attracted him strongly, and he was a regular attendant at the scientific lectures given for seniors. His contemporaries testified to his thorough acquaintance with the classics of English literature. In history, particularly the history of Connecticut and of New England, he was a recognized authority, and in this field he contributed frequently to periodicals. His *Historical Discourse Delivered . . . on the Two Hundredth Anniversary of the Settlement of New Haven* (1838) was an authoritative work, and his articles on the history of Yale College (*American Quarterly Register,* August 1835, February 1836, and *American Biblical Repository,* July, October 1841, January 1842) were for many years standard accounts. He contributed a biography of Ezra Stiles [*q.v.*] to Jared Sparks's *Library of American Biography* (2 ser., vol. VI, 1845). In the field of Latin his competence was great, but his publications few, consisting of several textbooks—an edition of Cicero's *De Oratore,* and two volumes of Latin selections. The purity and elegance of his Latin style was justly admired, and few have excelled him in mastery of the subtleties of the language. The bent of his mind was critical rather than creative, however, and his most characteristic work was done on reviews in periodicals, mostly published anonymously. The temper of the age favored controversy, and here Kingsley's enormous fund of accurate knowledge and his gift of keen satire made him a formidable adversary. His review of Stuart's *Select Classics* in the *American Monthly Review,* April 1833, is an excellent example of his critical and scholarly powers at their best.

[W. R. Cutter, *New Eng. Families* (1913), vol. II, and Leroy Brown, *Kingsley Geneal.* (1907), for Jonathan Kingsley's ancestry; F. B. Dexter, *Biog. Sketches Grads. Yale Coll.,* vol. V (1911); T. A. Thacher, *A Discourse Commemorative of Professor James L. Kingsley, to Which is Prefixed the Address at the Funeral by Theodore D. Woolsey* (1852); *Memorial Biogs. of the New-Eng. Historic Geneal. Soc.,* vol. I (1880); *Congregational Quart.,* Apr. 1863.] H. M. H.

KINGSLEY, NORMAN WILLIAM (Oct. 26, 1829–Feb. 20, 1913), dentist, sculptor, a son of Nathaniel and Eliza (Williams) Kingsley, was born in Stockholm, St. Lawrence County, N. Y. He received his early education in the public school of Poultney, Vt., and at an academy in Troy, N. Y. After serving as a clerk in several stores in Elmira and Troy, in 1848 he paid for a course of instruction in dentistry with his uncle, Dr. A. W. Kingsley, of Elizabeth, N. J., who stipulated that the then secret process of making porcelain teeth was not to be included in the course; but young Kingsley soon mastered the process without assistance and otherwise demonstrated his native mechanical and artistic abilities. In 1850 he began the practice of dentistry with B. C. Leffler in Owego, N. Y., where he shortly established an independent office. In 1852 he removed to New York City, practised about a year in partnership with Solyman Brown [*q.v.*] and Samuel Lockwood, and then established himself independently at 858 Broadway. For his artificial teeth on gold plates he received a gold medal from the world's fair at the Crystal Palace in 1853, and other medals from the Paris exposition of 1855. In 1858 he published the first of his many articles on the correction of irregularities of the teeth and thenceforth specialized largely on oral deformities. Beginning in 1860, he perfected the gold obturator and artificial velum of soft rubber for cleft palate cases, for which he received several medals, diplomas of merit, and honorary memberships in dental and medical societies at home and abroad. His first articles on artificial vela and obturators appeared in 1863 and 1864.

Kingsley visited Europe in 1864 and was cordially received by the medical and dental societies of Great Britain and France. Shortly afterward he invented and patented the first portable gas blowpipe for dentists' use. He was one of the founders of the New York College of Dentistry and served as its first dean and first professor of dental art and mechanism from 1866 to 1869. He originated several ingenious methods and appliances for regulating teeth and in 1880 published *A Treatise on Oral Deformities as a Branch of Mechanical Surgery,* in which he gave a comprehensive review of the scattered knowledge of the subject, together with descriptions of his own improvements. For many years it was the only standard textbook on orthodontia as well as oral deformities. A German version was published at Leipzig in 1881. Kingsley wrote the long article on "Surgery of the Teeth and Adjacent Parts" in *The International Encyclopædia of Surgery* (vol. V, 1884), edited by John

Ashhurst. In 1886 and 1887 he was president of the New York State Dental Society.

He had considerable reputation as a modeler of portrait-busts in clay, and he also worked in other media of art. In his youth, while a clerk at Elmira and Troy he was known locally as a clever engraver on copper and wood, and he did some creditable paintings in oil. When he removed to New York in 1852, he tried his hand at sculpture. In 1861 he modeled an idealized female head, called the "Evening Star." His finest work in this line is a bust of Christ, made in 1868, a steel engraving of which appears as the frontispiece of Howard Crosby's *Jesus, His Life and Work* (1871). Kingsley's best-known portrait-bust was that of Whitelaw Reid, presented to the Lotos Club. He finally became interested in pyrography, in which art heated iron instruments were then employed; but he substituted a modification of the dentists' blowpipe, which he had invented, and used it successfully in making his "flame-paintings" on wood, including numerous copies of Rembrandt's portraits. Kingsley was married, in 1850, to Alma W. Shepard. They had two daughters. He died in his eighty-fourth year at Warren Point, N. J., and was interred in Woodlawn Cemetery, N. Y.

[The best sketch of Kingsley is that by R. Ottolengui, in the dental *Items of Interest*, Apr. 1913. See also the sketch by B. L. Thorpe, in C. R. E. Koch, *Hist. of Dental Surgery* (1910), vol. III; *Who's Who in America*, 1912–13; *Dental Cosmos, Dental Register*, Apr. 1913.] L. P. B.

KINKEAD, EDGAR BENTON (Mar. 14, 1863–Apr. 9, 1930), jurist, son of Isaac Benton and Hannah A. (Thornburg) Kinkead, was born in the little village of Beverly, Washington County, Ohio. His paternal ancestors came from Ireland and remotely from Scotland, while his maternal ancestors were of Scotch-English origin. His father was a captain and later a colonel of the Ohio volunteers during the Civil War. He received his early education at the common schools of the village in which he lived and at Marietta Academy and was for two years (1880–82) at Marietta College where his record as a student was high. On Jan. 20, 1883, he married Nellie M. Snyder, a native of Canada. In 1884 he became deputy clerk of the probate court of Washington County, Ohio, at the same time beginning by himself the study of law. He continued his study while holding successively the positions of deputy clerk of the Ohio supreme court and of assistant librarian of the Ohio supreme court law library. He was admitted to the bar in 1889 and began practice in Columbus. In 1890 he was editor of the *Ohio Law Journal* and from 1898 to 1900 was special counsel in the office of the attorney-general of Ohio. While holding this position he was especially engaged in the preparation of important anti-trust cases against the Standard Oil Company. In 1908 he was elected a judge of the common pleas court of Ohio, was reëlected in 1914, in 1920, and for a fourth time in 1926.

Though in the active practice of law for eighteen years, he is best known as a teacher, writer, and judge. For twenty years he was a professor of law at the college of law of Ohio State University, teaching common law and code pleading. Not trained in modern methods of legal education he taught law in the older fashion, using lectures and textbooks as his means of instruction. He was a prolific writer on legal subjects and was the author of *The Law of Pleading in Civil Actions and Defenses under the Code* (2 vols., 1895); *Forms of Instructions to Juries* (1897), part of which was enlarged and republished in 1914 as *Approved Forms . . . of Instructions to Jury, both Civil and Criminal; Exposition of Common Law and Equity Pleading* (1900), a historical comparison with the code; *A Treatise on the Law of Court Practice and Procedure* (1900); *The Probate Law and Practice of the State of Ohio* (1901); *Commentaries on the Law of Torts* (2 vols., 1903); and *Procedure in Civil Trials and on Appeal and Error* (1915), some of which had already appeared in 1897 in the *Forms of Instructions to Juries.* These books were the product of careful accurate labor and have been for many years of great value to the practising lawyers and judges of Ohio. His ablest writing was done in the field of procedure. When he ventured from this field as he did in his *Commentaries on the Law of Torts* he was not so successful. His extended article on "Libel and Slander" for the *Cyclopedia of Law and Procedure* (vol. XXV, 1907) was, however, well done.

Kinkead was a judge of the common pleas court of Ohio for twenty-two years and it was probably here that he did his best work. He was noted for his painstaking industry and for his originality and independence of thinking. "Everyone makes mistakes sometimes" was his favorite remark as expressing his attitude toward precedents in legal cases. In his willingness to refuse to follow precedent he was thought by some to be almost iconoclastic, but in spite of his independent opinions he was rarely overruled by the higher courts. Among the outstanding cases which he tried during his term as judge were the "Slaymaker" case (his opinion in the case was later published in a separate volume) which was a suit involving over a million dollars brought by the minority shareholders of the Columbus Railway & Light Company against the Clark interests of Philadelphia and resulted in the ouster of these interests from their control of the local company; the "Bribery Cases" involving bribery charges against several members of the Ohio State Senate resulting in their conviction and penitentiary imprisonment; the libel suit brought by a United States federal judge against a Toledo newspaper which was decided in favor of the newspaper; and an injunction suit brought to prevent the Federal Gas & Fuel Company from turning off the supply of gas from the city of Columbus, resulting in favor of the city. Kinkead was known as a particularly able and fearless judge in the trial of criminal cases. He tried thirty-two murder cases, almost all of which resulted in conviction. He did not live to complete his last judicial term. He died in Atlanta, Ga., at the home of his daughter and only child. Though he was not a great jurist or great research scholar or great teacher of the law, he was a careful, indefatigable worker, and gave valuable service to his state.

[*Who's Who in America,* 1912–13; *Atlanta Jour., Ohio State Journal* (Columbus), Apr. 10, 1930; Franklin County court records.] A. H. T.

KINLOCH, CLELAND (1760–Sept. 12, 1823), rice planter, was born in Charleston, S. C. His parents, Anne Isabella (Cleland) and Francis Kinloch, of "New Gilmerton," "Wehaw," "Kensington," and "Rice Hope" plantations, were both of Scotch ancestry and of families prominent in South Carolina. His great-grandfather was Sir Francis Kinloch of Gilmerton, Scotland, whose second son, James, came to the province in 1703, prospered, and acquired "New Gilmerton" on Goose Creek. Upon his father's death, he was left at the age of seven to the guardianship of Gov. Thomas Boone. Five years later he entered Eton, where his exercises were frequently "sent up to the Doctor for being particular good ones." His "long & pretty" letters gave pleasant pictures of schooldays and visits to cousins at Gilmerton House. Wishing to be a merchant, he later went to Holland for his commercial education. The American Revolution delayed his homecoming until after the South Carolina Confiscation Act of 1782, which lists him to be amerced. He seriously considered returning to England; but upon the partition of his father's estate in 1784, when "Wehaw" fell to him, he energetically began its restoration. He is said to have been relieved from amercement, yet as late as 1790 his factor, John White, was trustee for his 300 slaves. He was a member of the convention which ratified the Federal Constitution. His votes on the Constitution and in the South Carolina convention of 1790, as well as in the legislature, 1791–93, suggest that he was in harmony with his class and probably a Federalist.

He was one of the first to adopt Gideon Dupont's system of flooding river ricefields by tide movement, using trunks and floodgates similar to those he had seen in Holland. On the plans of Jonathan Lucas, he erected and improved one of the first tidal rice-pounding mills, operated like those of Bordeaux and Holland by the rise and fall of the tide, and so complete that it threshed, husked, and barreled the grain. He enlarged "Wehaw" to some 5,000 acres, using many oxen and animals for its operation, and imported a Scotch gardener for the grounds. He also began embankments on new lands along the Wateree. On Apr. 15, 1786, he married Harriott, daughter of Ebenezer Simmons of Charleston. For several years they summered at Newport, R. I., and in 1804 he returned to Europe; but in 1807, he bought 611 acres in the High Hills of Santee and erected a three-story summer residence, surmounted by a rotunda, which he named "Acton." Benevolent and genial in his manners, he was popular with his neighbors and enjoyed conversing upon "the inexhaustible subjects of winter-grass, English & Latin prosody, the properties of the lever & the law of Nations." He was a handsome man, with blond coloring, regular features, and tall, robust figure. Industrious and economical, he prospered until in the great storm of 1822 his tide-water plantations suffered damages estimated at $30,000. The year following this disaster, he died at "Acton" and was buried in the Episcopal churchyard at Statesburg, S. C.

[Manuscript sketch of Cleland Kinloch by Langdon Cheves; extracts from Kinloch family papers in possession of Langdon Cheves; United States census of 1790; David Ramsey, *Hist. of S. C.,* vol. II (1809); the *Charleston Courier* and *Southern Patriot and Commercial Advertiser* (Charleston), Sept. 17, 1823.] A. K. G.

KINLOCH, ROBERT ALEXANDER (Feb. 20, 1826–Dec. 23, 1891), surgeon, was born at Charleston, S. C., to Dr. George Kinloch and Charlotte Granby, the former a native of Scotland and the latter of Wales. After graduating from Charleston College in 1845 and taking his degree in medicine at the University of Pennsylvania in 1848, he spent two years in the hospitals of London, Edinburgh, and Paris. With this unusual preparation, he returned to his native city and established himself in practice. The advent of the Civil War brought him into the Confederate army as a surgeon. He served at various times upon the staffs of Generals Lee, Pemberton, and Beauregard and upon medical examining boards at Norfolk, Richmond, and Charleston. Later he held the position of inspector of hospitals for South Carolina, Georgia, and Florida. Following the close of the war he returned to his practice in Charleston. His teaching career began in 1866 with his election to the chair of materia medica in the Medical College of the State of South Carolina. Three years later he was transferred to the chair of the principles and practice of surgery and finally to that of clinical surgery, which he occupied to the time of his death. He was elected dean of the faculty in 1888 and continued in that position for the remainder of his life.

As professor and as dean he was always an advocate of higher standards of education for the school and was deeply disappointed with the scant success attainable. It is as an operating surgeon, however, that Dr. Kinloch is best remembered. From the beginning of his career he was a bold and self-reliant operator with a manual dexterity and resourcefulness in emergency that soon put him in the forefront of the profession of his locality. He is credited with being the first American surgeon to perform a resection of the knee-joint for chronic disease and to treat fractures of the lower jaw and of other bones by wiring together the fragments. He was one of the first to open the abdomen and suture perforations of the intestines following gunshot wounds. His medical writings, mainly surgical case reports, were usually contributed to the *Charleston Medical Journal* of which he acted as editor for a short time. He was a member of the Medical Society of South Carolina and of the American Surgical Association and an associated fellow of the Philadelphia College of Physicians. He died in his native city of influenzal pneumonia during the influenza pandemic of 1891. Kinloch was tall with a slight, erect figure. His portrait shows a handsome face with kindly eyes. His professional skill, combined with his attractive personality, brought him a very large general practice, and he was for decades the leading medical man of Charleston. Though rather abrupt in his manner he won the devotion of his patients and the admiration of his pupils. He was married to Elizabeth Caldwell of Fairfield County, S. C., in 1856, and had four sons and four daughters. Two sons followed him in the practice of medicine.

[*Trans. Am. Surgic. Asso.*, vol. X (1892); *Medic. Record*, Jan. 2, 1892; H. A. Kelly and W. L. Burrage, *Am. Medic. Biogs.* (1920); the *News and Courier* (Charleston), Dec. 24, 1891.] J. M. P—n.

KINNE, LA VEGA GEORGE (Nov. 5, 1846–Mar. 16, 1906), jurist, was born in Syracuse, N. Y., the son of Æsop and Lydia (Beebe) Kinne. His father was a farmer of moderate circumstance. Desirous that their son should have the full advantage of the educational opportunities of their community the parents sent him through high school and to Ames Business School before he began the study of law in a Syracuse office. In 1865, he went to Mendota, Ill., where he continued his study of law in private while working in an implement store. He was admitted to the bar the following spring, but, being discontented with a mere law-office preparation, he enrolled in the law school of the University of Michigan. He received the degree of LL.B. in the spring of 1868, returned to Mendota, and entered the practice of law. On Sept. 23, 1869, he married Mary E. Abrams, of Peru, Ill., and moved to Toledo, Iowa, where in 1869 he became the junior member of the law firm of Crawford & Kinne. He continued in the practice of law until 1886 when he was elected judge of the seventeenth judicial district. Except for a few months while editor of the *Des Moines Leader,* he served as district judge until he was elected to the state supreme court in 1891. In 1897 he became chief justice.

Because he had abandoned the Republican party in 1869 and become a stanch Democrat his election to the supreme court caused great apprehension in the state. He had taken an active part in opposing a state prohibitory act which a Republican majority had adopted; and his political enemies, consequently, questioned his ability impartially to administer a law which he had so strongly opposed. His vigorous support of all laws not only silenced his political opponents but demonstrated to the state that political belief need play no part in judicial decision. His success in public life was indeed remarkable considering that as a Democrat he was representative of the minority group. He was twice candidate for governor (1881, 1883), and once for United States senator, and on each occasion ran well ahead of his party's ticket. A leader of his party, he was for many years a member, and several times chairman, of the Democratic state central committee and twice a delegate to the national convention (1876, 1884).

He was also the recipient of many offices of a non-political nature. He was a law lecturer at the State University of Iowa from 1888 to 1898, served for a time as law lecturer at the Iowa College of Law, Des Moines, and wrote *Iowa Pleading, Practice and Forms in Actions and Special Proceedings at Law and Equity* (1888), which became the standard procedural text for Iowa lawyers. He was president of the Iowa Bar Association in 1896 and appointed as representative from Iowa on the commission for uniform state laws. He served as an officer of the National Conference of Charities and Corrections, and was the Iowa representative of the International Prison Association. In 1898 Iowa reorganized the administration of its penal and charitable institutions by the creation of the board of control of state institutions, consisting of three members appointed by the governor. Kinne was named as the Democratic member of the board, serving until his death. As senior member he gave the greatest measure of service to his state. His sympathetic insight into human relations coupled with courageous executive abilities made him the creator of policies rather than administrator of details. He died in Des Moines.

[*The Bench and Bar of Iowa* (1901); Board of Control of State Institutions, *Bull. of Iowa Institutions*, Apr. 1906; E. H. Stiles, *Recollections and Sketches of Notable Lawyers and Public Men of Early Iowa* (1916); B. F. Gue, *Hist. of Iowa* (1903), vol. IV; *Proc. of the Twelfth Ann. Meeting of the Iowa State Bar Asso.* (1906); *Register and Leader* (Des Moines), Mar. 16, 17, 1906; *Who's Who in America*, 1906–07.]

F. E. H—k.

KINNERSLEY, EBENEZER (Nov. 30, 1711–July 4, 1778), teacher and physical experimenter, was born at Gloucester, England, the son of William Kinnersley, who came to America in 1714 to take the position of assistant pastor of the Pennepek Baptist Church, Lower Dublin, near Philadelphia. Ebenezer spent most of his early life at Lower Dublin, studying at home under his father's direction. As a young man he went to Philadelphia, where he established a small school. In 1743 he was ordained to the Baptist ministry, but never held a pastorate, though he was one of the constituent members of the Philadelphia Baptist Church and remained connected with it until his death. Attracted by the popular and spectacular experiments which Franklin was carrying on with the little known "electric fluid," he became associated with the group that was responsible for the "Philadelphia Experiments" in electricity. Of him Joseph Priestley wrote: "We must by no means overlook what was done by Mr. Kinnersley, the Doctor's [Franklin's] friend. . . . Some of his observations . . . are very curious; and some later accounts . . . seem to promise, that, if he continue his electrical inquiries, his name, after that of his friend [Franklin], will be second to few in the history of electricity." Concerning the exact nature of Kinnersley's contributions Priestley continues: "He first distinguished himself by re-discovering Mr. Du Faye's two contrary electricities of glass and sulphur, with which both he and Dr. Franklin were at that time wholly unacquainted. But Mr. Kinnersley had a great advantage over Mr. Du Faye; for, making his experiments in a more advanced state of the science, he saw immediately, that the two contrary electricities of glass and sulphur were the very same positive and negative electricities which had just been discovered by Dr. Watson and Dr. Franklin" (*The History and Present State of Electricity, post,* pp. 178–79). This discovery was made in Boston in 1751 where Kinnersley had gone (with a letter to Gov. James Bowdoin from Franklin) to deliver a series of lectures at Faneuil Hall. These lectures were a repetition of his series, "The Newly Discovered Electric Fire," the first to be given in America or Europe (advertisement in *Pennsylvania Gazette,* Apr. 11, 1751), delivered at Philadelphia the same year. Kinnersley was next at Newport, R. I., where he repeated his experiments and lectures in March 1752, and suggested methods of protecting buildings from lightning. He then lectured at New York and returned to Philadelphia in 1753 when he was elected chief master in the College of Philadelphia. He was appointed professor of English and oratory in 1755. About this time he demonstrated that heat could be produced by electricity and invented an electrical air thermometer, upon which most of his fame rests. His experiments in this connection he described in a letter to Franklin, dated Mar. 12, 1761, which Franklin read before the Royal Society of London (*Philosophical Transactions,* vol. LIII, 1763). In his *Experiments and Observations on Electricity Made at Philadelphia in America* (1769), Franklin wrote: "That the electric fire thus actually passes through the water, has . . . been satisfactorily demonstrated to many by an experiment of Mr. Kinnersley's, performed in a trough of water about ten feet long. The hand being placed under water in the direction of the spark (which always takes the strait or shortest course) is struck and penetrated by it as it passes" (A. H. Smyth, *The Writings of Benjamin Franklin,* 1905, II, 410–11). In 1757 Kinnersley received the degree of M.A. from the College of Philadelphia. In 1764 he published a syllabus of his lectures on electricity in which he described an orrery propelled by electricity and suggested that perhaps the solar system might be sustained by electricity (*A Course of Experiments in that Curious and Entertaining Branch of Natural Philosophy Called Electricity*). His "On Some Electrical Experiments Made with Charcoal" was published in *Philosophical Transactions* (London, vol. LXIII,

1773). It is said that at the time Kinnersley was better known as an electrical experimenter in America than was Franklin. He was a member of the American Philosophical Society. Resigning from the faculty of the College in 1772–73 because of failing health, he died at Philadelphia a few years later, leaving a wife, Sarah Duffield, whom he married in 1739, a daughter, and a son.

[Joseph Priestley, *The Hist. and Present State of Electricity* (2nd ed., London, 1769), and *Familiar Introduction to the Study of Electricity* (London, 1768); A. H. Smyth, *The Writings of Benjamin Franklin* (1905), vol. I; J. L. Chamberlain, *Univ. of Pa.*, vol. I (1901); E. J. Houston, *Electricity One Hundred Years Ago and Today* (1894); P. L. Ford, *Franklin Bibliog.* (1889); Park Benjamin, *The Intellectual Rise in Electricity* (1895); W. B. Sprague, *Annals Am. Pulpit*, vol. VI (1860).] F. A. T.

KINNEY, ELIZABETH CLEMENTINE DODGE STEDMAN (Dec. 18, 1810–Nov. 19, 1889), poet, essayist, was a native of New York City. She was the daughter of David Low Dodge [*q.v.*], a prominent New York merchant, and Sarah (Cleveland) Dodge. Her maternal grandfather was the colonial poet Aaron Cleveland [*q.v.*]. In March 1830 she married Col. Edmund Burke Stedman—Edmund Clarence Stedman [*q.v.*] was a child of this marriage—of Hartford, Conn., where she lived until the death of her husband in 1835. She then moved to her father's country estate, "Cedar Brook," near Plainfield, N. J. From here she contributed poems and articles to numerous magazines including *Graham's, Sartain's,* and the *Knickerbocker.* Her second marriage, in November 1841, connected her even more firmly with the world of letters as she became the wife of the well-known publicist and writer, William Burnet Kinney [*q.v.*], at that time editor of the *Newark Daily Advertiser,* of which he was the founder. Some of her best essays and critical articles appeared in the pages of the *Advertiser* during the ten years succeeding her marriage. In 1850 Mr. Kinney was appointed chargé d'affaires at Sardinia, and from 1850 to 1853 the Kinneys made their residence in Turin where both were popular in social and literary circles. In 1853, the Sardinian mission having ended, the Kinneys moved to Florence where they lived for more than ten years. Here they were members of the circle which included the Brownings, the Tennysons, the Trollopes, Hiram Powers, the American sculptor, and others. It was during this period that Mrs. Kinney wrote *Felicità* (1855), a metrical romance based on an incident in Italian history. In 1865 she and her husband returned to Newark. Two years later Mrs. Kinney's poems, which were widely scattered throughout English and American periodicals, were collected and published (*Poems,* 1867), and met with both critical and popular approval. *Bianca Cappello,* a second Italian romance in verse, was published in 1873. This like all of Mrs. Kinney's poetical works is marked by a virile romantic quality. Many of her poems were in reality tales of adventure, in verse full of color and action but couched in the "poetic" diction of the late nineteenth century. Her nature poetry is simple in manner and expresses a very sincere love of the world. Her essays and critical articles are as a rule sharply to the point in subject matter but softened in the presentation by lightness of treatment and a witty style.

[See: E. C. Stedman and Ellen McKay Hutchinson, *A Lib. of Am. Lit.*, vol. XI (1890); T. B. Read, *The Female Poets of America* (1849); John S. Hart, *The Female Prose Writers of America* (1852); E. A. and G. L. Duyckinck, *Cyc. of Am. Lit.* (ed. 1875); E. J. and H. G. Cleveland, *The Geneal. of the Cleveland and Cleaveland Families* (1899), vol. II; obituary in the *Newark Daily Advertiser,* Nov. 20, 1889. Mrs. Kinney's "Reminiscences" are unpublished.] G. G.

KINNEY, WILLIAM BURNET (Sept. 4, 1799–Oct. 21, 1880), journalist, diplomat, was born in Speedwell, Morris County, N. J., the youngest son of Abraham and Hannah (Burnet) Kinney and the grandson of Sir Thomas Kinney, an English baronet, who settled near Morristown prior to the Revolution. On his mother's side he was a descendant of William Burnet [*q.v.*], colonial official. At the age of thirteen he was the constant companion of his father, a colonel in the War of 1812, and on several occasions acted as a dispatch bearer. It was his father's intention that he should pursue a military career and accordingly he was sent to the Military Academy at West Point. While William was studying there his father died and at the wish to his mother he resigned from the institution and studied under the direction of private tutors. Two years later he entered upon the study of law in the office of his brother, Thomas T. Kinney, working under the guidance of his cousin, Joseph C. Hornblower [*q.v.*], later chief justice of the state of New Jersey. His tastes were so decidedly in the direction of a literary calling, however, that he gave up the law without being admitted to the bar and went into journalism. In 1820 he became editor of the *New Jersey Eagle,* a weekly paper of Newark. In 1825 he moved to New York to become literary adviser to Harper & Brothers. While there he took an active part in the organization of the Mercantile Library, serving for a time as the librarian. After ten years in New York City he returned to Newark to assume the editorship of the *Newark Daily Advertiser,* at that time the only daily paper in the state. He became the largest stockholder of this paper and united with it the *Sentinel of Freedom.*

In 1843, he entered actively into politics as the Whig candidate for Congress from the fifth district but was defeated. The next year he represented his party as the delegate-at-large from New Jersey to the Whig Convention in Baltimore, where he was instrumental in procuring the vice-presidential nomination for Theodore Frelinghuysen [*q.v.*]. For his stanch support of the Whig party in his newspaper, he was appointed by President Taylor the representative of the United States to the court of Sardinia at Turin. He was commissioned chargé on Apr. 22, 1850, and served until Oct. 8, 1853. It was during these years that the Sardinian government was being reconstructed along constitutional lines and he was often consulted by Cavour and other Italian leaders as to the practical workings of the American governmental system. His influence was continually being exercised in the interest of liberal and humanitarian measures, an instance of which was his success in procuring toleration for the Waldensian sect which was given permission to erect a place of worship in Turin, the first church building they had ever been allowed to own in that city. His services were recognized by his being chosen to lay the corner-stone.

The episode of Louis Kossuth's visit to the United States occurred during Kinney's service as chargé at Turin, and his letters to Secretary Daniel Webster and to Commodore Charles W. Morgan, in command of the United States Mediterranean Squadron, aided in preventing the American government from establishing any official connection with Kossuth's cause which would have involved grave international complications. He remained abroad after the expiration of his term as chargé, removing from Turin to Florence where he became well acquainted with the Brownings and began a history of the Medici family, which he did not live to complete. In 1865 he returned to Newark but was not actively engaged again in journalism. He died in New York and was buried in the churchyard of the First Presbyterian Church of Newark. His first wife was Mary Chandler Kinney who died in 1841, leaving two children. His second wife, whom he married in November 1841, was Elizabeth Clementine (Dodge) Stedman Kinney [*q.v.*]. There were two children of this marriage.

[*A Hist. of the City of Newark, N. J.* (1913), vol. III; W. H. Shaw, *Hist. of Essex and Hudson Counties, N. J.* (1884), vol. I; E. J. and H. G. Cleveland, *The Geneal. of the Cleveland and Cleaveland Families* (1899), vol. II; *Daily State Gazette* (Trenton), Oct. 22, 1880; *Newark Daily Advertiser,* Oct. 21, 23, 25, 1880; and Kinney's diary in the possession of W. B. Kinney, II, Newark, N. J.]

C. R. E., Jr.

KINNICUTT, LEONARD PARKER (May 22, 1854–Feb. 6, 1911), educator, chemist, sanitary engineer, was born in Worcester, Mass., the youngest of the six children of Francis Harrison and Elizabeth Waldo (Parker) Kinnicutt. His father, a prosperous hardware merchant, was descended in the seventh generation from Roger Kinnicutt who emigrated from Devon, England, about 1650. On his mother's side he was descended in the eighth generation from Samuel Lincoln, who came to Hingham, Mass., from Hingham, England, in 1637. Young Kinnicutt received his early education in the schools of Worcester, graduating from the high school in 1871. He went at once to the Massachusetts Institute of Technology, where he devoted himself chiefly to the study of chemistry. Following his graduation in 1875, he spent four years in professional studies in Germany. At Heidelberg he came under the inspiring influence of Bunsen, from whom he acquired an appreciation of the value of careful and accurate analysis. Here also under Bunsen's guidance he was initiated into the refinements of gas analysis. At this time organic chemistry was developing with tremendous rapidity especially in Germany. Bunsen had passed the zenith of his career and was not in sympathy with the new tendency which was manifesting itself in chemistry. It is not surprising, therefore, to find young Kinnicutt leaving Heidelberg and matriculating at Bonn, where Kekulé was lecturing with such success that Kinnicutt was captivated by the spirit and beauty of organic chemistry and devoted himself diligently to its study. He was fortunate in being accepted into the private laboratory of the master, where he became associated with Richard Anschütz, at that time lecture assistant, but later, after the retirement of Kekulé, director of the Chemical Institute at Bonn. In collaboration with Anschütz he published a number of papers, chiefly on phenyl-glyceric acid. This association ripened into a lasting friendship. Returning to the United States in 1879, he spent a year in study with Ira Remsen at the Johns Hopkins University, and then three years at Harvard, where he served as instructor in quantitative analysis and as private assistant to Wolcott Gibbs, at that time Rumford Professor of Chemistry. In 1882 he received from Harvard the degree of doctor of science and in September of the same year accepted an appointment as instructor of organic chemistry at the Worcester Polytechnic Institute. In the following January he became assistant professor of chemistry, three years later he was made full professor, and from 1892 he was director of the department.

As early as 1885 Kinnicutt began to give attention to the question of sewage disposal and sanitary problems. He became an authority on the sanitation of air, water, and gas; on the methods of analysis; and on the disposal of wastes. He paid particular attention to the examination of water and water-sheds, the contamination of rivers and ponds by trade wastes and sewage, and made numerous reports on private and public water supplies. After 1894 he visited England on an average every other year, familiarizing himself with the work done in that country, and the results were embodied in various articles which he published on the subject. He paid special attention to the subject of the pollution of streams by wool-washings, and made a careful study of this problem at Bradford, England, where a greater amount of wool was washed annually than in any other city in England or in the United States. He was employed as an expert in numerous cases regarding the pollution of streams and ponds, and was one of the experts in the case of the pollution of the Mississippi River at St. Louis by the sewage of Chicago. In 1903 he was appointed consulting chemist of the Connecticut sewage commission, a position which he retained up to the time of his death. He was a frequent contributor to scientific periodicals and the proceedings of learned societies upon topics relating to his specialty. In 1910, in collaboration with Prof. C. E. A. Winslow of the Massachusetts Institute of Technology, and R. Winthrop Pratt of the Ohio state board of health, he published a book entitled *Sewage Disposal* which is considered to be one of the best treatises on the subject in the English language.

He was deeply interested in the sanitary problems of his native city, Worcester, and kept a careful watch upon the city's water supply. During the "water famine" of the winter of 1910–11 he directed from his sick-bed the tests to be made, had daily reports brought to him, and outlined the policy by which, in his opinion, the city's health might be best safeguarded. He also devoted a great deal of time and money to secure a pure milk supply in summer for the babies in needy families, and at the time of his death he was a member of the Worcester Medical Milk Commission.

While a student in Germany he had discovered that he had incipient tuberculosis. For a long time it seemed to have been arrested, but at length it developed and after a lingering illness he died in his fifty-seventh year. He was twice married but had no children. His first wife was Louisa Hoar Clarke, daughter of Dr. Henry Clarke, whom he married June 4, 1885. On July 9, 1898, he married Frances Ayres Clarke, daughter of Josiah Clarke, and a cousin of his first wife.

[Charles Nutt, *Hist. of Worcester and Its People* (1919), vol. IV; W. L. Jennings, in *Science*, Apr. 28, 1911; *Proc. Am. Acad. Arts and Sciences*, vol. LIII, no. 10 (Sept. 1918); R. Anschütz, *Berichte der Deutschen Chemischen Gesellschaft*, vol. XLIV (1911); *Jour. of the Worcester Polytechnic Institute*, Mar., July 1911; *Technology Rev.*, Apr. 1911; *Jour. of the Asso. of Engineering Societies*, May 1911; *Jour. of the New Eng. Water Works Asso.*, Mar. 1911; *Proc. Am. Antiquarian Soc.*, n.s., vol. XXI (1911); *Who's Who in America*, 1910–11.]

W. L. J—s.

KINO, EUSEBIO FRANCISCO (*c.* 1645–Mar. 15, 1711), Jesuit missionary, explorer, cartographer, was born at Segno, Italy. The Italian spelling of his name was Chini or Chino. In America he generally wrote it Kino or Quino. He was baptized on Aug. 10, 1645. On Nov. 16, 1680, he wrote that he was thirty-seven years old, which would seem to put his birth date in 1643 or 1644, but this was apparently an inadvertence on his part. At an early age he made a vow that he would become a missionary. He entered the Jesuit order at Freiburg in 1665 and received his higher education in Upper Germany, where he spent many years. He showed a great predilection for mathematics and studied it assiduously with the hope of going to China, where Jesuit mathematicians had found official favor. After many petitions to the Father General, in 1678 he was assigned to a foreign mission that was being organized in Spain. His dream for years had been of a career in China, but he drew lots with a friend and chance assigned him to Mexico. Sailing from Genoa to Cádiz in 1678, he was delayed in Spain over two years. Meanwhile the Duchess of Aveiro y Arcos became his friend and patron, and a long correspondence between them followed.

Late in December 1680, he sailed from Cádiz to Vera Cruz, where he landed in May 1681. Soon after arrival in Mexico City he published a little book about the comet of 1680, which he had observed and studied while in Cádiz. His treatise, *Exposición Astronómica de el Cometa* (Mexico, 1681) was vigorously attacked by the Mexican Jesuit scholar Sigüenza y Góngora, in another little book. Still hoping to go to the Orient, in 1682 Kino joined the Atondo expedition to Lower California, as the head of the Jesuit mission. After a few months' trial at La Paz (1683), they moved north to San Bruno, near the place where Loreto was later founded. Here

Kino explored, wrote diaries and letters, made maps, and succeeded admirably with missionary work, but drought caused the abandonment of the enterprise in 1685. Returning to Mexico City, Kino two years later went to Pimería Alta, to work among the Pimas, in a district now embraced in northern Sonora and southern Arizona. Laboring for nearly a quarter century (1687–1711), with headquarters at Mission Dolores, he founded missions in the San Miguel, Magdalena, Altar, Sonóita, Santa Cruz, and San Pedro river valleys. A score of present-day towns began as missions that he established. He was the pioneer cattleman of the district, for in all these places he made the beginnings of stock raising.

From Dolores he made numerous expeditions on horseback north, northwest, and northeast, covering many thousand miles and several times reaching the Gila and Colorado rivers. He discovered and wrote the first description of the Casa Grande (unless it be the Red House of the Coronado expedition). He was instrumental in the return of the Jesuits to the California peninsula in 1697. He was named by the Spanish king to go there with Father Salvatierra, but he was too useful to be spared from the mainland. From his mission ranches he often shipped cattle and supplies across the Gulf to the new settlements. Finally, he conceived the idea of opening a road around the head of the Gulf to save the difficult water passage. California had commonly been regarded as an island, but as a result of two expeditions which he made to the lower Colorado River he concluded that it was a peninsula. His map showing it thus was several times published in Europe and became widely known. On Mar. 15, 1711, Kino died at Magdalena, one of the missions he had founded, and was buried in the chapel "on the Gospel side" by Father Agustín de Campos (original burial register).

[The chief printed source for Kino's career is his autobiography (*Favores Celestiales*) discovered, edited, and published in English by H. E. Bolton as *Kino's Historical Memoir of Pimería Alta* (2 vols., 1919). In this work the editor has supplied a long biographical sketch. Three years later the original of the *Favores Celestiales* was published by the Archivo General y Público of Mexico (*Las Misiones de Sonora y Arizona*, Mexico, 1922). Juan Matheo Manje's (Mange) *Luz de Tierra Incógnita* (Mexico, 1926) is a contemporary narrative by Kino's chief traveling companion. Early Jesuit accounts are in José de Ortega, *Apostólicos Afanes* (Barcelona, 1754), and Francisco Javier Alegre, *Historia de la Compañía de Jesús en Nueva-España* (Mexico, 3 vols., 1841–42). Brief sketches in English are in H. E. Bolton, *The Spanish Borderlands* (1921) and *The Padre on Horseback* (1932), and in H. H. Bancroft, *North Mexican States*, vol. I (1883). Eugenia Ricci has written the first extensive sketch in Italian, *Il Padre Eusebio Chini, Esploratore Missionario della California e dell' Arizona* (Milano, 1930). H. E. Bolton is preparing for the press three additional volumes of unpublished letters and diaries of Father Kino.]

H. E. B.

KINSELLA, THOMAS (Dec. 31, 1832–Feb. 11, 1884), editor, politician, was born in County Wexford, Ireland, from which place, in his seventeenth year, he emigrated to New York. After learning the printer's trade, he worked on the Cambridge *Post*, a weekly Whig newspaper in western New York. The publisher gave the lad free access to his library, and Kinsella read and studied eagerly to complete his grammar-school education. Editorial work attracted him and in addition to his compositor's duties he attempted articles for the paper. When the death of Henry Clay occurred, the editor being absent, Kinsella wrote an editorial on the statesman, and was much elated by the commendation it received.

Leaving the Cambridge *Post*, Kinsella in 1854 went South to familiarize himself with conditions there. Returning North in 1858, he obtained employment as a typesetter on the *Brooklyn Daily Eagle*. From the first, however, he contributed material to the paper. His ambition and ability attracted the attention of the proprietor, Isaac Van Anden, who promoted him to the position of law reporter. The Civil War found the *Eagle* under the editorship of Henry McCloskey, whose sympathies were with the South. So pronounced were his editorials that the government took notice of their treasonable character. McCloskey was forced to resign and Van Anden appointed Kinsella editor, Sept. 7, 1861. That position he held, with short interruptions, until his death. As editor, he made a marked success. He was a clear, forcible, and effective writer, and he supervised all departments of the paper, at the same time giving proper independence to those who won his confidence. The *Eagle* gained in prestige, in circulation, and in wealth under his leadership.

In 1865, the paper actively supported President Johnson, and in 1866 the President gave Kinsella a recess appointment as postmaster of Brooklyn, in which capacity he served for several months. The Senate, however, failed to confirm the appointment and he was displaced May 1, 1867. In 1868 he became a member of the Brooklyn board of education. In this connection his name is identified with two reforms: first, open bidding for supplies; and second, free opportunity and equal pay for women in the schools. A year later, he was appointed one of the three commissioners for the newly organized water and sewerage board. Finding that his duties consisted largely of "peddling out jobs" at the insistence of politicians, he resigned after a few months. In 1870, he was elected to Congress for the 2nd District as a Democrat. He took a conspicuous part in the organization of the Liberal Republican movement (1871–72), and influenced the New York Democratic convention to instruct for Horace Greeley. In the 1880 campaign Kinsella, in the *Eagle,* was the first to propose General Hancock as a candidate. After election, convinced that the Kings County Democratic organization had not given Hancock wholehearted support, he opened up a bitter contest with "Boss" McLaughlin.

His health failed in 1883 and he traveled abroad, returning in the autumn apparently much improved. In December, however, he broke down again, and from this attack he never rallied. After three months' illness, he died at his home in Brooklyn, a splendid example of the immigrant Irish boy rising to wealth and honored position in the country of his adoption. With only a fair education as a foundation, his eagerness for learning, his industry, his honesty, and sincerity of purpose gained him a multitude of friends. He was divorced from his first wife, by whom he had four daughters (*New York Tribune,* Feb. 12, 1884), and later he married Emiline Van Siclen, the divorced wife of Thomas W. Field [*q.v.*].

[H. R. Stiles, *The Civil, Political, Professional and Ecclesiastical Hist. . . . of the County of Kings and the City of Brooklyn, N. Y., from 1683 to 1884* (1884); *Biog. Dir. Am. Cong.* (1928); *N. Y. Times,* Feb. 12, 1884; *Evening Post* (N. Y.), Feb. 11, 1884.]

L. H. H.

KINSEY, JOHN (1693–May 11, 1750, o. s.), lawyer, politician, jurist, was born in Burlington, N. J., the son of John and Sarah (Stevens) Kinsey. His paternal grandfather was one of the commissioners sent out from England in 1677 by the West Jersey proprietors to buy land from the Indians and to lay out a town. His father was a prominent lawyer, member of the New Jersey legislature, for some time its speaker, and a Quaker preacher. John had the advantages of a good school education, studied law, was admitted to the bar, and after practising his profession several years was elected to the assembly, succeeding his father as speaker (1730). Conspicuous there for his sound judgment and knowledge of law, he led the opposition to Gov. William Burnet [*q.v.*], and the movement for a separate governor for New Jersey, and was largely responsible for the acts establishing Quaker affirmation and biennial assemblies (*New Jersey Archives,* 1 ser., V, 261–64).

Kinsey first attracted attention in Philadelphia in 1725 as a lawyer in the court of Gov. William Keith [*q.v.*]. Addressing the court with his hat on, he was ordered to take it off, but refused on conscientious grounds; whereupon the governor ordered the court officers to remove it. Quaker protests against this attack on their religious liberty moved Keith to issue an order allowing Friends thereafter to speak in court without uncovering. In 1730 Kinsey moved to Philadelphia, apparently seeking wider political opportunities. The following year he was elected to the assembly, holding this post, with the exception of one year, until his death. After 1739 he was speaker. In the contests with the governor over defense appropriations, bills of credit, taxation of proprietary lands, and other questions, his shrewd political management and adroit arguments generally steered the Quaker party to success at the polls and in the legislature. Invariably he succeeded in defeating the requests of Governor Thomas (1739–47) for appropriations for frontier defenses, and by withholding the governor's salary finally forced him to follow the assembly's suggestion that he raise a force of men personally. Although opposing direct war aid and compulsory military service, Kinsey sanctioned the voting of funds "for the King's use," which usually went for military purposes. He was a stout defender of the system of raising money by issuing bills of credit rather than by direct taxes, and was a trustee of the loan office entrusted with issuing these bills. From 1738 to 1741 he was attorney-general of the province and from 1743 to 1750, chief justice of the supreme court of Pennsylvania. He was one of the commissioners appointed in 1737 with a view to improving the relations between Pennsylvania and Maryland. Anxious to preserve the friendship of the Indians but opposed to arming them, he was influential as a member of the commission sent to Albany by the colonies in 1745 to reach an agreement with the Six Nations in temporarily averting a war with the French.

Kinsey died suddenly from a stroke of apoplexy at Burlington where he had gone to plead a case in court. His great learning, professional skill, and probity, his agreeable disposition, generosity, and simplicity of life made him greatly esteemed. He was influential in the yearly meeting of the Friends, and for many years was clerk of the Philadelphia Meeting. He was prominent in the Quaker social circle of Philadelphia and possessed a beautiful estate, "Plantation," on the east bank of the Schuylkill. His last years were saddened by the accidental death of his son, John, a young lawyer of great promise. Another son, James, was a distinguished lawyer and chief justice of the supreme court of New Jersey. While speaker of the New Jersey assembly Kinsey prepared for publication *The Acts of the General Assembly of the Province of New Jersey . . .* (1732), the first compilation of New Jersey laws.

[J. S. Walton, *John Kinsey* (1900), and a sketch in Isaac Sharpless, *Political Leaders of Provincial Pa.* (1919), give the most adequate accounts of Kinsey's political life. See also J. H. Martin, *Martin's Bench and Bar of Phila.* (1883); *N. J. Archives*, 1 ser., vols. V (1882), XI (1894), XII (1895), XIV (1890); *Pa. Colonial Records*, vol. IV (1851); *Pa. Mag. of Hist. and Biog.*, Jan. 1903; and *Votes and Proc. of the Pa. Assembly*, 1739–50.] J. H. P.

KINTPUASH [See CAPTAIN JACK, 1837?–1873].

KINZIE, JOHN (Dec. 3, 1763–Jan. 6, 1828), a fur-trader on the site of Chicago, was born at Quebec. His father, John McKenzie, had come thither as a surgeon with the British army and had there married Anne, the widow of William Haliburton, an army chaplain. When McKenzie died soon after their son was born, Anne McKenzie took as her third husband William Forsyth, who removed to Detroit and there opened the first tavern. Young John, who changed his name to Kinzie, left home early and learned the trade of silversmith, from which he received the Indian name, "Shaw-nee-aw-kee," the Silver Man. When about eighteen, he began trading with Indians on the Maumee River, at Fort Wayne, then on the site of Defiance, Ohio. Here he lived with Margaret McKenzie, an Indian captive, whose legal marriage to him has been often asserted and as often denied. In 1795 she found her own family and went home to Virginia. The next year Kinzie moved to St. Joseph River, where in 1798 he brought his bride, Eleanor (Little) McKillip, whose first husband Daniel McKillip, an officer in the British militia, had fallen at Wayne's battle of 1794. The Kinzies removed, in 1804, to the mouth of the Chicago River, a site Kinzie had visited and traded on years earlier, where in 1803 Fort Dearborn had been built. Here business prospered and three of their four children were born. In 1812 Kinzie had a quarrel with Jean Lalime, a French trader, whom he killed, supposedly in self-defense. In the massacre of Fort Dearborn troops in August of that year, Kinzie and his family were saved by friendly Indians. They retreated first to St. Joseph and then to Detroit, where Kinzie, suspected of American sympathies, was arrested by the British and for some time imprisoned. He never recovered from the effects of the war either in his property or person. In 1816 he returned to Chicago and lived there until his death. In 1821 he aided the commissioners who came to make an Indian treaty, and in 1825 was commissioned justice of the peace. He was remembered as a kindly, pleasant man, devoted to his family, shrewd at trade, and always popular with his Indian customers. A subdivision and a street in Chicago bear his name.

[Letters and account books in the Chicago Hist. Soc.; J. A. Kinzie, *Wau-Bun* (1856 and later editions, latest one 1930); E. L. K. Gordon, *John Kinzie* (copr. 1910); M. M. Quaife, *Chicago and the Old Northwest* (copr. 1913), and "Eleanor Little, Pioneer," *Burton Hist. Coll. Leaflet*, Jan. 1930; *The John Askin Papers*, ed. by M. M. Quaife, vol. I (1928).] L. P. K.

KIP, WILLIAM INGRAHAM (Oct. 3, 1811–Apr. 7, 1893), first bishop of the Protestant Episcopal Church in California, was born in New York, the eldest son of Leonard and Maria (Ingraham) Kip. The Kip family was originally French. Ruloff de Kype was forced during the religious wars of the sixteenth century to flee to the Low Countries. He returned to France to die in battle in 1569; but one of his sons remained, settled in Amsterdam, and became a Protestant. About 1637 Hendrick, the then head of the family, came to New Amsterdam where he and his sons secured large properties and from that time on the family, now known as Kip, was prominently identified with the social and business life of Manhattan Island. They were Loyalists during the Revolution and lost much of their property but Leonard reëstablished the family fortunes. William's boyhood was spent in New York. He studied at Rutgers College, then went to Yale, where he graduated in 1831. He began the study of law; but his interest turned to the ministry. After a short time at the Theological Seminary in Virginia, at Alexandria, he entered the General Theological Seminary, New York. Graduating there in 1835, he was ordained deacon on July 1 and priest in the following November. He married, July 1, 1835, Maria Elizabeth Lawrence, daughter of Isaac Lawrence of New York. He was successively rector of St. Peter's Church, Morristown, N. J., assistant minister of Grace Church, New York, and rector of St. Paul's Church, Albany. He was elected missionary bishop of California by the General Convention of 1853, was consecrated on Oct. 28, and reached San Francisco on Jan. 29, 1854.

The Episcopal Church in California at the time of his arrival was very weak. There were only two completed church buildings and only three regularly settled clergymen. In spite of their small numbers the Episcopalians had organized as a diocese, which, according to the law of the church, had a right to elect its own bishop. It had had no hand in the election of Bishop Kip. He came as a "missionary," and for three years by mutual consent acted as bishop, finally in 1857 accepting the election of the diocese and becoming its bishop in name as well as fact. His work was for many years difficult pioneering. It took three or four days by steamer to reach Los Angeles. River boats and horses took him into the mining camps. The population was shifting everywhere. Work flourishing one day had vanished the next. The bishop traveled constantly, laid foundations, acted as pastor to people scattered over the vast area of the state, and, when in San Francisco, ordinarily served as rector of one of the churches there. In 1862 he accepted formally the rectorship of Grace Church, San Francisco, and with the approval of the vestry and congregation established it as his cathedral. This was the first cathedral of the Episcopal Church in America. Under his administration the diocese grew, parishes were established in the permanent centers, church schools, St. Luke's Hospital in San Francisco, and other church institutions appeared. Although travel had become easier and the northern part of the state had been turned over to another bishop, the infirmities of age pressed heavily upon Bishop Kip and in 1890, in response to his request for assistance, the diocese elected Dr. William Ford Nichols of Philadelphia as his assistant and successor.

Kip was a scholar of the old-fashioned type, an able preacher, and a man of great social gifts. In theology he was an orthodox High Churchman, but neither in his ecclesiastical position nor as a citizen was he of an aggressive type. He was a man of distinguished bearing, tall, handsome, aristocratic; in character a simple Christian gentleman who met with devoted courage pioneering problems and tasks which must often have been distasteful to his scholarly habit of mind. Among his published writings are: *The Double Witness of the Church* (1843); *The History, Object, and Proper Observance of the Holy Season of Lent* (copr. 1843), which went through many editions; *The Early Jesuit Missions in North America* (1846); *The Christmas Holydays in Rome* (1846); *The Early Conflicts of Christianity* (1850); *The Catacombs of Rome* (1854); *The Unnoticed Things of the Scripture* (1868); *The Olden Time in New York* (1872); *Historical Scenes in the Old Jesuit Missions* (1875); *The Early Days of My Episcopate* (1892). He was also the author of *Historical Notes of the Family of Kip of Kipsburg and Kip's Bay, N. Y.* (privately printed, 1871).

[F. E. Kip, *Hist. of the Kip Family in America* (1928); W. S. Perry, *Hist. of the Am. Episcopal Ch.*, vol. II (1885); H. G. Batterson, *A Sketchbook of the Am. Episcopate* (1878); *A Calif. Pilgrimage, Being an Account of the Observance of the Sixty-fifth Anniversary of Bishop Kip's First Missionary Journey through the San Joaquin Valley, together with Bishop Kip's Own Story of the Event Commemorated* (1921); *Obit. Record Grads. Yale Univ.*, 1930; *Morning Call* (San Francisco), Apr. 7, 1893.]

E. L. P—s.

KIRBY, EPHRAIM (Feb. 23, 1757–Oct. 20, 1804), lawyer, law reporter, was born in Litchfield County, Conn., the eldest of the twelve children of Abraham and Eunice (Starkweather) Kirby, and a descendant of Joseph Kirby who emigrated from Warwickshire, England, and was one of the early settlers of Hartford, Conn. Leaving his father's farm in Litchfield at the age of nineteen, he joined a company of volunteers which participated in the battle of Bunker Hill. He was a private in the 5th Company, 7th Connecticut Regiment, from July 10 to Dec. 19, 1775; reënlisted in the 2nd Continental Dragoons on Dec. 24, 1776, and, serving until Aug. 7, 1779, was with Washington's army in New Jersey and Pennsylvania. He took part in the battles of Brandywine, Monmouth, and Germantown, and in the last action was left for dead on the field. Subsequently he served as ensign in Olney's Rhode Island battalion (Aug. 23, 1782–Dec. 25, 1783). After the close of the war, Kirby studied law in Litchfield in the office of Reynold Marvin, formerly King's Attorney, and on Mar. 17, 1784, married his daughter Ruth, by whom he had eight children. One of these, Frances, was the mother of Edmund Kirby-Smith [*q.v.*]. Kirby practised law in Litchfield until 1803, and quickly became a leading citizen with varied interests. In 1787 the honorary degree of M.A. was conferred upon him by Yale College. He was secretary of St. Paul's Masonic Lodge, Litchfield, and was an organizer and officer both of the Grand Lodge of Connecticut and of the Grand Chapter of Royal Arch Masons of the United States. He was an original member of the Connecticut Society of the Cincinnati, its secretary for three years, and a delegate to the meeting of the National Society at Philadelphia in 1796.

His political career began in 1791 when he served the first of his fourteen semi-annual sessions in the state legislature. President Jefferson, in January 1802, appointed him supervisor of the national revenue for the state of Connecticut. He had been successful in business, having been a director of the company organized in 1795 to purchase Connecticut lands in the Western Reserve; but in 1802 he lost his entire fortune in a Virginia land venture. His appointment by President Jefferson, on July 14, 1803, as a commissioner on the Spanish Boundary, to receive and determine the titles of lands held on the east side of Pearl River, offered him an opportunity for a new start. He had reached Fort Stoddart,

Mississippi Territory, and had begun hearings, when he fell sick and died at the age of forty-seven.

Kirby made a permanent place for his name in the annals of American law by publishing, in Litchfield, his *Reports of Cases Adjudged in the Superior Court and Court of Errors of the State of Connecticut, From the Year 1785 to May, 1788* (1789). It was the first fully developed volume of law reports published in the United States and in American legal literature holds a place comparable to that which Plowden's *Commentaries* holds in English legal literature. In a remarkable preface, Kirby demonstrated that a system of law reporting was essential to the development of American law. As a lawyer, he is said to have been "remarkable for the frankness and downright honesty of his advice to clients, striving always to prevent litigation" (P. K. Kilbourne, *post,* p. 105). Starting out with few opportunities for education, he rose to a position of leadership by sheer force of character, and won the friendship and respect of many national figures of his time.

[Date of death is authenticated by a letter from Chambers to Thomas Jefferson, Oct. 27, 1804, in the Lib. of Cong.; service in the 7th Conn. Regt. is verified by copies of letters in the possession of F. C. Hicks, New Haven. The original MS. of Kirby's *Reports* is in the custody of the Litchfield Hist. Soc. Published sources include: P. K. Kilbourne, *A Biog. Hist. of the County of Litchfield* (1851) and *Sketches and Chronicles of the Town of Litchfield, Conn.* (1859); P. L. Ford, *The Writings of Thomas Jefferson* (10 vols., 1892–99); M. E. Dwight, *The Kirbys of New Eng.* (1898); G. C. Woodruff, *A Geneal. Register of the Inhabitants of the Town of Litchfield, Conn.* (1900); D. C. Kilbourn, *The Bench and Bar of Litchfield County, Conn., 1709–1909* (1909). F. B. Heitman, *Hist. Reg. of Officers of the Continental Army* (1914).] F. C. H.

KIRBY, J. HUDSON (Apr. 3, 1819–1848), actor, gave through his robustious method of acting in tragedy and melodrama a lasting phrase to the annals of the American theatre. So admired was he by the gallery gods who frequented the theatres of New York, where the heyday of his brief life on the stage was passed, that "Wake me up when Kirby dies" has become historic as their favorite expression. He was born aboard ship near Sandy Hook while his parents were on their way to America, and little is known about him until at the age of eighteen he made his first appearance in subordinate characters at the Walnut Street Theatre in Philadelphia. The greater part of his professional career, which extended over a period of only ten years, was passed in the Bowery, the National, the Chatham, and other New York theatres of the cheaper grade. As early as the spring of 1838 he was acting in leading supporting rôles with James W. Wallack and Thomas S. Hamblin, and he soon acquired an extensive repertory of characters in plays that have endured and in plays now long forgotten, among the latter being *Six Degrees of Crime, The Siege of Tripoli, The Surgeon of Paris,* and *The Carpenter of Rouen.*

One after another he supported the leading stars of his day as they came to New York, perhaps his most notable efforts of that kind being made with Edwin Forrest in May 1842 at the Chatham Theatre, when he acted Pythias to that actor's Damon, Icilius to his Virginius, De Mauprat to his Richelieu, and Friar Lacy to his Jack Cade. Despite his strenuous acting, he was neither large in stature nor powerful in appearance, being of medium height and slight figure. His complexion and hair were rather dark. For his effects upon his audiences he relied mainly upon his voice, which had a melodious quality and strength that enabled it to rise above the turmoil of the people in the audience of that day who put no restraint upon either their approval or their disapproval of a play or an actor. The note of approval in his case was distinctly dominant, and he is an excellent example of the ephemeral vogue and popularity of many an actor. His occasional acting in cities other than New York widened his repute, and in 1845 he went to England, repeating his success in tragedy and melodrama at the Surrey and other London theatres of the popular type. He died in London in 1848, on the eve of his projected return to the United States. His wife, who was known on the stage as Mrs. J. Hudson Kirby, was a favorite actress during Hudson's lifetime and for some years after his death.

[F. C. Wemyss, *Wemyss' Chronology of the Am. Stage* (1852); J. N. Ireland, *Records of the N. Y. Stage,* vol. II (1867); T. A. Brown, *Hist. of the Am. Stage* (1870) and *A Hist. of the N. Y. Stage* (1903), vol. I; H. P. Phelps, *Players of a Century: A Record of the Albany Stage* (1880); Abram C. Dayton, *Last Days of Knickerbocker Life in N. Y.* (1882); Arthur Hornblow, *A Hist. of the Theatre in America* (1919), vol. II; G. C. D. Odell, *Annals of the N. Y. Stage,* vol. IV (1928).] E. F. E.

KIRBY-SMITH, EDMUND (May 16, 1824–Mar. 28, 1893), Confederate soldier, educator, was born in St. Augustine, Fla. His father, Joseph Lee Smith, a native of Connecticut, had a distinguished career as a soldier in the War of 1812, as a lawyer, and as a judge. He married Frances Marvin Kirby, daughter of Ephraim Kirby [*q.v.*] of Litchfield, Conn., and gave her surname to each of their children. After the death of an older brother, Ephraim Kirby Smith, in the Mexican War, Edmund, until that time known as Edmund K. Smith, began to use his full name, and a generation later the family name had become Kirby-Smith.

Of warrior stock on both sides of his house, Edmund early chose a military career. In 1836 he went to Alexandria to be prepared for the United States Military Academy by Benjamin Hallowell [*q.v.*], then famous as a teacher of boys. He entered the Academy in 1841 and was graduated four years later, having been a cadet at the period during which the majority of West Point trained general officers of both the Union and the Confederate armies received their preparation. Assigned to the 5th Infantry upon graduation, he took part in the war with Mexico, first under Taylor and later under Scott, participating in the battles of Palo Alto, Resaca de la Palma, Monterey, Vera Cruz, Cerro Gordo, Contreras, Molino del Rey, and Chapultepec. He was brevetted for gallantry at Cerro Gordo and at Contreras. After the war he was stationed at Jefferson Barracks, and in 1849 became assistant professor of mathematics at West Point. He rejoined his regiment in 1852 and served on the frontier for three years, during which time he was in command of the military escort for the Mexican Boundary Commission, and was himself botanist of the expedition. His report of his observations was published by the Smithsonian Institution.

In 1855 he was promoted to captain, and assigned to the famous 2nd Cavalry, which was at once sent to Texas, where at frequent intervals during the next few years it was operating against hostile Indians. Kirby-Smith exulted in the life, both as a soldier in active service and as an ardent hunter in a sportsman's paradise. In 1858, on leave, he spent several months in Europe, touring England, Wales, France, Germany, Austria, and Italy. Upon his return he rejoined his regiment, then in New Mexico on the Wichita Expedition, and was wounded at the battle of Nescatunga, June 13, 1859. For some months after the battle he commanded the expedition. Later he was in command of the regiment, stationed for a time at Camp Cooper, and in 1860 he was promoted to major.

The secession of Florida found him fully decided as to his own course, and he resigned from the army on Mar. 3, 1861. Before resigning, however, he had declined to surrender Camp Colorado, then under his command, to the Texas militia under General McCulloch, and had expressed his readiness to fight to hold it. Returning to Florida, he was at once commissioned colonel of cavalry and sent to Lynchburg to organize, muster into service, and equip the regiments as they arrived in Virginia. He was chief of staff to Joseph E. Johnston at Harper's Ferry, aided in organizing the army of the Shenandoah, and, promoted to brigadier-general in June, was placed in command of the 4th Brigade of that army. He was severely wounded at Manassas, where he had a part in turning the tide of battle in favor of the Confederates. While recuperating at Lynchburg he met and married (Sept. 24, 1861) Cassie Selden, the daughter of Samuel S. Selden. Returning to service in October, he was promoted major-general and placed in command of a division of Beauregard's army. Early in 1862 he was given command of the department of East Tennessee, Kentucky, North Georgia, and Western North Carolina. In June, in order to recover the Cumberland Gap, and in cooperation with Bragg to crush the Federal force under Buell and recover Nashville, he invaded Kentucky, fought and won the battle of Richmond, cleared the Gap of Federal troops, and occupied Lexington, threatening Cincinnati. He withdrew only after Bragg's retirement. The Confederate Congress thanked him, and in October he was promoted lieutenant-general. Disgusted with Bragg, he asked that his own command be detached, but this request was refused.

In January 1863 he was ordered to Richmond to assist in reorganizing the army and in February was placed in command of the Trans-Mississippi Department, consisting of Texas, Louisiana, Arkansas, and Indian Territory. Cut off from the East after the fall of Vicksburg, he became the virtual civil and military ruler of the whole region, which wags now called "Kirby-Smithdom." At once he set out to learn the resources of the country. Such communication as he had with Richmond was through the blockade, so he usually acted upon his own responsibility, sending great quantities of cotton abroad and selling it at high prices, bringing in machinery for factories and shops. Untouched by Federal troops, Texas produced great crops of grain and huge quantities of meat for supplying the rest of the department. The only military movement of importance was the Federal expedition under Banks which Kirby-Smith repulsed at Mansfield on Apr. 8, 1864. In February of that year he had been commissioned general. On June 2, 1865, he surrendered the last military force of the Confederacy.

After the surrender, Kirby-Smith went into Mexico and thence to Cuba. A plan to settle in Mexico was soon abandoned, and in November he returned to the United States. For a brief period he was president of an insurance company and of the Atlantic and Pacific Telegraph Company. He was an active layman in the Protestant Episcopal church, and longed to enter the ministry, but deciding, finally, that he was too old to be ordained, he turned to teaching and established a short-lived military school in Kentucky. In 1870 he became president of the University of Nashville, resigning in 1875 to accept the professorship of mathematics at the University of the South, where he taught happily and with distinction for eighteen years. He contributed an article on "The Defense of the Red River" to *Battles and Leaders of the Civil War* (vol. IV, 1888). The last surviving full general of either army, he died at Sewanee, Tenn., at the age of sixty-eight. He had five sons and six daughters.

[A. H. Noll, *General Kirby-Smith* (1907); *Confed. Mil. Hist.* (1899), I, 655; G. W. Cullum, *Biog. Reg. Officers and Grads. U. S. Mil. Acad.* (3rd ed., 1891); *Twenty-fourth Ann. Reunion Asso. Grads. U. S. Mil. Acad.* (1893); P. F. Hammond, "Campaign of Gen. E. Kirby-Smith in Kentucky in 1862," *So. Hist. Soc. Papers*, vols. IX, X (1881–82); *War of the Rebellion: Official Records (Army)*; *Battles and Leaders of the Civil War* (4 vols., 1887–88); G. R. Fairbanks, *Hist. of the Univ. of the South* (1905); *Confed. Veteran*, Apr. 1893; *Daily American* (Nashville), Mar. 29, 1893.]
J. G. deR. H.

KIRCHHOFF, CHARLES WILLIAM HENRY (Mar. 28, 1853–July 22, 1916), editor of technical journals, was born in San Francisco, son of Charles and Virginia (Siemsen) Kirchhoff. The father was in the German consular service. A few years after the boy's birth the family moved to Hoboken, N. J. He attended school in this country and in Germany, entered the Prussian Royal School of Mines in Clausthal in 1870, and was graduated in 1874 as a mining engineer and metallurgist. For the next three years he was chemist for the Delaware lead refinery in Philadelphia. During the Centennial Exhibition in that city he acted as correspondent for a number of British, German, and South African papers, and thus began his career in technical journalism, for which he was especially fitted both by education and by his careful discrimination in evaluating statistics. In 1877 he formed a connection with David Williams, an important figure in technical publishing, and served as assistant editor of his *Metallurgical Review*, a well-written but short-lived monthly. Williams transferred him to the editorial staff of *The Iron Age* as assistant editor in 1878. In 1881 he went to the *Engineering and Mining Journal* as managing editor and for a three-year period was under the inspiring direction of R. W. Raymond and R. P. Rothwell [*qq.v.*], but returned to *The Iron Age* as associate editor in 1884. He became editor-in-chief in 1889, succeeding James C. Bayles [*q.v.*], and served until 1910, when he retired because of poor health. For several years before his retirement he also acted as vice-president and manager for the David Williams Company, publishers of *The Iron Age*. Combining knowledge of foreign languages, understanding of the important metallurgical processes that were being developed, and commercial acumen, he made *The Iron Age* the recognized authority on the American iron and steel industry. Some of his articles in that journal were reprinted as a book in 1900 under the title *Notes on Some European Iron-Making Districts*. In connection with his work as a technical editor, he also acted from 1883 to 1906 as special agent for the United States Geological Survey in the gathering of statistics connected with the production of lead, copper, and zinc. He thoroughly understood the collection of such data and won the cooperation of producers. Among his many associates in the iron trade was Andrew Carnegie, who was interested in the publicity regarding consolidations mentioned by editorial writers. Kirchhoff's policy with respect to new developments and consolidations in the steel trade was quietly constructive and well informed but never sensational or irresponsible. A man of slight build and of professional appearance, he participated in many conferences with the great ironmasters of this formative period. He was one of the distinguished group of American editors who made modern technical journalism respected throughout the world. The American Institute of Mining Engineers, of which he was an early and active member, did him the unusual honor of electing him president on two widely separate occasions, in 1898–99 and in 1911–12. His presidential address in 1899 on "A Decade of Progress in Reducing Costs" showed his discernment and ability at their best. He also belonged to many other organizations, both in the United States and abroad, including the American Society of Mechanical Engineers, the Iron and Steel Institute of Great Britain, and the Century Club of New York. In 1908 he was awarded a decoration by the French government for his work in industrial safety and hygiene. On Feb. 26, 1912, he was married to Erwina Diepenbrock. His death occurred at his summer home near Asbury Park, N. J.

[R. W. Raymond in *Trans. Am. Inst. Mining Engineers*, vol. LVI (1917); *The Iron Age*, July 27, 1916; *Engineering and Mining Jour.*, July 29, 1916; *Iron Trade Rev.*, July 27, 1916; *Trans. Am. Soc. Mechanical Engineers*, vol. XXXVIII (1917); *Jour. Iron and Steel Inst.* (London), vol. XCIV (1916); *Engineering Record*, July 29, 1916; *Who's Who in America*, 1916–17; *N. Y. Times*, July 24, Aug. 3, 1916.]
P. B. M.

KIRCHMAYER, JOHN (*c.* 1860–Nov. 29, 1930), wood-carver, was born in Bavaria, presumably at Oberammergau, where he had training which, combined with artistic genius, made him one of the most remarkable sculptors in wood since Veit Stoss and Tillmann Riemenschneider. He may have been illegitimate (Sinclair, *post*). His certificate of death at Cambridge, Mass., records his age at death as seventy years; his father, John Kirchmayer; his mother, unknown. Circumstances of his early life are difficult to establish since, though often talkative, he was not always explicitly communicative in the family circle which he entered upon his first American marriage, to Frances Leclair in 1904. According to his own story, "as long ago as 1870 he played the part of Joseph in the Passion Play at Oberammergau, his birthplace" (Cram, *post,* p. 87). The cast of the play of 1870–71, however, names no Kirchmayer. He would then have been, according to the age given on his death certificate, ten or eleven years old. His name does not appear among the casts of 1880, 1890, or 1900. He plausibly told others (Bergengren, Tower, and Coburn, *post*), that his father was a revolutionist and a "realistic" wood-carver, one who made souvenirs for tourists, and that he himself began to carve in his father's shop at six years. He learned to make pottery with the Langs and he had drawing lessons at the village school, his teacher nominating him successfully for a scholarship at Munich. He later, so he said, had training and professional employment at Paris and London.

Arriving at New York, Kirchmayer was specially befriended by Stanford White [*q.v.*]. Cram describes his appearance at Boston about 1895, "a big, raw-boned, heavily bearded Bavarian." Architects then desperately needed intelligent and inspired artist craftsmen. Kirchmayer, creative and productive, one of the indubitably great artists of his era, found abundant encouragement from Henry Vaughan, from Cram, Goodhue & Ferguson, and other architects, and from the management of the Boston Society of Arts and Crafts of which he became a master craftsman. Working for wages in the shops of Irving & Casson and W. F. Ross & Company, "philosopher, churchman and artist combined," he produced such carvings as the great reredos of St. Paul's Cathedral, Detroit; the doors and other decorations of the Henry H. Rogers Memorial Church, Fairhaven, Mass.; important carvings at St. Paul's School, Concord, N. H.; Madonna and Child, All Saints' Church, Boston; the St. Patrick reredos, St. Vincent Ferrer Church, New York; St. Augustine of Hippo, Washington Cathedral; mantel wood sculptures at the United States Military Academy, West Point, and many more. His latest ecclesiastic works were the reredos of All Saints' Church, Peterboro, N. H.

In middle life Kirchmayer gave up journeyman's work and took at his unpretentious home, 379 Cambridge St., East Cambridge, only such commissions as he cared to execute. Many of his carvings were made for "Cranbrook," the country home of George G. Booth, publisher of the *Detroit* (Mich.) *News.* Kirchmayer's first wife having died, his studio for some years was in his kitchen to which only a few intimates were admitted. A devout Catholic by rearing and profession he had a mystical philosophy which animates his exquisite panels and detached figures. A contest over his will brought into print in 1930–31 peculiarities of his daily life which must interest students of abnormal psychology. Asserting himself a thorough American, devoted to American institutions, he frequently acclaimed his "American Gothic" as his own special contribution to American civilization. He married in 1929 Elizabeth Burdett, of Florida, to whom he left his property except such of his unsold carvings as she might give to the Boston Museum of Fine Arts. This will, after considerable publicity had been given to the testator's personal characteristics, was settled by compromise out of court.

[Sources include: Ralph Adams Cram, "John Kirchmayer, Master Craftsman," *Architecture,* Feb. 1931; Livingston Wright, "A Door Carved by I. Kirchmayer," *Art World,* July 1917; L. L. Tower, "The Wood Carvings of I. Kirchmayer," *Internat. Studio,* Nov. 1913, pp. lxxxix–xciii; Anne Webb Karnaghan, "Ecclesiastical Carvings in America," *Ibid.,* Oct. 1926; Ralph Bergengren, "I. Kirchmayer, Wood Carver," *House Beautiful,* Mar. 1915; F. W. Coburn, "Woodcarving and Architecture—Work by I. Kirchmayer and Others," *Internat. Studio,* Sept. 1910, pp. lxiii–lxv; *Boston Herald,* Nov. 30, 1930, Feb. 13, 1931; *Boston Globe,* Mar. 26, 1931. Information as to certain facts was supplied by Mrs. Marion Sinclair, Kirchmayer's sister-in-law, who understands that Johannes Kirchmayer, from whom the artist took his name, was his maternal grandfather.]

F. W. C.

KIRK, EDWARD NORRIS (Aug. 14, 1802–Mar. 27, 1874), clergyman, pastor of Presbyterian and Congregational churches and promoter of revivals, was born in New York. His father, George, a Scotchman, came to that city when eighteen years old, and married for his second wife Mary Norris, of Welsh and Irish ancestry, daughter of Thomas and Mary (Wade) Norris of Princeton, N. J. Edward was the third of her four children, and her only son. The head of the family was a store-keeper, without much ambition, but displaying all the stubbornness and piety commonly attributed to his race. After he was ten years old, Edward made his home with an uncle and aunt at Princeton, Robert and Sarah (Norris) Voorhees, the former a merchant of some means. At fifteen he was enrolled in the sophomore class of the College of New Jersey, and after his graduation in 1820 entered a New

York law office. He had not been particularly studious at college, and lived a care-free life until his conversion in 1822. Thereafter the spiritual welfare of his fellow men absorbed him utterly. He immediately entered the Princeton Theological Seminary, where he spent four years, and in June 1826 was licensed to preach.

After two years' service in the Middle and Southern states as agent of the American Board of Commissioners for Foreign Missions, he accepted an invitation to supply the Second Presbyterian Church, Albany, N. Y., during the ill health of its pastor, Dr. John Chester. Intensely evangelistic, plain-spoken, sometimes denunciatory, always uncompromising, his preaching was not acceptable to a fashionable congregation which included Martin Van Buren, Benjamin F. Butler, and William L. Marcy, and he was soon summarily dismissed. Some of his sympathizers then organized the Fourth Presbyterian Church of which he was installed pastor on Apr. 21, 1829, having been ordained in the Second Presbyterian Church, New York, Oct. 24, 1828. In the eight years that followed the new church grew rapidly and its pastor became widely known as a promoter of revivals and a lecturer in behalf of missions, temperance, and the anti-slavery movement. He also prepared young men for the ministry, uniting his class with that of Dr. Nathaniel S. S. Beman [*q.v.*] of Troy in 1833 and establishing the Troy and Albany Theological School, first located at Port Schuyler, later at Troy, and discontinued in 1837, when Kirk resigned his pastorate. From April of this year until September 1839 he was in Europe, studying conditions there and frequently preaching and lecturing. Upon his return he became secretary of the Foreign Evangelical Society (American and Foreign Christian Union) and helped to conduct revivals in the principal cities of the East, attracting crowds wherever he spoke. Calls to pastorates came to him from many places, and in 1842 he consented to settle in Boston where a Congregational church was organized for him.

For more than a quarter of a century he was one of the outstanding preachers of the city, and under his leadership the Mount Vernon Church became an aggressive agency of evangelism and reform. In 1846 he was prominent in the gathering at London which gave birth to the Evangelical Alliance. He was sent to Paris by the American and Foreign Christian Union in 1857 to establish an American chapel there, a mission which he successfully performed. Throughout the Civil War he was a fiery supporter of the Union, and when in 1865 the American Missionary Association was free to extend its work among the colored people of the South he was elected president. Besides scores of sermons and addresses which appeared in periodicals or in pamphlet form, he published: *Sermons Delivered in England and America* (1840); *Theopneusty, or the Plenary Inspiration of the Holy Scripture* (1842) and *The Canon of the Holy Scriptures* (1862), both translations from the French of Louis Gaussen, the latter an abridgment; *Louis Fourteenth and the Writers of His Age* (1855), a translation from the French of Jean Frédéric Astié; *Lectures on the Parables of Our Saviour* (1856); *Discourses Doctrinal and Practical* (1857). He also edited and compiled *Songs for Social and Public Worship* (1868). His *Lectures on Revivals*, edited by D. O. Mears, appeared in 1875. He never married, and died at his home in Boston.

[D. O. Mears, *Life of Edward Norris Kirk, D.D.* (1877); Justin Winsor, *The Memorial Hist. of Boston* (1881), vol. III; F. G. Beardsley, *A Hist. of Am. Revivals* (1904); John Ross Dix, *Pulpit Portraits . . . of Distinguished Am. Divines* (1854); *Princeton Theolog. Sem. Gen. Cat.* (1894); *Boston Transcript* and *Boston Daily Advertiser*, Mar. 28, 1874.] H. E. S.

KIRK, JOHN FOSTER (Mar. 22, 1824–Sept. 21, 1904), author, editor, born at Fredericton, New Brunswick, was the son of Abdiel and Mary Kirk. His family moved to Halifax and he was educated under a clergyman, an Oxford graduate, at Truro, Nova Scotia. He left Halifax in 1842 and, after a short period in Quebec, came to New England and settled in Boston. Here for several years he continued his studies, undecided what career to enter. An actor friend, Macready, advised him to go on the stage. When, however, another friend, Robert Carter, who had served the historian, William H. Prescott [*q.v.*], as secretary, recommended him for that position, Kirk accepted and remained with Prescott from 1848 until the death of the latter in January 1859. His broad background of European history, facility with its languages, and capacity for unwearied research made him invaluable to Prescott, who, in the preface to his *History of the Reign of Philip the Second, King of Spain* and elsewhere, generously acknowledged the value of Kirk's criticism and assistance. Kirk accompanied Prescott to England in May 1850 and, after visiting France, Holland, and Belgium, returned to America in September. Prescott's splendid library gave him opportunities for his own researches and he supplemented his secretarial work by contributing critical and historical papers to the *North American Review*. From Barante's *Histoire des Ducs de Bourgogne de la Maison de Valois* he had become deeply interested in the career of Charles the Bold of Burgundy; this interest was encouraged and materially assisted by both Prescott and Francis Parkman [*q.v.*], who was himself indebted to Kirk's scholarship. The death of Prescott in 1859 gave him the time necessary to complete the first two volumes of his *History of Charles the Bold, Duke of Burgundy,* published in 1864. Before the appearance of the third and final volume in 1868 he spent many months in a detailed study of the French and Swiss manuscript sources and in a careful examination of the scene of Charles's defeat. Edward A. Freeman in reviewing the volumes gladly hailed him as "a welcome recruit to the small band of real historians" (*Historical Essays,* p. 315) and "a worthy accession to the same company as . . . Prescott and Motley" (*Ibid.,* p. 372). His viewpoint was essentially that which De Gingins, the Swiss historian, had already developed and set forth. Founded as it was upon years of careful research, *Charles the Bold* was marked by a sane scholarship and was written with narrative power. The work, however, was marred by certain infelicities of style and by an extravagance that sometimes bordered on the sensational; nor was Kirk able to relate his story to the historical events that came before and after.

In 1870 he moved to Philadelphia to edit *Lippincott's Magazine* and to prepare a new edition of Prescott's historical works. He remained as editor of the *Magazine* for sixteen years; his editions of Prescott's *Works* were published at various times from 1873 to 1902. He married in 1879 Ellen Warner Olney, a prolific popular novelist under the pseudonym of "Henry Hayes." From 1885 to 1888 he was lecturer on European history at the University of Pennsylvania. He was engaged from 1886 to 1891 in editing the two-volume *Supplement to Allibone's Critical Dictionary of English Literature* (1891). The remaining years of his life, though varied by an occasional contribution to *Lippincott's Magazine* and the *Atlantic Monthly,* were devoted to the preparation of *Lippincott's New Dictionary.*

[J. F. Kirk, "A Slender Sheaf of Memories," in *Lippincott's Monthly Mag.,* Nov. 1902; "J. F. Kirk: An Appreciation," *Ibid.,* Feb. 1905; *Who's Who in America,* 1903–05; Geo. Ticknor, *Life of William Hickling Prescott* (1864); E. A. Freeman, *Hist. Essays* (London, 1871).]
F. M—n.

KIRKBRIDE, THOMAS STORY (July 31, 1809–Dec. 16, 1883), physician, was born on a farm on the Pennsylvania bank of the Delaware River, near Trenton, the son of John and Elizabeth (Story) Kirkbride. His parents were Friends, his paternal ancestors having come to America with William Penn. He received a classical education under Jared D. Tyler of Trenton, studied under the mathematician, John Gummere [*q.v.*], at Burlington, and later began his medical preparation with Dr. Nicholas Belleville of Trenton. Subsequently, he enrolled at the University of Pennsylvania and in 1832 received the degree of M.D.

Soon after his graduation he became resident physician at the Friends' Asylum for the Insane, at Frankford, a suburb of Philadelphia, and in 1833 he was appointed resident physician of the Pennsylvania Hospital, where he supervised the treatment of the mentally diseased. After two years there, he engaged in general practice in Philadelphia until October 1840, when he was elected physician-in-chief and superintendent of the Pennsylvania Hospital for the Insane, a department of the Pennsylvania Hospital, for which a separate building had just been erected. This position he held until his death, forty-three years later. Here he met novel problems with such executive ability and sympathetic understanding as to make his influence in the field of mental disorders a lasting one. The period in which he flourished has been termed "the Renaissance in psychiatry," and Kirkbride put into his institution the advanced ideas that insanity is a disease to be treated in a hospital (not in an asylum); that occupational therapy would "restore mental health, tranquilize the restlessness and mitigate the sorrows of disease"; and that patients should be individualized and respected as persons who appreciate libraries, lectures, and courtesy. He prepared and published in 1844 a set of rules for those employed in the care of the insane. In 1847 he issued a small work, *Remarks on the Construction and Arrangements of Hospitals for the Insane*; a larger work, *On the Construction, Organization and General Arrangements of Hospitals for the Insane,* appeared in 1854; and a more extensive edition, with some remarks on insanity and its treatment in 1880. The "Kirkbride plan" for building hospitals for mental cases was widely adopted. He also contributed to the *American Journal of Insanity* and the *American Journal of the Medical Sciences.* With other specialists he established in 1844 the Association of Medical Superintendents of American Institutions for the Insane, was its secretary for eight years, and its president for a like term. He also served as trustee of the first state hospital in Pennsylvania, and of the Pennsylvania Institute for the Blind.

His life was one of laboriousness in a wide field of interests. To Quaker inheritance and training may be ascribed his tranquility and his tenacity in holding to a course which was guided by an inner light. He was "gentle as a woman, firm as adamant." Among his most conspicuous qualities were continuing enthusiasm and the power to formulate his ideas definitely and clearly. Kirkbride was a man of medium height with a rather frail body. He was twice married: first in 1839 to Ann West Jenks of Philadelphia, who died in 1862, and four years after her death, in 1866, he married Eliza Butler.

[Ann. reports of the Pa. Hospital for the Insane, 1841 to 1883, esp. a memorial notice in the report of 1883; *Am. Jour. of Insanity,* Jan. 1884; T. G. Morton and Frank Woodbury, *Hist. of the Pa. Hospital* (1897); H. A. Kelly and W. L. Burrage, *Am. Medic. Biogs.* (1920); *Phila. Record* and *Public Ledger,* Dec. 18, 1883.]
E. D. B.

KIRKLAND, CAROLINE MATILDA STANSBURY (Jan. 12, 1801–Apr. 6, 1864), author, mother of Joseph Kirkland [*q.v.*], was born in New York City, the daughter of Samuel Stansbury, a bookseller and publisher, and the grand-daughter of the Loyalist poet, Joseph Stansbury [*q.v.*]. After her father's death she moved with her mother, Elizabeth (Alexander) Stansbury, to the western part of the state, where in 1827 or 1828 she married William Kirkland (1800–1846), a grand-nephew of Samuel Kirkland [*q.v.*] and for a time a member of the faculty of Hamilton College. The Kirklands conducted a seminary in Geneva for several years, then one in Detroit. Later they were among the earliest settlers of the village of Pinckney, Mich.

The trials of a housewife on the untutored frontier prompted Mrs. Kirkland to written expression. Having gone to the West with conceptions derived from such books as Châteaubriand's *Atala,* where no "vulgar inconvenience is once hinted at," she viewed with amusement and dismay the idiosyncrasies of life on the border and sketched with vivid pen the varying character types that surrounded her. Her first book, *A New Home—Who'll Follow* (1839; published in England as *Montacute;* and in 1874, with illustrations by Darley, as *Our New Home in the West: or, Glimpses of Life among Early Settlers*), was issued under the pseudonym of Mrs. Mary Clavers. The false pride of the rustic belles, the exterior coarseness of the pioneers and their utilitarianism—together with their hospitality and their innate delicacy in periods of trial—the delusive charms of the paper cities and the misery caused by the failure of the paper banks, the sufferings due to the ague, the crude merrymakings, and the frontier ideas of equality and communal property rights, all are painted with unusual boldness and humor. Her *Forest Life* (2 vols. in 1, 1842), a series of essay-like disquisitions, and the loosely woven stories which make up *Western Clearings* (1845) likewise bear out the author's claim of presenting "more minute and life-like representations of a peculiar people, than can well be given in a grave, straightforward history" (*Western Clearings,* p. vi). Faults of diffuseness and *préciosité* of style as well as the constraint caused by Western critics and the sentimentality characteristic of the period mark the later books.

In 1843 the family moved to New York City, and thereafter Mrs. Kirkland's work lost its distinctive flavor. She still wrote a few essays on Western life, but they were published in such conventional and didactic collections as *The Evening Book: or, Fireside Talk on Morals and Manners* (copr. 1851), and *A Book for the Home Circle* (copr. 1852). Meantime the death of her husband in 1846 forced her to support herself and her children by teaching, by acting as editor, 1847–48, and associate editor, 1849–51, of the *Union Magazine* (called *Sartain's Union Magazine* after 1849), and by miscellaneous writing. Her taste for reading, shown in frequent allusion and quotation in her Western sketches, found outlet in *Spenser and the Faëry Queen* (1847), with a reprint of a portion of the poem, in her anthologies, *Garden Walks with the Poets* (1852) and *The School-Girl's Garland* (2 ser., 1864), as well as in her discussion of Bryant written in 1853 for Putnam's *Homes of American Authors* (reprinted by that publishing house as *Little Journeys to the Homes of American Authors,* 1896). Her *Holidays Abroad* (2 vols., 1849) is the conventional series of travel letters, as *Memoirs of Washington* (1857) is the stereotyped biography.

According to Poe (*post*), Mrs. Kirkland was "frank, cordial, yet sufficiently dignified—even bold, yet especially ladylike; converses with remarkable accuracy as well as fluency; is brilliantly witty, and now and then not a little sarcastic, but a general amiability prevails." In 1845 she had contributed an introduction to Mrs. Hugo Reid's *A Plea for Woman: Being a Vindication of the Importance and Extent of Her Natural Sphere of Action.* Her interest in welfare work is shown by her pamphlet, *The Helping Hand* (1853), in behalf of discharged female convicts, and by the fact that the night before her death she was actively engaged at the Metropolitan Fair in aid of the United States Sanitary Commission. She died of apoplexy, Apr. 6, 1864. Among her pall-bearers were Peter Cooper, Nathaniel Parker Willis, and William Cullen Bryant.

[D. A. Dondore, *The Prairie and the Making of Middle America* (1926); Edna H. Twamley, "The Western Sketches of Caroline Mathilda (Stansbury) Kirkland," *Mich. Hist. Colls.*, vol. XXXIX (1915); F. B. Streeter, *Mich. Bibliog.* (1921), vol. II; V. C. Sanborn, *The Kirkland or Kirtland Family* (1894); E. A. Poe, "The Literati of New York," *Godey's Magazine*, Aug. 1846, repr. in *The Complete Works of Edgar Allan Poe* (17 vols., 1902), ed. by J. A. Harrison, vol. XV; J. S. Hart, *The Female Prose Writers of America* (1852); *Evening Post* (N. Y.), Apr. 6, 7, 11, 1864, notice of Apr. 6 repr. in *Littell's Living Age*, Apr. 30, 1864; E. A. and G. L. Duyckinck, *Cyc. of Am. Lit.*, 1875, vol. II; Thomas Powell, *The Living Authors of America* (1850).] D. A. D.

KIRKLAND, JOHN THORNTON (Aug. 17, 1770–Apr. 26, 1840), president of Harvard College, was a child of the frontier: one of twin sons born to the Rev. Samuel Kirkland [*q.v.*], missionary to the Oneida Indians, in General Herkimer's house near Little Falls, N. Y. The Indians called the child Agonewiska, or Fair Face. His mother (Jerusha Bingham, a niece of Eleazar Wheelock) took the children to Stockbridge, Mass., during the Revolution. In 1784 John entered Phillips Academy, Andover; and in the spring of 1786, Harvard College. He served as volunteer against Shays and graduated in 1789, the second scholar in his class, and a general favorite for his social qualities. After teaching a year at Andover, he studied divinity under an extreme Calvinist, and in reaction returned to Harvard to study the works of liberal divines. While he was still so engaged, the College appointed him (Nov. 19, 1792) tutor in logic and metaphysics. "A complete gentleman in his manners," wrote one of his pupils, "he aimed to treat the students as gentlemen that, if possible, he might make them so" (Pierce, *post*, pp. 145–46). In 1793, Kirkland was chosen pastor of the New South Church on Church Green, Boston, and ordained Feb. 5, 1794. As a preacher, he made religion attractive, and was successful in winning back the young and the sophisticated from "French infidelity." As a social companion he was a favorite of the gentry. His Phi Beta Kappa oration of 1798 against French infidelity and his sermon on the death of Washington (1800) made him a public character and earned him the degree of D.D. at Princeton. Without mentioning the then dreaded name Unitarian, he tactfully guided his congregation into that fold. He was one of the group who founded the *Monthly Anthology* (November 1803), and the Boston Athenæum. When the Harvard presidency became vacant in 1810, Kirkland had become the personified ideal of a New England gentleman and scholar. He was chosen without opposition, taking office Nov. 14.

During Kirkland's administration Harvard College became definitely a university, in the American sense of a congeries of professional schools (Law, Medicine, and Divinity) grouped about an arts college, which in turn became national rather than local in its clientele. No Harvard president was ever more popular, or equally beloved. Of fine presence and dignity, yet tolerant of the foibles of youth; a fervid preacher yet a man of the world; he attracted many students from outside New England, especially from the South, although the college was under constant attack on the grounds of impiety and aristocracy. Kirkland, working in complete harmony with the College corporation, increased the standard of teaching and study, secured the young Göttingen group—Bancroft, Everett, Ticknor, and Follen [*qq.v.*]—as instructors, introduced the lecture method and the first electives. It was hardly chance that graduates of such future distinction as Emerson, Prescott, Motley, Holmes, and Sumner were educated under Kirkland.

About 1823 he began to lose his grip, though not his popularity. Student disorders culminated in the "Great Rebellion" of 1823, when half the senior class were expelled just before Commencement. The loss of the state grant in 1824, when Massachusetts went Republican, made a serious deficit in college finances. Nathaniel Bowditch [*q.v.*], elected fellow of the Corporation in 1826, forced a retrenchment which undermined the president's authority. In 1827 Kirkland suffered a slight paralytic stroke. An outburst of Bowditch against him on a point of student discipline caused his sudden resignation on Apr. 2, 1828. With Mrs. Kirkland (Elizabeth, daughter of George Cabot, whom he married Sept. 1, 1827), he then visited the South, where he was warmly received by former pupils, and proceeded on an extended tour to Europe and the Near East. Returning to Boston in 1832, he lived there quietly until his death on Apr. 26, 1840. A lively tradition of his personality remained, and his administration was known as the "Augustan Age" of Harvard until long after his death.

[*A Discourse on the Life and Character of the Rev. John Thornton Kirkland* by J. G. Palfrey, and another with the same title by Alexander Young, both published in 1840; sketch by John Pierce, with bibliography of Kirkland's writings (sermons, addresses, and articles in the *Monthly Anthology*) in *Proc. Mass. Hist. Soc.*, 2 ser., IX (1895); C. M. Fuess, *Men of Andover* (1928); S. E. Morison, "The Great Rebellion in Harvard College and the Resignation of President Kirkand," *Pubs. Colonial Soc. of Mass.*, XXVII (1932), 54–112. The portrait by Gilbert Stuart, painted in 1816, is reproduced in the last two items.] S. E. M.

KIRKLAND, JOSEPH (Jan. 7, 1830–Apr. 29, 1894), writer, received from his mother, Caroline Matilda (Stansbury) Kirkland [*q.v.*], the torch of Middle-Western realism and handed it on to his distinguished disciple, Hamlin Garland. Born in Geneva, N. Y., where his parents were conducting a seminary, he spent the impressionable years of boyhood in the "backwoods" of Michigan and his young manhood in pioneer Illinois. He received little formal schooling, but had the benefit of excellent home training; he went to sea for about a year for the benefit of his health; after the death of his father, William Kirkland, in 1846, he probably assisted his mother in the support of the family—although only the fact that he was a clerk in the office of *Putnam's Monthly* about 1852 is fixed. Shortly after arriving in Chicago in 1856 he was employed in the auditing department of the Illinois Central Railroad.

His novels are based almost entirely upon his own experiences and observations. The best of them, *Zury: The Meanest Man in Spring County* (1885), depicts the terrible toil and privations of those first settlers who, granted land as a bonus for their war services or going West to make their fortunes, were destitute of funds and markets during the hard period of breaking and settling. It was the lesson learned in his childhood—that money was life, and the lack of money, death—that gave Zury his title; and it was doubtless the observation of such struggles as Zury's that prompted Kirkland to write to Garland, "You're the first actual farmer in American fiction,—now tell the truth about it" (Garland, *A Son of the Middle Border,* 1917, p. 371). The general truth of the novel is attested by the fact that its plot, in a Kansas background, was reproduced almost exactly by Emanuel and Anna M. Haldeman-Julius in their novel, *Dust* (1921). Their hero, however, lacks the redeeming factor of Kirkland's novel, a wife who has strength to overcome the miserliness and sordidness of outlook engendered by her husband's early struggles. Kirkland's second volume, *The McVeys* (1888), thinner and more forced and uneven than its predecessor, has only a slight interest today because of its sketches of local types and the fact that it is almost the only work of fiction to portray, however pallidly, the mining districts of the upper Mississippi. *The Captain of Company K* (issued in book form in 1891) won the first prize in the novel contest conducted by the *Detroit Free Press,* and was published serially in 1890. It is a chronicle of the Civil War, in which Kirkland himself took part from 1861 until 1863, as private, lieutenant, captain, and major, in the line and on the staffs of Generals McClellan and Fitz-John Porter. True to his earlier realistic code, he strips the conflict of its glamor by showing the misery and bitterness of the private soldier and line officer, helpless pawns in a tragic game they neither can nor wish to understand.

These volumes are Kirkland's chief claims to literary recognition, for *The Story of Chicago* (2 vols., 1892–94), completed after his death by his daughter Caroline, and *The Chicago Massacre of 1812* (1893), belong to the field of local history and are no better and no worse than scores of similar volumes; his periodical contributions are scattered and not particularly outstanding; and his dramatization with James B. Runnion of Daudet's *Sidonie* as *The Married Flirt* is notable chiefly for the protests it aroused among the moralists. The novels themselves save for *Zury,* a noteworthy realistic novel, have certain marked defects. Their plots lack smoothness and effectiveness of structure; they bear traces of toil rather than inspiration. As Kirkland himself realized, he could not emotionalize contemporary Western life.

In estimating his work, however, it must be remembered that he was not primarily a man of letters. After the Civil War he engaged in business in Central Illinois and Chicago. From 1875 until 1880 he was in the United States revenue service. In the latter year he was admitted to the Illinois bar and formed a partnership with Mark Bangs. He practised as an attorney until 1890. It was not until he was over fifty years old that he made himself known as a writer and not until he was about sixty that he served on the staff of the *Chicago Tribune* as special correspondent, reviewer, and literary editor. Small wonder, then, that in the significant interview with Hamlin Garland, which did much to shape the latter's career, he stated simply, "I began too late" (*A Son of the Middle Border,* p. 355).

Kirkland was married in 1863 to Theodosia Burr Wilkinson, a belle from Syracuse, N. Y. His wife's charm and his own wit, kindness, and enthusiasm made not only a pleasant home circle for their four children but a center in Chicago for men of intellect and imagination.

[The most complete account of Kirkland's life is to be found in a thesis by Winifred Wilson, in the Northwestern University library. See also V. C. Sanborn, *The Kirkland or Kirtland Family* (1894); *In Memoriam,* published by the Chicago Literary Club in 1894; *Chicago Daily Tribune,* Apr. 30, 1894; and D. A. Dondore, *The Prairie and the Making of Middle America* (1926).]

D. A. D.

KIRKLAND, SAMUEL (Nov. 20, 1741–Feb. 28, 1808), missionary to the Oneida Indians, was born in Norwich, Conn., the son of Rev. Daniel and Mary (Perkins) Kirtland, Samuel later changing the spelling of the name to Kirkland. He was a descendant of Nathaniel Kyrtland, or Kertland, of Sherrington, Bucks, England, who was in Lynn, Mass., in 1635. Samuel's father, a graduate of Yale College in the class of 1720, was for many years the pastor of the Parish of Newent, now Lisbon, in the town of Norwich. Young Kirkland, having determined to devote himself to missionary work among the Indians, prepared for college at Eleazar Wheelock's school at Lebanon, Conn., where he began his lifelong friendship with Joseph Brant [*q.v.*] and other Indian pupils, and acquired some knowledge of the Mohawk language. He entered the College of New Jersey as a sophomore in 1762, and received his degree *in absentia* in 1765, having set out on his first mission to the Indians in the autumn of 1764. With recommendations from Wheelock and Sir William Johnson he proceeded to Canadasaga, the principal village of the Senecas. Here he was adopted into the family of the chief sachem and remained until May 1766, learning the language, instructing his neighbors, and making acquaintances throughout the tribe. In spite of the loyalty of his friends, many of the Senecas, still excited on account of the late war, were suspicious and hostile. His life was often in danger, but his courage and tact gradually won for him general confidence. He returned to Lebanon in the spring of 1766 to be ordained (June 19), and, yielding to the advice of his friends, determined to establish his permanent mission among the Oneidas. He settled at Canowaroghare (Oneida Castle), their chief village, in August 1766, and carried on his mission in this vicinity for forty years. Receiving no regular financial support, he endured extreme poverty, living as an Indian. He soon gained the affection and confidence of the Oneidas to such a degree that they looked to him for counsel in all their affairs. He established a vigorous church, taught the people habits of industry, and persuaded them to prohibit the sale of liquor in their territory. During this period Wheelock gave full accounts of Kirkland's activities in the successive *Narratives* which he printed for his English contributors, and early in 1769 there came a gift of £30 from an admirer in Scotland, almost the first money Kirkland had received since he came among the Oneidas. Much of this went for relief of the Indians in a famine.

He passed the summer of 1769 in New England to regain his health, which had broken down from exposure and hardships. He was married to Jerusha Bingham, a niece of Wheelock's, Sept. 19, and at once returned with his wife to his mission. In 1770 a disagreement with Wheelock, who was now engaged in the establishment of Dartmouth College, induced Kirkland, with Wheelock's consent, to place himself under the charge of the Boston commissioners of the Honorable Society in Scotland for Propagating Christian Knowledge. He now received a salary of £100 from the Society and from Harvard College. He found means to erect a church, set up mills, and obtain oxen and tools for the Indians.

From Kirkland's papers, it appears that he was instrumental in preventing Lord Dunmore's War from becoming a general Indian uprising in 1774–75. The Shawnees of Virginia, infuriated by encroachments upon their lands and the murder of several of their tribesmen and a number of Senecas, sent messengers to the Six Nations to inform them of the facts and to incite them to take the lead in a general war against the colonists, assuring them that the Indians of the Ohio region were pledged to join in a great alliance on condition that the Six Nations would give their support. A council was called at Onondaga, and continued for more than a month before a decision was reached. Largely on account of the vigorous opposition of the Oneidas and Tuscaroras, the Six Nations refused to enter the war and advised the Shawnees to make peace with the Virginians. A general Indian war at that time might well have forced the colonists to look to Britain for aid and have suppressed the revolutionary movement.

Kirkland's second great service to the colonists followed in 1775. He persuaded the Oneidas to issue a formal declaration of neutrality (May 1775) and soon afterward obtained a general declaration of neutrality from the Six Nations. The authorities in Albany were unable, however, to complete the work which Kirkland had begun; the western tribes of the Confederacy, like the Mohawks, were unwilling to remain mere spectators when a war was in progress; and the Loyalists, with the aid of Brant, were unable to break the League of the Iroquois at a council held near Niagara. Only the Oneidas and Tuscaroras remained loyal to the colonies. During the war the Oneidas were scattered and Kirkland's mission was suspended. He directed Oneida scouts, securing valuable information of the movements of the enemy; served as chaplain at Fort Schuyler (Stanwix) and with Sullivan's expedition; and performed other services. His aid was formally recognized by Congress and by the legislatures of Connecticut, Massachusetts, and New York. At the close of the war he returned to Canowaroghare. He assisted at the treaty of Fort Stanwix (1784) and helped in persuading the Senecas to accept the terms laid down by the government. He rebuilt the church and found encouragement in the rapid progress of his people. In the summer of 1788 he made a tour through the Seneca country, discussed with Brant plans for the welfare of the Indians, and counseled the Six Nations in the business of the Phelps and Gorham purchase. In recognition of his services the Indians and the state of New York made him a grant of some 4,000 acres of wild land along the boundary of the Oneida territory a few miles east of Utica. During the following summer he journeyed through the entire country of the Six Nations, making an elaborate census of the Indians by families.

Hostile demonstrations of the Ohio Indians were causing anxiety in 1790. Kirkland proposed to the government in Philadelphia that a delegation be sent from the Six Nations to the Miamis to persuade them against war. But on account of delays, and the unwillingness of the government to treat with all the Indians in one great council, the embassy failed. Shortly afterward the victory of the Miamis over St. Clair so excited the Senecas that there was prospect of a further uprising under their leadership. At the request of Gen. Henry Knox, secretary of war, Kirkland went through the western part of the state in the winter of 1792 to convince the Indians, if possible, that such a policy would destroy them. He succeeded in bringing together a council of the Six Nations in spite of the threats of the western Indians and the intrigues of hostile whites, and persuaded the council to send a large delegation of chiefs to Philadelphia to negotiate with the federal government. As a result, the Six Nations continued friendly with the United States. Kirkland now set about the accomplishment of a plan which he had long cherished: the equipment of an academy on the boundary between the Indian lands and the white settlements for the coeducation of Indian and white boys. With the approval of President Washington and the promise of support from Alexander Hamilton, he obtained a charter for the Hamilton Oneida Academy in January 1793. He was the most liberal contributor to the school both in lands and in funds, and supported several Indian pupils; but the public had lost faith in the possibility of civilizing the Indians, and the school proved of more value to the white settlements. In 1812 it received a new charter as Hamilton College. The last years of Kirkland's life were uneventful. Despite painful illnesses and personal misfortunes he continued his missionary labors among the Oneidas until shortly before his death. Kindly, wise, and brave, he was respected and loved by the Oneidas and throughout the Iroquois Confederacy as a father and faithful counselor. John Thornton Kirkland [*q.v.*] was his son.

[V. C. Sanborn, "The Kirkland or Kirtland Family," *New-Eng. Hist. and Geneal. Reg.*, Jan. 1894, reprinted separately, with some additional matter, the same year; *Vital Records of Norwich 1659–1848* (1913); S. K. Lothrop, *Life of Samuel Kirkland* (1848); *Documentary History of Hamilton Coll.* (1922); F. B. Dexter, *Biog. Sketches Grads. Yale Coll.*, vol. I (1885); letters and journals of Kirkland, in the Hamilton Coll. Lib.; letters to Wheelock, at Dartmouth Coll.; Pickering Papers and letters of Kirkland, in the library of the Mass. Hist. Soc.]

J. D. I.

KIRKMAN, MARSHALL MONROE (July 10, 1842–Apr. 18, 1921), railroad executive, author, was born on a farm in Morgan County, Ill., the son of Thomas and Catherine (Sweet) Kirkman. After receiving only the most elementary schooling he entered the employ of the Chicago and North Western Railroad Company in 1856 as a messenger boy on the Chicago-Oshkosh line. He continued with the company until his retirement in 1910, at which time he held the office of vice-president in charge of receipts and disbursements. He was thus connected with the road from almost the beginning of its history. Personally, Kirkman was precise and meticulous, both in appearance and utterance. "Few men so polemic and positive as Mr. Kirkman have so many warm friends and admirers," wrote a contemporary (*Railroad Gazette*, Nov. 1, 1889, p. 722). His primary interest was railroad finance, particularly the accounting of operating receipts and expenditures. He held the position of auditor of freight accounts as early as 1861, and by 1881 had been promoted to the rank of comptroller of the entire line. This latter office he retained until his retirement, although the name was twice changed prior to 1910. He was active in advocating the simplification and standardization of railroad accounting, and many of his published works were written with that end in view. He was instrumental in the formation of the Association of American Railway Accounting Officers in 1888, and was the first president of that body. He was chairman of a committee of railway accounting officers which worked with representatives of the Interstate Commerce Commission to obtain a greater uniformity in railroad accounting. The most important contribution of Kirkman, however, was his numerous publications. Starting in 1877, he published many pamphlets and books touching all phases of the railroad business, but emphasizing the financial. Among them he included treatises on interstate commerce, railway disbursements, railway revenue, baggage car traffic, railway service, track accounts, maintenance of railways, rates, legislation, and the handling of supplies.

His most pretentious work was *The Science of Railways* (12 vols., 1894; many later editions). Also of considerable value was his *Classical Portfolio of Primitive Carriers* (1895), which was profusely illustrated. After 1900 his published works were all historical novels, except for *A History of Alexander the Great* (1913). Possibly the change was due in part to his contact with the World's Columbian Exposition at Chicago in 1893, for he was one of its early sponsors and served for two years on the committee on transportation. His first novel was *The Romance of Gilbert Holmes* (1900), which dealt with a boy prodigy who knew all of the important men who lived in Illinois, during the thirties and forties, and survived numerous wrecks, attacks, murders, explosions and other harrowing experiences with unblemished character and unshaken nerves. Kirkman's later fiction dealt entirely with the life and times of Alexander the Great, which he described in five novels, two of which he later revised and republished under different titles. His fiction was in no sense excellent, but it was better done than might have been expected in view of his temperament and background. His wife was Fannie Lincoln, by whom he had two children. He died in Chicago.

[*Who's Who in America,* 1920–21; *Railway Age Gazette,* May 6, 1910; *Railway Age,* Apr. 22, 1921; *Chicago Tribune* and *N. Y. Times,* Apr. 19, 1921; *Report of the President to the Board of Directors of the World's Columbian Exposition* (1898); information as to certain facts from Mrs. M. M. Kirkman.]

R. E. R.

KIRKPATRICK, ANDREW (Feb. 17, 1756–Jan. 6, 1831), jurist, third child of David and Mary (McEowen) Kirkpatrick, was born at Minebrook, N. J., on the old homestead established by his grandfather, Alexander, who had emigrated from Belfast, Ireland, in 1736. His grandfather, who was a strict Scotch-Presbyterian, had been exiled for taking part in the rebellion of the Old Pretender to the throne of England in 1715. Andrew, who was intended for the ministry by his devoutly religious father, graduated from the College of New Jersey in 1775, and began reading theology under a Scotch minister, Rev. Samuel Kennedy, residing about two miles from the Kirkpatrick home. Six months' trial was enough to convince Andrew that the ministry was not his calling, and without hesitation he suffered expulsion from his father's home as punishment for deserting theology for the law. Having no money, he was forced to teach for a while, but shortly entered the law office of William Paterson [*q.v.*], later governor of New Jersey, and was admitted to the New Jersey bar in 1785. Practice in Morristown not proving sufficiently profitable, he moved to New Brunswick in 1787. On Nov. 1, 1792, he married Jane Bayard, daughter of Col. John Bubenheim Bayard [*q.v.*], by whom he had seven children. Kirkpatrick and his wife were said to be the handsomest couple in New Brunswick, and the most popular.

In 1797 he was elected to the lower house of the New Jersey legislature, but resigned in January 1798, to become associate justice on the New Jersey supreme court. Six years later he was elevated by the legislature to the office of chief justice. He was twice reëlected, filling the office till 1824, when, as a result of a combination of political influences and opposition to his judicial conservatism, the legislature appointed another justice in his place. He was generally reputed to be an able judge, and in the law of real estate, profoundly learned. "He was the *beau ideal* of a minister of justice. . . . His enunciation was slow and distinct; his voice full and musical; and his opinions, when not previously prepared, were delivered with fluency and clearness; when written, the language . . . was marked by great purity and precision" (J. G. Wilson, *post,* pp. 19, 20). Two of the more important cases that he decided were *Arnold* vs. *Mundy* (1 *Halsted,* 1), and *Johnson* vs. *Morris* (2 *Halsted,* 6). Although eminently qualified for his office, Kirkpatrick had defects, not so grave then as they would be in a chief justice of today. He was a worshipper of the Common Law of England, especially that developed before 1776, and preferred the learning of Coke to the "modern innovations," regarding them as not worthy of his study. "He was a firm believer in capital punishment and the whipping post, and had little faith in the efficacy of confining criminals in state prisons" (Wilson, p. 26), because he believed it was too easy for them to escape or to secure release. After leaving the bench he spent his remaining years in retirement at his home in New Brunswick, where he died. He was one of the original trustees of Princeton Theological Seminary and chairman of the board from 1822 to 1831; and a trustee of the College of New Jersey from 1807 to 1831.

[J. G. Wilson, *Memorials of Andrew Kirkpatrick and His Wife Jane Bayard* (1870), an enlargement of sketch in *Proc. N. J. Hist. Soc.,* 2 ser., vol. II (1872); John Whitehead, *The Judicial and Civil Hist. of N. J.* (1897); F. B. Lee, *Geneal. and Memorial Hist. of the State of N. J.* (1910), vol. II; S. F. Bigelow, and G. J. Hagar, *The Biog. Cyc. of N. J.* (n.d.); *The Biog. Encyc. of N. J. of the Nineteenth Century* (1877); L. Q. C. Elmer, *The Constitution and Government of the Province and State of N. J.* (1872); W. C. Armstrong, *Capt. John Kirkpatrick of N. J. 1739–1822* (1927); *Emporium and True Advertiser* (Trenton, N. J.), Jan. 15, 1831.]

D. V. S.

KIRKWOOD, DANIEL (Sept. 27, 1814–June 11, 1895), astronomer, teacher, probably a first cousin of Samuel Jordan Kirkwood [*q.v.*], was born in Harford County, Md. His grandfather was an emigrant from Ireland who settled in Delaware; his parents were John and Agnes (Hope) Kirkwood. Daniel spent his early life on a farm and attended school in his native county. He began his career as a teacher in 1833, at Hopewell, York County, Pa. Since one of his pupils wished to study algebra, the two of them worked through Bonnycastle's Algebra together. The following year Kirkwood entered the York County Academy, and in 1838 was appointed mathematical instructor. In 1843 he accepted the principalship of the Lancaster High School and later became principal of the Pottsville Academy. In 1845 he married Sarah A. McNair of Newton, Bucks County, Pa.

His first college position was in Delaware College, Newark, Del., where he was professor of mathematics from 1851 to 1856, during the last two years serving also as president of the college. In conversation with his friends he intimated that he did not enjoy being a college president. He was an enthusiastic teacher and ready to serve the institution of which he was a member in any way he could, but apparently shrank from public notice. In 1856 he was called to Indiana University as professor of mathematics, and served there for thirty years, with the exception of a two-year interval (Aug. 2, 1865–Dec. 18, 1867) as professor of mathematics and astronomy at Jefferson College, Canonsburg, Pa. In 1891 he was appointed lecturer in Leland Stanford, Jr., University. He died at Riverside, Cal., in his eighty-first year.

Kirkwood's intellectual interests lay chiefly in mathematical astronomy. In the course of his career he contributed well over a hundred articles to the *American Journal of Science and Arts, Proceedings of the American Philosophical Society, The Analyst,* the *Sidereal Messenger, Monthly Notices of the Royal Astronomical Society* (London), and other scientific periodicals. Writing at a time when interest in the nebular hypothesis of Kant and La Place was strong, he criticized this theory in detail and worked out many ingenious consequences of it. In the *Proceedings of the American Association for the Advancement of Science* for 1849, he first published his formula for the rotation periods of the planets. In the same *Proceedings* for 1866, when only about fifty asteroids had been discovered, he confidently pointed out gaps among them where periods of revolution would bear simple ratios to that of Jupiter. He further attributed the gaps in the rings of Saturn similarly to perturbations and collisions. In 1861 he published a masterly article on comets and meteors (*Danville Quarterly Review,* December 1861), following this in 1867 with a book entitled *Meteoric Astronomy: A Treatise on Shooting Stars, Fire-Balls, and Aerolites* and, in 1873, with *Comets and Meteors: Their Phenomena in All Ages, Their Mutual Relations, and the Theory of their Origin.* Olivier, in his treatise on *Meteors* (1925), says that in these writings of Kirkwood "we see the first sound argument, based upon philosophical grounds, which was given to prove the connection between comets and meteors" (p. 50). His writings show both clear thinking and lucid style. "In intellect he was keen, logical, and far-seeing. In integrity he was without reproach. . . . He was as natural as a child. . . . The laws of Nature were to him the laws of God" (Swain, *post,* p. 147).

[Robt. J. Aley, memoir in *Indiana School Jour.,* Mar. 1896; Jos. Swain, memoir in *Pubs. of the Astronomical Soc. of the Pacific,* vol. XIII, no. 80 (Oct. 1, 1901); bibliography of Kirkwood's writings in *Circulars of Information of the Bureau of Education, No. 4–1873* (1873), and in S. B. Harding, *Indiana Univ.* (1904); T. A. Wylie, *Indiana Univ.* (1890); W. W. Payne, in *Popular Astronomy,* Dec. 1893; *The Observatory* (London), Sept. 1895; A. M. Clerke, *A Popular Hist. of Astronomy during the Nineteenth Century* (1886); C. P. Olivier, *Meteors* (1925); *San Francisco Chronicle,* June 12, 1895.] R. S. D.

KIRKWOOD, SAMUEL JORDAN (Dec. 20, 1813–Sept. 1, 1894), secretary of the interior, senator, and "war governor" of Iowa, was born in Harford County, Md., the son of well-to-do Scotch-Irish parents, Jabez Kirkwood and his second wife, Mary (Alexander) Wallace. His grandfather, Robert Kirkwood, coming from Londonderry, Ireland, had settled at Newcastle, Del., in 1731. Jabez Kirkwood, a farmer and blacksmith, was so desirous that his sons should have a thorough education that he sent Samuel to school when he was so small his older brothers had to carry him. In 1823 he went to Washington and for four years studied Latin and Greek in the private school of a family connection, John McLoed. After teaching a year and working for a time as a drug clerk, he returned to his family, who had met with financial reverses and were starting west in an effort to regain their fortunes. The family settled in Richland County, Ohio, and young Kirkwood spent his first few years there in clearing land for the new farm and occasionally teaching school or acting as deputy county assessor. In 1841 he moved to the county seat and after two years' study was admitted to the bar. In 1843 he married Jane Clark, whose people soon moved to Iowa City, Iowa. Twelve years later, after much urging from his wife's relatives, Kirkwood also moved to Iowa and purchased an interest in the Clark grist and flour mill.

In Ohio he had served as prosecuting attorney of Richland County, 1845–49, and had been a member of the state constitutional convention of 1850–51. Becoming established in his new home just as the Iowa Republican party was being organized, he was immediately accepted as a leader. After a term in the state Senate, he was nominated for governor in 1859. In one of the hottest campaigns ever conducted in Iowa, the unpolished miller-farmer triumphed over his Democratic rival, Augustus Cæsar Dodge [*q.v.*], just returned from the Court of Spain. Two years later he was reëlected. Kirkwood's office brought to him the responsibility of directing a state lacking in financial strength and divided by the political issue of the day. Before the end of his first term the nation was plunged in civil war. Rising to the situation, Kirkwood called a special session of the legislature, pledged his personal fortune, and borrowed from his friends to equip volunteers in the Union cause with the necessary arms and supplies. During his second term the pro-slavery element, or "Copperheads," gained great strength and at several times threatened insurrection, but the Governor's prompt dispatch of home-guard troops so successfully quelled internal dissension that the seriousness of the situation in Iowa at that time has often been overlooked. Kirkwood's vigor and promptness in action won him a place of prominence among the Northern war governors. In March 1863 he was appointed minister to Denmark, but fearing that it was a move to keep him from the United States Senate, he declined the appointment. With his term as governor completed, he returned to private life and the practice of law; but he was soon called to fill the unexpired term (1866–67) of James Harlan [*q.v.*], who left the Senate to become secretary of the interior.

Against his wishes, Kirkwood was again nominated in 1875 for governor, and in an uneventful campaign was returned to office for a third term by an overwhelming majority. In the following year, however, he was elected to the Senate, and consequently relinquished the governor's office in 1877. In 1881 he was appointed secretary of the interior. He held the office commendably but not brilliantly until some months after the death of Garfield, resigning Apr. 17, 1882. His last political adventure was unsuccessful; in 1886 he was Republican candidate for the United States House of Representatives and was defeated by Walter I. Hayes, who won his victory through a split in the Republican party that even the old War Governor could not mend. This was the last political activity of the now aging man, who spent the remaining years of his life at his home in Iowa City, where he died.

[Dan E. Clark, *Samuel Jordan Kirkwood* (1917); H. W. Lathrop, *The Life and Times of Samuel J. Kirkwood* (1893); B. F. Shambaugh, *The Messages and Proclamations of the Governors of Iowa*, vols. II, IV (1903); Civil War letters of Kirkwood in *Iowa Hist. Record*, July, Oct. 1886, Jan. 1887, Oct. 1890, Jan. 1891; biog. sketch, *Ibid.*, Oct. 1894; *Annals of Iowa*, Oct. 1873, Oct. 1894, Jan. 1898, Oct. 1900; *Biog. Dir. Am. Cong.* (1928).]

F. E. H—k.

KIRLIN, JOSEPH LOUIS JEROME (Mar. 20, 1868–Nov. 26, 1926), Catholic priest, writer, son of Patrick and Anne Kirlin, immigrants from Ulster, Ireland, was born in Philadelphia. Trained by the Christian Brothers at St. Paul's School and at La Salle College (A.B., 1886), he studied theology at the Seminary of St. Charles Borromeo in Overbrook and at the Catholic University of America in Washington, D. C., where he earned a theological degree (1893). He was ordained, Dec. 17, 1892, by the papal delegate, Cardinal Satolli, and appointed to curacies at Ivy Mills, at St. Joachim's Church, Frankford (1894–1901), and at St. Patrick's Church in Philadelphia (1901–1907). During these years, he won commendation as a preacher, as a social worker among the poor, as an advocate of temperance, and as a promoter of temperance and parochial societies. In 1903 he wrote a *Life of the Most Rev. Patrick John Ryan*, which gave him entrée into literary circles and whetted his interest in local church history, with the result that he published *Catholicity in Philadelphia* (1909), an example of what can be done in diocesan history. In 1907 he organized the new parish of the Most Precious Blood, Philadelphia, and soon built a large church and school. While continuing as rector, he was named in 1912 diocesan director of the Priests' Eucharistic League. In 1920 he was made a private chamberlain to the Pope. As a result of his devotional studies, he became sufficiently known to merit a place as a preacher and a reader of a paper at the international Eucharistic Congress at Chicago (1926). Despite ill health, he maintained an interest in civic affairs to the last, serving on one of the Philadelphia Sesqui-Centennial committees. A contributor to Catholic periodicals, he wrote in 1920 a series of meditative, doctrinal articles for *Emmanuel*, published in book form as *Christ the Builder* (1929). He was also the author of three devotional books: *One Hour with Him* (1923), *Our Tryst with Him* (1925), and *With Him in Mind* (1926). He left an unfinished manuscript which was published after his death under the title, *Priestly Virtue and Zeal, a Study of the Life of St. John Baptist Vianney, the Curé d'Ars and Patron of Priests, Applied to the Sacerdotal Life of Today* (1928).

[*Am. Cath. Who's Who* (1911); Katherine Brégy in *Records of the Am. Cath. Hist. Soc.*, June 1927; *Evening Bulletin* (Phila.), Nov. 26, 27, *Public Ledger*, Nov. 27, 1926.] R. J. P.

KIRTLAND, JARED POTTER (Nov. 10, 1793–Dec. 10, 1877), physician, naturalist, public servant, was born at Wallingford, Conn., the son of Turhand and Mary (Potter) Kirtland and a descendant of Nathaniel Kyrtland, immigrant from Buckinghamshire, England, who settled in Lynn, Mass., about 1635. His father, a stockholder and general agent of the Connecticut Land Company, moved to the Western Reserve in 1803, leaving Jared in Wallingford with his maternal grandfather. The boy received his early education in the academies of Cheshire and of Wallingford, and under the stimulating influence of his grandfather, Dr. Jared Potter, reputed to be the best-educated physician in the state, he developed a deep interest in natural history and horticulture. At the age of fifteen he discovered parthenogenesis in the moth of the silkworm, a phenomenon previously unknown in that insect. This was his first scientific contribution.

In 1811, having inherited his grandfather's medical library and money enough to finance his professional education, he began the study of medicine under preceptors. With the opening, in 1813, of the Medical Institution of Yale College, he became a member of the first class matriculated there. In the same year he was a private pupil of Professor Eli Ives in botany and of the elder Silliman in geology and mineralogy. The next year, at the Medical Department of the University of Pennsylvania, he came in contact with Benjamin S. Barton in botany and Benjamin Rush in medicine. He returned to Yale and received the degree of M.D. in 1815. On May 22, 1815, he married Caroline Atwater of Wallingford, who died in 1823. From 1815 to 1818 he practised medicine at Wallingford, and from 1818 to 1823 at Durham, Conn. At the age of twenty-five he was chosen probate judge in Wallingford.

In 1823, following the death of his wife, he moved to Poland, Mahoning County, Ohio, where his father had settled twenty years before; and was soon reputed the best-informed physician in that part of the state. Two years later he married Hannah Fitch Tousey of Newton, Conn. He was sent to the Ohio legislature in 1828 and was reëlected twice, holding office for six years. His especial service was a reformation of the penitentiary system by which industrial work for the inmates was substituted for the previous confinement in idleness.

In 1837 he removed from Poland, Ohio, to a farm near Cleveland, but in the same year assumed the chair of theory and practice of medicine in the Medical College of Ohio at Cincinnati, which he occupied until 1842. In 1839 he was president of the Third Ohio Medical Convention. In 1842–43 he gave a course of lectures in the Willoughby (Ohio) Medical College, and in 1843 he became one of the founders of the Cleveland Medical College, the medical department of Western Reserve College. Here he was professor of the theory and practice of medicine until 1864 and professor emeritus until his death. In this institution over two thousand students came under his stimulating instruction. He contributed to leading medical journals, and in 1849 was fourth president of the Ohio State Medical Society.

Throughout his life he assiduously continued his observations and collections in natural history. He discovered that the bivalve freshwater mollusks are bisexual, although previously described as hermaphroditic. He also discovered the byssus, an embryonic organ of the mollusks. These discoveries, published in the *American Journal of Science and Arts* in 1834 and 1840, brought him international notice. When the geological survey of Ohio was organized in 1837, he was given charge of zoölogy. He made extensive collections, and in the *Second Annual Report of the Geological Survey of the State of Ohio* (1838) published a checklist, with descriptive notes, containing the names of 585 Ohio animal species which he had assembled. In 1839 he became a member of the Boston Society of Natural History and subsequently published in its *Journal* several papers on climatology, insects, birds, and, notably, the fishes of Ohio.

From 1812 to his death his interest in experimental floriculture and horticulture was unabated. He developed many improved varieties of flowers and fruits, some of which are still popular, and made important improvements in apiculture. He was keenly interested in ornithology, trained himself to be an expert taxidermist, and instructed many in the art. He accumulated a large collection of birds and some of his personally prepared specimens went into leading European museums. That he might interest others in natural history, in 1845 he organized the Cleveland Academy of Natural Science, which was active until the Civil War. He was one of its officers throughout this period. In 1869 it was reorganized as the Kirtland Society of Natural Science, of which he was president until 1875. The present Cleveland Museum of Natural History is the continuation of these earlier organizations. Throughout his career he carried on an extensive correspondence with American and European scientists. His correspondence with Louis Agassiz was frequent. He accompanied Spencer F. Baird as a member of a natural history exploration to the regions around Lake Superior in 1853 and made an independent exploration to Florida in 1869. The bibliography of his published articles includes nearly two hundred titles.

His public service was unusually extensive. Besides his work in legislature, geological surveys, and medical schools, he was a trustee of Western Reserve College from 1833 to 1835, and a trustee of the Ohio Agricultural College until 1870. For several years, beginning in 1851, he was editor of the *Ohio Family Visitor,* a paper devoted to domestic affairs and agriculture. Although nearly seventy, he was an examining surgeon for several months during the Civil War. He was a member in its first year (1848) of the American Association for the Advancement of Science, a member of the National Academy of Sciences, of the American Philosophical Society, and of many other scientific and horticultural organizations. Personally he was a man of commanding and dignified presence, of a benevolent nature, and of a friendly disposition. One of his biographers, a personal acquaintance, writes of "his universal and unextinguishable cheerfulness, the result of an enthusiasm in the pursuit of knowledge and an enjoyment of nature which kept him fresh and green and youthful to the very last. Sorrow and bereavement . . . neither soured his feelings nor chilled his interest in men and things" (Newberry, *post,* pp. 137–38). The same biographer characterizes Kirtland's life as not only "one of the most admirable and useful" but also "the happiest of which I have any knowledge" (*Ibid.*). He died at Rockport, near Cleveland, a month after his eighty-fourth birthday, survived by one daughter and a family of grandchildren.

[*New-Eng. Hist. and Geneal. Reg.,* July 1860; *Cleveland Leader,* Dec. 11, 1877; *Obit. Record Grads. Yale Coll.,* 1878; Maurice Joblin, *Cleveland Past and Present* (1869); E. Cleave, *A Biog. Cyc. of Ohio* (1875); Benjamin Silliman, in *Am. Jour. Sci. and Arts,* Jan. 1878; M. P. Wilder, in *Trans. Mass. Horticultural Soc.,* 1878; Charles Whittlesey, in *Mag. of Western Hist.,* May 1885; J. S. Newberry, in *Biog. Memoirs of the Nat. Acad. of Sci.,* vol. II (1886); S. P. Orth, *Hist. of Cleveland* (1910), vol. I; H. A. Kelly and W. L. Burrage, *Am. Medic. Biogs.* (1920).] F. C. W.

KITCHIN, CLAUDE (Mar. 24, 1869–May 31, 1923), congressman, was born near Scotland Neck, N. C. His father, William Hodges Kitchin, noted for his power as a political campaigner, was a member of the Forty-sixth Congress. He married Maria F. Arrington, and lived to see two sons, William Walton [*q.v.*] and Claude, elected to the House of Representatives. Claude Kitchin was graduated (B.L.) from Wake Forest College in 1888 and on Nov. 13 following was married to Kate, the daughter of Luther R. Mills, a professor at Wake Forest. He studied law, was admitted to the bar in 1890, began practice, and was quickly successful. In 1900, as a result of his work in the white-supremacy campaigns of 1898 and 1900, he was elected to Congress and served until his death.

In Congress Kitchin won, rather quickly, recognition as a ready, spirited, and effective speaker, and, in the course of time, the accepted reputation of being the most powerful debater in the House. Attractive in appearance, full of vigor and strength, possessed of a fine voice, a ready wit, and a fluent ease in speaking, moved always by passionate conviction, he was at once a valuable champion of a cause and an opponent to be dreaded. His favorite weapon was ridicule, which he employed effectively but never with malice, for his good nature was so abounding as to become well-nigh proverbial. Presently his colleagues found that he was always prepared with respect to the subject matter of his speeches, especially when a tariff question was under discussion, and after a particularly able speech on the Payne-Aldrich tariff bill, he was placed on the ways and means committee. In 1915 he became its chairman. By virtue of this appointment he was majority leader, a position at that time perhaps second only to the presidency in power and influence. An earnest supporter of President Wilson, he nevertheless opposed and voted against the declaration of war with Germany. "My conscience and judgment," said he in an impressive explanation of his position, "after mature thought and fervent prayer for rightful guidance, have marked out clearly the path of my duty and I have made up my mind to walk it, if I go barefooted and alone" (*Congressional Record,* 65 Cong., 1 Sess., p. 332, Apr. 5, 1917). At the same time, however, he made clear his intention, when once war was declared, of giving to its prosecution his full support. Upon him as majority leader and chairman of the ways and means committee fell a tremendous burden of labor and responsibility, into which he threw himself with all his forces, working without rest day and night, until, in the words of Representative Clarence Cannon of Missouri, he "fell as truly a casualty of the war as if he had died leading the charge upon the crimson fields of France" (*Memorial Addresses,* p. 83). He supported actively the administration measures, and after aiding in the preparation of the two great war revenue bills, he directed their passage through the House. His vote on the declaration called forth bitter criticism which was intensified presently by a false newspaper report that he had declared his intention of so framing the revenue measures as to place the financial burden of the war upon the Northern states. In spite of the entreaties of his colleagues he declined to dignify the slander by an answer (*Ibid.,* p. 15), and it found wide acceptance. His active career ended on Apr. 9, 1920, when, after closing a powerful speech against making peace with Germany by joint resolution, he suffered a cerebral hemorrhage from which he never recovered sufficiently to resume his place in the House. He died three years later at Wilson, N. C.

Kitchin was a man of unusual power and ability. Clarence Cannon, in the speech already mentioned, said that he had "the strength and courage of a gladiator, the wisdom and vision of a statesman, and with them all the intuition and tenderness of a woman" (p. 81). Woodrow Wilson described another side, "I never knew a man who could state his position more lucidly or state yours more fairly" (*News and Observer,* June 1, 1923). Honest, utterly frank and sincere, he commanded the respect and affection of his colleagues regardless of party.

[*Claude Kitchin: Memorial Addresses* (1925), and *Cong. Record,* 68 Cong., 1 Sess., pp. 753–69; *Biog. Dir. Am. Cong.* (1928); *Who's Who in America,* 1922–23; *News and Observer* (Raleigh, N. C.), June 1, 1923; *N. Y. Times,* June 1, 1923; *Outlook,* June 13, 1923; Claude Kitchin papers in library of the Univ. of N. C.]

J. G. deR. H.

KITCHIN, WILLIAM WALTON (Oct. 9, 1866–Nov. 9, 1924), congressman, governor of North Carolina, brother of Claude Kitchin [*q.v.*], was born near Scotland Neck, N. C., the son of William Hodges and Maria F. (Arrington) Kitchin. At Wake Forest College, where he graduated (A.B.) in 1884, he was studious and of a retiring disposition—like his mother rather than his father, who had come up from Alabama, bought rich farming lands, fought through the Civil War to a captaincy, and then to a seat in Congress from a district theretofore heavily Republican. By 1890, after brief periods of teaching and editing the *Scotland Neck Democrat,* young William had established himself as a lawyer in Roxboro and had become chairman of the county Democratic executive committee. By 1893, having been defeated the previous year for the state Senate, he was a legislator, interested in fiscal affairs, education, and charities (*House Journal,* 1893, *passim*). In 1896 came his first great success. Nominated for Congress as a forlorn hope, he met his Republican opponent in joint debate and had the distinction of being the only Democratic congressman elected in the state, in that year of rampant Populism and consequent Republican opportunity. The grateful Democracy of the fifth district continuously reelected him until 1908. No particular distinction was derived from this service; his best assignments were to the committee on naval affairs and to that on manufactures; on the first he did good work, especially in 1901–02.

Twice, in 1902 and 1906, Kitchin had swung Democratic state conventions to continued support of W. J. Bryan and his platforms, which the "machine" wing of the party seemed inclined to abandon. Now, in 1908, he sought from the people the governorship on an anti-machine and anti-trust platform. Handsome, mellow-voiced, inclined to reason with his hearers, he impressed men as able, fearless, honest; and in the memorable June convention of that year he won, though the great leaders were against him. In the capacity of governor, 1909–13, he recommended direct primaries as being fairer to poor men, strict regulation of corporations, strict obedience to the new prohibition law, experiments in drainage and careful study of the road problem before adopting comprehensive construction policies, progressive but cautious factory legislation, support of schools and charities, and a budget balanced by assessing property at its real value. In 1912, resuming the contest of 1908, he entered the primary against Senator Furnifold M. Simmons, leader of the "machine" and protagonist of industrial and commercial development. Kitchin had not been sufficiently radical for some, however, while others thought him too radical; times were now good; the Simmons machine was working smoothly. Consequently he was overwhelmed, lost his bid for party leadership, and passed from public life. For five years he practised law in Raleigh; then, prematurely invalided, he retired to Scotland Neck, where he died. His wife, Musette (Satterfield) Kitchin, whom he had married Dec. 22, 1892, and five children survived him. Looking back, men said that as a political speaker he was equaled in his generation only by Charles Brantley Aycock [*q.v.*], and that he spoke for the economic needs of the common man as Aycock did for his education.

[Brief outlines of Kitchin's life appear in *Who's Who in America,* 1924–25, and *Biog. Dir. Am. Cong.* (1928); sketches and estimates, in the Wake Forest

Student, Jan. 1909, the *News and Observer* (Raleigh), Nov. 10, 1924, and *Proc. . . . N. C. Bar Asso.,* 1925. R. D. W. Connor, in *North Carolina* (1929), vol. II, gives an excellent though unsympathetic general account. None of Kitchin's important speeches appear to have been preserved.] C. C. P.

KITTSON, NORMAN WOLFRED (Mar. 5, 1814–May 10, 1888), fur-trader, promoter of transportation, was born at Chambly, Lower Canada, the son of George and Nancy (Tucker) Kittson. His grandfather, John George Kittson, was a native of England and, according to family tradition, served under Wolfe at Quebec. Kittson obtained a limited education at the Sorel Grammar School. Fired by the tales of William Morrison, a retired fur-trader, he began, at sixteen, an apprenticeship with the American Fur Company and served as clerk at various posts in the region which includes the present Wisconsin, Minnesota, and Iowa.

Since 1834 Henry Hastings Sibley [*q.v.*] had been the chief agent of the American Fur Company at St. Peter's (later Mendota, Minn.), opposite Fort Snelling. In 1843 Sibley admitted Kittson as one of his special partners and assigned him the still profitable valleys of the upper Minnesota and the Red River of the North as far as the British possessions. Sibley supplied the merchandise; Kittson was manager, and profits and losses were equally shared. Although the boundary between the United States and the British possessions had been established in 1818 at the Forty-ninth parallel, the Hudson's Bay Company, with headquarters at Fort Garry (later Winnipeg), still traded on United States soil. Kittson resolved to expel the intruder. In 1844 he established a trading post at Pembina, near the international boundary. Eastward and westward on a frontier of 300 miles he planted smaller posts. The winter he devoted to trade; the summer, to transportation. In June a train of ox-drawn, peltry-laden carts began a 400-mile trip to civilization; in August the carts came creaking back with supplies. During ten strenuous years Kittson carried on a spirited trade war with the Hudson's Bay Company, each side bidding for the trade of the Indians and half-breeds. The Company rehabilitated its posts and cut prices ruinously. Kittson competed shrewdly, sometimes bought furs on British soil, but frowned upon the use of liquor. Handicapped by limited capital, distance from his base, and inferior American supplies, and finally convinced that his opponent would not buy him out, he withdrew in 1854. His total profits "in this rascally fur business" were not large, but he had prompted the extension of *de facto* American government to the boundary.

Kittson was member for the Pembina district in the legislative council of Minnesota Territory, 1852–55, thrice making the arduous trip to the capital in winter by dog-train. In 1854 he moved to St. Paul, where he owned real estate that was rapidly increasing in value, and in 1858, although he hated politics, he was elected mayor as a Democrat. When the Hudson's Bay Company began importing supplies by way of Minnesota for the Fort Garry trade, it made Kittson, in 1860, its purchasing and forwarding agent—a remarkable tribute. In 1861 the Company placed a steamboat on the Red River of the North, thereby shortening the journey by ox-train. For years Kittson directed overland and river traffic, both for the Company and for private individuals. In 1871 James J. Hill [*q.v.*] began a steamboat service in opposition; but the following year Kittson and Hill wisely combined, and formed presently the highly remunerative Red River Transportation Company, with "Commodore" Kittson as manager.

In 1873 the St. Paul & Pacific Railroad, which was expected to open the Red River Valley to settlement and to connect with a Canadian line from Winnipeg, became insolvent. Kittson, Hill, and Donald A. Smith (later Lord Strathcona), an influential Scotch-Canadian interested in Manitoba, watched proceedings closely and, in 1878, in association with George Stephen (later Lord Mount Stephen), a Montreal magnate, secured control, reorganizing the line strongly (1879) as the St. Paul, Minneapolis & Manitoba Railway. To consummate the transaction, Hill and Kittson pledged $280,000—almost everything they had. "I did not dare to tell you," Kittson later told his best friend, Sibley, "because you would have thought that I was mad." This solid achievement made Kittson enormously wealthy.

His health was failing, however, and he shortly retired from business, to become one of the large horse-fanciers of the country, with stables in Midway Park, St. Paul, and Erdenheim, Pa. His sudden death in 1888 removed the oldest white settler in Minnesota and Dakota. Tall, energetic, straightforward, unassuming, warm in friendship with a few, respected by the many, he ranked high among the pioneer leaders and did much to open the Red River Valley to settlement.

[C. W. Rife, "Norman W. Kittson, a Fur-Trader at Pembina," *Minn. Hist.,* Sept. 1925, based largely upon Kittson's letters in the Sibley Papers (Minn. Hist. Soc.); information as to certain facts from Kittson's son, Rev. Henry Kittson; C. C. Andrews, *Hist. of St. Paul* (1890), pt. II; *Defendant's Exhibits* and *Defendant's Testimony* in *Jesse P. Farley* vs. *James J. Hill et al.,* in U. S. circuit court, district of Minnesota, in equity; W. W. Folwell, *A Hist. of Minn.,* vol. III

(1926), App. 10; J. G. Pyle, *The Life of James J. Hill* (1917), I, *passim;* T. M. Newson, *Pen Pictures of St. Paul* (1886); *Daily Pioneer Press* (St. Paul), May 11, 1888.] C. W. R.

KLEIN, BRUNO OSCAR (June 6, 1858–June 22, 1911), pianist, composer, and teacher, was born in Osnabrück, Hanover, Germany, the third of five children of Karl and Mathilde von Warnecke Klein. His father, a distinguished musician—conductor, pianist, and organist at the cathedral at Osnabrück—instructed his children in music. An older son, Bernhard, became a prominent organist in Philadelphia and a composer of much Catholic Church music. At the age of twelve, Bruno Oscar played the Mozart sonatas from memory and was able to read almost any music at sight. He was graduated from the Gymnasium, where he took special honors in Latin and Greek, but he decided to follow music as a profession and entered the Munich Conservatory in 1875. He became a student of Carl Baermann in piano, of Rheinberger in counterpoint, and of Wüllner in orchestration. Upon the completion of his studies in 1877 he visited his brother in Philadelphia and was so impressed with the new country that, after spending a short time in Germany, he decided to make America his home. He returned in 1878 and for five years toured the country as a concert pianist, in 1879 with the violinist Wilhemj. On Jan. 31, 1880, he married Emmy Schaefer, a German pianist, a graduate of the Leipzig Conservatory. In 1884 he took up permanent residence in New York and for many years was organist of Jesuit churches (St. Francis Xavier's, 1884–94, and St. Ignatius', 1904–11). From 1884 until his death he was head of the piano department of the Convent of the Sacred Heart, New York City. From 1887 to 1892 he was professor of counterpoint and composition at the National Conservatory, to which position he was called on recommendation of Rafael Joseffy and William Mason. During 1894–95 he gave concerts in Germany.

While he wrote numerous small pieces before going to New York, his first large work was a well-written sonata for piano and violin (*opus* 10), which was composed in 1883 and dedicated to William Mason. Thereafter he produced numerous works, among them a piano concerto in E minor (four movements), dedicated to Rafael Joseffy (who had performed many of Klein's works), a "Conzertstück" for piano and orchestra dedicated to Emil Liebling, a suite for piano (*opus* 25) in five movements, "Five Fantasy Pieces" (*opus* 20) for piano, after poems by Heine, and "Album Poétique" (*opus* 40), a group of six pieces for piano. His orchestral works include two overtures and several violin compositions with orchestral accompaniment ("Romanza" and "Spinnlied," and "Ballade" in D minor). He composed also many short piano pieces, all of poetic content, but he was most prolific as a song writer, having published eighty or more separately in addition to three song volumes. His quintet for soprano, violin, 'cello, horn, and piano (accepted by the Kneisel Quartet) ranks especially high as a representative work and is probably unique in form. His largest work was his one opera, *Kenilworth,* after Scott's novel, which had its first performance in Hamburg on Feb. 13, 1895, with a splendid cast including Katharina Klafsky in the rôle of Amy Robsart. He composed much music for the Catholic Church, including six masses. While his compositions appeared often on programs during the eighties and nineties they lost their popularity, though many of them remain useful teaching pieces. As a pianist, he had an adequate technique and a fine quality of tone and was among the best performers in America; as an accompanist he excelled, for he could make any transposition at sight.

[*Who's Who in America,* 1910–11; *Neue Berliner Musiczeitung,* Jan. 16, 1896; *Music,* May 1895; *Musical Record,* Jan. 1, 1900; *Musical Courier,* July 4, 1898, June 28, July 5, 1911; information as to certain facts from Mrs. Bruno Oscar Klein.] F. L. G. C.

KLEIN, CHARLES (Jan. 7, 1867–May 7, 1915), dramatist, began his association with the theatre as an actor but soon gave up that branch of the profession for the writing of plays. He was born in London, the son of Hermann and Adelaide (Soman) Klein, and was one of four brothers: Hermann, musician and teacher of singing; Alfred, actor; and Manuel, musician and composer; and Charles. He came to the United States in 1883 and for a time acted the title rôle in *Little Lord Fauntleroy,* and parts in *The Messenger from Jarvis Section* and *The Romany Rye,* for which he was especially fitted by his diminutive stature. While appearing in *The Schatchen* in New York (1890), he was commissioned by M. B. Curtis to rewrite that play, and thus he began his labors as a dramatist that continued uninterruptedly for the rest of his life. His next work was the construction, in collaboration with Charles Coote, an English actor, of a melodrama for Minnie Palmer, *A Mile a Minute,* its inspiration being two large lithographic pictures in the possession of her manager. Thereafter his plays followed one another so rapidly that there was scarcely a theatrical season which did not bring to the stage from him at least one play, some of them written by his own unassisted hand, and others in collaboration. Among the most popular of the latter were *The District Attorney* with Harrison Grey Fiske (1895), *Heartsease* with J. I. C. Clarke (1897), and *The Auctioneer* with Lee Arthur (1901), the last especially prepared for David Warfield when he was beginning his career as a star under the direction of David Belasco. Its popularity led to the writing of another play of Jewish character for the same actor, *The Music Master* (1904), a sentimental comedy that succeeded through Warfield's personality and dramatic skill rather than on account of any merits of its own. Among the better known of his plays that followed are *The Lion and the Mouse* (1905), *The Third Degree* (1909), *The Gamblers* (1910), and *Maggie Pepper* (1911). These and many of his other plays were as timely and as transitory as the first page of a daily newspaper. As Arthur Hobson Quinn (*post,* p. 104) has said: Klein "belongs in our dramatic history mainly by the fact that his plays were concerned frequently with themes of contemporary life in the United States. He had a theory of playwriting which was higher than his practice." Klein's personal attitude toward his work is clearly shown by his remark: "I cannot see how Bernard Shaw, who denies everything from pure love to pure music, can be a public benefactor; only the man who affirms what is good tells the whole truth." (Quoted by Montrose J. Moses in *The American Dramatist,* ed. 1925, pp. 15–16.) He was not unversatile, however, for he made an English version of Pierre de Courcelles's French melodrama, *Les Deux Gosses,* under the title of *Two Little Vagrants* (1896), and he wrote the librettos of two light operas, *El Capitan* (1896) with music by John Philip Sousa, acted with De Wolf Hopper in the title rôle, and of *Red Feather* (1903), with music by Reginald de Koven. He served for a time as play reader and censor on the staff of Charles Frohman, with whom he was one of the victims of the sinking of the *Lusitania* by the Germans in the second year of the World War. His theory of the dramatist's work was that it is primarily a reportorial task that took the ideas of the moment for texts, and that it was an artifice rather than an art. Thus his plays are not so much reproductions of real life as they are shrewd and clever constructions designed to hold the attention of the audience as it may also be held by the reading of a daily newspaper or timely magazine article. His wife was Lillian Gottlieb of New York, to whom he was married on July 10, 1888.

[*Who's Who in America,* 1912–13; Montrose J. Moses, *The Am. Dramatist* (2nd ed., 1917, 3rd ed., 1925); A. H. Quinn, *A Hist. of the Am. Drama from the Civil War to the Present Day* (1927), vol. II; the *N. Y. Dramatic Mirror,* Dec. 12, 1896, Nov. 2, 1910, May 12, 1915; *Harper's Weekly,* Dec. 8, 1906; *Theatre,* June 1915; *N. Y. Times,* May 8, 9, 1915.] E. F. E.

KLEIN, JOSEPH FREDERIC (Oct. 10, 1849–Feb. 11, 1918), mechanical engineer and teacher, was born at Paris, France, the son of Wilhelmina and Frédéric Musé. His father was a saddler and served for a time in the French cavalry. A year or two after Joseph was born his father died, his mother was married again—to Theobold Klein, and Joseph was given his stepfather's name. In 1852 the family came to America and settled at Bridgeport, Conn., where Joseph attended the public schools. In 1858 they moved to New Haven, and he attended the Eaton Grammar School. After completing the grammar-school course, he worked a short time in the shops of the New York, New Haven & Hartford Railroad, and then (1866–67) attended the preparatory school of William Russell, at New Haven. The next year he worked with Sargent & Company and with the W. & E. T. Fitch Company as salesman and shipping clerk, but in 1868, at the suggestion of a friend, J. Willard Gibbs [*q.v.*], later a professor in Yale University, he registered at the Sheffield Scientific School in the course of dynamic (mechanical) engineering. The same year he became an instructor in an evening school in New Haven, a position that he was able to fill while attending college. He received the degree of Ph.B. in 1871, and from then until 1873 he served as assistant to Professor W. P. Trowbridge at the University and continued his course in mechanical engineering to receive the degree of D.E. In 1873 he entered the employ of the Colt Company at Hartford as a draftsman, remaining with them four years and rising to the position of assistant to the chief engineer. In 1877 he returned to Yale as an instructor in the mechanical engineering department. While a member of the Yale faculty he engaged in experimental research in the application of the laws of thermodynamics and published "The Absolute Zero of Temperature" (*Van Nostrand's Engineering Magazine,* April 1880) and "Concerning (Tî-Tô) /Tî, or the Limit of Efficiency of Heat Engines" (*Journal of the Franklin Institute,* March, April 1879). At this time he also published "Tables and Diagram for Determining the Diameters of Speed Cones when Connected by an Open Belt of Constant Length" (*Ibid.,* May 1880).

In 1881 he went to Lehigh University to establish a course in mechanical engineering, and remained at Lehigh until his death. Almost as important, however, as the work that he did there in creating and developing one of the foremost engineering schools in America, are his contributions to engineering literature. He translated into English many of the standard German texts on machine design and thermodynamics and wrote as many more of his own based on the research that he carried on in the kinematics and mechanics of machines. He translated *Mechanics of Machinery Transmission* by J. Weisbach and G. Hermann in 1883, G. A. Zeuner's *Treatise on Valve Gears* in 1884, and Zeuner's *Technical Thermodynamics* in 1906. He was the author of *Mechanical Technology of Machine Construction* (1889); *Elements of Machine Design* (1889); *Tables of Co-ordinates for Laying out Gear Teeth* (1889); *The Design of a High-Speed Steam Engine* (1892); and *The Physical Significance of Entropy or of the Second Law* (1910). In addition to his work as head of the mechanical engineering department, he was secretary of the faculty, 1887–88, dean of the faculty from 1907 to his death, and acting president of the University from February to April 1910. He was a member of the American Society of Mechanical Engineers. Klein married Ada Louise Warner of Thomaston, Conn., Dec. 30, 1879. He died at Bethlehem, Pa.

[*Trans. Am. Soc. Mech. Engrs.*, vol. XL (1919); *Who's Who in America*, 1916–17; *Obit. Record Grads. Yale Univ.*, 1918; *The Brown and White* (Bethlehem, Pa.), Feb. 12, 1918; biographical sketch in the possession of Klein's son, A. W. Klein, who also furnished several interesting facts.] F. A. T.

KLINE, GEORGE (*c.* 1757–Nov. 12, 1820), frontier newspaper editor and book publisher, was born in Germany. At an early age he emigrated to America and worked at his trade of printer in Philadelphia, where in 1781 he published the *Allied Mercury*. Evidence of the thoroughness of his separation from the old country appears in his voluntary rearrangement of the letters of his name from Klein to Kline, in order to avoid the implication of alien birth. His social acceptability is indicated by his marriage, one year after his arrival in Philadelphia, to Rebecca, daughter of Judge Lewis Weiss, who became the mother of his eleven children.

In 1785 Kline removed to Carlisle, Pa., then scarcely more than a frontier settlement but already a place of considerable culture and the seat of Dickinson College. For thirty-five years thereafter Carlisle was the locus of his life and labors as a journalist and a purveyor of serious literature. In the same year that he arrived he started a Federalist weekly, *The Carlisle Gazette, and the Western Repository of Knowledge,* the first newspaper in Pennsylvania west of the Susquehanna River. It was a small four-page sheet on very blue paper, well printed and executed, and sold for six cents a copy or fifteen shillings for one year's subscription. With several changes of title, it was issued without interruption until 1817, when it was absorbed by the Carlisle *Spirit of the Times.*

Kline had an individual style and was a capable editor. In his paper events and movements characterizing the first decades of the history of the United States under the Constitution were viewed from the frontier rather than from the center of political and social activities. The *Gazette's* columns carried real news from the little but ambitious and growing towns of Cincinnati, Detroit, and St. Louis. Accounts of Indian attacks on the Ohio kept its readers conscious of the perils of the not-distant wilderness and forest. The embarrassment caused by delinquent subscribers was tacitly acknowledged in the editor's announcement of his willingness to receive "flour, wheat, corn, wood, pork, or spirits" in lieu of cash.

Thoroughly public spirited, George Kline was sympathetic with every project which promised to promote civic improvement, particularly the quality of public reading. His press issued, in 1797, *Rules of the Carlisle Library Company; with a Catalogue of Books Belonging thereto,* and he reprinted among other works Isaac Watts's *Scripture History* (1797), John Brown's *Westminster Assembly of Divines* (1797), Charlotte Smith's *Montalbert, a Novel* (*c.* 1800), vol. I, *Twenty Sermons* (1803) of Jonathan Edwards, and James Hervey's *Meditations and Contemplations* (2 vols., 1806). He died at Carlisle, after ten days of illness, and was buried in the Old Graveyard there. His wife survived him nearly fourteen years, dying July 13, 1834, at the home of a son in Harrisburg.

[See Leonore E. Flower, *Early Hist. of the Cumberland Valley* (1923); Sarah W. Parkinson, *Local Hist.: A Few Early Carlisle Publications* (1910); C. P. Wing, *Hist. of Cumberland County, Pa.* (1879); C. S. Brigham, "Bibliography of American Newspapers," *Proc. Am. Antiq. Soc.*, n.s. XXX, pt. 1 (1920); *Poulson's Am. Daily Advertiser* (Phila.), Nov. 21, 1820; *Harrisburg Chronicle,* July 21, 1834. Broken files of *Kline's Weekly Gazette* are preserved in the Hamilton Library at Carlisle and in the library of the Am. Antiq. Soc.; the Library of Congress possesses a complete file from the first issue of Aug. 10, 1785, to July 30, 1788; and the Dauphin County Historical Society of Harrisburg, a file complete from Aug. 8, 1787, to Oct. 23, 1817, believed to be Kline's office file.] L. C. P.

KLINGELSMITH, MARGARET CENTER (Nov. 27, 1859–Jan. 19, 1931), librarian and author, was born in Portland, Me. Her parents, Isaac Henry and Caroline How (Evans) Center, both belonged to old and prominent New England families. She attended private schools at Newton, Mass., and Portland, Me. In 1884 she was married to Joseph M. Klingelsmith at Atlanta, Ga. She entered the law school of the University of Pennsylvania in 1896 and soon made a record for herself as a student. Her essay on "The Tendency of Common Law in Crimes and Torts" won honorable mention for the Meredith Prize. She graduated in 1898, receiving the degree of bachelor of laws. Having been one of the first women admitted to the law school, she was also one of the first admitted to the Philadelphia bar. In 1899 she was appointed librarian of the Biddle Law Library of the University of Pennsylvania law school, a position which she held until her last illness, serving for nearly thirty-two years. When she undertook this work the library contained only seven or eight thousand volumes. With the assistance and support of the faculty, especially former Dean William Draper Lewis, she was able to develop it until it numbered nearly 80,000 volumes and was one of the leading law libraries in the country. Her unusual talent as well as knowledge in her line of work was often shown during her frequent trips abroad in the interest of the library, when she purchased many rare and valuable books.

When the law school was moved from its temporary quarters in old Congress Hall, at Sixth and Chestnut Streets, to its new building at Thirty-fourth and Chestnut Streets, Mrs. Klingelsmith wrote a history of the school which was published in the *University of Pennsylvania: The Proceedings at the Dedication of the New Building of the Department of Law* (1900). Meanwhile paleography was attracting her, and she became widely known as an authority in that field. She was also recognized as being unusually well informed on the subject of early English year books. In 1915 she published under the title *Statham's Abridgment of the Law* (2 vols.), a translation of a fifteenth-century work in Norman French. The University recognized this scholarly achievement in 1916 by conferring upon her the honorary degree of master of laws, the first time that the institution had conferred this distinction upon a woman. She was the author of a number of essays and biographies, including lives of James Wilson and Jeremiah Sullivan Black in volumes I and VI (1907, 1909) of William Draper Lewis' *Great American Lawyers.* Her writings reflected much of the charm and originality of her character. She contributed frequently to legal magazines and did much work on William Draper Lewis' and George Wharton Pepper's *Digest of Decisions and Encyclopaedia of Pennsylvania Law 1754–1898* (23 vols., 1898–1906) and on the second edition of *Pepper and Lewis's Digest of Laws* (1910).

During 1912 and 1913 she was vice-president of the American Association of Law Libraries. She was a member of the Woman's Suffrage Association and took an active interest in politics. At one time she received the support of the Democratic state organization as a candidate for justice of the superior court of Pennsylvania. She was one of the leading members of the First Unitarian Church of Philadelphia. Undoubtedly no other woman was so well known to the Philadelphia bar and her kindly, helpful spirit endeared her to several generations of law students. After her death the faculty of the law school and other friends erected a tablet to her memory in the Biddle Law Library.

[*Pa. Gazette,* Feb. 4, 1931; *Index to Periodicals and Law Library Jour.,* Apr. 1931; *Univ. of Pa. Law Rev.,* Nov. 1931; *Evening Public Ledger,* Jan. 20, 1931; *Phila. Inquirer,* Jan. 21, 1931; *Woman's Who's Who of America,* 1914–15; information from George E. Nitzsche, Esq., recorder of the Univ. of Pa.] A. L. L.

KLIPPART, JOHN HANCOCK (July 26, 1823–Oct. 24, 1878), agricultural writer and for nearly twenty-two years secretary of the Ohio State Board of Agriculture, was born near Canton, Stark County, Ohio, son of Henry and Eve (Henning) Klippart. His forebears were German, though they had been citizens of the United States for two or three generations. His parents were poor and were able to give him only the elementary education of the common schools. In his tenth year he went to live with an aunt to help her in her work of weaving. At thirteen he was an errand boy in a store in Louisville, Stark County. A few months later he became a drug clerk, working at first in a store in Canton and afterwards in Massillon and in Mount Eaton, Wayne County. In 1847 he married Emeline Rahn of Canton. During the next nine years he tried being a merchant, a railroad contractor, and an editor, but for some cause or other failed in all these ventures. Then, near the close of 1856, after a brief employment on the *Ohio Farmer,* he was elected corresponding secretary of the Ohio State Board of Agriculture. In this work he was successful, being reëlected to the office year after year until his death.

He also received numerous other appointments, mostly from his native state. In 1860 he was one of the state commissioners to visit Massachusetts to examine and make a report on the pleuro-pneumonia of cattle. The following year he was designated a member of the American Board of Commissioners of the London International Exhibition of 1862. He went abroad in

1865 with a commission from the Ohio State Board of Agriculture to examine the European institutions for teaching theoretical and practical agriculture and to observe the systems of agriculture practised in Europe and Great Britain. In 1869 he was appointed one of the assistant geologists of the Ohio Geological Survey, being assigned to the section dealing with agriculture. He was one of the delegates from Ohio to the National Agricultural Convention held at Washington, D. C., Feb. 15–17, 1872, and the next year was appointed one of the three state fish commissioners to take measures for restocking the waters of Ohio with food fish.

He was a frequent contributor to the agricultural press. The reports of the Ohio State Board of Agriculture from 1857 to 1877, which he edited, were among the best state agricultural reports of that time. He contributed to them numerous articles on agricultural and scientific subjects, among the more important of which were the following: "An Essay on the Origin, Growth, Diseases, Varieties, etc., of the Wheat Plant" (1857); "An Essay on Practical Drainage" (1860); "An Essay on the Varieties of Sheep and Sheep Culture in Ohio" (1862); "Report on an Agricultural Tour in Europe" (1865); "Address on Agricultural Education" (1865); "An Essay on Dairy Husbandry" (1870). Two of the articles were enlarged and subsequently published in book form: *The Wheat Plant* (1860) and *Principles and Practice of Land Drainage* (1861). His report on the agricultural survey of Ohio is contained in the *Geological Survey of Ohio: Report of Progress in 1870* (1871). His writings were for the most part in the nature of compilations.

Klippart was self-trained and brought to his office of corresponding secretary of the Board of Agriculture no practical knowledge of any branch of farming, but he had a passion for knowledge and an intense desire for improvement. He was an indefatigable worker, and was earnestly devoted to the interests of agriculture. He thus was able through his own efforts to acquire quite an extensive store of information, not only on agriculture but also on geology, botany, and archeology, and he learned to read several foreign languages. He used all this knowledge to advantage in his work, but he scattered his energies. Some of his contemporaries felt that he might have profited by greater concentration and greater moderation. He died of paralysis of the throat, probably brought on by overwork. His wife and one daughter survived him.

[L. H. Bailey, *Cyc. of Am. Agriculture,* IV (1909), 590; Ohio State Board of Agric., *Thirty-third Ann. Report . . . for 1878* (1879); *Cincinnati Daily Gazette,* Oct. 25, 1878.] C. R. B.

KLIPSTEIN, LOUIS FREDERICK (Jan. 2, 1813–Aug. 20, 1878), philologist, the first American to publish works on Anglo-Saxon, was born at Winchester, Va., the son of Peter and Frances (Kimmelmyer) Klipstein. His mother came from Baltimore. His father, who is described as a "gentleman of leisure," was a son of Philipp Klipstein, born in 1751 at Darmstadt, Grand Duchy of Hesse, who came to America as a surgeon with a regiment of Hessian troops and settled at Winchester after the close of the Revolution. Klipstein graduated in 1832 from Hampden-Sydney College and was enrolled in 1832–35 as a student at Union Theological Seminary, now at Richmond but then located at Hampden-Sydney. He was absent on leave, however, from December 1833 to November 1834 to teach in a school at Charlottesville. While there he could hardly fail to meet Prof. George Blättermann of the University of Virginia, who was prepared to give instruction in Anglo-Saxon; it is possible, therefore, that Klipstein's interest in the language began at this time. He was licensed Oct. 17, 1835, by the Winchester Presbytery and during part of that year, at least, was stated supply at Leesburg. Since he was in poor health, he went to South Carolina in 1839 and secured a position of some sort as tutor or teacher. On Oct. 3, 1840, he was dropped from the rolls of the Presbytery for having gone over to the New School, and in 1842 he became a candidate for orders in the Episcopal Church. In April 1844 the *Southern Literary Messenger* announced that Klipstein had started at Charleston a periodical, the *Polyglot,* devoted to the study of French, Italian, Spanish, Portuguese, German, and English. The *Polyglot* was soon abandoned, but its editor salvaged its contents for republication in his first book, *The Study of Modern Languages* (New York, no date—not seen). On Sept. 10, 1845, the University of Giessen conferred on him, *in absentia,* the degree of Ph.D., ostensibly in recognition of his work in Anglo-Saxon but actually, it would appear, as the result of pressure exerted by his distant cousin, August von Klipstein, professor of mineralogy in the university. As yet none of his works on Anglo-Saxon had been published, and the university authorities had not even received proof sheets. It is a curious fact, too, that the university library, in 1927, was still without a copy of any of his books.

He was employed about this time as tutor in the household of Mrs. Rebecca Jerman in the upper part of St. James's Parish, Santee, S. C., and married Allston Cahusac Jerman, a daughter of Mrs. Jerman. His sister Cornelia, who had come with him to South Carolina, married Edward Dupré Jerman. Having thus come into money, Klipstein thought himself able to realize his ambition to publish a series of textbooks on Anglo-Saxon. He issued, through the firm of George P. Putnam in New York, *A Grammar of the Anglo-Saxon Language,* which went into two editions in 1848, was revised and enlarged in 1849, and reprinted in 1853, 1857, and 1859; a reprint of Benjamin Thorpe's *Tha Halgan Godspel on Englisc* (1848); *Natale Sancti Gregorii Papae: Aelfric's Anglo-Saxon Homily on the Birthday of St. Gregory* (1848), which he dedicated to the Rev. Samuel Gilman [*q.v.*]; and *Analecta Anglo-Saxonica: Selections in Prose and Verse from the Anglo-Saxon Literature* (2 vols., 1849). In addition he announced that he was preparing "A Glossary to the Analecta Anglo-Saxonica"; "The Anglo-Saxon Paraphrase of the Book of Psalms"; "Anglo-Saxon Metrical Legends"; "The Anglo-Saxon Poem of Beowulf"; "The Rites, Ceremonies, and Polity of the Anglican Church"; and "A Philosophical Grammar of the Anglo-Saxon Language as Exemplified in the Monuments of the Language Chronologically Arranged." Klipstein drew heavily, but with proper acknowledgment, on the work of Kemble, Thorpe, Wright, Bosworth, Rask, and Ebeling, and took his texts from them, but he displayed a good deal of independence in regularizing spelling and inflectional endings. Apparently he counted on the proceeds from the sales of his first books to pay for the later ones, but in this expectation he was disappointed cruelly. Losses on his books cut into his wife's inheritance and led to a family quarrel. Overworked, disillusioned, unhappy, he took to drinking heavily, left home, and lived among negroes. Finally his wife sold her plantation on Hog Island, across the Cooper River from Charleston, and removed to Florida, where she died in 1897. Klipstein, destitute and disreputable, haunted Charleston and its vicinity for many years. In 1878 he was begging for food on the streets of the city, and that same year he wandered to Florida, perhaps in search of his wife, and died there.

[J. B. Henneman, "Two Pioneers in the Historical Study of English—Thomas Jefferson and Louis F. Klipstein," *Pubs. Mod. Lang. Asso.*, VIII (1893), xliii–xlix; Walther Fischer, "Aus der Frühzeit der Amerikanischen Anglistik; Louis F. Klipstein (1813–79)," *Englische Studien* (Leipzig), LXII (1927–28), 250–64; further information from Miss Ida K. Briggs of Warrenton, Va.; Prof. Wm. H. Whiting, Jr., of Hampden-Sydney College; H. M. Brimm of Union Theol. Sem., Richmond, Va.; Prof. Edwin B. Setzler of Newberry College, Newberry, S. C.; and Miss Katherine Walsh of Charleston, S. C.] G. H. G.

KLOPSCH, LOUIS (Mar. 26, 1852–Mar. 7, 1910), publisher, humanitarian, was born at Lübben, a suburb of Berlin, Germany. His father, Dr. Osmar Klopsch, was a physician by profession, and a liberal in politics. Louis's mother died shortly after his birth, and when he was two years old his father emigrated, arriving in New York with him in 1854. The family fortunes did not prosper in the new home; Louis received a scanty education in the New York City public schools, and at an early age was employed in advertising and publishing establishments. When he was twenty (1872) he launched out for himself with a four-page publication entitled *Good Morning,* to be distributed among customers by retail merchants. This he followed with the *Daily Hotel Reporter* (begun in 1877), and shortly afterward he was able to purchase a printing establishment.

Young Klopsch was of an essentially religious nature and devoted much time to evangelistic work, through which he was brought into contact with the Rev. T. DeWitt Talmage [*q.v.*], of the Brooklyn Tabernacle. Klopsch conceived the idea of syndicating Talmadge's sermons to several hundred newspapers (1885), and this syndication, together with another original idea, the Pictorial Associated Press, brought prosperity and success. Klopsch traveled with Talmage through Europe and the Holy Land in 1889–90, and on this journey took over the management of the American edition of the *Christian Herald.* Thereafter he relinquished his other publishing interests and purchased control of the *Herald.*

At last he had found his life work. Under his editorship the *Christian Herald* rapidly became a national and even an international influence, and "a medium of American bounty to the needy throughout the world" (Pepper, *post*). Through its pages he appealed to the American public for funds to support a wide variety of philanthropic and religious undertakings. In eighteen years a total of $3,365,648.14 was thus raised. Approximately half this sum went to famines in China (1901, 1907), India (1897, 1900), Japan (1906), Russia (1892), and Cuba (1897). To Klopsch may be given much of the credit for teaching the American people large-scale public charity. He twice visited India, and was awarded the Kaiser-I-Hind medal by King Edward VII for his services to the people of that land. While more than eighty charities are listed as having been supported by him, dearest to his heart of all were the Children's Homes at Nyack, founded in June 1895 with money left over after the relief of recent famines. He established his residence at

Tarrytown, across the river, that he might be near them. In 1895 he became president of the Bowery Mission, which long continued one of his major interests.

In 1886 he married Mary Merritt, daughter of the Rev. Stephen Merritt. His wife shared his enthusiasms, and their union was a most happy one. To them four children were born, three sons and one daughter, all of whom survived him. He was a man of broad sympathies and limited by no narrow creed. Irving Bacheller (*post*) said of him, "He preached with bread; he prayed with human kindness; he blessed with wheat and corn. His best missionaries were loaded ships; his happiness was in mitigated pain. His week-day was as holy as his Sabbath, his office as consecrated as his church." His untimely death, following an operation, was mourned from the White House to the poorest tenements. Messages of sympathy were received from the Viceroy of India and representatives of many foreign governments.

[C. M. Pepper, *Life-Work of Louis Klopsch, Romance of a Modern Knight of Mercy* (1910), with foreword by Irving Bacheller; files of the *Christian Herald*, particularly articles on Mar. 16 and 23, 1910; *Who's Who in America*, 1908–09; *N. Y. Times*, Mar. 9, 10, 1910.] H. A. M.

KNAB, FREDERICK (Sept. 22, 1865–Nov. 2, 1918), entomologist, was born in Würzburg, Bavaria, the son of Oscar and Josephine Knab, who came to America and settled at Chicopee, Mass., in 1873. Oscar Knab was an engraver and painter, and one of Frederick's uncles was also an artist. Young Knab devoted himself to painting at an early age, and in 1889 went to Munich for two years to study art. On his return to the United States he made landscape painting his profession for nearly ten years. As a boy he had been interested in natural history, especially entomology, and had begun a collection of insects which he kept up. In 1885–86 he spent sixteen months on a collecting trip up the Amazon. In 1903 he was employed under a grant by the Carnegie Institution of Washington as a regional collector and observer of mosquitoes for the northeastern section of the United States. During this work he made some important discoveries which revolutionized knowledge concerning the biology of the more northern mosquitoes. After a brief employment with the Natural History Survey of Illinois, he was called to Washington in 1904 and employed permanently as an entomologist, particularly as a student of mosquitoes. In 1905 he traveled extensively in Central America, studying mosquitoes, and in 1907 he did field work in Saskatchewan. He was not only co-author of the four-volume monograph, *The Mosquitoes of North and Central America and the West Indies* (4 vols. in 3, 1912–17), published by the Carnegie Institution of Washington, but he prepared many of the illustrations. His plates of mosquito larvae are the most admirable of their kind that have ever been done. Aside from this work on the monograph, he published extensively. He was a keen observer and had a philosophical turn of mind that made all of his published writings of much value. His bibliography includes 177 titles. He never married.

[The best biography will be found in the *Proceedings of the Entomological Society of Washington*, vol. XXI (1919), with portrait and bibliography.] L. O. H.

KNABE, VALENTINE WILHELM LUDWIG (June 3, 1803–May 21, 1864), piano manufacturer, was born in Kreuzburg, Prussia, Germany, the son of Martin Friedrich Traugott Knabe, a pharmacist, and his wife, Ernestine Christiane Dorothea Köhler. Wilhelm was apprenticed to a cabinet and piano maker in Meiningen and there met and became engaged to Christiana Ritz, whose brother was projecting a German settlement in America. When this company of colonists set sail in March 1833, she accompanied them. Most of these expected to settle somewhere on the Missouri River; but after a wearisome voyage, during which sickness took its toll of the wayfarers, they paused in the port of Baltimore to recuperate. There Wilhelm overtook them and there he married Christiana Ritz, Aug. 18, 1833. If he had ever intended to turn farmer in the Middle West, he changed his mind, for he found work with a piano repairer by the name of Henry Hartye. He became a naturalized citizen of the United States Sept. 12, 1840, and about the same time entered into a partnership with Henry Gaehle to manufacture pianos. When this partnership was dissolved in 1854, he continued the business alone. By 1860 he had established a reputation as one of the best piano-makers in the country and at the outbreak of the Civil War he practically controlled the piano business in the Southern states. The conflict between the states, however, ruined the market for Knabe pianos. Wilhelm Knabe died in the year preceding Lee's surrender, but his sons William (d. 1889) and Ernest (d. 1894) continued the business and developed a new market in the Northern and Western states.

[Alfred Dolge, *Pianos and Their Makers* (1911), vol. I; Daniel Spillane, *Hist. of the Am. Pianoforte* (1890); *Musical Courier*, Nov. 14, 1906; *Baltimore Clipper, Baltimore Daily Gazette*, May 23, 1864; manuscript and newspaper clippings lent by Mrs. S. Kennedy Brown of Germantown, Ohio.] F. H. M.

KNAPP, GEORGE (Sept. 25, 1814–Sept. 18, 1883), St. Louis journalist, for forty-six years a proprietor of the *Missouri Republican,* was born in Montgomery, Orange County, N. Y., the son of Edward and Frances (Flood) Knapp. His father was a native of Orange County, N. Y.; his mother, of County Donegal, Ireland. When he was six his parents moved to St. Louis, where the father died in 1823. To aid his widowed mother, young Knapp at the age of twelve became an apprentice in the business office of the *Missouri Republican,* then owned by Messrs. Charless and Pachall. The *Republican* was the successor of the *Missouri Gazette,* a Jeffersonian paper established in 1808 by Joseph Charless, postmaster at St. Louis. Familiarly known as "Old 1808," the *Republican* was the oldest newspaper in English west of the Mississippi River. In 1836 Knapp became part proprietor of its book and job printing department, and in 1837 one of the proprietors of the newspaper in connection with Messrs. Chambers and Harris. He continued as a publisher of the *Republican* until his death, making it the most influential regional journal in the Middle West and one of the leading newspapers of the country. After 1830 the *Republican* supported the Whigs until the disintegration of the Whig party in the fifties, when it became Democratic. During the Civil War it upheld the Union cause but was critical of the Lincoln administration, and after the war it continued to support Democratic candidates and policies.

In 1835 Knapp took a prominent part in the organization of the volunteer militia that for twenty-five years prior to the Civil War was the city's pride. In 1846 he went to Mexico as a lieutenant in the St. Louis Grays of the St. Louis Legion, and upon the regiment's return, he became a captain and subsequently lieutenant-colonel. In 1862 he organized and captained a company called the Missouri Republican Guards, composed of his employees. He was an earnest advocate of public improvements in St. Louis, was in considerable measure responsible for the building of the first Mississippi bridge at that city, the erection of the Southern Hotel, a famous hostelry, and the erection of the Chamber of Commerce building. Though of somewhat retiring disposition, he gained through travel, which he greatly enjoyed, such wide knowledge of the laws, customs, and manners of other peoples that he was much sought after in social company. He died Sept. 18, 1883, on the steamship *Pennland,* bound from Antwerp to New York, while returning from a European tour undertaken for the benefit of his failing health. At the time of his death he was the oldest newspaper man in St. Louis and for years afterward his family continued to direct the policies of the *Republican.* Knapp was married on Dec. 22, 1840, to Eleanor McCartan, daughter of Thomas McCartan of St. Louis. They had three daughters and nine sons, seven of the children surviving their father.

[L. U. Reavis, *St. Louis, the Future Great City of the World* (1875), pp. 705–06; W. B. Davis and D. S. Durrie, *An Illus. Hist. of Mo.* (1876); J. T. Scharf, *Hist. of St. Louis City and County* (2 vols., 1883); F. L. Billon, *Annals of St. Louis in Its Territorial Days, 1804–21* (1888); H. L. Conard, *Encyc. of the Hist. of Mo.* (1901), vol. III; *Boonville Weekly Advertiser,* Oct. 5, 1883; *Jefferson City Daily Tribune,* Sept. 29, 1883; *Missouri Republican,* Sept. 27, 1883.]

W. W.

KNAPP, HERMAN (Mar. 17, 1832–Apr. 30, 1911), ophthalmologist, was born in Dauborn, a village near Wiesbaden, Germany, where his ancestors had been well-to-do farmers for many generations. His father, Johann Knapp, was a member of the German Reichsrath in Berlin. Named Jakob Hermann, Knapp later dropped the first name. His early education, received in the school of his birthplace, was supplemented by private instruction from the parish minister. He took his medical degree at the University of Giessen in 1854, about the time that Helmholtz invented the ophthalmoscope, thus opening a new world to physicians of that day. It was not unnatural, therefore, that Knapp should be attracted to ophthalmology. After sitting at the feet of Helmholtz, Graefe, Donders, Desmarres, Bowman, and Critchett in the medical centers of Germany, France, and England, he was admitted in 1859, at the age of twenty-seven, to the medical faculty at Heidelberg, his admission thesis on "Optical Constants of the Eye" being given full credit by Donders in 1866 (*Die Anomalien der Refraction und Accommodation des Auges*) for its share in developing the new subject of physiological optics. Here Knapp labored and shared a friendship with Helmholtz until the latter's death. In 1865, during his thirty-third year, Knapp became professor at Heidelberg and founded his first ophthalmic clinic there. He had already made his impress upon European medicine to the degree that few men make before midlife.

Following a visit to America, Knapp in 1868 decided that New York City offered a larger field of usefulness, and he promptly relinquished home honors and took up abode here. He soon overcame the obstacle of language, and provided himself with a proper workshop by the establishment of the Ophthalmic and Aural Institute, the maintenance deficit of which he had to cover regularly with his own funds. To a large extent, this clinic was modeled after that of Von Graefe of

Berlin, its doors being open to rich and poor alike. The Institute was Knapp, and Knapp was the Institute. Under his direction, it acquired the good will of physicians and of laymen, and it soon grew to be a tradition, making its influence felt throughout the continent. Knapp's life in New York testifies that his absorbing ambition was to serve: he served his patients by affording efficacious treatment to all who came, and his colleagues through educating them in the science and art of diagnosis and treatment. He loved to teach and was particularly apt in presenting his subject matter clearly, especially with the aid of diagrams. He was possessed of unmatched diagnostic ability, of great surgical skill, and he was above all a man of scrupulous intellectual honesty. His most severe critic was himself. He was always ready to help the young man. Consequently, his clinic became a Mecca for budding American specialists. From 1882 to 1888 he was professor of ophthalmology in the medical department of the University of the City of New York, and from 1888 to 1902 held a similar chair in the College of Physicians and Surgeons.

His educational work did not stop with his clinic and lecture room but reached out wherever a medical journal can go. In establishing (1869) the *Archives of Ophthalmology and Otology*, which he edited for many years, Knapp rendered a great service. He conducted this organ on a very high standard, both in subject matter and in illustrations. An omnivorous reader, he kept himself and his readers acquainted with every advance of ophthalmology and otology, both at home and abroad. In addition to his editing, he was the author of over two hundred scientific papers, written out of the fund of his large clinical experience.

Knapp's early years on a farm and his regular habits endowed him with unusual health and with almost unlimited working power. He seemed to require little relaxation. He belonged to no clubs and gave almost no time to games and recreations, but never broke down under his arduous program. Apart from his life work, his chief delight seemed to be visiting old friends in the European clinics and observing how he might improve his own. To this end he always kept detailed notes of his observations on tours, so that he might upon a later date recall each event vividly. He was twice married: in 1864 to Adolfine Becker, who died in 1874, and in 1878 to Hedwig Sachsowsky. By the first marriage there were three children. Knapp died of pneumonia, at Mamaroneck, N. Y., in his eightieth year.

[Th. Leber in *Verhandlungen des Naturhistorisch-Medizinischen Vereines zu Heidelberg*, July 1911; E. Gruening, in *Archives of Ophthalmology*, July 1911; *The Am. Encyc. and Dict. of Ophthalmology*, vol. IX (1916); T. H. Shastid, in H. A. Kelly and W. L. Burrage, *Am. Medic. Biogs.* (1920), with additional references; *Who's Who in America*, 1910–11; *N. Y. Tribune*, May 2, 1911; information as to certain facts from Dr. Arnold Knapp, son of Herman Knapp.] J. H. W.

KNAPP, MARTIN AUGUSTINE (Nov. 6, 1843–Feb. 10, 1923), jurist, son of Justus Norton and Polly (McKay) Knapp, was born on a farm at Spafford, Onondaga County, N. Y. His early education was acquired at the common schools; later he entered Wesleyan University, winning his bachelor's degree as an honor man in 1868. He then taught in a country school while studying law. In 1869 at the age of twenty-six he was admitted to the New York bar, and on Dec. 29 of the same year he was married to Marian Hotchkiss, of Middletown, Conn. He engaged actively in the practice of law at Syracuse, N. Y. In 1877 he was made corporation counsel of the city of Syracuse, which post he held until 1883. The efforts of the West Shore Railroad to establish a line through the center of the state engaged much of his time and upon his retirement he came into a line of practice which strengthened his interest in transportation problems generally. Developing a reputation as a specialist in that field, he was appointed by President Harrison in 1897 a member of the Interstate Commerce Commission. The following year he became its chairman and remained a member of the commission for nineteen years, gaining reappointment by successive presidents regardless of party differences. During this period as *ex-officio* mediator under the Erdman Act of 1898 he aided in settling numerous railroad labor disputes, some of which were of considerable importance.

Upon the creation of the Commerce Court (June 18, 1910), the object of which was to relieve the federal judiciary at large of railway cases, and to place them in the hands of a tribunal versed in interstate commerce law, Knapp was appointed by President Taft a circuit judge, assigned to the court as presiding judge. Three years later, when the Newlands Act, creating the Board of Mediation and Conciliation, superseded the Erdman Act, he was appointed by President Wilson a member of the board. Upon the dissolution of the Commerce Court on Dec. 31, 1913, he was assigned to the court of appeals, fourth circuit, which position he retained until his death. His first wife having died in 1904, he was married on Aug. 10, 1907, to Nellie (Maynard) Gardner, of Syracuse, whom he survived. Knapp was short in stature, being only five feet in height.

He was quiet by nature but friendly and pleasant. He had a receptive mind on questions within his judicial activities and worked in harmony with other men. These traits together with his knowledge of railway problems made him an able mediator. There was no question concerning the fairness and wisdom of his settlement of a dispute. His correspondence with Joseph Nimmo, Jr., relative to the provisions of the Cullom Bill, gives evidence of the competence of his opinions on legal and constitutional questions, and of his firmness in upholding his convictions. He was an active member of many associations and clubs before which he appeared from time to time to deliver addresses upon railway and transportation questions.

[*Who's Who in America*, 1922–23; *Harper's Weekly*, June 10, 1905; *Am. Rev. of Revs.*, Jan. 1911; the *Nation*, Apr. 13, 1916; *Outlook*, Aug. 23, 1916; *Correspondence Between Hon. Martin A. Knapp, Chairman of Interstate Commerce Commission, and Jos. Nimmo, Jr.* (1900); the *Evening Star* (Wash., D. C.), Feb. 10, 1923; *N. Y. Times*, Feb 11, 1923.] L. H. S.

KNAPP, PHILIP COOMBS (June 3, 1858–Feb. 23, 1920), neurologist, the son of Philip Coombs Knapp and Sally Harriette (Moore) Knapp, was the ninth in direct descent from William Knapp who came to America from England in 1630. Born at Lynn, Mass., Knapp attended the Lynn High School and later Harvard College, from which he was graduated with the degree of A.B. in 1878, at the age of twenty—the youngest in his class. He went directly to Harvard Medical School and received his A.M. and M.D. degrees in 1883. After serving as house officer at the Boston City Hospital and the Boston Lunatic Hospital, he studied abroad for a brief period in Vienna and in Germany, returning to Boston in 1884 to practise in his chosen field of neurology. In 1885 he was appointed assistant physician for diseases of the nervous system to out-patients at the Boston City Hospital, and in 1886 was promoted to physician in that department. At that time there was no regular service inside the hospital for diseases of the nervous system, and it was largely through his efforts that the neurological department was given a house service of fifty beds and a fully equipped ward for mental cases. At the time of his death he was senior physician. He was also neurologist to the Boston Dispensary from 1886 to 1888. In 1888 he became clinical instructor in diseases of the nervous system at Harvard, a post he held until 1913.

Knapp was thus one of the pioneers of American neurology. He wrote the first treatise to be published in the United States on tumors of the brain, *The Pathology, Diagnosis and Treatment of Intra-Cranial Growths* (1891). Though Horsly had just begun to make his early operations on the brain, Knapp foresaw the possibilities of surgical treatment of brain tumors, and in a subsequent paper, "The Treatment of Cerebral Tumors," *Boston Medical and Surgical Journal*, Oct. 5, 12, and 19, 1899, he favored surgical intervention, especially when it was possible to save vision. Knapp had an unusual knowledge of neurological literature and himself contributed to many of its branches. He wrote the section on "Nervous Affections Following Railway and Allied Injuries," in F. X. Dercum's *Text-book on Nervous Diseases by American Authors* (1895), "Feigned Diseases of the Mind and Nervous System" in *A System of Legal Medicine* (2 vols., 1894), by A. M. Hamilton and Lawrence Godkin, and "Traumatic Neurasthenia and Hysteria," in *Brain*, Autumn 1897. In 1887, 1893, 1901, 1911, and 1912 he acted as editor and co-translator of Adolf von Strümpell's *Textbook of Medicine*. He was a gifted linguist, familiar with French, German, and, especially, Italian. For twenty years he was a councilor of the Dante Society. Knapp was an ardent bibliophile and an authority on the art of cooking. He appeared many times in court as medical expert, and because of his wide knowledge and experience as well as his unbiased decisions his judgment was highly respected by his legal associates. He showed also a special interest in the legal aspects of nervous and mental disease, and was a member of the Massachusetts Medico-Legal Society and the American Association of Medical Jurisprudence.

A certain reserve and taciturnity kept him from being very popular as a teacher: he was thorough in his methods, exacting in details, and possessed such a remarkable memory that he seemed to expect too much of his pupils. To the few, however, who did come to know him well, he was a stimulating teacher. He rarely imparted much of his great fund of knowledge voluntarily, but to those who were interested enough to ask questions he gave freely. Among his intimates he was known as a witty and entertaining conversationalist. He died in his sixty-second year as a result of cerebral thrombosis.

In 1893 (Dec. 12) he married Isabel (Williams) Stebbins, a widow of Springfield, who survived him.

[H. A. Kelly and W. L. Burrage, *Dict. of Am. Medic. Biog.* (1928); T. F. Harrington, *The Harvard Medic. School* (1905), vol. III; A. M. Knapp, *The Knapp Family in America* (1909); H. R. Stedman, "Philip Coombs Knapp, A.M., M.D.," *Archives of Neurology and Psychiatry*, May 1920; J. J. Thomas, "Philip Coombs Knapp," *Jour. of Nervous and Mental Disease*, May 1920; W. L. Burrage, "Philip Coombs Knapp, M.D.,"

Boston Medic. and Surgic. Jour., Mar. 11, 1920; *Boston Transcript*, Feb. 24, 1920.] J.F.F.

KNAPP, SAMUEL LORENZO (Jan. 19, 1783–July 8, 1838), miscellaneous writer, was born in Newburyport, Mass., the fifth of the six children of Isaac and Susanna (Newman) Knapp, and the fifth in descent from William Knapp, who settled in Watertown in 1630. His father was a sea-captain. Knapp graduated from Dartmouth College in 1804, read law with Theophilus Parsons, and opened an office in Newburyport in 1809. He may be the "Samuel Knapp of Haverhill, gentleman," who changed his name June 10, 1808, to Samuel Lorenzo Knapp (*Essex Antiquarian,* June 1900, p. 91). His first book, *Letters of Shahcoolen, a Hindu Philosopher, Residing in Philadelphia; to His Friend El Hassan, an Inhabitant of Delhi* (1802), was dedicated to John Quincy Adams. To Montesquieu and Goldsmith it owes little except its title; Shahcoolen's lucubrations on Mary Wollstonecraft and woman's rights, American poetry, American landscape, and other topics are steeped in juvenile solemnity. On July 18, 1814, Knapp married Mary Ann, daughter of Amasa Davis of Boston, by whom he had two daughters. Having little real aptitude for the law, he readily deviated into politics and the militia. He sat as a representative in the General Court, 1812–16, acquired the title of colonel by service in the Second Division of the militia, and became the leading spread-eagle orator of the town, but in 1816 his Newburyport career ended abruptly with his imprisonment for debt. While in jail he wrote another pseudonymous volume, *Extracts from the Journal of Marshal Soult* (Newburyport, 1817). On his release he went to Boston, endeavored with some success to build up a law practice, but soon turned to the more congenial occupation of writing. He contributed to the *New England Galaxy and Masonic Magazine* of his client, Joseph Tinker Buckingham [*q.v.*]; succeeded Alden Bradford [*q.v.*] as editor of the *Gazette,* 1824–26; launched the *Boston Monthly Magazine* in June 1825 and kept it alive for fourteen impecunious months; delivered, Aug. 2, 1826, the official Boston eulogy on Jefferson and Adams; received, through the influence of his friend Bishop Cheverus [*q.v.*], the degree of LL.D. from a French university; and started a newspaper, the *National Republican,* which failed in 1827. For some time thereafter he edited the *National Journal* in Washington. Later he lived in New York and was connected with the *Commercial Advertiser*. During a period of comparative affluence he rebuilt his father's farmhouse in Sanbornton, N. H., as a summer home. Although he published a number of orations, two volumes of tales, and some other matter, his specialty was biography. *Biographical Sketches of Eminent Lawyers, Statesmen, and Men of Letters* (1821), *Memoirs of General Lafayette* (1824), "Memoir of Bishop Cheverus" (*Boston Monthly Magazine,* June 1825), *A Discourse on the Life and Character of DeWitt Clinton* (1828), *Sketches of Public Characters* (1830), which he issued under the pseudonym of Ignatius Loyola Robertson, *A Memoir of the Life of Daniel Webster* (1831), *American Biography* (1833), *Life of Thomas Eddy* (1834), *Female Biography* (1834), *Life of Aaron Burr* (1835), and *Life of Timothy Dexter* (1838) were his harvests in this field. As a biographer he is ornate, laudatory, and patriotic, and wholly untrustworthy. His *Lectures on American Literature* (1829) was the first attempt to weigh and measure the national literature. Since the country had not produced a sufficient quantity of literature for his purposes, Knapp had to piece out his book with chapters on "the naval character of our country" and numerous other irrelevancies; his pages glow with the patriotism of the Jacksonian era. In 1835 he returned to Massachusetts in poor health and settled in Hopkinton, where he died in 1838.

[G. T. Chapman, *Sketches of the Alumni of Dartmouth Coll.* (1867); M. T. Runnels, *Hist. of Sanbornton, N. H.*, vol. II (1881); A. M. Knapp, *The Knapp Family in America* (1909); J. S. Loring, *The Hundred Boston Orators* (1852); E. V. Smith, *Hist. of Newburyport* (1854); J. J. Currier, *Hist. of Newburyport* (1906–09), with bibliography; J. T. Buckingham, *Personal Memoirs* (1852), I, 73–78, 118–20; *Mass. Reg. and U. S. Calendar*, 1813–17; *Boston Courier* and *Boston Transcript*, July 9, 1838; *Boston Statesman*, July 14, 1838.] G. H. G.

KNAPP, SEAMAN ASAHEL (Dec. 16, 1833–Apr. 1, 1911), agriculturist, teacher, was born at Schroon Lake, Essex County, N. Y., eighth and youngest child of Dr. Bradford and Rhoda (Seaman) Knapp. While he was still young his parents moved to Crown Point on Lake Champlain, where he attended the village school. He prepared for college at the Troy Conference Academy, Poultney, Vt., and entered Union College, Schenectady, in 1852, graduating with honors in 1856. In August of that year he married Maria Elizabeth Hotchkiss of Hampton, N. Y., a woman of marked literary attainment. Soon after their marriage they began teaching in Fort Edward Institute, in which Knapp became junior partner. In 1863 he purchased a half interest in the old Troy Conference Academy, subsequently called Ripley Female College.

In 1866, he met with a serious accident which

crippled him for several years and compelled him to give up teaching. Moving to Benton County, Iowa, he bought a small farm at Big Grove. For two years he was pastor of a Methodist church in Vinton, Iowa, and for five years, beginning in 1869, he was superintendent of the state school for the blind. He then went back to his farm. In 1872 he had begun to publish the *Western Stock Journal and Farmer,* at Cedar Rapids, Iowa. On his own place he used improved seed and he brought in better livestock. He was one of the organizers and the first president of the Iowa Improved Stock Breeders' Association. In 1879 he was elected professor of agriculture and manager of the farm of the Iowa State College. Three years later he drafted the first experiment-station bill, introduced into the Forty-seventh Congress by Representative C. C. Carpenter [*q.v.*], a bill which opened the way for the passage of the Hatch Act in 1887. In 1884 he became president of the Iowa State College.

He resigned the presidency in 1886 to take charge of a large colonization experiment at Lake Charles, La. In order to interest the native population in improved methods of agriculture, he offered very favorable terms to farmers from Iowa and other northern states who would settle, one to a township, and demonstrate what could be done by good farming. This plan was so successful that thousands of other northern farmers were attracted to the region and the natives also improved their practices. In searching for profitable crops, Knapp developed the rice industry of the Southwest. The Rice Growers' Association was formed, and he served it as president for several years.

In 1898 his friend James Wilson, then secretary of agriculture, appointed Knapp as a special agent of the department for the promotion of farming in the Southern states. He was sent to Japan, China, and the Philippines to investigate rice varieties, production, and milling, and his findings resulted in a great expansion of the rice industry. In 1901 he went again to the Orient as an agent for the Department of Agriculture and in the following year investigated the agricultural resources of Puerto Rico. In 1903 the Mexican boll weevil appeared in Texas. The condition of panic and despair which prevailed gave Knapp his great opportunity. In the spring of that year he so impressed a gathering of business men and farmers at Terrell, Tex., by the soundness of his argument that the way to fight the weevil was to practise general allround good farming, that he was asked to supervise a demonstration of such methods. This first farm demonstration made a big impression throughout east Texas. In November, the secretary of agriculture and the chief of the bureau of plant industry attended a field meeting on the demonstration tract and agreed to devote $40,000 of the money appropriated by Congress for fighting the boll weevil to the employment of men under Knapp's supervision to make similar farm demonstrations. Thus was inaugurated the Farmer's Co-operative Demonstration Work in the United States Department of Agriculture, the aim of which was, according to Knapp's words in 1909, to place a practical object lesson before the farm masses. The methods of carrying on this work were rapidly crystallized and simplified and were later applied to practically all of the Southern states. Knapp formulated and directed the development of the whole system, including the boys' and girls' club work. At first he had only a few assistants, but under his able management additional funds were secured from the government and other sources and at the time of his death hundreds of experienced agents were employed, scattered throughout the South from Virginia to Texas.

Knapp wrote no books but contributed frequently to the periodical press and was the author of many Department of Agriculture bulletins. One of his most important addresses was that delivered at the Ninth Conference for Education in the South, at Lexington, Ky., in 1906, and published in its *Proceedings.* Knapp died in Washington and was buried in Ames, Iowa. The Seaman A. Knapp School of Country Life, in connection with the George Peabody College for Teachers at Nashville, Tenn., was established as a memorial to him. His son, Bradford Knapp, continued the Farmers' Cooperative Demonstration Work until 1914, when by the Smith-Lever Act it was merged with the extension work of the states, carried on in cooperation with the United States Department of Agriculture.

[A. C. True, *A Hist. of Agric. Extension in the U. S.* (1928), and *Hist. of Agric. Educ. in the U. S.* (1929); O. B. Martin, *Demonstration Work, Dr. Seaman A. Knapp's Contribution to Civilization* (1921); *Dr. Seaman A. Knapp: Proc. of the Fourth Ann. Conv. of the Southern Commercial Cong. . . . Apr. 9, 1912* (1914), also *Sen. Doc. 537,* 63 Cong., 2 Sess.; *Yearbook U. S. Dept. of Agric., 1911* (1912); U. S. Dept. Agric. *Official Record,* Feb. 7 and 28, 1929; *Rev. of Revs.* (N. Y.), June 1911; *Farm and Ranch,* Feb. 2, 1929; *Wallace's Farmer,* Apr. 14, 1911; Mr. and Mrs. A. M. Mayo, *Dr. Seaman A. Knapp* (pamphlet, pub. by Supt. of Public Schools, Calcasien Parish, La.); *Southern Workman,* Sept. 1929; *U. S. Dept. of Agric. Ann. Reports,* 1904/05–1912/13; *Sunday Star* (Washington, D. C.), Apr. 2, 1911.] C. R. B.

KNAPP, WILLIAM IRELAND (Mar. 10, 1835–Dec. 6, 1908), teacher, scholar, author, son of the Rev. Henry R. Knapp and of Mary (Centre) Knapp, was born in Greenport, N. Y., where his father was pastor of the Baptist church. He was prepared for college at the Grammar School, later known as Colgate Academy, and graduated from Colgate University with the degree of B.A. in 1860. That same year on Dec. 25, he married Adeline Roberts, daughter of William Albert Roberts, a captain in the merchant service who had died many years before.

From 1860 to 1865, Knapp was professor of French and German at Colgate University where, in 1862, he took the degree of M.A. He left Colgate to become professor of ancient and modern languages in Vassar Female College (1865–67), where he is still remembered as "a very brilliant linguist . . . strikingly handsome," with a "delightful personality." These traits are constantly mentioned by those who knew him at various periods of his career. In 1867 he resigned his professorship and went to Europe, where he spent the next eleven years, chiefly in Spain, doing important research in Spanish literature of the sixteenth century. His editions of the works of Juan Boscan (Madrid, 1875) and the poems of Diego Hurtado de Mendoza (2 vols., Madrid, 1876, 1877) won him the official recognition of the Spanish government and in 1877 he was made Knight Commander of the Royal Order of Isabella the Catholic.

Upon his return to the United States in 1879 he joined the faculty of Yale University as "temporary instructor" in French and Spanish, and in June 1880 received an appointment to a permanent chair, becoming Street Professor of Modern Languages. He remained at Yale until June 1892, when he resigned to follow his colleague, William Rainey Harper [*q.v.*], to the newly founded University of Chicago, where he became the first professor of Romance languages and literature. In 1895, Knapp withdrew permanently from teaching and settled in Europe again in order to devote his entire time to literary pursuits. He spent the last years of his life in Paris.

Knapp was an able and versatile teacher of Romance languages as well as a scholar. Besides the works mentioned, he published grammars and elementary textbooks for the study of French and Spanish. His literary reputation rests chiefly, however, upon his famous biography of George Borrow and his editions of Borrow's works. The first manifestation of a special interest in this talented wanderer he gave in a nine-page article published in *The Chautauquan,* November 1887. During the next twelve years, "with patient industry he collected a perfect mountain of material. . . . He lived where Borrow lived; he followed Borrow's footsteps in England as in Spain . . . he . . . tracked the most notable of Borrow's schoolfellows, he . . . [drew] a ground-plan of the Borrow house at Norwich" (*Blackwood's Edinburgh Magazine,* April 1899, p. 724). The keenly awaited larger study, in two volumes, *Life, Writings and Correspondence of George Borrow,* was published in London (J. Murray) in 1899, and was followed, in 1900, by the promised editions of Borrow's *Lavengro* and *The Romany Rye.* Shortly after the publication of the *Life, Writings and Correspondence,* a collection of Borrow's letters, which Knapp had believed lost, was discovered in the crypt of the Bible House. While it is regrettable that he did not have access to these documents, which would have made his work complete, due credit must be granted him for having produced the first scholarly and authoritative biography of George Borrow.

[Sources include letters from Mrs. W. I. Knapp, Miss Cornelia M. Raymond, the Rev. Chauncey Goodrich; minutes of the Permanent Officers of Yale College, 1879, 1880, 1892; biographical data from the Secretary's Office, Yale Univ.; *Who's Who in America,* 1908–09; *Colgate Univ. Gen. Cat.* (1905); *Blackwood's Edinburgh Magazine,* Apr. 1899; *Saturday Review* (London), Apr. 15, 1899; *Athenæum* (London), Mar. 25, 1899; *Bookman* (N. Y.), Aug. 1899; *Nation* (N. Y.), Dec. 10, 1908; *Publishers' Weekly,* Dec. 12, 1908; Paris edition of the *N. Y. Herald,* Dec. 7, 1908.]

J. S—e.

KNEASS, SAMUEL HONEYMAN (Nov. 5, 1806–Feb. 15, 1858), civil engineer and architect, brother of Strickland Kneass [*q.v.*], was a son of William Kneass [*q.v.*] and Mary Turner (Honeyman) Kneass. He was born in Philadelphia. When he was fifteen he was placed in the office of William Strickland [*q.v.*] to learn the profession of architect and engineer. Strickland was at that time engaged upon several notable projects, one of them the Bank of the United States (now the Philadelphia Custom House). Making rapid strides in his new profession, Kneass was called upon to design one of the triumphal arches which were erected in Philadelphia to honor General Lafayette when he visited that city in 1824. The original drawing is in the collection in Independence Hall. He was also in charge of the field work, under his preceptor, of the survey for the Chesapeake & Delaware Canal. When Strickland was commissioned, in 1825, by the Pennsylvania Society for the Promotion of Internal Improvements, to report upon the public works in England, he selected young Kneass as his assistant, and all the drawings which illustrate Strickland's *Reports on Canals, Railways, and Other Subjects* (1826) were made for it by Kneass. Years later the plates and copyright were secured by an Englishman, F. W. Simms, who combined the material with new matter of his own and published it in London, under the title, *Public Works of Great Britain* (1838). Upon his return from Europe, Kneass was made principal assistant engineer in the corps organized by Strickland for the construction of the Susquehanna division of the Pennsylvania State Canal. In 1828 he was transferred to the Delaware division, and the following year became chief engineer of the Mine Hill & Schuylkill Haven Railroad, which position he occupied until 1831, when he left to commence work on the first of the western railroads, between Lexington and Frankfort, Ky. After a year he resigned to accept the position of chief engineer of the Philadelphia & Trenton Railroad.

He was engaged successively with various transportation companies, working on the Feliciana Railroad in Louisiana, the Philadelphia & Wilmington Railroad, and the Delaware & Schuylkill Canal. In 1836 he was elected engineer of the Philadelphia & Wilmington Railroad, which he completed. He remained with this company until 1840, when he revisited England and familiarized himself with the improvements made since his first visit. Upon his return he was immediately engaged on surveys and improvements for the southern districts of his native city, as well as upon some construction projects of the municipality. In 1845 he was appointed United States consul at Carthagena, New Grenada (Colombia). At the same time he had a contract for the construction of a canal from Carthagena to the river Magdalena. Returning the following year, he took charge of the Wisconisco Canal, and subsequently was engaged upon the Pennsylvania Central Railroad. In 1848 he resigned to take a position with the Northern New York Railroad, between Ogdensburg and Rouses Point. After a year in New York state, he went back to Philadelphia, having been elected city surveyor. During his term of office he constructed a new bridge across the Schuylkill River at Market Street, designed to carry, in addition to the ordinary traffic, the tracks of the Western Railroad, which was thus given direct connection with the city. In building this bridge he managed to remove the old structure and construct the new one without interrupting traffic, which was heavy at this point—a feat then regarded as a noteworthy piece of engineering.

Being primarily a railroad and canal builder, Kneass left the city's employ in 1853 and after a brief season with the Franklin & Warren Railroad in Ohio, became chief engineer of the North Western Railroad of Pennsylvania, which connected the Pennsylvania Railroad with the Cleveland & Mahoning. He remained in this employ until his death four years later in Philadelphia. He was married on Mar. 14, 1837, to Anna Arndt Lombaerdt.

[C. B. Stuart, *Lives and Works of Civil and Military Engineers of America* (1871); Anna J. Magee, "Memorials of the Kneass Family of Phila.," *Pubs. Geneal. Soc. of Pa.*, vol. VII, no. 2 (Mar. 1919); W. B. Wilson, *Hist. of the Pa. R. R. Co.* (1899); *Phila. and Wilmington R. R. Guide* (1856); Joseph Jackson, *Early Phila. Architects and Engineers* (1923); *Public Ledger* (Phila.), Feb. 16, 1858.]

J. J.

KNEASS, STRICKLAND (July 29, 1821–Jan. 14, 1884), civil engineer and railroad official, brother of Samuel Honeyman Kneass [*q.v.*] and son of William [*q.v.*] and Mary Turner (Honeyman) Kneass, was born in Philadelphia, where he received his first schooling in the classical academy of James P. Espy [*q.v.*]. About the time he had completed his studies in Espy's academy, his brother Samuel was laying out the Delaware & Schuylkill Canal, and was soon engaged in constructing the Philadelphia & Wilmington Railroad. Since the younger Kneass had determined to become an engineer, his brother took him as an assistant on both these projects, and thus he received practical training in his profession before he had taken a collegiate course. When the railroad to Wilmington was completed, he entered the Rensselaer Polytechnic Institute, Troy, N. Y., where he was graduated in 1839 with the degree of civil engineer, taking the highest honors in his class.

His first position after graduation was as assistant engineer and topographer on the Pennsylvania state survey for a railway between Harrisburg and Pittsburgh. This project proving premature, he went to Washington, where he became a draftsman in the bureau of engineering of the United States Navy. In 1842 he prepared maps for the special British commission on the northeast boundary between the United States and the Canadian provinces, and subsequently was employed by the federal government on the general map of the boundary survey. When, in 1847, the survey across Pennsylvania for the laying of the Pennsylvania Railroad was begun, he was chosen by the chief engineer of the road, J. Edgar Thomson [*q.v.*], as one of his assistants. In this capacity he displayed exceptional technical skill in constructing the road over the most difficult grade of the line, that from Altoona to the summit of the Alleghanies.

After the construction of the railroad was completed he was promoted to be principal first assistant engineer, and designed the shops and engine-house erected by the company at Altoona. In 1853 he resigned to become associate engineer on the North Pennsylvania Railroad, but remained only two years, accepting in 1855 the position of chief engineer and surveyor of the consolidated City of Philadelphia. He was twice reëlected for periods of five years, and to him fell the work of organizing the department and designing an entirely new drainage system for the enlarged city. He also designed new bridges to span the Schuylkill River, notably those at Chestnut Street and Callowhill Street. Following closely upon the extension of the city limits came numerous projects for street railways in the city, and for many of these companies Kneass acted as chief engineer. During the Civil War, in 1862, when it was feared that Lee would invade Pennsylvania, he was called upon to make surveys of the Susquehanna River between Duncan's Island and Havre de Grace, and to assist Alexander Dallas Bache [*q.v.*] in the preparation of maps of the environs of Philadelphia with a view to locating fortifications.

In 1872 he was persuaded by J. Edgar Thomson, then president of the Pennsylvania Railroad Company, to accept the position of assistant to the president. Six years later, 1878, he was elected president of the Eastern Railroad Association, and in 1880 was chosen president of the Pennsylvania & Delaware Railroad Company, the Trenton Railroad Company, the Columbia & Port Deposit & Western Railroad Company, and a director of the Pittsburgh, Cincinnati & St. Louis line. A member of various technical and scientific societies, he was for a period president of the Engineers' Club of Philadelphia. On Aug. 17, 1853, he married Margaretta Sybilla Bryan, a grand-daughter of George Bryan [*q.v.*]. He died of heart-disease in his sixty-third year.

[F. W. Leach, in J. T. Scharf and Thompson Westcott, *Hist. of Phila.* (1884), III, 1749; Anna J. Magee, "Memorials of the Kneass Family of Phila.," *Pubs. Geneal. Soc. of Pa.*, vol. VII, no. 2 (Mar. 1919); Frederic Graff, in *Proc. Am. Phil. Soc.*, vol. XXI (1884); H. B. Nason, *Biog. Record Officers and Grads. Rensselaer Poly. Inst.* (1887); W. B. Wilson, *Hist. of the Pa. R. R. Co.* (1899); obituary in *Phila. Press*, Jan. 15, 1884, repr. in *Railroad Gazette*, Jan. 18, 1884; *Phila. Inquirer*, Jan. 15, 1884.]

J. J.

KNEASS, WILLIAM (Sept. 25, 1780–Aug. 27, 1840), engraver and die-sinker, was born in Lancaster, Pa. A grandson of Johan Christian Kneass, probably a native of the Palatinate, who arrived in Philadelphia in 1753, William was the son of Christopher and Anna Justina (Feltman) Kneass. He received his education in Philadelphia, in which city he learned the art of engraving. In 1804 he set up in business for himself. He not only engraved in line, which was his specialty, but was proficient in stipple engraving, and also made use of aquatint. In the exhibition of the Pennsylvania Academy of the Fine Arts in 1813, he showed an aquatint engraving of "A View of Quebec," after a sketch by William Strickland [*q.v.*]. This plate appeared in the *Port Folio* for April of that year. Kneass engraved plates for the *Analectic Magazine,* usually in line, and for the American edition of Abraham Rees's *Cyclopædia* (1820–24). These engravings were principally in the department of mechanics. Several portraits in stipple by Kneass are listed in Stauffer's *American Engravers,* among them those of Joseph Black, Benjamin Lay, and William Penn. He also engraved vignettes for title-pages and for commercial purposes, but his most ambitious plate probably is the line-engraving of Masonic Hall, Philadelphia, after a drawing by Strickland. This is of large folio size.

In 1817 Kneass formed a partnership with James H. Young, another line engraver, under the style of Kneass, Young & Company, which continued until 1820. Later he formed a partnership with George Delleker. On Jan. 29, 1824, he was appointed engraver and die-sinker to the United States Mint, and held that office until his death. For the gold coinage in 1834 and 1838 and for the silver coinage in 1836, 1837, and 1838, he engraved many of the dies. His name appears on a pattern half-dollar of 1838, but the silver dollar of 1836 and another pattern half-dollar of 1838 were the work of his assistant, Christian Gobrecht [*q.v.*].

During the War of 1812, Kneass was a volunteer associate of the Field Engineers who constructed fortifications on the western front of Philadelphia. In 1815 he engraved a plan of this work, after a drawing by Strickland. He took a general interest in science and was one of the earliest members of the Academy of Natural Sciences, joining in 1814. Ten years later, in a rather jocular and irregular manner, he suggested to Samuel Vaughan Merrick [*q.v.*] the founding of the Franklin Institute. Young Merrick took him seriously, and, after an earnest conference with Kneass, called the meeting which led to the Institute's formation. Kneass was a member of the Beef Steak Club of Philadelphia, an organization of artists, wits and literary characters of that city who frequented his studio, then in Fourth Street, near Chestnut.

He was twice married: first on June 23, 1804, to Mary Turner Honeyman, by whom he had six children, among them Samuel Honeyman Kneass [*q.v.*], engineer and architect, and Strickland Kneass [*q.v.*], engineer. His first wife died in 1826, and subsequently he was married to Jane Kramer, who left no issue. A portrait of Kneass, by Sully, was exhibited in 1841 by the Artists' Fund Society, Philadelphia.

[Anna J. Magee, "Memorials of the Kneass Family of Phila.," *Pubs. Geneal. Soc. of Pa.*, vol. VII, no. 2 (Mar. 1919); *Commemorative Exercises at the Fiftieth Anniversary of the Franklin Institute* (1874); D. M. Stauffer, *Am. Engravers upon Copper and Steel* (1907); G. G. Evans, *Hist. of the U. S. Mint* (1885); *North American and Daily Advertiser* (Phila.), Aug. 29, 1840.] J. J.

KNEELAND, ABNER (Apr. 7, 1774–Aug. 27, 1844), Universalist clergyman, antitheist, was descended through his father from Edward Kneeland who settled at Ipswich, Mass., about 1630; and through his mother, Moriah Stone, from Capt. John Stone, an early member of the Plymouth colony. His father, Timothy Kneeland, was a soldier in the Revolution. Abner was born in what became Gardner, Mass. After attending the common schools he spent one term in Chesterfield (N. H.) Academy. He joined the Baptist Church at Putney, Vt., doing some preaching. On Apr. 9, 1797, he married Waitstill Ormsbee, and subsequently moved to Alstead, N. H. In 1803 he became a Universalist and the following year was licensed to preach. In 1805 the Congregationalists united with the Universalists in making him the town minister at Langdon, N. H. During this pastorate, his first wife having died in 1806, he married Lucinda Mason. He represented the town in the legislature (1810–11), and published *A Brief Sketch of a New System of Orthography* (1807), setting forth a phonetic system. He also brought out spelling books which had some vogue. In 1812 he became minister of a Universalist Society at Charlestown, Mass., and in August 1813, again a widower, he married Mrs. Eliza Osborn of Salem. The following year he went into business in that town.

He had commenced to doubt the divine origin of the Scriptures, and about this time undertook a somewhat extensive correspondence on the subject with his friend Hosea Ballou [*q.v.*]. This correspondence was published in 1816 as *A Series of Letters in Defence of Divine Revelation.* In 1817, his doubts being somewhat allayed, he resumed preaching at Whitestown, N. Y., and in the fall of the following year was settled over the Lombard Street Universalist Church in Philadelphia. There he edited successively the *Christian Messenger,* 1819–21, the *Philadelphia Universal Magazine and Christian Messenger,* 1821–23, and the *Gazetteer* (1824), in all his papers championing liberal views. He also published, among other works, a translation of the New Testament (1822). In 1825 his preaching and editorial activity were transferred to New York where for two years he served the Prince Street Universalist Society, resigning after a controversy with the trustees and becoming pastor of the newly organized Second Universalist Society. He began editing the *Olive Branch* in May 1827 (in 1828 the *Olive Branch and Christian Inquirer*), a paper devoted to "free inquiry, pure morality and rational Christianity." During this period he became intimate with Robert Dale Owen and Frances Wright [*qq.v.*], and was a frequent contributor to the *Free Enquirer.* His radicalism gradually estranged him from the Universalists, and at the meeting of the Southern Association in Hartford, May 1829, upon the advice of Hosea Ballou, he asked and was granted permission to suspend himself from fellowship.

Kneeland then went to Boston where he became the leader of a group known as the First Society of Free Enquirers, lectured frequently on Rationalism, and in 1831 began to expound his pantheistic views in the *Boston Investigator,* probably the first Rationalist journal in the United States. In the issue of Dec. 20, 1833, he used language and illustrative material which led to his indictment for publishing "a certain scandalous, impious, obscene, blasphemous and profane libel of and concerning God." Tried in January 1834, he was convicted, but appealed. In two further trials the juries disagreed, but conviction was again secured at the fourth trial, November term, 1835. The appeal was postponed from term to term until 1838, when James T. Austin [*q.v.*], attorney-general of Massachusetts, obtained a confirmation of the judgment, and sentence of sixty days was pronounced (20 *Pickering,* 206–46). When the Governor's Council met a few days later, a petition for pardon bearing about 170 names and a remonstrance signed by some 230 citizens were referred to the committee on pardons. The petition for pardon was signed by such men as William Ellery Channing, George Ripley, George W. Briggs, A. Bronson Alcott, Theodore Parker, William Lloyd Garrison, and Ralph Waldo Emerson. Three eminent pastors of Boston Baptist churches, though men of conservative theological views, also signed. The committee took no action, however, and sentence was enforced. Theodore Parker wrote: "Abner was jugged for sixty days; but he will come out as beer from a bottle, all foaming, and will make others foam" (Sanborn and Harris, *post,* I, 281).

About 1838 the First Society of Free Enquirers had planned to found a colony in the West, and in the spring of 1839, some months after his release from jail, Kneeland emigrated to the chosen site, which he had named Salubria, on the Des

Moines River some two miles from Farmington, Iowa. Here, although the colony project did not materialize, he made his home for the remaining five years of his life. In 1840 he was a Democratic candidate for the territorial council, and in 1842 was chairman of the Democratic convention of Van Buren County, but in both instances the "infidel ticket" which he supported was defeated by a combination of Whigs and "church Democrats."

Though he was anathema to the straitly orthodox churchmen, Kneeland was held in high esteem by free-thinkers. Sincere to the point of fanaticism—he "saw in every effort made by those who differed with him a determination to bind his conscience" (Frederick Hancock, quoted by Whitcomb, *post,* p. 355)—he was a man of indisputable courage and purity of character. Personally he was refined and sensitive, with a calm, courteous manner. For some months after he moved to the West he taught school at Helena, Ark., and was remembered by a former pupil for his noteworthy kindness and gentleness. He died at Salubria in his seventy-first year. By his four marriages—the last in 1834 to Mrs. Dolly L. Rice—he was the father of twelve children.

[S. F. Kneeland, *Seven Centuries of the Kneeland Family* (1897); L. C. Browne, *Review of the Life and Writings of M. Hale Smith* (1847); Voltaire Paine Twombly, sketch of Kneeland in the *State Line Democrat* (Keosauqua, Ia.), Aug. 27, 1903; Mary R. Whitcomb, "Abner Kneeland: His Relations to Early Iowa History," *Annals of Iowa,* Apr. 1904; Thos. Whittemore, *Life of Rev. Hosea Ballou* (4 vols. 1854–55); F. B. Sanborn and W. T. Harris, *A. Bronson Alcott, His Life and Philosophy* (1893); A. C. Thomas, *A Century of Universalism in Phila. and N. Y.* (1872); *Memoirs of the Life of Nathaniel Stacy* (1850); W. D. Herrick, *Hist. of the Town of Gardner, Worcester County, Mass.* (1878); *Hist. of Van Buren County, Ia.* (1878); J. M. Wheeler, *A Biog. Dict. of Freethinkers of All Ages and Nations* (London, 1889); S. P. Putnam, *400 Years of Freethought* (1894); Jos. McCabe, *A Biog. Dict. of Modern Rationalists* (London, 1920); obituary in *Boston Investigator,* Sept. 25, 1844; records of trials in the office of the clerk of the superior court of Massachusetts; papers relating to the petitions for pardon and the remonstrance against it in the Mass. Archives.]

W. H. A.

KNEELAND, SAMUEL (Jan. 31, 1697–Dec. 14, 1769), printer, publisher, was born in Boston, Mass., the son of John and Mary (Green) Kneeland. His mother was a grand-daughter of the early colonial printer, Samuel Green [*q.v.*]. Samuel Kneeland served his apprenticeship with his uncle Bartholomew Green [*q.v.*], and about 1718 established a shop of his own. In 1721 he married Mary Alden, great-grand-daughter of John and Priscilla Alden. He had a large family, for he was survived by four sons and five daughters. From 1720 to 1727 he printed the *Boston Gazette,* the second newspaper in the colonies, first issued in 1719 from the press of James Franklin [*q.v.*]. On Mar. 20, 1727, Kneeland began to publish as well as to print *The New England Weekly Journal,* the fourth newspaper to be established in New England. Some three months after starting this publication, he formed a partnership with his cousin Timothy Green; and, according to Isaiah Thomas (*post*), the chief authority on Kneeland's career, Green managed the affairs of the printing office for the next four or five years while Kneeland devoted himself to conducting a bookstore on King (now State) Street. In 1736 Kneeland and Green again became printers of the *Boston Gazette,* and in 1741 they purchased the ownership of it and merged it with their other publication, the *Weekly Journal.* At the end of 1752 Green withdrew from the firm and Kneeland continued alone. He published the paper under the title, *The Boston Gazette, or Weekly Advertiser* till 1755, when the provincial tax on printed paper made it unprofitable to do so any longer; but publishing this newspaper was far from being his chief activity. He was for many years official printer for the provincial government, and many public documents still exist that were issued from his press. He was the printer of many books, and the claim has been made that he printed the first edition of the Bible in English in North America. This claim has been vigorously denied by George Bancroft and others, but the opinion of those who have most recently investigated the matter seems to be that the tradition of a Bible surreptitiously printed in Kneeland's shop and sold under the imprint of Thomas Baskett, king's printer, has some basis in fact (Nichols, *post*). Another claim that seems to have more in the way of direct evidence to sustain it is that Kneeland also printed the first religious periodical in America. This was the *Christian History,* which Kneeland and Green printed in 1743 for Thomas Prince, Jr. His distinction, however, does not result from these more or less hypothetical achievements, for he was active and industrious for more than half a century, and he is an important figure in the history of American printing and perhaps no less important as a pioneer in newspaper publishing.

[Isaiah Thomas, *The Hist. of Printing in America* (2 vols. 1810), 2nd ed., printed in *Trans. and Colls. of Am. Antiq. Soc.,* vols. V, VI (1874); E. B. O'Callaghan, *A List of the Editions of the Holy Scriptures . . . Printed in America Previous to 1860* (1861); C. L. Nichols, "Is there a Mark Baskett Bible of 1752?," in *Pubs. Col. Soc. of Mass.,* vol. XXI (1920); C. S. Brigham, "Bibliography of American Newspapers," pt. 3, in *Proc. Am. Antiq. Soc.,* n.s. XXV (1915); *Pubs. Col. Soc of Mass.,* IX (1907), 442–43, 446–48; S. F. Kneeland, *Seven Centuries in the Kneeland Family* (1897); *Mass. Gazette: and Boston Weekly News-Letter,* Dec. 21, 1769.]

S. G.

KNEELAND, SAMUEL (Aug. 1, 1821–Sept. 27, 1888), Boston physician and zoölogist, the son of Samuel and Nancy (Johnson) Kneeland, was born in Boston, where his ancestors had lived for several generations. His great-grandfather was a brother of Samuel Kneeland [*q.v.*], the printer. Kneeland obtained his early education at the Boston Latin School, and received from Harvard the degrees of A.B. in 1840 and A.M. and M.D. in 1843; he then went abroad for two years, spending the greater part of his time in the hospitals of Paris. His thesis for the degree of M.D., "On the Contagiousness of Puerperal Fever," took the Boylston Prize in 1843, and was subsequently published in the *American Journal of the Medical Sciences* for January 1846. It is a remarkable paper, stating the germ theory of puerperal infection in no uncertain terms, but it undoubtedly had its origin from Kneeland's contact with Oliver Wendell Holmes [*q.v.*], whose celebrated essay on the same subject was first published in 1843. Kneeland again received the Boylston Prize in 1844 for his paper on "Hydrotherapy" (*American Journal of the Medical Sciences,* July 1847).

In 1847 he became associated with a group of young Boston physicians who were seeking to reform the medical profession. To this end the Boylston Medical School was organized, and incorporated by the legislature in 1847. The objective of the founders, as they expressed it, was: "To send out none but thorough students . . . to instil into the gentlemen of their school an ardent love for their profession, as well as to make them practically acquainted with it" (Harrington, *post,* II, 501). The institution flourished for a time, but its reputation rapidly dwindled when some of the leading professors of the new school were finally induced to join the faculty of the Harvard Medical School. Kneeland was for two years (1845–47) physician to the Boston Dispensary, and in 1851 he was appointed demonstrator in anatomy at the Harvard Medical School, a position which he held until 1853. In 1862 he left his practice in Boston to become a surgeon in the Federal army. He served under Burnside in the North Carolina campaign and was later in charge successively of the University Hospital, New Orleans, and the general hospitals of Mobile, Ala. He was mustered out of the service in 1866 with the brevet rank of lieutenant-colonel of volunteers.

Kneeland was a member of the Massachusetts Institute of Technology from its foundation in 1865, serving as professor of zoölogy and physiology, 1869–78, and as secretary, 1865–78. Although a practising physician, he was an enthusiastic zoölogist and collector, and he made collecting expeditions to Brazil, to the Lake Superior copper region, to Iceland, and, finally, in 1882, to the Hawaiian and Philippine Islands. He kept careful diaries and as a result of his travels he wrote a number of books and pamphlets: *The Wonders of the Yosemite Valley* (1871), *An American in Iceland* (1876), *The Philippine Islands* (1883). Among his other contributions were a translation of Felix Andry's *Manual of Diagnosis of Diseases of the Heart* (1846) and an edition of Charles H. Smith's *Natural History of the Human Species* (1851). From 1866 to 1871 he was one of the editors of *The Annual of Scientific Discovery,* and he contributed many articles (over a thousand) to Appletons' *American Cyclopædia* (16 vols., 1873–76). In addition he published many medical papers. He was secretary of the American Academy of Arts and Sciences and of the Boston Society of Natural History, and a member of the American Association for the Advancement of Science and the Boston Society for Medical Improvement. In 1849 he married Eliza Maria Curtis of Cambridge, Mass. He died at Hamburg, Germany.

[See *Proc. Am. Acad. Arts and Sci.,* n.s. XVI (1889); *Proc. Boston Soc. of Natural Hist.,* vol. XXIV (1890); T. F. Harrington, *The Harvard Medical School* (1905), vols. II and III; W. B. Atkinson, *Physicians and Surgeons of the U. S.* (1878); H. A. Kelly and W. L. Burrage, *Am. Medic. Biogs.* (1920); S. F. Kneeland, *Seven Centuries in the Kneeland Family* (1897); historical records of the Mass. Inst. of Technology. Kneeland presented a complete collection of his writings to the Library of the Boston Society of Natural History.]

J. F. F.

KNEELAND, STILLMAN FOSTER (May 17, 1845–Aug. 30, 1926), lawyer, author, was descended from Edward Kneeland who settled at Ipswich, Mass., soon after 1630. The fourth son of Gardner and Julia (Castle) Kneeland, he was born at South Stukely, Quebec, a few miles north of the Vermont line. His mother died when he was two months old, and his father shortly remarried, having one daughter and six sons by his second wife, Susan Goddard, "making in the aggregate the traditional Kneeland complement of eleven children." When he was eleven, the boy was apprenticed to a printer; he studied in his leisure time, and at sixteen was prepared to enter McGill University, Montreal. The Civil War across the border in the United States lured him away from his studies, however. Enlisting in the 11th Vermont Volunteers, he fought under Sheridan in the Shenandoah Valley, took part in the Wilderness campaign, and received a severe wound near the end of the war in the fierce fighting before Petersburg. At the close of the war he was discharged as a corporal. Throughout his life he maintained a keen interest in military affairs, serving many years in the National Guard of Vermont and of New York. He is said to have written a treatise on rifle practice and he was a co-inventor of the Briggs-Kneeland rifle.

With the coming of peace he turned to the study of law, and, after completing his work at the Albany Law School, was admitted to the bar in 1869. He began to practise at Albany, but in 1872 moved to New York and in a comparatively short time established himself as an authority on commercial law. Original in his methods and bold in his line of argument, he trusted to his mastery of detail and his fertility of resource to win his cases. He first brought himself into prominence when he represented certain persons who, claiming to be next of kin, attempted to break the will of the New York merchant, Alexander T. Stewart [*q.v.*]; though he lost to the powerful firm which opposed him (G. W. Travers, in *Magazine of Western History,* February 1891). Another case which served to establish his reputation as a commercial lawyer was that of *Claflin* vs. *Gordon* (39 *Hun,* 54) in which he won $200,000 for his client, not an insignificant sum in those days. During these busy years he published a *Commercial Law Register* (1873), *A Treatise upon the Principles Governing the Acquisition and Enforcement of Mechanics' Liens* (1876), and *A Treatise upon the Law of Attachments in Civil Cases* (1884).

In 1886 he acted as chairman of a committee of citizens of New York City which framed and secured the passage of a bill abolishing perpetual imprisonment for debt, and he was later instrumental in securing the passage of a law limiting imprisonment for civil contempt to six months. In 1894, running as a Republican, he was elected to the legislature from a Democratic district in Brooklyn in a contest so close that it had to be decided by the legislature. He was judge-advocate general under Governor Black, 1896–98, receiving the rank of brigadier-general.

Outside of his professional life Kneeland found time to develop considerable proficiency as an artist, and exhibited several paintings at various places over the country. He was a vice-president of the department of painting of the Brooklyn Institute of Arts and Sciences. Other interests are shown by his publication of *Seven Centuries in the Kneeland Family* (1897); by two volumes of verse, *Law, Lawyers and Lambs* (1910) and *Random Rhymes of a Busy Barrister* (1914); and by his fellowship in the Royal Geographical Society of London. He was married twice: on Nov. 29, 1871, to Mary Stuart Wilson of Albany, and in July 1922, some time after the death of his first wife, to Mrs. Eastman Johnson.

[In addition to references in the text and to Kneeland's history of his family, see *Encyc. of Contemporary Biog. of N. Y.* (1887); *New International Yearbook,* 1926; *Who's Who in America,* 1916–17; *N. Y. Herald Tribune,* Aug. 31, 1926. Information as to certain facts has been supplied by relatives.] D. V. S.

KNEISEL, FRANZ (Jan. 26, 1865–Mar. 26, 1926), violinist, teacher, and founder of the Kneisel Quartet, was born in Bucharest, Rumania, of Moravian parentage, the youngest of eleven children of Martin and Victoria (Lukas) Kneisel. His father, an able musician, was the leader of a military band and he began early to give his son violin lessons. The boy's progress was so marked that he was sent to the Conservatorium in Bucharest to study with Louis Wist. He completed the course and took the first prize in violin playing before he was fifteen years of age. Thereupon he entered the Vienna Conservatorium as a special student of Grün in violin and Hellmesberger in chamber music. He completed the three years' course in two years, graduating in July 1882 with highest honors and again taking the first prize. He continued the study of chamber music for one more year with Hellmesberger. On Dec. 31, 1882, he played the Joachim "Hungarian Concerto" at a Philharmonic concert and was immediately appointed solo violinist at the Hofburg Theatre, Vienna, as successor to Jacob Dont. In 1884 he was called to Berlin as concertmaster of the Bilse Orchestra, but he remained only one season, for in the autumn of 1885 he came to America to accept the position of principal and solo violinist in the Boston Symphony Orchestra which had been tendered him by its conductor, Wilhelm Gericke.

Though he was a youth of only twenty years when he came to Boston to succeed Bernhard Listemann, he possessed a flawless technique and a rich, resonant quality of tone. With this equipment he proved himself wholly adequate for his new position when he made his Boston début in a masterly performance of the Beethoven violin concerto on Oct. 31, 1885. He brought all the enthusiasm of youth to his work and for eighteen years officiated continuously and successfully in this position. Almost immediately upon his arrival in Boston he conceived the idea of forming a quartet and brought together in what he named the Kneisel Quartet, four men from the Symphony Orchestra who thus had the best training and had opportunity for daily rehearsing. Their Boston début took place on Dec. 28, 1885, and after 1891 every visit that the Orchestra made to

New York was the occasion for a Kneisel Quartet concert in Mendelssohn Hall. Artists of highest merit assisted frequently at these concerts and when a woodwind instrument was needed, it was easily supplied from the Orchestra. Much pioneer work was done in familiarizing the public, not only with the standard quartets, but also with quintets and septets, such as the Brahms "Clarinet Quintet" and the "Beethoven Septet." Also new works were presented, among them several American quartets. They became a symbol of excellence. "It would, indeed, be impossible," said one critic (Lahee, *post*, pp. 363–64), "to conceive greater perfection in the matter of ensemble, precision, delicacy, and all the proper interpretation of chamber music."

Kneisel resigned from the Boston Symphony Orchestra in May 1903 in order to devote himself entirely to the leadership of his Quartet. The original four were Kneisel, first violin, Emanuel Fiedler, second violin, Louis Svečenski, viola, and Fritz Giese, violoncello. Kneisel and Svečenski were members for the entire thirty-two years of its existence, but there were numerous changes among the other players. In 1904 he took the Quartet to England to give two of the Bradford concerts. In 1905 he became head of the violin department of the newly formed Institute of Musical Art and he retained this position up to the time of his death. In 1917, realizing the need of more time for the organization of his growing department at the Institute, he disbanded his Quartet and gave two farewell concerts, on Mar. 13 in Boston and on Apr. 3 in New York. They had appeared regularly in Boston for thirty-two seasons and for twenty-five in New York, besides touring regularly from coast to coast. Kneisel also possessed ability as an orchestral conductor. While still a youth in Bucharest he had conducted the Philharmonic (instrumental) Society. In the absence of Nikisch, he conducted the concerts of the Boston Symphony Orchestra at the World's Columbian Exposition in Chicago in 1893 and took the Orchestra on a concert tour in western cities in the early summer of that year. From 1897 to 1909 he was conductor of the orchestra at the Worcester (Mass.) Festivals. In 1912, as president of the Bohemians (New York), he established within this organization the Foundation for Needy Musicians. Many honors were bestowed on him—in 1911 Yale University conferred on him the honorary degree of Mus.D. and in 1915 Princeton University conferred the same degree. In 1918 the Harvard Musical Society (Pierian Sodality) made him an honorary member. Kneisel was married in Boston on Sept. 29, 1888, to Marianne Thoma, a Viennese violinist who like himself was a graduate of the Vienna Conservatorium and winner of the first prize for violin playing. They had several gifted children. Among his publications are the *Kneisel Collection of Violin Pieces* (1900, Church), *Advanced Studies for the Violin* (1910, Schirmer), and a "Concert Étude" (Schirmer). In collaboration with Harold Bauer he published in 1918 Brahms Sonatas for piano and violin.

[*Who's Who in America*, 1924–25; H. C. Lahee, *Famous Violinists of Today and Yesterday* (1899); Richard Aldrich, *Musical Discourse* (1928); Paul Rosenfeld, *Musical Chronicle (1917–23)* (1923); *Musical Record*, Nov. 1, 1898; the *Violinist*, June 1924, Apr. 1926; *Musical Leader*, July 22, 1926; the *Baton*, Apr. 1926; *N. Y. Times*, Mar. 27, 1926; information as to certain facts from Kneisel's daughter, Mrs. Willem Willeke.]

F. L. G. C.

KNICKERBOCKER, HERMAN (July 27, 1779–Jan. 30, 1855), lawyer and congressman, was a great-great-grandson of one of the original Dutch colonists of New Amsterdam, Harmen Jansen Knickerbocker, who came to the new world about 1674 and in 1682 purchased a large tract of land nineteen miles north of Albany, N. Y. Harmen's grandson, Johannes (1723–1803), a colonel in the Revolutionary army, was the father of Johannes (or John, Jr.) who married Elizabeth Winne, and to them was born a son Harmen, or Herman, on July 27, 1779. The boy received a classical education, studied law under John Bird and John V. Henry, was admitted to the bar in 1803, and started practice in Albany. He became senior partner in the law firm of Knickerbocker & Pierson, with an excellent practice. The wealth and social prominence of his family, combined with his own attractive personality and his ability, rapidly placed him among the foremost in his community. Inheriting great wealth, he moved from Albany to Schaghticoke, a part of his family estate just north of Troy. There he lived so perfectly the part of "lord of the manor," dispensed hospitality with so lavish a hand, and showed himself so liberal in his charities, that he became widely known as "The Prince of Schaghticoke."

Knickerbocker was town clerk in Troy, 1802–04, and supervisor, 1805–06. In 1809 he was elected as a Federalist to the Eleventh Congress (Mar. 4, 1809–Mar. 3, 1811) but did not stand for reëlection. During Jackson's administration he became a Democrat. During these years, too, he had taken an interest in the militia. In January 1801 a new troop of cavalry was raised in Rensselaer County in the 2nd Squadron of the 3rd Regiment of Cavalry, and Knickerbocker was made captain. In 1810 he was promoted major, and in 1818 he was commissioned colonel.

On returning from Washington to his home community after his term in Congress, he again served as supervisor of the city of Troy in 1813, and followed this with a term in the state assembly in 1816. From 1818 to 1823, and again from 1825 to 1829 he served as supervisor. In 1828 he was listed as first judge of the court of common pleas for Rensselaer County and served as judge for many years. In 1844 he was chosen justice of the peace at the annual town meeting. He was married three times: first to Ariantie, daughter of Abraham A. and Elsie (Van Rensselaer) Lansing, Oct. 10, 1801; second, to Rachel, daughter of John Hermen and Cathaline (Van Benthuysen) Wendell, Dec. 6, 1814; and third, to Mary, daughter of David and Rachel (McNeil) Buel, July 20, 1826. By his first wife he had five children; by his second wife five; and by his third wife four. He was a man of great charm, fine courtesy, and dignity, a worthy representative of one of the foremost families of New York state. He was a friend of Washington Irving, who, in introducing him on one occasion to President Madison in Washington, referred to him facetiously as "my cousin Diedrich Knickerbocker, the great historian of New York." His cordiality, hospitality, love of good cheer, and many social graces endeared him to a wide circle of friends. These he retained until the end of his life, even during those later years when much of his fortune was gone. He died at Williamsburg, now a part of New York City, at the age of seventy-five.

[See: Joel Munsell, *The Annals of Albany*, vol. VII (1856); Kathlyne Knickerbacker Viele, *Sketches of Allied Families: Knickerbacker-Viele* (1916); Wm. B. Van Alstyne, "The Knickerbocker Family," *N. Y. Geneal. and Biog. Record*, Jan.–Oct. 1908; David McAdam and others, *Hist. of the Bench and Bar of N. Y.* (1897), vol. I; *Biog. Dir. Am. Cong.* (1928); John Woodworth, *Reminiscences of Troy* (1853); Alden Chester, *Courts and Lawyers of N. Y.: A Hist.* (1925), vol. III; N. B. Sylvester, *Hist. of Rensselaer County, N. Y.* (1880); *N. Y. Times*, Jan. 31, 1855. Many members of the family have preferred to spell the name Knickerbacker.] L. H. H.

KNIGHT, AUSTIN MELVIN (Dec. 16, 1854–Feb. 26, 1927), naval officer, son of Charles Sanford and Cordelia (Cutter) Knight, was a native of Ware, Mass., but was appointed to the Naval Academy from Florida in 1869. After graduation in 1873, he served for three years in the Pacific on the *Tuscarora, Kearsarge, Palos,* and *Saco,* and then returned to the Naval Academy as an instructor in English, history, and law. From 1878 to 1883 he served in the European and South Atlantic squadrons on the *Quinnebaug* and *Galena.* His leaning toward the scientific work of the navy resulted in his being assigned in 1883 to the ordnance proving ground at Annapolis, of which he was in charge from 1885 to 1889. For three years he was again on sea duty and in 1892 became instructor in physics and chemistry at the Naval Academy. He served on the *Lancaster* and *Castine,* South Atlantic Station, from 1895 to 1897. At the outbreak of the Spanish-American War he was a lieutenant on the monitor *Puritan,* and did blockade duty off the north coast of Cuba and took part in the expedition for the occupation of Porto Rico. Becoming head of the department of seamanship at the Naval Academy in 1898, he served in that capacity until 1901. While here he decided to supply something more modern than Luce's *Seamanship,* which had been the chief work on that subject since the Civil War but did not give adequate instruction in the maneuvering of ships propelled entirely by steam. As a result he published in 1901 *Modern Seamanship.* His next cruises were in command of the *Yankton* surveying the south coast of Cuba (1901–03), and in command of the *Castine* (1903–04). During the years 1904 to 1907 he was president of a special board on naval ordnance, and of the joint army and navy board on smokeless powder. Promoted to the rank of captain in 1907, he was in command of the armored cruiser *Washington* for two years, during which time the Pacific fleet visited Samoa and was entertained by the native chiefs with characteristic ceremonies. In 1911 he was appointed rear admiral, and from 1913 to 1917 he was president of the Naval War College.

In April 1917 he was sent to command the Asiatic fleet, with the rank of full admiral, and was in charge during the first part of American operations at Vladivostok and in Siberia. According to Ackerman and Dennis (*post*), Admiral Knight, Gen. William S. Graves, commanding the United States troops in Siberia, and Roland S. Morris, ambassador to Japan, sent a report to President Wilson in October 1918 which he is said to have characterized as "the most convincing document" he had read on the Russian situation. It proposed that small American forces should be sent to the Ural front, accompanied by other Allied detachments, to assist the Czecho-Slovaks and give moral support to anti-Bolshevist forces; but the War Department, believing in concentrating all its energies on the western front in France, disapproved the suggestion. On Dec. 9, 1918, Knight was relieved of his command because he was soon to reach retiring age. He was placed on the retired list, Dec. 16, but continued on active duty till February of the next year. He was married twice: in 1878, to Alice Phinney Tobey, of Milwaukee, who died the next year, and in 1886, to Elizabeth Harwood Welsh, of Annapolis, who died in 1911. His ten years of retirement were spent mostly in Annapolis and Washington. He died at the Naval Hospital, Washington, and is buried in the Naval Academy Cemetery at Annapolis.

[L. R. Hamersly, *The Records of Living Officers of the U. S. Navy and Marine Corps* (7th ed., 1902); *Who's Who in America*, 1926–27; C. W. Ackerman, *Trailing the Bolsheviki* (1919); A. L. P. Dennis, *The Foreign Policies of Soviet Russia* (1924); W. S. Graves, *America's Siberian Adventure, 1918–1920* (1931); *Army and Navy Jour.* and *Army and Navy Reg.*, Mar. 5, 1927.] W. B. N.

KNIGHT, DANIEL RIDGWAY (Mar. 15, 1840–Mar. 9, 1924), painter, was born in Philadelphia. From 1861 to 1863 he studied at the Pennsylvania Academy of the Fine Arts. In 1872 he left America for France, where, in the outskirts of Paris, he soon established residence, and where he continued his tuition under Charles Gleyre and at the École des Beaux-Arts. This period of instruction was followed by eight months in Italy, but in 1875 he worked with Meissonier in his studio at Poissy. As early as 1873 he began exhibiting with the Société des Artistes Français, an association which was not broken until a few years before his death.

The story-telling picture of peasant life was much in vogue in Paris, both Bastien Le Page and Jules Breton exerted a certain influence upon the formative period of Ridgway Knight's art. He found many of his subjects in and about Poissy, painting its countryside, its harvest scenes, and its human types. "The Fugitives," which he sent to the Paris Salon of 1873, "Washerwomen" (1875), and "Repast during the Harvest" (1876), belong to this period of his career. His début as a full-fledged exhibiting artist was made almost simultaneously on both sides of the Atlantic, the year 1873 marking also the display of "The Veteran" and "Othello in the House of Brabantio" at the National Academy of Design in New York. His first public recognition came in 1884, when, like many another artist destined for fame, he received an honorable mention at the Paris Salon. In Paris honor followed honor. In 1888 he won a gold medal of the third class at the Salon, and the next year a silver medal at the Paris Exposition. Three years later he became recipient of the cross of the Legion of Honor of France, and was successively a knight and an officer of that body. Germany recognized him with a gold medal at Munich in 1888; America with a medal at the World's Columbian Exposition held in Chicago in 1893, and with the coveted grant of the medal of honor of his art Alma Mater, the Pennsylvania Academy of the Fine Arts. At the Antwerp international exposition of 1894, he again added a medal to his laurels. He was also a favorite in England: his painting, "The Year's Economies," was chosen in 1890 by the British Post Savings Bank as its New Year's card for all its depositors.

The story-telling character of his art and its resultant popularity rendered notable service to France during the World War, when Knight was made one of its official propagandists and his picture, "Bas de Laine," was distributed throughout the country in 1917 to push the third French war loan. Throughout his career he held a dual allegiance to the land of his birth and the land of his inspiration. As he had become an art propagandist for France, so, also, he became a member of the committee of the American Relief Clearing House. He died at his home, Les Terrasses, Rolleboise par Bonniers, in the department of Seine-et-Oise, France. His wife, before her marriage, was Rebecca Morris Webster. Two sons, growing up under their father's influence, became artists: one a painter, the other an architect. Ridgway Knight's works have found places in the permanent collections of various American museums. "Hailing the Ferry" may be found at the Pennsylvania Academy of the Fine Arts, "The Shepherdess" in the Brooklyn Museum, "The Shearer" in the Boston Museum, and other examples in museums at Milwaukee and Omaha.

[*Who's Who in America*, 1922–23; Ulrich Thieme and Felix Becker, *Allgemeines Lexikon der Bildenden Künstler*, vol. XX (1927); *L'Art*, June 5, 1881, Aug. 13, 1882, June 1, 1884, Oct. 15, 1885, July 1, 1887, May 1, 1888, and new ser. vol. II (1894), pp. 155–58; Eugene Montrosier, *Les Artistes Moderns*, vol. IV (1884); C. E. Clement and Laurence Hutton, *Artists of the Nineteenth Century and Their Works*, vol. I (1884); Emmanuel Benezit, *Dictionnaire Critique et Documentaire des Peintres, Sculpteurs*, vol. II (1913); J. D. Champlin and C. C. Perkins, *Cyc. of Painters and Paintings*, vol. II (1886); Clarence Cook, *Art and Artists of Our Time*, vol. III (1888); *Am. Art Annual*, 1924; *N. Y. Herald* (European edition); *N. Y. Times*, Mar. 10, 1924; date of birth from son.] D. G.

KNIGHT, EDWARD COLLINGS (Dec. 8, 1813–July 21, 1892), capitalist, inventor, was born on a farm in Collingswood, Gloucester (now Camden) County, N. J., the son of Jonathan and Rebecca (Collings) Knight. He was of Quaker stock, being descended from Giles Knight of Gloucestershire, England, who came to America on the *Welcome* with Penn's first colonists in 1682. When he was only ten his father died, leaving five other children, and the family went to live with the maternal grandfather. At fifteen, Edward commenced a period of eight years as a grocery clerk, the first half in New Jersey and the rest in Philadelphia, which thereafter was his home. In 1836, he went into the wholesale and retail grocery business with his mother. She soon withdrew, and he subsequently formed the firm of E. C. Knight & Company, with his former clerk, Charles A. Sparks, as partner. The firm became sole agents for the large Philadelphia sugar-refining firm of Kusenberg & Bartol, whom Knight later joined, about 1861, in establishing the extensive Southwark Sugar Refinery. Twenty years later this plant had a capacity of 1,500 barrels a day.

While sugar was the basis of his fortune, Knight had many other irons in the fire. He was a shipowner and conducted an extensive foreign trade—to Cuba and the West Indies for sugar, and to Chile and California with general groceries. In 1849, he was interested in the venture of sending to California on the deck of a bark the little steamer *Islander,* the pioneer steamboat in the river above Sacramento. He invested heavily and shrewdly in Philadelphia real estate, building several profitable business structures and owning numerous others. His most original achievement resulted from a business trip to New Orleans. The discomforts of the railroad journey prompted him to ponder the idea of a sleeping car, and in 1859, while Pullman was experimenting at Chicago, Knight contracted with Murphy & Allison to build a sleeper with a fixed triple tier of berths along one side. He took out patents (No. 24563, June 28, 1859; No. 25570, Sept. 27, 1859; No. 27297, Feb. 28, 1860), formed a company, and sold many of his "Knights," as they were punningly termed, to the Baltimore & Ohio and the Camden & Amboy railroads. About 1868 he sold out to Pullman, for some two million dollars.

Knight became president of the American Line of steamships, formed by a group of Philadelphians in 1873 under the auspices of the Pennsylvania Railroad to revive the American merchant marine and the port of Philadelphia. This concern ran four liners between Philadelphia and Liverpool, and finally merged with the Inman Line. He promoted the construction of the Delaware & Bound Brook Railroad (opened 1876), which provided a new line between New York and Philadelphia by joining the Central Railroad of New Jersey at Bound Brook with the North Pennsylvania just above Trenton. He was its president from its organization in 1874 until his death. In 1879, the road was leased on very profitable terms to the Philadelphia & Reading. In 1887, Knight became president of the North Pennsylvania Railroad, also leased by the Reading. He helped to develop coal properties at West Pittston, Pa., and the Camden Woolen Mills at Camden, N. J., and was at one time or another director of several banks and several railroads, including the Pennsylvania. He received an unsolicited nomination for Congress in 1856, but was defeated. In 1860, he was a Republican presidential elector, and in 1873, sat in the Pennsylvania constitutional convention. He was a member of the Philadelphia Park Commission and was an active promoter of the Centennial Exhibition of 1876 and the Pennsylvania bi-centennial celebrations of 1882. Knight was described as "quiet, persevering, steady-going." He was married, July 20, 1841, to Anna Marie Magill, and had five children. He died at Cape May, N. J.

[S. N. Winslow, *Biogs. of Successful Phila. Merchants* (1864); *Phila. and Popular Philadelphians* (1891); Charles Morris, *Makers of Phila.* (1894); J. W. Jordan, *Colonial Families of Phila.* (1911), vol. II; L. V. Poor, *Manual of American Railroads,* 1876–92; *Report of the U. S. Commissioner of Patents,* 1859, 1860; Joseph Husband, *The Story of the Pullman Car* (1917); *North American* and *Press,* both of Phila., July 22, 1892.] R. G. A.

KNIGHT, EDWARD HENRY (June 1, 1824–Jan. 22, 1883), mechanical expert, patent attorney, author, was born in London, England, the son of George and Sarah (Harris) Knight, who were of Irish and Welsh ancestry respectively. Until he came of age Edward lived with his parents in London, was educated there, and upon completing the school curricula learned the art of steel-plate engraving. He was employed in this work for a number of years and also undertook the study of medicine, specializing in surgery, but never completed the course, for in 1845 with seven of his brothers he migrated to America with the intention of settling in Canada. He went directly to Cincinnati, Ohio, however, whither an older brother had preceded him. Here he began the study of law, was admitted to the bar, and began to practise his profession, concentrating his attention more and more on patent law. On May 29, 1848, he married Maria Janet Richards of Cincinnati, and on Apr. 5, 1851, became a naturalized citizen of the United States. During the Civil War he served as a surgeon in relief work and at its close returned to his law practice in Cincinnati.

From this time on, Knight's activities became more and more varied. He began to collect data looking toward the publication of an encyclopedia of mechanical inventions. He established a reputation as a mechanical expert, and was called upon to serve as expert witness in patent lawsuits of many kinds. He engaged, too, in a variety of literary activities, compiling in 1870, *A Library of Poetry and Song,* which was published under the name of William Cullen Bryant, who edited it and wrote the introduction. He later assisted Bryant in compiling an enlarged edition in two volumes, entitled, *A New Library of Poetry and Song* (1876). He was for many years a contributor to the *Atlantic Monthly* and *Harper's Monthly* and *Weekly,* the titles of his writings including "Crude and Curious Inventions at the Centennial Exhibition" (*Atlantic Monthly,* May 1877–Apr. 1, 1878) and "The First Century of the Republic" (*Harper's New Monthly Magazine,* December 1874–March 1875). He also wrote "A Study of the Savage Weapons at the Centennial Exhibition" (*Annual Report of the Board of Regents of the Smithsonian Institution,* 1879). His massive three-volume work entitled *Knight's American Mechanical Dictionary* appeared between the years 1874 and 1876. It is a digest of mechanical appliances and processes and a general technological dictionary much used as a reference work. Later a supplement to this appeared, *Knight's New Mechanical Dictionary* (one volume in four parts, 1882–84). He was granted seven patents which included three on steam governors, one on a sewing machine guide, and another on a process for molding articles from paper pulp. From 1872 to 1876 he was connected with the United States Patent Office, having been appointed a patent examiner. He did not serve long in this capacity, however, but instead originated and edited the *Official Gazette of the United States Patent Office,* a weekly digest of patents issued, the first number of which appeared Jan. 3, 1872. He also devised the present system of classification of inventions and introduced the method of purchasing copies of patents by coupons. He was in charge of the Patent Office exhibit at the Centennial Exhibition at Philadelphia in 1876 and following the completion of this work he returned to Ohio. In 1878 he was appointed by President Hayes as a commissioner to the Universal Exposition at Paris, France, and served as one of the judges of machinery. He also wrote the official report on agricultural implements (*House Executive Document No. 42,* 46 Cong., 3 Sess.). In recognition of his *American Mechanical Dictionary,* the French government made him a chevalier of the Legion of Honor. His legal residence was at Bellefontaine, Ohio, where he died survived by his wife and five children. He left unfinished a work, "Development of the Mechanic Arts," which he was preparing for the Smithsonian Institution.

[U. S. Nat. Museum records; Patent Office records; Knight family records (MSS.); preface to W. C. Bryant, *A New Library of Poetry and Song* (1876); *Ann. Report of the Board of Regents of the Smithsonian Institution* (1883); *Evening Star* (Washington, D. C.), Jan. 24, 1883.] C. W. M.

KNIGHT, FREDERICK IRVING (May 18, 1841–Feb. 20, 1909), physician, laryngologist, son of Frederick and Anne (Goodwin) Knight, was born in Newburyport, Mass. He received his preliminary education in the Newburyport high school and graduated from Yale College in 1862. After receiving the degree of M.D. from Harvard in 1866, he served as an interne in the Boston City Hospital, and then went to New York, where he worked for a year under Austin Flint [*q.v.*]. Returning to Boston, he became assistant to Dr. Henry I. Bowditch [*q.v.*]. His association with these eminent authorities was due to his early and continued interest in diseases of the chest, and to these men he owed much of his subsequent success as a diagnostician in diseases of the respiratory tract. In 1871 he gave up his work with Bowditch and went abroad to pursue his studies in Berlin and Vienna.

Four years previously Dr. H. K. Oliver, one of the visiting physicians to the Massachusetts General Hospital, had instituted instruction in laryngology as a branch of clinical medicine in the Harvard Medical School, and while Knight was yet in Europe in 1872, he was appointed instructor in auscultation, percussion, and laryngoscopy in that institution. On his return to the United States a few months later he established a clinic at the Massachusetts General Hospital in order to obtain clinical material for his classes. Several years later laryngoscopy had so developed that the teaching of percussion and auscultation was taken out of Knight's province and thenceforth he taught laryngology solely. In 1882 his title was changed from instructor to assistant professor, and in 1886 he was appointed clinical professor. A brilliant younger man, Dr. Franklin H. Hooper, was associated with him as instructor in laryngology. Hooper developed a malignant growth of the tongue and neck, and in 1892 in order that his younger colleagues might be promoted before his death, Knight resigned his professorship in Hooper's favor, although he knew that when Hooper died he himself would probably not be able to resume the position. This proved to be the case and Knight never taught publicly again. He was one of the founders of the American Laryngological Association in 1878, and at its first regular meeting in 1879 read the first paper on the program, a discussion of retro-pharyngeal sarcoma. He was the third man elected to the presidency of the Association and until his death took the deepest interest in its affairs. When the *Archives of Laryngology* was founded in 1880, he was one of the most active of its promoters and one of the four men who composed the editorial staff. He also served as president of the American Climatological Association and of the Boston Society for Medical Improvement. He was a pioneer in the early days of the war against tuberculosis. On Oct. 15, 1871, while in Berlin, he married Louisa Armistead Appleton, daughter of William Stuart Appleton of Baltimore. They had one daughter.

[D. B. Delavan, *A Memorial of Frederick Irving Knight* (1909); *Proc. Am. Acad. Arts and Sciences*, vol. XLVII (1912); *Boston Medic. and Surgic. Jour.*, June 9, 1910; *Obit. Record Grads. Yale Univ.*, 1909; *Boston Transcript*, Feb. 23, 1909.] F. R. P.

KNIGHT, HENRY COGSWELL (Jan. 29, 1789–Jan. 10, 1835), writer, Episcopal clergyman, was born probably in Newburyport, Mass., the first child of Joseph and Elizabeth (Cogswell) Knight. He was the seventh in line of descent from John Knight, who settled in Newbury in 1635, and from John Cogswell who settled in Ipswich in 1636. His father was engaged in marine insurance and the West Indian trade. Before Henry was three years old his mother died, about a year after the birth of a second son, Frederick (Oct. 9, 1790). Some two years later, the father married Mary Treadwell of Ipswich, who bore a son, Antonio (Nov. 2, 1795), and died when he was about a month old. When Henry was nine, his father died, and he and his brother Frederick were taken to the home of their maternal grandfather, Dr. Nathaniel Cogswell, in Rowley. After attending Dummer Academy Henry entered Phillips Academy, Andover, in September 1806, and in 1808 was admitted to Harvard College. He was an indifferent student, preferring reading of his own choice to a definite program of study. In 1809 he published in Boston a pamphlet of poems, *The Cypriad,* virtually all of which was frankly imitative, although the versification is well handled. One poem in this collection, "The Little Sweep," so strongly resembles Blake's two poems on the same subject that it has been concluded that Knight saw a copy of the *Songs of Innocence and Experience,* although no known copy was in the United States in or before 1809; nor did Knight ever go to Europe. During 1809 he published a few poems in the *Monthly Anthology* (Boston), chiefly in Latin and decidedly in the classical spirit.

In 1811, without completing his course at Harvard, Knight left and went to Brown University. He was graduated there in 1812 with the degrees A.B. and A.M., and was the recognized class poet. A contemporary poem described him as, "the woe-begone, rabbit-eyed, fur whiskered knight." In 1814 he was in Philadelphia about to begin an extended journey through the South. Nothing further than what is afforded by his sprightly *Letters from the South and West* is known of this journey. In 1815 he published his second volume of poems, *The Broken Harp,* in Philadelphia. These are much more romantic than his earlier works. The first poem, "Earl Kandorf and Rosabelle," resembles Coleridge's unpublished "Christabel" so strongly in atmosphere, character of the heroine, and versification that, although none of the five known "Christabel" manuscripts could have reached America in or before 1815, it seems incredible that Knight had not read the poem.

In 1816 Knight was in Washington, Richmond, and Petersburg. Thence he traveled farther inland to Kentucky (1818), thence down the Ohio and Mississippi rivers to New Orleans, at which place he arrived July 4, 1818. He left the Gulf of Mexico in 1819 and returned to Massachusetts by boat. He was probably in Boston once more in 1821, for there in this year he published anonymously a pamphlet poem, *Fights of Faith,* which, under the title "The Crusade," appeared also in the two-volume edition of *Poems* ("Second Edition"), published in the same year in Boston. This collection comprised, chiefly, reprints of the pieces included in *The Cypriad* and *The Broken Harp.* In 1824 Knight published at Boston *Letters from the South and West, by Arthur Singleton, Esq.* These are a mine of information, written in a witty and very readable style—undoubtedly his best work. During the year 1826 he published, both under his pseudonym and under his own name, several articles in the *New England Galaxy* (Boston).

On May 6, 1827, he was ordained a deacon of the Protestant Episcopal church by Bishop Griswold of Massachusetts. In 1829 he became rector of Prince George's and St. Bartholomew's parishes in Montgomery County, Md., but the following year returned to Massachusetts, and for the rest of his life apparently resided in or near Boston. In 1831 he published *Lectures and Sermons,* in two volumes, stating in the dedication that he had preached these sermons in Maryland and Virginia. He died in Rowley, of scarlet fever. His brother Frederick, with whom Knight had probably made his home during his last years, survived until Nov. 20, 1849, when he died of consumption, having been long a recluse. *Thorn Cottage, or The Poet's Home: A Memorial of Frederick Knight, Esq.,* was published in 1855. In addition to the biographical material concerning Frederick, the volume contains a meager collection of his poems and a fragment of Henry Knight's autobiography. The half-brother, Antonio, lived some thirty-two years longer, dying in an insane hospital in 1882.

[*Anthology Soc.: Jour. of the Proc. of the Soc. Which Conducts the Monthly Anthology & Boston Rev.* (1910), with intro. by M. A. DeW. Howe; J. T. Buckingham, *Personal Memoirs* (2 vols., 1852); J. J. Currier, *Hist. of Newburyport* (1909), vol. II; E. A. and G. L. Duyckinck, *Cyc. of Am. Lit.* (1875), vol. II; *Jours. Proc. Conventions, Prot. Episc. Ch. in Mass.*, 1831–34; Mildred Elsie Williamson, "Henry Cogswell Knight, Frederick Knight, Antonio Knight," A.M. thesis (MS.), Brown Univ.; Helena H. Witherow, "Brown Poets," A.M. thesis (MS.), Brown Univ.; records of Dummer Academy, Phillips Academy, Harvard University, Brown University, and Salem Probate Court.]

M. E. W.

KNIGHT, JONATHAN (Nov. 22, 1787–Nov. 22, 1858), civil engineer, was born in Bucks County, Pa., the son of Abel and Ann S. Knight. His father, a weaver, from time to time practised surveying or taught school. Jonathan was largely self-educated, though he studied surveying under his father and was tutored in algebra by a local teacher. Throughout his life he displayed an aptitude for the exact sciences. In 1801 the family moved to East Bethlehem, Washington County, Pa., and here he afterward resided. When he was twenty-one he began teaching school and surveying land on his own account, and the following year he married Ann Heston, who became the mother of ten children. In the spring of 1815, he purchased a farm, but continued to be in demand as a surveyor. In 1816 he was appointed by the State of Pennsylvania to survey and map Washington County, and as soon as this work was completed he was elected county commissioner, serving three years. He then assisted in the preliminary surveys for the Chesapeake & Ohio Canal and for the National Road between Cumberland, Md., and Wheeling, Va. (now W. Va.). From 1822 to 1828 he served in the Pennsylvania legislature. In 1825 the federal government appointed him a commissioner to extend the National Road from Wheeling through the states of Ohio and Indiana to Illinois. This was one of the important engineering undertakings of the day.

His work in connection with the National Road brought him into prominence as an engineer, and with Col. Stephen H. Long he was chosen in 1827 by the newly organized Baltimore & Ohio Railroad Company to survey the parts of Maryland and northwestern Virginia through which the road was to pass. In the fall of 1828 he accompanied two other engineers of the company to England, where they made a careful examination of two railroads which were already in operation there, giving special attention to track construction and the development of the steam locomotive. Upon his return from this mission he was appointed chief engineer of the Baltimore & Ohio, which position he held until 1842, having charge of the location of the road, the planning of structures and machinery, and the letting of contracts, but not the actual construction work. In this position he made a number of scientific studies, among others an exhaustive investigation of the elements of resistance to cars moving upon railroads. Some of his investigations and reports were published in the early annual reports of the company. His location work was particularly remarkable, more so at the start because few people knew what a railroad was or should be and he was exploring a virgin field.

Upon leaving the Baltimore & Ohio Railroad Company he became a consulting engineer, being frequently employed by that company and others. In 1844–47 he cooperated with the city of Wheeling in its controversy with the Baltimore & Ohio in regard to the route of the railroad to that point. He was also very largely engaged in agriculture and became secretary of the first agricultural society organized in Washington County. At the same time he took an active interest in politics, and was elected as a Whig to the Thirty-fourth Congress (1855–57). He was a candidate for reëlection in 1856 and again in 1858 but was unsuccessful both times. He died after a brief illness, at East Bethlehem, Pa., on the seventy-first anniversary of his birth.

Knight was one of the notable civil engineers of his time. His career was somewhat marred by his tendency to engage in bitter disputes and acrimonious word battles with his associates; but despite this fact he remains a commanding figure of the first days of railroading in the United States.

[C. B. Stuart, *Lives and Works of Civil and Military Engineers of America* (1871); E. Hungerford, *The Story of the Baltimore & Ohio Railroad 1827–1927* (1928), vol. I; W. P. Smith, *Hist. and Description of the B. & O. Railroad* (1853); *Biog. Dir. Am. Cong.* (1928).]

J. H. F.

KNIGHT, JONATHAN (Sept. 4, 1789–Aug. 25, 1864), physician, a founder of the American Medical Association and of the Yale Medical School, was born in Norwalk, Conn. His father was Dr. Jonathan Knight of Norwalk, a former Revolutionary army surgeon, and his mother was Ann Fitch, the daughter of Dr. Asahel Fitch of Redding, Conn. At the age of fifteen Knight entered Yale College, and graduated four years later. He then for two years taught in the Chelsea Grammar School, at Norwich, Conn. Following this experience, beginning in the fall of 1809, he taught for a year at the Union School in New London, and in 1810 he returned to his Alma Mater as a tutor. During these years he carried on the study of medicine, and in August 1811 was granted a license to practise by the Connecticut Medical Society. About this time the establishment of the medical department at Yale was being discussed, and Benjamin Silliman the elder [*q.v.*], then professor of chemistry in the College, suggested that Knight resign his tutorship and spend a winter or two in Philadelphia, studying anatomy and physiology at the University of Pennsylvania. After receiving his master's degree in the summer, he followed the suggestion and spent the winters of 1811 and 1812 in Philadelphia. In 1813 he returned to New Haven as assistant professor of anatomy and physiology, and for the next twenty-five years lectured to the students in anatomy. In October 1813 he was married in Greenwich to Elizabeth, the daughter of James Lockwood, a graduate of Yale College in 1766.

Early in his career as a practitioner, Knight took an active interest in the Connecticut Medical Society. In 1817 he served on a committee to compile a pharmacopeia and in the same year he was elected secretary of the society. In the following year, Yale College conferred upon him the honorary degree of M.D. In 1826 he was one of the founders of the General Hospital Society of Connecticut, which was established to raise funds for a hospital in New Haven. In 1838, on the death of Dr. Thomas Hubbard, he was transferred to the chair of surgery in the College, a position which he held until shortly before his death.

His interest and activity in the Connecticut Medical Society and his capacity for organization led to his choice as president at both meetings (1846, 1847) of the National Medical Convention which formed the American Medical Association. In 1853 he was elected president of that body, and was subsequently reëlected. After the death of his predecessor in the chair of surgery at Yale, he became the leading surgeon in Connecticut. His successor in this chair, Dr. Francis Bacon, said of him: "It is enough to say that Dr. Knight's operations, comprising almost every one of modern surgery, were guided by a thorough anatomical knowledge, and that, without special dexterity or nimbleness of manipulation, they were carefully and successfully performed" (*The Beloved Physician, post,* p. 24). Though he wrote little, he reported the cure of a popliteal aneurysm, and to him belongs the credit of employing digital compression for this purpose. He died in August 1864, of peritonitis. When the New Haven Hospital was taken over by the Federal government during the Civil War, by order of the surgeon general the institution was designated as the Knight United States General Hospital.

[H. S. Burr, "Jonathan Knight and the Founding of the Yale School of Medicine," *Yale Jour. Biol. Med.*, July 1929; H. A. Kelly and W. L. Burrage, *Am. Medic. Biogs.* (1920); Leonard Bacon, *The Beloved Physician* (1864), a discourse delivered in the First Church in New Haven, with which are published remarks by Prof. Francis Bacon in his lecture introductory to the course on surgery; Francis Bacon, *Some Account of the Medic. Profession in New Haven* (1887); W. L. Kingsley, *Yale College, a Sketch of Its History* (1879), vol. II; *Trans. Am. Medic. Asso.*, vol. XVI (1866); *Obit. Record Grads. Yale Coll.*, 1865; *Morning Jour. and Courier* (New Haven), Aug. 26, 1864.] H. T.

KNIGHT, RIDGWAY [See KNIGHT, DANIEL RIDGWAY, 1839–1924.]

KNIGHT, SARAH KEMBLE (Apr. 19, 1666–Sept. 25, 1727), teacher, diarist, was born in Boston. Her father, Thomas Kemble, a merchant, is mentioned as living in Charlestown in 1651, but he moved to Boston shortly before his daughter's birth. Her mother was Elizabeth Trerice, whose father had a residence in Charlestown as early as 1636. Kemble was Cromwell's agent in selling prisoners of war, and there is a tradition that he was put in the stocks for "lewd and unseemly conduct" in kissing his wife on the Sabbath, when he met her at his door after an absence of three years. Some time before Kemble's death, which occurred in 1689, his daughter married Capt. Richard Knight, a widower much older than herself, who was a shipmaster, and of whom there is no record after 1706. Mrs. Knight seems to have succeeded her father as the head of the household and to have acted as the adviser of a number of relatives living with her. She was employed in connection with the recording of public documents, and more than a hundred official papers bear her signature as a witness, while many court records dating from the vicinity of 1700 are thought to be in her hand. She also kept a writing-school that Benjamin Franklin is said to have attended, although he does not mention her in his *Autobiography.* She was generally known as "Madam Knight" because of her educational and quasi-legal activities, for court records show that she was sometimes paid to assist in settling estates. Apparently her energy, ability, and knowledge of legal procedure led to her being entrusted with the management of considerable business, and in 1704 some of this required her presence in New York. The journey was a serious undertaking in those days, and it was an unheard of thing for an unaccompanied woman to attempt it, but Madam Knight accomplished it successfully and left in her diary an account of it that gives a vivid picture of the people and conditions she encountered. The diary also displays a sense of humor, and, beneath much vigorous abuse, a tolerance not commonly associated with her time. This diary did not make her prominent in her lifetime, but her other activities did. In 1712 her mother died, and the next year her daughter Elizabeth married Col. John Livingston of New London, Conn. Madam Knight thereupon sold her house in Boston and moved to Connecticut, where she occupied or operated property in the towns of Norwich and New London from 1714 till her death. She speculated in Indian lands, conducted several farms, and kept a shop and house of entertainment. In 1718 she was indicted and fined for selling liquor to the Indians, but she blamed a servant for the offense, and it does not seem to have affected her public repute. Her material affairs prospered, for she left an estate of £1,800 and gave valuable property to her daughter before she died. She was buried in New London.

Madam Knight's diary remained in manuscript till 1825, when it was printed in New York and elicited much notice (*The Journals of Madam Knight and Rev. Mr. Buckingham,* 1825). The diary next appeared serially in the *Protestant Telegraph of Boston* in 1847, and in 1858, in *Littell's Living Age* for June 26, it was reprinted with notes and commentary by W. R. Deane. Editions have since appeared in Albany, N. Y. (1865); Norwich, Conn. (1901); and Boston (1920).

[Besides the notes in the various editions of her diary, and by Mrs. Crocker, *Hist. Mag.,* Mar. 1865, the chief sources of information regarding Madam Knight's career and personality are: F. M. Caulkins, *Hist. of New London* (1852); Geraldine Brooks, *Dames and Daughters of Colonial Days* (1900); *Bostonian Soc. Pubs.,* vol. IX (1912); *Dedham Hist. Reg.,* Jan. 1891; *Hist. Mag.,* Aug. 1858; and unpublished material collected by W. R. Deane in the Mass. Hist. Geneal. Soc.] S. G.

KNOTT, ALOYSIUS LEO (May 12, 1829–Apr. 18, 1918), lawyer, politician, son of Edward and Elizabeth Sprigg (Sweeney) Knott, was born near Newmarket, Frederick County, Md. His father was a successful farmer and tobacco planter of Montgomery and Frederick counties, Md.; his first ancestor in America was James Knott who came from England about 1617 and settled in Accomac County, Va., whence, about 1642, his descendants moved to Maryland. At eight years of age, Aloysius, who as soon as he reached the age of discretion dropped the Aloysius and always afterwards signed himself A. Leo, was sent for three years to St. John's Literary Institution, a Jesuit school. In 1842 he moved with his parents to Baltimore where he graduated with honors from St. Mary's College in 1847. After three years of teaching, he entered the law offices of William Schley, a powerful Baltimore attorney, and in 1855 was admitted to practice in the courts of Baltimore.

Knott first became prominent in Maryland politics in the bitter struggle of 1864–67 to free the state from the rule of the Unconditional Unionist party. Following the seizure of the government by this party in 1861 with the aid of the Federal military forces, he had refused to take any part in public affairs; but he was finally aroused to action, along with the other Democratic leaders, in June 1864, by the threat of the imposition of a new and drastic constitution, and he led the movement in Baltimore to revive the Democratic party. He was elected a delegate to the city, state, and national conventions, but as a candidate for Congress was defeated. His own vote was challenged at the polls because of an accusation that he was a Confederate sympathizer, and his arrest prevented only by the interposition of one of the judges of the election. He was active in the formation of the new Conservative-Democratic party, consisting of the reorganized Democrats and the Johnson Republicans, and on Nov. 6, 1866, in a bitter and exciting struggle in which the new party secured a two-thirds majority in both Houses, he was elected to the lower house of the legislature. In the ensuing session he took an aggressive lead in securing the passage of the enfranchisement bill, the bill for a new constitution, and the military bill, a group of acts resulting in the liberation of Maryland from military rule.

From 1867 to 1879 Knott served as state's attorney of Baltimore. He was second assistant postmaster-general under Cleveland, 1885–89. He was secretary of the state Democratic convention in 1864, delegate to three Democratic National Conventions (1864, 1872, and 1900), and a member of the Democratic National Executive Committee from 1872 to 1876. He was a member of the Maryland legislature a second time in 1899. In 1900 he became a professor in the Baltimore Law School, and in 1905 was elected dean, which position he filled till a short time before his death. His wife was Regina M. Kenan, whom he married in Baltimore in 1873.

Knott stood high as a criminal and constitutional lawyer. He was an easy speaker, a ready debater, and so well posted as rarely to be thrown off guard by an opponent. Though a loyal Democrat all through his public career, he supported Roosevelt in 1904, considering the Democratic party to be "without an issue and without a man" (*Men of Mark in Maryland,* vol. II, 1910, p. 412). In addition to law and politics he was interested in history and research, being a member of the Maryland Historical Society and a president of the Maryland Original Research Society. Among other articles, he wrote a history of the Roman Catholic Church in Maryland for the *Catholic Encyclopedia* (vol. IX, copr. 1910).

[*Who's Who in America*, 1918–19; J. T. Scharf, *Hist. of Baltimore City and County* (1881); H. E. Shepherd, *Hist. of Baltimore, Md., 1729–1898* (1898); C. C. Hall, *Baltimore, Its Hist. and Its People* (1912), vol. III; *New International Yearbook*, 1918; M. P. Andrews, *Hist. of Md.* (1929); *A Biog. Sketch of Hon. A. Leo Knott with a Relation of Some Political Transactions in Md., 1861–67* (1898); *The Sun* (Baltimore), Apr. 1, 2, 1885, Apr. 19, 1918.] D. V. S.

KNOTT, JAMES PROCTOR (Aug. 29, 1830–June 18, 1911), lawyer, congressman, governor of Kentucky, was the son of Joseph Percy and Maria Irvine (McElroy) Knott. He was born near Raywick, Marion County, Ky., and was educated in Marion and Shelby counties. In 1846 he began the study of law, and continued his studies after he moved to Missouri in 1850. In the spring of 1851 he was admitted to the bar at Memphis, Scotland County, Mo. He served in the circuit and county clerk's offices and in 1857 was elected to the state legislature to represent Scotland County. In the legislature he served as chairman of the judiciary committee and conducted the impeachment of Judge Albert Jackson. The following year Gov. Robert M. Stewart appointed Knott to be attorney-general to fill out the unexpired term of Ephraim B. Ewing. In 1860, Knott was the nominee of the Democratic party for attorney-general and was elected on the ticket headed by Claiborne F. Jackson [*q.v.*].

Missouri at this time was a pro-slavery state but did not favor secession. The legislature in January 1861 called a convention to consider the relations of the state to the nation, and the secessionist party, although backed by Governor Jackson, lost the election by a popular majority of 80,000. The convention which met Feb. 28 voted not to secede, and Missouri was divided into two warring groups. Attorney-General Knott sympathized with the Southern cause but opposed the extreme measures of the secessionists. He failed to bring the two groups together, and in 1862 resigned his office, refusing to take the test oath of allegiance to the Federal government. After a short time in prison because of his Southern sympathies, he returned to his native state, Kentucky.

Knott opened his office for the practice of law at Lebanon, Ky., in 1863. After the war he was elected six times to the national House of Representatives, serving 1867–71 and 1875–83. In 1876 he was one of the managers appointed by the House to conduct the impeachment of W. W. Belknap [*q.v.*], secretary of war. He was several times chairman of the judiciary committee, and his oratorical powers secured for him a national reputation. His most famous effort was his speech on Duluth, Jan. 27, 1871 (*Congressional Globe*, 41 Cong., 3 Sess., App., pp. 66–68), in which he opposed a bill authorizing an extensive land grant to a railroad proposed to run along the St. Croix River to Duluth, Minn., then a wilderness village. His weapons were ridicule and humor, and so well did he employ them that not only was the bill killed but the speech has continued to be cited as a specimen of satire and —such is the irony of life—to enhance the fame of Duluth, which attributes to this oration its patronymic of "the zenith city of the unsalted seas." Years later Knott visited Duluth at the city's request, and was given a most gracious and enthusiastic reception.

In 1883 he was elected governor of Kentucky and served four years. He gave the state a wise and effective administration, marked by special progress in educational matters and in taxation. During his governorship, a state board of equalization was created which raised and equalized the tax assessments and paid off a large deficit which the state had incurred. After the expiration of his term of office in 1887, he resumed the practice of law, remaining in Frankfort, the capital, for the next five years. In 1891, he was a delegate to the state constitutional convention. In 1892, he accepted the professorship of civics and economics at Centre College, Danville, Ky., and in 1894, he and President William C. Young organized the law department of Centre College, of which he became the first dean and professor of law. After seven years' brilliant service as dean and lecturer, he was forced by ill health to retire in 1901, and he returned to his old home in Lebanon, Ky., where he lived quietly until his death. He married a Miss Forman of Missouri, and after her death he married, June 14, 1858, Sarah R. McElroy of Bowling Green, Ky. Knott County, formed during his administration, was named after him.

[Z. F. Smith, *The Hist. of Ky.* (1886); D. S. Barry, *Forty Years in Washington* (1924), vol. I; *Half Hours with the Best Am. Authors* (4 vols., 1887), ed. by Charles Morris; *Proceedings of the Joint Meeting of the Mo. Hist. Soc. and the Ky. Soc. of St. Louis on the Presentation of the Picture of Hon. J. Proctor Knott to the Mo. Hist. Soc.*, Oct. 28, 1927 (1927); *Centre College Mag.*, July 1928; J. M. Gresham, *Biog. Cyc. of the Commonwealth of Ky.* (1896); *Biog. Encyc. of Ky.* (1898); H. Levin, *The Lawyers and Lawmakers of Ky.* (1897); *Washington Herald*, June 19, 1911.] C. J. T.

KNOWLES, LUCIUS JAMES (July 2, 1819–Feb. 25, 1884), inventor and manufacturer, a descendant of Richard Knowles, immigrant, who came to Cape Cod before 1653, was born at Hardwick, Mass., the son of Simeon, Jr., and Lucetta (Newton) Knowles. Simeon was a farmer and a carriage maker, maintaining for the latter work the small shop which furnished Lucius the opportunity to develop an interest in mechanical construction and invention. Lucius attended the public schools at Hardwick and then spent three years at the Academy at Leicester, Mass. At seventeen he went to Shrewsbury to work in the country store of John Newton, his mother's brother, who in 1838 took him into the business which became John C. Newton & Company. But Knowles's interest was not in store-keeping. He spent more time constructing models of machines than in attending customers, and in 1841 he withdrew from the partnership and went to Worcester, Mass., where he began a daguerreotype business, the first in that city. Here, too, he continued to dabble with mechanics and when he made an improvement in thread-spooling equipment he set up a small business for spooling thread which he bought from a mill in Worcester. He then spent two years experimenting with cotton spinning in the attempt to equal the quality of the English thread of that time. For lack of capital he abandoned this and in 1846 formed a partnership with Harrison H. Sibley to operate the Old Draper Mill at Spencer, Mass., for the manufacture of cotton warp. In 1849 they secured a small mill at Warren, Mass., on the Quinebaug River, transferred their cotton business there, and in 1853 extended their activities to include a woolen mill which they built below the first. Still Knowles continued his experiments with mechanical improvement, receiving two patents for improvements in looms in 1856 and one for an improved method of operating the valves of pumping engines (1859). In 1860 the partnership was dissolved and the business divided so that Knowles might devote more of his time to the invention and manufacture of machinery. In 1862 he erected a building near his cotton factory and began to manufacture a boiler-feed water regulator, and (1863) steam pumps and experimental looms. From this building grew the Knowles Steam Pump Company and the L. J. Knowles & Brother Loom Works. The pump company became one of the largest in the business and was in 1879 sold to the Blake Manufacturing Company of Boston. The loom firm was moved to Worcester in 1866 where it expanded very rapidly to a leading position in the trade, being in 1897 consolidated with the Crompton Works as the Crompton & Knowles Loom Works. Though Knowles's inventions were responsible for much of the success of the two companies, few are outstanding or fundamental. He developed the steam pump to an advanced stage of refinement but so did other companies at the same time. An instance of his work in this connection is his adoption of the steam-actuated valve, for designs of which he received patents, though the invention is credited to H. R. Worthington. Similarly in looms he invented improvements tending to make manufacture more rapid and more economical of power. In this connection the open-shed principle of operation is an outstanding invention. Knowles was also active in civic affairs. He represented Warren, New Braintree, and West Brookfield in the Massachusetts House of Representatives, and the third Worcester district in the Senate. In 1871 he became a trustee of the Worcester Free Institute of Technology (Worcester Polytechnic Institute) and in 1873 was a member of the common council of Worcester. He was married first to Eliza Ann Adams of Shrewsbury, who died in 1873, and then to Helen Cornelia (Strong) Hayward of Boston. He died suddenly in Washington, D. C.

[J. D. Van Slyck, *Representatives of New Eng.* (1879); E. B. Crane, *Hist. Homes and Institutions and Geneal. and Personal Memoirs of Worcester County, Mass.* (1907); C. G. Washburn, *Manufacturing and Mechanical Industries of Worcester* (1889); A. M. Greene, *Pumping Machinery* (1911); *Bull. of the Nat. Asso. of Wool Manufacturers,* 1901; *Reports of the Commissioner of Patents* 1856–85; *Manufacturer's Rev. and Industrial Record,* Mar. 15, 1884; *Worcester Daily Spy,* Feb. 27, 1884.] F. A. T.

KNOWLTON, CHARLES (May 10, 1800–Feb. 20, 1850), physician, born in Templeton, Worcester County, Mass., was the son of Stephen and Comfort (White) Knowlton and was descended from English forebears who emigrated to America in the seventeenth century. He spent his early life on his father's farm, ardently desiring a medical education. He was mainly self-taught beyond the early grades except for his studies with various practitioners in Massachusetts and New Hampshire. Continuing his studies after his marriage on Apr. 17, 1821, to Tabitha F. Stewart (Stuart?) of Winchendon, Mass., he received the degree of M.D. from the medical department of Dartmouth College in 1824. He did little practising in western Massachusetts during the next few years, being mainly interested in preparing his *Elements of Modern Materialism* (1829), one of the earliest books on philosophical materialism, perhaps the first by an American author, issued in this country. Almost unreadable now, it nevertheless contains interesting anticipations of many modern views. The work which made his reputation was the anonymous publication in New York of the

Fruits of Philosophy; or, the Private Companion of Young Married People (1832). A second edition, not anonymous, was brought out in Boston in 1833 undoubtedly by Abner Kneeland, editor of the *Boston Investigator.* This was followed by other American editions up to the ninth (1839), which was reprinted by subscription (1877) on the initiative of a group of physicians at the Harvard Medical School.

Though a temperate discussion of the desirability of birth control, on medical, economic, and social grounds, the treatise, flaunting many accepted conceptions and values of the period, did not escape court action. The author was prosecuted and fined at Taunton, Mass., in 1832, and in Cambridge, Mass., he was sentenced on Dec. 10, 1832, to three months' imprisonment at hard labor in the House of Correction. Prosecution did not stop the sale of the work, however, and at Greenfield, Mass., Knowlton was again haled into court; but in this instance the prosecution, originating with an Ashfield clergyman, resulted in a *nolle prosequi,* the jury having been unable to agree on two previous occasions. In this trial, Knowlton's medical partner, Dr. Roswell Shephard, was a codefendant.

Reprinted in England from 1834 on by various Freethought publishers, the *Fruits of Philosophy* circulated quietly until it became the subject of the famous test case, *The Queen* vs. *Charles Bradlaugh and Annie Besant* (2 *Law Reports, Queen's Bench Division,* 569, reversed in 3 *Law Reports, Queen's Bench Division,* 607. See also the special report of the trial: *In the High Court of Justice, Queen's Bench Division, June 18, 1877. The Queen* v. *Charles Bradlaugh and Annie Besant,* 1877). The effect of the prosecution, eventually successful for the defendants, was electric. Circulation, which previously had not exceeded a thousand a year, reached a quarter of a million within a few years. It attained half a million if one includes the circulation of several provincial editions and of Annie Besant's *Law of Population,* which first appeared in January 1879 to replace the somewhat antiquated text of the *Fruits of Philosophy.* Dutch and French editions show that Knowlton exerted an influence on the Continent as well. Moreover the prosecution undoubtedly created a market for the development of a new contraceptive technique (introduced into England probably by Dr. Henry A. Allbutt) which has since revolutionized modern clinical procedure in the western world. Between 1876 and 1891 probably two million books and tracts furnishing elaborate contraceptive information were disseminated in England. Knowlton's other writings include: *Two Remarkable Lectures Delivered in Boston, by Dr. C. Knowlton, on the Day of his Leaving the Jail at East Cambridge, Mar. 31, 1833, Where he Had Been Imprisoned for Publishing a Book* (1833); *Address of Dr. Charles Knowlton, Before the Friends of Mental Liberty, at Greenfield, Mass., and Constitution of the United Liberals of Franklin County, Mass.* (1845); and *A History of the Recent Excitement at Ashfield,* part I (1834), the second part of which appeared in the *Boston Investigator,* Sept. 25, 1835.

[For an obituary and incomplete autobiographical sketch see the *Boston Medic. and Surgic. Jour.,* Sept. 10, 24, 1851. See also Norman E. Himes, "Charles Knowlton's Revolutionary Influence on the English Birth-Rate," *New Eng. Jour. of Medicine,* Sept. 6, 1928.]
N. E. H.

KNOWLTON, FRANK HALL (Sept. 2, 1860–Nov. 22, 1926), paleontologist and botanist, was born on a farm at Brandon, Vt., the son of Julius Augustus Knowlton and his wife, Mary Ellen Blackmer, of old New England lineage. He was sent to Middlebury College where Ezra Brainerd and Henry Martin Seeley taught all sciences and gave a permanent direction to his interest in natural history. Graduating with the degree of B.S. in 1884 he soon joined the United States National Museum, where he became assistant to Lester F. Ward, the paleontologist. In 1887 he was made assistant curator in botany and assistant paleontologist in 1889. In 1900 he was appointed paleontologist and later (1907) geologist on the United States Geological Survey. In 1889 he published "The Fossil Wood and Lignites of the Potomac Formation" (*American Geologist,* February 1889). Other papers followed, including "A Review of the Fossil Flora of Alaska" (*Proceedings of the United States National Museum,* vol. XVII, 1894). To satisfy a practical need he compiled *A Catalogue of the Cretaceous and Tertiary Plants of North America* which was published in 1898 and was later (1919) expanded into an invaluable reference book, *A Catalogue of the Mesozoic and Cenozoic Plants of North America.* As he acquired experience an ever increasing series of memoirs and special papers on the Cretaceous and Tertiary floras flowed from his pen, dealing for the most part with the Rocky Mountain region, interior Oregon, and Alaska. In all such monographs as the *Flora of the Montana Formation* (1900), *Fossil Flora of the John Day Basin* (1902), and on down to the *Fossil Floras of the Vermejo and Raton Formations of Colorado and New Mexico* (1918), many new species, based almost entirely on leaf impressions, were described. One of the pioneers in his field, he made little effort to homologize material; specimens from different horizons were described as distinct species, often indeed as distinct when from the same horizon if the impressions seemed unlike. It is probable that his species will suffer much reduction by the paleobotanist with the viewpoint perhaps of ecologic assemblages. Nevertheless Knowlton possessed a keen chronologic sense and through his determinations of the age of formations and their stratigraphic relations rendered important service to Western geology.

Knowlton was one of the founders of the Paleontological Society of America and in 1917, as its president, he read a paper on the "Relations between the Mesozoic Floras of North and South America" (*Bulletin of the Geological Society of America,* Dec. 30, 1918). He held that no demonstrable relationship exists between the Jurassic and Triassic floras of North and South America, but that there is direct and positive evidence of a relationship between the Upper Cretaceous floras of the two continents, the Dakota flora of the central and western United States having spread south by a land bridge as far as Argentina in Upper Cretaceous time. Ideas upon the geologic climates which had been long stirring in his mind found full expression in a paper, "Evolution of Geologic Climates" (*Ibid.,* December 1919), in which he held that previous to the Pleistocene epoch the earth was continuously enveloped by clouds, and that the oceans, permanently cooled in the Pleistocene, were warm from pole to pole, and that this high temperature was derived from the earth's inner heat and not from solar radiation which dominates existing climatic distribution. He believed that a relative uniformity and mildness of temperature, accompanied by high humidity, had prevailed over the greater part of the earth, extending to the polar circles—since, at least, the Middle Paleozoic. Knowlton admitted glaciation, but with the exception of three periods (Huronian, Permo-Carboniferous and Pleistocene) regarded these refrigerations as local and without widespread effect on temperature or the distribution of life. His thesis, while adversely criticized by A. P. Coleman, C. Schuchert, and G. R. Wieland, was acknowledged as entitled to serious consideration.

During his early years in Washington, 1887–96, he was professor of botany in the Columbian (now George Washington) University, which conferred on him the Ph.D. degree in 1896. He gave much time and energy to writing that could be appreciated by laymen. In 1897 he founded *Plant World,* a popular journal of botany, and was its editor until 1904; in 1909 he published a large and popular but authoritative work, *Birds of the World,* and in 1927 an excellent popular book, *Plants of the Past.* He took part in writing the definitions in botany for the *Century Dictionary,* for the 1900 edition of *Webster's Dictionary,* and for the *Standard Dictionary;* and he wrote the botanical matter for the *Jewish Encyclopædia.* He was married, on Sept. 27, 1887, to Annie Stirling Moorehead. She died in 1890 and on Oct. 3, 1893, he was married to Rena Genevieve Ruff. For many years he lived in Laurel, Md., but his last years were spent in Ballston, Va., where he died.

[For biographical information see the notices in the *Am. Jour. Sci.,* Mar. 1927, and in *Science,* Jan. 7, 1927, and the memoir by David White in the *Bull. of the Geol. Soc. of America,* Mar. 1927, which includes a bibliography of Knowlton's papers. For criticisms of his views on geologic climates see the *Am. Jour. of Science,* Apr. 1921.]
W. L. J—n.

KNOWLTON, MARCUS PERRIN (Feb. 3, 1839–May 7, 1918), jurist, was born in Wilbraham, Mass., the son of Merrick and Fatima (Perrin) Knowlton, and a descendant of William Knowlton who died on a voyage from London to Nova Scotia about 1633. He spent his boyhood on his father's farm at Monson and got his schooling in the Monson Academy. From 1856 to 1860 he attended Yale College, teaching school to defray his expenses and yet graduating with a creditable record. He read law and on Sept. 24, 1862, was admitted to the bar of Hampden County, Mass. Opening an office in Springfield, he soon had a large general practice. His reputation was gained not so much from the actual trial of causes as from the wisdom of his counsel and his "inclination for extended intellectual labor." He was a Republican, and though "never forthputting" or politically ambitious, he was elected to several offices: president of the Springfield common council (1872–73), representative in the Massachusetts House (1878), and state senator (1880–81). In 1881 Governor Long appointed him to the bench of the superior court, an office to which he proved singularly adapted. He had a broad working knowledge of the law, was prompt in his rulings, and lucid in instructing a jury. After coming to the bench he learned shorthand and was thereby aided in preparing his opinions with expedition—a characteristic for which he was noted throughout his career.

On Sept. 14, 1887, he was promoted to the Massachusetts supreme bench, and on Dec. 17, 1902, he succeeded Oliver Wendell Holmes as chief justice. An impairment of vision, which proved to be temporary, obliged him to leave the bench in September 1911. He had written the opinion of the court in 1,570 cases, a record exceeding that of any of his predecessors except Chief Justice Shaw. In twenty-nine cases he had written dissents—only four of which were during his chief justiceship. His successor, Chief Justice Rugg, declared that "no other magistrate in the history of Massachusetts has contributed so much to the visible fabric of our jurisprudence, . . . with the single exception of Chief Justice Shaw" (*Memorial, post,* p. 49). In writing his opinions the chief justice sought no "literary adornment, unless it be that which is inherent in the proper expression of accurate and original thought" (Knowlton's remarks on Justice Horace Gray, 182 *Mass.,* 624). Knowlton was of dignified appearance, grave but kindly, especially toward inexperienced counsel. Though somewhat removed from the crowd, he never lost his touch with plain people nor his humility of spirit. He bore an interested part in the life of his community. In his political philosophy he was orthodox but discriminating. After his retirement, when the financial difficulties of the Boston & Maine Railroad were felt throughout New England, he became chairman of the board of trustees charged with the reorganization. He was twice married: on July 18, 1867, to Sophia Ritchie, of Springfield, Mass., who died in 1886, and on May 21, 1891, to Rose M. Ladd of Portland, Me. He died in Springfield.

[See *Marcus Perrin Knowlton, Late Chief Justice of the Supreme Judicial Court of the Commonwealth of Mass.: A Memorial* (1919); *Obit. Record of Yale Grads. Deceased During the Year Ending July 1, 1918* (1919); A. P. Rugg, "Memoir of Hon. Marcus P. Knowlton, LL.D.," *Colonial Soc. of Mass. Pubs.,* vol. XXVI (1927); the *Green Bag,* Oct., Nov. 1911; C. H. W. Stocking, *The Hist. and Geneal. of the Knowltons of England and America* (1897); *Boston Transcript,* Sept. 8, 1887, Dec. 17, 1902, Sept. 6, 1911, May 7, 8, 1918. Knowlton's judicial opinions are reported in 145–209 *Mass. Reports.*] C. F.

KNOWLTON, THOMAS (November 1740–Sept. 16, 1776), Revolutionary soldier, was born at West Boxford, Mass., the son of William and Martha (Pinder) Knowlton. He was descended from Capt. William Knowlton of Kent, England, who died about 1633 during a voyage from London to Nova Scotia. The widow and children settled in Ipswich, Mass. Thomas Knowlton's youth was spent in Ashford, Conn., where his father had settled on a four-hundred-acre farm. In 1755 he enlisted for service in the Seven Years' War. He was successively promoted to sergeant, ensign, and lieutenant. On Apr. 5, 1759, he was married to Anna Keyes of Ashford. During the brief hostilities between England and Spain he accompanied General Lyman to Cuba and took part in the siege of Havana (1762). After peace had been declared he resumed farming at Ashford. Following the battle of Lexington he was elected captain of an Ashford company and marched to the defense of Massachusetts. At the battle of Bunker Hill (June 17, 1775) Prescott ordered Knowlton to leave the intrenchments and take up a position at the base of the hill, where he was to prevent the British right wing from flanking the Continental troops. Knowlton hastily fortified a rail and stone fence by building a second fence and filling the intervening space with new-mown hay. Stark's regiment extended the fortification and the breastwork was the scene of severe fighting. When the Continentals were forced to fall back Stark and Knowlton remained at the breastwork to protect the line of retreat. This task accomplished, they withdrew in relative good order. For his valuable services in preventing the destruction of the main body of Continental troops Knowlton received from a Boston admirer a gold-laced hat, a sash, and a gold breast-plate. He was commissioned major of the 20th Continental Infantry on Jan. 1, 1776.

On the night of Jan. 8, 1776, Knowlton made a daring sally into Charlestown. The British officers in Boston were attending the production of a farce written by General Burgoyne entitled *The Blockade of Boston.* The character burlesquing Washington—accoutred with an enormous wig and sword and attended by a ragged orderly bearing a rusty musket seven or eight feet long—had just appeared on the stage when a breathless runner brought word of Knowlton's raid. Howe and his entourage left at once "amidst fainting and shrieking among the females." Knowlton burned the houses in Charlestown quartering the British and captured five prisoners. He was promoted lieutenant-colonel by Congress on Aug. 12, 1776, and after the battle of Long Island he organized a small corps of picked men called "Rangers." In the battle of Harlem Heights (Sept. 16, 1776) Knowlton, commanding the "Rangers," was sent out to encircle a detachment of about 300 British Light Infantry, attack their rear, and effect their capture. Unfortunately he attacked too soon—a flank attack instead of an assault upon the enemy's rear as Washington intended—and the British escaped. Knowlton pursued and was killed.

[Ashbel Woodward, memoir of Knowlton and genealogical data in *New-Eng. Hist. and Geneal. Reg.,* Jan., Oct. 1861; Chas. Coffin, *The Lives and Services of Maj.-Gen. John Thomas, Col. Thos. Knowlton . . .* (1845); C. H. W. Stocking, *Hist. and Geneal. of the Knowltons of England and America* (1897); Richard Frothingham, *Hist. of the Siege of Boston* (1849); P. H. Woodward, "Historical Address," in *Statue of*

Col. Thos. Knowlton: Ceremonies at the Unveiling (1895); H. P. Johnston, "The Campaign of 1776, around New York and Brooklyn," *Memoirs of the Long Island Hist. Soc.*, vol. III (1878), and *The Battle of Harlem Heights* (1897); Jared Sparks, *The Writings of Geo. Washington* (12 vols., 1834–37).]

F. E. R.

KNOX, GEORGE WILLIAM (Aug. 11, 1853–Apr. 25, 1912), theologian, writer, and educator, was born in Rome, N. Y., the son of William Eaton Knox (1820–1883) and Alice Woodward (Jenckes) Knox. From his father, a distinguished Presbyterian pastor, he acquired an early religious bent, and in 1874, on graduation from Hamilton College, he entered Auburn Theological Seminary, specializing in missionary work. On May 11, 1877, he married Anna Caroline Holmes, of Auburn, daughter of Judge Jacob Holmes, and within a month was ordained by the Chemung Presbytery at Elmira. He sailed immediately for Japan as a Presbyterian missionary.

The tall, spare, wide-browed young pastor preferred the study of the Japanese language and the analysis and interpretation of Japanese religious systems to routine pastoral work among prospective converts, and, after passing his courses at the language school in Tokyo, gave over active parish work in favor of teaching homiletics at the Union Theological Seminary there. This post he retained from 1881 until 1893, serving, in addition, as professor of philosophy and ethics at the Tokyo Imperial University from 1886 until 1893. Meanwhile he was devoting his efforts to discerning the inner spirit of the Japanese as shown by the Japanese adaptations of Buddhism and Confucianism. In recognition of his scholarship in Japanese Confucianism he was elected to the vice-presidency of the Asiatic Society of Japan (1891–92), and in 1908 was awarded the decoration of the Order of the Rising Sun.

Returning to the United States in 1893, he became stated supply, and subsequently pastor, of the Presbyterian Church at Rye, N. Y., and three years later was appointed lecturer on apologetics at Union Theological Seminary. In 1899 he became full professor of philosophy and the history of religions at that institution. As a widely recognized authority in this field, he was selected to write the article on "Christianity" in the eleventh edition (1910–11) of the *Encyclopædia Britannica.* Certain statements made in this article stirred up resentment among Roman Catholics, and a series of controversial tracts were issued in protest, one of the more widely circulated being entitled, *Poisoning the Wells.* Although the article was subsequently revised and amended, much of the section on "Christianity" in the fourteenth edition (1929) of the *Britannica* remained his work. In 1911, he was commissioned by the Seminary to lecture on its behalf in China, Japan, India, and Korea, but his tour was cut short by his death, from pneumonia, in Seoul, Korea.

Knox's writings are scholarly, lucid and analytic. In Tokyo he published, in Japanese, textbooks of ethics, theology, and homiletics, and a work on "Christ the Son of God," and in English: *Japanese Systems of Ethics* (1886), *The Mystery of Life* (1890), and *A Japanese Philosopher* (1891). After returning to America he published: *The Direct and Fundamental Proofs of the Christian Religion* (1903), being the Nathaniel William Taylor Lectures at Yale Divinity School; *Japanese Life in Town and Country* (1904); *Imperial Japan: The Country and Its People* (London, 1905); *The Spirit of the Orient* (1906); *The Development of Religion in Japan* (1907); and *The Gospel of Jesus* (1909).

[*N. Y. Times* and *N. Y. Herald,* Apr. 27, 1912; *Who's Who in America,* 1912–13; "Three Educators," in *Outlook,* May 11, 1912; Shailer Mathews in *Am. Jour. Theol.,* July 1912; brief criticisms of Knox's writings, in *Chautauquan,* July 1906, *Nation* (N. Y.), Nov. 17, 1904, *Dial,* Dec. 1, 1904.]

H. E. W.

KNOX, HENRY (July 25, 1750–Oct. 25, 1806), major-general and secretary of war, was of Scotch-Irish descent, his father, William Knox, and his mother, Mary Campbell, having landed in Boston in 1729 from the north of Ireland. Married in February 1735, they had ten children, all sons, of whom Henry was the seventh. The father, a shipmaster by occupation, suffered financial reverses and died in the West Indies at the age of fifty, and Henry, then but twelve years old, was the sole support of his mother. Leaving the grammar school, the boy found work in the bookstore of Wharton & Bowes, in Cornhill, Boston. On his twenty-first birthday he opened for himself "The London Book-Store," which became a resort of British officers and brought him a fair income ("Henry Knox and the London Book-Store in Boston, 1771–74," in *Proceedings of the Massachusetts Historical Society,* vol. LXI, 1928, pp. 227ff.). His mother died a few months later, on Dec. 14, 1771.

A robust and enterprising youth, Knox was early interested in military affairs and enlisted in a local company when he was only eighteen. At the "Boston massacre," Mar. 5, 1770, he endeavored to restrain Captain Preston from firing on the mob. Through the bursting of a fowling-piece on a hunting expedition, he lost the third and fourth fingers of his left hand. He joined in 1772 the crack "Boston Grenadier Corps" as second in command under Capt. Joseph Pierce and made a study of military science and engineering. His martial bearing is said to have attracted the attention of Lucy Flucker, daughter of Thomas Flucker, royal secretary of the province, whom he married, June 16, 1774, against her family's wishes.

With the outbreak of the Revolution, Knox, although urged to adhere to the Royalist cause, withdrew with his wife from Boston in June 1775. He promptly offered himself as a volunteer to Gen. Artemas Ward and entered upon a career of unceasing activity, participating in nearly every important engagement of the war. His rise in the American army is like a tale of romance. The Patriots gladly accepted his experience as an artillerist; he soon, through his talents and personality, became one of General Washington's closest friends and advisers; and, although he had never been in a battle, he was commissioned colonel, Nov. 17, 1775, in charge of the artillery of the army. At his own suggestion and with the approval of Washington, he went with his brother William on a hazardous expedition to Fort Ticonderoga and brought back to Boston the supply of British ordnance captured on May 10, 1775, by Ethan Allen. His arrival in late January 1776, dragging "a noble train of artillery" over the snow, strengthened his reputation for daring and resourcefulness; and the fortification of Dorchester Heights with these guns compelled General Howe to evacuate Boston with eleven hundred Loyalists, including the Fluckers.

After laying out defenses at exposed points in Connecticut and Rhode Island, Knox joined Washington at Long Island, where he took part in the battles around New York. He reported, June 10, 1776, that he had available 120 cannon, but only 520 officers and men to handle them. The business of organizing the artillery was very arduous, and he wrote, Sept. 19, 1776, "I have not had my clothes off o' nights for more than forty days" (Brooks, *post,* p. 68). He was critical of the American officers and wrote on Sept. 5, 1776, "We want great men who, when fortune frowns, will not be discouraged." When most Patriots were despondent he remained optimistic, constitutionally incapable of being down-hearted. Under his direction Washington's troops on Christmas night, 1776, crossed the Delaware River, filled with floating ice, and, marching on Trenton, captured more than 1200 Hessian prisoners. For his services on this occasion, he was thanked in public orders by Washington and received his commission as brigadier-general, dated Dec. 17, 1776. At the battle of Princeton in January 1777 his regiment was conspicuous for its aggressiveness. When the army went into winter quarters at Morristown, the indefatigable Knox was sent to Massachusetts, where he started a government arsenal at Springfield. In the ensuing May, Ducoudray, a French officer, arrived in the colonies expecting to be made commander-in-chief of artillery. Deeply grieved, Knox addressed Congress on the subject, and Washington joined with Generals Greene and Sullivan in objecting to the substitution of Ducoudray for Knox. Washington, in his protest, described Knox as "a man of great military reading, sound judgment, and clear conceptions" (Sparks, *post,* IV, p. 446). As a consequence, the latter was retained in his position.

In the autumn campaigns of 1777, Knox's regiment took an active part, especially at Brandywine (Sept. 11), where a contemporary account said that they behaved "with their usual coolness and intrepidity," and at Germantown (Oct. 4). During the terrible winter at Valley Forge, he was allowed a leave of absence to visit his wife in Boston. At the battle of Monmouth (June 28, 1778), he expressed himself as delighted with the "coolness, bravery, and good conduct" of his men, and Washington wrote that the enemy had acknowledged "that no artillery could have been better served than ours" (Brooks, *post,* p. 124). In 1779 he made the first move for the establishment of the military academy which later became West Point. In 1780, when Pennsylvania troops mutinied, he was selected by Washington to present to the New England states the grievances of the army and secured some monetary relief from Massachusetts and New Hampshire. Later in the year he sat on the court-martial which tried Maj. John André. At the siege of Yorktown in the autumn of 1781 he placed the American cannon, and Washington declared that "the resources of his genius supplied the deficit of means." During the siege, Mrs. Knox was the guest of Mrs. Washington at Mount Vernon.

Knox's commission as major-general was dated Nov. 15, 1781, shortly after the surrender of Yorktown. At the close of hostilities he was named on a board to arrange with the British for an exchange of prisoners, but no agreement could be reached. For some months he was stationed at West Point and on Aug. 29, 1782, was placed in command of that post. When the neglected army grew restless, Knox, heading a committee of officers, petitioned Congress for aid. In May 1783 he conceived and organized the Society of the Cincinnati, composed of Revolutionary officers, and was made its first secretary, under Washington as president. He became vice-president of the order in 1805. During the autumn of 1783 the army was disbanded, and, after Washington had said farewell to his staff on Dec. 4, it was to Knox that he first extended a parting handclasp. Resigning in January 1784, Knox moved to Boston, where he was appointed by the General Court on a commission to treat with the Penobscot Indians. On Mar. 8, 1785, he accepted an election by Congress as secretary of war, at a salary of $2,450, out of which he paid an assistant. A "furious Federalist," he denounced the "State systems" and sent to General Washington, Jan. 14, 1787, a "rude sketch" for a general government. He was a stanch supporter of the new Constitution, and, when the cabinet was formed, was retained as secretary of war.

The army at that time numbered only 700 men, but when Knox prepared in 1790 a comprehensive plan for a national militia, it was rejected by Congress. He was also defeated in a controversy with Alexander Hamilton, secretary of the treasury, as to which department of the cabinet should purchase military stores and supplies. He promoted the negotiation of treaties with the Indian tribes, and urged both an adequate navy and a chain of coast fortifications. On Dec. 28, 1794, he retired to private life. While he was in the cabinet, he and his wife entertained elaborately, both in New York and Philadelphia, spending much more than their income and maintaining an expensive establishment. Manasseh Cutler once dined at Knox's table with forty-four other gentlemen and described the entertainment as being "in the style of a prince." His luxurious habits gave him the title of the "Philadelphia nabob."

In June 1796 Knox settled on the estate inherited by Mrs. Knox from her maternal grandfather, Gen. Samuel Waldo, near Thomaston, Maine, where he had just finished building an imposing mansion, called "Montpelier," at the head of the St. George's River. Here he carried on a great variety of projects, such as brickmaking, cattle-raising, ship-building, and lumber-cutting. As early as 1791, he had been engaged with William Duer in extensive land speculation in Maine, which led them into heavy borrowing. The amount of money involved was large, and Knox was drawn into many law-suits which kept him from having an easy mind. He lived, however, in state and entertained many distinguished foreigners, including Talleyrand, Louis Philippe, and Alexander Baring. From time to time he sat in the General Court and on the Governor's Council, and he served on several commissions, among them one for the adjustment of the northeastern boundary. In 1798, during the diplomatic crisis with France, he was appointed by President John Adams as major-general but was mortified by the fact that Hamilton and Charles C. Pinckney were given precedence over him. He died very unexpectedly, at the age of fifty-six, as the result of the lodging of a chicken bone in his intestines, and was buried at Thomaston, with military honors. A shaft of limestone still marks his grave.

Knox was a full-blooded, florid man, who, in 1783, weighed nearly three hundred pounds. Maclay, who did not like him, referred to his "Bacchanalian figure," and contemporaries ridiculed his pompous, self-complacent walk. He was forceful, often profane, in his language, and expressed himself very freely on most subjects. Although his sanguine disposition was an asset on the battle-field, it led him into hazardous business ventures. He was both generous and hospitable, and had qualities which endeared him to such different men as Greene, Lafayette, and Washington. Madam Knox, as she was commonly called, was almost as corpulent as her husband, and they were known in New York as "the largest couple in the city." She was described as "a lively and meddlesome but amiable" woman, but she had domineering ways, to which Knox was often obliged to yield, and her "lofty manners" led him occasionally to reprove her. Her tactless remarks and social blunders caused much amusement, but her position as a hostess, and her influence with Mrs. Washington, were undeniable. Of her twelve children, nine died young—two of them on the same day in 1796—and only three survived their parents. She herself died in 1824. The best portrait of Knox, by Gilbert Stuart, shows him in uniform, with his crippled left hand resting upon a cannon. It is in the Museum of Fine Arts in Boston.

[The extensive Knox papers, most of them not yet published, are preserved in the New-England Historic Genealogical Society in Boston. The best biography is *Henry Knox, A Soldier of the Revolution* (1900), by Noah Brooks. Another biography is Francis S. Drake's *Life and Correspondence of Henry Knox* (1873). See also Edward Channing, *Hist. of the U. S.*, vol. IV (1917); Jared Sparks, *The Writings of George Washington* (12 vols., 1834–37); C. F. Adams, *The Works of John Adams* (10 vols., 1850–56); J. C. Hamilton, *The Works of Alexander Hamilton* (7 vols., 1850–51); *Columbian Sentinel* (Boston), Nov. 5, 1806.]

C. M. F.

KNOX, JOHN JAY (Mar. 19, 1828–Feb. 9, 1892), financier, comptroller of the currency, was of Scotch-Irish ancestry on his paternal side, the great-grandson of John Knox, who emigrated to America in 1760 from Strabane, County Tyrone, Ireland. The seventh child of John J. Knox and Sarah Ann Curtiss, he was born in the village of Augusta, Oneida County, N. Y. Here his childhood was passed in healthful surroundings. He attended the Augusta Academy and the Watertown Classical Institute, then entered Hamilton College from which he graduated in 1849 after having made the Phi Beta Kappa Society. He began his business career as teller of the Bank of Vernon of which his father was president. In 1852 he was made teller of the Burnet Bank in Syracuse and in 1856 cashier of the Susquehanna Valley Bank at Binghamton, both of which institutions he helped to organize. From 1857 until 1862 he and his younger brother, Henry Martyn Knox, carried on a private banking business in St. Paul, Minn. In the latter year John Jay Knox contributed a carefully prepared article to the February issue of *Hunt's Merchants' Magazine and Commercial Review* in which he urged the establishment of a national banking system with a safe, elastic, convertible, and uniform paper currency. The essay attracted the attention of Secretary Chase, who appointed Knox to a clerkship in the Treasury Department. This office he held until 1865 when he became cashier for a short time of the Exchange National Bank at Norfolk, Va. Reëntering the government service he was placed in charge of the mint and coinage correspondence. In 1866 he made a report on the branch mint at San Francisco, which was published in Secretary McCulloch's annual report with a flattering reference. The same year he investigated a defalcation of $1,000,000 in the office of the assistant treasurer of the United States at New Orleans. On Oct. 10, 1867, he was made deputy comptroller of the currency and promoted to comptroller on Apr. 24, 1872, by President Grant.

In 1870 Congress ordered printed a report made by a committee of which Knox was a member, together with a proposed bill codifying the mint and coinage laws. After having been debated and considered for three years the measure known as the Coinage Act of 1873 was passed with few changes on Feb. 12, 1873. It discontinued the coinage of the silver dollar and made the gold dollar the unit of value. The subsequent unfounded charge of the free-silver advocates that the act had been surreptitiously passed Knox refuted in his published interview with the House committee on coinage, weights and measures on Feb. 20, 1891. Reappointed by President Hayes and President Arthur in 1877 and 1882 respectively, he remained comptroller until May 1, 1884, when he resigned to become president of the National Bank of the Republic in New York City, a position he held until his death. While comptroller he served as a member of the Assay Commission, helped to make the United States assistant treasurer a member of the New York Clearing House, took the necessary steps for the resumption of specie payments on Jan. 1, 1879, and negotiated with bankers for the issuance of 3-½ per cent. government bonds. He delivered various addresses before the American Bankers' Association and similar bodies, and lectured for several years on banking and finance at various universities.

Genial and gentle of disposition, Knox was a charming conversationalist, an art lover, fond of music, and familiar with the poets. Of sound judgment, he was a constructive financier and a leading authority in framing legislation relating to the government monetary system. Besides the works and addresses already mentioned, he wrote twelve annual reports as comptroller of the currency which were replete with information concerning currency questions of the day. He published a valuable monograph on *United States Notes; A History of the Various Issues of Paper Money by the Government of the United States* (1884) and contributed the nucleus to a *History of Banking in the United States* published in 1900. He also wrote articles on banking for magazines and encyclopedias. Knox was married, on Feb. 7, 1871, to Caroline E. Todd of Washington, D. C., by whom he had three sons and three daughters. He died in New York City.

[Sources include: *The Fiftieth Anniversary of the Marriage of John J. and Sarah A. Knox* (1863); *The Sixtieth Anniversary of the Marriage of John J. and Sarah Ann Knox* (1873); *Tribute of the Chamber of Commerce of the State of N. Y. to the Memory of John J. Knox, Mar. 3, 1892* (1892); J. L. Laughlin, *The Hist. of Bimetallism in the U. S.* (1886); *N. Y. Times*, Feb. 10, 1892. Knox's papers and correspondence were destroyed in 1923.] H. G. V.

KNOX, PHILANDER CHASE (May 6, 1853–Oct. 12, 1921), lawyer, senator, secretary of state, the son of David S. and Rebekah (Page) Knox, was born at Brownsville, Fayette County, Pa. His grandfather was a Methodist Episcopal clergyman, his father was a banker. The boy attended local schools, and in 1872 received the degree of A.B. from Mount Union College, in Ohio. While a student he began a lasting friendship with William McKinley, then district attorney of Stark County. After three years spent in reading law in the office of H. B. Swope of Pittsburgh, he was admitted to the bar of Allegheny County in 1875. Following a brief service as assistant United States district attorney for the western district of Pennsylvania, in 1877 he formed a law partnership with James

H. Reed of Pittsburgh. For twenty years Knox devoted himself to the practice of his profession, attaining recognition as among the ablest lawyers of the country, both as a counselor and as an advocate. In 1880 he married Lillie Smith, daughter of Andrew D. Smith of Pittsburgh. His talents were in constant demand in the controversies incident to the industrial development of the Pittsburgh region and in the organization and direction of the corporations which brought it about. In 1897 he served as president of the Pennsylvania Bar Association and in 1899 was offered the position of attorney general of the United States by his long-time friend, President McKinley. He declined the offer, probably because he was deeply engrossed in the formation of the Carnegie Steel Company, organized in 1900; but in 1901, when, upon the resignation of John W. Griggs, McKinley again offered him the appointment, he accepted it, and entered upon his office Apr. 9, 1901.

Within a year he initiated suit under the Sherman Anti-Trust Act of 1890 against the Northern Securities Company, through which James J. Hill, J. Pierpont Morgan, and their associates had attempted to merge the Great Northern, the Northern Pacific, and the Chicago, Burlington & Quincy railroads. Knox gave his personal attention to the litigation through all its stages up to the Supreme Court, before which he made the argument for the United States. He won a decision against the company on Apr. 9, 1903, and a confirmation of the judgment on Mar. 14, 1904. While attorney general, Knox was sent to Paris to examine the title of the New Panama Canal Company, successor of De Lesseps' company, which had offered to sell its property and interests in the Isthmus to the United States for forty million dollars. Upon his certification of clear title, the offer of the French company was accepted. He drafted legislation which created the Department of Commerce and Labor in 1903, and was partly responsible for drafting that giving the Interstate Commerce Commission effective control of railroad rates.

On June 10, 1904, Governor Pennypacker of Pennsylvania appointed Knox to fill the vacancy caused by the death of United States Senator Matthew S. Quay. He took his seat on July 1 and subsequently was elected for a full term of six years. As senator he was active and influential, especially in railroad-rate legislation; he served on the judiciary committee, took a prominent part in the Panama Canal tolls debate, and for a time was chairman of the committee on rules. He resigned the senatorship on Mar. 4, 1909, and became secretary of state under President Taft, with whom he had formed an intimate friendship which continued through the Roosevelt-Taft feud until Knox's death.

During the Taft administration, the cabinet was dominated by Knox, who had had a large share in its selection. Within his own portfolio, in order that the business with different groups of countries might pass through officials who had an intimate knowledge of those countries, and that foreign-service officers might keep in touch with the home viewpoint, the Department of State was reorganized on a divisional basis and the merit system of selection and promotion extended by an executive order to the diplomatic service up to the grade of chief of mission. In the conduct of foreign relations one of Knox's chief policies was the encouragement and protection of American investments abroad, or as it is popularly and somewhat opprobriously termed, "dollar diplomacy." This policy was first applied in the Far East in 1909, in the suggested "neutralization" of all the railways in Manchuria. Knox proposed that Russia, Japan, and other nations join in supplying China with the money necessary to enable the Chinese government to assume ownership of the Manchurian railroads. Both Russia and Japan objected, because of their alleged special interests there, and the project failed. More successful were the efforts of the United States government to secure the participation of American banks in railway and currency loans for China proper. The four-power consortium of 1910, increased in 1911 to six-power by the admission of Russian and Japanese banks, though hindered by President Wilson's withdrawal of support and subsequently by the World War, paved the way for the new four-power consortium of 1920.

Dollar diplomacy was also extended to Nicaragua and Honduras, by treaties signed in 1911. The purpose was to stabilize the governments by reorganizing their finances and removing the custom-houses from the possible attainment of prospective revolutionists. The treaties, which were to have made possible loans from American bankers, failed of ratification, but subsequently formed the basis of the Bryan-Chamorro Treaty with Nicaragua, which was ratified with amendments in 1916. In 1912 Knox visited the Caribbean republics to allay any suspicions that the United States had imperialistic aims. About the same time the proposal of a Japanese syndicate to buy a large tract of land in Lower California, including Magdalena Bay, led to the extension of the Monroe Doctrine to Asiatic as well as European nations.

During Knox's administration as secretary of

state, the Bering Sea controversy and the North Atlantic fisheries controversy were amicably settled by treaty and arbitration respectively, and an attempt was made to establish a reciprocity agreement with Canada to offset the bad feeling engendered in that country by the Payne-Aldrich tariff. The reciprocity project was approved by the House and Senate but was rejected by the Dominion Parliament. Attempts to secure ratification of general arbitration treaties with Great Britain and France and to establish a Court of Arbitral Justice at The Hague were also unsuccessful, although these failures paved the way for the ultimate adoption of both projects in subsequent administrations.

After Mar. 5, 1913, Knox returned to the practice of law at Pittsburgh, but after three years the hankering for public service led him again to become a candidate for the Senate, and on Nov. 6, 1916, he was elected for the term 1917–23. In the Senate, he took a leading part in the successful fight against the ratification of the Treaty of Versailles. His opposition, which was based primarily on the contention that the treaty of peace and the constitution of the League of Nations should be separated, was made public in a "round robin" on Mar. 4, 1919, before President Wilson's return to Paris for final negotiations. This "round robin" was drafted by Knox and signed by thirty-seven Republican members of the new Senate. The Treaty of Versailles was signed on June 28 and submitted to the Senate on July 10. Knox supported reservations on the ground that, if the negotiators understood the Treaty as President Wilson interpreted it to the senators, there should be no objection to embodying these interpretations in the resolution of ratification; but he voted against ratification on the ground that the Treaty, although the reservations tended to make it less "obnoxious to our Constitution," nevertheless imposed "obligations upon the United States which under our Constitution cannot be imposed by the treaty-making power" (*Congressional Record,* 66 Cong., 1 Sess., p. 8768). In all these proceedings against the Treaty, while Senator Henry Cabot Lodge generally appeared as spokesman, it was Knox who was chiefly consulted by the opposition and who drafted such resolutions and other documents as were necessary. The Treaty failed of ratification on Nov. 19, 1919, and again on Mar. 19, 1920. Its rejection necessitated a separate peace with Germany, a proposal which Knox had supported from the beginning: in the "Knox Resolutions" of June 10, 1919, and again on Nov. 18. After the failure of the Treaty, therefore, he offered a resolution (May 21, 1920) to repeal the declaration of war against Germany and Austria. The resolution was passed, but President Wilson vetoed it on May 27, on the ground that it did not seek to accomplish any of the objects for which the United States had entered the war. Less than eight weeks after the end of the Wilson administration, a joint resolution declaring the war at an end was introduced, passed, and, on July 2, 1921, signed by President Harding. A separate peace was thereupon negotiated and signed with Germany (Aug. 25, 1921) and submitted to the Senate Sept. 21. Three weeks later, on Oct. 12, 1921, shortly after leaving the Senate chamber, though apparently in good health, Knox was suddenly stricken with paralysis and died. His interment took place at Valley Forge, Pa., where he had made his country home for a number of years.

Knox has been justly characterized as an agreeable, generous, upright man, a shrewd corporation lawyer, with the restraints imposed by judicial training and traditions. Himself free of unworthy motives, he found it difficult to impute such motives to others. As secretary of state he sometimes failed in due consideration for the feelings of the weaker nations. He was bored with detailed routine but tremendously interested in great state policies.

[The private papers of Knox, in the possession of his daughter, Mrs. James R. Tindle, are not available to the public. A biography by Herbert F. Wright appeared in S. F. Bemis, *The Am. Secretaries of State and Their Diplomacy,* vol. IX (1929). The Taft papers in the Library of Congress are important for the relationship between Knox and Taft. Knox's public addresses, apart from those in the *Congressional Record,* are available in separate prints privately issued. His public papers as secretary of state, so far as published, are printed in the *Foreign Relations of the United States* and congressional documents. His public papers as attorney general, so far as published, are printed in the publications of the Dept. of Justice and congressional documents. The Northern Securities Case is ably presented by B. H. Meyer, "Hist. of the Northern Securities Case," *Bull. Univ. of Wis., Econ. and Pol. Sci. Ser.,* vol. I, no. 3 (1906). For Knox's Far East policy, see W. W. Willoughby, *Foreign Rights and Interests in China* (2nd ed., 2 vols., 1927); S. K. Hornbeck, *Contemporary Politics in the Far East* (1916); and T. W. Overlach, *Foreign Financial Control in China* (1919). "Dollar Diplomacy" in the Caribbean is adequately presented by Dana Gardner Munro, *The Five Republics of Central America* (1918). Juan Leets, *U. S. and Latin America: Dollar Diplomacy* (1912), is a criticism. More extended bibliographical references will be found in the Appendix to the published biography mentioned above.] H. F. W.

KNOX, SAMUEL (1756–Aug. 31, 1832), Presbyterian minister and educator, was the eldest son of Samuel Knox, a farmer descendant of the reformer, living in the County of Armagh, Ireland. His mother's name is unknown. Of his early life little can be said; even the date of his birth is disputed. Though it has been asserted that he first came to America in 1795, it is apparent, from references in the *Maryland Journal and Baltimore Daily Advertiser* (1786 and 1787) that he was at Bladensburg, Md., as early as 1786. Returning to Scotland (1789), he entered the University of Glasgow where he distinguished himself by diligent scholarship, was awarded prizes in Greek and Latin, and received the degree of M.A. (1792). After preparing for the ministry, and being licensed by the Presbytery of Belfast, he came to the United States, presented his credentials at Baltimore, and received a pastorate in Bladensburg (1795) which he held two years. At Frederick (1797–1803) and Soldiers' Delight (1804–09) he served as supply minister; but his clerical services were constantly hampered by political activities and quarrels. Several powerful polemical sermons and essays came from his pen. The most notable of these, "Some Prefatory Strictures on the lately avowed Religious Principles of Joseph Priestley" (1798) and "A Vindication of the Religion of Mr. Jefferson and a Statement of his Services in the Cause of Religious Liberty" (1800), suggest that politics may have influenced his religious thinking.

As a teacher, Knox occupied many stations: at Bladensburg Grammar School, 1788–89; first principal of Frederick Academy, 1797–1803; and head of a private academy, merged (1808) into Baltimore College, with Knox as principal, a position which he held till 1820. From 1823 to 1827 he was principal of the Frederick Academy and then taught a private school. In 1817 the Central College (later University of Virginia) Visitors decided to offer him the professorship of languages and belles-lettres, but the plan was never consummated. His claim to distinction as an educator rests primarily upon his *Essay on the Best System of Liberal Education, Adapted to the Genius of the Government of the United States* (1799) which was submitted in a prize contest instituted by the American Philosophical Society; and on his essay advocating a system of education in Maryland. The United States, he said in his prize essay, needed a national system, having a "wide extent of territory, inhabited by citizens blending together almost all the various manners and customs of every country in Europe" (p. 71). Nothing could better effect harmony than this "uniform system of national education," including both arts and sciences. Theological instruction should be left to each denomination, exclusion from the national system being justified by the principle of separation of church and state. His system embraced elementary schools for both sexes, county schools or academies for pupils (boys) who had completed four years in the elementary school and had passed an examination; a college in every state, with uniform plan and charges; and, finally, a national university, which would "constitute the fountain head of science." Uniform textbooks, supervision, professional training for teachers, equalized salaries, promotion on merit and a university press were other novel features proposed. Though austere and despotic as a teacher, and often embroiled with those who disagreed with him, Knox was a discerning and forceful advocate of education. Jefferson regarded him highly, and was probably influenced by his *Essay* in planning the University of Virginia. Though judged a "ripe scholar" and esteemed by contemporaries, it is not so much by his actual achievements as by his projects that he may rightly be considered a pioneer of American education. He married twice: first, Grace Gilmour by whom he had four daughters; second, Zeraiah McCleery of Frederick, Md.

[U. S. Bureau of Educ., *Report of the Commissioner of Educ. for the Year 1898–99* (1900), vol. I; Basil Sollers' chapter on secondary education in B. C. Steiner, *Hist. of Educ. in Md.* (1894); two manuscript sketches lent to the writer by the family; *Md. Hist. Mag.*, Sept. 1907, Sept. 1909; *Daily Nat. Intelligencer*, Sept. 4, 1832; and numerous pamphlets by Knox.]

T. W.

KNOX, THOMAS WALLACE (June 26, 1835–Jan. 6, 1896), traveler, journalist, author, inventor, was born at Pembroke, N. H., the son of Nehemiah and Jane Wallace (Critchett) Knox. His father was a shoemaker and said to be a descendant of John Knox, the Scotch reformer. Apprenticed early to his father's trade, he appears to have made his way independently to Boston where he attended the public schools. Returning to New Hampshire he worked for some years on a farm, while at the same time he educated himself with persistent determination. At eighteen he became a teacher and at twenty-two he had established an academy of which he was the principal at Kingston, N. H. In 1860 the gold rush in Colorado lured him to Denver where he became a special reporter and then city editor of the *Daily News.* At the outbreak of the Civil War he enlisted as a volunteer aide, serving through two campaigns in the Southwest and receiving a wound during a skirmish in Missouri. Somewhat later the governor of California appointed him lieutenant-colonel on the staff of the state National Guard. In 1863, as war correspondent for the *New York Herald,* he came under the displeasure of General Sherman and was court-martialed. He was convicted of disobedience to orders and excluded from the military department under Grant's command.

Failing to gain a revocation of the sentence, he returned to New York. In 1865 he published some of his military dispatches in a volume entitled *Camp-Fire and Cotton-Field.* In 1866 he traveled across Siberia as correspondent for the *Herald* with an American company engaged in establishing a telegraph line for the Russian government. The following year he was granted a patent, No. 68,088, for transmitting plans of battlefields by telegraph. Out of his adventurous experience in Russia came his book *Overland Through Asia* (1870) and his lucrative lifelong interest in foreign travel. On a journey abroad in 1875, in connection with an international rifle match at Dollymount, Ireland, he invented a device for telegraphing by Morse signals the spot where each bullet struck the target.

Knox's most productive tour was undertaken in 1877, when he explored many unfrequented parts of the Orient and secured materials for a large number of volumes of travel. His visit to the King of Siam resulted in the adoption by that country of a system of public instruction modeled upon the ideals and methods of American education, as Knox had described them. For his book, *The Boy Travelers in the Far East: Part Second: Adventures of Two Youths in a Journey to Siam and Java* (1881), which the King declared to be the best description of that country ever written, Knox received the decoration of the Order of the White Elephant. Encouraged by the favorable reception of his lively accounts of foreign lands, he settled in New York and began the prolific production of the books which, from 1879 up to his death, he published at the rate of two a year. Among these, a series of nearly forty travel books for boys represents his most distinctive efforts. A list of his other works includes *The Lives of James G. Blaine and John A. Logan* (1884), *Life and Work of Henry Ward Beecher* (1887), *Decisive Battles Since Waterloo* (1887), and *The Republican Party and its Leaders* (1892). None of these volumes survives the test of time; the name of their author does not appear in *The Cambridge History of American Literature,* yet they represent an honest attempt to meet the needs of Knox's generation. At the height of his career in the eighties he was one of the popular literary figures of New York. At the time of his death he is said to have traveled more widely, with the exception of Frank Vincent, than any other American.

[See obituaries in the *N. Y. Herald, N. Y. Times,* and *N. Y. Tribune,* Jan. 7, 1896; D. B. Sickels, *Memorial Address: Col. Thos. Wallace Knox,* Apr. 6, 1896; the *Critic,* Jan. 11, 1896; article in *Book News,* Feb. 1892, reprinted from *Harper's Young People,* Oct. 18, 1891; and N. F. Carter, *Hist. of Pembroke, N. H.* (2 vols. bound together, 1895). For the details of his court-martial see *War of the Rebellion: Official Records (Army),* 1 ser., XVII, pt. 2.] P. K.

KOBBÉ, GUSTAV (Mar. 4, 1857–July 27, 1918), critic, music historian, and author, son of William August Kobbé and Sarah Lord Sistare, was born in New York. There he attended public school until, as a boy of ten, he went to Wiesbaden, Germany, where he studied at the Gymnasium and was the pupil of Adolf Hagen in piano and composition. Returning to New York in 1872, he entered Columbia College in 1873 and was graduated from the school of arts in 1877 and from the law school in 1879. At the same time he continued his musical studies with Joseph Mosenthal. Almost immediately upon the completion of his college education, he began his career as a writer, choosing the journalistic road by preference. One of the editors of the *Musical Record and Review* (1879–80), he acted as assistant music-critic of the New York *Sun* (1880–82), and in the latter year was chosen by the New York *World* to report the first *Parsifal* performance in Bayreuth as a special correspondent. On Nov. 11, 1882, he was married to Carolyn Wheeler of Scarsdale, N. Y. He was successively music critic of the New York *Mail and Express,* the New York *World,* and the *New York Herald,* and contributed articles on musical and other subjects to such magazines as the *Century, Scribner's,* and the *Forum.* He also wrote a weekly article on art for the Sunday edition of the *Herald.* His literary activities in general covered a wide range of subjects. Included in his written works are *New York and Its Environs* (1891); *Plays for Amateurs* (1892); *My Rosary and Other Poems* (1896); *Famous Actors and Actresses and Their Homes* (1903); and *A Tribute to the Dog* (1911). His novels include *Miriam* (1898); *Signora, a Child of the Opera-House* (1902), an example of the genre known as "the musical novel"; *Modern Women* (1915); and *All-of-a-Sudden Carmen* (1917).

Written in a pleasantly direct and informal style, Kobbé's contributions to musical literature represent the most significant portion of his output. His *Loves of Great Composers* (1905) is a volume of romanticized biography. *Famous American Songs* (1906) and *How to Appreciate Music* (1906) are popularizations of their subjects for the general reader. He was an enthusiastic Wagnerian, however, and may be said to have done his best work in this special field. *Wagner and His Isolde* (1905), the Wagner-Wesendonk letters and the story of the friendship which inspired *Tristan,* is secondary in importance to *Wagner's Life and Works* (2 vols.,

1890), containing extended analyses of the music dramas, with note-examples of the leading motives. In spite of the enormous volume of Wagner literature extant, the work has been widely read. Kobbé was a genial person and he enjoyed many friends. He was interested in sports and had made a hobby of boating. It was while sailing a catboat near his summer home at Bayshore, L. I., that he was accidentally struck and killed by the wing of a naval hydroplane maneuvering in the waters of Great South Bay.

[*Who's Who in America*, 1918–19; the *Musician*, Sept. 1918; *Musical Courier*, Aug. 1, 1918; *Musical America*, Aug. 3, 1918; the *N. Y. Times*, *N. Y. Herald*, *Sun*, and *World*, July 28, 1918.] F. H. M.

KOBER, GEORGE MARTIN (Mar. 28, 1850–Apr. 24, 1931), physician, active in public welfare work, was born at Alsfeld, Hesse-Darmstadt, Germany, the son of Johann Jacob and Johanna Dorothea (Bär) Kober. He received his early education at the *Realschule* of his native town. His father was one of those whose souls were stirred by the ferment of liberty in the fifth decade of the nineteenth century, and he resolved that no son of his should serve under any German prince or potentate. George therefore emigrated to the United States in 1866. He found that his brother Charles, who had preceded him, was a soldier at Carlisle Barracks and there he enlisted also. Assigned to duty at the hospital in August 1867, he excited the interest and received the help of the surgeon, Dr. Joseph J. B. Wright, and by January 1870 he was appointed a hospital steward and had fixed his mind upon medicine as a career. Ordered to Frankford Arsenal, he began study under a preceptor, Dr. Robert Bruce Burns, an Edinburgh graduate. In 1871 Kober was ordered to Washington for duty and he entered the medical school of Georgetown University, taking an evening course. He received his degree in 1873 and the following year was appointed an acting assistant surgeon in the army and ordered to California. His career as an army doctor continued until November 1886, when he left the service, for which he always cherished a warm friendship. Frugal habits, civil practice, and wise investments made him financially comfortable, and by 1893 he had given up private practice and was devoting his time to teaching, public health work, and philanthropy. In 1901 he was made dean of the medical department of Georgetown University, which position he held until 1928.

Kober never married: his great love was for mankind, particularly the poor and afflicted. He gave liberally to the cause of public welfare and served on many commissions and committees dealing with it. He was a pioneer in the crusade against tuberculosis and designed the Tuberculosis Hospital in Washington; he called attention to the pollution of the Potomac River as a cause of typhoid in Washington, and was instrumental in securing the means of purification adopted; and he is credited with the first published report on the use of iodine as an antiseptic. He was a prolific writer, his published articles numbering about two hundred. They deal principally with hygiene, disease prevention, and philanthropy, among the more important being *Urinology and Its Practical Application* (1874), *Milk in Relation to Public Health* (1902), *Industrial Hygiene and Social Betterment* (1908). The medical corps of the army and Georgetown University were special objects of his regard. At the latter institution in 1923 he created an endowment fund of $16,000, the income of which was to be used for the creation of a scholarship in the medical school, a gold medal for the best student in hygiene, a gold medal to be awarded annually to a member of the Association of American Physicians who had contributed to the progress and achievement of the medical sciences or preventive medicine, and an annual course of lectures by men who had contributed to the progress and achievement of the medical sciences or preventive medicine. He was a fellow of the American Medical Association and of the Association for the Advancement of Science, secretary of the Association of American Physicians (1909–16), president of the Association of American Medical Colleges (1906), of the National Association for the Study and Prevention of Tuberculosis (1915), of the National Housing Association (1889), and an active member of numerous other societies.

He was a man of pleasing personality and gracious manners. His acquaintance with men of prominence was large. Despite his learning, he always spoke English with a marked German accent. At the time of his death, he was engaged in writing his *Reminiscences*, one volume of which had appeared in 1930. It deals more with his friends and his manifold interests than with himself. His seventieth, eightieth, and eighty-first birthdays were honored by testimonials by Georgetown University and various medical and scientific societies. On the occasion of the eightieth birthday he was presented with a bronze plaque bearing his portrait in relief and inscribed "George Martin Kober, Physician, Patriot, Philanthropist."

[F. A. Tondorf, *Biog. and Bibliog. of George M. Kober* (1920); *Military Surgeon*, Feb. 1924; *Am. Jour.*

of *Physical Anthropology*, Jan.–Mar. 1920; *Trans. of the Asso. of Am. Physicians*, 1927; *Hist. of the Medic. Soc. of the District of Columbia 1817–1909* (1909); F. A. Tondorf, *The Fiftieth Anniversary of the Graduation in Medicine of George Martin Kober, M.D., LL.D. March 6, 1923* (1923); *In Commemoration of Dr. George Martin Kober's Eightieth Birthday, March 28, 1930*; *Georgetown Coll. Jour.*, March 1920, June 1931; *Who's Who in America*, 1928–29; *Evening Star* (Washington), Apr. 24, 1931.] P. M. A.

KOCHERTHAL, JOSUA von (1669–Dec. 27, 1719), Lutheran clergyman, was the leader of the Palatine emigration to the province of New York. If the inscription on his gravestone has been rightly understood, he was born in or near Bretten, Melanchthon's birthplace, then part of the Palatinate but since 1803 of Baden. In the first years of the new century he was pastor at Landau in the Bavarian Palatinate. In 1704, a year after the French invasion, he went to London to inquire about the feasibility of emigrating to America. In his *Aussführlich und Umständlicher Bericht von der Berühmten Landschafft Carolina in dem Engelländischen America Gelegen* (1706; 4th ed., Frankfurt-am-Main, 1709) he described the Carolinas as a land of freedom, peace, and plenty and invited prospective emigrants to join his expedition. Although Kocherthal had not overlooked entirely the risks and hardships of emigration, his friend, the Rev. Anton Wilhelm Boehme [*q.v.* in the *Dictionary of National Biography*], thought it wise to publish another pamphlet, *Das Verlangte Nicht Erlangte Canaan* (Frankfurt and Leipzig, 1711) as a warning against being too sanguine. Meanwhile Kocherthal, with his family and almost fifty destitute followers, returned to London in 1708 and petitioned the Board of Trade to send his party to one of the plantations. By his piety and gentle manners he won the personal interest of Queen Anne, and his petition was granted. On Dec. 31, 1708, he and his people reached New York, where they found a generous benefactor in Lord Lovelace. In the spring they settled on the Hudson at the mouth of Quassaik Creek (Chambers River) and named their settlement Newburgh. Lovelace's death in May left them helpless, and Kocherthal immediately sailed for England to consult with the Queen. Again he was successful, and in 1710 he returned with ten shiploads of exiled Palatines. Of this great company, which numbered 3,086, according to Boehme, when it left England, 600 died on the voyage and 250 more after landing. In conformity with the plans of the new governor, Robert Hunter, the Palatines were shipped up the Hudson to East Camp and West Camp, where they were expected to repay the cost of their transportation and keep by gathering naval stores. There were, however, no naval stores to gather; Hunter had been deceived by Robert Livingston. So far as the Palatines were concerned, the one result of this unfortunate enterprise was to reduce them to the condition of slaves. By 1714 the scheme was given up. That the Palatines did not fare even more miserably was due in good measure to Kocherthal, who had intelligence and fortitude as well as piety and gentleness. In 1711 he established himself at Newtown in the West Camp area and from there made regular visits to congregations in East Camp, at Newburgh, and along the Mohawk and the Schoharie. He was on terms of friendship with Justus Falckner [*q.v.*] and with John Frederick Häger, who was of German Reformed antecedents but had received Episcopal ordination in England. Kocherthal's wife, Sybilla Charlotte, died Dec. 13, 1713, and he himself died six years later, when about to depart on another voyage to England. He was buried in West Camp. Benigna Sybilla, the eldest of his five children, married Wilhelm Christoph Berkenmeyer [*q.v.*].

[The notes on Kocherthal by W. J. Mann and B. M. Schmucker in their edition of the *Hallesche Nachrichten*, Erster Band (Allentown, Pa., 1886), are precise and detailed and furnish sufficient direction to their authorities. See also A. L. Gräbner, *Geschichte der Luth. Kirche in America* (St. Louis, 1892); F. R. Diffenderffer, "The German Exodus to England in 1709," *Proc. Pa.-German Soc.*, vol. VII (1897); H. E. Jacobs, "The German Emigration to America, 1709–40," *Ibid.*, vol. VIII (1898); *Pa. Mag. of Hist. and Biog.*, Jan. 1902; four articles on the Palatines in *Olde Ulster*, vol. III (Kingston, N. Y., 1907); Kocherthal's church records, *Ibid.*, vols. III and IV (1907–08).] G. H. G.

KOEHLER, ROBERT (Nov. 28, 1850–Apr. 23, 1917), painter, art-school director, was born in Hamburg, Germany, the son of Ernst Theodor Koehler and Louise Büter. When Robert was three years old the family emigrated to America, Herr Koehler establishing a machine shop in Milwaukee. In the German schools there the boy excelled in drawing and later learned the trade of lithography. At the outset of his career he was threatened with blindness but an operation averted calamity and he plunged energetically into commercial engraving, working first in Milwaukee and later in Pittsburgh and New York. In New York he earned his living by day in Arthur Brown's lithographic establishment on Thames Street, in the shadow of Old Trinity, and studied nights at the National Academy of Design, finally attracting the attention of George Ehret, a wealthy New York brewer, who bought his pictures and sent him to Munich in 1873 to study. Although his ambition at first ran no higher than to become a fine commercial lithographer, he studied with the best masters Munich afforded, Piloty, Löfftz, and Defregger, and decided to devote himself to painting. Forced by lack of funds to return to New York in 1875, he worked as pupil at the Academy and at the Art Students' League, returning to Munich four years later. This time he remained as student and finally as teacher for thirteen years. In 1886 he painted his most ambitious canvas, "The Strike," a large and rather dry picture of industrial life. It brought him the Order of St. Michael from Prince Regent Leopold of Bavaria, with a court reception, and honorable mention at the Exposition Universelle at Paris, 1889. As president for many years of the American Artists' Club and chairman of the American section of the international exhibitions in Munich he brought Whistler's work to the Bavarian capital and later met the great American artist in Venice.

Koehler returned to New York in 1892 and the following year was persuaded to succeed Douglas Volk as director of the Minneapolis School of Fine Arts. Against the advice of friends he accepted the post and spent the remainder of his life there, twenty-one years as director and three as director emeritus. Although his talent as an artist was negligible, his devotion to the school in the face of many discouragements was heroic. As a pioneer of art instruction and appreciation in the Northwest he exerted an influence which can hardly be overestimated. He was a trustee of the Minneapolis Society of Fine Arts and president of the Minneapolis Art League. He persuaded Eastern artists to send their pictures west for exhibition and arranged that at least one picture should be bought each year to become the property of the parent organization, the Society of Fine Arts. He lectured endlessly and wrote the major portion of the *Bulletin* of the society, contributing to its pages a delightful series, "Chapters from a Student's Life" (September 1906–Midsummer 1907), which describes his years in Munich. He founded and for seven years directed the Minnesota State Art Society, which, through the medium of traveling exhibitions of prints, sent echoes of the masters through farm district and isolated town. Although academic by training, he did not close his mind entirely to modernism. Koehler was married, in 1895, to Marie Franziska Fischer, who with one son survived him. His paintings are owned by the *Kunstverein*, Munich, the Academy of the Fine Arts, Philadelphia, the public libraries of Minneapolis and Duluth, and the museums of Minneapolis and Milwaukee.

[In addition to the "Chapters from a Student's Life," see *Who's Who in America*, 1916–17; M. D. Shutter and J. S. McLain, *Progressive Men of Minn.* (1897); A. N. Marquis, *The Book of Minnesotans* (1907); Charlotte Whitcomb, "Robert Koehler, Painter," *Brush and Pencil*, Dec. 1901; *Bull. of the Minneapolis Inst. of Arts*, June 1917; *Am. Art Annual*, 1917; *Minneapolis Jour.*, *Minneapolis Morning Tribune*, Apr. 24, 1917.]

H. L. V–D.

KOEHLER, SYLVESTER ROSA (Feb. 11, 1837–Sept. 15, 1900), museum curator, writer, artist, was born in Leipzig, Germany. He emigrated to the United States with his parents when a boy of twelve, having received only the rudiments of an education. His father was an artist and his grandfather a musician, hence he was naturally inclined to the artistic career which he followed throughout his life. He went to Boston in 1868, entering the establishment of L. Prang & Company, where he remained as technical manager for ten years. With Charles C. Perkins and William C. Prime, he started in 1879 the *American Art Review*, a scholarly periodical designed to awaken interest in art in the United States. The circle to which it appealed was small and after two years it ceased publication. Koehler contributed constantly to American, German, and English periodicals, writing chiefly on the subject of the graphic arts. He held for a time the position of curator of the section of graphic arts in the United States National Museum at Washington. He was appointed acting curator of the print department of the Boston Museum of Fine Arts in October 1885 and became regular curator in February 1887, a position he held until his death. His previous work with the Prang Company gave him mastery of the details of the technical processes and his years of study of the history of art made him invaluable as an authority and critic. The many catalogues of exhibitions of important etchers held in the Museum were prepared by him with introductions and copious descriptions. Notable among these was the catalogue for an exhibition in 1892, "illustrating the technical methods of the reproductive arts from the XV century," for which there was a constant demand for museums and collectors.

The building up of the print department of the Museum was regarded as the most important part of Koehler's life work. He frequently went to Europe in the interest of the Museum and was well known as a scholarly writer and lecturer. He delivered a course of nine lectures on "Old and Modern methods of Engraving" before the Lowell Institute in 1893 and later repeated them in Washington. He died suddenly at Littleton, N. H., of heart failure, while attempting to leave a train. He was buried from the home of Charles Biewald in Roxbury (now a part of Boston), Mass. His valuable library, and many prints, he gave to the Museum. In 1859 he married Amelia Susanna Jaeger. His published works include: *The Theory of Color in its Relation to Art and Art Industry* (1876), translated from the German of Wilhelm von Bezold; *Illustrations of the History of Art* (1879), an authorized American edition of the work of E. E. A. H. Seemann; *Original Etchings by American Artists* (1883); *Etching* (1885); *American Art* (1886); *Frederick Juengling* (1890); and an edition of T. Tokuno's *Japanese Wood-cutting and Wood-cut Printing* (1894).

[*Who's Who in America,* 1899–1900; *Trustees of the Museum of Fine Arts, Twenty-fifth Ann. Report,* 1900; *Internat. Studio,* Nov. 1900, Supp. pp. i–ii; *Boston Transcript,* Sept. 17, 1900.] H. W.

KOEMMENICH, LOUIS (Oct. 4, 1866–Aug. 14, 1922), musician, composer, was born in Elberfeld, Prussia, Germany, the son of Ludwig and Henrietta (Hasenkamp) Koemmenich. He showed a pronounced musical bent from childhood. For several years he studied with Anton Krause, at Barmen, a pianist, composer, and teacher of repute in his day, and at the age of nineteen he went to Berlin, where from 1885 to 1887 he attended the Kullak Academy, studying with Franz Kullak, Alexis Holländer, and William Tappert. He emigrated to the United States in 1890 and settled in New York. In a comparatively short space of time, he established his reputation as a teacher of singing and the pianoforte, and as a conductor of singing societies. In 1894 he became conductor of the Brooklyn *Sängerbund,* and in 1898 he organized an Oratorio Society in Brooklyn. From 1902 to 1910, while living in Philadelphia, he acted as conductor of the *Junger Männerchor* and in 1910 he conducted in the German Theatre. In 1912 he succeeded Frank Damrosch as conductor of the New York Oratorio Society, which post he retained until 1917. He also served as conductor of the Mendelssohn Glee Club (1913–19); the Beethoven Society (1916); and the New Choral Society of New York (1917–22). While active in these capacities, in which he became a well-known and respected figure in the musical life of New York, he found time to keep up with his work as a teacher of singing and to compose. His original works included a number of songs and choruses, with and without accompaniment, which are meritorious and pleasing. As a choral conductor he deserves credit, in particular, for presenting new works of musical importance by the organizations he had in charge. Thus he gave the first productions in New York of Otto Taubmann's *Eine Deutsche Messe,* Georg Schumann's oratorio, *Ruth,* and Enrico Bossi's secular cantata, *Jeanne d'Arc,* for soli, chorus, and orchestra. Koemmenich was married, Apr. 15, 1891, to Maria Dreibholz of Barmen, Prussia. She and three children survived his death by suicide in the summer of 1922.

[*Musical Courier,* July 4, 1898, Aug. 24, 1922; *Musical America,* Aug. 19, 1922; *N. Y. Times,* Aug. 15, 1922; information as to certain facts from Mrs. Louis Koemmenich.] F. H. M.

KOENIG, GEORGE AUGUSTUS (May 12, 1844–Jan. 14, 1913), chemist, mineralogist, was born at Willstätt, Grand Duchy of Baden, Germany, the son of Johannes and Margaretha (Pfotzer) Koenig. His early education was acquired at the public schools, the progymnasium at Kork, and the School of Moravian Brothers at Lausanne, Switzerland. He studied at the polytechnikum at Karlsruhe from 1859 to 1863, receiving the degree of mechanical engineer. He was at the University of Heidelberg two years, 1863–65, and at the University of Berlin a like period, 1865–67. His degrees of A.M. and Ph.D. were conferred by Heidelberg in 1867. He spent the year 1867–68 at the school of mines at Freiberg. In October 1868 he came to America and in Philadelphia began to manufacture sodium stannate from tin scrap. This he soon abandoned to become chemist at the Tacony Chemical Works in the same city. Here he remained until 1872, except for the winter of 1870–71, which he spent in mine examinations in Mexico under trying conditions, owing to primitive transportation methods and the activity of hostile Indians. His long college career began with his appointment in 1872 to an assistant professorship of chemistry and mineralogy in the University of Pennsylvania. In 1879 he was made professor of mineralogy and geology, which position he held until 1892, thus completing two decades of service in the university. During this period he was active in the general affairs of the institution, serving on several important investigating committees, one of which was the committee which examined the once famous Keely motor.

In 1892 Koenig resigned his chair at the University of Pennsylvania to accept the professorship of chemistry and metallurgy at the Michigan College of Mines. Later, as the college grew, a separate department was created for metallurgy, but Koenig remained at the head of the department of chemistry until his death. During the entire period of over twenty years, though he made many examinations and investigations in states other than Michigan, he was rarely absent from his classroom for a regular lecture or recitation. He relinquished active charge of his department the Sunday but one before he died. His mind was that of an investigator. He usually had one or more problems under investigation. To his colleagues or advanced students who were fortunate enough to drop into his laboratory when such investigations were in progress, his buoyant enthusiasm in the face of obstacles and negative results was inspiring. He was first to discover diamonds in meteoric iron. In the course of his examinations of minerals, he discovered and described some thirteen new species. His fine collection of type specimens he presented to the Michigan College of Mines. To the layman one of his most interesting and spectacular achievements was the preparation of artificial crystals of the copper arsenids, which grew out of his discovery of Mohawkite. His manipulation in obtaining these beautiful crystals never before known, and most of them not as yet found in nature, seemed wizard-like.

Results of his researches were published from time to time in the American and German journals of chemistry and mineralogy. His latest publication, dated Mar. 21, 1912, entitled "New Observations in Chemistry and Mineralogy," is a part of the elaborate hundredth-anniversary volume of the *Journal of the Academy of Natural Sciences of Philadelphia.* For many years he was interested in chemical and metallurgical methods. He developed quantitative methods of blowpipe analysis, to which he gave the name of chromometry. In 1881 he patented a process for the chlorination of silver and gold ores, and in 1897 an assay furnace dispensing with a muffle. Two years before his death he took out a patent for separating vanadium from some of its ores. His continuous hydrogen-sulfid generator obtained considerable vogue in chemical laboratories. He was a member of the American Philosophical Society, the Academy of Natural Sciences of Philadelphia, the Franklin Institute, the American Institute of Mining Engineers, and the Lake Superior Mining Institute. On Oct. 7, 1869, he was married to Wilhelmina Marquart of Willstätt, who with two of their children survived him.

[*Who's Who in America,* 1912–13; *Old Penn,* Jan. 25, 1913; *Am. Men of Science* (1910); *Engineering and Mining Jour.,* Jan. 25, 1913; *Mich. Coll. of Mines Alumnus,* Jan. 1913; *Pub. Ledger* (Phila.), Jan. 16, 1913; Koenig's unpublished autobiography and information as to certain facts from members of his family.]

J. F.

KOERNER, GUSTAVE PHILIP [See KORNER, GUSTAV PHILIPP, 1809–1896].

KOHLER, KAUFMANN (May 10, 1843–Jan. 28, 1926), rabbi, eldest child of Moritz and Babette Löwenmayer Kohler, was born in Fürth, Bavaria, into a family and community of stanchly orthodox Jewish traditions. In Talmudical academies in Mayence and Altona, he attained a mastery of Talmudic knowledge. At twenty he became a disciple of the dynamically ardent orthodox leader, Samson Raphael Hirsch, to whose influence he attributed much of his Jewish idealism. But in the universities of Munich (1864–65), Berlin (1865–67), and Erlangen (Ph.D., Nov. 13, 1867), he broke with orthodox Judaism. The critical methods of his university studies told him that Judaism was a historic growth, not every part of which was of equally divine character and value, and in his doctoral dissertation, *Der Segen Jakob's,* he made a strong plea for modernizing religion. This thesis limited exceedingly his prospects of obtaining a rabbinical position in Germany, and after two years of post-graduate study in the University of Leipzig, he was called to the Beth-El Congregation in Detroit, arriving in the United States on Aug. 28, 1869. Exactly a year later he married Johanna, daughter of David Einhorn [*q.v.*]. After two years in Detroit, during which time he led his congregation farther from its orthodox background, he was called to Sinai Temple, Chicago, where he introduced many elements of radical reform. At the beginning of 1874, he instituted Sunday services besides the regular Saturday exercises, an innovation which evoked violent criticism and denunciation. In September 1879, on the retirement of his father-in-law, David Einhorn, Kohler succeeded him as rabbi of Temple Beth-El, New York, where again he introduced supplementary Sunday services, and continued to battle lustily with his conservative critics and orthodox denouncers, maintaining his right to decide what was permanent and vital in Judaism, and what ephemeral. In 1885, in a series of lectures published as *Backwards or Forwards,* he attacked Alexander Kohut's definition of traditional Judaism.

This polemic led both men, the leading Jewish scholars in America, to action. On Kohut's side, it resulted in the foundation of the Jewish Theological Seminary of America (Jan. 2, 1887) to defend and strengthen traditional Judaism. On Kohler's side, it led him to call the Pittsburgh Conference, with the adoption of the radical Pittsburgh Platform (November 1885), at first repudiated even by some reform Jews, but later accepted as a statement of principles of American reform Judaism. Kohler was one of the founders, and for many years president, of the

New York Board of Jewish Ministers. Succeeding Isaac M. Wise [*q.v.*] as president of the Hebrew Union College at Cincinnati on Feb. 19, 1903, he raised its academic standards notably, himself teaching homiletics, theology, and Hellenistic literature. His seventieth, seventy-fifth, and eightieth birthdays were widely celebrated by American reform Jewry. Retiring in 1921 at the age of seventy-eight, he returned to New York, where he died in his eighty-third year.

The bibliography of Kohler's writings in *Studies in Jewish Literature,* issued in celebration of his seventieth birthday, contained at that time 801 items. He took a prominent part in the preparation of the Union Prayer Book, and of the Jewish Publication Society's English translation of the Bible. He wrote textbooks of reform Judaism, edited the *Sabbath Visitor* (1881–82), and the *Jewish Reformer* (1886), and was editor of the department of theology and philosophy of the *Jewish Encyclopedia.* His principal single work was his well-ordered and fully documented *Grundriss einer systematischen Theologie des Judentums auf geschichtlicher Grundlage* (1910), published in English in 1918 as *Jewish Theology Systematically and Historically Considered,* a work which mingles a reform treatment of Judaism with conservative Jewish apologetics. Highly valuable are Kohler's numerous studies on the Jewish origins of Christianity, on Hellenistic, apocryphal, and pseudepigraphic literature, on the origin of the Jewish liturgy, and on comparative religious folklore. These reveal consummate scholarship. At eighty he published *Heaven and Hell in Comparative Religion* (1923), tracing the remote folklore origin of Dante's eschatology, and at the time of his death, he was working on *The Origins of the Synagogue and the Church,* published posthumously in 1929. A collection of his papers, with a supplemental bibliography, was published in 1931 as *Studies, Addresses, and Personal Papers* and included his "Personal Reminiscences of my Early Life." The pen of scholarship was the most effective instrument of Kohler's self-expression. Though an earnest teacher and preacher inspired by religious idealism and the quest of truth, Kohler lived and lives principally through the written word. He will be remembered less as the opponent of Zionism and as the vigorous, learned protagonist of fading doctrinal battles, than as a productive, mature, and fearless scholar.

[See *Studies in Jewish Lit. in Honor of Kaufmann Kohler* (1913), pp. 1–38; H. G. Enelow, article in *Am. Jewish Year Book,* XXVIII (1926), pp. 235–60, reprinted as the introduction to Kohler's *Origins of the Synagogue and the Church;* David Philipson, article in *Central Conference of Am. Rabbis: Thirty-seventh Ann. Convention,* vol. XXXVI (1926); *Hebrew Union Coll. Monthly,* May 1918, Dec. 1921; the *Am. Hebrew, Jewish Exponent, Jewish Tribune,* Feb. 5, 1926; *Cincinnati Enquirer,* Jan. 29, 1926.] D. deS. P.

KOHLMANN, ANTHONY (July 13, 1771–Apr. 10, 1836), priest, educator, and missionary, was born in Kaiserberg, Alsace. He believed that the priesthood was his vocation, and with this in mind he began his preliminary studies at his native place. The anti-clerical character of the later developments of the French Revolution caused him to leave home and seek refuge in Fribourg, Switzerland. He matriculated at the university and after finishing his theological studies was ordained in 1796. Attracted to community life, he became a member successively of two communities that were patterned somewhat after that of the Jesuits. For a time he ministered to the sick at Hagenbrunn, Austria, during a plague, then he spent two years in the military hospital at Pavia. Finally, taking up the work that appealed to him most, he taught theology at various places in Europe. In 1803 he entered the Society of Jesus and was among the first to go as a missionary to the United States, sailing from Hamburg on Aug. 20, 1806. He was first stationed at Georgetown, then a small college, and when opportunity offered, he made missionary journeys to the scattered German congregations in Pennsylvania. In 1808 he was appointed by Archbishop Carroll administrator of the Diocese of New York and with Benedict Joseph Fenwick [*q.v.*] took charge of St. Peter's Church. He held the post of administrator until 1814. New York at this time had a Catholic population of about 14,000. Among these were some French and Germans. Kohlmann's fluency in languages made his ministry to these people more effective. The material assets of the New York diocese consisted of one church building, one school, and a cemetery. During Kohlmann's administration St. Patrick's pro-Cathedral was planned, a school for boys was started, and an academy for girls provided. His stay in New York was made memorable through a court decision rendered upon the subject of the seal of confessional. Through his offices as confessor, he was able to restore certain stolen goods to their rightful owner. The owner, however, insisted that the names of the guilty be divulged and brought suit to this end. The district attorney tried to solve the difficulty by a declaration of *nolle prosequi.* The board of trustees of St. Peter's Church insisted upon a court decision. This was rendered in favor of the clergyman and was later written into the law of the state, being made part of the revised statutes of

1828. Kohlmann looked upon the case as an opportunity to explain the Catholic position in the matter of the Sacrament of Penance, and upon it he wrote a brief treatise which attracted considerable notice at the time.

Kohlmann returned to Georgetown in 1815 where he served his society as master of novices. From 1818 to 1820 he was president of Georgetown College. With the restoration of the Jesuit University, the Gregoriana, in Rome, he was called to occupy the chair of theology. He left America in 1824, spending his last years in teaching. Among his pupils, many of whom rose to high offices in the church, was Joachim Pecci, who became Pope Leo XIII. His publications were controversial and occasional. *Unitarianism Philosophically and Theologically Examined,* which appeared first as a series of thirteen pamphlets, was published in 1821 in book form. It called forth considerable comment as it was directed against the views of certain influential Unitarian ministers, including Jared Sparks. J. M. Finotti in his *Bibliographia Catholica Americana* (1872) attributes to Kohlmann *The Blessed Reformation, Martin Luther, Portrayed by Himself* (Philadelphia, 1918), although it was published under the name of John Beschter. It is regrettable that the variety of Kohlmann's activities obscure somewhat the greatness of his administrative gifts. His services were of the utmost value to the Church during these critical years, both at Georgetown and in New York.

[Wilfrid Parsons, S. J., has written an authoritative sketch of Kohlmann's life and work in *Cath. Hist. Rev.,* Apr. 1918. Peter Guilday's *Life and Times of John Carroll* (2 vols., 1922) contains a brief sketch of Kohlmann and a number of extracts from his letters. *The Woodstock Letters,* vol. IV (1874) and vol. XII (1883), published privately by the Jesuits at Woodstock College, Md., contain valuable material. *The Souvenir of the Centennial Celebration of St. Patrick's* (N. Y., 1909, privately printed) contains a biographical note by Thomas F. Meehan. Further notices of Kohlmann's life and work may be found in J. R. Bayley, *Brief Sketch of the Cath. Ch. on the Island of N. Y.* (1870); J. G. Shea, *Memorial of the First Centenary of Georgetown Coll.* (1891), and *Cath. Churches of N. Y. City* (1877); John, Cardinal Farley, *Hist. of St. Patrick's Cathedral* (1908); and Wm. H. Bennett, *Cath. Footsteps in Old N. Y.* (1908).]

P. J. F.

KOHLSAAT, HERMAN HENRY (Mar. 22, 1853–Oct. 17, 1924), restaurateur and editor, the son of recent immigrants, Reimer and Sarah (Hall) Kohlsaat, was identified with Galena, Ill., in his youth, although he had been born at Albion on the other side of the state. With scanty formal education, he undertook his living in Chicago, and so throve that he married at the age of twenty-seven Mabel E. Blake, daughter of E. Nelson Blake, the president of the Chicago board of trade. Before he was forty he had bestowed upon his adopted town, Galena, a striking statue of General Grant, and a painting of Lee's surrender, by Thomas Nast; and he had brought Governor McKinley of Ohio to that town on Grant's birthday, to deliver a commemorative address (*Daily Inter Ocean,* Apr. 28, 1893). Kohlsaat was one of the little group of friends that had rescued him from bankruptcy when he was involved in the failure of Robert L. Walker in February 1893 (C. S. Olcott, *The Life of William McKinley,* 1916, I, 288). His fortune came from his interest in a wholesale baking concern, in which he had first worked as an errand boy and drummer, and from a chain of low-price lunch rooms in Chicago. Thus was explained, if not justified, the epithet of John J. Ingalls, who called him in a moment of exasperation "that d—d pastry cook" (J. B. Foraker, *Notes of a Busy Life,* 1916, I, 480).

Kohlsaat was a devoted Republican, going to the convention of 1888 as an alternate, and bringing to the party the support of the *Daily Inter Ocean,* of which he was part owner from 1891 until May 3, 1894. He was a devoted Chicagoan, too, using his journal for the advancement of the interests of the world's fair of 1893. And he had now become a devoted admirer of William McKinley. After the sale of his interest in the *Inter Ocean,* Kohlsaat took the first vacation of his life (*Chicago Tribune,* May 4, 1894), and for the remaining thirty years of his career he permitted himself to do as he pleased in business, politics, and travel. He searched for another metropolitan newspaper, looking into the affairs of the *Chicago Tribune,* the *New York Tribune,* and the *New York Times*; but he came to it by the accident of the unexpected death of his old friend James W. Scott. Scott had combined the *Chicago Times* with the *Chicago Herald,* Mar. 4, 1895, but had dropped dead in New York six weeks later. On Apr. 21, 1895, Kohlsaat appeared as editor and publisher of the *Chicago Times-Herald,* converting it immediately into an independent journal devoted to a protective tariff and the gold standard. On Mar. 28, 1901, he renamed it the *Chicago Record-Herald,* having bought the *Chicago Record* from Victor Lawson. The *Chicago Evening Post,* which had been part of the *Times-Herald* property, he released in 1901 to John C. Schaffer.

As the aggressive antagonist of free silver, Kohlsaat increased his prominence among western Republicans. He pressed upon McKinley the necessity for an emphatic stand upon gold, and he was with Hanna in the preconvention conferences of 1896, when the leaders agreed that the Democrats should be met squarely upon this issue. It irked him to hear that anyone else claimed to be the author of the gold plank, and he carried on a prolonged fight in defense of his own claim from the time he announced it when a journalist (*Chicago Times-Herald,* June 17, 1896) until he published his reminiscences in the *Saturday Evening Post* from May 13, 1922, to Jan. 13, 1923. He had no desire for office for himself, but his brother Christian was made a federal judge by McKinley, and he secured the Treasury for Lyman J. Gage of Chicago. He had great satisfaction in knowing the presidents and acting as their "brutal friend." For several years after 1902 he took a vacation from journalism, interesting himself in Chicago real estate; but he was back in the editorial chair of the *Record-Herald* from Jan. 1, 1910, until Sept. 7, 1911, directing that journal alongside the *Chicago Tribune* in the fight to unseat William Lorimer as senator from Illinois. A little later he had a year with the *Inter Ocean* again, before James Keeley merged it and the *Record-Herald* into the *Chicago Herald,* which first bore the new name June 14, 1914. In 1912 Kohlsaat was driven by rough misrepresentation by Roosevelt into an active support of Taft, and he could not resume his intimacy with Roosevelt until war made it seem to be an imperative duty. His death came suddenly in Washington, whither he had gone on invitation of Judge K. M. Landis to see the world series, and where he was a guest in the house of Herbert Hoover, then secretary of commerce. His two daughters survived him.

[The best obituaries are in the *N. Y. Times,* and *N. Y. Herald Tribune,* and the *Chicago Tribune,* all of Oct. 18, 1924. Kohlsaat's amiable vanities and his loyalty in friendship are revealed in his book of reminiscence *From McKinley to Harding: Personal Recollections of Our Presidents* (1923).] F. L. P.

KOHUT, ALEXANDER (Apr. 22, 1842–May 25, 1894), rabbi and lexicographer, born in Félégyhaza, Hungary, was one of the thirteen children of Jacob and Cecelia (Hoffman) Kohut. His only brother, Adolph, became one of Germany's best-known writers. Alexander, a beautiful child, was once kidnapped by gypsies. Since there was no school in his native village and his parents were too poor to pay a teacher, he was still unable to read or write at the age of eight. The family moved to Ketskemet, however, and here his secondary schooling progressed rapidly, being completed at the high school in Buda Pesth *summa cum laude.* In 1861 he entered the famous Jewish Theological Seminary in Breslau, where he lived a life of extreme poverty and assiduous study, gaining his rabbinical diploma in 1867. Three years later he received the degree of Ph.D. at Leipzig, *honoris causa,* for a thesis *Ueber die jüdische Angelologie und Daemonologie in ihrer Abhängigkeit vom Parsismus.* He served as preacher in Tarnowitz (1866), and rabbi at Stuhlweissenburg (1867), Fünfkirchen (1872), and Grosswardein (1880). The excellence of his public service and his brilliant oratory secured his election to the Hungarian parliament, though he did not take his seat, because, in the year he was elected, Congregation Ahawath Chesed called him to New York, where he arrived May 3, 1885.

Kohut was shocked at the extravagant vagaries of radical reform Judaism in America, and three weeks after his arrival began a series of sermons on "The Ethics of the Fathers," the theme of which was that "a reform which seeks to progress without the Mosaic-rabbinical tradition is a deformity. . . . Suicide is not reform." They were published in the same year. Conservative Jewry rallied around their new leader, and reform, put on the defensive, replied through Kaufmann Kohler [*q.v.*] in a series of addresses, *Backwards or Forwards,* and through the Pittsburgh Program of American Judaism. Kohut's reply, in cooperation with Sabato Morais and others, was the organization of the Jewish Theological Seminary of America, in which he was professor of Talmud. In 1891 he was appointed examiner in rabbinics in Columbia College. In Hungary he had married Julia Weissbrunn, who died in New York in 1886, by whom he had ten children, eight of whom survived her. On Feb. 14, 1887, he married Rebekah, daughter of Rabbi A. S. Bettelheim, who has become a leader of American and international Jewish womanhood. His early privations and excessive study had undermined his health, and the tall, commanding, alert, handsome man with white skin, blue-black hair, and flashing eyes, became a premature physical sufferer. He continued to work in his library, however, and even taught his students from his sick bed. In March 1894, when the death of his friend Kossuth was announced, he left his bed, went to synagogue, and against strict orders not to speak entered the pulpit and gave a flaming address on Kossuth's relation to Judaism, at the end of which he collapsed. He was carried home and after lingering a few weeks, died at the age of fifty-two, and was buried with the last volume of his *Aruch Hashalem* in his hand.

The *Aruch,* the basis of all subsequent rabbinical dictionaries, is the Talmudic dictionary compiled in the eleventh century by Nathan ben Jechiel of Rome. For twenty-five years, while caring for a large family on a modest salary,

Kohut worked unceasingly on an encyclopedic modernizing of this work. After immense effort and persistence in the field of Judeo-Persian and Yemenite Jewish literature, he published four volumes while in Hungary, the final four—including the supplement of references, indexes, addenda, etc.—appeared during his American period, the whole comprising more than 4,000 double-column pages. This monumental work of superlative scholarship, patient philological research, and textual criticism (1878–92) was republished in 1926.

A profound scholar who abhorred superficiality, he was also a brilliant orator in several languages. A lover of peace and unity who modestly fled personal recognition, he yet became the leader of an historic controversy. Giving a quarter of a century of unremitting toil to fine lexical points, he had nevertheless a deeply poetic soul and a moving piety and reverence. In keeping with his sentimental Jewish traditionalism he always carried with him a little of the earth of Palestine. His ideal home life was charmingly depicted by his widow in *My Portion.* In his memory his family established the Kohut Foundation, which has presented to Yale University the Alexander Kohut Memorial Hebrew and Rabbinnic books, the Alexander Kohut Publication Fund for publishing texts issued by its Semitic Department, and the Alexander Kohut Research Fellowship in Semitics. There have also been established by his son, George A. Kohut, similar Kohut Foundations in Vienna, Berlin, Budapest, and New York for publishing works in Jewish literature, especially in the fields of grammar, lexicography, folk-lore, and the history of religion.

[A bibliography of 115 items concerning Kohut, by his son, G. A. Kohut, appears in the *Festschrift zum 50jährigen Bestehen der Franz-Josef-Landesrabbinerschule in Budapest* (1927); a bibliography of his publications is in the *Proceedings of the Fourth Biennial Convention of the Jewish Theological Seminary Association* (1894), and is reprinted in *Tributes to the Memory of Alexander Kohut* (1894), ed. by G. A. Kohut; see also B. A. Elzas, Gotthard Deutsch, M. H. Harris, and Max Cohen in Kohut's *The Ethics of the Fathers* (1920); *Jewish Quart. Rev.*, Oct. 1921; J. D. Eisenstein, *Ozar Yisrael* (10 vols., 1907–13); vol. IX; *Am. Hebrew*, June 1 and July 6, 1894; Adolph Kohut, in *Semitic Studies in Memory of Rev. Dr. Alexander Kohut* (Berlin, 1897); *Jewish Encyc.*, vol. VII; Rebekah Kohut, *My Portion* (1925); *N. Y. Times*, May 27, 1894.]

D. deS. P.

KOLB, DIELMAN (Nov. 10, 1691–Dec. 28, 1756), Mennonite preacher, was born in the Palatinate. He belonged to a family distinguished for honest industry and sincere religious faith. The father, Dielman Kolb, Sr., and the mother, daughter of Peter Schumacher who had emigrated to Germantown, Pa., in 1685, both died in the Palatinate, but five of the next generation, including three preachers, eventually followed the example of the grandfather and migrated to Pennsylvania. Dielman Kolb, Jr., became a preacher among the Mennonites of Mannheim in the Palatinate while continuing, as was customary, his trade of weaving. He received religious exiles from Switzerland and helped them on their way until the position of Mennonites in the Palatinate became insecure, whereupon he followed his brothers to America. On Aug. 10, 1717, with his wife, Elizabeth Schnebli, a widow whom he had married in 1714, he landed at Philadelphia. They were soon settled in the district of Salford, later included in Montgomery County, where the thrifty Kolb, farming and continuing to ply his trade of weaving, became an important landholder.

Assured of his own position in the New World, Kolb continued to assist others. He corresponded with the Committee on Foreign Needs at Amsterdam, which supplied funds for transporting Swiss and German exiles to America, and he may have visited the Netherlands on this business (list of arrivals on the *Mortonhouse* from Rotterdam, Aug. 19, 1729, *Pennsylvania Archives,* 2 ser., vol. XVII, 1890, p. 15). He and his brothers were among the Germans who in 1731 secured a bill of naturalization from the Assembly of Pennsylvania, thus acquiring the right to hold and transfer property (*Votes and Proceedings of the House of Representatives of the Province of Pennsylvania,* vol. III, 1754, pp. 131, 135, 153). Unusually well educated for his day, he was interested in extending both educational and religious opportunities in Pennsylvania. He preached at Salford, at Goshenhoppen, and in other neighboring communities. In 1738 he was one of four who secured a tract of land on which the people of Salford erected a church and school. Kolb was a friend of the schoolmaster, Christopher Dock [*q.v.*], whom he persuaded to write a treatise on his teaching methods. In 1745, with Bishop Heinrich Funck, in behalf of the Mennonites of their section who wished to strengthen their children in the ancient principles of their faith, he arranged for a German translation of Tieleman Jans Van Braght's *Bloedigh Tooneel* (*Der Blutige Schau-platz,* 2 parts, 1748–49), a history of Christian martyrdom, with special emphasis on the Mennonites. Although the work of translating and printing was done by the Brotherhood of Dunkers at Ephrata, Kolb and Funck were responsible for reading the 1,512 pages of proof, word by word, comparing the German and Dutch to be sure that no errors were made.

He died in his sixty-sixth year, survived by his wife and an only child, Elizabeth, the wife of Andrew Ziegler.

[D. K. Cassel, *A Geneal. Hist. of the Kolb, Kulp or Culp Family* (1895); R. B. Strassburger, *The Strassburger and Allied Families of Pa.* (1922); S. W. Pennypacker, "A Noteworthy Book," *Pa. Mag. of Hist. and Biog.*, vol. V, No. 3 (1881); J. D. Souder, "The Life and Times of Dielman Kolb, 1691–1756," *Mennonite Quart. Rev.*, Jan. 1929.] D. M. C.

KOLB, REUBEN FRANCIS (Apr. 15, 1839–Mar. 23, 1918), Alabama planter and farm leader, was born at Eufaula, Ala., the son of Davis Cameron and Emily Frances (Shorter) Kolb. His father's ancestors came originally from Germany to South Carolina. He was educated in the public schools of Eufaula and at the University of North Carolina, graduating from the latter institution in 1859, at the age of twenty. From college he turned to cotton planting in his native county. On Jan. 3, 1860, he was married to Mary Caledonia Cargile, the daughter of a Barbour County planter. He represented Barbour in the secession convention, voted for secession, and joined the Confederate army at the outbreak of hostilities. He rose quickly from the rank of lieutenant to captain and distinguished himself on the battlefield of Chickamauga, where a memorial now stands to "Kolb's Battery." After the war he resumed his plantation activities and developed the "Kolb Gem" watermelon which became a favorite variety. In the movement for a scientific agriculture and for cooperation among the farmers he became a conspicuous figure. He was appointed state commissioner of agriculture in 1886 and in that capacity expanded greatly the services of the department and in various ways advertised the resources of the state abroad. He exhibited "Alabama on Wheels"—on a car furnished and operated by the Louisville & Nashville Railroad—to a quarter of a million people in the Central West. Vegetable and fruit farming profited especially from his advertising.

In youth Kolb had revealed a penchant for politics and had won his political spurs in the movement to rid the south of Carpet-baggers. He possessed all of the arts of a popular spokesman. He steered the farmers adroitly, and when the Alliancemen decided to go into politics they thought of no leader but him. In the heated battles that followed he became to the farmers "Our Patrick Henry." He stood for governor in the campaigns of 1890, 1892, and 1894, and threw the state into a tournament of debate and agitation. He made partisans of all—partisans who did not respect the good names of men or observe the canons of decent combat. Northern Republicans discussed the probability of his overthrowing the Democratic machine in Alabama. He accepted gracefully his defeat for governor and for United States senator in 1890, but when the party convention rejected him for governor in 1892 he carried the fight to the people, styling himself and his followers "Jeffersonian Democrats." The Jeffersonians and Populists nominated him for governor in 1894 and he engaged William C. Oates, candidate of the "Organized Democrats," in the most colorful campaign in the history of Alabama politics. The "Organized" labeled him a tool of Republican bosses of the North and the leader of those who desired to pillage and plunder. By scandalous manipulations they defeated him. Through the columns of his paper, the *People's Tribune* (Birmingham), Kolb continued for a while to thunder against election frauds. In 1910 he was again elected commissioner of agriculture, and in 1914 he was once more a candidate for governor, reminding many persons of his quondam name, suggested by his initials, "Run Forever Kolb." Eliminated in the first primary, he threw his support to the conservative candidate, Charles Henderson, in the second primary. This was a pathetic ending for one who had worn himself out fighting for progressive democracy in the state. His motives in supporting Henderson have often been questioned, but, whatever else may be said, he was an exponent of the new forces that began to shape the nation's life at the turn of the century. He died in Montgomery in his eightieth year.

[*Alumni Hist. of the Univ. of N. C.* (2nd ed., 1924); J. B. Clark, *Populism in Ala.* (1927); *Memorial Record of Ala.* (1893), vol. II; A. B. Moore, *Hist. of Ala.* (1927), vol. I; T. M. Owen, *Hist. of Ala. and Dict. of Ala. Biog.* (1921), vol. III; J. Sparkman, "The Kolb-Oates Campaign of 1894" (Univ. of Ala. thesis, 1924); Chas. G. Summersell, "Life of Reuben F. Kolb" (Univ. of Ala. thesis, 1930); *Montgomery Advertiser*, Mar. 24, 1918.] A. B. M.

KOLLE, FREDERICK STRANGE (Nov. 22, 1872–May 10, 1929), physician, pioneer in radiography and modern plastic surgery, was born in Hanover, Germany, the son of Johann A. and Bertha (Schaare) Kolle. Having received a German common-school education he emigrated to Brooklyn, where he entered the Long Island College Hospital Medical School, from which he received the degree of M.D. in 1893. Before graduation he had served as assistant in the ear department of the Brooklyn Eye and Ear Hospital and in 1893–94 he was interne in the Kings County Hospital. During 1894 he was also an assistant physician to the Brooklyn Hospital for Contagious Diseases. In the same year he opened an office in Brooklyn.

He became so familiar with the medical uses of electricity that in 1896 he was engaged to teach this branch in the Electrical Engineering Institute of Brooklyn and in the following year was made associate editor of the *Electrical Age,* a position which he held for five years. In 1896 he became interested in the then recent discovery of Röntgen rays and in 1898 published a booklet, *The X-Rays; Their Production and Application,* and received the appointment of radiographer to the Methodist Episcopal Hospital of Brooklyn. He did much to develop the technique of the new art and invented numerous devices, comprising a radiometer, the Kolle X-ray switching device, the dentaskiascope, folding fluoroscope, an X-ray printing process, the Kolle focus tube, and a direct-reading X-ray meter. At a somewhat later period he developed an interest in subcutaneous paraffin injections for cosmetic purposes and in 1908 published *Subcutaneous Hydrocarbon Prostheses.* This resource did not become a permanent one and Kolle was influenced in the direction of plastic and cosmetic surgery, in which he made numerous technical advances and devised new instruments and apparatus. In 1911 he published his major work, *Plastic and Cosmetic Surgery,* which gave him a wide reputation. The World War greatly enhanced the interest in this subject and Kolle's technique was largely employed by the military surgeons. In 1913 he compiled *The Physicians' Who's Who,* a reference work for the profession, which he dedicated to the memory of his former surgical teacher George Ryerson Fowler.

After 1914 Kolle withdrew entirely from public notice. He made no attempt to issue successive editions of his surgical and reference works and during and after the World War was conspicuous only by his absence from medical literature. It is known that his health failed and that he removed to Los Angeles, where he seems to have engaged only in general practice, if at all. Having developed a cancerous affection of the stomach, he came East and his death took place in St. Luke's Hospital, New York. Early in his career he showed a penchant for writing, published several books for children, among them *Fifty and One Tales of Modern Fairyland* (1905, 1910), and wrote a scientific novel, "Olaf." In 1899 he married Loretto Elaine Duffy, by whom he had two sons and a daughter.

[The date of birth is that given in *The Physicians' Who's Who* (1913); *Who's Who in America,* 1912–13, gives 1871; see also *Brooklyn Eagle,* and *N. Y. Times,* May 11, 1929; *Jour. Am. Medic. Asso.,* June 15, 1929.]

E. P.

KOLLOCK, SHEPARD (September 1750–July 28, 1839), journalist, publisher, was born at Lewes, Del., the youngest of the seven children of Shephard and Mary (Goddard) Kollock. He learned the printing business under his uncle William Goddard [*q.v.*] in the office of the *Pennsylvania Chronicle,* but when twenty years old he went for his health to St. Kitts and worked there at his trade until the news of Lexington and Concord sent him hurrying home to join the patriot forces. He is said, while in the West Indies, to have made the acquaintance of Alexander Hamilton and to have set type on Hamilton's narrative of the hurricane. After a short term in the artillery company of which Hamilton was captain, Kollock was commissioned Jan. 1, 1777, a first lieutenant in the 2nd Regiment (Col. John Lamb's) of Continental Artillery. On June 5 of that year he married Susan, daughter of Isaac Arnett, by whom he had eight children. He resigned from the army Jan. 3, 1779, in order to issue a newspaper in the Revolutionary cause, and on Feb. 16, 1779, published the first number of the *New Jersey Journal* at Chatham, N. J., where he was safely within Washington's lines but close enough to hear whatever news might transpire from the enemy. He also published the *United States Almanac* (1779–83), *Poems on the Capture of General Burgoyne* (1782), and twelve items of a religious character. In all twenty-two of his Chatham imprints have been discovered. He suffered frequently from a shortage of paper and sometimes received supplies from the Continental quartermaster. On the evacuation of New York he moved thither and launched on Dec. 3, 1783, the *New York Gazetteer,* which he published for three years. On Oct. 14, 1783, he also began, in partnership with his brother-in-law Shelly Arnett, the *Political Intelligencer* at New Brunswick, N. J. This partnership was dissolved within a year; in April 1785 Kollock moved the *Intelligencer* to Elizabethtown, N. J.; and on May 10, 1786, he renamed it the *New Jersey Journal.* Kollock continued to publish the *Journal* until with the issue of Sept. 8, 1818, he sold it to Peter Chatterton. Both in New York, where he issued the first directory of the city, and in Elizabeth he was a book publisher of importance. Most of his imprints are religious books; it is likely that he was influenced in his selection of titles by his pastor, the Rev. David Austin [*q.v.*]. From April–May 1789 to February–March 1791 he also issued the *Christian's, Scholar's, and Farmer's Magazine,* which was largely made up of serials. He was, in spite of his early association with Hamilton and Henry Knox, a good democrat and gave his enthusiastic support to Presidents Jefferson, Madison, Monroe, and

John Quincy Adams. He was an aide-de-camp to two governors of New Jersey, postmaster of Elizabeth, 1820–29, and a lay judge of the court of common pleas of Essex County for thirty-five years. To the end of his long life he remained pious, patriotic, vigorous, and serene, and was held in honor throughout the state. He died in Philadelphia while on a visit to one of his daughters and was buried in Elizabeth.

[E. J. Sellers, *Geneal. of the Kollock Family of Sussex County, Del.* (1897); F. B. Heitman, *Hist. Reg. of Officers of the Continental Army* (ed. 1914); Wm. Nelson, "Some New Jersey Printers and Printing in the 18th Century," *Proc. Am. Antiquarian Soc.*, new ser., vol. XXI (1911); C. S. Brigham, "Bibliog. of Am. Newspapers, 1690–1820," pt. VI, New Jersey, pt. VIII, New York City, *Ibid.*, new ser., vols. XXVI–XXVII (1916–17); C. H. Humphrey, "Check-List of N. J. Imprints to the End of the Revolution," *Papers of the Bibliog. Soc. of America*, vol. XXIV (1930); *Elizabeth Daily Jour.*, Feb. 26, 1929; E. F. Hatfield, *Hist. of Elizabeth, N. J.* (1868); Mary Kollock, sketch in the *Spirit of '76* (N. Y.), Jan. 1898; W. P. Tuttle, *Bottle Hill and Madison* (Madison, N. J., 1916); A. E. Vanderpoel, *Hist. of Chatham, N. J.* (1921); *Newark Daily Advertiser*, July 30, 1839.] G. H. G.

KOOPMAN, AUGUSTUS (Jan. 2, 1869–Jan. 31, 1914), painter and etcher, was born in Charlotte, N. C., son of Bernard and Johanna Koopman. He began his art studies at the Pennsylvania Academy of the Fine Arts, in Philadelphia, going later to Paris, where he entered the École des Beaux-Arts. For some time he also studied under Bouguereau and Robert-Fleury. Like many American artists he practically made France his home, wintering in Paris and spending the spring and summer in Étaples and in the near-by village of Equihen, where he found inspiration in the ocean, with its wind storms, disasters, and its boats. His "Horses Running to Meet a Boat," now in the St. Paul Art Institute, is a vigorous depiction of his subject. Full of movement also are "The Wind Storm" and "A Windy Day." In contrast to these pictures is the "Return of the Shrimpers," a quiet group trudging home from work. For this picture he received a medal at the St. Louis Exposition and he was especially invited to exhibit it at the Venice International Art Exposition in 1910. "Hoisting Sails" is rich in color with strong contrasts of light and shadow. His early work had many of the qualities characteristic of the modern Dutch artists, especially the marine painters Mesdag and Blommers. Later he came under the influence of the impressionists and the post-impressionists, without attaching himself to either school.

Koopman's work covered a wide range of themes. Besides marines, he painted some clever figure pictures and a notable decoration, "Industrial Arts," for the United States government pavilion at the Paris Exposition in 1900. Among his figure pictures "The Crystal Gazers" and the "Old Troubadour," the latter in the Philadelphia Art Club, are painted with great charm of pose and color. His dry-points and etchings were usually of fishermen, scenes in cafés, and figures, all done in careful line. He taught painting in Paris from 1896 to 1899 and was elected an associé of the Société Nationale des Beaux-Arts in 1912. From 1902 to 1906 he lived in London, where he specialized in portraits. He received many awards, medals, and prizes, among which were the special silver medal for his decoration at the Paris Exposition, bronze medals at the Pan-American Exposition at Buffalo in 1901 and at the St. Louis Exposition, and a silver medal at the Appalachian Exposition at Knoxville in 1911. His pictures gained favor for their marked individuality. He was in Étaples at the time of his death, working hard, in spite of a lingering illness. He had married, on May 6, 1897, Louise Lovett Osgood of Cohasset, Mass.

[J. W. Pattison, "Augustus Koopman—Painter of Emotions," *Fine Arts Jour.*, June 1913; E. A. Taylor, "The Paintings of Augustus Koopman," *Internat. Studio*, May 1914; *Who's Who in America*, 1912–13; *Am. Art Annual*, 1914; *N. Y. Times*, Feb. 3, 1914.] H. W.

KOOWESKOWE [See Ross, John, *c.* 1790–1866].

KOREN, JOHN (Mar. 3, 1861–Nov. 9, 1923), clergyman, statistician, was the son of Ulrik Vilhelm Koren [*q.v.*], a young Lutheran minister, who with his bride, Else Elisabeth (Hysing), arrived in the United States from Bergen, Norway, in November of 1853, and settled at Washington Prairie, near Decorah, Iowa. Here Bøicke Johan Rulffs, as he was named, was born. He received his education at Luther College, from which he graduated with the degree of A.B. in 1879, and proceeded to Concordia Seminary in St. Louis to prepare for the ministry. After his ordination in 1882 he held some minor pastorates in Chicago and Cleveland and in 1884 went to Boston, where for six years he served a small Lutheran church, preaching in Norwegian and German with equal proficiency. He left the ministry in 1890 never to return. Through the influence of Carroll D. Wright, whose niece, Katherine Orne Harnden, Koren married in 1894, he was appointed special representative of the Department of Labor and made two journeys abroad, in 1891 and 1893, to study the Gothenburg System of liquor control. To the end of the century he was engaged in the study of the liquor question for the Committee of Fifty and wrote a number of articles and monographs on the results of his investigations. His studies may have led to the interest in criminal statistics which he maintained for the rest of his life. Upon the resignation of Roland P. Falkner as expert special agent of the Bureau of the Census, Koren in 1903 was made his successor, a post he retained until 1912. In this capacity he planned the treatment of the statistical material and wrote the text analysis of the 1904 census of the population in penal institutions, hospitals for the mentally incompetent, almshouses, and benevolent institutions. He later planned the ill-fated and never published inquiry into criminal judicial statistics, the first undertaken by the Census Bureau. As chairman of the committees on statistics of the American Prison Association and the American Institute of Criminal Law and Criminology he constantly worked for the development of better and more nearly uniform data in criminal statistics. His association with the American Statistical Association was particularly fruitful. Member, and later chairman, of its committee on publications, he became in 1911 the first editor of its quarterly publications. As president of the Association in 1913–14, he made plans for an impressive symposium on the history of statistics, which, though delayed by the World War, finally appeared in 1918 (*The History of Statistics. Their Development and Progress in Many Countries,* 1918). In 1915 President Wilson appointed him American member of the International Prison Commission, a post which he retained until his death. Recognition of his ability as a statistician had also come to him in his home city where in 1914 he was appointed one of the trustees of the city department of statistics, later serving as chairman.

He was a man of simple life. His chief avocation was reading, which brought him a keen insight into national and international economic and social problems. The World War was a great blow to his peace-loving nature and the balanced view he took of the conflict caused some to regard him as unpatriotic. The petty persecutions to which he was subjected led him to withdraw from social contacts which his friendly nature had regarded as the boon of existence. Grown bitter as a result of his experiences, he suffered a nervous breakdown which ultimately led to his death. He disappeared one night from an Atlantic steamer nearing the American shore.

[For Koren's family background, J. M. Rohne, *Norwegian Am. Lutheranism up to 1872* (1926), and in particular his mother's diary, *Fra Pioneertiden: Uddrag af Fru Elisabeth Korens Dagbok og Breve fra Femtiaarene,* Udgivet af hendes Børn (Decorah, 1914); for personal data, Rasmus Malmin, O. M. Norlie, and O. A. Tingelstad, *Who's Who Among Pastors in all the Norwegian Lutheran Synods of America, 1843–1927* (1928); *Who's Who in America,* 1922–23; *Boston Transcript,* Nov. 17, 1923; *Nation,* Nov. 28, 1923; and *Jour. Am. Statistical Asso.,* Mar. 1924.] T. S.

KOREN, ULRIK VILHELM (Dec. 22, 1826–Dec. 20, 1910), Norwegian Lutheran clergyman, was born at Bergen, Norway, son of Paul Schonvig and Henriette Christiane (Rulffs) Koren. In the absence of the father who was a sea-captain until his death in 1842, the boy's mother supervised his education through the Lancaster school, the *Real* school and the Latin school of his native city. In 1844 he entered the university at Christiania (now Oslo), and in the course of eight difficult years he received the degrees of bachelor of arts, master of arts, and candidate of theology. After teaching a year at Nissen's Latin school, Christiania, Koren emigrated with his bride, Else Elisabeth Hysing, and reached the frontier settlement at Washington Prairie, near Decorah, Iowa, on Dec. 24, 1853. The next day he preached in a log hut the first of fifty-six annual Christmas sermons to the same congregation. He soon made his influence felt in the Norwegian Synod which had been organized by seven pastors and twenty-eight congregations a few months before his arrival. In 1857 the synod held its convention with his congregation and here steps were taken which led to the founding of Luther College in 1861. Koren not only selected the site for the school, at Decorah, Iowa, but forestalled the efforts that were made to move the school elsewhere after the fire in 1889. He engaged in extensive debates in the press concerning the principles and policies of the synod. These writings, now comprising the third volume of his works, collected and edited by his son Paul (*Samlede Skrifter,* 4 vols., 1912), cover a wide range of topics, chief among them being the question of predestination, which eventually split the synod. As its president (1894–1910) he had occasion to repair some of the damage done by these controversies. Clear, incisive, and polished in utterance, he was a powerful figure in the pulpit or on the platform, ranking among the best preachers in the Norwegian American Lutheran group. Throughout his published works it is the eloquent preacher and keen dialectician that speaks.

As pastor of the Little Iowa Congregation, as his vicinage was called, Koren ministered to his countrymen scattered over a large stretch of territory. As the land was taken up, this "congregation" was divided until it came to comprise about twenty separate congregations. For fifty-seven years he served the mother church at

Washington Prairie, which continued to be one of the most important of the Norwegian Lutheran congregations in America, both in point of membership and of influence. Besides the presidency of the synod, he held other important offices: secretary of the synod (1855), vice-president (1871–76), president of the Iowa district (1876–94). He was a member of the church council (1861–1910) and trustee of the synod (1887–1910). One of his sons was John Koren [*q.v.*], clergyman and statistician.

[J. Arndt Bergh, *Den Norsk Lutherske Kirkes Historie I Amerika* (1914); J. Magnus Rohne, *Norwegian American Lutheranism up to 1872* (1926); J. C. Jensson (Roseland), *Am. Lutheran Biogs.* (1890); O. N. Nelson, *Hist. of the Scandinavians and Successful Scandinavians in the U. S.* (1897); *Who's Who Among Pastors in All the Norwegian Lutheran Synods of America, 1843–1927* (1928); O. M. Norlie, O. A. Tingelstad and K. T. Jacobsen (ed. Comm.), *Luther College Through Sixty Years* (1922); Harold M. Tolo, "U. V. Koren," unpublished thesis for degree of M.A. at Univ. of Minn., copy at Luther College, Decorah, Iowa; *Dubuque Times-Jour.*, Dec. 21, 1910; *Sioux City Jour.*, Dec. 22, 1910.] J. M. R.

KÖRNER, GUSTAV PHILIPP (Nov. 20, 1809–Apr. 9, 1896), jurist, statesman, historian, son of Bernhard and Marie Magdelena (Kämpfe) Körner, was born in the free city of Frankfurt-am-Main where his father, an ardent German patriot, was a bookseller and dealer in works of art. Gustav received his early instruction in the model school (*Musterschule*) of Frankfurt and continued his preparation in the Gymnasium. In 1828 he entered the University of Jena to study jurisprudence. Here he joined forthwith the flourishing *Burschenschaft,* the patriotic student society which aimed at the unity and freedom of Germany, and which had its members in most German universities. Continuing his studies at the universities of Munich and Heidelberg, where he received his doctorate, he returned to Frankfurt where for a time he practised law. He took part in the revolutionary movements which had broken out in many parts of Germany. In the Frankfurt revolt of 1833 he was wounded, fled to France, and at Havre joined a number of friends who were about to sail for America. They arrived in New York on June 17, 1833, and proceeded at once to St. Louis, then the goal of many German immigrants who were attracted thither by Gottfried Duden's glowing description of Missouri. Körner and his party were, however, keenly disappointed when they discovered that the institution of slavery prevailed in this state. They therefore decided to settle in St. Clair County, Ill., where a number of their relatives and friends, mostly men and women of education and culture, had already purchased land. This colony, frequently known as the "Latin settlement," gradually became a cultural center which exerted a decided influence upon the intellectual and political life of the state, and eventually, under the leadership of Körner, upon national politics. On June 17, 1836, Körner was married to Sophie Engelmann, with whose family he had come to the United States.

To become acquainted with American law and to improve his English, Körner took a law course at Transylvania University at Lexington, Ky. Returning to Belleville, Ill., his future permanent residence, he practised his profession but soon found himself drawn into local and national politics, taking an active part in the campaigns of 1840 and 1844. In 1845 he was appointed justice of the Illinois supreme court, a post which he held until 1850. After the new constitution of Illinois, adopted in 1848, had made all state offices elective and reduced the salary of supreme court judges to the ridiculously small sum of $1,200, Körner refused the nomination for the position. In 1852 he was, however, nominated and elected lieutenant governor, which office he occupied until 1856.

In the meantime, the growing antislavery movement was engaging Körner's attention. Though originally a Democrat, like most of the older generation of Germans of this period, he did not hesitate to join the new Republican party, and by his example as well as by his eloquent speeches in the campaign of 1856 he did much to win over his countrymen to the Republican cause. A close friend of Abraham Lincoln, he took over some of the latter's law cases at Springfield and was consulted occasionally on important matters. Finally, in recognition of the many services which Körner had rendered the Union cause at the beginning of the Civil War, Lincoln, in 1862, appointed him minister to Spain, to succeed Carl Schurz. His chief task in this position was to counteract English and French attempts to bring about a joint recognition of the Confederacy, and to cultivate the traditional friendly relations with Spain. Difficult as his tasks were, Körner, with delicate diplomatic tact and fine understanding of the Spanish national character and culture, succeeded remarkably well. His book on Spain (*Aus Spanien,* 1867) shows how thoroughly he had studied and appreciated Spanish art, the natural beauties of the country, and the ethnic characteristics of its diverse population.

After his return from Spain (1864) he took little or no interest in active politics for a number of years. When the corruption of the Grant administration was growing more and more intolerable, however, he joined the Liberal Republican movement in 1872 and supported, though reluctantly, Horace Greeley. Again in 1876 he asserted his political independence as well as his steadfast devotion to the principles of the liberal movement by advocating the candidacy of Samuel Tilden against Hayes. Disappointed by the course of events following the election of 1876, he retired from his former active participation in politics and devoted the remaining years of his life almost exclusively to literary work. It was then that he wrote his valuable historical study entitled *Das Deutsche Element in den Vereinigten Staaten von Nordamerika* (1880). A keen observer of men, a profound and sympathetic student of American institutions, politics, and life in general, and a man of calm judgment, he was exceptionally qualified to write the history of one of the great constituent parts of the composite American population during a period the greater part of which he had followed as an eye witness. His object was "to show how strongly and to what extent the arrival of the Germans in large numbers since 1818 had influenced this country politically and socially." He was one of the first thus to recognize the importance of the ethnic problem in American historiography.

While it may be regretted that Körner did not include the German immigration of 1848 and the subsequent years in his history, the omission is partly compensated for by his autobiography which he finished shortly before his death. Although these reminiscences were written at the suggestion of his children and, therefore, record many matters pertaining to his immediate family, they unfold at the same time a fascinating picture of the cultural and political life of the nation and the important part which the German element played in it during the nineteenth century.

[The chief source of information is Körner's autobiography published under the title, *Memoirs of Gustave Koerner, 1809–1896: Life Sketches Written at the Suggestion of His Children* (1909), ed. by Thomas J. McCormack. H. A. Rattermann's German biography, *Gustav Körner, Deutsch-Amerikanischer Jurist, Staatzmann, Diplomat und Geschichtschreiber* (1902), is based essentially upon Körner's "Memoirs," the manuscript of which was placed at the author's disposal by the family. Other sources include: J. M. Palmer, *Bench and Bar of Ill.* (1899), vol. I; Newton Bateman and others, *Hist. Encyc. of Ill. and Hist. of St. Clair County* (1907), vol. I; *St. Louis Globe-Democrat*, Apr. 10, 1896.]

J. G.

KOŚCIUSZKO, TADEUSZ ANDRZEJ BONAWENTURA (Feb. 12, 1746–Oct. 15, 1817), Revolutionary soldier and Polish patriot, was born in the Palatinate of Breesc in the Grand Duchy of Lithuania (now Palatinate of Polesie, Poland). His father, an impoverished member of the small gentry, was a notary and cultivated part of the estate of Count Flemming. An aged uncle taught the youthful Kościuszko drawing, mathematics, and French. Alone he read Plutarch and became enamored of the heroes of antiquity. In his thirteenth year his father died and he was sent to the Jesuit College at Breesc; there he remained until he entered the Royal School at Warsaw in 1765. Four years later he graduated with the rank of captain and received a scholarship to France where, at Mézières, he studied engineering and artillery. Returning to Poland in 1774, he found few opportunities for his talents; and after an unfortunate love affair with Ludvika Sosnowska, in the course of which he almost lost his life at the hands of her father's retainers, he returned to Paris. There the announcement of the American Revolution stirred his imagination: he borrowed money and came to America. He arrived in Philadelphia in August 1776 and applied to various committees for appointment to service. The Pennsylvania Committee of Defense employed him, with Payne and De Lisle, to draw up plans for fortifying the Delaware River. The success of this work gained him a commission as colonel of engineers in the Continental Army (Oct. 18, 1776). In the spring of 1777 he joined the Northern Army under General Gates at Ticonderoga, where he advised the fortification of Mount Defiance. The failure to fortify this hill and its occupation by Burgoyne lost Ticonderoga to the Americans. Kościuszko's choice of battlefields and his erection of fortifications contributed greatly to the brilliant victory of the American forces over Burgoyne at Saratoga. In the spring of 1778 he was placed in charge of the building of fortifications at West Point, where he remained from March 1778 to June 1780. During his residence at West Point he formed an intimate friendship with Gates, and when the latter became commander in the South, he asked to have Kościuszko accompany him as chief of engineers. Before Kościuszko could join the army, however, Gates, following the battle of Camden, was removed and was replaced by Nathanael Greene [*q.v.*]. During the winter of 1780–81 Kościuszko explored the Catawba River. During Greene's masterly retreat before Lord Cornwallis in the campaign of 1781 Kościuszko was in charge of transportation. During the winter of 1782 he was stationed near Charleston, S. C., where he was more conspicuous as an officer of cavalry than as an engineer. He was among the first of the Continentals to enter Charleston after its evacuation by the British. He returned north with Greene in the spring of 1783 and at Newburgh, N. Y., was one of the founders of the Society of the Cincinnati. On Oct. 13, 1783, Congress made him a brigadier-general.

In July 1784 he left New York for Paris and from there went to Poland. After four years of rural retirement, in October 1789 he became major-general of the Polish army. During the spring of 1792 he led his tiny army in its brave resistance against the Russians; when the King succumbed to Russian intrigue, Kościuszko resigned his commission and determined to return to America. He went to France but in March 1794 returned to Poland to lead the famous rising. After several brilliant successes he became dictator, promulgated a series of liberal reforms, but at last, in October 1794, was defeated and captured by the Russians in the battle of Maciejowice. After two years of captivity he was released by Czar Paul I and in August 1797 he and several companions reached Philadelphia. Congress appropriated over fifteen thousand dollars which was due him and made him a land grant of five hundred acres in Ohio. While in America he visited Gates, Gen. Anthony W. White, and Jefferson. The traditional friendship between Washington and Kościuszko has no historical foundation; their infrequent relations were very formal. In May 1798 he secretly left America and returned to France. In 1800 at the request of Gen. William R. Davie he wrote in French his *Manoeuvres of Horse Artillery,* a translation of which was published in New York in 1808. He continued his brave but futile efforts for Polish freedom until his death in Switzerland in 1817. The funds arising from the sale of his Ohio lands were used to found the Colored School at Newark, N. J., one of the first educational institutions for negroes in America.

[*Memorial Exhibition: Thaddeus Kościuszko* (1927), catalogue of the memorial exhibition at the Anderson Galleries, New York, containing unpublished letters, introduction, etc.; Monica M. Gardner, *Kościuszko* (London, 1920); C. A. Manning, "Kościuszko et les États-Unis," in *Le Monde Slave* (Paris, Nov. 1925); J. Michelet, *La Pologne Martyr* (Paris, 1863); Karl Falkenstein, *Thaddäus Kościuszko* (ed. of 1834); S. Kunasiewicz, *T. Kościuszko w Ameryce* (Lwow, 1876).]

F. M—n.

KOYL, CHARLES HERSCHEL (Aug. 14, 1855–Dec. 18, 1931), civil engineer, was born in Amherstburg, Ontario, the son of Rev. Ephraim Lillie and Frances (Culp) Koyl. His early life was spent in Ontario, and in 1877 he graduated from Victoria College, Coburg. He continued his education at Johns Hopkins University, where, after two years' study, he was made a fellow in physics. After teaching mathematics and physics at various places in the United States and Canada, in 1887 he became instructor in physics and electrical engineering at Swarthmore College. On June 5, 1888, he patented a parabolic semaphore for use in railway signaling, and the following year was awarded the John Scott Legacy Medal of the Franklin Institute for this invention. In 1890 he began the practice of engineering in New York City. During this period he was for some time president of the National Switch & Signal Company, as well as the National Drying Company. In 1895–96 he was scientific assistant to the commissioner of street cleaning of New York City, and in this capacity did notable work, becoming an authority upon the disposal of municipal wastes.

While at Johns Hopkins he had become interested in municipal water treatment and he later became a pioneer in the treatment of industrial water supplies. In 1910 he was engaged by the Great Northern Railroad as engineer of water service to lessen, if possible, the cost to the road of procuring non-alkaline water for use in the locomotive boilers. He was extraordinarily successful in this undertaking and developed many ingenious schemes for softening water. Through his efforts he was able to effect a further saving of about $4000 per locomotive per year, by systematic removal of injurious matter from the water before it was put into the boilers.

This work continued to interest Koyl and in 1920 he became engineer of water service for the Chicago, Milwaukee & Saint Paul Railroad. His activities involved not only consideration of the location and design of suitable water-supply and treatment plants, but also the important feature of intensive education and check of employees in the proper handling of the work. Here again he was remarkably successful, and he continued his association with this railroad for the remainder of his life. He was a frequent contributor to technical journals on subjects in his special fields, among his notable papers being the following: "Municipal Refuse Disposal," a letter discussing a paper by J. T. Fetherston (*Transactions of the American Society of Civil Engineers,* vol. LX, 1908); "Prevention of Pitting in Locomotive Boilers by Exclusion of Dissolved Oxygen from Feedwater" (*Journal of the American Water Works Association,* August 1929); "The Preparation of Water for Railroad Use" (*Ibid.,* July 1930).

Koyl was married at Washington, D. C., Nov. 6, 1885, to Georgiana Thatcher Washburn. After her death, he married Adele T. Sanford, Apr. 27, 1901. He died at Evanston, Ill.

[*Who's Who in Engineering,* 1931; *Who's Who in America,* 1928–29; *Jour. of the Franklin Inst.,* Jan.,

Aug. 1889; *Specifications and Drawings of Patents Issued from the U. S. Patent Office,* June 1888; *Water Works and Sewerage,* Jan. 1932; *Engineering News-Record,* Dec. 24, 1931; *Chicago Daily Tribune,* Dec. 19, 1931.] H. K. B—s.

KRAEMER, HENRY (July 22, 1868–Sept. 9, 1924), botanist, pharmacognosist, was born in Philadelphia, Pa., the only son of John Henry and Caroline Kraemer, both of whom died when he was four years old. At the age of nine he entered Girard College, from which he graduated in 1883. Three years later, while serving his apprenticeship in the drugstore of C. B. Lowe, he entered the Philadelphia College of Pharmacy. He completed the course in 1889 and was awarded the John M. Maisch and Henry C. Lea prizes for his thesis, "A Microscopical and Chemical Study of White Oak Bark," in which he demonstrated, already, a leaning toward pharmacognosy. During his senior year he had been assistant to Prof. Samuel P. Sadtler, in chemistry, at the University of Pennsylvania, and the year after his graduation he was appointed instructor in botany and pharmacognosy in the New York College of Pharmacy. In 1891 he matriculated in the school of mines of Columbia University, from which he received the degree of bachelor of philosophy in 1895. He was appointed professor of botany, pharmacognosy, and materia medica in the school of pharmacy of Northwestern University in the same year, but was granted a year's leave before taking up his teaching work. This time he spent at the University of Marburg, Germany, where he studied botany under Prof. Dr. Arthur Meyer and attended lectures on philosophy, chemistry, and physics. He received the degree of doctor of philosophy *cum laude,* the title of his inaugural dissertation being *"Viola tricolor L., in morphologischer, anatomischer and biologischer Beziehung."* Returning to the United States, he took up his duties at Northwestern University, but after a year was elected to the chair of botany and pharmacognosy in the Philadelphia College of Pharmacy. He held this position until 1917, when he accepted the chair of pharmacognosy and pharmacy in the school of pharmacy at the University of Michigan. Two years later he was appointed dean of the school, but retired in 1920 and devoted his few remaining years to research in his chosen field. On Dec. 26, 1894, he married Theodosia Ernest Rich of Asheville, N. C. Although a daughter was born to this union, it was not entirely happy, and there was a separation in 1919. In 1922, Kraemer married Minnie Behm of Mount Clemens, Mich., who had been his secretary and assistant at the University of Michigan. He was a loyal member of many scientific societies and served actively on their committees. He was editor of the *American Journal of Pharmacy,* 1899–1917, reporter on the progress of pharmacy for the American Pharmaceutical Association, 1892–95; and collaborator on the *Pharmaceutical Review.* He was the author of *A Text Book of Botany and Pharmacognosy* (1902), *Applied and Economic Botany* (1914), *Scientific and Applied Pharmacognosy* (1915), and was botanical editor of *The Dispensatory of the United States of America* (20th edition, 1918). Kraemer was not only a true scientist and inspiring teacher, but also a philosopher, whose clear thinking has enriched pharmaceutical literature by many valuable contributions of an ethical and cultural nature as well as by pure scientific dissertations.

[*Who's Who in America,* 1924–25; *Am. Jour. Pharmacy,* July 1895; *The First Century of the Phila. Coll. of Pharmacy* (1922); *Am. Druggist,* LXXII (1924), 58; *Jour. Am. Pharmaceutical Asso.,* Oct. 1924; *Druggists' Circular,* Oct. 1924; *Modern Druggist,* XIII (1924), 19; *Jour. Nat. Asso. Retail Druggists,* Sept. 18, 1924; *Nat. Druggist,* LIV (1924), 480; *Practical Druggist and Pharmaceutical Rev.,* XLII (1924), 58; *Detroit Free Press,* Sept. 11, 1924.] A. G. D–M.

KRANTZ, PHILIP [See Rombro, Jacob, 1858–1922].

KRAUS, JOHN (Feb. 2, 1815–Mar. 4, 1896), educator, was the son of Jacob Kraus, a farmer of considerable means in Nassau, Germany, and of Margaretha (Herbst) Kraus, who died when John was still a child. He attended the public schools of Nassau and distinguished himself for his proficiency in mathematics. At the age of twenty he was assigned to military duty at Wiesbaden. Later he entered a teachers' seminary at Idstein. He was induced to prepare for teaching because of his interest in the principles of pedagogy advanced by Pestalozzi. After meeting Froebel in 1844 he became an ardent advocate of his kindergarten theory, and as a disciple of Froebel soon gained national prominence and governmental recognition. This recognition brought him into contact with various educators in different parts of Germany as well as in other European countries.

In 1851 he came to the United States. Here he established schools and through his lecturing and teaching spread the educational principles of both Pestalozzi and Froebel. He was among the first to write for publication on the principles of the kindergarten. His clarity of expression and forcefulness attracted attention, and in 1867 he was invited by Henry Barnard [*q.v.*], the first United States commissioner of education, to become associated with his organization. Kraus accepted, primarily in order to promote his kindergarten theories on a national scale. His publications in the daily press aroused much interest in kindergarten work. In 1872 he was a member of a committee of the National Education Association which, after study of the problems involved, urged the application of Froebel's principles of education not only to the kindergarten but also to the primary and advanced grades of the elementary schools of America. In 1873 Kraus was married to Maria Boelté [see Kraus-Boelté, Maria], whose work as a kindergarten specialist he had studied both in Germany and in England. He resigned his position in the United States Bureau of Education and with his wife organized a seminary for kindergarten teachers in New York City, which, with her cooperation, he conducted until his death in 1896. In 1877 they published a two-volume work entitled *The Kindergarten Guide*. Kraus's character reflected the early religious training which he received from his father. His life was free from selfishness and devoted to his educational ideas. He died in New York City.

[See introduction to *The Kindergarten Guide* (2 vols., 1877); *Kindergarten News*, Apr. 1896; Laura Fisher, "The Kindergarten," in *U. S. Bur. of Educ., Report of the Commissioner, 1903* (1905); Paul Monroe, *A Cyc. of Educ.*, vol. III (1912); Mary Lee Williams, "The Kindergarten in the United States," *Educ. Exchange*, Dec. 1912; H. S. Tarbell, "John Kraus," in *Addresses and Jour. of Proc. of the Nat. Educ. Asso.*, 1896, pp. 229–30; *N. Y. Tribune*, Mar. 6, 1896.]

N. H. D.

KRAUS-BOELTÉ, MARIA (Nov. 8, 1836–Nov. 1, 1918), educator, was a native of Hagenow in the Duchy of Mecklenburg-Schwerin, Germany. She was the daughter of Johann Ludwig Ernst Boelté, a lawyer of distinction, known for his wide learning, and of Louise (Ehlers) Boelté. Her girlhood was spent in a home marked by high standards of esthetics and morals; her early education was extensive and thorough. An account of Froebel's kindergarten awakened her interest in the education of young children. Later she studied with Froebel's widow (his second wife) and with Dr. Wichard Langé. During this time she also studied at a seminary for teachers, and on the completion of her work there went to London where she assisted Madame Bertha Rongé, a pupil of Froebel's, in her kindergarten and school. Then, thrown on her own resources, she taught various subjects including German and Swedish gymnastics and kindergarten methods in the family of Chief Justice Lord Denman. Her methods included studies of plants and animals, garden work, and excursions for the purpose of studying nature. In 1862 at the London International Exhibition she had charge of kindergarten work done by her own pupils. In 1867 she became a student in the South Kensington School of Art. Late that year she went to Hamburg and taught in the Froebel Union. Her work here was interrupted by severe illness, but she subsequently organized a successful kindergarten school at Lübeck, and developed a program for preparing kindergarten teachers. Froebel's widow visited her at Lübeck and commended her highly for exemplifying the Froebel theory of kindergarten education. She returned to England in 1870 and in 1872 came to America, where she began her kindergarten work under the sponsorship of Henrietta B. Haines.

In 1873 she married John Kraus [*q.v.*], whose writings on the kindergarten had led to a lively correspondence between them. Together they organized in New York the Normal Training Kindergarten with its model schools. It is reported that hundreds of students attended the institution and that over two thousand children came under its teaching. After her husband's death in 1896, Maria Kraus-Boelté carried on the work for some time, retiring in 1913 to devote herself to lecturing and writing. In 1903, 1904, and 1907 she lectured at the New York University Summer School. A woman of unusual personal charm, she left an indelible stamp on education in America. In addition to her lecturing and teaching, she wrote several monographs and articles and with her husband prepared *The Kindergarten Guide* (2 vols., 1877). She died in Atlantic City, N. J.

[The chief sources of information are: *The Kindergarten Guide*; Mrs. Kraus-Boelté's "Reminiscences of Kindergarten Work," in *Papers on Froebel's Kindergarten* (1881), ed. by Henry Barnard; and her paper on "The Kindergarten and the Mission of Women: My Experience as Trainer of Kindergarten Teachers in this Country, with Illustrations of the Work of the Latter," in *Addresses and Proc. of the Nat. Ed. Asso.* (1877), pp. 207–13. See also Susan Elizabeth Blow, "Kindergarten Education," in *Monographs on Educ. in the U. S.* (1900), ed. by N. M. Butler; C. P. Dozier, "Hist. of the Kindergarten Movement in the United States," *Educ. Bi-monthly*, Apr. 1908; *Who's Who in America*, 1906–07; "Mme. Maria Kraus-Boelté and her Training Work," *Kindergarten Magazine and Pedagogical Digest*, Apr. 1907; J. B. Merrill, in *Kindergarten Mag.*, Dec. 1918; *Kindergarten Messenger*, June 1874; *N. Y. Tribune*, *N. Y. Times*, Nov. 3, 1918.]

N. H. D.

KRAUSKOPF, JOSEPH (Jan. 21, 1858–June 12, 1923), rabbi, was born at Ostrowo, Prussia, to Hirsch Krauskopf and his wife, *née* Gilderslede. In his will he tells us that he made his own way in life from the age of twelve. Coming to the United States as a lad of fourteen, he was employed as a grocery clerk in Fall River, Mass. On the opening of the Hebrew Union College in Cincinnati in 1876, he entered it and graduated as rabbi in its first class, 1883. He began his rabbinical career with Congregation Benai Jehuda in Kansas City. On Oct. 22, 1887, he accepted a call to Congregation Keneseth Israel, Philadelphia, to which he ministered for the rest of his life. Under him the congregation grew from 150 to 1,500 families. In contrast to his scholarly predecessor, Samuel Hirsch, Krauskopf was from the beginning the energetic, practical, public rabbi. He at once made Sunday services a regular feature, and his topical addresses, which attracted large audiences, were often quoted in the local press and were regularly printed and widely disseminated for thirty-six years. Some of his first lectures led in 1888 to the formation of the Jewish Publication Society of America. He published *The Union Hebrew Reader* (1883) and *Bible Ethics* (1884), both in collaboration with H. Berkowitz; *The Service Manual* (1892), often reprinted; *The Service Ritual* (1888), revised as *The Service Hymnal* (1904); and *A Rabbi's Impressions of the Oberammergau Passion Play* (1908).

Among his innumerable public activities were his share in the establishment of stations for relief of distress in 1893, his efforts to have Philadelphia's old tenements replaced by model dwellings, his service as one of the three special field commissioners in the Spanish-American War, his work as member of the Pennsylvania Child Labor Committee, as founder of the Patriotic Society of Philadelphia, and as a director (1901–19) of the Philadelphia Federation of Jewish Charities. His outstanding monument is the National Farm School at Doylestown, Pa. This grew out of his desire to study the conditions in Russia, which were then driving multitudes of Jews to America. In 1894 he resolved to visit Russia, but Russia granted to Jews no permits to enter the country. Krauskopf insisted on his rights as an American citizen, and while they were becoming a matter of international discussion and proposed legislative action, he set out, and, though without the necessary visa, he was permitted to enter. The Jewish agricultural school at Odessa impressed him deeply. Tolstoy warned him against urban exploitation of Jews in America, urging their settlement on the undeveloped soil of the new land. With this inspiration Krauskopf founded in 1896, and through a quarter of a century of untiring devotion fostered the growth of, the National Farm School, a non-sectarian institution. In recognition of these services, he was appointed by the United States Department of Agriculture, in 1900, special commissioner to the Paris Exposition to report on exhibits of agricultural schools and to investigate agricultural education and agricultural conditions in Europe; he also served as director of the Jewish Commission of Herbert Hoover's department of food administration in 1917. A leader in reform Judaism, he was elected vice-president of the Pittsburgh Conference in 1885, and president of the Central Conference of American Rabbis in 1903. In that year, as director general of the Isaac M. Wise Memorial Fund for the Hebrew Union College, he raised over $300,000 almost singlehanded.

Krauskopf's death was hastened by his intense application to work. He was a large-hearted humanitarian, interested in men, understanding their needs, and possessing a gift for public service. As a master of clear, incisive and vivid discourse, he was in Philadelphia the recognized spokesman of his people, popularizing Jews and Judaism in circles beyond the confines of the synagogue. Finally, through methodical, efficient application, executive capacity, and indomitable will, he made his dreams come true. He was that rare combination, a practical idealist, preacher and organizer, visionary and publicist, dreamer and builder. His first wife, Rose, sister of his colleague Henry Berkowitz, bore him three children; his second, Sybil Feinman, who survived him, a daughter.

[*Jewish Exponent* (Phila.), June 15 and 22, 1923; Abraham J. Feldman in *Am. Jewish Year Book*, vol. XXVI (1924); *Central Conference of Am. Rabbis, Thirty-fourth Ann. Convention*, vol. XXXIII (1923); *Who's Who in America*, 1920–21; *Am. Hebrew* and *Jewish Tribune*, June 15, 1923; *Public Ledger*, June 13, 1923; information as to certain facts from Mrs. Krauskopf.]

D. deS. P.

KRAUTH, CHARLES PHILIP (May 7, 1797–May 30, 1867), Lutheran clergyman, college president, was born at New Goshenhoppen, Montgomery County, Pa., the second of the eight children of Charles James and Katherine (Doll) Krauth. His father, who was then parish teacher and church organist under the Rev. F. W. Geissenhainer, was born in Germany and is said to have been proud and handsome, like his wife, who was a native of Pennsylvania. During Krauth's boyhood and youth the family lived successively in Philadelphia, York, Baltimore, Winchester, and Norfolk, always poor but always respected. Krauth began the study of medicine in Norfolk under William Boswell Selden [*q.v.*] and at the University of Maryland but was compelled to desist for lack of funds. On the way to Frederick, Md., to borrow from his uncle, he met the Rev. David Frederick Schaeffer [*q.v.*] on the stagecoach, and Schaeffer soon had young Krauth for a pupil. Later he sent him to Winchester, Va., where the Rev. Abraham Reck was ill and needed a helper. Krauth was licensed in Baltimore in 1819 by the ministerium of Pennsylvania, was pastor at Martinsburg and Shepherdstown, Va. (now W. Va.) 1819–27 and of St. Matthew's, Philadelphia, 1827–33; first president of Pennsylvania (now Gettysburg) College 1834–50; and professor in Gettysburg Theological Seminary 1850–67. On Dec. 7, 1820, he married Catharine Susan Heiskell of Staunton, Va., who died in January 1824, leaving him with a daughter and a son, Charles Porterfield Krauth [*q.v.*]. On his removal to Gettysburg he married Harriet Brown of that place, who also bore him a daughter and a son. From the beginning of his long ministry Krauth was a man of mark. He was one of the founders of the Synod of Maryland and Pennsylvania in 1820 and of the Gettysburg Theological Seminary in 1825. As a young man he aided his teacher, D. F. Schaeffer, in editing the *Lutheran Intelligencer*; in later life he was an editor (1850–61) of the *Evangelical Review*. In Philadelphia, where he enjoyed the quickening friendship of Charles Rudolph Demme [*q.v.*] and had access to good libraries, he studied languages and theology assiduously, acquired a respectable knowledge of several fields, and made himself the best Hebraist in his denomination. Though largely self-educated, he proved to be a wise and capable college president. In spite of a weak voice he won a reputation as a preacher. He was president of the General Synod in 1848. In theology he was more conservative than his friend and colleague, Samuel Simon Schmucker [*q.v.*], but he regarded only the Augsburg Confession as authoritative, made use of revivals and other "new measures," and cared more for Christian fellowship than for complete uniformity in doctrine. In the controversy between the Old and the New Lutherans he maintained friendly relations with members of both parties, was claimed by both, and gave his full sympathy to neither. His one singularity was long remembered; in saluting a person he would raise his hat from behind instead of from in front; friends chided him in vain, he never gave up the habit. During the battle of Gettysburg his house was used as a Confederate hospital. To John Gottlieb Morris [*q.v.*], and to many others who knew him, he seemed the perfect embodiment of the ideal of the Christian scholar and gentleman. He taught in the Seminary until ten days before his death.

[M. L. Stoever, memoir in *Evangelical Quart. Rev.*, Jan. 1868; J. G. Morris, *Fifty Years in the Luth. Ministry* (1878); E. S. Breidenbaugh, *Pa. Coll. Book, 1832–82* (1882); A. Spaeth, *Charles Porterfield Krauth* (2 vols., 1898–1909); *Doc. Hist. of the Evangelical Luth. Ministerium of Pa.* (1898); A. R. Wentz, *Hist. of the Evangelical Luth. Synod of Md.* (1920) and *Hist. of Gettysburg Theol. Seminary* (1926); S. G. Hefelbower, *The Hist. of Gettysburg Coll.* (1932).] G. H. G.

KRAUTH, CHARLES PORTERFIELD (Mar. 17, 1823–Jan. 2, 1883), Lutheran clergyman, theologian, educator, and author, was born in a Lutheran manse at Martinsburg, Va. (now W. Va.). His mother, Catharine Susan Heiskell, was of English descent, a member of a family of culture and prominence. His father, Charles Philip Krauth [*q.v.*], of German and French ancestry two generations removed, was one of Lutheran America's brilliant leaders of that century. To follow the events in the life of Charles Porterfield Krauth is to trace the course of Lutheranism in America of the Mühlenberg tradition as it turned away from a developing American type of liberalism to a resuscitation of an older European form of confessional conservatism. Not only was he the epitome of that change but in a very real way was he identified with it as its most conspicuous champion. Surrounded by an academic environment, he developed early in life studious habits and a taste for books and learning which culminated in a library of some fifteen thousand carefully selected and rare books, notably of the kind "out of which other books are made." At the age of sixteen, he graduated from the college over which his father presided and two years later (1841) from the seminary. One of his teachers was the great champion of liberal Lutheranism in America, Samuel Simon Schmucker [*q.v.*], against whose theological views the pupil was later to set up a school. While still in his teens he was licensed and ordained (1842) to the Lutheran ministry.

One could hardly say that his pastoral ministry was especially eventful. His parishes at Canton and Baltimore, Md., Shepherdstown and Martinsburg, Va. (now W. Va.), were small; his quiet ministry in Winchester, Va., he regarded as the happiest period of his life (1848–55); then followed pastorates of increasing responsibilities in Pittsburgh and Philadelphia. The seclusion of his study, meanwhile, brought to his pulpit and pen messages of increasing power; it became evident that through his rigorous and systematic study he was marked for theological and ecclesiastical leadership. In the early years of his career he openly defended the rather broad platform of the General Synod which had declared that "the fundamental doctrines of the Word of God are taught in a manner substantially correct in the doctrinal articles of the Augsburg Confession." His reaction against such a platform in favor of a return to a close allegiance to the symbolical books of an older European Lutheranism can be traced to the influence which the Great Immigration, bringing with it many conservative German Lutherans to America, had in bringing to light an almost unknown tradition among native Lutherans. Already, through the repeated admonitions of his father, Krauth had entered upon an intensive study of German theological literature, especially the earlier dogmaticians together with the confessional books themselves. In time he became convinced that an unequivocal stand upon the confessional standards was the *sine qua non* of Lutheranism.

When the crisis came to a head in the so-called Platform controversy in the fifties, and later, when a native Lutheranism protested against a European, the leading figures in opposite camps were S. S. Schmucker and Krauth. Through his support of and contributions to the *Evangelical Review,* a journal set up to counteract the more radical influence of Kurtz's *Lutheran Observer,* as well as other literary expressions, through his recognized ability as a public debater of unusual strength both in logical argumentation and skilled diplomacy, through a growing recognition of his knowledge and successful executive leadership, he soon stood above his fellow ministers and won from them an unquestioned place of leadership. In the heat of controversy, questions of debate were with him kept separate from those of personal friendship; he was able to win and keep the admiration of his opponents. Conservative Lutheranism in America has hardly had since his day a champion of its cause to match him.

As editor-in-chief of *Lutheran and Missionary* (1861–67) he wielded tremendous influence for his cause. As first professor of "systematic divinity" in the newly formed theological seminary (1864) at Mt. Airy, Philadelphia (established in opposition to that of Gettysburg), over a period of nearly two decades, and by the product of his prolific pen, especially by that collection of papers published under the title, *The Conservative Reformation and Its Theology* (1871), his *magnum opus,* he set the stamp of his own theology upon a whole generation and more of American Lutheran ministers. He was consulted upon matters not only of doctrine but those of polity, liturgical art, and practice. The conservative character of the General Council (organized, 1867, in opposition to the General Synod) was in reality the child after his own heart. For two years (1866–68) he was a trustee of the University of Pennsylvania; from 1868 to his death he served on its faculty as professor of "moral and intellectual philosophy"; and in 1873 he was elected vice-provost of the university. With the establishment in 1882 of the *Lutheran Church Review,* a theological journal expressing the Mt. Airy theology, he became its editor-in-chief. He was a valued member of the American Revision Committee of the Old Testament from its organization in 1871 until his death. Krauth was twice married: in 1844 to Susan Reynolds and in 1855 to Virginia Baker. Two notable voyages took him away from the tasks set up by a self-imposed rigorous discipline and routine, in 1852–53 to St. Thomas and Santa Cruz where he came into close fellowship with Protestant communions other than his own; and, in 1880, through the generous provision of friends, he made a hurried visit in Europe collecting material for a contemplated biography of Luther. He died in Philadelphia.

[Sources include: Adolph Spaeth, *Chas. Porterfield Krauth* (2 vols., 1898–1909), containing a comprehensive bibliography of Krauth's publications; *Documentary Hist. of the Gen. Council of the Evangelical Luth. Ch. in North America* (1912); *Phila. Seminary Biog. Record* (1923); *Luth. Ch. Rev.,* Apr., July 1883; *Proc. Am. Philosophical Soc.,* vol. XX (1883), *Bible Soc. Record,* Feb. 15, 1883; *Press* (Phila.), Jan. 3, 1883. For the immediate background of the Krauthian development of American Lutheran theology, see Vergilius Ferm, *The Crisis in Am. Luth. Theology* (1927).]

V. F.

KREHBIEL, CHRISTIAN (Oct. 18, 1832–Apr. 30, 1909), Mennonite preacher, colonizer, was born at Weierhof in the Palatinate, the son of Johannes and Katharina (Krehbiel) Krehbiel. His formal education was limited. When, at the age of eleven, he removed with his parents to Klein Schwabhausen, Bavaria, he received compulsory religious education an hour a week for three years. Possessed of keen observation and a retentive memory, he soon gained a wide range of practical information. When he arrived at the age of eighteen, his parents, who were non-resistants, sold their property at a great sacrifice and came to America in order that their sons might escape compulsory military service. Young Krehbiel first worked on a farm at Hayesville, Ohio, but soon went westward by water via Cincinnati, Cairo, Ill., and Keokuk, to Lee County, Iowa, on the frontier. Here he lived in a log house, wielding the axe and the cradle, and receiving for his services as farmhand one hundred dollars a year. In 1858 he married Susanna A. Ruth, who became the mother of sixteen children and shared his life for over fifty years. In 1860 they removed to Summerfield, Ill., a new settlement, where he farmed successfully for nineteen years, at the same time extending his sphere of usefulness to wider fields. In 1864 he was elected to the Mennonite ministry, in which capacity he served forty-five years without pay. In the same year, though at that time he had four small children, he was drafted to serve in the Federal army, but was relieved by hiring a substitute.

Krehbiel was one of the earliest members of the General Conference of the Mennonite Church of North America. He preached the dedicatory sermon at the founding (1866) of the first Mennonite institution for higher learning, which was opened at Wadsworth, Ohio, Jan. 2, 1868. Plain, intensely practical, with strong convictions and unswerving faith, he was at this time a man of impressive physical strength. Though he was not tall, his muscular body, his deep, resonant voice, his untrimmed, black beard and unruly hair combined to suggest his vigorous personality. In 1872 he began an agitation for a settlement of Mennonites in Kansas. He bought land in the central part of the state, and, as president of the Mennonite Board of Guardians, interested co-religionists in the eastern states and in southern Russia, with the result that in 1874 about six thousand Mennonites settled in Harvey, Marion, MacPherson, Butler, and Reno counties. The success with which the immigrants from Russia raised the Turkey-red hard winter wheat that they had brought with them was instrumental in giving Kansas its position as the leading wheat state of the Union. Krehbiel was co-organizer and first president (1872) of the Foreign Mission Board of his denomination, an office which he held for twenty-four years. During that period missions were established among the Arapaho and Cheyenne Indians in the Indian Territory and among the Hopis in Arizona. In 1879 Krehbiel removed to Kansas, where in the early eighties he was one of the leaders in establishing the Mennonite Academy at Halstead, from which developed Bethel College at Newton. From 1886 to 1896 he superintended an Indian industrial mission school on his own 640-acre farm near Halstead, where thirty to forty Indians were trained annually. For ten years after that he made his farm an orphan home through the medium of which eighty-seven children were placed in Christian homes. In 1908 he organized the Mennonite Charite, an organization which owned the Halstead Hospital, now an institution with 140 beds. On Apr. 29, 1909, while he was working on his farm, a strong wind hurled a large barn door upon him, injuring him so badly that he died the next day.

[H. P. Krehbiel, *The Hist. of the Gen. Conf. of the Mennonites of North America* (1898); C. Henry Smith, *The Mennonites of America* (1910); *Mennonite Year-Book*, 1910; *Jubilaums-Fest der Allg. Konferenz* (1909); G. Harder, *Ein Ueberblick ueber die Missionstaetigkeit* (1915); *A Biog. Hist. of Central Kan.* (1902), vol. II; H. F. Weber, *Centennial Hist. of the Mennonites of Ill., 1829–1929* (1931); *Topeka State Jour.*, May 3, 1909.] E. E. L.

KREHBIEL, HENRY EDWARD (Mar. 10, 1854–Mar. 20, 1923), music critic, historian, author, and lecturer, was the third of nine children born to Jacob and Anna Marie (Haacke) Krehbiel. The father was born in Wachenheim, Hesse-Darmstadt, Germany, but came to America when a very young child with his parents, who settled in Cleveland, Ohio. The mother was born in southern Germany and came to America at the age of seventeen. Jacob Krehbiel entered the German Methodist ministry as a young man and became a circuit rider through southern Michigan. For one year (1853–54) he lived in Ann Arbor and there Henry Edward was born. In 1864 the elder Krehbiel was sent to Cincinnati by the Central German Conference and his children attended the public schools of that city. As a boy Henry Edward displayed unusual musical talent. He had a few violin lessons and was able to lead the choir in his father's church, where he developed an interest in church music. Aside from his public-school training he was largely self-educated and he rose to a place of influence chiefly through his own efforts. He had no college training, but he was by instinct a student. For a time he studied law, but he soon dropped this for journalism, which field he entered as a reporter for the *Cincinnati Gazette*. Before long he became a "star reporter," with varied experiences with murder cases, base-ball news, boat-races, and the like. In his leisure moments he devoted himself to the study of music and in time he became the music editor of the *Gazette*, which position he filled from 1874 to 1880. Upon the invitation of Whitelaw Reid he went to New York to succeed the veteran music critic of the *Tribune*, John R. G. Hassard, who was not well and desired to be relieved, but was filled with uncertainty as to the young man's abilities. For a time Krehbiel did general work on the *Tribune*, as he had done in Cincinnati. Meantime he prepared himself more solidly in his chosen field, so that when Hassard's health made his retirement imperative, he took over the full duties of music critic, a position which he held for forty-three years.

Though at heart a classicist, Krehbiel was the champion of Wagner and did much to awaken an appreciation not only for this master, but for all things new at that time. He had a warm appreciation for Brahms, whom he valiantly defended against the attacks of fellow critics. He was quick to recognize the merits of Dvořák's "New World Symphony" at its first performance, of

Tschaikowsky's Sixth Symphony, and indeed, his judgment as a critic was remarkably just and accurate, for he was open-minded and generous. The weakest link in his critic's armor was his strange dislike for Theodore Thomas, notwithstanding the conductor's contribution to American music life. Krehbiel was a man of rare culture and possessed a remarkable memory which was of value to him in building historical backgrounds for his criticisms. He spoke German and English with equal fluency and acquired a reading knowledge of French, Italian, Russian, and Latin. In addition to his familiarity with the whole literature of music he had a deep fondness for folk music, especially negro folk tunes, and made a large collection of "Spirituals." He held that since they emanated from one group in America, they were entitled to be classified as American folksongs, and, though not the product of the dominating race, they had qualities that appealed to any race. He also did much research work in Indian music, some of the results of which he presented at the congress of musicians during the World's Columbian Exposition at Chicago. He was a member of the international jury of awards in Paris, at the Exposition Universelle in 1900, and in acknowledgment of his services received the decoration of chevalier of the Legion of Honor.

Krehbiel's greatest literary achievement was no doubt his edition of Alexander Wheelock Thayer's *Life of Ludwig van Beethoven* (1921) in three volumes. The work is not a translation of the German version (in which language it was first published), but it was built upon the mass of original material which Thayer had accumulated and which came into Krehbiel's hands from both Thayer and Hermann Deiters, the German translator. The third and last volume is almost entirely Krehbiel's own interpretation of the voluminous notes which Thayer collected but never used. He also made use of material which had more recently come to light. His other works include: *Studies in the Wagnerian Drama* (1891); *A Book of Operas* (1909); *Chapters of Opera* (1908, 1911); *The Pianoforte and its Music* (1911); *A Second Book of Operas* (1917); *Afro-American Folk-Songs* (1914); *More Chapters of Opera* (1919); and an English version of *Parsifal* (1919). He was twice married. His first wife, whom he married in Cincinnati in 1880, was Helen Osborne of Derby, Conn., an organist and writer. In Cincinnati she wrote under the pen name of "Solomon Owl" for the children's magazine, *Golden Hours.* Later she wrote for New York papers under the name of "Rolling Stone." His second wife, whom he married in Brooklyn, N. Y., in 1896, and who survived him, was Marie Van of Cincinnati, a professional singer of American birth but of French parentage.

[L. C. Elson, *The Hist. of Am. Music* (1904); H. E. Krehbiel, "Alexander Thayer and His Life of Beethoven," *Musical Quart.*, Oct. 1917; the *Baton,* Dec. 1922; *Music and Letters,* July 1923; *Musical Courier,* Mar. 29, 1923; the *Sun* (N. Y.), Mar. 20, 1923; *N. Y. Times, N. Y. Tribune,* Mar. 21, 1923; information as to certain facts from Mrs. Charles Krehbiel, Krehbiel's sister-in-law, and from Mrs. Henry Edward Krehbiel.]

F. L. G. C.

KREZ, KONRAD (Apr. 27, 1828–Mar. 9, 1897), poet, was born at Landau, Rhenish Bavaria, the son of Jean Baptiste and Luise Henrietta (Naas) Krez. His father had been an officer in the Bavarian army; when Prince Otto was made King of Greece in 1832, he accompanied him to Athens and died there in 1839. Konrad inherited his father's martial spirit and picked up all the romanticism and republicanism with which the winds of the time were laden. Having completed the course in the Gymnasium at Speyer, in the spring of 1848 he joined Gen. Ludwig von Tann's expedition to aid the Schleswig-Holsteiners in their revolt against Danish rule. On July 3, 1848, he matriculated as a student of law at the University of Heidelberg, and before the end of the year he published in his native town a small volume of verse, *Dornen und Rosen von den Vogesen.* He tried vainly to join an expeditionary force to raise the siege of Montevideo and in the spring of 1849 was in the midst of the uprising in Baden and the Palatinate. The movement collapsed in July, and Krez, like many another future citizen of the United States, scuttled over the border into Switzerland, and went thence to France. The preface of his second volume of verse, his *Gesangbuch* (Strasbourg, 1850), was dated from Nancy on May 22. The book itself embodies the *Zeitgeist* with amusing completeness and is gay, sentimental, satirical, patriotic, anti-monarchical, and anti-clerical by turns. Though he wrote with his head full of Schiller, Heine, and the poets of the War of Liberation, Krez possessed a real gift for melodious verse, a lively fancy, and a sharp sense of humor.

In January 1851 he emigrated to New York, where he found employment and continued his study of law. In 1852 he married Addie, daughter of Judge John A. Stemmler, who with six of their seven children survived him. In 1854 he settled in Sheboygan, Wis., began the practice of his profession, and soon became prominent in civic affairs. On Mar. 7, 1863, he was commissioned colonel of the 27th Wisconsin Infantry. The regiment saw little actual fighting, but its losses by disease were heavy. Krez was a capable officer and toward the close of the war was brevetted brigadier-general. In August 1865, when his regiment was mustered out, he returned to Sheboygan and the next day opened his law office. Unable to stomach a second Grant administration, he left the Republican party in 1872, and was collector of the port of Milwaukee on President Cleveland's appointment from 1885 to 1889. Passionately devoted to the German language as the vehicle of German culture, he became in 1889 the fiery, militant leader of the Germans and Scandinavians of the state in their protest against the Bennett Law, an act to compel attendance at schools where the teaching was in English. For several terms he was a member of the state assembly and in 1892 was city attorney of Milwaukee. Poetry as a profession he had abandoned, but from time to time he wrote poems for his own delectation. Two of them, "Entsagung und Trost" and "An Mein Vaterland," were published in the *Gartenlaube* (1868, p. 116; 1870, p. 4) and were widely read. "An Mein Vaterland" is almost perfect as the expression of the patriotism of the exiled forty-eighters. *Aus Wisconsin* (New York, 1875; enlarged edition, Milwaukee, 1895) is a collection of both his youthful and his later work, and is one of the most interesting volumes of verse written in German by an American. Though he could not fulfill the promise of his early work, he was a poet of genuine, unforced feeling and, at times, of considerable technical skill. Most of his verse is autobiographical. He died in Milwaukee after a short illness.

[M. A. W. Brown, ed., *Soldiers' and Citizens' Album of Biog. Record* (1890), pp. 597–99; G. A. Zimmermann, *Deutsch in Amerika: Beiträge zur Geschichte der Deutsch-Amerikanischen Literatur—I. Episch-Lyrische Poesie* (1894); Franz Brümmer, *Lexikon der Deutschen Dichter und Prosaisten des Neunzehnten Jahrhunderts* (Leipzig, n.d.); H. E. Legler, "A Wisconsin Group of German Poets," *Trans. Wis. Acad. of Sciences,* XIV (1904), 471–84; *Milwaukee Jour.,* Mar. 9, 11, 1897; *Milwaukee Sentinel,* Mar. 10, 12, 1897; *97 Wis. Reports,* pp. xxxiv-xxxix; Gustav Toepke, *Die Matrikel der Universität Heidelberg,* Sechster Teil (Heidelberg, 1907), p. 69; Wilhelm Hense-Jensen, *Wisconsin's Deutsch-Amerikaner* (2 vols., 1900–02); F. B. Heitman, *Hist. Reg. U. S. Army,* vol. I (1903); *War of the Rebellion: Official Records (Army)*, 1 ser., vols. XXII, XXIV, XXXIV, XLI, XLVIII, XLIX; Alb. Becker, "Konrad Kretz, ein Prälzer Dichter in Amerika," *Prälzische Heimatkunde* (1912), pp. 40–41; E. Fried, "Konrad Krez, ein Pfälzer Dichter in Amerika," *Der Pfälzerwald* (1914), pp. 86–87; K. Reisert, "Konrad Krez," *Ibid.* (1915), pp. 51–54.]

G. H. G.

KRIMMEL, JOHN LEWIS (1789–July 15, 1821), painter, styled by his contemporaries "the American Hogarth," was born at Ebingen, in Württemberg, Germany. He emigrated to the United States in 1810 to join his brother, George Frederick Krimmel, who, frowning upon his younger brother's artistic leaning, clapped him into his Philadelphia counting-house. This occupation pleased Krimmel so little that before many months he left his brother's home as well as his commercial establishment, took lodgings, and devoted himself to the more congenial business of portrait painting. His first portrait, that of his landlady and her family, stirred sufficient interest among acquaintances to enable the young artist to continue portrait painting as a livelihood, though at times an uncertain one. His eyesight was so abnormally keen and his observation so quick that his work, whether executed upon canvas or ivory, was that of a born miniaturist. At one time, having married, and incurred the responsibility of a growing family, he accepted a position as professor of drawing in a young ladies' seminary. His tenure of office was short, however. The mistress of the school, desiring to curry favor with the parents of her charges, demanded that her drawing professor execute the work for his pupils. To Krimmel the artist, any such proposition was intolerable: he refused point blank, and found himself jobless.

In America he had found his center of interest. His first painting to be exhibited, "Pepper-Pot" (1811), was typical of Philadelphia and marked the beginning of his long association with the Columbian Society of Artists who held yearly exhibitions at the Pennsylvania Academy of the Fine Arts. With kindly humor and a keen eye he painted American scenes and American types, from the young girl of humble parentage returning home a finished prig from the fashionable boarding school to crowds of Americans celebrating the Fourth of July; gathering in Center Square, Philadelphia, by the city water works, or watching the demolition by fire of the old Masonic Hall. Always his interest lay in contemporary events and individuals; he was one of the few painters of his generation in America to chronicle the life of his day. The purchasing public did not consider the American scene of any importance, however, and Krimmel was forced to eke out his living as portraitist and miniaturist. Much of his work, owing, probably, to the apathy of the public, is preserved not in the original but through engravings made from the originals by his friend and patron, Alexander Lawson.

He went to Germany in 1817 for a short stay, but after his sojourn in America found little to interest him in the land of his nativity and returned to his adopted country. When he left America he had been an unknown and struggling painter. When he returned he found himself "discovered" by the country's chief literary organ, the *Analectic Magazine,* which in the issue for February 1820 reproduced in outline engraving his painting, "Country Wedding," now to be found in the permanent collection of the Pennsylvania Academy of the Fine Arts. The growing popularity of his genre creation, and especially of his "Procession of Victuallers" and "The Burning of Masonic Hall," brought him an order to paint an historical picture depicting Penn's treaty with the Indians. This work, which was to have been his masterpiece, was never completed, since Krimmel was drowned in a mill pond near Germantown in the summer of 1821, the same year in which he had become president of the Association of American Artists.

The works of Krimmel are sadly scattered, with scant record as to their whereabouts. Among the best known of them are his "Fourth of July Celebration at the State House, 1819," "The Burning of Masonic Hall," and "Centre Square, Philadelphia, in 1812." The original sketch for his "Election Day," together with several other works, is in the possession of the Pennsylvania Historical Society.

[Wm. Dunlap, *Hist. of the Rise and Progress of the Arts of Design in the U. S.* (1834), vol. II; Joseph Jackson, "Krimmel: The American Hogarth," *International Studio,* June 1929; Ulrich Thieme and Felix Becker, *Allgemeines Lexikon der Bildenden Künstler,* vol. XXI (1927).] D. G.

KROEGER, ADOLPH ERNST (Dec. 28, 1837–Mar. 8, 1882), journalist, translator, a minor figure in the St. Louis philosophical movement, was born at Schwabstedt, near Husum, Duchy of Schleswig, the eldest child of the Lutheran pastor, Jacob Kroeger. Having assisted at the insurrection against the Danes in 1848, the father found it wholesome to quit the country and settled with his family on a farm near Davenport, Iowa, whither a brother had preceded him. There, till his death in 1857, he bore the hardships of a "Latin farmer" but spent happy hours instructing his son, who learned Greek, Latin, French, German, and English and became an enthusiast for music, poetry, and philosophy. When fifteen years old young Kroeger secured a place as assistant bookkeeper in a Davenport bank. He went East in 1858 and found work on the *New York Times,* was sent as its correspondent to St. Louis, attracted attention by his political articles, married Eliza Curren in 1861, was appointed to a lieutenancy on the staff of Gen. John C. Frémont, and after Frémont's displacement returned to St. Louis to live by journalism, with municipal politics for a side line and philosophy for the real business of his life. He wrote in German and English for several newspapers and periodicals, was elected city treasurer in 1865 for a two-year term, and was one of the mainstays, from its founding in 1867, of William Torrey Harris' *Journal of Speculative Philosophy.* He had a faculty for conveying German philosophy into fathomable English, his most notable work being his translations of Fichte's *New Exposition of the Science of Knowledge* (1868; 1889), *The Science of Rights* (1869; 1889), and *The Science of Ethics as Based on the Science of Knowledge* (1897). He also translated parts of Leibnitz and Kant and wrote frequently on philosophical topics. Much of his musical and literary criticism, including essays on *Hamlet* and Poe, is buried in the files of the *Missouri Republican.* In 1870 his promising career ended in a cruel downfall. The December before, as unofficial deputy for the city treasurer, M. E. Susisky, Kroeger had given his own personal check for $6,000 to a creditor of the city and had reimbursed himself with a treasury check that Susisky had signed in blank. No money was misappropriated, vouchers covered the full amount, but when Susisky later defaulted the transaction fell under suspicion; Kroeger was indicted, tried, convicted of forgery in the third degree, and sent to the penitentiary on a five-year sentence. In 1872 his friends, led by Henry C. Brokmeyer, convinced Gov. Benjamin Gratz Brown of his innocence, and his pardon followed. Kroeger returned to St. Louis, exonerated in due form but humiliated, impoverished, sick, and in disrepute. In 1873 he published a little volume on *The Minnesinger of Germany.* He strove gallantly to support his family by writing for newspapers, completed a romance, a history of the Civil War in Missouri, and other work that never found a publisher, and solaced himself with medieval German poetry and romantic philosophy. His vitality, however, was sinking; late in 1881 he took to his bed, and the next spring he died, leaving his wife and four children in narrow circumstances. His elder son, Ernest Richard, became a musician of prominence in St. Louis; his elder daughter, Alice Bertha, was a well-known reference librarian.

[*St. Louis Globe-Democrat,* Mar. 9, 1882; D. H. MacAdam, "Adolph E. Kroeger—A Study," *Missouri Republican,* Apr. 16, 1882; H. A. Rattermann, "Adolph E. Kröger," *Der Deutsche Pionier,* Oct. 1882; W. T. Harris, "Adolph E. Kroeger—Obituary," *Jour. of Speculative Philosophy,* Oct. 1882, with list of publications; T. A. Post, *Reports of Cases . . . in the Supreme Court of the State of Mo.,* vol. XLVII (1888); A. P. Richter, *Geschichte der Stadt Davenport und des County Scott* (Davenport, Iowa, 1917), pp. 354–59; D. H. Harris, *A Brief Report of the Meeting Commemorative of the Early St. Louis Movement* (copyright 1922).] G. H. G.

KROL, BASTIAEN JANSEN (1595–1674), colonial official, was born at Harlingen, in Friesland, and before his coming to America was a *caffawercker,* or velours worker, by trade. In 1615 he resided with his mother, Annetjen Egberts, at Amsterdam, where, shortly after Feb. 7, he married Annetjen Stoffels, from Esens, in East Friesland. On Oct. 12, 1623, he applied to the consistory of the Dutch Reformed Church at Amsterdam to be sent as a comforter of the sick to the West Indies. He was not accepted at that time, but on Dec. 7 received his instructions, and on Jan. 25, 1624, sailed for New Netherland. He was back in Holland on Nov. 14 of the same year, when he reported to the consistory that the people in New Netherland desired to have a minister and that provision should be made for the baptism of children. A week later the consistory decided not to send a minister, but authorized Krol, in addition to his duties as a comforter of the sick, to perform the ceremonies of baptism and marriage, on condition that he should observe the formulas of the Reformed authors and not use words of his own composition. He sailed with Willem Verhulst, the newly appointed director of New Netherland, on the ship *Orangenboom,* and on Aug. 1, 1626, was appointed commissary at Fort Orange, to take the place of Daniel van Krieckenbeeck, who had been killed by the Indians. He was chosen for this post because "he was well acquainted with the Indian language," showing that he had previously been stationed at Fort Orange, rather than at Manhattan, as has been supposed. Two years later, when the Rev. Jonas Michaëlius arrived at New Amsterdam and formally organized the first church in New Netherland, Krol was made a member of the consistory. He returned to Holland in 1629, but in March 1630 was again sent out as commissary of Fort Orange, where, with the consent of the West India Company, he also acted as an agent of Kiliaen van Rensselaer, the patroon of Rensselaerswyck, and purchased land for him from the Indians in the vicinity of the fort. In 1631 through the influence of Van Rensselaer, Krol was promoted to the directorship. He assumed his new office on Minuit's departure in March 1632, but retained it only a year. He then, at Van Twiller's request, returned for a short time to Fort Orange to prevent Jacob Eelkens from trading there and finally sailed for Holland. On June 30, 1634, at the request of the patroons, he appeared at Amsterdam before Notary Justus van de Ven and in the course of an interrogatory made certain statements about his various voyages to New Netherland and about the conduct of Hans Jorissen Hontom, his successor at Fort Orange, whose dealings with the Indians were giving much trouble and were detrimental to the patroons' interests. Doubtless as a result of these circumstances, he was once more sent to New Netherland, in 1638, to fill the position of commander of Fort Orange, where, in September 1642, he was instrumental in ransoming some French prisoners from the Indians. On Nov. 8, 1644, he and his wife resided on the Lindegracht, at Amsterdam, and jointly made their last will. A little more than two months later Annetjen Stoffels died and was buried in the churchyard of the Noorderkerk. By her Krol had three children. On Oct. 7, 1645, he declared his intention to enter into marriage with Engeltie Baerents, from Norden, widow of Abram Valentijn. Little is known of his further career. Ten years later he was still living at Amsterdam, but suffering from the effects of a stroke. He died shortly before Mar. 14, 1674, and was buried on that date in the churchyard of the Noorderkerk.

Krol must have possessed more than ordinary skill and sagacity. From the first he had considerable influence over the Indians around Fort Orange and it was largely due to his tact and judgment in dealing with them that their friendly relations with the Dutch, which more than once threatened to be disturbed, were not broken as long as he held office in New Netherland.

[N. Y. colonial mss. in State Lib.; A. J. F. van Laer, *Van Rensselaer Bowier MSS.* (1908) and *Docs. Relating to New Netherland 1624–1626* (1924); records of the consistory and the notorial records at Amsterdam; A. Eekhof, *Bastiaen Jansz, Krol, Krankenbezoeker, Kommies en Kommandeur van Nieuw-Nederland 1595–1645* (1910), *Jonas Michaëlius, Founder of the Church in New Netherland* (1926), and sketch in *Nieuw Nederlandsch Biografisch Woordenboek* (1911), vol. I, cols. 1252–54.] A. J. F. v—L.

KRUELL, GUSTAV (Oct. 31, 1843–Jan. 2, 1907), wood-engraver, son of Ludwig and Franziska Kruell, was born in Grafenberg, a small village near Düsseldorf, Germany. His boyhood was spent on his father's farm until, at the age of fifteen, he was apprenticed to an engraver in Düsseldorf, with whom he remained for five years. He then went to Leipzig for study and in 1864 established himself in Stuttgart, becoming a member of the firm of Kühn & Company. In 1867 (Smith, *post*) he married Clara Cecilia Kühn, daughter of his partner. Financial reverses following a panic led Kruell in 1873 to emigrate to America. Here he entered the office of Harper & Brothers in New York, working at the same time, outside, for other publishers. In 1874 he was joined by his wife and four children. They lived in Jersey City, N. J., then in

East Orange. With Timothy Cole, Henry Wolf, Frederick Juengling [*q.v.*], and Elbridge Kingsley [*q.v.*], Kruell formed the Society of American Wood-Engravers. The ancient craft of wood-engraving, practised for five hundred years, had been partially eclipsed by the rise of the newer art of engraving on copper, but the art once more came into its own in the hands of this "new school" of artists. Kruell was frequently praised for his cleverness in drawing. He was particularly successful in portraiture, in which he evinced great vigor and distinction, reproducing the portraits from his own drawings. The most striking of his cuts were portraits that possessed strong individuality, such as those of Lincoln, two of which appeared in the *Portfolio of National Portraits* (1899) and one in *Harper's New Monthly Magazine* for April 1885. His engraving after the photograph used by Augustus Saint-Gaudens in modeling his statue for Lincoln Park, Chicago, is considered by many the finest portrait of the Great Emancipator. Kruell made many portraits of the officers of the Civil War, both Union and Confederate, which became well known through the nation-wide circulation of the weekly and monthly periodicals in which they were published. He also engraved portraits of Jefferson, Webster, Beecher, Bryant, Hawthorne, Darwin, Wendell Phillips, Lowell, and many others. That of Lowell, it is said, was accepted by the poet's family and intimate friends as the best of his later years. One of his most interesting portraits is that of Arthur P. Stanley, a thoughtful, earnest, and striking portrayal. His work was not confined to portraiture, however. His "Flight of Night," after William Morris Hunt, and "Phorcydes," after Elihu Vedder, appeared in the *American Art Review* (January, June 1880). He engraved blocks for Owen Meredith's "Lucile" and for Alfred Tennyson's "Dream of Fair Women." "The Princes in the Tower" (*St. Nicholas,* February 1880) was done delicately yet with strength and depth of color. He raised his wood-engraving to the dignity of a fine art. Over five hundred blocks engraved by Kruell have been listed (R. C. Smith, *post*). He received awards at expositions in Paris, Chicago, Buffalo, and St. Louis and honors in Vienna, Berlin, and Paris. His prints are in the British Museum, the Fogg Art Museum at Harvard University, the Museum of Fine Arts, Boston, the National Museum at Washington, and in many private collections. He died at San Luis Obispo, Cal.

[R. C. Smith, *Gustav Kruell* (1929); *Am. Art. Annual,* 1907–08; W. J. Linton, *The Hist. of Wood-engraving in America* (1882); Frank Weitenkampf, *Am. Graphic Art* (1912); *Studio,* June 20, 1891; *Scribner's Mag.,* Feb. 1895; *Who's Who in America,* 1906–07; *Evening Post* (N. Y.), Jan. 3, 1907.] H. W.

KRUESI, JOHN (May 15, 1843–Feb. 22, 1899), mechanical expert, inventor, was born in Speicher, Canton Appenzell, Switzerland. While he was still an infant, his parents died and Kruesi was placed in the local orphan asylum, where he lived the difficult life of such institutions, until he was able to take care of himself. He then went to St. Gall, Switzerland, as an apprentice learned the locksmith's trade, and later proceeded to Zurich, where he worked as a journeyman machinist. During the following three years (1867–70), he followed his trade in Holland, Belgium, and France. Believing that his greatest opportunity lay in the United States, in 1870, after a visit with his relatives in Switzerland, he sailed from England for New York. There he found work with the Singer Sewing Machine Company and quickly indicated his superior mechanical knowledge not only by improving the action of the sewing machine, but by making changes in the manufacturing methods. In the meantime he became deeply interested in Edison's experimental work and in 1871, despite attractive monetary inducements, he left the Singer Company and went to work for him in Newark, N. J. From that time until his death he was closely associated with Edison and was responsible for the mechanical execution of many of the latter's ideas. He was with him in 1877 at Menlo Park, N. J., as foreman of the machine shop, and that year built the first Edison phonograph. During the next two years he had an intimate part in perfecting the incandescent lamp and dynamo and devised much of the machinery for the manufacture of electric lighting equipment. With the establishment of the Edison Machine Works in New York in 1881, Kruesi was made superintendent, and there began the manufacture of Edison dynamos. He was active, too, in the installation of the electric lighting system in New York City, developing a water-tight and insulated underground method of distributing electricity, the feature of which was the placing of gangs of wires in iron tubes and filling them with hot tar. In connection with this work he obtained ten patents, the first granted Oct. 24, 1882, and the last, July 5, 1887. The Kruesi tube, as it was called, and all other equipment used in the installation of the system was made subsequently by a subsidiary organization, the Electric Tube Company, in New York. By 1886 the capacity of the Edison Machine Works was overtaxed and the plant was established in Schenectady, N. Y., with Kruesi as general manager and chief mechanical engineer. He directed its affairs most successfully for the succeeding nine years, but in 1895, after the consolidation of the company with the Thompson-Houston Electric Company as the General Electric Company, he was relieved of the heavy burden of the the two-fold office and continued as chief engineer for the remainder of his life. In 1871 he married Emily Zwinger of Allegheny, Pa. He died in Schenectady, survived by eight children.

[*Specifications and Drawings of Patents Issued from the U. S. Patent Office,* Oct. 1882, Apr. and Nov. 1883, Apr. 1884, July 1885, Jan. 1886, July 1887; J. W. Howell and H. Schroeder, *The Hist. of the Incandescent Lamp* (1927); W. B. Kaempffert, *A Popular Hist. of Am. Invention* (1924); records of Edison Pioneers, N. Y.; Thomas C. Martin, *Forty Years of Edison Service, 1882–1922* (1922); *Engineering Record,* Mar. 4, 1899; *Trans. of the Am. Soc. of Mech. Engineers,* vol. XX (1899); *Am. Machinist,* Mar. 2, 1899.]

C. W. M.

KRÜSI, HERMANN [See KRÜSI, JOHANN HEINRICH HERMANN, 1817–1903].

KRÜSI, JOHANN HEINRICH HERMANN (June 24, 1817–Jan. 28, 1903), educator, was born in Yverdon, Switzerland, the son of Hermann and Catherine (Egger) Krüsi. His father had been a teacher in Pestalozzi's school at Yverdon, but shortly before Hermann's birth had established his own private school there. While Hermann was still a child the family moved from Yverdon to Trogen, where the elder Krüsi assumed charge of the Cantonal School. Here the boy's formal education began. His autobiography gives doubtful praise to the instruction he received: the formality practised by some of his teachers seems to have been unsuited to his independent nature and inquiring mind. Later he attended the normal school at Gais, to which his father had been transferred, and he received instruction in religious education at Yverdon under Johannes Niederer, a colleague of Pestalozzi. In 1838 he went to Dresden, Germany, where he studied two years in the Blochmann-Vizthum Institute, a private *Gymnasium.* While here his education was expanded by travel and outside study and by visits to German normal schools. After a year at the Bunzlau Normal School in Prussia, he returned to Gais in 1841, and for the next five years was a student and an instructor in his father's school there. During this time he produced three plays and wrote some poems to which he himself attached little importance except as natural steps in the development of his intellectual life and in the expression of his emotional nature. After his father's death in 1844, and the closing of school in the fall of 1845, he went to England and taught in a private school for boys at Cheam. He possessed strong republican principles, however, and soon became dissatisfied with the aristocratic Cheam school. Accordingly, at the end of one term he resigned and took a teaching position in the Home and Colonial Infant Training School at King's Cross, London, a school founded and conducted by English Pestalozzians. Here he labored happily until 1852, publishing in 1850 *A Progressive Course of Inventive Drawing on the Principles of Pestalozzi.*

After a year's visit in Switzerland, he then came to the United States, where he became well acquainted with his countrymen, Louis Agassiz and Arnold Guyot. He began his work in America at the so-called New England Normal College in Lancaster, Mass., where he remained two years as a teacher of German, French, and drawing. He then lectured in the Massachusetts and New Hampshire institutes for teachers, gave private instruction, and for two years (1857–59) taught in the Trenton (New Jersey) Normal School. In the summer of 1862 Edward Austin Sheldon, principal of the Oswego (New York) State Normal School, invited him to a position on the faculty, because of his well-known advocacy of Pestalozzian principles. He accepted and began his notable work in Oswego in the fall of that year. He remained in the Normal School for twenty-five years, and there made his professional contribution in Object Teaching. In 1887 he retired, to spend the last sixteen years of his life in travel, study, and writing. He died at Alameda, Cal.

Krüsi was a strong character, a man of high ideals, patient, persevering, courageous, and an ardent apostle of Pestalozzi. He was a prolific writer and a versatile scholar, although comparatively few of his productions were published. In 1875, however, he published *Pestalozzi: His Life, Work, and Influence,* and in 1907, his own autobiography, *Recollections of My Life.* Among the papers he left at his death were many articles, lectures, and essays dealing with religious, political, literary, and educational topics.

[The most important source is Krüsi's *Recollections of my Life* (1907); his *Pestalozzi* contains some autobiographical information, and details of his life and of his educational philosophy are found in most of his writings. See also W. S. Monroe, *Hist. of the Pestalozzian Movement in the U. S.* (1907); N. H. Dearborn, *The Oswego Movement in American Education* (1925); and Paul Monroe, *A Cyc. of Educ.,* vol. III (1912). Unpublished letters and personal interviews with Krüsi's colleagues at Oswego supplement the information obtained from the foregoing sources.]

N. H. D.

KUGELMAN, FREDERICK BENJAMIN [See KAYE, FREDERICK BENJAMIN, 1892–1930].

KUHN, ADAM (Nov. 17, 1741–July 5, 1817), physician, botanist, was born at Germantown,

Pa., the son of Adam Simon Kuhn and his wife, Anna Maria Sabina Schrack. Under his father, a native of Swabia who had immigrated to Pennsylvania in 1733, young Kuhn began his first studies in medicine. In the autumn of 1761 he set out for Sweden and continued his medical studies at the University of Upsala, where he fell under the tutelage of Linnæus in botany. A picture of his life there has been preserved by a fellow-pupil, Johann Christian Fabricius, who writes of the enjoyment derived from the lectures and confidential friendship of the great Swedish botanist: "In summer we followed him into the country. We were three, Kuhn, Zoega and I, all foreigners. In winter we lived directly facing his house, and he came to us every day" (Stoever, *post,* p. 273). After his course at Upsala, Kuhn went to London in 1764, studying there for a time, and then going to the University of Edinburgh where he took the degree of M.D. in 1767. During his stay in England he came under the notice of John Ellis, English botanist and correspondent of Linnæus. The latter, in a Latin letter to Ellis in 1765, pronounced Kuhn "one of the most worthy and industrious young men I ever knew" (Smith, *post,* I, 165).

Returning to the Province of Pennsylvania, Kuhn became, in January 1768, professor of materia medica and botany in the College of Philadelphia. There he fell under the appraising eye of Dr. Charles Caldwell, who drew a word portrait of him which is deeply etched with strong feeling: "He was, by far, the most highly and minutely furnished specimen of old-school medical production . . . His hair . . . of which nature had furnished him with an exuberant abundance, . . . his hairdresser so arranged as to give it the resemblance of a fashionable wig, well pomatumed, stifly curled, and richly powdered . . . His breeches were black, his long-skirted waistcoat white or buff, and his coat snuff-colored. In his hand he carried a gold-headed cane and a gold snuff-box, and his knee and shoe buckles were of the same metal. . . . He entered the sick-room at a given time, spent a given number of minutes . . . and never suffered deviation to be made from his directions" (*Autobiography, post,* p. 121). With his foibles and his pomposity, a good deal of a precisian and thus arousing antagonisms and resentments, he was nevertheless strong in sense and discreet in judgment. Lacking powers of imagination, he had a capacity for accurate observation. In addition he possessed the homely virtues of punctuality, faithfulness, and diligence. He was made physician to the Pennsylvania Hospital, and in 1786 consulting physician to the Philadelphia Dispensary; he was one of the founders, and in 1808, president, of the College of Physicians of Philadelphia; he was chosen professor of the theory and practice of medicine in the University of the State of Pennsylvania in 1789; and on the union of the medical schools of the College and the University, he was appointed professor of the practice of physics. This chair he held from 1792 to 1797. In addition he was a member of the American Philosophical Society.

Kuhn was the first professor of botany in the American colonies, but he did nothing to advance the science of botany, though a virgin vegetation lay at his doors. He did, however, carry with him a new plant of North America in a living state to Linnæus. It represented a new genus and the Swedish botanist named it *Kuhnia.* Through *Kuhnia eupatorioides,* a widely distributed species of the family *Compositae,* all field students of the eastern United States recall his name.

When he was thirty-nine years of age Kuhn married Elizabeth (Hartman) Markhoe, widow of Francis Markhoe and daughter of Isaac Hartman, of St. Croix. By her "he had two sons, respectable characters." At the age of seventy-three he gave up medical practice, and three years later died in Philadelphia, after a brief illness without pain.

[S. P. Griffiths, in the *Eclectic Repertory and Analytical Rev.,* Apr. 1818; D. J. H. Stoever, *Life of Sir Charles Linnaeus* (1794), tr. from the German by Joseph Trapp; James Edward Smith, *A Selection of the Correspondence of Linnaeus,* (1821), vol. I; *Autobiography of Charles Caldwell* (1855), ed. by H. W. Warner; J. W. Harshberger, *The Botanists of Phila. and Their Work* (1899); H. A. Kelly, *Some Am. Medic. Botanists* (1914); *"Autobiographie des Naturforschers Fabricius,"* in *Linne und Fabricius* (1928), ed. by Julius Schuster; J. W. Jordan, *Colonial and Revolutionary Families of Pa.* (1911), vol. I; *Poulson's Am. Daily Advertiser,* July 9, 1817.]
W. L. J—n.

KUMLER, HENRY (Jan. 3, 1775–Jan. 8, 1854), bishop of the United Brethren in Christ, was born in Lancaster County, Pa., the son of Jacob and Elizabeth (Young) Kumler. The former, son of John Kumler, was a native of the county of Basel, Switzerland, and was brought to America by his parents when he was about seven years old. Henry grew up on his father's farm with very ordinary educational advantages, married Susanna Wingert, Sept. 5, 1797, and in 1810 bought property near Greencastle, Franklin County, Pa., and settled there. His early connections had been with the German Reformed Church, but in 1814, having passed through a severe spiritual struggle and experienced a call to preach, he became a member of the Eastern conference of the United Brethren in Christ. He was at this time well on toward middle age, but he threw himself into the work of this young denomination with whole-hearted devotion and extraordinary energy. The year after his admission he was a delegate to the first General Conference of the church, which revised the Confession of Faith and the Discipline; and he was a delegate to every subsequent General Conference until 1825, when he was elected bishop. Much of his life was spent in the saddle. The first five years of his ministry were in the East. In 1815 he traveled a large circuit near Greencastle; in 1816 he was appointed to the Virginia circuit, on which he covered 370 miles every four weeks; in 1817 he was made presiding elder. For some time the Pennsylvania Germans had been migrating westward in large numbers, and the valley of the Miami had become a center for the work of the United Brethren. In 1819 Kumler transferred his activities to that section. Acquiring a fertile farm near Trenton, Butler County, Ohio, he made it his home for the rest of his life. Adjoining his house he built a large room, where regular services were held for many years. His home became a stopping place for preachers, and conferences were frequently entertained there. First elected bishop in 1825, he served in that office for five successive terms, twenty years in all. By the end of this period age had made it difficult for him to endure the extended horseback journeys required. In addition to his services, being a man of some means, he gave liberally to the needs of the work, and to him as much as to any other person, perhaps, the planting and nurture of the churches of the United Brethren in southwestern Ohio was due. He had twelve children, one of whom, Henry Kumler, Jr., also became bishop. Bishop Daniel Kumler Flickinger [*q.v.*] was his grandson.

[Daniel Berger, *Hist. of the Church of the United Brethren in Christ* (1897); A. W. Drury, *Hist. of the Church of the United Brethren in Christ* (1924); Henry A. Thompson, *Our Bishops* (1889); R. E. Flickinger, *Flickinger Family Hist.* (1927).] H. E. S.

KUNZE, JOHN CHRISTOPHER (Aug. 5, 1744–July 24, 1807), Lutheran clergyman, was born in Saxony at Artern on the Unstrut, the son of an innkeeper and tradesman. He was educated at the Halle Orphanage, then under Gotthilf August Francke, at Rossleben and Merseburg, and at the University of Leipzig, where he matriculated Sept. 21, 1763. After teaching for three years at Kloster Bergen near Magdeburg, he became inspector of an orphanage at Greitz. In 1770, through his connections at Halle, he was called to Philadelphia as coadjutor to Henry Melchior Mühlenberg [*q.v.*]. Accompanied by F. A. C. and G. H. E. Muhlenberg [*qq.v.*], he left Halle on May 5, was ordained at Wernigerode, and landed at New York Sept. 22, 1770. On July 23, 1771, he married Mühlenberg's second daughter, Margaretta Henrietta. In 1779 he succeeded his father-in-law as chief pastor in Philadelphia, and J. H. C. Helmuth [*q.v.*] became his colleague. In 1784 he removed permanently to New York as pastor of Christ Church, with which he united the remnants of the old Dutch congregation. As a scholar Kunze had few equals in the United States, and in his own denomination his influence was second only to Mühlenberg's. He had a minute knowledge of Greek, Latin, Hebrew, Arabic, and Italian literature, and was a student also of medicine, astronomy, and numismatics. Although he never mastered the pronunciation of English and was compelled to abandon his attempts to preach in that language, he realized that English would become the language of the Lutheran Church in America, and the chief ambition of his life was to provide adequately for the education of Lutheran ministers who could use both German and English. His first attempt in this direction was his Seminarium, a pre-theological school, which he started in Philadelphia in 1773. In spite of many handicaps it managed to thrive, but the outbreak of the Revolution closed its doors. In 1779 he tried to establish a German Institute in the University of Pennsylvania, but the movement never received any support. As professor of Oriental languages in Columbia College, 1784–87 and 1792–99, he again failed for lack of students. In 1797 he became professor of theology on the Hartwick Foundation, the bequest of Johann Christoph Hartwig [*q.v.*], which paid him a yearly stipend of $500. In all, he did succeed in preparing a number of students for ordination. They became the first English Lutheran clergymen in the United States. In New York society he was a general favorite. John Daniel Gros [*q.v.*] and Rabbi G. M. Seixas were among his intimate friends. A much less intimate friendship with Aaron Burr scandalized some of his Episcopal colleagues.

His publications include: *Einige Gedichte und Lieder* (1778); *Ein Wort für den Verstand und das Herz vom Rechten und Gebanten Lebenswege* (1781); *Von den Absichten und dem Bisherigen Fortgang der Privilegirten Deutschen Gesellschaft* (1782); a sermon on the conclusion of peace (1783); *Rudiments of the Shorter Catechism of Luther* (1785), of which no copy is known to be extant; *Elisas Betränter Nachruf bei der Hinwegnahme seines Gottesmannes Elias* (1878), being a sermon on the death of Mühlenberg; *King Solomon's Great Sacrifice at the Dedication of His Temple: A Sermon* (1801); *Statement of a Case Concerning the Establishment of a Professorship of Divinity in the German Lutheran Church in the State of New York* (1805), reprinted by William Hull in the *Lutheran Church Review,* July 1898; and *A Table of a New Construction for Calculating the Great Eclipse, Expected to Happen on the 16th of June, 1806* (1806). With the help of his assistant, George Strebeck, he prepared *A Hymn and Prayer Book for the Use of Such Lutheran Churches as Use the English Language* (1795). It is the first Lutheran hymn book in the English language and contains the earliest surviving American translation of Luther's Shorter Catechism. The six sermons by his deceased pupil, Lawrence Van Buskirk, which he published with a brief introduction in 1797 are the first English Lutheran sermons published in America. During his last years he was much disquieted by the growing spirit of rationalism. He was survived by his wife, four daughters, and a son who died the following year.

[*Nachrichten von den vereinigten Deutschen Evangelisch-Lutherischen Gemeinen in Nord-America* (2 vols., 1886–95), ed. by W. J. Mann and B. M. Schmucker, usually cited as the "Hallesche Nachrichten"; W. J. Mann, *Life and Times of Henry Melchior Mühlenberg* (1887); A. L. Gräbner, *Geschichte der Lutherischen Kirche in America* (1892); *Doc. Hist. Ev. Luth. Ministerium of Pa.* (1898); C. F. Haussmann, *Kunze's Seminarium* (1917); J. W. Francis, *Old New York* (1866); Anton Eickhoff, *In der Neuen Heimath* (1884), pp. 138–39; Georg Erler, *Die Jüngere Matrikel der Universität Leipzig 1559–1809*, III (1909), 223; H. M. M. Richards, "Descendants of Henry Melchior Mühlenberg," *Pa.-Ger. Soc. Proc. and Addresses,* vol. X (1900); H. M. Oakley and J. C. Schwab, *The Muhlenberg Album* (privately printed, 1910); *N. Y. Herald,* July 29, 1807.]
G. H. G.

KUNZE, RICHARD ERNEST (Apr. 7, 1838–Feb. 7, 1919), physician and naturalist, was born in Altenburg, Germany, the youngest of six sons. His father, Johann Jacob Kunze, came of an old Thuringian family and was court horticulturist to the reigning duke. His mother, Adelaide Callen, was the daughter of a refugee of the French Revolution who had belonged to the household of Louis XVI. Since the boy showed a scholarly aptitude for the classics, his schooling continued until he was fifteen; but his strongest interest turned towards natural history, in which he gained instruction and help from local entomologists and ornithologists. Disappointed in his desire for college, he entered a counting house, but at sixteen, on the death of his father, he struck out boldly and alone for the New World. For a time he worked as a laborer on estates and farms in New Jersey and New York, learned the ways of the people in the new land, and acquired fluency in English speech. His acuteness attracted the attention of Dr. Charles J. Stearns, under whom he began the study of medicine. Later he attended lectures at the Metropolitan Medical College, and in 1859 began practice in New York City as a physician and pharmacologist. With an ever deepening interest in plant drugs, he took a course in the College of Pharmacy of the City and County of New York, and graduated in 1868 from the newly founded Eclectic Medical College. During the next twenty years he contributed many papers upon remedial plants to the eclectic medical journals. He stressed the importance of cactaceen drugs to the profession and investigated their therapeutic value in cardiac disturbances, researches which involved *Cereus Macdonaldiae, nycticalus,* and *serpentinus,* as well as other species of the same genus.

In 1857 he had married Ann McNamee, an Irish woman and efficient helpmeet, who died in 1888, after an illness of several years. When an accident to his right hand interfered with the delicacy necessary to operations, he gave up his medical practice, and in 1896 settled near Phoenix, Ariz. Here he began a cactus plantation a half-mile south of the city limits. Enthralled by the peculiar structure and color of the desert topography and its strange plant forms, he wandered over Arizona and into northern Mexico with a camping outfit of wagon and horses, studying the unique vegetation, the reptiles, and the insects of the region and collecting cacti and spiny xerophytes for his new garden. As the unusual collection grew, it became the resort of the curious and the objective of botanical travelers. A source of cactus stock for botanical gardens, it furnished him a means of subsistence while he carried on his studies of all desert life. His living was made precarious by the World War, which interrupted valuable shipments of cactus stock destined for European institutions; but no discouragement lessened his enthusiasm for the desert, which sustained him until death came in the beloved garden to which he had given over twenty years of devotion.

While his interests as a naturalist were rather widely scattered, one of his special predilections centered on the study of poisonous reptiles and poisonous plants, a subject which was the basis for a number of his published papers on toxins. In the field of pharmacology, his writings exhibit both erudition and practical value. Thorough and painstaking in his work, persistent in his ideals, impatient of injustice, courageous in opposition to evil, he held the respect and affection of his colleagues in the medical profession and of those cultivated persons who gained his friendship.

[Alexander Wilder, in *Am. Medic. Jour.*, June 1908, more eulogistic than critical; J. A. Munk, in *Cal. Eclectic Medic. Jour.*, Mar. 1919, an appreciation; *Am. Inventor*, Oct. 1905; *Arizona Republican* (Phoenix), Feb. 10, 1919; newspaper clippings and reminiscences of Kunze's friends.] W. L. J—n.

KURTZ, BENJAMIN (Feb. 28, 1795–Dec. 29, 1865), Lutheran clergyman, editor, was born in Harrisburg, Pa., the son of Benjamin and Elizabeth (Gardner) Kurtz. His grandfather, John Nicholas Kurtz, the son of a parochial teacher near Giessen, was sent from Halle to Pennsylvania as a catechist in 1745 and was the first minister ordained (1748) by the Ministerium of Pennsylvania. At fifteen Kurtz was employed as an assistant in the Harrisburg Academy and three years later began to study theology under John George Lochman [*q.v.*] at Lebanon. He was licensed at Frederick, Md., in 1815 by the Ministerium of Pennsylvania; was assistant to his uncle, John Daniel Kurtz, in Baltimore for a short time; was pastor at Hagerstown, Md., 1815–31, and at Chambersburg, Pa., 1831–33, and was editor of the *Lutheran Observer* in Baltimore, 1833–58. Kurtz was one of the most prominent men in the General Synod and, next to his close friend Samuel Simon Schmucker [*q.v.*], the chief exponent of "American Lutheranism." He was one of the founders of the Synod of Maryland and Virginia (1820), of the General Synod (1820), which was organized in his church and which he twice served as president, and of the Gettysburg Theological Seminary (1825). As a pastor and preacher he was extraordinarily successful, and his position in Washington County, Md., was almost that of a bishop. In spite of much opposition he advocated temperance reform and introduced English services, prayer meetings, revivals, Sunday schools, and educational and benevolent societies into his congregations. In 1826 he went to Europe to collect money and books for the Gettysburg Seminary. For a time he was stranded in London without funds. In Germany he was received with interest and respect and secured contributions from the Crown Prince of Prussia, the King of Württemberg, and the Dukes of Cumberland and Cambridge. Among the clergymen who sought him out was Martin Stephan [see article on Carl Ferdinand Wilhelm Walther], who was to lead a colony of Saxon Lutherans to Missouri. Kurtz's mission realized $10,000, gifts of fine needlework that sold for an additional $2,000, and some 6,000 books.

When hemorrhages of the lungs forced him out of the active ministry, he accepted the invitation of John Gottlieb Morris [*q.v.*] to assume the editorship of the *Observer* and made that paper a power in the church. His knowledge of theology was limited, but he was strongly evangelical, plain-spoken, and fearless, and against liturgical worship and the Lutheran confessions he waged a vigorous polemical war. He advocated a union of the Lutheran and German Reformed Churches. His doctrinal position is fully set forth in his chief book, *Why Are You a Lutheran?* (1843), which went through ten editions. In 1846 he visited Europe again as a delegate to the first meeting of the Evangelical Alliance. He championed S. S. Schmucker's "Definite Synodical Platform" in 1855 and was the first to admit any knowledge of its origin. When the Maryland Synod grew too orthodox for him, he withdrew, together with a handful of followers, and on Dec. 1, 1857, at Middletown, Md., organized the Melanchthon Synod, which was reabsorbed into the parent body in 1868. Kurtz wrote the Melanchthon Synod's "Declaration of Faith," in which baptismal regeneration, the Real Presence in the Eucharist, and other "errors" of the Augsburg Confession were repudiated. In 1858 he made his most grievous mistake, the founding of the Missionary Institute at Selinsgrove, Pa., which poured into the Lutheran Church a stream of quarter-educated ministers. In person he was lank and cadaverous, with a huge, hawk-like nose, and a forbidding manner. He was a witty, entertaining talker, but could not listen to the talk, or the sermons, of other ministers. By the Old Lutherans he was feared, disliked, and denounced; by his own party he was admired. He was married three times: to Ann Barnett of Washington County, Md., to Mary Catharine Baker of Winchester, Va., and to Mary Calhoun of Chambersburg, Pa. Of his ten children only five survived him. He died in Baltimore after a lingering illness.

[E. W. Hutter, *Eulogy on the Life and Character of Rev. Benjamin Kurtz, D.D., LL.D.* (1866); M. L. Stoever, memoir in *Evangelical Quart. Rev.*, Jan. 1867; J. G. Morris, *Fifty Years in the Luth. Ministry* (1878); C. A. Hay, *Memoirs of Rev. Jacob Goering, Rev. George Lochman, D.D., and Rev. Benj. Kurtz, D.D., LL.D.* (1888), with a list of publications; Adolph Spaeth, *Charles Porterfield Krauth* (2 vols., 1898–1909); A. R. Wentz, *Hist. Ev. Luth. Synod of Md.* (1920) and *Hist. Gettysburg Theol. Sem.* (1927); *Doc. Hist. Ev. Luth. Ministerium of Pa.* (1898); Vergilius Ferm, *The Crisis in Am. Luth. Theology* (1927); *Cat. of Books . . . &c in the Lib. of the Luth. Hist. Soc., Gettysburg, Pa.* (1890), pp. 21 and 39; M. A. Cruikshank and B. K. Miller, *Life of Johann Nicolaus Kurtz* (privately printed, 1925).] G. H. G.

KUSKOV, IVAN ALEKSANDROVICH (1765–October 1823), commercial counselor, founder and first manager of the Russian settlement called "Fort Ross," in California, was born in the city of Totma, Vologda Government, Russia. In 1787, at the age of twenty-two, he left for Siberia, to "find happiness." There, in 1790, he met A. A. Baranov [*q.v.*], who had just agreed to become resident director of the Alaskan fur-trading establishments of the Golikov and Shelekhov company. Baranov persuaded Kuskov to go with him as an assistant. They reached "Russian America" in 1791. During his thirty-two years of service Kuskov was often obliged to take the place of Baranov in the latter's absence. He was obliged to travel a great deal, organizing the work of building the new Russian settlements and promoting the building of ships. In 1806 he directed all the structural work in Novo-Arkhangel'sk (the present Sitka, founded in 1804), having been appointed by Baranov as commander in chief of the fortress there. He is chiefly noted for his establishment of a Russian settlement in California. He had several times visited that region for purposes of trade and to find a site for a settlement, and in 1812, quietly and peacefully, he built "Fort Ross," some fifty miles from the port of San Francisco, in a land inhabited for years by Spanish colonists. From 1812 to 1821 he managed the fort; he built a shipyard and constructed three merchant ships and many smaller vessels. Near by he started cattle breeding, gardening, and farming. During the course of his career in spite of his exceptional good nature and upright character, many attempts were made on his life by the Alaskans and Californians. All his dangers were shared by his wife, Ekaterina Prokhorovna, who was popular with the natives. She learned their language and customs easily and understood how to handle them. She was the daughter of a burgess of the city of Ustug, near Totma, in the Vologda Government, and after the death of her parents, in India, she went to Alaska, where she married Kuskov. He left Russian America in 1822, and returned to his native city, Totma, where in October of the following year he died.

[*Russkiĭ biograficheskiĭ slovar'*, vol. IX (St. Petersburg, 1903), pp. 613–14, contains an article on Kuskov, in which he is called Kusov. Elsewhere, however, his name is spelled Kuskov, and he always signed his name thus. In addition to this article, see *Russkiĭ arkhiv* (Moscow), 1898, no. 10; K. Khliebnikov, *Zhizneopisanie Aleksandra Andreevicha Baranova* (St. Petersburg, 1835); P. Tikhmenev, *Istoricheskoe obozrienie obrazovaniia Rossiĭsko-Amerikanskoĭ kompanii* (2 vols., St. Petersburg, 1861–63), and K. Khliebnikov, "Zapiski o Amerikie" (in *Materialy dlia istorii russkikh zaseleniĭ*, supplement to *Morskoĭ sbornik*, St. Petersburg, Mar. 1861); H. H. Bancroft, *Hist. of Alaska* (1886), and *Hist. of Cal.*, vol. II (1885); Rev. A. Kashevaroff, "Fort Ross," in *Alaska Mag.* (Juneau, Alaska), May 1927.]

M. Z. V.

KYLE, DAVID BRADEN (Oct. 11, 1863–Oct. 23, 1916), laryngologist, the youngest son of Samuel W. Kyle and his wife, *née* Cross, was born at Cadiz, Ohio. After graduating from Muskingum College, he studied medicine at Jefferson Medical College, Philadelphia, from which he graduated in 1891, receiving a gold medal for a thesis on "The Pathology and Treatment of Tetanus." All his life Kyle was deeply interested in pathology and shortly after graduating he opened a private laboratory in which he gave extramural teaching in clinical microscopy, pathology, and bacteriology. In 1896 he was appointed to fill the chair of pathology *ad interim* at Jefferson Medical College. At the expiration of this term of duty, he was elected clinical professor of laryngology and in 1904 was made professor of laryngology, which position he held until his death. He was also on the staff of St. Mary's and St. Agnes' hospitals. He was active in the work of the scientific societies devoted to his speciality, contributing many articles to their transactions. In 1900 he was president of the American Laryngological, Rhinological, and Otological Society, and of the American Laryngological Association in 1911. He was a fellow of the College of Physicians of Philadelphia and served several terms as chairman of its section on laryngology and otology. His *Text-book of Diseases of the Nose and Throat,* first published in 1899, went through five editions and was widely adopted in various medical colleges. A special feature of the work was the attention given in it to the pathology underlying manifestations of disease in the nose and throat. It also contained an unusually large number of original illustrations. He was a tireless worker and not only had a very large private practice but also did a great deal of hospital work in addition to his teaching. On Dec. 19, 1900, he married Jeanette E. Smith, daughter of Col. Thomas J. Smith, of Philadelphia. They had no children.

[*Trans. Am. Laryngological Asso.*, 1917; *Trans. Am. Laryngological, Rhinological, and Otological Soc.*, 1916; *Trans. Am. Climatological and Clinical Asso.*, vol. XXXII (1916); H. A. Kelly and W. L. Burrage, *Am. Medic. Biogs.* (1920); *Who's Who in America*, 1916–17; *Public Ledger* (Phila.), Oct. 24, 1916; personal acquaintance.]

F. R. P.

KYLE, JAMES HENDERSON (Feb. 24, 1854–July 1, 1901), Congregational clergyman, United States senator, was descended from a Scotch-Irish family of culture and ample fortune. An ancestor, Samuel, came to America in 1738 and settled at Chambersburg, Pa., where he built "Clifton Hall," which for more than a century was the chief seat of the family. One of his seven sons migrated to Ohio after the Revolution and his grandson Thomas B. Kyle married Margaret Henderson and became the father of James Henderson Kyle, who was born near Xenia, Ohio. In 1865 Thomas Kyle, who had been a captain of volunteers in the Civil War, removed with his family to a farm near Urbana, Ill., where James spent his youth. He attended classes at the University of Illinois, 1871–73, thence went to Oberlin College where he graduated from the classical course in 1878. He then studied law, but after two years turned to theology, and in 1882 was graduated from the Western Theological Seminary (Presbyterian) at Allegheny, Pa. Upon completing his course he was given charge of the educational program of the Presbyterians in the Synod of Utah, but in 1884 accepted a call to the Congregational Church of Salt Lake City. In the autumn of 1885 he went to Dakota and organized the Congregational churches of Ipswich and Aberdeen, of which he was pastor until 1890. In that year he was made financial secretary of Yankton College, and was serving in that capacity when he entered politics.

His introduction to politics was unique. In 1890, when the Populist movement was at its height, the Populist party had called a mass convention for the nomination of legislators, to meet at Aberdeen on July 4. A local celebration of Independence Day had also been planned. As the hour for the celebration approached it was discovered that the man invited to deliver the oration had failed to keep his appointment. The committee in charge visited Kyle and invited him to speak. He accepted, but having no time to prepare an address, read to the "embattled farmers" a copy of an address delivered in 1877 by Prof. John M. Gregory of the University of Illinois. It was an extreme arraignment of the federal government and of the tariff and financial policies of the United States. Nothing could have better fitted the situation in view of the excited political temper of his hearers. Immediately following the address they went into mass convention and, without consulting him, nominated Kyle for the state Senate. He was elected, and in the ensuing session of the legislature, after a prolonged deadlock, he was accepted as a compromise candidate and elected to the United States Senate.

One other unique circumstance contributed to his political fortune at this time. In the South Dakota legislature a fusion of the Democrats, Populists, and independent Republicans would have had a majority of one vote over the regular Republicans. In the Illinois legislature there were 101 Democrats, 100 Republicans and three Populists. Congressman Jerry Simpson of Kansas was first to see the possibilities, through adroit manipulation, of securing from normally Republican states two senators of Democratic sympathies. A plan was consummated by which the Illinois Populists joined the Democrats and elected General Palmer, and the South Dakota Democrats joined the Populists in electing James H. Kyle. Throughout his first term Senator Kyle generally supported Democratic policies. When the time for his reëlection came in 1897 a fusion of Populists and Republicans sent him back to the Senate and thereafter he generally supported Republican policies.

In the Senate Kyle interested himself mainly in educational matters, and made a respectable record. His chief service, however, was as chairman of the National Industrial Commission, a body created by Congress to investigate the industrial status of the country. Although the nineteen-volume report published by the Commission was chiefly prepared by experts, Kyle gave to it his constant attention and in a broad way determined its direction. He was industriously engaged upon it when death came unexpectedly to him, at his home in Aberdeen.

Kyle married, Apr. 27, 1881, Anna Isabel Dugot of Medina, Ohio, a classmate in the Oberlin preparatory school. Two children survived them.

[*Memorial and Biog. Record, Central S. D.* (1899); *Biog. Dir. Am. Cong.* (1928); *Memorial Addresses on the Life and Character of James H. Kyle*, 57 Cong., 1 Sess. (1902); *Who's Who in America*, 1899–1901; *Congreg. Year-Book*, 1902; Jours. of the S. Dak. legislature, 1891; *Chicago Tribune*, Feb. 10, 1891; W. P. Butler, "A True Story of the Election of James H. Kyle," MS. in S. Dak. Dept. of Hist. files; *Reports of the Industrial Commission* (19 vols., 1900–02); *Daily Argus-Leader* (Sioux Falls, S. Dak.), July 2, 1901.]

D. R.

KYNETT, ALPHA JEFFERSON (Aug. 12, 1829–Feb. 23, 1899), Methodist Episcopal clergyman, reformer, was born in Adams County, Pa., youngest of the eight children of John and Polly (Peterson) Kynett. In 1832 his parents moved to Ohio, in 1838 to Indiana, and in 1842 to Iowa, where they had their part in the exploits of the pioneer settlers. Kynett's early education was necessarily limited, but he pursued relentlessly a course of self-culture that yielded advantages far in excess of those conferred by the ordinary college training of his day. When he was twenty-two years old he entered the ministry of the Methodist Episcopal Church by joining the Iowa Conference. He was ordained deacon by Bishop Scott in 1853, and elder by Bishop Simpson in 1855. In 1854 he married Althea Pauline, daughter of the Rev. James Gilruth of Davenport, Iowa, where Kynett had been pastor for two years. In 1860 he was appointed presiding elder of Davenport district, a position of heavy responsibility for so young a man. During the Civil War he became a member of Governor Kirkwood's staff, and aided in raising and equipping troops for the front. In 1864 he was elected for the first time a delegate to the Methodist General Conference, and was reëlected successively every four years. He soon rose to prominence in this body and became a dominant factor in the molding of legislation. In the General Conference of 1864 he was the directing force in the establishment of the Church Extension Society, formulating the legislation that initiated it and writing its constitution. This organization was the outgrowth of the Church Extension Society of the Upper Iowa Conference, which was formed in 1864 at Kynett's suggestion and of which he was corresponding secretary. In 1867 he became secretary of the general organization and in that office he remained until his death. He gave to his denomination an administration of remarkable efficiency, aiding, in the thirty-two years of his incumbency, over eleven thousand churches with loans and donations that aggregated over six millions of dollars, and securing the erection of hundreds of churches all over the country, especially in the developing areas of the West. In connection with this work he edited the bi-monthly, *Christianity in Earnest,* from 1889 until his death. He was a stalwart in the advocacy of many notable causes, such as lay representation in the General Conference, equal lay and ministerial representation in the same body, and the admission to it of women as members. He was one of the founders of the Anti-Saloon League, the plan of arraying the various church denominations in a determined crusade against the liquor traffic having been put into effective operation by him while he was a young pastor in Iowa. He organized in 1893, as a non-partisan movement, the Interdenominational Christian Temperance Alliance of Ohio, and in 1895 he joined Luther B. Wilson of Washington, D. C., in calling the convention that created the Anti-Saloon League of America. It was largely through his energetic direction that what is now the Board of Temperance, Prohibition and Public Morals of the Methodist Episcopal Church was formed, and he was an influential factor in its earlier onslaughts against the liquor traffic. It was while delivering an address before a convention of the Anti-Saloon League of Pennsylvania at Harrisburg that he sustained the stroke that was followed by his death. He was buried in West Laurel Hill Cemetery, Philadelphia.

[*Jour. of the Gen. Conference of the M. E. Ch., Held ... May 1900* (1900); S. N. Fellows, *Hist. of the Upper Iowa Conference of the M. E. Ch.* (copr. 1907); G. M. Hammell, *The Passing of the Saloon* (copr. 1908); E. H. Cherrington, *Hist. of the Anti-saloon League* (1913) and *Standard Encyc. of the Alcohol Problem,* vol. IV (1928); *Meth. Rev.,* Nov. 1899; *Christianity in Earnest,* Mar.–Apr. and May–June, 1899; *The Christian Advocate,* Mar. 2, 1899; information as to certain facts from a son, Rev. A. G. Kynett, Philadelphia.]

S. J. H.

LA BARGE, JOSEPH (Oct. 1, 1815–Apr. 3, 1899), Missouri River navigator, fur-trader, was born in St. Louis, the son of Joseph Marie and Eulalie (Hortiz) La Barge. After some schooling in St. Louis he was sent, at the age of twelve, to St. Mary's College, in Perry County, but at fifteen was expelled. His mind was set on steamboating and fur trading, and in the fall of 1831 he got a place as clerk on the American Fur Company's boat, the *Yellowstone,* which had just returned from the upper river and was proceeding to New Orleans. On its return the following spring he signed a three years' contract with the company. Most of this period was spent as an Indian trader in the Omaha region. He was on the *Yellowstone* during its upward voyage of 1833, when a cholera epidemic caused its temporary abandonment by officers and crew, leaving him for a time in charge and giving him his first experience as a navigator. On the completion of his contract he worked for a time as a trader for one of the Robidou brothers, and for the next four years served as a clerk, pilot, and master on different boats on the lower river. In 1841 he entered the fur trade in opposition to the company, but was soon forced out. He was married in the following year (Aug. 17) to Pelagie Guerette. In 1843, as pilot of the company's boat, *Omega,* he made the voyage that carried Audubon to the upper Missouri. For the next twelve years, as pilot or master, sometimes of his own boat, at other times of a company boat, he continued in the perilous upper river traffic. In 1856 he parted with the company for good, and for the next few years was on the lower river. In the winter of 1861–62 he organized the firm of La Barge, Harkness & Company, to engage in the Fort Benton trade, but after heavy losses the venture was abandoned. When he foresaw in the middle sixties the ultimate conquest of the steamboat by the railway, his judgment told him to retire; but his inclination prompted him to keep on, and he lost his entire fortune. From 1880 to 1885 he was in government service as a pilot, and from 1890 to 1894 he held a municipal office in St. Louis. His last gainful work was done in 1896–97 for the Missouri River Commission, when he compiled a valuable list of all the steamboat wrecks on the Missouri River from the opening of the river to navigation down to 1897 ("Report of the Chief of Engineers," 1897, pt. 6, pp. 3870–92, *House Executive Document No. 2,* 55 Cong., 2 Sess.). He died suddenly at his home in St. Louis and after an imposing funeral in the Cathedral was buried in Calvary cemetery.

Though he had rivals to fame in his brother John and in Grant Marsh, Joseph La Barge was the most widely known of the Missouri River boatmen. His working life spanned the whole era of commercial steamboating on the upper river: as a clerk he served in 1831 on the boat which in that year made the first voyage to Fort Tecumseh (later Fort Pierre), and as a master he made the last through voyage (1878) between St. Louis and the head of navigation at Fort Benton. He is described by his biographer as one of the most distinguished-looking men of the West in his time. He was five feet ten in height, well proportioned, erect and muscular, with sharp, alert eyes and a quiet energy in all his movements. His manner was sociable, his voice pleasant, and he talked entertainingly. Though French was his mother tongue, he acquired a facile command of English. His ethical standards were high, and though he was often the victim of unscrupulous acts of others, he was known for his scrupulous integrity.

[H. M. Chittenden, *Hist. of Early Steamboat Navigation on the Missouri River: Life and Adventures of Joseph La Barge* (2 vols., 1903); "Diary of Jas. Harkness of the Firm of La Barge, Harkness and Co.," *Contributions of the Hist. Soc. of Mont.*, vol. II (1896); *Forty Years a Fur Trader on the Upper Missouri: The Personal Narrative of Chas. Larpenteur* (2 vols., 1898), ed. by Elliott Coues; Wm. Hyde and H. L. Conard, *Encyc. of the Hist. of St. Louis* (1899), vol. II.]

W. J. G.

LA BORDE, MAXIMILIAN (June 5, 1804–Nov. 6, 1873), physician, writer, educator, was born in Edgefield, S. C., the son of Pierre LaBorde, a native of Bordeaux, France, and his wife Sarah Crane, of Edgefield. Pierre LaBorde had inherited an estate in Santo Domingo; but, fleeing from the slave insurrection of 1791, he landed penniless in Charleston, where he became the leader of a theatre orchestra as violinist. Later he settled in Edgefield as a merchant. Maximilian, an agile, precocious child, full of drollery and wit, attended Edgefield Academy, and was later taught by James Caldwell. In 1821 he graduated from South Carolina College and entered the law office of Simkins & McDuffie in Edgefield. After two years, however, he turned to medicine, graduated with the first class from the Medical College of South Carolina in Charleston, and began to practice in Edgefield. On Sept. 28, 1826, he married Sophia Parsons Carroll, daughter of James P. Carroll, of Charleston. In 1836 he was one of the founders of the *Edgefield Advertiser,* of which he soon became sole editor and owner, and the same year was elected to the South Carolina legislature, where he served on the committee on education. The next year he was appointed trustee of South Carolina College, and two years later he was elected secretary of state and removed to Columbia. In 1841 his wife died, and on Dec. 27, 1843, he married her younger sister, Elizabeth.

At the age of thirty-eight LaBorde began his teaching career as professor of logic and belles-lettres at South Carolina College, and in 1845 he was transferred to the chair of metaphysics. In his relations with students he "conciliated their regard, and showing himself to be their friend, secured an unusual measure of their personal esteem and friendship in return" (J. L. Reynolds, "Memoir" in *History of South Carolina College,* ed. 1874, p. xxiii). He always had one or more beneficiaries in the college. Successful also as a popular lecturer, he was one of the founders of the Columbia Athenæum. He was interested in church and welfare work, became warden of Trinity Episcopal Church, and served as president of the board of regents for the state insane asylum. The summer of 1861 he spent in Virginia, establishing wayside hospitals, and when war left the college without students, he gave his entire time to relief work, helping to organize and becoming chairman of the Central Association for the Relief of South Carolina Soldiers. When Columbia was occupied by Sherman, he helped save the college from fire. In the spring of that year, his son Oscar was killed at the battle of Averysboro.

When South Carolina College became the state university after the war, LaBorde was made professor of rhetoric, criticism, elocution, and English language and literature. This position he held until he resigned on Oct. 9, 1873. He then accepted a position as South Carolina secretary of the Southern Historical Society; but developing bronchitis, he died on the campus where he had been associated for more than fifty years as student, trustee, and professor. In accordance with his wish, his library was given to the University of the South. Impulsive, he yet had exquisite tact, independence, and open-mindedness, as well as a peculiar gift for repartee. His first major publication was a textbook, *Introduction to Physiology* (1855), but his best-known work is the *History of South Carolina College* (1859), valuable for its lifelike character sketches. He also wrote the *Story of Lethea and Verona* (1860); *A Suburban House and an Old Lady* (1861); and articles for the Columbia press, agricultural journals, *Russell's Magazine,* and the *Southern Quarterly Review.* Probably his last publication was a pamphlet, *Tribute to Hon. J. B. O'Neall* (1872).

[*Alumni Directory, Univ. S. C.* (1826); J. W. Davidson, *The Living Writers of the South* (1869); *News and Courier* (Charleston), Nov. 8, 1873; family records.] A. K. G.

LACEY, JOHN (Feb. 4, 1755–Feb. 17, 1814), Revolutionary soldier, public official, was born in Buckingham, Bucks County, Pa., of Quaker stock. His father was John Lacey, whose grandfather, William, came from the Isle of Wight with William Penn; his mother was Jane (Chapman) Lacey, whose father, Abraham, was the son of an original settler from England. Lacey attended a country school and always regretted his inadequate education. At fourteen he began work in his father's grist mill. The chief event of his youth was a trip with his great-uncle in 1773 to visit the Indians at "New Commers Town," beyond Pittsburgh. In 1775, as the Revolution approached, he warmly espoused the American cause, and despite disownment by the Quakers in February 1776, and opposition from family and friends, he held to his course with tenacity. He was commissioned captain (Jan. 5, 1776), raised a company in Bucks County, and took part in the Canadian campaign of that year as captain in the 4th Regiment of the Pennsylvania line, returning home in December. On Mar. 22, 1777, he was appointed sub-lieutenant in Bucks County, a civil position for organizing men and supplies, and on May 6 was appointed lieutenant-colonel of militia. He took part in fighting near Gulf Mills Road in November 1777. On Jan. 9, 1778, he was offered the appointment of brigadier-general (at the age of twenty-three) and accepted, at a time when the cause of the Americans was at its lowest and many were withdrawing from the army. Though he sometimes had as few as sixty men under him, he was energetic in his efforts to check the Loyalists and prevent British raids in the country north of Philadelphia. At Crooked Billet, May 1, 1778, he was surprised by the enemy, but succeeded in extricating himself. On May 11 he turned over his command to General Potter and on June 5, returned to his home. He continued as sub-lieutenant, and was appointed commissioner of confiscated estates for Bucks County. In August 1780, he resumed command of the militia called for service because of a threatened British attack, and in the fall of 1781, he was again in command of the militia until the British surrendered at Yorktown.

In politics, Lacey was a vigorous and energetic partisan, opposing not only the Loyalists but also (as a Democrat, or "Constitutionalist") the aristocratic party called Republicans. He was elected to the Assembly from Bucks County in October 1778. In October 1779 he was elected to the Supreme Executive Council for three years, and served except for the periods of 1780 and 1781 when he was in command of the militia. In the election of October 1781 he marched the militia in military formation to the polls. This action resulted in charges against him of undue influence over the soldiers and intimidation of the populace. After long consideration, however, the Council decided (in March 1782) that the proceedings had been proper and the election was confirmed. Lacey's action was much condemned but was also strongly supported by his party.

On Jan. 18, 1781, Lacey married Anastasia Reynolds, daughter of Colonel Thomas Reynolds of New Mills, now Pemberton, N. J. Four children were born to them. In 1782 he moved to New Mills, and engaged in iron manufacturing with his father-in-law. He held a place of prominence in the community, was elected justice of the peace, and member of the state Assembly in 1801. His positive character continued to make enemies, however, and his impeachment as justice was narrowly averted. He was of a type the Revolution brought forth; an unlettered man of natural abilities, energetic but far from tactful, needed in time of war to consolidate the patriots and crush the opposition. He died at New Mills, in his sixtieth year.

[Lacey wrote his memoirs, down to Jan. 1778, at the solicitation of his son-in-law, William Darlington [*q.v.*], whose copy of the MS., annotated, together with a mass of letters and documents, is in the library of the Pa. Hist. Soc. The memoirs were published in *Pa. Mag. of Hist. and Biog.*, Apr. 1901–July 1902. See also a biography by W. H. H. Davis, in *Graham's Mag.*, Feb.–May 1854, privately printed under the title, *Sketch of the Life and Character of John Lacey* (1868); *Pa. Archives,* 1 ser. V, VI, VIII (1853), IX (1854); *Minutes of the Provincial Council of Pa.*, vols. X–XIV, XVI (1852–53); *Poulson's Am. Daily Advertiser,* Feb. 23, 1814.] A. H. S.

LACEY, JOHN FLETCHER (May 30, 1841–Sept. 29, 1913), soldier, lawyer, congressman, was born in a one-room log cabin on the Ohio River near New Martinsville in what is now West Virginia. One of the boy's formative experiences was seeing a negro slave barely escape his pursuers by crossing the river in a skiff. When he was fourteen his parents, John Mills and Eleanor (Patten) Lacey, moved to a farm near Oskaloosa, Iowa. During the next six years he helped his father as a brick mason, worked on the farm, attended various local academies, and taught two winter schools. At the outbreak of the Civil War he enlisted in the Federal army, but was soon captured at Blue Mills, Mo., and paroled. Until exchanged in 1862, he read law with the attorney general of Iowa, Samuel A. Rice. He then enlisted under Rice in the 33rd Iowa Volunteers and rose to the rank of assistant adjutant-general of his brigade. Vivid descriptions of his experiences are to be found in his sketches of Generals Rice and Steele (*Annals of Iowa,* April 1895 and April–July 1898).

The war over, Lacey was admitted to the bar and on Sept. 19, 1865, married Martha Newell. He then proceeded to make up for his deficiencies in education by studying law twelve to sixteen hours a day, by reading widely in history and literature, and by extensive travel at home and abroad. In 1869 he began his public career in the House of the Thirteenth General Assembly as a member of the judiciary committee. The following year he published the Third Iowa Digest and in 1875 and 1884 respectively, the first and second volumes of *A Digest of Railway Decisions.* The latter work covered all railway cases in the English language and established his reputation as an authority on railway law. Between 1889 and 1907, he represented the Sixth District of Iowa in Congress continuously, except for the Fifty-second Congress (1891–93). An ardent student of Indian affairs, public lands, and forestry, he was one of the earliest conservationists. As chairman of the committee on forests, he helped to frame most of the legislation of that period on the preservation of forests and wild life. His work won the approval of President Roosevelt who declared that, when there was "a matter . . . of consequence to the nation as a whole," Lacey could be relied upon to "approach it simply from the standpoint of public service" (*Memorial Volume, post,* p. 43). As a strong but conservative Republican of the "stand pat" school he had little patience with the "progressive movement" for tariff revision and corporation regulation as advocated by Gov. Albert B. Cummins [*q.v.*] in the "Iowa Idea." In consequence he lost his seat in Congress in 1907 and was defeated by Cummins for the Senate in 1908. Lacey's political career was then over and he devoted the rest of his life to the practice of law in Oskaloosa.

As a lawyer and statesman his strength lay in persistence, tireless energy, and a practical mind. He was an able debater and an accomplished speaker. Always a student, he was equaled by few in understanding of public affairs. Medium in height and physique, he was a gentleman of the old school, always polite, dignified, and well dressed. While kindly, witty, and approachable in personal relations he was a grim political fighter who always knew exactly where he stood; nevertheless he commanded the respect even of his enemies, because of his high conception of public service.

[The Lacey Papers, Hist. Dept., Des Moines, Iowa; *Major John F. Lacey, Memorial Vol.* (1915); E. H. Stiles, *Recollections and Sketches of Notable Lawyers and Pub. Men of Early Iowa* (1916); *Biog. Dir. Am. Cong.* (1928); *Who's Who in America,* 1912–13; *Oskaloosa Daily Herald,* Sept. 29, Oct. 4, 1913.] C. E. P.

LACLEDE, PIERRE (*c.* 1724–June 20, 1778), trader, founder of St. Louis, was born in the village of Bedous, in the lower Pyrenees, France. His surname was Liguest—the form Laclede Liguest appearing in all legal documents bearing his signature—but he chose to be known as Laclede. He is said to have been of good family and to have been trained for commercial pursuits. He arrived in New Orleans in 1755, and after a time became a member of the trading firm of Maxent, Laclede & Company. In 1857 he formed a union, unsanctioned by church or state but approved by society, with Marie Thérèse (Bourgeois) Chouteau, a highly respected woman who had left her husband, taking her infant son, (René) Auguste Chouteau [*q.v.*], with her. By Laclede she had a son, (Jean) Pierre Chouteau [*q.v.*], and three daughters, all of whom, in observance of French law, bore the surname of the undivorced husband. In 1762 Maxent, Laclede & Company obtained an eight years' monopoly of the trade with "the savages of the Missouri," and in August of the following year Laclede with his family started north, arriving at Fort de Chartres, on the Illinois side of the river, exactly three months later.

The transfer of the territory east of the Mississippi to the British determined him to establish his trading post on the western side. In February 1764, he put his young stepson in command of a party of thirty men and sent them across the river to a location he had already selected, with instructions to plat the ground and erect a storehouse and cabins. In April he followed and named his village St. Louis, in honor of Louis IX. Until the installation of civil government, more than eighteen months later, he was the sole ruler of the community. He was, however, a benevolent dictator, who dispensed justice with an even hand and distributed the land fairly, keeping little for himself. His village grew, and though his monopoly was revoked, his trade expanded. His commercial methods, however, proved faulty, and he accumulated a mass of worthless paper which left him heavily in debt to his firm. In the fall of 1776 he left for New Orleans, where he spent nearly two years in the effort to straighten out his tangled finances. On his homeward voyage, when near the mouth of the Arkansas, he died. The place of his burial was marked, but efforts made some time afterward to discover it were unsuccessful.

Laclede was the founder of a great family which does not bear his name and of a great city which for many years suffered his memory to be wholly eclipsed. Historical research has restored him to his place. He appears as a man of vision, who saw in his little village a future metropolis; a man of initiative, energy, and daring, just in his dealings, and, though a trader, less devoted to his own interests than to those of his community.

[F. L. Billon, *Annals of St. Louis in Its Early Days under the French and Spanish Dominations* (1886); Wm. Hyde and H. L. Conard, *Encyc. of the Hist. of St. Louis* (1899); J. T. Scharf, *Hist. of St. Louis City and County* (1883); articles on the founding of St. Louis in *Mo. Hist. Soc. Colls.*, vol. III, nos. 3 and 4 (1911), vol. IV, no. 2 (1913).]
W. J. G.

LACOCK, ABNER (July 9, 1770–Apr. 12, 1837), farmer, representative, senator, canal-builder, was born on Cub Run, near Alexandria, Va., the son of William and Lovey Lacock. His father was a native of England and his mother of France. When Abner was quite young the family moved to Washington County, Pa., and settled on a farm. Young Lacock lacked the advantages of early education, but native ability, careful observation, and extensive reading, helped to overcome this handicap. In 1796 he moved to the sparsely settled region of Beaver (then in Allegheny County), Pa. The same year he was appointed justice of the peace, and later became an innkeeper. In 1801 he was elected to the legislature, and continued his services there until 1803, when he was appointed the first associate judge of Beaver County. He resigned his judgeship a year later to reënter the legislature. Here (1804–08) he was identified with the radical Republicans in their attacks on the judiciary, and as one of "the puppets of Leib's machine" (*Freeman's Journal,* Philadelphia, Aug. 14, 1807), was conspicuous in the impeachment proceedings against Gov. Thomas McKean [*q.v.*]. From 1808 to 1810 he was a member of the state Senate.

Elected to Congress as a "war candidate" in 1810, Lacock supported President Madison and the war measures. From 1813 to 1819 he was in the United States Senate. A bitter enemy of A. J. Dallas, he acquiesced in that gentleman's appointment as secretary of the treasury only because of the country's desperate financial condition (Henry Adams, *History of the United States,* vol. VIII, 1891, p. 243). His greatest activity in the Senate was manifested in the promotion of internal improvements. In a committee report on Feb. 14, 1817 (*Annals of Congress,* 14 Cong., 2 Sess., pp. 120–22), he recommended an extensive program of roads and canals, and the use of the bank bonus for this purpose. He interested himself in pensions and bounty lands for soldiers and in higher salaries for government clerks and secretaries. He favored popular election of the president, under which method, he argued (Mar. 20, 1816), "there could be no fear of corruption" (*Annals of Congress,* 14 Cong., 1 Sess., p. 220). The investigation of Jackson's conduct in the Seminole campaign was instigated by Lacock, and his report (Feb. 24, 1819) in the capacity of chairman of the investigating committee severely censured the General's actions in raising and organizing armed forces and in attacking Spanish territory as violations of the Constitution and of international law (*Ibid.,* 15 Cong., 2 Sess., pp. 256–68). He was also a member of the committees on naturalization, post roads, appropriations, rules, foreign relations, military affairs, accounts, and pensions. Between terms of Congress he cultivated his farm.

Lacock was one of the first men to push actively the plan for connecting the Delaware and Ohio rivers by a state line of canals, and after leaving the Senate he devoted himself wholeheartedly to this project. He was one of five commissioners appointed on Apr. 11, 1825, to survey a route for the contemplated improvements, was a member of the board of canal commissioners, and after the legislature had authorized construction, supervised the building of the western division of the canal, from Pittsburgh to Johnstown. The first canal boat to run west of the Alleghanies, a freight and passenger packet, was the *General Abner Lacock.* In 1829 his services as canal commissioner terminated. From 1832 to 1835 he was again in the state legislature, this time a Clay Whig and conspicuous for his advocacy of free popular education. In 1836 he was appointed commissioner to survey and construct the Pennsylvania and Ohio canal, known as the "crosscut canal," connecting the Erie division of the Pennsylvania canal with the Portsmouth and Ohio canal. Illness brought on by exposure while working on this project subsequently caused his death at his residence near Freedom, Pa.

Lacock derived his title of "General" from his service as brigadier-general of the Pennsylvania militia. He was an expert surveyor, an accomplished writer, and a good public speaker.

His library, well selected and one of the largest in western Pennsylvania, was destroyed by the Ohio floods in 1832. His wife was Hannah Eddy. He had three sons and four daughters, and left a considerable estate consisting largely of land.

[Biographical sketch by J. M. Swank in *Pa. Mag. of Hist. & Biog.*, IV (1880), 202–08; J. H. Bausman, *The Hist. of Beaver County, Pa.* (2 vols., 1904); *Hist. of Beaver County, Pa.* (1888); and Samuel Hazard, *Register of Pa.*, Apr. 25, 1829; *Pa. Reporter* (Harrisburg), Apr. 27, 1837; *Western Argus* (Beaver, Pa.), Apr. 19, 1837; information from Mrs. Curtis C. Noss, Rochester, Pa., and Mrs. A. G. Matthews, Richmond, Ind.]

J. H. P.

LACY, DRURY (Oct. 5, 1758–Dec. 6, 1815), educator, clergyman, was the son of William Lacy, a farmer of Chesterfield County, Va., and his wife Elizabeth Rice. When ten years old he lost his left hand by the explosion of an overloaded gun which a soldier at a county muster asked him to fire. Debarred from manual pursuits, he was placed by his father in the then celebrated school conducted by Rev. Christopher Macrae, of Littleton Parish in Cumberland County, Va., who had been educated in Edinburgh, Scotland. The boy's mother died when he was ten years old, his father when he was sixteen; and being without patrimony, he was soon compelled to leave school and to seek work. At eighteen he became a tutor in the family of Daniel Allen, a prominent planter and elder in the Presbyterian Church, Cumberland County, and there came under the influence of President John Blair Smith of Hampden-Sydney College, a graduate of the College of New Jersey, who was supplying the Cumberland Church at that time. He next became a tutor in the family of Col. John Nash of Prince Edward County, the father-in-law of President Smith.

Of a vigorous mind, and with the encouragement and guidance of President Smith, he continued his studies in Latin, Greek, the sciences, and mathematics, receiving the degree of B.A. in 1788. He had studied theology under Smith, was licensed to preach in September 1787, and was ordained the following year. His proficiency was such that in his twenty-sixth year he was employed as a tutor in the college, and while holding this office he preached in neighboring congregations—Hat Creek and Concord in Campbell County, and Cub Creek in Charlotte County. He is said to have had a voice of extraordinary range and beauty, which enabled him to speak to vast crowds out-of-doors, where much of his preaching was done. He took an active part in the revival of 1787–88 in southern Virginia.

To lighten the burdens of the President, who was also teacher and preacher, young Lacy was elected vice-president of the college, and on Smith's resignation to go to Philadelphia, he became for several years acting president (1789–97). At the end of this time, resigning his position in the college, he established an academy at his home, "Ararat," a short distance from Hampden-Sydney, and there taught for the rest of his life. He had many students who afterward became eminent in their professions, among them Hugh Blair Grigsby [*q.v.*], historian, author, and publicist, who said of him: "I bear my testimony to his thorough teaching. . . . Though 61 years have passed since I was under his care, I feel the influence of his teaching on my mind and character at this moment, and pointing the very thought which I am now pressing." He continued his active interest in the affairs of the college as a member of the board of trustees. In 1809 he was moderator of the General Assembly of the Presbyterian Church and was often a delegate from his presbytery to the Assembly, which in those days usually met at Philadelphia. He had married, on Dec. 25, 1789, Anne, daughter of William Smith of Powhatan County, Va., whom he survived but a few days. His death occurred in Philadelphia, following a surgical operation, and he was buried in the graveyard of the Third Presbyterian (Pine Street) Church of that city.

[P. H. Hoge, *Moses Drury Hoge: Life and Letters* (1899); A. J. Morrison, *Coll. of Hampden Sidney: Dict. of Biog., 1776–1825* (n.d.); Minutes of Hanover Presbytery, in the library of Union Theological Seminary, Richmond, Va.; H. B. Grigsby, *Discourse on the Lives and Characters of the Early Presidents and Trustees of Hampden-Sidney Coll.* (1913); W. B. Sprague, *Annals of the Am. Pulpit*, vol. III (1858); W. H. Foote, *Sketches of Va., Hist. and Biog.* (1850); sketch in *Watchman of the South*, Jan. 10, 1839; *Poulson's Am. Daily Advertiser*, Dec. 8, 1815.]

J. D. E.

LACY, ERNEST (Sept. 19, 1863–June 17, 1916), poet, playwright, educator, was born at Warren, Pa., the son of Barnet W. and Martha M. (Maclean) Lacy, of English and Scotch-Irish ancestry. The father, a well-known Pennsylvania attorney, suffered financial reverses and at his death left the family in straitened circumstances that early threw the boy on his own resources. Ernest and his older brother, William, attended Hastings Academy and studied law in the office of a Philadelphia attorney. Both showed unusual precocity, and Ernest qualified for the bar before he was twenty-one. William's *An Examination of the Philosophy of the Unknowable as Expounded by Herbert Spencer* (1883), set up and printed by the two brothers in the garret of their home because they could not find a publisher, attracted international attention and was reprinted by Ernest in 1912 after the author's death.

Earning his livelihood by preparing students for the bar examinations, and with his brother working on a revision of Kent's *Commentaries,* published under William's name in four volumes (1891–92), Lacy revealed the true bent of his genius in his *Rinaldo,* a romantic five-act tragedy in blank verse written while he was still in his teens. In order to get into touch with actors who wanted plays he gave up the law for the theatre. After considerable work as a theatrical press-agent he became manager of the old Walnut Street Theatre in Philadelphia. Nearly all of the leading plays came to this house, and through William B. Gross he was introduced to Joseph Haworth, Robert B. Mantell, Julia Marlowe, Richard Mansfield, and other well-known actors. After several years spent as a reviser of plays at the Walnut, he became business-manager of the Park Theatre. When the Paris Winter Circus came to Philadelphia, Lacy became manager, and it is characteristic of his versatility that he thoroughly enjoyed his job.

In 1894 Julia Marlowe produced, in Chicago, Lacy's *Chatterton,* a one-act play, and it immediately won the public and the critics by the poetic beauty of its blank verse and the dramatic effectiveness of its close. *Rinaldo* was produced by Joseph Haworth in 1895. It is in the tradition of the older romantic drama with a strong Elizabethan flavor. Though a juvenile production, it has passages of gripping power, and its blank verse often rises to a high level. The last scene "represents the virtues and defects of the romantic tragedy" (Quinn, *post,* I, 208). Lacy also had a knack for writing Irish comedy. His *Crom-a-Boo* and *Black-Thorn Sceptre* were never produced but he won a popular success with *The Ragged Earl,* in which Andrew Mack appeared in 1899, and which was later turned into a popular screen play. *Japhet in Search of a Father,* a dramatization of Marryat's novel, was written for Richard Mansfield, but not produced by him. Unfinished plays on which Lacy was at work at his death are *Earl George,* suggested by a note in Blackstone on an ancient penance, and *Montezuma,* a romantic tragedy dealing with the Aztec civilization. *The Bard of Mary Redcliffe,* written for E. H. Sothern, is his best work and in the judgment of competent critics is the foremost poetic drama written in America. He devoted years to the study of Chatterton, and spent his summer vacations in England studying in the archives of Bristol and absorbing the atmosphere of the place and the surrounding country. Chatterton became his patron saint. Furthermore, his chivalric devotion to his brother, his memories of their common struggles for recognition, and his consciousness of his own power and genius are poured into this play.

In 1893, Lacy, who was then in London reading at the British Museum and doing dramatic coaching, was invited to join the faculty of the old Philadelphia Central High School, chiefly for the purpose of developing the courses in public speaking. In 1896 he became assistant professor, in 1900 full professor, and in 1907 he succeeded Albert H. Smyth as head of the English department. He was a pioneer in developing debating in the public schools, his legal training standing him in good stead, and in transforming the older formal work in "elocution" into vital training in self-expression. His profound knowledge of Shakespeare and his first-hand acquaintance with dramatic technique made his Shakespeare courses unique. Because of his poetic sensibility and his rich emotional nature he was a rare interpreter of the Romantic poets. Two of his best sonnets are those to Wordsworth and Byron. He considered Shelley's *Cenci* the greatest English drama of the nineteenth century. His strength as a teacher of literature did not lie in the presentation of facts, but in critical insight into the poetic mind and in the relating of poetry to life.

Lacy was of medium height and powerful build, with finely chiseled features and a well-poised head, his sensitiveness hidden behind a challenging air. He had a rich musical voice and his reading of Shakespeare was for generations of high school students the best part of their education in English literature. The failure of his muse in his later years was partly due to the drain upon his vitality caused by the drudgery of teaching, and partly to his growing sense of alienation from the realistic trends of the drama. His *Plays and Sonnets* (1900) contained *Rinaldo, Chatterton,* and sixty-one sonnets, marked by depth of feeling and mastery of form. This volume was reprinted in 1910, and another added, which contained *The Bard of Mary Redcliffe*; both volumes were reprinted by N. S. Brown in 1916. In 1917 appeared a one-volume memorial edition. On June 18, 1885, he married Hattie C. Dugan, who survived him.

[A. H. Quinn, *A Hist. of the Am. Drama from the Civil War to the Present Day* (2 vols., 1927); F. S. Edmonds, *Hist. of the Central High School of Phila.* (1902); *Who's Who in America,* 1914–15; *Phila. Press* and *N. Y. Times,* June 18, 1916; information furnished by Mrs. Lacy, E. H. Sothern, Chester N. Farr, Jr., Louis Mann, and others; personal recollections.]

J. D. S.

LADD, CATHERINE (Oct. 28, 1808–Jan. 30, 1899), schoolmistress and writer of fugitive prose and verse, was born in Richmond, Va., where her father James Stratton had married her mother, Ann Collins, in 1807, a year after his arrival from Ireland. Six months after her birth, he fell from a vessel off the coast and was drowned. She was educated in the schools of Richmond and is said to have been a playmate of Edgar Allan Poe. One of her most treasured recollections of Richmond was her meeting with Lafayette at the public reception given for him there in 1824. In September 1828 she married George Williamson Livermore Ladd, born in Plymouth, N. H., who had been a seaman ten years before; but having studied with S. F. B. Morse in Boston, he was then in the South as a portrait painter. Accompanied by her mother, she went with him to Charleston, S. C., where they arrived in time to witness the jubilee for the election of Andrew Jackson. From Charleston they went to Augusta, Ga., where they remained until burned out in the great fire of 1829. They then returned to South Carolina but later removed to Macon, Ga., where for three years Mrs. Ladd was principal of Vineville Academy. In 1839 she learned that a building had been erected in Winnsboro, S. C., for a girls' school but had never been opened, and she "determined to give it a trial." On Jan. 1, 1840, she opened the Winnsboro Female Institute, which in 1850 had nine teachers and about a hundred students, and she remained principal until it was closed by the Civil War.

She took a keen interest in public affairs and is said to have published as early as 1851 articles on the encouragement of manufacturing in South Carolina. She is also said to have submitted a design for the first Confederate flag. As permanent president of the Ladies' Relief Association of Fairfield, she did much for the sick and wounded Confederate soldiers. Her son Albert Washington Ladd was wounded at the battle of Seven Pines; her husband died on July 14, 1864; and she lost everything in 1865 when her home was burned by Sherman's troops. In 1870 she reopened her boarding and day school, including among her subjects art, music, and dancing. Probably because of failing eyesight, she retired in 1880 and went to live on "Buena Vista Plantation," nineteen miles from Winnsboro, where she spent most of her time in her garden. On July 1, 1891, she became totally blind. She died at "Buena Vista" in her ninety-first year, and although she had been a member of the Episcopal Church, she was buried in the neighboring Salem Presbyterian churchyard. Mrs. Ladd's poems are characterized by religious feeling and love of nature. Her occasional letters of reminiscence and later poems, which appeared in the Winnsboro press, are signed Mrs. C. Ladd; but her earlier pen names are said to have been Minnie Mayflower, Arcturus, and Alida. Two poems of little merit, signed by her pseudonym Morna, appear in the second volume of the *Southern Literary Messenger*. She is said to have been a regular contributor to the Charleston *News and Courier* and to have published articles on art and education, as well as tales, essays, plays, and news-letters.

[Printed sources include: Ida Raymond, *Southland Writers* (2 vols., 1870); Mrs. Thomas Taylor and others, *S. C. Women in the Confederacy*, vol. I (1903); the *State* (Columbia, S. C.), Mar. 7, 1906, Apr. 12, 1912. Mrs. Ladd's scrapbook is in the possession of Mrs. Joe Fee, Blair, S. C. It contains undated newspaper clippings, family papers, and an autobiographical letter dictated by Mrs. Ladd, probably in 1898.]

A. K. G.

LADD, EDWIN FREMONT (Dec. 13, 1859–June 22, 1925), chemist, United States senator, was born at Starks, Me., the son of John and Rosilla (Locke) Ladd. He traced his ancestry to Daniel Ladd of Ipswich, Mass., who came from England in 1634. He was educated in Somerset Academy, in Maine, and graduated from the University of Maine in 1884. Having majored in chemistry, upon his graduation he was employed by the New York Experiment Station and soon became chief chemist of the institution, continuing in the position until called in 1890 to the department of chemistry of the North Dakota Agricultural College at Fargo, N. D. There he almost immediately came into public notice for his campaign against the adulteration of food. At that period foods were adulterated with coal-tar products, sulphites, copper, alum, and other harmful matter; glucose was substituted for sugars, cheap vegetable matter for coffee, inferior meats and waste tissue for potted ham and chicken; meats were embalmed with chemicals. Dyspepsia and stomach disorders were alarmingly frequent and directly attributable to these adulterated foods. Ladd's fight for pure food came into conflict with the interests of extensive organizations supplying national food products but he combated them successfully and helped to drive them from North Dakota. He was made the administrator of the pure-food law and by his courageous enforcement of it attained wide recognition. He became the chief ally of Harvey W. Wiley, chief chemist of the federal Department of Agriculture, and they worked together in their efforts to provide the American people with pure food products. When Ladd died Wiley wrote a comprehensive and touching tribute to the man and his work (*Congressional Record,* 69 Cong., 1 Sess., pp. 9016–17). For a quarter of a century (1899–1925), Ladd was editor of the *North Dakota Farmer.*

During Ladd's years as pure-food administrator, North Dakota farmers enjoyed a special market for white wheat which made a superior brand of flour. In time a bleaching process was devised and came into general use by which equally white flour could be made from inferior grain, but the bleaching agent was a poison unfit for human consumption. Ladd, turning his attention to this evil, secured laws requiring that all sacks and containers for flour made from bleached wheat be plainly marked, giving the name of the bleaching agent employed. He made a less successful fight for the better grading of storm-damaged wheat which his investigations informed him had greater flour-producing value than the milling trade admitted. His efforts in this direction added to his popularity. In recognition of his work and ability, in 1916 he was made president of the North Dakota Agricultural College, and four years later he was elected to the United States Senate. Although he was a Republican candidate for the senatorship, he was supported by the Non-Partisan League. During his years in office he was best known for his advocacy of various measures for farm relief. In 1924 he supported LaFollette and as a result was deprived of party rank for committee assignments. In 1923 he visited Russia for the purpose of obtaining first-hand information regarding social and economic conditions and proved himself a painstaking and unprejudiced investigator. Some of the agricultural and food bulletins which he published attained the dignity of scientific treatises and his *Manual of Quantitative Chemical Analysis* (1898) was an authority in its field. He was a member of many scientific societies. He was married on Aug. 16, 1893, to Rizpah Sprogle of Annapolis, Md., who survived him.

[*Who's Who in America,* 1924–25; *Biog. Dir. Am. Cong.* (1928); *Cong. Record,* 68 Cong., 2 Sess., pp. 1285–95, 69 Cong. 1 Sess., pp. 9008–19; the *Sun* (Baltimore), and *Fargo Forum,* June 23, 1925; letters from Mrs. Edwin F. Ladd in the Archives of the South Dakota Department of History.] D. R.

LADD, GEORGE TRUMBULL (Jan. 19, 1842–Aug. 8, 1921), psychologist, philosopher, theologian, was the son of Silas Trumbull and Elizabeth (Williams) Ladd, being a descendant of Daniel Ladd who came from London to New England in 1634. Through his paternal grandmother he was related to Elder William Brewster and Gov. William Bradford [*qq.v.*]. He attended a private school at his birthplace, Painesville, Ohio, but for the most part prepared himself for college. In 1864 he was graduated from Western Reserve College (now Western Reserve University), and in 1869 from Andover Theological Seminary. In December of the same year, 1869, he married Cornelia Ann, daughter of John C. Tallman of Bellaire, Ohio, and began his ministry at Edinburg, Ohio. Two years later he became pastor of the Spring Street Congregational Church, Milwaukee, Wis., and continued there until he accepted the chair of philosophy at Bowdoin College (1879). Removing to New Haven in 1881, for forty years he maintained a connection with Yale University, often conducting courses in other institutions, notably at Harvard, Western Reserve University, and the State University of Iowa. On invitation from the Imperial Educational Society and the Imperial University of Tokyo, he visited Japan in 1892, 1899, and 1906, lecturing at Doshisha, Kyoto, Tokyo, and Kobe; and on the second of these visits he extended his journey to India, lecturing on philosophy in the University of Bombay, and on the philosophy of religion at Calcutta, Madras, Benares, and elsewhere.

Ladd's claim to distinction lay neither in the creating of a system of philosophy, nor in original work as a psychological investigator. He was an interpreter and systematizer. His own view in philosophy seems to have been determined largely by Hermann Lotze, whose lecture notes, in six small volumes, he began to translate and publish in 1884. Like Lotze he sought to reconcile the opposing claims of the realists and the idealists, to attain a realistic spiritualism, monistic yet verging on personalism. With almost equal thoroughness graduate students studied under him the works of Hegel and Wundt in the original. One of his main efforts was directed toward acquainting America with German thought as exhibited in the post-Kantian idealists. Another and greater service was his part in introducing from Germany the study of psychology as an experimental science grounded on physiology. His *Elements of Physiological Psychology* (1887) was the first, and with its revision (1911), the most encyclopedic handbook on its subject in the English language. Its appearance coincided with the rise of the "new" psychology in America, and to its influence extending through the nineties is partly attributable the installation of psychological laboratories here in greater numbers than in all the rest of the world. On the speculative and introspective side of the science, there appeared in 1894 the companion volume, *Psychology, Descriptive and Explanatory.* Together they are a fitting monument to Ladd's faithful workmanship. He was a prolific writer in many fields. The character of his interests is best shown in *The Doctrine of Sacred Scripture* (1883), *Philosophy of Mind* (1895), *A Theory of Reality* (1899), *Philosophy of Conduct* (1902), *The Philosophy of Religion* (2 vols., 1905), and *Knowledge, Life and Reality* (1909, 1918). In later years he wrote *What Can I Know?* (1914), *What Ought I to Do?* (1915), *What Should I Believe?* (1915), *What May I Hope?* (1915), and *The Secret of Personality* (1918). Some of his works have been translated into Japanese, some printed for the blind, and some have been adopted as textbooks in Russia, India, and Japan.

With William James, J. McKeen Cattell, J. Mark Baldwin, G. Stanley Hall, Joseph Jastrow, and others, he founded in 1892 the American Psychological Association, and was its second president the following year. In 1895 he married again, his second wife being Frances V. Stevens, daughter of Dr. George T. Stevens of New York. Aside from his literary activity, his work in the closing years of the nineteenth century was mainly with graduate students in philosophy and psychology. To this end he relinquished the Clark Professorship of Metaphysics and Moral Philosophy at Yale in 1901 and accepted a university professorship that placed him in charge of the graduate work in philosophy. In 1899 the Emperor of Japan conferred upon him the Order of the Rising Sun, third class, and on his visit to Japan in 1907 he received the same order, second class, also the gold medal of the Imperial Educational Society of Japan. The same year he was guest and unofficial adviser of Prince Ito in Korea. At the comparatively early age of sixty-two he became professor emeritus, but continued his literary labors with undiminished energy almost to the time of his death at the age of seventy-nine.

[*Who's Who in America,* 1920–21; Warren Ladd, *The Ladd Family* (1890); obituary notices by Carl E. Seashore in *Science,* Sept. 16, 1921; by A. C. Armstrong in the *Philosophical Rev.,* Nov. 1921; and by G. Dawes Hicks in *Nature,* Sept. 1, 1921; *New Haven Journal-Courier,* Aug. 9, 1921.] E. M. W.

LADD, JOSEPH BROWN (July 7, 1764–Nov. 2, 1786), physician and poet, was the eldest son of William and Sarah (Gardner) Ladd, and was descended from Joseph Ladd who was in Portsmouth, R. I., in 1644. He was born in Newport, R. I., and educated in private schools in that city. His father was a soldier in the American Revolution, a member of the Rhode Island legislature, a member of the convention that ratified the Constitution, and a charter member of the Marine Society of Newport. At the age of fourteen the son was placed in a mercantile establishment, which he disliked and soon left. He then spent a year working in a printing office in Newport, and while employed there wrote some ballads and satirical verses. A satire on Dr. Hopkins, the eminent theologian, offended that gentleman, and Ladd was removed by his father from the office. He decided to study medicine and was placed with Dr. Isaac Senter. In the next four years he not only prepared for his chosen profession but also read widely in philosophy and literature. He began to write serious poetry, inspired by his love for an orphan heiress whose guardians would not consent to her marrying him. Licensed to practise medicine in 1783, he was advised by Gen. Nathanael Greene, who had recently returned to Rhode Island, to go to Charleston, S. C. Ladd did so and soon established himself in that community both as a doctor and as a man of letters. He wrote considerable verse and some prose on literary and scientific subjects, and he also took part in political discussion. On July 4, 1785, he delivered before Governor Moultrie and the Cincinnati of South Carolina an address on the principles of the American Revolution. In the autumn of 1786 he accepted a challenge to a duel and died from his wounds. A book of verse, *The Poems of Arouet,* was published in the year of his death.

Although very little of Ladd's poetry possesses today any particular freshness or force, he perhaps deserves more attention than he has received as one of the earliest of American writers to show the influence of the English pre-romantic poets. He wrote, it is true, various patriotic pieces in the heroic couplet, and his translations, also in heroic couplets, of the Bible and Homer are typical of the eighteenth century. On the other hand, he paraphrased several poems of Ossian's in rhymed verse and attempted the modernization of one of Chatterton's Rowley poems. His work contains references to Collins and Goethe, and his descriptions have some of the flavor of Gray and Goldsmith. The love poems addressed from Arouet to Amanda are so extremely sentimental that S. M. Tucker has suggested (*Cambridge History of American Literature,* I, 1917, p. 178) that they may have been influenced by the Della-Cruscan school. This is doubtful, for, though the poems are not dated, many of them must have been written before *The Florence Miscellany* appeared in 1785; but it is undeniable that their insipidity, which may be forgiven on the ground of the author's youth, does resemble the tone of much Della-Cruscan verse. What is important, in any case, is that Ladd was experimenting, and that he was sensitive to new influences some time before they were generally felt in America.

[The chief source is *The Literary Remains of Jos. Brown Ladd, M.D.* (1832), edited by Ladd's sister, Mrs. Elizabeth Haskins, with a biographical sketch by W. B. Chittenden. See also Warren Ladd, *The Ladd Family* (1890), and J. N. Arnold, *Vital Record of R. I.*, XIV (1905), 35.] G. H.

LADD, WILLIAM (May 10, 1778–Apr. 9, 1841), "apostle of peace" and pioneer in the theory of international organization, was born at Exeter, N. H., and died at Portsmouth. He was the third of ten children of Abigail Hill and Col. Eliphalet Ladd, a wealthy sea-captain and ship-builder, and was descended from Daniel Ladd who settled in New England in 1634. At twenty he had taken his degree at Harvard with distinction and was commanding one of the largest brigs that Portsmouth, N. H., boasted. Until 1812 he followed the sea, with the exception of a few years spent in Florida, where he lost part of his fortune in a free-labor experiment designed to point the way to the peaceful abolition of slavery. Then he settled down with his wife at Minot, Me., where he prospered as the scientific cultivator of a large farm. He had married Sophia Ann Augusta Stidolph in London in 1799. In 1819 this bluff, florid, robust, and almost excessively good-humored man by sheer chance became interested in the struggling cause of international peace. The handful of peace societies were so pitifully weak that it was a question whether they would survive. Ladd spared no pains to give them energy and strength: he founded new groups; he enlisted able lieutenants; he devoted a forceful pen and a winning voice to peace propaganda, to which he gave, by witty anecdotes and illustrations, a practical turn (*A Brief Illustration of the Principles of War and Peace, by Philanthropos,* Albany, 1831, *passim*). He was the first to point out some of the most significant relationships between pacifism and feminism (*On the Duty of Females to Promote the Cause of Peace,* Boston, 1836). He made and so far as possible executed careful and practical plans for enlisting the press and pulpit, the college and school. A sincerely religious man, he became a licensed Congregational clergyman in 1837, the better to reach worshipers, seminaries, and synods. Against great obstacles he founded, in May 1828, the American Peace Society, edited its periodical, and by painful journeys carried its message to state legislatures, Congress, and the White House. By showing his colleagues the value of the delegation and the petition he not only contributed to the technique of pacifist propaganda, but was the first to try to bring the peace question into the sphere of politics.

Peace circles were agitated by debates regarding the fundamental principles and philosophy of pacifism, and Ladd contributed tactfully but cogently to a clarification of opinion (Curti, *post*). Believing that the non-resistance principle was "the only solid and substantial foundation," and holding that no ultraism was as bad as ultraconservatism, he succeeded in 1837 in committing the American Peace Society to a condemnation of all war, defensive as well as offensive. Yet he desired the cooperation of friends of peace of all shades of opinion, and he was too much an actualist to follow William Lloyd Garrison and Henry Clarke Wright [*qq.v.*] in all the vagaries of the Non-Resistance Society. Only his letters can adequately testify to his zeal, devotion, and sacrifice. His incessant activity was "meat and drink" to him, and he grudged every minute that he did not devote to the cause of peace. He was too joyous and clear-visioned to be a fanatic, yet he felt it necessary to act every day as if the peace of the world depended upon his efforts and those of his coworkers. It was his greatest regret that he had but one life to give the cause. He refused to obey his physician who warned him, after partial paralysis, to spare himself. With legs so badly ulcered that he was forced to preach from a stool, he held out to the very night before his death. He was the St. Francis of the peace movement, giving up worldly goods as well as life itself to an ideal.

Ladd was not only a martyr to peace; he was one of its greatest architects. Prior to the appearance of *An Essay on a Congress of Nations* (Boston, 1840), the peace movement, both in America and Europe, was essentially a negative opposition to war. While many of the ideas in Ladd's *Essay* were to be found in earlier projects, notably that of Jeremy Bentham, these projects lacked a definite basis for permanent international organization and required radical changes in standards of conduct and modes of thought (James Brown Scott, Introduction to Ladd's *Essay on a Congress of Nations,* N. Y., 1916, p. xxxviii). Ladd's plan was on the contrary systematic, concrete, and practical. His scheme for the organization of the world consisted, briefly, in the establishment of two distinct but correlated institutions: a congress of nations for formulating the principles of international law, and for providing for the general welfare of the nations; and a court of nations for settling differences by judicial decision or by diplomatic arbitration, according to the nature of the case. Thus, like Kant, he associated the realization of peace with the securing of justice. By providing for two distinct institutions, Ladd anticipated the common objection that an international court would be controlled by a diplomatic body. This was a contribution to international thought, and, related as it was to the American doctrines of the separation of powers and judicial supremacy, it has played an important rôle in subsequent international thought and organization. The American quality of Ladd's plan was further evident in his emphasis on public opinion as the only necessary sanction for both jurisdiction and consent to the award of the court. Popularized by Elihu Burritt [*q.v.*] in both America and Europe, Ladd's plan, in its essential features, has been realized in The Hague Conferences, the World Court, and the League of Nations. If it be thought that Charles Sumner was over-enthusiastic in believing that William Ladd had enrolled himself among the benefactors of mankind, there is little question that he prophesied more clearly than any American of the nineteenth century the subsequent development of international organization.

[John Hemmenway, *The Apostle of Peace: Memoir of Wm. Ladd* (Boston, 1872) is an uncritical eulogy which fails to do its subject justice. For Ladd's activities and significance see M. E. Curti, *The Am. Peace Crusade, 1815–60* (1929). Other accounts include: A. D. Call, "The Revival of Wm. Ladd," *Advocate of Peace*, Apr. 1927, and "Wm. Ladd," *Ibid.*, Nov. 1927, which contains an excellent bibliography; J. W. Penney, "Capt. Wm. Ladd, the Apostle of Peace," *Colls. and Proc. of the Me. Hist. Soc.*, 2 ser. X (1899), pp. 113–38; G. C. Wing, Jr., "Wm. Ladd," *Sprague's Jour. of Me. Hist.*, Apr.-May-June, 1823; and the *Kennebec Jour.* (Augusta), Apr. 17, 1841. The Ladd MSS. are in the possession of the American Peace Society, Washington, D. C.] M. E. C.

LADD, WILLIAM SARGENT (Oct. 10, 1826–Jan. 6, 1893), merchant, banker, business leader, was born in Holland, Vt., son of Nathaniel Gould and Abigail (Mead) Ladd and a descendant of Daniel Ladd who emigrated from England in the seventeenth century. The father, a physician, moved to New Hampshire in 1830 where William at fifteen worked on a farm, at nineteen taught a village school, and afterward became station agent for the Boston, Concord & Montreal Railroad at Sanbornton Bridge (Tilton). This position he held until 1851, when he was attracted to Portland, Ore., by stories of the opportunity to make money by outfitting and provisioning the California miners. At this time Portland had a population of about seven hundred and had become the metropolis of the Pacific Northwest. Here Ladd with a small stock of goods became a merchant, prospered, erected the first brick building in 1853, was elected mayor in 1854, and in 1859 established the first bank north of San Francisco under the name of Ladd & Tilton, an institution that weathered successfully the panics of the succeeding years. He was married in 1854 to Caroline A. Elliott, a New Hampshire schoolmate.

Ladd was the principal financial supporter and the leading promoter of many transportation and industrial enterprises, including the Oregon Steam & Navigation Company (1862), which enjoyed a monopoly of transportation on the upper Columbia River during the boom times of the Idaho gold rush and made fortunes for its owners; its successor the Oregon Railroad & Navigation Company (1879); the Oregon Iron & Steel Company (1866); Oregon Telegraph Company (1862); Oregon Central Railroad Company (1866); Oregon & Idaho Telegraph Company (1868); and the Portland Flouring Mills (1883), described in 1890 as "the largest manufacturing corporation in the Northwest states." He took over Villard's unfinished Portland Hotel in 1887 and in three years completed it, giving his city the finest hotel of its day in the region. He also helped to form companies for the manufacture of furniture and cordage and established model farms for raising high-bred stock and for conducting agricultural experiments.

Ladd was also known for his public interests and philanthropies. He made gifts to churches and schools, gave $50,000 to the Presbyterian Theological Seminary of San Francisco (1866); was an early member of the public-school board and the Portland Library Association, giving the library free quarters in his bank building for twenty years; set aside one tenth of his yearly income for charity and beneficence, and by his will set up a trust fund of a half-million dollars to be used for charitable purposes. At his death, he was worth more than ten million dollars. Paralyzed in his lower limbs at the age of forty-nine, he continued in the face of this handicap an active direction of his varied interests. "The biography of William S. Ladd," wrote the editor of the *Oregonian* (Jan. 7, 1893), "wants but little of being also the history of Portland. . . . He has been foremost, or with the foremost, in every work through which character is given to city and state."

[H. H. Bancroft, *Chronicles of the Builders of the Commonwealth*, vol. I (1891); H. W. Scott, *Hist. of the Oregon Country* (1924), vol. II; Jos. Gaston, *Portland, Ore., Its Hist. and Builders* (1911), vol. III; Warren Ladd, *The Ladd Family* (1890); *Oregonian* (Portland), Jan. 7, 15, July 12, 1893.] R. C. C—k.

LADD-FRANKLIN, CHRISTINE (Dec. 1, 1847–Mar. 5, 1930), logician and psychologist, was born in Windsor, Conn., a descendant of Daniel Ladd who emigrated to New England in 1634. Her father, Eliphalet Ladd, was a nephew of William Ladd [*q.v.*], the founder of the American Peace Society, and her mother, Augusta (Niles) Ladd, was a niece of John Milton Niles [*q.v.*], postmaster-general under Van Buren. Christine Ladd's childhood was passed largely in her native village, but partly in New York City and partly (after the death of her mother) in Portsmouth, N. H. Her playmates were her brother and a neighbor boy, and she later attributed her long-continued physical vigor to "playing with the boys." Her last two years as a schoolgirl were spent at Wilbraham Academy, where she was permitted to study Greek and mathematics with the pupils who were preparing for Harvard, and from which she was graduated as valedictorian of her class. She had already set her heart upon going to Vassar, and through the kindness of her aunt, Juliet Niles, she was enabled to realize her dream. She first expected to stay only one year, but after spending the succeeding year in teaching and private study, she persuaded her aunt to send her back to Vassar for a second year, at the end of which, in 1869, she was graduated.

Her most inspiring teacher at college was the astronomer, Maria Mitchell, though her own preference was for a career in physics. This being denied her, since no graduate laboratories were open to women, she devoted herself instead to mathematics and published a number of short mathematical papers during the next few years, while teaching the sciences in secondary schools. The new opportunities for research offered by the Johns Hopkins University, founded in 1876, led her to seek admission as a graduate student. Though women were not admitted, it so happened that the English mathematician, J. J. Sylvester, then at Johns Hopkins, had noted some of her published work. He persuaded the University to admit her on a special status, and even to grant her a fellowship which she held for three years, or till 1882. By that time she had qualified for the degree of Ph.D., but the University did not grant her the degree until 1926. While engaged in mathematical study at Johns Hopkins she became specially interested in symbolic logic as taught by the eminent C. S. Pierce, and she published in his volume, *Studies in Logic by Members of the Johns Hopkins University* (1883), an original method for reducing all syllogisms to a single formula, which she called the "antilogism" or the "inconsistent triad" of propositions, and which is still regarded as a major contribution to logic.

On Aug. 24, 1882, Miss Ladd was married to Fabian Franklin, then a young professor of mathematics at Johns Hopkins, later prominent as an editor and publicist, and continued to live in Baltimore till 1909, being herself lecturer in psychology and logic at Johns Hopkins for the last four years of this period. Thereafter, her husband becoming associate editor of the New York *Evening Post,* she resided in New York and lectured on logic and psychology at Columbia University, holding the title of lecturer in psychology from 1914 until 1927. Comparable in importance to her work on logic was that on vision, in which her publications began to appear in 1887. Her interest in the subject was intensified in 1891–92 by a year of study in Germany, where she succeeded, though the rules excluded women from the universities, in receiving instruction from the psychologist G. E. Müller of Göttingen and in working in Helmholtz' laboratory in Berlin. Müller was a supporter of Hering's well-known theory of color vision, while Helmholtz had his own still more famous theory. Mrs. Ladd-Franklin, poring over these opposed theories, saw merits but also defects in each of them, and was able to formulate a theory of her own which was consistent with all the facts and had the additional merit of indicating how the complete color sense of man might have evolved from the rudimentary brightness sense of certain lower animals, and how color-blindness in man could be understood as an incomplete development. Helmholtz had been compelled by the exigences of his theory to regard yellow as a blend of red and green; and Hering, while doing justice to yellow as a unitary color sensation, had been forced to regard the primary red and green as exactly complementary colors. The Ladd-Franklin theory avoids both of these defects by regarding the red sense and the green sense as developed out of the more primitive yellow sense, and as coalescing into the yellow sense when aroused together.

Color theories have been hotly debated for many years, and the Ladd-Franklin theory, entering the arena in 1892, became a center of controversy, in which its author, always eager for argumentative logic, continued to the end of her life to take an active part. She was always seeking converts to her theory and never gave a wavering sinner a chance to escape while conviction appeared at all possible. Late in her career, when nearly eighty years old, she rediscovered a curious visual phenomenon known as the "blue arcs," which had in fact been discovered and forgotten some eight times during the preceding hundred years, but of which she made much more use than her predecessors. She used it as evidence for the emission of faint light by active nerve fibers. Till her death she was actively engaged in developing this new idea and debating it with the doubters. She also published in 1929 a collection of her principal writings on *Colour and Colour Theories.* Aside from her two specialties, Mrs. Ladd-Franklin had other important interests and published many articles on philosophical and general subjects. She was interested in opening to women such academic opportunities as fellowships and university professorships from which women were being kept, as she once expressed it, merely by "prejudice on the part of the unfair sex." She was interested also in the campaign for woman's suffrage. She had a wide circle of friends and was remarkable to an advanced age for her activity and alertness.

[J. M. and Jaques Cattell, *Am. Men of Sci.* (4th ed., 1927); Warren Ladd, *The Ladd Family* (1890); Carl Murchison, *The Psychological Reg.* (1929); *N. Y. Times,* Mar. 6, 1930.] R. S. W.

LA FARGE, JOHN (Mar. 31, 1835–Nov. 14, 1910), painter, worker in stained glass, and writer, though intensely an American was all his life proud of his French blood. His father, Jean-Frédéric de la Farge, born in 1786 at Bussac, Charente Inférieure, grew up during the transition from the old régime to the new and at an early age embraced an adventurous career. Bred in the Napoleonic wars, he had both military and naval experiences. In December 1801, he embarked as an ensign on the expedition under General Leclerc to apprehend Toussaint l'Ouverture in Santo Domingo. A wound received during the passage of his ship through the British blockade seems only to have increased his love of action. He gave up his post as ensign for a lieutenancy in the army, was captured by Guerrier, and narrowly escaped massacre when he finally contrived to leave the island and board a ship that took him to Philadelphia. There his martial proclivities fell from him. Starting without capital, he developed such effective business traits that he succeeded in shipping, banking, and real-estate ventures, aided by connections with France. He forthwith dropped his French style, including the particle, and became John La Farge. Removing to New York, he established a hotel and engaged in numerous other enterprises. He acquired properties in Louisiana and in Jefferson and Lewis counties in New York. The village not far from Watertown, on the edge of which he built a mansion, came ultimately to be known as Lafargeville. This energetic man of affairs married a Frenchwoman, Louisa, the daughter of M. Binsse de Saint-Victor. They were living in New York, at No. 40 Beach St., when the future painter was born.

John La Farge came into a suave, gracious environment, in a neighborhood about midway between the Battery and Washington Square. With but few brief periods farther north, he dwelt always within easy reach of Washington Square—in Clinton Place, Washington Place, Ninth Street, Tenth Street, lower Fifth Avenue. All his life he maintained his studios in the famous building at 51 West Tenth St. There was always something about him, in his reticence, his dignity, his whole air of breeding, reminiscent of "Old Washington Square." But his upbringing was essentially French. He was steeped in the French language, in French manners and ways of family life, in the French care for religion and for the things of the mind. An English governess drilled him in the language and looked closely to his behavior. "I think I was a good boy," he once said, and "very innocent" (Cortissoz, p. 54). Also he "supposed" he went to school. At six he was reading *Robinson Crusoe,* and not much later pretty nearly everything from Homer to Voltaire. His education as the years went on was received from various sources —the grammar school of Columbia, St. John's College (now part of Fordham University), and Mount St. Mary's College at Emmitsburg, Md., where he was graduated in 1853.

A sheaf of letters that passed between him and his father when he was first at St. Mary's throws light upon his character and aptitudes, and upon the paternal understanding which fostered both. His father adjured the boy of fifteen to keep guard over his three younger brothers, to "give them good counsel and give it to them in such manner that they do not think you act as master. . . . Read them when you can the fables of Fontaine. Take the moral in it which is excellent in all the courses of life, and show them the application" ("Schoolboy Letters," *post,* p. 76). Greatly pleased with his son's progress, the father wrote, late in 1850: "I am persuaded that you advance always because you understand or seek to understand everything you read—that you have an excellent memory and all the good judgment that a boy of your age can have" (*Ibid.,* p. 93). Some idea of what that phrase, "everything you read," involved may be gathered from a bald enumeration of the authors La Farge demanded of his father —Cicero, Catullus, Herodotus, Homer, Landor, Coleridge, Dryden, Goldsmith, and even twelve numbers of the *Encyclopédie Iconographique.*

The letters chiefly reveal a devouring curiosity, foreshadowing the man who was, in his way, to take all knowledge for his province. Meanwhile, what of the arts? In his own words, "the influences which I felt as a little boy were those of the paintings and works of art that surrounded me at home. . . . There were on the walls a sea piece by Vernet; some imitation historical story, that of Daniel, charming, however, in color, by Lemoyne; . . . a large painting of Noah and his sons, ascribed to Sebastiano del Piombo; . . . many Dutch paintings of various authors and excellence, among them a beautiful Solomon Ruysdael. . . . All this and the very furniture and hangings of the Empire parlor did not belong to the Victorian epoch in which I was growing up. It so happened that my first teachings were those of the eighteenth century and my training has covered a century and a half" (Cortissoz, pp. 63–64).

As early as six he had "a mere boy's wish" to learn how to draw and paint and he had lessons from his maternal grandfather, Binsse de Saint-Victor, who appears to have been a good miniaturist. Later an English water colorist also gave him lessons. The reading of Ruskin withdrew him for a time from the atmosphere of the eighteenth century, interesting him in medievalism instead, but this mood passed. Art attracted him but not yet as a vocation. In so far as any specific bent declared itself on the termination of his college days it was intellectual rather than esthetic. The mood in which he faced the future is reflected in this autobiographical passage: "In the early part of 1856, . . . I went to Europe, having already passed some little while in a lawyer's office—enough to make me doubt whether my calling lay in that direction, . . . Europe was to be a manner of amusement, and, for me, of taking up also some family connections" (*Ibid.*, p. 73). He sailed in the celebrated side-wheeler, the *Fulton,* and, arriving in Paris, plunged into experiences which in the long run were to determine his career.

His sponsors, of course, were his relatives, the Saint-Victors. He saw much of the famous Paul de Saint-Victor, a man of letters occupying a place of high importance in Paris, and was often in the house of his grand-uncle, Paul's father. All about him was the stimulating world of Gautier, Victor Hugo, and Baudelaire. Romanticism was at its apogee but if La Farge needed a corrective for its redundancies he could always find it in the eighteenth-century gait of grand-uncle Saint-Victor. He visited the academic Gérôme, then a promising young artist, and at the house of Chassériau he found raging all the time the war between things academic and things romantic. "At once one was asked what one held in regard to M. Ingres and M. Delacroix" (*Ibid.,* p. 85). Presently, as an onlooker upon the mêlée, he had to make something like a decision for himself. His father advised him to study painting, "of which I was rather fond," as La Farge mildly put it, and American friends in Paris helped him to make choice of a master. They were "very much inclined" to Couture, so to Couture he went. His mode of establishing himself in the studio was characteristic. "I explained to him what I wished, which was to get a practical knowledge of painting, as practised by him. I also made him understand that I was doing this as a study of art in general and had no intention of becoming a painter. This he at first thought preposterous and was probably somewhat astonished at the youngster who laid out this programme in such an unusual manner. But I argued with him, and won his good graces, so that the next day in the early morning I entered the studio and took my place with the others. I was given, in the usual manner, by the student in control, a seat and place, paper, etc., and I began drawing from the model before me. There being no one to guide me, and feeling that the way the others drew was not mine, I went on my own way. That day or next came in the great man, who, instead of objecting to my work having so little in common with those following his system, was pleased to say, on the contrary, that mine was the only one that really gave the motion of the model" (*Ibid.,* pp. 91–92).

In its suggestion of a certain thoughtful independence this points to La Farge's whole evolution as an artist. Even Couture's appreciative treatment was not enough to hold him. He was in the studio only about a fortnight, frequenting the drawings of the old masters in the Louvre instead, on Couture's advice, and then hunting them down in Munich and Dresden. His travels took him as far as Copenhagen, and there he made a careful study of Rembrandt's "Supper at Emmaus." In Belgium he developed a profound feeling for Rubens, tracking down practically every painting of his in the country, and after that thrilling experience he spent the autumn in England, where he saw the great Manchester exhibition of 1857, admiring the Rokeby "Venus" of Velasquez and finding much interest in the juxtaposition of that master with Titian and Rubens. In England he was also for a time in the company of some of the Pre-Raphaelites. Returning to America in 1858, he went back to reading law.

He had not yet made up his mind. But he had architects and painters among his friends, he dabbled with brush and pencil, and in another year he was studying at Newport with one of his friend Couture's pupils, William Hunt. In 1860 he was married to Margaret Mason Perry, by whom he had nine children. Though for a moment the Civil War threatened to dislocate all plans, the fates willed otherwise. La Farge wanted to enlist but his shortsightedness unfitted him for the profession of arms and he was obliged, willy-nilly, to stay at home. There his vision answered for the pursuit of experimental activities, half artistic, half scientific, in which a new-found friend, John Bancroft, proved enormously stimulating and helpful. "He was a student," wrote La Farge, "almost too much of one, and we plunged into the great questions of light and color which were beginning to be laid out by the scientific men and which later the painters were to take up. This was the cause of a great deal of work but of less painting, if I may say so, less picture-making, because of an almost incessant set of observations and comments and inquiries supplemented by actual work in painting. All that I have done since then has been modified by those few years of optical studies, and the last realistic painting which may have shown it is the 'Paradise Valley,' which belongs to '66–'67–'68." (*Ibid.*, pp. 121–22).

Not only chronologically but also in other more important ways the "Paradise Valley" supplies a perfect point of departure for consideration of La Farge's development as an artist. It was energized primarily by the operation of that mysterious force which is called genius but it was conditioned also by a factor not always noticeable among artists, a steady play of mind. The foregoing passage is prophetic. The optical studies to which he refers were fortified by others in many fields. Side by side with his investigations into science went research into nature. The "Paradise Valley" was in advance of its time. French impressionism was yet to make its impact upon American art but in this landscape La Farge, animated by his own inquisitiveness, reveals his own discoveries and anticipates the formula of Monet. "I wished," he said, "to apply principles of light and color of which I had learned a little. I wished my studies of nature to indicate something of this, to be free from *recipes,* as far as possible, and to indicate very carefully in every part, the exact time of day and circumstance of light" (*Ibid.*, p. 112). He delighted in his association with Hunt and appreciated the latter's idolization of Millet but he adhered to his already ingrained habit of thinking his own way through the production of a picture. At the same time he was slow to yield to the purely creative impulses half unconsciously stirring within him and his later memories of that formative period were those of a young experimentalist much preoccupied with the ponderable problems of a craft. Referring to certain of his early landscapes, he dwells upon the effort that he made in them to achieve sheer accuracy: "They are studies out of the window to give the effect and appearance of *looking out* of the window and our not being in the same light as the landscape. And also to indicate very exactly the time of day and the exact condition of the light in the sky. . . . I aimed at making a realistic study of painting, keeping to myself the designs and attempts, serious or slight, which might have a meaning more than that of a strict copy from nature. I painted flowers to get the relation between the softness and brittleness of the flowers and the hardness of the bowl or whatever it might be in which the flowers might be placed. Instead of arranging my subject, which is the usual studio way, I had it placed for me by chance, with any background and any light, leaving, for instance, the choice of flowers and vase to the servant girl or groom or any one. Or else I copied the corner of the breakfast table as it happened to be" (*Ibid.*, p. 116). In other words, the technician was finding himself, under self-imposed discipline.

From all this cogitation and experimentation there emerged a painter of equal proficiency and distinction, the kind of painter whose labors have a strange inner support, from which they draw most of their validity. Logical ratiocination—incurably characteristic of him—might be at the bottom of his work. He might say, as a thinker, recurring to the "Paradise Valley," that his program was "to paint from nature a portrait," but he went on to explain that it was also his purpose to "make distinctly a work of art which should remain as a type of the sort of subject I undertook, a subject both novel and absolutely 'everydayish'" (*Ibid.*, p. 129). Being what he was now proving himself to be, an instinctive artist, in his paintings he subordinated the "everydayish" element to his originality. What made him ultimately a commanding figure in the American school was the fact that he saw his subjects beautifully as well as veraciously, that he had breadth of vision as well as control over the minute, passing effect, that he was a fine colorist and draftsman, and a skilful man with his hands. He was also versatile and industrious. His career, once inaugurated, was one of prodigious activities. At the outset he painted landscapes, flower subjects, and a few figure subjects. Incidentally he dipped into illustration. When the *Riverside Magazine* was started by Ticknor and Fields he made numerous drawings for it, taking his motives from Browning and other poets. In these he showed the quality of inventive imagination which was ever to stand him in good stead. He liked to tell of a piquant incident flowing from one of his early illustrations, "The Wolf Charmer." Long afterward he met in Japan a court painter, Hung Ai, and that luminary immediately exclaimed: "Oh, you are the wolf man!" (*Ibid.*, p. 143). The old engraving had lodged itself in his mind for years. From the "stroke" Hung Ai had guessed the truth, that La Farge had used a Japanese brush on the design.

La Farge went on painting easel pictures for some time but even while landscape thus occupied him he had "become tempted and then drawn to work in the lines of architecture" (*Ibid.*, p. 156); and, in 1876, he was invited by H. H. Richardson, who was then carrying Trinity Church in Boston to completion, to decorate the interior. There was then practically no such thing as mural decoration in the United States. The only pioneer in the field was La Farge's friend William Hunt, painting his charming designs in the Capitol at Albany. La Farge, however, so richly fertilized by his European travels and so apt in the logic of art, fearlessly tackled the huge walls in Boston, improvised a staff of helpers, and, working amid the crudest of conditions and under much pressure as to time, left the church astonishingly unified in a scheme of great warmth and dignity. It was the forerunner of divers important commissions, of panels in the Church of the Incarnation in New York, of others in St. Thomas's in the same city (which were destined to be destroyed by fire), of the lovely "Music" and "Drama" for the music room in the residence of Whitelaw Reid in New York, and many other notable achievements, "The Ascension," in the Church of the Ascension, New York, looming above all the rest.

This great painting had a curious origin. Dr. Donald, the rector, first consulted La Farge with a view to placing a stained-glass window in the altar wall. Then the painter had the idea of getting Augustus Saint-Gaudens to fill the space with a big bas-relief. Neither of these plans prospered and when Stanford White undertook the architectural renovation of the church the upshot of all their deliberations on the subject was La Farge's execution of his vast picture. At the moment of signing the contract, in 1886, he had agreed to go with Henry Adams to Japan and there, with characteristic freedom from convention, he found his background. "I had a vague belief," he said, "that I might find there certain conditions of line in the mountains which might help me. Of course the Judean mountains were entirely out of the question, all the more that they implied a given place. I kept all this in mind and on one given day I saw before me a space of mountains and cloud and flat land which seemed to me to be what was needed. I gave up my other work and made thereupon a rapid but very careful study, so complete that the big picture is only a part of the amount of work put into the study of that afternoon" (*Ibid.*, pp. 164–65). In other words, "The Ascension," indubitably the greatest mural painting of a religious subject produced anywhere in La Farge's time, is in essentials the result of a sudden burst of white-hot inspiration, a fact which might be inferred from the spiritual force and pure beauty vitalizing it in a well-knit, soundly structural design. He impressively adorned other walls, especially those of the supreme court room in the state Capitol of Minnesota, at St. Paul, where he illustrated in four great lunettes "The Moral and Divine Law," "The Relation of the Individual to the State," "The Recording of Precedents," and "The Adjustment of Conflicting Interests." The deep student of religion, philosophy, and statesmanship, as well as the authoritative artist, is apparent in these compositions. The figure of Moses on Mount Sinai, in the first of these lunettes, is especially eloquent of La Farge's command of the grand style.

All through his mural period La Farge was also much occupied with work in stained glass. It was due to his genius that one of the great crafts of the Middle Ages was in America revived and lifted to a high plane. When he exhibited one of his windows, the Watson Memorial, at the Paris Exposition of 1889, the insignia of the Legion of Honor was conferred upon him by the Government, and his fellow artists, assembled as a jury, added to a medal of the first class this expression of their admiration: "His work cannot be fully gauged here, where a single window represents a name the most celebrated and widely known in our Sister Republic. He is the great innovator, the inventor of opaline glass. He has created in all its details an art unknown before, an entirely new industry, and in a country without tradition he will begin one followed by thousands of pupils filled with the same respect for him that we have ourselves for our own masters. To share in this respect is the highest praise that we can give to this great artist" (*Ibid.*, p. 184).

La Farge treasured this tribute as one of the greatest strokes of good fortune in his life—taking it, too, as in some sort a ratification of his French blood. The beginnings of his glass were promoted casually enough. He was rather at a loose end, painting pictures that did not sell any too rapidly. In despair of finding a satisfactory market in New York, he was considering a proposal from Durand-Ruel to exploit his work in Paris and London. An architectural friend commissioned him, just then, to design a window for Memorial Hall, at Harvard, and as contact with the Pre-Raphaelites in England had interested him in glass he agreed to go on with the project. When he had made the window he liked it so little that he promptly destroyed it. During a convalescence in bed the secret of success came to him. A colored glass container of tooth powder on his toilet table caught his eye at the moment when light was passing through it. His imagination leapt to the suggestion and shortly afterward, with a Luxemburg glass-maker in Brooklyn for an aid, he had developed the "opalescent glass" on which much of his fame was to rest. He produced thenceforth thousands of windows, not only for churches but for private houses, and at least one renowned design, the "Peacock Window," which might be described as glass created for its own sake, the embodiment of the very genius of an artistic medium. La Farge was a born colorist. This is made plain by his early paintings, by the later works commemorating his travels in Japan and amongst the islands of the South Seas, and by his mural decorations. Yet it may be said that in his glass as nowhere else La Farge the colorist comes definitively into his own, investing his beautiful designs, whether based on the figure or on purely decorative motives, with a kind of orchestral piercingness and power.

It was an inordinately busy life that he led. He drew and painted; he made his glass; he traveled not only to Europe but to the far places of the earth; he lectured and he wrote. All the time he was dogged by ill health. He suffered from a slight lameness, he had had lead poisoning, he knew all about the pains of neuritis, he was often obliged to take to his bed from exhaustion, yet even there he was active with pencil or brush. He was six feet tall, deep-chested, with long and slender hands and feet. His dark brown hair, only subdued with touches of gray in his last years, crowned a magnificent head. His green-gray eyes were set in deep sockets; his nose was long, straight, and aristocratic; his skin was fine-textured and, while fairly warm in tint, had a certain parchment-like quality. A shrewd observer found him in his youth "picturesque." He was that always but the term requires a little qualification. Clothed usually in black and consistently fastidious in all his wear and ways, ceremonious without stiffness, he somewhat fused the traits of the artist with those of the man of the world. He had something of the aloofness, the mystery, characteristic of his great French contemporary, Puvis de Chavannes, and could be, when he chose, extremely difficult to approach. Also, when he chose, he could be most humanly accessible, sympathetic with young people, knowing how to laugh and to chuckle, delighting in a good limerick, and foregathering with a friend over a cigar with all the humor in the world. With all his scholarship, he had an extraordinary imagination and an almost mystical feeling for recondite ideas. In his talk he was as distinguished, as creative, as in his art, having—as in all things—a way of his own, very deliberate, elaborately parenthetical, and altogether fascinating.

When with Henry Adams he visited Japan and later went to the South Seas, he studied life with the directness of the explorer and with the more complex passion of the philosopher. *An Artist's Letters from Japan* (1897), and *Reminiscences of the South Seas* (1912), with illustrations from his own paintings and drawings, are a record not only of what he saw but also of the myriad thoughts evoked by his exotic surroundings. Writing of the *siva* dance, in the latter book, he says: "If I do not refrain and cut short at once, I shall become entangled in trying to give you word pictures that are utterly inadequate. I feel, too, that the drawings and paintings I have made are so stupid from their freezing into attitudes the beauties that are made of sequence" (*Reminiscences,* p. 119). As a matter of fact, his travel books, like his travel pictures, remain among the most typical things he did in color and in eloquence. Somewhere in his strange cosmos was the instinct of the poet; he had, indeed, a great literary gift. His earliest published writing was "An Essay on Japanese Art," prepared to accompany Raphael Pumpelly's *Across America and Asia* (1870). In 1893 appeared his pamphlet, *The American Art of Glass.* With A. F. Jaccaci, he edited *Noteworthy Paintings in American Collections* (1904), to which he contributed an exhaustive survey of Mrs. Gardner's collection at Fenway Court. Lectures that he gave at the Metropolitan Museum in New York in 1893 were later brought together in a volume entitled *Considerations on Painting* (1895). Those on the Barbizon school with which he inaugurated the

Scammon Course at the Art Institute of Chicago were afterwards published as *The Higher Life in Art* (1908). In his *Great Masters* (1903) he recorded his critical interpretations of Michael Angelo, Raphael, Rembrandt, Rubens, Velasquez, Dürer, and Hokusai. *One Hundred Masterpieces of Painting* (1912) has specifically to do not only with the giants of the art but also with the subjects that they treated. He writes of allegories, of portraits, of decorations. In the preface, written as the end of his life was drawing near, he said: "The contemplation of art is a form of study of the history of man and a very certain one. Its records are absolutely disinterested from any attempt at proving anything. . . . We have before us (in works of art) the mirror of life at a given moment. . . . I have chosen masterpieces or beautiful examples, not only because they are beautiful, which in itself is all sufficient, but because they escape, in that way, the touch of the bad taste of fashion." In all his writings, down to the very last, *The Gospel Story in Art* (1913), which was prepared for the press after his death in Providence, R. I., by his old friend Mary Cadwalader Jones, his mind was set on the eternal verities. In these writings he is careful of facts, faithful to history, a learned expert, and, above all things, the reverent student of truth and beauty.

La Farge was unique in the Protean nature of his genius and in the operation of its multifarious activities in a peculiarly rarefied atmosphere. He had a kind of Leonardesque wisdom, an intellectuality which gave balance to everything he did and encrusted it with rich, subtle implications. His sensibility and his depth were matched by the delicate French precision with which he defined a thought in words or in the language of art. "In conversation La Farge's mind was opaline, with infinite shades and refractions of light, and with color toned down to the finest gradations" (*The Education of Henry Adams,* 1918, p. 371). He worked in paint or in glass, so far as his refractory mediums permitted, very much as he talked, and so he used a pen. He could be very simple and intimate, both in his early and late periods, and he could paint in the grand style when the theme called for it. In all his moods he painted with a certain authority. "The Ascension" and the "Peacock Window," two totally different conceptions, are alike in their demonstration of his command over mass and over nuance. He came indeed, in some quarters, to be regarded before he died as an old master born out of his time.

This was the feeling and the judgment of many of his contemporaries, in and out of his profession. His fellow artists held him in honor and valued his opinion. He had a devoted following amongst collectors. The adverse criticism that was occasionally directed against his work was never sufficient in point or in volume to lessen the prestige which gave him, finally, a sort of Olympian relation to his coevals as well as to his juniors. On what, specifically, is to be based any surmise as to the endurance of his high repute? In his earlier period he painted landscapes of great distinction but they do not place him in the category of landscape painters as Innes, say, is placed there. They are vitalized and beautiful but they are not numerous enough, he did not "follow them up" enough, for them to give him outstanding rank in their field. His flower subjects are so extraordinarily fine that they are always likely to retain a salience of their own. But neither the flower subjects nor the smaller figure pieces which he painted from time to time will give him his distinctive place. That he will probably owe to his stained glass and to his mural painting. He was the first American master of the fusion of decorative art with architecture and he remains the greatest, a colorist and a designer who developed remarkable powers as a collaborator with the builder. Both as a designer and a colorist he could make the easel picture a memorable thing. In the continuation of a wall, whether in glass or on canvas, he reached his highest level. To this more or less recondite claim upon the attention of the student of American art, giving new life to old tradition, he added imagination, extraordinary play of mind, and grace of style, attributes stamped with originality and distinction.

[The "Schoolboy Letters between John La Farge and His Father," were published in *Hist. Records and Studies* of the U. S. Catholic Hist. Soc., March 1928. The same volume contains "Some Records of the La Farge Family," by Thos. F. Meehan. Cecilia Waern wrote *John La Farge: Artist and Writer* (1896) from acquaintance with the painter and his works and from information that he gave her. The official biography is *John La Farge: A Memoir and a Study* (1911) by Royal Cortissoz, produced out of collaboration with La Farge, who supplied much autobiographical matter for the purpose. For comments immediately after his death, see *N. Y. Herald-Tribune, N. Y. Times,* Boston *Transcript,* and other papers.] R. C.

LAFAYETTE, MARIE JOSEPH PAUL YVES ROCH GILBERT DU MOTIER, Marquis de (Sept. 6, 1757–May 20, 1834), French statesman and soldier, was born in the château of Chavaniac, between Brionde and Le Puy, in Auvergne, France, the son of Gilbert, Marquis de Lafayette, colonel in the French grenadiers, and Marie Louise Julie de la Rivière, both of notable and ancient French families. His father was killed at the battle of Minden, Aug. 1,

1759. The boy was brought to Paris in 1768 and entered the fourth form at the Collège du Plessis, where he remained four years. His mother died Apr. 3, 1770, and his grandfather several weeks later. Lafayette inherited the fortune of the latter and found himself, at the age of thirteen, possessed of an income of 120,000 livres. He yearned for a military career, agreeable to the strong tradition in his family, and on Apr. 9, 1771, he was entered in the second company of the King's Musketeers, from which he was transferred, Apr. 7, 1773, to the regiment commanded by Noailles, where he became a second lieutenant. A marriage between Lafayette and Marie Adrienne Françoise de Noailles had already been arranged; this took place Apr. 11, 1774, and henceforth the fortunes of the shy, awkward youth, not yet seventeen, were allied to those of one of the most powerful French families of the old régime. Shortly after his marriage he was promoted to a captaincy and joined his regiment at Metz, returning in September to participate in the court life at Versailles. Here he suffered considerable mortification, since he drank poorly and danced so badly that he provoked Marie Antoinette to laughter.

During the summer of 1775 he returned to barracks at Metz; on Aug. 8 he attended a dinner given by the Comte de Broglie to the Duke of Gloucester. Here the Duke spoke freely and sympathetically of the American insurgents and Lafayette's enthusiasm and imagination were first stirred. During the weeks that followed, vague aspirations slowly crystallized. By aiding the insurgents he saw the possibility of crushing "perfidious Albion" and avenging the defeat of the Seven Years' War, in which his country had been humiliated and his father had lost his life. He partook of that current romantic enthusiasm for a regenerated world which had been engendered by the writings of Rousseau and Raynal, and saw himself in the garb of a modern Plutarch's hero, a rôle proper to satisfy his own love of *la gloire*. Thus motivated, he made the first and most important decision of his life, to aid the American colonists. Concealing his plans from his family, he confided in the Comte de Broglie, who tried to dissuade him, but who later introduced him to John Kalb [*q.v.*]. Lafayette withdrew from active service in the French army, June 11, 1776, and after the announcement of the Declaration of Independence he entered into relations with Silas Deane and Arthur Lee [*qq.v.*]. Two agreements were signed, during December 1776 and February 1777, between them. Kalb and Lafayette were promised commissions, and the latter agreed to serve the colonies with the greatest zeal without compensation, reserving only the right to return to France, if called by his king or family. He sent Du Boismartin, a friend, to purchase and fit out a vessel for the passage to America. To allay all suspicions Lafayette spent several weeks in London with the French ambassador, the Marquis de Noailles, his uncle. Returning to Bordeaux he embarked with Kalb in *La Victoire*. The vessel put in at Los Pasajes, where Lafayette was ordered by Louis XVI to accompany the Duc d'Ayen on a tour in Italy. Lafayette hesitated and Kalb thought that the venture was given up. To satisfy the British ambassador a *lettre de cachet* had been launched against Lafayette. News of this determined him and, having rejoined Kalb at Los Pasajes, he sailed for the United States, Apr. 20, 1777. The commotion created by his departure was excellent publicity for the cause of the Americans.

On June 13 they disembarked near Georgetown, S. C., where they were entertained by Major Benjamin Huger. Within a week Lafayette wrote his wife a letter of boyish enthusiasm relating many impressions that he had already formed of men and affairs in America. After six weeks of arduous travel he and his companions arrived in Philadelphia, where he presented his credentials to a committee of Congress. Congress was weary of foreign adventurers and his first reception was more like a dismissal than a welcome. Undaunted, he wrote a petition requesting two things: to serve at his own expense, and to begin as a volunteer. This modest and unusual proposal secured attention; his credentials were examined, and on July 31 Congress voted him the rank and commission of major-general, but gave him no active command. The situation was one that Lafayette never completely understood. On Aug. 1 he met General Washington in Philadelphia. This was the beginning of a historic friendship. The young major-general, not yet twenty, was virtually adopted by Washington, whose staff he joined as a volunteer. He received his baptism of fire in the battle of the Brandywine, Sept. 11, when he was slightly wounded in the leg. Kalb called this an excellent bit of good fortune, for it established Lafayette in the eyes of his American comrades. He recuperated at the Moravian settlement at Bethlehem, Pa., and in October rejoined Washington in camp at Whitemarsh. At Gloucester he led a successful skirmishing party against the Hessians. Partly because of his personal qualities and partly from political considerations, Congress on Dec. 1 voted him command of the division of Virginia light troops with full authority as major-general. During the winter he remained at Valley Forge, sharing hardships and privations and earning the title of "the soldier's friend." He warned Washington of the Conway Cabal and urged him to protect himself. At the end of January 1778, the Board of War placed Lafayette in command of the proposed "irruption into Canada," a fantastic scheme to capture Canada with a handful of men in the dead of winter. He immediately had visions of restoring the lost provinces of France and wrote to his friends in Europe of his glorious anticipations. When, on Feb. 19, he arrived at Albany and understood that nothing had been done he was humiliated and enraged. He wrote to Washington denouncing those who had led him astray, adding: "I well know that you, my dear general, will do everything possible to get me the one thing for which I thirst: glory" (Charavay, p. 29). Other letters to Washington and Laurens described his "painful and ridiculous situation" (Sedgwick, p. 61) in what Laurens called "that indigested romantic scheme" (E. C. Burnett, *Letters of Members of the Continental Congress,* III, 1926, p. 124). By April, Lafayette, chagrined and disappointed, was back at Valley Forge. Bitter memories were forgotten during the celebrations which followed the arrival, May 1, of the news of the French alliance; Lafayette was again a center of attention. On May 18 at Barren Hill, by skilful maneuvering, he escaped capture by a larger force commanded by Sir Henry Clinton. He participated in the battle of Monmouth, June 28, with distinction but without success. He was active in preparations for the combined land and sea attack against Newport, R. I., to be carried out with the aid of the French fleet under D'Estaing. He was valuable as a liaison officer between the two armies, and, following the wretched failure of the expedition early in August, he did much to calm the jealousies and recriminations of both French and Americans.

In October 1778, Congress granted him a furlough that he might return to France, voted him an elegant sword, and wrote a letter to Louis XVI extolling his merits. He sailed Jan. 11, 1779, in the *Alliance,* manned by British prisoners and deserters, whose mutiny he later subdued. In Paris and Versailles he was welcomed and acclaimed, received by the King and Queen, consulted by all the ministers, and kissed by all the ladies. He was discussed, toasted, entertained; meanwhile he proposed to Vergennes an invasion of Great Britain, a descent upon Ireland, a conquest of Canada, and other projects having a common end, for, he declared, "the thought of seeing England humiliated and crushed makes me tremble with joy" (Whitlock, I, 194). He advocated hiring part of the Swedish navy for service in America; tried to float an American loan in Holland; and urged a French army for expeditionary service in the United States, proposing himself as commander of it. He acquiesced in the appointment of the Comte de Rochambeau as commander and, early in March 1780, sailed on the *Hermione* to prepare for the arrival of the French army. Arriving at Boston, Apr. 28, he was given a triumphal welcome at Governor Hancock's house. After considerable delay he found Washington at Morristown, in great need of troops and money. He visited Congress to discuss the necessary measures to be taken to cooperate with the French fleet, and was restored to his old command of the Virginia light troops. The French fleet arrived at Newport, R. I., during July and Lafayette met Rochambeau July 25 to advocate an offensive campaign, which was declined by Rochambeau. When, during September, Washington first conferred with Rochambeau, Lafayette was invaluable as an intermediary. He returned with Washington to West Point, where they learned of Arnold's treason. As a member of the court martial at Tappan he voted for the death penalty for André. Following this he went into winter headquarters at Philadelphia.

Meanwhile, Washington planned a combined land and sea attack to capture Gen. Benedict Arnold who was at Hampton Roads. For this purpose he entrusted 1,200 New England troops to Lafayette, who marched to Head of Elk, on Chesapeake Bay, where he arrived Mar. 3, 1781. The French fleet did not arrive and the opportunity of capturing Arnold was lost. Early in April he received orders to join General Greene in the Carolinas. Rallying his men by a personal appeal, he marched southward, reaching Richmond on Apr. 29, just in time to prevent its occupation and destruction by the British army under General Phillips. Lafayette now asked assistance from General Wayne and Pennsylvania troops. When Lord Cornwallis marched northward and was joined by the troops formerly under Phillips, Lafayette, with his thousand effective troops, slowly retreated before the advance of the superior forces of the British. "The boy can not escape me," wrote Cornwallis (Whitlock, I, 236). Lafayette retired until he met Wayne at the Rapidan River, then returned to harass Cornwallis. The latter slowly retired to the sea, finally reaching Portsmouth, where he dispatched some of his troops to New York. Washington now told Lafayette of the proposed concerted action with De Grasse and the French fleet and ordered him to prevent the escape of Cornwallis to the southward. With the arrival of De Grasse, of Rochambeau's army, and Washington's Continental Army, Cornwallis was besieged at Yorktown, where he capitulated, Oct. 19. "The play is over," Lafayette wrote the Comte de Maurepas, "the fifth act is just ended" (*Ibid.,* I, 260). During all the Virginia campaign, Lafayette had demonstrated tact, caution, and a superior knowledge of military tactics.

Lafayette sailed for France in the *Alliance* in December. He was enthusiastically received by populace and court. Incessantly fêted and consulted, he basked in the thunderous acclaim. Meanwhile, he aided the American agents in seeking supplies and a loan. He was at Cadiz, ready to sail with a new expedition, when news of the signing of the preliminary articles of peace reached him. He now returned to his ancestral estates in Auvergne, where he won great popularity with the peasants by his distribution of grain. He then established himself at his hôtel in Paris, rue de Bourbon, where he held salon and discoursed on America and republican principles. He was made a member of the Society of the Cincinnati. He returned to America in August 1784, arriving at New York, where he received a tremendous ovation. During the following six months he visited his old colleagues in arms and was affectionately welcomed from Mount Vernon to Boston. On Dec. 8 Congress gave him a distinguished reception at Trenton and on the 21st he sailed from New York on *La Nymphe.*

Lafayette returned to France with a renewed enthusiasm and a new vision. He would give France her charter of liberties and would establish them. In his salon and his utterances his ardent republicanism asserted itself; he engaged in various philanthropic and humanitarian enterprises, for the manumission of negro slaves and the abolition of slavery, and for the restoration of the civil rights of the French Protestants. With Jefferson [*q.v.*], now minister to France, he labored for the readjustment of American frontiers with Spain. During 1785–89, his services to the United States, while not dramatic, were invaluable. He attacked the tobacco monopoly of the farmers-general in an effort to eliminate the middle profits of the British merchants; he sought to find a large French market for the New England fisheries, for the United States, a debtor nation, could pay the French debt only by building up credits from an excess of exports. Through the activity of Jefferson and Lafayette, the United States was gaining the position of the most favored nation in the French market. When Jefferson, in 1786, contemplated a combined blockade of the Barbary pirates Lafayette at once offered his services as chief of operations. He urged upon the French government the postponement of the first payments of the American debt that the United States might first care for its internal finances. Early in 1789, he was instrumental in securing the recall of De Moustier, who, although he had been sent to America as French minister at Jefferson's request, had made himself obnoxious to the American government. In 1787, Lafayette had been a member of the Assembly of Notables; his enthusiastic republicanism had alarmed Jefferson, who suggested the British constitution rather than the American as a model for the French. When Jefferson left France in October 1789, Lafayette was already well launched in that revolution in which he became a prominent figure.

His activities, his successes, and his blunders in that movement belong to French rather than to American history. In 1790 he was the most popular figure in France; from 1792 to 1797 he was incarcerated in foreign prisons, from which Congress, Washington, and Gouverneur Morris vainly sought to effect his release. Liberated at length through French influence, he and his family remained in exile until late in 1799, when they returned and settled at La Grange, about forty miles from Paris. The Revolution had shattered his fortune. Congress had, in 1794, voted him $24,424, his emoluments as a brigadier-general, which he had refused to accept during the American Revolution. It was estimated that he spent more than $200,000 of his private funds in assisting the colonies; he never solicited repayment, but in 1803 Congress voted him a grant of 11,520 acres. These lands were eventually located in Louisiana, but it was a dozen years before he realized any financial assistance from them. Lafayette remained aloof from politics, cultivating his lands at La Grange. He acknowledged Napoleon, though he later broke with him; he remained a liberal, upheld by faith in the ultimate triumph of representative government. He never ceased to hold up the United States as an example and promise to mankind; he was a good friend and counselor of the American legation in Paris.

In 1824 President Monroe invited him to visit the United States; he arrived at Staten Island Aug. 15 and began an epochal tour which Charles Sumner said "belongs to the poetry of history." "The Marquis," "the soldier's friend," had returned, the venerable symbol of a past heroic age. For more than a year his triumphal tour of the

United States provoked demonstrations of frenzied enthusiasm without precedent or parallel in American history. This was one of the happiest years of his life, for he had never lost his one great foible, as Jefferson had described it, "a canine appetite for popularity and fame" (*The Writings of Thomas Jefferson,* 1903, VI, 70). On Sept. 8, 1825, he sailed for France and on Oct. 9 reached La Grange, where he was given a brilliant fête attended by four thousand people. He reëntered politics and played a conspicuous part in the July Revolution of 1830 but by his indecision lost the opportunity of establishing the republic of which he had long dreamed. One of his last speeches in the Chamber was in 1833, favoring ratification of the Franco-American treaty signed July 4, 1831. His last speech was one attacking the reactionary policies of Louis-Philippe, whom he had assisted to power. He died May 20, 1834, and was buried in Picpus Cemetery in Paris. His grave was covered with earth from Bunker Hill.

[For the extensive materials concerning Lafayette, consult Stuart W. Jackson, *La Fayette; a Bibliography* (1930), detailed but uncritical, and Louis R. Gottschalk's critical bibliographical article in *Jour. of Mod. Hist.,* June 1930, pp. 281–87. The best source for his life is the *Mémoires . . . du général La Fayette . . .* (6 vols., Paris, 1837–38), of which the first three volumes have been translated into English (London, 1837). B. F. Stevens, *Facsimiles . . .* (25 vols., London, 1889–98), Henri Doniol, *Histoire de la participation de la France à l'établissement des États-Unis d'Amérique* (5 vols., Paris, 1886), and Charlemagne Tower, *The Marquis de La Fayette in the Am. Revolution . . .* (2 vols., 1895) are the best sources for his activities in the American Revolution. *The Letters of Lafayette and Jefferson* (1929), ed. by Gilbert Chinard, reveal his services to the United States after his return to France. Étienne Charavay, *Le général Lafayette . . .* (Paris, 1898), the best biography, has never been translated into English. Brand Whitlock, *La Fayette* (2 vols., 1929), is the most complete biography in English, but see Bernard Faÿ's review, *Saturday Rev. of Lit.,* Oct. 19, 1929. A. Levasseur, *La Fayette in America in 1824 and 1825* (2 vols., 1829), is a detailed history of his last American visit. Lida Rose McCabe, *Ardent Adrienne . . .* (1930), is an interesting biography of Madame de Lafayette. Louis R. Gottschalk has in preparation a volume of unpublished letters of Lafayette.]

F. M—n.

LAFFAN, WILLIAM MACKAY (Jan. 22, 1848–Nov. 19, 1909), journalist and art connoisseur, was born in Dublin, Ireland, the son of Michael and Ellen Sarah FitzGibbon Laffan. He was educated at H. T. Humphrey's school at Blackrock and prepared for Dublin University at French College, Booterstown. After leaving Trinity College, Dublin University, he studied for a short time at St. Cecilia's School of Medicine. His interest in art had already shown itself and he was artist to the Pathological Society of Dublin. At the age of twenty he was attracted by journalism and went to San Francisco, where as a reporter he exhibited a knack for humorous description. He became the first city editor of the *San Francisco Chronicle* when it was established in the latter part of 1868. With his own pencil he provided for the *Chronicle* the first illustrated journalism on the Pacific Coast. His service on the *Chronicle* and later as managing editor of the San Francisco *Bulletin* made him quickly familiar with many angles of practical newspaper work.

In 1870 Laffan went to Baltimore, where he worked as a reporter and soon became editor of the Baltimore *Daily Bulletin,* the ownership of which he later acquired. This newspaper, which became the *Evening Bulletin,* was devoted largely to art, literature, and science. In 1877 he moved to New York City and was taken on the *Sun* by Charles A. Dana as dramatic critic. From that time until his death, with the exception of two years spent as art editor and general representative of Harper Brothers in London, his literary career was with the *Sun.* He became its publisher in 1884 and in 1887 he started the *Evening Sun.* Dana died in 1897 and on Feb. 22, 1902, Laffan's name appeared in the *Sun's* editorial masthead as proprietor. Through his friendship with J. Pierpont Morgan he had been able to buy the control of the newspaper. Although the editorial direction of the paper remained with Edward Page Mitchell [*q.v.*], who had been Dana's chief editorial writer for many years, Laffan was active in the supervision of every department. He wrote occasionally for the editorial columns, usually some brief and striking paragraph. In 1904 he announced the *Sun's* support of President Roosevelt, whom the *Sun* had frequently opposed, in five words:

"Theodore, with all thy faults—."

Except to his intimates he was a mysterious figure. His pride was so great as to exclude the ordinary vanities. He disliked publicity and avoided public appearances. He had a "Celtic temperament that boiled at low temperature, boiling behind a physiognomy betokening a habit of control imperturbable as ice at zero. His hatreds were so passionate that he could discern precious little good in the fiercely hated; no woman could be more tenderly considerate when affection existed" (Mitchell, *post,* p. 353).

In art Laffan won high rank. His *Engravings on Wood* was published by Harpers in 1887. In 1897 he published *Oriental Ceramic Art* and in 1907 he edited the *Catalogue of the Morgan Collection of Chinese Porcelains.* He was one of the group of connoisseurs assembled by J. P. Morgan when the latter became president of the

Metropolitan Museum of Art in 1904. Laffan was elected a trustee in 1905. "There was no department of art to which he was not sympathetic and no department in which he had not expert knowledge" (R. W. De Forest, "Mr. Laffan's Part in the Development of the Metropolitan Museum," the *Sun,* Nov. 20, 1909, p. 6). As the principal art adviser of J. P. Morgan and Henry Walters, Laffan was responsible for the purchase of millions of dollars worth of treasures that were sent from Europe to American collections. He had much to do with the Metropolitan Museum's first archeological campaign in Egypt and when seized with his last illness was planning similar explorations in Mesopotamia. J. P. Morgan's will established in his honor the Laffan Professorship of Assyriology and Babylonian Literature at Yale University. In 1872 Laffan married Georgiana Ratcliffe of Baltimore.

[E. P. Mitchell, *Memoirs of an Editor* (1924); *Who's Who in America,* 1908–09; *The Metropolitan Museum of Art: Fortieth Ann. Report,* 1909; *Bull. of the Metropolitan Museum of Art,* Dec. 1909; F. M. O'Brien, *The Story of The Sun* (1918); news and editoral articles in the *Sun* (N. Y.), Nov. 20, 1909; personal acquaintance.]

F. M. O.

LAFFITE, JEAN (fl. 1809–1821), adventurer and outlaw, was probably born in Bayonne, France, shortly before 1780. The many stories of his ancestry and early life are confused and contradictory. It seems likely that he followed the sea from his early youth, and he may have been the "Captain Lafette" of the French privateer *La Soeur Chérie* when, in April 1804, she put into the Mississippi for repairs and provisions (*Official Letter Books of W. C. C. Claiborne,* II, 97–98). Before 1809 he was established in New Orleans as joint owner, with his brother Pierre, of a blacksmith shop, which was operated by slave labor and was probably used as a depot for goods and slaves brought into Louisiana by a band of privateers and smugglers. Shortly afterward—probably in 1810—Jean Laffite became the chief of this band at their establishment on the secluded islands of Barataria Bay. Under his shrewd direction, ten or a dozen ships sailed with commissions from the young republic of Cartagena to prey on the Spanish commerce of the Gulf. The goods and slaves they brought in Laffite sold to New Orleans merchants and Louisiana planters in flagrant violation of the United States revenue laws. His men were also accused by British and American officials of attacking neutral merchantmen; but in spite of proclamations by the governor of Louisiana and ineffective expeditions against, and conflicts with, the Baratarians, they continued to flourish. The United States government was occupied by the War of 1812, and Louisiana was profiting by the work of Laffite.

On Sept. 3, 1814, three officers of the British army and navy visited Laffite, and offered him rewards in lands, pardon for past offenses, and a captaincy in the British army in return for aid in the impending attack on New Orleans. Laffite, having adroitly secured as much information as possible, put the British off with promises to consider the question. Then he promptly informed the Louisiana officials of the whole affair, although Pierre Laffite was even then in jail in New Orleans. In spite of this patriotic act, a force under command of Commodore Daniel T. Patterson of the American navy and Col. George T. Ross of the United States army arrived at Barataria Sept. 16, and, meeting with no resistance, destroyed the establishment, took the ships found there to New Orleans, and arrested the men. When this blow fell, Laffite was in hiding with his brother, who had escaped from jail. Immediately, he offered the services of the Baratarians to the American cause, and, Dec. 17, 1814, Gov. W. C. C. Claiborne [*q.v.*] issued a proclamation of invitation to the Baratarians. Many of them responded and served in the battle of New Orleans. As a reward, President Madison, on Feb. 6, 1815, pardoned them for past crimes.

The Laffites were not long in returning to their evil ways. They were interested in the privateering establishment at Galveston even before Luis de Aury left it, but it was not until September 1817 that Jean Laffite founded there his new establishment, Campeche (*American State Papers, Foreign Relations,* vol. IV, 1834, pp. 132–38). As president of the commune of Campeche (manuscript, Galveston), he commanded an increasing number of privateers, while Pierre made frequent, mysterious journeys to the United States. The privateers flew the flags of the countries revolting from Spain, and Jean Laffite was in 1819 appointed governor of Galveston under the short-lived republic founded by the American filibuster, James Long [*q.v.*]. He never rendered any considerable aid to the revolutionists, however, and his men worked solely for their own profit. They were, in fact, usually denominated pirates, and sixteen of them were convicted as such in New Orleans, Nov. 22, 1819. Another band of them in the same year raided the coast of Louisiana, causing an American cruiser to come to Galveston. Laffite hanged the leading offender, and pacified the Americans, but in 1820 an American merchantman was captured and scuttled in Matagorda Bay, and the United States government acted. In spite of the fact that Galveston had been acknowledged as Spanish territory by the treaty of 1819, Lieut. Lawrence Kearny [*q.v.*] was sent in the brig *Enterprise* to break up the Galveston establishment early in 1821. Laffite acquiesced quietly, and burning his town, sailed away.

The Laffites were known on the Spanish Main for several more years, but disappeared before 1825. They were probably already dead, one killed in a battle at sea, the other by fever in a Yucatan village; but of their deaths no facts are established. In life, Jean Laffite was a romantic figure, a criminal leader with gentlemanly manners, noted for his hospitality, handsome, and ruthless. Legend has heightened this romance, obscuring the fact that he was a shrewd, successful merchant as well as the last of the great freebooters.

[See Charles Gayarré, "Hist. Sketch of Pierre and Jean Lafitte, the Famous Smugglers of La., 1809–1814," in *Mag. of Am. Hist.*, Oct., Nov. 1883; *Official Letter Books of W. C. C. Claiborne* (1917), esp. VI, 216–17, 232–33, 279–80; A. L. Latour, *Hist. Memoir of the War in West Fla. and La. in 1814–15* (1816); "Life of Jean Lafitte, the Pirate of the Mexican Gulf," in *Colburn's United Service Mag.* (London), Oct., Nov. 1851, reprinted in *Littell's Living Age*, Mar. 1852; *De Bow's Rev.*, Oct. 1851, Aug. 1855; H. Yoakum, *Hist. of Tex.* (1855), vol. I; *Papers of Mirabeau Buonaparte Lamar*, vols. I (1921), IV, pt. II (1925); William Kennedy, *Texas* (London, 1841), vol. I; Lyle Saxon, *Lafitte, the Pirate* (1930); *Niles' Weekly Reg.*, Nov. 19, 1814, Feb. 5, 1820. The spelling of the name here adopted is that of signature to documents in the Rosenberg Library, Galveston, and letters published in Latour and in the Lamar Papers. The archives of St. Louis Cathedral, New Orleans, contain the baptismal records of Laffite's illegitimate children by his quadroon mistress.] W. B.

LAFITTE, JEAN [See LAFFITE, JEAN, fl. 1809–1821].

LA FLESCHE, SUSETTE [See BRIGHT EYES, 1854–1903].

LA FOLLETTE, ROBERT MARION (June 14, 1855–June 18, 1925), governor of Wisconsin, United States senator, Progressive candidate for the presidency, was born in a log-cabin in the town of Primrose, Dane County, Wis. His father, Josiah LaFollette, and his mother, Mary (Ferguson) Buchanan LaFollette, had moved into the new state of Wisconsin from Indiana; to Indiana they had gone from Kentucky, where the father of Josiah had lived on a farm adjacent to that of Thomas, the father of Abraham Lincoln. The LaFollette family, which was much like that of Lincoln in status and objective, derived its name from a French Huguenot founder who arrived in New Jersey about 1750 (L. A. Warren, "The Lincoln and LaFollette Families in Pioneer Drama," *Wisconsin Magazine of History*, June 1929, p. 359). Robert was born to the hard labor that went with pioneer poverty. He remained on the farm at Primrose until he worked his way into, and through, the University of Wisconsin at Madison, where he came under the influence of President John Bascom and was graduated with the degree of B.S. in 1879. After studying law a few months, in a private office and in the law school of the university, he was admitted to the bar in February 1880 and began practice in Madison.

He was already a prominent figure in the community. Though he was short of frame and at this time slender, his upstanding hair and resonant voice drew attention to him. He yearned to be an actor but took instead to declamation, preparing an Iago that won him the championship of an interstate oratorical contest in 1879, and that often had to be repeated before admiring friends (*Wisconsin State Journal*, May 12, 1879). He won also as a wife his classmate, Belle Case (Apr. 21, 1859–Aug. 18, 1931), who took up the study of law, receiving the degree of LL.B. from the state university in 1885, and who worked with him in law and politics. It early became a tradition, in which LaFollette wholeheartedly concurred, that her sound judgment was the most valuable of the family assets. Neither he nor she, then or later, showed an interest in legal practice for the sake of money; and the abundant time which the young lawyer had on his hands in the early years was invested in political friendships. He canvassed Dane County in 1880, and was elected district attorney without the permission of the local leader, Col. E. W. Keyes [*q.v.*]. Upon his renomination in 1882, he was the only Republican elected on the county ticket.

That year, in his district, there was controversy over the Republican nomination for Congress; this resulted in the election of a Democrat but made it easier for LaFollette, on his own initiative, to secure the Republican nomination in 1884. The older leaders underestimated his industry and charm. He was elected in November 1884, in spite of the activity of a third candidate, a Prohibitionist, who drew away nearly two thousand votes. Twice again he was nominated and elected, his service in the House of Representatives thus covering the six years 1885–91. While he was establishing himself in Congress, where his industry and power in debate served him well, the control of the Republican party in Wisconsin was vested in Senator Philetus Sawyer [*q.v.*] of Oshkosh, a lumberman of great wealth and a business politician of unusual sagacity. Sawyer was aided after 1885 by the junior senator, John Coit Spooner [*q.v.*], a railroad lawyer from the western side of the state, and with them was associated Henry Clay Payne [*q.v.*], whose position at various times as postmaster of Milwaukee, chairman of the state central committee, and national committeeman, gave him great political opportunities. LaFollette was a younger man and at first an outsider, but during his six years in Washington he gained a place on the committee on ways and means, and did valiant service as a junior in the preparation of the McKinley tariff. Still relatively a conservative, he was headed for greater responsibilities when the political landslide of 1890 separated him from his office.

The reaction against the protective tariff, which was the chief cause of the Republican defeat of that year, was felt in Wisconsin as elsewhere; but in Wisconsin the feeling against the Republicans was embittered by the Bennett Law, enacted by the last legislature, which prescribed that all schools in the state should give a portion of their instruction in the English language. The adherents of the foreign-language parochial schools were inflamed by this legislation and for the moment they outrode every other political force in Wisconsin. Only one of the Republican representatives, Nils P. Haugen, was returned to Congress, and a Democratic state government was installed at Madison. Sawyer and Spooner, in their struggle to survive and to retain control of the Republican state organization, were disposed to discard those whom the Bennett Law had struck and to abandon LaFollette with the rest.

LaFollette returned to the practice of law in Madison. He found himself outside politics, not pliant enough to retain the active support of the leaders, and less available for new favors than men who had not been caught among the animosities of 1890. Before the time came for the nominations of 1892, he had given additional reasons for his abandonment by the leaders, and had acquired a new point of view. In the autumn of 1891 Senator Sawyer summoned him to Milwaukee to offer him law business in defending certain former state treasurers (whose bondsman Sawyer was) against a suit brought by the Democratic state government to compel them to account for the interest they had received on state moneys in their charge. The case was about to open in the Madison court of Judge Robert G. Siebecker, the Democratic brother-in-law of LaFollette, when the latter startled the political world by announcing that Senator Sawyer had tried, through him, to bribe Judge Siebecker, offering him large contingent fees payable after the case had been "decided right" (*Milwaukee Sentinel*, Oct. 29, 30, 1891). Judge Siebecker at once withdrew from the case. Sawyer, though conceding that in ignorance of the family connection he had offered the work to LaFollette, disclaimed an intent to bribe and denied that LaFollette had instantly and indignantly repulsed his advances. LaFollette, however, adhered to his charge, and was convinced that this effort at bribery was only a small evidence of the political corruption practised by the party managers.

It is not possible to measure with precision the relative degrees in which resentment for his abandonment after 1890 and determination to clean up politics now entered his life. Both influenced him; and as his campaign against the bosses advanced, his vision of a new political system grew in definiteness. The caucus and convention system he believed to be unrepresentative and corrupt, and a means of maintaining political control in the hands of industrial, railroad, and financial interests so that they might escape their due share of taxation and reap illicit profit. In the ten years that elapsed between his retirement from Congress and his inauguration as governor in 1901 he elaborated a definite program of reform, comprising: (a) a system of direct-primary nominations protected by law; (b) an equalization of taxation of corporate property with that of other similar property; (c) the regulation of charges by railroads and other corporations to ensure fair play and to prevent them from passing on their taxes to the public; and (d) the erection of commissions of experts for the regulation of railroads and for other public interests. His first steps as a reformer were directed toward the reclaiming of the state government from boss control.

LaFollette found himself an unwelcome aid in the Republican canvass of 1892, but he assisted as a free-lance speaker, for he was and continued to be a Republican. He toured the state for followers in his crusade, finding them most numerous in the western sections where the farmers had been permeable to Granger ideas and those of Populism, and in northern counties where railroad dominance and the power of the timber barons had aroused real animosities. In the more populous southeast, from Milwaukee on the east to Janesville, on Rock River, he made the fewest of his converts. In 1894, through the medium of a Wisconsin Republican League, he and his friends pushed the candidacy of a Scandinavian congressman, Nils P. Haugen, for the nomination as governor; but the organization procured with ease the selection and election of Major W. H. Upham, an up-state business man. It now became easier, however, to make way against the Republican managers, for both Sawyer and Spooner were out of the Senate. In 1896 LaFollette sought the nomination as governor, and went to the state convention in Milwaukee believing that he had a majority of the delegates pledged to his candidacy. When they failed him, and nominated an Oconto lumberman, Edward S. Scofield, on the sixth ballot, LaFollette believed that a corrupt use of money had accomplished his defeat. In 1898 he returned to the attack, but again Scofield was nominated and elected.

There were reasons to suppose that the struggle of LaFollette was now hopeless. McKinley was president; Payne was in high favor; Spooner was back in the Senate, where a Milwaukee "Stalwart" joined him. The Democratic interlude was over, and the conservative Republicans had seemed to meet one of the leading LaFollette demands by setting up a tax commission (1899). In 1900, however, he found new recruits in the persons of Joseph W. Babcock [*q.v.*], congressman and chairman of the Republican congressional committee in 1894, who had been passed over for senator in favor of Spooner, and Isaac Stephenson [*q.v.*], a wealthy lumberman whose senatorial aspirations had been similarly checked. With this new backing, the campaign against the Wisconsin bosses was so successfully resumed that all open resistance was withdrawn. LaFollette found himself nominated by acclamation in 1900; but his associates were the conservative associates of Governor Scofield who were renominated, and in the legislature the "Stalwart" Republicans had surrendered nothing. He took the office of governor in January 1901, committed to a program of direct-primary legislation, tax reform, and railroad control. This was partly reminiscent of Populism, partly anticipatory of Progressivism; but nowhere else was such a program so aggressively presented in a Republican state, and before the trend of the times was fully realized elsewhere the "Wisconsin Idea" had taken a place at the head of liberal political thought (Charles McCarthy, *The Wisconsin Idea,* 1912; Frederic C. Howe, *Wisconsin: An Experiment in Democracy,* 1912).

LaFollette attacked, as corrupt and greedy political manipulators, the leaders whom he had found in power and created a deep and lasting schism in the party in the state. When his opponents blocked him, as they did at every step, he countered by going to the people, whom he understood. They listened to him for long hours at county fairs, or in a thousand Chautauqua audiences, when he recited in full his statistical proofs of the unfair system of taxation and the need for a public control of railroad rates. His labors racked his body to its permanent injury, but assembled a loyal following of common people who remained his until, and after, death. The legislature of 1901 did none of the things that he had urged in his campaign, and he believed that its recalcitrance was another proof of the plot of the bosses against reform. They had allowed him the empty shell of office, but had retained the reality of legislative control. At about this time one of the wealthy "Stalwarts," Charles F. Pfister, secured control of the Milwaukee *Sentinel,* upon which LaFollette had relied for support, and turned into its columns a persistent attack upon his aims and motives. To fight the *Sentinel,* the Milwaukee *Free Press* was soon set up as a new daily by Isaac Stephenson, who differed from most of LaFollette's associates in having money (Isaac Stephenson, *Recollections of a Long Life, 1829–1915,* 1915, p. 219). The conservatives responded to LaFollette's charge of treachery by denouncing his "rule-or-ruin" ambition, and his refusal to cooperate. In 1902 the governor made a thorough canvass not only for his own renomination but also for the election of a legislature that would work with him. He was so successful that his own lieutenant, Irvine L. Lenroot, was chosen speaker of the Assembly, and his primary law was enacted in 1903, subject to a popular referendum the next year. He had removed the Republican state convention of 1902 from the hostile influences of Milwaukee to the friendly atmosphere of the university gymnasium at Madison (Barton, *post,* p. 201). When Lenroot began the keynote speech before the convention of 1904, the prospect of victory for the primary law was so good that he was warranted in reminding his auditors that they constituted "the last republican convention in Wisconsin" (*Wisconsin State Journal,* May 18, 1904).

In the legislature of 1903 the conservative forces had blocked the passage of railroad and taxation laws acceptable to LaFollette, and after the session they had set to work to put him out of politics. They contested every step in the campaign of 1904, but a majority of the state central committee were now LaFollette men, and these decided to nominate a state ticket and to select delegates at large to the Republican National Convention in a single state convention to be held in May. The selection of the delegates to this convention was a matter of warm partisanship, and gave rise to many contests which the state central committee was disposed to settle in favor of the LaFollette contestants. There was rumor of an intended seizure of the gavel by "Stalwarts," and the gymnasium hall was policed by University athletes and so fenced as to keep physical control in the hands of the friends of the governor. The precautions were so complete that the convention renominated LaFollette with ease, and chose him to lead the delegates at large in Chicago; whereupon the "Stalwart" delegations and contestants held a rival convention in the opera house, nominated their own state ticket, and chose a set of delegates for the national convention with Payne and Spooner at their head.

The Republican National Convention at Chicago seated the anti-LaFollette delegation in spite of the fact that they were the choice of a bolting faction. The president designate, Roosevelt, made no opposition to the seating of the "Stalwarts," thereby arousing in LaFollette a conviction that his progressivism was neither genuine nor dependable. In spite of the schism, the Republican party carried Wisconsin in 1904, and LaFollette met a friendly legislature in 1905. A railroad commission was set up, the bill erecting it receiving constructive support from the railroad politicians who now accepted it as inevitable. The Progressive movement and the "Wisconsin Idea" were fully launched, to be elaborated during the next few years by the lieutenants of LaFollette. He himself was elected to the United States Senate in 1905, replacing Quarles. He deferred his resignation as governor and his qualification as senator until January 1906, in order to complete the work in hand. For the next ten years men trained as civil servants in Wisconsin found unusual opportunities in the federal service, although LaFollette, who had been the leader of many of them, was "alone in the Senate."

Thrice after 1905 LaFollette was elected to succeed himself. His popular following in Wisconsin defied any attempt to break his hold upon it, but at no time did his associates in the Republican party recognize his right to lead, or accept cheerfully his direction in those fields in which he could qualify as expert. His speeches continued to be elaborate statistical treatises, and he revealed on the floor of the Senate the same qualities of vision, courage, and persistence that had enabled him to organize and direct his crusade against the bosses in Wisconsin. Undependable as a unit in the Republican organization, he insisted upon a right to dominate that was not accorded him and a freedom to stigmatize his opponents that was bitterly resented. As the years went on, however, a surprising number of the measures advocated by him were enacted. Before the World War checked the movement for reform, the direct primary was established by law in most of the states of the nation. This served to break in a measure the tight grip of party bosses on the personnel in office, but resulted also in the bringing to Washington and into the state governments of men as stubborn and refractory as LaFollette himself, to the destruction of party coherence. His reforms in taxation made Wisconsin a leader in fair assessment and in the adoption of the income tax, which soon became national. In the matter of railroad control, LaFollette advocated in the Senate physical valuation as a basis for rate-making, and was generally dissatisfied with any measure that could command a majority of votes. Regulatory commissions, advocated by him as means to the bridging of the gap between the electorate, which can pass intelligent judgment only on general propositions, and technical experts, who can strive for scientific exactitude, rebuilt his state and to some extent changed the whole aspect of American government. Because of its dependence upon laboratory men in economics, law, and science, the movement toward government by commissions gave definitive impulses to the University of Wisconsin, which was perhaps the object of LaFollette's greatest affection, and through his influence that institution rose to national prominence.

Unalterably at variance with the dominant wing of the Republican party that represented industry and finance, LaFollette regarded himself and was regarded by his followers as the logical man to take over the principles of the Roosevelt administration and translate these into enactment. They failed to perceive that the "Stalwart" faction, with which Roosevelt himself had not been able to maintain more than an armed truce, would not have tolerated a genuine Rooseveltian. LaFollette's name was presented to the Republican National Convention of 1908, but it was Taft who secured the nomination, while Roosevelt gave no sign of seeing in LaFollette more than a progressive local leader. The latter, remembering his own rebuff of 1904 and perceiving Roosevelt's willingness to find a working basis with the "stand-pat" wing of the party, became deeply convinced that Roosevelt was not a genuine reformer. The Taft administration could never convince him that it was progressive. LaFollette led the Senate opposition to the Payne-Aldrich tariff, and espoused the cause of conservation. His hopes for the nomination to succeed Taft in 1912 were advanced by the Democratic gains of 1910. The schism that had been scarcely concealed in the Republican party since 1901 broke out in open warfare.

In the opinion of LaFollette the foundation of

American society was imperiled by the unrestrained greed of business, which he felt would inevitably engender Socialism. He was no Socialist, but he feared for the continuance of the "American principle" unless democracy could develop agencies powerful enough to overcome the selfish power of wealth. He founded a personal organ for maintaining contact with his followers when, on Jan. 9, 1909, appeared the first number of *LaFollette's Weekly Magazine,* carrying the caption: "Ye shall know the truth and the truth shall make you free." Believing that in the nation, as previously in Wisconsin, it was necessary to gain control over the organization before reforms could be attained, he drafted the manifesto upon which the National Progressive Republican League was organized in his Washington residence in 1911. The League aimed at such mechanical reforms as direct primaries and the direct election of senators, and hoped to bring about the nomination of a Progressive candidate to succeed Taft. It was generally conceded that LaFollette was the logical leader of this insurgent group, although defeat was expected to be the immediate reward of its activities. He was encouraged to fight by many who would have preferred to support Roosevelt, but who believed that the latter was outside the contest. He thought that Roosevelt was himself one of his backers. But, by the end of 1911, the revolt against Taft ceased to appear hopeless and Roosevelt, in secrecy, became convinced that it might be won, if only he took the lead. In February 1912, a temporary breakdown of LaFollette on a public occasion (Owen Wister, in "Roosevelt and the 1912 Disaster," *Harper's Magazine,* May 1930) gave the pretext for many of his supporters to switch to Roosevelt. LaFollette believed for the rest of his life that he had been used only as a decoy and never forgave either Roosevelt or the deserters among his own followers. He remained in the race at the Chicago convention, but to no avail. His prominence as a Progressive soon threw him into close contact with the Wilson administration when the latter undertook to enact progressive measures with Democratic votes. On numerous occasions the Democrats received LaFollette's support, paying for it by joining with him in the passage of a seaman's act in 1915. His strong sympathy with labor, too, brought him close to much of the activity of the Democrats; but he broke away when the problems of the World War and neutrality began to require American attention.

Such positive testimony as LaFollette's private correspondence may contain with reference to the reasons for his war attitude has not yet become available. Roosevelt's early and vigorous support of the Allies may have helped to fix his attitude. He retained throughout his life that critical attitude toward Great Britain that was nearly universal during his service in the House of Representatives. The German or Scandinavian origin of many of his constituents did not tend to soften it. When imperialism began to be discussed during his senatorial career, his sympathies were with the people of the dependencies. His characteristic hostility to the larger agencies of wealth made him critical of the profits which some Americans derived from the munitions trade, and made it easy for him to believe that the drift of the United States into the World War was the result of a conspiracy of Wall Street to protect its loans to the Allies. Really anti-British, he could not avoid the reputation of being pro-German. Never a man to conceal his sentiments or to take cover in a fight, he became an open critic of the diplomatic course of President Wilson. He engineered the filibuster that prevented the passage of the armed merchant-ship legislation at the close of the short session in 1917, and he spoke and voted against the declaration of war against Germany. In the latter debate he used the almost fatal words: "Germany has been patient with us" (*Congressional Record,* 65 Cong., 1 Sess., p. 234). After the declaration, he "supported all other war measures because if we were to send an army in a foreign war at all, it was right and necessary to send them perfectly equipped and amply supplied in every way" (*LaFollette's Magazine,* July 1919, p. 1). He used every effort, however, to make the war a charge upon the current income of the rich, rather than a bonded obligation upon posterity. In September 1917, the incorrect press version of one of his speeches at a Non-Partisan League meeting in St. Paul exaggerated his unpopularity, and directed against him a movement for his expulsion from the Senate. There was no ground for an expulsion, but the Senate evaded compliance only by protracting its proceedings. LaFollette continued to be the scapegoat for excited patriots. No piece of criticism wounded him more deeply than an adverse memorial from members of the faculty of his university, and a censure by the legislature of his state. But when his partisans later wished to retaliate upon those who had censured him it was his hand that restrained them. Active as he was in criticism of the avowed aims of the war, his activity was lessened by the long and desperate illness of his eldest son. He opposed the ratification of the Covenant of the League of Nations, and the accession of the United States to the World Court. He strove to organize farmer and labor opinion, to protect these classes against the consequences of deflation, and to prevent "big business" from entrenching itself in the legislation of the post-war period.

LaFollette had been reëlected easily in 1916; and at the next senatorial election, in 1922, the war was over, the reaction had set in, and he was stronger than ever among his constituents. In the Senate from 1919 to 1925, he and his "little group of willful men," as Wilson had previously characterized them, were able to hold a balance of power. His Republican associates resented his independence but dared not risk the consequences of turning him out of the party. His hold on liberal opinion was steadily becoming stronger, and his character stood every test in the trying years of the Harding administration. He was the author of the resolution which authorized the senatorial investigation of the Teapot Dome and other naval oil leases. There was no chance that his party would ever accept him for the presidency, but there was in 1924 a possibility that the forces in revolt might be welded into a new party of liberalism, and that a third candidate might throw the election into the House of Representatives, where on the vote by state delegations the insurgents might hold a balance of power and determine the choice. "Coolidge or chaos" was the phrase of George Harvey, who exaggerated the possibility of this to the advantage of the Republican candidate. A conference for Progressive political action, meeting at Cleveland in July 1924, invited La Follette to run independently; this he did, selecting his vice-presidential associate, Senator Burton K. Wheeler, from among the progressive Democrats. He carried out as active a canvass against both Coolidge and Davis as his health would permit, and received nearly 5,000,000 votes in November, or one-sixth of the votes cast; whereas the Populist ticket of 1892 had received only one vote in twelve. It was his last campaign. He had long worked against physical disabilities which now got the better of him. He died in Washington during the following summer, but the magnetism of his name placed his eldest son and namesake in his Senate seat. His widow and three other children also survived him.

[In the files of *LaFollette's Weekly* and of the Madison *Capital Times* may be found expression of LaFollette's views, and an approving exposition of them. See also the compilation of Ellen Torelle, *The Polit. Philosophy of Robt. M. LaFollette as Revealed in his Speeches and Writings* (1920). He prepared for serial use in the *American Magazine* in 1911–12 the personal chapters that became *LaFollette's Autobiography; A Personal Narrative of Political Experiences* (1913), reprinted and enlarged in later years. A friendly sketch of his work is Albert O. Barton, *LaFollette's Winning of Wisconsin 1894–1904* (1922). Among numerous articles may be cited: Bruce Bliven, "Robt. M. LaFollette," *New Republic*, July 1, 1925, and "Robt. M. La Follette's Place in Our Hist.," *Current Hist.*, Aug. 1925; F. A. Ogg, "Robt. M. LaFollette in Retrospect," *Current Hist.*, Feb. 1931. For Mrs. LaFollette, see *N. Y. Times*, Aug. 19, 20, 1931. Shortly after his death his wife and children executed an agreement whereby his voluminous papers will eventually become the property of the State Historical Society of Wisconsin.]

F. L. P.

LAFON, THOMY (Dec. 28, 1810–Dec. 22, 1893), negro philanthropist, was born in New Orleans, La., the son of Pierre Laralde and Modest Foucher. How he came by the name Lafon is not known. His father was part French; his mother was of Haitian extraction. Both were free persons of color. In some way young Lafon acquired sufficient education to begin life as a school teacher. Then, about 1850, he began to operate a small store in Orleans Street, in his native city. Just before the Civil War he began to lend his savings at advantageous rates of interest and to invest in real estate. Possessed of excellent judgment and great sagacity, he quickly accumulated a comfortable fortune, which grew with the years, and which enabled him to leave an estate valued at approximately half a million dollars at the time of his death.

Lafon was physically weak and almost emaciated in appearance, but his carriage was erect and dignified, and his manners courteous and affable. His fluency in the use of French and Spanish led many, apparently without reason, to believe that he had been educated in Europe. He was devoted to art and especially fond of music. His olive complexion, regular features, and straight steel-gray hair, would have enabled him to pass as a Caucasian in most communities, but he made no effort to conceal his race. He was of a retiring nature and averse to notoriety of any kind. Although he owned pretentious houses in many sections of the city, he preferred a humble abode, a small, shabby-looking cottage at the corner of Ursuline and Robertson Streets. He never married, but lived here with his sister, his sole companion and adviser, who possessed the same traits and characteristics as himself. He shunned all extravagances and lived like a miser, but, while he carefully investigated all requests for assistance, he was never known to refuse financial aid to deserving persons or causes. A devoted Roman Catholic, he became greatly attached, toward the end of his life, to Archbishop Janssens, who possibly influenced his later philanthropies. These extended to all classes of society with no distinction in regard to color or race, sex or age. By his will, dated Apr. 3, 1890, he provided for his aged sister and some friends, but left the bulk of his estate to charitable, educational, and religious institutions of New Orleans. Among them were the Charity Hospital, the Lafon Old Folks Home, the Society of the Holy Family, the Shakespeare Almshouse, Straight University (now Straight College) and one or two other colored educational institutions, and the Eye, Ear, Nose, and Throat Hospital. In recognition of his charities the city of New Orleans has named one of its public schools after him. He died at his home, and was buried in St. Louis Cemetery on Esplanade Avenue.

[Records at St. Louis Cathedral and at the City Hall, New Orleans; *Jour. of Negro Hist.*, Jan. 1917, Apr. 1922; R. L. Desdunes, *Nos Hommes et Notre Histoire* (Montreal, 1911); *Daily Picayune* (New Orleans), Dec. 23 and 24, 1893; copy of Lafon's will (will No. 41,124) in the office of the Clerk of the Civil District Court for the Parish of Orleans, New Courthouse Building, New Orleans.] M. J. W.

LAGUNA, THEODORE DE LEO DE (July 22, 1876–Sept. 22, 1930), philosopher, was born at Oakland, Cal., the son of Alexander de Leo and Frederica Henrietta (Bergner) de Laguna. His father was a French citizen of Spanish descent who came to the United States during the political revolution of 1848. His mother was born in Saxony. Alexander de Laguna married her in Philadelphia in 1850. In the same year they sailed for San Francisco by way of Cape Horn. Theodore, who was the youngest of nine children and a rather frail child, attended the public schools of Oakland and was graduated from the University of California in 1896. From the same University he received the degree of M.A. in 1899. In 1900–01 he was fellow in philosophy in Cornell University and at the end of that year was granted the doctorate in philosophy. From 1901 to 1903 he taught school in the Philippine Islands and traveled in the Orient. Although his health suffered from this experience, he regarded it as an important factor in the later formulation of his sociological views. During the years 1903–05 he resumed his studies in philosophy at Cornell University where he held office as honorary fellow and assistant in philosophy. On Sept. 9, 1905, he married Grace Mead Andrus, then a graduate student in Cornell University. From the time of his marriage his wife was closely associated with him in his philosophical studies, teaching, and publication. In the autumn of 1905 they went to the University of Michigan where De Laguna had been appointed assistant professor of education. From 1907 until his death at Hardwick, Vt., in September 1930, he was professor of philosophy at Bryn Mawr College.

De Laguna's interests were not confined to technical philosophy, but included also the fields of literature and music. Reared in the rigorous pietism of a Lutheran home, he sought, even in his undergraduate years, freedom of thought by shaking off the trammels of the constraining faith in which he had been bred, but more than a touch of that faith lingered on to his last days (*Contemporary American Philosophy,* vol. I, pp. 420 ff.). His philosophical life was spent largely in the processes of analysis and criticism. He gave his allegiance to no school of thought, although at different periods of his life he acknowledged the spell of neo-Hegelianism and welcomed certain aspects of the pragmatism of William James, such as the evolutionary view of knowledge and the emphasis laid on belief. He was disposed to reject the traditional empiricism and rationalism in their dogmatic forms. Between these, on the one hand, and the new theories of social and organic evolution on the other, he wrote as a mediator. He characterized his own philosophy as "The Way of Opinion." Not only is knowledge in constant process of growth and modification, according to De Laguna's view, but there is no such thing as truth in general; there are only truths of particular propositions. There is no science of the universe, but only particular sciences. Cosmologies are merely figures of speech. He is not an agnostic nor is he a skeptic in any ordinary connotation of these terms. While he denies the validity of induction, and accords to deduction alone logical validity as a method, he finds in science a healthy condition. "Scientific knowledge has the best claim to the title that any beliefs can have" (*Contemporary American Philosophy,* vol. I, p. 411); it (scientific knowledge) is the most authoritative "opinion," the nearest approximation to certainty, and in this respect is superior to speculative philosophy in its present state. De Laguna's publications include the following: *Dogmatism and Evolution: Studies in Modern Philosophy* (1910), written in collaboration with his wife; *Introduction to the Science of Ethics* (1914); *Factors of Social Evolution* (1926); "The Way of Opinion" (in *Contemporary American Philosophy,* vol. I, 1930); and numerous articles and discussions of current philosophical literature published principally in the *Journal of Philosophy* and the *Philosophical Review.*

[*Who's Who in America,* 1930–31; Addresses at a Memorial Service for Theodore de Leo de Laguna at Bryn Mawr College, Nov. 16, 1930, delivered by Marion Edwards Park, Brand Blanchard, W. P. Montague, and Helen H. Parkhurst (unpublished); *N. Y. Times,* Sept. 25, 1930.] W. A. H.

LAHONTAN, LOUIS-ARMAND DE LOM D'ARCE, Baron de (June 9, 1666–*c.* 1713), a noted traveler in the New World and author of a popular volume of description and travel, was a native of the south of France, where the village of Lahontan still stands on the banks of the Garonne. His father, Isaac de Lom d'Arce, was a noted engineer who bought the barony of Lahontan and bequeathed it to his only son, the child of his old age and of a second marriage with Jeanne-Françoise le Fascheux de Couttes. Isaac Lahontan died in 1674 after having had financial losses that left his estate greatly depleted. Louis, following the custom of his time, entered the army at an early age, held first a commission in the Bourbon regiment, and then transferred to the marine corps, which had charge of colonial defense. In 1683 he embarked with his regiment for New France, where the governor, La Barre, had asked for troops to aid him against the Iroquois. Lahontan's first military service was in La Barre's futile expedition of 1684 to Lake Ontario, which failed to reach or punish the Iroquois Indians, with whom the governor was forced to make an ignominious peace. For this he was recalled. The Marquis Denonville, who came in his place, undertook in 1687 an expedition which was more effective. In the interval between the two excursions Lahontan was in garrison, where he devoted much time to hunting and to observing his surroundings. Meanwhile he was summoned to France on affairs of his estate. Needing every available soldier, the governor would not allow him to go and, after the campaign was finished, sent him west with Duluth and Tonty because he understood the Indian languages and the Indian methods of diplomacy. He was left as commandant at Fort St. Joseph, on St. Clair River above Detroit. This post he abandoned the next year on pretext of danger, visited Mackinac, and thence went somewhere into the farther west to spend the winter. In his book he claimed to have ascended the Mississippi, to have found the River Long, and there to have wintered among tribes whose names and customs are unknown to history.

In the summer of 1689 he returned to Quebec and joined the new governor, Count de Frontenac, by whom the young baron was held in such esteem that he was sent to France in 1690 to bear the good news of the defeat of the English fleet on the lower St. Lawrence. Lahontan's reward was a promotion to a captaincy and the gift of a place in the order of Notre Dame. By September 1691 he was again in Canada, a member of the gay court of Frontenac at Château St. Louis. There he had an *affaire du coeur* with a Canadian girl, whom he finally refused to marry, apparently from caprice. The next year he again embarked for France and, on the way, aided in the repulse of a large British squadron at Plaisance, Newfoundland. In reward for this service he was made royal lieutenant for the last-named colony, whence in 1693 the erratic soldier deserted the service, and made himself an exile from French domains. Thereafter he wandered about Europe, from Portugal to Holland and, later, from Hamburg and Copenhagen to Spain. In 1703 he published at The Hague his famous book, *Nouveaux Voyages de Mr. le Baron de Lahontan dans l'Amérique Septentrionale,* which ran through many editions and translations. It was accompanied by a map showing the River Long and a number of illustrations of the manners and customs of the Indians, a brief vocabulary, and much interesting material on the New World. In the first English edition, the same year, the author published a series of "Dialogues" with the Huron Indian he called "Adario," wherein he discussed the philosophy of primitive life as contrasted with civilization. His last years were spent at the court of Hanover, where he was befriended by the philosopher, Leibnitz, and where he is believed to have died.

Lahontan was a caustic spirit with a cynical outlook on life; his favorite authors were Lucian and Petronius and he had a deep aversion for ecclesiastics of all kinds. His "Dialogues Curieux" depicted the "natural man" so important to eighteenth-century philosophers, and his influence on the growth of primitivism both in England and France has been lately traced by Chinard (*post*). Addison, Steele, and preëminently Swift derive from Lahontan, while his work was a source for LeSage, Montesquieu, Voltaire, and Châteaubriand. He wrote well, even charmingly, and his descriptions of Canada and the West add to the knowledge of primitive conditions, of flora, fauna, and the life of the savages. His accounts of historical events and personages are accurate, except where he wilfully misled his readers. His imaginary River Long has discredited his book of travels, which in many particulars is the best account of New France in the late seventeenth century.

[*New Voyages to America,* ed. by R. G. Thwaites (1905) with critical biography and bibliography; introduction of Gilbert Chinard, *Dialogues Curieux, par Baron de Lahontan* (1931); F. C. B. Crompton, *Glimpses of Early Canadians: Lahontan* (1925); *Proc. and Trans. of the Royal Soc. of Canada,* vol. XII (1895); L. P. Kellogg, *The French Régime in Wis. and the Northwest* (1925).] L. P. K.

LAIMBEER, NATHALIE SCHENCK (Dec. 4, 1882–Oct. 25, 1929), banker and financial writer, was born in New York City, the daughter of Spotswood and Effie (Morgan) Schenck. Her interest was first aroused in finance, she said, when as a child she accompanied her grandmother to the bank. Sometimes she was permitted to clip coupons from bright orange bonds, and she then determined that her first purchase would be securities of similar color. During the Spanish-American War, when she was but fifteen, she collected $25,000 in dimes for the American Red Cross for the construction of an ice plant in Cuba. She did not prepare for a business career, however, and for many years devoted her abilities entirely to social and charitable enterprises. She was married in 1904 to Capt. Charles Collins of the British Army, by whom she had one son and from whom she was later divorced. In 1909 she married William Laimbeer of New York, and to them two daughters were born. In 1913 her second husband was killed in an automobile accident on Long Island and as a result of the same accident she was for some time a semi-invalid.

Her first outstanding public work was done as a volunteer in the United States Food Administration during the World War, when she assisted in devising plans for the canning and conservation of food. Following in the line of this experience, in November 1918, she became manager of the Bureau of Home Economics of the New York Edison Company, giving many lectures and demonstrations at various colleges and schools. In 1919, she entered upon her banking career as manager of the women's department of the United States Mortgage & Trust Company. Less than a year later she was appointed assistant secretary of that organization in charge of those Manhattan branches which were organizing women's departments. She was called to the National City Bank of New York in 1925 as assistant cashier, being the first woman employed by that bank ever to be given a title. As head of the women's department, until poor health forced her to retire in 1926, she became nationally known as a banker of ability and sound judgment. From January 1928 to July 1929 she was editor of the department on finance of the *Delineator,* and she contributed many articles on finance to the New York *World* and other papers. She was one of the founders of the Association of Bank Women, served as its national vice-president from 1921 to 1923, and was elected to the presidency for the three years following. In this office she made, it is said, a definite contribution to the cause of bank women, securing for them recognition as an integral part of the banking profession. Coincident with, and perhaps owing to, her work in the Association of Bank Women, came a change in the conception of banks: heretofore considered as credit institutions primarily, they came to be regarded as organized agencies for public service, and women's departments increased in number and effectiveness.

Mrs. Laimbeer died in New York, as a result of acute cardiac dilatation, and was buried in Woodlawn Cemetery.

[*N. Y. Times,* Oct. 26, 1929; *Delineator,* Jan. 1928–July 1929, esp. Mar. 1928; letter from W. P. Williams, personnel director of the National City Bank of N. Y., June 20, 1930; interview with the president of the Asso. of Bank Women, June 26, 1930; records of the Department of Health, N. Y. City.] I. V–F.

LALOR, ALICE [See TERESA, MOTHER, 1766–1846].

LAMAR, GAZAWAY BUGG (Oct. 2, 1798–Oct. 5, 1874), ship-owner, banker, cotton merchant, and Confederate agent, was born in Richmond County, Ga., the son of Basil and Rebecca (Kelly) Lamar and a descendant of Thomas Lamar who, coming from France, settled in Maryland before 1663. His first wife was Jane Meek Creswell, to whom he was married in Augusta, Ga., Oct. 18, 1821. He manifested a keen aptitude for business and rose quickly to a place of prominence in the financial circles of Augusta and Savannah. Quick to discern the trends of the time, he rarely missed an ascending movement in commerce. He introduced the first iron steamship in American waters, building the *John Randolph* in Savannah in 1834 from plates and structural shapes fabricated in England (commemorative tablet, City Hall, Savannah). The next year he was one of the incorporators of the Iron Steam-Boat Company of Augusta, which established a line of steamers on the Savannah River. He was financially interested in the Mechanics' Bank of Augusta, of which his brother, George Washington Lamar, was cashier. In 1838 he bought the Centre Street toll bridge over the Savannah River at Augusta, selling it two years later to the municipality. He is said to have rendered financial assistance to the Republic of Texas, when his cousin Mirabeau B. Lamar [*q.v.*] was president; and at another time to have assisted in the floating of a Mexican bond issue. His ship *Mary Summers* served as an American transport in the Mexican War.

On the night of June 14, 1838, his steamship *Pulaski* went down off the Carolina coast, and though Lamar himself and his eldest son were rescued from the water, his wife and six children were among the 140 who were lost. The surviving son later came into prominence in the affair of the slave ship *Wanderer,* and as a lieutenant-colonel in the Confederate army was killed in one of the last engagements of the Civil War. A few years after his first wife's death Lamar married Harriet, daughter of Charles Antoine de Cazenove, a native of Switzerland, and his wife, Anne Hogan of Alexandria, Va. By his second marriage Lamar had two sons and three daughters.

In 1845 he removed to New York, becoming president of the Bank of the Republic. In November 1860 he bought 10,000 muskets at the Watervliet Arsenal, N. Y., and shipped them to Georgia, where they arrived just after the secession of South Carolina. On Jan. 22, 1861, New York police took from the steamer *Monticello* at her North River pier 200 muskets consigned to Savannah; and the Georgia authorities seized five New York vessels lying at Savannah as a reprisal. Lamar acted as agent for the state of Georgia in the settlement of the affair, which was effected, with restitution, on Mar. 18. He remained in New York until well after the commencement of hostilities, acting as a Confederate intelligence and postal agent.

Returning to Savannah as head of the Bank of Commerce, he was elected president of the Bank Convention of the Confederate States, held at Atlanta in July 1861. For the next three and a half years he was actively engaged in banking and blockade running. In October 1863 he incurred considerable popular disfavor through the exposure of overtures he had addressed to Fernando Wood, former mayor of New York and then member of Congress, looking toward a copartnership in blockade running. Lamar proposed to finance and manage the venture if Wood could "grease" the blockade so that their ships could pass freely at Ossabaw Inlet. The proposals were intercepted and printed in the *New York Times,* and were reprinted in many Confederate papers. Lamar vigorously defended his proposition on the basis that the end justified the means: that to loosen up the blockade it was as consistent with the public good to use bribes as gunpowder. He considered the war over when Sherman occupied Savannah, and immediately took the oath of allegiance to the United States in order to save as much of his property in the occupied area as possible. After many disputes with Federal officers, however, over property which they claimed as "captured and abandoned," he was arrested by the military authorities on charges of conspiring with his nephew, G. B. Lamar, Jr., and others, to appropriate government cotton and to bribe various military and civil officials. He was confined for a time in the Old Capitol Prison at Washington; but was released by President Johnson. He retained Gen. Benjamin F. Butler to press his claims against the government. Considerable sums have been recovered by his heirs and legatees.

Though an astute politician and trader, Lamar was a generous man. He endowed hospitals for negroes in Augusta and Savannah; and was one of the endowers of the Young Men's Library Association of Augusta. He died in New York; and was buried at Alexandria, Va., among the Cazenoves.

[C. C. Jones and Salem Dutcher, *Memorial Hist. of Augusta, Ga.* (1890); I. W. Avery, *The Hist. of the State of Ga.* (1881); *War of the Rebellion: Official Records (Army),* 1 ser. IV, 2 ser. III (*Navy*), 1 ser. XXVIII (pt. 2), LIII, supp., 3 ser. I, 4 ser. I; A. D. Candler, *The Confed. Records of the State of Ga.*, vol. IV (1910); Edward Mayes, *Geneal. Notes on a Branch of the Family of Mayes and on the Related Families* (1928?); W. H. Lamar, "Thomas Lamar of the Province of Maryland and a Part of His Descendants," *Southern Hist. Asso. Pubs.*, July 1897; *Daily Chronicle and Sentinel* (Augusta), Oct. 28, 29, 1863; *Savannah Republican,* Oct. 24, 27, 1863; *N. Y. Tribune,* Oct. 6, 1874; *Atlanta Constitution,* Oct. 8, 1874.]

W. M. R., Jr.

LAMAR, JOSEPH RUCKER (Oct. 14, 1857–Jan. 2, 1916), jurist, a descendant of Thomas Lamar, who emigrated from France to Virginia in the seventeenth century, was born at "Cedar Grove," the plantation home of his maternal grandfather in Elbert County, Ga. His father, James Sanford Lamar, was educated for the bar but having come under the influence of Alexander Campbell, entered the ministry of the Disciples of Christ. His mother, Mary Rucker, was the youngest child of Joseph Rucker of Ruckersville, Ga., a planter of wealth and unusual mental force. Joseph Lamar's early childhood was spent at "Cedar Grove" but after his mother's death in 1864 he went to live in Augusta, where his father was pastor of the Disciples' Church. There at the academy of Joseph T. Derry he was a schoolmate of Woodrow Wilson. After completing his secondary education at Martin Institute, Jefferson, Ga., and the school conducted by Col. Richard Malcolm Johnston at Penn Lucy, Md., he entered the University of Georgia. At the request of his father—who had been called to a pastorate in Louisville, Ky.—he transferred to Bethany College, West Virginia, where he graduated in 1877. After studying law at Washington and Lee University, and in the office of Henry Clay Foster in Augusta, he was admitted to the bar of Georgia in 1878. He then returned to Bethany, taught Latin for a year, and on Jan. 13, 1879, was married to Clarinda Huntington Pendleton, a daughter of the president of the college. In 1880 he moved to Augusta to practise law in partnership with Foster, and there he made his home until elevated to the United States Supreme Court.

Lamar was an indefatigable worker and rose rapidly at the bar. He also took an interest in public questions and served two terms in the state legislature (1886–87, 1888–89). An interest, early developed, in the history of the jurisprudence of his native state led him to write many papers on the subject. His talent for research was given recognition in 1893 by his appointment as one of three commissioners to recodify the laws of Georgia. To Lamar was assigned the major task of preparing the civil code. This compilation, *The Code of the State of Georgia* (2 vols., 1896), enhanced his reputation and eight years after its completion he was appointed an associate justice of the state supreme court. He found the duties of the court congenial, but his health suffered from the exacting and confining nature of the work, and after serving two years he resigned. He resumed the practice of law in Augusta and was soon retained in important litigation. It was during this period that he gained a favorable decision, on final appeal to the United States Supreme Court, in the case of *Central of Georgia Railway Company* vs. *Wright, Comptroller-General of Georgia* (207 *U. S.*, 127). His argument, that the Georgia statute providing the method of assessing railroad property for taxation violated the "due process" clause of the Constitution, was considered masterly. Nominated by President Taft an associate justice of the Supreme Court of the United States, he was unanimously confirmed by the Senate and sworn into office Jan. 3, 1911.

Lamar's opinions, on both the state and federal benches, have distinct literary merit and reveal unusual judicial ability. Terse, clear, and logical, they yet leave little to be said upon controlling questions. They also show that he had a profound sense of justice, as in *Oliver* vs. *Oliver* (118 *Ga.*, 362), where he held that a director of a corporation, who purchases shares in the company without informing the seller of a contemplated transaction which would enhance the value of the stock, must rescind the sale or give the seller other appropriate relief. Perhaps his most widely discussed decision was rendered in *Gompers* vs. *Bucks Stove & Range Company* (221 *U. S.*, 418), in which the conviction of Samuel Gompers and other labor leaders was set aside because of defective procedure, but where the power of courts to punish for violations of injunctions restraining boycotts was upheld. His most far-reaching decision was probably *United States* vs. *Midwest Oil Company* (236 *U. S.*, 459) in which it was held the president of the United States had the right, without express authority of Congress, to withdraw public oil lands from private entry.

Lamar was sent by President Wilson as one of the commissioners to represent the United States at the mediation conference at Niagara Falls, Canada, in May–June 1914, sponsored by Argentina, Brazil, and Chile, to adjust the differences between the American and Mexican governments growing out of Wilson's refusal to recognize Huerta as president of Mexico. His tact and ability so impressed Wilson that the President wished to appoint him a delegate to the Pan American Conference to be held in Chile the following October, but Lamar felt he could not absent himself so long from his judicial duties; moreover, his health was beginning to fail. At the end of the next term he sought to regain his strength at various watering places. He did not improve, however, and, returning to Washington, died just five years after becoming a member of the Supreme Court. Lamar was a companionable man with much charm of manner. Lord Bryce, who knew him in Washington, said of him, "He seemed to me to have an eminently just and wide mind, always seeking for the truth in a spirit of perfect candour, and penetrating deep to the true reasons of political principles and legal rules" (*Life of Joseph Rucker Lamar, post,* p. 282). Several of Lamar's papers are scattered through the reports of the Georgia Bar Association.

[See: Clarinda Pendleton Lamar, *The Life of Jos. Rucker Lamar* (1926); W. J. Northen, *Men of Mark in Ga.*, vol. IV (1908); memorials in 241 *U. S.*, App. ii, and 146 *Ga.*, 841; *Evening Star* (Washington), Jan. 3, 1916; *N. Y. Times*, Jan. 4, 31, 1916. Lamar's opinions are to be found in 117–21 *Ga. Reports* and in 220–38 *U. S. Reports.*] B. F.

LAMAR, LUCIUS QUINTUS CINCINNATUS (Sept. 17, 1825–Jan. 23, 1893), Mississippi statesman, senator, associate justice of the United States Supreme Court, was born in Putnam County, Ga., fourth of eight children of Lucius Quintus Cincinnatus and Sarah Williamson (Bird) Lamar. The Lamars, who were of French Huguenot ancestry according to tradition, settled in Maryland prior to 1663, moved to Georgia about 1755, and, following the advancing frontier, became established in Putnam County about 1810. The elder L. Q. C. Lamar was a distinguished Georgia lawyer who served as judge of the Ocmulgee circuit. His brother,

Mirabeau B. Lamar [*q.v.*], was the second president of the Republic of Texas. Young L. Q. C. Lamar was connected on his mother's side with the distinguished Williamson, Bird, Clarke, and Campbell families.

Prepared in the schools of Baldwin and Newton County, he was graduated from Emory College, Oxford, Ga., in 1845. The president of that institution was the notable A. B. Longstreet [*q.v.*], whose daughter Lamar later married. He studied law in Macon, Ga., under Absalom Chappell, a kinsman, and was admitted to the bar in Vienna, Dooly County, in 1847. After a short-lived partnership with Judge Chappell, he began practice in Covington, Newton County. On July 15, 1847, he married Virginia Longstreet. In November 1849, thinking the newer country more promising for a young man, he followed his father-in-law, who had become president of the University of Mississippi, to Oxford, Miss. Here he practised law, served as adjunct professor of mathematics in the University, and entered politics. He returned to Newton County, Ga., in 1852, and served that county in the legislature in 1853. In 1854 he moved to Macon, Ga., but resided there only one year, returning to Mississippi for personal and professional reasons in October 1855.

He now became permanently identified with Mississippi. In 1857 he was elected to Congress from the first district as a Democrat, and was returned to the Thirty-sixth Congress in 1859. During these turbulent years he acted with the Southern Democrats on slavery and party questions. He was conservative in temperament and loved the Union, but was determined to preserve what he understood to be the rights of the Southern states. It was this spirit which animated him in the secession crisis. As a member of the Charleston Democratic Convention in 1860 he opposed the withdrawal of the Southern delegates, but was over-ruled. He had never questioned the theoretical right of secession, and after Lincoln's election he became convinced that only the dissolution of the Union could preserve the rights and liberties of the slave-holding states. Resigning his seat in Congress and returning to Mississippi he drafted and reported the Mississippi ordinance of secession.

He assisted in raising the 19th Mississippi Regiment for the Confederacy, and served as its lieutenant-colonel in Virginia until his health, never robust, forced his retirement from active service in May 1862 and his resignation in the following October. In November he was appointed special commissioner of the Confederacy, to Russia, and proceeded to Europe, arriving in London, Mar. 1, 1863. He passed several months in London and Paris, but when the events of 1863 had demonstrated the futility of his mission he was recalled, before setting out for St. Petersburg. He reached Richmond Jan. 9, 1864. In the last year of the Confederacy he labored to sustain the Davis administration against its critics. From December 1864 to the surrender he served as judge-advocate of the III Army Corps of the Army of Northern Virginia.

Lamar's activities in the first years of peace were confined to his law practice and professorships, first of metaphysics and then of law, in the University of Mississippi. His political life seemed closed. In 1872, however, receiving some Liberal Republican support, he was elected to Congress, winning the first Democratic victory in Mississippi since the beginning of Congressional Reconstruction. Soon his chivalrous eulogy of Charles Sumner, delivered April 1874 (*Congressional Record,* 43 Cong., 1 Sess., pp. 3410–11), attracted national attention, and did much to bind up sectional wounds. The following year, conditions in Mississippi being intolerable, Lamar led the victorious fight which accomplished redemption from radical misrule. He was now the foremost political figure in the state, and his stanch national patriotism and personal integrity were winning the admiration of Congress and the country. He pleaded for sectional reconciliation and good will. In a spirit of moderation he supported the electoral compromise settlement of 1876 which made Hayes president. Elected to the Senate in January 1876, he took his seat Mar. 6, 1877.

In the Senate he took high rank at once as orator and statesman. He wished to face new issues, to represent a "New South," but his former Confederate affiliations subjected him to badgering by Conkling, Blaine, Hoar, and others, with whom he engaged in frequent spirited colloquies from which he emerged with increased renown. In 1878 his opposition to the free-silver movement, contrary to the instructions of his state legislature, attracted much attention, and his independence evoked some adverse criticism in Mississippi. He believed that the free coinage of silver under existing conditions was an unsound policy, and that payment of national bonds in silver constituted a violation of faith to the bond-holders.

In 1885 Cleveland tendered Lamar appointment as secretary of the interior, a post which he accepted with misgivings. His acceptance, he wrote to Jefferson Davis, was actuated by the wish to "impress the country with a desire of the South faithfully to serve the interests of a common country" (Mayes, *post,* p. 471). He administered his department in a manner highly satisfactory to the president, who on Dec. 6, 1887, nominated him to the coveted place on the Supreme Court bench made vacant by the death of Justice Woods. The nomination met some political and factious opposition, on the score of Lamar's age and previous Confederate activities, but was confirmed by the Senate on Jan. 16, 1888. He served on the Court until his death five years later. Of him, Chief Justice Fuller said: "He rendered few decisions, but was invaluable in consultation. His was the most suggestive mind that I ever knew, and not one of us but has drawn from its inexhaustible store" (*Ibid., post,* p. 546).

By his first marriage, Lamar had one son and three daughters. His wife died, Dec. 30, 1884, and on Jan. 5, 1887, he married Henrietta (Dean) Holt of Macon, widow of William S. Holt. No issue came of this union. Lamar died at Macon, Ga. He represented the best of the old and the new South. He was a leader in both orders. In him were united scholarship and the gifts that produce political leadership: the combination made him a powerful figure.

[Edward Mayes, *Lucius Q. C. Lamar, His Life, Times and Speeches* (1896) is the basis of all subsequent accounts. It is filial and somewhat uncritical, but contains a store-house of Lamar materials. See also H. L. Carson, *Hist. of the Supreme Court of the U. S.* (1891), vol. II; "In Memoriam: Lucius Q. C. Lamar," 148 *U. S. Reports,* 707–11; *War of the Rebellion: Official Records (Army),* 1 ser. XI (pt. 1), XV, XXVI (pt. 2), LI, LIII, 4 ser. II, III; H. P. Judson, in *Rev. of Rev.* (N. Y.), Mar. 1893; *Atlanta Constitution,* Jan. 24, 1893; scattered material in official documents and the contemporary press. A number of letters from L. Q. C. Lamar are in the Confederate, James Murray Mason, and Cleveland MSS. at the Lib. of Cong.]
H. J. P., Jr.

LAMAR, MIRABEAU BUONAPARTE (Aug. 16, 1798–Dec. 19, 1859), second president of the Republic of Texas, was born in Warren County, Ga. He was a cousin of Gazaway Bugg Lamar and uncle of Lucius Q. C. Lamar [*qq.v.*]. His parents, John and Rebecca (Lamar) Lamar were cousins descended from Thomas Lamar who emigrated from France to Virginia and then settled in Maryland before 1663. Mirabeau was the second of a family of nine children, more than one of whom later reached positions of distinction. The unusual names were due to the eccentricity of an uncle. John Lamar was a thrifty farmer who gave his children a sound common-school education. After an unsuccessful venture as a merchant in Alabama, Mirabeau Lamar, in 1823, became the private secretary to Gov. George M. Troup of Georgia. In this position he took an active part in the movement to secure the expulsion of the Creeks and Cherokees against the opposition of the national government. After his marriage, on Jan. 1, 1826, to Tabitha B. Jordan, of Perry, Ala., Lamar became the editor of the *Columbus Enquirer* at Columbus, Ga., the organ of the state-rights party. His wife died in 1833. Defeated for Congress, he soon afterward became interested in Texas and took a short trip there in 1835. Late in March 1836, he returned to Texas, borrowed a horse, and was soon on his way to join Houston's army at Groce's ferry (*The Papers of Mirabeau Buonaparte Lamar,* I, 346). In the battle of San Jacinto, Lamar distinguished himself as the commander of the cavalry and soon after became secretary of war in the provisional cabinet of President Burnet. He advocated the execution of Santa Anna and was bitterly opposed to the more lenient policy of Austin and Houston. In the election of 1836, Lamar was chosen vice-president of Texas, and two years later, after a curious campaign marked by the suicide of two leading opponents, he became president for the full constitutional period of three years (December 1838–December 1841). The new president was an excellent horseman and had a reputation as a ready orator and writer. His habit of writing verses after the fashion of Byron, some of which he later brought together in a volume entitled *Verse Memorials* (1857), strengthened the belief of his opponents that he was a dreamer rather than a statesman. But the simplicity of his manners, his honesty and generosity in money matters, his hospitality, and his complete devotion to the welfare of Texas were generally recognized by a pioneer community which did not always read his poems. (Anson Jones, *Memoranda and Official Correspondence Relating to the Republic of Texas,* 1859, p. 34, and Kendall, *post,* I, 69, are typical unfriendly and friendly portraits.)

President Lamar regarded the recent rejection of Texas by the United States as on the whole fortunate and laid all his plans for the creation of a great independent republic. He advocated a national bank and planned a comprehensive system of education beginning with the common schools and ending with a state university, both to be supported by generous grants of land. He commenced successful negotiations to secure recognition by France, England, and Holland. Mexico had been compelled by foreign war and internal dissensions to grant a virtual truce to the rebellious Texans, but all efforts to gain a recognized independence failed. One reason was Lamar's plan to extend the sovereignty of Texas to the whole region north and east of the Rio Grande. For this purpose he secured the expulsion of the Cherokees from eastern Texas (1839) and sent a successful punitive expedition against the troublesome Comanches in the west. He had personally selected a capital for the nation on the extreme limit of settlement and in 1840 became the founder of the new city of Austin on the Colorado. In the closing months of his administration he opposed a scheme of Houston to grant great areas in the west to a colonizing French company, and without authority from Congress, he organized an expedition of 265 soldiers and 38 civilians to open trade with distant Santa Fé and to persuade the New Mexicans by peaceful means to accept the sovereignty of Texas. The distance had been miscalculated; the unfriendly influence of the Mexican governor Armijo had been underestimated; and the members of the expedition were easily captured and sent as prisoners on a long march to Mexico. Lamar had been successful in many things, but he was unable to solve the growing financial difficulties of Texas. His Indian policy was ruthless and effective, but also expensive. When Houston was reëlected president at the close of 1841, Texas had a paper currency depreciated almost to the vanishing point and a debt of more than seven millions with no immediate likelihood of solvency.

Lamar's closing years were relatively uneventful. In 1844 he reversed his former attitude and became an advocate of annexation on the frank ground that such a measure was necessary to the preservation of slavery and the safety of the South (*Papers,* IV, 1924, pt. I, p. 113). After services during the Mexican War at Monterey and Laredo, he spent most of his time in the management of his plantation at Richmond. He was bitterly opposed to Clay's compromise measures of 1850. After remaining a widower for many years, in 1851 Lamar was married to Henrietta Maffitt of Galveston, sister of John Newland Maffitt [*q.v.*]. In the fifties he took an active interest in various commercial conventions for the South. In 1857 his financial difficulties were partially relieved by an appointment as minister to Nicaragua, but he found it impossible to gain the ratification of a proposed treaty which would have given the United States a virtual protectorate over the isthmus, and his capacity for a diplomatic post was bitterly criticized by papers unfriendly to the Democratic administration (*Papers, post,* IV, pt. 2, pp. 201–04). In July 1859, he was recalled and died at his home in Richmond before the close of the year.

[*The Papers of Mirabeau Buonaparte Lamar* (6 vols., 1920–27) were published by the Texas State Library. See also: A. K. Christian, *Mirabeau Buonaparte Lamar* (1922), reprinted from the *Southwestern Hist. Quart.,* Jan. 1920–Apr. 1921; W. C. Binkley, *The Expansionist Movement in Texas* (1925), which contains an excellent bibliography; W. H. Lamar, "Thomas Lamar of the Province of Maryland, and a Part of his Descendants," *Southern Hist. Asso. Pubs.,* July 1897, G. W. Kendall, *Narrative of the Texan Santa Fé Expedition* (2 vols., 1844), and Edward Mayes, *Geneal. Notes on a Branch of the Family of Mayes and on the Related Families* (1928?).]
R. G. C.

LAMB, ISAAC WIXOM (Jan. 8, 1840–July 14, 1906), Baptist clergyman, inventor, the son of Rev. Aroswell and Phebe (Wixom) Lamb, was born in Hartland, Livingston County, Mich. He was descended from Valentine Wightman, first of the family of pastors of Groton Church, Groton, Conn. Lamb's early life was that of the pioneer farmer's son, and included a common-school education in the district schools followed by a preparatory-school course at Kalamazoo, Mich. He then entered the Baptist Theological Seminary at Rochester, N. Y. As a boy he had earned his spending money by braiding whip lashes by hand, and while attending the seminary he was in the habit, while poring over his books, of not only braiding lashes but doing all sorts of knitting as well. He had always shown an aptitude in mechanics and an interest in invention, and upon returning to his home in West Novi, Mich., he began to work seriously upon a machine to braid whip lashes. For this device he secured patent No. 24,565 on June 28, 1859. He thereupon began working on the perfection of a knitting machine, and in order to expedite his work, removed about 1861 to Detroit, Mich. On Sept. 15, 1863, he secured patent No. 39,934 for a knitting machine capable of knitting not only tubular goods such as the legs and feet of hosiery, but flat, single-ribbed or plain work as well. This was the first successful flat, as contrasted to circular, knitting machine to be designed in the United States. Furthermore, it could knit fine or coarse yarn with equal ease. In 1864 Lamb removed to Rochester, N. Y., where he sold an interest in his invention and in the following year organized the Lamb Knitting Machine Manufacturing Company. About the same time a second company to manufacture the machine was established at Chicopee Falls, Mass. Going to Europe, he secured patents in France, England, and Belgium, and in 1866 established factories in Paris and in Covet, Switzerland. He had meanwhile continued improving his machine and in 1865 had secured three patents which when added to his original machine made it capable of producing thirty different kinds of knitted goods. The machine, too, could be operated at the rate of 4,000 knots a minute. Upon his return to the United States in 1869, he gave up his business connections and was ordained in the Baptist ministry; and until 1899 he was engaged in active pastoral work in various localities throughout Michigan. He still devoted his leisure to invention, however, and secured more than fifteen patents, chiefly for further improvements of his knitting machine. While a resident of Dansville, Mich., in 1879, he also perfected and patented leaf turning paper, and in 1883 while living in Parshallville, Mich., he devised an improved windmill and derrick. In 1895 he organized the Perry Glove & Machine Company in Perry, Mich., to manufacture gloves with machines of his own design. He was president of this company and mill superintendent at the time of his death. In the disposal of his knitting machine patents Lamb realized comparatively little financially. He gave much to church and charitable causes. He was twice married: first, on Sept. 25, 1861, to Caroline Smith of Hartland, Mich.; and after her death, to Mrs. Elizabeth L. Phelps on Mar. 21, 1880. He died in Perry, Mich., survived by his widow and two step-children.

[*Senate Ex. Doc. No. 12,* 36 Cong. 1 Sess.; *House Ex. Doc. No. 60,* 38 Cong. 1 Sess.; *House Ex. Doc. No. 52,* 39 Cong. 1 Sess.; *Specifications and Drawings of Patents Issued from the U. S. Patent Office,* Aug. 1879, Aug. 1882, May 1883, Dec. 1884, Jan. 1887, Nov. 1891, Dec. 1893, Mar. 1897, Apr., Sept., Oct. 1898, May 1900, Mar. 1904, May 1905; W. B. Kaempffert, *A Popular Hist. of Am. Invention* (1924); John Chamberlain, "The Technology of Knitting," in *The Textile American* (Boston), Oct. 1923; *Who's Who in America,* 1906–07; Lamb family records; *Textile World Record* (Boston), Aug. 1906; *Detroit News,* July 16, 1906; *Detroit Journal,* July 17, 1906.] C. W. M.

LAMB, JOHN (Jan. 1, 1735–May 31, 1800), Revolutionary patriot, soldier, was born in New York City. His father, Anthony Lamb, a native of England, was apprenticed to Henry Carter, a mathematical instrument maker near St. Clement's Church, London, but in July 1724 became an accomplice of Jack Sheppard, one of the most noted burglars in history. Sheppard died on the gallows at Tyburn, Nov. 16, 1724, but because it was Lamb's only offense, he received "a favourable prosecution" (Borrow, *post*) and was sentenced to be transported to the American colonies. In Virginia he served out his time, then settled in New York City, where he worked at his trade, married a Dutch lady named Ham, and became a respectable citizen. John Lamb joined his father in the manufacture of mathematical instruments, then became prosperous as a wine merchant. On Nov. 13, 1755, he married Catherine Jandine, of Huguenot descent. After the passage of the Stamp Act in 1765 he was a leader of the Sons of Liberty, was active in haranguing the populace, corresponded with patriots in the other colonies, and continued to be an irrepressible agitator during the next decade. He signed the non-importation agreement, wrote articles for the patriot press in New York and Boston, and published anonymous handbills. In December 1769 he publicly denounced the New York Assembly for its subserviency to the royal governor. The Assembly, suspecting Lamb of being the author of two handbills which were considered libels on the house, ordered him to its bar. He was examined, but dismissed for lack of evidence. During the excitement over the tea tax he was a member of the committee of the Sons of Liberty chosen to correspond with similar committees elsewhere. When news of the battle of Lexington reached New York, Lamb and Isaac Sears [*q.v.*] seized the custom house and prevented vessels from leaving the harbor. Lamb and his men seized the military stores at Turtle Bay. He was commissioned captain of an artillery company in July 1775 and joined the army of Gen. Richard Montgomery for the invasion of Canada. At the siege of St. Johns he aroused the displeasure of Montgomery, who wrote (Nov. 24, 1775) to Gen. Philip Schuyler, that Lamb was "a restless genius" and had "a bad temper. . . . He has been used to haranguing his fellow-citizens in New York, and can not restrain his talent here." Brave, intelligent and active he was, "but very turbulent and troublesome" (B. J. Lossing, *The Life and Times of Philip Schuyler,* 1860, I, 469). Wounded and captured during the assault on Quebec (Dec. 31, 1775), Lamb was released on parole a few months later. Congress appointed him major of artillery in command of the northern department (Jan. 9, 1776) but he remained inactive because of his parole. On Nov. 29, 1776, Congress ordered Washington to include Lamb in the next exchange of prisoners. In January 1777 he was exchanged and appointed colonel of the 2nd Continental Artillery. He was wounded at Compo Hill in April 1777 while assisting Benedict Arnold in harassing the British retreat following the British attack on Danbury, Conn. He commanded the artillery at West Point in 1779 and 1780, and was brevetted brigadier-general (1783) by virtue of the general act for promotions passed by Congress at the close of the Revolution. In 1784, the New York legislature, of which he was a member, appointed him collector of the customs for the port of New York. He was chairman of an association of "Federal Republicans" opposed to the ratification of the federal Constitution and corresponded with Anti-Federalist leaders—Patrick Henry, Richard

Henry Lee, William Grayson, and others. A Federalist mob took note of his activities by threatening his house, which he hastily fortified. The Constitution ratified, Washington promptly appointed Lamb to the collectorship at New York. A few years later a large shortage occurred, and although it is supposed that Lamb's deputy, a former criminal, was guilty, Lamb, held responsible by the government, sold his lands to cover the lost funds, resigned his office (1797), and died in poverty.

[Lamb MSS., N. Y. Hist. Soc.; I. Q. Leake, *Memoir of the Life and Times of Gen. John Lamb* (1850); H. B. Dawson, *The Sons of Liberty in N. Y.* (1859); Thos. Jones, *Hist. of N. Y. during the Revolutionary War* (2 vols.), written between 1783 and 1788 but first published in 1879; *Jour. . . . of the Gen. Assembly of the Colony of N. Y.*, Dec. 20, 21, 1769; *Jours. of Cong.*, Jan. 9, Nov. 29, 1776; *Names of Persons for whom Marriage Licenses were Issued by the Secy. of the Province of N. Y. previous to 1784* (1860); John Schuyler, *Institution of the Soc. of the Cincinnati* (1886); John Villette, *The Annals of Newgate; or the Malefactors Register* (1776), I, 258–59; Jas. Mountague, *The Old Bailey Chronicle* (1788), I, 315–16; G. H. Borrow, *Celebrated Trials and Remarkable Cases of Criminal Jurisprudence* (1825), III, 378–79; *Commercial Advertiser* (N. Y.), May 31, 1800.]

F. E. R.

LAMB, MARTHA JOANNA READE NASH (Aug. 13, 1829–Jan. 2, 1893), author, editor, daughter of Arvin and Lucinda (Vinton) Nash, was born in the little town of Plainfield, Mass., close to the Berkshire Hills, "blessed with an abundance of rock and forest and fresh air," as she once characterized it. Her grandfather, Jacob Nash, was a Revolutionary soldier, and her grandmother, Joanna (Reade) Nash, had ancestors on the *Mayflower* and was of the same family as Charles Reade, the English novelist. While Martha was still a child her mother died. Her father, she says, was a severe critic of newspapers and of people who wrote for them. At the age of fifteen, when on a visit to her mother's birthplace, she wrote an unsigned letter to a Northampton paper, which the editor, having discovered the identity of his contributor, published over her signature. Fearing her father's wrath, she locked herself in her room until she was assured that she would not be "scolded for her first literary effort." In school her favorite subject was mathematics, and it was that and allied subjects to which she later devoted herself during a brief teaching career. Her article, "The Coast Survey" (*Harper's New Monthly Magazine,* March 1879), reveals her grasp of a technical subject.

On Sept. 8, 1852, she was married to Charles A. Lamb, of Ohio, and lived for some years thereafter in Chicago, where her husband was salesman for a furniture house. While there she aided in the movement which led to the foundation of the Half-Orphan Asylum and the Home for the Friendless. In 1866 she made New York City her residence and plunged into literary work. At first she wrote several books for children, then a novel, *Spicy* (1873), which had the Chicago fire for a background, then short stories for magazines. While thus engaged she saw an opportunity to indulge the taste for historical study which had always possessed her. Though Washington Irving had written his burlesque *History of New York* in 1809, and Mary L. Booth, a single-volume *History of the City of New York* in 1859, neither had used to any extent the wealth of source material that was available. With the aid of the colonial documents published by the State of New York, of newspapers, and of manuscript collections, she was able to write a *History of the City of New York: Its Origin, Rise, and Progress* (2 vols., 1877–81), which for accuracy, clearness, and precision of statement was far superior to any earlier work on the subject. Both humor and pathos appear in her treatment of what to some others would have seemed but dry facts. The work won acclaim for her as "one of the most advanced women of the century" (New York *World*, Jan. 3, 1893). In May 1883 she was chosen as editor of the *Magazine of American History,* at that time in its seventh year, and the only periodical in the country that was devoted to American history. This publication absorbed her attention for the rest of her life. She secured for its columns contributions from talented writers in all parts of the country and herself contributed scores of articles, some of which were subsequently reprinted, among them, *Wall Street in History* (1883), *Unpublished Washington Portraits* (1888). With untiring energy she gave her personal attention to the most minute details in connection with each issue, and her readers realized they were profiting by the work of an accomplished, patient, industrious, and painstaking student. Invited to a meeting of the Royal Society of Canada in 1891, she was "the guest of Montreal," an honor never previously bestowed upon a woman not of royal blood. Her death occurred in New York City, but she was buried in the Berkshire Hills from which she came.

[Daniel Van Pelt, "Mrs. Martha J. Lamb," in *Mag. of Am. Hist.*, Feb. 1893; Mrs. F. H. Pierson, "Martha J. Lamb, the Historian," in *Proc. N. J. Hist. Soc.*, 2 ser. X (1890), 115–20; *New-Eng. Hist. and Geneal. Reg.*, July 1893; N. Y. *World,* Jan. 3, 1893; *N. Y. Herald*, Jan. 4, 1893; *N. Y. Geneal. and Biog. Record,* Apr. 1893; *Publishers' Weekly,* Jan. 7, 1893; W. B. Gay, *Gazetteer of Hampshire County, Mass., 1654–1887* (1887); Jacob Porter, *Topog. Description and Hist. Sketch of Plainfield in Hampshire County, Mass.*

(1834); *Confession of Faith, Covenant, and List of Members of the Cong. Ch., Plainfield, Mass.* (1893); C. N. Dyer, *Hist. of the Town of Plainfield, Hampshire County, Mass.* (1891); F. E. Willard and M. A. Livermore, *A Woman of the Century* (1893).] A. E. P.

LAMBDIN, JAMES REID (May 10, 1807–Jan. 31, 1889), painter, was born in Pittsburgh, Pa., the son of James and Prudence Lambdin. At the age of twelve he spent most of his free time drawing, carving, and engraving on wood. He discovered his life-long passion for painting when, over the door of a coffee house opposite his mother's home in Pittsburgh, he chanced to see, painted as a sign, a full-length copy of one of Stuart's portraits of Washington. Spurred by his new ambition he went to Philadelphia in 1823, and there began to study under Edward Miles, an English painter and miniaturist. After six months he was accepted as a pupil by Thomas Sully, with whom he worked for several years, returning to his native city in 1826. At that time friends interested in his career endeavored to collect sufficient funds to send him to Europe, and Lambdin hurried to New York for embarkation. The funds, however, did not materialize, and the disappointed young painter returned to Pittsburgh. In a zealous endeavor to acquaint the West with works of art, he opened a museum and gallery of paintings in Pittsburgh at Fourth and Market streets. Assisted by popular subscription, he enlarged his collection to include, besides fifty pictures—historical and otherwise—twenty quadrupeds, 200 foreign and American birds, 500 minerals, 400 fossils, 150 marine shells, marine plants, and Indian curios.

For four years Lambdin remained in his native city, but in 1832 he moved his museum and family to Louisville, Ky., seeking a wider field for his prospects as a painter. Although he resided in Louisville for several years, he spent the greater part of his time visiting the large cities between Pittsburgh and Mobile, Ala. During this period of restless roving, he painted (1833) a portrait from life of Chief Justice Marshall. By 1837, having tired of an itinerant existence, he had settled in Philadelphia, where he soon became a member of the Artists' Fund Society, in which organization he served as corresponding secretary in 1838 and 1844, as vice-president from 1840 to 1843, and as president from 1845 to 1867. From 1845 to 1864 he was a director of the Pennsylvania Academy of the Fine Arts, and for some time chairman of that institution's committee on instruction. In 1858 he presided over the convention of American artists at Washington, and was appointed by President Buchanan to serve as one of the United States art commissioners. He served as professor of fine arts at the University of Pennsylvania from 1861 to 1866.

Lambdin achieved recognition through portrait painting. Among his canvases are portraits of every president of the United States from John Quincy Adams to James A. Garfield, the majority having been executed in Washington at the Executive Mansion. He painted a self portrait which is owned by the Pennsylvania Academy of the Fine Arts. He was also an accomplished miniaturist. His "Miniature of an Artist" was shown at the Pennsylvania Academy in 1845, and his miniature of "Polly Vincent" is also well known. He was married to Mary Cochran of Pittsburgh, and they had six children, five of whom lived to maturity. He died of heart failure on the train between Philadelphia and his home in the suburbs.

[*Public Ledger* (Phila.), Feb. 1, 1889; school catalogues of the Univ. of Pa., 1861–66; catalogue of the Sesquicentennial Hist. Exhibition of the Pa. Acad. of the Fine Arts, 1926; catalogue of the Loan Exhibition of Hist. Portraits at the Pa. Acad. of the Fine Arts, Dec. 1, 1887, to Jan. 15, 1888; *Standard History of Pittsburg, Pa.* (1898), ed. by Erasmus Wilson; Theodore Bolton, *Early Am. Portrait Painters in Miniature* (1921); H. B. Wehle, *Am. Miniatures, 1730–1850* (1927); *Art in America,* June 1922; Ulrich Thieme and Felix Becker, *Allgemeines Lexikon der Bildenden Künstler,* vol. XXII (1928); Wm. Dunlap, *Hist. of the Rise and Progress of the Arts of Design in the U. S.* (2 vols., 1834), rev. ed. (3 vols., 1918), ed. by F. W. Bayley and C. E. Goodspeed; information from the Md. Hist. Soc.; *Pittsburgh Mercury,* Oct. 4, 1826.] D. G.

LAMBERT, LOUIS ALOISIUS (Apr. 13, 1835–Sept. 25, 1910), Roman Catholic clergyman and author, was born at Charleroi, Pa. His father, William Lambert, had come from Ireland in 1811; his mother was Lydia Jones, a Quakeress who had entered the Catholic Church. Educated at St. Vincent's College, Westmoreland County, Pa., and subsequently at the archdiocesan seminary, Carondelet, Mo., Lambert was ordained a priest in 1859, for the diocese of Alton, Ill. He was then stationed at Cairo and served missions in several counties. When the Civil War broke out he was commissioned chaplain of the 18th Regiment, Illinois Infantry, by Governor Yates. With the rank of a captain of infantry, he saw service in Missouri, Kentucky, Tennessee, and Mississippi. When peace came he returned to Cairo, but went to New York in 1868 to become professor of philosophy in the novitiate of the newly established Congregation of St. Paul. On May 20, 1869, he received official excardination from the diocese of Alton, and on Oct. 16, 1869, was appointed pastor at Waterloo, N. Y. There in the next twenty years he began and virtually completed the building of a church. Meanwhile, however, he deepened his interest in writing and lecturing. During 1877 he founded the *Catholic Times,* a weekly, which was merged some time later in the *Catholic Times* of Rochester. In 1892 he founded and until 1894 edited the *Catholic Times* of Philadelphia, which in its third year was combined with its rival as the *Catholic Standard and Times.* Meanwhile an unusual opportunity had presented itself. In August 1881, the *North American Review* had published a debate between Robert G. Ingersoll and Judge Jeremiah S. Black [*qq.v.*]. A new wave of agnostic rationalism was gaining momentum at the time, and the circumstances under which the Ingersoll-Black debate was conducted lent strength to the atheist argument. Father Lambert took up the cudgels in a series of papers contributed to the *Catholic Union and Times* of Buffalo, N. Y. These were reprinted as *Notes on Ingersoll* (1883) and ran through many editions, the book appealing to Catholics and Protestants alike. The method was a form of literary dialogue, in which passages from Ingersoll's addresses were quoted and commented upon. Lambert's *Tactics of Infidels* (1887) continued the argument, in the same manner. Thus Lambert became the champion of orthodoxy in the United States, and as such was bitterly attacked in such "infidel" pamphlets as B. W. Lacy's *Reply to Rev. L. A. Lambert's Notes on Ingersoll* (1885) and Charles Watts's *Orthodox Criticism Tested* (Toronto, n.d.). Lambert's other published writings include: *Thesaurus Biblicus* (1880), the first Catholic Biblical concordance in English, adapted from a German work by Philip Merz; and *Christian Science at the Bar of Reason* (1908). He also edited *Catholic Belief* (1884), by Joseph Faà di Bruno, and *Indifferentism* (1917), by Rev. John MacLaughlin. During these years he was widely termed the "American Newman" and he was certainly the first American Catholic apologist to reach a wide audience outside his own communion, but his writings are so closely identified with controversies peculiar to a definite era that they have not lasted beyond their day. He must be judged primarily as a journalist, and here his most important achievement, apart from his books, was his editorship of the New York *Freeman's Journal* from 1894 to 1910. During several years he was involved in a bitter quarrel with his ordinary, Bishop Bernard J. McQuaid of Rochester. The charges against Father Lambert were these: that he had written in a spirit of opposition to the bishop; that he was the leader of a group of rebellious priests, who sought unjustifiable control over a "clergy fund" and other matters; and that his attitude with regard to certain Irish patriotic demonstrations had been antagonistic to episcopal authority. The Bishop summarized these charges in a letter to Cardinal Simeoni, of the Propaganda (Feb. 18, 1888), adding that he had been "shamefully deceived" about Father Lambert's character and claiming that the latter had been dismissed from Alton diocese for bad conduct. These personal accusations were quite mistaken, as the facts prove, but the Bishop had some cause for complaint. He was, no doubt, a little autocratic, but he faced the problem of maintaining discipline among frequently recalcitrant priests. Father Lambert was, perhaps, spoiled in a measure by his literary and oratorical successes, so that he failed occasionally to pay the Bishop due respect. The controversy was carried to Rome, elicited the interest of many other clergymen and prelates, was tentatively decided several times, and finally settled (Jan. 22, 1890) after both Bishop McQuaid and Lambert had journeyed to the Vatican. The terms were that Lambert should remain in the diocese of Rochester, but be transferred from Waterloo to Scottsville. During these years his popularity had increased, and crowds gathered to listen to his addresses. After a period of decline, he died at Newfoundland, N. J., and was buried at Scottsville, N. Y.

[Archdiocesan archives, New York and Baltimore; F. J. Zwierlein, *The Life and Letters of Bishop McQuaid,* vol. III (1925); J. T. Smith, in *Ave Maria,* Dec. 3, 1910; *Cath. World,* Nov. 1910; *Cath. News* (N. Y.), Oct. 1, 1910; *Freeman's Journal* (N. Y.), 1894–1910; *Cath. Encyc.,* vol. XVI (copr. 1914); *Newark Evening News,* Sept. 26, 1910; date and place of birth and names of parents from *Who's Who in America,* 1910–11.]

G. N. S.

LAMBERTON, BENJAMIN PEFFER (Feb. 25, 1844–June 9, 1912), naval officer, the son of James Findlay and Elizabeth (Peffer) Lamberton, was born in Cumberland County, Pa. After attending Carlisle high school and Dickinson preparatory school, in 1858 he entered Dickinson College and continued there until the end of his junior year. His imagination having been fired by contact with the army post at Carlisle, his first desire had been for a military career, and it was this that finally led to his securing an appointment as midshipman in the navy. He entered the Naval Academy in 1861 with a large war class and was graduated at the end of three years in the upper section. On Feb. 25, 1873, he married Elizabeth Marshall Stedman of Boston. After various assignments in the Atlantic and Pacific squadrons, in 1885 he attained the grade of commander and was ordered to Charleston as lighthouse inspector. There must have been something in this service that had unusual interest for him, since he had four assignments under the Lighthouse Board, covering ten years.

In the spring of 1898, on being ordered to the Asiatic Station, he succeeded in reaching the American squadron at Hong Kong just before it sailed for Manila. He had been detailed to command the cruiser *Boston,* but Commodore Dewey created for him the position of chief of staff. "Thus," Dewey wrote, "I secured the aid of a most active and accomplished officer . . . when there was positive need of his services; but not until later did I realize how much I owed to the sympathetic companionship of Lamberton's sunny, hopeful, and tactful disposition" (*Autobiography, post,* pp. 193–94). As the American force engaged the Spanish in Manila Bay, he was standing next to Dewey on the bridge. The following morning when the Spanish flag was flying over the arsenal at Cavite, he went in the *Petrel* to demand its surrender. Later he was given charge of removing the sick and wounded Spaniards to the captured steamer *Isabel* and of taking them to Manila. When the American army arrived, and the Spaniards in Manila capitulated, he was the naval representative on the joint commission that determined the details of surrender. He had been highly commended by Dewey in his report of the battle of Manila Bay, and Congress advanced him seven numbers. On the 17th of May he was promoted to the rank of captain, and later was given command of the *Olympia.* In 1903 he was promoted to the rank of rear-admiral and made commander-in-chief of the South Atlantic Squadron, but this duty was cut short by a serious eye trouble that had its origin in his close proximity to the large guns of the *Olympia* during the firing in Manila Bay. In 1905 he was made chairman of the Lighthouse Board, holding this office until he was retired for age, Feb. 25, 1906. His last years were spent in Washington, where he died.

His letters show that home ties meant much to him. His father died when Lamberton was a boy, and out of his naval pay he provided for his mother. His cheerfulness was contagious, for it was the expression of good health and abounding vitality. He was fond of walking and outdoor sports. Often he was the companion of President Cleveland in duck shooting and fishing, and their friendship continued to the end.

[*Autobiography of George Dewey* (1913); F. E. Chadwick, *Relations of the U. S. and Spain—The Spanish-American War* (2 vols., 1911); *Annual Report of the Light-House Board* (1905); L. R. Hamersly, *The Records of Living Officers of the U. S. Navy and Marine Corps* (7th ed., 1902); *Army and Navy Jour.*, June 15, 1912; *Army and Navy Reg.*, June 22, 1912; *Evening Star* (Washington), June 10, 1912.] C. S. A.

LAMBING, ANDREW ARNOLD (Feb. 1, 1842–Dec. 24, 1918), Roman Catholic clergyman and historian, was born in Manorville, Pa., the son of Michael Anthony and Anne (Shields) Lambing. His father was a descendant of Christopher Lambing, who in 1740 emigrated to America from Alsace, France; his mother was of Irish ancestry. Educated at St. Michael's Seminary, Pittsburgh, he was ordained a priest on Aug. 4, 1869. He held the following pastorates in Pennsylvania: Loretto, 1869; Cameron Bottom, 1870; Kittanning, 1870–73; Pittsburgh (St. Paul's Orphan Asylum and Church of St. Mary of Mercy), 1873–85; and Wilkinsburg, 1885–1918. He served the Pittsburgh diocese as fiscal procurator, as president of the diocesan school board, and as censor of books. After having written two manuals, *The Orphan's Friend* (1875) and *The Sunday School Teacher's Manual* (1877), he definitely entered the field of historical study and writing. In 1880 he published *A History of the Catholic Church in the Dioceses of Pittsburg and Allegheny* and five years later, *The Baptismal Register of Fort Duquesne, 1754–1756* (1885), translated from the French and accompanied by an introductory essay and notes. His interest in the Fort likewise led him to dedicate an altar to Our Lady of the Assumption at the Beautiful River, as a memorial of the eighteenth-century shrine. Father Lambing's other publications include: *The Sacramentals of the Holy Catholic Church* (1892); *Come, Holy Ghost* (1901); *The Immaculate Conception of the Blessed Virgin Mary* (1904); *The Fountain of Living Water* (1907); and *Foundation Stones of a Great Diocese: Brief Biographical Sketches of the Deceased Bishops and Priests Who Labored in the Diocese of Pittsburgh from the Earliest Times to the Present* (1912). In addition he contributed to *The Standard History of Pittsburg* (1898), edited by Erasmus Wilson, and helped to edit *A Century and a Half of Pittsburg and Her People* (1908). In so far as his historical books are concerned, they must be judged as pioneer efforts, carried through without the preparation which modern research demands, therefore faulty, but nevertheless useful as first digests of the records. When Pope Leo's encyclical on the study of history was published (1883), Father Lambing tried to organize a historical society, but the result of his efforts was a publication which later became *American Catholic Historical Researches* and was ultimately merged (1912) with the *Records of the American Catholic Historical Society of Philadelphia.* As a serious attempt to promote study of the past by Catholics it has its place among journals of a former day. Having won the personal friendship of Andrew Carnegie, Father Lambing was made one of the trustees of the Carnegie Institute and of the Carnegie Technical School, Pittsburgh. For many years he was president of the Historical Society of Western Pennsylvania, and in 1893 he prepared the Pittsburgh diocesan school exhibit for the World's Columbian Exposition at Chicago. His last years were spent in such complete retirement that virtually no notice was taken of his death, which occurred at Wilkinsburg, where he is buried.

[A. A. Lambing, *Michael Anthony and Anne Shields-Lambing* (1896); *The Am. Cath. Who's Who* (1911); *Records of the Am. Cath. Hist. Soc. of Phila.*, June 1920.] G. N. S.

LAMBUTH, JAMES WILLIAM (Mar. 2, 1830–Apr. 28, 1892), missionary of the Methodist Episcopal Church, South, was of missionary lineage. His grandfather, William Lambuth, had been sent by Bishop Asbury from the Baltimore Conference to labor among the Indians "in the wilds of Tennessee," and his father, John Russell Lambuth, a member of the Kentucky Conference, had volunteered for service among the Indians of Louisiana. In 1830, the latter was holding a camp meeting in Greene County, Ala. Without any explanation he left the meeting but soon returned with this announcement, "I was called home by the birth of a baby boy. In heartfelt gratitude to God I dedicated the child to the Lord as a foreign missionary, and I now add a bale of cotton to send him with" (Pinson, *post*, p. 17).

The family early moved to Mississippi. James graduated from the University of Mississippi in 1851 and became a preacher chiefly to the negroes gathered in their cabins. In 1854 he joined the Mississippi Conference and was immediately appointed by Bishop Andrew to aid in founding the China Mission of his Church. After he had mastered the Chinese language he began preaching on the streets of Shanghai and in the villages along the canals and creeks of the Shanghai area. He made it his policy to spend two weeks of each month on a preaching tour, living in a houseboat and sharing his faith and life with the Chinese. This plan of work, which called for constant and prolonged absence from home, was made possible by the fact that his wife, Mary I. (McClellan) Lambuth, was as truly a missionary as her husband, and had not only the skill to care for her home but also the courage and wisdom to initiate a work for the women and children of China which continues to bear the imprint of her genius. When the outbreak of the Civil War interfered with missionary enterprises, Lambuth returned to Mississippi, but went back to China in 1864 and resumed his former activities.

As time went on, however, he came to look with uneasiness upon what he felt was a disproportionate amount of time, money, and effort spent on educational endeavors as compared with that given to evangelistic work. Partly from this cause and partly for health reasons, after thirty-two years of pioneering service in China, he and his son, Dr. Walter R. Lambuth [*q.v.*], accepted a commission to lay the foundation of Southern Methodist missions in Japan. The son was appointed superintendent, but the father had virtually an equal influence in selecting the territory around the Inland Sea as that upon which they would concentrate their efforts. By this choice the mission came to occupy a territory which has a strategic place in the industrial growth and resources of Japan. While the work had its center in the great industrial cities of Kobe and Osaka, it spread to the surrounding country. The elder Lambuth's travels by boat around the Inland Sea earned for him the title "Father of the Inland Sea Mission." After some sixteen years of service in Japan he died at Kobe with the appeal: "I die at my post; send more men."

[*Hist. Cat. of the Univ. of Miss., 1849–1909* (1910); W. W. Pinson, *Walter Russell Lambuth, Prophet and Pioneer* (1924); *In Memoriam: J. W. Lambuth* (Kobe, Japan, 1892); James Cannon III, *Hist. of Southern Meth. Missions* (1926); *Christian Advocate* (Nashville), May 5, 1892.] O. E. B.

LAMBUTH, WALTER RUSSELL (Nov. 10, 1854–Sept. 26, 1921), missionary and bishop of the Methodist Episcopal Church, South, was born in Shanghai, China, where his father and mother, James William Lambuth [*q.v.*] and Mary Isabella (McClellan) Lambuth, were missionaries. He lived in China during his first six years, occasionally going with his father on his houseboat journeys to the cities and villages of the Shanghai area. From 1859 to 1864 he was in America; a portion of the time in Tennessee and Mississippi with relatives and friends of his father, the remainder of the time with his mother's people in Cambridge, N. Y. During the Civil War his parents were in the United States and in 1864 the boy returned with them to China, where he remained until 1869.

Two years later he entered Emory and Henry College, Washington County, Va. Prior to his graduation in 1875, he decided to devote his life to the Christian ministry and the practice of medicine in China. From 1875 to 1877 he studied theology in the Biblical department of Vanderbilt University, pursuing at the same time a course in the medical school. In 1877 he was ordained elder in the Tennessee Conference of the Methodist Episcopal Church, South; received the degree of M.D. from Vanderbilt University; was married to Daisy Kelley of Nashville, Tenn.; and was sent as a missionary to China, where he began work in Shanghai and the adjacent village of Nanziang. While in the United States on leave in 1881, he studied in Bellevue Hospital Medical College, receiving the degree of M.D. from that institution, and the next year continued his studies in Edinburgh and London. Returning to China in 1882, he laid the foundations of the hospital and medical service in Soochow. In 1884 he resigned his duties there and established for the Methodist Episcopal Church the medical work in Peking. With his father in 1885–86 he inaugurated the missionary enterprise of the Methodist Episcopal Church, South, in Japan. He was appointed superintendent with headquarters at Kobe. While in China he had stressed evangelistic and medical activities, but in Japan he found it needful to develop educational facilities, founding the college and theological school known as Kwansei Gakuin, and the Hiroshima Girls' School.

In 1891 Lambuth returned to the United States, where he was assigned to field service at home, and edited the *Methodist Review of Missions.* He was elected general secretary of the Board of Missions in 1894, serving in that capacity with marked efficiency until 1910. He was a vital factor in 1907 in uniting the Canadian Methodist Church, the Methodist Episcopal Church, and the Methodist Episcopal Church, South, in Japan into what is now known as the Japan Methodist Church. At the General Conference of 1910 he was elected a bishop. His first assignment included superintendence of the mission activities in Brazil and the projection of a new work in tropical Africa. His adventurous journey with a view to founding a Methodist mission in the Congo, involving 2,600 miles by boat and rail and 1,500 miles on foot through the jungles of tropical Africa, brought him election as a fellow of the Royal Geographical Society of London. It was fitting that his last official service should be in the Orient, where it was his privilege to open a new work for the Koreans in Siberia.

Bishop Lambuth also had an influential part in enterprises which involved the cooperative effort of the various Christian churches. He participated actively in the Ecumenical Conferences, held an official place in the World Missionary Conference at Edinburgh in 1910, and was made a member of the continuation committee of that body, which did so much to make the principle of cooperation dominant in the policies of the missionary societies of Europe and America. In addition to his many other achievements, he was the author of the following books: *Side Lights on the Orient* (1903), *Winning the World for Christ* (1915), and *Medical Missions* (1920). He died in Yokohama, and, as he had requested, his ashes were taken to Shanghai and buried beside those of his mother.

[W. W. Pinson, *Walter Russell Lambuth, Prophet and Pioneer* (1924); MS. journal and diary; files of the *Methodist Review of Missions,* 1890 to 1900; *Christian Advocate* (Nashville), Nov. 18, 1921; *Jour. of the Gen. Conf. of the M. E. Ch. South* (1922); *The Japan Times and Mail* (Tokyo), Sept. 27, 28, 1921; *Who's Who in America,* 1920–21.] O. E. B.

LAMME, BENJAMIN GARVER (Jan. 12, 1864–July 8, 1924), engineer, inventor, was born on his father's farm near Springfield, Ohio, the son of James Given and Sarah (Garver) Lamme. His early life was that of the normal healthy farmer's boy, consisting of play, work, and school. The play, however, centered about "making things" with the farm tool kit and collecting Indian artifacts, while school satisfied an unusual taste for mathematics with which he was endowed. In 1883 he entered Ohio State University at Columbus, taking the course in mechanical engineering, and graduating in 1888, having lost a year owing to the illness and death of his father. During his college career his analytical sense developed to such an extent that he was able to picture a mathematical problem in his mind with full diagrams, produce the necessary equations, and carry them through to a final result without touching pencil to paper. This facility in mental computations he applied equally well in mechanics, physics, and other similar subjects. In his senior year he devised a series of formulae covering the flow of natural gas through long pipe lines, and these were later adopted by the state of Ohio.

After spending a few months at home following his graduation, early in 1889 he obtained work with the Philadelphia Natural Gas Company in Pittsburgh, a newly formed enterprise of George Westinghouse; but in May of that year he gave up this position and became an apprentice in the testing department of the Westinghouse Electric Company. With this organization he remained connected until his death. In the course of his first year's work he rose to be foreman of tests and at the same time, because of his skill in computing, he was given the task of making the calculations for electrical machinery. The unusually satisfactory results which he obtained in this latter work marked the beginning of his career as electrical engineer and inventor. Before the close of 1889 the Westinghouse Company produced from Lamme's calculations a double-reduction-gear direct-current railway motor, and the following year there was constructed from his design the single-reduction-gear motor, the direct ancestor of the now universally adopted street-railway motor. As a result of his success Lamme soon confined all of his attention to analytical work and the design of electrical machinery for his company. In increasing numbers, year after year, he obtained patents, being credited with a total of 162 at the time of his death. He was the leader in direct-current railway motor developments with respect to types of apparatus; a pioneer in designing the rotary converter, of which he became the champion; and to him is due most of the credit for the leading position which this machine holds in the electrical field. The alternating-current generators which inaugurated hydro-electric power at Niagara Falls, N. Y., were the product of his brain; he established many of the fundamental features of the direct-current generator; and he was among the first to produce a commercially successful induction motor. It was he who transformed the great creative ideas of Nikola Tesla into commercial form and created the single-phase railway system, including the first practical twenty-five-cycle commutator motor. This system, in 1905, was incorporated into the electrification of the New York, New Haven & Hartford Railway; and it is equipment of Lamme's design which supplies power to the elevated and subway systems of New York. In 1900 he became assistant chief engineer of the Westinghouse Company and in 1903, chief engineer, which position he held at the time of his death.

Aside from his own work, Lamme was much interested in training young engineers who came to the Westinghouse Company and he established a design school in which he was the much loved and respected teacher. During the World War he was a member of the naval consulting board, serving as chairman of the inventions committee. He was awarded the Thomas A. Edison gold medal in 1919 by the American Institute of Electrical Engineers for "invention and development of electrical machinery"; and in 1923 he received the initial award of the Joseph Sullivant gold medal, provided for the alumnus of Ohio State University who "has made the most notable contribution to the liberal, the fine, or the mechanic arts." He wrote over a hundred articles concerning his electrical studies, which appeared in technical journals and in the *Transactions* of the American Society of Electrical Engineers. A collection from these was published in 1919 under the title, *Electrical Engineering Papers.* Outside of his electrical work Lamme's chief interests were archeology, mathematical puzzles, of which he patented several, photography, and automobiling. He never married and made his home with a sister in Pittsburgh, where his death occurred.

[*Reg. of Grads. and Members of the Ohio State Univ. Asso. 1879–1917* (1917); *Benjamin Garver Lamme, Electrical Engineer: An Autobiog.* (1926); *Jour. Am. Inst. Electrical Engrs.,* Aug. 1924; *Electrical World,* July 12, 1924; *Scientific American,* Sept. 1924; *Industrial Engineer,* Aug. 1924; *Illustrated World* (Chicago), Jan. 1922; *Who's Who in America,* 1922–23; *Gazette Times* (Pittsburgh) and *N. Y. Times,* July 9, 1924.]

C. W. M.

LAMON, WARD HILL (Jan. 6, 1828–May 7, 1893), lawyer, the son of George and Elizabeth (Ward) Lamon, was born in Frederick County, Va., but lived as a boy at Bunker Hill, Berkeley County, now in West Virginia, where he received a common-school education. He settled in Danville, Ill., in 1847, studied law in Louisville, Ky., and returned to Danville, where he was soon admitted to the bar. In 1852 he became the Danville partner of Lincoln, whose circuit-riding life he shared and whose friendship he enjoyed to a marked degree. By 1859 he had moved to Bloomington. Having joined the Republican party, he campaigned for Lincoln and was chosen to accompany the President-Elect to Washington in February 1861, being particularly responsible for Lincoln's safety when rumored assassination plots caused the scheduled itinerary to be changed to a secret night journey from Harrisburg to Washington. In March 1861 he was sent as Lincoln's personal agent to Charleston, S. C., where he found himself the target of popular derision. After conferring with Governor Pickens and Major Anderson, both of whom received from him the impression that Fort Sumter would be evacuated, he reported to Lincoln the inflamed condition of Southern sentiment.

On Apr. 6, 1861, Lincoln appointed him marshal of the District of Columbia. After the outbreak of war he tried to raise a "loyal" brigade in Virginia; took in Illinois troops to fill up his incomplete organization; served briefly in the field; and then returned to the marshalship at the capital. His giant frame, handsome appearance, and exuberant, swashbuckling air made him a conspicuous figure as he made arrests, executed the orders of the circuit court of the District, and performed such ceremonial duties as introducing people to the President at levees. Intense in his hatred of abolitionists, he was drawn into controversies over escaping slaves and figured in various conflicts between the military and civil authorities. Out of this situation grew various senatorial attacks upon him and the court he served, as well as clashes with the military governor of the district of Washington (H. G. Pearson, *James S. Wadsworth,* 1913, pp. 136–39). The radical onslaughts upon the marshal reacted upon Lincoln, who was criticized for keeping a Southern pro-slavery man in a position so responsible and so personally close to himself. When plots were suspected on every hand in 1864, Lamon slept next to Lincoln's bed-chamber and supervised the patrolling of the White House grounds. It was the regret of his life that he was absent from Washington (on a mission to Richmond) on the night of the assassination.

Resigning as marshal in June 1865, he became a law partner of Jeremiah S. Black [*q.v.*]. In 1872 there was issued *The Life of Abraham Lincoln from His Birth to His Inauguration as President,* by Ward H. Lamon. This book was written by Chauncey F. Black and was based chiefly upon material that Lamon bought from W. H. Herndon [*q.v.*]. It was intended as the first volume of an extended biography; but public dissatisfaction with its realistic treatment of Lincoln caused the project for the second volume to be dropped. From 1879 to 1886, his partnership with Black having been dissolved, he lived in Colorado, chiefly Denver, seeking health and practising law. His later years were spent mainly in Washington and in European travel. He died near Martinsburg, W. Va. His first wife, Angelina (Turner) Lamon, had died in April 1859, leaving one daughter. His second wife, Sally (Logan) Lamon, daughter of Stephen T. Logan [*q.v.*], had died in Brussels, Belgium, in 1892.

[Lamon MSS. in Huntington Lib., San Marino, Cal., including documentary material collected both by Herndon and by Lamon for biography of Lincoln, an extensive unpublished account of Lincoln's administration intended for the second volume of *The Life of Abraham Lincoln,* and about 2,300 letters; a few letters in Univ. of Ill. Lib.; Black Coll. in Lib. of Cong.; manuscript biography by E. M. Prince in McLean County Hist. Soc. Lib. at Bloomington, Ill.; information from Lamon's daughter, Mme. Xavier Teillard of Murat, Cantal, France; memoir in W. H. Lamon, *Recollections of Abraham Lincoln* (1895), ed. by Dorothy Lamon; *Harper's Weekly,* July 22, 1911; C. C. Tilton in *Trans. Ill. State Hist. Soc.,* vol. XXXVIII (1931); W. E. Barton, *The Soul of Abraham Lincoln* (copr. 1920); *World's Work,* Feb. 1911; *N. Y. Herald,* May 9, 1893, p. 14.]

J. G. R.

LAMONT, DANIEL SCOTT (Feb. 9, 1851–July 23, 1905), secretary of war and financier, was the able lieutenant of more prominent principals. He was of Scotch-Irish descent, son of John B. and Elizabeth (Scott) Lamont, and was born in Cortland County, N. Y., on his father's farm. He attended Union College, Schenectady, partly supporting himself, but failed to graduate with his class in 1872. A job was found for him, first as engrossing clerk and then as assistant journal clerk, in the Capitol at Albany, where he attracted the attention of Samuel J. Tilden and John Bigelow [*qq.v.*], and became their protégé in the Democratic faction that was at war with Tammany. Tilden gave him a clerkship on the state central committee (1872), which he retained for many years; and from 1875 to 1882 he was chief clerk of the New York department of state. Daniel Manning, who came to know him on the state central committee, employed him on the *Albany Argus* (1877–82), in which Lamont finally acquired a financial interest. When Cleveland was brought forward in 1882 by Manning, Lamont was assigned to him as political prompter, beginning a connection that was to last and grow more intimate through fifteen years. He was private and military secretary with rank of colonel on the staff of the Governor in 1883; and he went to Washington as private secretary to the President in 1885. Here he raised his office to a new dignity and importance, acting as buffer for his chief, speeding business by direct reference to the departments, and serving to advance the aims of the President by devotion and forethought. The newspaper men jested of the necessity to "see Lamont" if action was to be secured; and this drew Lamont closer to Cleveland, who welcomed the connection. Lamont came to know intimately the secretary of the navy, William C. Whitney, who gave him a financial job after 1889 in connection with his own large ventures in the street-railway matters; and here Lamont began the construction of a family fortune. In 1893 Cleveland recalled him as secretary of war, and Lamont reluctantly accepted the post, retaining it through the administration. He handled it effectively, without bringing it into political prominence. He noted correctly in his first year that "it may be assumed that Indian warfare is virtually at an end" (*Annual Report,* 1893, I, 5); he urged repeatedly and in vain the reorganization of the infantry on the basis of the regiment of three four-company battalions (*Ibid.,* 1896, I, 7); he directed the policing of Chicago during the Pullman strike. In 1897 he went back willingly to private life, and although he was occasionally mentioned in connection with political posts, he passed the remainder of his life outside politics. He was now elected vice-president of the Northern Pacific Railway Company (1898–1904), coming into close and profitable contact with

James J. Hill [*q.v.*]; and he acquired directorships in many other corporations and banks. He died at Millbrook, Dutchess County, N. Y., in 1905, leaving a wife, Juliet (Kinney) Lamont, and two daughters.

[Lamont was mentioned in innumerable paragraphs for twenty years, the notice being generally jocular and friendly, and treating him primarily as political manipulator. A good obituary is in the *Brooklyn Daily Eagle*, July 24, 1905. See also Robert McElroy, *Grover Cleveland* (2 vols., 1923); G. F. Parker, *Recollections of Grover Cleveland* (1909); *Who's Who in America*, 1903–05.]
F. L. P.

LAMONT, HAMMOND (Jan. 19, 1864–May 6, 1909), educator, editor, was born in Monticello, Sullivan County, N. Y., the son of Rev. Thomas Lamont, a Methodist minister, and Caroline Deuel (Jayne) Lamont. On his father's side he was of Scotch-Irish lineage, being a descendant of Robert Lamont, who came to America from County Antrim, Ireland, about 1750 and settled in North Hillsdale, N. Y. His mother's ancestral line ran back to William Jayne, an Englishman, who crossed the Atlantic in 1678 and made his home in New Haven, Conn. Hammond prepared for college in Albany and went to Harvard, where he graduated in 1886, having taken high rank as a scholar and achieved prominence as an undergraduate journalist. From 1887 to 1890 he was engaged in newspaper work in Albany and in the latter year joined the staff of the *Post Intelligencer*, Seattle, Wash. On May 14, 1891, at Nyack, N. Y., he married Lillian Mann. The able manner in which he reported a speech of President Eliot at Seattle in 1892 led to his being invited to Harvard as instructor in English. After serving in this capacity for three years, he became associate professor of rhetoric at Brown University, where in 1898 he was made professor. During his teaching career he edited *Specimens of Exposition* (1894, 1896), and *Edmund Burke, Speech on Conciliation with America* (1897); his work, *English Composition*, however, was not published until 1906. The arrival of Lamont at Brown was the beginning of a revolution in the teaching of English composition there, and his stay was a tonic to the whole university. Surrounding himself with assistants whom he inspired with his own spirit, he made the courses of his department the most conspicuous in the curriculum. Since they were required courses, directly and indirectly he touched the whole student body. Its first reaction was one of undisguised hostility. He had a keen, critical mind; he wielded a ruthless, slashing red pencil; his criticisms were often clothed in most discomforting irony; he despised sham, superficiality, and dishonesty in any form. Furthermore, the students found him a rigorous disciplinarian. Themes two minutes late were not received whatever the accompanying excuse; unfortunate youths who forgot to bring their work to class were marked zero. "If you are two minutes late for a train," he would say, "you miss the train; if you forget your theater ticket, you don't get into the theater. You'll do well to learn that lesson now." Under his instruction, however, men learned to think clearly, to distinguish truth from fallacy, the essential from the irrelevant, and to write, clearly, concisely, and correctly. His honesty, fearlessness, and competence, together with the kindly, helpful interest he took in all who were worthy of such interest, at length won for him the students' enthusiastic loyalty, and before he left the university he was probably the most popular of its professors. After his death two of his former classes purchased his library of twenty-seven hundred volumes of English literature and presented it to Brown as a memorial.

In 1900 he returned to journalism, becoming managing editor of the New York *Evening Post*. "His tireless industry, his broad grasp of political principles, his thorough knowledge of the newspaper and political worlds made him at once the foremost member of the *Evening Post* staff" (*Evening Post*, May 7, 1909). In June 1906 he succeeded Wendell Phillips Garrison as editor of the *Nation*. His knowledge of educational matters was so extensive and his judgment was so sound that educators were continually seeking his advice. Calls to professorships in several leading colleges he declined. His career terminated when he was in his prime. Failing to rally from an operation, he died in the Roosevelt Hospital, New York, in his forty-sixth year.

[Thomas Lamont, *A Brief Account of the Life at Charlotteville of Thomas William Lamont and of His Family* (1915); *Nation*, May 13, 1909; *Harvard Grads. Mag.*, June 1909; *Brown Alumni Monthly*, June 1909; *Who's Who in America*, 1908–09; personal acquaintance.]
H. E. S.

LA MOUNTAIN, JOHN (1830–Feb. 14, 1870), aeronaut, was born in Wayne County, N. Y. He has sometimes been confused with another aeronaut, Edward Lamountane, who was killed at Ionia, Mich., on July 4, 1873, while making an ascension with a Montgolfier paper balloon. John LaMountain seems to have been a sailor, but he became interested in ballooning at an early age. He made several ascensions, one at Bennington, Vt., in company with O. A. Gager; and in 1859 he and Gager became associated with the veteran John Wise, who had appealed to Congress for an appropriation of $15,-

000 to build a balloon of sufficient gas capacity to cross the Atlantic. Under the leadership of Wise, LaMountain and Gager constructed the balloon *Atlantic* for rapid transportation of mails and passengers from the United States to Europe. It was a spheroid fifty feet in diameter, carrying a wicker car above a light wooden boat. The Trans-Atlantic Balloon Company as organized consisted of Wise, LaMountain, Gager, and Messrs. Johnson and Gilbert. On July 1, 1859, just before 7:00 P. M., Wise, LaMountain, Gager and a reporter named William Hyde, left St. Louis, Mo., hoping to reach New York City, and the next day passed over Lake Erie, crossing near Niagara Falls at a height of 10,000 feet. They journeyed on over Lake Ontario, gradually falling. All ballast had been used and the weather became very unsettled. It was impossible to make a landing on the ground, owing to high wind. They therefore decided to swamp the balloon in the lake; but the attempt failed. After crossing the lake, the balloon crashed into trees and the aeronauts climbed down to earth at Henderson, Jefferson County, N. Y., about 2:35 P. M. on July 2. They had traveled over a thousand miles (850 in an air line), the longest air voyage on record to that date. LaMountain with one other companion, J. A. Haddock, made a second trip in the *Atlantic,* starting from Watertown, N. Y., Sept. 22, 1859. Drifting into Canada, they were forced to land in the wilderness about a hundred and fifty miles north of Ottawa and were finally rescued by trappers.

Early in 1861 LaMountain joined the Army of the Potomac and was able to give General McClellan important information regarding the position of the enemy, inasmuch as his balloon on one occasion, Aug. 10, 1861, passed over the enemy's lines at a height of one mile and a half. Recognizing that he was in some danger of being captured if the voyage continued in that direction, and aware of a west wind at greater altitude, he threw out ballast until he reached a height of nearly three miles. The wind direction at this height, as he had anticipated, brought the balloon back and he was able to make a landing in Maryland and to report what he had seen to Major-General Butler. General McClellan was much impressed with the possibilities of this use of the balloon, and four additional balloons were ordered for service. Later several officers of high rank made ascensions of moderate height under LaMountain's direction; but for various reasons, largely connected with the difficulty of transporting the balloons, the aeronautic section did not develop as had been expected.

LaMountain's companions on his aerial voyages give him credit for his good judgment at critical moments and speak of him as a daring and brave aeronaut. His name is sometimes spelled LaMountane, which may have been the original form.

[John Wise, *Through the Air* (1873); *War of the Rebellion: Official Records (Army),* 1 ser., IV, 600–01; *Daily Missouri Republican* (St. Louis), July 2–7, 1859; *N. Y. Herald,* Sept. 29, Oct. 4, 6, 1859; *Scientific American,* Apr. 18, 1863; *Am. Ann. Cyc.,* 1870.]

A. M.

LAMOUREUX, ANDREW JACKSON (Mar. 20, 1850–Feb. 25, 1928), journalist and librarian, was born in Iosco, Mich., the son of Thomas L. and Elizabeth (Carver) Lamoureux. He was a descendant of André Lamoureux, a Huguenot ship-master and pilot of Meschers, on the west coast of France, who after the Revocation of the Edict of Nantes escaped to Bristol, England, and, toward the end of the century, emigrated to New York. Prepared for college in the little village of Howell, Mich., Andrew entered Cornell University with the class of 1874 but, because of ill health, was obliged to leave before the completion of his course. During his university days, however, he was prominent in student activities. Upon leaving the university, he engaged in newspaper work, first in Utica, later in Ithaca, New York, and, at the time of the Centennial Exhibition at Philadelphia, he represented the newspaper directory at the newspaper exhibition held there. Not long after this, in 1877, he went to Rio de Janeiro, Brazil, to become editor of an English paper, the *British and American Mail,* published there and known as the official organ of the Brazilian coffee industry. Later, upon reorganization, it became the *Rio News* and acquired considerable political importance and a wide circulation both in Brazil and abroad. In its pages, as editor and owner, he took up the fight against slavery. This had theoretically been abolished, so far as the children of slaves were concerned, in 1871, but the fact that the older generations were still in bondage and that the new law was evaded aroused the young American to continue the struggle against the institution. When, in 1888, slavery was completely abolished, the people of Rio, realizing the important part he had played in its downfall, publicly acknowledged their appreciation and presented him with a diamond-studded gold pen. In addition to his journalistic activities, not only in connection with his own publication but also with several New York and London papers for which he acted as correspondent, he compiled in 1887 a *Handbook of Rio de Janeiro.* He was, likewise, one of the founders, and, for seven years, the secretary, of the "Strangers' Hospital" in Rio, one of the first modern public hospitals in Brazil. It was here he met, and on June 7, 1897 married, Sarah Cross, who was a graduate nurse, trained at the Swansea General and Eye Hospital, Birmingham, England.

Because he was the champion of the liberal cause and bent his efforts toward progressive welfare work, his life was often threatened and, at one time, it was necessary for him to leave the country for a period of eight months. In 1902, having disposed of his interest in the newspaper, he left Brazil and returned to the United States in broken health. Several years later he became reference librarian in the College of Agriculture, Cornell University, where he remained until his death. The most important literary work of his later years was his contribution of seventeen scholarly articles to the eleventh edition of the *Encyclopaedia Britannica*. Several of these cover the geography and statistics of certain Latin-American countries; others deal with the more important cities; all reveal the wide acquaintance of Lamoureux with South American conditions.

[*Ithaca Journal-News,* Feb. 25, 1928; *Cornell Alumni News,* Mar. 8, 1928; *New York Times,* Feb. 26, 1928; *Times* (London), Apr. 26, 1928; *The Delta Upsilon Decennial Cat.* (1902); A. J. Lamoureux, "André Lamoureux, the Huguenot Emigrant and Family," *Lamoureux Record,* Oct. 1919.] R. S. H.

LAMPSON, Sir CURTIS MIRANDA (Sept. 21, 1806–Mar. 12, 1885), merchant, was the fourth son of William and Rachel (Powell) Lampson and was born in New Haven, Vt. He received an ordinary school education. Being averse to farming with his father, he went to work as clerk in the general store of his native town. After spending several years there, but before he had reached his majority, he went to New York for further experience as a merchant and gradually worked into the exporting business. In view of the fact that he dealt largely in trade with England, he presumably decided that the business could be conducted to better advantage in England, and in the year 1830 he removed with his wife to that country. Beginning alone in London, he gradually built up a successful importing business which in the course of time he reorganized as the C. M. Lampson Company, with himself as senior partner. Having decided, too, to remain in England, he became a naturalized citizen of Great Britain on May 14, 1849, and purchased the estate of "Rowfant" in the parish of Worth and county of Sussex. By this time he had became a wealthy man and in addition to his own business was an active deputy-governor of the Hudson's Bay Company. In 1856 he met Cyrus W. Field who had gone to England from the United States for the purpose of interesting British capital in the project of establishing telegraphic communication by cable between England and America. Field was successful in this undertaking and brought about the organization of the Atlantic Telegraph Company of which Lampson was a most interested member of the board of directors, both financially and otherwise. He was one of the five directors who held out for continuing the attempt to lay a cable after the first failure in 1858 and was even more active after being made vice-chairman of the company.

Lampson worked almost seven years to build up sufficient confidence to attempt another laying of a cable. He was rewarded for his labors when with the refinancing and reorganization of the original company as the Anglo-American Company and with the aid of the steamship *Great Eastern* in laying the cable, a transatlantic telegraph service was finally established in 1865–66. For the great aid which he rendered to this undertaking Queen Victoria created him a baronet on Nov. 16, 1866, the citation of Her Majesty reading, "To whose resolute support of the project, in spite of all discouragements, it was in a great measure owing that it was not at one time abandoned in despair." Lampson was one of the trustees of the fund that was given by his friend George Peabody for the benefit of the poor of London. He was married on Nov. 30, 1827, in New York, to Jane Walter Sibley of Sutton, Mass., and at the time of his death in London he was survived by a son and daughter.

[*Illustrated London News,* Dec. 8, 1866; *Times* (London), Mar. 13, 1885; Jos. Foster, *The Baronetage of England, Scotland, and Ireland,* 1880; H. M. Field, *Hist. of the Atlantic Telegraph* (1867) and *The Story of the Atlantic Telegraph* (1892); I. F. Judson, *Cyrus W. Field, His Life and Work* (1896); C. F. Briggs, *The Story of the Telegraph* (1858); and *Dict. of Nat. Biog.*] C. W. M.

LAMY, JOHN BAPTIST (Oct. 11, 1814–Feb. 13, 1888), Roman Catholic prelate, was born at Lempdes, France, of a family which had given many servants to religion. His parents, Jean and Marie Dié Lamy (the name was originally l'Amy), sent him to the Seminary of Montferrand, and he was ordained a priest at Clermont-Ferrand by Bishop Louis Charles Ferron, Dec. 22, 1838. The next year, having been made assistant to the rector of a parish in his native diocese, he volunteered to join Bishop J. B. Purcell [*q.v.*], of Cincinnati, in mission work in lower Ohio. Upon reaching the United States, he was stationed at Wooster and Danville, Ohio, and later at Covington, Ky. When Mexico ceded the southwest territory in 1848, the bishops of the United States petitioned Rome for a transfer of the ecclesiastical jurisdiction. Accordingly Father Lamy was named vicar apostolic of New Mexico and consecrated bishop of Agathon. The ceremony took place at Cincinnati on Nov. 24, 1850, the celebrant being Bishop M. J. Spalding [*q.v.*]. Though the trip west was made via New Orleans and thence in company with a government caravan, it was hazardous and the Bishop almost lost his life in a serious accident. He arrived to find the Catholics of his territory (which included all of what is now New Mexico, the greater part of Arizona, a section of Colorado, and some districts in Nevada and Utah) scattered and inclined to resent, with the native clergy, the coming of an American bishop. Thereupon Bishop Lamy rode on horseback to Durango, Mexico, to visit Bishop Zubiria and to establish friendly relations. In order to forestall further trouble and to secure financial assistance, he then journeyed to France and Rome (1853). On July 29, 1853, he was named bishop of Santa Fé, and in 1875, archbishop. Laboring with great vigor and kindliness to spiritualize a somewhat turbulent population of Spanish and Indian Catholics, he undertook almost incredibly difficult journeys, preaching and catechizing. During 1852 he had attended the First Plenary Council of Baltimore, and on his way had induced the Sisters of Loretto, Kentucky, to send six of their number westward into New Mexico. One died on the way and another, becoming ill, went back, but the rest established a school in Santa Fé. Seven years later the Christian Brothers likewise made a foundation in the city, and the Jesuits arrived in 1867. Meanwhile, the Gadsden Purchase (1854) had added the southern part of Arizona to the diocese, and in 1860 Denver and the adjoining section of Colorado were also annexed. Much of the administrative work was confided to the Rev. Joseph Machebeuf, an indefatigable missionary, whom Bishop Lamy had appointed his vicar general. Apart from one or two brushes of minor importance, the Civil War did not affect the diocese. A report to Propaganda in 1865 revealed progress in every sense, and estimated the number of Catholics at 100,000, with flourishing churches and schools. On July 18, 1885, Bishop Lamy resigned to become titular bishop of Cyzicus. He died in Santa Fé. Few men are more representative of the pioneer Catholic missionary in the United States. He was simple of heart, generous and resolute, and his spare frame and austere profile testified to the hardships he had endured. During recent years his memory has been revived in *Death Comes for the Archbishop* (1927), a novel by Willa Cather which is largely based upon the records of his career.

[Archdiocesan archives, Santa Fé; W. J. Howlett, *Life of the Rt. Rev. Joseph P. Machebeuf, D.D.*, (1908); J. H. Defouri, *Hist. Sketch of the Cath. Ch. in New Mexico* (1887); J. G. Shea, *Hist. of the Cath. Ch. in the U. S.* (1892); *Commercial Gazette* (Cincinnati), Feb. 14, 1888; *The Commonweal*, Sept. 28, 1927.]

G. N. S.

LANDAIS, PIERRE (*c.* 1731–Sept. 17, 1820), naval officer, was born in St. Malo, Brittany. Early in life he entered the French navy and during the years 1766–69 accompanied the celebrated navigator Bougainville in a voyage of discovery around the world. Later he served as captain of a fireship and as a lieutenant at Brest. Dissatisfied with his prospects in the French service, he sought employment in the Continental navy and readily accepted a captain's commission therein, proffered to him on Mar. 1, 1777, by Silas Deane, the American commissioner at Paris, who placed a high estimate upon his professional abilities. Deane authorized him to take command of the French merchantman *Flamand* at Marseilles and transport to America a cargo of military supplies. On Dec. 1, 1777, he arrived at Portsmouth, N. H., after having quelled a serious mutiny on shipboard. Thence he proceeded to Philadelphia, taking with him letters of recommendation from Deane and from Baron von Steuben, one of his passengers on the *Flamand*. Favorably impressed by the Frenchman, the Continental Congress confirmed his appointment as captain and gave him command of the frigate *Alliance,* one of the best berths in the navy. On Oct. 15, 1778, the Massachusetts legislature passed an act naturalizing him as a citizen of that state. With Lafayette as a passenger, he returned to France where he arrived in February 1779, with a considerable number of his crew in irons, as a result of a plot against their commander.

In these two cruises, Landais disclosed that he had little aptitude for dealing with men and that his eccentricities more or less disqualified him for a naval command. John Adams, who saw him frequently at this time, reported that he was disappointed and moody, indecisive, jealous, and artless, and predicted that he would die poor and despised (C. F. Adams, *The Works of John Adams,* III, 1851, pp. 200, 204, 206). In April the *Alliance* was attached to the fleet of John Paul Jones [*q.v.*] and as next in rank to that officer her commander might have achieved great professional distinction, but animated by jealousy and petty pride he chose to disobey orders and assert his independence of his superior. Sulking, or fearful through timidity, he took but little part in the battle off Flamborough Head. The few shots fired by the *Alliance* did more damage to the flagship than to the enemy. After the cruise, Jones formally accused Landais of gross insubordination and of firing intentionally into the *Bon Homme Richard.* Franklin, the American minister at Paris, investigated the dispute, but unable to settle it, referred it to the Continental Congress in America. He placed Jones in command of the *Alliance* and warned her former commander not to meddle with the ship. In direct violation of these orders, encouraged by Arthur Lee, Landais went aboard the *Alliance* during the absence of Jones, took command of her, and sailed for America, leaving in France part of the cargo allotted to her. On this voyage the crew twice mutinied and Landais had frequent quarrels with his officers and passengers. Finally he retired to his cabin and declined to give commands or receive communications, and the *Alliance* was placed in charge of her lieutenant who brought her into Boston. A court-martial, presided over by Commodore John Barry [*q.v.*], that inquired into Landais's conduct in France and during this voyage sentenced him in January 1781 to be broken and rendered incapable of serving in the American navy.

Landais now became a resident of New York City and a chronic claimant for money alleged to be due him from the federal government. When early in the French Revolution the French navy was reorganized, he returned to his native land and again entered its naval service. In the Sardinian war of 1792–93 he is said to have displayed on one occasion much gallantry. In the latter year, ranking then as a rear-admiral, he commanded first a small fleet in the Mediterranean and later a larger fleet with the *Côte d'Or,* 110 guns, as his flagship, in the Atlantic. Several of his ships took part in the famous mutiny of 1793, and when he asked to resign his command, his request was readily granted. He returned to New York City in 1797. The twenty-three years of life that remained to this unfortunate officer were spent in "proud, solitary, and honourable poverty." He often visited the federal capital to prosecute his claims for prize money and a restitution of rank. In 1806 Congress voted him $4,000 on account, to be deducted from his share of prize money, in case of a final settlement. Two years before he died he erected in the cemetery of St. Patrick's (Old) Cathedral a monument to himself, with an inscription in French, which may be translated thus: "To the memory of Pierre de Landais, formerly rear-admiral in the service of the United States, who disappeared June, 1818, aged 87 years." He died in the New York City Hospital and is said to have been buried in the potter's field, then at Washington Square.

[Some more or less reliable information on Landais is found in the *Mag. of Hist.,* Sept. 1905. G. C. Verplanck's article in *Miscellanies* (1833), II, 329–33, is romanticized. Other sources are: J. H. Sherburne, *Life and Character of John Paul Jones* (ed. 1851); Papers of Continental Congress, No. 41, vol. V; No. 193, vol. II; *Report of the Secretary of State on the Memorial of Peter Landais* (1806); E. E. Hale, *Franklin in France* (1887), I, 319–41; L. E. Chevalier, *Histoire de la Marine sous la Première Republique* (1886), pp. 98, 100, 102, 119; C. H. Lincoln, *Naval Records of the Am. Revolution* (1906); C. O. Paullin, "Admiral Pierre Landais," in *Cath. Hist. Rev.,* Oct. 1931; and *N. Y. Gazette and Gen. Advertiser,* Sept. 19, 1820.]

C. O. P.

LANDER, EDWARD (Aug. 11, 1816–Feb. 2, 1907), jurist, was born in Salem, Mass., the eldest son of Edward and Eliza (West) Lander. His brother, Frederick W. Lander [*q.v.*], was a soldier and engineer; his sister, Louisa Lander, was a sculptress. He was graduated from Harvard in 1835, took the degree of M.A. in 1838, and that of LL.B. in 1839. After practising in his own state, he emigrated in 1841 to Indianapolis, Ind., where he became district attorney for several counties. During the Mexican War, he became captain of the 4th Indiana Volunteers but did not see active fighting. Soon after his return to civil life, he received an *ad interim* appointment and was subsequently elected judge of the court of common pleas. His next public office, to which he was appointed by President Pierce in 1853, was that of justice of the supreme court of Washington Territory. As a resident of the Puget Sound country he interested himself in means of communication with the transmontane hinterland, urging the building of railroads and participating in expeditions to explore trails.

More in harmony with his profession was his excellent work as member of a commission to draft a code of law for the territory. During the Indian wars of 1856–58, Lander was made captain of Company A of volunteers but became involved in a legal, rather than military, combat. The territorial authorities accused some settlers, former employees of the Hudson's Bay Company, of affording aid and comfort to the enemy, and therefore ordered them to Fort Steilacoom for surveillance. Local attorneys prepared writs of *habeas corpus* which were to be laid before the district court of Pierce County, Lander presiding for his colleague, Judge

Chenoweth, who was ill. To forestall the release of the suspects, Gov. Isaac Ingalls Stevens, on Apr. 3, 1856, proclaimed martial law in Pierce County and ordered Lander's arrest when the latter attempted to hold court. Later, the judge tried to bring Stevens before his own bench, in Olympia, Thurston County, on charges of contempt. The federal marshal and posse failed in the attempt to arrest Stevens who had now proclaimed martial law in Thurston County and had ordered Lander rearrested. The alleged emergency had passed before Judge Chenoweth secured the release of his colleague, who thereupon fined the executive, represented by attorney, the nominal sum of fifty dollars, merely to vindicate the supremacy of civil law. The national administration upheld the judge's position on the mooted question of martial law. Lander declined renomination for his position in 1858. As independent candidate for territorial delegate in 1861, he was defeated by a substantial majority. After receiving an injury which invalided him for the remainder of his life, he made his residence at Washington, D. C., where he represented Hudson's Bay Company and its subsidiary, the Puget Sound Agricultural Company, also the claimants in the French spoliation claims. He was married but had no children. He died at Washington.

[Elwood Evans and others, *Hist. of the Pacific Northwest: Ore. and Wash.* (1889), vol. I; F. T. Gilbert, *Hist. Sketches of Walla Walla, Whitman, Columbia, and Garfield Counties, Wash. Territory* (1882); F. J. Grant, *Hist. of Seattle, Wash.* (1891); E. S. Meany, *Hist. of the State of Wash.* (1909); Ezra Meeker, *Pioneer Reminiscences of Puget Sound* (1905); *New-Eng. Hist. and Geneal. Reg.*, Apr. 1851; the *Oregonian* (Portland), Feb. 3, 1907; *Pioneer and Democrat* (Olympia), May, June 1856; C. A. Snowden, *Hist. of Wash.* (1909), vol. III; Hazard Stevens, *The Life of Isaac Ingalls Stevens* (1900), vol. II; *Who's Who in America*, 1903–05.] H. J. D.

LANDER, FREDERICK WEST (Dec. 17, 1821–Mar. 2, 1862), transcontinental explorer, soldier, poet, was born at Salem, Mass., the son of Edward Lander and Eliza West. Edward Lander [*q.v.*] was his brother and Louisa Lander, the sculptress, was his sister. His paternal grandfather was interested in foreign trade, while his mother's father, Nathaniel West, served for a time as midshipman in the British navy and later commanded a noted American privateer, the *Black Prince,* distinguishing himself in the Revolution. Young Lander received his early education at Franklin and Dummer academies and was noted for physical strength and love of sports. Later he studied engineering at South Andover and at Norwich, Vt., then practised his profession for a time in survey work on several eastern railroads, in which he established a reputation for ability and thoroughness. In 1853 he served as a civil engineer on the staff of Isaac I. Stevens [*q.v.*] during the survey of the Northern Pacific Railroad route. In this capacity he made a reconnaissance of "the several crossings of the Mississippi." His report is printed in *Senate Executive Document 29* (33 Cong., 1 Sess.). In the spring of the year 1854 he headed a party of exploration to report upon the feasibility of a projected railroad from Puget Sound to the Mississippi River (see "Report of the Reconnaissance of a Railroad Route from Puget Sound via the South Pass to the Mississippi River," *House Executive Document 129,* 33 Cong., 1 Sess., vol. III), and during the four years following, he served as superintendent and chief engineer of the overland wagon road. This involved considerable arduous service and hazardous duty; and in 1858, Lander's party of seventy were attacked by Piute Indians in a spirited engagement. The Indians were repulsed. Lander submitted a report as to the advisability of a main line railroad from the Mississippi River to Salt Lake City, with branches to San Francisco and Puget Sound (*House Executive Document 70,* 35 Cong., 1 Sess.). Altogether, he led or participated in five transcontinental surveys, and for his accomplishments received high praise from the secretary of the interior. In October 1860 he was married to Jean Margaret Davenport [see Lander, Jean Margaret Davenport], an actress, born at Wolverhampton, England, who had come to the United States in 1838.

Upon the outbreak of the Civil War, Lander was entrusted with a secret and confidential mission to Governor Houston of Texas, with full authority to order Federal troops then in Texas to support Houston if thought advisable. Later he served with credit as an aide on General McClellan's staff in the engagements at Philippi and Rich Mountain; and on May 17, 1861, he was appointed brigadier-general of volunteers, taking over in July, command of a brigade of Gen. C. P. Stone's division on the upper Potomac. In the serious engagement of Edwards Ferry, he was severely wounded in the leg, after which he was authorized to reorganize his brigade into a division, with which command, on Jan. 5, 1862, he successfully defended the town of Hancock, Md., against a superior force of the enemy. On Feb. 14, 1862, while still suffering from his wound, he led a brilliant charge at Blooming Gap, for which gallant conduct he received a special letter of commendation from the secretary of war. About this time, ill-health due in large part to the severity of the winter campaign, compelled a leave of absence; and on Mar. 2,

1862, while preparing to move his division into the Shenandoah Valley to cooperate with General Banks, he died suddenly in the division camp on the Cacapon River, in Virginia, of a congestive chill, brought on by fatigue and exposure. General McClellan announced his death to the army in a special order, the day following. Lander was survived by his wife, by whom he had no children. Besides being a successful and intrepid explorer as well as a soldier of marked ability, Lander was a vigorous and forceful writer and was the author of many patriotic poems of the war period.

[See F. B. Heitman, *Hist. Reg. and Dict. of the U. S. Army* (1903), vol. I; *Battles and Leaders of the Civil War*, vol. II (1888); A. S. Webb, *The Peninsula: McClellan's Campaign of 1862* (1881); G. M. Dodge and W. A. Ellis, *Norwich Univ.* (1911), vol. II; *War of the Rebellion: Official Records (Army)*; *N. Y. Times*, Mar. 3, 1862; and *Boston Morning Jour.*, Mar. 4, 1862. Lander's name is given in the Salem vital records as Frederick William Lander. In later life he apparently used the name given above.] C. D. R.

LANDER, JEAN MARGARET DAVENPORT (May 3, 1829–Aug. 3, 1903), actress, was born at Wolverhampton, Staffordshire, England. Her father, Thomas Donald, at first a lawyer, was later manager of the Richmond (England) Theatre. Her mother, formerly Miss Danby, was well known in British provincial theatres. Under the name Jean Davenport the child made her first professional appearance at the Richmond Theatre in 1837, in the title part of Shakespeare's *King Richard the Third,* and next as Little Pickle in *The Spoiled Child.* Exploited as an infant prodigy, she played these characters in other cities of Great Britain, winning special success in London and Dublin. In 1838 she came to America, making her début at the National Theatre, New York City, on May 21, as Richard the Third and Little Pickle. Afterward she gave performances in all the large Eastern and Southern cities, playing in addition to the two parts mentioned, Sir Peter Teazle, Shylock, Sir Giles Overreach, the Dumb Boy of Manchester, Young Norval, and others, with great success. She returned to Europe in 1842, traveled in England and France, and studied under private tutors. In 1844 and 1845, in London, she appeared as Shakespeare's Juliet, Julia in *The Hunchback,* the Countess, in *Love,* and became a great favorite. From 1846 to 1848 she won further success in Holland and Germany. On her return to England in 1848, she made her appearance as a public reader. Her Shakespearian readings were especially notable.

During her second visit to America in 1849 her professional success on her tour of the country was so great that she decided to make America her home. Besides Juliet, the Countess, and Julia, she played Meeta, in *The Maid of Mariendorpt,* Horatia, in *The Roman Father,* Pauline, in *The Lady of Lyons,* and Peg Woffington in *Masks and Faces.* In December 1853, during her engagement at the Broadway Theatre, New York City, she appeared in adaptations from the French of *Adrienne Lecouvreur* and *La Dame aux Camélias,* having the distinction of introducing these two hapless heroines to the American public. In 1855 she went to California; in 1856–57 and in 1859 she was again in England. In October 1860, in San Francisco, she was married to Frederick West Lander [*q.v.*]. General Lander died in March 1862 from the effects of wounds received in the American Civil War. Mrs. Lander then served as a hospital nurse, coming out of her retirement from the stage to appear in *Mésalliance* (her own adaptation from the French) at Niblo's Garden, New York, Feb. 6, 1865. The critic of the *New York Herald* (Feb. 7, 1865), writing of this performance said in part: "Mrs. Lander is a small, beautifully formed lady, with a sweet, expressive face, and a voice as clear as a silver bell. Her motions are very graceful. . . . She carries us back to those old, delightful days when it required brains, not brass, to be a star." Shortly after this, Mrs. Lander added to her repertoire such parts as Queen Elizabeth, Mary Stuart, and Marie Antoinette, with all the success attending her former efforts. With Comte de Najac, she dramatized Hawthorne's *Scarlet Letter,* in which she made her last appearance as Hester Prynne at the Boston Theatre on Jan. 1, 1877. Thereafter she resided in Washington and Lynn, Mass. Her death occurred at her summer home in the latter city. Judged by the standards of the day she was undoubtedly an actress of great talent, taste, and intellectual attainment.

[T. A. Brown, *Hist. of the Am. Stage* (1870); J. N. Ireland, *Records of the N. Y. Stage* (1866), vol. II; G. C. D. Odell, *Annals of the N. Y. Stage,* vol. IV (1928); Lawrence Hutton, *Plays and Players* (1875); Wm. Winter, *The Wallet of Time* (1913), vol. I; Arthur Hornblow, *Hist. of the Theatre in America* (1919), vol. II; Eugene Tompkins and Quincy Kilby, *The Hist. of the Boston Theatre, 1854–1901* (1908); *N. Y. Dramatic Mirror,* Aug. 8, 15, 1903; *N. Y. Herald,* Sept. 24–29, 1849, Dec. 6, 1853, Feb. 7, 1865; *N. Y. Times,* Aug. 4, 1903.] L. H. F.

LANDON, MELVILLE DE LANCEY (Sept. 7, 1839–Dec. 16, 1910), humorous lecturer and writer under the pen-name Eli Perkins, was born on his father's farm at Eaton, Madison County, N. Y., son of John and Nancy (Marsh) Landon, both of old New England stock. After study in the district school and local academy he attended Madison (later Colgate) University and then Union College, graduating in 1861. At the outbreak of the Civil War he joined the battalion organized by Cassius M. Clay for the defense of Washington. At the same time he served as a clerk in the Treasury Department. In 1863 he served with the rank of major on Gen. A. L. Chetlain's staff in Tennessee. At the request of Secretary Chase he resigned and took up cotton growing in Louisiana and Arkansas with free labor, 1864–67, cultivating 1,700 acres in 1867. Subsequently he traveled in Europe, visiting Paris, Rome, Athens, and St. Petersburg, and in the last-named capital was for a short time secretary to his former commander Clay, then minister to Russia. Returning home in 1870, he prepared a compact digest, *The Franco-Prussian War in a Nutshell* (1871), and then took up journalism. His humorous correspondence from Saratoga for the New York *Commercial Advertiser,* which he signed "Lan" and later "Eli Perkins" (stated by Landon to have been applied to him by Artemus Ward) made him a reputation, and was collected under the title *Saratoga in 1901* (1872). In 1875 he published *Eli Perkins at Large: His Sayings and Doings.* After conducting a lecture tour for Josh Billings, he turned himself to platform humor, and in the ten years up to 1887 "delivered a thousand humorous and philosophical lectures through the Union." While his success on the platform is thus abundantly evidenced, his humor in print appears feebler and more largely anecdotal than that of some of his contemporaries; the "philosophical" element consists of plentifully illustrated distinctions between humor, wit, and satire. These popular readings and lectures he continued for many years. In 1879 he edited the *Complete Works of Artemus Ward* with a biographical introduction. He also published several collections, including *Wit and Humor of the Age* (1883); *Wise, Witty, Eloquent Kings of the Platform and Pulpit* (1890), and *Thirty Years of Wit* (1891). Many of his books were republished under varying titles. His book entitled *Money: Gold, Silver, or Bimetalism* (1895) was a campaign document against free silver. During his later years he frequently visited Europe and also toured the Orient, writing travel letters for New York and Chicago newspapers. He was president of the New York News Association, possessed considerable wealth, and at his residence in New York entertained many artistic and literary celebrities. His death from locomotor ataxia occurred at Yonkers, where he had made his home shortly before. He was married in Grace Church, New York, Mar. 22, 1875, to Emily Louise, daughter of the Rev. Edward Smith of Port Chester, N. Y., and was survived by his wife and one daughter.

[*Who's Who in America,* 1908–09; *N. Y. Times,* Dec. 17, 1910; J. O. Landon, *Landon Geneal.* (1928); biographical material in *Thirty Years of Wit* (eds. 1891 and 1899).] A. W.

LANDRETH, DAVID (Sept. 15, 1802–Feb. 22, 1880), merchant, agriculturist, and writer, was the only son of David Landreth, a native of Haggerston, near Berwick-on-Tweed, Northumberland County, England, and of Sarah (Arnell) Landreth, a native of Lewes, Del. The elder David Landreth was a tree grower, seedsman, and nurseryman, who came to Canada in 1781 and in 1783 removed to Philadelphia, where he established a nursery and seed business in 1784. The family name, according to Thomas C. Gentry's *Family Names* (1892), was of Anglo-Saxon origin, meaning a field stream or spring. David Landreth the younger was born in Philadelphia, received his education in private schools, and while a very young man entered his father's business. This enterprise at that time was being conducted under the partnership of his father and his uncle, Cuthbert Landreth. David was made manager of a branch store in Charleston, S. C., which prospered under his direction and continued to thrive with a succession of leaders until the period of the Civil War, when it was confiscated (Apr. 22, 1862) by act of the Confederate States. After successfully launching this branch he returned to Philadelphia, and in 1828 became proprietor of the firm, which now had a prosperous, well-established business. In 1847, the Landreth nursery and seed farm was removed to "Bloomsdale Farm," at Bristol, Pa. There Landreth planned and planted a nursery, arboretum, and vegetable variety trial grounds which were for a time the most complete in the United States. He engaged also in the breeding of Alderney cattle; in 1872–73 experimented with steam-plowing, trying both a Scotch and an American engine; and later conducted tests of steam digging and chopping. He served as vice-president of the United States Agricultural Society, a manufacturing company which was one of the first to make sowing and reaping machines.

Besides his business pursuits, he had numerous literary and public interests. He was one of the founders of the Pennsylvania Horticultural Society, organized in 1827, and served it as corresponding secretary, 1828–35, and as vice-president, 1829–36. In 1856 he became president of the Philadelphia Society for the Promotion of Agriculture, serving in this capacity for two years. He was president of the Agricultural

Section of the United States Sanitary Fair, and was one of the organizers (1847) of the Farmers' Club of Pennsylvania. His literary endeavors were expressed in the founding in 1832 and subsequent publishing of the *Illustrated Floral Magazine,* which was noted for the clearness, beauty, and accuracy of its descriptions and illustrations. In 1847 he published an American edition with additional notes of George W. Johnson's *Dictionary of Modern Gardening,* a classic of horticultural writing.

He was married twice: first, in 1825, to Elizabeth Rodney of Delaware, by whom he had five children; and second, in 1842, to Martha Burnet of Philadelphia, by whom he had three children. He died at his home at "Bloomsdale," Bristol, Pa. The seed firm which he conducted ably for so long a period was continued by his descendants, and is the oldest of its kind in America.

[Burnet Landreth, "David Landreth," in L. H. Bailey, *Cyc. of Am. Horticulture* (1900); S. F. Hotchkin, *The Bristol Pike* (1893); "An Early Methodist of Philadelphia," *Pa. Mag. of Hist. and Biog.*, XII (1888), 488–89; *Phila. Record,* Feb. 24, 1880; communication from Burnet Landreth, Jr., 1929.] W. B. M—k.

LANE, FRANKLIN KNIGHT (July 15, 1864–May 18, 1921), interstate commerce commissioner, secretary of the interior, the eldest of the four children of Christopher S. and Caroline (Burns) Lane, was born near Charlottetown, Prince Edward Island, Canada. His father at this time was a Presbyterian minister, but later, when recurrent attacks of bronchitis affected his voice, became a dentist. From his mother, a woman of direct Scotch descent, Lane derived many of his physical and mental traits. To escape the rigor of the Canadian climate, his father moved with the family to California in 1871, settling in Napa. From boyhood Lane was thoroughly American in his democratic outlook in his emphasis upon equality of economic opportunity, and in his restless, ambitious spirit. He attended a grammar school at Napa, and later a private school called "Oak Mound." In 1876, the family moved to Oakland, where the boy entered high school. He attended the University of California, 1884–86, as a special student, putting himself through college by working during vacation and after hours. Philosophy and economics were the subjects which appealed to him most strongly, and he became one of the leading spirits in a political science club.

The readable, effective style that characterizes Lane's public papers he himself attributed to his early newspaper training. He did newspaper work to help pay his way through college, and, after studying law in San Francisco at the Hastings College of the Law (part of the University of California), he was admitted to the bar in 1888. He then became a special correspondent in New York for the *San Francisco Chronicle.* In 1891, he bought an interest in the *Tacoma Daily News,* and became editor of that journal. In April 1893 he married Anne Wintermute. Though the editorship of a newspaper gave him an opportunity to exert an influence on local affairs and to express his views on public questions, the venture was not financially successful. The paper became bankrupt and Lane sold it at auction in 1894, turning with undampened ardor to new fields of activity. In the fall of that year, he entered into an association for a few months with Arthur McEwen, publisher of *Arthur McEwen's Letter,* a weekly political journal in San Francisco which attacked civic corruption, and more especially the Southern Pacific Railroad, then the colossus that dominated the affairs of the state. About the same time, he and his brother, George W. Lane, established a law partnership. In 1898, Lane made his formal entry into politics, accepting membership on a committee to draft a charter for San Francisco and stumping the city in behalf of the charter. Accepting the Democratic nomination for city and county attorney, he was elected in 1898 and reëlected the next year and in 1901. None of his opinions as city attorney were reversed by the supreme court. In 1902, he was nominated as the Democratic and Non-Partisan candidate for governor of California, but was defeated. Reluctantly yielding to his friends, he accepted the Democratic nomination for mayor of San Francisco in 1903, only to suffer defeat again.

The vigor of his democracy, however, and his fighting spirit, had already made Lane a national figure. In December 1905, President Roosevelt nominated him to the Interstate Commerce Commission. The Senate was slow to act, for the conservatives in that body regarded Lane as a radical, and the nomination was not confirmed until June 29, 1906. Lane quickly became recognized as one of the ablest members of the Commission. A champion of the "plain people," he held that if men had made great fortunes out of privileges granted by the common people it was possible to correct the evil by a change in law. His "radicalism" went no further than this. The decisions written by Lane as interstate commerce commissioner "were among the most important, and probably the most important, that determined the constitutional powers of the Government in the regulation of common carriers" (Hemphill, in *North American Review,* August 1917, p. 252). Some of his decisions involved nice questions of constitutional law, but they were all sustained by the Supreme Court. He undertook several pieces of constructive work while a member of the Commission. Notable among these was the installation of a uniform system of demurrage laws. Intellectual independence, breadth of vision, and a fine mastery of details characterized his seven years' service.

Lane was somewhat reluctant to leave the Commission, of which he had recently been made chairman, to accept Woodrow Wilson's offer (February 1913) of the secretaryship of the interior. Dependent almost entirely on his salary, he dreaded the added social and financial demands of a place in the cabinet. Nevertheless, he obeyed the summons of the draft. Though the post of secretary of the interior is one of the most exacting in the cabinet, Lane could hardly have asked for one better adapted to his talents, or enabling him to draw more effectively upon the stores of his experience in the West. A conservationist, he consistently maintained that the resources of the West should be used to develop the West. To show his practical interest in the welfare of Alaska, he nominated an Alaskan as its governor. He recommended the construction of a railway line from Seward to Fairbanks. The objective of his Indian policy was the release of every Indian from the guardianship of the government as soon as he gave evidence of his ability to care for his own affairs. Lane plunged with enthusiasm into a study of all the many activities carried on by the Department of the Interior. He was an indefatigable first-hand investigator, and his inspection trips covered reclamation projects, national parks, and Indian reservations.

To the employees who worked under him in Washington, as to the men and women in the field, he was the inspirational leader. He aimed to kindle in them the glow of his own enthusiasm for public service. To promote fellowship, and to foster the spirit of teamwork in the Department, he organized the "Home Club." His address to his staff on Flag Day, 1914, later published as a small pamphlet, *Makers of the Flag* (1916), has been described as a classic in its field, while his annual reports disclose his philosophic grasp of the problems of his Department and his high conception of his duties as a cabinet officer. He found time to continue his correspondence with an extraordinarily wide circle of friends. In *The Letters of Franklin K. Lane* (1922), a selection published after his death, the human qualities of the man are abundantly revealed. In 1916, he served as chairman of the American-Mexican joint commission; in 1918, he was made chairman of the railroad wage commission; and the following year he was chairman of the industrial conference. When the United States declared war against Germany in 1917, Lane threw himself, with his characteristic enthusiasm, into the work of rallying public support behind the war effort of the administration. To this end, he made numerous public speeches, many of which were published in 1918 in a book entitled *The American Spirit.* As the war drew to a close, he proposed that part of the public domain be set aside for returning soldiers who wished to go back to the land, but Congress did not accept the suggestion.

Lane resigned from the cabinet on Mar. 1, 1920, to become vice-president of the Pan-American Petroleum Company, at a salary said to have been $50,000 a year. His health was declining, and his private means were so small that he felt it incumbent upon him to accept private employment, and to build up an estate to safeguard the financial future of his wife and two children. He told close friends that on leaving Washington he would not have money enough to buy railroad tickets for himself and his family back to California, and to move there the little furniture he owned (Sullivan, *post,* p. 610). His hopes, however, were not to be realized, for he died on May 18, 1921, at Rochester, Minn., following an operation.

[Valuable biographical material is contained in *The Letters of Franklin K. Lane* (1922), ed. by Anne W. Lane and Louise H. Wall. Some of these were published as "Letters of a High Minded Man, Franklin K. Lane," in *World's Work,* Mar.–Sept. 1922. Among articles on him may be cited: Jas. C. Hemphill, "Franklin Knight Lane," *North Am. Rev.,* Aug. 1917; Wm. E. Smythe, "Franklin K. Lane, American," *Rev. of Revs.,* (N. Y.), Apr. 1920; Lawrence Abbott, "A Passionate American," *Outlook,* June 1, 1921. See also *Nation,* June 1, 1921; Mark Sullivan, "Public Men and Big Business," *World's Work,* Apr. 1924; *N. Y. Times,* May 19, 1921.]
O. M., Jr.

LANE, GEORGE MARTIN (Dec. 24, 1823–June 30, 1897), classicist, was descended from William Lane who settled in Dorchester, Mass., about 1635. His parents, Martin Lane of Northampton, Mass., and Lucretia Swan of Boston, removed to Cambridge shortly after the birth of their son. The boy was probably first inspired to classical scholarship in the school of Charles Stearns Wheeler, later instructor at Harvard. Graduating with high distinction from Harvard in 1846, Lane was appointed to conduct the upper Latin classes during the absence of Professor Charles Beck. In 1847 he went to Germany in order to devote himself to classical philology, a subject in which no American college then offered systematic instruction. After four years of study abroad, he received the degree of Ph.D.

at Göttingen, in 1851. Upon the resignation of Professor Beck in that year, Lane was elected University Professor of Latin with no intervening period of probation as a teacher—an unusual procedure, but (as President Eliot said) never better justified. On the establishment of the Pope Professorship in Latin in 1869, he was transferred to that position. Resigning in 1894 he was made professor emeritus. During forty-three years he was in the active service of Harvard College, of which he was one of the very ablest teachers. His pupils recalled with admiration his originality of thought, never disabled by his seemingly exhaustless memory; his power to inspire them with the love of truth; his insistence on scrupulous accuracy; his felicity of expression, born of his delicate literary taste; and an abounding wit and humor that gave life to every subject of his instruction.

Lane was preëminently a teacher—a great teacher through the spoken word. He wrote relatively little. He contributed articles to the *Nation,* to the *Bibliotheca Sacra* and the *North American Review,* and to the *Harvard Studies in Classical Philology.* His *Latin Pronunciation* (1871) extirpated the traditional "English" pronunciation of Latin almost everywhere throughout the United States. He corrected the proof of much of the large *Harpers' Latin Dictionary* (1879); his counsel and assistance made Charlton T. Lewis' *Latin Dictionary for Schools* (1889) a more original and trustworthy book. His scholarly fame is chiefly secured by his posthumously published *Latin Grammar for Schools and Colleges* (1898). Highly trained as was his linguistic sense, he was not content unless he could fortify his every statement by his own examination of the materials in all their details. So great indeed was his passion for precision that, after nearly thirty years of labor, the book was completed only after his death, by his pupil, Professor Morris Morgan. Of special importance is the Syntax, in the treatment of which the author showed that he had imbibed the very spirit of the Latin language and could reproduce in idiomatic translation the shifting tone and the character of the original. Of the *Latin Grammar,* Professor Gildersleeve said that it "will abide not only as a repertory of important facts and a repository of acute observations but as a monument of literary art and sympathetic interpretation" (Morison, *post,* p. 39).

Lane was distinguished for great personal charm, geniality, courtliness, and humor. Of his humor one specimen is still remembered—the "Lay of the Lone Fishball," a ballad of which he was himself the hero. He was married in 1857 to Frances Eliza Gardiner, who died in 1876; in 1878 to Mrs. Fanny (Bradford) Clark.

[*Am. Jour. of Philology,* July, Oct. 1897, Oct. 1898; *Harvard Studies in Classical Philology,* VII (1896), 374–81, IX (1898), 1–12; *Pubs. of the Col. Soc. of Mass.,* vol. VI (1904); *Nation* (N. Y.), July 8, 1897; J. H. Fitts, *Lane Geneals.,* vol. II (1897); S. E. Morison, *The Development of Harvard Univ. . . . 1869–1929* (1930); J. L. Chamberlain, *Harvard Univ.* (1900); F. O. Vaille and H. A. Clark, *The Harvard Book* (1875), vol. I.]

H. W. S—h.

LANE, HENRY SMITH (Feb. 24, 1811–June 18, 1881), representative and senator from Indiana, was born on a farm near Sharpsburg, Bath County, Ky., the son of James H. Lane, a colonel of militia and Indian fighter. He studied law and was admitted to the bar, in 1832, at Mt. Sterling, Ky. In 1834 he moved to Crawfordsville, Ind., where he practised his profession until he became a banker there, in 1854, with his father-in-law, Isaac C. Elston. He was a Whig member of the state House of Representatives (1838–39) and took an active part in the campaign of 1840. Elected to the twenty-sixth federal House of Representatives to fill a vacancy caused by resignation and reëlected to the next Congress, he served from Aug. 3, 1840, to Mar. 3, 1843. When Tyler succeeded Harrison and vetoed bills to charter a new federal bank Lane, like most of his party, broke with the President and denounced him in bitter terms. He greatly admired Henry Clay and campaigned ardently for him in 1844; the defeat of his idol was one of the great disappointments of his life. Unlike many northern Whigs he strongly supported the Mexican War, raised a company of volunteers, became its captain, and subsequently rose to be major and then lieutenant-colonel of the 1st Indiana Regiment. He went to Mexico but was mainly engaged in guarding supply trains and in garrison duty, and he did not participate in any battles. After his return home he again ran for Congress but was defeated by one of the leading Indiana Democrats, Joseph E. McDonald.

Early in his life, he recognized that slavery was out of harmony with the spirit of the age, but he opposed the methods of the active abolitionists. However, when the Republican party was founded upon the principle of opposition to slavery in the territories, he became one of its leaders in Indiana. He presided over the national convention of 1856 and made an impassioned speech that gave him a national reputation. In 1859, holding that the election of Bright and Fitch in 1857 had been irregular, the Republicans and "Americans" or old Whigs, who now controlled both houses of the state legislature, chose Lane and Monroe McCarty for the United States Senate, but they were not allowed to take the seats because the Democratic majority in that body supported Bright and Fitch. In the Republican National Convention of 1860 he energetically opposed the candidacy of Seward and played a large part in bringing about Lincoln's nomination. He was nominated for governor by the Indiana Republicans, with Oliver P. Morton as the candidate for lieutenant-governor. The two campaigned vigorously and were elected. Two days after his inauguration, in accordance with a previous understanding, he was elected United States senator and resigned the governorship in favor of Morton. In the Senate he was a member of the committee on military affairs and of the committee on pensions, of which latter he became chairman. He gave zealous support to the Union cause and, later, to the congressional plan of reconstruction, but he originated few measures and rarely spoke at any length, his talents "being better suited to the hustings than to a legislative body" (Woolen, *post,* p. 124). His influence was, however, much greater than the record of his activities in the *Congressional Globe* indicates.

He declined to be a candidate for reëlection and upon the expiration of his term in 1867 returned to Crawfordsville to take up again his banking interests. In 1869 he became special Indian commissioner and, in 1872, served as commissioner for the improvement of the Mississippi River. He was a delegate to the Republican national conventions of 1868 and 1872 and for many years a trustee of Asbury College (now De Pauw University). He was fond of telling how in the days of attending court in Fountain County before the war, he approached a group that included Abraham Lincoln. "Here," said Lincoln, "comes an uglier man than I am." As a stump speaker he had few equals, but his oratory was of the impassioned type, and he was not a logical speaker nor a good debater. Unlike his fellow partisan, Oliver P. Morton, he made few enemies, being popular even with most of his political opponents. He was twice married, first, to Pamelia Bledsoe Jameson of Kentucky, who died in 1842, and, second, on Feb. 11, 1845, to Jonna Elston, of Crawfordsville, a sister of the wife of Lew Wallace [*q.v.*].

[Files of the Congressional Joint Committee on Printing; *Encycl. of Biog. of Ind.*, ed. by G. I. Reed, vol. I (1895); *A Biog. Hist. of Eminent and Self-Made Men of the State of Indiana* (1880), vol. I; W. W. Woolen, *Biog. and Hist. Sketches of Early Ind.* (1883); *Indianapolis Journal,* June 20, 1881; *Indianapolis News,* Apr. 6, 1914, Aug. 8, 1914.] P. L. H.

LANE, HORACE M. (July 29, 1837–Oct. 27, 1912), missionary educator in Brazil, was born at Readfield, Me., the son of Rufus King Lane by his second wife Electa (Davis) Lane, both of New England stock. At nineteen he went to Brazil to take a commercial position. While he was prospering in business he became interested in Christian missions and education, and finally went into teaching. The understanding of the people and the mastery of their language gained in these years qualified him for his later achievements among Brazilians. Returning to the United States, he studied medicine and, settling in Missouri, entered upon the life of a physician. In 1863 he married Ellen Williams. A letter from a Presbyterian missionary in São Paulo, Brazil, in 1886, contained the request that he take charge of a school there. Though he had a large practice, and his wife's death had just left him with eight children to care for, he immediately went to São Paulo with his family, under appointment from the Presbyterian Board of Foreign Missions.

In his Escola Americana he adapted the essential features of American school practice to Brazilian conditions and showed a unique gift for educational method. This school was the first co-educational institution in the country, the first to receive students without distinction of race or color, and the first to provide manual training. Lane was inexhaustibly energetic and ceaselessly active. He had a rare faculty for winning friends, unusual administrative ability, and "a wizard's mastery of school finance in a Latin land." As the school developed it produced a demand for higher education, and in 1891 an independent non-sectarian institution named Mackenzie College was organized. For twenty-one years Lane presided over the college and the school, and created one of the most valuable educational forces in South America. Mackenzie graduates became prominent in engineering, business, public-school teaching, and intellectual leadership. Students were sent for advanced training to the United States, for Lane had a vision of Pan-American unity of spirit. During his presidency more than fifteen thousand students entered the college and the school. They felt his friendliness and to many he communicated his spirit. They were "scattered" he said, "throughout the land to aid in its regeneration." The wholesome religious influence of the college was a recognized power in Brazilian life. To this life he contributed in other ways than through his students. His methods and textbooks were the model for public schools throughout the nation, and he took a large part in the organization of an independent Brazilian Presbyterian Church. His character and services won the confidence of the leading men of São

Paulo and he was undoubtedly the most influential foreigner and educator in Brazil. In the physical weakness of his last years he held to his work with characteristic resolution and fidelity, and died at his post after a short illness.

[Jacob Chapman and J. H. Fitts, *Lane Geneals.*, vol. I (1891); *Ann. Reports of the Board of Foreign Missions of the Presbyt. Ch. in the U. S. A.*, 1886–1912; manuscript records of the Board; *Assembly Herald* (Phila.), June 1907, Jan. 1913; *The Continent* (Chicago), Dec. 12, 19, 1912; *Jornal do Commercio* (Rio de Janeiro), Oct. 29, 1912; information as to certain facts from Rev. George Alexander.] R. H. N.

LANE, JAMES HENRY (June 22, 1814–July 11, 1866), soldier and Kansas political leader, was the son of Amos and Mary (Foote) Howes Lane. His father, a native of New York, emigrated to Indiana in 1808, became an itinerant attorney, a member of the legislature (speaker in 1817), and congressman from the fourth Indiana district during Jackson's second term. His mother was born in Connecticut, acquired a good education, and imparted the fundamentals of learning to her son. Lane's birthplace was probably Lawrenceburg, Ind., although when it gave him political advantage he claimed Kentucky as his native state. He was a product of the frontier, and like his father, a Democrat of the Jackson school. He studied law in his father's office, was admitted to the bar, and practised his profession occasionally. In 1841 he married Mary E. Baldridge of Youngstown, Pa., a grand-daughter of Gen. Arthur St. Clair; they were divorced some fifteen years later and remarried in 1857. In the Mexican War he served as colonel of the 3rd Indiana Regiment, and as a volunteer commander without previous military experience acquitted himself creditably at Buena Vista. Later he commanded the 5th Indiana, which he led to Mexico City. Military achievement brought political advancement: he served as lieutenant-governor, 1849–53, and as member of Congress, 1853–55, where he voted for the Kansas-Nebraska Bill.

Refusing to stand for reëlection, he emigrated to Kansas Territory in April 1855 and soon attempted to organize the Democratic party there. Failing in this endeavor, he joined the Free-State movement, and as chairman of the platform committee of the Big Springs convention, in September 1855, he advocated a broad and constructive program designed to unite anti-slavery factions in the Territory. At the "People's Convention" two weeks later he was made chairman of the "Executive Committee of Kansas Territory," and as such directed the activities of the party in its quest for statehood. Posing as the spokesman of Stephen A. Douglas [*q.v.*], he assured Free-State men that they had only to frame a constitution and it would command the support of the Illinois Senator. In October he was elected president of a convention assembled at Topeka which framed and adopted a constitution ratified a month later by the voters of the party. The "Topeka Movement" was interrupted by the Wakarusa War in December, during which Lane fortified Lawrence against pro-slavery Missourians and, had it not been for the cautious Robinson (Charles Robinson [*q.v.*], leader of the anti-slavery forces), might have taken the offensive. This crisis was a turning point in Lane's career. He was essentially a conservative until the hysteria of exciting events produced the proper background for radical leadership. A "state" government was organized in March 1856, and Lane and Andrew H. Reeder [*q.v.*] were elected to the Senate by the would-be legislature.

Lane immediately went to Washington to labor for the admission of Kansas, armed with a memorial framed by the "Senators and Representatives of the General Assembly of the State of Kansas." It was favorably received in the House but was rejected by the Senate, where Douglas and other Administration leaders pronounced it a fraud and a forgery, largely upon technical grounds. Douglas refused to be drawn into a duel, and Lane toured the Northwest to lay the cause of Kansas before the people. Since the Missouri River had been closed to emigrants from the Northern states he opened a new route via Iowa and Nebraska, and through this channel "Lane's Army of the North" invaded Kansas. Arriving in August 1856 he attacked pro-slavery strongholds, and his men committed depredations fully as atrocious as those of the "border ruffians." Peace was restored upon the arrival of Gov. J. W. Geary [*q.v.*] in September.

After spending the following winter in the East, Lane returned to the Territory in March 1857. He opposed participation in the Lecompton movement but favored contesting the October election for members of the territorial legislature. This policy was adopted, and the Free-State party gained control of the General Assembly, which immediately elected Lane major-general of militia. Following the homicide of Gaius Jenkins, June 3, 1858, Lane retired from politics, but emerged in 1859 to become a Republican candidate for the Senate, and when the state was admitted in 1861 he reached the goal of his ambition.

Arriving in Washington in April 1861, he immediately raised a "Frontier Guard" which bivouacked in the East Room of the Executive Mansion for a few days. This episode marked the beginning of an intimate friendship with Lincoln which gave Lane influence and prestige in the management of Kansas affairs in Washington. In June 1861 Lincoln appointed him brigadier-general of volunteers with authority to raise two regiments. During September and October this "Kansas Brigade" operated against Confederate forces under Gen. Sterling Price in western Missouri and "jayhawked" property of both Union and Confederate sympathizers. Returning to the Senate in December, Lane demanded an aggressive winter campaign. The President, who admired his tireless activity and infectious enthusiasm, tendered him the command of an expedition from the department of Kansas into Arkansas and the Indian country, but a controversy with Gen. David Hunter, the departmental commander, prevented the "Great Southern Expedition" from materializing.

Although Lane had expressed anti-slavery convictions as a member of Congress from Indiana, he went to Kansas declaring that his attitude toward the institution there would depend upon the suitability of the soil and climate for hemp production. In 1857, however, he announced himself a "crusader for freedom." At the outbreak of war he asserted that "slavery would not survive the march of the Union Army," and his brigade assisted many blacks in escaping from Arkansas and Missouri. As recruiting commissioner for Kansas he assembled a regiment of negroes which was mustered Jan. 13, 1863, perhaps the second to be officially received into Union service.

The Lane-Robinson feud which began in the territorial period continued with credit to neither of the principals. In the Kansas election of 1862 indorsement of Lane became the chief issue, and dissatisfied Republicans, supported by Democrats, bolted the regular ticket. He was denounced as an "infamous demagogue" with "an insatiable thirst for power," but the result of the election was regarded as a Lane triumph. His enemies increased and in the legislative session of 1864 they sought to end his political career by electing Gov. Thomas Carney [*q.v.*] to the Senate. Since Lane's term would not expire for over a year the premature election was branded "a fraud upon the people." Lane stumped the state the following summer and, aided by opportune military events, secured the election of a friendly legislature which returned him to the Senate by an almost unanimous vote. As early as December 1863 Lane advocated the reëlection of Lincoln, and his Cooper Institute speech a few months later was a timely review of the Administration's successes. He was a delegate to the Baltimore convention, and in the Grand Council of the Union League which assembled the evening before, he defended the President's record. In the campaign which followed he represented Kansas on the National Committee, and as chairman of the "National Union Committee for the West," he urged northwestern radicals to support Lincoln. He was a strong advocate of western expansion and gave the Homestead and Pacific Railroad bills his undivided support. He secured a grant of land to Kansas to aid the construction of the Leavenworth, Lawrence & Fort Gibson, and the Atchison, Topeka & Santa Fé railroads. In the reconstruction of seceded states he deserted the radicals and reverted to conservatism. Accepting the perdurance theory, he advocated a "Topeka Movement" for Arkansas, Louisiana, and Tennessee as the best method of combating "bogus authority." His support of President Johnson's veto of the Civil Rights Bill caused almost universal condemnation in Kansas as "misrepresenting a radical constituency." Depressed by his cold reception at home, overworked, mentally deranged, charged with financial irregularities connected with Indian contracts, he shot himself on July 1, 1866, but lingered ten days, dying July 11.

Lane's great service to Kansas in the territorial period lay in his organization of various anti-slavery factions into a compact Free-State party. Albeit the movement which he led for statehood was destined to fail, it gave the members of that party a common purpose which united them until the pro-slavery legislature was overthrown. Furthermore, Northern men in Kansas had implicit faith in Lane's military capacity which gave them confidence in contests with "border ruffians." After the beginning of the Civil War, he was a pioneer in advocating emancipation and enlistment of negroes. Indigent, ambitious, provocative, magnetic, he was primarily an agitator. His "demoralized wardrobe," his unkempt hair and beard, his "lean, haggard, and sinewy figure," all contributed to his success in a frontier political canvass. His use of sarcasm and invective, his crude gestures and his long, bony fore-finger, his harsh and raspy voice made him an effective stump orator. "That he loved Kansas, and that Kansas loved him, is undeniable."

[John Speer, *Life of Gen. James H. Lane* (1896), is eulogistic; Wm. E. Connelley, *James Henry Lane* (1899), is fragmentary; W. H. Stephenson, "The Political Career of General James H. Lane" (*Kan. State Hist. Soc. Pubs.*, vol. III, 1930), emphasizes his political activities but devotes some attention to the military background. See also R. G. Elliott, "The Big Springs Convention," *Trans. Kan. State Hist. Soc.*, vol. VIII (1904); L. W. Spring, "The Career of a Kansas Politician," *Am. Hist. Rev.*, Oct. 1898; W. O. Stoddard, "The Story of a Nomination," *North Am. Rev.*, Mar. 1884; Jacob Stringfellow (N. V. Smith), "Jim Lane," *Lippincott's Mag.*, Mar. 1870; *Kan. State Hist. Soc. Colls.*, vol. XIII (1915); D. W. Wilder, *The Annals of Kansas* (1886); W. H. Stephenson, "Amos Lane, Advocate of Western Democracy," *Ind. Mag. of Hist.*, Sept. 1930; *Cong. Globe*, 1853–66; *War of the Rebellion: Official Records*, ser. I, II, III; *Leavenworth Daily Conservative*, July 12, 1866. The "Webb Scrap Book" (17 vols.), preserved in the Kan. State Hist. Lib., contains copious clippings from a wide range of newspapers, May 1854–Sept. 1856.]

W. H. S.

LANE, JAMES HENRY (July 28, 1833–Sept. 21, 1907), Confederate soldier, educator, was born at Mathews Court House (now Mathews), Va., the son of Walter Gardner and Mary Ann Henry (Barkwell) Lane. His great-grandfather, Ezekiel Lane, had been one of the earliest settlers in Mathews County and the family had been actively associated with political and military affairs in Virginia. His grandfather, William Lane, was a sergeant in the War of 1812, and his father served as a member of the Virginia legislature and as colonel of the Mathews County militia during the Civil War. James Henry received his education in private schools and from tutors on his father's plantation until 1851 when he entered Virginia Military Institute at Lexington, Va., as a sophomore. He graduated July 4, 1854, second in a class of fourteen. Three years later he graduated from the University of Virginia in the scientific course and immediately returned to the Virginia Military Institute, where he was commissioned lieutenant and served as assistant professor of mathematics and assistant instructor in tactics. Subsequently he taught in various private schools and when the Civil War began was serving as professor of natural philosophy and instructor in military tactics in North Carolina Military Institute. He immediately responded to the governor's call for men to serve for one year and was elected major of the 1st Regiment, North Carolina Volunteers. These troops proceeded at once to Virginia; on June 10, 1861, Lane led the scouting party which brought on the battle of Bethel and won for the regiment the title of "Bethel Regiment." He was elected lieutenant-colonel Sept. 1, 1861, and a fortnight later when D. H. Hill [*q.v.*] was made brigadier-general he became colonel of the 28th North Carolina infantry, having reorganized his volunteers into the "state troops" enlisted for the duration of the war. He served with the Army of Virginia during the entire war, participating in all the important engagements. He was twice wounded in the battles of the Peninsular campaign and dangerously wounded at the second battle of Cold Harbor. "For gallant and meritorious conduct" he was recommended for promotion by Generals Lee, Jackson, and Hill, and upon the death of General Branch at Sharpsburg that officer's brigade petitioned that Lane might be assigned to command them. The promotion was made Nov. 1, 1862. He was then twenty-nine years old and was popularly believed to be the youngest brigadier in the army. His brigade promptly dubbed him the "Little General" and presented him with a sword, sash, saddle, and bridle in honor of his promotion. The command of the rear guard on the retreat from Sharpsburg was intrusted to him. At Gettysburg he took active part in Pickett's charge, and again commanded the rear guard in Lee's retreat into Virginia. He surrendered with his brigade at Appomattox.

Lane returned to civil life to find his parents in want and the family plantation wasted. He borrowed $150 and sought employment as a teacher once more. For seven years he taught in private schools in North Carolina and Virginia. In 1872 he became professor of natural philosophy and commandant of the Virginia Polytechnic Institute, where he spent eight years. After a year in the Missouri School of Mines as professor of mathematics he became professor of civil engineering in the Alabama Polytechnic Institute, remaining in this school until June 1907 when he became professor emeritus. He was married in 1869 to Charlotte Randolph Meade.

[T. M. Owen, *Hist. of Ala. and Dict. of Ala. Biog.* (1921), vol. IV; C. A. Evans, *Confed. Mil. Hist.* (1899), vol. IV; *The South in the Building of the Nation* (1909), vol. XII; manuscript material relating to his life in the files of the Dept. of History and Archives, Montgomery, Ala.; W. R. Cox, *Address on the Life and Services of Gen. James H. Lane, Army Northern Va.* (n.d.); *Who's Who in America*, 1907–08; *Montgomery Advertiser*, Sept. 22, 1907.]

H. F.

LANE, JOHN (Apr. 8, 1789–Oct. 10, 1855), Methodist clergyman, and a founder of Vicksburg, Miss., son of William and Nancy Lane, was born in Fairfax County, Va., but when only two years of age was taken by his parents to Elbert County, Ga. His mother, a devout Methodist, so influenced his early life that he often testified that because of her teaching and example, "he had no recollection of having ever sworn a profane oath, uttered a willful falsehood, played a game of cards, drank a dram of ardent spirits as a beverage, or taken a chew of tobacco" (Jones, *post*, p. 400). He spent one year and a half in Franklin College, Ga. While there he decided to enter the Methodist itinerancy, and on

Jan. 12, 1814, was admitted on trial in the South Carolina Annual Conference. In 1815 when Bishop McKendree hesitated, because of Creek uprisings, to send preachers to the Mississippi territory, Lane volunteered for that frontier work and the following year he was a member of the first formal Mississippi Annual Conference of the Methodist Episcopal Church. On Oct. 27, 1819, he was married to Sarah, eldest daughter of Newet Vick.

In 1821 Lane was forced temporarily to leave the itinerancy. His father-in-law, a local Methodist minister, died in 1819, leaving a family of ten children, all of them too young to administer their father's estate. Prior to his death Vick had purchased the land upon which the greater part of the city of Vicksburg, Miss., is now situated. Seeing the commercial possibilities of the site, he had planned to start a city there. Although instructed by Vick's will to carry out his wish, the original executor of the estate felt that it would be more profitable to cultivate cotton on the land and refused to survey and sell the land as building lots. As a result, Lane was appointed to administer the estate. In this work he showed remarkable business ability and despite much litigation executed the plans of his father-in-law and thereby shares with him the honor of being the founder of Vicksburg. Lane became one of the leading merchants of the young city, was a director of the Railroad Bank of Vicksburg, and for a number of years was probate judge of Warren County. In time he was a man of some wealth.

Returning to the itinerancy in 1832, for the next twenty-three years he was an outstanding leader in Mississippi Methodism. He served sixteen years as a presiding elder and was five times sent as a representative to the General Conferences of the Church. As a member of the General Conference of 1844, he was active in the movement that resulted in the schism in the Methodist Episcopal Church and the formation of the Methodist Episcopal Church, South. He was largely responsible for the founding (1839) of Centenary College and was for many years the president of its board of trustees. As president of the Missionary Society of the Mississippi Conference he promoted religious work among the negro slaves. His home in Vicksburg has been described as a "sort of hotel of hospitality." He donated the land for the first Methodist church in Vicksburg, gave horses to many circuit-riders, and often entertained in his own home an entire Methodist annual conference. He contributed liberally to all benevolent causes. His beneficiaries, however, took advantage of his generosity. It is estimated that during his lifetime he paid one hundred thousand dollars of security money. His death came as a result of exposure while nursing members of his family during the yellow-fever epidemic in Vicksburg in 1855.

[T. O. Summers, *Biog. Sketches of Eminent Itinerant Ministers* (1859); W. B. Sprague, *Annals Am. Pulpit*, vol. VII (1859); John G. Jones, *A Complete Hist. of Methodism as Connected with the Miss. Conference of the M. E. Ch. South*, vol. I (1887); *Minutes of the Ann. Conferences of the M. E. Ch. South for the Year 1855* (1878); Dunbar Rowland, *Mississippi* (1907), vol. II; *Vicksburg Weekly Sentinel*, Oct. 17, 1855.]

P. N. G.

LANE, JOSEPH (Dec. 14, 1801–Apr. 19, 1881), soldier, governor, legislator, was born in Buncombe County, N. C., second son of John and Elizabeth Street Lane who soon bore him away to the frontier in Henderson County, Ky. There he attended the common school, but having to support himself took employment under the clerk of the county court. At fifteen he crossed the Ohio and worked as a clerk in a store in Warrick County, Ind. There in 1820 he was married to Polly Pierre. He then settled in Vanderburg County on a river-bank farm which he managed, also buying produce and conducting a flatboat commerce with New Orleans. Here he prospered for twenty-four years, becoming almost at once a prominent community and state leader. He was elected to the lower house of the Indiana legislature as early as 1822 and was reëlected frequently. From 1844 to 1846 he was a member of the Senate. In the Mexican War he led his brigade at Huamantla and in other engagements with such bravery and genius as to emerge one of the outstanding heroes of the war, brevetted major-general.

Returning home in August 1848, he was commissioned in the following December by President Polk to be governor of the Territory of Oregon. He made a winter journey, by the Santa Fé route, to California and on Mar. 2, 1849, arrived at Oregon City, where on the following day he proclaimed the new government. As superintendent of Indian affairs he forced the Cayuse to deliver up the Whitman murderers and began the negotiations with the truculent Rogue River tribe which finally ended with the peace at Table Rock in September 1853. Resigning the governorship June 18, 1850, he was at once chosen delegate in Congress from the territory, was reëlected three times, and when Oregon became a state, Feb. 14, 1859, entered the upper house as United States senator where he remained till Mar. 3, 1861. His public career was now ended. As candidate for vice-president on the Breckinridge ticket, as an open and avowed partisan of the secession movement, he lost his hold upon Oregon, which had become a Republican state in 1860. He retired to his farm near Roseburg and lived in semi-seclusion for twenty years. Nevertheless, his character for honest and fair dealing, his charm of manner and highmindedness, won for him the personal good will and even the friendship of many Oregonians who had become his relentless political enemies.

One much-touted episode of his later career belongs to legend rather than history; namely, his relation to the "Pacific Republic" in aid of the Confederacy. Because he brought home a box containing four rifles, made for him and for three neighbors by a Cincinnati gunmaker, rumor reported that he had brought military equipment to arm co-conspirators in southern Oregon. His accidental wounding by the premature discharge of a horse-pistol carried in the wagon in which a neighbor drove him south from Portland gave rise to all sorts of dramatic embellishments; and the ransacking of his effects while he lay ill at a neighbor's house may have revealed correspondence with men engaged in rebellion. But Lane, while ardently sympathizing with the South, was too much the political realist to undertake the dismemberment of southern Oregon and northern California—especially from Portland as a base! He was one of the ablest and most vivid personalities of his time in western history. His conversational powers were extraordinary; he was an effective public speaker, and an independent thinker on public questions.

[About 2,000 letters of Lane's are in the archives of the Oregon Historical Society. The best general descriptive sketch of his life to 1860 is in John Savage, *Our Living Representative Men* (1860). *Biog. Sketches of Hon. John C. Breckinridge and Gen. Joseph Lane* (1860) is a campaign document. Albert G. Brackett, *Gen. Lane's Brigade in Central Mexico* (1854), illustrates his military career. For Indian affairs his reports to the Indian office are invaluable. Other sources include: G. H. Williams, "Political History of Oregon from 1853 to 1865," *Quart. of the Ore. Hist. Soc.,* Mar. 1901; "Extract of a Letter from Gen. Lane to Senator Nesmith," *Ibid.,* June 1906; C. F. Coan, "The First Stage of the Federal Indian Policy in the Pacific Northwest," *Ibid.,* Mar. 1921; *Biog. Dir. Am. Cong.* (1928); information as to certain facts from Lane's son, Simon Lane.]

J. S—r.

LANE, LEVI COOPER (May 9, 1830–Feb. 18, 1902), surgeon, was born on a farm near Somerville, Butler County, Ohio, the eldest of the nine children of Ira and Hannah (Cooper) Lane. He attended Farmers College, near Cincinnati, and later Union College, Schenectady, N. Y. He graduated in medicine from Jefferson Medical College in 1851 and for the following four years served at Ward's Island, N. Y., as interne and house physician. He passed the examination for entrance to the United States Navy in 1855 and was assigned to duty at the hospital at Quarantine, Staten Island, N. Y. Later he had a tour of sea duty in Central American waters. Resigning from the navy in 1859, he joined his uncle, Dr. Elias Samuel Cooper [*q.v.*], in practice in San Francisco, and was at once appointed professor of physiology in the recently established medical school of the University of the Pacific. This school closed its doors in 1864 following the death of Dr. Cooper, and Lane accepted the chair of physiology in the Toland Medical College, which was started the same year. In 1870 a group from this faculty revived the old Medical College of the Pacific, and Lane became professor of surgery. In 1882 he built and gave to the school a fine brick building, at which time the name was changed to Cooper Medical College in honor of his uncle. He later gave a second building to the school and he began the negotiations which finally resulted in its amalgamation with Stanford University in 1909. He built the Lane Hospital in 1894 as an adjunct to the school.

Lane was a surgeon with original ideas and excellent judgment. For years he had the best of the surgical practice on the Pacific coast, his patients coming from as far as Alaska and Chile. He is credited with having performed the first vaginal hysterectomy in America, with having originated an operation for craniectomy for microcephalus, and he devised improvements in the surgical treatment of harelip. He brought to his surgical practice an exact knowledge of anatomy and excellent judgment of surgical risks. Aseptic surgery was introduced late in his career and he was never able to master its technique. He sought to balance this defect by absurd measures to preserve aseptic conditions in Lane Hospital. He was essentially a student and read Greek and Latin, as well as French, German, and Spanish. He submitted a Latin thesis on external urethrotomy for his examination for the navy. He had a profound knowledge of the history and literature of surgery and made a translation from the German of Billroth's *Surgical Pathology.* He projected an elaborate textbook on surgery in three volumes, but lived only to finish the first, the *Surgery of the Head and Neck* (1896), a work containing a wealth of material with its value greatly affected by poor arrangement. Among his other notable publications are *Ligations for the Cure of Aneurism* (1884), reprinted from the *Pacific Medical and Surgical Journal,* and *Rudolph Virchow* (1893), reprinted from the *Occidental Medical Times.* In 1896 he founded the Lane Lectures, a series designed to introduce to the California profession the most progressive minds of Europe and the eastern United States.

His whole career was handicapped by a frail physique and frequent illness. Asthmatic as a youth, he later suffered from a chronic bronchitis. His physical ills prevented him from taking great part in public affairs, though he was at one time a member of the city and state boards of health and a president of the state medical society. He was married in the early seventies to Mrs. Pauline Cook; they had no children. Lane's name is carried by the main building and by the library of the college that he refounded.

[*Am. Medicine,* Mar. 1, 1902; *Pacific Medic. Jour.,* Mar. 1902; H. A. Kelly and W. L. Burrage, *Am. Medic. Biogs.* (1920); *Annals of Surgery,* Sept. 1928; *San Francisco Call,* Feb. 19, 1902; information from family.]

J. M. P—n.

LANE, Sir RALPH (*c.* 1530–October 1603), colonist, was the second son of Sir Ralph Lane of Horton, Northamptonshire, and his wife Maud, daughter of William, Lord Parr. Of his early life nothing is known. He may have represented Higham Ferrers in the Parliament of 1558 and Northampton in that of 1562 (*Names of Members Returned to Serve in Parliament,* 1878, pt. I, pp. 397, 405). About 1563 he entered the service of Queen Elizabeth as equerry. He engaged in various maritime activities, receiving a commission in 1571 to search certain ships of Brittany reputed to be laden with unlawful goods, permission in 1573 to transport iron guns overseas, a license in 1574 to bring in ships with Portuguese commodities, and a patent in 1576 for searching for and seizing bullion and jewels transported contrary to statute. Active in the struggle between England and Spain, he suggested a plan for raising 10,000 men for service in Flanders, prepared seven ships for action against Spain, and asked to be commissioned "General of the Adventurers" in 1572. He asked to serve against the Spaniards in Ireland, in 1579, or to have the Queen's letters to the "Kings of Fez and Algiers." He was sent into Ireland to erect fortifications in 1583 and remained there for two years. He was appointed sheriff of Kerry but relieved of the office to go with Sir Richard Grenville on a voyage to Virginia for Sir Walter Raleigh. Grenville, Lane, and 107 colonists sailed from Plymouth in seven ships, Apr. 9, 1585, arrived off Cape Fear June 23, and finally settled on Roanoke Island. Lane was left in command of the colony when Grenville sailed for England, Aug. 25. He explored the surrounding country and sent glowing reports of Virginia to Walsingham and to Hakluyt. Realizing that a better harbor was necessary, he favored removal to Chesapeake Bay, but the hostility of the Indians was incurred, supplies failed to arrive, and removal was postponed. Sir Francis Drake, whose fleet appeared off the coast June 8, 1586, offered to outfit Lane with shipping and supplies to last through the summer or to carry the colonists back to England. Lane accepted the first proposition but almost immediately the ship Drake gave him was driven to sea in a four-day storm. Drake offered to furnish another ship, but the discouraged colonists asked to be taken back to England. They embarked June 18 and sailed the following day, arriving at Portsmouth July 27, 1586. Only four men had been lost during the year. Lane wrote an account of Virginia published by Hakluyt in *The Principall Navigations . . . of the English Nation* (1589). After his return to England, he resumed his activities against Spain. He submitted a plan for the defense of the coast in 1587 and was sent into Norfolk to view the forces of the county in the same year. He served as muster master of the camp at West Tilbury in Essex in 1588 and as muster master general of the army sent under Drake and Norris to the coasts of Spain and Portugal in 1589. Through the mediation of Lord Burghley he was made muster master general and clerk of the check of the garrisons in Ireland, Jan. 15, 1592, and remained in Ireland for the duration of his life. He was knighted by the lord deputy, Sir William Fitzwilliam, Nov. 17, 1593 (W. A. Shaw, *The Knights of England,* 1906, II, 90). He asked, Feb. 14, 1595, for the surveyorship of parish clerks in Ireland in order that he might "cess" himself upon them "for chickens and bacon while travelling about the musters." He was wounded in 1594 and from that time on suffered from ill health. Probably for that reason he was unable to perform his duties and charges of negligence were numerous in the years which followed. He seems never to have married. He died and was buried at Dublin.

[*Calendar of State Papers, Domestic Ser.*; *Calendar of State Papers, Ireland*; *Calendar of State Papers, Colonial Ser.*; *Acts of the Privy Council*; Alexander Brown, *The Genesis of the U. S.* (2 vols., 1890); Richard Hakluyt, *Collection of the Early Voyages . . . of the English Nation,* III (1810), 307–40, IV (1811), 26; F. L. Hawks, *Hist. of N. C.,* vol. I (1859); E. E. Hale, in *Trans. and Colls. Am. Antiq. Soc.,* vol. IV (1860); I. N. Tarbox, *Sir Walter Ralegh and His Colony in America* (1884) and H. S. Burrage, *Early English and French Voyages* (1906), both of which reprint Lane's account; Thomas Blore, *The Hist. and Antiquities of the County of Rutland,* I (1811), 169; W. C. Metcalfe, ed., *The Visitations of Northampton-*

shire Made in 1564 and 1618–19 (1887), pp. 185–86; sketch by J. K. Laughton, in *Dict. Nat. Biog.*]

I. M. C.

LANE, TIDENCE (Aug. 31, 1724–Jan. 30, 1806), pioneer Baptist minister of Tennessee, was born near Baltimore, Md., the son of Richard and Sarah Lane. He was the great-grandson of Major Samuel Lane, an officer in the King's service, who was in Maryland as early as 1680; his paternal grandparents were Dutton and Pretitia (Tidings) Lane. At his christening he was given his grandmother's maiden name, Tidings, but in some way or other this was changed to Tidence. The Lanes were typical frontiersmen. They migrated first into Southwestern Virginia, then pushed down into the Yadkin River country, North Carolina. Here, apparently, May 9, 1743, Tidence married Esther Bibbin (or Bibber). Sometime about 1754 Shubael Stearns [*q.v.*], a Separate Baptist evangelist with all the zeal and methods of the New Light persuasion, came into what is now Randolph County, N. C., and established the Sandy Creek Church. What Lane's religious connections up to that time had been is not known except that he had been christened in St. Paul's Church, Baltimore. From what he had heard of Stearns, he had not formed a favorable impression of him, but curiosity led him to make a forty-mile journey to hear him. Stearns had a magnetic influence over his audiences and an eye that exerted almost magical power. He fixed it on Lane, and Lane succumbed. He tried to quit the place, but was drawn back. "Shunning him," he said, "I could no more effect than a bird can shun a rattlesnake when it fixes its eyes upon it" (Burnett, *post*, p. 319). Lane underwent a thorough conversion and was thereafter an effective Baptist preacher after the pattern of Stearns.

The defeat of the Regulators at the battle of Alamance, 1771, led many of the North Carolinians to seek relief from oppression by pushing through the mountains into what is now eastern Tennessee. Among these were a considerable number of the Sandy Creek Church, who settled on Boone Creek, in the present county of Washington. Lane went thither about 1776, and by 1779 at the latest had organized the recent comers into the Buffalo Ridge Baptist Church. By so doing he became the first pastor of the first permanent church body of any denomination in Tennessee. A few years later he moved still farther westward and established himself on Bent Creek, near the present town of Whitesburg, Hamblin County. Here with Rev. William Murphy he organized the Bent Creek Baptist Church in June 1785, which he served as pastor for the remainder of his life. When the Holston Association was instituted in October, the first ecclesiastical association to be formed in Tennessee, Lane became its moderator. He is said to have been "much sought in counsel by the churches. He was not so hard in doctrine as some of his brethren, his doctrinal belief being a modified Calvinism" (Burnett, pp. 321–22). He had seven sons and two daughters. Four of the sons were in the battle of King's Mountain, three of them under Col. John Sevier [*q.v.*].

[J. J. Burnett, *Sketches of Tennessee's Pioneer Baptist Preachers* (1919); S. C. Williams, "Tidence Lane—Tennessee's First Pastor," in *The Baptists of Tenn.* (1930); B. F. Riley, *A Hist. of the Baptists in the Southern States East of the Mississippi* (1898); *N. C. Baptist Hist. Papers*, vol. II (Oct. 1897–July 1898).]

H. E. S.

LANE, WALTER PAYE (Feb. 18, 1817–Jan. 28, 1892), Texas and Confederate soldier, was born in County Cork, Ireland. Some four years after his birth, his parents, William and Olivia Lane, determined to emigrate to America. In 1821 they landed at Baltimore and found their way to Fairview, Guernsey County, Ohio. At the age of eighteen, Lane made a visit to an elder brother who was in business in Louisville, Ky. There he met the Texas commissioners, Austin and Archer, and was soon on his way to Texas, armed with a letter of introduction to Houston. So poor that he traveled part of the way on foot, he arrived in time to join the little army at Groce's ferry and to participate in the memorable campaign of San Jacinto. From this time, an almost insatiable desire for adventure was the mainspring of his career. After a short visit to his home, he was again in Texas, where he joined the crew of the privateer *Thomas Toby,* which, with seven guns and one hundred men, made rich prizes of Mexican vessels in the waters of the Gulf. When the *Thomas Toby* ended her voyages as a wreck in the shoals of Galveston Bay, he was reduced to making his living, for one winter, as a teacher of forty children in a typical neighborhood school. His attempt to take up land on the frontier in Robertson County, Tex., was checked by the Indians, who killed almost all the party of about twenty-four. He was badly wounded and barely escaped with his life. In the comparatively quiet days that followed, he was for two years a clerk in a village store, relieving the monotony of life by joining the army to expel the Cherokees from their homes in north-eastern Texas. At the outbreak of the Mexican War, he organized a company of Texas rangers, which saw much active service in the campaigns of Taylor in northern

Mexico, gained distinction in September 1846 at the capture of Monterey, and was sent on a number of hazardous scouting expeditions, one of which led two hundred miles into the heart of the enemy country. On this occasion, he showed his romantic spirit by going out of his way to gather with pious zeal the bones of the seventeen Mier prisoners who had been shot and buried at Salado three years before. The bodies were sent back for burial in Texas. According to his own account, in his attitude toward the Mexicans he was ruthless and careless of property; on one occasion he defied an order for his arrest delivered in person by his commanding general; but he was so brave and efficient as a scout that he made himself indispensable, and his lapses from military discipline were soon forgotten and forgiven.

After the discovery of gold in California, he alternated between the life of a miner and a merchant, making and losing more than one small fortune in California, Nevada, Arizona, and Peru. At the beginning of the Civil War, he had been living for three years in Marshall, Tex. He promptly enlisted and was at once elected lieutenant-colonel of the 3rd Texas Cavalry. His command saw hard fighting at Wilson's Creek, Pea Ridge, Corinth, where he gained the special praise of Beauregard, and in the closing campaigns against Banks in Louisiana. Before the end of the war, he had become a brigadier-general. He retired to take up again the life of a merchant in Marshall, where he remained a bachelor and made his spacious house a home for numerous nephews and nieces. As the years passed, the old soldier became the symbol of the heroic age in Texas history, and when he died he had long been the idol of the Daughters of the Confederacy and of the Daughters of the Republic of Texas.

[*The Adventures and Recollections of General Walter P. Lane* (copr. 1928); *The Encyclopedia of the New West,* ed. by W. S. Speer and J. H. Brown (1881); *War of the Rebellion: Official Records (Army),* ser. 1, III, VIII, X, pt. 2, XXVI, pt. 1, XXXIV, pt. 1 (1881–91); Alex. Dienst, "The Navy of the Republic of Texas," *The Quarterly of the Texas State Hist. Asso.,* Jan. 1909; *Galveston Daily News,* Jan. 29, 1892.]

R. G. C.

LANE, WILLIAM CARR (Dec. 1, 1789–Jan. 6, 1863), physician, first mayor of St. Louis, governor of New Mexico Territory, was born in Fayette County, Pa., on the farm of Presley Carr and Sarah (Stephenson) Lane, third son among their eleven children. After attending country school in the section where his father was a man of importance, he spent two years in Jefferson College and a year in a prothonotary's office. At twenty-one he matriculated in the two-year course in Dickinson College, and then studied medicine in Louisville and Shelbyville, Ky. In 1813 he volunteered against Tecumseh and was stationed at Fort Harrison, where he became surgeon's mate. Desiring fuller medical knowledge, he resigned from the army to attend lectures, 1815–16, at the University of Pennsylvania, during which time President Madison appointed him post surgeon. On returning to the military service, he joined the operations along the Mississippi, but again soon tired of army routine. While on furlough, he married, Feb. 26, 1818, Mary Ewing of Vincennes, and the next year, at her urging, withdrew from the army to practise in St. Louis. In 1821 Carr Lane, as the settlement of 600 dwellings knew him, was chosen aide-de-camp to Gov. Alexander McNair [*q.v.*], and in successive years named quartermaster-general of Missouri and elected (Apr. 5, 1823), first mayor of St. Louis. His vote, 122, against 70 for Auguste Chouteau and 28 for Marie Philip Leduc, indicated decline of the French influence.

Lane's prophetic message to the aldermen urged the establishment of a free school, and that "a suitable system of improvements may always be kept in view" (Darby, *post,* p. 343). During his first year, wards were established, assessors and health officers appointed, streets defined, and one block even graded and paved. So pleased were the voters they reëlected him annually five times, and nine years later, after they had called him to fill an unexpired term, reëlected him twice more—a record unequaled in St. Louis history. In addition, in 1826, he was elected representative in the legislature as a Democrat. According to a contemporary (*Ibid.,* p. 344), Lane, had he so desired, might, at this time, have been United States Senator in place of Thomas Hart Benton [*q.v.*], with whom he had joined in establishing the first Episcopal church in St. Louis; but he preferred to stand for the national House of Representatives, since in that body there was only one member from Missouri. His party, however, chose Spencer Pettis as its candidate in his stead. Later Lane opposed Jackson and became a Whig. During the Black Hawk War he served again as army surgeon.

In 1852 President Fillmore appointed him governor of New Mexico Territory. The non-coöperation of the military forces at first made it difficult for him to restore order to the chaos, but his administrative ability and energy eventually won the support of influential citizens. He urged stock raising, objected to the enactment of laws in two languages, and made treaties with the Indians. He revived the policy formerly practised by the Mexican and Spanish authorities of keeping the Indians quiet by giving them food, but this policy was not upheld by the government at Washington, and its cessation resulted in an increase of Indian outbreaks. Although desirous of obtaining parts of what later became the Gadsden purchase, Lane took no steps toward expansion. Believing he could do more for the territory as its delegate to Congress, he stood for that post, to miss it by a few votes. At Pierce's election he resigned and returned to St. Louis. His Southern sympathies later made him many enemies.

Lane was large, handsome, warm-hearted and high-tempered. It is said that, challenged to a duel, he called for lighted powder kegs for the contestants to sit upon to see who would be blown the highest. In his last years he urged a municipal waterworks for St. Louis and published a pamphlet, *Water for the City* (1860), in which he recommended the Chain of Rocks site which was later adopted. Survived by his widow and two daughters, he died in his seventy-fourth year and was buried in Bellefontaine Cemetery, leaving a record as lustrous as that of any St. Louisan of the years before the Civil War.

[See John F. Darby, *Personal Recollections* (1880); "Hist. Sketch of Gov. William Carr Lane together with Diary of his Journey from St. Louis, Mo., to Santa Fe, N. M., July 31st, to Sept. 9th, 1852," with annotations by Ralph E. Twitchell, *N. Mex. Hist. Soc. Pubs., No. 20* (1917); "Letters of Willam Carr Lane, 1852–1854," ed. by R. P. Bieber, in *N. Mex. Hist. Rev.*, Apr. 1928; H. H. Bancroft, *Hist. of Ariz. and N. Mex.* (1888); Louis Houck, *A Hist. of Mo.* (1908, vol. III); F. L. Billon, *Annals of St. Louis in its Territorial Days* (1888); Wm. Hyde and H. L. Conard, *Encyc. of the Hist. of St. Louis* (1899); W. B. Stevens, *St. Louis, the Fourth City* (1909); James Cox, *Old and New St. Louis* (1894); information from Mrs. Sarah Glasgow Wilson, Lane's grand-daughter, Dr. Presley Carr Lane, his grand-nephew, and Wm. G. B. Carson, his great-grandson, all of St. Louis. Lane's portrait by Chester Harding [*q.v.*] hangs in the St. Louis Art Museum.]

I. D.

LANG, BENJAMIN JOHNSON (Dec. 28, 1837–Apr. 4, 1909), conductor, composer, pianist, educator, was a son of Benjamin and Hannah (Learoch) Lang, the former of Scottish origin, a successful organist and pianoforte teacher at Salem, Mass., where Benjamin Johnson was born. He was educated in the public schools. His musical education, under his father, began early and in 1850 he played a church organ at Danvers. A year later he was the regular organist at Crombie Street Church, Salem. Thence he went to the First Baptist Church in Boston. In 1855 he continued his studies in Germany as a pupil of Alfred Jaell and a personal protégé of Franz Liszt, who gave him valuable advice. Returning to Boston the young musician began a lifetime of arduous teaching, at first in cooperation with his father and afterward in his own studio. He made his premier concert appearance in 1858 with the Mendelssohn Quintet Club in the first Boston performance of Beethoven's C minor trio, *opus* 1, number 3. He then began to acquire a reputation, which he sustained, for introducing previously unheard music. The list of his "firsts in Boston" grew to be prodigious.

Having become organist of the Old South Church in May 1862, Lang made his début as a conductor at a concert for the first Boston presentation of Mendelssohn's *First Walpurgisnight* with chorus, soli, and full orchestra. He thereafter found himself rapidly advancing as conductor and concert pianist, and in spite of personal handicaps, notably his shyness and somewhat brusque and dictatorial platform manner, he became the foremost New England musician of American birth. One of his triumphs was the Jubilee concert of Jan. 1, 1863, in the Music Hall, celebrating President Lincoln's Emancipation Proclamation. On this occasion he shared the musical honors with Carl Zerrahn. When the Apollo Club, of male singers, was formed in 1871, Lang was engaged as its first conductor. Its programs, deposited in the Boston Public Library, attest the enterprise with which "B. J.," as he was familiarly known in Boston, sought out new musical works and trained his amateur vocalists to present. In 1874 Lang took on also the conductorship of the Cecilia Society, a mixed chorus. These societies, under his baton, gave New England many remarkable concerts.

When Hans von Bülow visited Boston in 1875 he quarreled with the conductor whom he had engaged. Lang was called in at short notice and with great éclat conducted the first performance on any stage of the Tschaikowsky B flat minor concerto. In June 1877, upon the request of the governor of Massachusetts, he organized and directed a concert in honor of President Hayes, presented by the Apollo Club. Such honors entitled him, so many of his friends thought, to be considered for the conductorship of the Boston Symphony Orchestra when it was founded, but this honor never came to him. In 1891 he made one of his most spectacular successes in bringing to Boston the orchestra of the Metropolitan Opera Company, with famous singers, for a concert performance of Wagner's *Parsifal*. In 1895 he became conductor of the Händel and Haydn Society. In addition to these activities he also composed various musical works, including the oratorio *David*, several symphonies and overtures, and many church pieces and songs. Lang was married, in 1861, to Frances Morse Burrage, by whom he had three children. He died of pneumonia in the spring of 1909 and was buried from King's Chapel, where he had been organist since 1885.

[See W. F. Apthorp, sketch in *Music,* Aug. 1893; Ethel Syford, "The Apollo Club of Boston," *New Eng. Mag.,* Apr. 1910; *Jour. of School Music,* May 1909; *Musical Courier,* May 22, 1901; *Boston Transcript,* Apr. 5, 7, 1909. Volumes II, III, and IV of clippings in the Allen A. Brown music library, Boston Public Library, contain many references to Lang, and there is an autobiographical sketch in the program of the Cecilia Society's memorial concert given on Apr. 18, 1909.]

F. W. C.

LANGDELL, CHRISTOPHER COLUMBUS (May 22, 1826–July 6, 1906), professor of law, legal author, the son of John Langdell, was born in New Boston, a small farming town of New Hampshire. His paternal ancestors were English, but it was from the family of his Scotch-Irish mother, Lydia Beard, that he inherited his intellectual power. His early education was in district schools, and he began to teach at the age of eighteen with no other equipment. Encouraged to believe that he could work his way through college, he entered Phillips Exeter Academy in 1845, and with the aid of his sisters succeeded in graduating there and entering Harvard as a sophomore in the class of 1851. In the winter of the next year he was given leave of absence in order to teach school, and did not return to college, but after a brief period of study in an Exeter law office, entered the Harvard Law School in 1851. He remained there for three years, being librarian as well as student most of the time. His ability was soon recognized, and Prof. Theophilus Parsons employed his assistance in the preparation of his treatise, *The Law of Contracts* (2 vols., 1853–55). Many of the most valuable notes in Parsons' book were written by Langdell. During his stay at the Law School, he saw something of Charles W. Eliot [*q.v.*], then a junior in the College. Eliot, years afterwards, recalling his talks with Langdell, said: "He was generally eating his supper . . . , standing in front of the fire and eating with good appetite a bowl of brown bread and milk. I was a mere boy, only eighteen years old; but it was given me to understand that I was listening to a man of genius" (Lewis, *post,* p. 475).

In December 1854, Langdell began practise in New York City. By chance, while studying in the Law Institute of that city, he was able to supply Charles O'Conor [*q.v.*] with a reference, and thereafter assisted O'Conor in several important cases. Langdell did not often appear in court, and was not widely known, but became recognized by a number of leaders of the bar as an able lawyer. In 1870 his old friend Eliot, then recently made president of Harvard, invited him to become Dane Professor (afterwards dean) in the Harvard Law School. He accepted and, in collaboration with Eliot, introduced striking changes. Theretofore no examination had been a prerequisite to the degree of bachelor of laws. Examinations were now insisted upon, and, though each instructor was allowed to adopt the mode of teaching he thought best, Langdell determined that the students in his own classes should be trained to use original authorities and to derive for themselves, under his guidance, the principles of the law. He published for this purpose *A Selection of Cases on the Law of Contracts* (1871), *A Selection of Cases on Sales of Personal Property* (1872), and *Cases on Equity Pleading* (1875). To these selections were added brief summaries of the principles developed by the cases. In two instances these summaries were afterwards enlarged and published separately: *A Summary of Equity Pleading* (1877) and *A Summary of the Law of Contracts* (1879). *A Brief Survey of Equity Jurisdiction* was published in 1905.

In the preface to the *Cases on the Law of Contracts* Langdell stated the theory of teaching on which he acted: "Law, considered as a science, consists of certain principles or doctrines. To have such a mastery of these as to be able to apply them with constant facility and certainty to the ever-tangled skein of human affairs, is what constitutes a true lawyer; and hence to acquire that mastery should be the business of every earnest student of law. Each of these doctrines has arrived at its present state by slow degrees; in other words, it is a growth, extending in many cases through centuries. This growth is to be traced in the main through a series of cases; and much the shortest and best, if not the only way of mastering the doctrine effectually is by studying the cases in which it is embodied. But the cases which are useful and necessary for this purpose at the present day bear an exceedingly small proportion to all that have been reported. The vast majority are useless and worse than useless for any purpose of systematic study. Moreover, the number of fundamental legal doctrines is much less than is commonly supposed; the many different guises in which the same doctrine is constantly making its appearance, and the great extent to which legal treatises are a repetition of each other, being the cause of much misapprehension. If these doctrines could be so classified and arranged that each should be found in its proper place, and nowhere else, they would cease to be formidable from their number."

The method of teaching used by Langdell, though accepted with enthusiasm by his pupils and soon adopted by his colleagues, met with vigorous criticism both from the bar and from teachers in other law schools. The quality of the student-body was improved by the examinations which weeded out idlers, but the number of students in the school for many years remained less than it had been under the former régime. It was only by degrees, as graduates of the new school proved their capacity, that criticism abated. Not until 1890 was the case method used in any other law school. In that year William A. Keener [*q.v.*], one of Langdell's pupils, resigned his Harvard professorship to join the faculty of the Columbia Law School, and introduced the method of teaching he had learned from Langdell. Thereafter the spread of this method of teaching and the growth of the Harvard Law School were rapid. Langdell was fortunate in having as one of his early pupils James Barr Ames [*q.v.*], whose success in applying his teacher's method did much to popularize it. From youth, Langdell suffered from weakness of the eyes, and before he had been teaching many years in Cambridge the infirmity increased so that he was obliged to employ a reader, and could not carry on colloquies with students as part of his method of teaching. This subjected him to a disadvantage in his later years. He continued, however, to give instruction until 1900, though resigning his position as dean in 1895. In spite of the facts that he was the originator of a striking change in the method of legal instruction, and was independent and original in his writings on the law, Langdell was by temperament strongly conservative. He sought his legal inspiration from the earlier decisions and disliked variations from older rules of law. He was modest and not overmuch given to speech, but tenacious of his opinions and capable of direct, simple, and logical statement concerning any matter to which he had given attention. Never abating in his work even after he ceased to teach, he carried out with rare consistency in spite of increasing infirmities the early purposes of his life. The Corporation of the University gave his name to the main building of the Harvard Law School and to a professorship. A portion of his fortune is held by the School in trust to devote the income to a purpose always dear to his heart, the aid of poor students of ability. He married on Sept. 22, 1880, Margaret Ellen Huson, who survived him a few years. They had no children.

[Sketches by James Barr Ames in W. D. Lewis, ed., *Great Am. Lawyers,* vol. VIII (1909), and *Harvard Grads. Mag.,* Dec. 1906; by S. F. Batchelder in *Green Bag,* Aug. 1906; by Jeremiah Smith in *Bull. Phillips Exeter Acad.,* Sept. 1906; article by Eugene Wambaugh in the *Nation* (N. Y.), July 12, 1906; *The Centennial Hist. of the Harvard Law School* (1918); S. F. Batchelder, *Bits of Harvard Hist.* (1924); *Harvard Law School Asso., Report of the Ninth Ann. Meeting at Cambridge, June 25, 1895, in Especial Honor of Christopher Columbus Langdell* (1895); *Harvard Law Rev.,* Nov. 1906.]
S. W.

LANGDON, COURTNEY (Jan. 18, 1861–Nov. 19, 1924), educator, was born at Rome, Italy, where his father, William Chauncy Langdon [*q.v.*], was founder and first rector of the American Episcopal Church. His mother was Hannah Agnes Courtney of Virginia. Returning to America in 1862, his father became a member of the joint committee of the American Episcopal Church on Italian Catholic reform, and was sent as a representative to Italy in 1867, residing at Florence from that date until 1873. Courtney was, therefore, educated from his seventh to his thirteenth year in Italian schools. In 1873 his father founded and was the first pastor of Emmanuel Church, Geneva, Switzerland. There his son attended school during his fourteenth and fifteenth years. The father became rector of Christ Church, Cambridge, Mass., in 1876, and there Courtney knew Longfellow as a neighbor. When he entered Harvard in 1878, he had, as he expressed it, three mother tongues, and he cultivated them all to the close of his life. He remained at Harvard three years.

He was an instructor in modern languages at Lehigh University (1882–84), a private tutor in Baltimore (1884–86), and an instructor in Romance languages at Cornell (1886–90). He was then called to Brown University as assistant professor of modern languages. His field was later narrowed to Romance languages and literatures, of which he was made professor in 1898. In 1891 Brown gave him the rare honorary degree of bachelor of arts. During his thirty-four years at Brown he was an important force in the cultural life of the University. In his lectures his chief effort was to interpret the thought of his author in its application to modern life. From another point of view, his lectures formed a review of the spiritual record of the human race, the authors whom he chiefly considered being Homer, Virgil, Dante, Shakespeare, Molière, Milton, and Browning. He paid very little heed to the technical limits of his subject, and many a Brown graduate found his mental awakening in Langdon's lecture room. Various Langdoniana made up of his classroom sayings have found their way into print. His interest in the life of the students went far beyond the college walls. He followed with enthusiasm all their activities and was a favorite speaker at student gatherings. As a public lecturer on many themes in literature and the philosophy of life he was in wide demand.

His thought on religious matters is represented by *A Plea for a Spiritual Philosophy,* published in pamphlet form a year after his death. The World War stirred him to the depths of his nature, and in 1917 he published *Sonnets on the War.* He made a translation of Rostand's *Chantecler,* but owing to copyright difficulties, it was never published. His great work was his translation of Dante (*The Divine Comedy of Dante Alighieri,* 3 vols., 1918–21), with the original and the translation on opposite pages. The translation was in blank verse, extremely clear and readable. He had passed his boyhood in Dante's city, and Dante's language to him had conversational values that not all scholars recognize. While he made his translation in the light of the best modern scholarship, what makes it distinctive is the introductory comment given in his interpretative analyses. These form his spiritual legacy to the world. During the last months of his life he was engaged upon a translation of Ferrero's *Roman Historians,* which he finished only half an hour before his death. His final visit to Italy, in 1924, was made in part for the purpose of conferring with Ferrero. At this time he was made a Commander of the Crown of Italy, an honor which he highly prized. In his spiritual development he acknowledged a deep obligation to his older Cornell associate, Hiram Corson [*q.v.*]; later he found in Bergson an elaboration of his own philosophy. In 1883 he married Julia H. Bolles, of Olean, N. Y., by whom he had a daughter who died in infancy. This marriage was terminated by divorce and, Aug. 1, 1894, he married Susan Hayward Taft, of Uxbridge, Mass. He died in Providence, R. I., survived by his widow and six sons.

[*Who's Who in America,* 1924–25; *Brown Alumni Mo.,* Dec. 1924; Brown University archives; *Providence Jour.,* Nov. 20, 1924; *Publishers' Weekly,* Dec. 6, 1924; information from his widow and a brother, W. C. Langdon.]

H. L. K.

LANGDON, JOHN (June 26, 1741–Sept. 18, 1819), merchant and politician, son of John and Mary (Hall) Langdon, brother of Woodbury Langdon [*q.v.*], and great-grandson of Tobias Langdon who came to America before 1660, was born at Portsmouth, N. H., where his father's family had settled in the preceding century. He attended a local grammar school, served an apprenticeship as a clerk, went to sea, and later engaged in commercial ventures on his own account. By the outbreak of the Revolution he had acquired considerable property. He was a supporter of the revolutionary movement from the beginning and in 1774 took part in one of the first overt acts against British authority, the seizure and removal of munitions from the Portsmouth fort.

In 1775 he was speaker in the legislature and attended the Continental Congress. The journals of the latter body show that he had numerous duties, being a member of committees on the purchase of woolen goods and ordnance, and with Franklin, John Adams, and other notables, of another committee "to make enquiry in all the colonies, after virgin lead, and leaden ore, and the best methods of collecting, smelting, and refining it." On June 25, 1776, he was appointed agent for Continental prizes in New Hampshire and throughout the war was active in varied duties connected with this post. The state and Continental records contain correspondence and reports which show his responsibility for securing lead, powder, gunlocks, flints, blankets, rum, and similar military supplies. He was among the first to appreciate the possibilities of naval operations against British commerce and built several ships of war for the government. His private ventures are reported to have been successful and he came through the period with his fortune unimpaired. On Feb. 2, 1777, he married Elizabeth, the sixteen-year-old daughter of John Sherburne.

In 1777 he began a period of four years as speaker in the legislature, and in the same year performed one of his greatest services by organizing and financing General Stark's expedition against General Burgoyne. Tradition has it that on this occasion he pledged his plate and sold seventy hogsheads of Tobago rum to secure the necessary funds. He led a body of militia in person and was present at the surrender of the British army at Saratoga. Later he also commanded a detachment of New Hampshire troops in the Rhode Island campaign. In 1783 he was again a delegate in Congress, in 1784 state senator, and a year later served his first term as chief executive or president of New Hampshire. In 1786–87 he was again speaker in the legislature and at the close of the session attended the Constitutional Convention in Philadelphia, paying his own expenses and those of his colleague Nicholas Gilman because of the depleted condition of the treasury. Much of the important work of the convention had been done before his arrival, but Madison's notes show that he was a strong advocate of adequate powers for the new government in the fields of commercial regulation, defense, and taxation. At the close of the convention he attended another session of Congress. In the following year he was a member of the New Hampshire ratifying convention and served another term as state president, resigning in

January 1789 to enter the United States Senate on the organization of the new government.

He served two full terms in the Senate, being president *pro tempore* throughout the First and the greater part of the Second Congress. Since he was a commercial leader, an extensive holder of Continental securities, and a friend of Washington, it is not surprising that for a time at least he showed Federalist predilections. He supported the funding system and the creation of the United States Bank, but opposed the assumption of state debts. It is not clear just when he began to backslide into the Republican ranks. Soon after his death Jefferson wrote, "We were fellow labourers from the beginning of the 1st to the accomplishment of the 2nd revolution in our government, of the same zeal and the same sentiments" (*Letters by Washington,* etc., *post,* p. 47). In 1794 there was considerable opposition to his reëlection, and when, in the following year he voted against the ratification of the Jay Treaty he was definitely placed in the opposition. He had decided French sympathies, a fact noted by the minister of France in 1788, and was naturally a strong opponent of the policies of President Adams in the embroglio of 1798–99.

After his retirement from the Senate in 1801, he declined President Jefferson's offer of the secretaryship of the navy, but was active in organizing the Republican party in New Hampshire. He served in the legislature from 1801 to 1805, the last two terms as speaker, and from 1802 on contested the governorship annually with John T. Gilman until in 1805 he was successful. He was reëlected thenceforth every year till 1811, with the exception of 1809 when his support of the Embargo cost him his place. In 1812 he retired from active politics, declining the Republican nomination for the vice-presidency, tendered him by the congressional caucus, on the ground that his faculties were becoming blunted and he could not face further responsibilities.

Although there is nothing in Langdon's record which indicates genius, he was unquestionably a man of good sense, thorough patriotism, and fine character. Contemporaries, friends and opponents alike, bear witness to his personal charm. Although he has been described as frugal and fond of money, he entertained on a generous scale. The Marquis de Chastellux, one of his guests, described him as "a handsome man and of a noble carriage" and his residence as "elegant and well furnished" (*Travels in North America in the years, 1780–81–82,* 1787, II, 232).

[J. L. Elwyn, "Some Account of John Langdon," in *Early State Papers of N. H.*, XX (1891), 850–80; brief sketch by Wm. Plumer, *Ibid.*, XXI (1892), 804–12; for portrait, E. S. Stackpole, *Hist. of N. H.* (1916), vol. II; *Letters by Washington, Adams, Jefferson and Others, Written during and after the Revolution to John Langdon* (1880); C. A. Beard, *An Economic Interpretation of the Constitution of the U. S.* (1913); W. R. Cutter, *New England Families* (1913), vol. II; E. C. Burnett, *Letters of Members of the Continental Cong.* (5 vols., 1921–31); Max Farrand, *The Records of the Federal Convention of 1787* (3 vols., 1927); *N. H. Gazette* (Portsmouth), Sept. 21, 1819.]

W. A. R.

LANGDON, SAMUEL (Jan. 12, 1723–Nov. 29, 1797), Congregational clergyman and president of Harvard College, was born in Boston, Mass. He was the youngest child of Samuel and Esther (Osgood) Langdon. Although his father was a housewright or builder in rather humble circumstances, Samuel was prepared for college at the South Grammar School, and entered Harvard in 1736. Upon graduating in 1740, in the same class with Samuel Adams, he went to Portsmouth, N. H., where he took charge of the grammar school and acquired a reputation for learning and piety. In 1745 he went to Louisbourg as chaplain of the New Hampshire regiment and in the same year he became assistant to the Rev. Jabez Fitch of the North Church in Portsmouth. Two years later he succeeded Fitch as pastor, in which capacity he continued to serve most acceptably until 1774. His sermons were prepared with great care and he was the recognized head of the Piscataqua Association of ministers.

For his services in the Louisbourg expedition Langdon was granted land near Conway, N. H. Possibly it was this incident that led him to become interested in the geography and resources of the province. In 1756 he drew for Gov. Benning Wentworth a map of New Hampshire which became the basis of one that Langdon and Col. Joseph Blanchard published in London in 1761. The latter was dedicated to Charles Townshend, secretary at war, and it is said that this compliment led directly to the degree of doctor of theological studies which Langdon received from the University of Aberdeen in 1762.

According to his kinsman, the Rev. John Eliot, Samuel Langdon was elected to the presidency of Harvard College more because of "his character, as a zealous whig" than because of "his reputation in the republick of letters." Several officers of the college were pro-British, and John Hancock, the treasurer, was convinced that an out-and-out Whig was needed for the presidency. Accordingly Langdon was elected in 1774. But he did not enjoy the years that followed. War conditions prevailed, nerves were overwrought, and Langdon "did not receive all that kindness from the students and officers, or legislature of the college, which his character, as a scholar and a christian, merited" (Eliot, *post,* pp. 291–92). In August 1780, he asked the Corporation to accept his resignation. It was unfortunate that he took this step just two days after an impudent committee of students had suggested that he do so.

During the remaining seventeen years of his life he was the beloved pastor of Hampton Falls, N. H. His term of service there was quiet, useful, and happy. In 1788 he was a member of the New Hampshire convention for ratifying the federal Constitution. He bequeathed his library to the church for the use of the ministers of Hampton Falls. He was buried in the old cemetery in that town. Langdon was married, in 1748, to Elizabeth Brown, daughter of the Rev. Richard Brown of Reading, Mass. Five of their children lived to maturity, and three of these left descendants. His chief literary production was *Observations on the Revelation of Jesus Christ to St. John* (1791).

[F. B. Sanborn's biographical sketch in *Mass. Hist. Soc. Proc.,* 2 ser., XVIII (1905), 192–232, is sympathetic and informing, and a good antidote to John Eliot's account of Langdon in his *Biog. Dict. of the First Settlers and Other Eminent Characters . . . in New England* (1809) and to some of Josiah Quincy's observations in his *Hist. of Harvard Univ.* (1840), II, 161–200, 509–22. See also *Catalogue of the Boston Public Latin School* (1886); W. B. Sprague, *Annals Am. Pulpit,* vol. I (1857); Nathaniel Adams, *Annals of Portsmouth* (1825); Warren Brown, *Hist. of Hampton Falls* (1900); *Literary Diary of Ezra Stiles* (3 vols., 1901), ed. by F. B. Dexter; *Extracts from the Itineraries of Ezra Stiles* (1916), ed. by F. B. Dexter; "Belknap Papers," in *Mass. Hist. Soc. Colls.,* 6 ser. IV (1891); *Columbian Centinel* (Boston), Dec. 6, 1797.]

L. S. M.

LANGDON, WILLIAM CHAUNCY (Aug. 19, 1831–Oct. 29, 1895), Protestant Episcopal clergyman, was born in Burlington, Vt., the son of John Jay Langdon and Harriet Curtis (Woodward), great-grand-daughter of Eleazar Wheelock [*q.v.*], founder of Dartmouth College. Because of the mother's health, the family moved first to Washington, D. C., where in 1835 the father was a clerk in the United States Treasury, and then to Louisiana, whence he went to the Mexican War as colonel of the 1st Louisiana Regiment. William graduated from Transylvania University, Lexington, Ky., in 1850, and for a year thereafter was adjunct professor of astronomy at Shelby College, Kentucky. In 1851 he was appointed assistant examiner in the United States Patent Office, Washington, becoming chief examiner in 1855. The next year he resigned, and went into the practice of patent law.

In 1852, with Thomas Duncan, William J. Rhees, and Zalmon Richards, he started the Washington Young Men's Christian Association. Two years later, at a convention in Buffalo, he took the lead in founding the American Confederation of Young Men's Christian Associations, of which he was chosen first general secretary. He also made influential contributions to the coördinating of the various Y.M.C.A. societies of Europe at the Paris meeting of 1855 and to the establishing of definite relations between the American and European organizations. Through this work he came to realize the practicability of cooperation among Christian denominations. In 1854 he organized and conducted a system of inter-denominational mission Sunday schools for boys and girls in Washington. Finding greater interest in these activities than in the patent law, he decided to enter the ministry, and on Feb. 28, 1858, was ordained deacon in the Protestant Episcopal Church. In the same year he married Hannah Agnes Courtney, daughter of Enoch Sullivan Courtney, a merchant of Richmond and Baltimore.

During a trip to Europe in 1857 his attention had been attracted to the Old Catholic Movement, an endeavor to restore in the Roman Catholic Church the principles and practice of the early Christian church. Seeing in such restored conditions of early Christianity the common ground on which the reunion of the Christian churches could be effected, he thenceforth took an active interest in the movement. In 1859, having been advanced to the priesthood, he went to Rome where he started an Episcopal church for American residents and tourists, which became St. Paul's Inside the Walls. He returned to America in 1862 and for three years during the Civil War was rector of St. John's Church, Havre de Grace, Md. He presented a memorial to the General Convention of the Protestant Episcopal Church of 1865 on conditions in Italy and was sent back to that country to be the representative of his Church among the Old Catholics. Settling in Florence, he lived there until 1873 and established an Episcopal church, St. James's, for American residents and tourists. Upon the death of the editor of *L'Esaminatore,* the official organ of the Old Catholics, he succeeded to his post. In 1873 he moved to Geneva, where he started Emmanuel Church for American residents and tourists. He attended the Old Catholic congresses at Cologne and Bonn in 1872, 1873, 1874, and 1875.

Returning to the United States, he became the rector of Christ Church, Cambridge, Mass., in 1876, but on account of failing health resigned two years later. From 1883 to 1890 he was rector of St. James Church, Bedford, Pa. He then moved to Providence, R. I., where he started a mission which afterward became St. Martin's.

During his last years he lived with his son, Courtney Langdon [*q.v.*], in Providence, and was connected as an honorary assistant with Grace Church there.

Throughout the latter part of his career he devoted himself mainly to an effort to reunite Catholic and Protestant churches on the basis of their common rule of faith, their common Catholic doctrine, their two common sacraments, and the historic ministry. He organized a group of scholars known as the Sociological Group, which developed into the League of Catholic Unity. These influential men tried to effect a union of the Episcopal, Presbyterian, and Congregational churches, but the retrogressive attitude taken by the Protestant Episcopal General Convention of 1895 put to an end for the time any progress in that direction. The keen disappointment over this result proved the last straw of burden on Langdon's exhausted strength. He died a few days thereafter, on Oct. 29, 1895. At his funeral in Grace Church, Providence, on All Saints' Day, some thirty-five clergy of eleven different churches were present and partook of the Holy Communion together.

[Papers in the possession of the Langdon family, the National Council of the Y.M.C.A., and the International Y.M.C.A. College at Springfield, Mass.; papers of the Old Catholic Church in America; Wm. Chauncy Langdon, "The Story of My Early Life" (MS.), and "The Early Story of the Confederation of the Y.M.C.A.," in *Year Book of the Young Men's Christian Associations of the U. S. and Canada*, 1888; L. Doggett, *Hist. of the Young Men's Christian Asso.* (1922), vol. II; *N. Y. Tribune*, Oct. 30, 1895; *Providence Jour.*, Oct. 30, 1895.] G. E. S.

LANGDON, WOODBURY (1738 or 1739–Jan. 13, 1805), merchant, was the elder son of John and Mary (Hall) Langdon, and the brother of Gov. John Langdon [*q.v.*]. The exact date of his birth is not known, but without doubt the place was Portsmouth, N. H., where the Langdon family had been established since the middle of the seventeenth century. His father, a farmer on the outskirts of the town, was now and then elected a selectman. His mother was descended from Gov. Thomas Dudley of Massachusetts-Bay. Woodbury attended the Latin grammar school, which was kept by an excellent master, Major Samuel Hale, and then entered the counting-room of Henry Sherburne, a prominent merchant of Portsmouth. In 1765 he married Sherburne's daughter, Sarah. His commercial ventures were successful and in 1770 he was accounted a rich man. As the dissensions with the British government increased, he took the conservative side. In 1770 he was influential in keeping Portsmouth out of the non-importation agreement (Portsmouth Town Records, MS., vol. II, folio 246), and in town meeting, Dec. 16, 1773, he registered his disapproval of a series of resolutions which were passed condemning the British government's new policy. Nevertheless, Portsmouth elected him to the provincial Assembly in the spring of 1774, to the revolutionary convention at Exeter in the following summer, and reëlected him to the Assembly in February 1775.

After war broke out Langdon went to England to conserve "a considerable sum of money" belonging to him there. Much of what he did during the next two years is a mystery. He visited France twice, and Lord George Germain believed that he was concerting a plan of trade between that country and the United States. When Langdon returned to America in the summer of 1777, he landed at New York and was held a prisoner within the British lines. In December 1777 he escaped and returned to Portsmouth (*Literary Diary of Ezra Stiles,* 1901, edited by F. B. Dexter, II, 240).

In the spring of 1779 Langdon was elected to the Continental Congress and he took his seat in the following autumn. In 1780, 1781, and 1785 he was reëlected, but on each occasion declined to serve. Instead, he remained in New Hampshire, where he held various offices. His appointment as a justice of the superior court in 1785 had unpleasant consequences. On June 17, 1790, he was impeached by the House of Representatives for neglecting his duty, specifically for not holding court at various places in 1789 and 1790. The trial was held in January 1791, but it came to naught, and Langdon was allowed to resign. Meanwhile he had been appointed one of the federal commissioners for settling the accounts between the United States and individual states. In 1796 and again in 1797 he ran for Congress as the Republican candidate, but was not elected.

Langdon was a handsome man, but he lacked the winning manners of his brother John. His contemporary, William Plumer, wrote of him (*post,* p. 815): "He was a man of great independence and decision—bold, keen, and sarcastic, and spoke his mind of men and measures with great freedom. . . . He was naturally inclined to be arbitrary and haughty, but his sense of what was right, and his pride prevented him from doing intentional evil."

[The best biographical sketch of Langdon is that by Wm. Plumer in *Early State Papers of N. H.*, XXI (1892), 812–15. The course of his impeachment and trial may be followed in vol. XXII (1893) of the same series. A few of his letters are included in the Langdon MSS. of the N. H. Hist. Soc. An obituary appeared in the *New Hampshire Gazette* (Portsmouth), Jan. 29, 1805.] L. S. M.

LANGE, ALEXIS FREDERICK (Apr. 23, 1862–Aug. 28, 1924), educator, was born in Lafayette County, Mo., the son of Alexander and Caroline (Schnegelsiepen) Lange, natives of Bavaria, Germany. His education was begun in local elementary and high schools. Entering the University of Michigan in 1882, he had, by 1885, attained with distinction both the baccalaureate degree and the degree of master of arts, specializing in German, English, and Anglo-Saxon. The period 1886–87 he spent in Europe as a student, first at the University of Marburg, then at the University of Berlin. Upon his return to America, he became successively instructor in English and professor of German and Anglo-Saxon at his Alma Mater. He also resumed his studies for the degree of Ph.D., completing the requirements in 1892, after he had joined the faculty of the University of California.

His California career began in 1890 with his appointment as assistant professor of English. From the outset he became known as one of the successful teachers of the University. In 1907 he was persuaded by President Benjamin Ide Wheeler to transfer his interest to the field of education and to assume the headship of that department, where he developed a philosophy of administration within the University, and, later, in the organization of the state school system. He acted as dean of the College of Letters from 1897 to 1909, during which time he laid the foundation for the present organization of this college, by providing for lower division work, in which students were required to lay a general cultural foundation through contacting a partially restricted curriculum; and upper division work, in which the student entered upon specialization. During 1909–10, he served as dean of the Graduate Division, and organized the graduate work along modern lines. From 1910 to 1913 he acted as dean of the faculties, a position equivalent to the vice-presidency in many universities. When the School of Education was organized in 1913, he was made its director, and in 1922, its dean.

He was a stanch advocate of the theory that the school must maintain close relationship with the people. To assure this connection, he insisted, the system should be under lay control but should have the leadership and guidance of professionally trained experts. He was the leading instrumentality in securing, in 1913, the reorganization of the California State Board of Education as a lay board. He also suggested the present system of financing public schools. Later he proposed the program for the organization of the California Teachers Association into a series of sectional bodies with a State Council acting as a clearing house.

It is in the field of secondary education, however, that his influence has been most notable. Long before the founding of junior high schools or junior colleges, he was advocating a plan that extended from the seventh grade of the older elementary school to the end of the sophomore year of college. He is unquestionably the father of the junior high school movement, and he shares with David Starr Jordan [*q.v.*] the honor of originating the junior-college movement. In his administration of the School of Education, Lange's chief attention was given to the training of high-school teachers. The program which he developed has not been surpassed in any other state and is responsible for the national recognition which the public high schools of California have received. He translated from the work of Johann Friedrich Herbart *Outlines of Educational Doctrine* (1901), and edited *The Gentle Craft* by Thomas Deloney (Berlin, 1903). He was the author of a number of valuable papers, the most important of which were collected after his death and published under the title, *The Lange Book: The Collected Writings of a Great Educational Philosopher* (1927), edited with an introduction by A. H. Chamberlain. Lange was married in September 1891 to Carolyn Crosby Penny, a graduate of the University of Michigan. He died in his sixty-third year.

["Alexis F. Lange—a Symposium," *Sierra Educ. News,* Oct. 1924; Francis Bacon, "Alexis Lange," *Western Jour. of Educ.,* Jan. 1925; introduction to *The Lange Book* (1927), ed. by A. H. Chamberlain; *Who's Who in America,* 1922–23; *San Francisco Chronicle,* Aug. 29, 1924; *N. Y. Times,* Aug. 30, 1924.]

W. W. K.

LANGE, LOUIS (Sept. 29, 1829–Sept. 25, 1893), editor and publisher, son of Andrew and Anna (Stiel) Lange, was born in a rural district of Germany in the Province of Hesse, and received his elementary training in country schools. When he was seventeen he came to America and became an apprentice in the composing rooms of the *New Yorker Staats-Zeitung,* where he received the greater part of his education. In the summer of 1855 he entered the employ of the *Michigan Staats-Zeitung* of Detroit and stayed about two years. He then went to Mexico. On his return, he took up his residence in St. Louis, Mo., where in 1859 he became printer and bookkeeper for Moritz Niedner. On Mar. 11, 1861, Niedner founded the *Daily Missouri State Journal,* with Lange as financial manager. The paper was sympathetic with the Confederate cause at the time of the outbreak of the Civil War, and on July 13, 1861, was suppressed by order of Gen. Nathaniel Lyon [*q.v.*]. A regiment of Home Guards surrounded the newspaper office and removed the forms, type, parts of the press, and the morning edition of the paper to the headquarters of the regiment. It appears, however, that Lange was not himself committed to the Southern cause, and after the war he was known as a Republican. After being connected with the *Missouri Republican* (Democratic in politics) for about a year, he started in business for himself. Niedner, in the meantime, had purchased a small literary magazine known as *Die Abendschule,* previously published in Buffalo, N. Y., and this unpromising journal he sold to Lange in the spring of 1863 for the sum of $200. In Lange's hands, however, it grew from this small beginning into a position of importance, becoming one of the leading German literary periodicals published in the United States. So well was it managed and edited that it gained wide circulation among German-Americans of the best class and attracted the patronage of Germans abroad.

In the early days Lange supported his journal from the proceeds of a job-printing office in the attic of his home. He gave the best years of his life to the development of this periodical, which he kept free from political views, feeling strongly that such matters had no place in a purely literary magazine. After it became firmly established and his corps of editorial writers well organized, he founded a small political paper called *Die Rundschau,* which was published for a short time in St. Louis. Later, transferred to Chicago, where it was edited and published by his eldest son, Louis Lange, Jr., it became an important factor in German-American politics, and its editor was appointed United States consul successively at Annaberg and at Bremen, Germany, by President Cleveland.

Lange married Margarethe Schmidt in 1851. Six children were born to them. Lange was an intimate of Carl Daenzer, Emil Preetorius [*q.v.*], and Carl Schurz [*q.v.*] and was accustomed to meet with them every Wednesday afternoon in a little social group. He was active in the affairs of the Lutheran Church, and took an interest in religious education. He died in St. Louis, and was buried there.

[Information as to certain facts from Lange's son, Theodore Lange of St. Louis; R. V. Kennedy, *St. Louis Directory* (1859); *Daily Missouri State Journal,* Mar. 11–July 12, 1861; *Missouri Republican,* July 13, 1861; Wm. Hyde and H. L. Conard, *Encyc. of the Hist. of St. Louis* (1899); *Westliche Post,* Sept. 26, 1893.]

S. M. D.

LANGFORD, NATHANIEL PITT (Aug. 9, 1832–Oct. 18, 1911), Vigilante, explorer, and first superintendent of the Yellowstone National Park, was the twelfth child of George Langford II, a bank cashier of Westmoreland, N. Y., by his wife Chloe, daughter of Nathaniel Sweeting of Oneida County, N. Y. His paternal ancestor, John Langford, settled at Salem, Mass., about 1660; and his mother's forebear, Zebiah Sweeting of Somerset, England, came to Rehoboth, Mass., some time before 1699. Each family contributed two generations of soldiers to the War of the Revolution. After receiving an elementary education in a rural school, Langford, in 1854, migrated with his three sisters and his brother Augustine to St. Paul, Minn., and remained there as cashier in various local banks till 1862. In that year, on account of his health, he joined Capt. James L. Fisk's Northern Overland Expedition to the Salmon River gold fields as second assistant and commissary. After traveling 1,600 miles, most of the party settled for a stormy winter in the Prickly Pear Valley, but Langford and a few companions pushed on to Bannack, a Montana outpost 400 miles from the nearest permanent settlement. Gold had been discovered there in 1861; news of the discovery reached the outside world late in 1862, and that winter and the following spring thousands flocked in. The mining community found itself thronged with thieves and ruffians of all descriptions. Since there were no police and no courts of law, any one suspected of having gold was likely to be ruthlessly murdered. To handle the situation a group of courageous men, all of the Masonic order, took it upon themselves to punish outlaws, and Langford was one of those who played a distinguished part in organizing this celebrated Vigilante method of law administration and enforcement. His *Vigilante Days and Ways* (2 vols., 1890) describes these stirring times with a lucidity and literary charm which entitles it to a permanent place in American literary history.

Upon the organization of Montana as a territory in 1864, Langford was appointed United States collector of internal revenue. In 1868 he was twice removed from office by President Johnson and twice reinstated by the Senate. In December 1868 Johnson appointed him governor of the territory, but the appointment was not confirmed by the Senate.

Langford is best known, perhaps, as one of the first to describe the curious natural formations in that remarkable geological district now known as Yellowstone Park. In 1869 D. E. Folsom had penetrated the district, but was driven back by Indians. He told Langford and a few other intimate friends what he had seen, with the result that Gen. H. D. Washburn [*q.v.*] then organized, with the assistance of Langford, Lieut. G. C. Doane, and Judge Cornelius Hedges, an exploring party of nineteen men, and on Aug. 17, 1870, they left Helena. These four kept diaries of the journey, each of which has been published, but Langford's is the most finished and complete and is a masterpiece of descriptive narrative (*Diary of the Washburn Expedition to the Yellowstone and Fire Hole Rivers in the Year 1870,* 1905). Folsom and Hedges had each suggested independently that the Yellowstone district should become a national park, but it was Langford who brought the Yellowstone district to the attention of the nation through lectures and popular magazine articles (see *Scribner's Monthly,* May, June 1871, June 1873). After the park was created by act of Congress, Mar. 1, 1872, Langford served for the first five years, without compensation, as its superintendent. During this period he protected the park from numerous attempts at unscrupulous exploitation, and he was thus largely responsible for its being what it is today. He held various public offices in Montana till 1884, although in 1876 he had returned to St. Paul, where he resided until his death. He was an active member of both the Montana and the Minnesota historical societies, being president of the latter body from 1905 until his death. He made many contributions to their publications, the most important being a long history of the Louisiana Purchase (*Collections of the Minnesota Historical Society,* vol. IX, 1900).

Langford married Emma, daughter of Charles Wheaton of Northfield, Minn., Nov. 1, 1876. She died soon afterwards, and on Sept. 14, 1884, he married her sister, Clara Wheaton.

[Family material; genealogical papers and diary preserved in Minn. Hist. Soc. (MS. division); letters and papers in Mont. Hist. Soc. (presented by Langford in 1905); *Vigilante Days and Ways* (1890); introduction to Langford's *Diary of the Washburn Expedition* (1905); appreciations in *Colls. Minn. Hist. Soc.,* vol. XV (1915); T. J. Dimsdale, *Vigilantes of Montana* (1915); H. M. Chittenden, *The Yellowstone National Park* (1895); J. F. Fulton, in *Minn. Mag.,* Mar. 1931; *St. Paul Dispatch,* Oct. 18, 1911.] J. F. F.

LANGLADE, CHARLES MICHEL DE [See De Langlade, Charles Michel, 1729–1801].

LANGLEY, JOHN WILLIAMS (Oct. 21, 1841–May 10, 1918), chemist, educator, was the son of Samuel and Mary Sumner (Williams) Langley and the brother of Samuel P. Langley [*q.v.*], astronomer and aeronautical pioneer. He was born in Boston, Mass., where his father was a wholesale merchant and in later life a banker. Educated in public and private schools there, he entered the Lawrence Scientific School of Harvard, from which he received the degree of B.S. in 1861. After working as a chemist for a year in Boston, he enlisted in the navy and because of his medical knowledge was assigned for a few months to the Charlestown Navy Yard as acting assistant examining surgeon. He was then transferred to the United States gunboat *Pampero,* stationed at the mouth of the Mississippi River, and saw service on this vessel for one and one-half years. Resigning Sept. 1, 1864, he returned to his parents' home in Newton, Mass., and for the succeeding three years engaged with his brother Samuel in the building of several refracting telescopes and finally, an eight-inch glass reflector. Scientific interest alone prompted this activity of the brothers, and following it they spent much of the year 1868 in Europe, visiting scientific institutions, observatories, and art galleries. Upon his return John was appointed assistant professor of chemistry at the Western University of Pennsylvania, now the University of Pittsburgh, where he remained for five years. He then accepted a call to the University of Michigan as acting professor of general chemistry and physics; in 1877 he became full professor, resigning in 1888 to take a position as chemist and metallurgist for the Crescent Steel Works, Pittsburgh, Pa. Four years later he returned to university work, this time as professor of electrical engineering at the Case School of Applied Science, Cleveland, Ohio, where he remained until his retirement in 1906. During his whole career he was engaged in chemical and metallurgical research in iron and steel, the results of which were published in scientific journals. Among his papers were "On the Relationship of Structure, Density and Chemical Composition of Steel" (*American Chemist,* November 1876); "On the Sub-aqueous Dissociation of Certain Salts," with C. K. McGee (*Proceedings of the American Association for the Advancement of Science,* 1883); and "The Use of Electrolysis in Technical Chemical Processes" (*Journal of the American Chemical Society,* January 1894), read before the World's Congress of Chemists in 1893. He was a consultant for several steel manufacturers and was employed as expert in some twenty patent cases involving metallurgical processes. In 1889 he organized the International Committee for Standards of Analysis of Iron and Steel, the Work of which was taken over later by the United States Bureau of Standards. He was awarded the honorary degree of M.D. by the University of Michigan in 1877. On Sept. 12, 1871, he married Martica Irene Carret of

Charlestown, Mass., and at the time of his death in Ann Arbor, where he made his home after his retirement, he was survived by his widow, two daughters, and a son.

[T. H. S. Hamersly, *General Reg. of the U. S. Navy and Marine Corps* (1882); E. D. Campbell, *Hist. of the Chemical Laboratory of the Univ. of Mich., 1856–1916* (1916); *Univ. of Mich. Cat. of Grads., Non-Grads., Officers, and Members of the Faculties 1837–1921* (1923); *Who's Who in America*, 1918–19; *In Memoriam* (Scientific Club of Ann Arbor, Oct. 26, 1918); H. A. Kelly and W. L. Burrage, *Am. Medic. Biogs.* (1920); *Detroit Free Press*, May 12, 1918; information from family; authority for date of marriage, *Boston Transcript*, Sept. 13, 1871.] C. W. M.

LANGLEY, SAMUEL PIERPONT (Aug. 22, 1834–Feb. 27, 1906), a pioneer in research concerning solar radiation and human flight in heavier-than-air machines, author, third secretary of the Smithsonian Institution, was born in Roxbury, Mass. He was the son of Samuel and Mary Sumner (Williams) Langley. His ancestors were almost exclusively of English stock, with some slight admixture of Welsh. Some of them emigrated to Massachusetts in the early part of the seventeenth century and experienced the struggles of the times. Among his forebears were Richard, Increase, and Cotton Mather, and Rev. John Cotton, and many men prominent in the history of Massachusetts—members of the Phillips, Sprague, Sumner, Howell, Williams, Pierpont, and Langley families. Among his less known ancestors were mechanics and artisans skilled in various trades, and substantial farmers, men of rugged health and severely upright moral fiber and probity.

His father was a wholesale merchant of Boston, but a man of liberal interests. He had a small telescope with which the young Samuel and his brother John Williams [*q.v.*] watched the building of Bunker Hill Monument. The boys constructed a complete telescope for themselves, grinding and polishing the mirror to an excellent optical figure, and making the entire mounting. With this instrument they made many amateur observations of the heavens. Langley wrote long afterward: "I cannot remember when I was not interested in astronomy. I remember reading books upon the subject as early as at nine, and when I was quite a boy I learned to make little telescopes, and studied the stars through them. . . . One of the most wonderful things to me was the sun, and as to how it heated the earth. . . . I asked many questions, . . . and some of these childish questions have occupied many years of my later life in answering." (Goode, *post*, pp. 203–04.) The family were omnivorous readers, and Samuel, as a boy, made frequent use of the excellent public libraries of Boston. As a man he surprised his intimates by his wide knowledge of the English, German, and French classics, his historical research, and his acquaintance with works on astronomical, physical, and mechanical science. His formal education comprised attendance at several private schools, the Boston Latin School, and the Boston High School, from which he was graduated in 1851; but he had no college or university training.

He was engaged in engineering and architecture from 1851 to 1864. In 1864 and 1865 he traveled in Europe with his brother John, visiting observatories and learned societies. In 1866 he was appointed assistant professor of mathematics in charge of the small observatory of the Naval Academy at Annapolis, but in the following year became director of the Allegheny Observatory and professor of physics and astronomy in the Western University of Pennsylvania, where he remained twenty years. Allegheny Observatory needed funds exceedingly when Langley assumed charge. He devised a method of regulating railroad time from the Observatory clock, and persuaded the Pennsylvania Railroad to contract with the Observatory for this service. This arrangement inaugurated a practice which later became universal, and was the Observatory's principal source of revenue during Langley's directorship. In his earlier years he made the classic drawings of sun-spots which have been standard textbook illustrations to this day. He observed the total solar eclipses of 1869, 1870, and 1878, and made valuable observations. He also made careful visual studies of the solar spectrum, and was much in demand as a popular lecturer and writer on astronomical subjects.

His great astronomical achievement, however, was in the field of spectral measurements of solar and lunar radiation. He had always been more interested in the new astronomy of the physical characteristics of the heavenly bodies than in the older astronomy of position. To measure the distribution of heat in the spectrum of the sun he invented the bolometer (1878). This is an electrical thermometer, the sensitive element of which is a thin, narrow, blackened metallic tape, adapted to absorb radiation in very narrow bands of the spectrum, and sensitive to a rise in temperature of the millionth of a degree. With the bolometer he began at Allegheny Observatory an epoch-making series of experiments on the distribution of radiation in the solar spectrum, the transparency of the atmosphere to the different solar rays, and the enhancement of their intensity at high altitudes and even outside the atmosphere altogether. He devised a new method of determining the "solar constant of radiation," that fundamental quantity which is the measure of the intensity of solar heat at mean solar distance.

Because of the turbidity of the atmosphere at Allegheny, he organized in 1881 an expedition to the then wilderness of Mount Whitney, California, the highest mountain in the United States. This famous expedition was under the auspices of the War Department, but was aided by the Pennsylvania Railroad and by Langley's life-long friend, William Thaw of Pittsburgh. In the clear atmosphere of Mount Whitney, Langley and his able assistant, James E. Keeler, measured the energy of solar radiation with the bolometer and carried the solar spectrum far beyond the then recognized limit in the dark regions beyond the red. Computations of the solar constant were made from the observations both at Lone Pine and Mountain Camp, and valuable new results on atmospheric transparency resulted. By an unfortunate error of theoretical deduction the value of the solar constant was stated as 3.0 calories per square centimeter per minute, a value long quoted in textbooks, although the observations themselves, properly reduced, indicated approximately 2.0 calories, which is very near the present accepted value.

After his return from Mount Whitney, Langley employed the bolometer in studies of the deep infra-red spectra of the sun and the moon, and of heated bodies. His work on the lunar spectrum has not even yet been repeated. It led to determinations of the lunar temperature of the same order as, though somewhat lower than, those now preferred. In his later years at Allegheny, he did considerable popular lecturing and writing on astronomical subjects. Some of these lectures were published by the *Century Magazine,* and later collected in a book entitled *The New Astronomy* (1888), which passed through several editions and became a classic in astronomical literature. It is difficult to exaggerate its charm, which culminates in a whimsical parable on the last page.

On Jan. 12, 1887, Langley was appointed assistant secretary of the Smithsonian Institution in charge of library and international exchanges. When Secretary Spencer F. Baird died later in the same year, Langley was elected to succeed him (Nov. 18, 1887), and retained the position until his death. Like his predecessors and those who came after him, he felt keenly the hampering poverty of this great institution. There was and is a misapprehension in the public mind that the Smithsonian is a government bureau liberally supported by public funds. This probably grew from the fact that the Institution administers eight important government bureaus, and fostered them in their early years from its private funds. In fact it is a private foundation under government guardianship. Its great mission, as stated by its founder, James Smithson, is "the increase and diffusion of knowledge among men." Nothing could be broader in science than this object. The world-wide prestige of the Institution brings to it opportunities for accomplishments which the slenderness of its disposable income precludes. The first considerable addition to Smithson's original foundation of $550,000 occurred during Langley's administration. This was a bequest of $200,000 from Thomas Hodgkins of Brooklyn. Among Langley's important administrative works were the establishment of the National Zoological Park and the Astrophysical Observatory.

At this Observatory, which was founded in 1890 by private funds, he carried forward his studies of solar radiation. He introduced continuous photographic registration of the indications of his bolometer, and in this way he was able to feel out the positions of Fraunhofer and terrestrial absorption lines in the infra-red solar spectrum. A map of this hitherto unknown dark region of spectrum was prepared under his direction, extending to a wave-length of 5.3 microns, or ten times the wave-length of green light. The favorable total solar eclipse of May 1900 was observed by Langley and others of the Astrophysical Observatory at Wadesboro, N. C. On that occasion the bolometer was first used to measure the heat of the solar corona. Soon after, his attention was again turned to the solar constant of radiation. Early results of 1903 indicated solar variability, and Langley cautiously announced these observations in the year 1904. This subject has largely engrossed the Observatory since Langley's death. Expeditions have been sent to foreign lands, and much progress has been made towards realizing his vision.

Shortly before leaving Allegheny Observatory, Langley commenced the series of investigations into the possibilities of flight in heavier-than-air machines which he continued with conspicuous results at Washington. The greatness of his contribution to aviation depends not only on his pioneering laboratory investigations and successful long-distance flights of large power-driven models, but on the very fact that a man of his reputation should have adventured it in a field at that time so much ridiculed. He devised and constructed novel instruments for measuring lift and drift of the moving plane surfaces

Langley

which he carried at considerable speeds on long-armed whirling tables. In 1891 he published results of these investigations under the title "Experiments in Aerodynamics" (see *Smithsonian Contributions to Knowledge,* vol. XXVII). In "The Internal Work of the Wind" (*Ibid.*), published in 1893, he suggested reasonable explanations of the source of power used in the flight of birds.

He then proceeded to incorporate his established principles of flight in power-driven models of about fourteen feet span, built on the general plan of the four-wing dragonfly. He used curved supporting surfaces in all of his machines, though the experiments which led him to this improvement are unpublished. (Herring and others have claimed that Langley did not employ curved wings prior to 1895. The original note-books, still at the Institution, show that Langley employed parabolic curvatures of 1 to 12 camber, alternately with planes, in his wing models as early as the spring of 1894.) It was necessary to devise light engines as well as wing surfaces, and he constructed petrol-heated, flash-boiler steam engines of about five pounds weight per horsepower for this purpose. The light gasoline engine did not then exist. On May 6, 1896, Langley's model No. 5, thus equipped, was catapulted from a houseboat at Quantico, on the Potomac, and flew with excellent stability for a distance of 3,000 feet, resting quite uninjured on the water when the propellant was entirely exhausted. In November of the same year model No. 6 made the even longer successful flight of 4,200 feet.

These were the first sustained free flights of power-propelled heavier-than-air machines ever made. They attracted world-wide fame and enthusiasm. Langley himself said: "I have brought to a close the portion of the work which seemed to be specially mine—the demonstration of the practicability of mechanical flight—and for the next stage, which is the commercial and practical development of the idea, it is probable that the world may look to others" ("The 'Flying Machine,'" *McClure's Magazine,* June 1897). Nevertheless, he was persuaded to undertake the construction of a man-carrying airplane, for which the War Department Bureau of Ordnance appropriated $50,000.

Not only was the large machine built and equipped with a five-cylinder radial water-cooled gasoline engine developed by Langley's assistant, Charles M. Manly [*q.v.*], but a quarter-size model of about the same dimension as Langley's steam-driven models was also prepared with a gasoline engine of similar design. This fourteen-foot model flew without pilot and with good stability on Aug. 8, 1903, for approximately 1,000 feet. The large machine was twice tried, on Oct. 8 and Dec. 8, 1903, catapulted from a large houseboat on the Potomac. On both occasions, according to the testimony of Manly and others, defects in the operation of the launching device brought disaster. On the first trial the front part of the machine apparently caught on a projecting pin, the front wings were deflected downwards, and despite all that could be done with the rudder, the machine plunged into the water 150 feet from the houseboat. On the second trial the rear wings collapsed, and the machine soared upwards, turned a complete somersault, and fell back near the houseboat. Newspaper ridicule and misunderstanding were added to failing health, exhausted funds, and vexatious administrative cares, and Langley failed to push forward by new trials to a successful issue. Yet he said after the December trial: "Failure in the aerodrome itself or its engines there has been none; and it is believed that it is at the moment of success, and when the engineering problems have been solved, that a lack of means has prevented a continuance of the work" (*Annual Report of the Board of Regents of the Smithsonian Institution, 1904,* 1905, p. 125). This view has the great weight of the considered judgments expressed in written statements, public or private, by Manly, Chanute, Curtiss, Zahm, Ames, Taylor, and Durand. The large machine, restored, is now on exhibition with the earlier models in the United States National Museum. An exhaustive account of it is given by C. M. Manly in the "Langley Memoir on Mechanical Flight" (*Smithsonian Contributions to Knowledge,* vol. XXVII), published in 1911. In recognition of Langley's contribution to aeronautics, the flying field near Norfolk, and the laboratory of the National Advisory Committee for Aeronautics, as well as certain naval vessels, have been named after him.

Langley was the recipient of many scientific honors. Among those deserving special mention are the Henry Draper gold medal of the National Academy of Sciences, the Rumford gold and silver medals of the American Academy of Arts and Sciences, the Janssen medal of the Institute of France, and the Rumford medal of the Royal Society of London. He was a member of the National Academy of Sciences, a correspondent of the Institute of France, foreign member of the Royal Society of London, of the Royal Society of Edinburgh, and of the Academia dei Lincei of Rome. Of his many valuable publications perhaps the most important are: "Minute Structure of the Solar Photosphere" (*American Journal of Science and Arts,* February 1874); "The Bolometer and Radiant Energy" (*Proceedings of the American Academy of Arts and Sciences,* vol. XVI, 1881); "The Selective Absorption of Solar Energy" (*American Journal of Science,* March 1883); "Experimental Determination of Wave-lengths in the Invisible Prismatic Spectrum" (*Ibid.,* March 1884); "Researches on Solar Heat and its Absorption by the Earth's Atmosphere: A Report of the Mount Whitney Expedition" (*Professional Papers of the Signal Service,* no. XV, 1884); "The New Astronomy" (*Century Magazine,* 1884–85); "On the Temperature of the Surface of the Moon" (*Memoirs of the National Academy of Sciences,* vol. III, pt. 1, 1885); "Observations on Invisible Heat Spectra and the Recognition of Hitherto Unmeasured Wave-lengths" (*Proceedings of the American Association for the Advancement of Science,* 1885, and *American Journal of Science and Arts,* January 1886); "On Hitherto Unrecognized Wave-lengths" (*London, Edinburgh and Dublin Philosophical Magazine,* and *American Journal of Science and Arts,* both August 1886); "The Temperature of the Moon" (*Memoirs of the National Academy of Sciences,* vol. IV, pt. 2, 1889); "Energy and Vision" (*American Journal of Science and Arts,* November 1888); *Annals of the Astrophysical Observatory of the Smithsonian Institution,* vol. I, 1900; "The Solar Constant and Related Problems" (*Astrophysical Journal,* March 1903).

In mature life Langley was a large man of florid countenance, who concealed a deep-seated shyness by a front of dignity. Irascible, often giving offense, he yet revealed to his intimates a great charm of character. He was witty, apt of speech and quotation, warm-hearted, a lover of children, and impressed all who knew him as a man of large pioneering mind, ornamented with the graces of familiar intercourse. He had unusual facility in free-hand and mechanical drawing. His writing was like copper-plate, and his signature was a thing of beauty. He spoke fluent French, and was accustomed to make yearly trips abroad, where his reputation was justly very high in scientific circles. He never married. His death occurred at Aiken, S. C., in his seventy-second year.

[G. Brown Goode, *The Smithsonian Institution, 1846–1896* (1897); *Who's Who in America,* 1903–05; *Evening Star* (Washington), Feb. 28, 1906; Cyrus Adler, "Samuel Pierpont Langley," in *Bull. Phil. Soc. of Washington,* Jan. 1907, repr. in *Ann. Report . . . Smithsonian Inst., 1906* (1907); C. G. Abbot, "Samuel Pierpont Langley," in *Astrophys. Jour.,* May 1906; "Samuel Pierpont Langley Memorial Meeting," *Smithsonian Misc. Colls.,* vol. XLIX, no. 4 (1907), accompanied by a partial bibliography of Langley's writings; C. D. Walcott, "Biog. Memoir of Samuel Pierpont Langley," *Nat. Acad. Sci. Biog. Memoirs,* vol. VII (1913); Henry Leffmann, "A Tribute, Samuel Pierpont Langley: A Pioneer in Practical Aviation," in *Jour. of the Franklin Inst.,* Jan. 1919; C. G. Abbot, "The Relations between the Smithsonian Institution and the Wright Brothers," *Smithsonian Misc. Colls.,* vol. LXXXI, no. 5 (1928); letter files of the Smithsonian Institution.]

C. G. A.

LANGSTON, JOHN MERCER (Dec. 14, 1829–Nov. 15, 1897), educator and diplomat, was born in Louisa County, Va. His father, Ralph Quarles, was the owner of the estate. His mother, Lucy Langston, of African and Indian blood, Quarles's favorite slave, was emancipated by him in 1806 and subsequently bore him three sons, who followed the condition of their mother and took her name. Ralph Quarles was a kind master, who believed that slavery should be abolished by the voluntary act of the owner. In 1834 both of Langston's parents died. By his father's will the principal slaves were emancipated and liberal provision was made for the three sons. Langston was sent by the executors to live with his father's friend, William D. Gooch of Chillicothe, Ohio, who became his guardian and who gave him the care and education of a son. When the boy was about ten, Gooch decided to move to Missouri, a slave state. Langston started with him, but the sheriff, at the instigation of his half-brother, William Langston, followed with a process requiring Gooch to answer to the charge of attempting to carry the boy beyond the jurisdiction of the court that had made him guardian. Allen G. Thurman, then a young lawyer, appeared for William Langston, and the court ruled that the boy could not leave Ohio. After spending two years in a Cincinnati private school, he returned to Chillicothe and, in 1844, entered the preparatory department of Oberlin College. In 1849 he graduated from the collegiate department and in 1853 from the theological department. However, he had studied theology only in order to prepare himself for law, and, not being able to gain admission to a law school, he read law under Philemon Bliss, of Elyria. In September 1854, he was admitted to the bar and, the next month, married Caroline M. Wall, who was then a senior in the literary department of Oberlin College.

He began practising law in Brownhelm but, two years later, located in Oberlin. In March 1855 he was nominated by the Liberty Party for clerk of Brownhelm township and was elected, probably the first negro to be chosen to an elective office in the United States. During the Civil War he served as an agent for recruiting colored troops; he helped raise the first colored regiment, the 54th Massachusetts and, later, the 55th Massachusetts and the 5th Ohio regiments. From 1865 to 1867 he was a member of the Council of Oberlin and, in 1867 and 1868, of the city Board of Education.

In 1868 he was called to Washington and appointed inspector-general of the Freedmen's Bureau. In this capacity he visited many sections of the South, where his tactful educational addresses were received with enthusiasm by both the colored and white population. Upon the termination of these activities he accepted the professorship of law in Howard University. As dean (1869–1876) and vice-president and acting president (1872) he organized and established the law department of this institution. For seven years he was a member of the Board of Health for the District of Columbia and its attorney. In 1877 he became minister-resident to Haiti and chargé d'affaires to Santo Domingo and, until 1885, was in the diplomatic and consular service, where his tact, easy manner, and diplomatic address made a favorable impression. In 1883 he published *Freedom and Citizenship,* a selection from the many addresses that had made his reputation as an orator of power and distinction. Upon his return to the United States he was elected president of the Virginia Normal and Collegiate Institute at Petersburg, Va. In 1888 he was the Republican nominee for Congress from his district, and, although his election was contested, he was seated by the House in 1890. He was an unsuccessful candidate for reëlection. He retired to his home in Washington, where he continued to interest himself in political affairs and wrote *From the Virginia Plantation to the National Capital* (1894) in which he told with real charm the story of his dramatic and useful life.

[Autobiography mentioned above; introductory sketch by J. E. Rankin in *Freedom and Citizenship* (1883); *Souvenir Journal of the 35th National Celebration at Culpeper, Va. . . . under Auspices of the Langston National Monument Hist. and Emancipation Asso.,* comp. by R. B. Robinson (1898); W. J. Simmons, *Men of Mark* (1887); J. W. Cromwell, *The Negro in Am. Hist.* (1914); B. T. Washington, *The Story of the Negro* (2 vols., 1909); *New York Tribune,* Nov. 16, 1897.]
R. C. M.

LANGSTROTH, LORENZO LORRAINE (Dec. 25, 1810–Oct. 6, 1895), apiarist, was born in Philadelphia, Pa., the son of John G. and Rebekah (Dunn) Langstroth. He graduated from Yale College in 1831 and from 1834 to 1836 he was tutor in mathematics at the same institution. During this time also he took a course in theology and in May 1836 he became pastor of the South Congregational Church at Andover, Mass.; but owing to ill health he was compelled to resign in 1838. He next became principal of the Abbot Academy in Andover, resigning in 1839 when he became principal of the Greenfield (Mass.) High School for Young Ladies, a position he held for five years. In 1844 he resumed his pastoral work, taking the Second Congregational Church at Greenfield. Four years later he resigned this position to become principal of a school for young ladies at Philadelphia. He remained in this work until 1852 when he moved to Oxford, Ohio. It was here that he took up the work in beekeeping for which he is best known.

Langstroth's invention of the movable-frame beehive revolutionized not only all hives but the methods for keeping bees. There had been other so-called movable-frame hives before his day, but the frames after being in use for a short time became almost immovable, making a hive little, if any, better than the old box hives or log gums. His invention consisted in the discovery of the bee space (approximately five-sixteenths of an inch) which bees keep open without filling with comb or honey. Around his frame, hanging on projections from the upper corners, he provided a bee space on all four sides between the hive and frame and between the frames themselves. As the bees would not fill these spaces, the frames were not fastened by combs or bee glue. Hence they were always movable.

Besides inventing a hive and frame, Langstroth was a pioneer in many of the methods of management that later came to be common practice in the production of carloads of honey. All of these are well set forth in his book, *Langstroth on the Hive and the Honeybee,* first published in 1853. After a revision by C. P. Dadant it was republished in 1888 under the title: *The Honey Bee.* Many of the practices and theories later supposed to be new were first set forth by Langstroth. But as has been the case with many other pioneers and inventors, he was ridiculed and then robbed of the fruits of his invention. So great was the persecution that he suffered severe mental distress. For months at a time he would refuse to see his friends, much less talk on the subject of bees. Fortunately, however, he recovered and lived to see the day when his invention received almost universal adoption. He was a man of commanding presence and a charming conversationalist. He could have distinguished himself in many fields but he chose beekeeping because it brought him close to nature. Langstroth was married, on Aug. 22, 1836, to Anne M. Tucker of New Haven, Conn., by whom he had three children. He died at Dayton at the home of one of his daughters.

[Sources include: "Langstroth Memorial," *Gleanings in Bee Culture,* Dec. 15, 1895; E. R. Root, *ABC and XYZ of Bee Culture* (ed. 1917); *Obit. Record of Grads. of Yale Univ.,* 1895–96; *Vital Records of New Haven, 1649–1850,* pt. 1 (1917); L. A. Brainard, *The Geneal. of the Brainerd-Brainard Family in America* (1908), vol. I; Langstroth's manuscript journal and other unpublished papers in the Langstroth Root Memorial Library at Cornell University.] E. R. R.

LANGWORTHY, EDWARD (*c.* 1738–Nov. 1, 1802), member of the Continental Congress, was born in or near Savannah, Ga. About all that is known of his own early life is that, left an orphan, he was placed in Whitefield's Bethesda Orphan House, where he received his early education, that he "kept a school" for a time in Savannah, that in January 1771 he was placed in charge of a school "for Academical Learning" just established in connection with the orphanage, that he married the sister of Ambrose Wright, and that she died (letter of James Habersham to the Countess of Huntington, Jan. 9, 1771, in *Collections of the Georgia Historical Society,* VI, 117; see also *Ibid.,* p. 124).

Langworthy's first appearance upon the political stage was as one of the signers of the Loyalist protest against the Savannah resolutions of Aug. 10, 1774 (*Georgia Gazette,* Sept. 7, 1774). A year later, however, he had so completely reversed his position that he was chosen secretary to the council of safety and served the succeeding Revolutionary bodies, provincial congress, council of safety, and convention, in the same capacity. In June 1777 he was chosen as a delegate to the Continental Congress and took his seat Nov. 17, following. He was reëlected Feb. 26, 1778. As a member of Congress he played, with one or two exceptions, no conspicuous part. His party affiliations were nevertheless early established. He stood firmly with the friends of Washington, and it was in defense of the commander-in-chief that he obtained his most conspicuous record in the *Journals of Congress.* When on the night of Apr. 10, 1778, in order to prevent the adoption of obnoxious passages in a proposed letter to General Washington, Thomas Burke [*q.v.*] of North Carolina resolved to break the quorum by leaving the floor, Langworthy followed him from the hall. The obdurate Burke refused to obey the order of Congress to return, but Langworthy did obey and offered a limping explanation of his course (see *Journals,* Apr. 10, 11, 24, 1778). Langworthy has also the distinction, though the act has no personal significance, of being one of the three Georgia delegates who signed the Articles of Confederation. He took his position with the pro-Deane party in Congress, his close association with that group continuing after his retirement, and he stood with the majority of the Southern delegates in opposing the inclusion of the right to the Newfoundland fisheries as an ultimatum in the peace negotiations. His votes on this question in particular roused Henry Laurens [*q.v.*], who was in the opposite camp, to point out, in April 1779 that the term for which Langworthy was elected had expired Feb. 26. This event ended his service in Congress. While he waited in Philadelphia, hoping to receive a new appointment, there appeared in the *Pennsylvania Gazette* articles signed "Americanus" criticizing Congress, or a faction therein, particularly for its course in the matter of the fisheries and the peace ultimata, and Langworthy was pointed to as the possible author of some of them. He probably was, and he may have been the author of other pseudonymous articles of the time.

On Jan. 25, 1785, he joined William Goddard in issuing the *Maryland Journal and Baltimore Advertiser,* but severed his connections with the paper at the end of one year. It was at this time that he came into possession of the papers of Gen. Charles Lee, recently deceased, selections of which, with a sketch of Lee's life, he published under the title, *Memoirs of the Life of the Late Charles Lee* (London, 1792). From 1787 to 1791 he was principal and teacher of classics in the Baltimore Academy. From 1791 to 1794 he resided at Elkton, Md., engaged in the preparation of a history of Georgia; but the work was never published, and the manuscript has been lost. After the death of a second wife in 1794, he obtained a clerkship in the customs office in Baltimore which he held until his death.

[George White, *Hist. Colls. of Ga.* (3rd ed., 1855); C. C. Jones, Jr., *The Hist. of Ga.* (2 vols., 1883), *Biog. Sketches of the Delegates from Ga. to the Continental Cong.* (1891); A. D. Candler, *The Revolutionary Records of the State of Ga.,* vol. I (1909); *Collections of the Ga. Hist. Soc.,* vol. V, pt. I (1901), vol. VI (1904); E. C. Burnett, *Letters of Members of the Continental Congress,* vols. III (1926), IV (1928), "Edward Langworthy in the Continental Congress," in *Ga. Hist. Quart.,* Sept. 1928; B. A. Konkle, "Edward Langworthy," *Ibid.,* June 1927; *Federal Gazette and Baltimore Daily Advertiser,* Nov. 2, 1802, which gives the date of Langworthy's death as "yesterday evening."] E. C. B.

LANGWORTHY, JAMES LYON (Jan. 20, 1800–Mar. 14, 1865), Iowa pioneer, was born in Windsor, Vt. His earliest American ancestor was probably Andrew Langworthy, who, according to tradition, emigrated from Essex, England, in 1634, and settled in Rhode Island (L. B. Langworthy, *post*). James was one of the eleven children of Stephen Langworthy, a physician, and Betsy (Massey) Langworthy. A few years after his birth the family moved to St. Lawrence County, N. Y., and about 1815 to Erie County,

Pa. Three years later, after a leisurely journey toward the farther West, they settled at Edwardsville, Ill., in the St. Louis region. Here the mother and one of the sons died. The family then moved north to Diamond Grove, near Jacksonville, where the father remarried. Young Langworthy appears to have picked up a fair education. About 1819 he went to St. Louis, where for three years he worked in a mill. In 1824 his adventurous spirit led him to ascend the Mississippi to the lead mines in the Galena neighborhood. With several other prospectors he opened the mines at Hardscrabble, near Hazelgreen, Wis. In 1827 he served in the brief campaign against the Winnebagos, and in the same year was joined by his brothers, Lucius Hart (1807–1865) and Edward (1808–1893), and later by another brother, Solon Massey (1814–1886). Becoming deeply interested in accounts of the rich lead mines across the river, he visited them in the spring of 1829; and though white men had been excluded therefrom by the Foxes after the death of Julien Dubuque in 1810, he seems to have been permitted to make a brief exploration. In the spring of 1830 the Foxes, frightened by the Sioux, temporarily abandoned the location, and James Langworthy, with his brother Lucius, at once crossed the river and began active work. Others followed, and on June 17 a committee of which James was the head drew up a miners' agreement which was the first civil regulation in the history of Iowa.

The Indians soon returned, and under orders of General Atkinson the miners were compelled to leave. In 1832 came the Black Hawk War, in which James and his three brothers saw service, followed by the cession by the Indians of a large strip of the eastern part of the present Iowa. Though the date of June 1, 1833, had been set for the opening of the lands, James and two of his brothers, with a number of other miners, at once reinvaded the region. A detachment of soldiers was sent to the scene, and on the promise of Lieut. Jefferson Davis that the location claims of each prospector would be respected on the formal opening of the territory, the miners peacefully withdrew. They returned on the first of June, headed by James and two of his brothers, Solon arriving a year later and the father some time afterward. On Mar. 17, 1840, James was married to Agnes Miln, a native of Edinburgh, Scotland. In the early forties, with his brother Lucius, he constructed the military road from Dubuque to the new territorial capital, Iowa City. Through all the early years of Dubuque he was a leader, indefatigable in efforts making for the development of the town, and perhaps its most prominent citizen. Though Lucius was the first sheriff of Dubuque County, Edward a member of the constitutional convention of 1844, and both of them members of the territorial legislature, James seems not to have cared for political distinction. He died at his home, survived by his wife and several children.

[Autobiographical articles by Langworthy's brothers in J. C. Parish, "The Langworthys of Early Dubuque," *Iowa Jour. of Hist. and Politics,* July 1910; W. J. Peterson, "Some Beginnings in Iowa," *Ibid.,* Jan. 1930; *Hist. of Dubuque County, Iowa* (n.d.), ed. by F. T. Oldt; "Memoirs of Lyman Barker Langworthy of Rochester, N. Y.," written 1869 (typescript, 1910, in Lib. of Cong., with corrections by C. F. Langworthy); *The Hist. of Dubuque County, Iowa* (1880).]

W. J. G.

LANIER, JAMES FRANKLIN DOUGHTY (Nov. 22, 1800–Aug. 27, 1881), financier, was the son of Alexander Chalmers Lanier and Drusilla (Doughty) Lanier. On his father's side he was of Huguenot ancestry, a distant relative of the poet Sidney Lanier [*q.v.*]. His grandfather fought in the Revolution as a captain in the regiment of light cavalry commanded by the dashing Col. William Washington and later served in General Wayne's victorious campaign against the Northwestern Indians. Lanier was born in Washington, Beaufort County, N. C., but in 1807 his parents moved to Eaton, Preble County, Ohio. There his father manumitted two valuable slaves, whom he had taken with him, although they constituted a considerable portion of his estate. A few years later Alexander C. Lanier served as a major under General Harrison in the War of 1812. In 1817 the family moved to Madison, then one of the most important towns in the new state of Indiana, and there opened a drygoods store, but the father's health was poor and in 1820 he died insolvent, leaving debts that were ultimately paid by his son.

While at Eaton young Lanier worked for a time as a clerk in the store of Cornelius Van Ausdall. For a year and a half he attended an academy at Newport, Ky. Shortly before his father's death he began to read law in the office of Gen. Alexander Meek and in 1823 completed a law course in Transylvania University. He began practice immediately. In 1824 he was appointed assistant clerk of the state House of Representatives, a post he continued to hold until 1827, when he became chief clerk. In this work he made acquaintances that were later to be of great service to him.

As a lawyer he was successful, but the profession proved too much for his strength. When the State Bank of Indiana was chartered in 1833, he took a larger share of the stock first subscribed than did any other individual and became the first president of the Madison branch, and a member of the general board of control with Hugh McCulloch [*q.v.*], later secretary of the treasury. When the panic of 1837 came, the Bank of Indiana was one of the few in the Mississippi Valley to weather the storm. As a result, its officers won a great and well-deserved reputation for honesty and financial ability. Since the bank at that time was a depository of $1,500,000 of United States funds, Lanier, as a representative of the board of control, set out for Washington with $80,000 in gold to report the condition of the institution to the secretary of the treasury. He was cordially received by Levi Woodbury, then secretary, who told him that his bank "was the only one that had offered to pay any part of its indebtedness in specie" (Lanier's autobiography, p. 15). The bank was permitted to retain the government deposits until they were exhausted through regular disbursements, and Woodbury insisted upon Lanier's accepting the post of pension agent for a part of the western region. A decade later Lanier went to Europe in the interest of his state and succeeded in making an arrangement that restored the financial credit of Indiana, which was badly in arrears in interest on its bonds.

During this period he aided in the resuscitation of the first railroad in Indiana, the Madison & Indianapolis. Late in 1848 he moved to New York City, where on Jan. 1, 1849, he helped to found the firm of Winslow, Lanier & Company. They were pioneers in the floating of railway securities, and since the time was opportune for such an enterprise their success was speedy and remarkable. Soon, Lanier later wrote, they "not unfrequently negotiated a million dollars of bonds daily," and their total for a year was, for that period, enormous. In the six years, 1849 to 1854 inclusive, in which they were engaged in this kind of business, 10,724 miles of new railroad were constructed, and Winslow, Lanier & Company were connected, in one way or another, with all the important lines. With their negotiation of bond issues they frequently coupled contracts for the purchase of rails; generally also the firm was the agent for the payment of interest in the bonds they had floated. After the panic of 1857 Lanier played a large part in managing the affairs of the Pittsburg, Fort Wayne, & Chicago Railroad, and from a state of impending bankruptcy he was able to restore it to a condition of great prosperity. It ultimately became a part of the Pennsylvania system.

Lanier's most striking public service was rendered during the Civil War. At the outbreak of that struggle the State of Indiana had no money in its treasury, but Lanier loaned Oliver P. Morton [*q.v.*], the Republican governor, over $400,000, with which he was able to equip Indiana's troops much more rapidly than would otherwise have been possible. In 1862 the Democrats won in the state election, gaining control of the legislature and most of the state offices; the legislature thereupon attempted to take the control of the militia away from the governor. To prevent the enactment of this and other dangerous measures, the loyal members withdrew, leaving the legislature without a quorum. This step enabled the governor to retain command of the militia, but left the treasury without the money to pay interest on its debt. In this grave crisis Lanier again came forward, advanced $640,000, and saved the financial reputation of the state, although he knew that the only hope of repayment lay in the patriotism and honesty of some future legislature. Repayment was, in fact, an issue in the campaign of 1864, and when the Union party under the leadership of Morton won the day, the new legislature reimbursed Lanier, with interest. Following the Civil War, while on trips to Europe, Lanier did much, as unofficial representative of the United States government, to convince European financial circles of the stability of the government and the desirability of its bonds.

Lanier was twice married: to Elizabeth Gardiner, in 1819; and after her death, to Mary McClure in 1848. There were eight children by the first marriage and at least one by the second. In the early forties he built at Madison a large mansion which now belongs to the State of Indiana and is preserved partly as a museum and example of the best architecture of the period and partly as a memorial to Lanier's public services. He died in New York and was buried in Greenwood Cemetery.

[Consult Lanier's own *Sketch of the Life of J. F. D. Lanier* (privately printed, 1870; 2nd ed., revised, 1877); G. S. Cottman, "James F. D. Lanier," *Ind. Mag. of Hist.*, June 1926; Blanche G. Garber, "The Lanier Family and the Lanier Home," *Ibid.*, Sept. 1926; G. L. Payne, "Lanier of Indiana," in *Hoosier Banker*, May, June 1922; G. S. Cottman, *The Lanier Memorial Home* (1927), issued by the Department of Conservation of Indiana; *N. Y. Tribune*, Aug. 28, 1881.] P. L. H.

LANIER, SIDNEY (Feb. 3, 1842–Sept. 7, 1881), poet, musician, critic, was probably a descendant of musicians who enjoyed the patronage of Queen Elizabeth, James I, Charles I, and Charles II. One of these, Jerome Lanier, had fled from France on account of the persecution of the Huguenots and availed himself of his accomplishments in music to secure a place in Queen Elizabeth's household. His son, Nicholas Lanier, wrote music for the masques of Ben

Jonson and Campion and for the lyrics of Herrick, and was the first marshal of a society of musicians organized by Charles I in 1626. After the Restoration, five of the Laniers were members of the Corporation of Music, the charter of which was confirmed by Charles II on Apr. 1, 1664. Pepys refers to one of these Laniers as the "best company for musique I ever was in in my life, and [I] wish I could live and die in it" (*Diary,* Dec. 6, 1665). The study of the records of the family confirmed the poet in the opinion that "if a man made himself an expert in any particular branch of human activity . . . a peculiar aptitude towards the same branch would be found among some of his descendants" (Mims, *post,* p. 12). There is more substantial authority for his descent from Thomas Lanier, who, along with a large number of other Huguenots, settled in Virginia in the early years of the eighteenth century at Manakin or Monacan-town, some twenty miles from Richmond (J. F. D. Lanier, *post,* appendix). One branch of the family went through Tennessee and Kentucky to Indiana; among their descendants were two of the leading bankers of New York City, J. F. D. Lanier [*q.v.*] and his son Charles D. Lanier, who befriended the poet. The other branch moved from Virginia into Rockingham County, N. C., and thence into Georgia and Alabama. Sterling Lanier, the poet's grandfather, had by the beginning of the Civil War amassed a moderate fortune as a hotel-keeper in Macon, Ga., and Montgomery, Ala. His son, Robert Sampson Lanier, became a fairly successful lawyer in Macon, known for his fine presence, his habit of methodical industry, his courtesy and refinement. He was well read in the classics that were the staple of a Southern gentleman's reading—Shakespeare, Addison, and Walter Scott. In 1840 he married Mary Jane Anderson, of Scotch-Irish descent, the daughter of Hezekiah Anderson, a Virginia planter, who had attained success in the political life of that state.

The three children, Sidney, Clifford, and Gertrude, were taught the strictest tenets of the creed of Calvin and were subjected to the Presbyterian discipline of those days. The seriousness of this life was broken by the kindly social relations of the home and the community, and, in the case of Sidney, by his rather precocious enjoyment of music. He did not remember a time when he could not play upon almost any musical instrument. When he was seven years old he made his first effort at music on an improvised reed cut from the neighboring river bank, with which he sought to emulate the trills and cadences of the song birds. One of his earliest Christmas gifts was a small, one-keyed flute; he soon organized an orchestra among his playmates. Among a people not noted for reading, he found delight in the romances of Froissart, the adventures of Gil Blas, and the romances of Scott. In the absence of public schools in the community he received his early education in a private academy. On Jan. 6, 1857, he entered the sophomore class of Oglethorpe University, near Milledgeville, Ga., a small denominational institution of the Presbyterian Church. Although he later referred to this as "a farcical college," he received a lasting inspiration from one of the teachers there, Dr. James Woodrow, a former pupil of Agassiz at Harvard and just returned from two years' study in German universities. Woodrow opened Lanier's mind to the value of science in modern thought and its relation to poetry and religion; he also revealed to him the meaning of real scholarship and awakened in him a desire to study in Germany. What Lanier lacked in adequate academic instruction he found in some of the more intellectual students with whom he read and talked and practised music. His reading of *The Anatomy of Melancholy,* Jeremy Taylor, Keats, Chatterton, and, among contemporary writers, Carlyle and Tennyson, was quite remarkable for that time and place. Graduating at the head of his class in 1860, he was appointed a tutor. He was then "a spare-built boy, of average height and underweight, mostly addicted to hard study, long reveries, and exhausting smokes with a German pipe" (Mims, p. 38). While he felt that his natural bent was toward music, he hesitated to follow a musician's career. The plan that he formed was to study in a German university, as preliminary to a professorship in a college, which might in turn give opportunity for creative work.

From such visions he was awakened by the guns of Fort Sumter. No one was more affected by the war spirit that swept through the South like a tidal wave. He dreamed with his people of a nation that might be the embodiment of all that was fine in government and society; he believed that the Confederacy "was to enter upon an era of prosperity such as no other nation . . . had ever enjoyed, and that Macon . . . was to become a great art center" (Mims, p. 47). In April 1861, he joined the Macon Volunteers, the first company that went out of Georgia to Virginia. With the exception of the seven days' fight at Chickahominy and Malvern Hill a year later, he did not participate in the more acute struggles of the war. He and his brother Clifford, in 1863 and 1864, served as mounted scouts along the James River, and, in August 1864, he was transferred to Wilmington, N. C., where he became a signal officer on blockade-runners. On Nov. 2 he was captured in a particularly hazardous adventure. He was taken to the prison at Point Lookout, Md., where he spent four months of dreary and distressing life under conditions afterwards described in his novel, *Tiger-Lilies.* All through the war his interest in music and poetry found expression. In the letters he wrote home we read of serenades, moonlight dashes, and parties in old Virginia homes; of the capture of his books including an edition of Coleridge, Shelley, and Keats; of the salvaging of his flute, which he always carried up his sleeve and which was a solace to his fellow prisoners. At Fort Boykin in 1863, he began to think of literary work as his probable vocation. While reading English and German poetry he wrote to his father: "Gradually I find that my whole soul is merging itself into this business of writing, and especially of writing poetry. I am going to try it" (Jan. 18, 1864, Mims, p. 56). Even amid the loathsome surroundings of prison he translated Heine's "The Palm and the Pine" and Herder's "Spring Greeting." Thus closed the war period. One scarcely knows which to admire most: the soldier, brave and knightly; the poet, preparing his wings for a flight; or the musician, inspiriting his fellow soldiers in camp and in prison.

Reaching Macon on Mar. 15, 1865, after a long and painful journey on foot through the Carolinas, he remained dangerously ill for two months, his mother during the same time dying of consumption. In the next eight years of his life he passed through every sort of tragic experience, well-summarized in his words to Bayard Taylor: "Pretty much the whole of life has been merely not dying" (Aug. 7, 1875, *Letters,* p. 121). Broken by disease, now a clerk in a hotel, now teaching under well nigh impossible conditions, again practising law in his father's office, discouraged by the suffering of the Southern people in what he called the "dark raven days" of Reconstruction, and all the while with the unfulfilled desire to follow a musical or literary career, he struggled hard to find some way out of his difficulties. The problem was still further complicated by his marriage to Mary Day on Dec. 21, 1867, and the quick growth of their family. Aside from the financial difficulties, it proved to be "an idyllic marriage, which the poet thought a rich compensation for all the other perfect gifts which Providence denied him" (Mims, p. 97).

A visit to New York in 1867 to arrange for the publication of *Tiger-Lilies* (1867), subsequent visits from 1869 to 1871 when he heard for the first time Theodore Thomas' orchestra play Wagner's music, a visit for his health to San Antonio, Tex., in 1873, that resulted in an encouraging verdict on his musical powers by a group of German musicians, had all kept alive his deepest passion. Finally, realizing that his time of life was short at best, he wrote on Nov. 29, 1873, to his father from Baltimore, whither he had moved, a letter that expressed his determination to follow the artistic career, in words so memorable that they deserve to live in American literary history: "Why should I, nay, how can I, settle myself down to be a third-rate struggling lawyer for the balance of my little life, as long as there is a certainty almost absolute that I can do some other thing so much better? . . . My dear father, think how, for twenty years, through poverty, through pain, through weariness, through sickness, through the uncongenial atmosphere of a farcical college and of a bare army and then of an exacting business life, through all the discouragement of being wholly unacquainted with literary people and literary ways,—I say, think how, in spite of all these depressing circumstances, and of a thousand more which I could enumerate, these two figures of music and of poetry have steadily kept in my heart so that I could not banish them. Does it not seem to you, as to me, that I begin to have the right to enroll myself among the devotees of these two sublime arts, after having followed them so humbly, and through so much bitterness?" (*Poems of Sidney Lanier,* pp. xx–xxi).

Fortunately, his father assented to the logic of his entreaty, and, in so far as he could, supported him in his efforts. Even then the way was not clear for concentrated work. The remaining eight years of his life were still to be divided between music and poetry; the continued ill health necessitated trips to Florida, Pennsylvania, Alleghany Spring, Va., and finally to western North Carolina; while the support of his wife and four boys necessitated every sort of hackwork in writing, teaching, and music. During the first winter in Baltimore he gave most of his time to playing the flute in the newly organized Peabody Orchestra under the direction of Asger Hamerik. Not satisfied with his natural genius, he studied the technique of music, and soon won the applause, not only of the general public but also of Thomas and Damrosch, and of various musical organizations in the city. While perfecting himself in the technique of the flute and of the orchestra, he became interested in the history of music, especially of Elizabethan music. Of much significance was his growing conception of the place of music in modern culture. In his letters and in his posthumously published *Music and Poetry* (1898) he maintained that music has a natural place in the education of every cultivated man; he advocated the establishment of chairs of music in universities. Holding an exalted view of the cultural and religious value of music, he believed that its future was immense in America, especially in the field of orchestral music. With real prophetic insight he said, "It only needs direction, artistic atmosphere, and technique in order to fill the land with such orchestras as the world has never heard" (Mims, p. 146).

All the while, however, he was eager to write poetry. In 1874 he wrote to a friend: "My head and my heart are so full of poems which the dreadful struggle for bread does not give me time to put on paper, that I am often driven to headache and heartache purely for want of an hour or two to hold a pen" (Baskervill, *post,* p. 211). His poem, "Corn," conceived on a visit to his family in Georgia, and published in *Lippincott's Magazine,* February 1875, and "The Symphony," published in the same magazine in June, represent the definite beginning of his poetic career. The praise of Gibson Peacock, Bayard Taylor, Charlotte Cushman, and others now strengthened his confidence in himself. Early in 1876 he was invited by Dudley Buck [*q.v.*] to write the words for the cantata to be rendered at the opening exercises of the Philadelphia Exposition. When the words were printed without the music, they were received with ridicule in all parts of the country, the critics failing to see that he had written, not a poem, but an interpretation of the music, corresponding to the libretto of an opera. The most significant fact about the work was its strong national spirit. It was immediately followed by the "Psalm of the West," which he called his Centennial Ode. These two, with a few short poems, were published in a volume in the fall of 1876, though it bore the date of 1877.

Having thus established himself as a musician worthy to be offered a place in Theodore Thomas' orchestra and as a promising man of letters, Lanier was again to be deflected from his course by the necessity of making a living for his family and by a new interest that developed through his study in the Peabody Library of Old and Middle English and of the literature of the Elizabethan age. With something of the spirit of research characteristic of the scholars of the newly founded Johns Hopkins University, he entered with zeal upon the investigation of certain problems in English studies. In lectures before groups of ladies at private homes and at the Peabody Institute, in which he anticipated modern efforts toward adult education—lectures published posthumously as *Shakspere and His Forerunners* (2 vols., 1902)—he prepared the way for the offer that came from President Gilman on Feb. 3, 1879, that he should accept the position of lecturer in English literature at Johns Hopkins. The results of his studies for university classes were *The Science of English Verse* (1880) and *The English Novel* (1883), the former being one of the permanent contributions of American scholarship to the technical consideration of the relations of poetry and music. Lanier believed that "versification has a technical side quite as well capable of being reduced to rules as that of painting or any other fine art" (*The Science of English Verse,* p. xv, quoting J. J. Sylvester). Though he perhaps over-stated the idea that the laws of music and of verse are identical, the book emphasizes a point of view that should be considered by both poets and students of poetry. His book is not only a scientific monograph, but also a philosophical treatise on a subject that has been discussed with increasing interest in recent years.

If Lanier had had a long life to live, one would not begrudge the time given by him to such studies, to his continued devotion to music, or to the series of boys' books that he wrote as "pot-boilers"—*The Boy's Froissart* (1879), *The Boy's King Arthur* (1880), *The Boy's Mabinogion* (1881), *The Boy's Percy* (1882). He would doubtless have in time worked out a synthesis of all his ideas and interests; as it was, he impresses one as blinded with excess of light and as rather feverishly passing from one interest to another. When to this variety of interests is added his constant search for health after periods of utter exhaustion, one wonders that he should have written as many excellent poems as he did. In the series on the marshes of his native Georgia, beginning with "The Marshes of Glynn," written in the full maturity of his powers, and ending with "Sunrise," written in the last months of his life with a temperature of 104 degrees, he revealed not only depth of spiritual passion but a melody and harmony of verse rare among modern poets. By the spring of 1880 he had won his fight over every obstacle that had been in his way—save one. He had a position which, supplemented by literary work, could support himself and his family. The years 1878 and 1879 had been his most productive. Finally, however, in the summer of 1880 he entered upon his last battle with his old enemy, the disease which he had inherited from both sides of his family and which had been accentuated by his prison life and by his habit of excessive work. In his book *Florida* (1876), written as a guidebook to the then unknown state, he had advised that consumptives "set out to get well, with the thorough assurance that consumption is curable" (*Florida*, p. 210). With characteristic optimism he had tried to follow his own advice, but Fate was against him in his heroic struggle. In June 1881, he went with his family to Asheville, N. C., and later to Lyon, a sheltered valley among the mountains of Polk County. He jotted down or dictated to his wife during his last days outlines or suggestions of poems which he hoped to write. One of these was a fitting close to his life, which came on Sept. 7, 1881:

"I was the earliest bird awake,
It was a while before dawn, I believe,
But somehow I saw round the world,
And the eastern mountain top did not hinder me,
And I knew of the dawn by my heart, not by mine eyes."
(Baskervill, p. 226).

With the spiritual endowment of a poet and an unusual sense of melody, Lanier never attained, except in a few poems which will hold their place in American anthologies, that union of sound and sense which is characteristic of the greatest poetry. Sickness, poverty, and hard work in other lines did not give him a chance to revise his poems and prevented him from that repose which is the proper mood of the artist. He had "the spontaneous overflow of powerful emotions," but his emotions were not "recollected in tranquillity." He suffered from a tendency to indulge in fancies; he was inoculated with "the conceit virus" of the metaphysical poets of the seventeenth century. He was hampered, too, by his theory of verse; often the music is present but not the inevitable word. But, not to mention some dozen others of his poems, "An Evening Song," "My Springs," "A Ballad of Trees and the Master," "The Song of the Chattahoochee," "The Revenge of Hamish," "The Symphony," some of the sonnets of the "Psalm of the West," "Sunrise," and, above all, "The Marshes of Glynn," will keep his fame alive.

[*Poems of Sidney Lanier* (1884), ed. by his wife, Mary Day Lanier, with a memorial by W. H. Ward; *Letters of Sidney Lanier: Selections from His Correspondence, 1866–1881* (1899), ed. by Henry W. Lanier, with a prefatory note by Chas. D. Lanier; Edwin Mims, *Sidney Lanier* (1905); Aubrey H. Starke, *Sidney Lanier* (1932); W. M. Baskervill, in *Southern Writers: Biog. and Critical Studies* (1896–97); M. H. Northrup, "Sidney Lanier: Recollections and Letters," in *Lippincott's Mag.*, Mar. 1905; D. C. Gilman, "Sidney Lanier: Reminiscences and Letters," in *S. Atlantic Quar.*, Apr. 1905; H. C. Thorpe, "Sidney Lanier—A Poet for Musicians," *Musical Quart.*, July 1925; J. F. D. Lanier, *Sketch of the Life of J. F. D. Lanier* (2nd ed., 1877); Baltimore *Sun*, Sept. 9, 1881.] E. M.

LANIGAN, GEORGE THOMAS (Dec. 10, 1845–Feb. 5, 1886), journalist, was born at St. Charles, on the Richelieu River, Canada, and is said to have been connected on his mother's side with the Webster family of New England. After attending high school in Montreal he learned telegraphy and worked on the government telegraph lines as operator and later as superintendent. His ambition to take up journalism, formed when as a boy he had contributed to the New York *Albion*, found opportunity during the Fenian disturbances in 1866, when he sent special correspondence to the *New York Herald*. With a group of associates he then started in Montreal a satirical and humorous paper, the *Free Lance*, which later became the *Evening Star*. Selling out his share in the *Free Lance*, he subsequently went to Chicago and became a special writer for the *Chicago Times*. About 1870 he moved to St. Louis, where he was employed on the *St. Louis Daily Globe*. His vivid articles on the smallpox ravages there are said to have aroused objections and lost him his position. He returned to Chicago, where he wrote for the *Chicago Tribune* and became western correspondent of the New York *World*. In 1874 he was asked to join the *World* editorial staff, on which he served for the next eight years. His command of French led to his specialization on foreign news, but he also wrote editorials, political and literary articles, and humorous sketches in verse and prose, showing remarkable facility and knowledge in the whole range of newspaper work. "He was," writes a fellow journalist, F. J. Shepard, "the best all-around newspaper man I ever knew—could do anything on a newspaper better than anybody else. He was a cherubic person, nearly as broad as he was long, wrote a hand that was copperplate, was an excellent French scholar who reviewed Hugo's *L'Art d'Être Grandpère* within twenty-four hours of its reception with long extracts in English verse." His Sunday *"Crême des Chroniques"* column was notably popular, as well as his satirical verse fables, published in book form in 1878 as *Fables of G. Washington Æsop, Taken "Anywhere, Anywhere Out of the World"* (1878). He also published a collection called *National Ballads of Canada* (Montreal, 1878). His celebrated "Threnody for the Ahkoond of Swat" and "The Amateur Orlando" are included in Rossiter Johnson's *Play-Day Poems* (1878) and other anthologies. In June 1883 he became editor of the Rochester *Post-Express* but resigned the next year, when he was not allowed to support Cleveland for President, and joined the staff of the *Philadelphia Record*. Here he remained until his death. His frequent changes of position are probably explained in part by his convivial habits. His brilliant talents in the general field of journalism were fully realized only by his more intimate associates, his popular recognition coming chiefly from his writings in lighter vein. His wife was Frances E. Barrett, whom he married in 1866, and by whom he had two sons and two daughters.

[*World* (N. Y.), *Buffalo Courier,* and *Philadelphia Record,* Feb. 6, 1886; information as to certain facts from F. J. Shepard, Buffalo, N. Y.] A. W.

LANMAN, CHARLES (June 14, 1819–Mar. 4, 1895), writer, amateur explorer, and artist, was a great-great-grandson of James Lanman who came from England to Boston about 1724, and a grandson of James Lanman of Norwich, Conn., who was United States senator from 1819 to 1825. The latter's son, Charles James, was one of the earliest emigrant lawyers from New England to the Territory of Michigan, where he married Marie Jeanne Guie, a French woman with Indian blood in her veins. Charles, their son, born in Monroe, Mich., was sent east in 1829 to his grandfather to be educated, and attended the Plymouth Academy near Norwich until 1835. At sixteen he entered an East India mercantile house in New York City, where he remained ten years. During this period he began exploring places in the eastern part of the United States, then more difficult of access, which have since become well-known vacation resorts. He was one of the first to use the canoe as a pleasure craft. Sketches which he published in papers and magazines, both in England and the United States, attracted the attention of Washington Irving, who once called him "the picturesque explorer of our country" (P. M. Irving, *The Life and Letters of Washington Irving,* vol. IV, 1864, p. 226). He also began exhibiting paintings and sketches from nature in oil, having studied under Asher B. Durand [*q.v.*], and although only an amateur was elected an associate of the National Academy of Design in 1846. Two of his books, *Essays for Summer Hours* (1842) and *Letters from a Landscape Painter* (1845), appeared before he returned to Monroe, Mich., in 1845, to take charge of the *Monroe Gazette.* The next year he became associate editor of the *Cincinnati Chronicle,* and in 1847 returned to New York to take a place on the editorial staff of the *Express.*

During these years he continued his fishing trips and explorations on foot, on horseback, and in canoes, which carried him through the Mississippi Valley, the region of the Great Lakes and the St. Lawrence, and over the whole of the Appalachian system from the Bay of Fundy to the Gulf states. From time to time he gathered his magazine articles into volumes: *A Summer in the Wilderness* (1847), *A Tour to the River Saguenay* (1848), *Letters from the Alleghany Mountains* (1849), and *Haw-ho-noo, or Records of a Tourist* (1850). The popularity of these volumes resulted in several reprints in England and America. A selection from them, and from his uncollected contributions to periodicals, was published in London under the title *Adventures in the Wilds of America* (1854) and reprinted with additions in Philadelphia (two volumes) in 1856.

In 1849 he was appointed librarian of the War Department at Washington and in the same year married Adeline Dodge. He resigned his office in 1850 to become private secretary to Daniel Webster. The fruit of this intimacy was the valuable, anecdotal *Private Life of Daniel Webster* (1852), first published the previous year as a pamphlet, with the title, *Personal Memorials of Daniel Webster.* Lanman reëntered public life in 1853, and from 1855 to 1857 was librarian and head of the returns office in the Interior Department. In 1859 he first published his well-known *Dictionary of the United States Congress,* revised at frequent intervals and finally taken over by the government and published by Congress as a document. After the author had been paid a regular royalty of one dollar a copy for a number of years, Congress deprived him of his rights under the copyright law; and he was unable to obtain any redress. He was librarian of the House of Representatives in 1861, and edited the *Journal of Alfred Ely, A Prisoner of War in Richmond* (1862). He again became head of the returns office in the Interior Department in 1865.

The next few years were spent in literary work at his home in Georgetown, interspersed with frequent fishing and exploring trips. He published a *Life of William Woodbridge* (1867) and *Red Book of Michigan* (1871). He was appointed American secretary of the Japanese legation in 1871, and held that position eleven years. As a result of this connection he edited the volume, *The Japanese in America* (1872), to which he contributed sections on "The Japanese Embassy," "The Japanese Students," and "Japanese Poetry." He was assistant assessor of the District of Columbia in 1885, and librarian of the Washington city library in 1888. The remainder of his life was spent in his Georgetown home, writing and painting. In all, he was the author of thirty-two distinct works. He was a handsome man of genial presence, popular in society, and an excellent raconteur. His wife survived him nine years. There were no children.

[Lanman papers in the Lib. of Cong.; recollections of distant relatives living in Norwich and New London, Conn.; *Am. Ancestry,* vol. III (1888); *Evening Star* (Washington), Mar. 5, 1895; *Washington Post,* Mar. 5, 6, 1895; *N. Y. Tribune,* Mar. 6, 1895.]

H. H. B. M.

LANMAN, JOSEPH (July 11, 1811–Mar. 13, 1874), naval officer, was born at Norwich, Conn., of old New England stock, son of Peter Lanman, a Norwich merchant and ship-owner, and Abigail Trumbull Lanman, a grand-daughter of Gov. Jonathan Trumbull. Recommended by his uncle, Senator James Lanman, as "much superior to lads of his age," and "of great zeal and ambition for naval life," he secured an appointment as midshipman, Jan. 1, 1825. His first cruise was the next year in the *Macedonian* to Brazil. Up to the Civil War his career followed the naval routine of sea and shore service. He was promoted lieutenant on Mar. 3, 1835. During the Mexican War he was on ordnance duty in the Navy Department, and then in the Pacific Squadron, 1847–48, from which he was detached in 1848 as bearer of special dispatches to Washington. He was in the *San Jacinto* of the Mediterranean Squadron, 1849–51; on special duty for three years; then, after promotion to commander, Sept. 14, 1855, at the Washington Navy Yard, 1855–56; and commander of the steamer *Michigan* on the Great Lakes, 1859–61. At the outbreak of the Civil War he was sent to the Mare Island Navy Yard, San Francisco, from which he was transferred in January 1862 to command the steam sloop *Saranac* of the Pacific Squadron. In August of that year he was made commodore and in September was shifted to the steam sloop *Lancaster* of the same squadron. Returning to the East coast in the summer of 1864, he was assigned to the steam frigate *Minnesota* and joined the North Atlantic Blockading Squadron under Porter, in which, on Oct. 12, he was given command of the second division. His ship led this division in both attacks on Fort Fisher, Dec. 24–25, 1864, and Jan. 13–15, 1865. Admiral Porter commended him in his report for "admirable judgment and coolness" and in a letter of Jan. 17, 1865, assigning him to command the vessels at Hampton Roads, expressed "high appreciation" of his work at Fort Fisher and "the gallant manner in which you, with your ship, have on several occasions led the fleet into action" (*War of the Rebellion: Official Records* (*Navy*), 1 ser. XI, p. 610). Lanman turned over his sea command two weeks later. On Dec. 8, 1867, he was made rear admiral, and after serving as head of the Portsmouth Navy Yard, 1867–69, he was during the next two years in command of the South Atlantic Squadron operating chiefly in Brazilian waters. Upon his retirement in July 1872, he returned to his home in Norwich, where he died two years later of pneumonia. A monument was erected by his townspeople on his grave in Yantic Cemetery, Norwich. Lanman was reputedly somewhat irascible, but an alert and able officer. He was fond of social life and had a host of distinguished friends. In appearance he was short and stout, with ruddy complexion and piercing grey eyes. His upper lip was clean-shaven, but, being troubled with asthma, he grew a heavy beard which in later years was braided and worn inside his clothing. He was married in Washington, Sept. 20, 1842, to Ann Cornelia, daughter of Capt. Job G. Williams of the United States Marine Corps, and had three daughters and a son.

[L. R. Hamersly, *Records of Living Officers of the U. S. Navy and Marine Corps* (ed. 1870); M. McG. Dana, *The Norwich Memorial: The Annals of Norwich, New London County, Conn., in the Great Rebellion of 1861–65* (1873); a letter-book of Lanman's last cruise, Sept. 1869–Aug. 1870, in the U. S. Naval Academy Museum; *Norwich Weekly Courier,* Mar. 19, 1874; *Army and Navy Jour.,* Mar. 21, 1874; information as to certain facts from members of Lanman's family.]

A. W.

LANSING, GULIAN (Feb. 1, 1825–Sept. 12, 1892), missionary in Egypt, was born at Lishaskill, Albany County, N. Y. His parents, John and Eliza Lansing, by ancestry were Dutch and of the Dutch Reformed Church. Lansing, however, having graduated from Union College in 1847, left the church of his fathers to study theology in the seminary of the Associate Reformed Church in Newburgh. In 1850 he was ordained in this church for missionary service, was married to Maria Oliver of Lishaskill, and went out to his church's mission to Jews in Damascus.

Returning in 1856 from a visit to America he stopped for reasons of health at Cairo, where two Associate Reformed missionaries had recently established themselves. He remained in Egypt all the rest of his life. In the first year he began preaching and teaching in Alexandria. The formation of the United Presbyterian Church of North America in 1858 by the consolidation of the Associate Synod and the Associate Reformed Church caused changes in missionary organization in Egypt. With the coming of new missionaries, the important United Presbyterian mission was established which devoted itself chiefly to the people of the degenerate Coptic church, though it reached out also to the less approachable Moslems. In 1860 Lansing moved to the mission's headquarters at Cairo, and bore a foremost part in the new developments. Active and sociable, he did much of his best work by direct contact with the people. He soon made a voyage up the Nile, in a boat which he procured for the mission, preaching and distributing Bibles. In this and later journeys he was accompanied by the fifth Lord Aberdeen, one of the many influential travelers whose interest he enlisted. Some of his journeys were described, in order to attract attention to the mission, in his *Egypt's Princes* (1864). They resulted in the establishment of several new missionary stations in the Nile Valley. To his courage and practical wisdom the mission mainly owed its first building in 1862 and the much larger quarters completed in 1881. He was a good Arabic and Hebrew scholar and taught in the mission's theological school. He assumed as his special responsibility the defense of converts against persecution, obtaining the help of the American consul-general and the United States government. In the systematic attempt of the Coptic hierarchy to destroy Protestantism, beginning in 1867, he undertook to gain from the khedive protection and redress. His sagacity, firmness and commanding bearing gave him success, and finally secured for Protestantism legal standing as a religion. For a quarter of a century he was a leader in all the concerns of the mission, always hopeful, farsighted and energetic.

In 1865 his wife died of cholera, and Lansing barely escaped alive. The following year he married Sarah B. Dales, also a leader in the mission. From 1886 his strength declined, and he spent much time in England and America, but his last year was passed in Cairo.

[Andrew Watson, *The Am. Mission in Egypt, 1854 to 1896* (1898); minutes of the Asso. Ref. Synod of N. Y.; reports of Board of Foreign Missions of United Presbyt. Ch., and manuscript biography of Lansing by J. B. Dales in archives of the Board; *Union Coll., A Record of the Commemoration . . . 1895, of the One Hundredth Anniversary* (1897); *United Presbyterian*, Sept. 22, 1892.]

R. H. N.

LANSING, JOHN (b. Jan. 30, 1754), jurist, born in Albany, N. Y., was the son of Gerrit Jacob and Jannetje (Waters) Lansing and was descended from Gerrit Lansing who had emigrated from the Netherlands about 1640 and was among the early settlers of the manor of Rensselaerwyck. Lansing studied law with Robert Yates in Albany and James Duane in New York and was admitted to practice in Albany in 1775. During 1776 and 1777 he served as military secretary to Gen. Philip Schuyler. Resuming his law practice in Albany he served in the New York Assembly six terms, 1780–84, 1786, and 1788. During the two latter years he was speaker. He was a member of Congress under the Articles of Confederation in 1784 and 1785. He was appointed mayor of Albany in 1786 and served four years. In 1786 he was one of the New York commissioners delegated to settle the territorial dispute with Massachusetts; and in 1790 and 1791 he served in a similar capacity in helping adjust the boundary dispute between New York and Vermont and the claims arising out of the settlement.

On Mar. 6, 1787, Lansing was chosen with Robert Yates and Alexander Hamilton as a delegate to the Philadelphia Convention. On July 10, believing that the convention was exceeding its instructions in drafting a new constitution instead of amending the Articles of Confederation, Lansing and Yates withdrew, setting forth their reasons for doing so in a joint letter to Gov. George Clinton (*Secret Proceedings and Debates of the Convention . . . at Philadelphia*, 1821, pp. 280–83. The *Secret Proceedings* were copied by Lansing from Yates's longhand notes). Lansing was a member of the New York ratifying convention of 1788 where he stoutly opposed the new federal constitution. His long judicial career began in 1790 with his appointment as a judge of the supreme court of New York where he served for eleven years, being chosen chief justice in 1798. In 1801 he became chancellor of the state and held that post until 1814 when he reached the constitutional age limit of sixty. James Kent [*q.v.*] was his successor. No regular system of reporting prevailed in either of these courts until after the period of Lansing's service. Such of his opinions as are available show him to have been learned, polished, and concise. The most striking incident of his judicial career occurred during his chancellorship when he imposed imprisonment for contempt upon John V. N. Yates, a distinguished member of the Albany bar. This led to a clash between Lansing and the supreme court of the state in which he was finally defeated and later was sued unsuccessfully by Yates for unlawful imprisonment. While chancellor he refused an injunction to restrain the violation of the Fulton-Livingston steamboat monopoly, on the ground that the monopoly violated the natural rights of citizens to the free navigation of state waters, rather than on the ground later used by Marshall of conflict with federal commercial regulations. His decision was overruled (9 Johnson's Supreme Court *Reports*, 507).

Much of Lansing's earlier political preferment had been due to the support of the powerful Clinton family. But he did not take orders meekly. In 1804, with Burr in the midst of his bitter fight with Jefferson and with Clinton seeking the vice-presidential nomination, the Jeffersonian-Republican legislative caucus at Albany nominated Lansing for the governorship. In the interest of party harmony he reluctantly accepted. Hamilton, who was in Albany at the time arguing the case of Harry Croswell, urged New York Federalists to support Lansing rather than Burr, if they had no candidate of their own (H. C. Lodge, *The Works of Alexander Hamilton,* VII, 1886, pp. 323–26). Burr was nominated and Lansing shortly thereafter withdrew his name. Two years later he made public his reasons for doing so alleging that George Clinton had "sought to pledge him to a particular course of conduct in the administration of the government of the state" (Alexander, *post,* I, p. 153). To Clinton's denial Lansing specified that Clinton had asked for the appointment of DeWitt Clinton as chancellor.

After his retirement from the bench Lansing resumed his law practice as one of the leaders of the bar. He became a regent of the University of the State of New York in 1817, and he also took an interest in the affairs of Columbia College. He had married, on Apr. 8, 1781, Cornelia Ray of New York City and had ten children, five of whom died in infancy. He was a large, handsome man, dignified and kindly in manner, a good conversationalist and a favorite in society. His death created a tremendous sensation. In December 1829 he went to New York on business connected with Columbia College and remained about a week. On Dec. 12 he left his hotel about nine in the evening to post some letters on the Albany boat at the foot of Cortlandt Street. He never returned and no trace of him was ever found. That he was murdered is supported by the statement of Thurlow Weed's biographer that many years later Weed received, under a pledge of secrecy, evidence as to the facts of Lansing's death with an injunction to publish them when those implicated were dead. While this latter condition was met in 1870 there remained alive those "sharing in the strong inducement which prompted the crime." Weed accordingly never made public the facts in his possession. (See T. W. Barnes, *Memoir of Thurlow Weed,* 1884, pp. 34–35.) Lansing published *Reports of Select Cases in Chancery and the Supreme Court of the State of New York in 1824 and 1826* (1826).

[A. B. Street, *The Council of Revision of the State of N. Y.* (1859); L. B. Proctor, "Chancellors Livingston, Lansing and Kent," *Albany Law Jour.*, Supp. to vol. XLV (Jan.–July 1892); C. G. Munsell, *The Lansing Family* (1916); Jonathan Pearson, *Contributions for the Geneals. of the First Settlers of the Ancient County of Albany from 1630 to 1800* (1872); *Daily Albany Argus*, Dec. 29, 1829; *N. Y. Mercury*, Dec. 30, 1829; D. S. Alexander, *A Pol. Hist. of the State of N. Y.*, vol. I (1906).] R. E. C.

LANSING, ROBERT (Oct. 17, 1864–Oct. 30, 1928), secretary of state, was born at Watertown, N. Y., the son of John and Maria Lay (Dodge) Lansing. His American ancestry reached far back into colonial times: on his father's side in New York and New Amsterdam, whither Gerrit Lansing had come about 1640 from Holland; on his mother's, in Rhode Island and Connecticut (C. G. Munsell, *The Lansing Family,* 1916; T. R. Woodward, *Dodge Genealogy,* 1904). Robert attended Amherst College, from which he was graduated in 1886, and read law in his father's office. In 1889 he was admitted to the bar and became the junior partner in the firm of Lansing & Lansing at Watertown. His life might have been spent in local practice but for his marriage, Jan. 15, 1890, to Eleanor Foster, daughter of John W. Foster [*q.v.*], distinguished diplomat and in 1892–93 secretary of state under President Harrison. The association with Foster opened to young Lansing the field in which he was to win distinction. The new career began in 1892 with his appointment as associate counsel for the United States in the fur-seal arbitration. From that date to 1914 he served frequently as counsel or agent of the United States before international arbitration tribunals. It was said on good authority in 1914 that he had "appeared more frequently before arbitral tribunals than any living lawyer" (*American Journal of International Law,* April 1914, p. 337). In addition, he represented private interests in several international cases and acted for some years as counsel for the Chinese and Mexican legations in Washington. He was instrumental in founding the American Society of International Law (1906) and in establishing (1907) the *American Journal of International Law,* of which he was an editor up to the time of his death. On Apr. 1, 1914, he became counselor for the Department of State, in which capacity he not only had to deal with the legal aspects of the numberless problems raised by the outbreak of the World War in the following August, but also served as acting secretary of state during the frequent absences of Secretary Bryan. It was an open secret that a large proportion of the official notes signed by Bryan were the work of Lansing (*World's Work,* August 1915, pp. 398–402).

Upon Bryan's resignation during the *Lusitania* crisis, Lansing was named secretary of state *ad interim* and shortly thereafter (June 23, 1915) was regularly appointed to the office. The selection for this post of an expert in international law without political prominence or importance, though very unusual, elicited some favorable comment (*Nation,* July 1, 1915). His technical knowledge was without doubt of great value, but he had little real opportunity to exhibit his ability in an independent fashion. Important matters of policy President Wilson himself determined, and, in general, negotiations of great delicacy were conducted informally through Col. Edward M. House. Ambassador Bernstorff's remark, "Since Wilson decides *everything,* any interview with Lansing is a mere matter of form" (*Official German Documents Relating to the World War,* 1923, II, 1017), was however, an exaggeration. Lansing had both ideas and definite policies. He was in advance of the President in visualizing the war as a struggle between democracy and autocracy and in foreseeing the eventual participation of the United States. Peace with Mexico and the recognition of Carranza were also quite as much his policies as Wilson's and in Lansing's mind were designed to keep the hands of the United States free for war with Germany. In the negotiations with Germany over the sinking of the *Lusitania, Arabic,* and *Sussex,* the President's hand was uppermost, whereas the protests against British blockade and contraband practices were almost entirely the work of Lansing. The latter were written in such strong language that they evoked bitter remonstrance from the American ambassador to Great Britain, Walter Hines Page, who described one of Lansing's notes as "an uncourteous monster of 35 heads and 3 appendices" (Hendrick, *post,* II, 78). Lansing, who had no thought whatever of a break with Great Britain, felt that strong protests were necessitated by the tremendous pressure of injured exporting interests, as well as by the fact that technically the British practices were as clearly violations of international law as were the German. On Nov. 2, 1917, Lansing signed with Viscount Ishii of Japan the so-called Lansing-Ishii agreement, by which, while both nations declared their adherence to the "open door" in China, the United States recognized "that Japan has special interests in China, particularly in the part to which her possessions are contiguous" (*United States Treaty Series,* no. 630, 1917). The negotiation resulting in this agreement took place some months after the United States had entered the war and at a time when some such concession to Japan seemed necessary to secure her continued participation as a belligerent. Aside from its apparent necessity, the best defense that can be made of it is that it had no permanently injurious effects upon China. At the time it did much to destroy Chinese confidence in the friendship of the United States.

Up to the close of hostilities Lansing and Wilson had apparently worked in complete harmony. With the opening of the Peace Conference they began to drift apart. Lansing's legalistic and prosaic habits of mind were entirely out of accord with the President's idealistic and imaginative conceptions, and this difference was glaringly apparent in their attitudes to the proposed League of Nations, which to Wilson was paramount, to Lansing unimportant. As a consequence Lansing, though nominally (under Wilson) chief of the American delegation, did not know the President's mind or possess his confidence. He was therefore in no position to make very important contributions to the work of the Conference. As chairman of the commission on responsibility for the war, however, he indorsed the report which held the Central Powers responsible for deliberately provoking the war. To substantiate their position he and his American colleague (Dr. James Brown Scott) published a portion of a report made in July 1914 by an Austrian investigator, von Wiesner, which appeared to be a complete exoneration of the Serbian government from all complicity in the Sarajevo assassinations. Whether Lansing and Scott were in possession of the entire report, which in reality held Serbia culpable, has never been revealed. While strongly disapproving some features of the treaty as finally adopted, Lansing signed it and later advocated the ratification of it as far better than no treaty at all.

Revelation during the Senate hearings on the treaty of Lansing's former opposition to certain features of it deepened the breach between him and Wilson, who at about this time was stricken with paralysis. During Wilson's illness Lansing took the responsibility of calling the cabinet together for occasional meetings, and this action on his part was seized upon by the President, in February 1920, as cause for demanding his resignation, which was accordingly submitted on Feb. 12. It was rather generally agreed by spokesmen of both political parties that the calling of cabinet meetings was entirely proper, that Wilson's ill health alone could excuse his peevish notes to the Secretary, and that the real cause of the break was to be found in the disagreements that had developed at the Peace Conference. After his resignation Lansing pursued the private practice of international law, with office in Washington, until his death on Oct. 30, 1928. A handsome man, of large build and rather impressive presence, he was noted for his courtesy and tact. Among other things, he found amusement in sketching, his pencil drawings of his colleagues in the cabinet being celebrated among their subjects.

His own view of the Peace Conference is given in his books, *The Big Four and Others of the Peace Conference* (1921), and *The Peace Negotiations: A Personal Narrative* (1921), the latter a detailed account of his relations with Wilson. He was also the author of *Notes on Sovereignty from the Standpoint of the State and of the World* (1921); and, with Gary M. Jones, of *Government: Its Origin, Growth, and Form in the United States* (1902).

[A brief sketch of Lansing's career prior to his entering the Department of State was printed in *Am. Jour. of International Law*, Apr. 1914. His work as secretary of state is described by J. W. Pratt in *Am. Secretaries of State and Their Diplomacy*, ed. by S. F. Bemis, vol. X (1929). Much of his official correspondence is printed in the official publications of the Department of State: *Dipl. Correspondence with Belligerent Governments Relating to Neutral Rights and Duties* (4 vols., 1915–18); the annual volumes of *Papers Relating to the Foreign Relations of the U. S.*, 1915–20; and the *Supplements* to those volumes for the same years. *The Intimate Papers of Col. House* (4 vols., 1926–28), ed. by Chas. Seymour; and Burton J. Hendrick, *The Life and Letters of Walter H. Page* (3 vols., 1922–25), contain many references to Lansing.]

J. W. P—t.

LANSTON, TOLBERT (Feb. 3, 1844–Feb. 18, 1913), inventor, was born on a farm at Troy, Ohio, the son of Nicholas Randall and Sarah Jane (Wright) Lanston. During his boyhood he moved with his parents to Iowa. He attended the district schools and helped with the farm work, in which he displayed a marked mechanical skill and inventive ability, until the outbreak of the Civil War, when he enlisted and served throughout that struggle. At its close he went to Washington, D. C., and obtained a clerical position in the United States Pension Office. For twenty-two years he continued in this service, meantime studying law and being admitted to the bar. He also found time to exercise his mechanical ingenuity. In 1870 he patented a padlock and in the following year a hydraulic dumbwaiter, a brush and comb, and a railroad car coupler. In 1874 he invented a locomotive smokestack; and in 1878 a sewing-machine chair. Later he was granted patents for a sewing machine, a water faucet, and a window sash. About 1883 he became greatly interested in machines for composing type, probably as a result of the work along this line which Ottmar Mergenthaler [*q.v.*] was then doing in Washington. Presumably Lanston devoted all of his available time between 1883 and 1887 to this subject, for he was rewarded on June 7, 1887, with a series of three patents for "producing justified lines of type," one for a "type forming and composing machine," and one for a new form of type. About the same time he obtained British patent No. 8183 on the same mechanisms. Resigning from the Pension Office, he organized the Lanston Type Machine Company, in Washington, and to it assigned all his patents. He then undertook the difficult task of converting his patented ideas into a practical machine for commercial work, and at the same time a machine which could be successfully manufactured. For ten years he labored on the problem and finally introduced in 1897 his perfected "monotype." The monotype consists really of two machines, one for composing type and one for casting it. On the composing machine is a keyboard much like that of a large typewriter: when each key is struck, two perforations are made in a paper ribbon, this ribbon then passes to the second or casting machine, and, as it runs through, air passing through its perforations causes letters to be cast, one by one, at the rate of 150 a minute. As each letter is cast it is pushed into a line and each line as finished is added to the last. Lanston at first worked on the idea of stamping the types in cold metal but about 1890 arranged his machine to cast them from melted metal. A few years prior to the introduction of his machine, he reorganized his company and, under the new name of Lanston Monotype Manufacturing Company, established a plant in Philadelphia, Pa. During the next thirteen years he not only assisted in the successful conduct of the business but also devoted much time to the further perfection of the monotype. Over and above his basic patents of 1887 he was granted further patents in 1896, 1897, 1899, 1900, 1902, and 1910. While the linotype composing machine antedated the monotype, there was apparently room for both: fully nine-tenths of all type setting in the United States is done on these machines. For his invention Lanston was awarded the Cresson gold medal by the Franklin Institute of Philadelphia in 1896. In 1899 he also patented an adding machine. Shortly after securing his last patent he was stricken with paralysis and was invalided until his death three years later. He was married in 1865 to Betty G. Heidel of Washington and a number of years after her death he married, in 1909, Alice H. Hieston of that city. She, with one son by his first wife, survived him. He died in Washington.

[*House Ex. Doc. No. 89*, 41 Cong., 3 Sess.; *House Ex. Doc. No. 86*, 42 Cong., 2 Sess.; *Specifications and Drawings of Patents Issued by the U. S. Patent Office*, Nov. 1874, Mar. 1875, May 1878, Sept. 1881, Oct. 1882, Dec. 1883, June 1887, Jan. 1888, Apr. 1896, Sept. 1897, Mar., Sept. 1899, July, Dec. 1900, May, June 1902, July 1903, and Mar. 1910; *Illustrated Journal of the Patent Office for the Year 1887* (London), Oct. 13, 1888; L. A. Legros and J. C. Grant, *Typographical Printing-Surfaces* (London, 1916); W. B. Kaempffert, *A Popular Hist. of Am. Invention* (1924); *Am. Printer* (N. Y.), Mar. 1913; *Inland Printer* (Chicago), May 1913; *Washington Post*, Feb. 19, 1913.] C. W. M.

LAPHAM, INCREASE ALLEN (Mar. 7, 1811–Sept. 14, 1875), the first Wisconsin scientist, was a native of New York state, where he was born at Palmyra, second son of Seneca and Rachel Allen Lapham. He was descended from John Lapham who emigrated from England in the seventeenth century and settled finally at Dartmouth, Mass. He was named for his mother's father, Increase Allen, and was reared in the Quaker faith. His father was a canal contractor and engineer. When Increase was thirteen years old, he was employed on the Erie Canal near Lockport, cutting stone and carrying a survey rod; he also drew plans at this early age for the locks in the canal and his first lessons in mineralogy and geology were from his observations of the fossils in the stone he cut. He had little formal education, but he attended the grammar school of Mann Butler, in Louisville, Ky., where he obtained some elements of culture. At that time he wrote his first scientific monograph, "A Notice of the Louisville and Shippingsport Canal and of the Geology of the Vicinity," which was accepted by Silliman's *American Journal of Science and Arts* (July 1828). From 1830 to 1833 he worked on a canal at Portsmouth, Ohio, and made so good a report of canal conditions and possibilities that he was appointed in the latter year secretary of the Ohio State Board of Canal Commissioners. About this time his father and family bought a farm near Mount Tabor, Ohio, and Increase published a paper on "Agriculture in Ohio," in which he advocated rotation of crops and other scientific ideas of farming.

During the years 1833–35 at Columbus the young man devoted all his spare time to scientific study, making a herbarium of plants and a good collection of minerals. He was offered a position in 1836 on the Ohio Geological Survey, but preferred to work as an assistant to Byron Kilbourn, one of the founders of Milwaukee, in his various enterprises of surveying, canal building, platting, and promoting. From this time for almost forty years he made his home at Milwaukee, one of its most modest, quiet citizens, but one of the most useful. The first Wisconsin imprint came from his pen in 1836, *A Catalogue of Plants and Shells found in the Vicinity of Milwaukee on the West Side of Lake Michigan.* In 1844 appeared *Wisconsin: its Geography and Topography, History, Geology, and Mineralogy,* in the preparation of which the author traveled widely over the territory. During these early years Lapham began a correspondence with many eminent scientists of his time and in 1852 Gray dedicated a new genus of plants to him under the term *Laphamia.*

Lapham was an expert map maker and his are among the first and best maps of Wisconsin and the vicinity of Milwaukee. During his surveys he became interested in the emblematic Indian mounds found on Wisconsin's surface and in 1855 his monograph, "The Antiquities of Wisconsin," published in the *Smithsonian Contributions to Knowledge* (vol. VII), attracted much attention. One of his last services to the state was the preparation of a number of models of Indian mounds for exhibition at the Centennial Exposition of 1876. He was interested in civic affairs and in Milwaukee held many local offices. As school commissioner he sought to promote higher education, giving land for a high school and traveling in the East to solicit a bond issue for the building. He aided in the establishment of a school for the normal training of girls, which in 1850 under the fostering care of Catherine Beecher became the Milwaukee Female College, later the Milwaukee-Downer College. Of this institution Lapham was president of the board of trustees for many years. He was one of a committee to draft the constitution of the State Historical Society of which he served as vice-president for twelve years and president for ten years. He was also a charter member of the Wisconsin Academy of Sciences, Arts, and Letters, and contributed a number of papers to its published *Transactions.*

At Lapham's urgent insistence the United States government passed a law in 1869 establishing the weather bureau. Lapham was offered its headship, but as the bureau was part of the Department of War, he would not compromise his Quaker principles by joining the army. In 1871, however, he accepted a temporary position at Chicago as observer and therein earned the first salary he had received for scientific employment. In 1873 the state of Wisconsin appointed him geologist with an adequate salary and assistants for a state survey. Two years later he was displaced for a political follower of the new governor. He retired to a farm at Oconomowoc and there died from heart disease while boating on the lake. His portrait hangs in the state capitol, and a peak in southern Wisconsin bears his name. He married in 1838 Ann M. Alcott, who died before him, leaving five children.

[S. S. Sherman, *Increase Allen Lapham* (1876), contains a bibliography of fifty titles. Other sources include: M. M. Quaife, "Increase Allen Lapham, First Scholar of Wisconsin," *Wis. Mag. of Hist.*, Sept. 1917; "Early Days in Ohio from Letters and Diaries of Dr. I. A. Lapham," *Ohio Archæol. and Hist. Quart.*, Jan. 1909; W. B. Lapham, *The Lapham Family Register* (1873); *U. S. Biog. Dict., Wis. Vol.* (1877). Lapham's papers, in the Wisconsin Historical Library, include an autobiography written in 1859].

L. P. K.

LAPHAM, WILLIAM BERRY (Aug. 21, 1828–Feb. 22, 1894), physician, journalist, and genealogist, was born in Greenwood, Oxford County, Me., the son of John and Louvisa (Berry) Lapham and a descendant of Thomas Lapham who settled in Massachusetts in 1634 or 1635. He entered Waterville (now Colby) College in 1851, but remained there only a year, leaving to study medicine. After receiving the degree of M.D. from the New York Medical College in 1856, he began to practise in Bryant's Pond, Me. At the outbreak of the Civil War he was appointed assistant surgeon, and later first lieutenant, in the 23rd Maine Volunteers. From 1863 to the close of the war he served with the 1st Maine Mounted Artillery, which he had helped to recruit, and in 1865 he received the brevet rank of major, although his rank in actual service had been that of senior first lieutenant of the 7th Battery. In 1867 he was a representative in the Maine legislature. He was examining surgeon for the pension board for a number of years, and trustee of the state insane hospital from 1867 to 1874. His literary interests led to his becoming, in 1872, editor of the *Maine Farmer,* which he continued to conduct till 1881. His chief distinction, however, was gained as an antiquarian. From 1875 to 1878 he edited the *Maine Genealogist.* He was a member of the Maine Historical Society and of the New-England Historic Genealogical Society, serving as chairman of the publication committee of the former, and contributing many papers to the proceedings of the latter. He was also a corresponding member of the Royal Historical Society of Great Britain. He wrote histories of the towns of Woodstock, Paris, Rumford, Bethel, and Norway, in Maine; and he compiled genealogies of the Lapham, Ricker, Chase, Chapman, Webster, Hill, and Knox families. He also wrote and published himself *My Recollections of the War of the Rebellion* (1892). He was recognized as an authority on genealogy and early New England history, and his researches in both these fields are respected by specialists.

Lapham received the honorary degree of A.M. from Colby College in 1871. On Nov. 27, 1866, he married Cynthia A. Perham of Woodstock, Me., by whom he had one son and two daughters. He died at the National Soldiers Home in Togus, Me.

[Autobiographical material in W. B. Lapham, *The Lapham Family Register* (1873), and *Hist. of Woodstock, Me.* (1882); H. D. Kingsbury and S. L. Deyo, *Illus. Hist. of Kennebec County, Me.* (1892); *New-Eng. Hist. and Geneal. Reg.,* July 1894; *Boston Transcript,* Feb. 23, 1894.] S. G.

LARAMIE, JACQUES (d. 1821), pioneer trapper, was born probably in Canada and was of French descent. Though few, if any, of the trapper-explorers have been so generously honored in the giving of place-names, of none among these adventurers who have attained fame is so little known. Even his real name is in doubt. It is usually said to have been La Ramée. There seems, however, a greater probability that it was Lorimier, and the man a relative of the Louis Lorimier who was a trader among the Indians in the Ohio Valley, and later, under the Spanish and American régimes, the commandant at Cape Girardeau, Mo. Among Americans at that time "Laramie" was the usual pronunciation and spelling of this name, and there is some significance in the fact that in Albert Gallatin's map of 1836 the mountain named for the trapper appears as Lorimier's Peak. Tradition makes Laramie an employee of the North West Company. In time he drifted to St. Louis and was probably among the trappers who as early as 1816 were ranging the Colorado foothills, and who gathered from time to time in rendezvous near the site of the present Denver. About 1819, perhaps earlier, with several companions, he entered the unknown country of southeastern Wyoming. He is reputed to have been the first white man to visit, along its upper course, the Laramie River, the mouth of which had been discovered by Robert Stuart's party of eastbound Astorians in the winter of 1812–13. Resolved on a solitary hunt, he separated from his companions in the fall or early winter of 1820 and explored the Laramie possibly as far as the mouth of the Sibylee (Sabille), where he built a cabin. His long absence prompted a search for him, and in the following spring his dead body was found. He had been killed, it is supposed, by a party of Arapahos.

In the legendry of the West he became an important figure, and districts that he never saw were soon associated with his name. The trading-post, Fort William, erected near the junction of the Laramie and the North Platte in 1834, was popularly known as Fort Laramie almost from the beginning; its successor, Fort John, was later formally renamed for the trapper in deference to popular usage, and the name was continued by the United States government when it bought the post in 1849. A branch of the river became the Little Laramie; a broad area of semi-desert, the Laramie Plains; a nearby mountain range (the "Black Hills" of Parkman and other early chroniclers), the Laramie Mountains; and the highest point of the range, Laramie Peak. While yet a great part of the present Wyoming belonged to Dakota Territory, Laramie County was organized, and in April 1868 the Union Pacific Railroad fixed a location for the present city of Laramie. The fame of the trapper has prompted considerable research as to his personal history, but little has been revealed, and most that has been written about him is purely speculative.

[Grace R. Hebard, "Jacques Laramie," *Midwest Review,* Mar. 1926; C. G. Coutant, *The Hist. of Wyoming* (1899), pp. 296–99.] W. J. G.

LARCOM, LUCY (Mar. 5, 1824–Apr. 17, 1893), author and teacher, a descendant of Mordecai Larkham (or Larcom), who was first recorded in Beverly, Mass., in 1681, was the ninth child in the family of Benjamin and Lois (Barrett) Larcom, of Beverly. She was born, as she said, "of people of integrity and profound faith in God" and with "an inheritance of hard work and the privilege of poverty." At the age of two the child's school education began and she learned to read with avidity, delighting especially in hymns. In this taste were combined the two deepest loves of her life, poetry and religion. After the death of Benjamin Larcom in 1835, Mrs. Larcom removed to Lowell, Mass., where her daughters worked in the mills and found companions who stimulated their already determined desire for development. About 1840 Lucy Larcom began to contribute to the *Operative's Magazine,* which, merged in 1842 with the *Lowell Offering,* became the *Lowell Offering and Magazine.* In 1846 she made the then long journey to Looking Glass Prairie, Ill., and for a few years experienced the pleasures and pains of a district school teacher in pioneer communities. Her ambition eventually carried her to Monticello Seminary near Alton, Ill., where she studied and taught (1849–52) and, in her own words, "learned what education really is." Later she taught (1854–62) in Norton, Mass., at Wheaton Seminary (later Wheaton College). Her love of literature and history and her genuine interest in her pupils made her an inspiring teacher and her personal influence went far outside her classrooms.

Her first book, *Similitudes from Ocean and Prairie,* published in 1854, was a series of prose poems which she justly characterized as "a very immature affair." In her youth an ardent abolitionist and throughout her life an intense patriot, she won her first poetic success with the "Call to Kansas," which in 1855 took the prize of the New England Emigrant Aid Company. The first collection of her verses, entitled merely *Poems,* appeared in 1869. Some of these, notably "Hannah Binding Shoes," had already gained for her a considerable reputation; and by 1884 her verses had become so popular that a complete collection was published in the "Household Edition" of Houghton, Mifflin & Company. Her poetry is simple and homely, with flexible rhythms and easy rhymes. Moral applications and spiritual analogues abound, and to her were the very heart of her writing. Her observation, especially of nature, was delighted but not discriminating; she felt with an enthusiasm which she was seldom able to convey to her readers. Seriously as she and her friends regarded her high calling as a poet, her verses were of the kind that pass with the generation to which they belong. The same could not be said of her reminiscent volume, *A New England Girlhood* (1889). As the conditions there recorded fade still farther into the background, this book emerges as a surprisingly successful reconstruction of New England village life. The chapters dealing with her years in Lowell make a definite contribution to American social and industrial history and likewise deserve praise as literature.

From 1865 to 1873 Miss Larcom was one of the editors of *Our Young Folks.* Many of her "Childhood Songs" (collected and published in 1873) were contributed to this magazine. Her sympathy with children and understanding of their tastes fitted her to assist her close friend, John Greenleaf Whittier, in the preparation of his verse anthology, *Child Life* (1871). This was followed by their collaboration in the more ambitious *Songs of Three Centuries* (1883). Independently she made many anthologies of writings on nature and religion. Her life after she left Wheaton was spent mainly in Beverly and Boston and was placidly busy. Her religious experiences deepened with the years and her writing took on a slightly mystical tone. *The Unseen Friend* (1892) was the final expression of her faith. The year after its publication she died in Boston and was buried in Beverly. She had outlived many of her generation and most of her closest friends. She had taken a part, not as a leader, but as an active participant, in the liberal movements of the century; perhaps it is as a type that one regards her finally.

[In addition to *A New England Girlhood,* see: D. D. Addison, *Lucy Larcom: Life, Letters, and Diary* (1894); Mary Larcom Dow, *Old Days at Beverly Farms* (1921); W. F. Abbott, "Geneal. of the Larcom Family," *Essex Inst. Hist. Colls.,* Jan., Apr. 1922; Frances Hays, *Women of the Day* (1885); *N. Y. Tribune,* Apr. 19, 1893.]

E. D. H.

LARD, MOSES E. (Oct. 29, 1818–June 17, 1880), minister of the Disciples of Christ, editor, was born in Bedford County, Tenn. When he was about eleven years old his father, Leaven Lard, of Scotch descent, moved with his wife and six children to Ray County, Mo., where soon afterwards he died of smallpox. From his father Moses inherited a tall, vigorous frame, determination, and courage; and from his mother, a pious Baptist, his religious tendencies. The father's death soon caused the breaking up of the family and the boy went to live in Liberty, Mo. When seventeen years old he had not yet learned to write, but in time he acquired that art by tearing down and copying old advertisements which had been posted in the town. Gen. Alexander W.

Doniphan [*q.v.*] became interested in him and with others made it possible for him in 1845 to enter Bethany College in what is now West Virginia. He was then nearly twenty-seven and had a wife, Mary, and two children; but he completed his course with high honors.

Returning to Missouri, he resided there until the Civil War, serving Disciples churches in Independence, Liberty, Camden Point, and St. Joseph, and also engaging extensively in evangelistic work. At Camden Point he was for a time president of the Female College established by Professor H. B. Todd. He soon became one of the leading Disciples and one of the most effective preachers in that section of the country. In 1854 Rev. Jeremiah B. Jeter [*q.v.*], a Baptist minister of Richmond, Va., published *Campbellism Examined,* a book that created much controversy. Alexander Campbell asked Lard to write a reply, and in 1857 he published *Review of Rev. J. B. Jeter's Book Entitled "Campbellism Examined."* Exhaustive, able, and caustic, it was widely regarded as a conclusive rebuttal of Jeter's principal representations, and it added much to Lard's prestige. After the outbreak of the Civil War, unwilling to take the oath of allegiance to the federal government imposed in 1862 by the Missouri state convention, he went to Canada. When he came back to the United States he took up his residence in Kentucky, living for a time in Georgetown and thereafter in Lexington. In the latter place he was pastor of the Main Street Church for a period; he also preached extensively throughout the state; but his influence was exerted most widely as an editor. He established *Lard's Quarterly,* which he published until the *Apostolic Times* was started in 1869. Of this periodical he became chief editor, with four associates. He was one of the leaders of the conservative group among the Disciples, whose attitude was set forth in the prospectus to the *Apostolic Times*: "To the primitive faith, and the primitive practice, without enlargement or diminution, without innovation or modification, the editors here and now commit their paper" (Moore, *Comprehensive History, post,* p. 556). He opposed anything approaching a creedal statement, open communion, the use of an organ in public worship, and the assumption of pastoral functions. He wrote with conciseness, vigor, and a certain picturesqueness that had its effect. Although conservative regarding ecclesiastical matters, he was independent, sincere, courageous, and, in some respects, radical. Toward the close of his life he issued a pamphlet in which he endeavored to show that the Greek word *aionios* does not in every case mean everlasting, and that its use in the Bible does not necessarily establish the fact of eternal punishment. This pamphlet subjected him to severe criticism on the ground that he had Universalist leanings, and some of the Disciples advocated withdrawal from fellowship with him. He also published a commentary on the Epistle to the Romans, into which he put much labor. He died of cancer at Lexington, Ky., and was buried in Mount Mora Cemetery, St. Joseph, Mo. Nine children survived him.

[J. T. Brown, *Churches of Christ* (1904); T. P. Haley, *Hist. and Biog. Sketches of the Early Churches and Pioneer Preachers of the Christian Ch. in Mo.* (1888); W. T. Moore, *The Living Pulpit of the Christian Ch.* (1869), and *A Comprehensive Hist. of the Disciples of Christ* (1909); *Christian Standard* (Cincinnati), June 26, 1880; W. E. Garrison, *Religion Follows the Frontier* (1931).] H. E. S.

LARDNER, JAMES LAWRENCE (Nov. 20, 1802–Apr. 12, 1881), naval officer, was born in Philadelphia, the grandson of Lynford Lardner, a native of England who came to Pennsylvania in 1740, and the son of John and Margaret (Saltar) Lardner. After a cruise to India in the merchant ship *Bengal* in anticipation of entry into the naval service, he became a midshipman May 10, 1820. He was in the *Dolphin* and the *Franklin* in the Pacific, 1820–24; and in the *Brandywine* which took Lafayette to France, 1825–26. After promotion to lieutenant, in 1828, he was for three years navigating officer in the *Vincennes,* during which time she cruised around the world. He was in the *Delaware,* Mediterranean Squadron, 1833–34, in the *Independence,* then the largest frigate in the world, on a cruise to England, Russia, and South America, 1837–38. During the Mexican War he was in the receiving ship at Philadelphia, and in 1850–53 he commanded the *Porpoise* on the African coast. In 1851 he was promoted to commander and just after the opening of the Civil War he was made captain in May 1861. In September following he was assigned to the steam frigate *Susquehanna,* which he commanded at Port Royal, S. C., Nov. 7, 1861, and in subsequent operations on the South Carolina and Georgia coast. The *Susquehanna* was next to the flagship in the Port Royal action, and after the battle Flag Officer Samuel F. Du Pont [*q.v.*] commended Lardner in general orders, stating that "your noble ship throughout the whole of the battle, was precisely where I wanted her to be, and doing precisely what I wanted her to do, and . . . your close support of this ship was a very gallant thing" (*Official Records,* 1 ser. XX, 286–87). In June 1862, Lardner took command of the East Gulf Blockading Squadron, receiving the rank of commodore in July, but in November he was invalided home with yellow fever, from which forty died on his flagship alone. In June 1863, he succeeded Charles Wilkes in command of the West India Squadron, which consisted of about ten ships, and was charged with the duties of protecting commerce and completing the blockade. Secretary of the Navy Welles spoke of Lardner at this time somewhat dubiously as "discreet, prudent, perhaps overcautious" (*Diary of Gideon Welles,* 1911, I, 319). Prudence was desirable in view of recent British complaints about questionable ship seizures in this area, and the Commodore's other qualities were not put to severe test, for at the end of his cruise, Oct. 3, 1864, he reported "no rebel cruiser in the West Indies for the last sixteen months" (*Official Records,* 1 ser. III, 249). He retired in November 1864. In July 1866, he was made rear admiral, and from 1869 to 1872 he was governor of the Naval Asylum in Philadelphia.

Lardner was married first, Feb. 2, 1832, to Margaret Wilmer, by whom he had five children, two of whom survived him. After his first wife's death in 1846, he married June 23, 1853, Ellen Wilmer, by whom he had two sons. He died in Philadelphia from a kidney ailment and was buried in Oxford Episcopal Church near Frankford, Pa. A destroyer launched in 1919 was named for him. Admiral Robley D. Evans [*q.v.*], who served under him in the Civil War, describes him as "one of the finest specimens of the old navy, . . . a splendid seaman, a courteous, kindly gentleman, brave to the point of recklessness." He continues: "To a naturally fluent tongue the admiral added a vocabulary of oaths so fine that it was musical, and when aroused he did not hesitate to speak his mind in the language all seamen understood. At the same time his black eyes shone like fireflies, and his white mustache bristled" (*A Sailor's Log,* 1901, pp. 61–62). The Secretary's Order at his death declared that "his whole career in the service was marked by purity of character, intelligence, and devotion to duty" (*Army and Navy Journal,* Apr. 23, 1881, p. 737).

[*War of the Rebellion: Official Records (Navy)*; Navy registers; L. R. Hamersly, *The Records of Living Officers of the U. S. Navy and Marine Corps,* 3rd ed. (1878); *Army and Navy Jour.,* Apr. 16, 1881, and *Phila. Inquirer,* Apr. 13, 16, 1881; J. W. Jordan, *Colonial Families of Phila.* (1911), vol. II; genealogical article by F. W. Leach, in the *North American* (Phila.), Jan. 31, 1909.]

A. W.

LARKIN, JOHN (Feb. 2, 1801–Dec. 11, 1858), Catholic educator and preacher, was born of Irish stock at Newcastle-upon-Tyne, England. He pursued his classical studies under the historian, Dr. John Lingard, at Ushaw College near Durham where Dr. Nicholas Wiseman, later cardinal, was a friend and school-fellow. On graduation, he traveled in the East with some thought of entering business, but the call of religion brought him to the Seminary of St. Sulpice in Paris where he joined the Sulpicians. As a deacon, he was assigned to St. Mary's Seminary in Baltimore, Md., where he taught mathematics, completed his theological studies, and was ordained (1827). Thereupon he instructed in mathematics and allied subjects at the Sulpician College in Montreal for twelve years. Challenged by the need of priests in the United States and the opportunity of broader and more intense service in the Society of Jesus, he left Canada for Kentucky where, at St. Mary's College, he enlisted as a Jesuit (1840). Even before he had completed his novitiate, he preached at retreats throughout Kentucky and Ohio. In 1841 he established St. Ignatius' Literary Institution at Louisville. As a preacher of marked ability and broad intellectual range he was in general demand at civic as well as at religious functions as far as Boston.

In 1846 Larkin was summoned to teach at St. John's College, Fordham, N. Y., which Bishop Hughes had just assigned to the Jesuits, and was placed in charge of the Society's academies and congregations in the New York region. The following year he founded the College of St. Francis Xavier in New York City and was its first president, 1847–49. In 1850 he was appointed bishop of Toronto. Determined to avoid the burdens of episcopal dignity and an enforced severance from the Society of Jesus, he refused the honor and journeyed to Rome, though he took pains to make his tertianship at Laon in France on the way. Through Jesuit influence, he was relieved of the appointment by Pope Pius IX and returned as president of Fordham (1851). As rector he won the students despite a considerable reform in the curriculum and an insistence upon better standards of scholarship. During the days of Know-Nothing agitation, when active threats were made to destroy the institution, he procured a dozen muskets from the civic authorities and the college suffered no damage. In 1854 he was again in England preaching through the north country, when he was commissioned as agent of the father-general to visit the Jesuit houses in Ireland. After his return to New York, about 1856, he served as missionary at the College of St. Francis Xavier until his death.

[B. J. Webb, *The Centenary of Catholicity in Ky.* (1884); *The Coll. of St. Francis Xavier, 1847–97* (1897); T. G. Taaffe, *A Hist. of St. John's Coll., Fordham, N. Y.* (1891); *Woodstock Letters,* vol. III (1874), vol. XXVI (1897); *N. Y. Freeman's Jour.,* Dec. 18, 1858, Mar. 3, 1887; *N. Y. Tribune,* Dec. 14, 1858.]

R. J. P.

LARKIN, THOMAS OLIVER (Sept. 16, 1802–Oct. 27, 1858), merchant, diplomatic agent, was United States consul at Monterey, early capital of California, at the time that country was acquired by the United States. He was born in Charlestown, Mass., the son of Capt. Thomas Oliver and Ann (Rogers) Cooper Larkin. After living for some years in North and South Carolina, he sailed from Boston for California in 1831, arriving at Monterey on Apr. 13, 1832. On ship-board during his voyage he met Rachel (Hobson) Holmes who, later widowed, became his wife on June 10, 1833. He refers to their first children as the first children born in California whose parents were both from the United States. Larkin built the first double-geared flour mill in that region, making the models for it himself. He soon became a successful merchant, operating a local store and trading with Mexico and the Sandwich Islands in lumber, flour, potatoes, beaver and sea-otter skins, and horses. He also set an early precedent of prosperity for land speculation in the far West.

Larkin's real claim to distinction lies in his brief but engaging activities in the field of diplomacy. He played a not unimportant part in the machinations that were preliminary to the acquisition of California by the United States. He served his government in several capacities; as consul, 1844–48; confidential agent, 1846–48; naval store-keeper, 1847–48; and navy agent, 1847–49. As consul he aided American seamen and immigrants in distress, protected them from the irregularities of the unstable Mexican régime in California, and promoted the interests of American commerce. His work as navy agent and naval store-keeper was largely routine and perfunctory. From the beginning of his consulate in 1844 he looked forward to the ultimate transfer of California from Mexico to the United States. He was jealous and watchful of the British and French diplomatic agents in California, fearing that their governments had designs upon the country. He reported his aspirations and suspicions insistently to the government at Washington and was encouraged in return to be diligent in his "watchful waiting."

President James K. Polk was eager to secure California for the United States. To that end a secret dispatch, dated Oct. 17, 1845, and signed by James Buchanan, secretary of state, was sent to Larkin. By this dispatch he was appointed "confidential agent in California." He was instructed to warn the Californians against any attempt to transfer them to the jurisdiction of England or France. Likewise he was to "arouse in their bosoms that love of liberty and independence so natural to the American Continent." The most significant lines of the instructions were as follows: "In the contest between Mexico and California we can take no part, unless the former should commence hostilities against the United States; but should California assert and maintain her independence, we shall render her all the kind offices in our power as a Sister Republic. . . . Whilst the President will make no effort and use no influence to induce California to become one of the free and independent States of this Union, yet if the People should desire to unite their destiny with ours, they would be received as brethren, whenever this can be done, without affording Mexico just cause of complaint" (original dispatch in the Bancroft Library, University of California). Under authority of this dispatch Larkin launched, in April 1846, a well-conceived campaign of propaganda looking toward the separation of California from Mexico. He seemed to be making good progress when the Mexican War opened and California was secured to the United States by conquest. His most important diplomatic work was in his confidential agency, the significance of which lies in the light it throws upon Polk's policy of territorial expansion. After serving as a member of the state constitutional convention in 1849, Larkin withdrew from public life and devoted himself to his business interests.

[The chief manuscript collection bearing upon Larkin's life and work was brought together by H. H. Bancroft and is now in the Bancroft Library, University of California. R. W. Kelsey, *The U. S. Consulate in Cal.* (1910), is based largely upon these manuscripts. See also J. B. Moore, *The Works of Jas. Buchanan* (12 vols., 1908–11); M. M. Quaife, *The Diary of Jas. K. Polk* (1910), vol. III; R. G. Cleland, *A Hist. of Cal.: The Am. Period* (1922); J. S. Reeves, *Am. Diplomacy under Tyler and Polk* (1907); J. H. Smith, *The War with Mexico* (2 vols., 1919); W. E. Lincoln, *Some Descendants of Stephen Lincoln . . . Edward Larkin . . . Thomas Oliver* (1930); *Century Mag.*, Aug. 1891; *San Francisco Herald*, Oct. 29, 1858.] R. W. K.